Financial Accounting

Fifth Edition

K. Fred Skousen
Brigham Young University

W. Steve Albrecht
Brigham Young University

Harold Q. Langenderfer
University of North Carolina, Chapel Hill

COLLEGE DIVISION South-Western Publishing Co.
Cincinnati Ohio

Sponsoring Editor: David L. Shaut
Developmental Editor: Linda Spang
Production Editor: Mark Sears
Production House: York Production Services, Inc.
Cover/Internal Design: Joseph M. Devine
Marketing Manager: Michael J. O'Brien
Cover Photo: © Richard DeWeese

AO75EA
Copyright © 1994
by South-Western Publishing Co.
Cincinnati, Ohio

ALL RIGHTS RESERVED
The text of this publication, or any part thereof, may not be reproduced or transmitted in any form or by any means, electronic or mechanical, including photocopying, recording, storage in an information retrieval system, or otherwise, without the prior written permission of the publisher.

Library of Congress Cataloging-in-Publication Data
The complete version of the text is catalogued as follows:

Skousen, K. Fred.
    Accounting principles and applications.—4th ed./K. Fred Skousen, Harold Q. Langenderfer, W. Steve Albrecht.
    p. cm.
    Rev. ed. of: Accounting/K. Fred Skousen . . . [et al.]. 3rd ed. c1987.
    ISBN 0-538-81163-3
    1. Accounting. I. Langenderfer, Harold Q. II. Albrecht, W. Steve. III. Accounting. 3rd ed. IV. Title.
HF5635.S618 1992
657—dc20   92-24772
                                                                     CIP

ISBN 0-538-82832-3

1 2 3 4 5 6 7 KI 9 8 7 6 5 4 3

Printed in the United States of America

Preface

Financial Accounting is a user-oriented one-semester or two-quarter text. The fifth edition of the textbook builds on and maintains the strengths of our first four editions. The overall objective of this edition is to provide introductory accounting students and their instructors with the most timely, relevant, and understandable textbook possible.

IMPORTANT FEATURES OF THE 5TH EDITION

Financial Accounting provides both practical and theoretical coverage of financial accounting topics. Following are some important distinguishing features and changes in the fifth edition that reflect the changes occurring in accounting education and in the business world.

User Orientation

In contrast to the traditional preparer approach, with its early emphasis on transaction analysis and recording, our textbook reflects a more user-oriented approach. Chapter 1 describes the purpose of accounting and the primary users of accounting information and explains essential concepts of financial accounting and reporting. Chapter 2 provides an overview of the general-purpose financial statements, using simple corporate illustrations. Transactions and recording procedures are first introduced in Chapter 3. Building on the concepts and financial statement elements explained in the first two chapters, Chapters 3 through 5 provide clear, concise coverage of the accounting cycle. Procedural topics, such as reversing entries, special journals, and worksheet entries for a periodic inventory system are presented in optional appendixes.

Corporate Emphasis

The text is written with an emphasis on corporations to reflect the real world of financial reporting. In Chapter 1, the entity concept is explained, and each type of business organization is defined and described briefly. In Chapter 2, the corporation is used to explain and illustrate financial statements, and the corporate emphasis continues in subsequent chapters. In Chapter 3, however, we explain and illustrate the basic differences between stockholders' equity and owners' equity for unincorporated businesses. A separate chapter (14) provides more detailed coverage of proprietorships and partnerships.

Focus on Ethics

Chapter 1 introduces the topic of ethics. A general decision model for resolving ethical issues is presented, along with a brief summary of the American Institute of Certified Public Accountants' *Code of Professional Conduct*. In addition, every chapter contains an ethics case relating to the topics covered in the chapter. The cases present ethical dilemmas that require students to think about behavioral and moral issues in business and accounting. Research in moral development suggests that students who are exposed to, and required to think about, ethical issues develop a stronger personal code of ethics than do those who are naive about the issues. We believe these ethics cases will provide a basis for rich classroom discussions.

Chapter Organization and Structure

Each chapter is carefully structured to help students focus on important ideas and remember them. Specific components found in each chapter include:

LEARNING OBJECTIVES. Each chapter begins with specific learning objectives to guide students in their study of the chapter. These objectives show students and instructors the organizational flow of the chapter and help students evaluate their understanding of the main points within each chapter. The objectives are integrated in the text margins and summarized at the end of the chapter.

SETTING THE STAGE. New in this edition, an interesting, real-life scenario "sets the stage" for each chapter. These scenarios tie directly to material covered in the chapter and help students relate chapter topics to actual business happenings.

BUSINESS ENVIRONMENT ESSAYS. The text contains numerous real-world examples, adapted from financial newspapers and publications, that illustrate important concepts being discussed. These examples enable students to see how the accounting topics they are studying are applied and interpreted in real-world situations.

KEY TERMS. Throughout each chapter, key terms are defined in the margins, making it easier for students to learn accounting, the language of business. A list of key terms (with page references) is presented at the end of each chapter to provide additional reinforcement, and all key terms are defined in a comprehensive glossary at the end of the book.

SUMMARIES. Several concise summaries are presented within each chapter to help students remember the important points just discussed, and each chapter concludes with a comprehensive summary, organized by learning objectives.

REVIEW PROBLEMS. A review problem, with solution, at the end of each chapter demonstrates the application of the major concepts and procedures covered in the chapter.

APPENDIXES. To allow greater flexibility of coverage, several optional topics are covered in appendixes at the end of selected chapters. These appendixes expand upon procedural aspects of chapter topics, describe alternative or more complex techniques, or simply provide additional coverage.

END-OF-CHAPTER MATERIALS. The end-of-chapter materials are designed to test and reinforce student understanding in various ways. The discussion questions are intended to refine students' understanding of specific accounting terms and concepts. The exercises deal with single concepts, and each can be completed fairly quickly (a maximum of 30 minutes). The problems generally take longer to complete than the exercises, and they probe for a deeper level of understanding. There are two sets of problems for each chapter to aid in class assignment decisions. Those problems identified as "unifying concepts" require students to analyze the computed results.

Two types of cases are included at the end of each chapter to help students develop analytical, problem-solving, and communication skills. The Business Analysis Cases demonstrate how accounting affects day-to-day business decisions and require students to interpret data, as well as solve problems. The Ethics Cases, new to this edition,

Preface

require students to consider behavioral and moral issues in accounting and business.

LEARNING AND TEACHING AIDS THAT ACCOMPANY THE TEXTBOOK

This textbook is part of a comprehensive and carefully prepared educational package that offers various forms of assistance to both instructors and students. Each of the supplementary items available for use with the text is described briefly.

Available to Students

STUDY GUIDE. The Study Guide provides a means for students to reexamine the concepts and procedures in each chapter from several different perspectives. This publication includes chapter outlines; learning objectives; detailed chapter summaries; discussions of topics that cause problems for students and suggestions for overcoming those problems; and tests for student self-assessment, including matching, true-false, multiple-choice questions, and computational exercises (all with solutions).

WORKING PAPERS. Appropriate printed forms for students to use in solving end-of-chapter problems are available for Chapters 2 through 16.

PRACTICE CASE, MOUNTAIN BIKES, INC., PREPARED BY JERRY G. KREUZE OF WESTERN MICHIGAN UNIVERSITY. The practice case covers the basic accounting cycle and is designed for use after students have completed Chapter 5 of the text. This case, which requires 8 to 10 hours to complete, can be solved manually or with the Solutions Software described below.

SOLUTIONS SOFTWARE, PREPARED BY WARREN W. ALLEN AND DALE H. KLOOSTER OF EDUCATIONAL TECHNICAL SYSTEMS. This software is a general ledger program tailored specifically to Financial Accounting. Available in IBM®[1] and Macintosh™[2] versions, the software may be used to solve selected end-of-chapter problems, which are identified with the symbol in the margin. It can also be used in completing the practice case (Mountain Bikes, Inc.).

ELECTRONIC SPREADSHEET APPLICATIONS FOR FINANCIAL ACCOUNTING PREPARED BY GAYLORD N. SMITH OF ALBION COLLEGE. This supplemental text-workbook with template diskette includes accounting applications and a Lotus® 1-2-3®[3] tutorial. It requires approximately 20–25 hours for completion and is available in IBM and Macintosh (Excel) versions.

Available to Instructors

SOLUTIONS MANUALS. The manual contains answers to all discussion questions and detailed solutions for exercises, problems, business analysis cases, and ethics cases.

INSTRUCTOR'S RESOURCE MANUAL. This manual contains chapter outlines, teaching suggestions, alternative examples for classroom use, and teaching transparency masters. The manual should be particularly helpful to new instructors or graduate teaching assistants who wish to use the teaching notes and examples.

TEST BANK. A collection of more than 1,000 examination problems, multiple-choice questions, true-false questions, and matching exercises, accompanied by solutions, is available in both printed and microcomputer (MicroSWAT III) versions. The Test Bank is designed to save time in preparing and grading periodic and final examinations. The printed version of the Test Bank also includes sample quizzes for each chapter and sample examinations for groups of chapters.

SPREADSHEET APPLICATIONS. These template diskettes are used with Lotus 1-2-3 for solving selected end-of-chapter problems that are identified in the textbook with the symbol in the margin. These diskettes, which also provide a Lotus 1-2-3 tutorial and "what if" analysis, are provided free of charge to instructors at educational institutions that adopt this text.

---

[1] IBM is a registered trademark of International Business Machines Corporation. Any reference to IBM refers to this footnote.

[2] Macintosh is a trademark of Macintosh Laboratory, Inc., and is used by Apple Computer, Inc., with its express permission. Any reference to Macintosh refers to this footnote.

[3] Lotus and 1-2-3 are registered trademarks of the Lotus Development Corporation. Any reference to Lotus or 1-2-3 refers to this footnote.

SOLUTIONS TRANSPARENCIES AND TEACHING TRANSPARENCIES. Transparencies of solutions to all end-of-chapter problems are available. The teaching transparencies are designed to aid the instructor in presenting key concepts and principles discussed in the text.

VIDEOS. Two videotapes for classroom use are available. "Setting the Stage" includes 19 brief role-play segments that bring the world of financial accounting to life. "Luca Pacioli: Renaissance Scholar" is a 25-minute documentary on the life of the father of accounting.

ACKNOWLEDGMENTS

Throughout the textbook, relevant publications of standard-setting and professional organizations are discussed, quoted, or paraphrased. We are indebted to the American Accounting Association, the American Institute of Certified Public Accountants, and the Financial Accounting Standards Board for material from their publications.

The fifth edition of Financial Accounting reflects many comments and suggestions from colleagues and students, all of which are deeply appreciated. In particular, we wish to thank Alice Sineath, Forsyth Technical Community College, and Donald MacGilvra, Shoreline Community College, for their reviews of the answers in the solutions manual, test bank, and study guide.

K. Fred Skousen
W. Steve Albrecht
Harold Q. Langenderfer

Contents in Brief

PART 1
Financial Reporting and the Accounting Cycle 1

1 Accounting and Its Environment 2
2 Financial Statements: An Overview 26
3 Introducing the Accounting Cycle 58
4 Adjusting Entries 100
5 Completing the Accounting Cycle 136
  Appendix A: Reversing Entries 155
  Appendix B: Special Journals 158

PART 2
Income Determination 203

6 Income Measurement and Reporting 204
  Appendix: Using a Work Sheet in Accounting for Inventory 233
7 Inventory and Cost of Goods Sold 258

PART 3
Reporting Assets, Liabilities, and Owners' Equity 299

8 Cash, Marketable Securities, and Receivables 300
  Appendix: Internal Control 327
9 Property, Plant, and Equipment; Intangible Assets; and Natural Resources 356

10 Liabilities 404
11 Bonds Payable 450
12 Long-Term Investments 482
13 Owners' Equity—The Corporation 516
   Appendix: Consolidated Financial Statements 541
14 Owners' Equity—Proprietorships and Partnerships 582

PART 4
Other Dimensions of Financial Reporting 621

15 Statement of Cash Flows 622
16 Financial Statement Analysis 664
   Appendix: International Aspects of Financial Reporting 692
17 The Impact of Income Taxes on Business Decisions 730

Illustrative Financial Statements 767

Glossary 783

Index 793

Contents

PART 1
FINANCIAL REPORTING AND THE ACCOUNTING CYCLE 1

1 Accounting and Its Environment 2

The Purpose of Accounting 4
   The Relationship of Accounting to Business 6
Users of Accounting Information 6
Basic Concepts and Assumptions Underlying Financial Accounting 9
   The Entity Concept 9
   The Assumption of Arm's-Length Transactions 11
   The Cost Principle 11
   The Monetary Measurement Concept 12
   The Going Concern Assumption 12
   Double-Entry Accounting 12
The Environment of Accounting 13
   The Significance and Development of GAAP 13
   International Business 16
   Ethics in Accounting 16
Career Opportunities in Accounting 19
   Public Accounting 19
   Industry 19
   Government and Other Nonprofit Organizations 21
   Educational Preparation 21

2 Financial Statements: An Overview 26

General-Purpose Financial Statements 28
   The Balance Sheet 28
   The Income Statement 33
   The Statement of Cash Flows 36
How the Financial Statements Tie Together 38
Notes to Financial Statements 39
The Audit Report 39

3 Introducing the Accounting Cycle 58

The Process of Transforming Transaction Data into Useful Accounting Information 60
The Basic Accounting Equation 61
   Using Accounts to Categorize Transactions 62
   Expanding the Accounting Equation to Include Revenues, Expenses, and Dividends 64
The First Four Steps in the Accounting Cycle 66
   Step 1. Analyze Transactions and Business Documents 66
   Step 2. Journalize Transactions 68
   Step 3. Post Journal Entries to Accounts 75
   Step 4. Determine Account Balances and Prepare a Trial Balance 78
Illustration of the First Four Steps in the Accounting Cycle 80

4 Adjusting Entries 100

Additional Characteristics of the Accounting Model 102
  Periodic Reporting 102
  Accrual Accounting 103
  Accrual—Versus Cash—Basis Accounting 104
Adjusting Entries (Step 5 of the Accounting Cycle) 105
  Unrecorded Revenues 106
  Unrecorded Expenses 108
  Prepaid Expenses 110
  Unearned Revenues 113
Alternative Approaches for Adjusting Entries 115
  An Alternative Approach to Adjustments for Prepaid Expenses 116
  An Alternative Approach to Adjustments for Unearned Revenues 117
  Concluding Comment 118

5 Completing the Accounting Cycle 136

The Work Sheet 138
  Preparing a Work Sheet 138
  Special Considerations in Using a Work Sheet 142
Preparing Financial Statements 147
The Closing Process 147
  Real and Nominal Accounts 147
  Closing Entries 148
  Using an Income Summary Account 149
  Closing the Dividends Account 150
  The Closing Process for Proprietorships and Partnerships 151
Preparing a Post-Closing Trial Balance 151
A Summary of the Accounting Cycle 152
Appendix A: Reversing Entries 155
Appendix B: Special Journals 158

PART 2
INCOME DETERMINATION 203

6 Income Measurement and Reporting 204

A Definition of Income 206
Methods of Measuring Income 207
Revenue Recognition 210
  Recognizing Revenue on Credit Sales 211
Recognizing Expenses 214
  The Cost of Goods Sold Expense 215
  The Perpetual Inventory Method 215
  The Periodic Inventory Method 219
  Taking a Physical Count of Inventory 223

  Closing Entries for Cost of Goods Sold 224
  Other Operating Expenses 226
The Income Statement 227
  Other Revenues and Expenses 230
  Extraordinary Items 230
  Earnings per Share 230
Appendix: Using a Work Sheet in Accounting for Inventory 233

7 Inventory and Cost of Goods Sold 258

The Proper Measurement of Inventory 260
  Inventory Cutoff 260
The Effects of Inventory Errors 260
  Other Factors in Accounting for Inventory 264
Inventory Cost Flows 265
  Specific Identification Inventory Costing 265
  Assumed Inventory Cost Flows 266
  Periodic Inventory Cost Flow Assumptions 267
  Perpetual Inventory Cost Flow Assumptions 271
  A Comparison of All Inventory Costing Alternatives 273
Reporting Inventory at Amounts Below Cost 274
  Inventory Valued at Net Realizable Value 274
  Inventory Valued at Lower of Cost or Market 275
Methods of Estimating Inventories 277
  The Gross Margin Method 278
  The Retail Inventory Method 279
Accounting for Inventories in Manufacturing Firms 280

PART 3
REPORTING ASSETS, LIABILITIES, AND OWNERS' EQUITY 299

8 Cash, Marketable Securities, and Receivables 300

Controlling and Accounting for Cash 302
  Control of Cash 302
  Accounting for Petty Cash 304
  Reconciling the Bank Account 306
Accounting for Short-Term Investments 311
  Recording Investments in Marketable Securities 312
  Valuing Marketable Securities at Lower of Cost or Market 313
Accounting for Receivables 315
  Accounts Receivable 315
  Notes Receivable 322
  Discounting Notes Receivable 324
  Other Receivables 325
Appendix: Internal Control 327

Contents

9 Property, Plant, and Equipment; Intangible Assets; and Natural Resources 356

Nature of Operating Assets 358
Accounting for Property, Plant, and Equipment 358
   Acquisitions of Property, Plant, and Equipment 359
   Allocating the Cost of Plant and Equipment to Expense 363
Repairing and Improving Plant and Equipment 374
Disposal of Property, Plant, and Equipment 375
   Discarding Property, Plant, and Equipment 375
   Selling Property, Plant, and Equipment 376
   Exchanging Property, Plant, and Equipment 377
Accounting for Intangible Assets 380
   Patents 380
   Franchises and Licenses 381
   Goodwill 381
Accounting for Natural Resources 382

10 Liabilities 404

Current Liabilities 406
   Short-Term Obligations to Creditors 406
   Payroll Liabilities 410
   Tax Liabilities 412
   Obligations to Provide Goods or Services 414
Long-Term Liabilities 415
   Measuring Long-Term Liabilities 415
   Accounting for Long-Term Liabilities 419
   Other Long-Term Liabilities 426
Contingent Liabilities 427

11 Bonds Payable 450

The Nature of Bonds 452
   Types of Bonds 452
   Characteristics of Bonds 453
Determining a Bond's Issuance Price 454
   Bonds Issued at Face Value 455
   Bonds Issued at a Discount 456
   Bonds Issued at a Premium 456
Accounting for Bonds Payable 458
   Accounting for Bonds Issued at Face Value 459
   Accounting for Bonds Issued at a Discount or at a Premium 460
   Effective-Interest Amortization 464
   Accounting for Bonds Issued Between Interest Dates 465
   Bond Retirements at Maturity 468
   Bond Retirements Before Maturity 468

12 Long-Term Investments 482

Accounting for Long-Term Investments in Bonds 484
   Accounting for the Acquisition of Bonds 485
   Accounting for Bonds Purchased Between Interest Dates 486
   Accounting for the Amortization of Bond Discounts and Premiums 487
   Accounting for the Sale or Maturity of Bond Investments 491
   Valuation of Long-Term Investments in Bonds 492
Accounting for Long-Term Investments in Stocks 493
   Acquisition of Stocks 493
   The Cost Method 495
   The Equity Method 496
   The Cost and Equity Methods Illustrated 497

13 Owners' Equity—The Corporation 516

Corporations and Corporate Stock 518
   Characteristics of a Corporation 518
   The Stock of a Corporation 520
Accounting for Stock 522
   Issuance of Par-Value Stock and No-Par Stock with Stated Value 522
   Issuance of No-Par Stock Without a Stated Value 524
   Accounting for Treasury Stock 525
   Reporting Stock on the Balance Sheet 528
Distributions to Stockholders 529
   Types of Dividends 530
   Accounting for Cash Dividends 531
   Accounting for Stock Dividends 534
   Stock Splits 536
Accounting for Retained Earnings 536
   Prior-Period Adjustments 537
   The Statement of Retained Earnings 537
   Retained Earnings Restrictions 537
Statement of Stockholders' Equity 539
Appendix: Consolidated Financial Statements 541

14 Owners' Equity—Proprietorships and Partnerships 582

Characteristics Shared by Proprietorships and Partnerships 584
   Ease of Formation 584
   Limited Life 585
   Unlimited Liability 585
Proprietorship Accounting 586

Characteristics Unique to Partnerships   588
    Mutual Agency   589
    Co-Ownership of Partnership Property   589
    Sharing of Partnership Profits   589
Basic Partnership Accounting   589
    Forming a Partnership   590
    Partners' Drawing Accounts   590
    The Statement of Partners' Capital   591
Accounting for Partnership Profits and Losses   592
    Stated Ratio   593
    Capital Investment Ratio   594
    Allowance for Salaries for the Remainder at Stated Ratio   595
Accounting for Changing Partnership Members   597
    Admitting a New Partner   598
    The Withdrawal of a Partner   601
    The Death of a Partner   604
The Liquidation of a Partnership   605

PART 4
OTHER DIMENSIONS OF FINANCIAL REPORTING   621

15 Statement of Cash Flows   622

Purposes of a Statement of Cash Flows   624
Information Reported in the Statement of Cash Flows   625
    Major Classifications of Cash Flows   625
    Noncash Investing and Financing Activities   627
The Direct and Indirect Methods of Reporting Operating Cash Flows   629
    The Indirect Method   629
    The Direct Method   631
    Recommendation of FASB Statement No. 95   633
Preparing a Statement of Cash Flows   635
    The Indirect Method Illustrated   635
    The Direct Method Illustrated   642
Usefulness of Cash Flow Statements   644
    Historical Perspective   644
    Importance of Cash Flow Analysis   645

16 Financial Statement Analysis   664

Reasons for Financial Statement Analysis   666
    Investment and Credit Decisions   666
    Managerial Decisions   667
    Regulating Decisions   667
Overview of Financial Statement Analysis   668
    Some Basic Techiques   668
    Key Relationships   668

Operating Performance   671
    Income Statement Vertical Analysis   672
    Income Statement Horizontal Analysis   673
Asset Turnover   674
    Balance Sheet Vertical Analysis   674
    Balance Sheet Horizontal Analysis   675
    Balance Sheet Ratio Analysis   676
Debt-Equity Management   681
Return on Stockholders' Equity   683
    Earnings per Share   683
    Price-Earnings Ratio   684
    Dividend Payout Ratio   685
    Book Value per Share   685
Return on Total Assets   687
Limitations of Financial Statement Analysis   689
    Uses of Estimates   689
    Changes in Values and Price Levels   691
    Ratios as a Basis for Comparison   691
Appendix: International Aspects of Financial Reporting   692

17 The Impact of Income Taxes on Business Decisions   730

The Federal Income Tax Liability   732
    Calculating the Tax Liability for an Individual Taxpayer   733
    Calculating the Tax Liability for a Corporation   738
    Some Considerations in Calculating Taxable Income   741
How Each Form of Business Is Taxed   743
    How Proprietorships Are Taxed   743
    How Partnerships Are Taxed   743
    How Corporations Are Taxed   744
    Choosing the Form of Organization   746
Tax-Planning Guidelines   746
Tax Considerations in Accounting for Inventories   747
Investments in Long-Term Operating Assets   749
    Tax Effects of Ways of Acquiring Long-Term Operating Assets   750
    Tax Effects of Alternative Ways of Depreciating Long-Term Operating Assets   751
    Tax Effects of Disposing of Long-Term Operating Assets   753

ILLUSTRATIVE FINANCIAL STATEMENTS   767

GLOSSARY   783

INDEX   793

Part 1

Financial Reporting and the Accounting Cycle

CHAPTERS

1. Accounting and Its Environment
2. Financial Statements: An Overview
3. Introducing the Accounting Cycle
4. Adjusting Entries
5. Completing the Accounting Cycle
   Appendix A – Reversing Entries
   Appendix B – Special Journals

Chapter 1

Accounting and Its Environment

Learning Objectives

After studying this chapter, you should be able to:
1. Describe the purpose of accounting and explain its role in business and society.
2. Identify the primary users of accounting information.
3. Explain the basic concepts and assumptions that underlie financial accounting.
4. Describe the environment of accounting, including the effects of generally accepted accounting principles, international business, and ethical considerations.
5. Identify various career opportunities in accounting.

SETTING THE STAGE

Meeks Brinkerhoff was a hay and cattle farmer in western Montana. Although he was an excellent farmer and had increased substantially the size of his cattle herd, Meeks's major interest was tinkering with various farm implements and tools trying to make them more effective and efficient. When Meeks was 48 years old, he successfully invented a hay rake that decreased significantly the amount of time it took to harvest hay. Excited about his invention, Meeks contacted several farm implement companies to see if they were interested in purchasing the rights to his rake. Several companies were very impressed, and one, Ford Harvester, agreed to pay Meeks $1 million plus 10 percent of the profits on all hay rakes sold.

Over the next 14 years, Meeks received substantial royalties from the hay rake. Meeks saved some of the money, but he also purchased additional farm land and made several other investments. At age 62, Meeks decided to retire and turn the farm and investments over to his three children. Because his daughter was living in California and because his second son had graduated from medical school and was a pediatrician, Meeks gave responsibility to manage the farm and investments to his oldest son, Mike. To ensure that everyone in his family would continue to receive income from the business, before retiring, Meeks formed a family partnership. Mike became the managing partner and was to receive an annual salary of $100,000, but each of the three children, as well as Meeks and his wife, were to own 25 percent of the partnership and share in the profits after paying Mike's salary. Believing things were in order, Meeks and his wife purchased a home in Arizona and left to enjoy their retirement years in the sun.

Although ownership was divided equally among the partners, no one except Mike paid much attention to the successes and failures of the family business. Meeks and his wife were having a great time in Arizona, the daughter loved her life in California, and the youngest son's medical practice was thriving.

Five years later, Joan, the daughter, was called back to the farm in Montana for an important family meeting. At that meeting, she discovered that Mike had made several bad investments and had lost millions of dollars. Not only had the family partnership lost all its assets, but Mike had incurred over $2 million in debt. Since Joan was a 25 percent partner, she was told that she now had a liability of $500,000.

Like her younger brother, Joan was incensed and hurt. Asking why she owed money, Joan was informed by Mike and his attorney that even though she didn't pay attention to what was going on, as a partner, she had "just as much liability as Mike or anyone else." "Besides," the attorney said, "at the end of every quarter, you were sent financial statements that showed how the business was doing, and together with the other partners, you signed all the loan documents and contracts."

Not only was Joan angry with Mike, she was also very upset with herself. How could she have been so dumb? How she wished she had paid attention to the financial affairs of the family business. But then, she thought, I don't even know what a financial statement is, let alone how to understand one. Why didn't I take the time to learn more about business and accounting? I didn't even know what a partnership was or recognize the extent of my potential liability.

Note: The facts in this scenario are real; the names and locations have been changed.

Problems like those described in this scenario happen every day in our society. Individuals, including extremely bright professionals, lose money because they don't understand accounting or financial statements or how to assess the well-being of a business entity. In this class, you will begin your study of accounting. You will learn what accounting is and why it is important. You will learn that accounting is the language of business and unless you have some understanding of it, business, investments, taxes, and money management will be like a foreign language to you. This chapter introduces you to accounting and provides a perspective by describing briefly the accounting profession, its past and present. This background should make it easier for you to understand the concepts and techniques that will be examined in later chapters.

THE PURPOSE OF ACCOUNTING

Objective 1

Describe the purpose of accounting and explain its role in business and society.

Making good decisions is critical for success in any business enterprise. When an important decision must be made, it is essential to use a rational decision-making process. The process is basically the same no matter how complex the issue. First, the problem or question must be clearly identified. Next, the facts surrounding the situation must be gathered and analyzed. Finally, several alternative courses of action should be considered before a decision is reached.

An economic, or financial, decision involves making the best allocation of available resources. For example, assume that you have $5,000 to invest. What factors would you consider in deciding among the alternative investment choices? One choice might be tuition, books, and other expenses for additional education. Another choice might be new clothes or a newer car. Still another choice might be to invest in a certificate of deposit (CD) at a bank where you could earn a return (called interest) on your investment. Obviously, your choice will depend on many factors, such as the specific alternatives available, current needs, long-term plans, other available resources, and the potential risks and rewards associated with each investment opportunity. These same factors must be weighed by businesses and other organizations in making decisions.

Accounting plays a vital role in providing information needed to make knowledgeable financial decisions. The information supplied by accounting is

business *an organization operated with the objective of making a profit from the sale of goods or services*

nonprofit organization *an entity without a profit objective, oriented toward providing services efficiently and effectively*

in the form of quantitative data, primarily financial in nature, and relates to specific economic entities. An economic entity may be an individual, a business enterprise, or a nonprofit organization. A **business,** such as a grocery store or a car dealership, is operated with the objective of making a profit for its owners. The goal of a **nonprofit organization,** such as a city government or a university, is to provide services in an effective and efficient manner. Every entity, regardless of its size or purpose, must have a way to keep track of its economic activities and to measure how well it is accomplishing its goals. Accounting provides the means for tracking activities and measuring results.

Without accounting information, many important financial decisions would be made blindly. Investors, for example, would have no way to distinguish between a profitable company and one that is on the verge of failure;

BUSINESS ENVIRONMENT ESSAY
It's a Competitive Business World

Accounting information is used to help make economic decisions. If good decisions are made, firms prosper. As the following excerpt from an article in *Business Week* illustrates, however, the business world is very competitive. Such factors as shifting market conditions and consumer demands can have a major impact on the outcome of decisions.

Quaker Oats' Pet Peeve
Its Gaines line is slipping in a dog-eat-dog world

These days, in the never-ending battle for the loyalty of pet owners, Quaker Oats Co. looks like, well, a dog. Marketing and operating blunders, made worse by red-hot competition, have scuttled the big plans the Chicago food giant had in late 1986, when it bought Anderson Clayton & Co. just to get its hands on the Gaines dog-food line.

After selling off the rest of Anderson Clayton, Quaker wound up paying $225 million for the dog-food operation. That seemed a fair price when pet food looked like a growth business. But now, Quaker is struggling simply to shore up the unit's U.S. operating margins, which sank from 8% in 1986 to 6% last year. . . .

Quaker started out with high expectations for pet food. The potential seemed huge: After cereals, pet food is the second-largest line for supermarkets, generating $5.5 billion in 1988 sales. In the heady early days after the deal, company executives predicted double-digit operating margins.

The Anderson Clayton deal, figured Quaker, would give it the momentum it needed to achieve those returns. By adding the Gaines and Cycle lines to Quaker's Ken-L Ration and Kibbles 'n Bits brands, the company doubled its market share to 14% and jumped from No. 5 to No. 2, behind Ralston Purina Co. It also boosted pet food to 25% of total company revenues.

But sales in dog food have been flat for several years. Cats have supplanted dogs as the pet of choice for Americans. At the same time, many dog owners are bypassing supermarkets to buy premium food in specialty stores. As a result, industry sales in dry and semi-moist dog food—Quaker's biggest niches—have dropped 8.6% and 28.9%, respectively, since 1986. And the Anderson Clayton lines didn't carry quite the cachet that Quaker expected.

Source: Lois Therrien, "Quaker Oats' Pet Peeve," *Business Week,* July 31, 1989, pp. 32–33.

bankers could not evaluate the riskiness of potential loans; corporate managers would have no basis for controlling costs, setting prices, or investing the company's resources; and governments would have no basis for taxing income. No list of examples could fully represent the pervasive use of accounting information throughout our economic, social, and political institutions. When accounting information is used effectively as a basis for making economic decisions, limited resources are more likely to be allocated efficiently. From a broad perspective, the result is a healthier economy and a higher standard of living.

Thus, **accounting** is a service activity designed to accumulate, measure, and communicate financial information to various decision makers, such as investors, creditors, and managers. Accounting involves a system of concepts and procedures that organizes and summarizes an entity's economic activities. This textbook focuses on accounting for business enterprises although many of the basic accounting concepts and procedures apply to nonprofit organizations as well.

accounting *a service activity designed to accumulate, measure, and communicate financial information about economic entities for decision-making purposes*

The Relationship of Accounting to Business

Business is the general term applied to the activities involved in the production and distribution of goods and services. Accounting is used to record and report the financial effects of business activities. As a result, accounting is often called the "language of business"; it provides the means of recording and communicating the successes and failures of business organizations.

All business enterprises have some activities in common. As shown in Exhibit 1-1, one common activity is the acquisition of monetary resources. These resources, often referred to as "capital," come from investors (owners) and creditors (lenders), and from the business itself in the form of earnings that have been retained. Once resources are obtained, they are used to buy land, buildings, and equipment; to purchase materials and supplies; to pay employees; and to meet any other expenses involved in the production and marketing of goods or services. When the product or service is sold, additional monetary resources (called "revenues") are generated. These resources can be used to pay off loans, to pay taxes, and to buy new materials, equipment, and other items needed to continue the operations of the business. In addition, some of the resources may be distributed to owners as a return on their investment.

The results of these activities are measured and communicated (reported) by accountants. In order to measure these results as accurately as possible, accountants follow a fairly standard set of procedures, usually referred to as the **accounting cycle**. The cycle includes several steps, which involve analyzing, recording, classifying, summarizing, and reporting accounting data. These steps are explained in detail in Chapters 3 through 5.

accounting cycle *the procedures for analyzing, recording, classifying, summarizing, and reporting accounting data*

USERS OF ACCOUNTING INFORMATION

Objective 2

Identify the primary users of accounting information.

The accounting cycle generates output in the form of financial reports. As shown in Exhibit 1-2, there are two major categories of reports—internal and external. Internal reports are used by those who direct the day-to-day operations of a business enterprise. These individuals are collectively referred to as

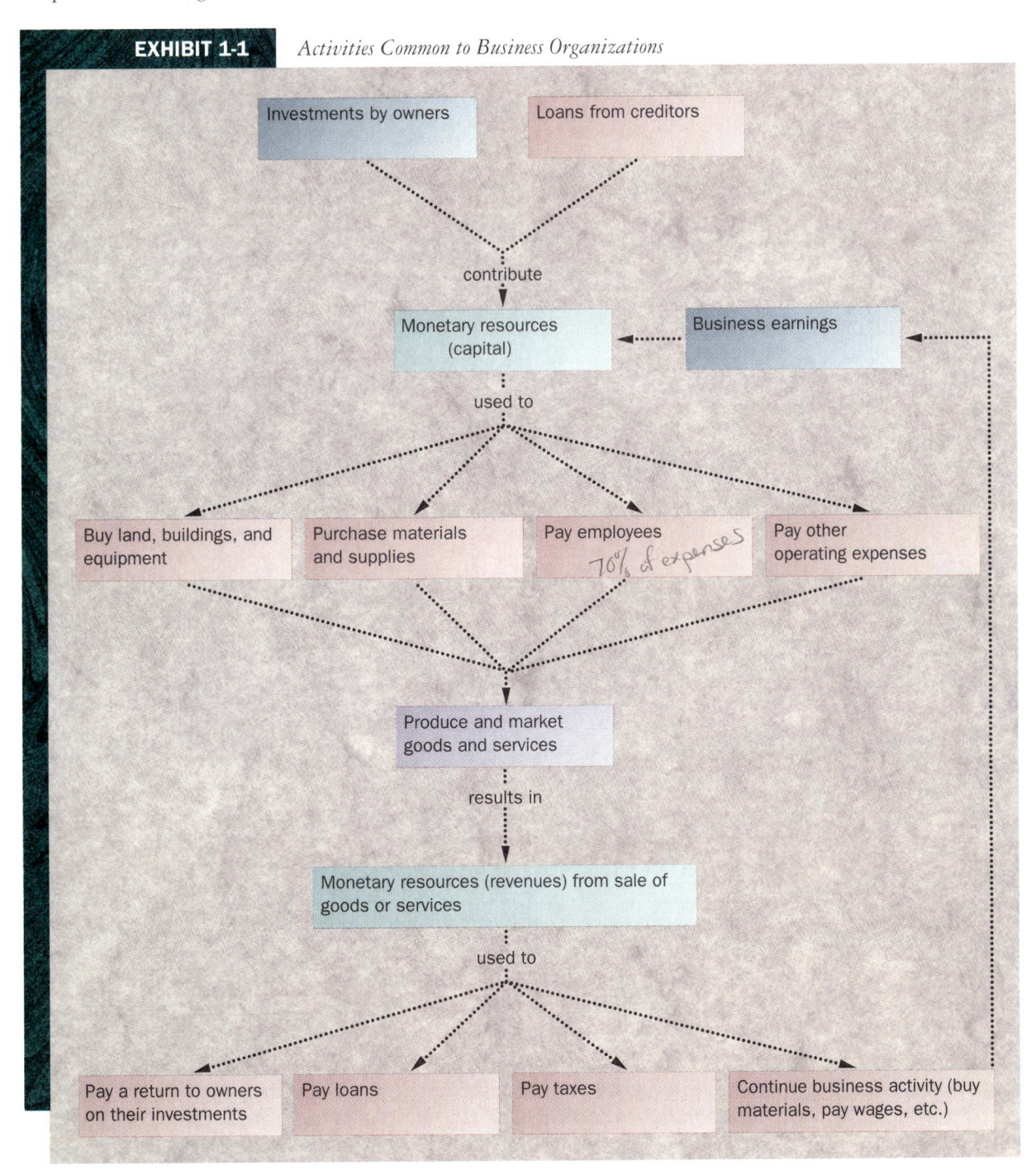

Chapter 1 *Accounting and Its Environment*

EXHIBIT 1-1 *Activities Common to Business Organizations*

```
        Investments by owners        Loans from creditors
                    \                 /
                     \               /
                      contribute
                          ↓
                 Monetary resources  ←······  Business earnings
                    (capital)
                          ↓
                       used to
          ┌──────────┬──────┴──────┬──────────┐
          ↓          ↓             ↓          ↓
    Buy land,   Purchase       Pay employees   Pay other
    buildings,  materials      70% of expenses operating
    and         and supplies                   expenses
    equipment
          └──────────┴──────┬──────┴──────────┘
                            ↓
                    Produce and market
                    goods and services
                            ↓
                        results in
                            ↓
                Monetary resources (revenues) from sale of
                goods or services
                            ↓
                         used to
          ┌──────────┬──────┴──────┬──────────┐
          ↓          ↓             ↓          ↓
    Pay a return  Pay loans    Pay taxes   Continue business
    to owners on                            activity (buy
    their investments                       materials, pay
                                            wages, etc.)
```

management accounting
the area of accounting concerned with providing internal financial reports to assist management in making decisions

"management," and the related area of accounting is called **management accounting.** In preparing financial reports that will enable management to decide which products to produce, what prices to charge, and which costs seem excessive, for example, management accounting focuses on the information needed for planning, implementing plans, and controlling costs.

EXHIBIT 1-2   *Output of the Accounting Cycle*

Internal Reporting (Management Accounting)

The Accounting Cycle

Financial reports for internal use by company management.
Examples: budgets, cost analyses, divisional performance reports.

External Reporting (Financial Accounting)

General-purpose financial statements for use by creditors, investors, and other external users.
Examples: the income statement, the balance sheet, the statement of cash flows.

Other external reports:
Special reports required by regulatory agencies, such as the SEC. Example: registration statements.
Income tax forms required by the IRS and state and local governments. Example: Corporate tax returns.

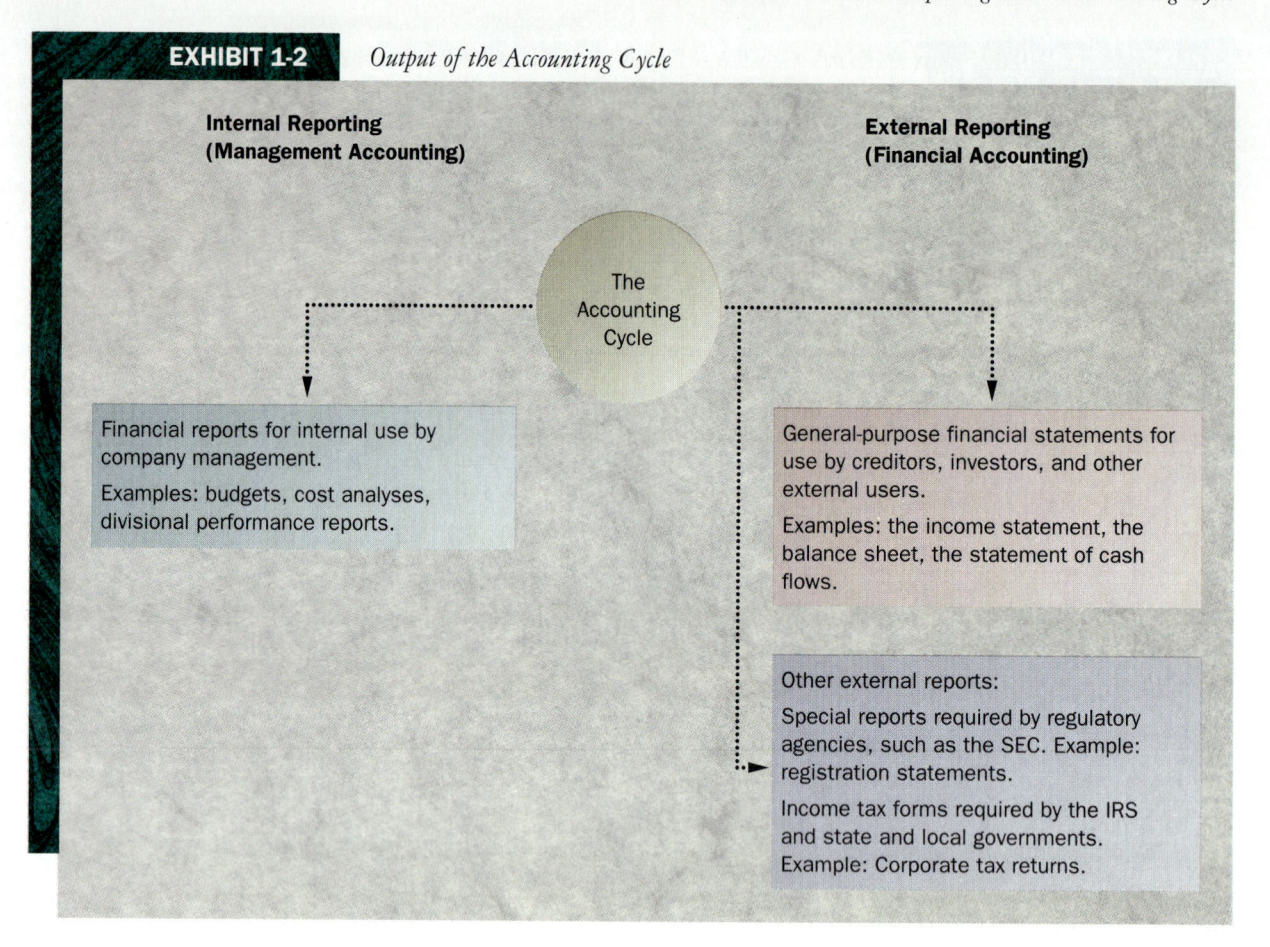

External financial reports are used by individuals and organizations who have an economic interest in the business but who are not part of its management. Information is provided to these "external users" in the form of general-purpose financial statements and special reports required by government agencies. General-purpose financial statements are prepared primarily to meet the needs of investors and creditors. These users of accounting information need to answer such questions as: Which company in an industry is likely to provide the best investment opportunity? Should a company's stock be held or sold? Should a loan be made to a company and for how much? In addition to general-purpose financial statements, other external reports are prepared as required by various regulatory agencies of the government, one of the most notable being the Securities and Exchange Commission (SEC). Further, income tax returns and other tax reports are supplied to the Internal Revenue Service (IRS) and state and local taxing authorities.

External financial reports come within the area of accounting referred to as **financial accounting.** Most of the data needed to prepare both internal and external reports is provided by the same accounting system. A major difference between management and financial accounting is the types of financial reports prepared. Internal reports are tailored to meet the needs of management and may vary considerably among businesses. General-purpose financial statements and other external reports, however, follow certain standards or guidelines and

financial accounting the area of accounting concerned with reporting financial information to interested external parties

are thus more uniform among companies. The general-purpose financial statements are discussed and illustrated in Chapter 2.

> **To Summarize** *Accounting is a service activity designed to accumulate, measure, and communicate financial information about economic entities—businesses and nonprofit organizations. Its purpose is to provide information used to make informed decisions about how to best use available resources. Accounting is often called the "language of business" because it provides the means of recording and communicating business activities and the results of those activities. Two major categories of reports are generated by the accounting cycle: internal and external. Management accounting focuses on providing reports for internal use by management to assist in making operating decisions and in planning and controlling a company's activities. Financial accounting provides information to meet the needs of external users. General-purpose financial statements are used by investors, creditors, and other external parties who are interested in a company's activities and results. Special reports are provided to government agencies, such as the SEC and IRS.*

BASIC CONCEPTS AND ASSUMPTIONS UNDERLYING FINANCIAL ACCOUNTING

Objective 3

Explain the basic concepts and assumptions that underlie financial accounting.

The basic concepts and assumptions of accounting form a theoretical foundation for current financial accounting practice. These ideas are so fundamental to any economic activity that they usually are taken for granted in conducting business. It is important to be aware of them, however, because these assumptions, together with certain basic concepts and procedures, determine the rules and set the boundaries of accounting practice. They indicate which events will be accounted for and in what manner. In total, they provide the essential characteristics of the traditional **accounting model.**

accounting model *the basic accounting assumptions, concepts, principles, and procedures that determine the manner of recording, measuring, and reporting an entity's transactions*

This section will describe the entity concept, the assumption of arm's-length transactions, the cost principle, the concept of monetary measurement, and the going concern assumption. It also will introduce double-entry accounting, the system upon which all accounting activity is built. Additional concepts and assumptions will be covered in later chapters. *Do not be concerned if you do not fully understand all the terms and concepts at this first encounter.* As noted, accounting is the language of business, and it takes time to learn a new language. The terms and concepts will become much more familiar as your study continues.

entity *an organizational unit (a person, partnership, or corporation) for which accounting records are kept and about which accounting reports are prepared*

The Entity Concept

Because business involves the exchange of goods or services between entities, it follows that accounting records should be kept for those entities. For accounting purposes, then, an **entity** is defined as the organizational unit for which accounting records are maintained—for example, IBM Corporation. It is a focal point for identifying, measuring, and communicating accounting data. Furthermore, the entity is considered to be separate from its individual owners.

An accountant records only the financial activities that occur between the entity being accounted for and other parties. The accountants for IBM Corporation, for example, would record all sales of IBM products to Companies A and B but not sales of Company A products to Company B. Accountants for these other firms would keep track of their own companies' activities. In addition, IBM's accountants would not be concerned with the personal activities and transactions of the owners (stockholders) of IBM Corporation.

There are three major types of business entities: a proprietorship, a partnership, and a corporation. Although the emphasis in this book is on corporations, most of the same principles also apply to proprietorships and partnerships. To explain the differences, we have a separate chapter on proprietorships and partnerships (see Chapter 14).

proprietorship *a business owned by one person*

PROPRIETORSHIP. A **proprietorship** is a business owned by one person. Usually, the owner of the business is actively involved in its operations. For example, many owners of small businesses—especially those that provide personal services—manage the day-to-day activities of, and receive the profits directly from, those businesses.

Because accountants view the business unit as a separate entity, care must be exercised to distinguish between the resources and records of the owner, or proprietor, and those of the accounting entity, the business. If the resources of the reporting entity (the entity for which the records are being maintained) are not accounted for separately, the financial success of the entity cannot be measured accurately. Although business records must be kept separate from the proprietor's personal records, the owner is ultimately responsible for all obligations of the proprietorship.

partnership *an association of two or more individuals or organizations to carry on economic activity*

PARTNERSHIP. A **partnership** is an association of two or more individuals or organizations to carry on economic activity. As in a proprietorship, the partners generally manage the business as well as own it.

A partnership should have a written agreement that specifies the ownership rights of the partners, as well as when and how the earnings of the business are to be distributed. Like a proprietorship, a partnership is not a separate legal entity, so the partners are ultimately responsible for any partnership obligations. For accounting purposes, however, the activities and records of the partnership are kept separate from the activities and records of the owners.

corporation *a legal entity chartered by a state, with ownership represented by transferable shares of stock*

CORPORATION. A **corporation** is a business that is chartered (incorporated) as a separate legal entity under the laws of a particular state. As such, a corporation has the same rights and obligations that individuals have: It can, for example, make purchases and investments, sell goods or services, and incur obligations, and it must pay income taxes. The bylaws of a corporation describe its scope of activity and specify the amount and type of ownership interests it can sell. These ownership interests are in the form of stock certificates, and the owners of a corporation are called **stockholders,** or **shareholders.** Within the constraints of the bylaws, stockholders can buy and sell freely their interests, thus allowing the corporate ownership to change without dissolving the business.

stockholders (shareholders) *individuals or organizations that own a portion (shares of stock) of a corporation*

The stockholders elect a board of directors, which, in turn, hires executives to manage the corporation. The managers, as employees of the corporation, may or may not be stockholders. This separation of ownership from management illustrates the need for two kinds of accounting information. As noted earlier, the internal users, management, need managerial accounting information; the external users, investors and creditors, need financial accounting information. Note that the investors of a corporation are the owners (stockholders), but they are considered external users because generally they are not actively involved in the corporation's operations and do not have direct access to the accounting records.

The Assumption of Arm's-Length Transactions

Accounting is based on the recording of economic transactions. Viewed broadly, **transactions** include not only exchanges of economic resources between separate entities but also events that have an economic impact on a business but do not involve other entities. The borrowing and lending of money and the sale and purchase of goods or services are examples of the former type. A fire loss and the deterioration of a piece of equipment are examples of the latter. Collectively, transactions provide the data that are included in accounting records and reports.

Accounting for economic transactions enables us to measure the success of an entity. The data for a transaction will not, however, accurately represent that transaction if any bias is involved. Therefore, unless there is evidence to the contrary, accountants assume **arm's-length transactions**. That is, they make the assumption that both parties—for example, a buyer and a seller—are rational and free to act independently, each trying to make the best deal possible in establishing the terms of the transaction. For example, suppose that you have saved to buy a car. You are willing to pay $2,000 for a certain used car but the owner wants to sell the car for $3,000. You haggle over the price and reach a market, or exchange, price of $2,500. The $2,500 is considered the accounting measurement of the transaction because it has been established through negotiation by independent parties acting in their own interests.

The Cost Principle

To further ensure objective measurements, accountants record transactions at **historical costs,** that is, at the amounts originally paid or received for goods and services in arm's-length transactions. The historical cost is assumed to represent the fair market value of the item at the date of the transaction because it reflects the actual use of resources by independent parties. Because of such factors as inflation (an increase in the general price level of goods and services), this amount may be quite different from the amount that would have to be paid at a later time to buy or replace the item.

To illustrate, assume that a company purchases land for $15,000 in cash in an arm's-length transaction. This transaction would be recorded at the historical cost of $15,000 and would be maintained in the records at that amount, no matter what the land might be valued at in the future. If, however, the company sells the land for $25,000 after 5 years, the $25,000 exchange price would be used to record this second transaction, recognizing the difference between

---

transactions *exchanges of goods or services between entities (whether individuals, businesses, or other organizations), as well as other events having an economic impact on a business*

arm's-length transactions *business dealings between independent and rational parties who are looking out for their own interests*

historical cost *the dollar amount originally exchanged in an arm's-length transaction; an amount assumed to reflect the fair market value of an item at the transaction date*

the original, or historical, cost and the current exchange price as a gain on the sale ($25,000 − $15,000 = $10,000 gain). In accounting, this convention of recording transactions at cost is often referred to as the **cost principle,** or cost concept.

When you read an accounting report, therefore, you should remember that the reported values are historical costs, reflecting exchange prices at various transaction dates. Although historical costs are useful in that they ensure objective accounting measurements, they have certain disadvantages. The most significant is that they do not necessarily reflect current values or current exchange prices.

cost principle *the idea that transactions are recorded at their historical costs or exchange prices at the transaction date*

The Monetary Measurement Concept

Accountants do not record all the activities of economic entities. They record only those that can be measured in monetary terms. Thus, the concept of **monetary measurement** becomes another important characteristic of the accounting model. For example, employee morale cannot be measured directly in monetary terms and is not reported in the accounting records. Wages paid or owed, however, are quantifiable in terms of money and are reported. In accounting, all transactions are recorded in monetary amounts, whether or not cash is involved. In the United States, the dollar is the unit of exchange and is thus the measuring unit for accounting purposes.

In using the dollar as the measuring unit to account for transactions, accountants have traditionally ignored the impact of inflation. Accountants record the dollar amount of a transaction using the number of dollars exchanged in the transaction; they do not consider the amount of goods or services that a dollar would have purchased last year or that it may purchase next year. If inflation becomes as significant in the United States as it is in some foreign countries, the accounting profession may be forced to provide data adjusted for inflation.

monetary measurement *the idea that money, as the common medium of exchange, is the accounting unit of measurement, and that only economic activities measurable in monetary terms are included in the accounting model*

The Going Concern Assumption

Another basic accounting assumption is that the entity being accounted for is a **going concern.** This means that, in the absence of evidence to the contrary, the entity is expected to continue in operation, at least for the foreseeable future. If accountants made the opposite assumption, that an entity was about to go out of business, they would record liquidation values (the generally lower prices that would be obtained if the entity were forced to sell all resources immediately) rather than the original exchange prices of transactions.

going concern *the idea that an accounting entity will have a continuing existence for the foreseeable future*

Double-Entry Accounting

The accounting model is built on a basic equation known as the **accounting equation:**

accounting equation *an algebraic equation that expresses the relationship between assets (resources), liabilities (obligations), and owners' equity (net assets, or the residual interest in a business after all liabilities have been met): Assets = Liabilities + Owners' Equity*

Assets	**=**	**Liabilities**	**+**	**Owners' Equity**
Resources		Obligations		Net Assets or Owners' Residual Interest
[Property rights of an entity expected to produce future benefits]		[Creditors' claims against assets]		[Resources less obligations; owners' claims against assets]

Since the accounting equation is an algebraic equation, both sides must always be equal. This is a very important point. An increase on one side of the equation must be matched exactly by an increase on the other side of the equation or by a decrease on the same side of the equation. To maintain this balance, accountants record all transactions with a double entry; that is, they balance the effect of each entry by making an offsetting entry. To illustrate, if a company borrows money from a bank, the transaction will be recorded on the company's books as an increase in cash (an asset) and a corresponding increase in the company's obligation (a liability) to the bank.

The accounting equation is presented here merely to give you a first glimpse of **double-entry accounting.** An in-depth discussion of the elements of the equation is reserved for Chapter 2. The mechanics of double-entry accounting are explained in detail in Chapters 3, 4, and 5.

double-entry accounting
a system of recording transactions in a way that maintains the equality of the accounting equation

> **To Summarize** *In conducting economic activities, entities enter into transactions that form the basis of accounting records. An accounting model has been developed for recording, measuring, and reporting an entity's transactions. This model is founded on certain basic concepts and several important assumptions, principles, and procedures. First, the organizational unit being accounted for is a separate entity. The entity may be small or large; a business or a nonprofit organization; a proprietorship, a partnership, or a corporation; but it is the organizational unit for which accounting records are kept and financial reports prepared. Second, the transactions are assumed to be arm's-length. Third, transactions are recorded at historical costs—the exchange prices at the transaction date. Fourth, transactions must be measurable in monetary amounts. Fifth, the accounting entity is assumed to be a going concern. Sixth, the accounting model uses a double-entry system that is based on the fundamental accounting equation: Assets = Liabilities + Owners' Equity.*

THE ENVIRONMENT OF ACCOUNTING

Objective 4
Describe the environment of accounting, including the effects of generally accepted accounting principles, international business, and ethical considerations.

Accounting functions in a dynamic environment. Changes in technology as well as economic and political factors can significantly influence accounting practice. Three particularly important factors are the development of generally accepted accounting principles, international business, and ethical considerations.

The Significance and Development of GAAP

As noted in the Business Environment Essay, the history of accounting can be traced several thousand years. Although the needs of early users were simple, their systems elementary, and their means of recording primitive (for example, the number of sheep inscribed with a stylus on a clay tablet), the cornerstone of accounting theory had been laid. Today is an age of electronic data processing. However, the requirement that prompted the first forms of accounting is still present: a need for reliable data as the basis for making economic decisions.

BUSINESS ENVIRONMENT ESSAY
The Evolution of Accounting

Accounting has evolved to meet the needs of those who use the information it provides. It can be argued that as a profession accounting is very young; however, as a service activity it dates back several thousand years. Among the earliest-known records are those of the Egyptians and Babylonians (from approximately 3000 B.C.), who recorded on clay tablets such transactions as the payment of wages and taxes. During the Roman period (which lasted from approximately 500 B.C. to A.D. 500), detailed tax records were maintained. In England under Henry I (around 1100), investigations of financial records similar to contemporary audits were conducted. And as early as 1494, an Italian Franciscan monk, Luca Pacioli, published a treatise containing the essential elements of the double-entry accounting system that is still in use today.

Early business activity centered on a barter economy. Instead of using cash (or credit cards) as a medium of exchange, people traded goods and services. The emphasis of accounting was on the receipt and disposition of these goods and services. As the means of transacting business changed, accounting also changed. The essential elements of the accounting process were maintained, but certain concepts and procedures were modified in order to serve the users of accounting information better.

The Industrial Revolution brought about changes in business, and therefore in accounting. Beginning in England in the mid-1800s, manufacturing processes started to evolve from individualized, handicraft systems to mass-production, factory systems. Technological advances not only provided new machinery but required new types of expenditures as well. Cost accounting systems had to be developed to analyze and control the financial operations of these increasingly complex manufacturing processes.

Also important to the evolution of accounting was the development of the corporate form of business. In a corporation, the owners of the business (the shareholders) often are not the managers of the business. This type of organization creates a need for accurate reporting of financial information to investors, creditors, security analysts, and the other external parties who have a direct interest in the company but who are not involved in its day-to-day management.

Governmental laws and requirements also have caused changes in the business environment and have stimulated the growth of accounting services. For example, the Companies Act in England in the 1850s established compulsory independent audits by chartered accountants. In the United States, the 1913 Revenue Act instituted the personal federal income tax, which created a need for income tax accounting. The 1934 Securities Exchange Act established the Securities and Exchange Commission (SEC), which monitors the reporting procedures of companies that sell stock publicly.

These and other factors have produced changes in the types of accounting services needed, and in many instances, they have affected the accounting procedures themselves. Thus, the profession of accounting has evolved to meet the needs of the people it serves in an ever-changing and increasingly complex business environment.

As this brief history makes clear, accounting is not an exact science. It is constantly evolving, changing to meet the needs of users and adapting itself to the economic environment in which it operates.

generally accepted accounting principles (GAAP) *authoritative guidelines that define accounting practice at a particular time*

Although business activity has changed and accounting principles have been modified accordingly, accounting practice is not subject to frequent and haphazard change. Accountants follow **generally accepted accounting principles (GAAP),** a body of standards or guidelines based on fundamental, time-tested accounting concepts. Only as concepts and principles prove useful are they incorporated into the body of knowledge referred to as generally accepted accounting principles.

It is particularly important to the external users of accounting information that GAAP be applied consistently in the preparation of financial reports. Unless the available data are somewhat comparable, investors and creditors cannot make good investing and lending decisions. Remember that individuals must constantly choose between alternatives—the investor between Company X and Company Y, and the banker between two loan applicants. Thus, GAAP enhances comparability and provides the foundation for sound decision making.

Development of GAAP has not been an overnight event; furthermore, it is an ongoing process. The first real period of interest in formally defining GAAP in the United States began in the early 1930s. It was sparked by several events, but particularly by the passage of the 1933 and 1934 Securities Acts and the establishment of the **Securities and Exchange Commission (SEC).** As part of this activity, the **American Institute of Certified Public Accountants (AICPA),** through its Committee on Accounting Procedures, began publishing Accounting Research Bulletins (ARBs), each of which identified and explained specific accounting principles. In 1959, the Accounting Principles Board (APB) was established by the AICPA, replacing the Committee on Accounting Procedures. The APB issued accounting opinions that were considered to be GAAP.

Securities and Exchange Commission (SEC) *the government body responsible for regulating the financial reporting practices of most publicly owned corporations in connection with the buying and selling of stocks and bonds*

American Institute of Certified Public Accountants (AICPA) *the national organization of CPAs in the United States*

Financial Accounting Standards Board (FASB) *the private organization responsible for establishing the standards for financial accounting and reporting in the United States*

In 1973, the **Financial Accounting Standards Board (FASB)** replaced the APB as the primary standard-setting body for accounting principles in the private sector of the United States. It is important to note that the FASB is not a part of the AICPA, as the APB was. It is an independent body, and its members are appointed by the Financial Accounting Foundation (representatives from a broad spectrum of the financial community). Furthermore, the seven members of the FASB are well paid, work full time on the Board, and must have severed all connections with their previous employers. The FASB is assisted by a large staff and by the Financial Accounting Standards Advisory Council (FASAC). Members of the Advisory Council serve on a part-time, voluntary basis for a period of one year, though they are often reappointed.

Though the FASB is currently recognized as the primary source of generally accepted accounting principles, it actually has been delegated this authority by the SEC, which has the legal right to determine accounting principles and procedures. The FASB issues *Statements of Financial Accounting Standards,* which establish new standards or amend those previously issued, and *Interpretations,* which clarify, explain, or elaborate on existing standards. Both the *Statements* and *Interpretations* are part of GAAP. The Board also issues *Statements of Financial Accounting Concepts,* which provide guidelines for solving problems and understanding the rationale behind the standards. They do not establish new standards or change existing standards and thus are not part of GAAP.

International Business

One of the significant environmental changes in recent years has been the expansion of business activity on a worldwide basis. As consumers, we are familiar with the wide array of products from other countries, such as electronics from Japan and clothing from Korea. On the other hand, many U.S. companies have operating divisions in foreign countries. Other American companies are located totally in the United States but have extensive transactions with foreign companies. The economic environment of today's business is truly based on a global economy.

As a result of the global economy, accounting practices often must be modified to reflect the international environment. For example, it was noted that the dollar is used as the measuring unit for accounting purposes in the United States. Naturally, other countries use their own currencies as measuring units, for example, pesos in Mexico or yen in Japan. For consistency, multinational U.S. companies must restate the results of overseas operations in terms of equivalent U.S. dollars. (The appendix to Chapter 16 discusses the mechanics of accounting for international operations and transactions.)

Accounting practices among countries vary widely. Attempts are being made to make those practices more consistent among countries. This is a slow, evolutionary process, and differences still exist. To the extent that accounting practices can be adopted uniformly on an international basis, the accounting reports of companies throughout the world will be more comparable.

Ethics in Accounting

Another environmental factor affecting accounting, and business in general, is the growing concern over ethics. This concern is highlighted as major incidents of improper acts are reported by the news media. Examples of impropriety are found in all areas of activity, for example, the Iran-Contra affair in government, the Pete Rose controversy in sports, the Jim and Tammy Bakker episode in religion, and the Ivan Boesky insider trading conviction in business.

Clearly, ethical considerations affect an entire society, not just accounting or business. However, ethics are especially important in accounting because of the trust placed in independent accountants to represent the public interest. The acceptance of this responsibility to the public is a distinguishing mark of the accounting profession.

Recognizing the importance of ethical behavior, the accounting profession has adopted a *Code of Professional Conduct,* which provides guidelines for the performance of services by its members (see Exhibit 1-3). For example, integrity, objectivity, and independence are key principles that are to be upheld by certified public accountants (CPAs). By accepting membership in the profession, CPAs assume an obligation of self-discipline above and beyond the requirements imposed by law. Adherence to the code calls for an unswerving commitment to honorable and ethical behavior, even at the sacrifice of personal advantage.

Accepting ethical responsibilities is as important for internal or management accountants as it is for independent CPAs. Ethical standards for management accountants have been established by the Institute of Management Accountants (IMA).

Chapter 1   *Accounting and Its Environment*   17

> **Exhibit 1-3**   *Highlights of AICPA Code of Professional Conduct**
>
> **SECTION I—PRINCIPLES**
>
> *Article I—Responsibilities* In carrying out their responsibilities as professionals, members should exercise sensitive professional and moral judgments in all their activities.
>
> *Article II—The Public Interest* Members should accept the obligation to act in a way that will serve the public interest, honor the public trust, and demonstrate commitment to professionalism.
>
> *Article III—Integrity* To maintain and broaden public confidence, members should perform all professional responsibilities with the highest sense of integrity.
>
> *Article IV—Objectivity and Independence* A member should maintain objectivity and be free of conflicts of interest in discharging professional responsibilities. A member in public practice should be independent in fact and appearance when providing auditing and other attestation services.
>
> *Article V—Due Care* A member should observe the professional's technical and ethical standards, strive continually to improve competence and the quality of services, and discharge professional responsibility to the best of the member's ability.
>
> *Article VI—Scope and Nature of Services* A member in public practice should observe the Principles of the *Code of Professional Conduct* in determining the scope and nature of services to be provided.
>
> **SECTION II—RULES**
>
> The Bylaws of the AICPA require that members adhere to the Rules of the *Code of Professional Conduct*. Any departures from the Rules must be justified. The current Rules are:
>
> Rule 101—Independence
> Rule 102—Integrity and Objectivity
> Rule 201—General Standards
> Rule 202—Compliance with Standards
> Rule 203—Accounting Principles
> Rule 301—Confidential Client Information
> Rule 302—Contingent Fees
> Rule 501—Acts Discreditable
> Rule 502—Advertising and Other Forms of Solicitation
> Rule 503—Commissions
> Rule 505—Form of Practice and Name
>
> Compliance with the AICPA *Code of Professional Conduct* depends primarily on a member's understanding and voluntary actions. However, there are provisions for reinforcement by peers and the public through public opinion, and ultimately by disciplinary proceedings, where necessary. Adherence to the *Code* helps ensure individual and collective ethical behavior by CPAs.
>
> * See, AICPA, *Code of Professional Conduct* (New York: American Institute of Certified Public Accountants, Inc., 1988).

You should not be so naive as to think that ethical dilemmas in business are rare. Such issues arise quite frequently. To help prepare you to enter the business world and to recognize and deal with ethical issues, we have included at the end of each chapter at least one ethics case. The decision model shown in Exhibit 1-4 may be useful in helping you learn to cope with ethical issues when they arise. Ethics is an important topic that should be considered carefully, with the ultimate goal of improving individual and collective behavior in society.

Exhibit 1-4 *Decision Model for Resolving Ethical Issues*

I. *Determine the facts:* What, where, when, how?
II. *Determine who the stakeholders are:* Identify each person affected by the decision, whether directly or indirectly (be all inclusive).
III. *Define the ethical issues:* State the Issues in Conflict form: Loyalty vs. confidentiality, integrity vs. job security, GAAP principles vs. personal benefit, good faith in negotiations vs. personal benefit, compliance with the law vs. short-term welfare, loyalty to superior vs. company policy, company policy vs. professional responsibility.
IV. *Identify the major principles, rules, values:* Integrity, quality, respect for persons, professional standards, professional responsibilities, respect for liberty, rights of others, job security, family welfare.
V. *Identify specific alternative courses of action:* List the major alternatives, including the extreme limits and reasonable interim or eventual compromises.
VI. *Compare the values and alternatives to determine if there is a clear decision:* Determine if there is one compelling principle or value that indicates the proper alternative.
VII. *Assess the consequences of each alternative:* Identify the short term and long term, positive and negative consequences for the major alternatives. Discuss each alternative with a trusted and objective person.
VIII. *Make your decision:* Balance the consequences against your primary principles and select the alternative that best fits.

To Summarize *Accounting functions in a dynamic environment. Generally accepted accounting principles (GAAP) have developed over time, and have been influenced by such events as the Securities Acts in 1933 and 1934. The primary standard-setting body for the private sector is the Financial Accounting Standards Board (FASB). The accounting environment includes business activity that is conducted on an international basis. Consequently, accounting practices often must be modified to reflect the accounting standards of different countries. Attempts are being made to establish comparable international accounting practices. There is increasing concern in society over ethics. High standards of ethical conduct are important, especially for certified public accountants who assume a special responsibility to the public. CPAs have adopted a* Code of Professional Conduct *that contains principles and rules as guidelines for the performance of accounting services. A similar code of ethics has been adopted by many management accountants.*

CAREER OPPORTUNITIES IN ACCOUNTING

Objective 5

Identify various career opportunities in accounting.

Accounting is not only a field of study—an academic discipline—it is also one of the fastest-growing professions in the United States and throughout the world, and it is playing an increasingly vital role in our economy. Accounting offers many attractive career opportunities. In addition, it provides an excellent educational background for anyone going into business.

Students who choose accounting as their major field of study in college may select from several career paths. These include working in public accounting, in industry, or for a nonprofit organization, including the government. In addition, accounting may be useful as a background for other careers. Some of these alternatives are shown in Exhibit 1-5.

Public Accounting

Most large CPA firms provide four services to clients: (1) auditing, (2) tax services, (3) management advisory services, and (4) small-business consulting. Smaller CPA firms also generally provide other accounting services; that is, they handle some or all of their clients' bookkeeping in addition to preparing their financial statements.

Auditing is the term generally used to describe the review and evaluation of a company's general-purpose financial statements and accounting procedures. The purpose of an audit is to investigate, test, and check the data prepared by the company and to analyze the appropriateness of its procedures. This review provides the basis for the auditor to issue a professional opinion as to the reliability of the information presented. Thus, independent audits add credibility to the financial statements.

A highly complex and technical field, *tax accounting* involves the use of data generated from the accounting process in the preparation of financial reports according to tax laws. These reports provide the basis for assessing an organization's tax liability. Tax accountants also become involved in tax planning and analyzing the tax consequences of managerial decisions.

A third main area of emphasis within CPA firms is *management advisory services,* which is a consulting activity generally provided on a project-by-project basis. For example, independent accountants may be asked by a client to make recommendations for improving a company's computerized information system or its procedures for safeguarding company resources.

Small-business consulting usually involves the analysis of a company's entire operation. In many ways, small-business consulting is similar to working as a general practitioner in medicine; that is, the accountant in this area must know something about all aspects of accounting and business and be able to perform a variety of tasks.

Industry

Within larger companies, there are at least three positions that offer major accounting career opportunities: (1) controller, (2) chief financial executive, and (3) internal auditor. Of course, no one begins in a top management position. However, entry-level accounting jobs are plentiful, and accounting majors are much in demand.

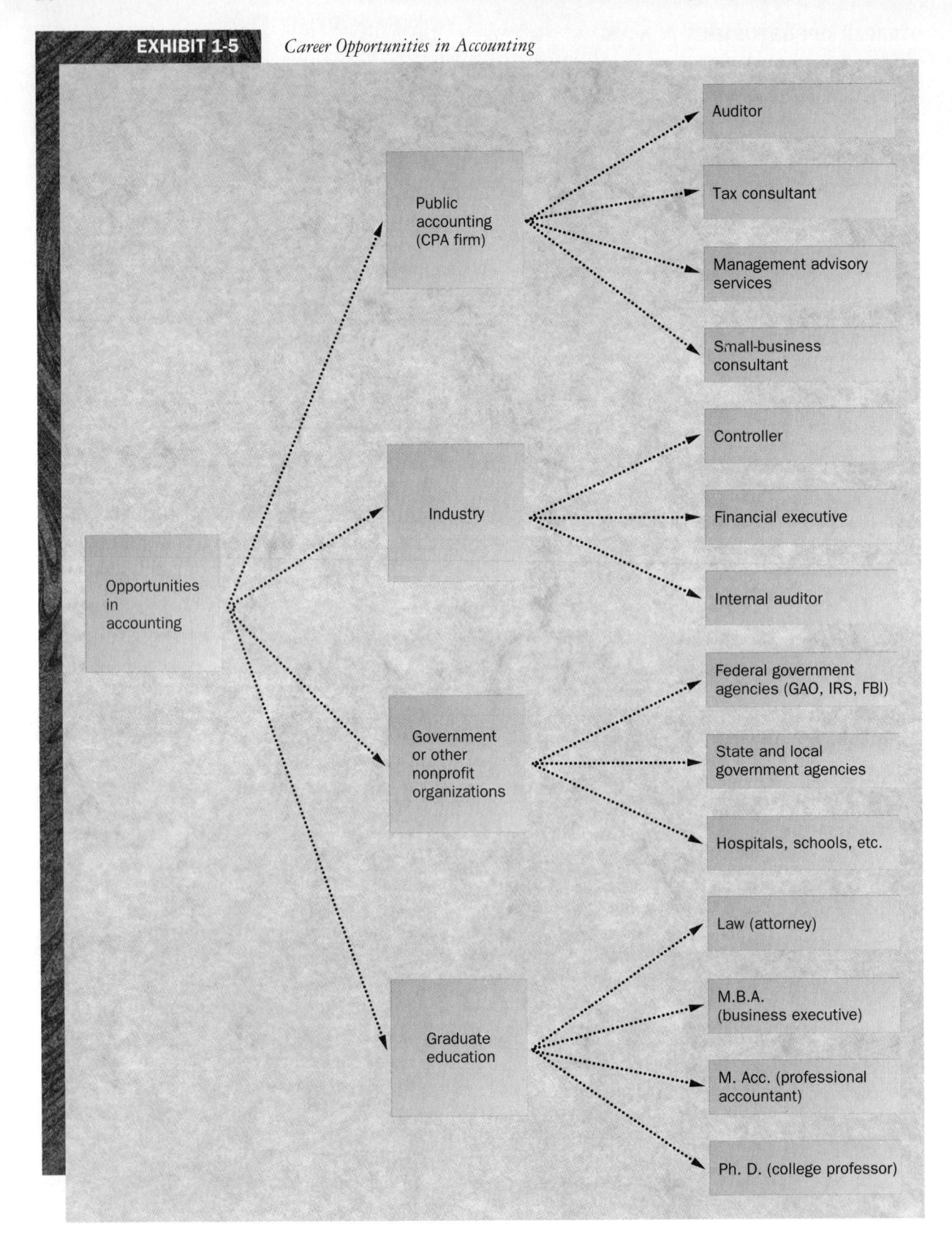

EXHIBIT 1-5 *Career Opportunities in Accounting*

Opportunities in accounting

- Public accounting (CPA firm)
  - Auditor
  - Tax consultant
  - Management advisory services
  - Small-business consultant
- Industry
  - Controller
  - Financial executive
  - Internal auditor
- Government or other nonprofit organizations
  - Federal government agencies (GAO, IRS, FBI)
  - State and local government agencies
  - Hospitals, schools, etc.
- Graduate education
  - Law (attorney)
  - M.B.A. (business executive)
  - M. Acc. (professional accountant)
  - Ph. D. (college professor)

As the title indicates, a controller is usually responsible for determining the costs of operating the business and for making sure they are not excessive. This includes projecting costs and revenues, comparing actual results with the projections, and determining whether and where the company needs better cost-control procedures. The controller also normally assumes at least some of the responsibility for preparing the external financial reports.

Employment as an accountant within a business may eventually lead to becoming the company's president or its chief financial executive. In the latter position, one is responsible for a broad range of activities, generally including all financial aspects of the company. More chief financial officers have backgrounds in accounting than in any other discipline.

Accountants employed by businesses also work as internal auditors. Generally, only larger organizations have internal audit staffs; smaller entities usually must rely more completely on independent CPAs. Internal auditing includes some of the same types of audit activity and the same kinds of challenges that exist in external auditing. However, internal auditing usually involves a more detailed investigation of the operations of a company, a function called operational auditing.

Government and Other Nonprofit Organizations

In the federal government, many agencies and units—such as the military, the Environmental Protection Agency (EPA), and the Federal Power Commission (FPC)—need audit staffs. Additional employers are the General Accounting Office (GAO), the Internal Revenue Service (IRS), and the Federal Bureau of Investigation (FBI). In addition, many accounting jobs are available in state and local government agencies and in nonprofit organizations such as schools, hospitals, and universities. All the financial and management accounting activities discussed earlier are applicable to nonprofit organizations. The reporting emphasis, however, is not on measuring income (or loss), but on determining how efficiently the organization is accomplishing its objectives. Consequently, different accounting concepts may be used. Accounting for nonprofit organizations is one of the fastest-growing segments of accounting practice.

Educational Preparation

Some college students decide to earn an undergraduate degree in accounting even though they have no intention of working as an accountant. This is particularly true for those who want to obtain a degree in law (J.D.) or a graduate degree in business administration (M.B.A.). Accounting is considered by many educators to be one of the two or three best prelaw majors.

Another alternative that should receive careful consideration is graduate study in accountancy. For those who would seek careers as professional accountants, a master's degree in accountancy (M. Acc.) is likely to provide an advantage; in fact, several states already have laws requiring that future CPAs have postbaccalaureate education.

Other students may want to consider a teaching career in accounting. To teach at the university level generally requires a Ph.D. degree and an interest in conducting research.

To Summarize *Career opportunities are plentiful for accounting majors. The general areas for employment are public accounting, industry, and nonprofit organizations. Accounting education is also useful as a background for other careers, such as banking, finance, and law.*

Review of Learning Objectives

Objective 1
Describe the purpose of accounting and explain its role in business and society. Accounting is a service activity designed to assist individuals and organizations in deciding how to allocate scarce resources and reach their financial objectives. It is used to accumulate, measure, and communicate economic data about organizations and to assist in the decision-making process.

Objective 2
Identify the primary users of accounting information. The primary users of accounting information are managers, creditors, investors, and other interested individuals and organizations. Management accounting deals primarily with the internal accounting functions of planning, implementing, and control. Financial accounting is concerned with reporting business activities and results to external parties. The objectives of both areas of accounting are measurement and communication of information for decision-making purposes.

Objective 3
Explain the basic concepts and assumptions that underlie financial accounting. The ground rules of accounting are established by basic assumptions and concepts. These include the entity concept, the assumption of arm's-length transactions, the cost principle, the concept of monetary measurement, the going concern assumption, and double-entry accounting, which is built on the fundamental accounting equation: Assets = Liabilities + Owners' Equity. Collectively, these concepts and assumptions determine the essential characteristics of the accounting model.

Objective 4
Describe the environment of accounting, including the effects of generally accepted accounting principles, international business, and ethical considerations. Accounting functions in a dynamic environment. The principles of accounting have evolved over time to meet the changing demands of the business environment. They are therefore not absolute. Only if they prove useful do they become generally accepted. Accounting principles provide comparable data for external users and need to be applied with judgment.

Since the 1930s, several organizations have been involved in the development of accounting principles. The American Institute of Certified Public Accountants (AICPA), the Securities and Exchange Commission (SEC), and the Financial Accounting Standards Board (FASB) are among the most prominent. The FASB is currently the primary standard-setting body for accounting principles in the private sector.

Accounting is practiced in an international environment. Accounting procedures in the United States sometimes must be modified to accommodate foreign operations. Attempts are being made to establish consistent and comparable accounting practices throughout the world.

Ethical considerations affect society and are particularly important for accountants, who have a special responsibility to the public. CPAs have adopted a *Code of Professional Conduct* to guide them in the performance of their duties.

Objective 5
Identify various career opportunities in accounting. Accounting offers many career opportunities. The broad categories include working for a CPA firm, a business, and the government or another nonprofit organization, or as an educator. Accounting also provides excellent background for other fields of endeavor, such as law.

Key Terms and Concepts

accounting *(6)*
accounting cycle *(6)*
accounting equation *(12)*
accounting model *(9)*
American Institute of Certified Public Accountants (AICPA) *(15)*
arm's-length transactions *(11)*
business *(5)*
corporation *(10)*
cost principle *(12)*
double-entry accounting *(13)*
entity *(9)*
financial accounting *(8)*
Financial Accounting Standards Board (FASB) *(15)*
generally accepted accounting principles (GAAP) *(15)*
going concern *(12)*
historical cost *(11)*
management accounting *(7)*
monetary measurement *(12)*
nonprofit organization *(5)*
partnership *(10)*
proprietorship *(10)*
Securities and Exchange Commission (SEC) *(15)*
stockholders (shareholders) *(10)*
transactions *(11)*

Discussion Questions

1. How does accounting provide a benefit to society?
2. What are the essential elements in decision making, and where does accounting fit into the process?
3. What types of personal decisions have required you to use accounting information?
4. What does the term *business* mean to you?
5. As you begin the study of accounting, what ideas do you have about its role and importance in the business world? Be specific by discussing your views of accounting in relation to marketing, finance, economics, and management.
6. In what ways are the needs of internal and external users of accounting information the same? In what ways are they different?
7. Explain why each of the following is important in accounting:
    (a) The entity concept.
    (b) The assumption of arm's-length transactions.
    (c) The cost principle.
    (d) The monetary measurement concept.
    (e) The going concern assumption.
8. Why is it important for financial reporting to be based on generally accepted accounting principles?
9. Of what significance is the growth of the Korean economy to accountants in the United States?
10. Why are ethical considerations so important to CPAs?
11. How is the *Code of Professional Conduct* intended to help CPAs fulfill their responsibilities?
12. Why is accounting one of the fastest growing professions?

Exercises

E1-1
The Role and Importance of Accounting

Assume that you are applying for a part-time job as an accounting clerk in a retail clothing establishment. During the interview, the store manager asks how you expect to contribute to the business. How would you respond?

E1-2
Accounting Information and Decision Making

You are the owner of Automated Systems Inc., which sells Apple computers and related data processing equipment. You are currently trying to decide whether to continue selling the Apple computer line or distribute the IBM personal computer instead. What information do you need to consider in order to determine how successful your business is or will be? What information would help you decide whether to sell the Apple or the IBM personal computer line? Use your imagination and general knowledge of business activity.

E1-3
The Benefits of Studying Accounting

Assume that one of the following describes your future occupation. How would knowledge of accounting benefit you?

1. Financial executive.
2. City manager.
3. Financial analyst.
4. Proprietor of a small business.
5. Politician planning to become a representative in Congress.

E1-4
The Entity Concept

Don Gifford lives in a small community where he is involved in a number of different business activities. He works for a real estate agency, is the mayor of the town, and prepares tax returns during the tax season. In accounting for the business activities of Mr. Gifford, which of the following items of information would be considered in determining how successful his businesses are?

1. Real estate commissions paid to Gifford.
2. The amounts paid for rent and utilities by the real estate agency.
3. Tax revenues for the town.
4. Salary paid to the mayor.
5. Fees paid for licenses to operate businesses in the town.
6. Parking tickets paid by citizens, including one by Gifford.
7. The amount of interest received by a client and reported on her tax return.
8. Supplies used in preparing tax returns.
9. Gas, oil, and related costs of operating the family car.
10. Fees received from tax clients.
11. City council expenditures.
12. Receipts from the sale of houses owned by the real estate agency.

E1-5
The Assumption of Arm's-Length Transactions

Kate Covey owns and manages a reception center. She has decided to build another center in a medium-sized town 50 miles away. Kate will manage both centers, and the new one will be built on some land she already owns. The land was purchased for personal use 10 years ago for $12,000. Would $12,000 be the appropriate value at which to record the land if it is used for the new reception center? Discuss.

E1-6
The Cost Principle

On January 1, 1994, Save-More Construction Company paid $150,000 in cash for a parcel of land to be used as the site of a new office building. During March, the company petitioned the City Council to rezone the area for professional office buildings. The City Council refused, preferring to maintain the area as a residential zone. After 9 months of negotiation, Save-More Construction convinced the Council to rezone the property for commercial use, thus raising its value to $200,000.

For accounting purposes, what value should be used to record the transaction on January 1, 1994? At what value would the property be reported at year-end, after the City Council rezoning? Explain why accountants follow the cost principle in recording transactions.

E1-7
The Monetary Measurement Concept

Many successful companies, such as Ford Motor Company, Exxon, and Marriott Corporation, readily acknowledge the importance and value of their employees. In fact, the employees of a company are often viewed as the most valued asset of the company. Yet in the asset section of the balance sheets of these companies there is no mention of the asset Employees. What is the reason for this oversight and apparent inconsistency?

E1-8
The Going Concern Assumption

Assume that you open an auto repair business. You purchase a building and buy new equipment. What difference does the going concern assumption make with regard to how you would account for these assets?

E1-9
Ethics in Accounting

The text has pointed out that ethics is an important topic, especially for CPAs. Derek Bok, former law professor and president of Harvard University, has suggested that colleges and universities have a special opportunity and obligation to train students to be more thoughtful and perceptive about moral and ethical issues. Other individuals have concluded that it is not possible to "teach" ethics. What do you think? Can ethics be taught? If you agree that we can teach ethics, how might the ethical dimensions of accounting be presented to students?

E1-10
Challenges to the Accounting Profession

Over 10 years ago, *Forbes* published an article calling accounting "the latest glamour profession." In May 1987, the same magazine published another article entitled, "Blood on the Ledger." In the more recent article, *Forbes* detailed some of the challenges confronting the accounting profession. From your general understanding of accounting and the current business environment, what are some of the challenges you see facing the accounting profession?

Ethics Case *Masters Building Supply*

You have been hired to prepare the financial reports for Masters Building Supply, a proprietorship owned by Charles Masters. You have encountered several payments made from the company bank account to a nearby university, and contact Charles Masters to find out how to classify these payments. Masters explains that those checks were written to pay his daughter's tuition and to purchase her textbooks and miscellaneous supplies. He then tells you to include the payments with other expenses of the business. "That way," he explains, "I can deduct the payments on my tax return. Why not, since it all comes out of the same pocket?"

How would you respond to Masters?

Chapter 2

Financial Statements: An Overview

Learning Objectives

After studying this chapter, you should be able to:
1. Understand the basic elements and formats of the general-purpose financial statements—balance sheet, income statement, and statement of cash flows.
2. Explain how the basic financial statements tie together.
3. Recognize the importance of the notes to the financial statements and the independent auditor's report.

• • • • • • • • • • • • •

SETTING THE STAGE

Not long ago, in a city of approximately 100,000 people, a family-owned muffler shop experienced a financial disaster. The muffler shop had operated in the city for over 45 years and had been quite successful. The owner of the shop, Dan Moosman, had five children, but only one, Rob, showed any interest in the business. Rob was an excellent mechanic and had worked installing mufflers during summer vacations while going to school. Rob's best friend was a boy named John Tuller. Unlike Rob, John was not a mechanic but instead had a passion for numbers. While Rob was assuming control of his father's muffler business, John was attending college and earning his degree in business. Even during this time, however, Rob and John (and their wives) socialized together often, usually playing tennis or cards or going out to dinner.

Upon graduation, John accepted a position with an accounting firm in a nearby state. Three years later, when the accountant for the muffler shop retired, Rob called John to see if he was interested in working for him in the muffler business. He offered John the position of accountant and business manager and promised him complete freedom to manage all accounting and business elements of the business. Rob was content to manage the 15 mechanics and make sure that the work performed was of the highest quality.

Over the next seven years, the business grew, and the shop replaced an increasing number of mufflers each year. However, after seven years, the business was so cash poor that Rob had to inform John he could no longer afford to employ him. Rob's wife, Becky, was recruited to perform the accounting and other business functions. It wasn't long until Becky realized that the accounting records didn't make sense and that money appeared to be missing. Rob and Becky retained a certified public accountant who prepared some financial statements and determined that their best friend, John, had stolen approximately $650,000 over the past seven years.

John's method of stealing was to embezzle approximately one-half of all the receipts that were paid in cash. If a customer paid with a check or by using a credit card, money was not stolen. However, when the payment was in currency, John would pocket half of the money and deposit the rest in the shop's bank account.

The method used by the CPA to determine how much money had been stolen by John was to prepare income statements, balance sheets, and statements of cash flow for each of the seven years. The income statements showed how much income the muffler shop should have made based on actual expenses and the number of muffler jobs performed; the balance sheets showed the amounts of assets the business should have had at the end of each year; and the statements of cash flows showed what the cash inflows and outflows should have been each year. Rob had not felt it necessary to have these kinds of financial statements prepared while his best friend was keeping the books.

Note: The facts in this scenario are real; the names of the individuals involved have been changed.

In this chapter, you will learn about these three primary financial statements. You will learn that the financial statements are summary reports that show how a business is doing and where it is having successes and failures. By reviewing the financial statements (the outputs of the accounting process) at the beginning of the book, we are trying to give you a sense of direction (a view of the forest) before we cover the details (so that you won't get lost in the trees). The financial statements covered in this chapter are the same ones used every day by millions of business owners, investors, and creditors as they attempt to evaluate how well or poorly organizations are doing.

As you study the financial statements, keep in mind that the purpose of financial reporting is to present as accurately and objectively as possible the financial position of a company and the progress it is making toward its goals. Do not be concerned if you do not yet fully understand all the items illustrated on the statements when you complete this chapter; it is meant only as an introduction. The income statement will be covered in depth in Chapters 6 and 7, the balance sheet in Chapters 8 through 14, and the statement of cash flows in Chapter 15.

GENERAL-PURPOSE FINANCIAL STATEMENTS

Objective 1
Understand the basic elements and formats of the general-purpose financial statements—balance sheet, income statement, and statement of cash flows.

general-purpose financial statements *the financial reports intended for use by a variety of external groups; they include the balance sheet, the income statement, and the statement of cash flows*

Because financial statements are used by so many different groups, they are called **general-purpose financial statements**. These statements provide users with the answers to three essential questions about a business entity.

1. What is the company's current financial status?
2. What were the company's operating results for the period?
3. How did the company obtain and use cash during the period?

The balance sheet shows an entity's financial position at a point in time. The income statement reports the results of operations for a period of time. The statement of cash flows shows the inflows and outflows of cash for the accounting period. The financial statements, along with notes and other information from management, are supplied to owners and others interested in the business, generally on an annual basis. This report is often referred to simply as the "Annual Report."

The Balance Sheet

balance sheet (statement of financial position) *the financial statement that shows the assets, liabilities, and owners' equity of an entity at a particular date*

The **balance sheet**, sometimes called the **statement of financial position**, provides a financial picture of an enterprise at a particular point in time. It shows a company's financial resources (assets) and the sources of, or claims against, those resources (liabilities and owners' equity). It is referred to as a balance sheet because total assets always equal the total of liabilities and owners' equity. This, you will recall, is in keeping with the basic accounting equation Assets = Liabilities + Owners' Equity. To help you understand a balance sheet, we will first describe briefly these three basic elements; then we will show how they are related by illustrating a simple balance sheet.

ASSETS. In general terms, **assets** may be defined as economic resources that are owned or controlled by an entity. To be included on the balance sheet, assets must be measured or estimated in monetary amounts. Assets include cash, accounts receivable (amounts owed from customers), inventory (goods held for sale), land, buildings, equipment, and even intangible items, such as copyrights and patents.

assets economic resources that are owned or controlled by an entity

LIABILITIES. The term **liability** is used to describe an entity's obligations to pay cash or transfer other economic resources to suppliers, banks, and other creditors. Liabilities represent creditors' claims against assets and are measured in monetary amounts. They generally indicate that economic resources such as cash, goods, or services will be transferred in the future to settle an obligation that has resulted from a past transaction. Some common liabilities are accounts payable (amounts owed to suppliers), notes payable (amounts owed to banks or others), and mortgages payable (amounts owed for purchased property, such as land or buildings).

liabilities obligations of an entity to pay cash or transfer other economic resources; liabilities represent claims against assets

OWNERS' EQUITY. If the basic accounting equation is restated in the form Assets − Liabilities = Owners' Equity, it becomes clear that the remaining claim against the assets of a business, after the liabilities have been deducted, is **owners' equity.** Thus, owners' equity is a residual amount; it represents the **net assets** (total assets minus total liabilities) available after all obligations have been satisfied. Obviously, if there are no liabilities (an unlikely situation, except at the start of a business), then the total assets are exactly equal to the owners' claims against those assets—the owners' equity.

owners' equity (net assets) the ownership interest in the assets of an entity; equals total assets minus total liabilities

Investors transfer resources, usually cash, to a business in return for part ownership of the business. Investments by owners increase total assets (resources) and thus increase owners' equity. If the business is a corporation, the amount contributed by investors is called **capital stock,** and the investor's ownership interest is represented by stock certificates. Thus, the owners of a corporation are called stockholders or shareholders, and the owners' equity section of the balance sheet is sometimes referred to as *stockholders' equity.* Owner investments in proprietorships and partnerships are identified simply as *capital* since no shares of stock are issued when investments are made by a proprietor or partner.

capital stock the portion of a corporation's owners' equity contributed by investors (owners) in exchange for shares of stock

Distributions to owners decrease total assets and therefore decrease owners' equity. A distribution involves the transfer of assets, usually cash, from the business to the owners. If the business is a corporation, distributions to the owners (stockholders) are called **dividends.** In a proprietorship or partnership, distributions to owners are usually referred to as withdrawals or *drawings.*

dividends distributions to the owners (stockholders) of a corporation

Owners' equity is also affected by the results of a company's operations. If a business is profitable, owners' equity is increased; if a business is not profitable, owners' equity is decreased. For a corporation, the amount of accumulated earnings of the business that have not been distributed to owners is called

retained earnings *the portion of a corporation's owners' equity that has been earned from profitable operations and not distributed to stockholders*

retained earnings. The amount of retained earnings plus capital stock equals the corporation's total owners' equity. In a proprietorship or partnership, past earnings are not shown separately. Instead, total owners' equity is reported as capital, which includes both owner investments and undistributed earnings. In a partnership, a capital amount is shown for each owner. Those elements dealing with profitability are included in the income statement and are discussed later in this chapter.

In summary, owners' equity and liabilities show the sources of assets committed to or invested in a business. As the accounting equation makes clear, those who made the commitment have claims against the resources of the entity. Creditors' claims are represented by liabilities, whereas owners' equity represents the amount of assets provided by owners or derived from operations, as shown in Exhibit 2-1.

THE FORMAT OF A BALANCE SHEET. A simple balance sheet for a corporation is shown in Exhibit 2-2. The heading includes the name of the company and the title and date of the statement. A balance sheet is presented for a particular date because it reports a company's financial position at a point in time. The balance sheet in Exhibit 2-2 presents the company's financial position as of December 31, 1994.

As illustrated, the balance sheet is divided into the three major sections we have described: assets, liabilities, and owners' equity. The asset section identifies the types of assets owned by a firm (land, for example) and the monetary amounts associated with those assets. The liability section defines the extent and nature of a firm's borrowings (through a mortgage, for example) and provides an indication of its financial stability.

Owners' equity completes the balance sheet. This section identifies the portion of a firm's resources that were contributed by owners in exchange for shares of stock and the amount of undistributed earnings the firm has earned since inception. Together with liabilities, owners' equity indicates how an entity is financed (whether by borrowing or by owner contributions and operating profits).

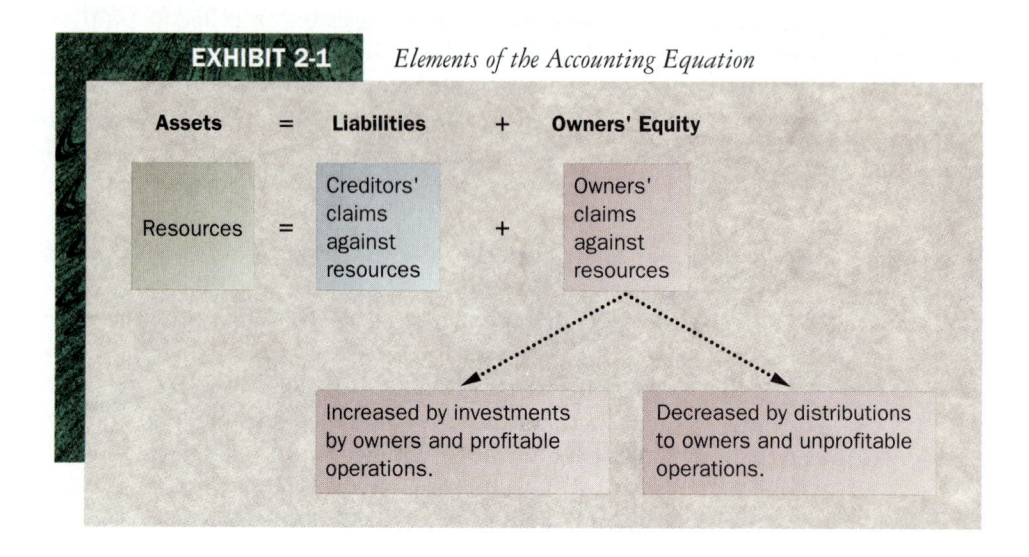

EXHIBIT 2-1 *Elements of the Accounting Equation*

Assets	=	Liabilities	+	Owners' Equity
Resources	=	Creditors' claims against resources	+	Owners' claims against resources

Increased by investments by owners and profitable operations.

Decreased by distributions to owners and unprofitable operations.

Exhibit 2-2

Professional Services, Inc.
Balance Sheet
December 31, 1994

Assets		Liabilities and Owners' Equity		
Cash	$2,600	**Liabilities:**		
Accounts receivable	2,500	Accounts payable	$ 4,200	
Office supplies	1,200	Mortgage payable	35,000	
Land	8,000	Total liabilities		$39,200
Buildings (net)*	40,000			
		Owners' equity:		
		Capital stock (500 shares)	$ 5,000	
		Retained earnings	10,100	
		Total owners' equity		15,100
		Total liabilities and		
Total assets	$54,300	owners' equity		$54,300

* Buildings and other long-term operating assets are reported "net" of depreciation, a concept that is explained later in the text.

People often think that because owners' equity represents the residual portion of the balance sheet equation—the remainder after liabilities have been subtracted from assets—it refers to the current value or the worth of a firm. If the assets were stated at current market values—the amounts that would have to be paid today to replace items purchased, say, 10 years ago—this would be the case. However, since assets are recorded at historical (original) costs, owners' equity merely shows two ways in which resources are brought into a firm (owner contributions and earnings of the business). A firm's actual worth would depend on how much it could be sold for in an arm's-length transaction, which may be more or less than the total owners' equity reported on the balance sheet.

A CLASSIFIED AND COMPARATIVE BALANCE SHEET. Readers of financial statements usually need to compare the statements of different companies. To facilitate that comparison, most companies prepare **classified balance sheets,** which means that assets and liabilities are subdivided into current and noncurrent categories. Classification assists readers in evaluating a company's financial position and in comparing a company's financial position to that of other companies.

To illustrate a classified balance sheet for a corporation, we again consider the balance sheet for Professional Services, Inc. In Exhibit 2-3, the assets are classified as current, or short term, and noncurrent, or long term. Current assets include cash and other assets that are expected to be converted to cash within a year. Current assets generally are listed in decreasing order of liquidity (convertibility to cash), and so cash is listed first, followed by the other current assets, such as accounts receivable. Long-term assets, such as land, buildings and equipment, include assets that a company needs in order to operate its business over an extended period of time.

classified balance sheet a balance sheet in which assets and liabilities are subdivided into current and noncurrent categories

Exhibit 2-3

Professional Services, Inc.
Comparative Balance Sheets
December 31, 1994 and 1993

Assets	1994	1993	Liabilities and Owners' Equity	1994	1993
Current assets:			**Current liabilities:**		
Cash	$ 2,600	$ 3,600	Accounts payable	$ 4,200	$ 4,500
Accounts receivable	2,500	2,100	**Long-term liabilities:**		
Office supplies	1,200	800	Mortgage payable	35,000	36,000
Total current assets	$ 6,300	$ 6,500	Total liabilities	$39,200	$40,500
Long-term assets:			**Owners' equity:**		
Land	$ 8,000	$ 3,000	Capital stock (500 shares)	$ 5,000	$ 5,000
Buildings*	40,000	42,000	Retained earnings	10,100	6,000
Total long-term assets	$48,000	$45,000	Total owners' equity	$15,100	$11,000
Total assets	$54,300	$51,500	Total liabilities and owners' equity	$54,300	$51,500

*As noted in Exhibit 2-2, buildings are reported net of depreciation; the $2,000 decrease in Buildings reflects depreciation for 1994.

Like assets, liabilities usually are classified as either current (obligations expected to be paid within a year) or long term. A particular account payable, for example, usually would be paid within 30 days or so, whereas a mortgage may remain on the books for 20 or 30 years until it is fully paid.

You will notice also that the balance sheet in Exhibit 2-3 includes financial information for both the current year and the preceding year. Most companies prepare such **comparative financial statements** so that readers can identify any significant changes in particular items. For example, Professional Services has increased its land holdings significantly this past year. (For a more complex illustration of a classified and comparative balance sheet, see the financial statements of General Mills at the back of the book.)

comparative financial statements *financial statements in which data for two or more years are shown together*

LIMITATIONS OF A BALANCE SHEET. Although the balance sheet is useful in showing the financial status of a company, it does have three primary limitations. First, as we have indicated, the balance sheet generally does not reflect the current value or worth of a company. All items are listed at their original cost, which may be very different from their current market values.

Second, a balance sheet reports only those resources that can be expressed in monetary (dollar) terms. This means that some items commonly considered to be assets or liabilities are omitted. The development of major new products, the discovery of new sources of materials, being situated in a strategic location, the presence of a staff of talented and loyal employees, high morale, good management, are all examples of assets that do not appear on the balance sheet because they are difficult to quantify. Similarly, the emission of pollutants into the air is not recorded on the balance sheet but could be considered a liability.

Third, two similar companies may use different accounting methods for the same types of transactions, or may categorize and report similar transactions differently, making comparisons between companies difficult. For example, one company may classify its assets as current, land and buildings, and other; another company may have only current and long-term assets. Without additional details, a reader would not be able to compare the land holdings of the two companies.

Despite its deficiencies, the balance sheet is a useful source of information regarding the financial position of a business. In fact, when a balance sheet is classified, and when comparative data are provided, the statement provides a relatively clear picture of a business's financial position.

> **To Summarize** *The balance sheet provides a summary of the financial position of an entity at a particular date. It helps external users assess the financial relationships between assets (resources) and the liabilities and owners' equity (claims against those resources). Assets and liabilities are usually classified as either current or long term and are presented in descending order of liquidity. For a corporation, owners' equity consists of capital stock and retained earnings; for a proprietorship or partnership, it contains a capital amount for each owner. Classified and comparative balance sheets provide useful information for readers of financial statements.*

The Income Statement

income statement (statement of earnings) *the financial statement that summarizes the revenues generated and the expenses incurred by an entity during a period of time*

The **income statement,** or **statement of earnings,** shows the results of an entity's operations for a period of time (a month, a quarter, or a year). It summarizes the revenues generated and the costs incurred (expenses) to generate those revenues. The "bottom line" of an income statement is net income or net loss, the difference between revenues and expenses. To help you understand an income statement, we must first define its elements—revenues, expenses, and net income or net loss.

revenues *increases in a company's resources from the sale of goods or services*

REVENUES. The term **revenues** refers to increases in the resources of an entity from the sale of goods or services. The increases are derived primarily from the normal operations of the business. Manufacturing and merchandising entities receive revenues from the sale of merchandise. A service enterprise (for example, a CPA firm) generates revenues from the fees it charges for the services it performs. Companies might also earn revenues from other activities, for example, from charging interest or collecting rent.

When goods are sold or services performed, the resulting revenue is in the form of cash or credit (a promise from the buyer to pay for the goods or services by a specified date in the future). Revenues thus represent an increase in total assets, which, in turn, increases owners' equity.

expenses *costs incurred in the normal course of business to generate revenues*

EXPENSES. The term **expenses** refers to the costs incurred in normal business operations to generate revenues. Employee salaries and utilities used during a period are two common examples of expenses. Like revenues, expenses represent flows of resources during a period of time, but expenses are outflows instead of inflows, and therefore decrease owners' equity.

In considering revenues and expenses, you should note that not all inflows of resources are revenues, nor are all outflows of resources considered to be expenses of the current period. For example, cash may be received by borrowing from a bank, which is an increase in a liability, not a revenue. Similarly, cash may be paid for supplies, which is an exchange of one asset for another asset, not an expense of the current period. This concept will be discussed further in Chapters 3 and 4.

NET INCOME (OR NET LOSS). Net income, sometimes called earnings or profit, is an overall measure of the performance of a business entity. It reflects the business's accomplishments (revenues) in relation to its efforts (expenses) during a particular period of time. If revenues exceed expenses, the result is called net income (Revenues − Expenses = Net Income); if expenses exceed revenues, the difference is called net loss. Because net income results in an increase in resources from operations, owners' equity is also increased; a net loss will decrease owners' equity.

It is important to note the difference between revenues and net income. Both concepts represent an increase in the net assets of a firm. However, revenues represent total resource increases; expenses are subtracted from revenues to derive income or loss. Thus, whereas revenue is a "gross" concept, income (or loss) is a "net" concept.

net income (or net loss) *a measure of the overall performance of a business entity; equal to revenues minus expenses for the period*

THE FORMAT OF AN INCOME STATEMENT. A simple income statement is presented in Exhibit 2-4. It begins with the name of the company, the title of the report, and the period covered. In contrast to the balance sheet, which is "as of" a particular date, the income statement refers to the "year ended." Remember, the income statement covers a period of time; the balance sheet is a report at a point in time. Also note that the income statement reports the resource inflows (revenues) and resource outflows (expenses) from operations, whereas the balance sheet reports the status of resources (assets) and claims against those resources (liabilities and owners' equity).

The income statement usually shows two main categories—revenues and expenses—although several subcategories may also be presented. Revenues are listed first. The expenses incurred to generate the revenues for the period are listed next. Typical operating expenses for most businesses are employee salaries, utilities, and advertising. As you will see in Chapter 6, an additional expense for the cost of the goods sold must be subtracted from sales revenue in the case of manufacturing and merchandising enterprises.

After all operating expenses are identified and totaled, they are subtracted from revenues. For a corporation, the resulting difference is called *income before taxes.* An income tax expense is then subtracted, resulting in the corporation's *net income.* Unlike corporations, proprietorships and partnerships are not taxed directly, and the difference between revenues and operating expenses is the net income of the business. This income is then reported by the individual owners in their tax returns.

earnings (or loss) per share *the amount of net income (or loss) related to each share of stock*

One final bit of information required on the income statements of corporations is **earnings per share** (EPS). This EPS amount is computed by dividing the net income (earnings) for the current period by the number of shares of

Exhibit 2-4

Professional Services, Inc.
Comparative Income Statements
For the Years Ended December 31, 1994 and 1993

	1994	1993
Revenues	$48,800	$45,100
Expenses:		
Salaries expense	$33,500	$31,200
Utilities expense	1,800	1,700
Advertising expense	3,400	2,900
Supplies expense	900	700
Miscellaneous expenses	2,600	2,800
Total expenses	$42,200	$39,300
Income before taxes	$ 6,600	$ 5,800
Income taxes*	2,000	1,750
Net income	$ 4,600	$ 4,050

Earnings per share
1993: $4,050 ÷ 500 shares = $8.10
1994: $4,600 ÷ 500 shares = $9.20

* Income statements for proprietorships and partnerships do not include income taxes since earnings are taxable to the individual owners and not to the business entity. See further details in Chapters 13 and 14.

---

stock outstanding during the period. If the company reported a net loss for the period, the income statement would show the **loss per share** (the net loss divided by the number of shares of stock outstanding). Earnings per share information tells readers whether net income is growing in relation to the size of the company's equity. Corporations are required to present the EPS figure because it is viewed by many analysts as an important measure of a company's profitability.

Like the balance sheet, the income statement usually shows the comparative results for two or more periods, which tells investors and creditors how profitable an enterprise has been during the current period as compared with earlier periods. Thus, as illustrated in Exhibit 2-4, the comparative income statement indicates trends and provides some basis for predicting the future success of a business. Such relationships as the ratio of expenses to revenues and of net income to owners' equity also provide useful information in interpreting the operating results of a company. These relationships are identified through financial statement analysis, which is covered in Chapter 16.

In addition to an income statement, corporations sometimes prepare a **statement of retained earnings.** This statement identifies changes in retained earnings from one accounting period to the next. As illustrated in Exhibit 2-5, the statement shows a beginning retained earnings balance, the net income for the period, a deduction for any dividends paid, and an ending retained earnings balance. For Professional Services, it is assumed that $500 of dividends were paid during 1994.

statement of retained earnings the report that shows the changes in retained earnings during a period of time

Exhibit 2-5

Professional Services, Inc.
Statement of Retained Earnings
For the Year Ended December 31, 1994

Retained earnings, January 1, 1994	$ 6,000
Add net income for the year	4,600
	$10,600
Less dividends	500
Retained earnings, December 31, 1994	$10,100

Corporations sometimes present a *statement of stockholders' equity* instead of a statement of retained earnings. The statement of stockholders' equity, illustrated in Chapter 13, is more detailed and includes changes in capital stock as well as changes in retained earnings.

> **To Summarize** *The income statement provides a measure of the success of an enterprise over a specified period of time. It shows the major sources of revenues generated and the expenses associated with those revenues, with the difference between revenues and expenses being net income or net loss. It matches efforts against accomplishments over a period of operating activity and helps external users evaluate the future success of a company. The income statements of corporations must also include earnings per share, which is a measure of the company's profitability. Like balance sheets, income statements are usually prepared on a comparative basis. A statement of retained earnings is often provided by corporations. Chapters 6 and 7 examine the income statement in detail.*

The Statement of Cash Flows

statement of cash flows
the financial statement that shows an entity's cash inflows (receipts) and outflows (payments) during a period of time

The **statement of cash flows** shows the cash inflows (receipts) and cash outflows (payments) of an entity during a period of time. As shown in Exhibit 2-6, companies receive cash primarily by selling goods or providing services, by selling other assets, by borrowing, and by receiving cash from investments by owners. They use cash to pay current operating expenses such as wages, utilities, and taxes; to purchase additional buildings, land, and otherwise expand operations; to repay loans; and to pay their owners a return on the investments that have been made. These cash flows are classified according to three main activities: operating, investing, and financing.

Because the statement of cash flows involves concepts and analytical procedures that have not yet been introduced, we will not discuss its preparation at this point. The preparation and interpretation of a statement of cash flows will

EXHIBIT 2-6   *Cash Flows*

Operating activities:
- Sell goods
- Provide services

Investing activities:
- Sell buildings
- Sell land

Financing activities:
- Borrow money
- Receive investments from owners

↓

Inflows of Cash (Receipts)

↓

CASH

↓

Outflows of Cash (Payments)

↓

Operating activities:
- Pay wages
- Pay utilities
- Pay taxes

Investing activities:
- Purchase buildings
- Purchase land

Financing activities:
- Repay loans
- Distributions to owners

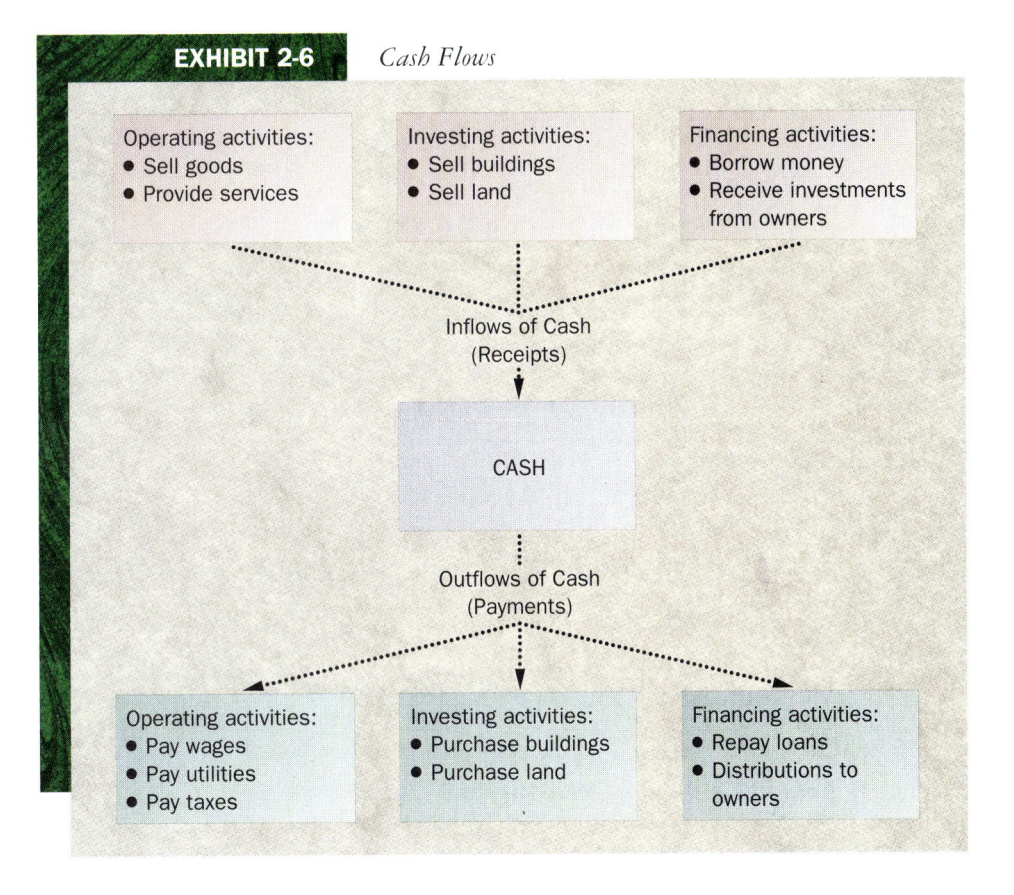

be explained in Chapter 15, when you are better able to see its importance and understand its complexities. For now, recognize that the statement of cash flows is one of the three major financial statements and that it shows the significant cash inflows and outflows of a company during a period of time. Exhibit 2-7 is provided as a simple illustration of a statement of cash flows for Professional Services, Inc. for the year ended December 31, 1994. As with the balance sheet and income statement, companies usually provide comparative statements of cash flows. However, we have elected not to show comparative statements of cash flows to keep this illustration simple. (The General Mills' financial statements at the back of the book provide comparative statements of cash flows.)

To Summarize *The statement of cash flows is one of the three major financial statements. It shows the significant cash inflows (receipts) and cash outflows (payments) of an entity for a period of time. These cash flows are classified according to operating, investing, and financing activities. Chapter 15 provides a more complete discussion of the statement of cash flows.*

Exhibit 2-7

Professional Services, Inc.
Statement of Cash Flows
For the Year Ended December 31, 1994

Cash Flow from Operating Activities

Cash receipts from:		
Customers		$48,400
Cash payments for:		
Salaries	$33,500	
Utilities	1,800	
Advertising	3,400	
Supplies & miscellaneous expenses	2,200	
Taxes	2,000	42,900
Net cash provided by operating activities		$ 5,500

Cash Flow from Investing Activities

Cash receipts	$ -0-	
Cash payments to purchase land	(5,000)	
Net cash used in investing activities		(5,000)

Cash Flow from Financing Activities

Cash receipts	$ -0-	
Cash payments for dividends	(500)	
Cash payments to repay mortgage principal	(1,000)	
Net cash used in financing activities		(1,500)
Net decrease in cash		$ (1,000)
Cash at beginning of year		3,600
Cash at end of year		$ 2,600

HOW THE FINANCIAL STATEMENTS TIE TOGETHER

Objective 2
Explain how the basic financial statements tie together.

articulation *the interrelationships among the financial statements*

Although we have introduced the general-purpose financial statements as if they were independent of one another, in fact they are interrelated and tie together; that is, they "articulate." In accounting language, **articulation** refers to the relationship between an operating statement (the income statement or the statement of cash flows) and comparative balance sheets, whereby an item on the operating statement helps explain the change in an item on the balance sheet from one period to the next.

For example, a change in owners' equity from one accounting period to the next is explained in large part by the addition of net income (or the subtraction of net loss). Any remaining difference would result from additional investments by or distributions to owners. Exhibits 2-3 and 2-4 can be used to illustrate this point. During 1994, Professional Services had net income of $4,600 (Exhibit 2-4). In 1993, total owners' equity was $11,000, and in 1994, it was $15,100 (Exhibit 2-3). The difference between the two amounts is $4,100 ($15,100 − $11,000). This net increase in owners' equity is the result of the increase from net income less the dividends paid ($4,600 − $500 = $4,100). As you study the financial statements, these relationships will become clearer and you will understand the concept of articulation better.

Chapter 2 *Financial Statements: An Overview* 39

> **BUSINESS ENVIRONMENT ESSAY**
> *Are Financial Statements Too Complex?*
>
> Financial statement data, including sales, earnings, and earnings per share numbers, are important for investors, creditors, and others who make investment and lending decisions. However, many people are becoming concerned that financial statements are so complicated that investors either don't read the statements or can't understand them. Lowe Co.'s vice president for investor relations summarized this fear when he said, "By the time most shareholders wade through 50 pages of an annual report, they don't care what the results are." To overcome this problem, Lowe Co. supplemented its 1984 annual report with the following postcard.
>
> Date March 1, 1984
> Dear Investor:
>
> - We want you to be the first to know Lowe's results for 1983.
> - Sales were $1.43 (billion, ~~million~~). This was a (record, ~~near record, not a record~~).
> - Earnings were $50.6 (~~billion~~, million). This was a (record, ~~near record, not a record~~).
> - Per share earnings were $1.40. This was a (record, ~~near record, not a record~~).
> - Dividends paid were $.32 per share.
> - Share price in the year (increased, ~~decreased~~) by 12%.
> - Prospects for the new year look to be (~~great~~, good, ~~about average, not so good, poor, just plain awful~~).
> - Full Annual Report will be mailed about April 25.
>
> Chairman Robert L. Strichland
> President Leonard G. Herring
>
> *Source:* Adapted from *Forbes*, April 30, 1984, p. 108.

NOTES TO FINANCIAL STATEMENTS

Objective 3
Recognize the importance of the notes to the financial statements and the independent auditor's report.

notes to financial statements *explanatory information considered an integral part of the financial statements*

The **notes to financial statements** are a required, integral part of those statements because they provide vital information that cannot be conveyed by the titles and dollar amounts of statement items. For example, liabilities are listed on the balance sheet at certain amounts, but a note is usually necessary to describe specific payable dates and any special circumstances. Thus, explanatory notes are necessary to provide a better understanding of the information in the statements.

The notes generally follow a standard sequence. The first note describes the accounting policies and principles followed by the business. Other notes refer to specific items in the statements; they are usually cross-referenced to those items and presented in the order in which the items appear in the statements. As illustrated by the General Mills' statements at the back of the book, a company usually will present the notes in a special section of the annual report adjacent to the statements themselves.

THE AUDIT REPORT

A company's financial statements are often audited by an independent **certified public accountant (CPA)**. A CPA firm will issue an **audit report** that expresses an opinion about whether the statements present fairly a company's

certified public accountant (CPA) *a special designation given to an accountant who has passed a national uniform examination and has met other certifying requirements; CPA certificates are issued and monitored by state boards of accountancy or similar agencies*

audit report *a report issued by an independent CPA that expresses an opinion about whether the financial statements present fairly a company's financial position, operating results, and cash flows in accordance with generally accepted accounting principles*

financial position, operating results, and cash flows in accordance with generally accepted accounting principles. Note that the financial statements are the responsibility of a company's management and not of the CPA. Although not all company records have to be audited, audits are needed for many purposes. For example, a banker sometimes will not make a commercial loan without first receiving audited financial statements from a prospective borrower. As another example, most securities cannot be sold to the general public until they are registered with the Securities and Exchange Commission, and the registration process requires inclusion of audited financial statements.

An audit report does not guarantee accuracy, but it does provide added assurance that the financial statements are not misleading since they have been examined by an unbiased and independent professional. However, the CPA cannot examine every transaction upon which the summary figures in the financial statements are based, so the accuracy of the statements must remain the responsibility of the company's management. The audit report for General Mills is presented immediately after the notes to the financial statements at the back of the book.

BUSINESS ENVIRONMENT ESSAY
Should Auditors Be Responsible for Detecting Fraud?

More lawsuits have been filed against CPAs in the last 15 years than during the entire previous history of the accounting profession. One possible reason is that the public expects auditors to discover fraud, if it exists, when conducting an audit.

Auditors maintain that an audit is not a guarantee and that audits are not conducted specifically to uncover fraudulent practices. Auditors claim further that the accounting procedures used and the resulting financial statements are the responsibility of company management. The auditor's responsibility is to express a professional opinion about those statements.

Recently, however, accountants have acknowledged a responsibility for catching "material fraud." For example, in their audit report, auditors state that the audit is conducted on a test basis to obtain reasonable assurance that the financial statements are free from material misstatement.

For some investors, this acceptance by auditors of a partial responsibility for detecting fraud is not sufficient. As a result, when an investment goes sour, especially when there is fraud involved, more and more investors are suing the auditors. To give just one example, late in 1988 the stock of Regina Co., a maker of vacuum cleaners, collapsed shortly after the issuance of its annual report with financial statements audited by one of the large CPA firms. The auditors had not detected management fraud and are now being sued by many investors in a class-action suit.

One such investor stated, "Unsophisticated investors like me just can't put a lot of faith in an auditor's opinion. It's not magic." A representative of the CPA firm countered, "We're only human and prefer to trust the people we're auditing." Other members of the firm expressed the belief that company management, bent on fraud, can fool the auditors.

The answer to the question—should auditors be expected to detect fraud—is not an easy one. It is a question that is being asked often in business and government circles. What do you think?

Source: Adapted from an article by Lee Berton, "Battle of the Books: Audit Firms Are Hit By More Investor Suits for Not Finding Fraud," *The Wall Street Journal,* January 24, 1989, p. 1 col. A.

Most audit reports will have at least three paragraphs as follows:

- The *introductory paragraph* explains what statements have been audited and describes the specific responsibilities of management and the auditors.
- The *scope paragraph* describes what an audit is, indicating that an audit is based only on tests of accounting records and transactions but that it does provide a reasonable basis for the audit opinion.
- The *opinion paragraph* gives the auditor's opinion about the financial statements and references conformity to generally accepted accounting principles (GAAP).

If there are exceptions to GAAP or if certain accounting procedures have changed from those employed in previous years, these would be noted in additional paragraphs of the audit report.

You will note that the audit report for General Mills refers to the **consolidated financial statements** of General Mills. This means that the statements represent the total economic picture of General Mills, including any companies that General Mills owns or controls. Most financial statements presented in the annual reports to stockholders are consolidated financial statements. This topic is discussed more fully in the appendix to Chapter 13.

<small>**consolidated financial statements** *statements that report the combined results, financial position, and cash flows of two or more legally separate but affiliated companies as if they were one economic entity*</small>

Review of Learning Objectives

Objective 1

Understand the basic elements and formats of the general-purpose financial statements—balance sheet, income statement, and statement of cash flows. The overall objective of financial reporting is to assist decision makers in allocating resources and meeting their goals. By providing information concerning an entity's financial position, the results of its operations, and its cash flows, the general-purpose financial statements satisfy the needs of a variety of users: creditors, stockholders, potential investors, financial analysts, and others.

The balance sheet shows an entity's financial position at a particular date. It discloses the relationships between the firm's economic resources (assets) and the sources of, or claims against, those resources. (Creditor claims are called liabilities, and ownership claims are called owners' equity.) Thus, the balance sheet reflects the basic accounting equation Assets = Liabilities + Owners' Equity. For ease of reading, the balance sheet usually is classified. Assets and liabilities are divided into current and long term and appear in decreasing order of liquidity. For a corporation, owners' equity (stockholders' equity) consists of capital stock and retained earnings. Most companies present comparative balance sheets.

The income statement reports the results of a company's operations in terms of its overall income or loss for a period of time. It itemizes revenues and expenses and shows the resulting net income (or net loss). Revenues reflect increases in a company's resources from the sale of goods or services. Expenses refer to the costs incurred in the normal course of business to generate revenues. Net income, or earnings, is a measure of the overall performance of a business. This measure includes all changes in owners' equity during a period except those resulting from investments by owners or distributions to owners. The income statement shows major categories of revenues and expenses and often presents comparative data for two or more years. For a corporation, the amount of earnings per share of stock also is reported on the income statement.

The statement of cash flows is one of the three main financial statements. It reports cash receipts and payments during a period. The cash inflows and outflows are classified according to operating, investing, and financing activities.

Objective 2

Explain how the basic financial statements tie together. The financial statements are interrelated and tie together. This concept is referred to as articulation. It helps explain the relationship between operating statement (the income statement or the statement of cash flows) and comparative balance sheets.

Objective 3

Recognize the importance of the notes to the financial statements and the independent auditor's report. In understanding financial statements, it is important to consider the accompanying notes. These explanatory notes provide additional information about certain items and dollar amounts in the statements. They are a required, integral part of the financial statements.

Another key item associated with financial statements is the audit report. This report contains the opinion of an independent CPA about whether the statements present fairly a company's financial position, operating results, and cash flows in accordance with generally accepted accounting principles. This professional opinion adds credence to management's representations as reported in the financial statements. Most financial statements presented in the annual report to stockholders are prepared on a consolidated basis.

Key Terms and Concepts

articulation *(38)*
assets *(29)*
audit report *(40)*
balance sheet (statement of financial position) *(28)*
capital stock *(29)*
certified public accountant (CPA) *(39–40)*
classified balance sheet *(31)*
comparative financial statements *(32)*
consolidated financial statements *(41)*
dividends *(29)*
earnings (or loss) per share *(34)*
expenses *(33)*
general-purpose financial statements *(28)*
income statement (statement of earnings) *(33)*
liabilities *(29)*
net income (loss) *(34)*
notes to financial statements *(39)*
owners' equity (net assets) *(29)*
retained earnings *(30)*
revenues *(33)*
statement of cash flows *(36)*
statement of retained earnings *(35)*

Review Problem

The Income Statement and the Balance Sheet

Pat Stewart, proprietor of The Style Shop, has come to you for help in preparing an income statement for 1994 and a balance sheet as of December 31, 1994. The company does not know the amount of its accounts receivable or net income. Several amounts determined as of December 31, 1994, are presented below.

Pat Stewart, Capital (12/31/94)	$68,000
Advertising Expense	2,000
Cash	17,000
Rent Expense	2,400
Building (net)	100,000
Interest Expense	700
Mortgage Payable	72,000
Accounts Payable	6,000
Land	24,000
Supplies	2,000
Salary Expense	20,000
Revenues	42,000
Other Expenses	1,300
Accounts Receivable	?

Required:
1. Prepare an income statement for the year ended December 31, 1994.
2. Prepare a classified balance sheet as of December 31, 1994.
3. Determine the correct amount of accounts receivable at year-end.

Chapter 2 Financial Statements: An Overview

Solution **1 and 2. Income Statement and Balance Sheet**

The first step in solving this problem is to separate the balance sheet items from the income statement items. Items that show the company's financial position appear on the balance sheet; revenues and expenses are reported on the income statement. Keep in mind that this is a proprietorship.

Balance Sheet Items	Income Statement Items
Pat Stewart, Capital	Advertising Expense
Cash	Rent Expense
Building (net)	Interest Expense
Mortgage Payable	Salary Expense
Accounts Payable	Revenues
Land	Other Expenses
Supplies	
Accounts Receivable	

After the items have been classified, the income statement and the balance sheet may be prepared using a proper format.

The Style Shop
Income Statement
For the Year Ended December 31, 1994

Revenues		$42,000
Expenses:		
Advertising expense	$ 2,000	
Rent expense	2,400	
Interest expense	700	
Salary expense	20,000	
Other expenses	1,300	26,400
Net income		$15,600

The Style Shop
Balance Sheet
December 31, 1994

Assets			Liabilities and Owner's Equity		
Current assets:			*Current liabilities:*		
Cash	$ 17,000		Accounts payable	$ 6,000	
Accounts receivable	3,000*				
Supplies	2,000	$ 22,000	*Long-term liabilities:*		
			Mortgage payable	72,000	
Long-term assets:			Total liabilities		$ 78,000
Land	$ 24,000				
Building (net)	100,000	124,000	*Owner's equity:*		
			Pat Stewart, capital		68,000
			Total liabilities and		
Total assets		$146,000	owner's equity		$146,000

*See item 3 for calculation

3. Accounts Receivable

Since total assets always must equal total liabilities and owners' equity, accounts receivable may be computed by subtracting, as shown below.

Total assets (total liabilities and owner's equity)		$146,000
Less: Cash.	$ 17,000	
Supplies	2,000	
Land.	24,000	
Building (net)	100,000	143,000
Equal accounts receivable		$ 3,000

Discussion Questions

1. As an external user of financial statements, perhaps an investor or creditor, what type of accounting information do you need?
2. What is the major purpose of:
   (a) A balance sheet?
   (b) An income statement?
   (c) A statement of cash flows?
3. Why are classified and comparative financial statements generally presented in annual reports to shareholders?
4. Why are owners' equity and liabilities considered the "sources" of assets?
5. Distinguish between:
   (a) Assets and expenses.
   (b) Revenues and net income.
6. Owners' equity is not cash; it is not a liability; and it generally is not equal to the current worth of a business. What is the nature of owners' equity?
7. What are the two main components of owners' equity in a corporation? Why are they reported separately?
8. Some people feel that the income statement is more important than the balance sheet. Do you agree? Why or why not?
9. How might an investor be misled by only looking at the "bottom line," the net income or EPS number, on an income statement?
10. Why is it important to classify cash flows according to operating, investing, and financing activities?
11. What is the purpose of the notes to the financial statements?
12. You are thinking of investing in one of two companies. In one annual report, the auditor's opinion states that the financial statements were prepared in accordance with generally accepted accounting principles. The other makes no such claim. How important is that to you? Explain.
13. Some people think that auditors are responsible for assuring the accuracy of financial statements. Are they correct? Why or why not?
14. What are consolidated financial statements? Why are consolidated statements often included in the annual reports to stockholders?

Exercises

E2-1
Accounting Equation

Compute the missing amounts for companies A, B, and C.

	A	B	C
Cash	$25,000	$ 9,000	$12,000
Accounts Receivable	20,000	15,000	7,000
Land and Buildings	50,000	?	40,000
Accounts Payable	?	6,000	14,000
Mortgage Payable	30,000	10,000	15,000
Owners' Equity	55,000	30,000	?

E2-2
Comprehensive Accounting Equation

Assuming no additional investments by or distributions to owners, compute the missing amounts.

	X Co.	Y Co.	Z Co.
Assets: January 1, 1994	$360	$?	$230
Liabilities: January 1, 1994	280	460	?
Owners' Equity: January 1, 1994	?	620	150
Assets: December 31, 1994	380	?	310
Liabilities: December 31, 1994	?	520	90
Owners' Equity: December 31, 1994	?	720	?
Revenues in 1994	80	?	400
Expenses in 1994	100	116	?

E2-3
Computing Elements of Owners' Equity

From the information provided, determine:

1. The amount of retained earnings at December 31.
2. The amount of revenues for the period.

Totals	January 1	December 31
Current assets	$ 5,000	$ 10,000
All other assets	150,000	160,000
Liabilities	25,000	30,000
Capital stock	50,000	?
Retained earnings	80,000	?

Additional data:
Expenses for the period were $35,000.
Dividends paid were $7,500.
Capital stock increased by $5,000 during the period.

E2-4
Balance Sheet Relationships

Correct the following balance sheet.

Transcontinental Company
Balance Sheet
December 31, 1994

Assets		Liabilities and Owners' Equity	
Cash	$ 7,000	Land	$ 5,000
Accounts payable	8,000	Accounts receivable	3,000
Supplies	2,000	Notes payable	10,000
Equipment	10,000		
Owners' equity	9,000		
	$36,000		$18,000

E2-5
Balance Sheet Preparation

From the following selected data, prepare a classified balance sheet for High Fashion, Inc., at December 31, 1994.

Accounts Payable	$ 31,000
Accounts Receivable	66,000
Buildings	217,000
Owners' Equity, 1/1/94	100,000
Cash	77,500
Distributions to Owners During 1994	12,500
Supplies	1,500
Land	110,000
Mortgage Payable	275,000
Net Income for 1994	78,500
Owners' Equity, 12/31/94	?

E2-6
Income Statement Computations

Given below are the operating data for an advertising firm for the year ended December 31, 1994.

Revenues	$175,000
Supplies Expense	45,000
Salaries Expense	70,000
Rent Expense	1,500
Administrative Expense	6,000
Income Taxes (25% of income before taxes)	?

For 1994, determine:

1. Income before taxes.
2. Income taxes.
3. Net income.

E2-7
Income Statement Preparation

The following selected information is taken from the records of Kroton Corporation.

Accounts Payable	$ 25,000
Accounts Receivable	49,000
Advertising Expense	7,500
Cash	15,500
Supplies Expense	23,000
Rent Expense	5,000
Utilities Expense	1,500
Income Taxes (30% of income before taxes)	?
Miscellaneous Expenses	2,200
Owners' Equity	125,000
Salaries Expense	88,000
Fees (revenues)	242,000

Prepare an income statement for the year ended December 31, 1994. (Assume that 5,000 shares of stock are outstanding.)

E2-8
Classification of Financial Statement Elements

Indicate for each of the following items whether it would appear on a balance sheet (BS) or an income statement (IS). If a balance sheet item, is it an asset (A), a liability (L), or an owners' equity item (OE)?

1. Accounts Payable
2. Sales Revenue
3. Accounts Receivable
4. Advertising Expense
5. Cash
6. Supplies
7. Consulting Revenue
8. Land
9. Capital Stock
10. Rent Expense
11. Equipment
12. Interest Receivable
13. Mortgage Payable
14. Notes Payable
15. Buildings
16. Salaries and Wages Expense
17. Retained Earnings
18. Utilities Expense

E2-9
Cash Flow Computations

From the following selected data, compute:

1. Net cash flow provided (used) by operating activities.
2. Net cash flow provided (used) by financing activities.
3. Net cash flow provided (used) by investing activities.
4. Net increase (decrease) in cash during the year.
5. The cash balance at the end of the year.

Selected data:

Cash receipts from:	
Customers	$135,000
Investments by owners	27,000
Sale of building	45,000
Proceeds from bank loan	30,000
Cash payments for:	
Wages	41,000
Utilities	1,500
Advertising	2,000
Rent	18,000
Taxes	33,500
Dividends	10,000
Repayment of principal on loan	20,000
Purchase of land	53,000
Cash balance at beginning of year	193,000

E2-10
Income and Retained Earnings Relationships

Assume that retained earnings increased by $240,000 from December 31, 1993, to December 31, 1994, for Becker Corporation. During the year, a cash dividend of $140,000 was paid.

1. Compute the net income for the year.
2. Assume that the revenues for the year were $920,000. Compute the expenses incurred for the year.

E2-11
Retained Earnings Computations

During 1994, Downy Corporation had revenues of $180,000 and expenses, including income taxes, of $100,000. On December 31, 1993, Downy had assets of $400,000, liabilities of $100,000, and capital stock of $250,000. Downy paid a cash dividend of $40,000 in 1994. No additional stock was issued. Compute the retained earnings on December 31, 1993, and 1994.

E2-12
Preparation of Income Statement and Retained Earnings Statement

Prepare an income statement and a statement of retained earnings for Big Sky Corporation for the year ended June 30, 1994, based on the following information:

Capital Stock (1,500 shares @$100)	$150,000
Retained Earnings, July 1, 1993	76,800
Dividends	6,500
Ski Rental Revenue	77,900

Expenses:

Rent Expense	$ 6,000	
Salaries Expense	38,600	
Utilities Expense	2,400	
Advertising Expense	7,500	
Miscellaneous Expenses	7,700	
Income Taxes	2,100	64,300

E2-13
Articulation: Relationships Between a Balance Sheet and an Income Statement

The total assets and liabilities of Pentex Company at January 1 and December 31, 1994, are presented below.

	January 1	December 31
Assets	$76,000	$112,000
Liabilities	26,000	28,800

Determine the amount of net income or loss for 1994, applying each of the following assumptions concerning the additional issuance of stock and dividends paid by the firm. Each case is independent of the others.

1. Dividends of $10,800 were paid and no additional stock was issued during the year.
2. Additional stock of $4,800 was issued and no dividends were paid during the year.
3. Additional stock of $62,000 was issued and dividends of $15,600 were paid during the year.

Problem Set A

P2A-1
Balance Sheet Classifications and Relationships

Happy Company sells greeting cards. As of December 31, 1994, its financial position is as follows:

Cash	$40,000
Accounts Receivable	25,000
Accounts Payable	21,000
Land, Buildings, and Equipment	98,000
Notes Receivable	6,000
Notes Payable	12,000
Interest Receivable	3,000
Retained Earnings	47,000
Capital Stock	?

Chapter 2 *Financial Statements: An Overview*

Required:
1. Compute the total amount of assets.
2. Compute the total amount of liabilities.
3. Compute the total amount of stockholders' equity.
4. Determine the amount of capital stock of Happy Company.

P2A-2
Preparation of a Classified Balance Sheet

The information presented here is taken from the records of Whaler Company.

Building	$50,000
Accounts Payable	15,000
Cash	15,000
Capital Stock	20,000
Retained Earnings	22,500
Supplies	6,500
Accounts Receivable	10,000
Notes Payable (long term)	30,000
Land	6,000

Required: Prepare a classified balance sheet for Whaler Company as of March 31, 1994.

P2A-3
Balance Sheet Preparation with a Missing Element

The following data are available for LeAnn's Bakery as of December 31, 1994.

Cash	$10,000
Accounts Payable	14,000
Capital Stock	35,200
Accounts Receivable	20,000
Building	28,000
Supplies	1,200
Retained Earnings	?
Land	10,000

Required:
1. Prepare a balance sheet for LeAnn's Bakery.
2. Determine the amount of Retained Earnings at December 31, 1994.

P2A-4
Income Statement Preparation

Use the following information for Pete's Pet Store for the month of December 1994.

Salaries Expense	$ 7,200
Revenues	51,000
Income Taxes	2,400
Miscellaneous Expenses	1,200
Rent Expense	10,800
Supplies Expense	18,600
Advertising Expense	2,000

1,000 shares of stock outstanding.

Required: Prepare an income statement for Pete's Pet Store for the month ended December 31, 1994.

P2A-5
Income Statement Preparation—Proprietorship

Tom Kline, a CPA, has worked for five years for a national CPA firm. On January 1, 1994, he began business as a sole proprietor in his hometown. During the first year of operations he received professional fees of $68,500 for his services and incurred the following expenses.

Secretarial Salaries	$20,000
Office Rent	6,000
Heat and Electricity	3,500
Telephone	750
Duplicating Services	500
Office Supplies	380
Professional Dues	220
Accounting and Tax Services	350
Travel and Entertainment	1,800
Total Expenses	$33,500

Required:
1. Prepare an income statement for the business for the year ended December 31, 1994.
2. Explain why no EPS figure is presented on your income statement.

P2A-6
Expanded Accounting Equation—Corporation

You are furnished only the following information for Dasey, Inc. for the year 1994.

(a) Except for net income and a $30,000 dividend payment deducted from retained earnings, no other additions to or deductions from retained earnings have been made.

(b) The only other accounts that were changed were those listed below. The amount of change for each account is shown as a net increase or decrease.

	Increase (Decrease)
Cash	$ 19,000
Accounts Receivable	(6,000)
Supplies	27,000
Accounts Payable	(23,000)
Mortgage Payable	40,000
Capital Stock	10,000

Required: Using the accounting equation, compute net income for 1994.

P2A-7
Statement of Cash Flows

The following selected data are available for Yammamoto Company for the year ended December 31, 1994.

Cash balance at beginning of year	$157,000
Cash receipts from the sale of land	43,000
Cash payments for wages and salaries	82,000
Cash receipts from customers	341,000
Cash receipts from a bank loan	12,000
Cash distribution to owners	52,000
Cash payments to purchase a building	89,000
Cash payments for operating expenses	124,000
Cash payments for taxes	38,000

Required: Prepare a statement of cash flows for Yammamoto Company for the year ended December 31, 1994.

P2A-8
Unifying Concepts: Net Income and Statement of Retained Earnings

A summary of the operations of Stellenbach Company for the year ended May 31, 1994, is shown below.

Advertising Expense	$ 2,760
Supplies Expense	37,820
Rent Expense	1,500
Salaries Expense	18,150
Miscellaneous Expenses	4,170
Dividends	12,400
Retained Earnings (6/1/93)	156,540
Income Taxes	21,180
Consulting Fees (revenues)	115,100
Administrative Expense	7,250

Required:
1. Determine net income for the year by preparing an income statement. (2,000 shares of stock are outstanding.)
2. Prepare a statement of retained earnings for the year ended May 31, 1994.
3. Prepare a statement of retained earnings assuming that Stellenbach had a net loss for the year of $25,000.

P2A-9
Unifying Concepts: Comprehensive Financial Statement Preparation—Corporation

SPREADSHEET PROBLEM

The following information was obtained from the records of Buy for Less, Inc. as of December 31, 1994.

Land	$ 25,000
Buildings	96,700
Salaries Expense	26,700
Utilities Expense	6,500
Accounts Payable	17,100
Revenues	265,200
Supplies	46,300
Retained Earnings (1/1/94)	181,700
Capital Stock (500 shares outstanding)	30,000
Accounts Receivable	31,000
Supplies Expense	138,600
Cash	?
Notes Payable	17,200
Rent Expense	17,100
Dividends in 1994	40,500
Other Expenses	8,700
Income Taxes	35,200

Required:
1. Prepare an income statement for the year ended December 31, 1994.
2. Prepare a statement of retained earnings for the year ended December 31, 1994.
3. Prepare a classified balance sheet as of December 31, 1994.
4. **Interpretive Question** Why is the balance in Retained Earnings so large as compared with the balance in Capital Stock?

P2A-10

Unifying Concepts: Elements of Comparative Financial Statements

The following report is supplied by Smith Brothers Company.

Smith Brothers Company
Comparative Balance Sheets
December 31, 1994 and 1993

Assets	1994	1993	Liabilities and Owners' Equity	1994	1993
Cash	$13,000	$15,000	Accounts payable	$ 5,000	$ 4,000
Accounts receivable	18,000	11,000	Salaries and commissions payable	8,000	8,000
Notes receivable	11,000	10,000	Notes payable	25,000	27,000
Land	38,000	38,000	Capital stock	20,000	20,000
			Retained earnings	22,000	15,000
Total assets	$80,000	$74,000	Total liabilities and owners' equity	$80,000	$74,000

Operating expenses for the year included utilities of $4,500, salaries and commissions of $44,800, and miscellaneous expenses of $1,500. Income taxes for the year were $3,000, and the company paid dividends of $5,000.

Required:
1. Compute the total expenses, including taxes, incurred in 1994.
2. Compute the net income or net loss for 1994.
3. Compute the total revenue for 1994.
4. **Interpretive Question** Why are comparative financial statements generally of more value to users than statements for a single period?

Problem Set B

P2B-1

Balance Sheet Classifications

Salazar Corporation has the following balance sheet elements as of December 31, 1994.

Land	$ 69,000
Cash	?
Building	178,000
Accounts Payable	100,000
Notes Payable (short term)	105,000
Equipment	350,000
Mortgage Payable	300,000
Capital Stock	135,000
Retained Earnings	88,000
Supplies	17,000
Accounts Receivable	88,000

Required: Compute the total amount of:

1. Current assets.
2. Long-term assets.
3. Current liabilities.
4. Long-term liabilities.
5. Stockholders' equity.

P2B-2
Preparation of a Classified Balance Sheet—Corporation

Following are the December 31, 1994, account balances for Circle M Company.

Cash	$ 1,950
Accounts Receivable	2,500
Supplies	1,800
Equipment	11,275
Accounts Payable	3,450
Wages Payable	250
Dividends Paid	1,500
Capital Stock	775
Retained Earnings, January 1, 1994	12,000
Revenues	10,000
Miscellaneous Expenses	1,550
Supplies Expense	3,700
Wages Expense	2,200

Required:
1. Prepare a classified balance sheet as of December 31, 1994.
2. **Interpretive Question** On the basis of its 1994 earnings, was this company's decision to pay dividends of $1,500 a sound one?

P2B-3
Preparation of a Classified Balance Sheet—Proprietorship

Bonnie Cash, a sole proprietor, sells personal computers and software packages. As of December 31, 1994, the following information was taken from the records of her company, BC Computer Systems.

Mortgage Payable (current portion)	1,500
Mortgage Payable (noncurrent portion)	15,000
Accounts Receivable	15,760
Cash	10,000
Building	100,000
Store Equipment	25,500
Land	18,000
Salaries Payable	880
Bonnie Cash, Capital	139,040
Accounts Payable	13,580
Office Supplies	740

Required: Prepare a classified balance sheet as of December 31, 1994.

P2B-4
Income Statement Preparation—Corporation

The following information is taken from the records of Rollins & Associates, Inc. for the year ended December 31, 1994.

Income Taxes	$ 10,800
Service Revenues	150,000
Rent Expense	5,500
Salaries Expense	35,000
Miscellaneous Expenses	380
Utilities Expense	1,230
Administrative Expense	12,300

Required: Prepare an income statement for Rollins & Associates, Inc. for the year ended December 31, 1994. (Assume that 4,000 shares of stock are outstanding.)

P2B-5
Income Statement Preparation—Corporation

Perfecto Corporation has been a leading supplier of magnetic storage disks for three years. Following are the results of Perfecto's operations for 1994.

Sales Revenue	$68,000
Advertising Expense	1,530
Income Taxes	4,360
Delivery Expense	480
Packaging Expense	355
Salaries Expense	18,350
Supplies Expense	8,410

EPS = $3.45

Required:
1. Prepare an income statement for the year ended December 31, 1994.
2. How many shares of stock were outstanding?

P2B-6
Expanded Accounting Equation—Proprietorship

On September 1, owner's equity for Sellers Company, a proprietorship owned by T. J. Sellers, was $17,000 and total assets equaled $25,000. During September owner's equity increased $20,000. Also during the month, total liabilities decreased $3,000, and T. J. Sellers withdrew $10,000 for personal use.

Required:
1. Compute the amount of net income for September, assuming that only income and drawings affected owner's equity during the month.
2. Compute the amount of total assets for Sellers Company at the end of September.

P2B-7
Statement of Cash Flows

The cash account for Kwon Enterprises shows the following for the year ended December 31, 1994.

Beginning cash balance	$?
Cash receipts during year from:	
Services	1,351,000
Investments by owners	82,000
Sale of land	135,000
Cash payments during year for:	
Operating expenses	963,000
Taxes	114,000
Purchase of building	326,000
Distributions to owners	55,000
Ending cash balance	850,000

Required: Prepare a statement of cash flows for Kwon Enterprises for the year ended December 31, 1994.

P2B-8
Unifying Concepts: Net Income and Statement of Retained Earnings

The following information is taken from the records of O'Hara Company for the year ended December 31, 1994.

Retained Earnings, December 31, 1994	$ 91,175
Rent Expense	12,670
Miscellaneous Expenses	540
Revenues	283,475
Income Taxes	72,010
Administrative Expense	90,240
Dividends	45,520

10,000 shares of stock are outstanding.

Chapter 2 *Financial Statements: An Overview*   55

Required:
1. Determine net income for the year by preparing an income statement.
2. Prepare a statement of retained earnings for the year ended December 31, 1994. (Note: You must compute the beginning retained earnings amount.)

P2B-9
Unifying Concepts: Preparation of Financial Statements

The Down Town Theatre had the following operating figures for August 1994.

Sale of Tickets	$75,000
Equipment Rental Expense	7,000
Utilities, Taxes, and Licenses Expense	11,400
Film Rental Expenses	14,600
Advertising Expense	4,000
Wages and Salaries Expense	13,000
Dividends Paid	10,000

End-of-the-month balance sheet figures were as follows:

Cash	$56,600
Supplies	3,600
Land	40,000
Buildings and Screen	60,000
Accounts Payable	24,400
Other Assets (long term)	12,000
Capital Stock	80,000
Retained Earnings, August 1, 1994	52,800

Required:
1. Prepare an income statement for August 1994. (Assume that 8,000 shares of stock are outstanding.)
2. Prepare a statement of retained earnings for August 1994.
3. Prepare a balance sheet as of August 31, 1994.

P2B-10
Unifying Concepts: Elements of Comparative Financial Statements

The following information has been supplied by Cash and Carry Company.

Cash and Carry Company
Comparative Balance Sheets
December 31, 1994 and 1993

Assets	1994	1993	Liabilities and Owners' Equity	1994	1993
Cash	$ 5,000	$ 8,000	Accounts payable	$11,000	$11,000
Accounts receivable	12,000	9,000	Mortgage payable	14,000	15,000
Office supplies	8,000	5,000	Capital stock	21,000	21,000
Building	44,000	44,000	Retained earnings	23,000	19,000
Total assets	$69,000	$66,000	Total liabilities and owners' equity	$69,000	$66,000

The company paid utilities of $3,500, miscellaneous expenses of $5,900, taxes of $2,300, and dividends of $2,000.

Required: 1. Compute the total expenses incurred in 1994.
2. Compute the net income or net loss for 1994.
3. Compute the total revenues for 1994.
4. **Interpretive Question** What benefits do comparative financial statements provide their users?

Business Analysis Case 1 *Photo Processing, Inc.*

Photo Processing, Inc. is a small company that has been in business for two years. Sara Gullind, the president of the company, has decided that it is time to expand, but she needs $10,000 to purchase additional equipment and to pay for increased operating expenses. She can either apply for a loan at First City Bank, or she can issue more stock (1,000 shares are outstanding) to new investors.

Required: 1. Assuming that you are the loan officer at First City Bank, what information would you request from Photo Processing before deciding whether to make the loan?
2. As a potential investor in Photo Processing, what information would you need to make a good investment decision?
3. What informational needs are common to creditors and investors? What is the primary source of that information?

Business Analysis Case 2 *Prime Properties, Inc.*

An investor may choose from several alternatives: for example, the stocks of different companies; rental property or other real estate; or savings accounts, money market certificates, and similar financial instruments. When considering an investment in the stock of a particular company, comparative financial data presented in the annual report to stockholders helps an investor identify key relationships and trends. As an illustration, comparative operating results for Prime Properties, Inc. from its 1994 annual report are provided. (Dollars are presented in thousands except for earnings per share.)

	Year Ended December 31		
	1994	1993	1992
Revenues:			
Property management fees	$ 58,742	$ 63,902	$ 66,204
Appraisal fees	55,641	60,945	62,320
Total revenues	$114,383	$124,847	$128,524
Expenses:			
Selling and advertising	$ 64,371	$ 75,403	$ 80,478
Administrative expenses	30,671	31,115	31,618
Other expenses	9,265	9,540	9,446
Interest expense	2,047	1,468	26
Total expenses	$106,354	$117,526	$121,568
Income before taxes	$ 8,029	$ 7,321	$ 6,956
Income taxes	2,409	2,196	2,087
Net income	$ 5,620	$ 5,125	$ 4,869
*Earnings per share	$2.25	$2.05	$1.95

* 2.5 million shares outstanding

Required: 1. What trends are indicated by the comparative income statement data for Prime Properties, Inc.? Which of these trends would be of concern to a potential investor?
2. What additional information would an investor need in order to make a decision about whether to invest in this company?

Ethics Case   *New Designs, Inc.*

Jerry Jones, the accountant for New Designs, Inc., is perplexed. It is the end of the fiscal year, and he is preparing the accounting records so that the financial statements can be presented to the Board of Directors and eventually to the stockholders in the annual report. Jerry's boss, the chief financial officer (CFO) of the company, has asked a "favor." He wants Jerry to include some revenues in this year's income statement that technically belong in the next accounting period. The CFO also wants some expenses that are actual expenses of this period deferred to the next period. Jerry knows that management is concerned over the net income number to be reported since managers' bonuses are based on annual net income.

Required: 1. What are the accounting issues involved in this case?
2. What are the ethical issues involved in this case?
3. What should Jerry do?

Chapter 3

Introducing the Accounting Cycle

Learning Objectives

After studying this chapter, you should be able to:
1. Understand the process of transforming transaction data into useful accounting information.
2. Explain the basic accounting equation.
3. Describe the first four steps in the accounting cycle: analyze transactions and business documents, journalize transactions, post journal entries, and prepare a trial balance.

SETTING THE STAGE

IBM is one of the largest corporations in the world. For the year ended December 31, 1990, IBM reported revenues of over $69 billion and net earnings of $6.02 billion. It paid cash dividends of over $2.7 billion to its 789,046 shareholders. At year-end, its assets totaled approximately $87.6 billion, and it employed 373,816 people in more than 70 countries all over the world.

Imagine the number of transactions a company the size of IBM has during a year. Every day it sells millions of computers and other information-processing products; it enters into millions of purchase transactions; it pays its employees wages and reimburses its salespeople for travel and other expenses; and it pays all its other operating costs, including rent, utilities, and so forth. And although some of these transactions are based in U.S. dollars, many are based in German marks, British pounds, Japanese yen, Mexican pesos, and other currencies. Imagine how difficult it must be to keep track of each of these transactions and summarize them into three basic financial statements for shareholders, various governmental agencies, and other interested parties.

IBM takes its financial reporting responsibilities seriously, as do most public companies. Even though it is very large, IBM is one of the first calendar-year-end companies to issue its annual report. On the 12th workday after the first of the year, IBM issues a press release providing year-end results. This means that in 12 days, IBM must get the results of its German, British, Japanese, Mexican, and other subsidiaries and summarize them, together with IBM's U.S. results. Then, in a few more days, but always before the end of January, IBM reviews a draft of its annual report with its Board of Directors. In early February, millions of copies of this annual report are issued to shareholders and others who want to analyze IBM and see how the company has performed.

accounting cycle *the procedures for analyzing, recording, classifying, summarizing, and reporting the transactions of a business*

What is the process by which IBM and other entities transform raw transaction data into useful information? Certainly, shareholders and others would not understand how IBM had performed if the company merely published volumes of raw transaction data. How do millions of transactions get summarized and eventually reported in general-purpose financial statements? The transformation process is referred to as the **accounting cycle** and is the subject of this and the next two chapters.

In the first two chapters, we provided an overview of financial accounting. We discussed the environment of accounting and its objectives; some basic concepts, principles, and procedures of accounting; and the general-purpose financial statements. With this chapter, we begin our study of the accounting cycle. This simply means that we will examine the procedures for analyzing, recording, classifying, summarizing, and reporting the transactions of an entity. Here we describe the first four steps in the cycle; the remaining steps are explained in Chapters 4 and 5.

THE PROCESS OF TRANSFORMING TRANSACTION DATA INTO USEFUL ACCOUNTING INFORMATION

Objective 1
Understand the process of transforming transaction data into useful accounting information.

Business entities buy and sell goods or services; borrow and invest money; pay wages to employees; purchase land, buildings, and equipment; distribute earnings to their owners; and pay taxes to the government. These activities are referred to as *exchange transactions* because the entity is actually trading (exchanging) one thing for another. A college bookstore, for example, exchanges textbooks for cash.

To determine how well an entity is managing its resources, the results of transactions must be analyzed. The accounting cycle makes the analysis possible by recording, classifying, and summarizing an entity's transactions and preparing reports that present the summary results. Exhibit 3-1 shows the sequence of the accounting cycle. Later, we will break these general categories down into specific steps.

Keeping track of a company's transactions requires a system of accounting that is tailor-made to the needs of that particular enterprise. Obviously, the accounting system of a large multinational corporation (a company with operations in several countries) with thousands of business transactions each month will be much more complex than the system needed by a small drugstore. And the more complex and detailed the accounting system, the more likely it is to be automated. Historically, of course, all accounting systems had to be maintained by hand. The image of the accountant with green eyeshade and quill pen, sitting on a high stool and meticulously maintaining the accounting records, reflects those early manual systems. Today, few accounting systems are completely manual. Even small companies generally use some type of automated equipment—cash registers, adding machines, typewriters, calculators, bookkeeping machines, and personal computers. Such equipment helps reduce the number of routine clerical functions and improve the accuracy and timeliness of the accounting records. Although the accounting records and reports generated by an automated or computerized system will usually look somewhat different from those of a manual system, the underlying accounting principles are the same. There is no difference in the accounting theory involved, only in

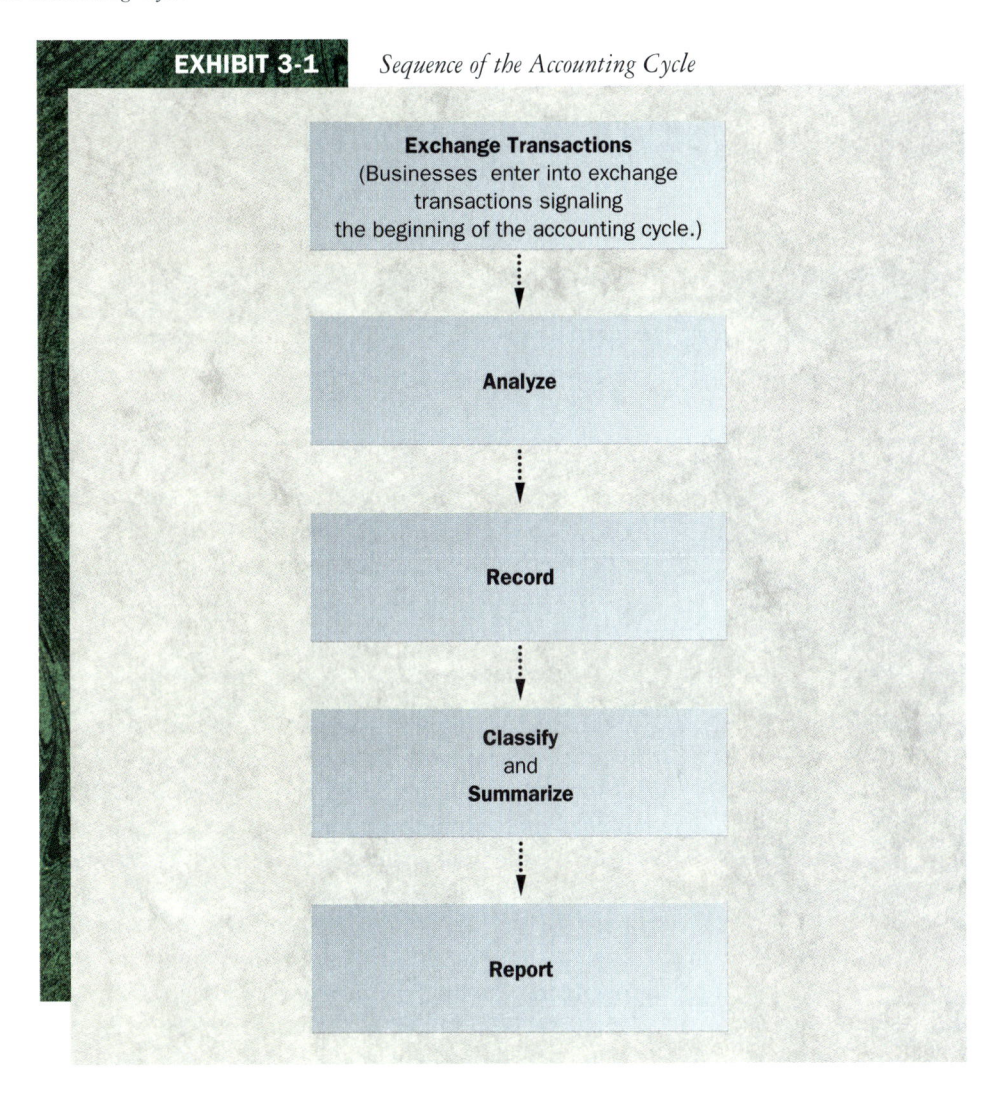

EXHIBIT 3-1 *Sequence of the Accounting Cycle*

Exchange Transactions
(Businesses enter into exchange transactions signaling the beginning of the accounting cycle.)

↓

Analyze

↓

Record

↓

Classify and Summarize

↓

Report

the mechanical aspect of the bookkeeping process. Because a manual accounting system is easier to understand, we will use a manual system for our examples in this text.

Regardless of the type or complexity of the business or the accounting system, the basic steps of the accounting cycle are the same. Before you study these steps, it is important that you understand double-entry accounting more fully. This concept was introduced briefly in Chapters 1 and 2. You will recall that the accounting model is built on a basic equation. You now need to learn how to use the equation in accounting for the transactions of a business.

THE BASIC ACCOUNTING EQUATION

Objective 2
Explain the basic accounting equation.

As you will recall, the fundamental accounting equation is:

$$\underset{[\text{Resources}]}{\textbf{Assets}} = \underset{\begin{bmatrix}\text{Creditors' claims}\\\text{against resources}\end{bmatrix}}{\textbf{Liabilities}} + \underset{\begin{bmatrix}\text{Owners' claims}\\\text{against resources}\end{bmatrix}}{\textbf{Owners' Equity}}$$

Since the accounting equation is an equality, it must always remain in balance. To see how this balance is maintained when accounting for business transactions, consider the following activities (transactions).

Business Activity (Transaction)	Effect in Terms of the Accounting Equation
1. Investment by owners	Increase asset (cash), increase owners' equity (capital stock): A↑ = OE↑
2. Borrow money from bank	Increase asset (cash), increase liability (notes payable): A↑ = L↑
3. Pay off bank loan (note)	Decrease asset (cash), decrease liability (notes payable): A↓ = L↓
4. Purchase equipment for cash	Decrease asset (cash), increase asset (equipment): A↓ = A↑

In each case, the equation remains in balance because an identical amount is added to both sides, or subtracted from both sides, or added to and subtracted from the same side of the equation. The terms in parentheses are the specific accounts affected by the transactions, as we will now explain.

Using Accounts to Categorize Transactions

account *an accounting record in which the results of transactions are accumulated; shows increases, decreases, and a balance*

An **account** is a specific accounting record that provides an efficient way to categorize transactions. Thus, we may designate asset accounts, liability accounts, and owners' equity accounts. Examples of asset accounts are Cash, Supplies, and Equipment; liability accounts include Accounts Payable and Notes Payable. The equity accounts for a corporation are Capital Stock and Retained Earnings; for a proprietorship or partnership, they are simply the owners' Capital accounts (for example, John Jones, Capital).

Accounts may be presented in a number of ways. The simplest, most fundamental format is the configuration of the letter **T**. This is called a **T-account**. Note that a T-account is an abbreviated representation of an actual account (described later) and is used as a teaching and learning tool. The following are examples of T-accounts, representing the transactions described previously.

T-account *a simplified depiction of an account in the form of a letter* **T**.

Cash		Equipment		Notes Payable		Capital Stock
debit	credit					

The account title (Cash, for example) appears at the top of the T. Transaction amounts are recorded either on the left, or debit, side or on the right, or credit, side. A **debit** is therefore defined as an entry on the left side of an account and a **credit** as an entry on the right side of an account. The appropriate debit (abbreviated DR) and credit (abbreviated CR) entries for the above T-accounts are:

debit *an entry on the left side of an account*

credit *an entry on the right side of an account*

Cash		Equipment		Notes Payable		Capital Stock
DR	CR	DR	CR	DR	CR	DR	CR

In representing the left and right sides of an account, debits and credits refer to increases or decreases that result from each transaction, depending on the type of account. *For asset accounts, debits refer to increases, and credits to decreases.* For example, to increase the Cash account, we debit it; to decrease the Cash account, we credit it. This debit–credit, increase–decrease relationship holds for any asset account. *The opposite relationship is true of liability and owners' equity accounts; they are increased by credits and decreased by debits.* For example, the Notes Payable account is increased by a credit; it is decreased by a debit. The effect of this system is shown here, with an increase indicated by (+) and a decrease by (−).

Assets	=	Liabilities	+	Owners' Equity
DR | CR		DR | CR		DR | CR
(+) | (−)		(−) | (+)		(−) | (+)

Keep in mind that in actual business practice, when a manual accounting system is used, the T-account is an integral feature of a more formal and complete account. Exhibit 3-2 is an example of such an account. Note that in addition to the debits and credits in the T-account portion (drawn in heavy lines in this example), the account has a title, Cash; an account number, 101; and columns for a transaction date, an explanation of the transaction, a posting reference (a cross reference to other records), and a balance.

As you have just seen, the terms *debit* and *credit* switch meaning from an increase to a decrease, and vice versa, in going from one side of the accounting equation to the other. To understand why this happens, keep in mind three basic facts regarding double-entry accounting:

1. For every transaction, there must be at least one debit and one credit.
2. Debits must always equal credits for each transaction.
3. Debits are always entered on the left side of an account and credits on the right side.

Exhibit 3-2 *Cash Account*

ACCOUNT: Cash					ACCOUNT NO. 101
Date	Item	Post Ref.	Debits	Credits	Balance

Now notice what this means for one of the business transactions shown earlier (page 62): investment by owners. An asset account (Cash) is increased; in other words, it is debited. An owners' equity account (Capital Stock) is also increased; in other words, it is credited. There is both a debit and a credit for the transaction, and we have increased accounts on both sides of the equation by an equal amount, thus keeping the equation in balance.

Be careful not to let the general, nonaccounting meanings of the words *credit* and *debit* confuse you. In general conversation, credit has an association with plus and debit with minus. But on the asset side of the accounting equation, where credit means decrease and debit means increase, this association can lead you astray. In accounting, debit simply means left, whereas credit means right. To make sure you understand the relationship between debits and credits, the various accounts, and the accounting equation, let us examine further the transactions listed on page 62.

Business Activity (Transaction)	Effect in Terms of the Accounting Equation			
	Assets	**= Liabilities**	**+**	**Owners' Equity**
1. Investment by owners ..	Cash DR(+)			Capital Stock CR(+)
2. Borrow money from bank	Cash DR(+)	Notes Payable CR(+)		
3. Pay off bank loan (note)	Cash CR(−)	Notes Payable DR(−)		
4. Purchase equipment for cash...............	Equipment DR(+) Cash CR(−)			

Note that every time an account is debited, other accounts have to be credited for the same amount. This is a major characteristic of the double-entry accounting system: *the debits must always equal the credits*. This important characteristic creates a practical advantage: the opportunity for "self-checking." If debits do not equal credits, an error has been made in analyzing and recording the entity's activities.

Expanding the Accounting Equation to Include Revenues, Expenses, and Dividends

revenues increases in a company's resources from the sale of goods or services

expenses costs incurred in the normal course of business to generate revenues

At this point, we must bring **revenues** and **expenses** into the picture. Obviously, they are part of every ongoing business. Revenues provide resource inflows; they are increases in resources from the sale of goods or services. Expenses represent resource outflows; they are costs incurred in generating revenues. Note that revenues are not synonymous with cash or other assets but are a specific source of cash and certain other assets. For example, cash received from the sale of a product would be considered revenue, whereas cash received by borrowing from the bank would not be revenue but an increase in a liability. By the same token, expenses are not synonymous with the expenditure of cash but constitute a particular type of expenditure. Thus, cash paid for interest on

Chapter 3 *Introducing the Accounting Cycle* 65

a loan is an expense, but cash paid to buy a building represents the exchange of one asset for another.

How do revenues and expenses fit into the accounting equation? Remember that revenues minus expenses equals net income and that net income is a major source of change in owners' equity from one accounting period to the next. Revenues and expenses, then, may be thought of as subdivisions of owners' equity; that is, these two types of accounts are temporary accumulation and storage compartments for operating transactions that affect the owners' equity accounts (the Retained Earnings account of a corporation or the Capital accounts of a proprietorship or partnership). Revenues increase owners' equity and so, like all owners' equity accounts, are increased by credits. Expenses reduce owners' equity and are therefore increased by debits.

Dividends account *the account used to reflect periodic distributions of earnings to the owners (stockholders) of a corporation*

Drawings account *the account used to reflect periodic withdrawals of earnings by the owner (proprietor) or owners (partners) of a proprietorship or partnership*

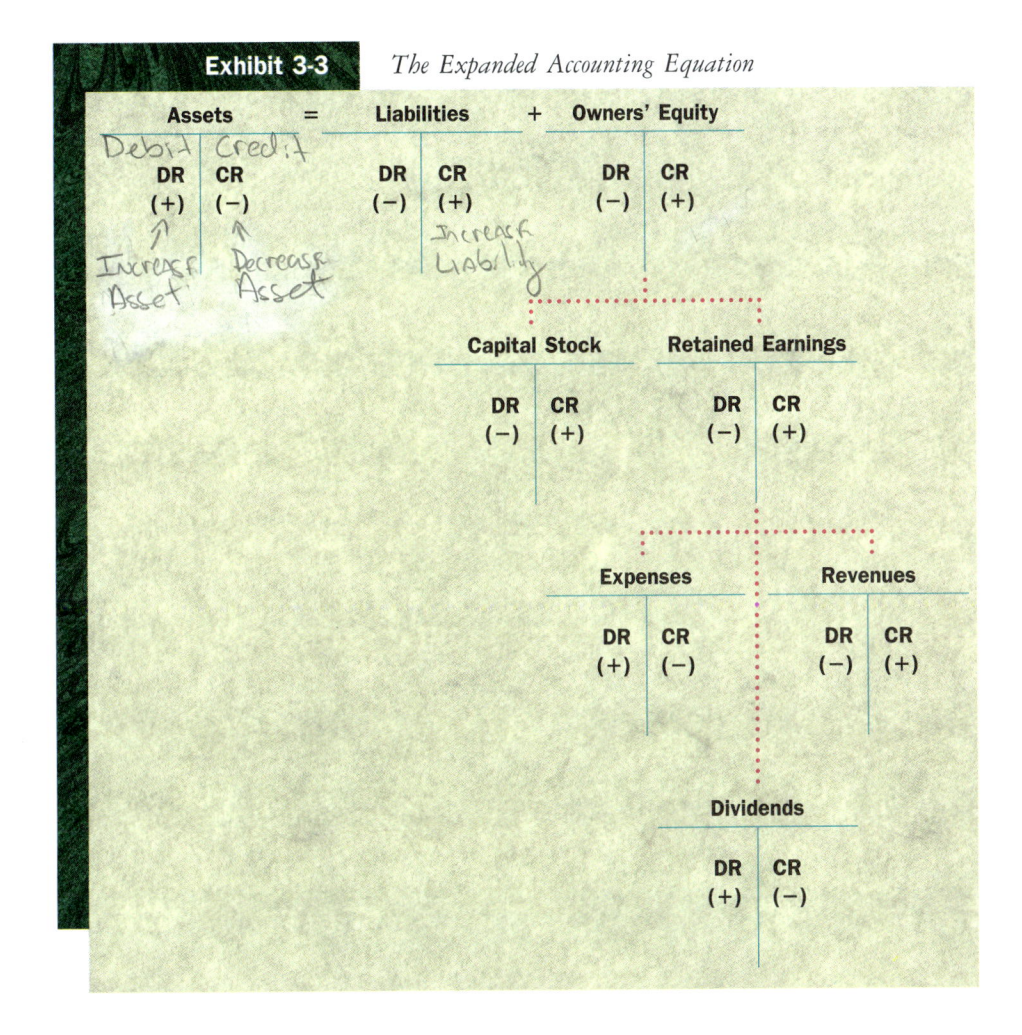

One other account affects owners' equity. It is the account that shows distributions of earnings to owners. This account is called the **Dividends account** for a corporation or the **Drawings account** for a proprietorship or partnership. Since dividends reflect payments to the owners, therefore reducing owners' equity, the Dividends account is increased by a debit and decreased by a credit. The same is true for the Drawings account.

Using the corporate form of business as an example, the accounting equation may be expanded to include revenues, expenses, and dividends, as shown in Exhibit 3-3.

Exhibit 3-3 *The Expanded Accounting Equation*

Assets	=	Liabilities	+	Owners' Equity
DR (+) / CR (−)		DR (−) / CR (+)		DR (−) / CR (+)

Capital Stock: DR (−) / CR (+)
Retained Earnings: DR (−) / CR (+)

Expenses: DR (+) / CR (−)
Revenues: DR (−) / CR (+)

Dividends: DR (+) / CR (−)

> **To Summarize** *Businesses enter into exchange transactions. Evidence of these transactions is provided by business documents. Accounting is designed to accumulate and report in summary form the results of an entity's transactions, that is, to transform the financial data into useful information for decision making. Regardless of the size or complexity of an entity, or the manner in which the records are maintained (manual or automated system), the steps of the accounting cycle are generally the same. The entire process is based on double-entry accounting and the basic accounting equation. Accounts accumulate the results of transactions. Debits are always entered on the left side of an account, and credits are always entered on the right side. Debits increase asset, expense, and dividend accounts and decrease liability, owners' equity, and revenue accounts. Credits decrease asset, expense, and dividend accounts and increase liability, owners' equity, and revenue accounts. Revenues increase owners' equity, whereas expenses and dividends decrease owners' equity. Therefore, under a double-entry system of accounting, it is always possible to check the accounting records to see that Assets = Liabilities + Owners' Equity, and that debits equal credits.*

THE FIRST FOUR STEPS IN THE ACCOUNTING CYCLE

Objective 3

Describe the first four steps in the accounting cycle: analyze transactions and business documents, journalize transactions, post journal entries, and prepare a trial balance.

Although some of the procedures may be modified or combined, the accounting cycle consists of the specific steps shown in Exhibit 3-4 on page 67. For ease of understanding, we will generally assume an annual accounting cycle, with financial statements being prepared at the end of each year. Note, however, that most large companies go through the cycle several times a year—for example, monthly. Furthermore, you should recognize that some steps in the cycle, such as analyzing and recording transactions, are continuous activities.

Step 1. Analyze Transactions and Business Documents

business documents *records of transactions used as the basis for recording accounting entries; includes invoices, check stubs, receipts, and similar business papers*

The first step in the accounting cycle is to analyze transactions and the **business documents**—the sales invoices, check stubs, and other records that are evidence of those transactions. Business documents confirm that a transaction has occurred and establish the amounts to be recorded. Exhibit 3-5 on page 68 shows an example of a business document: a sales invoice. This exhibit shows that sales of $2,293.50 were made to the University Bookstore by Campus Supplies, Inc. The invoice also indicates the terms of the sale and shows that the purchase price is due to be paid within 30 days of the invoice date.

The analysis of a transaction is a key step in accounting. The accountant must determine the most appropriate way to record each transaction and to recognize its economic impact on the accounting equation. Though many transactions are straightforward, others are complex or unfamiliar, and accountants must have a thorough understanding of accounting theory in order to analyze them correctly. It is this understanding that allows accountants to make important judgments as they record and report on the activities of business enterprises.

Chapter 3 *Introducing the Accounting Cycle*

EXHIBIT 3-4 *Steps in the Accounting Cycle*

Step 1. Analyze transactions and business documents

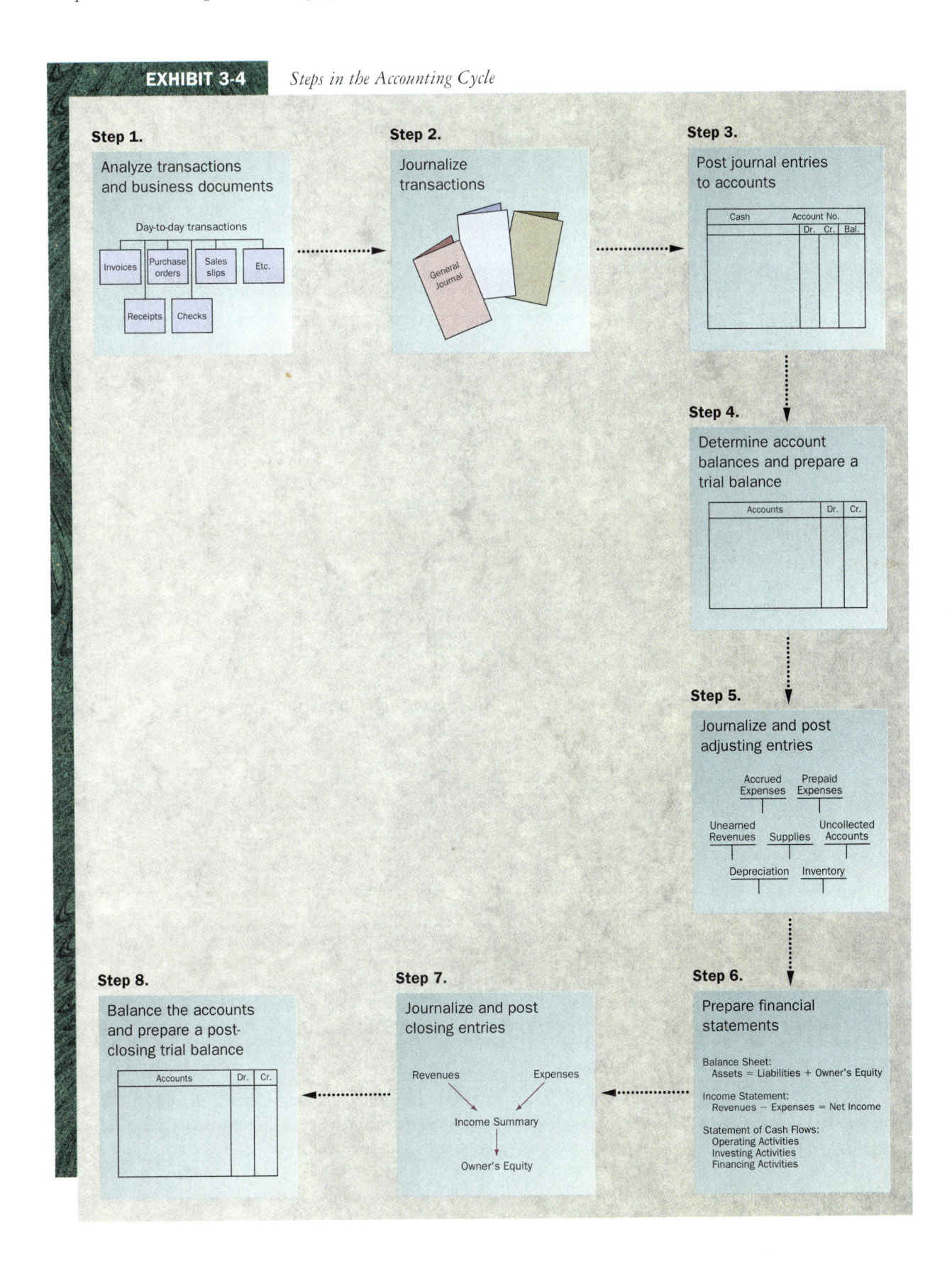

Day-to-day transactions
- Invoices
- Purchase orders
- Sales slips
- Etc.
- Receipts
- Checks

Step 2. Journalize transactions

General Journal

Step 3. Post journal entries to accounts

Cash	Account No.
	Dr.	Cr.	Bal.

Step 4. Determine account balances and prepare a trial balance

Accounts	Dr.	Cr.

Step 5. Journalize and post adjusting entries

- Accrued Expenses
- Prepaid Expenses
- Unearned Revenues
- Supplies
- Uncollected Accounts
- Depreciation
- Inventory

Step 6. Prepare financial statements

Balance Sheet:
   Assets = Liabilities + Owner's Equity

Income Statement:
   Revenues − Expenses = Net Income

Statement of Cash Flows:
   Operating Activities
   Investing Activities
   Financing Activities

Step 7. Journalize and post closing entries

Revenues → Income Summary ← Expenses
Income Summary → Owner's Equity

Step 8. Balance the accounts and prepare a post-closing trial balance

Accounts	Dr.	Cr.

EXHIBIT 3-5 Sales Invoice

CAMPUS SUPPLIES, INC.

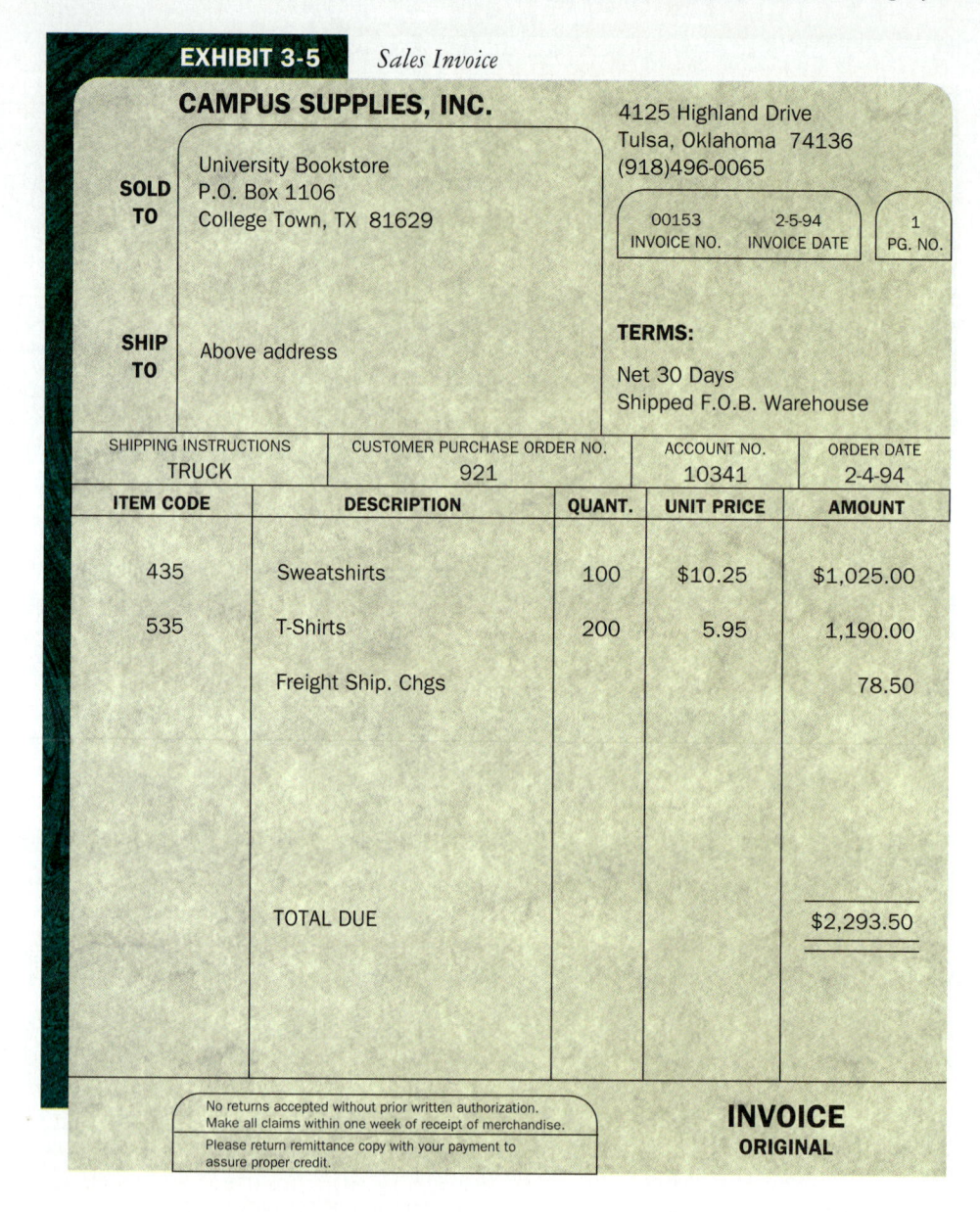

4125 Highland Drive
Tulsa, Oklahoma 74136
(918)496-0065

SOLD TO: University Bookstore, P.O. Box 1106, College Town, TX 81629

INVOICE NO. 00153　INVOICE DATE 2-5-94　PG. NO. 1

SHIP TO: Above address

TERMS: Net 30 Days
Shipped F.O.B. Warehouse

SHIPPING INSTRUCTIONS	CUSTOMER PURCHASE ORDER NO.	ACCOUNT NO.	ORDER DATE
TRUCK	921	10341	2-4-94

ITEM CODE	DESCRIPTION	QUANT.	UNIT PRICE	AMOUNT
435	Sweatshirts	100	$10.25	$1,025.00
535	T-Shirts	200	5.95	1,190.00
	Freight Ship. Chgs			78.50
	TOTAL DUE			$2,293.50

No returns accepted without prior written authorization.
Make all claims within one week of receipt of merchandise.
Please return remittance copy with your payment to assure proper credit.

INVOICE
ORIGINAL

Step 2. Journalize Transactions

The second step in the accounting cycle is to record the results of transactions in a **journal**. Known as "books of original entry," journals provide a chronological record of all entity transactions. They show the dates of the transactions, the amounts involved, and the particular accounts affected by the transactions. Usually, an explanation of the transaction is also included.

This chronological recording of transactions provides a company with a complete record of its activities. If amounts were recorded directly in the accounts, it would be difficult, if not impossible, for a company to trace a transaction that occurred, say, six months previously.

Smaller companies, such as a locally owned pizza restaurant, may use only one book of original entry, called a General Journal, to record all transactions.

journal an accounting record in which transactions are first entered; provides a chronological record of all business activities

Chapter 3 *Introducing the Accounting Cycle*

Larger companies having thousands of transactions each year may use special journals (for example, a Cash Receipts Journal) as well as a General Journal. Special journals are described in an appendix to Chapter 5.

A specific format is used in journalizing (recording) transactions in a General Journal. The debit entry is listed first; the credit entry is listed second and is indented to the right. Normally, the date and a brief explanation of the transaction are considered essential parts of the journal entry. Dollar signs usually are omitted. Unless otherwise noted, this format will be used whenever **journal entries** are presented.

journal entry *a recording of a transaction where debits equal credits; usually includes a date and an explanation of the transaction*

General Journal Entry Format

```
Date    Debit Entry ..................................................  xx
             Credit Entry ............................................       xx
        Explanation.
```

Exhibit 3-6 is a partial page from a General Journal, showing typical journal entries. Study this exhibit carefully because the entire accounting cycle is based on journal entries. If journal entries are incorrect, the resulting financial information will not be accurate.

To give you additional exposure to analyzing transactions and recording journal entries, we now discuss the entries used to record some common transactions of a business enterprise. These transactions fit into the following four

Exhibit 3-6 *General Journal*

JOURNAL Page 1

Date	Description	Post Ref.	Debits	Credits
Jan. 1994 1	Cash		5,000	
	Consulting Fee Revenue			5,000
	Received cash for consulting services.			
4	Supplies		1,500	
	Accounts Payable			1,500
	Purchased supplies on account.			
10	Accounts Payable		1,500	
	Cash			1,500
	Paid for supplies purchased on account.			

general categories: acquiring cash, acquiring other assets, selling goods or providing services, and collecting cash and paying obligations. Obviously, we cannot present all possible transactions in this chapter. In studying the illustrations, strive to understand the conceptual basis of transaction analysis rather than memorizing specific journal entries. Pay particular attention to the dual effect of each transaction on the entity in terms of the basic accounting equation, that is, in terms of its impact on assets and on liabilities and owners' equity. Remember that business activity involves revenues, expenses, and distributions to owners as well and that these accounts eventually increase or decrease an owners' equity account (Retained Earnings for a corporation and Proprietorship or Partnership Capital for proprietorships and partnerships).

ACQUIRING CASH, EITHER FROM OWNERS OR BY BORROWING. One of the first tasks of any business is to acquire cash, either through owners' investments or by borrowing. Once a business is established, it normally generates cash from operations—by selling goods or services.

Example 1. The following transactions for two types of organizations—a proprietorship and a corporation—illustrate contributions (investments) by owners:

assets (+)	Cash	50,000	
owner's equity (+)	M. Rhodes, Capital		50,000
	Received $50,000 cash investment from M. Rhodes, proprietor.		
assets (+)	Cash	50,000	
owners' equity (+)	Capital Stock		50,000
	Issued 5,000 shares of capital stock at $10 per share.		

These two transactions are similar in that each increased cash as a result of owners' investments. In the first case, a proprietor contributed the cash; in the second case, capital stock of a corporation was issued (sold) to investors (stockholders). In both instances, the investment, and hence the ownership interest, was increased. The Cash account was debited, and the Capital Stock (or Capital) account was credited. The economic impact of these situations may be summarized as:

Assets	= Liabilities	+ Owners' Equity
(increase $50,000)	(no change)	(increase $50,000)

Example 2. In this example, cash is obtained by borrowing.

assets (+)	Cash	25,000	
liabilities (+)	Notes Payable		25,000
	Borrowed $25,000 from First National Bank, signing a 6-month note at 12% interest. (The interest is entered into the accounting records later, generally when the note is paid; see Example 3, page 74.)		

Here, the Cash account was debited, and the Notes Payable account was credited. The accounting model would capture the economic impact of borrowing the money as follows:

Assets = Liabilities + Owners' Equity
(increase $25,000) (increase $25,000) (no change)

ACQUIRING OTHER ASSETS. Cash obtained from owners' investments, borrowings, or revenues can be used to acquire other assets needed to operate the business. Such assets include supplies, buildings, and equipment. They may be purchased with cash or on credit. Credit purchases require payment after a period of time, for example, 30 days. Normally, interest expense is incurred when assets are bought on a time-payment plan that extends beyond two or three months. (To keep our examples simple here, we will not include interest expense. We will show how to account for interest on page 74, where we discuss the payment of obligations.) Examples of transactions involving the acquisition of noncash assets follow.

Example 1. Supplies costing $1,250 are purchased for cash; an increase in one asset (supplies) is accompanied by a decrease in another asset (cash).

assets (+) Supplies 1,250
assets (−)   Cash 1,250
Purchased supplies for cash.

The accounting equation is:

Assets   = Liabilities   + Owners' Equity
(increase $1,250; (no change)   (no change)
decrease $1,250)

Example 2. Supplies costing $4,500 have been purchased "on account," which means that the buyer has used credit instead of cash to make the purchase and has an obligation (liability) to pay for the supplies at some future date.

assets (+)   Supplies 4,500
liabilities (+)   Accounts Payable 4,500
Purchased supplies on account.

The accounting equation shows:

Assets   = Liabilities   + Owners' Equity
(increase $4,500) (increase $4,500) (no change)

When the company pays for its supplies, cash will be reduced, and the liability, Accounts Payable, will also be reduced, thus keeping the equation in balance. Supplies and similar items purchased on account are generally paid for within 30–60 days and normally do not require an interest charge.

Example 3. An asset (for example, a building) has been acquired, a cash down payment has been made, and a long-term obligation has been incurred for the balance of the asset's cost. As the journal entry illustrates, more than two accounts can be involved in recording a transaction. This type of entry is called a **compound journal entry**. Notice how the explanation clarifies the entry.

compound journal entry *a journal entry that involves more than one debit or more than one credit or both*

assets (+)
liabilities (+)
assets (−)

Building...	63,000	
Mortgage Payable		53,000
Cash		10,000

Purchased building for $63,000, making a $10,000 down payment and signing a 10-year, 12% mortgage for the balance.

The accounting equation is:

Assets = Liabilities + Owners' Equity
(increase $63,000; (increase $53,000) (no change)
decrease $10,000)

SELLING GOODS OR PROVIDING SERVICES. The next category of common transactions involves the sale of merchandise or services. Revenues are generated and expenses incurred during this process. Sometimes merchandise or services are sold for cash; at other times, they are sold on credit (on account) and a receivable is established for collection at a later date. Therefore, revenues indicate the source not only of cash but of other assets as well, all of which are received in exchange for the merchandise or services provided. Similarly, expenses may be incurred and paid for immediately by cash, or they may be incurred on credit—that is, they may be "charged," with a cash payment to be made at a later date. Illustrative transactions follow. Note that the effect of revenues and expenses on owners' equity is indicated in brackets for each transaction.

Example 1. Cash is received for services provided.

assets (+)
revenues (+) [equity (+)]

Cash	17,000	
Consulting Fee Revenue		17,000

Received cash for consulting services.

Because revenues increase owners' equity, the accounting equation is:

Assets = Liabilities + Owners' Equity (Revenues)
(increase $17,000) (no change) (increase $17,000)

Example 2. Merchandise is sold to customers on account, establishing a receivable. In this case, the company is allowing a customer 30 days to make payment. As with short-term credit purchases, interest is generally not charged on short-term credit sales. When payment is received, Accounts Receivable is reduced, and Cash is increased by the same amount.

Sales, whether made on account or for cash, require entries that reflect not only the sales but also the cost of the **inventory** sold. The **cost of goods sold** is

inventory *goods held for resale*

cost of goods sold *the expense incurred to purchase the merchandise sold during a period*

an expense and, as such, is offset against the sales revenue to determine the profitability of sales transactions. The special procedures for handling inventory are described in Chapters 6 and 7. It is sufficient here to show an example of the impact of the transactions on the accounting equation.

assets (+)	Accounts Receivable	75,000	
revenues (+) [equity (+)]	Sales Revenue		75,000
	Sold merchandise on account.		
expenses (+) [equity (−)]	Cost of Goods Sold	60,000	
assets (−)	Inventory		60,000
	To record the cost of merchandise sold and to reduce inventory for its cost.		

In this example, merchandise costing the company $60,000 is being sold for $75,000. The effect on the accounting equation for each transaction would be:

Sales on Account

Assets   = Liabilities   + Owners' Equity (Revenues)
(increase $75,000)   (no change)   (increase $75,000)

Cost of Goods Sold

Assets   = Liabilities   + Owners' Equity (Expenses)
(decrease $60,000)   (no change)   (decrease $60,000)

Example 3. Expenses other than cost of goods sold are also incurred in operating a business, as the following entries for advertising and wages expense illustrate:

expenses (+) [equity (−)]	Advertising Expense	500	
assets (−)	Cash		500
	Paid advertising expense.		
expenses (+) [equity (−)]	Wages Expense	22,500	
assets (−)	Cash		22,500
	Paid wages expense.		

The effect on the accounting equation of the advertising expense would be:

Assets   = Liabilities   + Owners' Equity (Expense)
(decrease $500)   (no change)   (decrease $500)

The entry for Wages Expense affects the equation in the same manner, the only difference being the amount, $22,500.

COLLECTING CASH AND PAYING OBLIGATIONS. Obviously, once merchandise or services are sold on account, the receivables must be collected. The cash received generally is used to meet daily operating expenses and to pay other obligations. Excess cash can be reinvested in the business or distributed to the owners as a return on their investment.

Example 1. The collection of accounts receivable is an important aspect of most businesses. Customers are allowed to purchase merchandise on charge accounts or with credit cards on the assumption that the availability of credit will increase total sales. If collections are not made, however, the seller may lose not only the cash but the merchandise as well. When receivables are collected, that asset is reduced, and cash is increased, as shown here.

assets (+)	Cash	75,000	
assets (−)	Accounts Receivable		75,000
	Collected $75,000 of receivables.		

The effect of collecting the receivables on the accounting equation is:

Assets = Liabilities + Owners' Equity
(increase $75,000; (no change)   (no change)
decrease $75,000)

Example 2. The entry to record the payment of obligations with cash is:

liabilities (−)	Accounts Payable	4,500	
assets (−)	Cash		4,500
	Paid $4,500 on account.		

After payment of accounts payable, the accounting equation shows:

Assets   = Liabilities   + Owners' Equity
(decrease $4,500)   (decrease $4,500)   (no change)

To help bring these two examples into clearer focus, remember that two parties are always involved in exchange transactions. What one buys, the other sells. When sales are on credit, the seller will record a receivable, and the buyer will record a payable. The two accounts are inversely related. The seller of merchandise records a receivable and a sale and simultaneously records an expense for the cost of goods sold and a reduction of inventory, as in Example 2 on pages 72–73. The buyer records the receipt of the merchandise and at the same time records an obligation to pay the seller at some future time. When payment is made, the buyer reduces Accounts Payable and Cash, as in Example 2, whereas the seller increases Cash and reduces Accounts Receivable.

Example 3. On page 70, we showed the entry required when cash is borrowed. As the following compound journal entry shows, a note payable or similar obligation requires an entry for payment, as well as for the interest due:

liabilities (−)	Notes Payable	25,000	
expenses (+) [equity (−)]	Interest Expense	1,500	
assets (−)	Cash		26,500
	Paid $25,000 note with interest ($25,000 × 0.12 × 6/12 = $1,500).		

Analysis of this transaction reveals that assets have decreased for two reasons. First, a liability of $25,000 has been paid with cash; second, interest expense at 12% for 6 months on the note payable has been paid. This relationship will generally be present in most long-term and some short-term liability transactions. Since the interest charge is an expense and decreases owners' equity, the impact of the entry on the accounting equation is:

Assets   = Liabilities   + Owners' Equity (Expense)
(decrease $26,500)   (decrease $25,000)   (decrease $1,500)

Example 4. Corporations that are profitable generally pay dividends to their stockholders. Put simply, dividends represent a distribution to the stockholders of part of the earnings of a company. The following entry illustrates the payment of a cash dividend:

owners' equity (−)
assets (−)

Dividends	12,000	
Cash		12,000
Paid a $12,000 cash dividend.		

As noted earlier, dividends, like revenues and expenses, affect owners' equity. Unlike revenues and expenses, dividends are a distribution of profits and, therefore, are not considered in determining net income. Because dividends reduce the retained earnings accumulated by a corporation, they decrease owners' equity. The payment of a $12,000 dividend affects the accounting equation as follows:

Assets   = Liabilities   + Owners' Equity
(decrease $12,000)   (no change)   (decrease $12,000)

The preceding entry relates to a corporation. When a proprietor or partner withdraws cash from the business, the entry would include a debit to the proprietor's or partner's drawings account, as shown in the following example:

owner's equity (−)
assets (−)

M. Rhodes, Drawings	12,000	
Cash		12,000
Withdrew cash from business.		

The net effect on the accounting equation is the same. Drawings reduce the equity in proprietorships and partnerships, just as dividends reduce the equity in corporations.

Step 3. Post Journal Entries to Accounts

Once transactions have been analyzed and recorded in a journal, it is necessary to classify and group all similar items. This is accomplished by the bookkeeping procedure of **posting** all the journal entries to appropriate accounts. As indicated earlier, accounts are records of like items. They show transaction dates, increases and decreases, and account balances. For example, all increases

posting *the process of transferring amounts from the journal to the ledger* and decreases in cash arising from transactions recorded in the journal are accumulated in one account called Cash. Similarly, all revenue transactions are grouped together in the Sales (or Service) Revenue account. Exhibit 3-7 shows how the January 1 transaction from the General Journal (Exhibit 3-6, page 69) would be posted to the Cash account.

All accounts are maintained in an accounting record called the General Ledger. A **ledger,** then, is a "book" of accounts. Exhibit 3-8 shows how the two cash transactions in the General Journal would be posted to the Cash account in the General Ledger, with arrows depicting the posting procedures. Observe that a number has been inserted in the "posting reference" column in both books. This number serves as a cross-reference between the General Journal and the accounts in the General Ledger. In the journal, it identifies the account to which the journal entry has been posted. In the ledger, it identifies the page on which the entry appears in the General Journal. For example, the GJ1 notation in the Cash account for the January 1 entry means that the $5,000 has been posted from page 1 of the General Journal.

A particular company will have as many or as few accounts as it needs to provide a reasonable classification of its transactions. The list of accounts used by a company is known as its **chart of accounts.** Exhibit 3-9 shows some accounts that might appear in a typical merchandising company's chart of accounts.

ledger *a book of accounts in which data from transactions recorded in journals are posted and thereby classified and summarized*

chart of accounts *a systematic listing of all accounts used by a company*

Exhibit 3-7 *Cash Account in General Ledger*

ACCOUNT: Cash
ACCOUNT NO. 101

Date		Item	Post Ref.	Debits	Credits	Balance
Jan. 1994	1	Balance				10,100
	1	Received cash for consulting services		5,000		15,100

Chapter 3 Introducing the Accounting Cycle

Exhibit 3-8 *Posting to the General Ledger*

JOURNAL — Page 1

Date	Description	Post Ref.	Debits	Credits
Jan. 1, 1994	Cash	101	5,000	
	Consulting Fee Revenue			5,000
	Received cash for consulting services.			
4	Supplies		1,500	
	Accounts Payable			1,500
	Purchased supplies on account.			
10	Accounts Payable		1,500	
	Cash	101		1,500
	Paid for supplies purchased on account.			

GENERAL LEDGER

ACCOUNT: Cash ACCOUNT NO. 101

Date	Item	Post Ref.	Debits	Credits	Balance
Jan. 1, 1994	Balance	✓			10,100
1	Received cash for consulting services	GJ1	5,000		15,100
10	Paid for supplies purchased on account	GJ1		1,500	13,600

Exhibit 3-9   *Chart of Accounts for a Merchandising Business*

Assets (100–199)

Current Assets (100–150):
101 Cash
103 Notes Receivable
105 Accounts Receivable
107 Inventory
108 Supplies

Long-Term Assets (151–199):
151 Land
152 Buildings
154 Office Furniture

Liabilities (200–299)

Current Liabilities (200–219):
201 Notes Payable
202 Accounts Payable
203 Salaries Payable
204 Interest Payable
206 Income Taxes Payable

Long-Term Liabilities (220–239):
222 Mortgage Payable

Owners' Equity (300–399)

301 Capital Stock
330 Retained Earnings

Sales (400–499)

400 Sales Revenue

Expenses (500–599)

500 Cost of Goods Sold
501 Sales Salaries and Commissions
523 Rent Expense
525 Travel Expense
528 Advertising Expense
551 Officers' Salaries
553 Administrative Salaries
570 Payroll Taxes
571 Office Supplies Expense
573 Utility Expense
578 Office Equipment Rent Expense
579 Accounting and Legal Fees

Step 4. Determine Account Balances and Prepare a Trial Balance

At the end of an accounting period, the accounts in the General Ledger are reviewed to determine each account's balance. *Asset, expense, and dividend accounts normally have debit balances; liability, owners' equity, and revenue accounts have credit balances.* In other words, the balance is normally on the side that increases the account.

To illustrate how to determine an account balance, consider the T-account below depicting several assumed transactions during the month of March.

The beginning balance in the Cash account plus all debit entries to Cash less all credit entries to Cash equals the ending balance in the Cash account.

Cash

Beg. Bal.	53,450		
3/1	11,200	3/2	4,200
3/7	2,900	3/3	575
3/30	6,350	3/9	1,200
		3/18	5,625
		3/23	16,050
		3/31	2,145
	73,900		29,795
	(29,795)		
End. Bal.	44,105		

trial balance *a listing of all account balances; provides a means of testing whether total debits equal total credits for all accounts*

After the account balances have been determined, a **trial balance** is usually prepared. A trial balance lists each account with its debit or credit balance. By adding all the debit balances and all the credit balances, the accountant can see whether total debits equal total credits. Even if the trial balance does show total debits equal to total credits, there may be errors. A transaction may be omitted completely, or it may have been recorded incorrectly or posted to the wrong account. These types of errors will not be discovered by preparing a trial balance; additional analysis would be required. A trial balance, using assumed data, is illustrated in Exhibit 3-10.

Exhibit 3-10

Pulman Corporation
Trial Balance
December 31, 1994

	Debits	Credits
Cash	$ 79,050	
Accounts Receivable	1,250	
Inventory	4,500	
Land	28,000	
Accounts Payable		$ 10,500
Notes Payable		25,000
Capital Stock		50,000
Retained Earnings		20,000
Sales Revenue		76,100
Cost of Goods Sold	60,000	
Advertising Expense	500	
Selling Expense	8,300	
Totals	$181,600	$181,600

To Summarize *The first four steps in the accounting cycle, as shown in Exhibit 3-4, are analyze transactions and business documents, journalize transactions, post journal entries to accounts, and determine account balances and prepare a trial balance. Exchange transactions between entities and related events provide the basis for all accounting records. The transactions are evidenced by source documents, such as an invoice, a bank note, or a check. Since the source documents provide the essential data of the transaction, they must be analyzed carefully to determine the proper entries in the General Journal or special journals. If the entries are not properly recorded, the entire accounting system will break down because the rest of the steps in the cycle are based on the journal entries. After transactions have been journalized, they can be classified and summarized by posting to the ledger accounts. At the end of the accounting period, the account balances are determined. Assets, expenses, and dividends usually have debit balances; liabilities, owners' equity, and revenues generally have credit balances. A trial balance is then prepared to see that total debits equal total credits.*

ILLUSTRATION OF THE FIRST FOUR STEPS IN THE ACCOUNTING CYCLE

We have introduced the first four steps in the accounting cycle. A simple illustration will help reinforce what you have learned about the relationship of assets, liabilities, and owners' equity, including revenues, expenses, and dividends, and the mechanics of double-entry accounting. Katherine Kohler established the Double K Corporation in 1994 with an initial capital contribution of $20,000, for which she received 1,000 shares of capital stock. Double K Corporation paid $10,000 cash for inventory. It also borrowed $20,000 from a bank to buy some land, signing a long-term note with the bank. Land was then purchased for $25,000 cash. During the accounting period, Double K Corporation sold 20 percent, or $2,000, of the inventory purchased. The company sold that inventory for $3,200, but in doing so incurred $200 in selling expenses and $100 in miscellaneous expenses. The sale of merchandise was originally made on credit; the company later collected the full amount in cash.

The inventory purchases are verified by invoices showing the actual items purchased, dates, amounts, and so forth. There is a $20,000 note payable to the bank. Other business documents indicate the sale of inventory and the expenses incurred. Through analysis of these transactions and supporting documents (step 1), the pertinent facts are obtained and the transactions are recorded in a journal (step 2).

In keeping with the entity concept, the transactions of Double K Corporation are accounted for separately from those of Katherine Kohler. The journal entries to record the transactions of Double K Corporation are as follows. (Note that letters are used in place of dates.)

			Debits	Credits
assets (+) owners' equity (+)	(a)	Cash 　Capital Stock *Issued 1,000 shares of capital stock for $20,000.*	20,000	20,000
assets (+) assets (−)	(b)	Inventory 　Cash *Purchased $10,000 of merchandise for cash.*	10,000	10,000
assets (+) liabilities (+)	(c)	Cash 　Notes Payable *Borrowed $20,000 from a bank.*	20,000	20,000
assets (+) assets (−)	(d)	Land 　Cash *Purchased land for cash.*	25,000	25,000
assets (+) revenues (+)	(e)	Accounts Receivable 　Sales Revenue *Sold $3,200 of merchandise on account.*	3,200	3,200
expenses (+) assets (−)		Cost of Goods Sold 　Inventory *To record the cost of merchandise sold.*	2,000	2,000

Chapter 3 Introducing the Accounting Cycle

expenses (+)	(f) Selling Expenses	200	
expenses (+)	Miscellaneous Expenses	100	
assets (−)	Cash		300
	Paid selling and miscellaneous expenses.		
assets (+)	(g) Cash	3,200	
assets (−)	Accounts Receivable		3,200
	Collected accounts receivable.		

Next, the transactions are posted to the ledger accounts (step 3). T-accounts are used to illustrate this process, with the letters a through g showing the cross-references to the journal entries. A balance is shown for the end of the period. (Where only one transaction is involved, the amount of the transaction is also the account balance.)

Cash					Accounts Receivable				Inventory				Land	
(a)	20,000	(b)	10,000	(e)	3,200	(g)	3,200	(b)	10,000	(e)	2,000	(d)	25,000
(c)	20,000	(d)	25,000										
(g)	3,200	(f)	300					Bal.	8,000				
Bal.	7,900												

Notes Payable			Capital Stock			Sales Revenue			Cost of Goods Sold	
	(c)	20,000		(a)	20,000		(e)	3,200	(e)	2,000

Selling Expenses		Miscellaneous Expenses	
(f) 200		(f) 100	

To see whether total debits equal total credits in the ledger, a trial balance may be prepared (step 4), as shown. The balances are taken from each ledger account.

Double K Corporation
Trial Balance
December 31, 1994

	Debits	Credits
Cash	$ 7,900	
Inventory	8,000	
Land	25,000	
Notes Payable		$20,000
Capital Stock		20,000
Sales Revenue		3,200
Cost of Goods Sold	2,000	
Selling Expenses	200	
Miscellaneous Expenses	100	
Totals	$43,200	$43,200

From the data in the trial balance, an income statement and a balance sheet can be prepared. Exhibit 3-11 shows these two financial statements for Double K Corporation in proper form. As you can see, total assets equal total liabilities and owners' equity. Thus, the accounting equation is in balance.

Exhibit 3-11

Double K Corporation
Income Statement
For the Year Ended December 31, 1994

Sales revenue		$ 3,200
Expenses:		
Cost of goods sold	$ 2,000	
Selling expenses	200	
Miscellaneous expenses	100	2,300
Net income		$ 900
EPS ($900 ÷ 1,000 shares of stock)		$ 0.90

Double K Corporation
Balance Sheet
December 31, 1994

Assets		Liabilities and Stockholders' Equity	
Cash	$ 7,900	Notes payable	$20,000
Inventory	8,000	Capital stock	20,000
Land	25,000	Retained earnings	900
Total assets	$40,900	Total liabilities and stockholders' equity	$40,900

Two final notes: First, the preparation of financial statements is rarely so simple. In reality, the procedure usually also involves the adjustment of some ledger accounts, which need to be brought current before they can be included in the balance sheet or the income statement. In Chapter 4, we will explain how accounts are adjusted (see step 5 on page 105) so that the financial statements will accurately reflect the current financial position and operating results of an enterprise.

Second, net income does not usually equal the ending retained earnings balance. Only in the first year of a company's operations would this be the case. Double K Corporation began operations in 1994 and paid no dividends during the year, so its $900 net income on the income statement equals the retained earnings figure on the balance sheet. In future years, the figures would be different since retained earnings is an accumulation of earnings from past years adjusted for dividends and other special items.

Chapter 3 Introducing the Accounting Cycle

Review of Learning Objectives

Objective 1

Understand the process of transforming transaction data into useful accounting information. The objective of the accounting process is to gather and transform transaction data into useful information that measures and communicates the results of business activity. The accounting system used to keep track of the many financial activities of an entity should be tailor-made for that entity, and may be a manual or an automated system, depending on the organization's needs.

Objective 2

Explain the basic accounting equation. The procedures for processing accounting data are based on double-entry accounting and the fundamental accounting equation Assets = Liabilities + Owners' Equity. Revenues increase retained earnings, whereas expenses and dividends decrease retained earnings. Thus, these accounts have a direct impact on the amount of owners' equity. In terms of the increase–decrease relationship of accounts, assets, expenses, and dividends are increased by debits; liabilities, owners' equity, and revenues are increased by credits. The double-entry system of accounting assures that the accounting equation will always balance because debit entries require equal credit entries; that is, total debits must always equal total credits when transactions are properly recorded.

Objective 3

Describe the first four steps in the accounting cycle: analyze transactions and business documents, journalize transactions, post journal entries, and prepare a trial balance. In conducting economic activities, businesses and other types of entities enter into exchange transactions. These transactions form the basis of accounting records. The procedures used in accounting for such transactions are known as the accounting cycle and include the following steps:

1. Analyze transactions and business documents.
2. Journalize transactions.
3. Post journal entries to accounts.
4. Determine account balances and prepare a trial balance.
5. Journalize and post adjusting entries.
6. Prepare financial statements.
7. Journalize and post closing entries.
8. Balance the accounts and prepare a post-closing trial balance.

This chapter has discussed the first four steps in the cycle; step 5 is explained in Chapter 4, and the remaining steps will be explained in Chapter 5.

Key Terms and Concepts

account *(62)*
accounting cycle *(60)*
business documents *(66)*
chart of accounts *(76)*
compound journal entry *(72)*
cost of goods sold *(72)*
credit *(62)*
debit *(62)*
dividends account *(65)*
drawings account *(65)*
expenses *(64)*
inventory *(72)*
journal *(68)*
journal entry *(69)*
ledger *(76)*
posting *(75)*
revenues *(64)*
T-account *(62)*
trial balance *(79)*

Review Problem

The First Four Steps in the Accounting Cycle

Journal entries are given below for October 1994, the first month of operation for Roadworthy Automotive, Inc.

```
1994
Oct.  1   Cash..................................................  40,000
              Capital Stock ......................................           40,000
          Issued capital stock for cash.
```

Oct.	1	Insurance Expense	500	
		Cash		500
		Purchased a 1-year insurance policy.		
	2	Rent Expense	750	
		Cash		750
		Paid the rent for the month of October.		
	3	Shop Equipment	8,000	
		Cash		8,000
		Purchased shop equipment for cash.		
	4	Supplies	3,000	
		Accounts Payable		3,000
		Purchased shop supplies on account.		
	5	Automotive Equipment	11,500	
		Cash		3,500
		Notes Payable		8,000
		Purchased a truck. Paid $3,500 cash and issued a 30-day note for the balance.		
	8	Cash	1,750	
		Service and Repair Revenue		1,750
		Received cash for repairs.		
	9	Advertising Expense	300	
		Cash		300
		Paid cash for radio spot announcements.		
	12	Automotive Expense	200	
		Cash		200
		Paid gas, oil, and service costs on the truck.		
	14	Accounts Payable	3,000	
		Cash		3,000
		Paid $3,000 on account.		
	16	Accounts Receivable	1,200	
		Service and Repair Revenue		1,200
		Repaired truck for Acme Drilling Company on account.		
	18	Telephone Expense	75	
		Cash		75
		Paid for installation and servicing of telephone for 1 month.		
	19	Automotive Expense	180	
		Cash		180
		Paid for minor repairs on the truck.		
	20	Cash	1,000	
		Notes Receivable	1,450	
		Service and Repair Revenue		2,450
		Collected $1,000 cash from Jones for truck repairs; accepted a 60-day note for the balance.		
	24	Repairs and Maintenance Expense	150	
		Cash		150
		Paid cleaning and painting expenses on the building.		

Chapter 3 *Introducing the Accounting Cycle*

Oct. 25	Cash...	1,500	
	Service and Repair Revenue		1,500
	Received cash for repairs and services from Hamilton, Inc.		
27	Supplies	2,500	
	Cash...		2,500
	Purchased shop supplies.		
29	Office Equipment......................................	1,250	
	Cash...		1,250
	Purchased a computer.		
30	Cash...	1,200	
	Accounts Receivable		1,200
	Collected receivables from Acme Drilling Company.		
31	Utilities Expense	900	
	Cash...		900
	Paid the monthly utility bill.		
31	Automotive Expense	350	
	Cash...		350
	Paid for gas, oil, and servicing of the truck.		

Required: Set up T-accounts, post all journal entries to the accounts, balance the accounts, and prepare a trial balance.

Solution The first step in solving this problem is to set up T-accounts for each item; then post all journal entries to the appropriate ledger accounts, as shown. Once the amounts are properly posted, account balances can be determined.

Cash		Notes Receivable		Accounts Receivable		Supplies	
10/1 40,000	10/1 500	10/20 1,450		10/16 1,200	10/30 1,200	10/4 3,000	
10/8 1,750	10/2 750			Bal. 0		10/27 2,500	
10/20 1,000	10/3 8,000					Bal. 5,500	
10/25 1,500	10/5 3,500						
10/30 1,200	10/9 300						
	10/12 200						
	10/14 3,000						
	10/18 75						
	10/19 180						
	10/24 150		Shop Equipment		Automotive Equipment		Office Equipment	
	10/27 2,500	10/3 8,000		10/5 11,500		10/29 1,250	
	10/29 1,250						
	10/31 900						
	10/31 350						
Bal. 23,795							

Notes Payable		Accounts Payable		Capital Stock		Service and Repair Revenue	
	10/5 8,000	10/14 3,000	10/4 3,000		10/1 40,000		10/8 1,750
			Bal. 0				10/16 1,200
							10/20 2,450
							10/25 1,500
							Bal. 6,900

Insurance Expense		Rent Expense		Advertising Expense		Automotive Expense	
10/1 500		10/2 750		10/9 300		10/12 200	
						10/19 180	
						10/31 350	
						Bal. 730	

Telephone Expense		Repairs and Maintenance Expense		Utilities Expense	
10/18 75		10/24 150		10/31 900	

The final step is to prepare a trial balance to see whether total debits equal total credits for all accounts. List all the accounts with balances in financial statement order; then enter the balance in each account.

Roadworthy Automotive, Inc.
Trial Balance
October 31, 1994

	Debits	Credits
Cash	$23,795	
Notes Receivable	1,450	
Supplies	5,500	
Shop Equipment	8,000	
Automotive Equipment	11,500	
Office Equipment	1,250	
Notes Payable		$ 8,000
Capital Stock		40,000
Service and Repair Revenue		6,900
Insurance Expense	500	
Rent Expense	750	
Advertising Expense	300	
Automotive Expense	730	
Telephone Expense	75	
Repairs and Maintenance Expense	150	
Utilities Expense	900	
Totals	$54,900	$54,900

Discussion Questions

1. What is the basic objective of the accounting cycle?
2. Assume you are asked to consult with company management on the type of accounting system to have. What factors would you likely suggest they consider?
3. In a double-entry system of accounting, why must total debits always equal total credits?
4. How are revenues and expenses related to the basic accounting equation?
5. In what ways are dividend and expense accounts similar, and in what ways are they different?
6. Explain the first four steps in the accounting cycle.
7. What purposes do business documents serve?
8. Distinguish between a journal and a ledger.
9. Assume that Company A buys $1,500 of merchandise from Company B. The merchandise originally cost Company B $1,000. What entries should the buyer and seller make, and what is the relationship of the accounts for this transaction?
10. Indicate how each of the following transactions affects the accounting equation.
    (a) Purchase of supplies on account.
    (b) Payment of wages.
    (c) Cash sales.
    (d) Payment of monthly utility bills.
    (e) Purchase of a building.
    (f) Cash investment by a stockholder.
    (g) Payment of a cash dividend.
    (h) Sale of goods for more than their cost.
    (i) Sale of land at less than its cost.
11. What is a chart of accounts? What is its purpose?
12. If a trial balance appears to be correct, does that guarantee complete accuracy in the accounting records? Explain.

Exercises

E3-1
Basic Accounting Equation

For each of the following transactions show how the fundamental accounting equation is kept in balance. Example: Borrowed money (increase assets, increase liabilities).

1. Purchased merchandise for resale by paying cash.
2. Paid off a note.
3. Collected a customer's account balance.
4. Sold merchandise on credit at a profit.
5. Paid the month's rent.

E3-2
Expanded Accounting Equation

Payless Department Store had the following transactions during the year:

1. Purchased inventory on account.
2. Sold merchandise for cash, assuming a profit on the sale.
3. Borrowed money from a bank.
4. Purchased land, making cash down payment and issuing a note for the balance.
5. Issued stock for cash.
6. Paid salaries for the year.
7. Paid a vendor for inventory purchased on account.
8. Sold a building for cash and notes receivable at no gain or loss.
9. Paid cash dividends to stockholders.
10. Paid utilities.

Using the following column headings, indicate the net effect of each transaction on the accounting equation (+ increase; − decrease; 0 no effect). Transaction 1 has been completed as an example.

Transaction	Assets	= Liabilities	+ Owners' Equity
1	+ (Inventory)	+ (Accounts Payable)	0

E3-3
Classification of Accounts

For each of the accounts listed, indicate whether it is an asset (A), a liability (L), or an owners' equity (OE) account. If it is an account that affects owners' equity, indicate whether it is a revenue (R), expense (E), or dividend (D) account.

1. Cash
2. Sales
3. Accounts Receivable
4. Cost of Goods Sold
5. Insurance Expense
6. Capital Stock
7. Mortgage Payable
8. Salaries and Wages Expense
9. Retained Earnings
10. Salaries Payable
11. Accounts Payable
12. Interest Revenue
13. Inventory
14. Interest Receivable
15. Notes Payable
16. Equipment
17. Office Supplies
18. Utilities Expense
19. Interest Payable
20. Rent Expense

E3-4
Normal Account Balances

For each account listed in E3-3, indicate whether it would normally have a debit balance or a credit balance.

E3-5
Journalizing Transactions

Record each of the following transactions in Chico's General Journal. (Omit explanations.)

1. Issue capital stock for $50,000 cash.
2. Borrowed $10,000 from a bank. Signed a note to secure the debt.
3. Purchased inventory from a supplier on credit for $8,000.
4. Paid the supplier for the inventory received.
5. Sold inventory that cost $1,200 for $1,500 on credit.
6. Collected $1,500 from customers.
7. Paid salaries and rent of $25,000 and $1,200, respectively.

E3-6
Journalizing Transactions

Silva Company had the following transactions:

1. Purchased a new building, paying $20,000 cash and issuing a note of $50,000.
2. Purchased $15,000 of inventory on account.
3. Sold inventory costing $5,000 for $6,000 on account.
4. Paid for inventory purchased on account (item 2).
5. Issued capital stock for $25,000.
6. Collected $4,500 of accounts receivable.
7. Paid utility bills totaling $360.
8. Sold old building for $27,000, receiving $10,000 cash and a $17,000 note (no gain or loss on the sale).
9. Paid $2,000 cash dividends to stockholders.

Record the above transactions in General Journal format. (Omit explanations.)

Chapter 3 *Introducing the Accounting Cycle*

E3-7
Journalizing and Posting Transactions

Given the following T-accounts, describe the transaction that took place on each specified date during July:

Cash		
7/4 9,500	7/1	3,420
7/28 8,000	7/23	2,000
	7/25	5,000
	7/30	5,500
Bal. 1,580		

Accounts Receivable	
7/14 18,000	7/4 9,500
	7/28 8,000
Bal. 500	

Inventory	
7/10 20,000	7/14 15,000
Bal. 5,000	

Equipment
7/30 1,500

Land
7/30 4,000

Accounts Payable	
7/25 5,000	7/10 20,000
	Bal. 15,000

Sales Revenue
7/14 18,000

Cost of Goods Sold
7/14 15,000

Rent Expense
7/23 2,000

Advertising Expense
7/1 3,420

E3-8
Trial Balance

The account balances in Dr. Margaret Katz's ledger as of July 31, 1994, are listed here in alphabetical order. The balance for the Capital account has been omitted. Prepare a trial balance, and insert the missing amount for M. Katz, Capital.

Accounts Payable	$ 8,600	Insurance Expense	$ 3,600
Accounts Receivable	2,000	Land............................	19,000
Buildings................	20,000	Miscellaneous Expenses	1,400
M. Katz, Capital	?	Mortgage Payable (due 1997)	24,000
Cash	19,600	Salary Expense	10,000
M. Katz, Drawings	3,000	Supplies	600
Equipment	16,000	Utilities Expense	400
Fees Earned	26,000		

E3-9
Accounting for Distributions to Owners

Give the entries to record the following two independent transactions:

1. The board of directors of ITEC Corporation paid to stockholders a $160,000 cash dividend on March 8, 1993.
2. Susan Schaffner withdrew $30,000 from her proprietorship on July 1, 1994.

E3-10
Relationships of the Expanded Accounting Equation

Char Bosk, Inc. had the following information reported. From these data, determine the amount of:

(a) Capital Stock at December 31, 1993.
(b) Retained Earnings at December 31, 1994.
(c) Revenues for the year 1994.

	December 31, 1993	December 31, 1994
Total assets	$250,000	$300,000
Total liabilities	60,000	70,000
Capital stock	?	50,000
Retained earnings	150,000	?
Revenues for 1994		?
Expenses for 1994		205,000
Dividends paid during 1994		5,000

Problem Set A

P3A-1
Journal Entries and Trial Balance

SOLUTIONS SOFTWARE

The balances in the Lopez Company General Ledger as of January 1, 1994, were:

	Debits	Credits
Cash	$15,000	
Accounts Receivable	200	
Inventory	26,000	
Equipment	3,000	
Salaries Payable		$ 4,000
Accounts Payable		2,500
Notes Payable		20,000
M. Lopez, Capital		17,700
Totals	$44,200	$44,200

Lopez Company had the following transactions in 1994. All expenses were paid in cash, unless otherwise stated.

(a) Purchased inventory for $17,500 cash. Accounts Payable as of January 1, 1994, were also paid.
(b) Sold $98,000 of merchandise, 90 percent for cash and 10 percent on credit.
(c) The cost of goods sold was $32,000.
(d) Paid electricity and other utilities of $12,000.
(e) Paid three high-school students $250 a month each to help out on a part-time basis. Record one entry for the full year's amount. (Ignore payroll taxes.)
(f) Paid $25,000 in wages earned in 1994 by full-time employees.
(g) Mary Lopez withdrew $1,500 a month for 12 months for living expenses. Record one entry for total withdrawals.
(h) Collected receivables of $9,500.

Required:
1. Prepare journal entries to record each of the above transactions. (Omit explanations.)
2. Prepare a trial balance for The Lopez Company at December 31, 1994.
3. **Interpretive Question** If the debit and credit columns of the trial balance are equal, does this mean that no errors have been made in journalizing the transactions? Explain.

P3A-2
Journalizing and Posting

Snow Flake Company had the following transactions during July 1994.

July 1 Issued capital stock for $40,000 cash.
 3 Paid a note of $10,000 owed since January 1, 1994, together with interest of $600.

Chapter 3 *Introducing the Accounting Cycle*

July 5 Paid $15,000 to employees for their July 1994 wages.
     9 Paid yearly property taxes of $1,800.
   17 Purchased $15,000 worth of tennis balls and racquets on account for resale.
   21 Sold all the tennis balls and racquets purchased on July 17 for $22,500, with $7,500 received in cash and the balance on credit.
   25 Paid $14,500 of obligations.
   29 Received $10,300 from customers as payments on their accounts.

Required:
1. Journalize each of the transactions for July. (Omit explanations.)
2. Set up T-accounts, and post each of the journal entries that you made in (1).
3. **Interpretive Question** If the owner of a business wanted to know at any given moment how much cash or inventory the company had on hand, where would the owner look? Why?

P3A-3

Journal Entries from Ledger Analysis

Given are a number of T-accounts. Transactions have been posted to the accounts and given a letter to indicate each transaction.

Cash			
(a) 100,000	(b) 40,000		
(d) 15,000	(c) 6,000		
(i) 12,400	(g) 13,000		
	(k) 10,000		
	(l) 3,350		

Accounts Receivable	
(e) 15,700	(i) 12,400

Accounts Payable	
(k) 10,000	(f) 1,850
(l) 3,350	(h) 10,000
	(j) 6,500

Delivery Equipment	
(b) 40,000	
(h) 10,000	

Capital Stock	
	(a) 100,000

Delivery Revenues	
	(d) 15,000
	(e) 15,700

Salaries Expense	
(g) 13,000	

Delivery Expense	
(f) 1,850	

Rent Expense	
(c) 6,000	

Heating Expense	
(j) 3,000	

Utilities Expense	
(j) 2,000	

Telephone Expense	
(j) 1,500	

Required: Describe the event that is probably being recorded with each entry.

P3A-4

Unifying Concepts: Journalizing, Posting, and Preparing a Trial Balance and Balance Sheet

SOLUTIONS SOFTWARE

The following transactions of Roylance Company (a proprietorship) occurred during May 1994:

May 1 Received $50,000 cash from the owner, John Roylance, as an investment in the company.
   10 Purchased land and a building for $20,000 cash and a 10-year $40,000 mortgage. The land was appraised at $15,000 and the building at $45,000.
   15 Purchased supplies from Hill Top Company for $5,000 on account.
   31 Sold half the land purchased on May 10 for $7,500, receiving $2,500 cash and a 60-day note in the amount of $5,000.

Required:
1. Journalize the above transactions.
2. Post to T-accounts.
3. Prepare a trial balance.
4. Prepare a balance sheet.

P3A-5
T-Accounts, Trial Balance, and Income Statement

SOLUTIONS SOFTWARE

The following list is a selection of transactions from Bennington Corporation's business activities during 1994, the first year of operations.

(a) Received $50,000 cash for capital stock.
(b) Paid $5,000 cash for equipment.
(c) Purchased inventory costing $18,000 on account.
(d) Sold $25,000 of merchandise to customers on account. Cost of goods sold was $15,000.
(e) Signed a note with a bank for a $10,000 loan.
(f) Collected $9,500 cash from customers who had purchased merchandise on account.
(g) Purchased land, $10,000, and a building, $60,000, for $15,000 cash and a 30-year mortgage of $55,000.
(h) Made a first payment of $2,750 on the mortgage principal plus another $2,750 in interest.
(i) Paid $12,000 of accounts payable.
(j) Purchased $1,500 of supplies on account.
(k) Paid $2,500 of accounts payable.
(l) Paid $7,500 in wages earned during the year.
(m) Received $10,000 cash and $3,000 of notes in settlement of customers' accounts.
(n) Received $3,000 in payment of a note receivable plus interest of $250.
(o) Paid $600 cash for a utilities bill.
(p) Sold excess land for its cost of $3,000.
(q) Received $1,500 in rent for an unused part of a building.
(r) Paid off $10,000 note, plus interest of $1,200.

Required:
1. Set up T-accounts, and appropriately record the debits and credits for each transaction. Leave room for a number of entries in the Cash account.
2. Prepare a trial balance.
3. Prepare an income statement for the period. (Ignore income taxes and the EPS computation.)

P3A-6
Analysis of Transactions

Pacific Motors, Inc. entered into the following transactions during the month of August:

(a) Purchased $1,500 of supplies on account from Major Supply Company. The cost of the supplies to Major Supply Company was $1,200.
(b) Paid $600 to Valley Electric for the monthly utility bill.
(c) Sold a truck to Fast Delivery, Inc. A $5,000 down payment was received with the balance of $12,000 due within 30 days. The cost of the delivery truck to Pacific Motors was $11,000.
(d) Purchased a total of 8 new cars and trucks from Japanese Motors, Inc. for a total of $96,000, one-half of which was paid in cash. The balance is due within 45 days. The total cost of the vehicles to Japanese Motors was $80,000.
(e) Paid $1,875 to Silva's Automotive for repair work on cars for the current month.

(f) Sold one of the new cars purchased from Japanese Motors to the town mayor, Ana Mecham. The sales price was $17,500, and was paid by Mecham upon delivery of the car. The cost of the particular car sold to Mecham was $12,100.

(g) Borrowed $10,000 from a local bank to be repaid in one year with 12% interest.

Required:
1. For each of the transactions, make the proper journal entry on the books of Pacific Motors. (Omit explanations.)
2. For each of the transactions, make the proper journal entry on the books of the other party to the transaction, for example, (a) Major Supply Company, (b) Valley Electric. (Omit explanations.)

P3A-7
Unifying Concepts: Journal Entries, T-Accounts, Trial Balance

Hugo Company, a retailer, had the following account balances as of April 30, 1994:

Cash	$10,100	
Accounts Receivable	4,900	
Inventory	16,000	
Land	26,000	
Building	24,000	
Furniture	4,000	
Accounts Payable		$12,000
Notes Payable		25,000
Capital Stock		30,000
Retained Earnings		18,000
Totals	$85,000	$85,000

During May, the company completed the following transactions.

May 3 Paid one-half of 4/30/94 accounts payable.
    6 Collected all of 4/30/94 accounts receivable.
    7 Sold inventory costing $7,700 for $6,000 cash and $4,000 on account.
    8 Sold one-half the land for $13,000, receiving $8,000 cash plus a note for $5,000.
   10 Purchased inventory on account, $10,000.
   15 Paid installment of $5,000 on note payable.
   21 Issued additional capital stock for $2,000 cash.
   23 Sold inventory costing $4,000 for $7,500 cash.
   25 Paid salaries of $2,000.
   26 Paid rent of $500.
   29 Purchased desk for $500 cash.

Required:
1. Prepare the journal entry for each transaction.
2. Post the entries to T-accounts.
3. Prepare a trial balance as of May 31, 1994.

Problem Set B

P3B-1
Journal Entries and Trial Balance

As of January 1, 1994, Raintop Roofing Company had the trial balance shown on the next page.

Raintop Roofing Company had the following transactions in 1994. Assume that expenses were paid in cash unless otherwise stated.

(a) Bought additional land for $4,000.
(b) Sold $10,000 of inventory on account. Cost of goods sold was $8,000.
(c) Purchased additional inventory for $20,000 on account.
(d) Mack Reed withdrew $20,000 during 1994.

(e) Sold $12,000 of inventory, 80 percent on account and 20 percent for cash. Cost of the goods sold was $10,000.
(f) Collected receivables of $8,900.
(g) Paid $3,000 principal on the mortgage.
(h) Paid off accounts payable of $3,500.

	Debits	Credits
Cash	$ 35,000	
Accounts Receivable	3,200	
Inventory	15,000	
Land	11,000	
Building	39,800	
Accounts Payable		$ 6,700
Mortgage Payable		35,000
M. Reed, Capital		62,300
Totals	$104,000	$104,000

Required:
1. Prepare journal entries to record each of the transactions. (Omit explanations.)
2. Prepare a trial balance for Raintop Roofing Company at December 31, 1994.

P3B-2
Journal Entries from Ledger Analysis

T-accounts for Ling Tech, Inc. are shown here.

Cash
(a) 6,000 | (c) 4,500
(b) 8,000 | (f) 3,700
(d) 9,000 | (g) 1,700
(i) 1,000 | (h) 2,000

Accounts Receivable
(d) 2,000 | (i) 1,000

Inventory
(c) 9,000 | (e) 7,500

Accounts Payable
(f) 3,700 | (c) 4,500

Notes Payable
 | (a) 6,000

Capital Stock
 | (b) 8,000

Sales Revenue
 | (d) 11,000

Cost of Goods Sold
(e) 7,500 |

Salary Expense
(g) 1,700 |

Rent Expense
(h) 2,000 |

Required: Analyze the accounts and prepare the appropriate journal entries that must have been made by the company. (Omit explanations.)

P3B-3
Journalizing and Posting Transactions

Pat Bjornson, owner of Pat's Beauty Supply, completed the following business transactions during March 1994.

March 1 Purchased $53,000 of inventory on credit.
      4 Collected $10,000 from customers as payments on their accounts.

Chapter 3 *Introducing the Accounting Cycle*

March 5   Purchased equipment for $3,000 cash.
      6   Sold inventory that cost $30,000 to customers on account for $40,000.
     10   Paid rent for March, $1,050.
     15   Paid utilities for March, $100.
     17   Paid a $300 monthly salary to the part-time helper.
     20   Collected $33,000 from customers as payments on their accounts.
     22   Paid $53,000 cash on account payable. (See March 1 entry.)
     25   Paid property taxes of $1,200.
     28   Sold inventory that cost $20,000 to customers for $30,000 cash.

Required: 1. For each transaction, give the entry that Pat would make to record it in the company's General Journal. (Omit explanations.)
2. Draw T-accounts, and post the journal entries to their appropriate accounts.

P3B-4

Unifying Concepts: Compound Journal Entries, Posting, Trial Balance

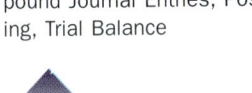

SOLUTIONS SOFTWARE

J&W Merchandise Company had the following transactions during 1994.

(a) Sam Jeakins began business by investing the following assets, receiving capital stock in exchange:

Cash	$ 20,000
Inventory	37,000
Land	25,500
Building	160,000
Equipment	12,500*
Totals	$255,000

* A note of $5,000 on the equipment was assumed by the company.

(b) Sold merchandise that cost $30,000 for $45,000; $15,000 cash was received immediately and the other $30,000 will be collected in 30 days.
(c) Paid off the note of $5,000 plus $300 interest.
(d) Purchased merchandise costing $12,000, paying $2,000 cash and issuing a note for $10,000.
(e) Exchanged $2,000 cash and $8,000 in capital stock for office equipment costing $10,000.
(f) Purchased a truck for $15,000 with $3,000 down and a 1-year note for the balance.

Required: 1. Journalize the transactions. (Omit explanations.)
2. Post the journal entries to a General Ledger, using T-accounts for each account listed.
3. Prepare a trial balance as of December 31, 1994.

P3B-5

Correcting a Trial Balance

The following trial balance was prepared by a new employee unfamiliar with accounting. It appears that some debit and credit balances are mixed up.

Required: Prepare a corrected trial balance for the company. (Assume that all accounts have "normal" balances and that the recorded amounts are correct.)

Riverdale Company
Trial Balance
June 30, 1994

	Debits	Credits
Cash	$ 16,500	
Accounts Receivable	6,000	
Accounts Payable	20,000	
Inventory		$ 22,500
Supplies		2,000
Supplies Expense	1,500	
Notes Receivable		10,500
Notes Payable	5,500	
Insurance Expense		3,000
Utilities Expense	800	
Advertising Expense	4,500	
Sales Revenue	148,900	
Cost of Goods Sold		108,300
Wages Payable	7,600	
Wages Expense	18,400	
Rent Expense		6,900
Land	15,000	
Buildings	75,000	
Equipment	10,000	
Capital Stock		60,000
Retained Earnings		58,900
Totals	$329,700	$272,100

P3B-6
Transaction Analysis and Journal Entries

The following is a list of some of the transactions of Benson Corporation during 1994.

(a) Purchased $7,000 of supplies on account; cost to creditor, $6,000.
(b) Received $1,600 for the office space rented out.
(c) Paid $15,400 of accounts payable.
(d) Paid $7,000 cash for equipment; cost to supplier, $6,200.
(e) Purchased $20,000 of inventory, paid 10 percent down and issued a note for the balance; cost to creditor, $18,600.
(f) Sold merchandise costing $59,000 for $70,000 cash.
(g) Received dividends of $600.

Required: Prepare the journal entries for each of the transactions for Benson Corporation and for each of the other parties to the transactions. Give an explanation with each entry.

P3B-7
Unifying Concepts: First Steps in the Accounting Cycle

The following balances were taken from the General Ledger of Brooke Company on January 1, 1994.

	Debits	Credits
Cash	$ 13,500	
Short-term Investments	10,000	
Accounts Receivable	12,500	
Inventory	15,000	
Land	25,000	
Buildings	75,000	
Equipment	20,000	

Chapter 3   *Introducing the Accounting Cycle*   97

	Debits	Credits
Notes Payable		$ 17,500
Accounts Payable		12,500
Salaries and Wages Payable		2,500
Mortgage Payable		37,500
Capital Stock (7,000 shares outstanding)		70,000
Retained Earnings		31,000

During 1994, the company completed the following transactions:

(a) Purchased inventory for $110,000 on credit.
(b) Issued an additional $25,000 of capital stock (2,500 shares) for cash.
(c) Paid property taxes of $4,500 for the year 1994.
(d) Paid advertising and other selling expenses of $8,000.
(e) Paid utility expenses of $6,500 for 1994.
(f) Paid the salaries and wages owed for 1993. Paid additional salaries and wages of $18,000 during 1994.
(g) Sold merchandise costing $105,000 for $175,000. Of total sales, $45,000 were cash sales and $130,000 were credit sales.
(h) Paid off notes of $17,500 plus interest of $1,600.
(i) On November 1, 1994, received a loan of $10,000 from the bank.
(j) On December 30, 1994, made annual mortgage payment of $2,500 and paid interest of $3,700.
(k) Collected receivables for the year of $140,000.
(l) Paid off accounts payable for $112,500.
(m) Received dividends and interest of $1,400 on short-term investments during 1994. (Record as Miscellaneous Revenue.)
(n) Purchased additional short-term investments of $15,000 during 1994. (Note: Short-term investments are current assets.)
(o) Paid 1994 corporate income taxes of $11,600.
(p) Paid cash dividends of $7,600.

Required:
1. Journalize the 1994 transactions. (Omit explanations.)
2. Set up T-accounts with the proper account balances at January 1, 1994, and post the journal entries to the T-accounts.
3. Determine the account balances, and prepare a trial balance as of December 31, 1994.
4. Prepare an income statement and a balance sheet. (Remember that the Dividends account and all revenue and expense accounts are temporary Retained Earnings accounts.)

Business Analysis Case   *Rollins Engineering Company*

As the proprietor (owner) of Rollins Engineering Company, you are looking for someone to fill the position of office manager. Part of the job description is to maintain the company's accounting records. This means that the office manager must be able to journalize transactions, post them to the ledger accounts, and prepare monthly trial balances. You have just interviewed the first applicant, Jay McMahon, who claims that he has studied accounting. As an initial check on his understanding of the basic mechanics of accounting, you give Jay a list of accounts randomly ordered and with assumed balances, and you ask him to prepare a trial balance. Jay prepares the following.

Trial Balance

	Debits	Credits
Accounts Payable		$ 450
Salaries Expense		17,500
Consulting Revenues	$26,900	
Cash	8,210	
Utilities Expense	1,200	
Accounts Receivable		4,400
Supplies	1,100	
Rent Expense	3,000	
Rollins, Capital		12,500
Supplies Expense	3,300	
Office Equipment	1,500	
Rollins, Drawings		2,400
Other Expenses	640	
Salaries Payable	3,400	
Totals	$49,250	$37,250

Required:
1. Based solely on your assessment of Jay McMahon's understanding of accounting, would you hire him as office manager? Explain.
2. Prepare a corrected trial balance that you can use as a basis for your discussion with Jay and future applicants.
3. Explain how the basic accounting equation and the system of double-entry accounting provide a check on the accounting records.

Ethics Case *Swain Corporation*

Swain Corporation is a small company that services farm equipment for ranchers in rural Rio Blanco County, Colorado. Buck Swain, the owner, manages the company with the assistance of an excellent mechanic and a part-time bookkeeper. On most jobs, parts must be specially ordered and shipped to the store. Most business is charged on open accounts to various ranchers. Cash is often received from the ranchers to pay those accounts.

The economy of Rio Blanco County has been especially tight since the closing of one mine and several oil-drilling operations. Swain's bookkeeper, because of financial pressures, has on three occasions taken some of the cash that has been paid on accounts. The theft has been covered by the bookkeeper adjusting the bank deposits and bank reconciliations and covering individual account receivables on a delayed basis, that is, using cash received from one customer to cover the account payment for another customer. The bookkeeper fully intends to make things right as soon as possible.

Required:
1. What is the normal journal entry for the receipt of cash in payment of an account receivable?
2. What entry is the bookkeeper making?
3. How might Mr. Swain detect the theft? What steps might Mr. Swain take to protect the company from such unethical practices?

Chapter 4

Adjusting Entries

Learning Objectives

After studying this chapter, you should be able to:
1. Understand two additional characteristics of the accounting model: periodic reporting and accrual accounting.
2. Explain the need for adjusting entries and describe how to make adjusting entries for unrecorded revenues, unrecorded expenses, prepaid expenses, and unearned revenues.
3. Describe alternative approaches for adjusting entries.

SETTING THE STAGE

Jeri Seamons was pleased. Her accountant had just finished preparing financial statements for the past year. The statements showed that her perfume company had made a profit of over $200,000 during the year. The financial statements still had to be audited by an outside CPA firm, as required under the terms of the company's loan agreement with First City Bank. The outside auditors were expected to arrive during the next week and would take two weeks to complete their audit.

At the conclusion of their work, the auditors met with Jeri. She was shocked when they informed her that the company had not made $200,000 last year but, instead, had a net loss of approximately $180,000. How could this be? Why was her accountant's assessment so different from that of the auditors?

In explaining to Jeri how they calculated the loss, the CPAs outlined the following points:

1. Jeri's accountant had forgotten to record certain liabilities that were owed at year-end. The accountant had failed to record rent, property taxes, interest, and wages payable.
2. Jeri's accountant had failed to write off certain assets that no longer had future value. In particular, the balance sheet prepared by the accountant had included some prepaid insurance whose coverage had expired and over $50,000 of perfume inventory that had to be discarded because it was not manufactured correctly.
3. Jeri's accountant had recorded as revenue a $30,000 advance payment by a customer for perfume that was still being manufactured and wouldn't be delivered until next year.

The auditors informed Jeri that the liabilities would have to be recorded, which would increase liabilities and expenses; that the expired assets would have to be written off, which would decrease assets and increase expenses; and that the revenue received in advance must be recorded as a liability until the perfume was delivered. The net result of these adjustments was a decrease in reported income of approximately $380,000. Jeri was angry and disappointed. Not only would these "adjustments" make her show a loss, but the poor performance would place the company in violation of the loan agreement with First City. Most likely, the bank would demand immediate repayment of the loans, and Jeri knew her company couldn't afford to repay them at the present time.

Confused and discouraged, Jeri asked the auditors, "Why can't we record things as expenses when we pay them and record receipts as revenue when we receive them? Isn't that the way the federal government keeps its books? By insisting on these adjustments, you are going to ruin my business. Isn't there some way to avoid having to reduce my net income so drastically?"

Note: Though the names and company setting have been changed, this situation actually happened with a client where one of the authors worked as an independent auditor.

As this scenario illustrates, adjustments are usually needed to bring account balances current so that financial statements will reflect accurate data. The nature of these adjustments and how they are calculated are explained in this chapter. To see why adjusting entries are necessary, you must first understand two additional characteristics of the accounting model: periodic reporting and accrual accounting.

ADDITIONAL CHARACTERISTICS OF THE ACCOUNTING MODEL

Objective 1

Understand two additional characteristics of the accounting model: periodic reporting and accrual accounting.

In Chapter 1, we described several characteristics of the accounting model: (1) an accounting entity is a separate economic unit and a going concern; (2) entities enter into arm's-length transactions, which become the basis for accounting entries and which are measured at their original, historical costs; (3) the equality of both sides of the accounting equation is maintained through use of the double-entry system; and (4) the dollar is the common unit used in the United States to measure and communicate the results of business transactions.

Periodic Reporting

Another characteristic of the accounting model is that accounting information is reported regularly, at least annually. This is called the **time period (or periodicity) concept**. It says that an accounting entity's life is divided into distinct and equal (comparable) periods, such as months, quarters, or years, in order to report financial information in a timely and regular manner. In practice, the size and complexity of many businesses require that reports be prepared on a monthly basis.

time period (or periodicity) concept *the idea that the life of a business is divided into distinct and relatively short time periods so that accounting information can be timely*

All businesses, large or small, issue their financial statements periodically so that users can make sound economic decisions. Current owners, prospective investors, bankers, and others obviously need up-to-date reports in order to compare and judge a company's financial position and operating results on a continuing, timely basis. In brief, they need to know the financial position of an entity (from the balance sheet), the relative success or failure of current operations (from the income statement), and the nature and extent of cash flows (from the statement of cash flows).

The financial picture of an entity—its success or failure in meeting its economic objectives—cannot really be complete until the "life" of a business is over. However, managers, owners, and creditors cannot wait 10, 20, or 100 years to receive an exact accounting of a business. Accordingly, the life of an enterprise is divided into distinct accounting periods, each generally covering

Chapter 4 Adjusting Entries

fiscal year *an entity's reporting year, covering a 12-month accounting period*

calendar year *an entity's reporting year, covering 12 months and ending on December 31*

12 months or less. The 12-month accounting period is referred to as the **fiscal year**. When an entity closes its books on December 31, it is said to be reporting on a **calendar-year** basis.

Most large corporations, and even many small companies, issue a report to stockholders as of a fiscal year-end. As noted in Chapter 2, this annual report includes the financial statements (balance sheet, income statement, and statement of cash flows) and other financial data, such as a 5-year summary of operations. Other financial reports are prepared more frequently, perhaps quarterly or monthly. Indeed, some reports, such as sales reports for use by management, may be prepared on a daily basis.

Although periodic reporting is vital to a firm's success, the frequency of reporting forces accountants to use some data that are based on judgments and estimates. As you will see, the shorter the reporting period (for example, a month instead of a year), the less exact are the measurements of assets and liabilities and the recognition of revenues and expenses. Ideally, accounting judgments are made carefully and estimates are based on reliable evidence, but the limitations of accounting reports should be understood and kept in mind.

Accrual Accounting

accrual-basis accounting *a system of accounting in which revenues and expenses are recorded as they are earned and incurred, not necessarily when cash is received or paid*

Closely related to the time-period concept is the concept of **accrual-basis accounting**. This important characteristic of the traditional accounting model simply means that revenues are recognized (recorded) when earned without regard to when cash is received, and expenses are recorded as incurred without regard to when they are paid. Accrual accounting requires that revenues and expenses be assigned to their proper accounting periods.

REVENUE RECOGNITION. How do we assign revenues to particular periods? First, how do we determine when revenues have actually been earned? The **revenue recognition principle** states that revenues are recorded when two main criteria have been met.

revenue recognition principle *the idea that revenues should be recorded when (1) the earnings process has been substantially completed and (2) an exchange has taken place*

1. The earnings process is substantially complete, which generally means that a sale has been made or services have been performed.
2. An exchange has taken place.

The first criterion ensures that the parties to the transaction have fulfilled their commitment or are formally obligated to do so. For example, a company generally records sales revenues when goods are shipped or when services are performed. If XYZ Company sold and shipped $80,000 of goods in 1994, but will not receive the cash proceeds until 1995, the $80,000 would still be recognized as revenue in 1994, when it was earned. If, on the other hand, the company is paid in 1994 for goods to be shipped in 1995, it does not record those payments as revenues until the goods are actually shipped. The second criterion ensures that there is objective evidence (documentation) by which to measure the amount of revenue involved.

matching principle *the concept that all expenses incurred in generating revenues must be recognized in the same reporting period as the related revenues*

THE MATCHING PRINCIPLE. Once a company determines which revenues should be recognized during a period, how does it identify the expenses incurred? The **matching principle** requires that all expenses incurred to generate the revenues recognized in an accounting period be matched with those revenues. The cost of the merchandise sold, for example, should be matched to the revenue derived from the sale of that merchandise during the period. Expenses that cannot be matched with revenues are assigned to the accounting period in which they are incurred. For example, the exact amount of electricity used to make a toaster generally cannot be determined, but since the amount used for a month or a year is known, that amount can be matched to the revenues earned during the same period.

As shown in Exhibit 4-1, this process of matching expenses with recognized revenues determines the amount of net income reported on the income statement. Net income is extremely important in determining how well a company is doing, that is, in assessing a company's accomplishments and efforts. The subject of income determination, including revenue recognition and expense matching, is discussed more completely in Chapters 6 and 7.

Accrual- Versus Cash-Basis Accounting

We have explained accrual-basis accounting because it is the foundation of accounting for most businesses today. However, since some small businesses record transactions and recognize revenues and expenses only when cash is received or paid, we will briefly describe **cash-basis accounting**. Most individuals also prepare their income tax returns on a cash basis. With the cash-basis approach, income is what is left after cash disbursements of a period are subtracted from cash receipts during that period.

cash-basis accounting *a system of accounting in which transactions are recorded and revenues and expenses are recognized only when cash is received or paid*

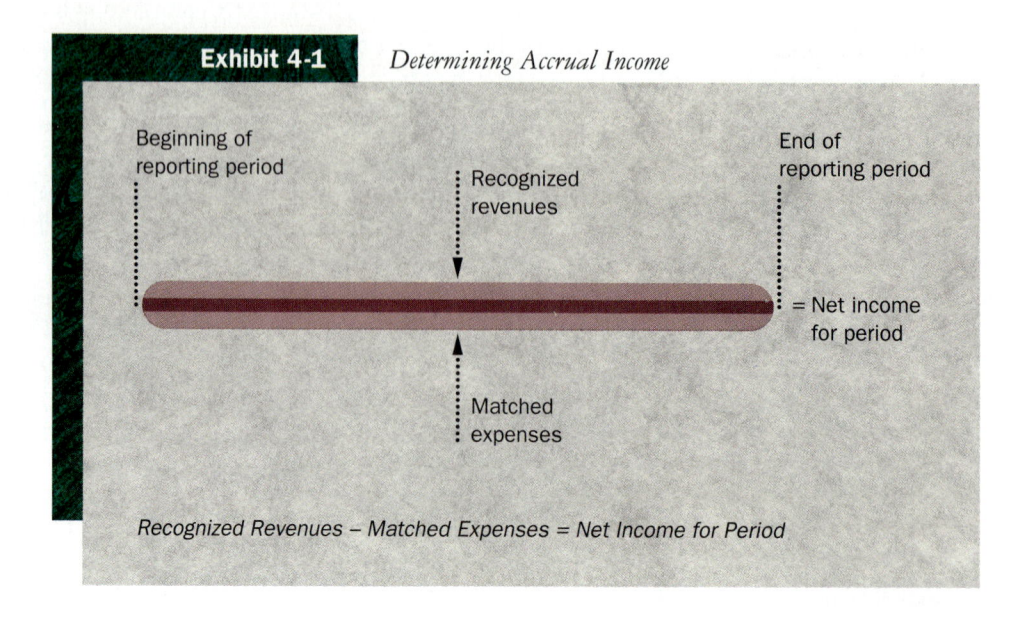

To illustrate the difference between cash- and accrual-basis accounting, and to demonstrate why accrual-basis accounting provides a more meaningful measure of income, assume that Karas Enterprises billed clients $50,500 for consulting services in 1994. By December 31, Karas had received $42,000, with the $8,500 balance expected in 1995. During the year, Karas paid $23,000 for staff-related expenses and $8,900 for various other expenses. At December 31, Karas still owed $1,200 for additional expenses incurred. These expenses will

Exhibit 4-1 *Determining Accrual Income*

Beginning of reporting period → Recognized revenues ↓ / Matched expenses ↑ → End of reporting period = Net income for period

Recognized Revenues – Matched Expenses = Net Income for Period

be paid during January 1995. How much income should Karas Enterprises report for 1994? The answer depends on whether cash-basis or accrual-basis accounting is used. As shown here, with cash-basis accounting, reported income would be $10,100. With accrual-basis accounting, reported income would be $17,400.

Karas Enterprises
Reported Income for 1994

Cash-Basis Accounting		**Accrual-Basis Accounting**	
Cash receipts	$42,000	Revenues earned	$50,500
Cash disbursements	31,900	Expenses incurred	33,100
Income	$10,100	Income	$17,400

How do we explain this $7,300 difference? Under cash-basis accounting, Karas Enterprises would report only $42,000 in revenue, the total amount of cash received during 1994. Similarly, the company would report only $31,900 of expenses during 1994. The additional $1,200 of expenses incurred but not yet paid would not be reported. However, using accrual-basis accounting, Karas earned $50,500 in revenues, which is the total increase in resources for the period (an increase of $42,000 in cash plus $8,500 in receivables). Similarly, Karas incurred a total of $33,100 in expenses, which should be matched with revenues earned to produce a realistic income measurement. The combined result of increasing revenues by $8,500 while increasing expenses by only $1,200 creates the $7,300 difference in net income ($8,500 − $1,200 = $7,300).

As this example shows, accrual-basis accounting provides a more accurate picture of a company's profitability. It matches earned revenues with the expenses incurred to generate those revenues. This helps investors, creditors, and others better assess the operating results of a company and make more informed judgments concerning its profitability and earnings potential. Accrual-basis accounting is required by generally accepted accounting principles.

> **To Summarize** *Users of accounting information need timely, periodic financial reports to make decisions. The revenue recognition and matching principles provide guidelines for assigning the appropriate amounts of revenues and expenses to each period under accrual accounting. Accrual-basis accounting provides a better measure of net income than cash-basis accounting does, and it is therefore the concept required by GAAP in reporting the results of company operations.*

ADJUSTING ENTRIES (STEP 5 OF THE ACCOUNTING CYCLE)

As we explained in Chapter 3, transactions generally are recorded in a journal as they happen, that is, in chronological order, and then posted to the ledger accounts. The entries are based on the best information available at the time.

Objective 2

Explain the need for adjusting entries and describe how to make adjusting entries for unrecorded revenues, unrecorded expenses, prepaid expenses, and unearned revenues.

Although the majority of accounts are up to date at the end of an accounting period, and their balances can be included in the financial statements, some accounts require adjustment to reflect current circumstances. In general, these accounts are not updated throughout the period because it is impractical or inconvenient to make entries on a daily or weekly basis. So, *at the end of each accounting period, in order to report all asset, liability, and owners' equity amounts properly, and to recognize all revenues and expenses for the period on an accrual basis, accountants are required to make any necessary adjustments prior to preparing the financial statements.* The entries that reflect these adjustments are called, as you would expect, **adjusting entries.**

adjusting entries *entries required at the end of each accounting period to recognize, on an accrual basis, revenues and expenses for the period and to report proper amounts for asset, liability, and owners' equity accounts*

Usually there will be no underlying documents to signal a need for adjusting entries. Rather, they are recorded on the basis of an analysis of the circumstances at the close of each accounting period. The areas most commonly requiring analysis to see whether adjusting entries are needed are:

1. Unrecorded revenues
2. Unrecorded expenses
3. Prepaid expenses
4. Unearned revenues

As we illustrate and discuss adjusting entries, remember that the basic purpose of adjustments is to bring account balances current in order to report all asset, liability, and owners' equity amounts properly, and to recognize all revenues and expenses for the period on an accrual basis. This is done so that the income statement and the balance sheet will reflect the proper operating results and financial position at the end of the accounting period.

Because adjusting entries are made to correct or update account balances, the adjustment process is one of analysis rather than mere recording. *This process involves three steps: (1) determining what entries, if any, were originally made to the accounts, (2) determining what the account balances should be, and (3) making the adjusting entries that are needed to bring existing balances to their appropriate amounts.* T-accounts are helpful in analyzing adjusting entries and will be used in the illustrations that follow.

Unrecorded Revenues

In accordance with the revenue recognition principle of accrual accounting, revenues should be recorded when earned, regardless of when the cash is received. At the end of each accounting period, an analysis should be made to see whether there are any revenues that have been earned but have not yet been collected or recorded. Such revenue items are referred to as **unrecorded revenues.** When we increase the revenue account for amounts earned but not yet recorded, the offsetting account in the adjusting entry is a receivable showing the corresponding obligation of the other party to pay for that revenue. The receivable is a valid asset representing an amount owed to the entity at the end of the accounting period.

unrecorded revenues *revenues earned during a period that have not been recorded by the end of that period*

Even though cash has not been received, the revenues are earned and should be reported as such. In order to recognize the total revenues earned and to report the corresponding receivables as assets, adjustments to the accounts are required.

To illustrate, we will assume that Super Value, Inc. reports on a calendar-year basis and has determined the following on December 31, 1993:

1. Rent revenue of $500 earned in 1993 has not been recorded and will not be received until January 10, 1994.
2. Interest revenue of $200 has been earned on a one-year $10,000 note issued to Super Value on November 1, 1993. The interest rate is 12 percent with interest due at the maturity date, October 31, 1994.

Following the three-step analysis, we observe that no original entry has been made. However, remember that under accrual-basis accounting, revenue is recorded when it is *earned,* not when the cash is received. Thus, the rent revenue must be recognized in 1993 (when earned) and not in 1994 (when received). The accounts involved and the correct balances as of December 31, 1993, are shown as follows in T-account form:

	Rent Receivable	Rent Revenue
Original entry.............	none	none
Correct balances (12/31/93)	500	500

Once the original entries and the desired ending balances are known, you can determine what adjusting entry is needed. For this transaction, the entry required at December 31 is one that increases Rent Receivable (an asset account) from $0 to $500 and Rent Revenue (a revenue account) from $0 to $500. The adjusting entry is:

Dec. 31	Rent Receivable	500	
	Rent Revenue		500
	To record earned rent not yet received.		

Item 2 (interest revenue) is another example of an unrecorded revenue. In this case, interest is to be received at the maturity date of the note. At the end of the year, the interest for 2 months, November and December, has been earned but not yet received or recorded. Accrual accounting dictates that unless an adjusting entry is made, the applicable revenue and asset accounts will not reflect the current circumstances, and the resulting financial statements will not be as useful to decision makers. In this case, the 2 months' interest revenue should be recognized and the related interest receivable recorded. The appropriate adjusting entry may be determined by following the same process used for the rent revenue example, as follows:

	Interest Receivable	Interest Revenue
Original entry.............	none	none
Correct balances (12/31/93)	200	200

The proper adjusting entry is:

> Dec. 31 Interest Receivable.. 200
>   Interest Revenue.. 200
>   To record interest[1] earned on a one-year, $10,000 note with interest at 12% due at maturity: $10,000 × .12 = $1,200; $1,200 ÷ 12 = $100 per month; $100 × 2 months (November and December) = $200.

Adjusting entries are recorded in the General Journal and are posted to the accounts in the General Ledger in the same manner as other journal entries. Note that each adjusting entry must involve one (or more) balance sheet accounts and one (or more) income statement accounts.

After the adjusting entries have been journalized and posted, the receivables appear as assets on the balance sheet, and the rent and interest revenues are reported on the income statement. Through the adjusting entries, the asset (receivable) accounts are properly stated and revenues are appropriately reported.

Unrecorded Expenses

Under accrual accounting, the matching principle requires that all expenses incurred to generate recognized revenues of a particular accounting period be recorded in that same period. Therefore, at the end of each accounting period an analysis should be made to see that expenses are properly recorded. The result will be a better measure of income.

Just as revenues can be earned before they are collected or recorded, expenses can be incurred prior to being paid or recorded. Expenses incurred in a particular period but not recorded during that time are referred to as **unrecorded expenses.** These expenses, along with their corresponding liabilities, should be recorded when incurred, no matter when they are paid. Thus, adjusting entries are required at the end of an accounting period to recognize any unrecorded expenses in the proper period of incurrence and to record the corresponding liabilities. As the expense is recorded (increased by a debit), the offsetting liability is also recorded (increased by a credit), showing the entity's obligation to pay for the expense. If such adjustments are not made, the net income measurement for the period will not reflect all appropriate expenses, and the corresponding liabilities will be understated on the balance sheet.

To illustrate, we will assume that at year-end, December 31, 1993, Super Value Inc. has determined the following:

1. Property taxes of $1,500 for this year will not be paid until January 3, 1994; income taxes of $22,000 for this year will not be paid until April 15, 1994.

unrecorded expenses *expenses incurred during a period that have not been recorded by the end of that period*

---

[1] As noted in Chapter 2, interest is the cost of using money. The amount borrowed or lent is the *principal.* The *interest rate* is an annual rate stated as a percentage. The *period of time* involved may be stated in terms of a year. For example, if interest is to be paid for 3 months, time is 3/12, or 1/4 of a year. If interest is to be paid for 90 days, time is 90/365 of a year. Thus, the formula for computing interest is Interest = Principal × Interest Rate × Time (fraction of a year).

2. Interest expense of $300 is owed on a 2-year, $12,000 bank note issued on October 1, 1993, by Super Value. The interest rate is 10 percent, and interest payments are due on September 30.

To represent its current financial position and earnings, Super Value must record the impact of these events in the accounts even though cash transactions have not yet occurred. Property and income taxes will not be paid until 1994. However, under accrual-basis accounting, these taxes are expenses of 1993 and should be recognized on this year's income statement, with the corresponding liability shown on the balance sheet as of the end of the year. The analysis and resulting adjusting journal entries required at year-end for the unrecorded property and income taxes would be as follows:

	Property Tax Expense	Property Taxes Payable
Original entry.............	none	none
Correct balances (12/31/93)	1,500	1,500

	Income Tax Expense	Income Taxes Payable
Original entry.............	none	none
Correct balances (12/31/93)	22,000	22,000

Dec. 31	Property Tax Expense.............................	1,500	
	Property Taxes Payable		1,500
	To record property taxes not yet paid.		
31	Income Tax Expense	22,000	
	Income Taxes Payable		22,000
	To record income taxes not yet paid.		

The first interest payment on the note is due September 30, 1994. However, at December 31, Super Value has incurred 3 months' interest expense (for October, November, and December) that should be recognized in the accounts for this period. Accounting for this interest is illustrated with T-accounts followed by the appropriate adjusting entry.

	Interest Expense	Interest Payable
Original entry.............	none	none
Correct balances (12/31/93)	300	300

Dec. 31	Interest Expense...	300	
	Interest Payable		300
	To record interest expense on a 2-year bank note of $12,000 at 10%: $12,000 × 0.10 = $1,200; $1,200 ÷ 12 = $100; $100 × 3 months (October, November, December) = $300.		

The property tax, income tax, and interest expenses would be shown on the income statement for the year ended December 31, and the payables—property taxes, income taxes, and interest—would be shown as liabilities on the balance sheet as of December 31. Because of the adjusting entries, both the income statement and balance sheet will more accurately reflect the financial situation of Super Value, Inc.

Prepaid Expenses

Payments that a company makes in advance for items normally charged to expense are known as **prepaid expenses**. An example would be the payment of an insurance premium for three years. Theoretically, every resource acquisition is an asset, at least temporarily. Thus, the entry to record an advance payment should be a debit to an asset account (Prepaid Expense) and a credit to Cash, showing the exchange of cash for another asset.

prepaid expenses payments made in advance for items normally charged to expense

Business enterprises do not acquire expenses. Expenses emerge as benefits are received from the assets acquired and the values of the assets decline. Therefore, an expense is a "used-up" asset, a resource whose value has been at least partly realized. For example, when supplies are purchased, they are recorded as assets; when they are used, their cost is transferred to an expense account. The purpose of making adjusting entries for prepaid expenses, then, is to show the complete or partial expiration of an asset's ability to help generate future revenues. That is, if the original entry is to an asset account, the adjusting entry reduces the asset to an amount that reflects its remaining future benefit and at the same time recognizes the actual expense incurred for the period.

The three-step analysis we have used for unrecorded revenues and expenses applies equally to the adjustments for prepaid expenses and unearned revenues (to be discussed next). The objective is the same: to ensure that the proper amounts of revenues and expenses are recognized during the period and that the appropriate asset and liability account balances are shown on the balance sheet. There is one difference. For unrecorded items, there is no original entry. For prepaid expenses and unearned revenues, this is not the case. Since cash has already been paid (in the case of prepaid expenses) or received (in the case of unearned revenues), an original entry has been made to record the cash transaction. Therefore, *the amount of the adjusting entry is the difference between what the correct balance should be and the amount of the original entry already recorded.*

To illustrate adjustments for prepaid expenses, we will assume the following about Super Value:

1. On September 1, 1993, Super Value rents office space in a building. The rent is $1,500 a month, and Super Value is required to pay 6 months' rent in advance.
2. On November 1, 1993, Super Value purchases a 2-year insurance policy, paying a $2,400 premium.
3. On December 15, 1993, Super Value purchases several months worth of supplies at a total cost of $750. At year-end, $575 worth of supplies were still on hand.

Using the three-step analysis for prepaid rent, we first determine the original entry. On September 1, Super Value would record the expenditure of $9,000 as follows:

Chapter 4 *Adjusting Entries*   111

Sept. 1	Prepaid Rent..	9,000	
	Cash...		9,000
	Paid 6 months' rent in advance: 6 × $1,500 = $9,000.		

This entry shows that one asset (Cash) has been exchanged for another asset (Prepaid Rent). Over the next 6 months, Super Value will use the office space, and the asset, Prepaid Rent, will become an expense.

At year-end, only those assets that still offer future benefits to the company should be reported on the balance sheet. Thus, an adjustment is required to reduce the Prepaid Rent account and to record the rent expense for the period. In this example, Super Value has used the rented office space for 4 months, September through December. Since this portion of the asset, Prepaid Rent, has been used up, it must be recorded in the Rent Expense account. The remaining 2 months of the prepaid rent have not been used up—the amount still has future benefits, and so it remains in the asset account. The correct amounts at December 31 should be Prepaid Rent, $3,000 (2 months × $1,500), and Rent Expense, $6,000 (4 months × $1,500).

The adjusting journal entry to bring the original amounts to their corrected balances at year-end would be:

Dec. 31	Rent Expense	6,000	
	Prepaid Rent		6,000
	To reduce the asset account and to record rent expense for 4 months: 4 × $1,500 = $6,000.		

When the adjusting entry is journalized and posted, the proper amount of rent expense ($6,000) will be shown as an expense on the income statement, and the proper amount of prepaid rent ($3,000) will be carried forward to the next period as an asset on the balance sheet, as illustrated in the following T-accounts:

	Prepaid Rent		Cash		Rent Expense	
Original entry (9/1/93)	9,000		9,000			
Adjusting entry (12/31/93)		6,000			6,000	
Correct balances (12/31/93)	3,000				6,000	
	To balance sheet				To income statement	

The entries and the analysis for the insurance transaction are similar to those for prepaid rent. The initial entry would be:

Nov. 1	Prepaid Insurance	2,400	
	Cash...		2,400
	Paid insurance premium for 2 years, $2,400.		

At year-end, an adjustment must be made to reflect the proper insurance expense for the period and to reduce the amount of prepaid insurance to be shown as an asset on the balance sheet. In the example, an adjusting entry would be required to update the accounts so that 2 months' worth of insurance expense ($2,400 ÷ 24 months = $100; $100 × 2 = $200) would be shown on the income statement. The remaining 22 months of insurance benefits ($100 × 22 = $2,200) would be shown as an asset on the balance sheet. The entries are summarized in T-account form as follows:

	Prepaid Insurance	Cash	Insurance Expense
Original entry 11/1/93	2,400	2,400	
Adjusting entry 12/31/93	200		200
Correct balances 12/31/93	2,200		200
	To balance sheet		To income statement

The adjusting entry would be:

Dec. 31	Insurance Expense	200	
	Prepaid Insurance		200
	To reduce the asset account and to record the insurance expense for 2 months: 2 × $100 = $200.		

supplies *materials used in a business that do not generally become part of the sales product and were not purchased to be resold to customers*

inventory *goods held for sale*

Supplies and **inventory** are often confused. Supplies include such items as paper, pencils, paper clips, soap, paper towels, and lubricants, which might be used in an office or a warehouse. These items are not classified as inventory since they have not been purchased for resale to customers (as is inventory in a merchandising firm) or for direct use in the manufacture of products (as are raw materials in a manufacturing firm).

When supplies are consumed in the normal course of business, the asset account (Supplies or Supplies on Hand) must be adjusted and the used-up portion charged as an operating expense (Supplies Expense) on the income statement. Thus, the adjustment for supplies is handled the same way as for any other prepaid asset.

Using the three-step analysis, Super Value initially recorded $750 of supplies as an asset, as follows:

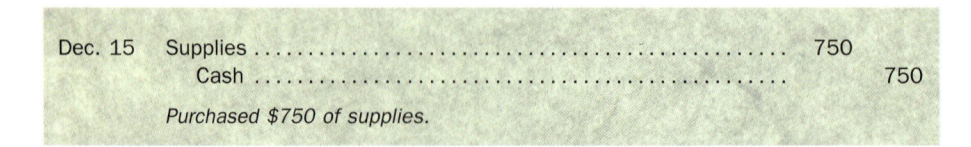

Dec. 15	Supplies	750	
	Cash		750
	Purchased $750 of supplies.		

At year-end, only $575 worth of supplies remains. An adjustment must be made to recognize that $175 ($750 − $575) of the supplies have been used and should be charged to expense. The entries are summarized in the following T-accounts:

Chapter 4 *Adjusting Entries*

	Supplies		Cash		Supplies Expense	
Original entry (12/15/93)...	750		750			
Adjusting entry (12/31/93)		175			175	
Correct balance (12/31/93)	575				175	
	To balance sheet				To income statement	

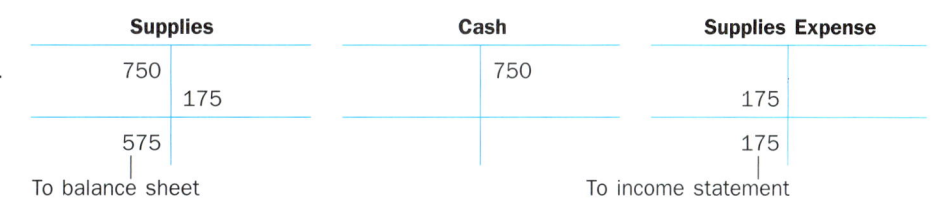

The adjusting entry would be:

> Dec. 31   Supplies Expense.. 175
>   Supplies 175
> *To reduce the asset account to $575 and to record the use of $175 of supplies as an expense.*

Unearned Revenues

unearned revenues
amounts received before they have been earned

Amounts received before the actual earning of revenues are known as **unearned revenues.** They arise when customers pay in advance of the receipt of goods or services. Since the company has received cash but has not yet given the customer the purchased goods or services, the unearned revenues are in fact liabilities. That is, the company must provide something in return for the amounts received. For example, a building contractor may require a deposit before proceeding to construct a house. Upon receipt of the deposit, the contractor has unearned revenue, a liability; that is, the contractor must construct the house to earn the revenue. If the house is not built, the contractor will be obligated to repay the deposit.

To illustrate the adjustments for unearned revenues, we will assume the following about Super Value:

1. On June 1, a tenant pays Super Value $3,600 for 1 year's rent in advance, covering the period from June 1 of the current year to May 31 of the next year.
2. On October 1, a client pays a consulting fee of $1,800 for regular monthly services to be rendered by Super Value during the next 9 months.

Following the three-step analysis, step 1 is to determine the original entry. Typically, the original entry to record unearned revenues involves a debit to Cash and a credit to a liability account. In our example of rent received 1 year in advance, the liability account would be Unearned Rent, as shown here.

> June 1   Cash 3,600
>   Unearned Rent...................................... 3,600
> *Received 12 months' rent in advance: $300 × 12 = $3,600.*

The credit to the liability account, Unearned Rent, is logically and technically correct; until the tenant uses the facility, the rent received in advance is unearned and is thus an obligation (liability) of Super Value.

The next step is to compute the correct balances at year-end. On December 31, $2,100, or 7 months' rent, has been earned (7 × $300 = $2,100) and should be reported as Rent Revenue on the income statement. Five months' rent (5 × $300 = $1,500) is still unearned and should be shown as a liability, Unearned Rent, on the balance sheet. Since the money was indeed received, the Cash amount is correct. Incidentally, Cash is seldom one of the accounts adjusted when adjusting entries are made. The Cash account needs to be corrected only when it is wrong because of errors in the original entries.

The last step is to prepare a journal entry that, when posted, will produce the correct balances in the accounts. In the Unearned Rent example, the adjusting entry to be journalized and posted would be:

Dec. 31	Unearned Rent	2,100	
	Rent Revenue		2,100
	To reduce the liability account and to record rent revenue for 7 months: $300 × 7 months = $2,100.		

These results may be illustrated in the following T-accounts:

	Unearned Rent	Cash	Rent Revenue
Original entry (6/1/93)	3,600	3,600	
Adjusting entry (12/31/93)	2,100		2,100
Correct balances (12/31/93)	1,500		2,100
	To balance sheet		To income statement

After the adjusting entry has been made on December 31, Super Value's accounts would show $3,600 of cash received. Of this amount, $2,100 had been earned (7 months' rent × $300) and would be reported as rent revenue on the income statement; $1,500 will not be earned until the next reporting period and would be shown as a liability on the balance sheet.

The same type of analysis can be used for the consulting transaction (item 2 on page 113). With step 1, we determine the original entry. In this case, the receipt of $1,800 for 9 months' consulting services would be recorded as follows:

Oct. 1	Cash	1,800	
	Unearned Consulting Fees		1,800
	Received 9 months' consulting fees in advance: $200 × 9 = $1,800.		

As before, in step 2, we compute the correct end-of-period balances. The proper amount of consulting revenue earned during this period is $600 ($200 × 3 months: October, November, and December). This amount should be reported on the income statement. The fees for 6 months are still unearned ($200 × 6 months = $1,200) and should be shown as a liability on the balance sheet.

Step 3 is to prepare an adjusting entry that will bring the accounts to their appropriate balances for reporting on the financial statements. In this example, the adjusting entry would be:

Dec. 31	Unearned Consulting Fees	600	
	Consulting Revenue		600

To reduce the liability account and to record consulting revenue for 3 months: $200 × 3 months = $600.

After the adjusting entry has been journalized and posted, the proper amount of consulting revenue ($600) will be shown on the income statement. The liability account, Unearned Consulting Fees (or, alternatively, Consulting Fees Received in Advance), will also be reported at its correct amount ($1,200). The entries are summarized in T-account form as follows:

	Unearned Consulting Fees	Cash	Consulting Revenue
Original entry (10/1/93)	1,800	1,800	
Adjusting entry (12/31/93)	600		600
Correct balances (12/31/93)	1,200		600
	To balance sheet		To income statement

> **To Summarize** *To present financial statements that accurately report the financial position and the results of operations on an accrual basis and for specific periods of time, adjusting entries must be made. The four main categories of adjustments are unrecorded revenues, unrecorded expenses, prepaid expenses, and unearned revenues. In analyzing accounts at the end of an accounting cycle, adjusting entries are made in order to recognize all earned revenues and all incurred expenses and to report the proper balances in the asset, liability, and owners' equity accounts. This requires a three-step analysis: (1) identifying the original entries, if any, (2) determining the correct end-of-period balances, and (3) preparing adjusting entries to bring the original account balances to their proper end-of-period amounts. With unrecorded revenues and unrecorded expenses there is no original entry. With prepaid expenses, the original entry includes a credit to Cash and a debit to either an asset or, as explained in the next section, an expense account. With unearned revenues, the original entry includes a debit to Cash and a credit to either a liability or, as you will soon learn, a revenue account.*

ALTERNATIVE APPROACHES FOR ADJUSTING ENTRIES

In our analysis of adjusting entries, we assumed that all companies follow the same procedure. For unrecorded revenues and expenses, this is the case. With prepaid expenses and unearned revenues, however, some companies use a differ-

Objective 3

Describe alternative approaches for adjusting entries.

ent approach from the one we have just described. In this section, we present these alternative approaches, explaining the reasons for their use.

An Alternative Approach to Adjustments for Prepaid Expenses

In our earlier discussion we assumed that the original entry for prepaid expenses involved an asset account, such as Prepaid Rent or Prepaid Insurance. This is called the *asset approach*. When it is likely that all the benefits of an expenditure will be received within the current accounting period, a company may, as a matter of expediency, initially use an expense account. This is called the *expense approach*. If, at the end of the accounting period, the entire amount is indeed an expense, no adjustment is necessary. If some of the benefit of an expenditure extends to the following year, an adjustment is necessary to record the amount as an asset.

To illustrate the expense approach, we will use the insurance example for Super Value, Inc. Assume that the original prepayment entry was debited to Insurance Expense as follows:

```
Nov. 1   Insurance Expense ........................................ 2,400
            Cash.................................................        2,400
         Paid insurance premium for two years.
```

An end-of-period adjustment must be made to reflect the proper insurance expense for that period and to record the amount of prepaid insurance to be shown on the balance sheet as an asset. The entries, in T-account form, are:

	Insurance Expense	Cash	Prepaid Insurance
Original entry (11/1/93)	2,400	2,400	
Adjusting entry (12/31/93)	2,200		2,200
Correct balances (12/31/93)	200		2,200
	To income statement		To balance sheet

The adjusting entry updates the accounts so that 2 months' worth of insurance expense ($2,400 ÷ 24 months = $100; $100 × 2 months = $200) will be reported on the income statement. The remaining 22 months of insurance benefits ($100 × 22 = $2,200) will be shown as an asset, Prepaid Insurance or Unexpired Insurance, on the balance sheet. The adjusting entry is:

```
Dec. 31  Prepaid Insurance........................................ 2,200
            Insurance Expense ...................................        2,200
         To recognize the proper asset amount and to reduce the expense account:
         $100 × 22 months = $2,200.
```

Note that the year-end account balances are exactly the same as they were under the asset approach. Regardless of how prepaid expenses are originally recorded—as assets or as expenses—if the three-step adjusting entry analysis is followed correctly, the income statement and balance sheet will include the proper amounts. It is therefore more important for you to understand the *process* of analysis for adjusting than the specific approach used. To repeat, first determine what original entries have been made, if any; next determine the correct end-of-period account balances; finally prepare an adjusting journal entry that will change the original account balances to the correct balances as of the end of the accounting period so that they will be reported properly on the income statement and the balance sheet.

An Alternative Approach to Adjustments for Unearned Revenues

In discussing adjusting entries for unearned revenues, we assumed that the original entry involved a liability (for example, debit Cash; credit Unearned Revenue). This procedure, called the *liability approach,* required that an adjusting entry be made at year-end to reduce the amount of the liability (unearned revenue) and to record the proper amount of revenue earned during the period.

Some companies prefer that the original entry involve a revenue account rather than a liability account. This is called the *revenue approach*. With this approach, the company records the receipt of cash paid for services to be performed in the future as revenue because it knows the revenue will be earned in the near future. And if all the revenue is earned by the end of the period, the company need not make an adjusting entry.

When the original entry involves a revenue account, the end-of-period adjustment is made to reduce the revenue account to the amount actually earned during the period and to record a corresponding liability for the amount not yet earned.

To illustrate the revenue approach, consider again the rent example for Super Value Inc. Upon receipt of the $3,600 for 1 year's rent in advance, Super Value may make the following original entry:

June 1	Cash	3,600	
	Rent Revenue		3,600
	Received 12 months' rent in advance: $300 × 12 = $3,600.		

At this point, no entry has been made to Unearned Rent, and it has a zero balance. Recall that step 2 in the analysis of adjusting entries requires that the correct account balances be determined. Since the total year's rent is $3,600, rent of $300 is earned each month ($3,600 ÷ 12 = $300). During 1993, Super Value should recognize 7 months' rent (June 1 through December 31), or $2,100 (7 × $300 = $2,100), as being earned. The balance of $1,500 ($3,600 − $2,100) is unearned. That is, on December 31, 1993, 5 months' rent has been received (5 × $300 = $1,500) that will not be earned until 1994. Thus, the correct balances in the accounts are $2,100 for Rent Revenue, to be shown on the income statement, and $1,500 for Unearned Rent, to be reported as a liability on the balance sheet. Since the money was received, the Cash account is correct.

Using the revenue approach, the results from the rent transaction are as shown in the following T-accounts:

	Rent Revenue		Cash		Unearned Rent
Original entry (6/1/93)		3,600	3,600		
Adjusting entry (12/31/93)	1,500				1,500
Correct balances (12/31/93)		2,100			1,500
		To income statement			To balance sheet

Given the preceding analysis, the correct adjusting entry can be made by debiting Rent Revenue for an amount ($1,500) that will decrease it from $3,600 to $2,100, and crediting Unearned Rent for an amount ($1,500) that will increase it from $0 to $1,500. The required adjusting entry at year-end would be:

Dec. 31	Rent Revenue	1,500	
	Unearned Rent		1,500

To recognize rent revenue earned for 7 months and to record the remaining obligation due: $300 × 5 months = $1,500.

Again, the approach used is less significant than the process of analysis. Both liability and revenue approaches produce exactly the same result: accurate recognition of revenues on the income statement and proper reporting of liabilities on the balance sheet.

Concluding Comment

Whether the asset or the expense approach is used depends on the accounting philosophy of the company, just as does the choice of the liability or revenue approach. A company will often use different approaches for different transactions, depending on the nature of the asset, expense, revenue, or liability item. Under either the asset or the expense approach, or the liability or the revenue approach, the objective is to report the proper amounts on the income statement and to show the appropriate account balances on the balance sheet.

Review of Learning Objectives

Objective 1

Understand two additional characteristics of the accounting model: periodic reporting and accrual accounting. In conducting economic activities, businesses and other types of entities enter into exchange transactions. These transactions form the basis of accounting records and must be analyzed, recorded, classified, summarized, and reported.

To facilitate the accounting process, an accounting model has been established. This model has several important characteristics, including the notion of a separate accounting entity that is a going concern and that uses double-entry accounting to record its arm's-length transactions. In the United States, these transactions are measured in monetary amounts using the U.S. dollar as the unit of measurement. Transactions generally are reported at historical cost.

The model further assumes that accounting information is needed on a timely basis for decision-making purposes. This requires that the total life of a business be divided into accounting periods, generally a year or less, for which reports are prepared. Some of the data presented in the periodic reports must be tentative because allocations and estimates are involved in dividing an entity's life into relatively short reporting periods.

The necessity for periodic reporting further requires that accrual accounting be used to provide accurate statements of financial position and results of operations for an accounting period. Accrual-basis accounting means that revenues are recognized as they are earned, not necessarily when cash is received, and that expenses are recognized as they are incurred, not necessarily when cash is paid. Accrual-basis accounting provides a more accurate picture of a company's financial position and operating results than cash-basis accounting although the latter is often used by small companies and by individuals, especially for tax purposes.

Objective 2

Explain the need for adjusting entries and describe how to make adjusting entries for unrecorded revenues, unrecorded expenses, prepaid expenses, and unearned revenues. One of the most important functions accountants perform is the proper matching of the revenues recognized during a reporting period with the expenses incurred to generate those revenues. This requires that adjusting entries be made at the end of each accounting period. Adjusting entries are the means of increasing or decreasing accounts so as to report proper end-of-period revenue and expense amounts on the income statement and appropriate balances for balance sheet accounts. The accounts that generally require adjustments may be classified under four headings: unrecorded revenues, unrecorded expenses, prepaid expenses, and unearned revenues. A three-step analysis may be used to determine the correct adjusting entries.

Objective 3

Describe alternative approaches for adjusting entries. Companies may use *either* the asset or the expense approach for recording prepaid expenses. If an asset is initially recorded, the adjusting entry will reduce the asset to its correct balance and establish the proper expense amount. If an expense is initially recorded, the adjusting entry will reduce the expense and set up an appropriate amount as an asset.

Companies may use *either* the liability or the revenue approach for recording unearned revenues. If a liability is intially established, the adjusting entry will reduce the liability and recognize an appropriate amount of revenue for the period. If a revenue is initially recorded, the adjusting entry will reduce the revenue and establish an appropriate liability at year-end.

Under either the asset or the expense approach, or the liability or the revenue approach, the objective is to report the proper amounts on the income statement and to show the appropriate account balances on the balance sheet.

Key Terms and Concepts

accrual-basis accounting *(103)*
adjusting entries *(106)*
calendar year *(103)*
cash-basis accounting *(104)*
fiscal year *(103)*
inventory *(112)*
matching principle *(103)*
prepaid expenses *(110)*
revenue recognition principle *(103)*
supplies *(112)*
time period (or periodicity) concept *(102)*
unearned revenues *(113)*
unrecorded expenses *(108)*
unrecorded revenues *(106)*

Review Problem

Adjusting Entries: Unrecorded Revenues and Expenses, Prepaid Expenses, and Unearned Revenues

Savmor, Inc., a service-oriented company, has completed operations for 1993. All regular transaction entries have been journalized and posted, a trial balance has been prepared, and an analysis has been made of the accounts to determine the required adjustments. The analysis reveals the following:

1. At the close of the year, two notes were uncollected. Interest of $370 had been earned by Savmor on these notes, as computed here, but had not yet been recorded.
   (a) Note 1: $10,000, 2-month, 12 percent note dated December 1, 1993. Interest revenue earned for December was $100 ($10,000 × 0.12 × 1/12 = $100).
   (b) Note 2: $7,200, 4-month, 15 percent note dated October 1, 1993. Interest revenue earned for 3 months (October, November, December) was $270 ($7,200 × 0.15 × 3/12 = $270).
2. Unbilled but earned service fees on an incomplete contract amounted to $875. The total amount to be received on the contract is $4,380.
3. At the close of the year, three short-term notes issued by Savmor were outstanding. (Amounts are rounded to the nearest dollar.)

Note Date	Face Amount	Note Period	Interest Rate	Unrecorded Interest Expense at December 31
10/17/93	$16,000	90 days	12%	$395[a]
11/1/93	12,000	75 days	10%	197[b]
12/16/93	7,200	120 days	15%	44[c]
				$636

[a] $16,000 × 0.12 × 75/365 = $395 (14 days in October + 30 days in November + 31 days in December = 75 days)
[b] $12,000 × 0.10 × 60/365 = $197 (29 days in November + 31 days in December = 60 days)
[c] $7,200 × 0.15 × 15/365 = $44 (15 days in December)

4. Unrecorded property taxes at year-end were $4,550; the property taxes are for 1993 and are due January 10, 1994.
5. Earned but unpaid employee salaries and wages totaled $9,600 at December 31, 1993. The next payroll will be made on January 15, 1994. (Ignore payroll taxes.)
6. Service fees on two contracts were received in full, but the contracts were incomplete as of December 31. When the fees were received, a liability account was credited for the total amount. The status of the two contracts is as follows:
   (a) Contract 1: $8,500; 80 percent complete.
   (b) Contract 2: $6,800; 40 percent complete.
7. IMB Company paid Savmor $10,800 on August 1, 1993, to lease some of the company's equipment. The 1-year lease period began August 1; receipt of the $10,800 was credited to Equipment Rent Revenue.
8. All advertising costs had been charged to expense as incurred. The Prepaid Advertising account had a zero balance on December 31. Advertising services paid for in 1993 to be received in 1994 amount to $5,400.

9. The company issued a long-term note for $36,000 on October 1, 1993. The note is to be paid at the end of 6 years; interest at 12 percent (a total of $4,320) is due annually each October 1 until the note is paid.
10. Estimated income taxes for the year were $28,200.

Required: Prepare appropriate adjusting journal entries for Savmor, Inc., at December 31, 1993.

Solution To solve this problem you must analyze each item and prepare the appropriate adjusting journal entry. The explanations for each entry help in understanding the entries made and why they are needed.

1. Interest Receivable 370
    Interest Revenue 370

    To record previously unrecorded interest revenue and interest receivable.

(The entry records interest earned to December 31, 1993, on notes 1 and 2 even though the interest has not been received. This is an example of an unrecorded revenue.)

2. Service Fees Receivable 875
    Service Fees Revenue 875

    To record previously unrecorded service fees revenue and service fees receivable to December 31, 1993.

(The service fees have been earned and should be recognized in 1993 even though they will not be received until 1994.)

3. Interest Expense 636
    Interest Payable 636

    To record previously unrecorded interest expense and interest payable to December 31, 1993, on three short-term notes.

(Interest will be paid when the notes mature in 1994. This is an example of an unrecorded expense.)

4. Property Tax Expense 4,550
    Property Taxes Payable 4,550

    To record property taxes payable and the related property tax expense for the period ending December 31, 1993.

(The property taxes must be recognized as expenses in 1993 even though they will not be paid until 1994.)

5. Salaries and Wages Expense 9,600
    Salaries and Wages Payable.............................. 9,600

    To record employees' salary and wage expense applicable to 1993 and the related liability at December 31, 1993.

(This entry is necessary to recognize the salary and wage expense in 1993 and the obligation that exists at December 31. The wages will be paid in 1994.)

6. Unearned Service Fees Revenue 9,520
    Service Fees Revenue 9,520

    To recognize service fees revenue earned in 1993 on contracts 1 and 2 and to reduce unearned service fees revenue recorded as a liability when fees were received. (Contract 1: $8,500 × 0.80 = $6,800; contract 2: $6,800 × 0.40 = $2,720)

[This is an example of an unearned revenue that was originally recorded as a liability (liability approach). The adjusting entry is needed to recognize partial satisfaction of the obligation (liability) by services provided on the contracts in 1993.]

7.	Equipment Rent Revenue	6,300	
	Unearned Equipment Rent Revenue		6,300

To reduce equipment rent revenue previously recorded and to recognize the obligation (liability) on the equipment lease to IMB Company. ($10,800 × 7/12 = $6,300)

[This is an example of an unearned revenue that was originally recorded as a revenue (revenue approach). Since all the revenue has not been earned by December 31, 1993, the amount not earned (7 months' rent) must be transferred from the revenue account, Equipment Rent Revenue, to the liability account, Unearned Equipment Rent Revenue.]

8.	Prepaid Advertising	5,400	
	Advertising Expense		5,400

To adjust the Advertising Expense and Prepaid Advertising accounts at December 31, 1993.

[This is an example of a prepaid expense that was originally recorded as an expense (expense approach). This entry recognizes that part of the recorded expenses should be shown as an asset, Prepaid Advertising, at December 31, 1993, since some of the advertising will benefit 1994.]

9.	Interest Expense	1,080	
	Interest Payable		1,080

To record interest expense and interest payable for 3 months to December 31, 1993, on a long-term note. ($4,320 × 3/12 = $1,080)

(Since no entry has been previously recorded, this adjustment is necessary to correctly report interest expense for 1993 and the obligation to pay the interest. The obligation and interest will be paid in 1994.)

10.	Income Tax Expense	28,200	
	Income Tax Payable		28,200

To record income tax expense on income earned during 1993, and the related liability (income tax payable) that will be paid in 1994.

(This adjustment recognizes a previously unrecorded expense of 1993 that is to be paid in 1994.)

Discussion Questions

1. Why are financial reports prepared on a periodic basis?
2. Distinguish between reporting on a calendar-year and on a fiscal-year basis.
3. When are revenues generally recognized (recorded)?
4. What is the matching principle?
5. Explain why accrual-basis accounting is more appropriate than cash-basis accounting for most businesses.
6. Why are accrual-based financial statements considered somewhat tentative?
7. Why are adjusting entries necessary?
8. Since there are usually no source documents for adjusting entries, how does the accountant know when to make adjusting entries and for what amounts?
9. Describe the three-step process used in determining the appropriate amounts of adjusting entries.
10. Explain the importance of step 2—determining the

Chapter 4 *Adjusting Entries*

appropriate account balances—in the three-step process of analyzing adjusting entries.
11. The Cash account is generally not one of the accounts increased or decreased in an adjusting entry. Why?
12. Why are supplies not considered inventory? What type of account is supplies?
13. Whether the asset or the expense approach is used in making adjusting entries for prepaid expenses, the result is the same. Explain.
14. Explain why there are alternative ways of recording certain transactions, either as assets or expenses, or as liabilities or revenues.

Exercises

E4-1
Cash-Basis Accounting

In which year would Patty Smith record the revenue or expense from each of the following transactions if Smith's accounting records are kept on a cash basis?

1. On January 5, 1994, Smith received and paid the December 1993 electricity bill.
2. On December 30, 1993, Smith paid an insurance premium for the year 1994.
3. Smith received $100 interest on January 3, 1994, on a note dated December 1, 1993. The principal on the note will be paid on December 1, 1994.
4. Smith paid state property taxes on January 10, 1994. The taxes were assessed on her property for the year 1993.

E4-2
Accrual-Basis Accounting

Refer to the preceding problem. Assume that Ms. Smith keeps her records on an accrual basis. For each situation, in which year would she record the revenue or expense?

E4-3
Reporting Income: Cash Versus Accrual Accounting

On December 31, Brian Pendleton completed the first year of operations for his new business. The following data are available from the company's accounting records:

Sales to customers	$145,000
Collections from customers	125,000
Interest earned and received on savings accounts	1,500
Amount paid for 1½ years' rent	3,600
Utility bill owed: to be paid next month	960
Cost of goods sold	80,000
Amount paid to suppliers for inventory	83,000
Wages paid to employees	47,500
Wages owed to employees at year's end	1,200
Interest due at 12/31 on a loan to be paid the middle of next year	800

1. How much net income (loss) should Brian report for the year ended December 31 according to (a) cash-basis accounting and (b) accrual-basis accounting?
2. Which basis of accounting provides the better measure of operating results for Brian?

E4-4
Reporting Revenues on an Accrual Basis

Galland Company, a proprietorship, receives revenue from many sources. In preparing year-end financial statements at December 31, 1993, Galland had trouble deciding how much revenue to report on the 1993 proprietorship income statement. Assuming accrual-basis accounting, for each revenue item listed indicate how much Galland should include as revenue for 1993.

1. Will receive interest revenue of $6,000 on short-term investments on February 1, 1994, for the 3-month period ending January 31, 1994.
2. Rented an office building to the Bateman Corporation. On July 1, 1993, Bateman paid Galland $50,000 rent for the year ended June 30, 1994.
3. Will receive a dividend check from Bik Company on January 22, 1994. Galland owns 10,000 shares of Bik Company stock. On December 30, 1993, Bik Company declared a cash dividend of $2 per share payable to those who owned its stock on that date.
4. Received a check from a client on December 1, 1993, for $18,000. The payment is for professional advice and counseling for the 12-month period ending November 30, 1994.

E4-5
Reporting Expenses on an Accrual Basis

Assuming accrual-basis accounting for each of the following situations, state how much expense should be reported by BOS Inc. for 1993.

1. On January 1, 1993, BOS borrowed $1,000 from a bank. The note is due, with annual interest of $160 ($1,000 × 0.16 = $160), on January 1, 1995.
2. BOS paid a car insurance premium of $240 in advance on October 1, 1993. The premium is for a 6-month period of insurance coverage.
3. BOS paid salaries of $12,000 on December 1, 1993. This amount represents salaries for December and January.
4. BOS signed an advertising contract for weekly radio spot announcements on August 1, 1993, paying $2,400 on that date for a 2-year advertising program.
5. BOS rented a storage shed, paying $3,600 on November 1, 1993, for a year's rent.

E4-6
Classifications of Accounts Requiring Adjusting Entries

For each type of adjustment listed, indicate whether it is an unrecorded revenue, an unrecorded expense, an unearned revenue, or a prepaid expense at December 31, 1993.

1. Property taxes that are for the year 1993, but are not to be paid until 1994.
2. Rent revenue earned during 1993, but not collected until 1994.
3. Salaries earned by employees in December 1993, but not to be paid until January 5, 1994.
4. A payment received from a customer in December 1993 for services that will not be performed until February 1994.
5. An insurance premium paid on December 29, 1993, for the period January 1, 1994, to December 31, 1994.
6. Gasoline charged on a credit card during December 1993. The bill will not be received until January 15, 1994.
7. Interest on a certificate of deposit held during 1993. The interest will not be received until January 7, 1994.
8. A deposit received on December 15, 1993, for rental of storage space. The rental period is from January 1, 1994, to December 31, 1994.

E4-7
Adjusting Entries: Unrecorded Revenues and Expenses

Hakala Enterprises has hired you to make the necessary adjusting entries at December 31, 1993, prior to preparing its financial statements. Through your analysis, you determine that the following independent transactions are not reflected in the accounts. For each item, give the adjusting entry that should be made at December 31, 1993.

1. Employees will be paid their December wages on January 5, 1994. The monthly wage expense is $10,000. (Ignore payroll taxes.)

Chapter 4 *Adjusting Entries*

2. Hakala owns 10,000 shares of Arizona Utility stock. On November 30, 1993, the utility company declared a $5 per share dividend to be paid to stockholders of record on December 15, 1993. The dividend check will be received by Hakala on January 10, 1994.
3. Hakala made a $20,000 loan to one of its officers on July 1, 1993. The loan will be repaid in one year with 10% interest.
4. Hakala has received notice of its property tax assessment for 1993. The $4,500 bill will actually be paid in March 1994.

E4-8

Adjusting Entries: Prepaid Expenses Using the Asset Approach

Carol Bigler owns and operates Bigler Signs, Inc. Bigler Signs uses the asset approach in recording all prepaid expenses. Give the entry that Carol would make to record each of the following transactions on the date it occurred, and prepare the adjusting entries needed on December 31, 1993.

1. On July 1, 1993, the company paid a 3-year premium of $7,200 on an insurance policy that is effective July 1, 1993, and expires June 30, 1996.
2. On February 1, 1993, Bigler Signs paid its property taxes for the year February 1, 1993, to January 31, 1994. The tax bill was $1,800.
3. On May 1, 1993, the company paid $180 for a 3-year subscription to an advertising journal. The subscription starts May 1, 1993, and expires April 30, 1996.

E4-9

Adjusting Entries: Prepaid Expenses Using the Expense Approach

Refer to the transactions outlined in E4-8. Assume now that Bigler Signs uses the expense approach in recording all prepaid expenses. Give the entry the company would make on the date of each transaction's occurrence as well as the adjusting entries it would make on December 31, 1993.

E4-10

Adjusting Entries: Unearned Revenues Using the Liability Approach

Mark Boswell is the owner/operator of Boswell Consulting Company. Mark uses the liability approach in recording all unearned revenues. Give the entry that Mark would make to record each of the following transactions on the date of occurrence, and assuming accrual-basis accounting, give the adjusting entries needed at December 31, 1993.

1. Boswell received $1,800 on September 15, 1993, in return for which the company agreed to provide consulting services for 18 months beginning immediately.
2. Boswell rented part of its office space to Bristle Brush Company. Bristle paid $1,200 on November 1, 1993, for the next 6 months' rent.
3. Boswell loaned $100,000 to a client. On November 1, the client paid $24,000, which represents 2 years' interest in advance (November 1, 1993, through October 31, 1995).

E4-11

Adjusting Entries: Unearned Revenues Using the Revenue Approach

Refer to the transactions outlined in E4-10. Assume now that Boswell Consulting Company uses the revenue approach in recording all unearned revenues. Give the entry that Boswell would make to record each of the transactions on the date it occurred as well as the adjusting entries needed on December 31, 1993.

E4-12

Adjusting Entries: Comprehensive

Shop Rite Stores is ready to prepare its financial statements for the year ended December 31, 1993. The following information can be determined by analyzing the accounts:

1. On August 1, 1993, Shop Rite received a $4,800 payment in advance for rental of office space. The rental period is for one year beginning on the date payment was received. Shop Rite recorded the receipt as rental revenue.

2. On March 1, 1993, Shop Rite paid its insurance agent $3,000 for the premium due on a 24-month corporate policy. Shop Rite recorded the payment as insurance expense.
3. Shop Rite pays its employee wages the middle of each month. The monthly payroll (ignoring payroll taxes) is $22,000.
4. Shop Rite received a note from a customer on June 1, 1993, as payment for merchandise. The amount of the note is $1,000 with interest at 12%. The note and interest will be paid on June 1, 1995.
5. On December 20, 1993, Shop Rite received a 2,500 check for merchandise. The transaction was recorded as unearned revenue. By year's end, Shop Rite had completed and shipped three-fourths of the merchandise order. The rest of the merchandise won't be shipped until at least the middle of January 1994.
6. During September, Shop Rite purchased $500 worth of supplies. At December 31, 1993, one-fourth of the supplies had been used. Shop Rite initially recorded the purchase of supplies as an asset.

Where appropriate, prepare adjusting journal entries at December 31, 1993, for each of these items.

Problem Set A

P4A-1
Cash- and Accrual-Basis Accounting

SPREADSHEET PROBLEM

In the course of your examination of the books and records of Hickory Company, you find the following data:

Salaries earned by employees	$ 53,000
Salaries paid	55,000
Total sales revenue	838,000
Cash collected from sales	900,000
Utility expense incurred	5,000
Utility bills paid	4,800
Cost of goods sold	532,000
Cash paid on purchases in 1993	411,000
Inventory at December 31, 1993	320,000
Tax assessment for 1993	5,000
Taxes paid in 1993	4,900
Rent expense for 1993	30,000
Rent paid in 1993	25,000

Required:
1. Compute Hickory's net income for 1993 using cash-basis accounting.
2. Compute Hickory's net income for 1993 using accrual-basis accounting.
3. **Interpretive Question** Why is accrual-basis accounting usually used? Can you see any opportunities for improperly reporting income under cash-basis accounting? Explain.

P4A-2
Adjustment of Accounts

Several of the account balances at January 1, 1993, for Universal Company are listed here.

Rent Payable	$1,000
Unearned Consulting Fees	1,200
Interest Receivable	300
Utilities Payable	100

The following information is pertinent:

(a) For the year 1993, the rent was $800 per month. At December 31, 1993, the December 1993 rent had not been paid. Rent payments are debited to expense.
(b) During 1993, Universal received payments totaling $10,000 for consulting fees. These receipts were credited to Consulting Fees Revenue. At December 31, 1993, Universal still owes clients services worth $700.
(c) The company received $5,500 during 1993 as payment in full on a $5,000, 1-year note. The interest received on the loan was credited to Interest Revenue. No notes receivable were outstanding on December 31, 1993.
(d) Utility expense in 1993 was $100 per month. The December 1993 utility bill amounting to $100 was paid on January 10, 1994. During 1993, all utility payments were debited to Utility Expense.

Required:
1. For each transaction, give the entry that would be made on December 31, 1993, to properly record the revenues and expenses for the calendar year 1993.
2. **Interpretive Question** Why is it important to know both the amount of a revenue or an expense and the method used to record its payment in order to make an adjusting entry?

P4A-3
Adjusting Entries

The information presented here is from Sun Marketing, Inc.

(a) Salaries for the period December 26, 1993, through December 31, 1993, amounted to $14,240. (Ignore payroll taxes.)
(b) Interest of $6,000 is payable for 3 months on a 15 percent $160,000 loan.
(c) Rent of $24,000 was paid for 6 months in advance on December 1 and charged to expense.
(d) Rent of $82,000 was credited to a revenue account when received. Of this amount, $33,400 is unearned at year-end.
(e) The unexpired portion of an insurance policy is $1,000. The Insurance Expense account was originally debited.
(f) Interest revenue of $300 from a $2,000 note has been earned but has not been collected or recorded.

Required: Prepare the adjusting entries that should be made on December 31, 1993. (Omit explanations.)

P4A-4
Adjusting Entries

You have just completed a trial balance and an analysis of the accounts of SOS Company, at December 31, 1993. Your analysis reveals the following information:

(a) The Prepaid Rent account shows a zero balance. Included in the Rent Expense account is an amount of $9,000, a payment of one year's rent for the period October 1, 1993, to September 30, 1994.
(b) The Prepaid Insurance account was debited as the following insurance was bought:

Policy No.	Purchase and Effective Date of Policy	Life of Policy	Premiums
1AX	Jan. 1, 1992	3 years	$2,400
2BX	June 1, 1992	2 years	960
3CX	Sept. 1, 1992	1 year	480
4DX	Sept. 1, 1993	1 year	600

(c) The balance in the Prepaid Advertising account is $3,600. This amount is for a series of radio spot announcements to be run for a 6-month period, beginning November 1, 1993.

(d) At the close of the year, the company had two notes receivable. The first, a 90-day, 12 percent note for $7,200, was dated December 16, 1993. The second, a 60-day, 9 percent note for $6,000, was dated December 1, 1993. Interest receivable on these two notes at December 31 is $80 ($36 + $44), rounded to the nearest dollar.

(e) At the close of the year, three short-term notes payable were outstanding.

Date of Note	Face Amount	Note Period	Interest Rate	Interest Expense Accrued
10/17	$ 8,100	90 days	8%	$133
11/1	12,000	120 days	10%	197
12/16	6,600	120 days	12%	33

(f) Property taxes not yet recorded at December 31, 1993, amount to $2,275.

(g) $21,600 was received on a 1-year equipment lease, effective August 1, 1993. The receipt was credited to Equipment Rent Revenue.

(h) Salaries and wages incurred but not yet recorded at December 31, 1993, total $3,500.

Required: Prepare the adjusting journal entries required at December 31, 1993.

P4A-5
Determining Adjusting Entries from General Journal Entries

Howard Barnes, the bookkeeper of Snyder & Sons, thinks that the following journal entries may lead to adjusting entries at December 31, 1993:

Feb. 1	Prepaid Insurance		1,200	
	Cash			1,200
Mar. 31	Cash		9,000	
	Rent Revenue			9,000
May 1	Legal Service Expense		1,800	
	Cash			1,800
Aug. 1	Property Tax Expense		6,000	
	Cash			6,000
Oct. 31	Prepaid Interest		700	
	Cash			700

Howard has discovered the following additional information:

(a) The insurance premium is for the 12-month period ending February 1, 1994.
(b) The rent revenue represents rent received from a tenant for the period March 31, 1993, to September 30, 1993.
(c) The legal service expense is for the services of Boyd Pack, attorney at law, for the 12-month period ending April 30, 1994.
(d) The property tax expense is for the state's fiscal year, which ends June 30, 1994.
(e) The prepaid interest represents interest on a loan for the last 3 months of 1993.

Required: Make adjusting entries required at December 31, 1993.

Chapter 4 Adjusting Entries

P4A-6
Year-End Analysis of Account Balances

Correct account balances for Gunther's Inc. at the beginning and end of 1993 are shown here:

		1/1/93	12/31/93
1.	Prepaid Insurance	$3,200	$4,600
2.	Wages Payable	1,700	1,200
3.	Prepaid Rent	700	500

Expense accounts associated with the preceding accounts for 1993 are listed as follows:

1.	Insurance Expense	$ 4,400
2.	Wages Expense	26,000
3.	Rent Expense	2,100

Required: Determine the amount of cash paid out during the year for each type of expense, (1) through (3).

P4A-7
Adjusting Entry Analysis

ESCO Consulting Company follows the asset and liability approaches in accounting for prepaid expenses and unearned revenues. The following information is provided for selected accounts at December 31, 1993:

	Account Balances Before Adjustment	Account Balances After Adjustment
Prepaid Rent	$2,400	$1,800
Salaries and Wages Payable	1,250	2,250
Unearned Consulting Fees	6,500	3,200
Interest Receivable	600	900

During 1993, $10,000 was paid for rent; $50,000 salaries and wages expense was paid; $24,000 was received for consulting fees; and $2,500 interest revenue was received.

Required: Give the adjusting entries that should be made at December 31, 1993, by ESCO Consulting Company (omit explanations), and indicate the proper amounts to be reported on the 1993 financial statements for:

(a) Rent Expense
(b) Salaries and Wages Expense
(c) Consulting Fees Revenue
(d) Interest Revenue

P4A-8
Unifying Concepts: Adjusting Entries and Financial Statements

The 1993 year-end financial statements of Kelly Company, a service business, are shown as follows. The company's accountants prepared the statements before making the necessary adjustments.

Kelly Company
Income Statement
For the Year Ended December 31, 1993

Revenue from services		$151,920
Operating expenses:		
Insurance expense	$ 5,480	
Rent expense	500	
Office supplies expense	2,960	
Salaries expense	55,000	63,940
Net income		$ 87,980

Kelly Company
Balance Sheet
December 31, 1993

Assets		Liabilities and Owner's Equity	
Cash	$ 22,000	Accounts payable	$ 54,800
Accounts receivable	40,000	Kelly Peterson, capital	200,000
Notes receivable	12,800		
Machinery	180,000		
		Total liabilities	
Total assets	$254,800	and owner's equity	$254,800

The following items are not reflected in the preceding financial statements:

(a) Salaries earned but not recorded or paid were $5,000. (Ignore payroll taxes.)
(b) Prepaid insurance premiums amounted to $1,950. Insurance Expense was originally debited for all insurance expenditures.
(c) Interest earned but not received or recorded was $700.
(d) Service revenue collected and recorded but not earned was $4,180.

Required:
1. Give the required adjusting entries. (Omit explanations.)
2. Prepare a revised income statement and balance sheet.
3. Prepare a schedule reconciling the revised amount of owner's equity with the amount shown on the original statement.

Problem Set B

P4B-1
Cash- and Accrual-Basis Accounting

High Five Company had the following transactions during the first month of its operations in 1993.

Jan. 1 Purchased $1,000 of supplies on account.
9 Billed Squires Company $3,000 for services performed during this month.
15 Received $2,400 from Squires for services performed.
20 Paid $800 for supplies purchased on account on January 1.
31 Supplies costing $400 were used during the period.

Chapter 4 *Adjusting Entries*

Required:
1. Prepare journal entries, assuming that High Five Company uses accrual-basis accounting.
2. Prepare journal entries using cash-basis accounting.
3. From the transactions given, what is the difference in the accrual-basis net income and the cash-basis net income?
4. **Interpretive Question** Which basis of accounting is generally more appropriate and why?

P4B-2
Adjustments to Correct Ending Balances

During the year, Samuelson Company records all cash receipts from revenues and all cash payments of expenses in appropriate income statement accounts. At year-end, required adjustments are made to correct the revenue, unearned revenue, expense, and prepaid expense account balances. The following balances, taken from the accounts, have not been changed since January 1, 1993.

Unearned Rent Revenue	$ 575
Prepaid Property Taxes	750
Interest Receivable	800
Salaries Payable	1,900

An analysis of the accounts indicates that the following are the correct balances at December 31, 1993.

Unearned Rent Revenue	$1,050
Prepaid Property Taxes	750
Interest Receivable	260
Salaries Payable	2,750

Required: In General Journal form, give the adjusting entries required to reflect the correct balances in the accounts at December 31, 1993.

P4B-3
Adjusting Entries

The information that follows is for UTEP Corporation:

(a) An 18-month note receivable from a customer is due January 1, 1995. The note was signed on July 1, 1993. Its face amount is $1,000, and the interest rate is 10 percent per year. The interest is not required to be paid until the note matures.
(b) UTEP paid $4,800 for 6 months' rent of a warehouse on October 1, 1993. Prepaid Rent was debited in recording the transaction.
(c) Property taxes in the amount of $8,000 for 1993 will be paid on January 15, 1994.
(d) On November 1, 1993, a customer paid UTEP $2,500 for services to be rendered over the next 5 months, beginning November 1. UTEP recorded the receipt of cash as Rent Revenue.
(e) The unexpired portion of an insurance policy is $800. The Insurance Expense account was originally debited.
(f) Consulting fees in the amount of $1,500 were received by UTEP on March 1, 1993. The account Consulting Fees Revenue was credited. The fees were for 6 months' consulting services.

Required: Prepare required adjusting entries at December 31, 1993. (Omit explanations.)

P4B-4
Adjusting Entries

In analyzing the accounts to prepare the financial statements for Balnforth Company at December 31, 1993, you observe the following balances for selected accounts:

Prepaid Advertising	$1,800
Unearned Rent	2,400
Insurance Expense	7,680
Service Revenue	1,200

In addition, you determine the following information:

(a) The Insurance Expense account was debited as the following insurance premiums were paid:

Policy Number	Purchase and Effective Date of Policy	Life of Policy	Premiums
101	January 1, 1993	3 years	$4,800
102	July 1, 1993	2 years	1,920
103	September 1, 1993	1 year	960

(b) The amount in Prepaid Advertising is for advertising copy to be run from September 1, 1993, through February 28, 1994.

(c) On December 1, 1993, $2,400 cash was received from a tenant for 1 year's rent paid in advance.

(d) Salaries and wages are paid on the 15th day of each month and amount to $3,600 per month.

(e) On July 1, 1993, Balnforth Company loaned $10,000 to its president. The president signed a 2-year note that calls for 12 percent annual interest. The note receivable plus interest is due on July 1, 1995.

(f) On August 1, 1993, Balnforth Company received $1,200 for services to be rendered over the next 8 months, beginning August 1. The account Service Revenue was credited upon receipt of the cash.

Required: Based on the preceding data, prepare appropriate adjusting journal entries required at December 31, 1993, for Balnforth Company. (Omit explanations).

P4B-5
Examination of Accounts and Adjusting Entries

During the course of your review of Zahas Company at December 31, 1993, you find that the company owes the following notes to its bank:

(a) A 2-year, $20,000, 10 percent note dated January 1, 1993, due December 31, 1994. Zahas Company is required to make semiannual interest payments of $1,000 to the bank on June 30 and December 31 of each year.

(b) A 6-month, 12 percent note dated November 1, 1993, due April 30, 1994. The face value of the note, $3,000, is payable on April 30, together with the interest.

Required:
1. For the first note, give the entries necessary to record the interest payments on June 30 and December 31, 1993; any adjusting entry that may be required on December 31; the interest payments on June 30, 1994, and December 31, 1994; and the payment of the note in full on December 31, 1994.
2. For the second note, give the entries necessary to record the receipt of the proceeds of the note on November 1, 1993; any adjusting entry that may be required on December 31, 1993; and the payment of the note in full on April 30, 1994.
3. What is Zahas Company's total interest expense for the calendar year 1993?

Chapter 4 *Adjusting Entries*

P4B-6
Year-End Analysis of Income Statement Accounts

An analysis of cash records and account balances of Wells, Inc. for 1993 is as follows:

	Account Balances January 1, 1993	Account Balances December 31, 1993	Cash Received or Paid in 1993
Wages Payable	$2,600	$3,000	
Unearned Rent	4,500	5,000	
Prepaid Insurance	100	120	
For wages			$29,600
For rent			12,000
For insurance			720

Required: Determine the amounts that should be included on the 1993 income statement for (1) wages expense, (2) rent revenue, and (3) insurance expense.

P4B-7
Adjusting Entry Analysis

Super Sales Company, a magazine distributor, follows the revenue and expense approaches when recording cash receipts and payments. The company also leaves the balance sheet account balances resulting from year-end adjusting entries unchanged until the end of the next year when the accounts are again adjusted. Four accounts, with their balances before and after adjustment at December 31, 1993, are as follows:

	Before Adjustment	After Adjustment
Unearned magazine subscriptions	$3,900	$3,500
Property taxes payable	2,450	2,700
Printing fees receivable	4,600	5,200
Prepaid advertising	1,200	900

Required: Give the adjusting entries that should be made at December 31, 1993, by Super Sales. (Omit explanations.)

P4B-8
Unifying Concepts: Analysis of Accounts

The following summary totals were taken from the accounting records of Electric Heating Company for the year ended December 31, 1993:

Assets	$125,400
Liabilities	53,000
Equity	72,400
Pretax income	26,900

The controller overlooked the following information and did not make the necessary adjustments as of December 31, 1993:

(a) On July 1, 1993, the company loaned $12,000 to the president. The president gave the company a 1-year note with a 15 percent interest rate. The loan was recorded properly on July 1. The president has not paid anything in 1993. (Interest on the note is $1,800 a year.)
(b) An insurance policy was purchased on November 1, 1993. The premium of $1,200 for the first year was prepaid and debited to Prepaid Insurance.

(c) On June 1, 1993, the company received 1 year's advance rent of $2,100 and credited Rent Revenue.
(d) Interest on a 12 percent, $10,000 note payable to the bank is due every July 1. (The interest was last paid on July 1, 1993.) Yearly interest on the note is $1,200.
(e) Accrued salaries for the period 12/29/93 to 12/31/93 were $2,524.
(f) Income taxes were 30 percent. (Round to the nearest dollar.)

Required: Determine the proper balances of assets, liabilities, owners' equity, and income as of December 31, 1993. Use the following format in working this problem:

Item	Assets	=	Liabilities	+	Owners' Equity		Pretax Income
Beginning balance	$125,400	=	$53,000	+	$72,400		$26,900
(a)							
(b)							
(c)							
(d)							
(e)							
Subtotal	$		$		$		$
(f)							
Correct balances	$	=	$	+	$		$

Business Analysis Case   *Fashion Design, Inc.*

Dian Karen and Kathy Gillen are considering forming a partnership in order to purchase a small business that specializes in interior decoration services. The business records show a modest profit over each of the past 5 years (approximately $5,000 net income per year). However, the past year's operating results appear to be much better, as shown by the unaudited income statement.

Fashion Design, Inc.
Income Statement
For the Year Ended December 31, 1993

Revenues:		
Consulting revenues	$51,000	
Commissions on furnishings sold	18,000	
Total revenues		$69,000
Expenses:		
Advertising expense	$ 1,200	
Rent expense	4,800	
Salaries expense	36,000	
Supplies expense	500	
Utility expense	1,800	
Other expenses	1,500	45,800
Income before taxes		$23,200
Income taxes (estimated at 25%)		5,800
Net income		$17,400

EPS: $17,400 ÷ 1,000 shares = $17.40 per share

Chapter 4 *Adjusting Entries*

In an attempt to verify what appears to be unusually high net income for 1993, Karen and Gillen hire a CPA to audit the records. The CPA discovers the following information:

(a) The company pays salaries on the 1st and 15th of each month. Salaries amounting to $2,500 have been earned by employees by December 31 but will not be paid until January 1.
(b) Of the $18,000 in commissions received by December 31, 30 percent will not be earned until completion of a job in mid-February of 1994. All commissions received have been recorded as revenues.
(c) A $10,000 payment was received on November 1 on a consulting assignment that is only one-half earned at December 31. The total amount was credited to Consulting Revenues when received.
(d) The rent is $400 per month and must be paid in advance on a 1-year lease. A check for $4,800 was given to the landlord on March 1, 1993, and recorded as rent expense on that date.

Except for these data, the income statement appears to the CPA to accurately reflect the operating results of Fashion Design.

Required:
1. Do the 1993 operating results offer encouragement to Karen and Gillen as potential investors? Explain.
2. What adjustments (if any) are required to make the income statement reflect more accurately the results of operations for the year?
3. What is the impact on the balance sheet (if any) of the data discovered by the CPA?

Ethics Case *Daisy Industries*

You are employed as the controller for Daisy Industries. Your assistant has just completed the financial statements for the current year and given them to you for review. A copy of the statements also has been given to the president of the company. The income statement reports a net income for the year of $50,000 and earnings per share of $2.50.

In reviewing the statements, you realize the assistant neglected to record adjusting entries. After making the necessary adjustments, the company shows a net loss of $10,000 instead of net income of $50,000. The difference is due to an unusually large amount of unrecorded expenses at year-end. You realize that these expenses are not likely to be found by the independent auditors.

You wonder if it would be better to delay the recording of the expenses until the first part of the subsequent year in order to avoid reporting a net loss on the income statement for the current year. A significant increase in revenues is expected in the coming year, and the expenses in question could be "absorbed" by the higher revenues.

Required:
1. What issues are involved in this case?
2. As the controller, what course of action would you take?

Chapter 5

Completing the Accounting Cycle

Learning Objectives

After studying this chapter, you should be able to:
1. Understand how to prepare and use a work sheet.
2. Explain how financial statements may be prepared from a work sheet or directly from the accounts.
3. Describe the closing process in the accounting cycle.
4. Explain how to prepare a post-closing trial balance.
5. Understand how all the steps in the accounting cycle fit together.

• • • • • • • • • • • • •

SETTING THE STAGE

Mack Taylor was the controller (chief accountant) for the 1st National Bank of Tennessee. Over a period of four years, he embezzled approximately $160,000 from the bank. He was able to conceal his thefts by manipulating the accounting records, always keeping in mind the basic accounting equation:

Assets = Liabilities + Owners' Equity

Mack realized that if he stole cash (an asset), he must manipulate the accounting records so that this equation remained in balance. He knew his manipulation would have to involve increasing another asset, decreasing a liability, or decreasing owners' equity. He reasoned that if he increased another asset, bank officers would want to know where the asset came from, and if he reduced liabilities, vendors who weren't paid would complain. Therefore, Mack decided to focus his concealment efforts on reducing owners' equity, consisting of common stock and retained earnings. He didn't want to mess with the stock accounts because they were managed by an outside transfer agent (a company that maintains stock records), so he decided to focus on retained earnings. Mack knew that retained earnings is decreased by dividends and increased by earnings. Mack rationalized that if he recorded fictitious dividends to reduce owners' equity, someone would notice because the same amount of dividends were paid each quarter. Therefore, he decided to focus on reducing net income.

How could net income best be manipulated, Mack wondered. He could reduce recorded revenues, but once revenues are recognized, they are rarely reduced (except with certain adjusting entries). Therefore, Mack decided to increase expenses. Increasing expenses would reduce net income, which would reduce retained earnings and stockholders' equity. Thus, the accounting equation would still balance.

To hide his fraud, Mack embezzled cash and recorded the following expenses:

Advertising Expense	XXX
Cash	XXX

No one in the company realized that advertising expense was higher than it should have been. And because expense and revenue accounts are brought to zero balances (closed) at the end of each accounting period so that income can be correctly measured next period, Mack's trail of theft was wiped out through the closing process. In essence, since advertising expense was brought to a zero balance at the end of each accounting period, if Mack's company didn't catch him before the end of the year, the trail was gone.

Mack used this scheme to perfection. Never once was he suspected until he got greedy and stole $10,000 when a company mistakenly paid the bank twice. When the company realized its error and came to the bank for repayment, the extra $10,000 was traced to Mack's personal bank account. Upon investigation, Mack admitted stealing approximately $160,000. (The actual amount stolen could have been much greater.)

Note: This scenario really happened, but the names have been changed. "Mack" has served prison time for his offense and now works for another company as an accountant.

In this chapter, you will learn how the accounting cycle is completed and how income statement accounts are closed or brought to zero balances at the end of each accounting period. You will learn that Mack's knowledge of accounting was accurate and that his concealment techniques were quite good. We will also show that completing the cycle can be facilitated by using a work sheet.

THE WORK SHEET

Objective 1
Understand how to prepare and use a work sheet.

work sheet *a columnar schedule used to summarize accounting data*

A **work sheet** is a tool used by accountants to facilitate the preparation of financial statements. Unlike the financial statements, work sheets are for internal use only; they are not distributed to "outsiders." Although the use of work sheets is optional, most accountants find them helpful for organizing large quantities of data. Many work sheets are now prepared on electronic spread sheets, using a software package such as Lotus 1-2-3, Excel, or Quatro Pro.

Preparing a Work Sheet

In preparing a work sheet, accountants first list the trial balance, then add any adjusting entries, and finally extend the combined amounts into the appropriate financial statement columns. The figures in these columns are used in preparing the income statement and the balance sheet. Additional analysis is required to prepare the statement of cash flows (see Chapter 15).

A work sheet will usually have a minimum of 8 columns, as shown in Exhibit 5-1 on page 140. The accounts are listed on the left side, and columns 1 and 2 indicate the account balances prior to adjustments; that is, this pair of columns contains the unadjusted **trial balance.** Columns 3 and 4 are for adjusting entries. It should be noted that even when a work sheet is used to prepare financial statements, the adjusting entries still must be journalized and posted to the ledger accounts.

trial balance *a listing of all account balances: provides a means of testing whether total debits equal total credits for all accounts*

The last four columns of a work sheet are used for extending the unadjusted trial balance figures, plus or minus adjustments, into the appropriate financial statement columns. Revenue and expense accounts are extended into the income statement columns, and asset, liability, and owners' equity accounts into the balance sheet columns. The exact form of a work sheet is flexible, and its content depends on the type of business and the way a company handles certain transactions.

To illustrate the use of a work sheet, we will examine the operating activities of ITEC, Inc. for 1 month. The purpose is to show you how a work sheet is used. Do not be concerned if you do not at first understand every adjustment. The work sheet for ITEC, Inc., using the 8-column format, is shown in Exhibit 5-1. The amounts in the trial balance columns are based on the following transactions. (Note that the company was organized on January 1, 1994.)

Jan.		
	1	Issued capital stock for $20,000 cash.
	2	Paid $4,800 cash to lease a truck for 1 year.
	5	Received $600 from a tenant for 6 months' rent ($100 per month).
	6	Paid $480 for a 1-year insurance policy.
	8	Purchased $250 of supplies for cash.
	12	Purchased inventory for $10,000 on account.
	14	Sold inventory for $15,000 on account; cost of the merchandise sold was $8,000.
	19	Collected $12,000 cash from customers' accounts receivable.
	20	Paid $7,000 cash for inventories bought on January 12.
	23	Paid $1,500 for sales representatives' salaries.
	27	Purchased $14,000 of inventory for cash.
	30	Sold inventory for $19,700 cash; cost of the merchandise sold was $13,000.

After all transactions have been journalized and posted, the balances in the accounts can be listed in the first two columns of the work sheet as the unadjusted trial balance (see Exhibit 5-1). The columns are then added to make sure that total debits equal total credits. Assuming an accounting period of one month, the following data are applicable to the necessary adjusting entries at January 31:

(a) Salaries payable, $700. On January 23, $1,500 was paid to sales representatives. By the end of the month, an additional $700 in sales salaries had been earned but not yet paid.

(b) Insurance expense, $40. On January 6, $480 was paid for insurance, debiting Prepaid Insurance. At the end of the month, only one-twelfth of this annual fee should be expensed ($480 ÷ 12 = $40); the balance ($440) should be shown as an asset, Prepaid Insurance.

(c) Monthly rent revenue earned, $100. See January 5 transaction.

(d) Supplies on hand, $110. Of the supplies purchased on January 8, some remain on hand, and some have been used. An explanation of this adjustment is given on page 140.

(e) Prepaid truck rental, $4,400. On January 2, a truck was leased for 1 year for $4,800, payable in advance. (A lease is a formal rental agreement.) At the end of January, eleven-twelfths of the annual lease should be shown as an asset, Prepaid Truck Rental ($4,800 ÷ 12 = $400; $400 × 11 months = $4,400); one-twelfth ($400) should be shown as an expense.

As illustrated in Exhibit 5-1, these adjustments appear in the adjustments columns and are identified as entries (a) through (e). A key for the adjustments is usually included at the bottom of the work sheet. Some accounts that are

Exhibit 5-1 Eight-Column Work Sheet

ITEC, Inc.
Work Sheet
January 31, 1994

Account Titles	Trial Balance Debits	Trial Balance Credits	Adjustments Debits	Adjustments Credits
Cash	24,270			
Accounts Receivable	3,000			
Inventory	3,000			
Supplies	250			(d) 140
Prepaid Insurance	480			(b) 40
Accounts Payable		3,000		
Unearned Rent Revenue		600	(c) 100	
Capital Stock		20,000		
Sales		34,700		
Cost of Goods Sold	21,000			
Salaries Expense	1,500		(a) 700	
Truck Rental Expense	4,800			(e) 4,400
	58,300	58,300		
Salaries Payable				(a) 700
Insurance Expense			(b) 40	
Rent Revenue				(c) 100
Supplies Expense			(d) 140	
Prepaid Truck Rental			(e) 4,400	
			5,380	5,380
Net Income (to balance)				

Adjustments:
- (a) Salaries Payable, $700
- (b) Insurance Expense, $40 ($480 ÷ 12 = $40 a month)
- (c) Rent Revenue Earned, $100
- (d) Supplies Expense, $140 ($250 − $110)
- (e) Prepaid Truck Rental, $4,400 ($4,800 ÷ 12 = $400; $400 × 11 months)

Chapter 5 Completing the Accounting Cycle

| Income Statement || Balance Sheet ||
Debits	Credits	Debits	Credits
		24,270	
		3,000	
		3,000	
		110	
		440	
			3,000
			500
			20,000
	34,700		
21,000			
2,200			
400			
			700
40			
	100		
140			
		4,400	
23,780	34,800	35,220	24,200
11,020			11,020
34,800	34,800	35,220	35,220

involved in the adjusting entries have a zero balance before adjustments and so are not included in the trial balance. These accounts are added below those listed on the trial balance. The adjustments are added to or subtracted from the preadjustment account balances. If an 8-column work sheet is used, as in Exhibit 5-1, the results are extended to the appropriate income statement or balance sheet columns as debits or credits, respectively.

As shown in Exhibit 5-2, if a 10-column work sheet is used, an adjusted trial balance pair of columns may be included. These amounts are then extended to the appropriate income statement and balance sheet columns. The totals for each set of columns must show the equality of debits and credits.

Note in Exhibits 5-1 and 5-2 that the income statement and the balance sheet column subtotals do not show this equality. A balancing figure must be added to both the income statement and the balance sheet to make total debits equal total credits for each pair of columns. If credits (revenues) exceed debits (expenses) for the income statement column subtotals, a balancing debit amount ($11,020 in this case) must be added, reflecting net income for the period. The same amount must also be added as a credit to the balance sheet columns, showing an increase in owners' equity. If debits exceed credits for the income statement subtotals, there is a net loss for the period. This would be presented as a balancing credit amount on the income statement and a balancing debit amount on the balance sheet, showing a reduction in owners' equity. In either case, a balancing figure is required to bring total debits equal to total credits for each set of columns.

The financial statements, as shown in Exhibits 5-3 and 5-4, generally are prepared directly from the work sheet. (Taxes have been ignored to simplify the example.)

Special Considerations in Using a Work Sheet

Two items relating to ITEC's work sheet (Exhibit 5-1) require additional explanation. In this section, we will explain: (1) the work sheet adjustment for income taxes and (2) reporting the ending retained earnings balance.

WORK SHEET ADJUSTMENT FOR INCOME TAXES. To keep the ITEC illustration simple, we ignored income taxes. However, when a corporation earns income, it must pay income taxes. As noted in Chapter 4, a year-end adjustment is required, debiting Income Tax Expense[1] and crediting Income Taxes Payable for the appropriate amount. When the taxes are actually paid, usually during the following year, Income Taxes Payable is debited, and Cash is credited.

The adjustment for income taxes presents a minor problem on the work sheet because the amount of income taxes to be paid cannot be determined until net income (net loss) has been computed. One way to solve this problem is to subtotal the work sheet columns, determine the balancing figure for income, multiply that figure by the tax rate to determine the amount of the tax, and then make the adjusting entry for Income Tax Expense and Income Taxes Payable the same way as other adjustments are made.

---

[1] Income Tax Expense is the complete account title. However, income statements often use the shorter form, Income Taxes.

With this approach, both income tax accounts—Income Tax Expense and Income Taxes Payable—are added on the work sheet following the column subtotals. To illustrate, we assume that ITEC, Inc. is subject to a tax rate of 25 percent. The work sheet shown in Exhibit 5-1 would be completed as follows:

	Adjustments		Income Statement		Balance Sheet	
	Debits	Credits	Debits	Credits	Debits	Credits
Subtotals	5,380	5,380	23,780	34,800	35,220	24,200
Income Tax Expense	2,755		2,755			
Income Taxes Payable		2,755				2,755
Totals	8,135	8,135	26,535	34,800	35,220	26,955
Net Income (to balance)			8,265*			8,265
Totals			34,800	34,800	35,220	35,220

* [$34,800 − $23,780 = $11,020 to balance the income statement columns: $11,020 × 0.25 = $2,755 Income Tax Expense and Income Taxes Payable; the balance ($11,020 − $2,755 = $8,265) is net income.]

REPORTING THE ENDING RETAINED EARNINGS BALANCE. We have explained and illustrated how the financial statements can be prepared from the income statement and balance sheet columns on the work sheet. To simplify the illustration (Exhibit 5-1), we assumed that ITEC, Inc. was organized on January 1, 1994, and therefore had no previous retained earnings balance. Normally, a work sheet will show the beginning retained earnings on the trial balance, which will be extended as a credit to the balance sheet columns. In addition, if a corporation has paid its stockholders dividends during the period, the Dividends account will be shown on the trial balance and extended as a debit to the balance sheet columns. When preparing the balance sheet, these amounts must be considered in determining the ending retained earnings balance. The beginning retained earnings amount is added to the net income balancing figure on the work sheet, and any amount shown for dividends is subtracted. The resulting figure is the amount of ending retained earnings to be reported on the balance sheet; thus:

```
   Beginning Retained Earnings
+  Net Income
−  Dividends
   Ending Retained Earnings
```

For the ITEC illustration, the beginning Retained Earnings balance was zero since the company had just been established. There also were no dividends paid. Therefore, the ending balance for retained earnings ($11,020; see Exhibit 5-4) was simply the amount of net income for the period.[2] For the next month, ITEC would start with a balance of $11,020 in its Retained Earnings account,

---

[2] Recall that income taxes were ignored in calculating the net income of $11,020. In practice, however, a corporation's net income *after taxes* is the amount that would be added in computing the ending balance for Retained Earnings.

Exhibit 5-2 *Ten-Column Work Sheet*

ITEC,
Work
January

Account Titles	Trial Balance Debits	Trial Balance Credits	Adjustments Debits	Adjustments Credits
Cash	24,270			
Accounts Receivable	3,000			
Inventory	3,000			
Supplies	250			(d) 140
Prepaid Insurance	480			(b) 40
Accounts Payable		3,000		
Unearned Rent Revenue		600	(c) 100	
Capital Stock		20,000		
Sales Revenue		34,700		
Cost of Goods Sold	21,000			
Salaries Expense	1,500		(a) 700	
Truck Rental Expense	4,800			(e) 4,400
	58,300	58,300		
Salaries Payable				(a) 700
Insurance Expense			(b) 40	
Rent Revenue				(c) 100
Supplies Expense			(d) 140	
Prepaid Truck Rental			(e) 4,400	
			5,380	5,380
Net Income (to balance)				

Adjustments:
(a) Salaries Payable, $700
(b) Insurance Expense, $40 ($480 ÷ 12 = $40 a month)
(c) Rent Revenue Earned, $100

Inc.
Sheet
31, 1994

Adjusted Trial Balance		Income Statement		Balance Sheet	
Debits	Credits	Debits	Credits	Debits	Credits
24,270				24,270	
3,000				3,000	
3,000				3,000	
110				110	
440				440	
	3,000				3,000
	500				500
	20,000				20,000
	34,700		34,700		
21,000		21,000			
2,200		2,200			
400		400			
	700				700
40		40			
	100		100		
140		140			
4,400				4,400	
59,000	59,000	23,780	34,800	35,220	24,200
		11,020			11,020
		34,800	34,800	35,220	35,220

(d) Supplies Expense, $140 ($250 − $110)
(d) Prepaid Truck Rental, $4,400 ($4,800 ÷ 12 = $400; $400 × 11 months)

Exhibit 5-3

ITEC, Inc.
Income Statement
For the Month Ended January 31, 1994

Sales revenue		$34,700
Rent revenue		100
Total revenues		$34,800
Expenses:		
Cost of goods sold	$21,000	
Insurance expense	40	
Salaries expense	2,200	
Supplies expense	140	
Truck rental expense	400	
Total expenses		23,780
Net income		$11,020

Exhibit 5-4

ITEC, Inc.
Balance Sheet
January 31, 1994

Assets		Liabilities and Owners' Equity		
Cash	$24,270	Liabilities:		
Accounts receivable	3,000	Accounts payable	$ 3,000	
Inventory	3,000	Salaries payable	700	
Supplies	110	Unearned rent		
Prepaid insurance	440	revenue	500	
Prepaid truck rental	4,400	Total liabilities		$ 4,200
		Owners' equity:		
		Capital stock	$20,000	
		Retained earnings	11,020	
		Total owners' equity		31,020
		Total liabilities and		
Total assets	$35,220	owners' equity		$35,220

add the net income balancing figure for that month, and subtract any dividends to determine the ending retained earnings balance to report on the balance sheet. The same process would be followed for a proprietorship or partnership. The net income would be added to the beginning capital balance for the period, any withdrawals would be subtracted, and the ending capital balance would be reported on the balance sheet.

Chapter 5 *Completing the Accounting Cycle*   147

> **To Summarize** *A work sheet is often used to analyze end-of-period adjustments and to facilitate the preparation of financial statements. It will usually have at least 8 columns, 2 for each category: unadjusted trial balance, adjusting entries, income statement, and balance sheet. Sometimes columns are added for an adjusted trial balance. The exact format and content of a work sheet will be determined by the special needs of a particular business. Work sheet adjustments may also have to be made for supplies and income taxes. The ending retained earnings balance for a corporation (or the capital accounts for proprietorships or partnerships) is computed from the amounts shown on the work sheet. The beginning balance is added to the net income balancing figure, any dividends (or withdrawals) are subtracted, and the resulting ending balance is reported on the balance sheet.*

PREPARING FINANCIAL STATEMENTS

Objective 2

Explain how financial statements may be prepared from a work sheet or directly from the accounts.

Once all transactions have been analyzed, journalized, and posted and all adjusting entries have been made, the accounts can be summarized and presented in the form of general-purpose financial statements. The information for the income statement and the balance sheet is taken directly from the work sheet, when one is used. All that is needed is to organize the data into appropriate sections and categories so as to present them as simply and clearly as possible. When a work sheet is not used, financial statements are prepared directly from the data in the adjusted ledger accounts.

THE CLOSING PROCESS

Objective 3

Describe the closing process in the accounting cycle.

We have almost reached the end of the accounting cycle. Thus far, the accounting cycle has included analyzing documents, journalizing transactions, posting to the ledger accounts, determining account balances and preparing a trial balance, making adjusting entries, and preparing the financial statements (either directly from the accounts or from a work sheet). Just two additional steps are needed: (1) journalizing and posting closing entries and (2) preparing a post-closing trial balance.

Real and Nominal Accounts

real accounts *accounts that are not closed to a zero balance at the end of each accounting period; permanent accounts appearing on the balance sheet*

nominal accounts *accounts that are closed to a zero balance at the end of each accounting period; temporary accounts generally appearing on the income statement*

To explain the closing process, we must first define two new terms. Certain accounts are referred to as **real accounts.** They report the cumulative increases and decreases in certain account balances from the date the company was organized. These accounts (assets, liabilities, and owners' equity) appear on the balance sheet and are permanent in that they are not closed to a zero balance at the end of each accounting period. Balances existing in real accounts at the end of a period are carried forward to the next period.

Other accounts are known as **nominal accounts.** These accounts (revenues and expenses) are temporary in that they are reduced to a zero balance through the closing process at the end of each accounting period. Thus, nominal ac-

closing entries *entries that reduce all nominal, or temporary accounts to a zero balance at the end of each accounting period, transferring their preclosing balances to a permanent balance sheet account*

counts begin with a zero balance at the start of each accounting cycle. Transactions throughout the period, generally a year, are journalized and posted to the nominal accounts, which are used to accumulate and classify all revenue and expense items for that period. At the end of the accounting period, adjustments are made, the income statement is prepared, and the balances in the temporary accounts are then closed to an owners' equity (permanent) account. These **closing entries** bring the income statement accounts back to a zero balance, which makes the accounts ready for a new accounting period and a new set of transactions. In addition, the closing entries transfer the net income or loss for the accounting period to owners' equity and reduce owners' equity for any distributions to owners. Without closing entries, revenue and expense balances would extend from period to period, making it difficult to isolate the operating results of each accounting period.

Closing Entries

The actual mechanics of the closing process are not complicated. *Revenue accounts normally have credit balances, so they are closed by being debited; expense accounts generally have debit balances and are closed by being credited.* The difference between total revenues and total expenses represents the net income (or net loss) of the entity. For a proprietorship or partnership, net income is credited to the owner's capital account(s) since income increases owners' equity; for a corporation, net income is credited to Retained Earnings. Conversely, a net loss would be debited to the owner's capital account(s) or to Retained Earnings since a loss decreases owners' equity.

To illustrate the closing process, we refer again to ITEC, Inc. If the data for the closing journal entry were taken from the income statement in Exhibit 5-3, the closing entry would be:

Jan. 31	Sales Revenue	34,700	
	Rent Revenue	100	
	Cost of Goods Sold		21,000
	Insurance Expense		40
	Salaries Expense		2,200
	Supplies Expense		140
	Truck Rental Expense		400
	Retained Earnings		11,020
	To close revenues and expenses to Retained Earnings.		

We need to explain a number of points related to this entry. First, the closing entries must also be posted to the appropriate ledger accounts. Second, books normally are closed at the end of a fiscal or calendar year, not at the end of each month, as in our example. A shorter period is used here to simplify the illustration.

Third, closing entries are generally made from data in the income statement columns of a work sheet rather than from the income statement itself. The income statement may not report each item of revenue or expense separately but may combine or summarize some of the items. In the closing process, it is not sufficient to close the balance in a combined or summarized income statement category, such as total expenses or total revenues. Each individual revenue and expense account balance must be reduced to a zero balance. Since the work sheet lists each individual revenue and expense account, the closing entries are more appropriately made from it.

Finally, the Cost of Goods Sold account is an expense account. Like other expense accounts, Cost of Goods Sold must be closed. If the cost of merchandise sold is not recorded after each sale, then cost of goods sold becomes a computed amount determined at the end of the accounting period. The computation of cost of goods sold is discussed in detail in Chapters 6 and 7.

Using an Income Summary Account

In the preceding example, the revenue and expense accounts were closed directly to Retained Earnings. An alternative approach involves using a special account called **Income Summary.** This account is a temporary "clearing account." Its function is to facilitate the process of combining all revenue and expense amounts into one figure—the net income or loss for the period. An Income Summary account is used in the following manner. Revenue accounts usually have credit balances, so they are closed by being debited, with the total credited to Income Summary. Expenses generally have debit balances, so they are closed by being credited, with the total debited to Income Summary. The balance in the Income Summary account, which now represents the income or loss for the period (the difference between revenues and expenses), is in turn closed to the appropriate owners' equity account(s).

Although the Income Summary account facilitates the closing process, it is not required, and many companies close revenues and expenses directly to Retained Earnings, as illustrated earlier. However, use of an Income Summary account keeps the owners' equity accounts from becoming cluttered; only the net income (or loss) and dividend closing entries are transferred to the equity accounts.

The closing journal entries for ITEC when an Income Summary account is used would be:

> **Income Summary** *a clearing account used to close all revenues and expenses at the end of an accounting period; the preclosing balance of the Income Summary account represents the operating results (income or loss) of an accounting period*

Jan. 31	Sales Revenue	34,700	
	Rent Revenue	100	
	Income Summary		34,800
	To close revenues to Income Summary.		
31	Income Summary	23,780	
	Cost of Goods Sold		21,000
	Salaries Expense		2,200
	Insurance Expense		40
	Supplies Expense		140
	Truck Rental Expense		400
	To close expenses to Income Summary.		
31	Income Summary	11,020	
	Retained Earnings		11,020
	To close Income Summary to Retained Earnings: $34,800 − $23,780.		

The final step, again, would be to close the Income Summary account to Retained Earnings. No matter how many entries are made, and whether or not an Income Summary account is used, the effect is the same. All nominal accounts will have a zero balance. Correspondingly, all real accounts, including the owners' equity accounts, will be stated at their appropriate balances.

Closing the Dividends Account

The Dividends account is a nominal (temporary) account that must be closed at the end of the accounting period. However, dividends are *not* expenses and will not be reported on an income statement; they are distributions to stockholders of part of a corporation's earnings. Thus, dividends reduce retained earnings. When dividends are declared by the board of directors of a corporation, the amount that will be paid is debited to Dividends and credited to a liability account, Dividends Payable, or to Cash if paid immediately. Since Dividends is a temporary account, it must be closed to Retained Earnings at the end of the accounting period. The Dividends account is closed by crediting it and by debiting Retained Earnings, thereby reducing owners' equity.

We omitted dividends from the ITEC example because they generally are not declared or paid on a monthly basis. However, if ITEC had declared dividends during January, the Dividends account would have to be closed on January 31 by crediting Dividends and debiting Retained Earnings for the declared amount. Again, note that dividends are not closed to Income Summary because dividends are not an expense but a distribution of earnings that directly reduces Retained Earnings. The Income Summary account is a clearing account used only for closing all revenues and expenses.

The books are now ready for a new accounting cycle. The closing process for the revenues, expenses, and dividends of a corporation is shown schematically in Exhibit 5-5.

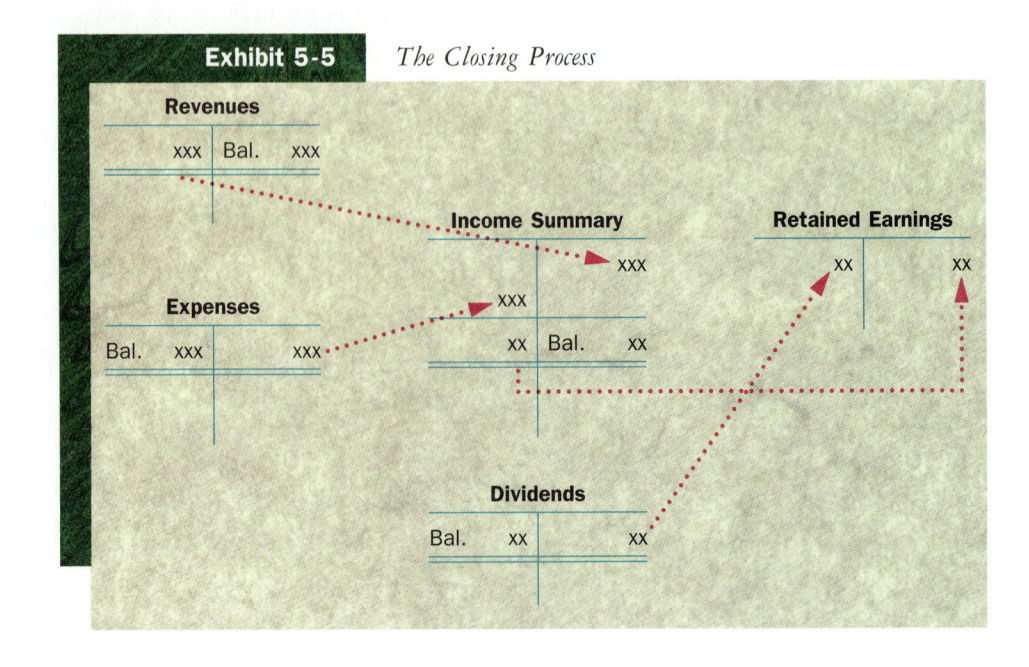

Exhibit 5-5 *The Closing Process*

The Closing Process for Proprietorships and Partnerships

We have illustrated the closing process for a corporation by debiting or crediting the difference between revenues and expenses directly to Retained Earnings or indirectly through an Income Summary account. If a business is a proprietorship or a partnership, the closing entry will be made to a proprietorship or partnership Capital account. For example, if ITEC were owned by Rhonda Fehlberg, a proprietor, the entry to close Income Summary to the Capital account would be:

Jan. 31	Income Summary	11,020	
	R. Fehlberg, Capital		11,020
	To close Income Summary to the capital account of R. Fehlberg.		

drawings *distributions to the owner(s) of a proprietorship or partnership: similar to dividends for a corporation*

Neither a proprietorship nor a partnership pays dividends. Instead, funds are withdrawn by owners in anticipation of, or after the realization of, earnings and are called **drawings** or withdrawals. The closing process for a proprietorship or partnership drawings account is the same as for a corporate dividends account. Each such account is closed to a proprietorship or partnership Capital account by crediting the Drawings account and debiting the respective proprietorship or partnership equity account. The owners' equity section of the balance sheet for proprietorships, partnerships, and corporations is explained fully in Chapters 13 and 14.

> **To Summarize** *After all accounts have been balanced and a trial balance prepared, adjusting entries are made and financial statements are prepared, generally from a work sheet. Next, all nominal, or temporary, accounts are closed to a zero balance. All real, or permanent, accounts (balance sheet accounts for assets, liabilities, and owners' equity) are carried forward to the new reporting period. All nominal accounts (revenues, expenses, and dividends) are closed to Retained Earnings. Revenue accounts are closed by being debited; expense accounts are closed by being credited. If Income Summary is used as a clearing account, the total amount debited to all revenue accounts is credited to Income Summary, and the total amount credited to all expense accounts is debited to Income Summary. The balance in Income Summary is then closed to Retained Earnings for a corporation. Alternatively, revenues and expenses may be closed directly to Retained Earnings. For a corporation, dividends also must be closed to Retained Earnings. For a proprietorship or partnership, the Drawings account must be closed to the proprietorship or partnership equity account. Although a few of the account titles are different, the closing process is the same for proprietorships, partnerships, and corporations.*

PREPARING A POST-CLOSING TRIAL BALANCE

Objective 4
Explain how to prepare a post-closing trial balance.

The last step in the accounting cycle is to balance the accounts and to prepare a **post-closing trial balance.** The accounts are to be balanced—that is, the debits and credits added and a balance determined—only after the closing

post-closing trial balance
a listing of all real account balances after the closing process has been completed; provides a means of testing whether total debits equal total credits for all real accounts prior to beginning a new accounting cycle

entries have been recorded and posted in the General Ledger. The information for the post-closing trial balance is then taken from the ledger. The nominal accounts will not be shown since they have been closed and thus have zero balances. Only the real accounts will have current balances. This step is designed to provide some assurance that the previous steps in the cycle have been performed properly, prior to the start of a new accounting period. Exhibit 5-6 illustrates a post-closing trial balance for ITEC, Inc.

A SUMMARY OF THE ACCOUNTING CYCLE

Objective 5
Understand how all the steps in the accounting cycle fit together.

We have now completed our discussion of the steps in the accounting cycle. By way of review, Exhibit 5-7 shows the material presented earlier as Exhibit 3-1. Many of the steps, such as analyzing transactions, occur continuously. Other steps, such as preparing the financial statements, generally occur once during the cycle.

The financial statements that result from the accounting cycle provide useful information to investors, creditors, and other external users. Generally, these statements are included in the annual reports provided to stockholders. As the Business Environment Essay below makes clear, careful interpretation of the information presented in these reports is important. The techniques for interpreting and analyzing financial statements are the subject of Chapter 16.

BUSINESS ENVIRONMENT ESSAY
Annual Reports to Stockholders—Read Carefully

Financial statements are the end product of the accounting cycle and report a company's financial position, results of operations, and cash flows. The financial statements of corporations are presented in the annual report to stockholders. Major U.S. corporations spend millions of dollars to publish annual reports that will impress their stockholders and potential investors. In fact, the annual report is to some extent a public relations document. In addition to the financial statements, these reports typically include several pages of discussion and analysis prepared by management to describe the company's operations, its past performance, and expectations for the future. As might be expected, this information tends to reflect an optimistic outlook. All the information in the annual report should be read and evaluated carefully, as the following examples illustrate:

- The Quantum Chemical Corporation reported a net loss of $123.3 million in 1991, down from 1990's net earnings of $21.2 million. The chairman said: "Despite these challenging operation conditions, the year was marked by achievements that hold promise for the future."
- Armco, Inc. posted a net loss of $336.5 million in 1991, 3.76 times of the net loss of 1990 ($89.5 million). The chairman said: "We lost $336.5 million. Still, Armco made great progress . . . Our strategy is in place. We have defined our future."
- The Fuqua Industries, Inc. reported a net loss of $51 million in 1991, which is 216 times of the loss of 1990 ($235,000). The president said: "A renewed company has emerged . . . poised for profitability . . . determined to create value . . ."

Exhibit 5-6

ITEC, Inc.
Post-Closing Trial Balance
January 31, 1994

	Debits	Credits
Cash	$24,270	
Accounts Receivable	3,000	
Inventory	3,000	
Supplies	110	
Prepaid Insurance	440	
Prepaid Truck Rental	4,400	
Accounts Payable		$ 3,000
Salaries Payable		700
Unearned Rent Revenue		500
Capital Stock		20,000
Retained Earnings		11,020
Totals	35,220	35,220

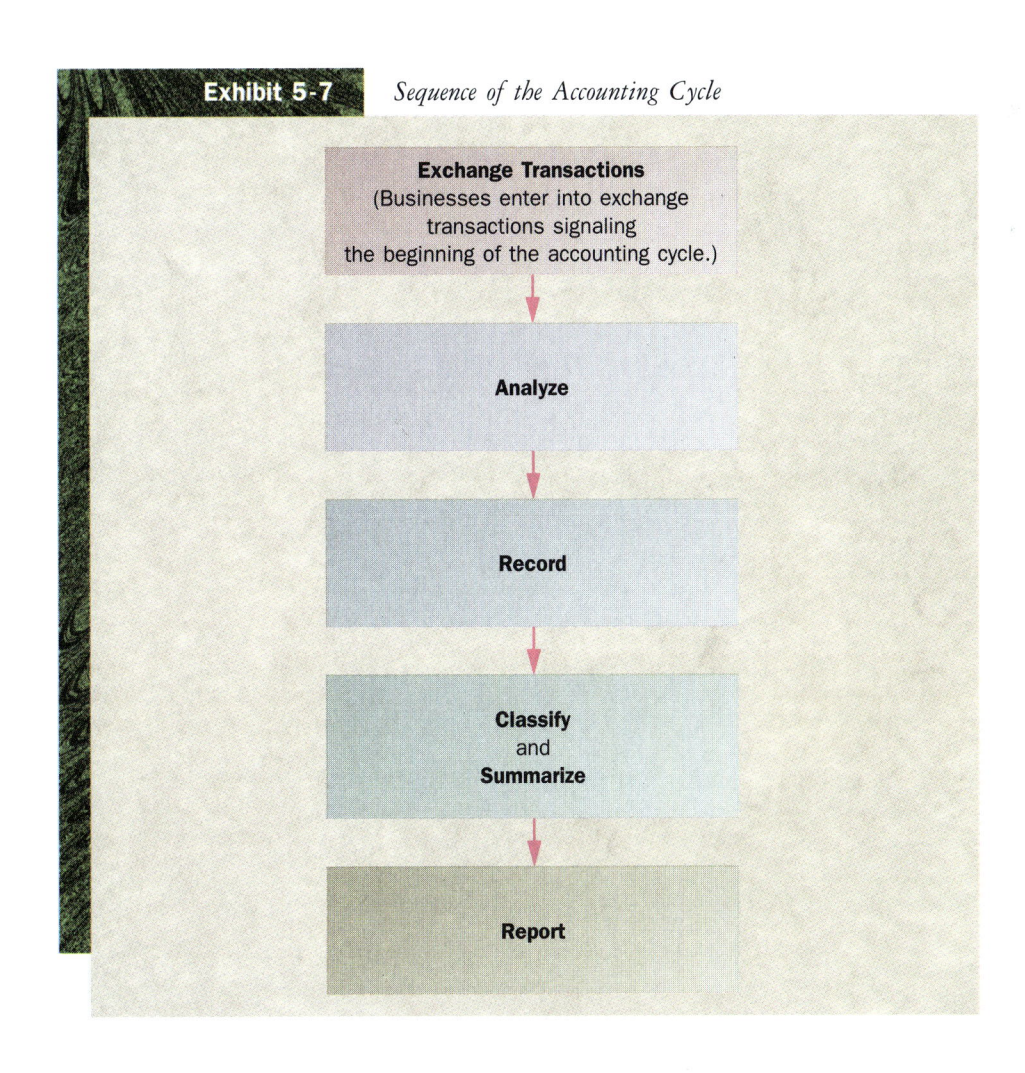

Exhibit 5-7 *Sequence of the Accounting Cycle*

Exchange Transactions
(Businesses enter into exchange transactions signaling the beginning of the accounting cycle.)

↓

Analyze

↓

Record

↓

Classify and Summarize

↓

Report

Chapter 5　Completing the Accounting Cycle

Appendix A

Reversing Entries

Adjusting entries at the end of an accounting period affect both the income statement and the balance sheet. All income statement accounts are reduced to a zero balance through the closing process. However, the balance sheet accounts are not closed. So what happens to the adjustment amounts posted to the balance sheet accounts? When and how are these amounts cleared from the accounts? This appendix answers these questions, and explains reversing entries, which are sometimes included as part of the accounting cycle.

PREPARING REVERSING ENTRIES

reversing entry *a journal entry made at the beginning of a year that exactly reverses an adjusting entry made at the end of the previous year*

A **reversing entry** is a journal entry made at the beginning of a year that exactly reverses an adjusting entry made at the end of the previous year. Reversing entries are never required—they are always optional—and they have no effect on the financial statements prepared for the previous period. In some instances, they facilitate the recording of expenses and revenues with routine entries. Thus, they may reduce the need for analyzing accounts to determine how much of a payment is expense, how much is settlement of a liability, and how much is revenue or asset collection.

To illustrate reversing entries, we will assume that Paula Smith, an employee, is paid a $2,000 salary on the 15th of each month. The entry for December 15 and the adjusting and closing entries at December 31, 1994, would be:

Dec. 15	Salaries Expense	2,000	
	Cash		2,000
	Paid monthly salary to Paula Smith for the period ending December 15, 1994.		
31	Salaries Expense	1,000	
	Salaries Payable		1,000
	To record salaries payable to Paula Smith for one-half month.		
31	Income Summary	24,000	
	Salaries Expense		24,000
	To close Salaries Expense to Income Summary ($2,000/month × 12).		

The following reversing entry could be made as of January 1, 1995, after Salaries Expense has been closed:

```
Jan. 1   Salaries Payable ..................................... 1,000
              Salaries Expense ............................... 1,000
         To reverse the adjusting entry made on December 31, 1994.
```

Note the effect of these entries on the companion accounts. The balance sheet account, Salaries Payable, set up to show the liability as of December 31, 1994, now has a zero balance. The Salaries Expense account shows a credit balance of $1,000. This amount will be deducted from the 12 monthly payments of $2,000. The addition of the $1,000 at December 31, 1995, will then result in the correct amount in the Salaries Expense account for 1995 [(12 × $2,000) − $1,000 + $1,000 = $24,000]. Here are the T-accounts for 1994, with reversing entries shown.

Salaries Expense		Salaries Payable	
Payments (Jan.–Nov. 1994) 22,000	Reversing entry (1/1/94 from (previous period)) 1,000		Adjusting entry (12/31/94) 1,000
Payment (12/15/94) 2,000			
Adjusting entry (12/31/94) 1,000			Balance (12/31/94) 1,000
		(1/1/95) 1,000	
	Closing entry (12/31/94) 24,000		
			Balance after reversing entry (1/1/95) 0
Balance (12/31/94) 0	(1/1/95) 1,000		

reversing entry

Reversing entries are appropriate for transactions that involve unrecorded revenues, unrecorded expenses (such as our example), prepaid expenses that are originally debited to an expense account, and unearned revenues that are originally credited to a revenue account. Stated more simply, *as a general guideline, if an adjusting entry increases a balance sheet account, then a reversing entry may be made.* (In our example, the adjusting entry on December 31, 1994, increased Salaries Payable.)

If a reversing entry is made on January 1, 1995, on January 15, 1995, when Paula Smith is paid, the entry would be as follows:

```
Salaries Expense ................................................ 2,000
    Cash ....................................................... 2,000
```

If a reversing entry is not made, the entry on January 15, 1995, is:

```
Salaries Expense ................................................ 1,000
Salaries Payable ................................................ 1,000
    Cash ....................................................... 2,000
```

Making reversing entries eliminates the need to remember how much of the payment is an expense and how much is a reduction in the payable. Instead, the full amount can be debited to Salaries Expense and credited to Cash; the balance is correct because of a credit to the expense account from the reversing entry. As noted, if a reversing entry is not used, the accounts must be analyzed at year-end (1995 in our example) and the three-step process for adjusting entries followed to determine the appropriate adjusting entry.

Appendix B

Special Journals

special journal *a book of original entry for recording similar transactions that occur frequently*

So far we have shown all journal entries in General Journal format. Many businesses have hundreds or even thousands of transactions every day, and so it is impractical and inefficient to use only one journal. Instead, they group transactions into similar classes and use a **special journal** for each.

COMPUTERIZED JOURNALS

In this electronic age, more and more companies have decided to maintain their special journals on a computer. Although a computer-based system is faster and requires less labor than a manual system, the steps in the process are basically the same in both: Transactions are recorded on source documents, they are then journalized and posted to the accounts, and the resulting information is summarized and reported. The difference lies in who (or what) does the work. With a computer-based system, operators enter data onto magnetic disks or tapes. Directed by special operating programs (software), the computer posts the journalized data to accounts in the ledgers, balances the accounts, and prepares trial balances, the financial statements, and other reports.

electronic data processing (EDP) *a term referring to the use of computers in recording, classifying, manipulating, and summarizing data*

A major advantage of computer use—collectively referred to as **electronic data processing (EDP)**—is its incredible speed. Most computers can make millions of calculations per second and produce more documents in a minute than a person could in an entire week. With a computer, then, accounts are always kept up to date, and reports can be printed on demand. A second advantage of computers is accuracy. If data are entered correctly, output errors are unlikely; generally, errors result only from hardware (equipment) or software defects. Finally, computers save time and effort. Once data are entered, they may be "massaged" (manipulated) for a variety of uses. Given all the data on accounts receivable, for example, a computer can be instructed to isolate all accounts 30 days overdue and print a list of them. Or, the list might focus on accounts owing more than a certain dollar amount.

Computers also have disadvantages. The term *GIGO* (garbage in, garbage out) refers to the problem that results when data are entered incorrectly. With incorrect input, all the related accounts and reports will be wrong. If bookkeepers or accountants had been doing the posting, an unlikely figure might have been caught and the mistake corrected at its source; computers accept data without question. A second disadvantage is the difficulty of tracing the steps in a calculation. As a result, a company's auditors will find it difficult, if not impossible, to properly review the documentation behind recorded transactions. A third disadvantage is the specialization required of computer operators. In a small company, for example, programmers who have complete access to the computer might be able to manipulate the company's programs for their

THE SALES JOURNAL

personal benefit. Most computer hardware and software, therefore, now have built-in controls, which limit access to data, define the kinds of transactions that can be processed, and cross-check all totals.

In this appendix, we refer to a manual system. We could just as well have demonstrated a computer-based system, for the basic principles are the same.

One of the most frequently occurring business transactions involves the sale of goods or services, either for cash or on credit. Cash sales, as you will soon learn, are generally recorded in a Cash Receipts Journal. When merchandise is sold on credit, a prenumbered sales invoice is prepared, specifying the date of the sale, the amount and kinds of merchandise sold, and the price. One copy of the invoice is sent to the accounting department to be used as the basis for an entry in the **Sales Journal**, which is a chronological listing of all credit sales, as shown in Exhibit 5-8.

Sales Journal *a special journal in which credit sales are recorded*

This sales journal page has no columns for sales discounts (reductions in price offered to customers who pay within a specified period), sales returns, or sales taxes. Antler Corporation records all credit sales at their gross amounts, noting sales discounts at the time of collection (in the cash receipts journal). Sales returns, which involve a debit to Sales Returns and Allowances and a credit to Accounts Receivable, are recorded by Antler in the General Journal. Many companies include sales discounts and returns in the Sales Journal, but we have omitted them here for the sake of simplicity. If Antler were operating

Exhibit 5-8 *A Sample Page in a Sales Journal for Antler Corporation*

SALES JOURNAL

Date		Customer	Invoice No.	Post Ref.	Amount
Jan. 1994	2	Lee Smith	125	105.7	600
	5	Roger Jameson	126	105.5	250
	6	Ralph Smith	127	105.8	315
	8	John Anderson	128	105.1	216
	9	Carl Hartford	129	105.4	822
	12	Mike Taylor	130	105.9	610
	16	Marvin Brinkerhoff	131	105.3	507
	23	Roy Avondet	132	105.2	125
	27	Jay Rasmussen	133	105.6	350
	28	Jerry Woolsey	134	105.11	816
					4,611
					(105) (400)

in a state with sales taxes, the taxes would be entered in a Sales Taxes Payable (credit) column, and the total would be posted to the Sales Taxes Payable account at the same time Accounts Receivable and Sales Revenue are posted.

The Sales Journal differs from the General Journal in several respects. First, since every transaction is similar, the entries do not require separate explanations. Second, there are no debit and credit columns because the total is always posted as a debit to Accounts Receivable (account 105) and a credit to Sales Revenue (account 400). Third, the Sales Journal includes a column for the sales invoice number for easy reference to a source of additional information.

Having a single total posted to Accounts Receivable saves time and keeps the General Ledger in manageable form but makes it difficult, if not impossible, for a company to monitor the activity of individual accounts. Maintaining a separate account for each customer within the General Ledger creates a different sort of problem—a voluminous General Ledger, which contains all these Accounts Receivable accounts, plus Cash, Inventory, and so forth. The same problem exists for accounts payable.

To handle this problem, companies generally keep at least three ledgers: the General Ledger, which contains all the balance sheet and income statement accounts; the Accounts Receivable **Subsidiary Ledger;** and the Accounts Payable Subsidiary Ledger. The subsidiary ledgers contain, in alphabetical order, separate accounts for each customer and creditor, respectively, showing all debits, credits, and a balance. They are called subsidiary ledgers because they back up, or support, the account balances in the General Ledger; that is, the total of all accounts in the Accounts Receivable Subsidiary Ledger, for example, equals the balance in Accounts Receivable in the General Ledger. Conversely, Accounts Receivable is called a **control account** because it summarizes the individual accounts in the Accounts Receivable Subsidiary Ledger. Exhibit 5-9 illustrates the relationship between the general and subsidiary ledgers.

As the Sales Journal entries are posted to the Accounts Receivable Subsidiary Ledger accounts, the individual account numbers are entered in the sales journal posting reference column. The number of the sales journal page and the date of the transaction are similarly entered as a posting reference in the subsidiary accounts. These cross-references quickly direct accountants to the source of additional information, while serving as a means of checking their work. Exhibit 5-10 shows the posting of the sales transactions to the Accounts Receivable Subsidiary Ledger and to the General Ledger. Note that the total posted to Accounts Receivable in the General Ledger equals the total of all postings to the Accounts Receivable Subsidiary Ledger.

subsidiary ledger *a grouping of individual accounts that in total equal the balance of a control account in the General Ledger*

control account *a summary account in the General Ledger that is supported by detailed individual accounts in a subsidiary ledger*

THE PURCHASES JOURNAL

A second frequently occurring transaction involves the purchase of merchandise for resale, either for cash or on credit. Cash purchases are recorded in a Cash Disbursements Journal and will be discussed later. Credit purchases are chronologically recorded in a **Purchases Journal.** The individual entries are posted to accounts in the Accounts Payable Subsidiary Ledger throughout the accounting period. At the end of the period, the total is posted to the Accounts Payable and Purchases accounts.

Purchases Journal *a special journal in which credit purchases are recorded*

Chapter 5 Completing the Accounting Cycle

Exhibit 5-9 *The General and Subsidiary Ledgers*

General Ledger
- XXX
- Notes Payable
- Accounts Payable
- XXX
- Inventory
- Accounts Receivable
- Cash

Accounts Payable Subsidiary Ledger
- White Co.
- United Company
- Tool Design Co.
- Palmer Supply Co.
- Mayberry Marketing
- Jackson Wholesale
- Equipment Supply
- Davies Wholesale

Accounts Receivable Subsidiary Ledger
- Jerry Woolsey 105.11
- Mike Taylor 105.9
- Ralph Smith 105.8
- Lee Smith 105.7
- Jay Rasmussen 105.6
- Roger Jameson 105.5
- Carl Hartford 105.4
- Marvin Brinkerhoff 105.3
- Roy Avondet 105.2
- John Anderson 105.1

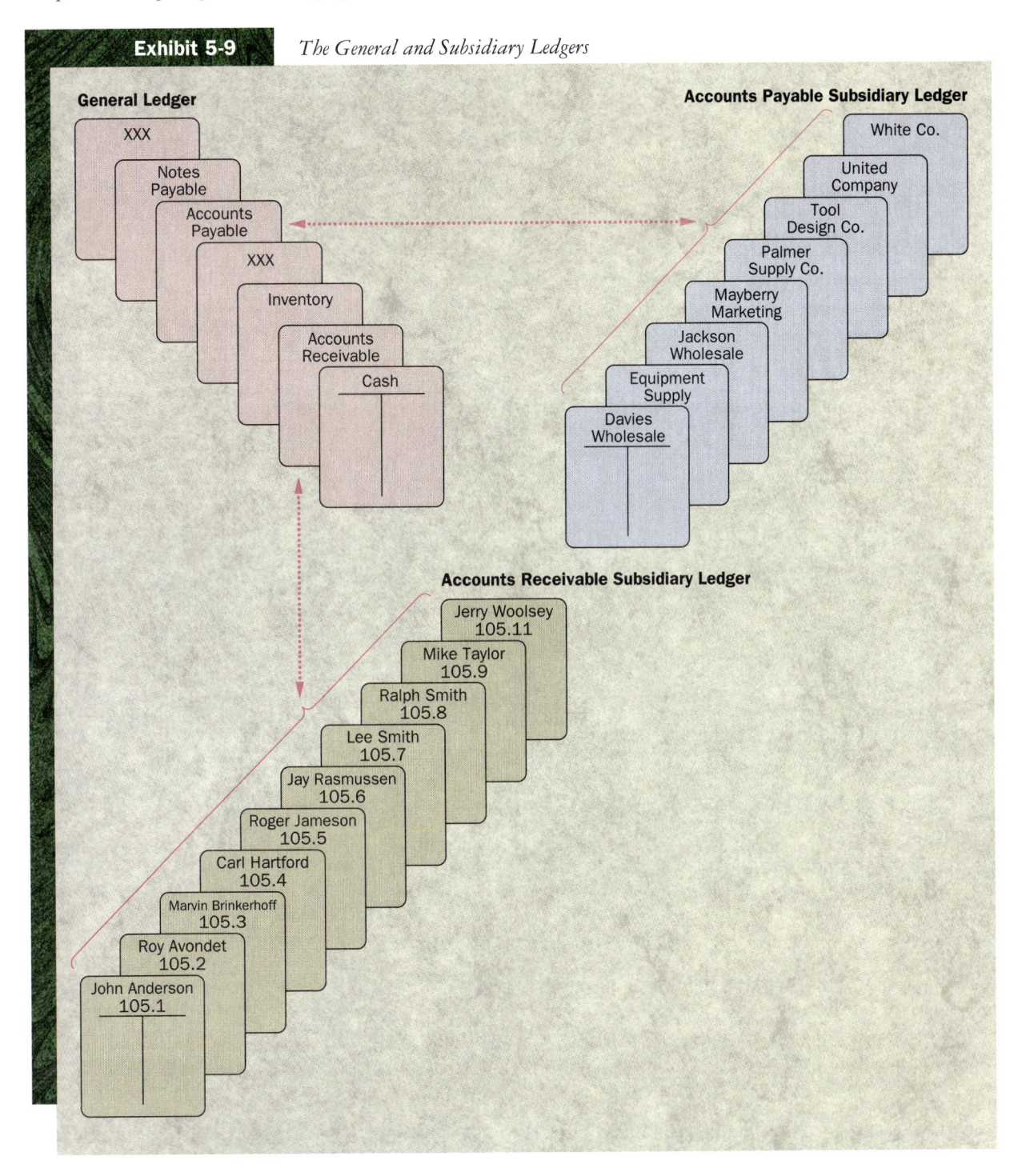

The Purchases and Sales Journals are similar, except that the Sales Journal includes invoice numbers, and the Purchases Journal includes invoice dates. Obviously, another company's invoice number would be meaningless. The date, on the other hand, is useful for identifying the beginning of a discount

Exhibit 5-10 Posting from the Sales Journal

SALES JOURNAL

Date	Customer	Invoice No.	Post Ref.	Amount
Jan. 2, 1994	Lee Smith	125	105.7	600
5	Roger Jameson	126	105.5	250
6	Ralph Smith	127	105.8	315
8	John Anderson	128	105.1	216
9	Carl Hartford	129	105.4	822
12	Mike Taylor	130	105.9	610
16	Marvin Brinkerhoff	131	105.3	507
23	Roy Avondet	132	105.2	125
27	Jay Rasmussen	133	105.6	350
28	Jerry Woolsey	134	105.11	816
				4,611
				(105) (400)

ACCOUNTS RECEIVABLE LEDGER

Lee Smith 105.7 — 1/2 600
Roger Jameson 105.5 — 1/5 250
Ralph Smith 105.8 — 1/6 315
John Anderson 105.1 — 1/8 216
Carl Hartford 105.4 — 1/9 822
Mike Taylor 105.9 — 1/12 610
Marvin Brinkerhoff 105.3 — 1/16 507
Roy Avondet 105.2 — 1/23 125
Jay Rasmussen 105.6 — 1/27 350
Jerry Woolsey 105.11 — 1/28 816

GENERAL LEDGER

Accounts Receivable (105) — 1/94 4,611
Sales Revenue (400) — 1/94 4,611

---

period. A sample page from a Purchases Journal is shown in Exhibit 5-11. As with the Sales Journal, Antler Corporation handles discounts at the time of payment.

This Purchases Journal is used for recording credit purchases of inventory only. Credit purchases of equipment, supplies, or other such items and purchase returns would be recorded in the General Journal. Exhibit 5-12 illustrates the posting of the Purchases Journal to the Accounts Payable Subsidiary Ledger and to the General Ledger.

Chapter 5 *Completing the Accounting Cycle*

Exhibit 5-11 *A Sample Page in a Purchases Journal for Antler Corporation*

PURCHASES JOURNAL

Date	Supplier	Invoice Date	Post Ref.	Amount
Jan. 1994 2	Mayberry Marketing	Jan. 1994 1	202.4	300
5	Jackson Wholesale Co.	4	202.3	616
6	Equipment Supply	5	202.2	485
12	Davies Wholesale	11	202.1	690
14	Jackson Wholesale Co.	12	202.3	150
15	Palmer Supply Co.	14	202.5	810
22	White Incorporated	22	202.8	800
29	United Co.	28	202.7	600
30	Tool Design Co.	29	202.6	400
				4,851
				(202) (450)

Each purchase is posted to the individual creditor's account in the Accounts Payable Subsidiary Ledger, and the total of $4,851 is posted to Accounts Payable (202) and Purchases (450) in the General Ledger. Again like the Sales Journal, the Purchases Journal is cross-referenced to the general and subsidiary ledgers, and the cumulative total of all balances in the Accounts Payable Subsidiary Ledger equals the balance in the Accounts Payable account.

THE CASH RECEIPTS JOURNAL

Cash Receipts Journal a special journal in which all cash received from sales, interest, rent, or other sources is recorded

Another special journal is the **Cash Receipts Journal,** which includes all cash received from sales, interest, rent, or other sources. Exhibit 5-13 shows a typical page from that journal and the posting of its entries.

The Cash Receipts Journal usually includes columns for Cash (DR), Sales Discounts (DR), Accounts Receivable (CR), and Sales Revenue (CR). In addition, an Other Accounts (CR) column is used to record all "irregular" cash transactions, that is, all items that do not fall naturally into a special column such as Cash or Accounts Receivable. Examples are collections of interest, rents, or notes receivable. The Other Accounts column is added for cross-checking purposes, and a check mark (✔) is placed below the total to indicate that the individual items have been posted.

Exhibit 5-13 shows that on January 7, $588 was received from Lee Smith in payment of $600 bill (debit Cash, credit Accounts Receivable). The $12 difference is a 2 percent discount ($600 × .02 = $12) offered by Antler to customers who pay within 10 days (debit Sales Discounts). The $125 cash sale on January 12 was debited to Cash and credited to Sales Revenue, and the interest revenue collected on January 18 was credited to Other Accounts. Mike

Exhibit 5-12 Posting the Purchases Journal

PURCHASES JOURNAL

Date	Supplier	Invoice Date	Post Ref.	Amount
1994 Jan. 2	Mayberry Marketing	Jan. 1	202.4	300
5	Jackson Wholesale Co.	4	202.3	616
6	Equipment Supply	5	202.2	485
12	Davies Wholesale	11	202.1	690
14	Jackson Wholesale Co.	12	202.3	150
15	Palmer Supply Co.	14	202.5	810
22	White Incorporated	22	202.8	800
29	United Co.	28	202.7	600
30	Tool Design Co.	29	202.6	400
				4,851
				(202) (450)

ACCOUNTS PAYABLE LEDGER

Mayberry Marketing 202.4
| | 300 | 1/2 |

Jackson Wholesale Co. 202.3
| | 616 | 1/5 |

Equipment Supply 202.2
| | 485 | 1/6 |

Davies Wholesale 202.1
| | 690 | 1/12 |

Jackson Wholesale Co. 202.3
| | 616 | 1/5 |
| | 150 | 1/14 |

Palmer Supply Co. 202.5
| | 810 | 1/15 |

White Incorporated 202.8
| | 800 | 1/22 |

United Co. 202.7
| | 600 | 1/29 |

Tool Design Co. 202.6
| | 400 | 1/30 |

GENERAL LEDGER

Accounts Payable (202)
| | 4,851 | 1/94 |

Purchases (450)
| 1/94 | 4,851 | |

Taylor did not receive a sales discount because he did not pay within the 10-day discount period.

In posting the entries from the Cash Receipts Journal to the General Ledger, only those amounts in the Other Accounts (CR) column are handled individually, with the number of each ledger account appearing in the Post Ref. column. For example, when the $150 payment was collected on January 9 and posted to Notes Receivable, the account number 103 was entered in the Post Ref. column. All other columns are posted to the General Ledger as totals at the end of each accounting period. The total of the debit columns is compared with the total of the credit columns to make sure that total debits equal total credits. As the totals are posted, their account numbers are entered just below the column totals. The individual entries in the Accounts Receivable (CR) column are posted to the customers' accounts in the Accounts Receivable Subsidiary Ledger. Subsidiary account numbers are placed in the Post Ref. column to indicate that these subsidiary postings have been made.

THE CASH DISBURSEMENTS JOURNAL

Cash Disbursements Journal *a special journal in which all cash paid out, for supplies, merchandise, salaries, and other items, is recorded*

The cash payments of a business are usually recorded in a separate **Cash Disbursements Journal,** as shown in Exhibit 5-14. The Cash Disbursements Journal contains Cash (CR), Purchase Discounts (CR), Accounts Payable (DR), Sales Salaries Expense (DR), General and Administrative Salaries Expense (DR), and Other Accounts (DR) columns. The Purchase Discounts and Accounts Payable columns are used to account for payments for merchandise previously purchased. The Sales and the General and Administrative Salaries Expense columns are used to record the payment of salaries if a separate payroll journal is not kept. The Other Accounts column is used to record cash purchases of merchandise and other payments for which there are no special columns. As with the other journals, the parenthetical numbers at the bottoms of the columns mean those column totals have been posted to their respective General Ledger accounts.

In reading Exhibit 5-14, notice that on February 1, the company made a $588 payment to satisfy the $600 payable to United Company. The 2 percent discount of $12 was taken because payment was made within 10 days of purchase. The payments to Equipment Supply and Mayberry Marketing were for the full amounts because they were not made within the 10-day discount period (see the Purchases Journal in Exhibit 5-12).

Exhibit 5-13 *The Cash Receipts Journal*

CASH RECEIPTS

Cash DR	Sales Discounts DR	Date	Receipt No.	Account Name
588.00	12.00	Jan. 1994 7	621	Lee Smith
150.00		9	622	Notes Receivable
125.00		12	623	Cash Sales
805.56	16.44	15	624	Carl Hartford
50.00		18	625	Interest Revenue
30.00		22	626	Cash Sales
122.50	2.50	29	627	Roy Avondet
610.00		29	628	Mike Taylor
2,481.06	30.94			
(101)	(404)			

GENERAL

Cash (101)
1/94   2,481.06

Notes Receivable (103)
                    1/94   150.00

Sales Revenue (400)
                    1/94   155.00

Sales Discounts (404)
1/94   30.94

ACCOUNTS RECEIVABLE

Roy Avondet (105.2)
1/29/94   125.00

Carl Hartford (105.4)
1/15/94   822.00

JOURNAL

Post Ref.	Accounts Receivable CR	Sales Revenue CR	Other Accounts Post Ref.	Amount CR
105.7	600.00			
			103	150.00
		125.00		
105.4	822.00			
			513	50.00
		30.00		
105.2	125.00			
105.9	610.00			
	2,157.00	155.00		200.00
	(105)	(400)		(✓)

LEDGER

Accounts Receivable (105)

1/94	2,157.00

Interest Revenue (513)

1/94	50.00

SUBSIDIARY LEDGER

Lee Smith (105.7)

1/7/94	600.00

Mike Taylor (105.9)

1/29/94	610.00

Exhibit 5-14 *The Cash Disbursements Journal*

CASH DISBURSE

Other Accounts		Cash CR	Purchase Discounts CR	Date	Check No.	Account Names
Post Ref.	Amount CR					
		588.00	12.00	Feb. 1, 1994	176	United Co.
		225.00		6	177	First Federal Co.
		3,000.00		8	178	Bell Telephone
		485.00		17	179	Equip. Supply
		2,100.00		24	180	Payroll
		300.00		28	181	Mayberry Mktg.
		6,698.00	12.00			
		(101)	(452)			

GENERAL

Cash (101)

2/94 6,698.00

Notes Payable (201)

2/6/94 225.00

Sales Salaries Expense (501)

2/94 1,400.00

General and Administrative Salaries Expense (550)

2/94 700.00

ACCOUNTS PAYABLE

Equipment Supply (202.2)

2/17/94 485.00

Mayberry Marketing (202.4)

2/28/94 300.00

...MENTS JOURNAL

Post Ref.	Accounts Payable DR	Salaries Expense Sales DR	Salaries Expense Gen. & Admin. DR	Other Accounts Post Ref.	Other Accounts Amount DR
202.7	600.00				
				201	225.00
				569	3,000.00
202.2	485.00				
		1,400.00	700.00		
202.4	300.00				
	1,385.00	1,400.00	700.00		3,225.00
	(202)	(501)	(550)		(✓)

LEDGER

Accounts Payable (202)
2/94   1,385.00

Purchase Discounts (452)
            | 2/94   12.00

Telephone Expense (569)
2/8/94   3,000.00

SUBSIDIARY LEDGER

United Company (202.7)
2/1/94   600.00

Review of Learning Objectives

Objective 1
Understand how to prepare and use a work sheet. A work sheet is often used to facilitate the preparation of financial statements. The accounts and their balances are listed on the work sheet, adjustments are made, and the adjusted balances are transferred to the appropriate financial statement columns. The data from the work sheet may then be used to prepare the financial statements.

Objective 2
Explain how financial statements may be prepared from a work sheet or directly from the accounts. When a work sheet is used, an accountant may prepare the financial statements from the data on the work sheet without having to refer to individual accounts in the ledger. When a work sheet is not used, adjustments must be made to individual accounts, as needed, and the adjusted ledger account balances are used to prepare the financial statements.

Objective 3
Describe the closing process in the accounting cycle. Once the financial statements have been prepared and the adjusting entries have been journalized and posted to the accounts, the accounting records should be made ready for the next accounting cycle. This is accomplished by journalizing and posting closing entries for all nominal accounts. Revenue accounts are closed by being debited; expense accounts are closed by being credited. An Income Summary account may be used or revenues and expenses may be closed directly to an owners' equity account. This is true for proprietorships, partnerships, and corporations. For a corporation, dividends are closed by being credited and are closed directly to Retained Earnings. Drawings for a proprietorship or partnership are similar to dividends and are closed to the owners' capital accounts.

Objective 4
Explain how to prepare a post-closing trial balance. The final step in the accounting cycle is to balance the accounts and prepare a post-closing trial balance. This provides some assurance that previous steps have been performed correctly and that the records are in order prior to the start of a new accounting cycle.

Objective 5
Understand how all the steps in the accounting cycle fit together. The accounting cycle consists of specific steps to analyze, record, classify, summarize, and report the exchange transactions of economic entities. By way of review, Exhibit 3-4, on page 67, identifies the steps in the accounting cycle. Note that Appendix A explains reversing entries, which are bookkeeping procedures sometimes used to clear the balance sheet accounts of the adjusting entries made at the end of an accounting period. Appendix B provides a discussion and some simple examples of special journals.

Key Terms and Concepts

Cash Disbursements Journal *(165)***
Cash Receipts Journal *(163)***
closing entries *(148)*
control account *(160)***
drawings *(151)*
electronic data processing (EDP) *(158)***

Income Summary *(149)*
nominal accounts *(147)*
post-closing trial balance *(152)*
Purchases Journal *(160)***
real accounts *(147)*
reversing entry *(155)**

Sales Journal *(159)***
special journal *(158)***
subsidiary ledger *(160)***
trial balance *(138)*
work sheet *(138)*

*Relates to Appendix A
**Relates to Appendix B

Review Problem

The Accounting Cycle

This review problem is longer than most. However, it provides a useful summary of the entire accounting cycle. The post-closing trial balance for Valley View Company as of December 31, 1993, is presented below:

Valley View Company
Post-Closing Trial Balance
December 31, 1993

	Debits	Credits
Cash	17,500	
Accounts Receivable	17,000	
Inventory	28,800	
Supplies	1,200	
Prepaid Building Rental	24,000	
Accounts Payable		18,000
Capital Stock (3,600 shares outstanding)		54,000
Retained Earnings		16,500
Totals	88,500	88,500

Following is a summary of the company's transactions for 1994.

(a) At the beginning of 1994, the company issued 1,500 new shares of stock at $20 per share.
(b) Total inventory purchases were $49,500; all purchases were made on credit and are recorded in the Inventory account.
(c) Total sales were $125,000; $102,900 were on credit, the rest were for cash. The cost of goods sold was $47,500; the Inventory account is reduced at the time of each sale.
(d) In December, a customer paid $3,500 cash in advance for merchandise that was temporarily out of stock. The revenue approach is used to record advance payments received from customers. The $3,500 is not included in the sales figures in (c) above.
(e) The company paid $66,500 on accounts payable during the year.
(f) The company collected $102,000 of accounts receivable during the year.
(g) The company purchased $600 of supplies for cash during 1994, debiting Supplies for the cost of each purchase.
(h) The company paid $850 for advertising during the year, debiting Advertising Expense.
(i) Total salaries paid during the year were $45,000.
(j) The company paid $650 during the year for utilities.
(k) Dividends of $7,500 were paid to stockholders in December.

On December 31, 1994, the company's accountant gathers the following information that is needed to adjust the accounts:

(l) As of December 31, salaries of $750 had been earned by employees but will not be paid until January 3, 1995.
(m) A count of the remaining supplies at December 31 shows $800 of supplies still on hand.
(n) The advertising expense paid during 1994 includes $400 paid on December 1, 1994 for a series of radio advertisements to be broadcast throughout December 1994 and January 1995.
(o) On December 31, 1993, the company rented an office building for 2 years and paid $24,000 in cash, the full rental fee for 1994 and 1995. The asset approach was used in recording the payment. No entries have been made for building rent in 1994.
(p) On December 20, 1994, a $150 bill was received for utilities. No entry was made to record the receipt of the bill, which is due to be paid on January 4, 1995.

(q) As of December 31, 1994, the merchandise paid for in advance (transaction (d)) was still out of stock. The company expects to receive the merchandise and fill the order by January 15, 1995.

(r) The company's income is taxed at a rate of 15%.

Required:
1. Make entries in the General Journal to record each of the transactions (items (a) through (k)).
2. Using T-accounts to represent the General Ledger accounts, post the transactions recorded in the General Journal. Enter the beginning balances in the accounts which appear in the December 31, 1993, post-closing trial balance before posting 1994 transactions. When all transactions have been posted to the T-accounts, determine the balance for each account.
3. Prepare a trial balance as of December 31, 1994, using the first pair of columns in an 8-column work sheet.
4. Make the necessary adjustments (items (l) through (r)) on the work sheet, and complete the work sheet.
5. Using the information in the completed work sheet, prepare an income statement and balance sheet.
6. Record adjusting entries and closing entries in the General Journal, and post these entries to the General Ledger (T-accounts).
7. Prepare a post-closing trial balance.

Solution

1. Journal Entries

Following are the journal entries to record the transactions for the year. Several of these are summary entries representing numerous individual transactions.

(a) Cash 30,000
     Capital Stock   30,000

The company issued additional shares of stock, so the Capital Stock account must be credited to reflect the increase in owners' equity. Since the company received cash of $30,000 (1,500 shares at $20 per share), the Cash account is also increased.

(b) Inventory 49,500
     Accounts Payable   49,500

The company purchased $49,500 of goods on credit. The Inventory account is increased (debited) for this amount. The Accounts Payable account is credited to show the increase in liabilities.

(c) Accounts Receivable 102,900
    Cash 22,100
     Sales Revenue   125,000

Total sales were $125,000, so the Sales Revenue account must be increased (credited) by that amount. Of this amount, $102,900 were on credit, and $22,100 were cash sales. We increase the asset accounts, Accounts Receivable and Cash, by debiting them.

(c) Cost of Goods Sold 47,500
     Inventory   47,500

The cost of the merchandise sold during the year was $47,500. The expense account, Cost of Goods Sold, must be increased (debited) by this amount. Since the goods were sold, the asset account, Inventory, must be reduced by a credit of $47,500.

(d) Cash 3,500
     Sales Revenue   3,500

The Cash account is debited (increased) by the amount received from the customer. Because the company uses the revenue approach to record advance payments for merchandise, the Sales Revenue account is credited.

(e) Accounts Payable 66,500
      Cash 66,500

The company's payments on its accounts reduce the amount of its obligation to creditors, so the liability account, Accounts Payable, is debited to decrease it by the amount paid. Since cash was paid, the Cash account must also be decreased or (credited).

(f) Cash 102,000
      Accounts Receivable 102,000

Since the company has collected some of its receivables from customers, the Accounts Receivable account is credited to show a decrease. Since cash was received, the Cash account is increased (debited).

(g) Supplies 600
      Cash 600

The company purchased $600 of supplies. By debiting Supplies, an increase is shown in that asset account. Since cash was paid, the Cash account must be credited to reduce it.

(h) Advertising Expense 850
      Cash 850

(i) Salaries Expense 45,000
      Cash 45,000

(j) Utilities Expense 650
      Cash 650

For transactions (h), (i), and (j), an expense account must be debited to show that expenses have been incurred. Since cash was paid in each transaction, the Cash account must be reduced (credited).

(k) Dividends 7,500
      Cash 7,500

The Dividends account must be debited to show a decrease in owners' equity resulting from a distribution of earnings. Since cash was paid, the Cash account must be reduced by a credit.

2. T-Accounts

T-accounts with the beginning balances and journal entries posted are shown here. (Note that accounts with more than one entry must be "balanced" by drawing a rule and entering the debit or credit balance below it.)

Cash				Accounts Receivable				Inventory			
Beg.				Beg.				Beg.			
bal.	17,500	(e)	66,500	bal.	17,000	(f)	102,000	bal.	28,800	(c)	47,500
(a)	30,000	(g)	600	(c)	102,900			(b)	49,500		
(c)	22,100	(h)	850	Bal.	17,900			Bal.	30,800		
(d)	3,500	(i)	45,000								
(f)	102,000	(j)	650								
		(k)	7,500								
Bal.	54,000										

Supplies		Prepaid Building Rental		Accounts Payable	
Beg. bal. 1,200 (g) 600		Beg. bal. 24,000		(e) 66,500	Beg. bal. 18,000 (b) 49,500
Bal. 1,800					Bal. 1,000

Capital Stock		Retained Earnings		Dividends	
	Beg. bal. 54,000 (a) 30,000		Beg. bal. 16,500	(k) 7,500	
	Bal. 84,000				

Sales Revenue		Cost of Goods Sold		Salaries Expense	
	(c) 125,000 (d) 3,500	(c) 47,500		(i) 45,000	
	Bal. 128,500				

Advertising Expense		Utilities Expense	
(h) 850		(j) 650	

3. Trial Balance

The balance of each account is entered in the Trial Balance columns of the work sheet (see page 176). Each column in the Trial Balance is totaled to determine that total debits equal total credits.

4. and 6. Recording Adjustments and Completing the Work Sheet

Adjustments are entered on the work sheet in the pair of columns adjacent to the Trial Balance, and the adjusted account balances are transferred to the appropriate Income Statement or Balance Sheet columns. (See page 177).

The adjusting entries for Valley View Company are presented in journal form and explained as follows:

(l) Salaries Expense.. 750
        Salaries Payable 750

As of December 31, there is an unrecorded liability of $750 for salaries owed to employees. Because the salaries were earned in 1994, the expense and related liability must be recorded in 1994.

(m) Supplies Expense... 1,000
        Supplies 1,000

The Supplies account (asset) has a debit balance before adjustment of $1,800 (the beginning balance of $1,200 plus $600 of supplies purchased during the year, transaction (g)). Since $800 of supplies are on hand at the end of the year, the Supplies account should be reduced (credited) by $1,000. The Supplies Expense account must be debited to show that $1,000 of supplies were used during the period.

(n) Prepaid Advertising 200
        Advertising Expense 200

The Advertising Expense account has a debit balance before adjustment of $850, the total amount paid for advertising during the year (transaction (h)). This amount includes $400 that was paid for advertising during December 1994 and January 1995. The portion that applies to 1995 should be shown as Prepaid Advertising since it is not an expense of the current year. Thus the asset account, Prepaid Advertising, must be debited for $200 ($400 ÷ 2 months), and the expense account must be reduced by a credit.

(o) Building Rent Expense 12,000
      Prepaid Building Rental 12,000

The original entry at the end of 1993 was a debit to the asset account, Prepaid Building Rental, and a credit to Cash. An adjusting entry is needed to record rent expense of $12,000 for 1994 ($24,000 ÷ 2 years). The expense account must be debited, and the asset account must be reduced by a credit. The remaining $12,000 in Prepaid Building Rental reflects the portion of the total payment that represents rent expense for 1995.

(p) Utilities Expense.. 150
      Utilities Payable 150

As of December 31, 1994, there is an unrecorded expense of $150 for utilities. Because the expense was incurred in 1994, an adjusting entry is needed to record the expense and related liability.

(q) Sales Revenue 3,500
      Unearned Sales Revenue 3,500

The original entry to record the advance payment from a customer was made using the revenue approach (transaction (d)). As of December 31, the revenue originally recorded had not been earned. An adjustment is needed to decrease (debit) Sales Revenue and show the obligation to the customer by crediting the liability account, Unearned Sales Revenue.

At this point, all necessary adjustments have been made except for income taxes. Before making the adjustment for income taxes, the account balances must be transferred to the appropriate Balance Sheet and Income Statement columns of the work sheet. Then subtotals are computed for the Adjustments, Income Statement, and Balance Sheet columns. The difference between total credits (revenues) and total debits (expenses) in the Income Statement columns is the amount of income before taxes, or $17,300. This is also the difference between the total debits and credits in the Balance Sheet columns.

The income before taxes is multiplied by the applicable tax rate of 15% to determine income taxes for the period. The final adjustment can now be recorded.

(r) Income Tax Expense...................................... 2,595
      Income Taxes Payable 2,595

The expense account is debited to show the income taxes incurred for the year and the liability account is credited to show the obligation to the government.

To complete the work sheet, the after-tax totals are computed, and the amount needed to balance the debits and credits—net income—is entered in both the income statement and balance sheet columns.

The income statement and balance sheet can now be prepared directly from the work sheet.

Valley View Company
Work Sheet
December 31, 1994

Account Titles	Trial Balance Debits	Trial Balance Credits	Adjustments Debits	Adjustments Credits
Cash	54,000			
Accounts Receivable	17,900			
Inventory	30,800			
Supplies	1,800			(m) 1,000
Prepaid Building Rental	24,000			(o) 12,000
Accounts Payable		1,000		
Capital Stock		84,000		
Retained Earnings		16,500		
Dividends	7,500			
Sales Revenue		128,500	(q) 3,500	
Cost of Goods Sold	47,500			
Salaries Expense	45,000		(l) 750	
Advertising Expense	850			(n) 200
Utilities Expense	650		(p) 150	
	230,000	230,000		
Salaries Payable				(l) 750
Supplies Expense			(m) 1,000	
Prepaid Advertising			(n) 200	
Building Rent Expense			(o) 12,000	
Utilities Payable				(p) 150
Unearned Sales Revenue				(q) 3,500
Subtotals			17,600	17,600
Income Tax Expense			(r) 2,595	
Income Taxes Payable				(r) 2,595
Totals			20,195	20,195
Net Income (to balance)				
Totals				

(l) Salaries Expense, $750
(m) Supplies Expense, $1,000
(n) Prepaid Advertising, $200
(o) Building Rental Expense, $12,000
(p) Utilities Expense, $150
(q) Unearned Revenue, $3,500
(r) Income Taxes, $2,595

Chapter 5 Completing the Accounting Cycle

| Income Statement || Balance Sheet ||
Debits	Credits	Debits	Credits
		54,000	
		17,900	
		30,800	
		800	
		12,000	
			1,000
			84,000
			16,500
		7,500	
	125,000		
47,500			
45,750			
650			
800			
			750
1,000			
		200	
12,000			
			150
			3,500
107,700	125,000	123,200	105,900
2,595			
			2,595
110,295	125,000	123,200	108,495
14,705			14,705
125,000	125,000	123,200	123,200

5. Income Statement and Balance Sheet

Valley View Company
Income Statement
For the Year Ended December 31, 1994

Sales revenue		$125,000
Expenses:		
Cost of goods sold	$47,500	
Salaries expense	45,750	
Advertising expense	650	
Utilities expense	800	
Supplies expense	1,000	
Building rental expense	12,000	107,700
Income before taxes		$ 17,300
Income taxes		2,595
Net income		$ 14,705

Earnings per share: $14,705 ÷ 5,100 shares = $2.88

Valley View Company
Balance Sheet
December 31, 1994

Assets

Cash	$54,000	
Accounts receivable	17,900	
Inventory	30,800	
Supplies	800	
Prepaid building rental	12,000	
Prepaid advertising	200	
Total assets		$115,700

Liabilities and Stockholders' Equity

Liabilities:		
Accounts payable	$1,000	
Salaries payable	750	
Utilities payable	150	
Income taxes payable	2,595	
Unearned sales revenue	3,500	
Total liabilities		$ 7,995
Stockholders' equity:		
Capital stock	$84,000	
Retained earnings*	23,705	
Total stockholders' equity		107,705
Total liabilities and stockholders' equity		$115,700

*Note that in preparing the balance sheet, net income must be added to the beginning balance in Retained Earnings and dividends must be subtracted ($16,500 + $14,705 − $7,500 = $23,705).

6. Journalizing and Posting Adjusting and Closing Entries

Journal entries for the adjustments were presented and explained earlier. The next step is to record the closing entries in the General Journal. Then, the adjusting and closing entries must be posted to the General Ledger (T-accounts). Closing journal entries are presented here. T-accounts with all adjusting entries and closing entries (items (s), (t), (u), and (v)) posted are also shown.

Chapter 5 *Completing the Accounting Cycle* 179

Although it is optional, an Income Summary account will be used for the closing entries. An alternative would be to close the accounts directly to Retained Earnings.

The first entry is to close the only revenue account, Sales Revenue. Since Sales Revenue has a credit balance, it is debited to reduce the balance to zero.

(s) Sales Revenue 125,000
      Income Summary   125,000

Next, we close out the expense accounts by crediting them.

(t) Income Summary 110,295
      Cost of Goods Sold   47,500
      Salaries Expense..   45,750
      Advertising Expense   650
      Utilities Expense   800
      Supplies Expense   1,000
      Building Rental Expense   12,000
      Income Tax Expense....................................   2,595

The balance in the Income Summary account, the company's net income, is next transferred to Retained Earnings. When the company has earned a profit, the Income Summary account will have a credit balance. It is closed to a zero balance by being debited.

(u) Income Summary   14,705
      Retained Earnings   14,705

Finally, Dividends, a nominal account, must be closed to Retained Earnings.

(v) Retained Earnings   7,500
      Dividends   7,500

Cash				Accounts Receivable				Inventory			
Beg. bal.	17,500	(e)	66,500	Beg. bal.	17,000	(f)	102,000	Beg. bal.	28,800	(c)	47,500
(a)	30,000	(g)	600	(c)	102,900			(b)	49,500		
(c)	22,100	(h)	850	End bal.	17,900			End bal.	30,800		
(d)	3,500	(i)	45,000								
(f)	102,000	(j)	650								
		(k)	7,500								
End bal.	54,000										

Supplies				Prepaid Building Rental				Prepaid Advertising			
Beg. bal.	1,200	(m)	1,000	Beg. bal.	24,000	(o)	12,000	(n)	200		
(g)	600			End bal.	12,000						
End bal.	800										

Accounts Payable			Salaries Payable		Utilities Payable	
(e) 66,500	Beg. bal.	18,000	(l)	750	(p)	150
	(b)	49,500				
	End bal.	1,000				

Income Taxes Payable		Unearned Sales Revenue		Capital Stock	
(r)	2,595	(q)	3,500	Beg. bal.	54,000
				(a)	30,000
				End bal.	84,000

Retained Earnings			Dividends		Sales Revenue			
	Beg. bal.	16,500	(k) 7,500	(v) 7,500	(q)	3,500	(c)	125,000
(v) 7,500	(u)	14,705			(s)	125,000	(d)	3,500
	End bal.	23,705						

Cost of Goods Sold		Salaries Expense		Advertising Expense	
(c) 47,500	(t) 47,500	(i) 45,000		(h) 850	(n) 200
		(l) 750	(t) 45,750		(t) 650

Utilities Expense		Supplies Expense		Building Rental Expense	
(j) 650		(m) 1,000	(t) 1,000	(o) 12,000	(t) 12,000
(p) 150	(t) 800				

Income Tax Expense		Income Summary	
(r) 2,595	(t) 2,595	(t) 110,295	(s) 125,000
		(u) 14,705	

7. Post-Closing Trial Balance

The final step in the accounting cycle is to prepare a post-closing trial balance as shown below. This procedure is a check on the accuracy of the closing process. It is a listing of all ledger account balances at year end. Note that only real accounts appear because all nominal accounts have been closed to a zero balance in preparation for the next accounting cycle.

Valley View Company
Post-Closing Trial Balance
December 31, 1994

	Debits	Credits
Cash	$ 54,000	
Accounts Receivable	17,900	
Inventory	30,800	
Supplies	800	
Prepaid Building Rental	12,000	
Prepaid Advertising	200	
Accounts Payable		$ 1,000
Salaries Payable		750
Utilities Payable		150
Income Taxes Payable		2,595
Unearned Sales Revenue		3,500
Capital Stock		84,000
Retained Earnings		23,705
Totals	$115,700	$115,700

Discussion Questions

1. What is the purpose of a work sheet?
2. Why is preparing a work sheet a useful but not a required step in the accounting cycle?
3. The first two columns in a work sheet are referred to as the unadjusted trial balance. What is meant by unadjusted? Explain.
4. After making the adjustments and preparing an adjusted trial balance on a 10-column work sheet, the income statement and balance sheet columns are completed. Explain the procedure used when adjusted trial balance columns are not included on a work sheet.
5. When a work sheet is completed, each pair of columns should balance; that is, each pair should have equal total debits and total credits. Explain the balancing procedure for the financial statement columns.
6. How are dividends treated on an 8-column work sheet? Explain how this treatment affects the financial statements taken from the work sheet.
7. In completing a work sheet, why does the adjustment for income taxes present a problem? How might this problem be solved?
8. How is the ending Retained Earnings balance determined from the information provided on a work sheet?
9. Which are prepared first, the year-end financial statements or the General Journal adjusting entries? Explain.
10. Distinguish between real and nominal accounts.
11. What is the purpose of closing entries?
12. Why must nominal accounts be closed at the end of each accounting period?
13. What is the purpose of the Income Summary account? Is its use required? Explain.
14. How would a corporation's closing process differ from that of a proprietorship or partnership?

Exercises

E5-1

Trial Balance

The following list of accounts was taken from the General Ledger of Quick Print Shop as of December 31, 1994:

Cash	$14,200
Notes Receivable	6,000
Accounts Receivable	16,800
Office Supplies	3,500
Printing Supplies	4,800
Prepaid Rent	6,800
Accounts Payable	17,200
Notes Payable	22,000
Property Taxes Payable	5,200
Lou Livingston, Capital	14,350
Lou Livingston, Drawings	33,000
Printing Revenue	53,720
Salaries and Wages Expense	25,000
Maintenance Expense	1,720
Heat, Light, and Power Expense	650

Prepare the trial balance columns of a work sheet for Quick Print Shop.

E5-2
Partial Work Sheet

The adjusted trial balance at December 31, 1994, of Rougely Company is presented here. Use the trial balance to prepare work sheet columns for adjusted trial balance, income statement, and balance sheet. Place the accounts in the order they would normally appear on a balance sheet and on an income statement, beginning with Cash.

Rougely Company
Adjusted Trial Balance
December 31, 1994

	Debits	Credits
Sales Revenue		$125,000
Cash	$ 37,700	
Accounts Payable		35,000
Salaries Expense	20,000	
Cost of Goods Sold	99,000	
Prepaid Insurance	2,800	
Accounts Receivable	15,000	
Lucky Heller, Capital		18,000
Salaries Payable		25,000
Rent Expense	12,000	
Inventory	16,500	
Totals	$203,000	$203,000

E5-3
Preparation of Financial Statements from a Work Sheet

Use the work sheet from E5-2 to prepare an income statement for the year ended December 31, 1994, and a balance sheet at December 31, 1994.

E5-4
Work Sheet to Correct a Trial Balance

The trial balance on the next page was prepared for Buck Company as of December 31, 1994. Although the trial balance is in balance, a review and analysis of the accounts reveal the following:

(a) Buck Company records Cost of Goods Sold and reduces Inventory each time a sale is made. On one sale, the cost and inventory reduction entry was not made. The merchandise sold cost $2,250.

(b) A payment on the mortgage of $2,000 was incorrectly recorded as a payment on the note.
(c) A policy to provide fire insurance for the year 1995 was purchased at the end of December 1994, at a cost of $480, which was debited to Insurance Expense.
(d) A note of $1,000 was collected in late 1994. The collection was incorrectly credited to Accounts Receivable.
(e) Interest of $300 on a note was received in advance and recorded as Interest Revenue; the $300 was unearned at December 31, 1994.

Given the preceding information, complete the following:

1. Prepare and complete a 6-column work sheet with columns for the unadjusted trial balance, adjustments, and adjusted trial balance.
2. Since both debits and credits total $271,400, why make any adjustments? Explain.

Buck Company
Trial Balance
December 31, 1994

	Debits	Credits
Cash	$ 23,875	
Notes Receivable	5,600	
Accounts Receivable	14,610	
Inventory	28,500	
Prepaid Insurance	1,260	
Land	18,000	
Accounts Payable		$ 12,430
Notes Payable		8,740
Mortgage Payable		16,000
Capital Stock		25,000
Retained Earnings		5,820
Sales Revenue		202,850
Interest Revenue		560
Cost of Goods Sold	132,890	
Wages Expense	36,150	
Selling Expense	4,865	
Insurance Expense	2,420	
Supplies Expense	480	
Interest Expense	2,750	
Totals	$271,400	$271,400

E5-5
Classifying Account Balances

For each of the following accounts, indicate whether it would be found in the income statement or in the balance sheet columns of a company's work sheet:

1. Cash
2. Inventory
3. Salary Expense
4. Prepaid Salaries
5. Retained Earnings
6. Office Supplies Expense
7. Accounts Receivable
8. Cost of Goods Sold
9. Maintenance Expense
10. Interest Receivable
11. Capital Stock
12. Accounts Payable
13. Buildings
14. Mortgage Payable
15. Interest Expense
16. Accounts Payable
17. Notes Receivable
18. Office Supplies
19. Sales Revenue
20. Insurance Expense
21. Machinery
22. Land
23. Salaries Payable
24. Prepaid Insurance
25. Notes Payable
26. Dividends

E5-6
Real and Nominal Accounts

Classify each of the following accounts as either a real account (R) or a nominal account (N):

1. Cash
2. Sales Revenue
3. Accounts Receivable
4. Cost of Goods Sold
5. Prepaid Insurance
6. Capital Stock
7. Retained Earnings
8. Insurance Expense
9. Salaries Payable
10. Interest Expense
11. Insurance Premiums Payable
12. Salary Expense
13. Accounts Payable
14. Prepaid Salaries
15. Utility Expense
16. Notes Payable
17. Inventory
18. Property Tax Expense
19. Rent Expense
20. Drawings
21. Interest Payable
22. Income Taxes Payable
23. Dividends
24. Buildings
25. Office Supplies
26. Income Tax Expense

E5-7
Closing Entries

Given is the income statement for Eriksen Enterprises for the year ended June 30, 1994.

Eriksen Enterprises
Income Statement
For the Year Ended June 30, 1994

Sales revenue	$187,000
Cost of goods sold	(122,000)
Selling and general expenses	(20,500)
Income before taxes	$ 44,500
Income taxes	17,800
Net income	$ 26,700

1. Prepare journal entries to close the accounts directly to Retained Earnings.
2. What problem may arise in closing the accounts if the information from the income statement is used?

E5-8
Closing Entries—Income Summary

Great Powder Ski Shop reported the following revenue and expense items on its 1994 income statement. Prepare all necessary entries to close the account balances, using an Income Summary account.

Revenues:	
Ski sales revenue	$400,000
Accessory sales revenue	150,000
Total revenues	$550,000
Expenses:	
Rent expense	$ 48,000
Utilities expense	19,000
Salaries expense	116,000
Interest expense	10,000
Property tax expense	4,000
Wax and supplies expense	1,600
Cost of goods sold	302,500
Total expenses	$501,100

E5-9
Closing Entries

Revenue and expense accounts of Rural Electric Company for September 1994 are presented below. Prepare the entries required to close the revenue and expense accounts to the Retained Earnings account.

	Debits	Credits
Sales Revenue		$55,000
Cost of Goods Sold	$26,000	
Salaries Expense	6,400	
Rent Expense	1,000	
Supplies Expense	200	
Insurance Expense	1,400	
Interest Expense	800	

E5-10
Closing Entries—Income Summary (Proprietorship)

Joe's Health Club is owned and operated by Joe Gott. The balances in the nominal accounts for Joe's Health Club are shown here. Make all necessary journal entries to close the accounts on December 31, 1994. Use an Income Summary account in the closing process.

Revenues	$192,640
Salaries Expense	82,000
Rent Expense	28,500
Interest Expense	12,200
Utility Expense	2,750
Insurance Expense	3,600
Miscellaneous Expenses	1,260
Office Supplies Expense	1,500
J. Gott, Drawings	36,000

E5-11
Closing Entries—Proprietorship, Partnership, and Corporation

Wild West Company shows a credit balance in the Income Summary account of $61,530 after closing all revenue and expense items to this account. Give the remaining entries to close the books, assuming that:

1. The business is a proprietorship, and the owner, Dave Stewart, has withdrawn $30,000 during the year; the amount is recorded in an account called Drawings.
2. The business is a partnership with two partners, Dave Stewart and Jane Stewart, who share profits equally. Dave has withdrawn $19,000 and Jane has withdrawn $16,000 during the year. These amounts are recorded in individual drawings accounts.
3. The business is a corporation, and the Dividends account shows that dividends of $32,000 have been paid during the year.

E5-12
Post-Closing Trial Balance

Before the final closing entries were made at December 31, 1994, a listing of account balances taken from the work sheet of Farmers' Co-Op showed the following:

Cash	$11,290
Accounts Receivable	28,240
Inventory	39,180
Prepaid Insurance	3,260
Land	68,000
Accounts Payable	14,320
Notes Payable	20,000
Salaries Payable	4,500

Taxes Payable	12,200
Unearned Rent	7,600
Mortgage Payable	45,000
Capital Stock	22,000
Dividends	10,000
Retained Earnings	14,000
Income Summary (credit balance)	20,350

Prepare (1) the closing entry or entries and (2) a post-closing trial balance.

E5-13
Adjusting and Reversing Entries (*Appendix A*)

Schensa Publishing Co., in preparation for issuing its annual report for fiscal year 1994, obtained the data listed here. Schensa does not reverse adjusting entries and records current transactions in income statement accounts. The company's fiscal year ends September 30.

(a) The Unearned Subscriptions Revenue account has an unadjusted balance of $18,750 at September 30, 1994. An analysis of collections received is as follows:

Date Received	Amount Received	Term of Subscription
July 1, 1993	$12,000	2 years
Sept. 1, 1993	9,000	1 year
Mar. 1, 1994	18,000	2 years
July 1, 1994	15,000	1 year

(b) At September 30, 1994, the Prepaid Insurance account showed a balance of $5,000. Schensa has the following policies in force:

Policy	Date	Term	Cost	Coverage
A	1/1/92	3 years	$7,200	Building
B	2/1/92	2 years	3,000	Printing equipment
C	4/1/94	1 year	2,400	Autos and trucks

(c) The balance in the Salaries Payable account is $9,500. Schensa pays its employees on the 5th and 20th of each month, based on salaries and wages earned through the 15th and last day of each month. Additional salaries and wages since September 15 total $6,750.

(d) Interest Payable has a balance of $400. Schensa owes two notes as follows:

	Unrecorded Interest
12%, 60-day note for $10,000 dated August 16	$145
15%, 90-day note for $24,000 dated September 10	200
	$345

(e) A physical count and pricing of supplies on hand reveals a total of $490. The Supplies account shows a balance of $940.

Given this information, complete the following:

1. Prepare adjusting entries as required.
2. Indicate which of the five adjusting entries, if any, could be reversed (following the general guidelines for reversing entries).

E5-14
Adjusting and Reversing Entries (*Appendix A*)

The trial balance of Dallas Company shows the following balances, among others, on December 31, 1994, the end of its first fiscal year:

Rent Revenue	$ 36,800
Office Supplies Expense	2,700
Mortgage Payable	130,000

Inspection of the company's records reveals that:

(a) Rent revenue of $2,800 is unearned at December 31, 1994.
(b) Interest of $7,800 on the mortgage is payable semiannually on March 1 and September 1.
(c) Office supplies of $500 are on hand on December 31. When purchases of office supplies were made during the year, they were charged to the Office Supplies Expense account.

Given this information, complete the following:

1. Prepare journal entries to adjust the books as of December 31, 1994.
2. Give the reversing entries that may be appropriately made at the beginning of 1995.

E5-15
Special Journals (*Appendix B*)

Brinkerhoff Implement Company uses five journals: Cash Receipts, Cash Disbursements, Sales, Purchases, and a General Journal. Assuming the same journal formats discussed in this appendix, indicate in which of the five journals each of the following transactions would be recorded:

1. Accrual of salaries payable (recognized by an adjusting entry).
2. Payment of property taxes.
3. Payment of salaries and other expenses.
4. Purchase of merchandise on account.
5. Purchase of merchandise for cash.
6. Sale of merchandise on credit.
7. Sale of merchandise for cash.
8. Purchase of supplies on account.
9. Purchase of a delivery truck for cash.
10. Cash refund to a customer who returned defective merchandise.
11. Return of merchandise purchased on account for credit.
12. Return of merchandise by a customer for credit.
13. Payment of a note payable.
14. Collection of a note receivable.
15. Expiration of a portion of prepaid insurance (recognized by an adjusting entry).

Problem Set A

P5A-1
Work Sheet and Financial Statements

The year-end trial balance of Music Land, Inc. is presented here.

Music Land, Inc.
Trial Balance
December 31, 1994

	Debits	Credits
Cash	$ 25,000	
Accounts Receivable	7,500	
Inventory	38,500	
Prepaid Insurance	500	
Prepaid Rent	1,100	
Land	85,000	
Notes Payable		$ 25,000
Accounts Payable		12,500
Salaries Payable		1,500
Capital Stock		32,000
Retained Earnings (1/1/94)		43,600
Sales Revenue		320,000
Cost of Goods Sold	210,000	
Salaries Expense	48,000	
Rent Expense	12,000	
Insurance Expense	3,000	
Property Tax Expense	2,500	
Office Supplies Expense	1,500	
Totals	$434,600	$434,600

Required:

1. Prepare a work sheet using the trial balance data. Assume that there are no adjusting entries, except for $18,000 of income taxes that will be paid next year.
2. Use the work sheet to prepare an income statement for the year ended December 31, 1994, and a balance sheet as of December 31, 1994.
3. **Interpretive Question** In what ways does a work sheet facilitate the preparation of financial statements?

P5A-2
Work Sheet, Adjustments, and Financial Statements

SOLUTIONS SOFTWARE

An inexperienced bookkeeper for Family Photo Company has prepared a list of account balances at the end of 1994. The following information is also provided for your use:

(a) An insurance premium of $1,200 was paid on July 1, 1994, for the period July 1, 1994, to June 30, 1995.
(b) No entry has been made to record the interest expense on a $5,000 note. The note was signed on October 1, 1994, and is due with $300 of interest on March 31, 1995.
(c) The salaries earned by company personnel in December have not yet been recorded. These salaries, totaling $5,000, will be paid on January 5, 1995.

Family Photo Company
Trial Balance
December 31, 1994

	Debits	Credits
Cash	$ 46,000	
Accounts Receivable	22,500	
Accounts Payable		$ 8,500
Inventory	63,250	
Salaries Expense	50,000	
Sales Revenue		300,000
Cost of Goods Sold	150,000	
Office Supplies Expense	2,500	
Interest Expense	1,000	
Retained Earnings		36,450
Interest Payable		-0-
Salaries Payable		-0-
Insurance Expense	-0-	
Rent Expense	45,000	
Property Tax Expense	3,000	
Prepaid Insurance	1,200	
Capital Stock		35,000
Rent Payable		500
Notes Payable		9,000
Dividends	5,000	
Totals	$389,450	$389,450

Required:
1. Prepare an 8-column work sheet with properly ordered accounts.
2. Make any necessary adjusting entries on the work sheet. (Ignore income taxes.)
3. Prepare an income statement for 1994 and balance sheet at December 31, 1994.

P5A-3

Classification and Analysis of Accounts

For each of the accounts listed, indicate (1) whether it is a real or a nominal account, (2) whether it will appear on an income statement or a balance sheet, (3) whether it will be "closed" or remain "open" at the end of the accounting period, and (4) if closed, whether it is normally closed by a debit or a credit. Use the format shown. (Two items have been completed as examples.)

Account Title	Real or Nominal	Income Statement or Balance Sheet	Closed or Open	Closed by Debit or Credit
Accounts Receivable	Real	B/S	Open	—
Advertising Expense	Nominal	I/S	Closed	Credit

1. Cash
2. Sales Revenue
3. Interest Expense
4. Office Supplies
5. Retained Earnings
6. Salaries Expense
7. Machinery
8. Income Taxes Payable
9. Accounts Payable
10. Interest Revenue
11. Prepaid Insurance
12. Salaries Payable
13. Dividends
14. Notes Payable
15. Office Supplies Expense
16. Cost of Goods Sold
17. Dividends Payable
18. Inventory
19. Capital Stock
20. Income Tax Expense
21. Drawings
22. Unearned Rent

P5A-4
Closing Entries

East Coast Company's trial balance as of August 31, 1994 and 1993 are shown as follows:

East Coast Company
Trial Balances
August 31, 1994 and 1993

	1994 Debits	1994 Credits	1993 Debits	1993 Credits
Cash	$33,400		$12,500	
Accounts Receivable	6,400		7,500	
Inventory	2,800		8,600	
Accounts Payable		$ 1,400		
Land			14,800	
Capital Stock		36,600		$36,600
Dividends			500	
Retained Earnings		6,800		-0-
Sales Revenue		22,000		34,000
Cost of Goods Sold	12,000		16,400	
Rent Expense	1,400		1,400	
Advertising Expense	800		500	
Salaries Expense	10,000		8,400	
Totals	$66,800	$66,800	$70,600	$70,600

Required:
1. Prepare journal entries to close the books as of August 31, 1993. Close nominal accounts directly to Retained Earnings.
2. In 1994, the company suffered a net loss, which reduced Retained Earnings. Prepare closing entries as of August 31, 1994. How much was the loss?

P5A-5
Closing the Books

The bookkeeper for Competition Company has prepared the trial balance and adjustments columns for a work sheet as of December 31, 1994.

	Trial Balance Debits	Trial Balance Credits	Adjustments Debits	Adjustments Credits
Cash	$ 5,500			
Accounts Receivable	2,200			
Inventory	5,600			
Supplies	800			$ 400
Prepaid Rent	2,400			1,800
Accounts Payable		$ 1,400		
Capital Stock		4,500		
Retained Earnings		3,000		
Sales Revenue		54,500		
Cost of Goods Sold	32,400			
Utilities Expense	1,800			
Salaries Expense	11,500		$1,000	
Insurance Expense	1,200			800
Totals	$63,400	63,400		
Supplies Expense			400	
Rent Expense			1,800	
Salaries Payable				1,000
Prepaid Insurance			800	
Totals			$4,000	$4,000

Chapter 5 Completing the Accounting Cycle

Adjustments:
(a) Supplies Expense, $400.   (c) Salaries Payable, $1,000.
(b) Rent Expense, $1,800.   (d) Prepaid Insurance, $800.

Required:
1. Complete the work sheet by extending the figures into the income statement and balance sheet columns, and in the process, determine the amount of net income or net loss.
2. Prepare the closing journal entries for the company using an Income Summary account.

P5A-6
Unifying Concepts: Adjusting and Closing Entries

Two trial balances of Roosevelt Company as of December 31, 1994, are presented here.

Roosevelt Company
Trial Balances
December 31, 1994

	Unadjusted Debits	Unadjusted Credits	Adjusted Debits	Adjusted Credits
Cash	$ 6,820		$ 6,820	
Supplies	585		800	
Prepaid Rent	1,350		945	
Prepaid Insurance	380		148	
Land	12,500		12,500	
Utilities Payable		$ 750		$ 865
Salaries Payable		-0-		750
Taxes Payable		-0-		148
Capital Stock		16,245		16,245
Service Fees Earned		11,300		11,300
Salaries Expense	2,750		3,500	
Rent Expense	-0-		405	
Supplies Expense	1,880		1,665	
Utilities Expense	470		585	
Taxes Expense	1,000		1,148	
Insurance Expense	-0-		232	
Miscellaneous Expenses	560		560	
Totals	$28,295	$28,295	$29,308	$29,308

Required:
1. Prepare the journal entries that were required to adjust the accounts at December 31, 1994.
2. Prepare the journal entries that are required to close the accounts at December 31, 1994.

P5A-7
Comprehensive Work Sheet—Proprietorship

The following account balances were taken from the General Ledger of Caroline Crocker, a proprietorship, at the end of the first year of business operations. The proprietorship has a fiscal year ending September 30, 1994.

Cash	$12,250
Notes Receivable	3,000
Accounts Receivable	5,300
Inventory	20,100
Store Supplies	500

Accounts Payable	6,600
Notes Payable	5,000
Caroline Crocker, Capital	15,100
Caroline Crocker, Drawings	3,000
Sales Revenue	95,000
Interest Revenue	200
Cost of Goods Sold	57,900
Sales Salaries Expense	7,500
General Expenses	10,900
Property Tax Expense	750
Interest Expense	700

The data for adjustments to be made at year-end are:

(a) Store supplies on hand, $310.
(b) Additional advertising, $105.
(c) Property taxes paid in advance, $300.
(d) Additional interest on notes payable, $145.
(e) Unrecorded interest on notes receivable, $212.

Ignore income taxes.

Required:
1. Prepare an 8-column work sheet.
2. Prepare adjusting and closing entries.

P5A-8

Unifying Concepts: Analysis of Accounts

The bookkeeper for Careless Company accidentally pressed the wrong computer key and erased the amount of Retained Earnings. You have been asked to analyze the following data and provide some key numbers for the Board of Directors meeting, which is to take place in 30 minutes. With the exception of Retained Earnings, the following account balances are available at December 31, 1994:

Cash	$122,000
Furniture	80,000
Accounts Payable	240,000
Land	520,000
Buildings (net)	480,000
Sales Revenue	830,000
Salaries Expense	100,000
Cost of Goods Sold	440,000
Accounts Receivable	98,000
Inventory	320,000
Notes Payable	500,000
Supplies	20,000
Capital Stock	600,000
Dividends	40,000
Retained Earnings	?

Required:
1. Compute the amount of total assets at December 31, 1994.
2. Compute the amount of net income for the year ended December 31, 1994.
3. After all closing entries are made, what is the amount of Retained Earnings at December 31, 1994?
4. What was the beginning Retained Earnings balance at January 1, 1994?

Chapter 5 Completing the Accounting Cycle

P5A-9

Unifying Concepts: The Accounting Cycle

SOLUTIONS SOFTWARE

The post-closing trial balance of Anderson Company at December 31, 1993 is shown here.

Anderson Company
Post-Closing Trial Balance
December 31, 1993

	Debits	Credits
Cash	$ 15,000	
Accounts Receivable	20,000	
Inventory	30,000	
Land	150,000	
Accounts Payable		$ 25,000
Notes Payable		35,000
Capital Stock		125,000
Retained Earnings		30,000
Totals	$215,000	$215,000

During 1994, Anderson Company had the following transactions:

(a) Inventory purchases were $80,000, all on credit (debit Inventory).
(b) An additional $10,000 of capital stock was issued for cash.
(c) Merchandise that cost $100,000 was sold for $180,000; $100,000 were credit sales, and the balance were cash sales. (Debit Cost of Goods Sold and credit Inventory for sale of merchandise.)
(d) The notes were paid, including $7,000 interest.
(e) $105,000 was collected from customers.
(f) $95,000 was paid to reduce accounts payable.
(g) Salary expenses were $30,000, all paid in cash.
(h) A $10,000 cash dividend was declared and paid.

Required:
1. Prepare journal entries to record each of the 1994 transactions.
2. Set up T-accounts with the proper balances at January 1994, and post the journal entries to the T-accounts.
3. Prepare a work sheet beginning with a trial balance as of December 31, 1994. Assume no adjusting entries.
4. Using your work sheet, prepare an income statement for the year ended December 31, 1994, and a balance sheet as of that date.
5. Prepare the entries necessary to close the nominal accounts, including Dividends.
6. Post the closing entries to the ledger accounts, and prepare a post-closing trial balance at 12/31/94.

P5A-10

Special Journals
(*Appendix B*)

Taylor Corporation began operations on January 1, 1994. Taylor's chart of accounts includes the following, among others:

Cash	101	Purchases	450
Marketable Securities	102	Purchase Returns and Allowances	451
Notes Receivable	103	Purchase Discounts	452
Supplies	112	Sales Salaries Expense	501
Notes Payable	201	General and Administrative	
Accounts Payable	202	Salaries Expense	550
Interest Payable	204	Telephone Expense	569
Sales Revenue	400	Interest Expense	601
Sales Returns and Allowances	402	Interest Revenue	701

Taylor used four special journals: Purchases, Sales, Cash Receipts, and Cash Disbursements.

Required: Record the following July 1994 transactions using the four special journals and a General Journal. Record purchases and sales at their gross amounts. Invoice, receipt, and check numbers have been omitted to simplify the problem.

July		
1	Purchased merchandise from Garn Company for $2,000, terms 2/10, n/30.
2	Purchased merchandise from Jacobs Company for $1,000, terms 2/10, n/30.
5	Sold $4,000 of merchandise to Bob Handy, terms 2/10, n/30.
6	Sold $3,000 of merchandise to Dave Harmon, terms 2/10, n/30.
7	Purchased $300 of office supplies on account from Utah Office Supply, terms n/30. (Supplies are to be used, not resold.)
7	Returned merchandise costing $150 to Garn Company.
8	Paid Garn Company amount owed for July 1 purchase (net of July 7 return). Discounts are given only on the net amount.
13	Paid Jacobs Company amount owed for July 2 purchase.
13	Collected full amount owed by Bob Handy for July 5 sale.
14	Collected full amount owed by Dave Harmon for July 6 sale.
15	Paid salaries for the first 2 weeks of July. Sales Salaries Expense, $700; General and Administrative Salaries Expense, $1,400.
17	Paid a $2,000 note plus $200 interest on the note to First Security Corporation. Interest has not previously been recognized.
19	Collected a note of $1,800 plus $180 interest from Greg Steinkopf.
25	Had cash sales of $300.
28	Paid telephone bill of $80 to Mountain Bell Telephone.
30	Sold merchandise costing $1,500 to Hillway Company, terms 2/10, n/30.

Problem Set B

P5B-1
Reconstruction of a Work Sheet

Shown here are the December 31, 1994, unadjusted and adjusted account balances taken from the work sheet of Plano Company.

	Unadjusted Account Balances	Adjusted Account Balances
Cash	$ 5,600	$ 5,600
Accounts Receivable	8,460	8,460
Store Supplies	800	1,200
Prepaid Insurance	3,600	1,800
Prepaid Rent	-0-	3,000
Accounts Payable	6,000	6,000
Wages Payable	1,500	1,700
Interest Payable	250	100
Notes Payable	5,000	5,000
Capital Stock	10,000	10,000
Retained Earnings	5,100	5,100
Dividends	6,000	6,000
Service Fees Revenue	52,810	52,810
Wages Expense	42,700	42,900
Store Supplies Expense	4,000	3,600
Insurance Expense	-0-	1,800
Rent Expense	9,000	6,000
Interest Expense	500	350

Required: Using the data provided, prepare a partial work sheet with trial balance, adjustments, and adjusted trial balance columns.

Chapter 5 *Completing the Accounting Cycle*

P5B-2

Ten-Column Work Sheet

SPREADSHEET PROBLEM

The following unadjusted trial balance is taken from the records of Hillcrest Company:

Hillcrest Company
Unadjusted Trial Balance
December 31, 1994

	Debits	Credits
Cash	$ 63,450	
Accounts Receivable	97,350	
Notes Receivable	72,000	
Office Supplies	4,800	
Land	111,000	
Notes Payable		$ 46,200
Capital Stock		225,000
Dividends	900	
Retained Earnings, December 31, 1993		60,300
Fees Earned		73,110
Rent Earned		4,290
Advertising Expense	4,380	
Office Expense	4,020	
Wages Expense	51,000	
Totals	$408,900	$408,900

Data for adjustments:

(a) Earned fees not yet recorded, $2,220.
(b) Interest on Notes Receivable not yet recorded, $720.
(c) Liability for Office Expense, $900.
(d) Interest on Notes Payable not yet recorded, $540.

Required: Using a 10-column work sheet, make any necessary adjustments, and extend the adjusted trial balance figures to the income statement and balance sheet columns.

P5B-3

Account Classifications and Debit–Credit Relationships

Using the format provided, for each account identify (1) whether the account is a balance sheet (B/S) or an income statement (I/S) account; (2) whether it is an asset (A), a liability (L), an owners' equity (OE), a revenue (R), an expense (E), or a clearing account (C); (3) whether the account is a real or a nominal account; (4) whether the account will be "closed" or left "open" at year-end; and (5) whether the account normally has a debit or a credit balance. The following example is provided:

Account Title	(1) B/S or I/S	(2) A,L, O/E,R, E,C	(3) Real or Nominal	(4) Closed or Open	(5) Debit/ Credit
Cash	B/S	A	Real	Open	Debit

1. Accounts Receivable
2. Accounts Payable
3. Prepaid Insurance
4. Mortgage Payable
5. Rent Expense
6. Sales Revenue
7. Cost of Goods Sold
8. Dividends
9. Capital Stock
10. Inventory
11. Retained Earnings
12. Drawings
13. Supplies
14. Utilities Expense
15. Income Summary
16. Interest Revenue
17. Notes Payable
18. Income Tax Expense
19. Dividends Payable
20. Unearned Rent Revenue
21. John Jones, Capital
22. Land
23. Unearned Consulting Fees
24. Interest Receivable
25. Consulting Fees

P5B-4
Closing Entries and Accounting for Dividends

The income statement for Home Light, Inc. for the year ended December 31, 1994, is as follows:

Home Light, Inc.
Income Statement
For the Year Ended December 31, 1994

Sales Revenue		$452,000
Less expenses:		
Cost of goods sold	$363,000	
Salaries expense	72,000	
Interest expense	5,250	
Office supplies expense	3,820	
Insurance expense	4,930	
Property tax expense	11,200	
Total expenses		460,200
Net Loss		$ (8,200)

Dividends of $20,000 were declared by the board of directors on December 30, 1994.

Required:
1. Give the entries required on December 31, 1994, to properly close the income statement accounts using an Income Summary account.
2. Give the entry required to record the declaration of dividends by the board of directors. Also give the entry required to close the Dividends account at December 31, 1994.
3. Give the entry required to record payment of the dividends declared on December 30, 1994. The payment is made on January 30, 1995.

P5B-5
Closing Entries—Income Summary

The income statement for the Meeker Co-Op is shown here.

Meeker Co-Op
Income Statement
For the Year Ended December 31, 1994

Revenues:		
Sales revenue	$300,000	
Interest revenue	2,250	
Rent revenue	3,000	
Total revenues		$305,250
Less expenses:		
Cost of goods sold	$187,500	
Sales salaries expense	25,000	
Sales supplies expense	500	
Rental expense, sales vehicles	1,000	
Officers' salaries expense	50,000	
Office supplies expense	1,000	
Postage expense	50	
Total expenses		265,050
Income before taxes		$ 40,200
Income taxes		12,060
Net income		$ 28,140

Chapter 5 *Completing the Accounting Cycle*

Required:
1. Give the journal entries to close the revenue and expense accounts to an Income Summary account.
2. Give the entries required to close the Income Summary account to Retained Earnings.
3. **Interpretive Question** Some companies prepare a post-closing trial balance after the accounts have been closed at year-end. What are the advantages of doing this?

P5B-6

Comprehensive Work Sheet—Corporation

Account balances taken from the General Ledger of Day Care Company on December 31, 1994, follow.

Cash	$ 10,030
Accounts Receivable	33,600
Inventory	34,760
Land	28,700
Accounts Payable	18,000
Notes Payable (short term)	12,000
Mortgage Payable	26,000
Capital Stock	25,800
Retained Earnings, January 1, 1994	6,470
Dividends	6,000
Sales Revenue	124,000
Selling Expense	21,220
Cost of Goods Sold	62,900
Insurance Expense	1,140
Supplies Expense	1,750
Property Tax Expense	3,320
Office Expense	8,100
Interest Revenue	480
Interest Expense	1,230

Adjustments required on December 31, 1994, are:

(a) Additional wages payable are $2,500.
(b) Supplies on hand total $350.
(c) Additional property taxes are $150.
(d) Additional selling expenses are $1,640.
(e) Prepaid insurance to be deferred to future years is $470.
(f) Interest on the mortgage is $1,820.
(g) The company estimates that income taxes will be 40 percent of income before taxes.

Required:
1. Prepare an 8-column work sheet.
2. Prepare adjusting and closing entries.
3. Prepare a post-closing trial balance.

P5B-7

Analysis of Accounts and Closing Entries

The following information is available:

Pantera, Inc.
Adjusted Trial Balance
December 31, 1994

	Debits	Credits
Cash	$ 2,000	
Supplies	500	
Prepaid Insurance	1,200	
Building (net)	40,000	
Land	20,000	
Accounts Payable		$ 1,600
Mortgage Payable		25,000
Capital Stock		13,000
Retained Earnings (1/1/94)		11,300
Dividends	1,000	
Sales Revenue		48,000
Cost of Goods Sold	22,000	
Wages Expense	7,000	
Utilties Expense	800	
Other Expenses	4,400	
	$98,900	$98,900

Required:
1. Compute the amount of Retained Earnings at December 31, 1994.
2. Assuming the use of an Income Summary account, prepare the journal entries that will close all revenue and expense accounts. Also prepare the closing entry for the Dividends account.
3. What is the total amount of debits (equal to credits) for the post-closing trial balance for Pantera, Inc.?
4. **Interpretive Question:** Why are revenues and expenses closed to a zero balance at the end of the accounting cycle?

P5B-8

Unifying Concepts: Analysis and Correction of Errors

At the end of November 1994, the General Ledger of Porridge Milling Company showed the following amounts:

Assets	$64,250
Liabilities	28,800
Owners' Equity	62,000

The company's bookkeeper is new on the job and does not have much accounting experience. Because the bookkeeper has made numerous errors, total assets do not equal liabilities plus owners' equity. The following is a list of errors made.

(a) Inventory that cost $42,000 was sold, but the entry to record cost of goods sold was not made.
(b) Credit sales of $12,100 were posted to the General Ledger as $21,100. The accounts receivable were posted correctly.
(c) $12,500 of inventory was purchased on account and received before the end of November, but no entry to record the purchase was made until December.
(d) November salaries payable of $5,000 were not recorded until paid in December.

Chapter 5 Completing the Accounting Cycle

(e) Common stock was issued for $18,500 and credited to Accounts Payable.
(f) Inventory purchased for $31,050 was incorrectly posted to the asset account as $13,500. No error was made in the liability account.

Required: Determine the correct balances of assets, liabilities, and owners' equity at the end of November.

P5B-9

Unifying Concepts: Trial Balance, Financial Statements, Closing Entries, Post-Closing Trial Balance

SOLUTIONS SOFTWARE

The following account balances were taken from the General Ledger of Fowler, Inc., at December 31, 1994, before closing the books.

Cash	$14,500
Supplies	4,250
Prepaid Insurance	3,750
Prepaid Rent	3,400
Land	30,000
Note Payable (long term)	15,500
Capital Stock	18,500
Retained Earnings	4,640
Dividends	2,500
Service Revenue	27,500
Concession Revenue	3,250
Salaries Expense	7,250
Repair Expense	1,600
Heat and Light Expense	1,450
Telephone Expense	180
Miscellaneous Expenses	510

Additional Data:

(a) A physical count and pricing of supplies showed $325 on hand.
(b) The Prepaid Insurance account is for a 2-year insurance policy premium. The policy covers 1994 and 1995 and became effective January 1, 1994.
(c) Rent expense for 1994 is $2,400.
(d) Employee salaries that were earned but unpaid at December 31 were $350.

Required:
1. Enter the account balances in the trial balance columns of an 8-column work sheet.
2. Record work sheet adjustments from the additional data. (Ignore income taxes.)
3. Complete the work sheet.
4. Prepare an income statement from the work sheet.
5. Prepare a balance sheet from the work sheet.
6. Make the closing entries. Use an Income Summary account.
7. Prepare a post-closing trial balance.

P5B-10

Purchases and Cash Disbursements (*Appendix B*)

Martin Company began operations on March 1, 1994. The chart of accounts used by Martin includes the following accounts, among others:

Cash	101		Purchases	501
Office Supplies	105		Purchase Returns & Allowances	502
Inventory	106		Purchase Discounts	503
Equipment	130		Salary Expense	512
Accounts Payable	202		Utilities Expense	513

March transactions relating to these accounts are listed as follows:

March 2 Purchased merchandise from Taylor Company for $2,000, terms 2/10, n/60. Invoice dated March 2.
    4 Purchased merchandise from Afflock Co. for $4,500, terms 2/10, n/60. Invoice dated March 3.
    5 Purchased merchandise from Afco Company costing $4,200, terms 2/10, n/30. Invoice dated March 4.
    9 Issued check to Afflock Co. for full payment.
   11 Issued check to Taylor Co. for full payment.
   12 Paid cash for office supplies costing $200.
   14 Purchased equipment for cash costing $1,000.
   19 Purchased merchandise for cash costing $2,100.
   20 Paid Afco for the merchandise purchased on March 5.
   22 Paid utilities for March costing $180.
   25 Paid March sales salaries of $2,800.

Required: Record the transactions in the appropriate journals using Purchases and Cash Disbursements Journals similar to those shown in Appendix B.

Business Analysis Case *Doctors, Inc.*

Doctors, Inc., a partnership, is considering the purchase of a small real estate business as an investment. Since you have some training in the mechanics of the accounting cycle, they have hired you to review the real estate company's accounting records and to prepare a balance sheet and an income statement for their use. In analyzing various business documents, you verify the following data.

1. The account balances at the beginning of the current year were as follows:

Cash in Bank	$ 7,800
Note Receivable from Current Owner	10,000
Supplies	750
Prepaid Office Rent	4,500
Accounts Payable	450
Owners' Equity	22,600

2. During the current year, the following summarized transactions took place:
   (a) The owner paid $1,200 to the business to cover the interest on the note receivable ($10,000 × 0.12 × 1 year). Nothing was paid on the principal.
   (b) Real estate commissions earned during the year totaled $45,500. Of this amount, $1,000 has not been received by year-end.
   (c) The company purchased $500 of supplies during the year. A count of the supplies at year-end shows $300 worth still on hand.
   (d) The $4,500 paid for office rental was for 18 months, beginning in January of this year.
   (e) Utilities paid during the year amounted to $1,500.
   (f) During the year, $400 of accounts payable were paid; the balance in Accounts Payable at year-end is $300, with the adjustment being debited to Miscellaneous Office Expense.

(g) The owner paid himself $1,500 a month as a salary and paid a part-time secretary $2,400 for the year. (Ignore payroll taxes.) The owner also withdrew $5,000 for personal use at year-end.

Required: Prepare a balance sheet and an income statement on the basis of the data for the real estate business.

Ethics Case *Year-Round Landscape, Inc.*

Sam and Julia Love are the owners of Year-Round Landscape, Inc., a small landscape and yard service business in Southern California. The business is three years old and has grown significantly, especially during the past year. To sustain this growth, Year-Round Landscape must expand operations.

In the past, the Loves have been able to secure funds for the business from personal resources and those of their family. Now those resources are exhausted and the Loves are seeking a loan from a local bank.

To satisfy bank requirements, Year-Round Landscape must provide a set of financial statements, including comparative income statements showing the growth in earnings over the past three years. In analyzing the records, Sam notices that the nominal accounts have not yet been closed for this year. Furthermore, Sam is aware of a major contract that is to be signed on January 3, only three days after the December 31 year-end for the business. Sam suggests that the closing process be delayed one week so that this major contract can be included in this year's operating results. Sam estimates that this contract will increase current year earnings by 20 percent.

Required:
1. What accounting issues are involved in this case?
2. What ethical issues are involved in this case?

Part 2

Income Determination

CHAPTERS

6 Income Measurement and Reporting
  Appendix – Using a Work Sheet in Accounting
      for Inventory
7 Inventory and Costs of Goods Sold

Chapter 6

Income Measurement and Reporting

Learning Objectives

After studying this chapter, you should be able to:
1. Understand economic, cash-basis, and accrual-basis income.
2. Explain the accounting for revenue and revenue-related accounts.
3. Contrast periodic and perpetual inventory methods.
4. Prepare a comprehensive accrual-basis income statement.

SETTING THE STAGE

ZZZZ Best was a Los Angeles-based company specializing in carpet cleaning and insurance restoration.[1] Prior to allegations of fraud and its declaration for bankruptcy in 1988, ZZZZ Best was touted as one of the hottest stocks on Wall Street. In 1987, after only 6 years in business, the company had a market valuation exceeding $211 million, giving its "genius" president a paper fortune of $109 million. Recent lawsuits, however, have alleged that the company was nothing more than a massive fraud scheme that fooled major banks, two large CPA firms, an investment banker, and a prestigious law firm.

ZZZZ Best was started as a carpet-cleaning business by Barry Minkow, a 15-year-old high school student, in 1981. Although ZZZZ Best appeared to be profitable and had impressive growth as a carpet-cleaning business, the growth was not nearly fast enough for the impatient Minkow. In 1985, ZZZZ Best supposedly expanded into the insurance restoration business, restoring buildings that had been damaged by fire, floods, and other disasters.

During 1985 and 1986, several insurance restoration projects were supposedly undertaken, including a $2.3 million job in an eight-story building, a $7 million contract in Sacramento, a $2.8 million job in San Diego, and a $13.8 million job in Dallas. The company reported high income from those jobs although none could later be verified. A public stock offering in 1986 stated that 86 percent of ZZZZ Best Corp.'s business was in the insurance restoration area.

Based on the company's high growth and reported income in 1987, a spokesperson for a large brokerage house was quoted in *Business Week* as saying that "Barry Minkow is a great manager and ZZZZ Best is a great company." He recommended that his clients buy their stock. That same year, the Association of Collegiate Entrepreneurs and the Young Entrepreneurs' Organization placed Minkow on their list of the 100 top young entrepreneurs in America, and the mayor of Los Angeles honored Minkow with a commendation that said the president had "set a fine entrepreneurial example of obtaining the status of a millionaire at the age of 18."

---

[1] This description is based on articles in *The Wall Street Journal* and investigative proceedings of the U.S. House of Representatives Subcommittee on Energy and Commerce hearings: *The Wall Street Journal*, July 7, 1987, p. 1; July 9, 1987, p. 1; August 23, 1988, p. 1; U.S. House of Representatives, Subcommittee on Oversight and Investigation of the Committee on Energy and Commerce, January 27, 1988; U.S. House of Representatives, Subcommittee on Oversight and Investigation of the Committee on Energy and Commerce, February 1, 1988.

Unfortunately, ZZZZ Best's insurance business, its impressive growth, and its high reported income were totally fictitious. In fact, the company never once made a legitimate profit. Barry Minkow, himself, later said that he was a "fraudster," who convincingly deceived almost everyone involved in the company.

In January 1988, a federal grand jury in Los Angeles returned a 57-count indictment charging 11 individuals—including ZZZZ Best founder and president, Barry Minkow—with engaging in a massive fraud scheme. Barry Minkow is presently serving a 25-year sentence in a federal penitentiary in Colorado.

How could a company such as ZZZZ Best report high income and fool knowledgeable accountants and other professionals? In this chapter, you will study the measurement of income and learn about revenues (which Minkow understood) and expenses. Because investment decisions are often made on the basis of a company's reported income, the subjects of this chapter are among the most important you will study in accounting.

In Chapter 2, we introduced the income statement, the balance sheet, and the statement of cash flows as end products, or outputs, of the accounting cycle. This chapter and subsequent chapters will help you understand these financial statements more fully. Specifically, Chapters 6 and 7 analyze the income statement, Chapters 8 through 14 cover the balance sheet, and Chapter 15 explains and illustrates the statement of cash flows.

First we briefly define income and describe the cash-basis and accrual-basis methods of measuring income. We then explain in some detail the accrual-basis method, which is currently required by generally accepted accounting principles.

A DEFINITION OF INCOME

Objective 1
Understand economic, cash-basis, and accrual-basis income.

economic income the maximum amount a person or a firm can consume during an accounting period and still be as well off at the end of the period as at the beginning

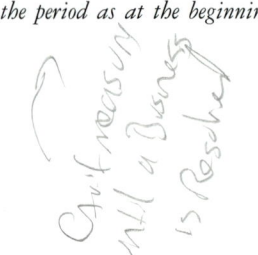

In an economic sense, income can be thought of as the increase in wealth experienced during a period. **Economic income** has been defined as the maximum amount a person or firm can consume during an accounting period and still be as well off at the end of the period as at the beginning. If a firm initially has $1,000 of purchasing power, its income during a period would be the amount it could spend and still have $1,000 of purchasing power at the end of the period (assuming that the owners of the firm have not invested or withdrawn any capital). Conceptually, this definition is appropriate; in practice, economic income is difficult to measure.

To illustrate the complexity of measuring economic income, we will assume that three individuals decide to open a clothing store and that each contributes $17,000 to the business. Let's say that they use the $51,000 (3 × $17,000) of invested funds to purchase a building for $50,000 and an inventory of 10 coats for a total cost of $1,000, or $100 each. If during their first month of business they sell all 10 coats at a price of $200 each and have no other operating expenses, how much income did they earn? Your first reaction may be to say that their income is $1,000 (10 coats × $100 profit on each coat). This answer, though logical, may or may not be correct. If the building is still worth exactly $50,000, their economic income is indeed $1,000. If, however, the building's value has increased or decreased, economic income may be something more or less than $1,000. How much more or less cannot be determined exactly unless the owners choose to sell the building at the end of the month.

Some accounting theorists would argue that income could be determined by valuing the building at either its replacement cost (the amount it would cost to purchase a similar building) or the amount at which it could be sold as determined by an appraisal. In reality, the only sure measure of the building's value is its sales price when it is actually sold.

When this single complexity is considered in relation to an actual business with numerous assets and transactions, the problems of measuring income multiply considerably. In fact, the income of a business can be determined accurately and objectively only at the end of the firm's life, after it has sold or otherwise disposed of all its operating and other assets and when cash is the only remaining asset. The cash can then be counted, and the increase over the beginning amount, adjusted for all owner withdrawals and investments since the firm was established, is income.

Since stockholders and others are unwilling to wait until the end of a firm's life to find out how well it has performed, firms report estimates of net income at regular intervals (at least annually and often monthly or quarterly). These periodic estimates are reported on the income statement. Although the income statement reports a precise net income amount, you should realize that there are usually several estimates and assumptions included in the calculation of this number.

METHODS OF MEASURING INCOME

In Chapter 4, we introduced cash-basis and accrual-basis accounting. The discussion there focused on the timing of revenue recognition and the expense matching process. We now extend our discussion to include the complexities of inventory and long-term assets such as buildings.

cash-basis accounting *a system of accounting in which transactions are recorded and revenues and expenses are recognized only when cash is received or paid*

Cash-basis accounting provides the simplest and most objective measure of income. Remember that with a cash basis, income is the difference between a business's cash receipts and its cash disbursements during an accounting period. Cash receipts and disbursements can be measured with a high degree of objectivity. To illustrate, we will assume that High Country Sporting Goods had the following transactions:

inventory *goods held for sale*

1. Started business on January 1, 1994. On that day High Country purchased a building for $100,000, as well as $50,000 of sporting goods **inventory**. At the time of purchase, it was estimated that the building would be used by the business for 20 years.
2. During 1994, High Country sold one-half the inventory for $60,000.
3. The only other expense incurred during 1994 was $20,000 paid for salaries.

Given these data, the cash-basis loss might be computed as follows:

Cash receipts		$60,000
Cash disbursements:		
Purchase of sporting goods inventory	$50,000	
Purchase of building	100,000	
Payment of salaries	20,000	
Total cash disbursements		170,000
Net loss		($110,000)

As you can see, there are some serious problems when income is computed strictly on a cash basis. First, did High Country really lose $110,000? Certainly, cash outflows exceeded cash inflows by $110,000. However, the major reason for the excess outflows was a $100,000 expenditure for a building that will benefit the company for many years and is more of an investment (asset) than an expense. Wouldn't it be better to allocate or assign a portion of the cost of the building to each of the periods in which it is used by the company? If the building can be used effectively for 20 years, for example, wouldn't it be preferable to charge only one-twentieth of the cost against revenues in the current year?

Furthermore, only half the inventory was actually sold. Shouldn't only the cost of the portion of inventory sold be an expense? And what if additional sporting goods had been sold on credit with payment yet to be received? Shouldn't such sales be recognized currently as revenues? And what if additional sporting goods inventory had been bought on credit near the fiscal year-end, with payment to be made 60 days later? Shouldn't such purchases be recognized currently as an asset? The answers to these and other questions indicate that the cash-basis income measurement method is not the most useful for determining income in most companies. However, some government and other nonprofit organizations, as well as many small businesses, rely heavily on some form of cash-basis accounting.

Because of the problems inherent in assessing income on a cash basis, generally accepted accounting principles require that financial statements be prepared using **accrual-basis accounting**. With this approach, the historical costs of operational assets (buildings, machines, and so forth) are allocated to expense over their estimated useful lives, and only the costs incurred in generating revenues during the current period are charged as an expense—for example, salaries, rent, and the cost of inventory actually sold. Net income is then equal to revenues earned minus expenses incurred. To illustrate the accrual-basis method, we again calculate the net income of High Country Sporting Goods for 1994.

accrual-basis accounting *a system of accounting in which revenues and expenses are recorded as they are earned and incurred, not necessarily when cash is received or paid*

Sales revenue		$60,000
Expenses:		
Cost of inventory sold (½ × $50,000 cost)	$25,000	
Salaries expense	20,000	
Building cost allocated to expense ($100,000 cost ÷ 20 years)	5,000	
Total expenses		50,000
Net income		$10,000

BUSINESS ENVIRONMENT ESSAY
When to Recognize Revenue

The decision of when to recognize revenue is a difficult one for some industries. Take the troubled savings and loan (S&L) industry for example. When loans are made, borrowers are required to pay loan origination fees, or "points," in order to obtain a loan. These fees usually total 1 to 3 percent of the amount borrowed, but some savings and loans have charged borrowers initial, one-time fees of 4 to 10 percent of the loan value in return for lower interest rates. Many S&Ls would report all or a substantial portion of the fees as revenue when loans were made, immediately boosting profits. It didn't matter that the loans might never be paid back or that the fees were paid in exchange for lower interest over the life of the loan.

The revenue from these fees is not trivial, as shown by the significant percentages of income that were comprised of loan origination fees for the following financial institutions in a recent year:

Company	Pretax Income (millions)	Loan Origination Fees (millions)	Percentage of Income from Fees
Financial Corp. of America	$ 63.2	$40.9	65%
HF Ahmanson & Co.	351.7	46.1	13
Great Western Fin. Corp.	335.4	67.8	20
Cal Fed Inc.	188.1	47.0	25
Meritor Financial Corp.	71.8	46.2	64
Glen Fed Inc.	112.0	60.4	54
Golden West Financial Group	242.7	21.6	9
First Federal of Michigan	79.9	10.5	13
Home Federal	117.2	46.8	40
Gibraltar Financial Corp.	61.8	30.3	49

Reporting these up-front fees as income when they are paid has enabled many S&Ls—including Financial Corp. of America—to report healthy profits even as they were heading toward financial collapse. As a result, the Financial Accounting Standards Board proposed new accounting rules requiring S&Ls to defer origination fees and recognize them as income over the life of the loan. Thus, a 3% fee on a 30-year, $100,000 mortgage would be recognized in the amount of $100 per year for 30 years (.03 × $100,000/30) instead of being reported as $3,000 income in the year the loan was made. The rationale is that these fees are part of the cost of borrowing money and should be recognized as income over the loan term, just like interest. The new rules eliminate the incentive to make high-risk, low-interest loans in order to show immediate income from origination fees.

Most large savings and loans, including many in the table, were already deferring a considerable amount of the loan fees paid by borrowers. Many others, however, were not. With the reported high, but illusory, profits from origination fees, some savings and loan executives paid themselves grand salaries and bonuses while their companies were going bankrupt. Don Dixon, former owner of Vernon Savings and Loan in Texas, for example, lived in a $2 million mansion and took company-paid trips to France to search for a chef. Centennial Savings of California kept a $48,000-a-year European chef on the payroll, a million-dollar penthouse on Telegraph Hill in San Francisco, a $750,000 airplane, a $30,000 chess set, and gave bonuses of $819,000 each to its two top executives. Sunbelt Savings in Texas spent $1.3 million on Halloween and Christmas parties.

Source: Adapted from John R. Hayes, "Party Pooping," *Forbes,* October 20, 1986, pp. 97–98.

inflation *an increase in the general price level of goods and services; alternatively, a decrease in the purchasing power of the dollar*

Since it is the method currently required for financial statements, accrual-basis accounting will be explained in greater detail in this chapter and used throughout the text. Note that this approach, like the cash-basis method, ignores the impact of **inflation.** There are other measurement methods that do attempt to adjust income for inflation and other factors causing changes in value, but they are not discussed in this book.

> **To Summarize** *Two methods of measuring income for financial reporting purposes are the cash-basis and the accrual-basis methods. These methods ignore inflation. Each has advantages and disadvantages. The method that will be used throughout this text, the accrual-basis method, is currently required for the financial statements of most organizations.*

REVENUE RECOGNITION

Objective 2
Explain the accounting for revenue and revenue-related accounts.

revenues *increases in resources from the sale of goods or services*

revenue recognition principle *the idea that revenues should be recorded when (1) the earnings process has been substantially completed and (2) an exchange has taken place*

Net income under accrual-basis accounting is equal to revenues earned minus expenses incurred. We will first discuss and illustrate the issues relating to revenue recognition. Then we will describe how expenses are measured and recognized.

Revenues, as you will recall from Chapter 2, are the increases in resources from the sale of goods or services. According to the **revenue recognition principle,** revenues are usually recorded when two important criteria have been met: (1) the earnings process has been substantially completed, generally meaning that a sale has been made or a service has been performed, and (2) an exchange has taken place.[2] As a practical matter, most companies record sales when goods are shipped to customers. Credit sales are recognized as revenues before cash is collected, and revenue from services is usually recognized when the service is performed, not necessarily when cash is collected.

To illustrate this principle, we will assume that on a typical business day Farm Land Products sells 30 sacks of fertilizer for cash and 20 sacks on credit, all at $10 per sack. Given these data, the $500 of revenue would be recorded as follows:

Cash	300
Accounts Receivable	200
Sales Revenue	500
Sold 30 sacks of fertilizer for cash and 20 sacks on credit.	

Although the debit entries are made to different accounts, the credit entry for the full amount is to a revenue account. Thus, accrual-basis accounting

---

[2] In some cases, revenue is recognized according to other criteria, such as upon production (when there is a ready market) or upon partial completion of the earnings process (for example, when a down payment has been made). However, these are exceptions to the general rule.

Chapter 6 *Income Measurement and Reporting*

allows the recognition of $500 in revenue instead of the $300 that would be recognized with the cash-basis method.

This example is a simple illustration of how sales are recorded and revenue is recognized. In reality, sales transactions are usually more complex, involving such things as discounts for prompt payment, returns of merchandise sold, and losses from uncollectible credit sales. Before we discuss these complexities, one note is appropriate. In many companies, the most frequent types of journal entries are those to record sales, cash collections, purchases, and payments to suppliers. Because such transactions are so frequent, most firms maintain four separate special journals. As was noted in the Special Journals Appendix at the end of Chapter 5, these are (1) the sales journal, (2) the purchases journal, (3) the cash receipts journal, and (4) the cash disbursements journal. However, in the following analysis of transactions, we will use only a few selected journal entries, and so we will continue to use the General Journal format.

Recognizing Revenue on Credit Sales

Many sales do not involve cash. Instead, they are made on credit, with the buyer usually having from 10 days to 2 months in which to pay the seller for the merchandise purchased. The asset that arises from this kind of transaction is called an **account receivable,** meaning that the buyer owes the seller for the merchandise purchased. An entry to record such a transaction and to recognize the sales revenue is shown here.

account receivable *a current asset representing money due for services performed or merchandise sold on credit*

```
Accounts Receivable ............................................. 1,000
    Sales Revenue .............................................         1,000
Sold $1,000 of merchandise to Adam Smith on account.
```

This entry shows that a customer, Adam Smith, purchased $1,000 of merchandise on credit. When the customer pays the full amount, the entry to record the receipt of cash and the canceling of the receivable will be:

```
Cash .......................................................... 1,000
    Accounts Receivable ........................................         1,000
Received payment in full from Adam Smith for merchandise purchased.
```

These two entries illustrate simple sales and collection transactions. Many companies, however, offer sales discounts and must deal with returns of merchandise and uncollectible accounts.

sales discount *a reduction in the selling price, allowed if payment is received within a specified period*

SALES DISCOUNTS. In many sales transactions, the buyer is given a discount if the bill is paid promptly. Such incentives to pay quickly are called **sales discounts,** or cash discounts, and the discount terms are typically expressed in abbreviated form. For example, 2/10, n/30 means that a buyer will receive a 2 percent discount from the selling price if payment is made within 10 days of the date of purchase, but that the full amount must be paid within 30 days or it will be considered past due. (Other common terms are 1/10, n/30 and 2/10,

EOM. The latter means that a 2 percent discount is granted if payment is made within 10 days after the end of the month.) A 2 percent discount is a strong incentive to pay within 10 days because it is equivalent to an annual interest rate of about 36 percent.[3] In fact, if the amount owed is substantial, most firms will borrow money, if necessary, to take advantage of a sales discount. This is because the interest rate they will have to pay a lending institution to borrow the money is considerably less than the effective interest rate of the sales discount.

If an account receivable is paid within a specified discount period, the entry to record the receipt of cash is different from the cash receipt entry shown earlier. Thus, if Adam Smith had purchased the $1,000 of merchandise on credit with terms 2/10, EOM and had paid within the discount period, the entry to record the receipt of cash would have been:

```
Cash .................................................... 980
Sales Discounts ($1,000 × 0.02) ...................... 20
    Accounts Receivable ..............................      1,000
Received payment from Adam Smith within the discount period.
```

contra account *an account that is offset or deducted from another account*

Sales Discounts is a **contra account,** specifically a contra-revenue account, which means that it is deducted from Sales Revenue on the income statement. This account is included with other revenue accounts in the General Ledger, but unlike other revenue accounts, it has a debit balance. Exhibit 6-1 summarizes the entries for sales discounts using the Adam Smith example.

SALES RETURNS AND ALLOWANCES. Customers often return merchandise, either because the item is defective or for a variety of other reasons. Most companies generally accept returned merchandise in order to maintain good customer relations. When merchandise is returned, the company must make an entry to

Exhibit 6-1 Accounting for Sales Discounts

Transaction	Journal Entry		
Sale	Accounts Receivable	1,000	
	Sales Revenue		1,000
Payment (if within discount period)	Cash	980	
	Sales Discounts ($1,000 × 0.02)	20	
	Accounts Receivable		1,000
Payment (if not within discount period)	Cash	1,000	
	Accounts Receivable		1,000

---

[3] This is calculated by computing an annual interest rate for the period that the money is "sacrificed." With terms 2/10, n/30, a buyer who pays on the 10th day instead of the 30th sacrifices the money for 20 days. Since 2 percent is earned in 20 days and there are just over 18 periods of 20 days in a year, earnings would be 18 times 2 percent, or approximately 36 percent annual interest.

reduce both the Accounts Receivable and the Sales Revenue accounts. A similar entry is required when the sales price is reduced because the merchandise was defective or damaged during shipment to the customer.

To illustrate the type of entry needed, we will assume that Adam Smith has returned $200 of the $1,000 of merchandise purchased. The entry to record the return of merchandise would be:

Sales Returns and Allowances	200	
Accounts Receivable		200
Received $200 of merchandise back from Adam Smith.		

Adam Smith would be sent a credit memorandum for the return, stating that credit has been granted and that the balance of his account is now $800. Like Sales Discounts, the **Sales Returns and Allowances** account is a contra account that is deducted from sales revenues on the income statement. Note also that when merchandise is returned, sales discounts are granted only on the selling price of the merchandise not returned.

It might seem that the use of offsetting contra accounts (Sales Discounts and Sales Returns and Allowances) involves extra steps that would not be necessary if discounts and returns of merchandise were deducted directly from the Sales Revenue account. Although such direct deductions would have the same final effect on net income, the separation of initial sales from all returns and allowances and discounts permits a company's management to analyze the extent to which customers are returning merchandise and taking advantage of discounts. If management finds that excessive amounts of merchandise are being returned, they may decide that the company's sales returns policy is too liberal or that the quality of its merchandise needs improvement.

A company's total recorded sales, before any discounts or returns and allowances, are referred to as **gross sales**. When sales discounts or sales returns and allowances are deducted from gross sales, the resulting amount is referred to as **net sales**.

Sales Returns and Allowances *a contra-revenue account in which the return of, or allowance for, reduction in the price of merchandise previously sold is recorded*

gross sales *total recorded sales before deducting any sales discounts or sales returns and allowances*

net sales *gross sales less sales discounts and sales returns and allowances*

LOSSES FROM UNCOLLECTIBLE ACCOUNTS. A third kind of complexity that can arise in the sales and collections cycle is the nonpayment of accounts. When companies sell goods and services on credit (as most do), there are usually some customers who do not pay for the merchandise they purchase. In fact, most businesses expect a small percentage of their receivables to be uncollectible. If a firm tries too hard to eliminate the possibility of losses from nonpaying customers, it usually makes its credit policy so restrictive that valuable sales are lost. On the other hand, if a firm extends credit too easily or to everyone, it may have so many uncollectible receivables that it goes bankrupt. Because of this dilemma, most firms carefully monitor their credit sales and accounts receivable to ensure that their policies are neither too restrictive nor too liberal. Methods of accounting for uncollectible receivables will be discussed in Chapter 8.

> **To Summarize** Revenue generally is accounted for according to the revenue recognition principle. That is, revenue is recognized when earned, which is at the time the earnings process has been substantially completed and an exchange has taken place. The entries to record revenue from the sale of merchandise or the performance of a service involve debits to Cash or Accounts Receivable and credits to Sales or Service Revenue. When accounting for revenue transactions, most businesses must also consider sales discounts, sales returns, and the uncollectibility of receivables resulting from credit sales.

RECOGNIZING EXPENSES

Objective 3
Contrast periodic and perpetual inventory methods.

expenses *costs incurred in the normal course of business to generate revenues*

Thus far our focus has been on the importance of measuring and recognizing revenues. **Expenses** are equally important and should be accounted for carefully. Expenses must be matched with the revenues they generate, which means that they are subtracted from, or charged against, revenues in computing net income *during the same time period that the related revenues are recognized.*

Some expenses can be matched directly with revenues generated, whereas other expenses are only indirectly related to specific revenues. Because the amount spent for merchandise sold can be related directly to specific revenues, it is separated from the other operating expenses. Usually called **cost of goods sold**, it appears as a separate section on the income statement immediately following the revenue section. As an example, consider a retail grocery store like Albertson's. The cost of goods sold would be the costs incurred in purchasing all vegetables, meats, canned goods, and other merchandise sold during the period. The other expenses would be the amounts incurred for rent, utilities, telephone, salaries, property taxes, and other operating items. Exhibit 6-2 shows the income statement for Albertson's Inc. for a recent year. On the statement, cost of goods sold is shown separately from other expenses and is deducted from revenues. The excess of revenues over cost of goods sold is labeled **gross margin** (sometimes called gross profit). This is a measure of how much a company "marks up" its merchandise over cost for resale to customers. In Albertson's case, for example, groceries and other merchandise that cost $5,260,459,000 were marked up $1,512,602,000, or 28.8 percent of cost, and were sold for $6,773,061,000. Gross margin represents the amount of profit available to cover the company's operating expenses and income taxes and to provide income to its owners. After paying operating expenses of $1,255,608,000 and income taxes of $94,449,000, Albertson's had net income of approximately $162.5 million which could be used to pay dividends or could be retained in the business.

cost of goods sold *the expenses incurred to purchase or manufacture the merchandise sold during a period*

gross margin *the excess of net sales revenue over the cost of goods sold*

multiple-step income statement *an income statement that separates cost of goods sold from other expenses and reports a gross margin figure*

single-step income statement *an income statement that lists all expenses together, including cost of goods sold*

The income statement format in Exhibit 6-2 is known as a **multiple-step income statement.** An alternative format that has become increasingly popular in recent years is the **single-step income statement.** Rather than separating cost of goods sold from other expenses and identifying gross margin, the single-step form lists costs of goods sold with other expenses and deducts total expenses (including cost of goods sold) from revenues. The General Mills Consolidated Statement of Earnings illustrates the single-step income statement format (see the illustrative financial statements at the back of the book).

Exhibit 6-2

Albertson's Inc.
Income Statement
(in thousands of dollars)

Sales revenue		$6,773,061
Less cost of goods sold		5,260,459
Gross margin		$1,512,602
Expenses:		
Operating, general and administrative	$1,190,337	
Interest expense	16,476	
Rent expense	48,795	
Total operating expenses		1,255,608
Income before income taxes		$ 256,994
Less income taxes		94,449
Net income		$ 162,545

The Cost of Goods Sold Expense

The measurement of cost of goods sold differs according to the type of business. In a retail or wholesale business, the cost of goods sold is simply the expenses incurred in purchasing the merchandise sold during the period. Manufacturing firms, however, produce the goods they sell, so cost of goods sold must include all manufacturing costs of the products sold. Because it is much easier to understand the concept of cost of goods sold in the context of a retail or wholesale firm, manufacturing firms will not be considered here.

Even in retail and wholesale firms, the measurement of cost of goods sold is complicated by the fact that not all inventory on hand is sold before new inventory is purchased. Indeed, a company's management would be foolish to deplete all inventory before ordering new merchandise. Such a practice would result in frequent out-of-stock situations, thus drastically reducing income due to lost sales.

In any given accounting period, a firm may purchase more inventory than it sells, sell more inventory than it purchases, or buy and sell exactly the same amount of inventory. No matter which situation occurs, a company records inventory as an expense only when it is sold. Until it is sold, inventory is classified as an asset on the balance sheet. Thus, it is possible for the cost of goods sold to be higher, lower, or the same as the amount of inventory purchased during an accounting period.

Up to this point, we have considered only one method of keeping track of inventory—the perpetual method. However, there are two principal methods of accounting for inventory and cost of goods sold: (1) the perpetual method and (2) the periodic method.

perpetual inventory method *a system of accounting for inventory in which detailed records of the number of units and the cost of each purchase and sales transaction are prepared throughout the accounting period*

The Perpetual Inventory Method

In previous chapters, examples involving inventory and cost of goods sold have assumed use of the **perpetual inventory method.** With this method, the Inventory account is increased (debited) when inventory is purchased and decreased (credited) when inventory is sold. Use of this method requires a company to maintain inventory records that identify the quantity and cost of all units purchased and sold at the time of each transaction. Accounting for inventory with the perpetual method is similar to accounting for cash. Because every inventory transaction is recorded in detail, the balance in the inventory account should represent the amount of inventory actually on hand.

To illustrate the perpetual inventory method, we will consider the case of All Seasons Equipment Company, which sells lawn mowers and snowblowers, and maintains a separate inventory record for each product. The 1994 inventory record for one type of snowblower is shown in Exhibit 6-3.

The mechanics of the perpetual method can be illustrated by examining the September transactions. The transaction on September 4 involved the purchase of 10 snowblowers for $250 each and would be recorded as follows:

```
Inventory..................................................... 2,500
    Accounts Payable (or Cash) ................................ 2,500
Purchased 10 snowblowers at $250 each.
```

Exhibit 6-3 1994 Perpetual Inventory Record—Snowblowers, Model 100

Maximum Stock 150
Minimum Stock 4

Date	Explanation	Purchased No. of Units	Cost per Unit	Total Cost	Sold No. of Units	Cost per Unit	Total Cost	Balance in Inventory No. of Units	Cost per Unit	Total Cost
Jan. 1	Beginning inventory....							32	......$200	$ 6,400
Jan. 28	Sold......				20	.....$200	$ 4,000	12	......$200	$ 2,400
Mar. 3	Sold......				8	.....$200	$ 1,600	4	......$200	$ 800
Aug. 2	Purchased...	100	$250	$25,000				104	4 at $200 100 at $250	$25,800
Aug. 8	Purchased...	30	$250	$ 7,500				134	4 at $200 130 at $250	$33,300
Sept. 4	Purchased...	10	$250	$ 2,500				144	4 at $200 140 at $250	$35,800
Sept. 6	Returned to manufacturer	(5)	$250	$(1,250)				139	4 at $200 135 at $250	$34,550
Sept. 20	Sold......				15	4 at $200* 11 at $250	$ 3,550	124	......$250	$31,000
Sept. 30	Returned from customer...				(1)	.....$250	$ (250)	125	......$250	$31,250
Nov. 20	Sold......				81	.....$250	$20,250	44	......$250	$11,000
Dec. 15	Sold......				24	.....$250	$ 6,000	20	......$250	$ 5,000
Dec. 31	Ending Inventory....							20	......$250	$ 5,000
Totals		135		$33,750	147		$35,150			

* In this example, the oldest units on hand are assumed to be sold first. Inventory flow alternatives are discussed in the next chapter.

On September 6, All Seasons returned five defective snowblowers to the manufacturer. Assuming that the snowblowers had not yet been paid for, the entry would be:

> Accounts Payable 1,250
>   Inventory 1,250
> *Returned 5 defective snowblowers, purchased for $250 each, to the manufacturer.*

If the returned snowblowers had been paid for, the manufacturer would probably refund the purchase price, and Cash would be debited instead of Accounts Payable.

On September 20, the company sold 15 snowblowers for $350 each. Since a sales transaction involves both the recognition of a sale and a reduction of inventory, two entries are needed. The two entries to record the sale would be:

> Accounts Receivable (or Cash) 5,250
>   Sales Revenue 5,250
> *To recognize the revenue from selling 15 snowblowers (15 × $350).*
>
> Cost of Goods Sold 3,550
>   Inventory 3,550
> *To recognize the expense from selling 15 snowblowers (4 at $200, 11 at $250).*

These entries illustrate that the cost of goods sold expense is incurred only when merchandise is sold. In this case, the merchandise that was sold for $5,250 cost the company $3,550. The difference between the revenue of $5,250 and the cost of goods sold of $3,550 represents a gross margin of $1,700.

Finally, on September 30 the company received one snowblower back from a customer. Assuming that a $250 snowblower sold on September 20 was returned, the entry to record the return would be:

> Sales Returns and Allowances 350
>   Accounts Receivable (or Cash) 350
> Inventory... 250
>   Cost of Goods Sold 250
> *Received 1 snowblower back from a customer.*

When using the perpetual method, a company can quickly determine its cost of goods sold as well as the amount of its ending inventory by examining the Inventory and Cost of Goods Sold accounts. In theory, the perpetual inventory method should eliminate the need to physically count the inventory. However, because of the possibility of clerical errors, spoilage, and theft, and because of income tax rules, even firms that maintain perpetual inventory records usually count their inventory at least once a year. After the inventory has been counted, the perpetual inventory records are adjusted, if necessary, to correct the balance in Inventory.

For example, the perpetual inventory record in Exhibit 6-3 shows 20 units on hand at December 31. If a physical count at year-end revealed two snowblowers were missing from inventory, the adjusting entry needed to record the shortage would be:

Inventory Shrinkage	500	
Inventory		500

To adjust the recorded inventory balance to the physical count, 18 snowblowers.

Because Inventory Shrinkage is an expense, at the end of the period it is closed to Income Summary.

For many small companies, the perpetual method involves too much clerical work and is too expensive to use. However, with the availability of computers to handle repetitive transactions, use of the perpetual inventory method has become feasible for many more companies, including department stores and other businesses with large inventories. Department stores often can maintain perpetual records by coding each inventory item and programming the cash register to adjust the records as each item is sold.

PURCHASE DISCOUNTS. Purchases are simply sales viewed from the other side of the transaction. That is, many purchase transactions include terms (such as 2/10, n/30) to encourage prompt payment. Just as sales discounts reduce gross sales, **purchase discounts** reduce the net cost of purchases. With the perpetual inventory method, the amount recorded in the Inventory account should reflect the actual cost of inventory on hand. Therefore, when a purchase discount is taken, the recorded amount of inventory must be reduced. To illustrate accounting for purchase discounts under the perpetual inventory method, assume that on September 9, All Seasons Equipment Company paid its supplier for the 10 snowblowers purchased on September 4. If the terms of the September 4 purchase were 2/10, n/30, the entry to record the payment would be:

purchase discount a reduction in the purchase price, allowed if payment is made within a specified period

Accounts Payable	2,500	
Inventory		50
Cash		2,450

Paid supplier for 10 snowblowers purchased on September 4 taking advantage of 2/10, n/30 terms. ($2,500 × .02 = $50 discount)

As you can see, this entry reduces the amount recorded for these 10 snowblowers from $2,500 to $2,450, which is their net cost.

TRANSPORTATION COSTS. Another factor that affects the recorded cost of inventory is the cost of transporting purchased merchandise. Because merchandise usually cannot be sold until it is on hand, the cost of transporting it into the firm is considered an addition to the cost of the inventory. When using the perpetual inventory method, this cost must be added to the Inventory account if the recorded inventory balance is to reflect the actual cost of acquiring inventory. To illustrate, assume that All Seasons Equipment Company pays a trucking company $350 to haul snowblowers from the supplier to its warehouse. The entry to account for this payment would be:

> Inventory... 350
>   Cash 350
> *Paid Trucks-R-Us Shipping Company $350 to deliver snowblowers to the warehouse.*

The Periodic Inventory Method

Although the perpetual inventory method provides excellent control over merchandise and allows for a quick determination of the amount of inventory on hand at all times, many businesses do not use this system because it is too time-consuming. For these firms, there is an alternative known as the **periodic inventory method.** It allows a company to determine Inventory and Cost of Goods Sold at the end of a period without recording the effect on Inventory of every sale and purchase transaction. A firm using the periodic inventory method can find out how much inventory it has remaining at the end of the period—and therefore how much its cost of goods sold is—only by physically counting and pricing goods on hand.

When using the periodic inventory method, a company initially records each inventory purchase in a **Purchases** account. During the period, the effects of sales are not reflected in either the Inventory or the Purchases account. At the end of the period, the company takes a physical count of all inventory on hand and determines the cost of goods sold for the period by making the following calculation (numbers are arbitrary):

>   Beginning inventory, January 1, 1994 .... $ 800
> + Purchases for the year 2,200
> = Cost of goods available for sale during 1994 .... $3,000
> − Ending inventory, December 31, 1994   300
> = Cost of goods sold for 1994 .... $2,700

periodic inventory method a system of accounting for inventory in which cost of goods sold is determined and inventory is adjusted at the end of the accounting period, not when merchandise is purchased or sold

Purchases an account in which all inventory purchases are recorded; used with the periodic inventory method

Exhibit 6-4 illustrates graphically the cost of goods sold calculation. The first item is the cost of the beginning inventory, $800, which is the ending inventory of the previous period as determined by a physical count.

The second item is the total amount of inventory purchased during the year, $2,200. This is added to the beginning inventory, and the total is the third item, the $3,000 cost of goods available for sale during the period. The label "cost of goods available for sale" is a useful one since all the inventory a firm sells must come either from units it had on hand at the beginning of the period or from units it purchased during the period. Fourth is the ending inventory, $300, which is determined by a physical count at the end of the current period. This amount is subtracted from the cost of goods available for sale, and the result is the cost of goods sold expense, $2,700. Since inventory available for sale generally has to be either included in the ending inventory or sold during the period, ending inventory and cost of goods sold are complementary amounts, and their sum must always equal the total cost of goods available for sale.

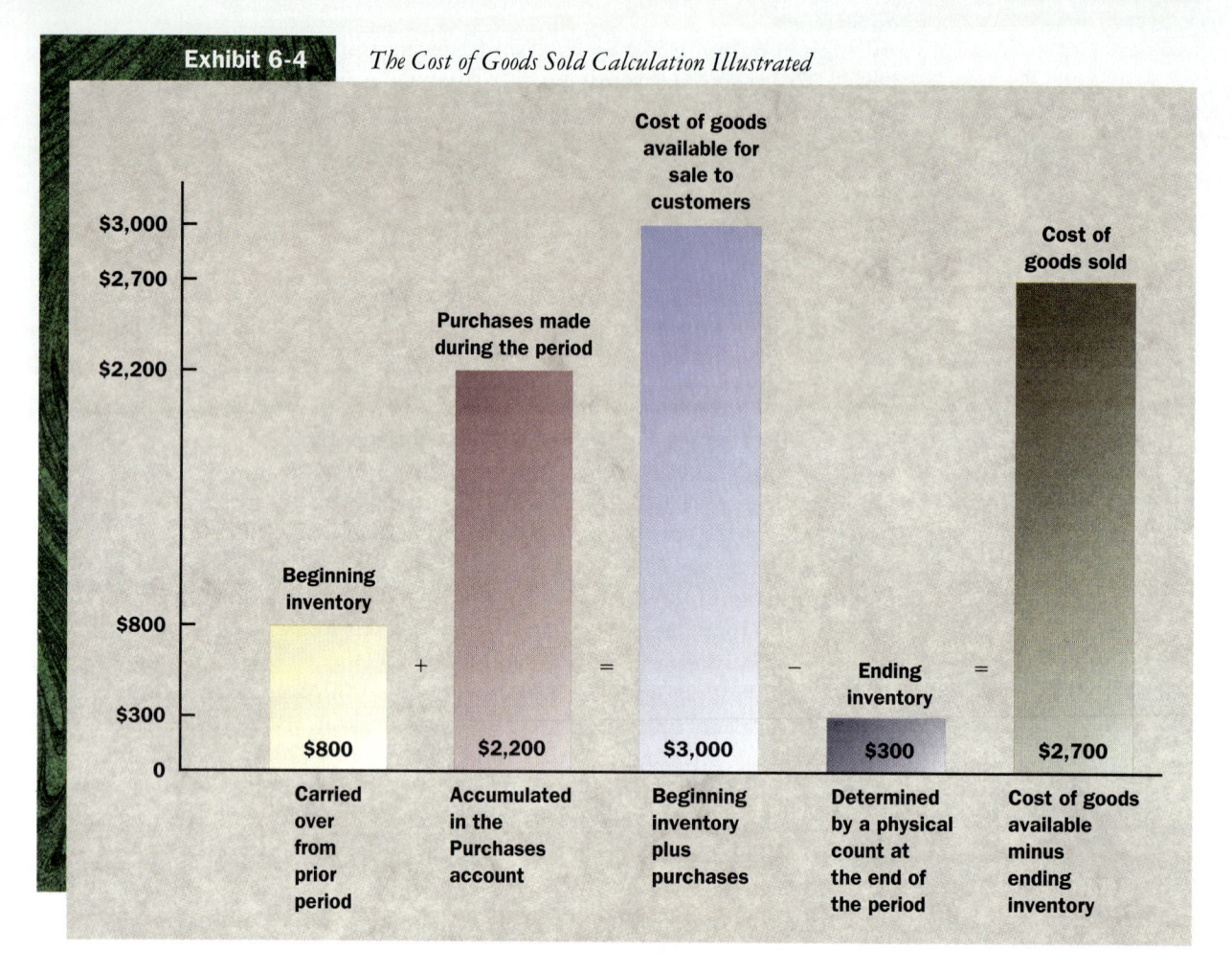

Exhibit 6-4 *The Cost of Goods Sold Calculation Illustrated*

Beginning inventory		Purchases made during the period		Cost of goods available for sale to customers		Ending inventory		Cost of goods sold
$800	+	$2,200	=	$3,000	−	$300	=	$2,700
Carried over from prior period		Accumulated in the Purchases account		Beginning inventory plus purchases		Determined by a physical count at the end of the period		Cost of goods available minus ending inventory

Although the simple periodic inventory method outlined here is correct, it is not complete. Other items—for example, purchase discounts, returns of merchandise purchased, and the cost of transporting merchandise into the firm—require that adjustments be made to this calculation.

PURCHASE DISCOUNTS. Purchase discounts are accounted for differently under the periodic method than under the perpetual method. When using the perpetual method, purchase discounts were recorded by crediting the Inventory account. When a company uses the periodic inventory method and records purchases at their gross amounts, a separate Purchase Discounts account is used. The balance in this account is subtracted from purchases in the cost of goods sold calculation. The Purchase Discounts account is a contra account—it is deducted from Purchases and has a credit balance.

To illustrate, assume that All Seasons Equipment Company does not maintain perpetual inventory records but instead uses the periodic inventory method. The purchase of 10 snowblowers on September 4 would be recorded as follows:

Purchases	2,500	
Accounts Payable		2,500
Purchased 10 snowblowers at $250 each.		

If the terms of the purchase were 2/10, n/30 and payment was made on September 9 (within the discount period), the payment would be recorded as follows:

Accounts Payable	2,500	
Purchase Discounts		50
Cash		2,450
Paid for merchandise purchased on September 4 taking advantage of 2/10, n/30 terms. (0.02 × $2,500 = $50 discount)		

If the payment had not been made within the 10-day discount period, the full $2,500 would have been paid.

As an alternative, many people argue that purchases should be initially recorded at their net-of-discount price ($2,450 in our example). They argue that this amount is the fair market value as evidenced by the cash paid for the item. When the discount is actually taken, there is no need to adjust Purchases or any other expense account. If the discount is not taken, the cash paid over and above the recorded cost of the goods is entered as an operating expense, usually called Purchase Discounts Lost. Advocates of this "net purchases" approach stress that the amount of discounts not taken is the more relevant number since it is an indication of management's efficiency, or lack thereof. Furthermore, this method shows rejected or missed discounts for what they really are—an additional expense of buying on credit.

Using the net approach, All Seasons Equipment Company would record its purchase of the 10 snowblowers, with terms 2/10, n/30, as follows:

Purchases	2,450	
Accounts Payable		2,450
Purchased 10 snowblowers costing $2,450 with terms 2/10, n/30.		
Accounts Payable	2,450	
Cash		2,450
Paid for 10 snowblowers purchased on September 4.		

If payment were not made within the discount period, the payment entry would be:

Accounts Payable	2,450	
Purchase Discounts Lost	50	
Cash		2,500
Paid for 10 snowblowers purchased on September 4.		

PURCHASE RETURNS AND ALLOWANCES. As indicated earlier, a firm may purchase merchandise for resale and find out that it is defective, does not meet specifications, or is otherwise unacceptable. This merchandise will be returned to the supplier, either for credit or for a cash refund. When using the periodic method, the company will account for the return by crediting a contra account called **Purchase Returns and Allowances,** which reduces the amount of purchases in the calculation of cost of goods sold.

Purchase Returns and Allowances *a contra-purchases account used for recording the return of or allowances for previously purchased merchandise*

To illustrate, assume again that on September 6, All Seasons returns 5 defective snowblowers that were purchased for $250 each. The entry to account for the transaction would be:

```
Accounts Payable (or Cash) .....................................  1,250
     Purchase Returns and Allowances ............................          1,250
Returned defective merchandise costing $1,250.
```

TRANSPORTATION COSTS. When using the perpetual method, transportation costs were accounted for by increasing or debiting the Inventory account. When using the periodic method, a separate **Freight-In** account is used. If, for example, All Seasons pays the trucking company $350 to deliver merchandise from its suppliers, the entry would be as follows:

Freight-In *an account used with the periodic inventory method for recording the costs of transporting into a firm all purchased merchandise intended for sale; added to Purchases in calculating cost of goods sold*

```
Freight-In......................................................    350
     Cash ......................................................           350
Paid freight on merchandise bought for resale.
```

CALCULATING COST OF GOODS SOLD WITH THE PERIODIC METHOD. Now that you are familiar with the purchase return, purchase discount, and freight-in entries, you are ready to calculate cost of goods sold as it is done using the periodic inventory method—with all factors accounted for. Using the data in Exhibit 6-3 for All Seasons Equipment Company and adding $350 paid for freight and a purchase discount of $50, the Cost of Goods Sold calculation is:

	Units	Costs
Beginning inventory	32 snowblowers	$6,400
Gross purchases	140 snowblowers[1]	$35,000
Less: Purchase returns	(5 snowblowers)	(1,250)
Purchase discounts (2/10, n/30)		(50)[2]
Add: Freight-in		350
Net purchases....................................	135 snowblowers	$34,050
Total snowblowers available for sale	167 snowblowers	$40,450
Less: Ending inventory	20 snowblowers	5,000
Cost of goods sold...............................	147 snowblowers	$35,450

[1] 100 on Aug. 2, 30 on Aug. 8, and 10 on Sept. 4.
[2] Assumes a discount only on the 10 snowblowers purchased on Sept. 4 (.02 × $2,500 = $50)

The cost of goods sold of $35,450 calculated here differs from the cost of goods sold of $35,150 reported in Exhibit 6-3 when using the perpetual method because here we added in a freight cost of $350 and deducted a purchase discount of $50. In that exhibit, we did not consider these factors; if they had been considered, the cost of goods sold amounts would be equal ($35,150 + $350 − $50 = $35,450).

In this cost of goods sold calculation, purchase discounts and purchase returns are subtracted from purchases, and freight-in is added to purchases to derive net purchases. Net purchases is then added to the beginning inventory amount to derive total cost of snowblowers available for sale. Then the cost of ending inventory is subtracted to arrive at cost of goods sold.

The perpetual and periodic methods should always result in the same balance for cost of goods sold. With the perpetual method, there is a Cost of Goods Sold account; with the periodic method, the preceding calculations must be made. This cost of goods sold calculation can be included on the income statement as a separate section after net sales, or the cost of goods sold amount only may be included on the income statement. Today, most companies merely report the total cost of goods sold number on their income statement.

Taking a Physical Count of Inventory

Whether a company is using the perpetual or the periodic method, the physical count is an important part of accounting for inventory. With the perpetual inventory method, the physical count confirms that the amount entered in the accounting records is accurate, or it highlights shortages and clerical errors. If, for example, employees have been stealing inventory, the theft will show up as a difference between the balance in the Inventory account and the amount physically counted. With the periodic inventory method, the physical count is the only way to determine the amount of ending inventory. Shortages and clerical errors will not be discovered unless they are significant.

A physical count of inventory involves two steps.

1. **Quantity Count** In most companies, physically counting all inventory is a time-consuming activity. Because sales transactions and merchandise deliveries can complicate matters, inventory is usually counted on holidays or after the close of business on the inventory day. An inventory form, such as the one shown in Exhibit 6-5, may be used. Special care must be taken to ensure that all inventory owned, wherever its location, is counted and that inventory on hand but not owned is not counted.

2. **Inventory Costing** When the physical count has been completed, each kind of merchandise is assigned a unit cost—generally, the amount paid for the merchandise. (In Chapter 7, we will explain the procedures used for assigning unit costs.) The quantity of each kind of merchandise is multiplied by its unit cost to determine the dollar value of the inventory. These amounts are then added to obtain the total ending inventory for the business. With both the periodic and perpetual methods, this is the amount reported as Inventory on the balance sheet. With the perpetual method, the ending balance in the Inventory account may have to be adjusted for any

Exhibit 6-5

All Seasons Equipment Company
Physical Inventory Form

Date of Inventory 12/31/94   Taken by NSA

Type of Merchandise	Date Purchased	Quantity on Hand	Unit Cost	Inventory Amount
Snowblowers, Model 100	8/8 and 9/4	20	$250	$ 5,000
Snowblowers, Model 200	9/15	8	300	2,400
Lawnmowers, Model 300	6/12	14	225	3,150
Total				$87,000

shortages discovered. The entry, as you will recall, involves a credit to the Inventory account and a debit to the expense account called Inventory Shrinkage.

Closing Entries for Cost of Goods Sold

In Chapter 5, we discussed the closing entries for several revenue and expense accounts. Since cost of goods sold is also an income statement account, it must be closed at the end of each accounting period. When the perpetual inventory method is used, Cost of Goods Sold is closed simply by crediting the account for its balance and debiting Retained Earnings directly or by debiting Income Summary, which is later closed to Retained Earnings. If in 1994, All Seasons Equipment Company had used the perpetual inventory method, as shown in Exhibit 6-3, the closing entry would be:

```
Income Summary (or Retained Earnings)..................... 35,150
    Cost of Goods Sold ........................................      35,150
To close the Cost of Goods Sold account for 1994.
```

This amount represents the sale of 32 snowblowers that cost $200 each and 115 snowblowers (116 less 1 returned) that cost $250 each.

With the periodic inventory method, the closing entries are somewhat more complex. As you will recall, when sales or purchases are recorded, no entry is made to the Inventory account. Instead, purchases of merchandise are recorded in an account called Purchases, and sales of merchandise are recorded only in the Accounts Receivable and Sales Revenue accounts. Therefore, for the periodic method, closing entries are needed to adjust the inventory balance and to close the Purchases, Purchase Discounts, Purchase Returns and Allowances, and Freight-In accounts. The closing entries for the model 100 snowblower line of All Seasons Equipment Company would involve three entries. The first entry, which eliminates the beginning balance of inventory from the accounts, would be:

Chapter 6 *Income Measurement and Reporting*

> Income Summary 6,400
>   Inventory (amount of beginning inventory, 32 units at $200)   6,400
> *To eliminate the beginning inventory balance.*

Since no debits or credits were made to the Inventory account during the period, this entry brings the inventory balance to zero. The second entry establishes the ending amount of inventory (per the physical count) in the Inventory account. That entry is:

> Inventory (amount of ending inventory, 20 units at $250)   5,000
>   Income Summary   5,000
> *To establish the ending inventory balance, per the 12/31/94 physical count, in the Inventory account.*

After the second entry, the inventory balance is correct, but the Income Summary account has been adjusted only for the beginning and ending inventory balances. It is now necessary to close the Purchases and Purchase Returns accounts. This entry would be:

> Income Summary   33,750
> Purchase Returns and Allowances   1,250
>   Purchases   35,000
> *To close the Purchases and Purchase Returns and Allowances accounts to Income Summary.*

In this entry, Purchase Returns and Allowances, which has a credit balance, is debited, and Purchases, which has a debit balance, is credited. This entry not only closes (brings to a zero balance) the Purchases and Purchase Returns accounts, it also transfers the net amount of purchases to the Income Summary account.

An examination of these three entries shows that the net balance closed to Income Summary is $35,150, the same amount obtained with the perpetual inventory method. The perpetual method simply reached that figure through a different route—using a Cost of Goods Sold account.

Income Summary
(Periodic Inventory Effects Only)

Beginning Inventory; see entry above	6,400	Ending Inventory; see entry above	5,000
Purchases; see entry above	33,750		
	$35,150		

Purchase discounts and transportation costs were not included in Exhibit 6-3. Under the perpetual inventory method, these items are recorded directly in the Inventory account and do not require any closing entries. With the periodic method, when there are balances in the Purchase Discounts and Freight-In accounts, these accounts have to be closed to Income Summary. Again, assuming discounts on purchases of $50 and transportation costs of $350, the entries to close these accounts would be:

Purchase Discounts	50	
Income Summary		50
To close the Purchase Discounts account to Income Summary.		
Income Summary	350	
Freight-In		350
To close the Freight-In account to Income Summary.		

Purchase Discounts, which has a credit balance, is debited in the closing process. Freight-In, which has a debit balance, is credited to bring that account balance to zero.

At the end of an accounting period, both the perpetual and the periodic inventory methods result in the same amounts for cost of goods sold and ending inventory. This is because both methods recognize inventory as an expense only when it is sold. The difference between the two methods is in the accounts used and in the timing of the entries to Inventory. With the perpetual method, entries are made to the Inventory and Cost of Goods Sold accounts with each purchase and sales transaction; with the periodic method, adjustments to Inventory and the cost of goods sold calculation are made only at the end of the period.

When using the periodic method, some people prefer to adjust inventory first and then close the purchases-related accounts to a Cost of Goods Sold account, and then close Cost of Goods Sold to Income Summary. Using an intermediate Cost of Goods Sold account is not as common in practice, however.

The importance of properly accounting for all purchases and sales transactions cannot be emphasized too strongly. Both affect cost of goods sold directly, and an error in accounting for these transactions affects income before taxes by the same amount.

Other Operating Expenses

You now know how to account for revenues, which are recognized when earned, and inventory, which becomes an expense only when it is sold. Other operating expenses—such as payments for salaries, advertising, rent, and insurance—must also be accounted for.

As we have already noted, expenses are recognized in accordance with the **matching principle;** that is, all expenses incurred in producing revenues should be identified with the revenues generated, period by period. Obviously, the matching principle is easier to apply to some expenses than to others. For example, sales commissions are easily associated with sales revenue, but the allocation of a building's cost over its useful life is not so closely tied to sales revenue. To solve this problem and still apply the matching principle, compa-

matching principle *the concept that all costs and expenses incurred in generating revenues must be recognized in the same reporting period as the related revenues*

Chapter 6 *Income Measurement and Reporting*

Exhibit 6-7

P & L Company
Income Statement
For the Year Ended December 31, 1994

Revenues:			
Gross sales revenue		$2,500,000	
Less: Sales returns and allowances		(12,000)	
Sales discounts		(13,000)	
Net sales revenue			$2,475,000
Cost of goods sold:			
Beginning inventory		$ 800,000	
Purchases	$1,200,000		
Add freight-in	36,000		
Less: Purchase returns and allowances	(26,000)		
Purchase discounts	(24,000)		
Net purchases		1,186,000	
Cost of goods available for sale		$1,986,000	
Less ending inventory		(900,000)	
Cost of goods sold....................			1,086,000
Gross margin			$1,389,000
Operating expenses:			
Selling expenses:			
Sales salaries expense	$ 200,000		
Sales commissions expense	60,000		
Advertising expense	45,000		
Delivery expense...................	14,000		
Total selling expenses		$ 319,000	
General and administrative expenses:			
Administrative salaries expense	$ 278,000		
Rent expense, office equipment	36,000		
Property tax expense	22,000		
Miscellaneous expenses	8,000		
Total general and administrative expenses		344,000	
Total operating expenses			663,000
Operating income			$ 726,000
Other revenues and expenses:			
Dividend revenue		$ 5,000	
Gain on sale of land		4,000	
Interest expense.....................		(85,000)	
Net other revenues and expenses			(76,000)
Income from operations before taxes ...			$ 650,000
Income taxes on operations (30%)			195,000
Income before extraordinary item			$ 455,000
Extraordinary item:			
Flood loss	$ (100,000)		
Income tax effect (30%)	30,000		(70,000)
Net income			$ 385,000
Earnings per share (100,000 shares outstanding):			
Income before extraordinary item			$4.55
Extraordinary loss....................			(0.70)
Net income			$3.85

goods sold, and operating expenses (which are separated into selling and general and administrative expenses on the income statement) have already been explained. The other revenues and expenses (including gains and losses), extraordinary items, and earnings per share need some clarification.

Other Revenues and Expenses

Other revenues and expenses are those items incurred or earned from activities that are outside of, or peripheral to, the normal operations of a firm. For example, a manufacturing company that receives dividends from its investments in the stock of another firm would show that dividend revenue as "Other Revenues and Expenses." This way, investors can see how much of a firm's revenue is from manufacturing—its major operating activity—and how much is from peripheral activities. The most common items reported in this section are interest and investment revenues and expenses. The Other Revenues and Expenses category also includes gains and losses from the sale of assets other than inventory, such as land and buildings.

Extraordinary Items

extraordinary items non-operating gains and losses that are unusual in nature, infrequent in occurrence, and material in amount

The **extraordinary items** section of an income statement is reserved for reporting special nonoperating gains and losses. This category is restrictive and includes only those items that are (1) unusual in nature, (2) infrequent in occurrence, and (3) material in amount. They are separated from other revenues and expenses so that readers can identify them as one-time, or nonrecurring, events. Extraordinary items can include losses or gains from floods, fires, earthquakes, and so on. For example, in 1980 when Mount St. Helens erupted, much of the Weyerhaeuser Company's timberlands were adversely affected by the mud slides and flooding. Weyerhaeuser reported an extraordinary loss of $66,700,000 in 1980 to cover standing timber, buildings, equipment, and other damaged items. Certain other types of gains and losses are required by generally accepted accounting principles to be reported as extraordinary items. These involve technical accounting issues that are discussed in more advanced texts.

If a firm has an extraordinary loss, its taxes are lower than they would be on the basis of ordinary operations. P&L Company, for example, actually paid only $165,000 ($195,000 − $30,000) in taxes. On the other hand, if a firm has an extraordinary gain, its taxes are increased. So that the full effect of the gain or loss can be presented, extraordinary items are always shown together with their tax effects so that a net-of-tax amount can be seen. Thus, an income tax expense may appear in two places on the income statement: below operating income before taxes and in the extraordinary items section.

Earnings per Share

earnings per share (EPS) net income divided by the average number of shares of stock outstanding during the period

As noted in Chapter 2, a company is required to show **earnings per share (EPS)** on the income statement. If extraordinary items are included on the income statement, a firm will report EPS figures on income before extraordinary items, on extraordinary items, and on net income. Earnings per share is calculated by dividing a firm's income by the average number of shares of stock

Chapter 6 *Income Measurement and Reporting*

BUSINESS ENVIRONMENT ESSAY
Are Earnings Up or Down?

When you look at the earnings-per-share figure on a company's income statement, can you be certain you know what it means? No. It depends on who computed the number and how "unusual" items were classified. For example, in a recent year, PepsiCo's earnings were $3.00 per share. According to the *Value Line Investments Survey,* the company's earnings had declined 7 percent from $3.23 in the preceding year. But readers of *Standard & Poor's Stock Reports* saw a gain of 25 percent from $2.40.

Why did *Value Line* and *S & P* report different figures? Simply explained, they treated a nonrecurring item—the write-down of the assets of some of PepsiCo's foreign bottling plants that, because of improper accounting techniques, had been overvalued—differently. *Value Line* decided that such nonrecurring items should be excluded from a company's earnings figure. *S & P,* on the other hand, left them in.

Whenever a company becomes involved in major litigation, discovers an accounting problem, or does anything out of the ordinary, the question arises: *Should this item be considered extraordinary?* If it is, the income statement shows separate per-share figures for the extraordinary item and for operating earnings. Otherwise, the number is generally lumped in with operating income. Investors are left to their own devices to figure out what's going on.

At one time, this was less of a problem. Under old accounting rules, almost all unusual items were classified as extraordinary and reported accordingly. Several years ago, however, accountants decided to cut down on the use of the extraordinary item classification. To qualify as extraordinary, an item now must be both "unusual and infrequent."

This would seem to be a reasonable requirement, until you consider that many different meanings can be applied to those two simple-sounding words. In PepsiCo's case, the write-off would seem to qualify as an extraordinary item. But PepsiCo's accountants apparently reasoned that write-offs in general, regardless of the reason, are a common and frequent occurrence. So, the write-off was not considered extraordinary.

Source: Adapted from *Forbes,* May 21, 1984, p. 186.

---

outstanding during the period. In Exhibit 6-7 it has been assumed that 100,000 shares of stock are outstanding. Earnings-per-share numbers are important because they allow potential investors to compare the profitability of all firms, whether large or small. Thus, the performance of a company earning $200,000 and having 200,000 shares of stock outstanding can be compared with the performance of a company that earns $60,000 and has 30,000 shares outstanding.

Chapter 6 *Income Measurement and Reporting*

Appendix

Using a Work Sheet in Accounting for Inventory

In Chapter 5, we explained how adjustments are presented on a work sheet so that account balances can be extended to the financial statements. The Inventory and Cost of Goods Sold accounts were omitted because we had not yet covered the accounting for inventory. Exhibit 6-8 shows how inventory accounts would be handled on a work sheet when the perpetual method is used; Exhibit 6-9 illustrates the periodic method.

You will note that the work sheet for the perpetual method shows three adjusting entries. Entry (a) is an adjustment to the Prepaid Insurance account, showing that $200 of the insurance coverage has expired, entry (b) accounts for a $2,000 shortage of inventory found when the physical count was taken ($82,000 recorded in inventory, $80,000 counted), and entry (c) records additional income tax expense of $5,000 for the period. If no shortage of inventory had been found, neither the Inventory nor the Cost of Goods Sold accounts would have to be adjusted because their balances would properly reflect the amount of inventory in the warehouse and the quantity sold during the period.

When the periodic method is used, the Inventory account must be adjusted, and the Purchases, Purchase Discounts, Purchase Returns and Allowances, and Freight-In accounts must be considered. With the exception of Inventory, all these accounts are treated the same way as revenue and expense accounts; that is, they are extended to the income statement columns on the work sheet. With Inventory, an adjusting entry is needed to eliminate the beginning balance and set up the ending balance.

Also with the periodic method, there is no shortage to account for because the company has not made any entries in the Inventory account during the period and has no total to indicate the amount that should be on hand. All that is known is that the ending inventory is $80,000 and the remainder was either sold, stolen, or misplaced. As we discussed in the chapter, the only entries relating to inventory required for the periodic method are closing entries.

After the trial balance columns have been totaled, the adjustments entered, and the equality of the columns proved, the balances are extended to the adjusted trial balance and to the income statement and balance sheet columns. As before, each account balance is cross-footed, and the net amount is entered in the adjusted trial balance columns. The only exception to this rule is that both the debit and the credit adjustments to Income Summary are extended to the same columns in the adjusted trial balance and income statement. The reason for this exception is that both the beginning and the ending inventory amounts are needed to prepare the cost of goods sold section of the income statement.

As was the case in Chapter 5, net income is determined as the difference between the debit and credit subtotal columns of the income statement and balance sheet. In this case, the company earned a net income of $17,800.

Exhibit 6-8 Work Sheet for a Company Using the Perpetual Inven-

Account Titles	Trial Balance Debits	Trial Balance Credits	Adjustments Debits	Adjustments Credits
Cash	42,100			
Accounts Receivable	35,000			
Prepaid Insurance	3,000			(a) 200
Inventory Dec. 31, 1994	82,000			(b) 2,000
Equipment	65,000			
Accum. Depr.—Equipment		15,000		
Accounts Payable		14,000		
Notes Payable		30,000		
Wages Payable		5,000		
Income Taxes Payable		6,000		(c) 5,000
Capital Stock		20,000		
Retained Earnings		112,100		
Sales Revenue		152,000		
Sales Discounts	2,000			
Cost of Goods Sold	100,000			
Expenses (not detailed)	25,000			
Insurance Expense			(a) 200	
Inventory Shrinkage			(b) 2,000	
Income Tax Expense			(c) 5,000	
	354,100	354,100	7,200	7,200
Net Income				

Chapter 6 *Income Measurement and Reporting*

tory Method

Adjusted Trial Balance		Income Statement		Balance Sheet	
Debits	Credits	Debits	Credits	Debits	Credits
42,100				42,100	
35,000				35,000	
2,800				2,800	
80,000				80,000	
65,000				65,000	
	15,000				15,000
	14,000				14,000
	30,000				30,000
	5,000				5,000
	11,000				11,000
	20,000				20,000
	112,100				112,100
	152,000		152,000		
2,000		2,000			
100,000		100,000			
25,000		25,000			
200		200			
2,000		2,000			
5,000		5,000			
359,100	359,100	134,200	152,000	224,900	207,100
		17,800			17,800
		152,000	152,000	224,900	224,900

Exhibit 6-9 Work Sheet for a Company Using the Periodic Inven-

Account Titles	Trial Balance Debits	Trial Balance Credits	Adjustments Debits	Adjustments Credits
Cash	42,100			
Accounts Receivable	35,000			
Prepaid Insurance	3,000			(a) 200
Inventory, January 1, 1994	70,000		(b) 80,000	(b) 70,000
Equipment	65,000			
Accum. Depr.—Equipment		15,000		
Accounts Payable		14,000		
Notes Payable		30,000		
Wages Payable		5,000		
Income Taxes Payable		6,000		(c) 5,000
Capital Stock		20,000		
Retained Earnings		112,100		
Sales Revenue		152,000		
Sales Discounts	2,000			
Purchases	114,000			
Purchase Returns & Allowances		3,000		
Transportation In	1,000			
Expenses (not detailed)	25,000			
Insurance Expense			(a) 200	
Income Tax Expense			(c) 5,000	
Income Summary			(b) 70,000	(b) 80,000
	357,100	357,100	155,200	155,200
Net Income				

Chapter 6 *Income Measurement and Reporting*

tory Method

| Adjusted Trial Balance || Income Statement || Balance Sheet ||
Debits	Credits	Debits	Credits	Debits	Credits
42,100				42,100	
35,000				35,000	
2,800				2,800	
80,000				80,000	
65,000				65,000	
	15,000				15,000
	14,000				14,000
	30,000				30,000
	5,000				5,000
	11,000				11,000
	20,000				20,000
	112,100				112,100
	152,000		152,000		
2,000		2,000			
114,000		114,000			
	3,000		3,000		
1,000		1,000			
25,000		25,000			
200		200			
5,000		5,000			
70,000	80,000	70,000	80,000		
442,100	442,100	217,200	235,000	224,900	207,100
		17,800			17,800
		235,000	235,000	224,900	224,900

Review of Learning Objectives

Objective 1
Understand economic, cash-basis, and accrual-basis income. Economic income is a concept based on the measurement of wealth. Because of such factors as changes in asset values, this concept is not used in practice to determine periodic income.

The two standard ways of measuring income for financial accounting purposes are cash-basis and accrual-basis historical cost. Each has its advantages and disadvantages, but the accrual-basis historical cost method is the one most commonly used for preparing the general-purpose financial statements.

Objective 2
Explain the accounting for revenue and revenue-related accounts. In general, revenues are recognized when the earnings process has been substantially completed and when an exchange has taken place. Revenue transactions can be straightforward or can involve complications, such as sales discounts, sales returns and allowances, or uncollectible credit sales.

Objective 3
Contrast periodic and perpetual inventory methods. The cost of goods sold section of an income statement reports the cost of the merchandise sold during a period. Inventory and cost of goods sold can be accounted for using either of two methods: perpetual or periodic. Although the accounting for each method is different, both produce the same ending balances for inventory and cost of goods sold. The differences between the two methods are in the control they provide over inventory and the amount of clerical effort required to maintain the inventory records. No adjustments are made to the inventory records during the year when the periodic inventory method is used. With the perpetual inventory method, inventory is adjusted for every sales or purchase transaction. Both methods take into consideration such things as discounts on purchases, returns of merchandise purchased, and the cost of transporting goods intended for resale into the firm.

Objective 4
Prepare a comprehensive accrual-basis income statement. The income statement is the means of reporting net income. Its major sections are revenues, cost of goods sold, operating expenses, other revenues and expenses, extraordinary items, net income, and earnings per share.

In addition to cost of goods sold expense, businesses incur many other expenses. With accrual accounting, these are recognized as they are incurred, not when they are paid for. Monies paid prior to the incurrence of an expense are called prepaid expenses. Expenses incurred before they are paid for give rise to liabilities. On the income statement, financial and other nonoperating revenues and expenses are classified separately. The income statement is not complete until all extraordinary items and earnings-per-share amounts have been included.

Key Terms and Concepts

account receivable *(211)*
accrual-basis accounting *(208)*
cash-basis accounting *(207)*
contra account *(212)*
cost of goods sold *(214)*
earnings per share *(230)*
economic income *(206)*
expenses *(214)*
extraordinary items *(230)*
Freight-In *(222)*
gross margin *(214)*

gross sales *(213)*
inflation *(210)*
inventory *(207)*
matching principle *(226)*
multiple-step income statement *(214)*
net sales *(213)*
periodic inventory method *(218)*
perpetual inventory method *(215)*
purchase discount *(218)*

Purchase Returns and Allowances *(222)*
Purchases *(218)*
revenue recognition principle *(210)*
revenues *(210)*
sales discount *(211)*
Sales Returns and Allowances *(213)*
single-step income statement *(214)*

Chapter 6 Income Measurement and Reporting

Review Problem

The Income Statement

From the following information prepare, in good form, an income statement for Neil Corporation for the year ended December 31, 1994. Assume that there are 200,000 shares of stock outstanding.

Sales Returns and Allowances	$ 50,000
Sales Discounts	70,000
Gross Sales Revenue	9,000,000
Flood Loss	80,000
Income Taxes on Operations	500,000
Administrative Salaries Expense	360,000
Sales Salaries Expense	800,000
Rent Expense (General and Administrative)	32,000
Utilities Expense (General and Administrative)	4,000
Supplies Expense (General and Administrative)	16,000
Delivery Expense (Selling)	6,300
Payroll Tax Expense (Selling)	6,000
Automobile Expense (General and Administrative)	3,800
Insurance Expense (General and Administrative)	34,000
Advertising Expense (Selling)	398,000
Interest Revenue	6,000
Interest Expense	92,000
Insurance Expense (Selling)	7,000
Entertainment Expense (Selling)	7,200
Miscellaneous Selling Expenses	15,000
Miscellaneous General and Administrative Expenses	10,800
Purchases	6,000,000
Purchase Discounts	30,000
Beginning Inventory	200,000
Ending Inventory	210,000
Purchase Returns and Allowances	20,000
Freight-In	10,000
Tax rate applicable to flood loss	30%

Solution

1. The first step in preparing a comprehensive income statement is classifying items, as follows:

Revenue Accounts

Sales Discounts	$ 70,000
Sales Returns and Allowances	50,000
Gross Sales Revenue	9,000,000

General and Administrative Expense Accounts

Administrative Salaries Expense	$ 360,000
Rent Expense	32,000
Utilities Expense	4,000
Supplies Expense	16,000
Automobile Expense	3,800
Insurance Expense	34,000
Miscellaneous General and Administrative Expenses	10,800

Miscellaneous Accounts

Income Taxes on Operations .... $ 500,000

Extraordinary Item Accounts

Flood Loss .... $ 80,000
Tax Rate 30%

Cost of Goods Sold Accounts

Purchases $6,000,000
Purchase Discounts 30,000
Beginning Inventory 200,000
Ending Inventory 210,000
Purchase Returns and Allowances 20,000
Freight-In 10,000

Selling Expense Accounts

Sales Salaries Expense .... $ 800,000
Delivery Expense 6,300
Payroll Tax Expense 6,000
Advertising Expense 398,000
Insurance Expense 7,000
Entertainment Expense 7,200
Miscellaneous Selling Expenses 15,000

Other Revenue and Expense Accounts

Interest Expense .... $ 92,000
Interest Revenue 6,000

2. Once the accounts are classified, the income statement is prepared by including the accounts in the following format:

          Net Sales Revenue (Gross Sales Revenue − Sales Returns and Allowances − Sales Discounts)
    − Cost of Goods Sold [Beginning Inventory + Net Purchases (Gross Purchases + Freight-In − Purchase Returns and Allowances − Purchase Discounts) − Ending Inventory]
    = Gross Margin
    − Selling Expenses
    − General and Administrative Expenses
    = Income from Operations
    +/− Other Revenues and Expenses (add Net Revenues, subtract Net Expenses)
    = Income Before Taxes
    − Income Taxes on Operations
    = Net Income Before Extraordinary Items
    +/− Extraordinary Items (add Extraordinary Gains, subtract Extraordinary Losses, net of applicable taxes)
    = Net Income

3. After net income has been computed, earnings per share is calculated and added to the bottom of the statement. It is important that the proper heading be included.

Neil Corporation
Income Statement
For the Year Ended December 31, 1994

Revenues:			
Gross sales revenue		$9,000,000	
Less: Sales returns and allowances		(50,000)	
Sales discounts		(70,000)	
Net sales revenue			$8,880,000
Cost of goods sold:			
Beginning inventory		$ 200,000	
Purchases	$6,000,000		
Less: Purchase returns and allowances	(20,000)		
Purchase discounts	(30,000)		
Plus freight-in	10,000	5,960,000	
Cost of goods available for sale		$6,160,000	
Less ending inventory		(210,000)	
Cost of goods sold			5,950,000
Gross margin			$2,930,000
Operating expenses:			
Selling expenses:			
Sales salaries expense	$ 800,000		
Delivery expense	6,300		
Payroll tax expense	6,000		
Advertising expense	398,000		
Insurance expense	7,000		
Entertainment expense	7,200		
Miscellaneous expenses	15,000		
Total selling expenses		$1,239,500	
General and administrative expenses:			
Administrative salaries expense	$ 360,000		
Rent expense	32,000		
Utilities expense	4,000		
Supplies expense	16,000		
Automobile expense	3,800		
Insurance expense	34,000		
Miscellaneous expenses	10,800		
Total and general and administrative expenses		460,600	
Total operating expenses			1,700,100
Operating income			$1,229,900
Other revenues and expenses:			
Interest revenue		$ 6,000	
Interest expense		(92,000)	
Total other expenses and revenues			(86,000)
Income from operations before taxes			$1,143,900
Income taxes on operations			500,000
Net income before extraordinary item			$ 643,900
Extraordinary item:			
Flood loss		$ (80,000)	
Income tax effect (30%)		24,000	(56,000)
Net income			$ 587,900
Earnings per share:			
Before extraordinary items		$3.22	($643,900 ÷ 200,000 shares)
Extraordinary loss		(0.28)	($56,000 ÷ 200,000 shares)
Net income		$2.94	($587,900 ÷ 200,000 shares)

Discussion Questions

1. Why is economic income so difficult to measure?
2. When is it theoretically possible to precisely determine the income of a firm?
3. When should revenues be recognized and reported?
4. When should expenses be recognized and reported?
5. Why is it usually important to take advantage of purchase discounts?
6. Why is it important to have separate accounts for Sales Returns and Allowances and Sales Discounts? Wouldn't it be much easier to directly reduce the Sales Revenue account for these adjustments?
7. Under what conditions will the dollar amount of cost of goods sold for a period be equal to the dollar purchases made during that period?
8. Why is it necessary to physically count inventory when the perpetual inventory method is being used?
9. Which inventory method (perpetual or periodic) provides the better control over a firm's inventory?
10. Is the accounting for purchase discounts and purchase returns the same with the perpetual and the periodic inventory methods? If not, what are the differences?
11. Are the costs of transporting inventory into and out of a firm treated the same way? If not, what are the differences?
12. What adjusting entries to the Inventory account are required when the perpetual inventory method is used?
13. What is the difference between a prepaid expense and an expense?

Exercises

E6-1
Recording Sales Transactions—Periodic and Perpetual Inventory Methods

On June 24, 1994, Hansen Company sold merchandise to Jill Selby for $80,000 with terms 2/10, n/30. On June 30, Selby paid $39,200 on her account. On July 20, Selby paid $24,000 on her account and returned $16,000 of merchandise, claiming that it did not meet contract terms.

1. Assuming that Hansen Company uses the periodic inventory method, record the necessary journal entries on June 24, June 30, and July 20.
2. Assuming that Hansen Company uses the perpetual inventory method, record the necessary journal entries on June 24, June 30, and July 20. The cost of merchandise to Hansen Company is 70 percent of its selling price.

E6-2
Recording Sales Transactions—Periodic and Perpetual Inventory Methods

Lopez Company sold merchandise on account to Atlantic Company for $4,000 on June 3, 1994, with terms 2/10, n/30. On June 7, 1994, Lopez Company received $200 of merchandise back from Atlantic Company and issued a credit memorandum for the appropriate amount. Lopez Company received payment for the balance of the bill on June 21, 1994.

1. Record these events on Lopez Company's books, assuming that the company uses the periodic inventory method.
2. Record these events assuming that Lopez Company uses the perpetual inventory method and that the cost of the merchandise is 60 percent of the selling price.

Chapter 6 *Income Measurement and Reporting* 243

E6-3
Income Statement Calculations

Complete the following cost of goods sold calculations by filling in all missing numbers:

	Company A	Company B	Company C	Company D
Sales revenue	$2,000	(4) $ ___	$480	$1,310
Beginning inventory	200	76	0	600
Purchases	(1) ___	423	480	249
Purchase returns and allowances	(20)	(19)	(0)	(8) (___)
Ending inventory	300	110	(6) ___	195
Cost of goods sold	1,200	370	(7) ___	(9) ___
Gross margin	(2) ___	(5) ___	155	(10) ___
Expenses	108	22	34	129
Net income (or loss)	(3) ___	107	121	546

E6-4
Cost of Goods Sold Calculations

Waukesha Company has provided the following information for the calendar year 1994:

Inventory balance, January 1, 1994	$100,000
Total cost of goods available for sale	300,000
Sales returns and allowances	13,000
Purchase returns and allowances	5,000
Freight-in	2,000
Sales (net of returns and allowances)	407,000
Operating expenses	27,000

The gross sales of Waukesha Company are 160 percent of cost of goods sold. Using the available information, compute the following. (Ignore income taxes.)

1. Gross sales for 1994.
2. Net purchases and gross purchases for 1994.
3. Cost of goods sold for 1994.
4. Inventory balance at December 31, 1994.
5. Gross margin for 1994.
6. Net income for 1994.

E6-5
Preparation of a Partial Income Statement

The following account balances were included in the ledger of Teasdale Company on December 31, 1994.

Name of Account	Balance
Cash	$ 1,600
Freight-In	3,840
Beginning Inventory, January 1, 1994	26,000
Purchases	328,000
Purchase Discounts	800
Purchase Returns and Allowances	4,480
Sales Revenue	372,000
Sales Discounts	1,200
Sales Returns and Allowances	5,600

The amount of inventory on hand on December 31, 1994, was $58,000. Prepare a partial income statement (through gross margin) from the available data for Teasdale Company for the year ended December 31, 1994.

E6-6
Cost of Goods Sold Calculation

The accounts of Meeks Company have the following balances for 1994:

Purchases	$260,000
Inventory, January 1, 1994	40,000
Purchase Returns and Allowances	7,640
Purchase Discounts	880
Freight-In	12,400
Freight-Out (selling expense)	2,400
Cash	4,000

The inventory balance on December 31, 1994, is $48,000.

Using the information given, construct the cost of goods sold section of the income statement for Meeks Company for 1994.

E6-7
Inventory: Adjusting and Closing Entries

In 1994, Deer Company had the following account balances.

Inventory, January 1, 1994	$120,000
Purchases	220,000
Purchase Returns and Allowances	4,000

Deer Company's electronic cash register shows cost of goods sold totaling $240,000. Assuming that a physical count of inventory on December 31, 1994, showed $92,000 of ending inventory, complete the following. (Note that this problem involves $4,000 of inventory shrinkage.)

1. Prepare the closing entries that are needed to adjust the inventory records and close the related purchases accounts, assuming that the periodic inventory method is used.
2. Adjust the inventory records and close the appropriate accounts, assuming that the perpetual inventory method is used but that the information regarding beginning inventory, purchases, and purchase returns and allowances is known.

E6-8
The Effects of Errors in Recording Expenses

An examination of the records of Twin Creeks Company early in 1994 revealed that the following errors and omissions had occurred during 1993 and 1994:

(a) Wages of $1,200 owed to employees at December 31, 1993, were not recognized as an expense in 1993, and were recorded as an expense when paid in 1994.
(b) All office supplies were charged to expense when purchased. Supplies of $300 were overlooked when the appropriate December 31, 1993, adjusting entries were made.
(c) A customer's payment of $500 in December 1993 for merchandise to be delivered in 1994 was recorded as a sale in 1993. No entry was made in 1994 when the goods were actually sold.

(d) Rent for January 1994 of $450 was paid in advance during 1993 and was charged to expense when paid.

Given this information, complete the following two requirements:

1. For each of the four errors state (a) whether 1993 net income would be under- or overstated and by how much and (b) whether 1994 net income would be under- or overstated and by how much.
2. If the reported net incomes for 1993 and 1994 were $20,000 and $30,000, respectively (before adjustment for the errors), what should the amount of net income have been for each of the two years?

E6-9
Completing an Income Statement

Jimmy Slow, the accountant for Parker Supply Company, forgot where he put the accounting records. After searching the premises, he did manage to find the following information for 1993 and 1994. The president of the company has requested comparative financial statements, and Jimmy needs your help in determining the missing numbers before he turns in his report to Mr. Parker.

	1993	1994
Sales revenue	$276,000	(5) $_____
Beginning inventory	65,000	(6) _____
Purchases	(1) _____	214,000
Cost of goods available for sale	273,000	(7) _____
Ending inventory	(2) _____	57,000
Cost of goods sold	224,000	(8) _____
Gross margin	(3) _____	61,000
Expenses	30,000	(9) _____
Income before taxes	(4) _____	24,000

E6-10
Preparing an Income Statement

Willow Company is preparing financial statements for the calendar year 1994. The following totals for each account have been verified as correct:

Office Supplies on Hand	$ 300
Insurance Expense	120
Gross Sales Revenue	6,000
Cost of Goods Sold	3,220
Sales Returns and Allowances	200
Interest Expense	100
Accounts Payable	120
Accounts Receivable	260
Extraordinary Loss	1,080
Selling Expenses	360
Office Supplies Used	80
Cash	300
Revenue from Investments	280
Number of Shares of Capital Stock	90

Prepare an income statement. Assume a 20 percent income tax rate on both income from operations and extraordinary items. Include EPS numbers.

Problem Set A

P6A-1
Different Concepts of Income

Jensen Retail Association is a new store in Bicknell, California, that sells hardware and other merchandise. During 1994, the store had the following information in its records:

(a) Started business on January 2, 1994. On that date, the company purchased a store building at a cost of $160,000. The building is expected to have a 20-year life.
(b) On January 3, 1994, inventory was purchased for $100,000. No other inventory purchases were made during the year.
(c) During the year, the store had the following transactions:
  (1) Sold merchandise that cost $60,000 for $140,000. Collected $120,000 in cash and accepted a receivable for $20,000.
  (2) Paid $44,000 in salaries and other expenses.
(d) All were cash transactions.
(e) On December 31, 1994, it was determined by appraisals that the current values of the store building and the remaining inventory were $200,000 and $52,000, respectively.

Required:
1. Compute the following:
   (a) Cash-basis income (or loss).
   (b) Accrual-basis income (or loss).
2. **Interpretive Question** Which of these net income numbers provides better information regarding the performance of the store during 1994? Why?
3. **Interpretive Question** Does either of these income measurement alternatives reflect the effects of increases or decreases in the values of assets and liabilities caused by inflation, technological advances, and so forth?

P6A-2
Concepts of Income—Cash and Accrual Accounting

SPREADSHEET PROBLEM

During its initial year of operation in 1994, Wells Company had the following transactions:

Sales revenue	$100,000 ($60,000 of which has been collected and $40,000 of which is still in receivables)
Purchases of merchandise	$ 60,000 ($52,000 of which has been paid for, and the remainder of which is still owed at year-end)
Expenses:	
Salaries expense	$ 32,000 ($30,000 of which has been paid)
Utilities expense	$ 2,000 (all of which has been paid)
Rent expense	$ 10,000 (all of which has been paid)
Other purchases (on December 31, 1994):	
Building	$ 22,000 ($5,000 of which has been paid)
Land	$ 6,000 ($2,000 of which has been paid)

Required:
1. Assuming that the amount of ending inventory is $4,000 and that there was no beginning inventory, compute the following:
   (a) Net income (using the currently required method) for 1994. (Ignore income taxes, depreciation, and interest expense.)
   (b) Net cash inflow (or outflow) for 1994.

Chapter 6 *Income Measurement and Reporting*

2. **Interpretive Question** Which of the statements required in part (1) better indicates the performance of the company during 1994?

P6A-3
Selling and Purchasing Transactions

Mercy Lawnmower Shop had the following transactions during the first nine days of March 1994:

March 1	Purchased 10 lawnmowers at $200 each, terms 2/10, n/30.
2	Returned 1 lawnmower to supplier because the frame was bent; received credit memorandum for $200.
5	Sold 5 lawnmowers for $400 each for cash.
8	One of the lawnmowers sold on March 5 was returned because of a defective motor; refunded in cash.
9	Paid supplier the net amount owed for the lawnmowers purchased on March 1.

Required:
1. Journalize these transactions using:
   (a) The periodic inventory method.
   (b) The perpetual inventory method.
2. **Interpretive Question** What types of companies are more likely to use the perpetual inventory method?

P6A-4
Income Statement Analysis

The following information is available for Morris Corporation for the year 1994:

	First Quarter	Second Quarter	Third Quarter	Fourth Quarter	Annual Statement
Revenues	$3,000	$4,000	$4,000	(13)$_____	$15,000
Beginning inventory	(1)_____	(5)_____	300	(14)_____	(24)_____
Purchases	1,000	1,500	2,000	(15)_____	6,500
Purchase discounts	15	(6)_____	(10)_____	(16)_____	100
Purchase returns and allowances	(2)_____	25	15	(17)_____	100
Net purchases	960	1,450	(11)_____	(18)_____	6,300
Cost of goods available for sale	(3)_____	(7)_____	2,250	(19)_____	6,600
Ending inventory	(4)_____	300	250	(20)_____	(25)_____
Cost of goods sold	1,110	(8)_____	2,000	(21)_____	6,200
Gross margin	1,890	2,700	2,000	2,210	8,800
Other expenses	1,500	1,500	(12)_____	(22)_____	5,200
Net income	390	(9)_____	1,000	(23)_____	3,600

Required:
1. Complete the income statement entries given by filling in all missing numbers in each quarter and in the annual statement.
2. **Interpretive Question** Ignoring the numbers and in general terms, if the beginning inventory of the first quarter were overstated by $100, what would be the amount and direction of the over- or understatement of net income in the second quarter?
3. **Interpretive Question** In general terms, if the ending inventory of the second quarter were understated by $200, what would be the amount and direction of the over- or understatement of net income in the third quarter?

P6A-5
Income Statement Calculations

Emco Corporation had the following data for the years 1991–1995:

	1991	1992	1993	1994	1995
Sales	$300,000	$350,000	$400,000	$450,000	$500,000
Beginning inventory	35,000	(5)_____	(10)_____	56,000	(19)_____
Purchases	(1)_____	(6)_____	260,000	240,000	270,000
Purchase discounts	500	1,000	(11)_____	1,500	(20)_____
Goods available for sale	(2)_____	228,000	299,000	(15)_____	(21)_____
Ending inventory	28,000	41,000	(12)_____	(16)_____	65,000
Cost of goods sold	180,000	(7)_____	243,000	237,500	(22)_____
Gross margin	(3)_____	(8)_____	(13)_____	(17)_____	240,000
Selling expenses	(4)_____	48,000	52,000	60,000	(23)_____
Administrative expenses	45,000	56,000	(14)_____	(18)_____	82,000
Net income	$40,000	(9)_____	$47,000	$90,500	$78,000

Required: Provide the missing income statement amounts.

P6A-6
Inventory Adjustment and Closing Entries

During 1994, the W. Whitman Company had the following transactions:

(a) Sold merchandise costing $50,000 for $120,000.
(b) Purchased merchadise costing $44,000.
(c) Returned merchandise costing $4,000 to the supplier.
(d) Received merchandise that was sold for $6,000 (cost $2,600) from dissatisfied customer.

Required: Assume that all are cash transactions and that inventory on hand at January 1, 1994, cost $58,000.

1. Journalize the above transactions using:
   (a) The periodic inventory method.
   (b) The perpetual inventory method.
2. Make all needed adjusting and closing entries related to the inventory and sales at December 31, 1994. (The ending inventory balance can be calculated by posting the perpetual inventory accounts.)

P6A-7
Unifying Concepts: The Income Statement

SOLUTIONS SOFTWARE

Use the following information to prepare an income statement for Fairchild Corporation for the year ending December 31, 1994. You should show separate classifications for revenues, cost of goods sold, gross margin, selling expenses, general and administrative expenses, income from operations, other revenue and expenses, income before taxes, income taxes, and net income. (Hint: Net income is $27,276.)

Sales Returns and Allowances	$ 4,280
Income Tax Expense	26,000
Interest Revenue	2,400
Office Supplies Expense (General and Administrative)	400
Utilities Expense (General and Administrative)	3,980
Office Salaries Expense (General and Administrative)	12,064
Miscellaneous Selling Expenses	460
Insurance Expense (Selling)	1,160
Advertising Expense	6,922
Sales Salaries Expense	40,088
Inventory, December 31, 1994	44,300
Purchases	230,560

Chapter 6 *Income Measurement and Reporting*

Sales Discounts	3,644
Interest Expense	1,170
Miscellaneous General and Administrative Expenses	620
Insurance Expense (General and Administrative)	600
Payroll Tax Expense (General and Administrative)	3,600
Store Supplies Expense (Selling)	800
Delivery Expense (Selling)	2,198
Purchase Discounts	3,050
Inventory, January 1, 1994	79,400
Sales Revenue	395,472
Average number of shares of stock outstanding	10,000

P6A-8
Work Sheet Using the Periodic Inventory Method *(Appendix)*

Flathead Wholesale Inc. uses the periodic inventory method. The work sheet given here has been completed through adjusting entries. A physical count at year-end (12/31/94) showed $65,000 of inventory on hand.

Required: Complete the work sheet. (Ignore income taxes.)

SPREADSHEET PROBLEM

Account Titles	Trial Balance Debits	Trial Balance Credits	Adjustments Debits	Adjustments Credits
Cash	51,400			
Accounts Receivable	22,800			
Prepaid Insurance	600			(a) 500
Inventory, January 1, 1994	60,000		(h) 65,000	(b) 60,000
Equipment	45,000			
Accum. Depreciation—				
Equipment		15,000		
Accounts Payable		16,000		
Interest Payable				(c) 400
Notes Payable—Long Term		20,000		
Capital Stock		100,000		
Retained Earnings		26,000		
Sales Revenue		153,000		
Sales Returns & Allowances	2,000			
Purchases	104,000			
Freight-In	4,000			
Purchase Discounts		2,200		
Operating Expenses				
(not detailed)	40,600			
Insurance Expense			(a) 500	
Interest Expense	1,800		(c) 400	
Income Summary			(b) 60,000	(b) 65,000
	332,200	332,200	125,900	125,900

Problem Set B

P6B-1
Different Concepts of Income

Nobel Corporation is a retail firm that sells videotapes in the home movie market. The company was formed on January 3, 1994, and during 1994 had the following cash transactions:

(a) On January 3, purchased a new building at a cost of $200,000, some furniture at a cost of $80,000, and inventory at a cost of $40,000. The building has a 50-year life and the furniture a 10-year life.
(b) During the year, sold $20,000 (one-half) of its inventory for $50,000, collecting $40,000 in cash with a receivable balance of $10,000, and paid salaries of $20,000. (No other expenses were recorded during the year.)

Required:
1. Given these data, compute:
   (a) Cash-basis income (or loss).
   (b) Accrual-basis income (or loss).
2. **Interpretive Question** Other than at the time of an exchange (sale or other arm's-length transaction), does either of these methods recognize changes in the values of assets and liabilities? Explain.

P6B-2
Net Income and Cash Flows

As the controller for Marywood Enterprises, you have just completed the annual report for 1994 and determined that net income for the year was $20,000. Notwithstanding the company's profitable operations, it is being plagued by a severe cash shortage. Helen Marywood, the company president, has asked you to find the reasons for the company's cash problems. In preparing your report, you discover the following with respect to this year's operation:

(a) Jonathan Corporation, a customer, was unable to pay for merchandise purchased during 1994. As a result, on November 1, 1994, Marywood accepted a 90-day, 15 percent note from Jonathan in the amount of $8,000.
(b) Accounts receivable were $24,000 on January 1, 1994, and $32,000 on December 31, 1994.
(c) Accounts payable were $18,000 on January 1, 1994, and $12,000 on December 31, 1994.
(d) During 1994, the company purchased a new building costing $200,000. Twenty percent of the purchase price was paid in cash, and the balance was borrowed from a local bank. (Ignore interest.) The building has a 40-year life. (One-fortieth of the cost should be expensed each year.)
(e) Inventory on hand totaled $42,000 on January 1, 1994, and $48,000 on December 31, 1994.
(f) Other payables totaled $2,000 on January 1, 1994, and $0 on December 31, 1994.
(g) Prepaid expenses increased $12,000 during 1994.
(h) Rent expense for 1994 of $7,000 was to be paid in 1995.
(i) Dividends paid during 1994 totaled $3,000.

Required:
1. Using this information, compute the net amount of cash inflow or outflow for 1994.
2. **Interpretive Question** Does the company have a critical cash shortage, or does it appear that its negative cash position is only a temporary problem?

P6B-3
Sales and Purchasing Transactions

This problem is designed to show how both the seller and the buyer account for cash discounts. Note the relationship between their entries for the same transaction—one party's sales discount is the other party's purchase discount.

Company R and Company S entered into the following transactions. Both companies use the periodic inventory method.

(a) Company R sold merchandise to Company S for $40,000, terms 2/10, n/30.
(b) Prior to payment, Company S returned $3,000 of the merchandise for credit.
(c) Company S paid Company R in full within the discount period.
(d) Company S paid Company R in full after the discount period.

Required:
1. Prepare journal entries to record the transactions for Company R (the seller).
2. Prepare journal entries to record the transactions for Company S (the buyer).

P6B-4
Income Statement Analysis

The following table represents portions of the income statements of United Company for the years 1992–1994:

	1992	1993	1994
Gross sales revenue	$25,800	(9) $_____	$42,000
Sales discounts	100	100	–0–
Sales returns and allowances	700	200	–0–
Net sales revenue	(1) _____	(10) _____	42,000
Beginning inventory	(2) _____	8,000	(15) _____
Purchases	15,000	(11) _____	24,800
Purchase discounts	500	300	700
Freight-in	500	–0–	(16) _____
Cost of goods available for sale	(3) _____	25,000	29,000
Ending inventory	(4) _____	(12) _____	3,800
Cost of goods sold	(5) _____	(13) _____	(17) _____
Gross margin	(6) _____	14,000	(18) _____
Selling expenses	(7) _____	(14) _____	4,000
General and administrative expenses	3,000	3,200	(19) _____
Income before taxes	4,000	8,000	9,000
Income taxes	(8) _____	4,000	4,500
Net income	2,000	4,000	(20) _____

Required: Fill in the missing numbers. Assume that gross margin is 40 percent of net sales revenue.

P6B-5
Cost of Goods Sold Calculations

The following data are available for 5 companies.

	Company A	Company B	Company C	Company D	Company E
Beginning inventory	$14,000	$24,800	(5) _____	(7) _____	$19,200
Purchases	26,500	(3) _____	43,000	89,500	(9) _____
Purchase returns and allowances	(1) _____	1,000	1,800	200	2,200
Cost of goods available for sale	40,100	(4) _____	56,300	(8) _____	81,500
Ending inventory	(2) _____	22,200	15,200	28,000	(10) _____
Cost of goods sold	31,400	67,200	(6) _____	93,400	68,400

Required: Complete the cost of goods sold sections for the 5 companies.

P6B-6
Inventory Closing Entries

In 1994, Linder Company had the following account balances:

Inventory, January 1, 1994	$360,000
Purchases	660,000
Purchase Returns and Allowances	12,000

Required:
1. Make the following required closing entries for the inventory-related accounts as of December 31, 1994, assuming the periodic inventory method:
   (a) Eliminate the beginning inventory balance.
   (b) Set up the ending inventory balance, assuming that sales revenue was $1,220,000 and cost of goods sold is 60 percent of the selling price.
   (c) Close the Purchases and Purchase Returns and Allowances accounts.
2. Suppose the company had been using the perpetual method instead of the periodic method and that cost of goods sold had a year-end balance of $720,000. Given the information in (1), how much inventory shrinkage was there?
3. Make the following adjusting and closing entries, assuming the perpetual inventory method:
   (a) Account for the shrinkage.
   (b) Close the Inventory Shrinkage and Cost of Goods Sold accounts.

P6B-7
Unifying Concepts: The Income Statement

From the following information, prepare an income statement for Notem Incorporated for the year ended December 31, 1994. (Hint: Net income is $119,100.) Assume that there are 10,000 shares of capital stock outstanding.

Gross Sales Revenue	$3,625,000
Income Tax Expense	140,000
Cost of Goods Sold	2,415,000
Sales Salaries Expense	410,000
Rent Expense (Selling)	16,000
Payroll Tax Expense (Selling)	3,100
Entertainment Expense (Selling)	2,000
Miscellaneous Selling Expenses	7,800
Miscellaneous General and Administrative Expenses	5,400
Automobile Expense (Selling)	3,500
Insurance Expense (General and Administrative)	1,900
Interest Expense	46,000
Interest Revenue	3,000
Sales Returns and Allowances	10,000
Advertising and Promotion Expense	199,000
Insurance Expense (Selling)	17,000
Delivery Expense (Selling)	3,100
Office Supplies Used (General and Administrative)	8,000
Utilities Expense (General and Administrative)	1,100
Administrative Salaries Expense	180,000
Fire Loss (net of tax)	40,000

P6B-8
Work Sheet Using the Perpetual Inventory Method (Appendix)

Nickel Retail Company, which uses the perpetual inventory method, is completing the year-end accounting work as of December 31, 1994. The work sheet given here has been completed through adjusting entries.

Required: Complete the work sheet. (Ignore income taxes.)

Chapter 6 Income Measurement and Reporting

Account Titles	Trial Balance Debits	Trial Balance Credits	Adjustments Debits	Adjustments Credits
Cash	84,200			
Accounts Receivable	76,000			
Inventory, December 31, 1994	160,000			(c) 1,000
Prepaid Insurance	4,000			(b) 300
Equipment	130,000			
Accum. Depreciation— Equipment		30,000		
Accounts Payable		28,000		
Notes Payable		66,000		
Wages Payable		10,000		
Interest Payable		6,000		(a) 400
Capital Stock		40,000		
Retained Earnings		224,200		
Sales Revenue		200,000		
Sales Discounts	4,000			
Cost of Goods Sold	96,000			
Expenses (not detailed)	50,000			
Interest Expense			(a) 400	
Insurance Expense			(b) 300	
Inventory Shrinkage			(c) 1,000	
	604,200	604,200	1,700	1,700

Business Analysis Case 1 Juan Alvarez

Juan Alvarez owns and operates a small furniture store that specializes in sofas and couches. He has made a profit in each of the last three years, but those profits are decreasing, and he is having real cash shortages. Customers are complaining that Juan's selection of couches is not as good as it used to be, but Juan does not have enough cash to restock his showroom. In an attempt to help him understand his problem, you have gathered the following data:

		1992	1993	1994
1.	Number of couches sold	15	13	11
2.	Average sales price	$ 500	$ 550	$ 600
3.	Number of couches purchased	14	12	10
4.	Average purchase price	$ 350	$ 450	$ 550
5.	Operating expenses (other than cost of goods sold and taxes)	$1,500	$1,000	$ 800
6.	Beginning inventory	6 @ $200 each		
7.	Income taxes (percentage of profits)	40%	40%	40%
8.	Amount taken out of business by Juan Alvarez	$ 450	$ 450	$ 450

Note that though Juan's purchase price of couches is increasing each year, his selling prices are also increasing.

Required:
1. Prepare income statements for each of the three years for Juan's furniture store. Assume that Juan sells all the $200 couches in beginning inventory before selling the $350 couches, the $350 couches before the $450 ones, and so on.
2. How many couches does Juan have in ending inventory?
3. Prepare cash-basis income statements, assuming that all of Juan's purchase and sales transactions are for cash.
4. What is the cause of Juan's cash shortages?

Business Analysis Case 2 *General Motors Corporation*

SPREADSHEET PROBLEM

Shown here are the income statements for General Motors Corporation for three recent years.

General Motors Corporation
Comparative Income Statement
(Dollars in Millions)

	Year 3	Year 2	Year 1
Net sales and revenues:			
Manufactured products	$95,268.4	$83,699.7	$74,581.6
Computer systems services	1,103.3	190.2	—
Total net sales and revenues	$96,371.7	$83,889.9	$74,581.6
Cost and expenses:			
Cost of sales	$81,654.6	$70,217.9	$60,718.8
Selling, general and administrative expenses	4,294.2	4,003.0	3,234.0
Depreciation of real estate, plants and equipment	2,777.9	2,663.2	2,569.7
Amortization of special tools	3,083.3	2,236.7	2,549.9
Amortization of intangible assets	347.3	69.1	.8
Total costs and expenses	$92,157.3	$79,189.9	$69,073.2
Operating income	$ 4,214.4	$ 4,700.0	$ 5,508.4
Other income less income deductions—net	1,299.2	1,713.5	815.8
Interest expense	(892.3)	(909.2)	(1,325.7)
Income before income taxes	$ 4,621.3	$ 5,504.3	$ 4,971.5

Chapter 6 *Income Measurement and Reporting*

	Year 3	Year 2	Year 1
United States, foreign and other income taxes	1,630.3	1,805.1	2,223.8
Income after income taxes	$ 2,991.0	$ 3,699.2	$ 2,747.7
Equity in earnings of nonconsolidated subsidiaries and associates (dividends received amounted to $100.5 in year 3, $706.1 in year 2 and $757.3 in year 1)	1,008.0	817.3	982.5
Net income	$ 3,999.0	$ 4,516.5	$ 3,730.2

Required: Based on these income statements, answer the following questions:
1. What was General Motors Corporation's gross margin for each of the three years?
2. If gross margin is approximately equal to markup, what is the percentage of cost that General Motors marked up its cars in the three years?
3. Was the percentage increase in sales greater from year 1 to year 2 or from year 2 to year 3? How about the percentage increase (decrease) in income?

Business Analysis Case 3 *Kroger Company*

The following are the sales, merchandise costs, and earnings data from Kroger Company for eight recent quarters:

	Sales (millions)		Merchandise Costs (millions)		Net Income (millions)	
	Year 2	Year 1	Year 2	Year 1	Year 2	Year 1
1st Quarter	$ 3,823	$ 3,633	$ 2,933	$ 2,787	$ 31.5	$ 18.8
2nd Quarter	3,991	3,796	3,042	2,886	46.7	43.2
3rd Quarter	5,061	4,623	3,872	3,549	45.0	38.6
4th Quarter	4,249	3,871	3,233	2,954	57.6	56.0
Total	$17,124	$15,923	$13,079	$12,176	$180.8	$156.6

The 1st, 2nd, and 4th quarters include 12 weeks of operating data, whereas the 3rd quarter includes 16 weeks.

Required: Based on these data, answer the following questions about Kroger, the second largest food retailer in the United States:

1. What was the average percentage markup on cost of merchandise during Year 2 and Year 1?
2. During which quarter in Year 2 and Year 1 were weekly sales the highest? The lowest? What do you think were the reasons?
3. What is the percentage of net income to sales in Year 2 and Year 1?
4. Do you think the markup and profit percentages calculated in requirements 1 and 3 are high compared to a furniture retailer? If food retailer markups are lower, how can they be as profitable as other types of retailers with higher markups?

Business Analysis Case 4 *Grumman Corporation*

Grumman Corporation is a defense contractor, manufacturing weapons for the armed services. Selected data from three recent years' financial statements are presented here (in thousands of dollars except per share data).

	Year 3	Year 2	Year 1
Provision for federal income taxes	$ 47,500	$ 70,500	$ 72,000
Interest expense	29,413	15,732	13,173
Other revenues	50,345	45,832	34,616
Cost of sales	2,780,660	2,256,309	1,944,279
Sales	3,048,520	2,557,807	2,220,162
Selling, administrative and other expenses	159,757	152,680	114,580
Earnings per share	2.65	3.62	3.82

Required:
1. Use the data to prepare income statements in good form for Grumman Corporation for Year 3, Year 2, and Year 1. The company does not compute a gross margin but instead groups cost of sales with other expenses and other revenues with Sales.
2. Approximately how many shares of stock must Grumman have outstanding in each year?
3. What is the major reason for Grumman's declining profitability?

Ethics Case *Meadow Creek Furniture Manufacturing Company*

You are an accountant working for Meadow Creek Furniture Manufacturing Company. The company has been in existence for twenty years and employs 200 people in Tupelo, Mississippi—a town of 30,000 people. At the present time, the national economy is in a recessionary period. The furniture industry as a whole is very adversely affected by recessions. Not surprisingly, Meadow Creek is experiencing some serious financial difficulties.

Because Meadow Creek needs cash, it is preparing financial statements to use in securing a bank loan. If the company does not receive the loan, it will be forced to liquidate. If the business is forced to liquidate, stockholders will suffer substantial losses, and many people will be unemployed.

The income statement that has been prepared shows a net income of $60,000. However, it does not take into account some financial concerns that you have about the company. First, you know that $100,000 of inventory recorded on the books consists of outdated and obsolete styles. An independent appraisal organization estimated that the inventory could probably be sold for $50,000.

Second, included in receivables is $50,000 owed by Rainbow Furniture Company. Currently, Rainbow is in bankruptcy and is expected to pay creditors $.10 on the dollar.

Third, Art Vance, a customer who purchased one of Meadow Creek's sofas in Michigan, is suing Meadow Creek for damages incurred while sitting down on the sofa. Mr. Vance, who is 6 1/2 feet tall and weighs over 300 pounds, alleges that he sat down on the sofa and the springs were of insufficient strength and quality to support his weight, thereby causing a permanent back injury. Mr. Vance claims that he has suffered physical pain, has missed work, and has experienced emotional distress as a result of the injury and is suing Meadow Creek for $500,000. Competent legal counsel to Meadow Creek has asserted that the probability is about 70 percent that Meadow Creek will lose an estimated $100,000. This problem has not been recorded as a liability or disclosed in the notes to the financial statements.

You are concerned that the financial statements, as prepared, overstate net income and assets because of these three problems.

Required:
1. How much could net income be overstated because of these three problems?
2. Should you remain quiet and let the financial statements be used to get the loan? How would you recommend that each problem be handled?
3. How far should an accountant go in pushing his or her opinions about ethical issues such as these?

Chapter 7

Inventory and Costs of Goods Sold

Learning Objectives

After studying this chapter, you should be able to:
1. Identify the items that should be included in inventory.
2. Explain the effects of errors in accounting for inventory.
3. Describe and apply the four inventory cost flow alternatives.
4. Describe and apply the lower-of-cost-or-market method of accounting for inventory.
5. Explain the gross margin and retail methods of estimating inventories.

SETTING THE STAGE

As you learned in Chapter 6, ending inventory is subtracted from cost of goods available for sale to arrive at cost of goods sold. Over the years, numerous unethical managers have discovered that by overstating the amount of ending inventory, cost of goods sold is lowered and gross margin and net income are increased. By fraudulently overstating net income in this manner, they have fooled auditors, investors, creditors, and others. Some of the more famous cases of overstated inventories and net income are McKesson & Robbins, Inc. (a Canadian drug manufacturer), Allied Crude Vegetable Oil Company (a salad oil company that filled storage tanks with ocean water), Crazy Eddie Inc. (a chain of electronic stores),[1] and Regina Company, Inc. (a manufacturer of vacuum cleaners).

Regina's problems started in 1985 when Donald Sheelen became chief executive officer. Through a process of (1) failing to record sales returns, (2) improperly recognizing revenues by creating fictitious sales invoices, and (3) overstating ending inventory and understating cost of goods sold, he increased reported net income over 300 percent from 1985 to 1988. Feeling the burden of the fraud, in 1988, Sheelen confessed the scheme to his priest, resigned from the company, and made a full confession to a U.S. attorney.

Inventory measurement plays an important role in income determination, and inventory misstatements—intentional or otherwise—can result in distorted financial statements. In this chapter, you will study how inventory affects net income and learn different ways to account for inventories. Building on your knowledge of the perpetual and periodic inventory methods discussed in Chapter 6, inventories and cost of goods sold will be examined in more detail. We will discuss (1) what items belong in inventory and the effects of errors in accounting for inventory, (2) inventory costing alternatives, (3) the valuation of inventories at lower of cost or market, and (4) the gross margin and retail methods of estimating inventories and cost of goods sold.

---

[1] Short descriptions of Crazy Eddie Inc. and Allied Crude Vegetable Oil Company are provided in a Business Environment Essay later in the chapter.

Source: The description of Regina, Inc. is based in part on "Regina Executives Consent to SEC Order," *Journal of Accountancy,* June 1989, p. 148.

THE PROPER MEASUREMENT OF INVENTORY

Objective 1
Identify the items that should be included in inventory.

One of the largest assets in retail or wholesale businesses is the inventory of merchandise. For such companies, inventory includes all goods owned and held for sale in the regular course of business. Inventory will normally be sold and converted into cash in less than one year and so is classified as a current asset. It is generally listed on the balance sheet immediately after accounts receivable.

A typical company's inventories are constantly in flux; at any given time, they are being bought, sold, and returned. As a result, it is sometimes difficult to keep track of which inventories on hand are owned, which are owned but not in stock, which have been sold but have not yet been shipped, and which have been purchased but have not yet arrived. For many companies, the key problem in computing net income is the proper measurement of inventory and cost of goods sold.

Inventory Cutoff

Although inventory is usually counted at the end of each accounting period, determining how much inventory is on hand is similar in many ways to measuring the amount of water in a sink that has the drain open and the tap on. The determination of which goods should be included in inventory at the end of a period is called **inventory cutoff.** The major factors to be considered in inventory cutoff are listed in Exhibit 7-1.

inventory cutoff the determination of which items should be included in the year-end inventory balance

A proper cutoff of inventory is critical because if the inventory balance is over- or understated, both the balance sheet and the income statement for the period will report incorrect amounts.

THE EFFECTS OF INVENTORY ERRORS

Objective 2
Explain the effects of errors in accounting for inventory.

Incorrect amounts for inventory on the balance sheet and cost of goods sold on the income statement can result from errors in counting inventories, recording inventory transactions, or both. If, for example, a purchase has been entered in the accounting records but the merchandise has not been physically counted and thus has been omitted from the ending inventory balance, cost of goods sold will be overstated, and net income will be understated. On the other hand, if a purchased item has been counted and included in the inventory balance but has not yet been recorded as a purchase, cost of goods sold is understated, and net income is overstated. To examine the effects of these types of inventory errors, we will assume that Richfield Company had the following inventory records for 1994:

Inventory balance, January 1, 1994	$ 8,000
Purchases through December 30, 1994	20,000
Inventory balance, December 30, 1994	12,000

Exhibit 7-1 *Inventory Cutoff Considerations*

1. Making sure that all goods (or merchandise) included in inventory have been purchased.
2. Making sure that all goods purchased are included in inventory.
3. Making sure that all goods sold during the period have been shipped (or at least not included in inventory).
4. Making sure that all shipped goods have been sold.

Chapter 7 Inventory and Cost of Goods Sold

We will further assume that on December 31 the company purchased and received another $1,000 of inventory. The following comparison shows the kinds of inventory situations that might result:

	Incorrect*	Incorrect	Incorrect	Correct
The $1,000 of merchandise was...	not recorded as a purchase and not counted as inventory	recorded as a purchase but not counted as inventory	not recorded as a purchase but counted as inventory	recorded as a purchase and counted as inventory
Beginning inventory	$ 8,000 (OK)**	$ 8,000 (OK)	$ 8,000 (OK)	$ 8,000 (OK)
Net purchases	20,000 (↓)	21,000 (OK)	20,000 (↓)	21,000 (OK)
Cost of goods available for sale	$28,000 (↓)	$29,000 (OK)	$28,000 (↓)	$29,000 (OK)
Ending inventory	12,000 (↓)	12,000 (↓)	13,000 (OK)	13,000 (OK)
Cost of goods sold	$16,000 (OK)	$17,000 (↑)	$15,000 (↓)	$16,000 (OK)

*This calculation produces the correct cost of goods sold but by an incorrect route—the errors in purchases and ending inventory offset each other.
** ↓ indicates that the amount is too low, ↑ means it is too high, and OK means it is correct.

From this example, you can see how inventory and cost of goods sold can be misstated by the improper recording or counting of inventory.

Similar errors can occur when inventory is sold. If a sale is recorded but the merchandise remains in the warehouse and is counted in the ending inventory, cost of goods sold will be understated, whereas **gross margin** and **net income** will be overstated. If a sale is not recorded but inventory is shipped and not counted in the ending inventory, gross margin and net income will be understated.

gross margin *the excess of net sales revenues over the cost of goods sold*

net income *a measure of the overall performance of a business entity; equal to revenues minus expenses for the period*

To illustrate these potential inventory errors, we will again consider the data of Richfield Company. Note that sales figures have been added and that the ending inventory and 1994 purchases now include the $1,000 purchase of merchandise made on December 31, 1994.

Sales revenue through December 30, 1994 (200% of cost)	$32,000
Inventory balance, January 1, 1994	8,000
Net purchases during 1994	21,000
Inventory balance, December 31, 1994	13,000

In addition, assume that on December 31, inventory that cost $1,000 was sold for $2,000. The merchandise was delivered to the buyer on December 31. The following analysis shows the kinds of situations that might result:

	Incorrect	Incorrect	Incorrect	Correct
The $2,000 sale was	not recorded and the merchandise was counted as inventory	recorded and the merchandise was counted as inventory	not recorded but the merchandise was excluded from inventory	recorded and the merchandise was excluded from inventory
Sales revenue	$32,000 (↓)*	$34,000 (OK)	$32,000 (↓)	$34,000 (OK)
Cost of goods sold:				
Beginning inventory	$ 8,000 (OK)	$ 8,000 (OK)	$ 8,000 (OK)	$ 8,000 (OK)
Net purchases	21,000 (OK)	21,000 (OK)	21,000 (OK)	21,000 (OK)
Cost of goods available for sale	$29,000 (OK)	$29,000 (OK)	$29,000 (OK)	$29,000 (OK)
Ending inventory	13,000 (↑)	13,000 (↑)	12,000 (OK)	12,000 (OK)
Cost of goods sold	$16,000 (↓)	$16,000 (↓)	$17,000 (OK)	$17,000 (OK)
Gross margin	$16,000 (↓)	$18,000 (↑)	$15,000 (↓)	$17,000 (OK)

* ↓ indicates that the amount is too low, ↑ means it is too high, and OK means it is correct.

To reduce the possibility of these types of inventory cutoff errors, most businesses close their warehouses while they count inventory. If they are retailers, they will probably count inventory after hours. During this period, businesses do not accept or ship merchandise, nor do they enter purchase or sales transactions in their accounting records.

As explained, an error in inventory results in cost of goods sold being overstated or understated. This error has the opposite effect on gross margin and hence on net income. For example, if at the end of the accounting period $2,000 of inventory is not counted, cost of goods sold will be $2,000 higher than it should be, and gross margin and net income will be understated by $2,000. (Ignore taxes for now.) Such inventory errors affect gross margin and net income not only in the current year but in the following year as well. An understatement in one year results in an overstatement in the next year, and vice versa.

To illustrate how inventory errors affect gross margin and net income, let us first assume the following correct data for Salina Corporation:

	1994		1995	
Sales revenue		$50,000		$40,000
Cost of goods sold:				
Beginning inventory	$10,000		$ 5,000	
Net purchases	20,000		25,000	
Cost of goods available for sale	$30,000		$30,000	
Ending inventory	5,000		10,000	
Cost of goods sold		25,000		20,000
Gross margin		$25,000		$20,000
Expenses		10,000		10,000
Net income		$15,000		$10,000

Now suppose that ending inventory in 1994 was overstated; that is, instead of the correct amount of $5,000, the count erroneously showed $7,000 of inventory on hand. The following analysis shows the effect of the error on net income in both 1994 and 1995:

	1994		1995	
Sales revenue		$50,000		$40,000
Cost of goods sold:				
Beginning inventory	$10,000		$ 7,000 (↑)	
Net purchases	20,000		25,000	
Cost of goods available for sale	$30,000		$32,000 (↑)	
Ending inventory	7,000 (↑)*		10,000	
Cost of goods sold		23,000 (↓)		22,000 (↑)
Gross margin		$27,000 (↑)		$18,000 (↓)
Expenses		10,000		10,000
Net income		$17,000 (↑)		$ 8,000 (↓)

* ↑ means the amount is too high, ↓ means it is too low.

As you can see, when the amount of ending inventory is overstated (as it was in 1994) both gross margin and net income are overstated by the same amount ($2,000 in 1994). If the ending inventory amount had been under-

BUSINESS ENVIRONMENT ESSAY
Inventory Fraud

One of the most common ways of committing major fraud is to overstate a company's inventory. If inventory is overstated, cost of goods sold is understated and net income is overstated. The overstatement of inventories and profits can lure investors and boost stock prices. In addition, since inventory can often be pledged as collateral to borrow money from banks, its overstatement increases a company's borrowing power. Each of these scenarios is illustrated by the following cases.

Crazy Eddie Inc.

Until recently Crazy Eddie Inc. was one of the hottest names in consumer electronics. What began in 1970 as a single store selling TVs, stereos, and other electronics products mushroomed into an empire with so many stores that *New Yorker* magazine once ran a cartoon in which all roads led to Crazy Eddie. The piercing slogan "C-r-r-r-azy Eddie! His prices are ins-a-a-a-ne." blurted incessantly on radio and TV stations and brought customers in droves. At one point, Crazy Eddie stock traded for as much as $43.25 per share.

Today, the company is under court-protected bankruptcy and its stock sells for $.25 per share on the over-the-counter market. Much of the blame for the company's spectacular crash is its inventory problems. As much as $65 million in inventory is inexplicably missing or phantom. When new management took over the company in a desperate rescue attempt in 1987, the $65 million inventory write-off more than erased all the earnings the company had ever reported. It seems that during the inventory counts, company officers had drafted phony inventory count sheets and improperly included merchandise so that the reported ending inventory and net income would be higher. The resulting artificially high profits and high stock price allowed its founder, Eddie Antar, to rake in $68.4 million from stock sales through 1986.

Source: Adapted from Jeff Tannenbaum, "Short Circuit." *The Wall Street Journal,* Monday, July 10, 1989, p. A1, Col. 6.

The Great Salad Oil Case

The Allied Crude Vegetable Oil (Great Salad Oil) Case is one of the most well-known inventory frauds of all time. Founded in 1957 by Tino De Angelis, the company was set up on an old petroleum tank farm in Bayonne, New Jersey. De Angelis used the soybean oil that was supposedly in the tanks as collateral to borrow money from financial institutions. He then hired American Express Warehousing, Ltd. (a subsidiary of American Express) to take charge of storing, inspecting, and documenting the oil. The warehousing receipts issued by the warehousers were used as evidence of the oil.

De Angelis handpicked 22 men to work at the tank farm, and they fooled the American Express inspectors with considerable ease. For example, one of them would climb to the top of a tank, drop in a weighted tape measure and then shout down to the inspector that the tank was full. In most cases, the tanks were empty, although some were filled with seawater, topped with a thin slick of oil. Moreover, the tanks were connected by a jungle of pipes which allowed the men to pump whatever oil there was from one tank to another.

These maneuvers gave De Angelis an "endless" supply of oil and endless borrowing power. If anyone had checked a statistical report issued by the U.S. Census Bureau, he or she would have found that the oil supposedly stored at the tank farm totaled twice as much as all the oil in the country. By the close of 1963, the warehouse receipts represented 937 million pounds of oil when actually only 100 million pounds existed.

> The salad oil scandal was revealed when De Angelis was unable to make payments on an investment. The ensuing investigation revealed a fraud that was conservatively estimated at $200 million. Most of the losses were borne by 51 major banking and brokerage houses in the United States and Europe, 20 of which collapsed.
>
> De Angelis pleaded guilty to four federal counts of fraud and conspiracy and was given a 20-year sentence. The millions of dollars loaned to De Angelis were never found, and it is generally believed that the missing oil never existed. In fact, when one oil tank that supposedly had $3,575,000 worth of oil was opened, seawater ran out for 12 consecutive days.
>
> *Source:* Marshall B. Romney and W. Steve Albrecht, "The Use of Investigative Agencies by Auditors." *The Journal of Accountancy,* October 1979, p. 61.

stated, net income and gross margin would also have been understated, again by the same amount.

Since the ending inventory in 1994 becomes the beginning inventory in 1995, the net income and gross margin for 1995 are also misstated. In 1995, however, beginning inventory is overstated, so gross margin and net income are understated, again by $2,000. Thus, the errors in the two years offset each other, and if the count taken at the end of 1995 is correct, income in subsequent years will not be affected by these errors.

Other Factors in Accounting for Inventory

In addition to miscounting goods on hand, at least two other factors complicate a company's attempt to determine the proper amount of inventory. One factor involves the issuing of goods on **consignment.** Sometimes the inventory a firm stocks in its warehouse has not actually been purchased from suppliers. With this arrangement, suppliers, known as the **consignors,** retain ownership of the inventory until it is sold, and the firm selling the merchandise, known as the **consignee,** merely stocks and sells the merchandise for the consignor and receives a commission on any sales as payment for services rendered. Some farm implement dealers, for example, do not actually own the tractors and other equipment they stock and sell.

It is extremely important that goods being held on consignment not be included in the inventory of the consignee even though they are physically on the consignee's premises. It is equally important that consignors properly include all such inventory in their records even though it is not on their premises.

Another factor that complicates the accounting for inventory has to do with shipping. The question is who owns the inventory that is on a truck or railroad car, the seller or the buyer? If the seller is bearing the shipping costs, the arrangement is known as **FOB (free-on-board) destination,** and the seller owns the merchandise from the time it is shipped until it is delivered to the buyer. If the buyer is bearing the shipping costs, the arrangement is known as **FOB shipping point,** and the buyer owns the merchandise during transit. Thus, in determining which inventory should be counted and included in the

---

consignment *an arrangement whereby merchandise owned by one party (the consignor) is sold by another party (the consignee), usually on a commission basis*

consignor *the owner of merchandise to be sold by someone else, known as the consignee*

consignee *a vendor who sells merchandise owned by another party, known as the consignor, usually on a commission basis*

FOB (free-on-board) destination *business term meaning that the seller of merchandise bears the shipping costs and maintains ownership until the merchandise is delivered to the buyer*

FOB (free-on-board) shipping point *business term meaning that the buyer of merchandise bears the shipping costs and acquires ownership at the point of shipment*

inventory balance for a period, a company must note the amount of merchandise in transit and the terms under which it is being shipped. In all cases, merchandise should be included in the inventory of the party who owns it.

> **To Summarize** *Inventory errors can have a significant effect on cost of goods sold, gross margin, and net income. Inventory errors affect cost of goods sold, gross margin, and net income on a dollar-for-dollar basis. That is, a $1 error in inventory results in a $1 error in the cost of goods sold, gross margin, and net income. In addition, a misstatement of an ending inventory balance affects net income, both in the current year and in the next year. Errors in beginning and ending inventory have the opposite effect on cost of goods sold, gross margin, and net income. Errors in inventory correct themselves after two years if the physical count at the end of the second year shows the correct amount of ending inventory for that period. This means that the records for the following year should show the correct amount of beginning inventory.*
>
> *When determining which goods should be included in inventory, consigned goods and shipping terms must be considered carefully to determine ownership of merchandise.*

INVENTORY COST FLOWS

Objective 3

Describe and apply the four inventory cost flow alternatives.

If all merchandise were purchased at the same unit cost, the determination of ending inventory and cost of goods sold for a period would not pose any problems once the quantity of goods on hand was determined. However, inventory almost always consists of units acquired at different costs. Thus, a firm must have a way to determine what costs are to be assigned to the inventory on hand and to the merchandise sold during the period. In the following sections, we will examine the different methods used by companies to determine inventories and cost of goods sold.

Specific Identification Inventory Costing

One alternative is to identify the cost of each unit that is sold. This approach, called **specific identification,** is often used by automobile dealers and other businesses that sell a limited number of units at a high price. To illustrate the specific identification inventory costing method, we will consider the September 1994 records of Nephi Company, which sells one type of bicycle.

specific identification *a method of valuing inventory and determining cost of goods sold, whereby the actual costs of specific inventory items are assigned to them*

Sept.	1	Beginning inventory consisted of 10 bicycles costing $200 each.
	3	Purchased 8 bicycles costing $250 each.
	5	Sold 12 bicycles at $400 each.
	18	Purchased 16 bicycles costing $300 each.
	20	Purchased 10 bicycles costing $320 each.
	25	Sold 16 bicycles at $400 each.

These inventory records show that during September the company had 44 bicycles (10 from beginning inventory and 34 that were purchased during the month) that it could have sold. However, only 28 bicycles were sold, leaving

16 on hand at the end of September. Using the specific identification method of inventory costing requires that the individual costs of the actual units sold be charged against revenue as cost of goods sold. To compute cost of goods sold and ending inventory amounts with this alternative, a company must know which units were actually sold and what the unit cost of each was.

Suppose that of the 12 bicycles sold by Nephi on September 5, 8 came from the beginning inventory and 4 from the September 3 purchase, and that all the 16 units sold on September 25 came from the September 18 purchase. With this information, cost of goods sold and ending inventory would be computed as follows:

	Bicycles	Costs
Beginning inventory	10	$ 2,000
Net purchases	34	10,000
Goods available for sale	44	$12,000
Ending inventory	16	4,600 (a)
Cost of goods sold	28	$ 7,400 (b)

The cost of ending inventory is the total of the individual costs of the bicycles still on hand at the end of the month, or:

```
 2 bicycles from beginning inventory at $200 each  = $  400
 4 bicycles purchased on September 3 at $250 each  =   1,000
10 bicycles purchased on September 20 at $320 each =   3,200
                         Total ending inventory    = $4,600 (a)
```

Similarly, the cost of goods sold is the total of the costs of the specific bicycles sold, or:

```
 8 bicycles from beginning inventory at $200 each  = $1,600
 4 bicycles purchased on September 3 at $250 each  =  1,000
16 bicycles purchased on September 18 at $300 each =  4,800
                         Total cost of goods sold  = $7,400 (b)
```

Assumed Inventory Cost Flows

For most companies, it is impractical, if not impossible, to keep track of specific units. When that is the case, an *assumption* must be made as to which units were sold during the period and which are still in inventory. Three commonly used cost flow assumptions are (1) units were sold in the order purchased, called *first-in, first-out (FIFO)*, (2) the most recently purchased units were sold first, called *last-in, first-out (LIFO)*, or (3) units sold reflect an *average* of the cost of all units available for sale.

It is very important to recognize that the assumed flow of goods for costing purposes does not have to match the actual physical movement of goods purchased and sold. In some cases, the assumed cost flow may be similar to the physical flow, but firms are not required to match the cost flow to physical flow. A grocery store, for example, usually tries to sell the oldest units first to minimize spoilage. Thus, the physical flow of goods would reflect a FIFO pattern, but the grocery store could use a FIFO, LIFO, or average cost assumption in determining its ending inventory and cost of goods sold. On the other hand, a company that stockpiles coal must first sell the coal purchased last since it is on top of the pile. That company might use the LIFO cost assumption, which reflects physical flow, or it might use one of the other alternatives.

In the next few sections, we will illustrate the FIFO, LIFO, and average inventory costing methods. Each alternative will be analyzed first in the context of the *periodic inventory method* and then in the context of the *perpetual inventory method*. (Remember that no matter which costing alternative is being used, the first step in valuing inventory is to identify the number of units left unsold at the end of the period.) Data for Nephi Company (page 265) will again be used in illustrating the different inventory cost flows.

Periodic Inventory Cost Flow Assumptions

As explained in Chapter 6, firms that use the periodic inventory method do not keep track of the cost of merchandise sold during the period. At the end of an accounting period, the merchandise on hand must be physically counted to determine the *quantity* of ending inventory. Then the *cost* of ending inventory is computed and subtracted from cost of goods available for sale to determine cost of goods sold. In the examples in Chapter 6, the ending inventory costs were given without explanation of how they were computed. Ending inventory cost could be computed using specific identification, as explained and illustrated previously. More often, however, the cost of ending inventory is determined using an assumed cost flow—FIFO, LIFO, or average costing.

FIFO (first-in, first-out)
an inventory cost flow whereby the first goods purchased are assumed to be the first goods sold so that the ending inventory consists of the most recently purchased goods

PERIODIC FIFO INVENTORY COSTING. The FIFO inventory costing alternative assigns the costs of the first items acquired to the first items sold; the periodic inventory method requires that all calculations be made at the end of the period. Thus, under periodic FIFO costing, Nephi Company would compute its ending inventory and cost of goods sold as follows:

	Bicycles	Costs
Beginning inventory	10	$ 2,000
Net purchases (8 at $250, 16 at $300, 10 at $320)	34	10,000
Goods available for sale	44	$12,000
Ending inventory	16	5,000 (c)
Cost of goods sold	28	$ 7,000 (d)

For inventory costing purposes, the 16 units on hand at the end of the period are assumed to be the last ones purchased since FIFO assumes that the first units purchased were the first ones sold. In order to determine the cost to be assigned to the 16 units on hand at the end of the period, Nephi Company will identify the cost of the last 16 bicycles purchased during the month. These were:

10 bicycles purchased on September 20 at $320 each = $3,200
6 bicycles purchased on September 18 at $300 each = 1,800
Total ending inventory cost = $5,000 (c)

Accordingly, the 28 bicycles sold are assumed to be the first ones purchased, or:

10 bicycles of beginning inventory at $200 each = $2,000
8 bicycles purchased on September 3 at $250 each = 2,000
10 bicycles purchased on September 18 at $300 each = 3,000
Total cost of goods sold = $7,000 (d)

LIFO (last-in, first-out) *an inventory cost flow whereby the last goods purchased are assumed to be the first goods sold so that the ending inventory consists of the first goods purchased*

PERIODIC LIFO INVENTORY COSTING. The **LIFO** inventory costing alternative is the opposite of FIFO; that is, LIFO assigns the costs of the last items purchased to the first items sold. With periodic LIFO costing, the cost of goods sold and the ending inventory for Nephi Company would be computed as follows:

	Bicycles	Costs
Beginning inventory	10	$ 2,000
Net purchases	34	10,000
Goods available for sale	44	$12,000
Ending inventory	16	3,500 (e)
Cost of goods sold	28	$ 8,500 (f)

The 16 bicycles remaining on hand at the end of the period are assumed to be from the beginning inventory and the first bicycles purchased this period.

10 bicycles of beginning inventory at $200 each = $2,000
6 bicycles purchased on September 3 at $250 each = 1,500
Total ending inventory cost = $3,500 (e)

Accordingly, the 28 bicycles sold are assumed to be the most recent ones purchased, or:

10 bicycles purchased on September 20 at $320 each = $3,200
16 bicycles purchased on September 18 at $300 each = 4,800
2 bicycles purchased on September 3 at $250 each = 500
Total cost of goods sold = $8,500 (f)

weighted average *a periodic inventory cost flow alternative whereby the cost of goods sold and the cost of ending inventory are determined by using a weighted-average cost of all merchandise available for sale during the period*

PERIODIC AVERAGE INVENTORY COSTING. An average cost approach is another alternative used to determine inventories and cost of goods sold. When the periodic inventory method is used, this approach is called **weighted average** inventory costing. This alternative uses the costs of neither the first nor the last inventory units purchased to determine cost of goods sold. Instead, a weighted-average cost per unit is computed and used to determine cost of goods sold and the cost of ending inventory. This alternative probably points up most clearly the difference between the flow of costs and the flow of goods through the firm. Although it may not be possible to mix the actual inventory items being sold (for instance, bicycles), it is perfectly acceptable to mix their costs to find the weighted-average cost of each item.

Using weighted-average costing, the cost of goods sold and ending inventory for Nephi Company would then be computed as follows:

	Bicycles	Costs
Beginning inventory	10	$ 2,000
Net purchases	34	10,000
Goods available for sale	44	$12,000
Ending inventory	16	4,364*
Cost of goods sold	28	$ 7,636

*Rounded.

In this case, a weighted-average cost per bicycle of $272.73 was used in computing both ending inventory and cost of goods sold. This weighted-average cost per unit is the total cost of goods available for sale divided by the total number of units available for sale, or:

$$\frac{\text{Cost of goods available for sale}}{\text{Total number of units available for sale}} = \frac{\$12,000}{44} = \$272.73 \text{ per bicycle}$$

The cost of the ending inventory is the weighted-average cost per unit multiplied by the number of units on hand at the end of a period, or 16 units × $272.73 = $4,364. And the cost of goods sold is the weighted-average cost per unit multiplied by the number of units sold, or $272.73 × 28 units = $7,636.

A COMPARISON OF COST FLOW ASSUMPTIONS USING THE PERIODIC INVENTORY METHOD. The cost of goods sold, gross margin, and ending inventory for Nephi Company under each of the three periodic cost flow assumptions are:

	FIFO	LIFO	Weighted Average
Sales revenue (28 bicycles @ $400 each)	$11,200	$11,200	$11,200
Cost of gross sold	7,000	8,500	7,636
Gross margin	$ 4,200	$ 2,700	$ 3,564
Ending inventory	$ 5,000	$ 3,500	$ 4,364

This comparison shows that the two extremes are FIFO and LIFO. This is the case when the cost of inventory items is either continually increasing (as in the example) or decreasing. Since in times of increasing prices FIFO assigns the highest value to ending inventory, a firm that wishes to report the highest possible net income (in order to attract investors or borrow money) would employ that alternative. Many firms, however, choose to report the lowest possible net income in order to minimize tax payments in the current year. Accordingly, they elect to use LIFO.

The LIFO method tends to report the oldest inventory costs on the balance sheet. In periods of rising prices, these costs can be much lower than the current cost of replacing the inventory. The income statement, however, is generally more realistic with LIFO. Since the most recent inventory costs are charged against revenues as cost of goods sold, the LIFO method is better than FIFO in matching current costs with current revenues. Whichever inventory costing method a firm uses, it must stick with that method for a reasonable period of time. Frequent changes from one inventory costing method to another are not allowed by the Internal Revenue Service or by generally accepted accounting principles.

Although in most instances where alternatives exist firms are allowed to use one accounting method for tax purposes and another for financial reporting, such is not the case in accounting for inventory costs. The Internal Revenue Service (IRS) has ruled that firms may use LIFO for tax purposes, but that if they do so, they must also use LIFO for financial reporting purposes. Therefore, companies must choose between reporting high profits and paying high taxes or reporting low profits and paying low taxes.

In the 1970s, many organizations switched from FIFO to LIFO, a trend that was accelerated by the high rate of inflation. And though the pace of inflation has slowed, many major companies still use LIFO. An annual survey of firms, for example, indicated that in 1987, 393 of the firms used LIFO, 392 used FIFO, and 216 used average costing for inventories.[2] Exhibit 7-2 shows recent LIFO inventory balances for three large corporations and how much different their inventory balances would have been if they had been using FIFO. Although FIFO and LIFO are the two most common procedures for costing inventory, specific identification is often used by companies with high-value inventory items, such as airplanes or diamonds, and weighted average is used by firms that have numerous small-value inventory items or have erratically fluctuating costs.

The use of different methods of inventory valuation creates more problems for readers than for preparers of financial statements. Readers must be careful in comparing the performances of companies. It is possible that differences in reported results are more a function of the inventory method used than of actual performance. To solve this problem, many people argue that the accounting profession should agree on a single method of inventory costing. The question is, which one. LIFO matches the most recent costs with current revenues, producing a more realistic income statement. FIFO, on the other hand,

Exhibit 7-2 *Comparison of LIFO and FIFO Inventory Values*

Company	Inventory Method Used	Amount of Inventory	Difference Between FIFO and LIFO
General Motors	LIFO	$8,269.7 million	If FIFO had been used, inventory would have been $2,196.3 million higher.
Kroger Company	LIFO	$1,472 million	If FIFO had been used, inventory would have been $223 million higher.
Ford Motor Co.	LIFO	$4,154 million	If FIFO had been used, inventory would have been $986 million higher.

[2] American Institute of Certified Public Accountants, *Accounting Trends & Techniques*, 1988, p. 110.

matches older costs with revenues but results in a more realistic inventory valuation on the balance sheet. Until the profession can agree on which method is best, and as long as there are differing income tax effects, each of these methods will continue to be used. You should recognize, however, that over the life of a firm (as all inventory is eventually sold), total income will be the same regardless of the inventory costing alternative used.

Perpetual Inventory Cost Flow Assumptions

So far, the four inventory cost flow alternatives have been illustrated only in the context of the periodic inventory method. A choice must also be made from among these same cost flows when the perpetual inventory method is used. Recall the basic difference between these two inventory methods: Under the periodic method all calculations are made at the end of a period, whereas under the perpetual method inventory costs are calculated throughout the period as inventory is purchased or sold.

PERPETUAL FIFO INVENTORY COSTING. The ending inventory and the cost of goods sold for Nephi Company using the perpetual FIFO inventory alternative would be:

	Bicycles	Costs
Beginning inventory	10	$ 2,000
Net purchases	34	10,000
Goods available for sale	44	$12,000
Ending inventory	16	5,000
Cost of goods sold	28	$ 7,000

The ending inventory of 16 bicycles at a cost of $5,000 is calculated as follows. Note that these same amounts were obtained with the periodic FIFO method. This is not a coincidence. Whereas the recording process is different, the amount of ending inventory, and thus the cost of goods sold and net income, will always be the same under the FIFO costing alternative, no matter which inventory method (periodic or perpetual) is used. This usually is not true of the LIFO or averaging cost flow alternatives.

	Purchased			Sold			Remaining		
Date	Number of Units	Unit Cost	Total Cost	Number of Units	Unit Cost	Total Cost	Number of Units	Unit Cost	Total Cost
Beginning inventory							10	$200	$2,000
Sept. 3	8	$250	$ 2,000				18	{10 at $200 / 8 at $250}	$4,000
5				12	{10 at $200 / 2 at $250}	$2,500	6	$250	$1,500
18	16	$300	$ 4,800				22	{6 at $250 / 16 at $300}	$6,300
20	10	$320	$ 3,200				32	{6 at $250 / 16 at $300 / 10 at $320}	$9,500
25				16	{6 at $250 / 10 at $300}	$4,500	16	{6 at $300 / 10 at $320}	$5,000
Totals	34		$10,000	28		$7,000			

PERPETUAL LIFO INVENTORY COSTING. Perpetual LIFO (like periodic LIFO) provides higher cost of goods sold, and hence lower ending inventory and net income, than FIFO when prices are rising. The difference between perpetual LIFO and FIFO is usually not so large as with the periodic method, however. The ending inventory for Nephi Company using perpetual LIFO would be determined as follows:

	Purchased			Sold			Remaining		
Date	Number of Units	Unit Cost	Total Cost	Number of Units	Unit Cost	Total Cost	Number of Units	Unit Cost	Total Cost
Beginning inventory							10	$200	$2,000
Sept. 3	8	$250	$2,000				18	{10 at $200, 8 at $250}	$4,000
5				12	{8 at $250, 4 at $200}	$2,800	6	$200	$1,200
18	16	$300	$4,800				22	{6 at $200, 16 at $300}	$6,000
20	10	$320	$3,200				32	{6 at $200, 16 at $300, 10 at $320}	$9,200
25				16	{10 at $320, 6 at $300}	$5,000	16	{6 at $200, 10 at $300}	$4,200
Totals	34		$10,000	28		$7,800			

The ending inventory amount of $4,200 is different from the $3,500 computed with the periodic LIFO costing method, as shown here.

Periodic LIFO $2,000 (10 @ $200) + $1,500 (6 @ $250) = $3,500
Perpetual LIFO $1,200 (6 @ $200) + $3,000 (10 @ $300) = $4,200

Since the perpetual LIFO method requires that computations be made as merchandise is sold or purchased, only the costs of the bicycles actually on hand can be recognized. Consider, for example, the September 5 sale of 12 units. On that date, only the units from beginning inventory and the September 3 purchase were available, so 4 units from beginning inventory (at $200 each) and all 8 units from the September 3 purchase (at $250 each) were sold (because they were the last ones in). Under the periodic LIFO method, no calculations are made until the end of the period, so the unit costs that remain in inventory are the oldest ones, no matter which units were actually available for sale on which dates.

With the perpetual LIFO method, the calculation for cost of goods sold would be:

	Bicycles	Costs
Beginning inventory	10	$2,000
Net purchases	34	10,000
Goods available for sale	44	$12,000
Ending inventory	16	4,200
Cost of goods sold	28	$7,800

Chapter 7 *Inventory and Cost of Goods Sold*

moving average *a perpetual inventory cost flow alternative whereby the cost of goods sold and the cost of ending inventory are determined by using a weighted-average cost of all merchandise on hand after each purchase*

PERPETUAL AVERAGE INVENTORY COSTING. The average costing alternative with the perpetual inventory method involves the computation of weighted averages at different times throughout the period. It is, therefore, referred to as the **moving-average** alternative. (With the periodic method, the average is computed only once, at the end of the period.) A company using the moving-average alternative would *compute a new average after each purchase transaction* and would derive its ending inventory as shown below for Nephi Company:

	Purchased			Sold			Remaining		
Date	Number of Units	Unit Cost	Total Cost	Number of Units	Unit Cost	Total Cost	Number of Units	Unit Cost	Total Cost
Beginning inventory							10	$200.00	$2,000
Sept. 3	8	$250.00	$2,000				18	$222.22	$4,000
5				12	$222.22	$2,667	6	$222.22	$1,333
18	16	$300.00	$4,800				22	$278.77	$6,133
20	10	$320.00	$3,200				32	$291.66	$9,333
25				16	$291.66	$4,667	16	$291.66	$4,667
Totals	34		$10,000	28		$7,333*			

*Rounding difference.

The moving-average cost of $222.22 on September 3, for example, is the total cost of all bicycles available on that date divided by the total number of units available, or $4,000 ÷ 18 units = $222.22.

With the moving-average alternative, cost of goods sold is calculated as follows:

	Bicycles	Costs
Beginning inventory	10	$ 2,000
Net purchases	34	10,000
Goods available for sale	44	$12,000
Ending inventory	16	4,667
Cost of goods sold	28	$ 7,333

A Comparison of All Inventory Costing Alternatives

The cost of goods sold and ending inventory amounts we have calculated in this chapter are summarized along with the resultant gross margins as follows:

	FIFO		LIFO		Weighted Average (Periodic)	Moving Average (Perpetual)	Specific Identification
	Periodic	Perpetual	Periodic	Perpetual			
Sales revenue	$11,200	$11,200	$11,200	$11,200	$11,200	$11,200	$11,200
Cost of goods sold	7,000	7,000	8,500	7,800	7,636	7,333	7,400
Gross margin	$ 4,200	$ 4,200	$ 2,700	$ 3,400	$ 3,564	$ 3,867	$ 3,800
Ending inventory	$ 5,000	$ 5,000	$ 3,500	$ 4,200	$ 4,364	$ 4,667	$ 4,600

This comparison points up several interesting facts. First, no matter which inventory costing alternative a company uses, during a period of rising prices, cost of goods sold is highest with LIFO and lowest with FIFO. As a result, gross margin, net income, and ending inventory are lowest with LIFO and highest with FIFO. Second, the difference between the FIFO and LIFO cost of goods sold is usually greater with the periodic method than with the perpetual method. Third, perpetual and periodic cost of goods sold amounts are always the same when FIFO is used.

It is impossible to conclude that any one of these alternatives is best even though in most circumstances there will be one method that is theoretically most appropriate given a company's physical flow of goods.

> **To Summarize** *There are four principal inventory costing alternatives: FIFO, LIFO, weighted (or moving) average, and specific identification. These alternatives can be used with either the perpetual or the periodic inventory method. During periods of inflation, periodic LIFO inventory results in the lowest net income, and FIFO (either periodic or perpetual) results in the highest net income.*

REPORTING INVENTORY AT AMOUNTS BELOW COST

Objective 4

Describe and apply the lower of cost or market method of accounting for inventory.

All the inventory costing alternatives we have discussed have one thing in common: They report inventory at cost. Occasionally, however, it becomes necessary to report inventory at an amount that is less than cost. This happens when the future value of the inventory is in doubt, usually when it is damaged, used, or obsolete, or when it can be replaced new at a price that is less than its original cost.

Inventory Valued at Net Realizable Value

net realizable value *the selling price of an item less reasonable selling costs*

When inventory is damaged, used, or obsolete, it should be reported at no more than its **net realizable value**. This is the amount the inventory can be sold for minus any selling costs. Suppose, for example, that an automobile dealer has a demonstrator car that originally cost $12,000 and now can be sold for only $10,000. The car should be reported at its net realizable value. If a commission of $500 must be paid to sell the car, the net realizable value is $9,500, or $2,500 less than cost. This loss is calculated as follows:

Cost		$12,000
Estimated selling price	$10,000	
Less selling commission	500	9,500
Loss		$ 2,500

To achieve a good matching of revenues and expenses, a company must recognize this estimated loss as soon as it is known that a loss will be realized (even before the car is sold). The journal entry required to recognize the loss and reduce the inventory amount of the car would be:

> Loss on Write-Down of Inventory (Expense).................... 2,500
>   Inventory.. 2,500
> *To write down demonstrator car to a net realizable value of $9,500.*

By writing down inventory to its net realizable value, a company recognizes a loss when it happens and is thus able to break even when the inventory is finally sold. Using net realizable values means that assets are not being reported at amounts that exceed their future economic benefits.

Inventory Valued at Lower of Cost or Market

Inventory also must be written down to an amount below cost if it can be replaced new at a price that is less than its original cost. Although the replacement cost of inventory seldom falls below original cost in an inflationary environment, this has happened in certain industries. In the electronics industry, for instance, the costs of computers and compact disc players have fallen dramatically in recent years. When goods remaining in ending inventory can be replaced with identical goods at a lower cost, the lower unit cost must be used in valuing the inventory, provided that the replacement cost is not higher than net realizable value or lower than net realizable value minus a normal profit. This is known as the **lower-of-cost-or-market (LCM) rule.** (In a sense, a more precise name would be the lower-of-actual-cost-or-replacement-cost rule.)

The **ceiling,** or maximum, market amount at which inventory can be carried on the books is equivalent to net realizable value, which is the selling price less estimated selling costs. The ceiling is imposed because it makes no sense to value an inventory item above what it can be sold for. For example, assume that a company purchased an inventory item for $10 and expected to sell it for $14. If the selling costs of the item amounted to $3, the net realizable value would be $11 ($14 − $3).

The **floor** is defined as the net realizable value minus a normal profit. The floor is imposed to avoid showing losses in one period and large profits in subsequent periods. The floor protects the normal profit margin but does not allow for larger profits. Thus if the inventory item costing $10 had a normal profit margin of 20 percent, or $2, the floor would be $9 (net realizable value of $11 less normal profit of $2).

In applying this LCM rule, you can follow certain basic guidelines.

1. Define market value as:
   (a) Replacement cost if it falls between the ceiling and the floor.
   (b) The floor if the replacement cost is less than the floor.
   (c) The ceiling if the replacement cost is higher than the ceiling.
   (As a practical matter, when replacement cost, ceiling, and floor are compared, market is always the middle value.)
2. Compare the defined market value with the actual cost and choose the lower amount.

The following chart gives four separate examples of applying the LCM rule; the resulting LCM amount is highlighted in each case.

---

lower-of-cost-or-market (LCM) rule *a basis for valuing certain assets at the lower of original cost or market value (current replacement cost), provided that the replacement cost is not higher than net realizable value or lower than net realizable value minus normal profit*

ceiling *the maximum market amount at which inventory can be carried on the books; equal to net realizable value*

floor *the minimum market amount at which inventory can be carried on the books; equal to net realizable value minus a normal profit*

Item	Number of Items in Inventory	Original Cost (LIFO, FIFO, etc.)	Market Replacement Cost	Net Realizable Value (Ceiling)	Net Realizable Value Minus Normal Profit (Floor)
A	10	$17	$16	**$15**	$10
B	8	21	**18**	23	16
C	30	26	21	31	**22**
D	20	**19**	16	34	25

The LCM rule can be applied in one of three ways: (1) by computing cost and market figures for each item in inventory and using the lower of the two amounts in each case, (2) by computing cost and market figures for the total inventory and then applying the LCM rule to that total, or (3) by applying the LCM rule to categories of inventory. For a clothing store, categories of inventory might be all shirts, all pants, all suits, or all dresses.

To illustrate, we will use the above data to show how the LCM rule would be applied to each inventory item separately and to total inventory. (The third method is similar to the second, except that it may involve several totals, one for each category of inventory.)

Item	Number of Items in Inventory	Original Cost	Market Value	LCM for Individual Items
A	10	$17 × 10 units = $ 170	$15 × 10 units = $ 150	$ 150
B	8	$21 × 8 units = $ 168	$18 × 8 units = 144	144
C	30	$26 × 30 units = $ 780	$22 × 30 units = 660	660
D	20	$19 × 20 units = $ 380	$25 × 20 units = 500	380
		$1,498	$1,454	$1,334

$44 ──────
$164 ──────

In the first situation—applying the LCM rule to individual items—inventory is valued at $1,334, a write-down of $164 from the original cost. In the second situation—using total inventory—the lower of total cost ($1,498) or total market value ($1,454) would be used, for a write-down of $44. The write-down is smaller when total inventory is used because the increase in market of $120 in item D offsets decreases in items A, B, and C. In practice, each of the three methods is acceptable, but once a method has been selected, it should be followed consistently.

The journal entry to write down the inventory to the lower of cost or market applying the LCM rule to individual items would be:

Loss on Write-Down of Inventory (Expense).............................. 164
    Inventory 164
To write down inventory to lower of cost or market.

The amount of this entry would have been $44 if the LCM rule had been applied to total inventory.

The lower-of-cost-or-market rule has gained wide acceptance because it reports inventory on the balance sheet at amounts that are in keeping with future economic benefits. With this method, losses are recognized when they occur, not necessarily when a sale is made.

> **To Summarize** *The recorded amount of inventory should be written down (1) when it is damaged, used, or obsolete and (2) when it can be replaced (purchased new) at an amount that is less than its original cost. In the first case, inventory is reported at its net realizable value, an amount that allows a company to break even when the inventory is sold. In the second case, inventory is written down to the lower of cost or market. When using the lower-of-cost-or-market rule, market is defined as the middle of the ceiling, replacement cost, and floor. Ceiling is defined as the net realizable value, and floor is net realizable value minus a normal profit margin. In no case should inventory be reported at an amount that exceeds the ceiling or that is less than the floor. These reporting alternatives are attempts to show assets at amounts that reflect realistic future economic benefits.*

BUSINESS ENVIRONMENT ESSAY
Reel Assets

The decision of when to write inventory down to a market value that is less than cost is a difficult one in many industries. Take the movie industry for example. Suppose a company spends $20 million to make a film. Financial accounting rules allow producers to record as an asset most of that cost, including production and national advertising and promotion, as film inventory. The cost of the inventory is then written off over the film's economic life. The tricky question is: "What is the economic life?"

Many film makers have been accused of carrying film inventory as assets long after the movies have bombed or become worthless. In 1985, for example, Orion Pictures finally wrote their film inventory down $16 million to account for 40 worthless films that had been released since 1982.

Source: Adapted from "Reel Assets," *Forbes,* December 29, 1986, pp. 64–66.

METHODS OF ESTIMATING INVENTORIES

Objective 5
Explain the gross margin and retail methods of estimating inventories.

We have assumed that the number of inventory units on hand is known, generally by a physical count that takes place at the end of each accounting period. As we indicated, for the periodic inventory method, this physical count is the only way to determine how much inventory is on hand at the end of a period. For the perpetual inventory method, the physical count verifies the quantity on hand or indicates the amount of inventory shrinkage. There are times, however, when a company needs to know the dollar amount of ending inventory, but a physical count is either impossible or impractical. For example, many firms prepare quarterly, or even monthly, financial statements, but it is too expensive and time-consuming to count the inventory at the end of each period. In such cases, if the perpetual inventory method is being used, the balance in the Inventory account is usually assumed to be correct. With the periodic inventory method, however, some estimate of the Inventory balance must be made.

There are two common methods of estimating the dollar amount of ending inventory. The first, the gross margin method, can be used by most types of firms; the second, the retail inventory method, is used primarily by department stores and other retail businesses.

The Gross Margin Method

gross margin method a procedure for estimating the amount of ending inventory; the historical relationship of cost of goods sold to sales revenue is used in computing ending inventory

With the **gross margin method,** a firm uses available information about the dollar amounts of beginning inventory and purchases and the historical gross margin percentage to estimate the dollar amounts of cost of goods sold and ending inventory.

To illustrate, we will assume the following data for Payson Brick Company:

Net sales revenue, January 1 to March 31	$100,000
Inventory balance, January 1	15,000
Net purchases, January 1 to March 31	65,000
Gross margin percentage (historically determined percentage of net sales)	40%

With this information, the dollar amount of inventory on hand on March 31 can be estimated as follows:

		Dollars	Percentage of Sales
Net sales revenue		$100,000	100%
Cost of goods sold:			
Beginning inventory	$15,000		
Net purchases	65,000		
Total cost of goods available for sale	$80,000		
Ending inventory ($80,000 − $60,000)	20,000 (3)*		
Cost of goods sold ($100,000 − $40,000)		60,000 (2)*	60%
Gross margin ($100,000 × 0.40)		$ 40,000 (1)*	40%

*The numbers indicate the order of calculation.

In this example, the gross margin was first determined by calculating 40 percent of sales (step 1). Next, the cost of goods sold was found by subtracting gross margin from sales (step 2). Finally, the dollar amount of ending inventory was obtained by subtracting cost of goods sold from total cost of goods available for sale (step 3). Obviously, the gross margin method of estimating cost of goods sold and ending inventory assumes that the historical gross margin percentage is appropriate for the current period. This assumption is a realistic one in many fields of business. In cases where the gross margin percentage has changed, this method should be used with caution.

The gross margin method of estimating ending inventories is also useful when a fire or other calamity destroys a company's inventory. In these cases, the dollar amount of inventory lost must be determined before insurance claims can be made. The dollar amounts of sales, purchases, and beginning inventory can be obtained from prior years' financial statements and from customers, suppliers, and other sources. Then the gross margin method can be used to estimate the dollar amount of inventory lost.

The Retail Inventory Method

retail inventory method
a procedure for estimating the dollar amount of ending inventory; the ending inventory at retail prices is converted to a cost basis by using a ratio of the cost and the retail prices of goods available for sale

The **retail inventory method** of estimating the dollar amount of ending inventory is similar to the gross margin method. It is widely used by department stores, chain stores, and other retail businesses to approximate the inventory balance between physical counts. In these types of organizations, all items—including beginning inventory and purchases—are recorded on both a cost and a selling-price basis. Then, total goods available for sale can be calculated at both cost and selling price. By deducting net sales revenue for the period from the goods available for sale at selling price, the ending inventory at selling price is derived. This number is converted to ending inventory at cost by using the appropriate markup ratio (which is total goods available for sale at cost divided by total goods at selling price).

To illustrate, we will consider the following data for Ream's Hardware Store:

	Cost	Selling Prices
Beginning inventory	$ 42,000	$ 63,000
Net purchases during the month	105,900	154,500
Total goods available for sale	$147,900	$217,500
Less net sales revenue for the month		160,000
Ending inventory at selling price		$ 57,500
Cost-to-selling-price ratio ($147,900 ÷ $217,500)		68%
Ending inventory at cost (0.68 × $57,500)	$ 39,100	

In this case, the cost-to-selling-price ratio of goods available for sale is 68 percent. This percentage is applied to the ending inventory at selling price to determine the cost of the ending inventory.

The major difference between the gross margin and the retail inventory methods is that the latter uses the percentage markup—that is, the cost-to-selling-price ratio for goods available for sale—*from the current period* (by keeping current records at both cost and retail), whereas the former uses the *historical gross margin rates.* To the extent that the gross margin percentages change over time, inventory estimates based on the retail method should be more accurate.

To Summarize *There are two common methods of estimating the dollar amounts of inventory: (1) the gross margin method and (2) the retail inventory method. The former uses a historical gross margin percentage to estimate the cost of ending inventory; the latter uses the current cost-to-selling-price ratio to estimate inventory levels in retail firms.*

ACCOUTING FOR INVENTORIES IN MANUFACTURING FIRMS

raw materials materials purchased for use in manufacturing products

work-in-process partially completed units in production

finished goods manufactured products ready for sale

In this chapter, we have focused on determining inventory and cost of goods sold for a merchandising firm, that is, a wholesale or retail business. Accounting for inventory in a *manufacturing* company, however, is quite different from accounting for inventory in a retail or wholesale firm. In the latter types of firms, inventory consists only of merchandise purchased from suppliers. In manufacturing companies, three types of inventory must be accounted for: (1) **raw materials,** (2) **work-in-process,** and (3) **finished goods.**

Raw material inventories are goods purchased from suppliers for use in manufacturing the product. In a tire manufacturing firm, for example, raw materials would include rubber, steel, and other items used in making a tire. Work-in-process inventories are those production units that are in the process of being manufactured, together with their related manufacturing costs. For the tire manufacturer, the work-in-process inventory would include raw materials, factory labor (called direct labor), and other production costs (called overhead). Finally, finished goods inventories represent those units that are completed and ready for sale. At this point, you need not be concerned about these different types of inventories. The specific techniques of accounting for inventory in a manufacturing firm will be covered when you study management accounting.

Review of Learning Objectives

Objective 1

Identify the items that should be included in inventory. Inventory represents one of the largest assets for wholesale, retail, and many manufacturing firms. Since inventory is constantly being purchased and sold, it is difficult to measure it accurately. Making sure the correct amount of inventory is reported at the end of each accounting period is known as inventory cutoff.

Objective 2

Explain the effects of errors in accounting for inventory. Obtaining an accurate inventory amount involves properly matching inventory counted with inventory purchased and sold as well as accounting for goods on consignments and shipping costs. When inventory is not correctly accounted for, both cost of goods sold and net income will be reported incorrectly. Inventory errors affect net income on a dollar-for-dollar basis and usually correct themselves after two periods.

Objective 3

Describe and apply the four inventory cost flow alternatives. The four major costing methods used in accounting for inventories are specific identification, FIFO, LIFO, and average. FIFO, LIFO, and averaging can be used with either the periodic or perpetual method. Periodic averaging is called the weighted-average method, and perpetual averaging is called the moving-average method. Each of these may result in different dollar amounts of ending inventory, cost of goods sold, gross margin, and net income. A firm may choose any costing alternative without regard to the way goods physically flow through that firm. Often the costing alternative selected will depend on tax considerations. During an inflationary period, LIFO provides the lowest income and therefore lower taxes.

Objective 4

Describe and apply the lower-of-cost-or-market method of accounting for inventories. Sometimes inventory must be reported at amounts below cost. This occurs (1) when inventory is damaged, used, or obsolete or (2) when the replacement cost drops below the original inventory cost. In the first case, inventory is valued at net realizable value, and in the second, it is valued at the lower of cost or market. When lower-of-cost-or-market valuation is used, market is defined as the replacement cost of the inventory, but in no case can it be greater than the item's net realizable value (the ceiling) or less than net realizable value minus a normal profit (the floor).

Chapter 7 Inventory and Cost of Goods Sold

Objective 5

Explain the gross margin and retail methods of estimating inventories. Although most firms take a physical count of inventory at the end of each year, they sometimes may need to estimate the value of inventory prior to year-end. To estimate the dollar amount of ending inventory, they generally use one of two common methods: the gross margin method, which can be used in almost any situation, or the retail inventory method, which is limited to retail firms, such as chain or department stores. The gross margin method estimates the amount of inventory on the basis of historical gross margin percentages; the retail method uses the cost-to-selling-price ratio from the current period.

Key Terms and Concepts

ceiling *(275)*
consignee *(264)*
consignment *(264)*
consignor *(264)*
FIFO (first-in, first-out) *(267)*
finished goods *(280)*
floor *(275)*
FOB destination *(264)*

FOB shipping point *(264)*
gross margin *(261)*
gross margin method *(278)*
inventory cutoff *(260)*
LIFO (last-in, first-out) *(268)*
lower-of-cost-or-market (LCM) rule *(275)*
moving average *(273)*

net income *(261)*
net realizable value *(274)*
raw materials *(280)*
retail inventory method *(279)*
specific identification *(265)*
weighted average *(268)*
work-in-process *(280)*

Review Problem

Inventory Cost Flow Alternatives

Lehi Wholesale Distributors buys printers from manufacturers and sells them to office supply stores. During January 1994, its inventory records showed the following:

Jan. 1 Beginning inventory consisted of 26 printers at $200 each.
    10 Purchased 10 printers at $220 each.
    12 Sold 15 printers.
    15 Purchased 20 printers at $250 each.
    17 Sold 14 printers.
    19 Sold 8 printers.
    28 Purchased 9 printers at $270 each.

Required: Calculate ending inventory and cost of goods sold, using:

1. Perpetual FIFO inventory.
2. Periodic FIFO inventory.
3. Perpetual LIFO inventory.
4. Periodic LIFO inventory.
5. Moving-average inventory.
6. Weighted-average inventory.

Solution When computing ending inventory and cost of goods sold, it is usually easiest to get an overview first. The following calculations are helpful:

Beginning inventory, 26 units at $200 each	$ 5,200
Purchases: 10 units at $220	$ 2,200
20 units at 250	5,000
9 units at 270	2,430
Total purchases (39 units)	$ 9,630
Cost of goods available for sale (65 units)	$14,830
Less ending inventory (28 units)	?
Cost of goods sold (37 units)	?

Given a beginning inventory, only ending inventory and cost of goods sold will vary with the different inventory costing alternatives. Because ending inventory and cost of goods sold are complementary numbers whose sum must equal total goods available for sale, you can calculate only one of the two missing numbers in each case, and then compute the other by subtracting the first number from goods available for sale. Thus, in the calculations that follow, we will always calculate ending inventory first.

1. Perpetual FIFO Inventory

With this alternative, records must be maintained throughout the period, as shown below. The final calculation is:

Cost of goods available for sale	$14,830
Ending inventory [(19 × $250) + (9 × $270)]	7,180
Cost of goods sold	$ 7,650

PERPETUAL FIFO CALCULATIONS

	Purchased			Sold			Remaining		
Date	Number of Units	Unit Cost	Total Cost	Number of Units	Unit Cost	Total Cost	Number of Units	Unit Cost	Total Cost
Beginning Inventory							26	$200	$5,200
January 10	10	$220	$2,200				36	{ 26 at $200 10 at $220 }	$7,400
12				15	$200	$3,000	21	{ 11 at $200 10 at $220 }	$4,400
15	20	$250	$5,000				41	{ 11 at $200 10 at $220 20 at $250 }	$9,400
17				14	{ 11 at $200 3 at $220 }	$2,860	27	{ 7 at $220 20 at $250 }	$6,540
19				8	{ 7 at $220 1 at $250 }	$1,790	19	$250	$4,750
28	9	$270	$2,430				28	{ 19 at $250 9 at $270 }	$7,180
Totals	39		$9,630	37		$7,650			

2. Periodic FIFO Inventory

With this alternative, calculations will be made at the end of the period. Since we know that 28 units are left in ending inventory, we look for the last 28 units purchased because the first units purchased would all be sold. The last 28 units purchased were:

9 units at $270 each on January 28 =	$2,430
19 units at $250 each on January 15 =	4,750
Ending Inventory	$7,180

Note that the periodic FIFO inventory amount is the same as that calculated with perpetual FIFO. This is always the case. In this example, ending inventory is $7,180, and cost of goods sold is $7,650.

Chapter 7 *Inventory and Cost of Goods Sold*   283

3. Perpetual LIFO Inventory

With this alternative, as shown below, the calculation is:

Cost of goods available for sale	$14,830
Ending inventory	6,230
Cost of goods sold	$ 8,600

PERPETUAL LIFO CALCULATIONS

	Purchased			Sold			Remaining		
Date	Number of Units	Unit Cost	Total Cost	Number of Units	Unit Cost	Total Cost	Number of Units	Unit Cost	Total Cost
Beginning inventory							26	$200	$5,200
January 10	10	$220	$2,200				36	{ 26 at $200 10 at $220 }	$7,400
12				15	{ 10 at $220 5 at $200 }	$3,200	21	$200	$4,200
15	20	$250	$5,000				41	{ 21 at $200 20 at $250 }	$9,200
17				14	$250	$3,500	27	{ 21 at $200 6 at $250 }	$5,700
19				8	{ 6 at $250 2 at $200 }	$1,900	19	$200	$3,800
28	9	$270	$2,430				28	{ 19 at $200 9 at $270 }	$6,230
Totals	39		$9,630	37		$8,600			

4. Periodic LIFO Inventory

With this alternative, calculations can again be made at the end of the period, and so the first 28 units available would be considered the ending inventory (since the last ones purchased are the first ones sold). The first 28 units available were:

Beginning inventory:	26 units at $200 =	$5,200
January 10 purchase:	2 units at $220 =	440
Ending inventory		$5,640

Thus,

Cost of goods available for sale	$14,830
Ending inventory	5,640
Cost of goods sold	$ 9,190

5. Moving-Average Inventory

With this alternative, a new average cost of inventory items must be calculated each time a purchase is made, as shown in the table on the next page.

Cost of goods available for sale		$14,830
Ending inventory		6,748
Cost of goods sold		$ 8,082

MOVING-AVERAGE CALCULATIONS

Date	Purchased	Sold	Remaining	Computations
Beginning inventory			26 units at $200 = $5,200	
January 10	10 units at $220 = $2,200		36 units at $205.56 = $7,400	$5,200 + $2,200 = $7,400; $7,400 ÷ 36 = $205.56
12		15 units at $205.56 = $3,083	21 units at $205.56 = $4,317	
15	20 units at $250 = $5,000		41 units at $227.24 = $9,317	$4,317 + $5,000 = $9,317; $9,317 ÷ 41 = $227.24
17		14 units at $227.24 = $3,181	27 units at $227.24 = $6,136	
19		8 units at $227.24 = $1,818	19 units at $227.24 = $4,318	
28	9 units at $270 = $2,430		28 units at $241 = $6,748	$4,318 + $2,430 = $6,748; $6,748 ÷ 28 = $241

6. Weighted-Average Inventory

With this alternative, the calculation again can be made at the end of the period. Thus, total units available for sale is divided into total cost of goods available for sale to get a weighted average cost.

$$\frac{\text{Cost of goods available for sale}}{\text{Units available for sale}} = \frac{\$14,830}{65} = \frac{\$228.15}{\text{per unit}}$$

Cost of goods available for sale	$14,830
Less ending inventory (28 units at $228.15)	6,388
Cost of goods sold (37 units at $228.15)	$ 8,442

Discussion Questions

1. When is the cost of inventory transferred from an asset to an expense?
2. Is net income under- or overstated when purchased merchandise is counted and included in the inventory balance but not recorded as a purchase?
3. Is net income under- or overstated if inventory is sold and shipped but not recorded as a sale?
4. What is the effect on net income when goods held on consignment are included in the ending inventory balance?
5. Who owns merchandise during shipment under the terms FOB shipping point?
6. Explain the difference between cost flows and the movement of goods.
7. Which inventory cost flow alternative results in paying the least amount of taxes when prices are falling?
8. Why might you expect to see a different inventory costing alternative used in smaller, owner-operated firms than in larger, publicly owned companies?
9. Would a firm ever be prohibited from using one inventory costing alternative for tax purposes and another for financial reporting purposes?
10. When should inventory be valued at its net realizable value?
11. When should inventory be valued at the lower of cost or market?
12. Why is it necessary to know which inventory cost flow alternative is being used before the financial performances of different firms can be compared?
13. Why is it more difficult to account for the inventory of a manufacturing firm than for that of a merchandising firm?

Chapter 7 Inventory and Cost of Goods Sold

Exercises

E7-1
The Effect of Inventory Errors

As the accountant for Mt. Pleasant Enterprises, you are in the process of preparing the income statement for the year ended December 31, 1994. In doing so, you have noticed that merchandise costing $2,000 was sold for $4,000 on December 31.

Before the effects of the $4,000 sale were taken into account, the relevant income statement figures were:

Sales revenue	$80,000
Beginning inventory	18,000
Purchases	44,000
Ending inventory (includes the $2,000 inventory)	13,000

1. Prepare a partial income statement through gross margin under each of the following four assumptions:
   (a) The sale is recorded in the 1994 accounting records but because the merchandise hasn't been shipped, it is counted in the ending physical inventory.
   (b) The sale is recorded in 1994 and the merchandise is not counted in ending inventory.
   (c) The sale is not recorded in the 1994 accounting records and merchandise is counted in ending inventory.
   (d) The sale is not recorded in the 1994 accounting records and the merchandise is not counted in the ending inventory.
2. Under the given circumstances, which of the four assumptions is correct?
3. Which assumption overstates gross margin (and therefore net income)?
4. Which assumption understates gross margin (and therefore net income)?

E7-2
The Effect of Inventory Errors

The accountant for Steele Company reported the following accounting treatments for several purchase transactions that took place near December 31, 1994, the company's year-end:

Date inventory was received	Was the purchase recorded in the company's books on or before December 31, 1994?	Amount	Was the inventory counted and included in the inventory balance at December 31, 1994?
1994:			
Dec. 26	Yes	$1,100	Yes
29	Yes	800	No
31	No	1,800	Yes
1995:			
Jan. 1	No	300	Yes
1	Yes	3,000	No
2	No	600	No

1. If Steele Company's records reported purchases and ending inventory balances of $80,800 and $29,800, respectively, for 1994, what should the proper amounts in these accounts have been?
2. What would the correct amount of cost of goods sold be for 1994 if the beginning inventory balance on January 1, 1994, was $20,200?
3. By how much would the cost of goods sold be over- or understated if the corrections in question (1) were not made?

E7-3
Goods on Consignment

Company A has consignment arrangements with Supplier B and with Customer C. In particular, Supplier B ships some of its goods to Company A on consignment, and Company A ships some of its goods to Customer C on a consignment. At the end of 1994, Company A's accounting records showed:

Goods on consignment from Supplier B	$ 8,000
Goods on consignment to Customer C	$10,000

1. If a physical count of all inventory revealed that $30,000 of goods were on hand, what amount of ending inventory should be reported?
2. If the amount of the beginning inventory for the year was $27,000 and purchases during the year were $59,000, what is the cost of goods sold for the year? [Assume the ending inventory from question (1).]
3. If, instead of these facts, Company A had only $4,000 of the goods on consignment with Customer C and $10,000 of consigned goods from Supplier B, and if physical goods on hand totaled $36,000, what would the correct amount of the ending inventory be?
4. With respect to question (3), if beginning inventory totaled $24,000 and the cost of goods sold was $47,500, what were the purchases?

E7-4
FIFO, LIFO, and Weighted-Average Calculations (Periodic Inventory Method)

The following transactions took place with respect to Model M computers in Alpha's Computer Store during April 1994:

Apr.	1	Beginning inventory	40 computers at $1,200
	5	Purchase of Model M computers	15 computers at $1,300
	11	Purchase of Model M computers	16 computers at $1,350
	19	Sale of Model M computers	20 computers at $3,000
	24	Purchase of Model M computers	10 computers at $1,400
	30	Sale of Model M computers	12 computers at $3,000

Assuming the periodic inventory method, compute the cost of goods sold and ending inventory balances using the following inventory costing alternatives:

1. Weighted average.
2. FIFO.
3. LIFO.

E7-5
Specific Identification Inventory Costing

Ercanbrack's Diamond Shop is computing its inventory and cost of goods sold for November 1994. At the beginning of the month, the following jewelry items were in stock:

Ring A	8 at $600 =	$ 4,800
Ring A	10 at 650 =	6,500
Ring B	5 at 300 =	1,500
Ring B	6 at 350 =	2,100
Ring B	3 at 450 =	1,350
Ring C	7 at 200 =	1,400
Ring C	8 at 250 =	2,000
		$19,650

During the month, the following rings were purchased: 4 type A rings at $600, 2 type B rings at $450, and 5 type C rings at $300. Also during the month, the following sales were made:

Ring Type	Quantity Sold	Sales Price	Cost
A	2	$1,000	$600
A	3	1,050	600
A	1	1,200	650
B	2	850	450
B	2	800	350
C	4	450	200
C	3	500	250
C	1	550	250

Because of the high cost per item, Ercanbrack uses specific-identification inventory costing.

1. Calculate cost of goods sold and ending inventory balances for November.
2. Calculate gross margin for the month.

E7-6
FIFO, LIFO, and Weighted-Average Calculations (Periodic Inventory Method)

On the last day of July 1994, the inventory records of Mario's Bookstore showed the following:

July	1	Beginning inventory	28,000 at $2.00 = $56,000
	5	Sold	4,000
	13	Purchased	6,000 at 2.25 = 13,500
	17	Sold	3,000
	25	Purchased	8,000 at 2.50 = 20,000
	27	Sold	5,000
			$89,500

Assuming the periodic inventory method, compute Mario's cost of goods sold and ending inventory balances for July using the following cost flows (round unit costs to the nearest cent):

1. FIFO.
2. LIFO.
3. Weighted average.

E7-7
FIFO, LIFO, and Moving-Average Calculations (Perpetual Inventory Method)

1. Using the figures in E7-6, compute the ending inventory and cost of goods sold balances with (a) FIFO, (b) LIFO, and (c) moving average, using the perpetual inventory method. Compute unit costs to the nearest cent.
2. Why are periodic LIFO and perpetual LIFO cost of goods sold amounts usually different?
3. Which of the three alternatives is best? Why?

E7-8
Lower of Cost or Market

Prepare the necessary journal entries to account for the purchases and year-end adjustments of the inventory of Payson Manufacturing Company. All purchases are made on account. Payson uses the periodic inventory method.

1. Purchased 50 standard widgets for $8 each to sell at $14 per unit.
2. Purchased 15 deluxe widgets at $20 per unit to sell for $30 per unit.

3. At the end of the year, the standard widgets could be purchased for $9 and are selling for $15.
4. At the end of the year, the deluxe widgets could be purchased for $10 and are selling for $16 per unit. Selling costs are $4 per unit, and normal profit is $6 per unit.
5. At the end of the second year, standard widgets could be purchased for $6 and are selling for $8. Selling costs are $1 per widget, and normal profit is $2 per widget.
6. At the end of the second year, the deluxe widgets could be purchased for $9 and are selling for $20. Selling costs and normal profit remain the same as in (4).

E7-9
Valuation of Inventory

Broderick Company sells lumber. Inventory cost data per 1,000 board feet of lumber for the Broderick Company are as follows:

Item	Quantity on Hand (per 1,000 board ft.)	Original Cost (per 1,000 board ft.)	Current Replacement Cost (per 1,000 board ft.)	Net Realizable Value (per 1,000 board ft.)	Net Realizable Value Minus Normal Profit
Plywood	25	$ 600	$ 600	$ 500	$ 400
Oak	20	2,000	1,800	1,900	1,850
Pine	43	800	700	800	600
Redwood	12	1,400	1,800	1,600	1,300

1. By what amount, if any, should each item, considered separately, be written down?
2. Make the appropriate journal entry (or entries):
   (a) Assuming that each inventory item is considered separately.
   (b) Assuming that LCM is applied to total inventory.

E7-10
Gross Margin Method of Estimating Inventory

Jason Company needs to estimate the inventory balance for its quarterly financial statements. The periodic inventory method is used. Records show that quarterly sales totaled $400,000, beginning inventory was $80,000, and purchases totaled $280,000; the historical gross margin percentage has averaged approximately 40 percent.

1. What is the approximate amount of ending inventory?
2. If a physical count shows only $100,000 in inventory, what could be the explanation for the difference?

E7-11
Retail Inventory Estimation Method

Beattle Clothing Store uses the retail inventory method to estimate ending inventory. During the first six months of 1994, the store had the following balances:

	At Cost	At Selling Price
Beginning inventory	$ 90,000	$130,000
Purchases	150,000	224,000
Sales revenue		236,000

Given these data, what is the cost of the inventory that Beattle should report on its March 31 quarterly financial statements? (Round the cost ratio to the nearest whole percent.)

Problem Set A

P7A-1
What Should Be Included in Inventory?

Demetrius is trying to compute the inventory balance for the December 31, 1994, financial statements of his automotive parts shop. He has computed a tentative balance of $52,600 but suspects that several adjustments still need to be made. In particular, he believes that the following could affect his inventory balance:

1. A shipment of goods that cost $3,000 was received on December 28, 1994. It was properly recorded as a purchase in 1994 but not counted with the ending inventory.
2. Another shipment of goods (FOB destination) was received on January 2, 1995, and cost $800. It was properly recorded as a purchase in 1995 but was counted with 1994's ending inventory.
3. A $2,800 shipment of goods to a customer on January 3 was recorded as a sale in 1995 but was not included in the December 31, 1994, ending inventory balance. The goods cost $2,000.
4. The company had goods costing $6,000 on consignment with a customer, and $5,000 of merchandise was on consignment from a vendor. Neither amount was included in the $52,600 figure.
5. The following amounts represent merchandise that was in transit on December 31, 1994, and was recorded as purchases and sales in 1994 but not included in the December 31 inventory.
    (a) Ordered by Demetrius, $1,800, FOB destination.
    (b) Ordered by Demetrius, $600, FOB shipping point.
    (c) Sold by Demetrius, cost $4,000, FOB shipping point.
    (d) Sold by Demetrius, cost $4,600, FOB destination.

Required:
1. Determine the correct amount of ending inventory at December 31, 1994.
2. Assuming purchases (before any adjustment, if any) totaled $86,400 and beginning inventory (January 1, 1994) totaled $31,600, determine the cost of goods sold in 1994.

P7A-2
Correction of Inventory Errors

The annual reported income for Salazar Company for the years 1992-1995 is shown here. However, a review of the inventory records reveals inventory misstatements.

	1992	1993	1994	1995
Reported net income	$30,000	$40,000	$35,000	$45,000
Inventory overstatement, end of year		3,000		2,000
Inventory understatement, end of year	4,000		1,000	

Required: Using the data provided, calculate the correct net income for each year.

P7A-3
Tax Effects of FIFO, LIFO, and Weighted Average (Periodic Inventory Method)

Tallow Corporation shows the following transactions in its 1994 books:

Beginning inventory	700 units at $ 6	= $4,200
Purchase	300 units at $ 8	= 2,400
Sale	400 units at $16 (sales price)	
Purchase	200 units at $10	= 2,000
Sale	300 units at $18 (sales prices)	
		$8,600

Required: 1. Assuming Tallow Corporation is taxed at 28 percent, determine its 1994 tax liability under each of the following three inventory alternatives. Assume that the only expense during 1994, other than cost of goods sold, was a $5,000 administrative expense. (Round income statement numbers to the nearest dollar.)
   (a) FIFO (periodic).
   (b) LIFO (periodic).
   (c) Weighted average (periodic).
2. Identify the alternative that results in the lowest tax liability. Explain.

P7A-4
Unifying Concepts: Inventory Cost Flow Alternatives

Dudley Wholesale buys canned pickles from canneries and sells them to retail markets. During August 1994 Dudley's inventory records showed the following:

Aug.			
1	Beginning inventory	4,100 cases at	$10.50
4	Purchase	1,500 cases at	11.00
9	Sale	950 cases at	19.95
13	Purchase	1,000 cases at	11.00
19	Sale	1,450 cases at	19.95
26	Purchase	1,700 cases at	11.50
30	Sale	1,900 cases at	19.95

Even though it requires more computational effort, Dudley uses the perpetual inventory method because management feels the extra cost is justified by the advantage of always having current knowledge of inventory levels.

Required: 1. Calculate the cost of goods sold and ending inventory using the following cost flow alternatives. (Calculate unit costs to the nearest tenth of a cent.)
   (a) FIFO.
   (b) LIFO.
   (c) Moving average.
2. **Interpretive Question** Why are the cost of goods sold amounts the same under the perpetual FIFO and the periodic FIFO costing methods?
3. Calculate the ending inventory and the cost of goods sold using the periodic LIFO costing method.
4. **Interpretive Question** In this particular case, why does LIFO result in the same amounts under both periodic and perpetual inventory methods?

P7A-5
The Perpetual and Periodic Inventory Methods

Mares Corporation had the following transactions relating to its inventory during November 1994:

Date		Units	Unit Cost	Total
Nov. 1	Balance on hand	200	$5.00	$1,000
5	Purchase	60	6.00	360
11	Sale	150		
14	Sale	50		
19	Purchase	120	6.50	780
21	Sale	30		
26	Purchase	50	7.00	350

Chapter 7 Inventory and Cost of Goods Sold

Required: Determine the ending inventory using each of the following costing methods:
1. Periodic FIFO.
2. Periodic LIFO.
3. Weighted average.
4. Perpetual FIFO.
5. Perpetual LIFO.

P7A-6
Inventory Cost Flow Alternatives

Stocks Inc. sells weight-lifting equipment. The sales and inventory records of the company for January through March 1994 were as follows:

	Weight-Lifting Sets	Unit Cost	Total Cost
Beginning inventory, January 1	460	$30	$13,800
Purchase, January 16	110	32	3,520
Sale, January 25 ($45.00 per set)	216		
Purchase, February 16	105	36	3,780
Sale, February 27 ($40.00 per set)	307		
Purchase, March 10	150	28	4,200
Sale, March 30 ($50.00 per set)	190		

Required:
1. Determine the amounts for ending inventory, cost of goods sold, and gross margin under the following costing alternatives:
   (a) FIFO.
   (b) LIFO.
   (c) Weighted average.
   Use the periodic inventory method. Round amounts to the nearest dollar.
2. **Interpretive Question** Which alternative results in the highest gross margin? Why?

P7A-7
Inventory Theft Loss

In November 1994, Staley Company had a significant amount of its inventory stolen. The company determined the cost of its inventory not stolen to be $16,000. The following information was taken from the records of the company:

	January 1, 1994 to Date of Theft	1993
Purchases	$ 85,000	$ 80,000
Purchase returns & allowances	1,000	1,200
Sales	110,000	118,000
Sales returns & allowances	3,000	3,200
Insurance expense	2,000	2,100
Salaries expense	28,000	32,000
Rent	6,000	7,000
Advertising expense	3,500	4,000
Depreciation expense	4,500	5,000
Beginning inventory	25,000	24,000
Purchase discounts	500	600

Required: Using the gross margin method, compute the cost of the inventory stolen. (Round the gross margin percentage to the nearest tenth of a percent.)

P7A-8
Unifying Concepts: Inventory Estimation Methods

Jamestown Clothing Store has the following information available:

	At Cost	At Selling Price	Other
Purchases during January 1994	$120,000	$170,000	
Inventory balance, January 1, 1994	48,000	62,000	
Sales during January 1994		180,000	
Average gross margin rate for the last three years			25%

Required:
1. On the basis of this information, estimate the cost of inventory on hand at January 31, 1994, using:
   (a) The gross margin method.
   (b) The retail inventory method.
   Round to the nearest whole percent.
2. **Interpretive Question** Which method is probably the more accurate? Why?

Problem Set B

P7B-1
The Effect of Inventory Errors

You have been hired as the accountant for Tracy Company, which uses the periodic inventory method. In reviewing the firm's records, you have noted what you think are several accounting errors made during the current year, 1994. These potential mistakes are listed as follows:

(a) A $3,000 purchase of merchandise was properly recorded in the Purchases account, but the related Accounts Payable account was credited for only $2,000.
(b) A $3,500 shipment of merchandise received just before the end of the year was properly recorded in the Purchases account but was not physically counted in the inventory and hence was excluded from the ending inventory balance.
(c) A $6,700 purchase of merchandise was erroneously recorded as a $7,600 purchase.
(d) A $500 purchase of merchandise was not recorded either as a purchase or as an account payable.
(e) During the year, $1,200 of defective merchandise was sent back to a supplier. The original purchase entry had been recorded, but the merchandise return entry was not recorded.
(f) During the physical inventory count, inventory that cost $400 was counted twice.

Required:
1. If the previous accountant had tentatively computed the 1994 gross margin to be $10,000, what would be the correct gross margin for the year?
2. If the company is taxed at 40 percent, how much additional tax will it have to pay when these errors are corrected?
3. If these mistakes are not corrected, how much will the 1995 net income be in error?

P7B-2
Computing Beginning Inventory from Ending Inventory

The Acosta Company sell widgets. During a recent fire, the inventory records were destroyed. The accountant has been able to piece together the following information concerning August purchases:

Chapter 7 Inventory and Cost of Goods Sold

Date	Quantity	Unit Price
Aug. 2	15,000	$5.00
8	20,000	5.20
15	10,000	5.10
23	13,000	5.30

Additional information:

On August 31, 14,000 units were on hand costing $74,000. Acosta Company has always used the periodic FIFO inventory costing system. Gross margin on sales for August was $245,100. In August, Acosta sold 50,000 widgets at $10 each.

Required: Reconstruct the beginning inventory amount in units and dollar value for the month of August.

P7B-3
Analysis of Inventory Costing Alternatives

For the years 1993 through 1995, Prothro Company reported the following ending inventories and net incomes. Prothro Company uses the LIFO inventory costing alternative.

Year	LIFO Ending Inventory	Net Income
1993	$ 66,000	$281,000
1994	99,000	274,000
1995	129,000	300,000

Required:
1. Ignoring the effects of income taxes, determine the amount of net income Prothro would have reported in 1994 and 1995 if it had used FIFO instead of LIFO. Assume FIFO ending inventories of $75,000 in 1993, $105,000 in 1994, and $140,000 in 1995.
2. Assuming the company's tax rate is 45 percent, determine the amount of additional tax that will have to be paid in 1995 if FIFO is used instead of LIFO.

P7B-4
Cost of Goods Sold Calculations

Complete the Cost of Goods Sold section for the income statements of the following five companies:

	Able Company	Baker Company	Carter Company	Delmont Company	Eureka Company
Beginning inventory	$16,000	$24,800	(5) $17,100	(7) $32,900	$19,200
Purchases	26,500	(3) 65,600	43,000	89,500	(9) 64,500
Purchase returns and allowances	(1) 400	1,000	1,800	200	2,200
Cost of goods available for sale	42,100	(4) 89,400	58,300	(8) 122,200	81,500
Ending inventory	(2) 8,700	22,200	15,200	28,800	(10) 13,100
Cost of goods sold	33,400	67,200	(6) 43,100	93,400	68,400

P7B-5
Inventory Cost Flow Alternatives

Robinson Cement Company sells two products: concrete mix in bags and plaster mix in bags. Beginning inventory for September 1, 1994, is as follows:

Item	No. of Bags	Unit Cost
Concrete	100	$16.00
Plaster	300	14.00

Purchases during March were as follows:

Date	Item	No. of Bags	Unit Cost
Sept. 5	Concrete	100	$16.60
5	Plaster..	200	14.20
16	Concrete	100	15.80
28	Plaster..	100	13.60

During September, the firm sold 150 bags of concrete at $22 each and 350 bags of plaster at $20 each.

Required:
1. Assuming the periodic inventory method, calculate separately for concrete and plaster the sales revenue, cost of goods sold, ending inventory, and gross margin as of September 30, 1994, using the following cost flow alternatives:
   (a) FIFO.
   (b) LIFO.
   (c) Weighted average.
2. **Interpretive Question** Which alternative would result in paying the lowest taxes? Why?

P7B-6
Estimating Cost of Goods Sold

Garber Company is located in San Francisco, California. During 1994 an earthquake damaged its building and destroyed many of the accounting records. The president of the company has requested that you prepare an income statement for the year ended December 31, 1994. In doing so, you have been able to gather the following information:

Inventory balance, January 1, 1994	$ 50,000
Purchases made during 1994	130,000
Sales made during 1994	210,000
Operating expenses incurred during 1994 (other than cost of goods sold)	18,000

Garber Company's cost of goods sold has been approximately 75 percent of sales for the past 5 years.

Required: Prepare an income statement for Garber Company for the year ending December 31, 1994, using the available information. (Ignore income taxes.)

P7B-7
Inventory Estimation Methods

The following information for Numeyer Company is available for the third quarter of 1994:

Income Statements

	July	August	Sept.	Totals 3rd Quarter
Sales revenue	$150,000	$106,000	$120,000	$376,000
Cost of goods sold	91,500	62,540	?	?
Gross margin	$ 58,500	$ 43,460	?	?
Operating expenses	48,000	32,000	34,000	114,000
Pretax income	$ 10,500	$ 11,460	?	$?
Gross margin ratio	0.39	0.41	0.40	(estimated)

Chapter 7 *Inventory and Cost of Goods Sold* 295

The company uses the periodic inventory method. Although monthly statements are prepared, a monthly inventory count is not made. Instead, the company uses the gross margin method to estimate ending inventory. Inventory estimates at July 31 and August 31 were $21,000 and $16,000, respectively.

Required: 1. Calculate the cost of goods sold for September given the following additional data:

Cost of goods sold:	Amounts	Computations
Beginning inventory	$26,000	From records
Purchases	54,000	From records
Goods available for sale	?	?
Ending inventory	?	?
Cost of goods sold	?	?

2. Fill in the missing figures for September and the third quarter totals in the income statements given. (Ignore income taxes.)

P7B-8

Unifying Concepts: Analysis of Inventory Costing Methods

This problem demonstrates the effect on income of using FIFO and LIFO when prices are (a) rising and (b) falling. Four different situations are evaluated as follows:

Situation A—FIFO is used when prices are rising.
Situation B—LIFO is used when prices are rising.
Situation C—FIFO is used when prices are falling.
Situation D—LIFO is used when prices are falling.

The basic data common to all four situations are sales, 500 units for $5,000; beginning inventory, 400 units; purchases, 500 units; ending inventory, 400 units; operating expense, $3,200. The following income statements have been prepared for each situation:

	Prices Rising		Prices Falling	
	Situation A FIFO	Situation B LIFO	Situation C FIFO	Situation D LIFO
Sales revenue	$5,000	$5,000	$5,000	$5,000
Cost of goods sold:				
Beginning inventory	$ 800	_____	_____	_____
Purchases	1,500	_____	_____	_____
Cost of goods available for sale	$2,300	_____	_____	_____
Ending inventory	1,200	_____	_____	_____
Cost of goods sold	$1,100	_____	_____	_____
Gross margin	$3,900	_____	_____	_____
Operating expenses	3,200	_____	_____	_____
Pretax income	$ 700	_____	_____	_____
Income tax expense (20%)	140	_____	_____	_____
Net income	$ 560	_____	_____	_____

Required: 1. Complete the income statement for each situation. In situations A and B (prices rising), assume the following: beginning inventory, 400 units at $2 = $800;

purchases, 500 units at $3 = $1,500. In situations C and D (prices falling), assume the opposite; that is, beginning inventory, 400 units at $3 = $1,200; purchases, 500 units at $2 = $1,000. Use periodic inventory procedures.

2. **Interpretive Question** Analyze the effects on pretax income, income taxes, and net income as demonstrated in question (1) when prices are rising and when prices are falling.
3. **Interpretive Question** Would you recommend FIFO or LIFO? Explain.

Business Analysis Case 1   *Adams Aviation Inc.*

Adams Aviation Inc. is a retail operation that buys Cessna 180 airplanes from manufacturers and sells them to individuals. Adams is the only airline dealer in a small Montana town and so has a monopoly on the market. Because of the high cost of airplanes and the low volume of sales, Adams maintains as small an inventory as possible. In fact, at the beginning of October, the company had no inventory or liabilities, as shown by the following balance sheet:

Adams Aviation Inc.
Balance Sheet
October 1, 1994

Assets		Stockholders' Equity	
Cash	$450,000	Capital stock	$250,000
		Retained earnings	200,000
Total assets	$450,000	Total stockholders' equity	$450,000

On October 8, Adams took delivery of an airplane purchased at a price of $200,000. On October 18, Adams sold the airplane for $250,000. On October 22, Adams purchased another airplane for $220,000. (There was a price increase.) During October, operating expenses were $18,000. All transactions were paid in cash. Adams uses the same inventory method for income-tax and financial-reporting purposes, and its income tax rate is 35 percent.

Required:
1. Prepare income statements for Adams for the month of October using:
   (a) The periodic FIFO inventory method.
   (b) The periodic LIFO inventory method.
   (c) The perpetual LIFO inventory method.
2. Prepare balance sheets as of October 31, using the three inventory costing methods.
3. Assume that Adams has a policy of paying dividends each period exactly equal to net income. What effect would the dividend payment have on the balance sheets prepared in question (2)?
4. Assume that the price of airplanes increases to $240,000 on November 1. Will Adams be able to pay cash for a new airplane?
5. Which method is more realistic in representing Adams's income?
6. Why do the periodic FIFO and perpetual LIFO methods give the same results?

Business Analysis Case 2 *Boulder Paint Company*

On December 15, 1994, a major fire destroyed the warehouse contents of Boulder Paint Company in Southern Idaho. To file a claim for an insurance reimbursement, the company needed to estimate the amount of inventory lost in the fire. In an attempt to estimate the fire loss, they gathered the following information:

(a) By consulting with suppliers, they determined that total purchases to the date of the fire amounted to $1,210,000.
(b) The December 31, 1993, balance sheet noted an inventory balance of $250,000.
(c) Commissions (for the sales staff) totaled $160,000 for the year. Of the $160,000 in commissions, 40 percent was paid at a commission rate of 5 percent, and the balance was paid at a rate of 10 percent. The company's gross margin rates during the previous several years have averaged about 45 percent.

Required: Answer the following questions based on the information provided:

1. How did the paint company determine its fire loss?
2. What is the estimated amount of the inventory destroyed in the fire?
3. If the insurance company thought the claim was too high, on what basis might it have argued that the paint company's calculations are not valid?
4. What would the estimate of the loss have been if the appropriate gross margin rate were 35 percent instead of 45 percent?

Ethics Case *XYZ Automobile Manufacturing Company*

Two years ago, the XYZ Automobile Manufacturing Company that you work for implemented a quality assurance program to test its new cars. Cars, with the odometers disconnected, were given to executives and other trusted employees to test drive to determine if the cars were ready for shipment to dealers. Before tested cars were shipped, the odometers were reconnected with no indication that the cars had been driven.

As the company controller, you had agreed initially with the testing concept. After all, the test-drive period was intended to last only a few days and was in the best interest of car buyers because "bugs" could be eliminated before the cars were shipped. Now, however, you have your doubts about the ethics of the program.

Many of the executives and employees have been driving the cars for weeks and even months, and you are sure that some of the cars have between 5,000 and 10,000 unrecorded miles on them before being shipped. You wonder if the company is really selling new or used cars.

Required: Answer the following questions based on the information provided:

1. Is this inventory testing program in the best interest of customers, or is the company taking advantage of dealers and consumers?
2. Do you believe this program of test-driving is legal and ethical?
3. If you believe the testing program is unethical or illegal, what should you do?

Part 3

Reporting Assets, Liabilities, and Owners' Equity

CHAPTERS

8 Cash, Marketable Securities, and Receivables
  Appendix – Internal Control
9 Property, Plant, and Equipment; Intangible Assets; and Natural Resources
10 Liabilities
11 Bonds Payable
12 Long-Term Investments
13 Owners' Equity – The Corporation
   Appendix – Consolidated Financial Statements
14 Owner's Equity – Proprietorships and Partnerships

Chapter 8

Cash, Marketable Securities, and Receivables

Learning Objectives

After studying this chapter, you should be able to:
1. Describe the procedures used to control and account for cash, including petty cash funds and bank reconciliations.
2. Explain the recording and valuation of marketable securities and other short-term investments.
3. Describe the accounting for accounts receivable, including losses from uncollectible accounts.
4. Explain the accounting for notes receivable.

SETTING THE STAGE

In recent years, many savings and loans in the United States have gone bankrupt, with their depositors being rescued by U.S. taxpayers. No savings and loan failure has received more coverage in the press than Lincoln Savings and Loan of California, the largest failure in the history of U.S. thrift institutions.[1] Lincoln was seized by federal regulators in April 1989. Since then, there have been both federal and state indictments against its owners (Charles Keating and others) alleging accounting abuses, including the manipulation of real estate transactions, accounts receivable, and net income. After purchasing Lincoln in 1984, Keating made significant changes. Instead of focusing on home mortgages, as had been done in the past, Keating and his cronies plunged into high-risk speculation in currency futures, junk bonds, corporate stock, hotels, and vast tracts of desert land in Arizona. To show high profits, they arranged several real estate "sales" just before the end of accounting periods. Most of these sales involved small down payments of cash and large receivables. A sample transaction might look like the following. (These numbers are representative but not exact.)

Cash	1,000,000	
Receivables	99,000,000	
Real estate		40,000,000
Income		60,000,000

After federal regulators seized Lincoln, they hired the CPA firm of Kenneth Leventhal & Co. to examine these real estate transactions and determine if the receivables and income should have been recognized. Leventhal investigated 15 transactions that accounted for $135 million in income—approximately half of Lincoln's income since the time Keating acquired it—and concluded that none of the profits should have been allowed. In their report they stated, "Seldom in our experience have we encountered a more egregious example of the misapplication of generally accepted accounting principles."

Essentially, the lawsuits allege that Keating significantly manipulated real estate transactions and receivables to make it appear that Lincoln was financially sound when, in fact, it never did make a profit. Like inventory, receivables can be manipulated to report higher profits. (In fact, most financial state-

---

[1] This description is based on articles in *The Wall Street Journal: The Wall Street Journal,* August 7, 1989, p. A10; November 20, 1989, p. A8; November 21, 1989, p. A20; November 24, 1989, p. A3; November 27, 1989, p. A10; January 8, 1990, p. A12.

ment frauds misstate either receivables or inventory.) Even Barry Minkow of ZZZZ Best (see "Setting the Stage" in Chapter 6) was known to say, "Receivables are a wonderful thing. All you need to do to increase income is create a receivable. Debit a receivable and credit revenue and zap, you've got income."[2]

With this chapter, we begin a detailed examination of the balance sheet. We will learn how to account for cash, marketable securities, accounts receivable, and notes receivable. When companies sell goods or services, they either receive cash or acquire receivables, which usually are converted to cash within a short period of time. Sometimes companies temporarily have cash in excess of the amount needed for current operations. To earn income with the excess cash, it is usually invested in marketable securities or other assets, such as certificates of deposit. We study these assets together because they are the most **liquid** assets, and they are all available for meeting current obligations. Other balance sheet accounts are discussed in Chapters 9 through 14.

liquid *readily convertible into cash*

CONTROLLING AND ACCOUNTING FOR CASH

Objective 1

Describe the procedures used to control and account for cash, including petty cash funds and bank reconciliations.

Cash is obviously the most liquid of all assets. It includes coins, currency, money orders and checks (made payable or endorsed to the company), and money on deposit with banks or savings institutions. All the various transactions involving these forms of cash are summarized and reported under a single balance sheet caption, Cash. On a recent balance sheet, for example, Rockwell International showed a cash balance of $756.9 million, of which $713 million comprised savings deposits, and only a small amount was actual operating cash in checking accounts. The cash does not, however, include postage stamps (prepaid expenses), IOUs (receivables), or postdated checks (receivables). Further, cash that is restricted for special purposes (such as the repayment of a long-term liability) or restricted by law (such as cash in foreign banks that cannot be taken out of those countries) is excluded from the cash balance and reported elsewhere.

The major elements in accounting for cash are (1) recording and processing cash transactions, (2) accounting for petty cash, and (3) preparing bank reconciliations.

In many companies, cash transactions are journalized, posted, and summarized by a computer. Accountants merely "input" the original data: The computer performs most of the accounting functions, including the preparation of special journals and the financial statements. In relatively small businesses, cash transactions are more likely to be entered manually, often in separate cash receipts and cash disbursements journals. These journals are discussed in the appendix on special journals in Chapter 5.

Control of Cash

Because of its value, and because it is the most liquid asset, cash must be carefully safeguarded. In particular, management must attempt to:

---

[2] From "Cooking the Books," a videotape produced by the National Association of Certified Fraud Examiners, Austin, Texas, 1991.

1. Prevent losses of cash by theft or fraud.
2. Provide accurate accounting of all inflows, outflows, and balances of cash.
3. Maintain a sufficient balance of cash on hand to provide for day-to-day requirements, finance current operations, and satisfy maturing liabilities.
4. Prevent large amounts of excess idle cash from accumulating on hand or in checking accounts.

Several control procedures have been developed to help management meet these objectives. In the appendix on internal control at the back of this chapter, we discuss in detail controls for cash and other assets. However, because cash is particularly vulnerable to loss or misuse, here we mention three important controls that are an integral part of accounting for cash.

One of the most important controls for cash is that the *handling* of cash be separated from the *recording* of cash. The purpose of this separation of duties is to make it difficult for theft or errors to occur unless two or more people are involved. As an example of what can happen without this safeguard, consider the case of an employee who both opens the mail and keeps the books. He or she could pocket a cash payment from one customer and not record the receipt until payment is received from a second customer. The recording of a second customer's payment could be made when a third customer pays, and so on. This type of delayed recording of payments is called **lapping** and allows an employee to use company money for extended periods of time.

lapping *a procedure used to conceal the theft of cash by crediting the payment from one customer to another customer's account on a delayed basis*

Separation of duties actually involves three procedures: (1) the separation of cash receiving from cash disbursing, (2) the clear identification and use of specific routines for cash receiving and cash disbursing, and (3) the assignment of each aspect of cash handling and accounting to different individuals.

A second cash control practice is to require that all cash receipts be deposited daily in bank accounts. Most cash comes from over-the-counter sales or accounts receivable collected through the mail. To ensure that all such sales are properly accounted for, businesses use cash registers that provide a tape of the day's sales. At the end of the day, all cash is counted, compared with the amount on the tape, and deposited in the bank. Payments received through the mail are controlled by separating the receiving, recording, and depositing functions. The person who receives the cash and checks makes a list, then forwards the cash and checks to the cashier for deposit in the bank. The list is also sent to the accounting department to be compared with the actual deposit slip from the bank and entered into the cash receipts journal. If all cash receipts are deposited on the day they are received, the likelihood of cash being lost or misused is minimized.

A third cash-control practice is to require that all cash expenditures (except those paid out of petty cash) be made with prenumbered checks. In addition, the person or persons who approve payment should be different from those who actually sign the checks. In companies where this system is used, no checks can be signed unless they are accompanied by an approved invoice that gives the purpose of the check and the justification and verification for the expenditure. Any check not actually used should be clearly marked "void," or otherwise mutilated, and filed in sequence in a convenient place so that all checks can be accounted for.

In addition to safeguarding and protecting cash, a business must ensure that cash is wisely managed. In fact, many businesses establish elaborate control and budgeting procedures for monitoring cash balances, working capital ratios, and estimated future cash needs. Companies also try to keep only minimum balances in no-interest or low-interest checking accounts, with other cash in more high-yielding investments such as certificates of deposit.

Accounting for Petty Cash

For control purposes, it makes sense to pay all bills by check since a check provides a permanent record of each transaction. However, most businesses find it too expensive and inconvenient to write checks for small miscellaneous cash expenditures. Instead, they usually pay for such items as minor delivery charges, stamps, and inexpensive supplies out of cash kept on hand in what is called a **petty cash fund.** The size of a petty cash fund depends on the number, magnitude, and frequency of these miscellaneous expenditures. Obviously, the petty cash funds of a multinational corporation will be much larger than those of a small business. Businesses want the fund to be large enough so that it does not have to be replenished too often but not so large that it tempts theft or misuse. Most firms keep enough cash on hand to cover about one month's miscellaneous expenditures. It is also common for firms to limit the amount that can be taken from the petty cash fund for a single expenditure.

Although a petty cash fund is more difficult to control than checks, potential losses can be minimized by handling the petty cash fund on an imprest basis. That is, any cash removed from the fund must be replaced by a prenumbered petty cash voucher accompanied by a receipt or invoice from the supplier of the item or service purchased. The receipt or invoice validates the type and amount of the expenditure. Thus, with an **imprest petty cash fund,** the balance can be easily checked. The total of unused cash and vouchers should always equal the imprest balance. Exhibit 8-1 is a voucher showing that a $42 delivery bill from Taylor Trucking Company was paid from petty cash.

To illustrate the accounting for an imprest petty cash fund, we will assume that on July 1, Cooper Company decided to establish a petty cash fund of $200.

petty cash fund *a small amount of cash kept on hand for making miscellaneous payments*

imprest petty cash fund *a petty cash fund in which all expenditures are documented by vouchers or vendors' receipts or invoices; the total of the vouchers and cash in the fund should equal the established balance*

Exhibit 8-1 *Petty Cash Voucher*

PETTY CASH VOUCHER

No. 22   DATE July 17

PAID TO Taylor Trucking

FOR Delivery Bill   AMOUNT $ 42 | 00

CHARGE TO ACCOUNT 616 (Freight-In)

SIGNATURE OF PERSON USING FUNDS *Janet Doan*

A check was made out to petty cash and cashed at the bank. The $200 cash was placed in a convenient but safe place. The journal entry would be:

July 1	Petty Cash	200	
	Cash		200
	Established a $200 petty cash fund.		

For each expenditure, a voucher (accompanied by a receipt) is prepared to account for the money spent. For example, if Cooper paid $40 for office supplies, $42 for freight, and $30 for postage, three vouchers would be placed in the fund. Petty cash expenditures are not recorded as they occur; instead a single entry is made when the petty cash fund is replenished. The entry to replenish Cooper's petty cash fund would be:

Aug. 1	Office Supplies	40	
	Freight-In	42	
	Postage Expense	30	
	Cash		112
	Replenished the petty cash fund.		

As this entry indicates, when the petty cash fund is replenished, a check is written for the total amount of all expenditures, Cash is credited, and the affected expense accounts are debited individually. The items in this entry are then posted to their respective accounts. At no time is the petty cash fund replenished by debiting or crediting the Petty Cash account. The only entries ever made to that account are those that permanently increase or decrease its original dollar amount. If, for example, Cooper decided to increase the imprest fund balance from $200 to $350, the increase would be recorded as shown in the following journal entry:

Petty Cash	150	
Cash		150
Increased petty cash fund imprest balance to $350.		

For control purposes, one person should have complete responsibility for the petty cash fund. A different person should be authorized to write the checks that replenish the fund. The custodian of the petty cash fund should be responsible for maintaining the fund's balance and should make sure that all petty cash vouchers are prenumbered and used only once.

If the actual balance is ever different from the amount that should be in the fund (usually because of an error in making change), the discrepancy should be recorded in an account called **Cash Over and Short**. This account is debited

Cash Over and Short *an account used to record overages and shortages in petty cash*

BUSINESS ENVIRONMENT ESSAY
Not so Petty Cash

Although the petty cash funds of most U.S. companies are quite small and only have a few transactions each month, they are not so small in many foreign companies. Take Japanese companies, for example. In Japan, checks are seldom used to pay bills. Payments are made either with wire transfers through banks or with petty cash. Petty cash funds are used for travel advances, entertainment expenses, small purchases, temporary loans to employees, and many other purchases. In one small Japanese company, for example, there are over 250 petty cash transactions each month. Obviously, such volume requires a larger fund balance and allows for a greater possibility of misuse or even fraud. In Japan, however, dishonest acts by employees are rarely a problem. Employees in Japan generally work for only one company throughout their lives and are very loyal to that company. In return, Japanese companies take care of their employees very well. In addition, as a Japanese executive once said, "If an employee were ever caught being dishonest, he would never work for another Japanese company again." In Japan, there are very few controls over petty cash. The petty cash custodian not only disburses petty cash funds but has complete responsibility to reimburse the fund and keep all fund records.

when there is a shortage and credited when there is an excess of cash. For example, if Cooper Company had found on August 1 that the petty cash fund had only $82 in cash (instead of the correct amount of $88) and $112 in validated expenditures, the entry to replenish the petty cash fund would have been:

Aug. 1	Office Supplies	40	
	Freight-In	42	
	Postage	30	
	Cash Over and Short	6	
	Cash		118

Replenished the petty cash fund and recognized a shortage of $6.

Cash Over and Short is an expense account reported with Other Expenses when it has a debit balance and a revenue account reported with Other Revenues when it has a credit balance.

At the end of an accounting period, an entry must be made to debit expenses and credit cash so that income will not be overstated. The result is that the petty cash fund should be replenished at the end of each accounting period so that all expenses for the period are recorded.

Reconciling the Bank Account

With the exception of petty cash, most cash is kept in various accounts at one or more banks. Generally, only a few employees are authorized to sign checks, and they must have their signatures on file with the bank.

Chapter 8 *Cash, Marketable Securities, and Receivables*

NSF (Not sufficient funds) check *a check that is not honored by a bank because of insufficient cash in the customer's account*

Every month, the bank sends the business a statement that shows the cash balance at the beginning of the period, the deposits, the amounts of the checks processed, and the cash balance at the end of the period. With the statement, the bank includes all of that month's canceled checks (or at least a listing of the checks) as well as debit and credit memos (for example, an explanation of charges for **NSF checks** and service fees). Keep in mind that a bank considers customers' deposits as a liability; hence, debit memos reduce the company's cash balance, and credit memos increase it.

The July bank statement for one of Hunt Company's accounts is presented in Exhibit 8-2. This statement includes four bank adjustments to Hunt's balance—a bank service charge of $7 (the bank's monthly fee), $60 of interest paid by First Security Bank on Hunt's average balance, a $425 transfer out of the account into another account, and a $3,200 direct deposit made by a

Exhibit 8-2 *Bank Statement*

First Security Bank
Helena, Montana 59601

Statement of Account

HUNT COMPANY
1900 S. PARK LANE
HELENA, MT 59601

Account Number 325-78126

Date of Statement JULY 31, 1994

CHECK NUMBER	CHECKS AND WITHDRAWALS	DEPOSITS AND ADDITIONS	DATE	BALANCE
			6/30	13,000
620	140		7/01	12,860
621	250	1,500	7/03	14,110
622	860		7/05	13,250
623	210		7/08	13,040
		2,140	7/09	15,180
624	205		7/10	14,975
626	310		7/14	14,665
	425 T		7/15	14,240
		3,200 D	7/18	17,440
628	765		7/19	16,675
629	4,825		7/22	11,850
630	420		7/24	11,430
632	326	1,600	7/25	12,704
		2,100	7/26	14,804
633	210		7/29	14,594
635	225		7/31	14,369
	7 SC	60 I	7/31	14,422
	9,178 TOTAL CHECKS AND WITHDRAWALS	10,600 TOTAL DEPOSITS AND ADDITIONS		14,422 BALANCE

NSF = Not Sufficient Funds
D = Direct Deposit
SC = Service Charge
I = Interest
MS = Miscellaneous
T = Transfer Out of Account
ATM = Automated Teller Machine Transaction

customer who regularly deposits payments directly to Hunt's bank account. Other adjustments that are commonly made by the bank to a company's account include:

1. *NSF (not sufficient funds).* The cancellation of a prior deposit that could not be collected because of insufficient funds in the check writer's (payor's) account. When a check is received and deposited in the payee's account, the check is assumed to represent funds that will be collected from the payor's bank. However, when a bank refuses to honor a check because of insufficient funds in the account on which it was written, the check is returned to the payee's bank and is marked "NSF." The amount of the check, which was originally recorded as a deposit (addition) to the payee's account is deducted from the account when the check is returned unpaid.
2. *MS (miscellaneous).* Other adjustments made by a bank.
3. *ATM (Automated Teller Machine) Transactions.* These are deposits and withdrawals made by the depositor at automated teller machines.
4. *Withdrawals for credit card transactions that are paid directly from accounts.* These types of cards, called debit cards, are like using plastic checks, and instead of getting a bill or statement, the amount charged is deducted from the user's bank balance.

BUSINESS ENVIRONMENT ESSAY
E. F. Hutton's Overaggressive Cash Management Practices

It is extremely important that companies (and individuals) manage their cash well. Too much money left in no-interest or low-interest checking or savings accounts can mean lost income. On the other hand, not having sufficient cash available to pay short- and long-term debts can mean late penalties, bad check charges, higher interest rates, and poor credit ratings.

Because cash management is so important, companies are always looking for ways to improve cash handling. Unfortunately, for at least one firm, cash management strategies turned from aggressive to fraudulent.

In the mid-1980s, E. F. Hutton & Company challenged its branch managers to invigorate their cash management practices. The managers responded by developing a way to use cash at no interest. In anticipation of the collection of receivables (or sometimes even without the receivables), branch managers would write checks on accounts they knew were insufficiently funded. Later on, before the checks cleared through the banking system, deposits would be made so that the bad checks would be covered. Using this method (known as kiting or using the float), the managers were able to use and earn interest on money that didn't even belong to the firm. E. F. Hutton commended managers who effectively used this technique, and before long, Hutton was kiting checks on four hundred of its banks.

Apparently, at the time, Hutton felt it was shrewdly taking full advantage of the banking system's check clearing procedures and tolerant bankers. However, in 1986 when their overaggressive cash management techniques netted them 2,000 counts of mail and wire fraud, E. F. Hutton agreed to pay millions of dollars in fines as well as all costs relating to the government investigation into the firm's banking practices. In the end, several of Hutton's officers found themselves without jobs, and the company lost credibility with many of its clients.

Source: Adapted from Gellerman, Saul W., "Why Good Managers Make Bad Ethical Choices," *Harvard Business Review,* July–August 1986, p. 85.

It is unusual for the ending balance on the bank statement to equal the amount of cash recorded in a company's Cash account. The most common reasons for differences are:

1. *Time period differences.* The time period of the bank statement does not coincide with the timing of the company's postings to the Cash account.
2. *Deposits in transit.* These are deposits that had not been processed by the bank as of the bank statement date usually because they were made at or near the end of the month.
3. *Outstanding checks.* These are checks that have been written and deducted from a company's Cash account but have not cleared as of the bank statement date.
4. *Bank debits.* These are deductions made by the bank that have not yet been recorded by the company. The most common are monthly service charges, NSF checks, and bank transfers out of the account.
5. *Bank credits.* These are additions made by a bank to a company's account before they are recorded by the company. The most common source is interest paid by the bank on the account balance.
6. *Accounting errors.* These are numerical errors made by either the company or the bank. The most common are transpositions of numbers.

bank reconciliation *the process of systematically comparing the cash balance as reported by the bank with the cash balance on the company's books and explaining any differences*

The process of determining the reasons for the differences between the bank balance and the company's Cash account balance is called the **bank reconciliation**. This usually results in adjusting both the bank statement and the book (Cash account) balances. If the balances were not reconciled—if the Cash balance were to be left as is—the figure used on the financial statements would probably be incorrect, and external users would not have accurate information for decision making.

We will use Hunt Company's bank account to illustrate a bank reconciliation. The statement shown in Exhibit 8-2 indicates an ending balance of $14,422 for the month of July. After arranging the month's canceled checks in numerical order and examining the bank statement, Hunt's accountant notes the following:

1. A deposit of $3,100 on July 31 was not shown on the bank statement. (It was in transit at the end of the month.)
2. Checks #625 for $326, #631 for $426, and #634 for $185 are outstanding. Check #627 was voided at the time it was written.
3. The bank's service charge for the month is $7.
4. A direct deposit of $3,200 was made by Joy Company, a regular customer.
5. A transfer of $425 was made out of Hunt's account into the account of Martin Custodial Service for the amount owed.
6. The bank paid interest of $60 on Hunt's average balance.
7. Check #630 for Thelma Jones's wages was recorded in the accounting records as $240 instead of the correct amount, $420.
8. The Cash account in the General Ledger shows a balance on July 31 of $13,937.

The bank reconciliation would then be as shown in Exhibit 8-3.

Exhibit 8-3

Hunt Company
Bank Reconciliation
July 31, 1994

Balance per bank statement		$14,422	Balance per books		$13,937
Additions to bank balance:			Additions to book balance:		
Deposits in transit		3,100	Direct deposit	$3,200	
Total		$17,522	Interest	60	3,260
			Total		$17,197
Deductions from bank balance:			Deductions from book balance:		
Outstanding checks: 625	$326		Service charge	$ 7	
631	426		Bank transfer	425	
634	185	(937)	Error in recording check (for		
			Jones's wages) #630	180	(612)
Adjusted bank balance		**$16,585**	**Adjusted book balance**		**$16,585**

Since the bank and book balances now agree, the $16,585 adjusted Cash balance is the amount that will be reported on the financial statements. If the adjusted book and bank balances had not agreed, the accountant would have had to search for errors in bookkeeping or in the bank's figures. When the balances finally agree, any necessary adjustments are made to the Cash account to bring it to the correct balance. The entries to correct the balance include debits to Cash for all reconciling additions to the book balance and credits to Cash for all reconciling deductions from the book balance. Additions and deductions from the bank balance do not require adjustments to the company's books since the deposits in transit and the outstanding checks have already been recorded by the company, and of course, bank errors are corrected by notifying the bank. The adjustments required to correct Hunt's Cash account would be:

Cash	3,260	
Accounts Receivable		3,200
Interest Revenue		60

To record the additions due to the July bank reconciliation (a $3,200 deposit made by Joy Company and $60 interest).

Custodial Expense	425	
Miscellaneous Expense	7	
Wages Expense	180	
Cash		612

To record the deductions due to the July bank reconciliation (service charge of $7, a $180 error in recording check #630, and the bank transfer of $425 to Martin Custodial Service).

> **To Summarize** *Cash is a company's most liquid asset and is the first asset listed on its balance sheet. Companies must carefully monitor and control the way cash is handled and accounted for. Common controls include (1) separation of duties in the handling of and accounting for cash, (2) daily deposits of all cash receipts, and (3) payment of all expenditures by prenumbered checks, except for the small miscellaneous expenses paid from a petty cash fund. The petty cash fund is usually maintained on an imprest basis.*
>
> *Because most payments are made by check, companies need to reconcile monthly bank statements with the cash balance reported on the company's books. This reconciliation process involves determining reasons for the differences and bringing the book and bank balances into agreement. Adjusting entries are then made for additions to and deductions from the book balance.*

ACCOUNTING FOR SHORT-TERM INVESTMENTS

Objective 2

Explain the recording and valuation of marketable securities and other short-term investments.

line of credit *an arrangement whereby a bank agrees to loan an amount of money (up to a certain limit) on demand for short periods of time, usually less than a year*

Most businesses are cyclical or seasonal; that is, their cash inflows and outflows vary significantly throughout the year. At certain times (particularly when inventories are being purchased), a company's cash supply is low. At other times (usually during or shortly after heavy selling seasons), there is excess cash on hand. A typical cash flow pattern for a retail firm is illustrated in Exhibit 8-4. The time line shows that the company has insufficient cash for inventory buildup for the Christmas rush, followed by large amounts of accounts receivable (from credit-card sales) and then an excess of cash immediately after Christmas.

To ensure that there is always cash available to meet current obligations, most firms have a **line of credit** with their bank. Such an arrangement allows a

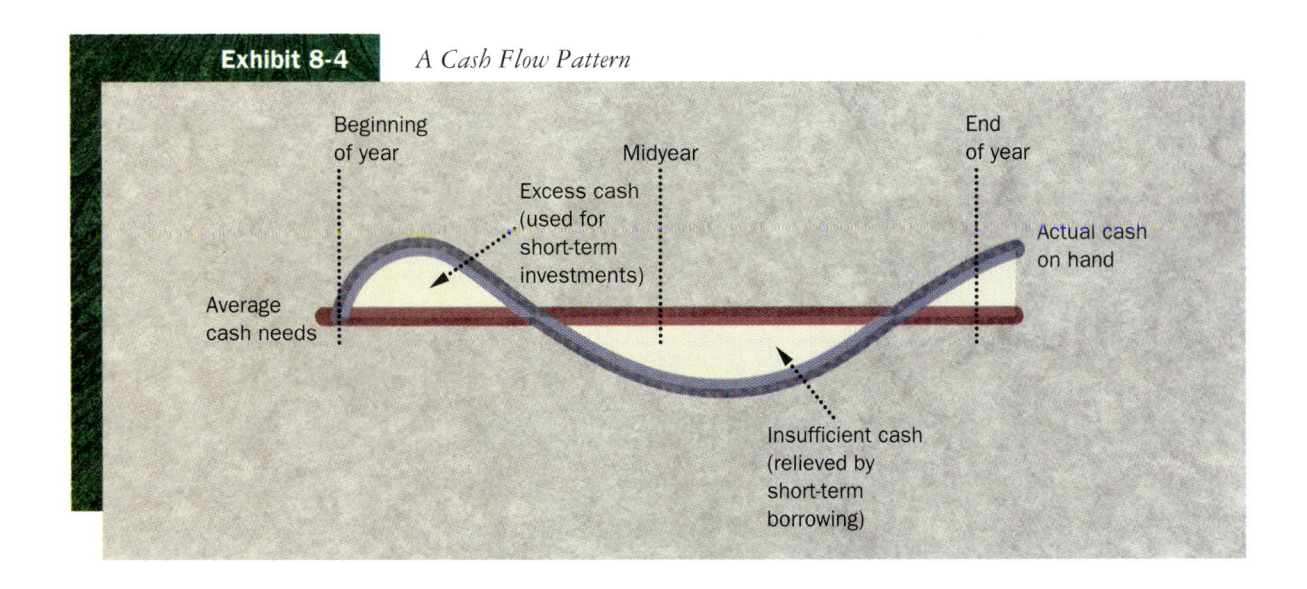

Exhibit 8-4 *A Cash Flow Pattern*

marketable securities
short-term investments in securities (stocks, bonds, and so on) made with temporarily idle cash to earn a return

company to borrow on demand up to a certain amount of cash on a short-term basis—usually for less than a year. Having a line of credit allows companies to maintain only enough cash on hand to meet their average cash needs. A credit line thus enables firms to invest in income-yielding assets when operations generate funds in excess of average cash needs.

Because money has a time value and can earn a return, these temporary excesses of cash are usually invested, in some cases for only 3 or 4 days. The most typical short-term investments are **marketable securities** of other companies or governmental agencies. There are two categories of marketable securities: debt and equity. Debt refers primarily to bond investments, and equity refers to stocks. Other short-term investments include commercial paper, certificates of deposit, money market funds, and treasury bills. Both commercial paper and certificates of deposit are investment contracts at guaranteed interest rates for specific periods; the former are short term and are issued by companies, and the latter are short or long term and are issued by financial institutions. Money market funds contain a variety of short-term securities; thus, their interest rates vary each week, depending on the market rate of interest and the investments purchased by the fund.

Next to cash, marketable securities and other short-term investments are the most liquid of all assets. As a result, they are classified as a current asset and listed just below Cash on the balance sheet. Investments in securities must be properly classified as either short term or long term because there are important differences in accounting for them. Here we will discuss short-term investments in marketable securities. Long-term investments will be covered in Chapter 12.

Recording Investments in Marketable Securities

Short-term investments in marketable securities, like all other assets, are recorded at cost when purchased. For accounting purposes, cost includes the market price of the asset plus any extra expenditures required in making the purchase (such as a stockbroker's fee).

To illustrate, we will assume that during a period of excess cash, Salem Corporation purchased 100 shares of Mohawk stock at $171 per share and paid a broker's commission of $500. The entry to record the investment would be:

Marketable Securities, Mohawk Stock	17,600	
Cash		17,600

Purchased 100 shares of Mohawk stock as a short-term investment at $171 per share plus $500 in commissions.

Obviously, Salem's managers invested in Mohawk because they thought the stock would earn a good short-term return, either from dividends or through a gain on the eventual sale of the stock. Assuming that Salem held the stock long enough to receive a quarterly dividend of $1.40 per share, the accounting entry would be:

```
Cash .......................................................... 140
    Dividend Revenue ............................................    140
Received dividend on the investment in Mohawk stock.
```

Now suppose that Salem sells the stock for $185 per share, less a $300 commission. The entry to account for the gain on the sale of Mohawk stock would be:

```
Cash ....................................................... 18,200
    Marketable Securities, Mohawk Stock ........................    17,600
    Gain on Sale of Marketable Securities.......................       600
Sold 100 shares of Mohawk stock at $185 per share, less a $300 commission.
```

Although the market price at the time of the sale is $185 per share, for a total of $18,500 for 100 shares, the company receives only $18,200; the $300 sales commission reduces the net cash collected and, hence, the gain on the sale. Note that increases in market price above the cost of a stock are not recognized until the stock is actually sold.

At the end of the accounting period, the gain on the sale of Salem's investment in marketable securities must be included on its financial statements. The Gain on Sale of Marketable Securities would be included with Other Revenue and Expenses on the income statement. The investment has been eliminated, and the proceeds are included in Cash on the balance sheet. Accounting for investments in bonds, treasury bills, and other marketable debt securities is the same as for stock, except the earnings are in the form of interest rather than dividends.

Valuing Marketable Securities at Lower of Cost or Market

Short-term investments are initially recorded at cost, and their recorded balance is never increased to an amount greater than cost to recognize increases in market prices until they are sold. On the other hand, when market values of marketable equity securities (stocks) drop below their original costs, they must be written down to market value. This practice of recording marketable securities at the **lower of cost or market (LCM)** represents an important departure from the usual procedure of reporting assets at cost. Technically, only marketable *equity* securities must be reported at the lower of cost or market; however, this procedure is appropriate and followed by many companies for all marketable securities, whether equity or debt. In this book, we will apply the lower-of-cost-or-market rule to all marketable securities.

Because marketable securities are bought and sold frequently, sometimes even daily, and their selling prices change frequently throughout the year, companies usually adjust investments to their lower-of-cost-or-market amounts only at year-end, when accurate amounts are needed for the financial statements. This adjustment to LCM ensures that investments are not reported at a cost figure that overstates their future benefits to the company.

lower of cost or market (LCM) a basis for valuing certain assets at the lower of original cost or market value (current replacement cost)

When accounting for investments at the lower of cost or market, a company considers all marketable securities (its entire short-term portfolio) as a unit. The recorded amount for a single stock that drops in selling price below its original cost will not be written down if the market value of the entire portfolio is still equal to or greater than the original cost. To illustrate, we will assume that Salem's portfolio of marketable securities includes the following:

	Cost	Market	Market Minus Cost
Stock of Mohawk Company	$17,600	$18,500	$ 900
Stock of ABC Company	21,000	19,000	(2,000)
Bonds of MMM Company	26,500	25,000	(1,500)
U.S. Government Bonds	13,200	14,100	900
Total	$78,300	$76,600	($1,700)

Because the portfolio's total market value is $1,700 less than its original total cost, marketable securities should be written down to $76,600. The entry to recognize the loss is:

Loss on Marketable Securities	1,700	
Allowance to Reduce Marketable Securities to LCM		1,700
To reduce marketable securities to lower of cost or market ($78,300–$76,600).		

Loss on Marketable Securities appears on the income statement under Other Revenues and Expenses, and Allowance to Reduce Short-Term Investments to LCM is a contra account on the balance sheet that is offset against Marketable Securities. The balance sheet presentation for the marketable securities of Salem would be:

Current assets:
Marketable securities	$78,300
Less allowance to reduce marketable securities to LCM	1,700
	$76,600

At the end of the next period, the cost and market values of the portfolio are again compared, and the reported balance is adjusted as appropriate to reflect the lower of cost or market for the securities portfolio as of that date. If the market value of the portfolio has increased, the account Allowance to Reduce Marketable Securities to LCM is debited, and Gain on Marketable Securities is credited. In no case, however, is the portfolio ever reported at market values that exceed cost.

When individual securities from the portfolio are sold, a gain or loss is recognized for the difference between the original cost of the securities and the selling price, without regard to previous portfolio adjustments to LCM. At the end of the period, the lower of cost or market is determined for the remaining securities, and the appropriate adjustment is made.

> **To Summarize** *Marketable securities and other short-term investments are very liquid assets, so they are listed just below Cash on the balance sheet. Revenues from marketable securities usually take the form of dividends, interest, or gains when selling the investments and are included under Other Revenues and Expenses on the income statement. Marketable equity securities must be written down to the lower of cost or market if the market value of the company's total portfolio drops below cost. If the portfolio subsequently increases in value to more than cost, the investments are written back up to their original cost.*

ACCOUNTING FOR RECEIVABLES

Objective 3

Describe the accounting for accounts receivable, including losses from uncollectible accounts.

receivables *claims for money, goods, or services*

The term **receivables** refers to a company's claims for money, goods, or services. Receivables are created through various kinds of transactions, the two most common being the sale of merchandise or services on credit and the lending of money. On a personal level, we are all familiar with credit. Because credit is so readily available, we can buy such items as refrigerators and sofas that perhaps we could not afford to pay cash for. Major retail companies such as Sears, K-mart, and J.C. Penney have made credit available to almost every responsible person in the United States. We live in a credit world, not only on the individual level but also at the wholesale and manufacturing levels.

In business, such credit sales give rise to the two most common types of receivables: accounts and notes receivables. Other receivables may result from loans to officers or employees of a company or from interest, for example. To identify and maintain the distinction between these receivables, businesses establish a separate General Ledger account for each classification. If the amount of a receivable is material, it is separately identified on the balance sheet. Those that are to be converted to cash within a year or the normal operating cycle are classified as current assets and listed on the balance sheet just below Cash and Marketable Securities. All other receivables are categorized as long-term assets (see Chapter 12). In this section, we will first discuss the accounting for accounts receivable and then consider the accounting for notes receivable.

Accounts Receivable

accounts receivable *money due from rendering services or selling merchandise on credit*

Accounts receivable are short term, liquid assets that arise from credit sales to customers. Sometimes called *trade receivables,* these assets are usually converted to cash within 10 to 60 days.

When companies sell goods or services on credit, the basic accounting entry involves a debit to Accounts Receivable and a credit to Sales Revenue. In most businesses, however, the accounting is not so straightforward. We have already mentioned sales discounts, returns, and freight charges. In addition, companies have to account for the possibility that some customers will not pay for the merchandise they purchase. In fact, most businesses expect a certain percentage of their sales to be uncollectible. If a firm tries too hard to eliminate all losses from nonpaying customers, it usually makes its credit policy so restrictive that valuable sales are lost. On the other hand, if a firm extends credit too easily or to everyone, it may have so many uncollectible sales that it has financial difficulties. Because of this dilemma, most firms evaluate the credit worthiness of each customer and carefully monitor credit sales to ensure that company policies are neither too restrictive nor too liberal.

bad debt *an uncollectible account receivable*

When an account receivable becomes uncollectible, a firm incurs a **bad-debt** loss. This loss must be recognized as a cost of doing business, so it is classified as an operating expense. There are two ways to account for losses from uncollectible accounts: the direct write-off method and the allowance method.

direct write-off method *the recording of actual losses from uncollectible accounts as expenses during the period in which accounts receivable are determined to be uncollectible*

With the **direct write-off method,** an uncollectible account is recognized as an expense at the time it is determined to be uncollectible. For example, assume that during the month of July, a certain store had credit sales of $30,000. These sales would be recorded as a debit to Accounts Receivable and a credit to Sales Revenue. If payments for all the sales except one for $150 to Jake Palmer are received in August, the total of the entries to record collections is $29,850 in debits to Cash and credits to Accounts Receivable. If after receiving several past-due notices, Palmer still does not pay, the company will probably turn the account over to an attorney or an agency for collection. Then, if collection attempts fail, the company may decide that the Palmer account will not be collected and write it off as a loss. The entry to record the expense under the direct write-off method would be:

Uncollectible Accounts (or Bad Debt) Expense	150	
Accounts Receivable		150
To write off the uncollectible account of Jake Palmer.		

matching principle *the concept that all costs and expenses incurred in generating revenues must be recognized in the same reporting period as the related revenues*

Although the direct write-off method is objective, in that the account is written off at the time it proves to be uncollectible, it may violate the **matching principle,** which requires that all costs and expenses incurred in generating revenues be identified with those revenues period by period. With the direct write-off method, sales made near the end of one accounting period may not be recognized as uncollectible until the next period. As a result, expenses and net income are misstated in both the current and the following period. This makes the direct write-off method unacceptable (from a theoretical point of view) unless bad debts involve only small amounts.

allowance method *the recording of estimated losses due to uncollectible accounts as expenses during the period in which the sales occurred*

The **allowance method,** on the other hand, satisfies the matching principle since it accounts for uncollectibles during the period in which the sales occurred. With this method, a firm uses its experience or industry averages to estimate the amount of receivables that will become uncollectible. That estimate is recorded as an uncollectible accounts expense in the period of sale. Although the use of estimates may result in a somewhat imprecise expense figure, this is generally thought to be a less serious problem than the understatement of expenses created by the direct write-off method. In addition, with experience, these estimates tend to be quite accurate.

To illustrate the allowance method, we will assume that during 1994 total credit sales for a small appliance store were $200,000. If management estimates that one-half of 1 percent (0.005) of these sales will be uncollectible, the entry to record the uncollectible accounts expense will be:

> Uncollectible Accounts Expense 1,000
>   Allowance for Uncollectible Accounts 1,000
> *To record the estimated uncollectible accounts expense for the current year ($200,000 × .005).*

Uncollectible Accounts Expense *an account that represents the portion of the current period's receivables that are estimated to become uncollectible*

Allowance for Uncollectible Accounts *a contra account, deducted from Accounts Receivable, that shows the estimated losses from uncollectible accounts*

Uncollectible Accounts Expense is an operating expense on the income statement, and **Allowance for Uncollectible Accounts** (sometimes called Allowance for Bad Debts) is a contra account that is offset against Accounts Receivable on the balance sheet. An allowance account is used because the company does not yet know which receivables will not be collected. In 1995, as actual losses are recognized, the balance in Allowance for Uncollectible Accounts is reduced. For example, if in 1995, the receivable of Jake Palmer for $150 could not be collected, the entry would be:

> Allowance for Uncollectible Accounts 150
>   Accounts Receivable 150
> *To write off the uncollectible account of Jake Palmer.*

Because both Allowance for Uncollectible Accounts and Accounts Receivable are balance sheet accounts, the entry to write off accounts as uncollectible does not affect net income in 1995. Instead, the net income in 1994 (when the sale was actually made) already reflects the uncollectible accounts expense. For example, assume the balance in Accounts Receivable was $50,000 before the Palmer account was written off. The net amount in Accounts Receivable after the $150 write-off is exactly the same as it was before the entry, as shown here.

Before Write-off Entry		**After Write-off Entry**	
Accounts receivable	$50,000	Accounts receivable	$49,850
Less allowance for uncollectible accounts	1,000	Less allowance for uncollectible accounts	850
Net balance	$49,000	Net balance	$49,000

net realizable value of accounts receivable *the net amount that would be received if all receivables considered collectible were collected; equal to total accounts receivable less the allowance for uncollectible accounts; also called the book value of accounts receivable*

The net balance of $49,000 reflects the estimated **net realizable value of accounts receivable,** that is, the amount of receivables the company actually expects to collect. This amount is sometimes referred to as the book value of accounts receivable.

Occasionally, a customer whose account has been written off as uncollectible later pays the outstanding balance. When this happens, the company reverses the entry that was used to write off the account and then recognizes the payment. For example, if the $150 were collected from Jake Palmer, the entries to correct the accounting records would be:

Accounts Receivable	150
Allowance for Uncollectible Accounts	150

To reinstate the balance previously written off as uncollectible.

Cash	150
Accounts Receivable	150

Received payment in full of previously written-off accounts receivable.

Because customers sometimes pay their balances after their account was written off, it is important for a company to have good control over both the cash collection procedures and the accounting for accounts receivable. Otherwise, such payments as the previously written off $150 could be pocketed by the person who receives the cash, and it would never be missed. This is one reason that most companies separate the handling of cash from the recording of cash transactions in the accounts.

ESTIMATING THE ALLOWANCE FOR UNCOLLECTIBLE ACCOUNTS. The amount recorded in Uncollectible Accounts Expense affects both the reported net realizable value of the receivables and the net income, so companies must be careful to use good estimation procedures. There are several methods of estimating uncollectible receivables.

1. As a percentage of total credit sales.
2. As a percentage of total accounts receivable balance at year-end.
3. As an amount based on an "aging" of accounts receivable.

To use these methods, a company must estimate the total amount of the loss on the basis of experience or industry averages. Obviously, a company that has been in business for several years should be able to make more accurate estimates than a new company. Many established companies will use a 3- or 5-year average as the basis for estimating current losses from uncollectible accounts.

Percentage of Sales Method. If a company were to use credit sales as a basis for its estimate, the amount of uncollectibles would be a straight percentage of the current year's credit sales. That percentage would be a projection based on experience and modified for the current period. For example, if credit sales for the year were $300,000 and if experience indicated that 1 percent of all credit sales would be uncollectible, the entry to record the estimate would be:

Estimate as a Percentage of Sales

Allowance for Uncollectible Accounts

Existing Balance	500
Percentage of This Year's Sales Estimated to be Uncollectible	3,000
New Balance	3,500

Uncollectible Accounts Expense	3,000
Allowance for Uncollectible Accounts	3,000

To record the estimated uncollectible accounts expense for the current year ($300,000 × 0.01).

When this method is used, the existing balance, if there is one, in Allowance for Uncollectible Accounts is not considered in the adjusting entry. The 1 percent of the current year's sales that is estimated to be uncollectible is calculated separately and then added to the existing balance. For example, as shown

Chapter 8 Cash, Marketable Securities, and Receivables

in the margin, if the existing balance were $500, the $3,000 would be added, making the new balance $3,500. The rationale for not considering the existing balance in Allowance for Uncollectible Accounts is that it relates to previous periods' sales and, as a strict interpretation of the matching principle suggests, should not affect the estimate for the current period.

Percentage of Receivables Method. If a company bases its estimates of losses on total accounts receivable, the amount of uncollectibles is a percentage of the total balance at the end of the period. Thus, if a company has a balance of $90,000 in Accounts Receivable and its management determines that 3 percent of the receivables will be uncollectible, the balance in Allowance for Uncollectible Accounts should be $2,700. However, if the account has an existing balance, only the net amount needed to bring the balance to $2,700 would be added. For example, as shown in the margin, an existing credit balance of $500 in Allowance for Uncollectible Accounts would require the following entry:

Estimate as a Percentage of Receivables
Allowance for Uncollectible Accounts

	Existing Balance 500
	Adjustment Needed 2,200
	Desired Balance 2,700

Uncollectible Accounts Expense	2,200	
Allowance for Uncollectible Accounts		2,200
To adjust the Allowance account to desired balance.		

When uncollectible accounts are estimated as a percentage of total accounts receivable, the matching principle is not a consideration because Accounts Receivable is a balance sheet account, and the balance of the receivables could relate to any period.

The Aging Method. The third method of estimating bad debt losses requires that a company base its calculations on how long its receivables have been outstanding. With this procedure, called **aging accounts receivable,** each receivable is categorized according to age, such as current, 1–30 days past due, 31–60 days past due, 61–90 days past due, 91–120 days past due, and over 120 days past due. Once the receivables in each age classification are totaled, each total is multiplied by the appropriate uncollectible rate (as determined by experience). Exhibit 8-5 shows how a company with $38,260 in Accounts Receivable typically would determine that $4,627 of its current receivables are likely to be uncollectible.

aging accounts receivable *the process of categorizing each accounts receivable by the number of days it has been outstanding*

If the existing credit balance in Allowance for Uncollectible Accounts is $500, the entry would be:

Estimate as an Amount Based on Aging of Accounts Receivables
Allowance for Uncollectible Accounts

	Existing Balance 500
	Adjustment Needed 4,127
	Desired Balance 4,627

Uncollectible Accounts Expense	4,127	
Allowance for Uncollectible Accounts		4,127
To adjust the Allowance account to desired balance.		

The aging of accounts receivable is probably the most accurate method of estimating uncollectible accounts. It also enables a company to identify its problem customers quickly. And because the method can identify such customers, even those companies that base their estimates of bad debts on credit sales or total outstanding receivables also often age their receivables as a way of monitoring the individual accounts receivable balances.

Exhibit 8-5 Aging of Accounts Receivable

| Customer | Balance | Current | \multicolumn{5}{c}{Days Past Due} |
			1–30	31–60	61–90	91–120	Over 120
A. Adams	$10,000	$10,000					
R. Bartholomew	1,500						$1,500
F. Christiansen	6,250	5,000	$1,250				
G. Dover	7,260			$7,260			
M. Ellis	4,000	4,000					
G. Erkland	2,250				$2,250		
R. Fisher	1,000					$1,000	
T. Francis	2,000		2,000				
E. Zeigler	4,000	4,000					
Totals	$38,260	$23,000	$3,250	$7,260	$2,250	$1,000	$1,500

Estimate of Losses from Uncollectible Accounts

Age	Balance	Percentage Estimated to Be Uncollectible	Amount
Current	$23,000	1.5	$ 345
1–30 Days Past Due	3,250	4.0	130
31–60 Days Past Due	7,260	20.0	1,452
61–90 Days Past Due	2,250	40.0	900
91–120 Days Past Due	1,000	60.0	600
Over 120 Days Past Due	1,500	80.0	1,200
Totals	$38,260		$4,627

credit card *a plastic card that represents an individual's right to make purchases on credit; examples are VISA, MasterCard, American Express, and store-issued cards*

credit card draft *the part of the multiple-page credit form that is sent by the retailer to the credit card company for reimbursement of the stated amount*

CREDIT CARD SALES. Our discussion so far has centered on the methods used by wholesale and manufacturing firms in accounting for credit sales. Many retail businesses also sell on credit. Because most of their customers are individuals, these companies accept nationally available **credit cards,** such as VISA, MasterCard, American Express, Diner's Club, Carte Blanche, and DISCOVER card as payment for purchases. Some businesses—major department stores and oil companies, for example—issue their own credit cards.

Credit cards provide advantages for both the customer and the retailer: They allow customers to shop without carrying large amounts of cash and to pay for their purchases over an extended period of time, and they enable retailers to increase sales while avoiding the risk of uncollectible accounts.

A credit card represents an agreement between a lender (a credit card company) and an individual, giving the individual the right to use the card to make purchases at any number of businesses. When an individual (the customer) uses a credit card, he or she must sign a multiple-copy form, which includes a **credit card draft** that the retailer sends to the credit card company for reimbursement of the stated amount. The credit card company is then responsible for collecting the amount on the draft from the customer. Because credit card companies assume the burden of approving customers' credit, collecting from customers, and worrying about uncollectibles, they usually charge businesses a 2-to-5 percent fee for their credit services.

Credit card companies generally follow one of two procedures for reimbursing retailers: (1) they require the retailer to submit the credit card drafts in order to receive payment, or (2) they allow retailers to deposit the drafts directly into a checking account for immediate credit. Generally, travel and entertainment cards such as American Express, Diner's Club, Carte Blanche, and DISCOVER use the first method, whereas VISA and MasterCard use the second. How a retailer accounts for credit card sales therefore depends on the reimbursement method used by the credit card company.

To illustrate the accounting for method 1, assume that Haskins Steak House has American Express drafts totaling $800 at the end of the day. These foods sales would be recorded as follows:

Accounts Receivable, American Express	800	
Sales Revenue		800
To record American Express credit card sales for October 13.		

Haskins Steak House would then mail the credit card drafts to American Express, which would then send payment for $760 (assuming a 5 percent credit card fee—0.95 × $800) to Haskins. At that time, Haskins would make the following entry:

Cash	760	
Credit Card Expense	40	
Accounts Receivable, American Express		800
Received payment for October 13 American Express drafts.		

Note that Credit Card Expense is a selling expense that would be reported on the income statement.

To illustrate the accounting for method 2, assume that on October 13, Haskins Steak House had VISA credit card sales of $1,200. Because MasterCard and VISA cards are generally issued by banks, depositing a bank draft in the checking account is equivalent to depositing a check in the account. If the issuing bank charges a 4 percent fee on a VISA transaction, Haskins would make the following entry when depositing credit card drafts in its account:

Cash	1,152	
Credit Card Expense	48	
Sales Revenue		1,200
To record VISA credit card sales for October 13 (0.96 × $1,200).		

> **To Summarize** Accounts receivable are short-term, liquid assets that arise from credit sales to customers. Even though companies monitor their customers carefully, there are usually some who do not pay for the merchandise they purchase. There are two ways of accounting for losses from uncollectible receivables: the direct write-off method and the allowance method. The allowance method is generally accepted in practice because it is consistent with the matching principle. The three ways of estimating losses from uncollectible receivables are (1) as a percentage of sales, (2) as a percentage of total outstanding receivables, and (3) as an amount based on an aging of accounts receivable. By using credit cards, retail businesses can avoid the problem of uncollectible accounts but must pay a fee (reported as a selling expense on the income statement) for processing credit card transactions.

Notes Receivable

Objective 4
Explain the accounting for notes receivable.

note receivable *a claim against a debtor, evidenced by an unconditional written promise to pay a certain sum of money on or before a specified future date*

maker *a person (entity) who signs a note to borrow money and who assumes responsibility to pay the note at maturity*

payee *the person (entity) to whom payment on a note is to be made*

principal on a note *the face amount of a note; the amount (excluding interest) that the maker agrees to pay the payee*

maturity date *the date on which a note or other obligation becomes due*

interest rate *the cost of using money, expressed as an annual percentage*

interest *the amount charged for using money*

A **note receivable** is a claim against a debtor, evidenced by an unconditional written promise to pay a sum of money on or before a specified future date. Depending on the length of time until the due date, the note may be classified as a current or a long-term asset. In addition, it may be either a trade note receivable or a nontrade note receivable. A trade note receivable represents an amount due from a customer who purchased merchandise. Businesses often accept notes receivable from customers because they are contractual obligations that usually earn interest. A nontrade note receivable arises from the lending of money to an individual or company other than a customer—for example, an employee. Exhibit 8-6 shows a typical note receivable.

There are several key terms associated with a note receivable. The **maker** of a note is the person who signs the note and who must make payment on or before the due date. The **payee** is the person to whom payment will be made. The **principal** is the face amount of the note. The **maturity date** is the date the note becomes due. The **interest rate** is the percentage of the principal that the payee annually charges the maker for the loan, and the **interest** is the dollar amount paid by the maker in accordance with this rate. Interest can also be thought of as the service charge, or rent, for the use of money. The formula for computing the interest on a note is:

principal × interest rate × time (in terms of a year) = interest

For example, if Komatsu Company accepted from Solomon Company a 12 percent, 90-day $2,000 note receivable, the interest would be calculated as:

$2,000 × 0.12 × 90/365 = $59.18

In calculating the time, we will use 365 days (rather than 360 as some texts do) because that is more common among financial institutions. We will always round the interest to the nearest penny and often to the nearest dollar. When determining the number of days a note is outstanding, the issuance or the maturity date is included but not both. For example, a note issued on June 5 and maturing on June 25 would be considered a 20-day note.

Chapter 8 Cash, Marketable Securities, and Receivables

Exhibit 8-6 *A Typical Note Receivable*

$2,000	Helena, Montana	July 15, 1994
PRINCIPAL	LOCATION	DATE

Ninety (90) days _____ AFTER DATE _____ Solomon Company _____ PROMISES

TO PAY TO THE ORDER OF _____ Komatsu Company _____
                                                              PAYEE

Two thousand and no/100 _____ DOLLARS

PAYABLE AT _____ First Security Bank _____

FOR VALUE RECEIVED, WITH INTEREST AT _____ 12 percent per annum.

Georgia Solomon
SIGNATURE OF MAKER

If the $2,000 note were accepted in settlement of Solomon's unpaid account with Komatsu Company, the journal entry to record the note in Komatsu's books would be:

```
Notes Receivable ...................................... 2,000
    Accounts Receivable .............................           2,000
Accepted 90-day, 12% note from Solomon Company in lieu of payment of its account
receivable.
```

When the note matures and payment is made (90 days later), Komatsu's entry to record the receipt of cash would be:

```
Cash .................................................. 2,059.18
    Notes Receivable ................................          2,000.00
    Interest Revenue ................................              59.18
Received payment from Solomon Company for $2,000 note plus interest.
```

maturity value *the amount of an obligation to be collected or paid at maturity; equal to principal plus any interest*

Principal plus interest ($2,059.18 in this example) is known as the **maturity value** of the note. If the note is not paid by the maturity date, negotiations with the maker usually result in the company's extending the period for payment, issuing a new note, or retaining an attorney or collection agency to collect the money. If the note eventually proves to be worthless, it is written off as a loss against Allowance for Uncollectible Accounts.

Often notes receivable are classified on the balance sheet as special receivables when an agency or attorney is attempting to make collection.

Discounting Notes Receivable

discounting a note receivable *the process of the payee's selling notes to a financial institution for less than the maturity value*

Because notes receivable are contractual promises to pay money in the future, they are negotiable. They can be sold, or **discounted,** to banks and other financial institutions. This means that the holder of a note who needs cash before a note matures can sell the note (simply by endorsing it) to a financial institution. The maker of the note, therefore, owes the money to the financial institution or other endorsee.

To financial institutions, the purchase of a note for cash is just like making a loan; that is, cash is given out now in return for repayment of principal with interest in the future. To a company selling a note, discounting is a way of receiving cash earlier than would be possible otherwise.

discount rate *the interest rate charged by a financial institution for buying a note receivable*

discount *the amount charged by a bank when a note receivable is discounted; calculated as maturity value times discount rate times discount period*

discount period *the time between the date a note is sold to a financial institution and its maturity date*

Several key terms are associated with the discounting of notes. The **discount rate** is the annual rate (percentage of the maturity value) charged by the financial institution for buying the note; the **discount** is the actual amount the bank will earn (in terms of interest) on the transaction; and the **discount period** is the length of time for which the note is discounted. The formula for computing the discount is:

maturity value × discount rate × discount period = discount

To illustrate the discounting of a note, we refer to the 90-day, 12 percent note for $2,000 that Komatsu Company accepted from Solomon Company. After holding the note for 15 days, Komatsu decides to discount it at 16 percent at First Security Bank. The discount would be $67.70, computed as follows:

maturity value × discount rate × discount period = discount
$2,059.18 × 0.16 × 75/365 = $67.70

net proceeds *the difference between maturity value and discount when a note receivable is discounted*

Since Solomon's note is worth $2,059.18 at maturity, Komatsu's **net proceeds** from the bank are $2,059.18 − $67.70, or $1,991.48. The calculations are:

Face of note	$2,000.00
Interest the note earns ($2,000 × 0.12 × 90/365)	59.18
Maturity value	$2,059.18
Discount ($2,059.18 × 0.16 × 75/365)	(67.70)
Net proceeds	$1,991.48

The entry to record the discounting of the note would be:

Cash	1,991.48	
Interest Expense	8.52	
Notes Receivable		2,000.00

To record the discounting of the 90-day, 12% $2,000 note from Solomon Company at 16% for 75 days.

Appendix
Internal Control

Roswell Steffen, chief teller at the Park Avenue branch of the Union Dime Savings Bank in New York City, earned a modest salary. A quiet man, he was well liked by his fellow workers and spent most evenings at home with his wife and two teen-age daughters in their small garden apartment in New Jersey. An investigation by federal, state, and local authorities into a large-scale, illegal bookmaking operation revealed that Steffen had another side. He had been betting thousands of dollars a day on horse races and professional sports. Because of the size of the bets, the investigators consulted with officials of the Union Dime Bank, who conducted an extensive review of their records and found that Steffen had embezzled $1,500,000 over a 3- to 4-year period. Steffen, a compulsive gambler, admitted that he had lost the entire sum.

When asked how he had embezzled the money, Steffen explained that he had been given daily, unregulated access to the cash vault and that many of the tellers he supervised were inexperienced. As part of his supervisory duties, he also had access to the computer terminals and the authority to modify the computerized data. This combination of circumstances allowed Steffen to take cash from deposits and manipulate computer inputs in order to conceal any shortages.

Steffen was not a computer "genius," and the mechanics of his crime were fairly simple. As the supervisor of tellers, he could override many of the basic controls on the bank's computerized accounting system. When a customer brought in a large deposit, Steffen would enter the amount in the customer's passbook. On the computer, however, he would record the deposit under the account number of a second passbook, which he later destroyed. Money was withdrawn periodically by Steffen from the second passbook account.

Steffen kept careful track of the fictitious deposits and constantly made corrections to juggle the more than fifty accounts he was manipulating. When this system became too complicated and time-consuming, he switched to 2-year certificates of deposit, which required manipulation only every 24 months. Occasionally, customers would discover an error in their accounts and march into the bank demanding a correction. The tellers would naturally refer these irate customers to Steffen, the chief teller, who would explain the difficulty as a computer error or a new teller's misposting. He would then make corrections, altering some other account to compensate for the "error."

These "errors" went undetected for almost four years because Steffen, who was not authorized to use the computer terminal except for administrative and clerical procedures, was in fact using it to enter transactions and manipulate the accounts so that they appeared to be correct. More important, Roswell Steffen was able to perpetrate this fraud because there was a serious breakdown of internal controls at the Union Dime Savings Bank. Although the bank had most of the features of a good accounting system (sound reporting practices, timely data, and so on), it lacked strength in an essential area: internal control.[1]

In Chapter 8, we briefly discussed the controls needed for cash and cash transactions. Here we explain internal control in more detail.

WHAT IS INTERNAL CONTROL?

The American Institute of Certified Public Accountants (AICPA) has defined *internal control* as "the policies and procedures established to provide reasonable assurance that an entity's established objectives will be met."[2] Most companies have the following five concerns in mind when they are designing internal controls:

1. That the accounting records and financial statements provide reliable data for business decisions.
2. That the assets and records are safeguarded. Most companies think of their assets as including their financial assets (such as cash or property), their employees, their confidential information, and their reputation and image.
3. That their operations run efficiently, without duplication of effort or waste.
4. That management policies are followed.
5. That the Foreign Corrupt Practices Act, which requires companies to maintain proper record keeping systems and controls, be complied with.

Although the independent auditor will always review a company's system of internal control, responsibility for establishing and maintaining that system belongs to a company's management. Until several years ago, this responsibility was only implied; there was no formal legal requirement. However, in the wake of illegal political campaign contributions, business frauds, and numerous illegal payments to foreign officials in exchange for business favors, Congress passed the *Foreign Corrupt Practices Act (FCPA) of 1977.* The result of this legislation is that all companies whose stock is publicly traded are required by law to keep records that represent the firm's transactions accurately and fairly. In addition, they must maintain adequate systems of internal accounting control.

Although a good system of internal control would probably have prevented the fraud perpetrated by Roswell Steffen, fraud prevention is not the main purpose. The real purpose of internal controls is to promote efficient operations. In fact, the concept of internal control is so basic that it affects every aspect of an organization, including the efficient acquisition, utilization, and conservation of all resources.

In a small coffee shop, for example, questions relating to internal control would include: Have the personnel been adequately trained? Is there a good refrigeration system to keep the food fresh? Do the waiters and waitresses have order booklets with serialized, preprinted numbers on them? Is there a cash register with an internal tape? Does the building have a fire sprinkler system? Is there good supervision of personnel? Are the duties of the cashier and of the waiters and waitresses adequately separated? Who makes the bank deposit of the day's receipts? Who has responsibility for the accounting records? In other

---

[1] Russell, Harold F., *Foozles and Frauds* (Altamonte Springs, Fla.: Institute of Internal Auditors, 1977).
[2] AU Section 320, par. 6, *AICPA Professional Standards,* Volume 1 (June 1, 1989).

words, internal control goes beyond the control of cash receipts and disbursements and the results of transactions as summarized in accounting reports; it extends to all phases of the operations of a business.

ELEMENTS OF INTERNAL CONTROL

A company's internal control system can be categorized into three basic categories of policies and procedures: (1) the control environment, (2) the accounting system, and (3) the control procedures.

The Control Environment

The control environment consists of the actions, policies, and procedures that reflect the overall attitudes of top management, the directors, and the owners about control and its importance to the company. In a strong control environment, management believes control is important and makes sure that everyone responds conscientiously to the control policies and procedures. The seven components of the control environment are described in the following sections.

1. MANAGEMENT PHILOSOPHY AND OPERATING STYLE. Does management set a good example by following controls, and do they stress the importance of controls to the other employees? Are they risk averse, dominated by one or two individuals, realistic about goals, and so forth?

An example of a company with a poor management philosophy and operating style was Equity Funding. In that company, top management was extremely dominant and dishonest, there was a lack of clear lines of responsibility, budgets were unrealistic, and there was a lack of organizational checks and balances. In that environment, top management wrote $2 billion of fictitious life insurance. Their dishonest actions spoke so loudly that a climate of moral decay filtered throughout the organization resulting in widespread cheating by employees on travel reimbursements and other abuses.

2. ORGANIZATIONAL STRUCTURE. Does the organizational structure identify clear lines of authority and responsibility? Is the organizational structure unduly complex so that dishonest transactions can be concealed?

An example of an organizational structure that was used to conceal a large fraud (approximately $300 million) from the external auditors was the ESM company in Ohio. ESM was a brokerage house that bought and sold government securities. Over a period of seven years, the officers of the company funneled cash to themselves until the company owed approximately $300 million more in payables than it had in receivables. This net payable was concealed by establishing a complex organization structure and reporting a fictitious receivable from an affiliated company. If the auditors would have investigated the receivable, they would have found that the company from which it was collectible was bankrupt.

A good organizational structure would also require that only one person in a department be responsible for each function, such as cash receipts, cash disbursements, purchasing, payroll preparation, or credit approval. It takes little

> **BUSINESS ENVIRONMENT ESSAY**
> *Are Controls Too Tight?*
>
> In 1982, 60,000 PepsiCo. shareholders received a letter from the company informing them that "significant financial irregularities" (fraud) had been discovered in Pepsi's foreign bottling operations. In recent years, similar problems have rocked such leading companies as Heinz, Coca Cola, J. Walter Thompson, Greyhound, and McCormick & Co. Why have large frauds been able to happen in those companies? Don't they have any internal controls?
>
> Well-run corporations such as these have always paid close attention to internal controls. However, internal controls are expensive, and all companies have to decide the appropriate level to control their employees. There's no point in spending $1 million in salaries to protect $500,000 of assets. Companies must make cost–benefit tradeoffs.
>
> In the real world, no controls are completely effective. The cost of internal controls, moreover, often can't be measured in dollars alone. Frequently the question relates more to lost productivity and creativity. For example, a person has a good idea for a product that's going to cost $10,000 to start development. In a highly controlled environment, a senior vice president's approval is required as well as that of several committees. Pretty soon the person with the idea gets exhausted. And after going through all this once, he decides it just isn't worth the fight next time.
>
> Controls must be tight enough to keep the crooks out but loose enough to encourage creativity. Such balancing is difficult and requires the collective effort of management and the accountants.
>
> *Source:* Adapted from "The Numbers Game," *Forbes,* February, 1984, pp. 121–122.

imagination to envision the confusion that would result if a business gave every employee unlimited purchasing authority. There would be overstocking, duplication of orders, loss of quantity discounts, and tremendous waste. By designating responsibility for the purchasing function, or any other function, the organization runs more smoothly, and control is maintained.

Normally, each company will have an organization chart that not only specifies the formal lines of authority but also indicates departmental responsibilities. In addition to formal lines of authority, each organization will have an informal hierarchy that depends on the personality of the individuals and on the group dynamics of the situation.

3. AUDIT COMMITTEE. Is there an audit committee comprised of outside board of director members that work with the internal and external auditors?

Companies listed on the New York Stock Exchange are required to have audit committees comprised entirely of outside directors who are not employees of the company. The audit committee is usually charged with oversight responsibility for the company's financial reporting process, including internal control and compliance with applicable laws and regulations.

4. GOOD COMMUNICATION METHODS. Are formal organizational and operating plans, job descriptions, and related policies and other control-related matters communicated adequately through memoranda, manuals, and the like?

5. MANAGEMENT CONTROL METHODS. Is there a good monitoring system, such as budgets, to ensure that internal controls are followed?

6. INTERNAL AUDIT FUNCTION. Does the company have an independent internal audit department that regularly provides independent checks on the adequacy of and compliance with internal controls?

A major concern of management and auditors is how well the system of internal control is functioning. In a large firm, operating results are generally being monitored constantly by a staff of internal auditors, as is the adherence of employees to management's policies. By reviewing the system of internal controls and making a periodic audit of operations, the internal audit department functions as an arm of management. To function properly, however, the internal audit staff should not be subordinate to any operating department; instead, they should report directly to top management.

Many frauds are detected and prevented by internal auditors who assess the risks of business operations and check to see if controls are being followed. In a sense, internal auditors are the eyes and ears of top management.

7. PERSONNEL POLICIES. Does the company have policies and procedures to ensure that honest, capable, and efficient people are hired?

Having competent and trustworthy employees is the most important characteristic of a satisfactory system of internal control, yet it is the most difficult to evaluate. The best-structured system will fail if the company's employees are incompetent or dishonest. People are an organization's most important resource, and for this reason good personnel policies are essential in achieving a good system of internal control. Perhaps the most important areas to consider in ensuring that an organization has competent and trustworthy personnel are employee selection, employee training, employee supervision, performance review, and fidelity bonding.

(a) Employee Selection. Prospective employees should be evaluated and screened through interviews, aptitude tests, background checks, and evaluation of references from past employers. Once a person's qualifications are confirmed, great care should be taken in matching jobs with talents.

(b) Employee Training. Training programs should be designed to accelerate employee development and to increase the number of competent individuals available to assume the various levels of responsibility. Employees should also be trained to perform a variety of jobs, for several reasons: (1) so that vacations and illnesses will not disrupt operations, (2) so that assignments can be rotated periodically to guard against errors and irregularities that might otherwise go unnoticed, and (3) so that employees will have no excuse not to take a vacation. Take the classic example of the bank clerk who had not taken a vacation in 20 years. An illness forced her to take a few weeks off, and her work was performed by another clerk, who discovered that for a number of years she had been embezzling large sums of money. She had been able to cover up the fraud only because she was always present.

(c) Employee Supervision and Performance Review. A qualified supervisor should assist in the day-to-day activities and conduct periodic performance reviews. These reviews help identify both the strengths and the weaknesses of the employee's performance. They also force employees to account for the assets under their control.

(d) Fidelity Bonding. Employees in charge of easily converted assets should be bonded. A *fidelity bond* is simply an insurance contract whereby a bonding company agrees to reimburse the employer for any theft, embezzlement, or fraud perpetrated by an employee covered by the agreement. Its purpose is really twofold: (1) The company is insured against the misappropriation of assets by its employees, and (2) employees, realizing that the bonding companies generally prosecute to the fullest extent to recover losses, are more hesitant to commit dishonest acts.

An example of the failure to hire competent and trustworthy personnel was the company who found that their controller had defrauded the company of several million dollars. After investigating the fraud, it was discovered that the controller had been fired from his five previous jobs, three for fraud. He was discovered in the defrauded company when the president appeared on the premises one night and found a stranger working in the accounting area. Upon investigation, it was learned that the nocturnal stranger was a phantom controller actually doing the work of the corporate controller, who wasn't even trained in accounting.

The Accounting System

The purpose of a company's accounting system is to identify, assemble, classify, analyze, record, and report the entity's transactions and to maintain accountability for assets. To be effective, the accounting system must make sure that seven internal control objectives are met.

1. That only valid transactions are recorded. If fictitious sales were recorded, for example, reported revenues would be too high and the integrity of the financial statements would be lost.
2. That all transactions are properly authorized.
3. That all legitimate transactions are recorded and that the records are complete. If, for example, all liabilities were not recorded, a company would report a financial condition much better than it really is.
4. That transactions are properly classified. Cash that is in a foreign country and can't be taken out should not be reported as cash, for example. To do so would overstate current assets.
5. That transactions are recorded in the proper time period. A company might try to make its revenues and income look better than it is by, for example, recording early January sales in December.
6. That all transactions are properly valued. For example, if a receivable is uncollectible, it should not be classified as a current asset.
7. That transactions are properly included in subsidiary records and correctly summarized.

The accounting system itself should contain adequate controls to ensure that these objectives are met.

Internal Control Procedures

Control procedures are those policies and procedures, in addition to the control environment and accounting system, that management has established to provide reasonable assurance that the company's established objectives will be met. Generally, control procedures fall into five categories: adequate segregation of duties, proper procedures for authorization, adequate documents and records, physical control over assets and records, and independent checks on performance.

1. ADEQUATE SEGREGATION OF DUTIES. A good internal control system should provide for the appropriate segregation of functional responsibilities. This means that no department should be responsible for handling *all* phases of a transaction. In some small businesses, of course, this segregation is not possible. However, there are three functions that should be performed by separate departments or by different people.

(a) Authorization. Authorizing and approving the execution of a transaction; for example, approving the sale of a building or land.

(b) Record keeping. Recording the transaction in the accounting journals.

(c) Custodial. Having physical possession of or control over the assets involved in a transaction, including operational responsibility—for example, having the key to the safe in which cash or marketable securities are kept or, more generally, having control over the production function.

By separating the responsibilities for these duties, a company realizes the efficiency derived from specialization and reduces the errors, both intentional and unintentional, that might otherwise occur.

An example of a problem resulting from the nonsegregation of the custody and record keeping functions was a young female employee of a wholesale candy distributor who both opened incoming mail and kept the accounts receivable file. Needing money, in a family emergency, she stole $300. After realizing how easy it was, she took another $76,000 before being caught.

2. PROPER PROCEDURES FOR AUTHORIZATION. A strong system of internal control requires proper authorization of every transaction. In the typical corporate organization, this authorization originates with the stockholders who elect a board of directors. It is then delegated from the board of directors to upper-level management and eventually throughout the organization. Whereas the board of directors and upper-level management possess a fairly general power of authorization, a clerk usually has limited authority. Thus, the board would authorize dividends, a general change in policies, or a merger, whereas a clerk would be restricted to the authorization of credit or a specific cash transaction.

3. ADEQUATE DOCUMENTS AND RECORDS. A key to good controls is an adequate system of documentation and recording. As explained in the text, documents are the physical, objective evidence of accounting transactions. Their existence allows management to review any transaction for appropriate authorization. Documents are also the means by which information is communicated throughout an organization. In short, adequate documentation provides evidence that the recording, classifying, and summarizing functions are being performed properly.

A well-designed document has several characteristics: (1) it is easily interpreted and understood, (2) it has been designed with all possible uses in mind, (3) it has been prenumbered for easy identification and tracking, and (4) it is formatted so that it can be handled quickly and efficiently.

A related but separate feature of sound documentation is a chart of accounts. As explained in Chapter 3, this is a written classification of a company's accounts. Typically, the accounts are grouped by type in the order of their appearance on the financial statements and other reports. By organizing the accounting records, the chart of accounts contributes to the consistent reporting of similar transactions and to the proper presentation of information on a company's financial statements.

4. PHYSICAL CONTROL OVER ASSETS AND RECORDS. Some of the most crucial policies and procedures involve the use of adequate physical safeguards to protect resources. For example, a bank would not allow significant amounts of money to be transported in an ordinary car. A company should not leave its valuable assets unprotected. Examples of physical security systems are fireproof vaults for the storage of classified information, currency, and marketable securities, and guards, fences, and remote control cameras for the protection of equipment, materials, and merchandise.

Records and documents are also important resources and must be protected. Recreating lost or destroyed records can be costly and time-consuming. The high cost of backup records (often on microfilm) is usually more than justified in protecting such valuable resources.

Providing proper safeguards reduces opportunities for employees to misappropriate assets. Each firm needs a comprehensive security program specifically engineered to protect its corporate assets.

An example of a fraud committed in a setting of poor physical safeguards was the crime against the Perini Corporation. Approximately $1,150,000 of checks were written on the company's accounts by an outsider. Access to the checks was easy because Perini kept its supply of unused checks in the same unlocked storeroom where the styrofoam coffee cups were stored. Every clerk and secretary had access to the storeroom. The checks had been written on a checkwriting machine which automatically signed the President's name. Despite inherent control procedures in the machine and Arthur Andersen's warning to implement them, the company found it inconvenient to use most control procedures. For example, the machine dumped signed checks into a box that was supposed to be locked; the key was supposed to be kept by an employee in a different department. No such employee was assigned, however, and the box was left unlocked. Nor did anyone pay attention to the machine's counter, which kept track of the number of checks written so that the number of checks written could be compared with vouchers authorized for payment.

5. INDEPENDENT CHECKS ON PERFORMANCE. Independent checks on performance are a valuable control technique. Independent checks incorporate external and internal audit functions, as well as the internal checks created from a proper segregation of duties.

The critical characteristic of an independent check is the impartiality of the reviewing party. It is for this reason that internal audit staffs technically report to the chief executive operating officer or, alternatively, the board of directors. It is also for this reason that the CPA profession establishes strict independence standards and guidelines for professional behavior.

There are many ways to independently check performance. Certainly using internal auditors is one of the most common. However, mandatory vacations, where another employee performs the vacationing person's duties; periodic rotations or transfers; or merely having someone independent of the accounting records reconcile the bank statement, for example, are all types of independent checks.

One of the best examples of a fraud that was perpetrated because of a lack of independent checks was that of Roswell Steffen, whose fraud was used as an illustration at the beginning of this appendix. When caught, he said, "If the bank would have coupled a two-week vacation with four weeks of rotation to another job, my embezzlement would have been impossible to cover up."[3]

The various elements of control are summarized in Exhibit 8-7.

Although the control environment elements affect the overall firm, there are specific control procedures for each type of financial statement account. For example, in Chapter 8, three controls for cash were mentioned: daily deposits, the use of prenumbered checks, and segregation of cash receipts from cash accounting. Likewise, there are specific internal controls for accounts receivable, inventories, and even liabilities to make sure they are accounted for accurately. Most accounting programs offer specialized courses on accounting systems and auditing in which controls are covered in more detail.

Exhibit 8-7 Elements of Control

Control Environment	Accounting System	Control Procedures
1. Management philosophy and operating styles.	1. Valid transactions.	1. Segregation of duties.
2. Organizational structure.	2. Properly authorized transactions.	2. Proper procedures for authorization.
3. Audit committee.	3. Completeness.	3. Adequate documents and records.
4. Communication methods.	4. Proper classification.	4. Physical control over assets and records.
5. Management control methods.	5. Proper timing.	5. Independent checks on performance.
6. Internal audit function.	6. Proper valuation.	
7. Personnel policies.	7. Correct summarization.	

THE EFFECTS OF COMPUTERS ON INTERNAL CONTROL

The elements of internal control we have discussed apply equally to a computerized accounting system. Computer operators are usually bonded, duties are generally rotated and segregated where possible, and physical safeguards are maintained. In addition, computers are valuable assets that require environmental controls, such as sprinkler systems, climate control, guards or restricted access, and fireproof libraries.

---

[3] Russell, Harold F., *Foozles and Frauds* (Altamonte Springs, Fla.: Institute of Internal Auditors, 1977).

For all its benefits, however, the computer can also be a source of problems in internal control in the following ways:

1. Although the decrease in human involvement with the data will eliminate many mechanical and mathematical errors, it may also obscure errors that would otherwise be discovered in manual systems. For example, the receipt of two identical refunds from one company would be processed in the normal manner by the computer. A person, on the other hand, might become suspicious and, by checking into the matter, discover that a duplication has been made.
2. Because computer systems require such specialized skills, it may be difficult for a company to achieve the degree of segregation of duties necessary for sound internal control. For example, programmers in a small company may be asked to operate the computer system, making it possible for them to manipulate their own programs for personal benefit.
3. Data must be converted to tapes or disks, so errors may be introduced into the system during the data-conversion process.
4. Less documentary evidence usually remains after certain functions have been performed by the computer. This means that the internal controls that rely upon a review of documentation may be less meaningful. Computers may destroy or conceal much of the "audit trail."
5. Because management, and even auditors, may not thoroughly understand the computer, dishonest employees can take advantage of this ignorance. People can steal with the aid of a computer without actually having to carry away goods or cash.

Because of these factors, internal checks and controls must be adapted to and built into computer systems. Computer-based internal control systems are often complex and may be difficult for management and auditors to work with, but they are necessary in many companies.

Chapter 8 Cash, Marketable Securities, and Receivables

Review of Learning Objectives

Objective 1

Describe the procedures used to control and account for cash, including petty cash funds and bank reconciliations. Cash is the most liquid of all assets. Therefore, stringent procedures for controlling cash must be established and maintained. Most cash is kept in bank accounts, which are reconciled each month. One exception is a petty cash fund, which is usually maintained on an imprest basis to cover small, miscellaneous expenditures. Bank reconciliations adjust the bank and book balances so that they are the same correct amount.

Objective 2

Explain the recording and valuation of marketable securities and other short-term investments. Temporary excesses of cash are usually invested in marketable securities [stocks (equity) and bonds (debt)] of other companies or government agencies, commercial paper, certificates of deposit, money market funds, treasury bills, or other interest-bearing items. These short-term investments are extremely liquid assets and so are listed on the balance sheet just below Cash. Marketable equity securities are accounted for on a lower-of-cost-or-market basis; that is, they are carried at cost unless the market value of a firm's total portfolio of short-term investments drops below cost, at which time the investments are written down to market. Gains and losses resulting from the sale of marketable securities or losses due to a reduction to the lower of cost or market are included in a firm's income statement with Other Revenues and Expenses.

Objective 3

Describe the accounting for accounts receivable, including losses from uncollectible accounts. Accounts receivable are short-term liquid assets that arise from credit sales to customers. Accounts receivable balances are generally collected from 10 to 60 days after the date of sale. There are two ways to account for losses from uncollectible receivables: the direct write-off and the allowance methods. Only the allowance method is generally acceptable because it matches expenses with revenues. Losses from uncollectible receivables can be estimated: (1) as a percentage of sales, (2) as a percentage of total outstanding receivables, and (3) as an amount based on an aging of accounts receivable. Most retailers accept credit cards from individuals because they enable them to avoid the problem of uncollectible accounts. Retailers who accept these cards usually have to pay a fee to the credit card companies.

Objective 4

Explain the accounting for notes receivable. A note receivable is a claim against a debtor, evidenced by an unconditional written promise to pay a sum of money on or before a specified future date. The amount of interest to be earned annually is equal to the principal times the interest rate times the time period (in terms of 1 year) of the note. Notes can be discounted at a bank or other financial institution. Discounting allows the original payee of a note to receive money prior to the maturity date. The discount is the note's maturity value times the discount rate times the discount period.

Key Terms and Concepts

accounts receivable *(315)*
aging accounts receivable *(319)*
Allowance for Uncollectible Accounts *(317)*
allowance method *(316)*
bad debt *(316)*
bank reconciliation *(309)*
Cash Over and Short *(305)*
credit card *(320)*
credit card draft *(320)*
direct write-off method *(316)*
discount *(324)*
discount period *(324)*
discount rate *(324)*

discounting a note receivable *(324)*
imprest petty cash fund *(304)*
interest *(322)*
interest rate *(322)*
lapping *(303)*
line of credit *(311)*
liquid *(302)*
lower of cost or market (LCM) *(313)*
maker *(322)*
marketable securities *(312)*
matching principal *(316)*
maturity date *(322)*

maturity value *(323)*
net proceeds *(324)*
net realizable value of accounts receivable *(317)*
note receivable *(322)*
NSF (not sufficient funds) check *(307)*
payee *(322)*
petty cash fund *(304)*
principal on a note *(322)*
receivables *(315)*
recourse *(325)*
Uncollectible Accounts Expense *(317)*

Review Problem

Accounts and Notes Receivable

Marvin Furniture Company sells living and dining room furniture. Approximately 10 percent of the company's sales are cash; the remainder are on credit. During the year ending December 31, 1994, the company had net credit sales of $2,200,000; as of December 31, 1994, total accounts receivable were $800,000 and Allowance for Uncollectible Accounts had a debit balance of $1,100. In the past, approximately 1½ percent of net credit sales have proved to be uncollectible. An aging analysis of the individual accounts receivable reveals that $32,000 of the accounts receivable balance appears to be uncollectible.

On June 10, 1994, Marvin Furniture Company received a $3,000, 14 percent, 90-day note receivable from R. Taylor for merchandise sold. On July 10, the note was discounted at 15 percent at the Tracey National Bank. On September 8, the maturity date of the note, Marvin was notified that R. Taylor had dishonored the note. Marvin paid the maturity value of the note plus a $20 fee. On September 9, Marvin received payment in full from R. Taylor.

Required:
1. Prepare journal entries to record uncollectible accounts expense, using:
   (a) The percentage of net credit sales method.
   (b) The aging of accounts receivable method.
2. Prepare all the necessary journal entries to account for the note from R. Taylor.

Solution

1. Journal Entries for Uncollectible Accounts Expense:

(a) Percentage of Net Credit Sales Method

1994
Dec. 31 Uncollectible Accounts Expense 33,000
            Allowance for Uncollectible Accounts   33,000

To record uncollectible accounts expense as 1½ percent of $2,200,000 ($2,200,000 × 0.015 = $33,000).

The debit balance is ignored when the percentage of sales method is used.

(b) Aging of Accounts Receivable Method

1994
Dec. 31 Uncollectible Accounts Expense 33,100
            Allowance for Uncollectible Accounts   33,100

To record uncollectible accounts expense using the aging of accounts receivable method.

When the estimate is based on receivables, which could come from any period, the existing balance in Allowance for Uncollectible Accounts must be adjusted to the desired amount. In this case, since we want to end up with $32,000 in the Allowance account, $33,100 must be entered in order to eliminate the $1,100 debit balance.

2. Journal Entries for the R. Taylor Note:

1994
June 10 Notes Receivable 3,000
            Sales Revenue   3,000

To record the note receivable and sale of merchandise to R. Taylor. The note is a 90-day, 14% note.

```
1994
July 10   Cash ...................................................   3,027.03
              Notes Receivable .................................              3,000.00
              Interest Revenue .................................                  27.03
          To record the discounting of the R. Taylor note at the Tracey National Bank at 15%.
```

Interest = $3,000 × 90/365 × 0.14 = $103.56
Maturity value = $3,000 + $103.56 = $3,103.56
Discount = $3,103.56 × 60/365 × 0.15 = $76.53
Proceeds = $3,103.56 − $76.53 = $3,027.03
Interest revenue = $3,027.03 − $3,000.00 = $27.03

```
1994
Sept. 8   Special Receivable, R. Taylor ........................   3,123.56
              Cash ...........................................                3,123.56
          To record payment to Tracey National Bank of R. Taylor's dishonored note
          ($3,103.56 + $20).
```

The entire amount is shown as a receivable because Marvin Furniture will attempt to collect all of it from R. Taylor.

```
1994
Sept. 9   Cash ..................................................   3,123.56
              Special Receivable, R. Taylor ....................              3,123.56
          To record receipt of payment from R. Taylor of previously dishonored note
          ($3,103.56 + $20).
```

Discussion Questions

1. What is generally included in the Cash figure reported on the balance sheet?
2. Why do companies usually have more controls for cash than for other assets?
3. What are three generally practiced controls for cash, and what are their purposes?
4. What is an imprest petty cash fund, and why is it important that petty cash be handled this way?
5. What are the major reasons that the balance of a bank statement is usually different from the Cash book balance (Cash per the General Ledger)?
6. Why don't the additions and deductions from the bank balance on a bank reconciliation require adjustment by the company?
7. Why are short-term investments in stocks written down if cost exceeds market price but not written up if the market price exceeds cost?
8. Why do most companies tolerate having a small percentage of uncollectible accounts receivable?
9. Why does the accounting profession require use of the allowance method of accounting for losses due to uncollectible accounts rather than the direct write-off method?
10. Why would a retail business accept credit cards as payment from customers if the credit card company keeps 2 to 5 percent of the sales price as a handling fee?
11. *"Internal control refers only to measures taken to prevent fraud and embezzlement." Do you agree? Explain.
12. *Who has primary responsibility for establishing and maintaining the internal control system within an organization? Discuss.
13. *What is the significance of the Foreign Corrupt Practices Act of 1977 with respect to internal accounting controls?
14. *What are the principal characteristics of an effective system of internal control?

* Relates to Appendix.

15. *The general principle of adequate segregation of duties recognizes that three basic functions should be segregated by department, or at least performed by different people. What are those three functions? Why is it important to separate them?

16. *With respect to internal control, identify the three most important areas to consider in evaluating a firm's personnel.

* Relates to Appendix.

Exercises

E8-1
The Definition of Cash

For each of the following separate cases, compute the amount that would be reported as cash on the balance sheet.

1. Balance in general checking account at Bank A, $20,000; IOU from company employee, $200; balance in savings account at Bank C, $2,000; balance in fund that can only be used to repay a bond debt, $7,000; balance in bank account in Libya, $5,000 (restricted).
2. Cash on hand, $1,850; petty cash fund, $250; overdraft (negative balance) in special checking account at Bank A, $100; NSF check for $500; postage stamps, $85; undeposited checks, $1,025.
3. Money orders, $800; short-term certificates of deposit, $5,000; money advanced to the company president, $2,000; note receivable left with the bank for collection, $2,500.

E8-2
The Definition of Cash

1. Determine which of the following items should be included in calculating the cash balance of a company:
   (a) A check returned by a bank (NSF).
   (b) Postage stamps.
   (c) IOUs signed by employees.
   (d) Money orders on hand (made payable to the company).
   (e) Petty cash on hand.
   (f) A deposit made with the telephone company.
   (g) A deposit in a foreign bank (unrestricted).
   (h) Postdated checks.
   (i) Money advanced to officers.
   (j) A note receivable left with a bank for collection.
   (k) The bank account balance at City Bank.
   (l) Cashier's checks payable to the company.
2. State how each of the noncash items would be accounted for.

E8-3
Control of Cash

Molly Maloney is an employee of Marshall Company, a small manufacturing concern. Her responsibilities include opening the daily mail, depositing the cash and checks received in the bank, and making the accounting entries to record the receipt of cash and the reduction of receivables. Explain how Maloney might be able to misuse some of Marshall's cash receipts. As a consultant, what control procedures would you recommend?

E8-4
Accounting for Petty Cash

The following transactions relating to petty cash were completed by Flamingo Corporation, a firm with a December 31 year-end:

Dec. 19 Established a petty cash fund of $400 with check #1135.
20 Paid a Union Trucking delivery bill of $350 for freight on merchandise purchased—used petty cash voucher #1.
21 A count of cash in the petty cash fund revealed $46. Replenished the fund with check #1240.
23 Decided to increase the fund permanently to $650 with check #1290.
27 Purchased stamps, $48 (petty cash voucher #2); paid newspaper carrier, $16 (petty cash voucher #3); purchased office supplies, $330 (petty cash voucher #4).
31 Replenished the fund with check #1335 for $394.

Where appropriate, prepare General Journal entries to account for these transactions.

E8-5
Bank Reconciliation Computations

Barnum Company has the following financial information. (Assume that all receipts and payments are by check.)

October 31, 1994, Bank Reconciliation

Balance per bank	$24,000
Add deposits in transit	5,100
	$29,100
Less outstanding checks	(6,500)
Balance per books	$22,600

November Results	Per Bank	Per Books
Balance, November 30	$21,340	$24,300
November Deposits	16,600	25,000
November Checks	24,900	23,300
November Note collected by bank	5,660	—
November Bank charges	20	—

From the information provided, compute the amount of:

1. Deposits in transit on November 30, 1994.
2. Outstanding checks on November 30, 1994.

E8-6
Preparing a Bank Reconciliation

Prepare a bank reconciliation for Oldroyd Company at January 31, 1994, using the information shown.

1. Cash per the accounting records at January 31 amounted to $72,802; the bank statement on this same date showed a balance of $64,502.
2. The canceled checks returned by the bank included a check written by the Oldham Company for $1,764 which had been deducted from Oldroyd's account in error.
3. Deposits in transit as of January 31, 1994 amounted to $10,928.

4. The following amounts were adjustments to Oldroyd Company's account on the bank statement:
   (a) Service charge of $26.
   (b) A NSF check of $1,400.
   (c) Interest earned on the account, $40.
5. Checks written by Oldroyd Company that have not yet cleared the bank include four checks totaling $5,778.

E8-7
Marketable Securities—Journal Entries

Prepare journal entries to account for the following Marketable Securities transactions of Morrell Company:

1994
July 1   Purchased 200 shares of Nickle Company stock at $36 per share plus brokerage fees of $450.
Oct. 31   Received a cash dividend of $1.50 per share on Nickle Company stock.
Dec. 31   At year end, Nickle Company stock had a market price of $33 per share.

1995
Feb. 20   Sold 100 shares of the Nickle Company stock for $37 per share.

E8-8
Marketable Securities—Investments in Stock

In June 1994, Jacobson Company had no short-term investments but had excess cash that would not be needed for 9 months. Management decided to use this money to purchase stock as a short-term investment. The following transactions relate to their short-term investments:

July 16   Purchased 4,000 shares of Eli Corporation stock. The price paid, including brokerage fees, was $41,880.
Sept. 23 Received a cash dividend of $.90 per share on the Eli stock.
      28 Sold 2,000 shares of Eli Corporation stock at $11 per share. Paid a selling commission of $160.
Dec. 31   The market value of Eli's stock was $11.25 per share.

Given these data, make the journal entries to account for Jacobson's investment in Eli Corporation stock.

E8-9
Computing and Recording Uncollectible Accounts Expense

During 1994, Wishbone Corporation has a total of $5,000,000 in sales, of which 80 percent are on credit. At year-end, the Accounts Receivable balance shows a total of $2,300,000, which has been aged as follows:

Age	Amount
Current	$1,900,000
1–30 Days Past Due	200,000
31–60 Days Past Due	100,000
61–90 Days Past Due	70,000
Over 90 Days Past Due	30,000
	$2,300,000

Prepare the journal entry required at year-end to record the uncollectible accounts expense under each of the following independent conditions. Assume, where applicable, that Allowance for Uncollectible Accounts has a credit balance of $5,500 immediately before these adjustments.

1. Use the direct write-off method. [Assume that $60,000 of accounts are determined to be uncollectible and are written off in a single year-end entry.]
2. Based on experience, annual uncollectible accounts are estimated to be approximately 1.4 percent of total credit sales for the year.
3. Based on experience, uncollectible accounts for the year are estimated to be approximately 3 percent of total accounts receivable.
4. Based on experience, uncollectible accounts are estimated to be the sum of:

   1 percent of current accounts receivable
   6 percent of accounts 1–30 days past due
   10 percent of accounts 31–60 days past due
   20 percent of accounts 61–90 days past due
   30 percent of accounts over 90 days past due

E8-10
Accounting for Credit Card Sales

On December 23, 1994, the Ratliff Department Store had American Express credit card drafts totaling $15,260 and VISA drafts totaling $46,820. On that day, they deposited the VISA drafts in their bank account and sent the American Express drafts to the credit card company for reimbursement. On December 29, 1994, Ratliff received payment of 96 percent of the total American Express drafts. Prepare the journal entries needed to account for these transactions on December 23 and December 29, assuming the store receives 95 percent of VISA sales.

E8-11
Accounting for Credit Card Sales

Pinnegar Clothing accepts two kinds of credit cards: Carte Blanche and VISA. Pinnegar can deposit its VISA drafts directly in its bank account at the First National City Bank, which is an issuer of VISA cards. However, the Carte Blanche drafts must be sent to Chicago, Illinois, for reimbursement. Given this information, account for the following transactions:

1. On October 15, 1994, sold $800 of clothing to VISA-paying customers. The VISA drafts were deposited in the bank account on this day. There is a 3 percent charge on VISA sales.
2. On October 16, 1994, sold $1,850 of clothing to Carte-Blanche-paying customers. The Carte Blanche drafts were sent to Chicago for reimbursement on that day.
3. Received payment from Carte Blanche for the October 16 sales. Carte Blanche charges a 4 percent handling fee.

E8-12
Journal Entries for Notes Receivable

Prepare journal entries for the following transactions for Stansworth Plumbing for 1994:

July 1   Installed a sprinkling system for Chuck's Engineering and billed $12,600 for the job.
Sept. 1 Chuck's had not paid for the sprinkling system yet. Stansworth agreed to accept a three-month note for the full amount with interest at an annual rate of 14%.
Oct. 1   Discounted Chuck's note at the bank at a 15% discount rate.
Dec. 1   Chuck's Engineering paid the bank in full.

E8-13
Separation of Duties
(Appendix)

The city of Moroni can afford to hire only one employee to give out parking tickets. This employee is also responsible for collecting fines and money from parking meters as well as for keeping records for all monies collected.

1. What are the internal control weaknesses of this arrangement?
2. If two employees are available, what arrangements might be made for better control?

E8-14
Reasons for Internal Control
(Appendix)

Discuss the reasons for each of the following control procedures:

1. Before the treasurer of Devonshire Company signs disbursement checks, she reviews the supporting data. Afterward, the supporting data are returned to the accounting department, and the checks are mailed by the treasurer's secretary.
2. Each clerk in a department store has a separate cash drawer and does not have access to the cash drawers of other clerks.
3. The ticket-taker at Ellett Theatre is required to tear each admission ticket in half. He drops half in a box, and presents the stub to the patron.
4. At Pacos Company, four copies of each purchase order are prepared. The fourth and final copy is sent to the receiving department. The form is designed in such a way that the quantity ordered does not appear on the fourth copy.
5. Volunteers who solicit contributions for a local charity are required to issue a receipt for any cash contributions. The receipt book is serially prenumbered and has a single carbon copy for each receipt.
6. Tom Truble, the cashier for Funk Manufacturing Company, is required to keep copies of all voided (invalidated) receipts.

E8-15
A Bank Fraud *(Appendix)*

Mac Faber was the controller of the Lewiston National Bank. In his position of controller, he was in charge of all accounting functions. He wrote cashier checks for the bank and reconciled the bank statement. He alone could approve exceptions to credit limits for bank customers, and even the internal auditor reported to him. Unknown to the bank, Mac had recently been divorced and was supporting two households. In addition, many of his personal investments had soured, including a major farm implement dealership that had lost $40,000 in the last year. Several months after Mac had left the bank for another job, it was discovered that a vendor had paid twice and that the second payment had been deposited by Mac in his personal account. Because Mac was not there to cover his tracks (as he had been on previous occasions), an investigation ensued. It was determined that Mac had used his position in the bank to steal $117,000 over a period of two years. Mac was prosecuted and sentenced to 30 months in a federal penitentiary.

1. What internal control weaknesses allowed Mac to perpetrate fraud?
2. What motivated Mac to perpetrate the fraud?

Problem Set A

P8A-1
Accounting for Petty Cash

On December 1, 1994, Hipple Company established a petty cash fund. Transactions for the fund during December, 1994, were as follows:

Dec. 1 Established the fund by cashing a company check for $1,500 and delivering the proceeds to the petty cash fund cashier.

Chapter 8 *Cash, Marketable Securities, and Receivables*

Dec. 19   A request for replenishment of the petty cash fund was received by the accounts payable department, supported by appropriate signed vouchers summarized as follows:

Advertising Expenses	$421
Administrative Expenses	195
Equipment	125
Delivery Expense	416

20   A check for $1,157 was drawn to reimburse the petty cash fund.
30   The company's auditors counted the fund and found the following:

Cash in petty cash fund	$ 498
Employee's checks with Jan. dates (post-dated)	295
Signed vouchers summarized as follows:	
Advertising Expense	221
Administrative Expense	183
Office Supplies	301
Total	$1,498

31   A check for $707 was drawn to reimburse the petty cash fund.

Required:
1. Prepare the appropriate journal entries on each of the preceding dates.
2. Discuss the appropriateness of using the petty cash fund as a temporary bank for employees who need loans.

P8A-2
Preparing a Bank Reconciliation

The records of Denna Corporation show the following bank statement information for December:

(a)	Bank Balance, December 31	$87,450
(b)	Service Charges for December	50
(c)	Rent Collected by Bank	1,000
(d)	Note Receivable Collected by Bank (including $300 interest)	2,300
(e)	December Check Returned Marked NSF (check was a payment of an account receivable)	200
(f)	Bank Erroneously Reduced Denna's Account for a Check Written by Denna Company	1,000
(g)	Cash Account Balance, December 31	81,200
(h)	Outstanding Checks	9,200
(i)	Deposits in Transit	5,000

Required:
1. Prepare a bank reconciliation for December.
2. Prepare the entry to correct the Cash account as of December 31.

P8A-3
Reconciling Book and Bank Balances

SPREADSHEET PROBLEM

Jensen Company has just received the September 30, 1994 bank statement summarized in the following schedule:

	Charges	Deposits	Balance
Balance, September 1			$ 5,100
Deposits Recorded During September		$27,000	32,100
Checks Cleared During September	$27,300		4,800
NSF Check, J. J. Jones	50		4,750
Bank Service Charges	10		4,740
Balance, September 30			4,740

Cash on hand (recorded on Jensen's books but not deposited) on September 1 and September 30 amounted to $200. There were no deposits in transit or checks outstanding at September 1, 1994. The Cash account for September reflected the following:

Cash

Sept. 1 Balance	5,300	Sept. Checks	28,000
Sept. Deposits	29,500		

Required: Answer the following questions. (Hint: It may be helpful to prepare a complete bank reconciliation.)

1. What is the ending balance per the Cash Account before adjustments?
2. What adjustments should be added to the depositor's books?
3. What is the total amount of the deductions from the depositor's books?
4. What is the total amount to be added to the bank's balance?
5. What is the total amount to be deducted from the bank's balance?

P8A-4
Unifying Concepts: Marketable Securities—Recording and Analysis

The following data pertain to the marketable securities of Howell Company during 1994, the company's first year of operations:

(a) Purchased 400 shares of Corporation A stock at $40 per share, plus brokerage fees of $200.
(b) Purchased $6,000 of Corporation B bonds.
(c) Received a cash dividend of 50 cents per share on the Corporation A stock.
(d) Sold 100 shares of Corporation A Stock for $46 per share.
(e) Received interest of $240 on the Corporation B bonds.
(f) Purchased 50 shares of Corporation C stock for $3,500.
(g) Received interest of $240 on the Corporation B bonds.
(h) Sold 150 shares of Corporation A Stock for $28 per share.
(i) Received a cash dividend of $1.40 per share on the Corporation C stock.
(j) Interest receivable at year-end on the Corporation B bonds amounts to $60.

Required: Prepare journal entries to record the preceding transactions. Post the entries in T-accounts, and determine the amount of each of the following for the year:

1. Dividend revenue.
2. Interest revenue.
3. Net gain or loss from selling securities.

P8A-5
Short-Term Investments in Stock

In December 1994, the treasurer of Marble Company discovered that the company had excess cash on hand and decided to invest in Sandy Corporation stock. The company intends to hold the stock for a period of 6 to 12 months. The following transactions took place:

Jan. 1 Purchased 5,500 shares of Sandy Corporation stock for $82,500.
April 15 Received a cash dividend of 65 cents per share on the Sandy Corporation stock.
May 22 Sold 1,500 shares of the Sandy Corporation stock at $20 per share for cash.
July 15 Received a cash dividend of 45 cents per share on the Sandy Corporation stock.

Chapter 8 Cash, Marketable Securities, and Receivables

Aug. 31 Sold the balance of the Sandy Corporation stock at $8 per share for cash.

Required: Give the appropriate journal entries to record each of these transactions.

P8A-6

Unifying Concepts: Aging of Accounts Receivable and Uncollectible Accounts

Delta Company has found that, historically, ½ percent of its current accounts receivable, 1 percent of accounts 1 to 30 days past due, 1½ percent of accounts 31 to 60 days past due, 3 percent of accounts 61 to 90 days past due, and 10 percent of accounts over 90 days past due are uncollectible. The following schedule shows an aging of the accounts receivable as of December 31, 1994:

	Current	Days Past Due 1 to 30	31 to 60	61 to 90	Over 90
Balance	$45,600	$9,850	$4,100	$850	$195

The balances at December 31, 1994, in certain selected accounts are as follows. (Assume that the allowance method is used.)

Sales Revenue	$120,096
Sales Returns	1,209
Allowance for Uncollectible Accounts	113 (credit balance)

Required:
1. Given these data, make the necessary adjusting entry (or entries) for uncollectible accounts on December 31, 1994.
2. On February 14, 1995, Lori Jacobs, a customer, informed Delta Company that she was going bankrupt and would not be able to pay her account of $46. Make the appropriate entry (or entries).
3. On June 29, 1995, Lori Jacobs was able to pay the amount she owed in full. Make the appropriate entry (or entries).
4. Assume that Allowance for Uncollectible Accounts at December 31, 1994, had a debit balance of $113 instead of a credit balance of $113. Make the necessary adjusting journal entry that would be needed on December 31, 1994.

P8A-7

Discounting a Note Receivable

Escondido Company frequently sells merchandise on promissory notes that are later sold (discounted) to a local bank to obtain cash prior to maturity date. The following transactions relate to one such note.

Feb. 1 Sold merchandise for $9,000 to Marta Tabor; accepted a 6-month, 11 percent note. Escondido Company uses a perpetual inventory system. The merchandise cost $6,250.
April 1 Discounted the note at the bank at a 13 percent discount rate.
Aug. 1 On this date (due date of the note), Marta Tabor did not make payment, and Escondido Company had to pay the note plus a $30 fee.
Oct. 1 Collected the maturity value of the note plus protest fee from Marta Tabor together with interest on the receivable of 15 percent from August 1.

Required: 1. Give the appropriate journal entries to account for the preceding transactions for Escondido Company. Round all calculations to the nearest dollar.
2. **Interpretive Question** Why did Escondido Company debit a receivable for the full $9,525 on August 1?

P8A-8
Discounting a Note Receivable

You are the accountant for Semper Fi Finance Company. The following transactions and events occurred in June 1994 and 1995:

SOLUTIONS SOFTWARE

1994
June 1 Semper Fi made a $30,000 loan to Rhonda Roades, who signed a note promising to pay the loan plus interest at 18 percent in 1 year.
June 16 Because of excessive loans made in the month of June, Semper Fi Finance discounted Rhonda's note at a local bank at 20 percent (with recourse).
1995
June 1 The local bank notified Semper Fi of the default by Rhonda and demanded immediate payment of the principal, accrued interest, and a $50 penalty fee.
July 1 Semper Fi collected the entire receivable from Rhonda plus 18 percent interest on the amount paid to the bank on June 1, 1995.

Required: 1. Prepare journal entries, assuming a 365-day year.
2. **Interpretive Question** Should any disclosure of the discounted liability on the note have been made on Semper Fi Finance Company's financial statements for December 31, 1994? If so, what type of disclosure?

Problem Set B

P8B-1
Accounting for Petty Cash

Stetler Company uses an imprest petty cash fund to pay for small, miscellaneous expenditures.

Required: 1. Prepare the necessary journal entries to record the following events:
(a) Establishment of a petty cash fund of $2,000 on March 1, 1994.
(b) On March 12, a disbursement from the petty cash fund of $130 is made to Pepsi Cola to pay for office drinks.
(c) On March 15, $60 is taken from the fund to pay for postage stamps.
(d) On March 18, because the company is short of cash, $1,200 of the fund is used to meet payroll expenses.
(e) On March 25, with the company cash position restored, the petty cash fund is replenished.
(f) On March 26, it is decided that only $1,000 is needed in the fund, and it is reduced accordingly.
2. **Interpretive Question** Explain why a petty cash fund should be handled on an imprest basis.
3. **Interpretive Question** Explain why one person is usually given complete responsibility for handling a petty cash fund. Doesn't that make it easy for that person to steal from the fund?

Chapter 8 Cash, Marketable Securities, and Receivables

P8B-2
Preparing a Bank Reconciliation

Milton Company has just received the following monthly bank statement for June.

Date	Checks	Deposits	Balance
June 1			$25,000
2	$ 150		24,850
3		$ 6,000	30,850
4	750		30,100
5	1,500		28,600
7	8,050		20,550
9		8,000	28,550
10	3,660		24,890
11	2,690		22,200
12		9,000	31,200
13	550		30,650
17	7,500		23,150
20		5,500	28,650
21	650		28,000
22	700		27,300
23		4,140†	31,440
25	1,000		30,440
30	50*		30,390
Totals	$27,250	$32,640	

* Bank service charge
† Note collected, including $140 interest.

Data from the Cash account of Milton Company for June are as follows:

June 1 balance $20,440

Checks written:
June		Deposits:	
June 1	$ 1,500	June 2	$ 6,000
4	8,500	5	8,000
6	2,690	10	9,000
8	550	18	5,500
9	7,500	30	6,000
12	650		$34,500
19	700		
22	1,000		
26	1,300		
27	1,360		
	$25,750		

At the end of May, Milton had three checks outstanding for a total of $4,560. All three checks were processed by the bank during June. There were no deposits outstanding at the end of May. It was discovered during the reconciliation process that a check for $8,050, written on June 4 for supplies, was improperly recorded on the books at $8,500.

Required:
1. Determine the amount of deposits in transit at the end of June.
2. Determine the amount of outstanding checks at the end of June.
3. Prepare a June bank reconciliation.
4. Prepare the journal entries to correct the Cash account.
5. **Interpretive Question** Why is it important that the Cash account be reconciled on a timely basis?

P8B-3
Determining Where the Cash Went

Kim Lee, the bookkeeper for Briton Company, had never missed a day's work for the past 10 years until last week. Since that time, he has not been located. You now suspect that Kim may have embezzled money from the company. The following bank reconciliation, prepared by Kim last month, is available to help you determine if a theft occurred:

Briton Company
Bank Reconciliation for August 1994
Prepared by Kim Lee

Balance per bank statement..	$162,442	Balance per books	$199,200
Additions to bank statement:		Additions to book balance:	
Direct total deposits	8,000	Deposits in transit	250
		Interest earned	600
Deductions:		Deductions:	
NSF check	(1,800)	Outstanding checks: #201..	(19,200)
Bank service charge..........	(48)	#204..	(5,000)
		#205..	(4,058)
		#295..	(195)
		#565..	(1,920)
		#567..	(615)
		#568..	(468)
Adjusted bank balance....... $168,594		**Adjusted book balance..... $168,594**	

In examining the bank reconciliation, you decide to review canceled checks returned by the bank. You find that checks #201, 204, 205, and 295 were voided when written. All other bank reconciliation data has been verified as correct.

Required:
1. Prepare a corrected bank reconciliation identifying the amount suspected stolen by Kim.
2. **Interpretive Question** Describe how Kim accounted for the stolen money. What would have prevented the theft?

P8B-4
Short-Term Investments in Stocks

Menlo Company often purchases common stocks of other companies as short-term investments. During 1994, the following events occurred:

July 1 Menlo purchased the common stocks listed here.

Corporation	Number of Shares	Price per Share
A..........................	400	$ 72
B..........................	600	46
C..........................	300	156
D..........................	200	84

Sept. 30 Menlo received a cash dividend of $2.50 per share on Corporation A stock.
Dec. 1 Menlo sold the stock in Corporation D for $74 per share.
Dec. 31 The market prices were quoted as follows: Corporation A stock, $64; Corporation B stock, $48; Corporation C stock, $150.

Required:
1. Prepare journal entries to record the events.
2. Illustrate how these investments would be reported on the balance sheet at December 31.
3. What items and amounts would be reported on the income statement for the year?

Chapter 8 Cash, Marketable Securities, and Receivables

4. **Interpretive Question** Why are losses from the write-down of short-term investments in stock to the lower of cost or market included in the current year's income, whereas most similar losses for long-term investments in stock are not?

P8B-5
Unifying Concepts: Short-Term Investments in Stocks and Bonds

Frederick Manufacturing Company produces and sells one main product. There is significant seasonality in demand, and the unit price is quite high. As a result, during the heavy selling season, the company generates cash that is idle for a few months. The company uses this cash to acquire short-term investments. The following transactions relate to Frederick's short-term investments during 1994.

Mar. 15		Purchased 800 shares of Lewis Corporation stock at $25 per share, plus brokerage fees of $624.
Apr.	1	Purchased $42,000 of 12 percent bonds of Martin Company, plus a brokerage fee of $225.
June	3	Received a cash dividend of $1.80 per share on the Lewis Corporation stock.
Oct.	1	Received a semiannual interest payment of $2,520 on the Martin Company bonds.
	10	Sold 600 shares of the Lewis Corporation stock at $29 per share less a $325 brokerage fee.
Dec. 31		Recorded $1,260 of interest earned on the Martin Company bonds for the period October 1, 1994 through December 31, 1994.
	31	The market price of the Lewis Corporation stock was $22 per share and the market price of the Martin Company bonds was $40,320.

Required: Prepare journal entries to record these transactions.

P8B-6
Estimating Uncollectible Accounts

Ulysis Corporation makes and sells clothing to fashion stores throughout the country. On December 31, 1994, before adjusting entries were made, it had the following account balances on its books:

Accounts Receivable	$ 2,320,000
Sales Revenue, 1994 (60% were credit sales)	16,000,000
Allowance for Uncollectible Accounts (credit balance)	4,000

Required:
1. Make the appropriate adjusting entry on December 31, 1994, to record the allowance for uncollectible accounts if uncollectible accounts are estimated to be 1 percent of credit sales.
2. Make the appropriate adjusting entry on December 31, 1994, to record the allowance for uncollectible accounts if uncollectible accounts are estimated to be 3 percent of accounts receivable.
3. Make the appropriate adjusting entry on December 31, 1994, to record the allowance for uncollectible accounts if uncollectible accounts are estimated on the basis of an aging of accounts receivable and the aging schedule reveals the following:

Balance of Accounts Receivable		Percent Estimated to Become Uncollectible
Not yet due	$1,200,000	½ of 1 percent
1–30 days past due	$ 800,000	1 percent
31–60 days past due	$ 200,000	4 percent
61–90 days past due	$ 80,000	20 percent
Over 90 days past due	$ 40,000	30 percent

4. Now assume that on March 3, 1995, it was determined that a $64,000 account receivable from Petite Corners is uncollectible. Record the bad debt, assuming that:
   (a) The direct write-off method is used.
   (b) The allowance method is used.
5. Further assume that on June 4, 1995, Petite Corners paid this previously written off debt of $64,000. Record the payment, assuming that:
   (a) The direct write-off method had been used on March 3 to record the bad debt.
   (b) The allowance method had been used on March 3 to record the bad debt.
6. **Interpretive Question** Which method of accounting for uncollectible accounts, direct write-off or allowance, is generally used? Why?

P8B-7
Discounting a Note Receivable

Required:
1. Record the following transactions in General Journal form in the books of Lyman Irrigation Company. Assume that Lyman Irrigation closes its books annually.

   Mar. 1   Sold sprinkling pipe to Federated Farms for $16,000, terms 2/10, n/30 (periodic inventory method).
   12   Accepted a $16,000, 90-day, 10 percent note from Federated Farms in payment of its account.
   Apr. 11 Discounted the note with recourse at the bank at a 14 percent discount rate.
   June 15 Notified by the bank that Federated Farms defaulted; the check was returned marked NSF. (Give the necessary entries in Lyman's books to record its payment of the note to the bank.)
   30   Wrote off the Federated Farms note as uncollectible.

2. **Interpretive Question** Why did Lyman have to pay off Federated Farms' note?
3. How would the note receivable have been accounted for on Lyman's April 30 financial statements?
4. How would Lyman account for the note if on July 7, Federated Farms paid the amount in full?

P8B-8
Discounting a Note Receivable

On May 1, your company accepted a $24,000, 3-month, 12 percent note from a customer. On May 31, your company discounted the note at a local bank at a 15 percent discount rate (with recourse).

Required:
1. As the accountant for the company, prepare appropriate journal entries to record the acceptance and discounting of the note.
2. Prepare the appropriate entry assuming that at maturity (July 31) the customer defaulted on the note. The bank charges a penalty fee of 0.25 percent of the maturity value for all defaulted notes discounted with recourse.
3. Prepare the appropriate entry assuming that on October 1 you collected the full amount (maturity value plus penalty fee) from the customer plus 18 percent interest on that amount from July 31.

Business Analysis Case 1   *Burton Company*

Burton Company has poor control over its cash transactions. On May 31, the accountant prepared the following bank reconciliation:

Balance per bank	$15,550.00	Balance per books	$19,066.62
Deposits in transit	3,794.41	NSF check	(150.00)
Outstanding checks	(442.79)	Bank service charge	(15.00)
Adjusted cash balance	$18,901.62	Adjusted cash balance	$18,901.62

It is now time to prepare the June bank reconciliation, but the accountant is in the hospital with injuries sustained in an automobile accident. You have been asked to prepare the June bank reconciliation for him.

As you review the June bank statement, you note that the following canceled checks, all written in May, are enclosed:

#62............	$116.25	#362............	$190.71
#183	250.00	#363............	106.80
#284	253.25	#364............	145.28

You decide to review the May bank statement as well, and you find a $100 bank credit (due to an incorrect charge) that the accountant ignored in his May 31 reconciliation.

The accountant you are replacing handles all incoming cash and makes the bank deposits personally. He also reconciles the monthly bank statement.

Required:
1. Prepare a corrected May 31 bank reconciliation in order to verify your suspicion that the accountant has stolen some money. (The theft will show up as a difference in the corrected bank and book balances.)
2. How much do you suspect the accountant has taken?
3. How did the accountant attempt to conceal the theft?
4. What internal control would you recommend to prevent future thefts of this type?

Business Analysis Case 2   *Anheuser-Busch and Exxon Companies*

Selected items from the recent balance sheets (in millions) of two major U.S. corporations are as follows:

	Anheuser-Busch Co.	Exxon
Cash	$ 49.7	$ 1,078
Marketable securities	119.9	1,396
Total current assets	965.5	17,355
Total assets	5,121.4	69,160

Required: On the basis of this information, answer the following questions:

1. Which company's cash and marketable securities total represents the larger percentage of its total current assets?
2. Which company's cash and marketable securities total represents the larger percent of its total assets?
3. What do you think accounts for the contrasting answers in parts 1 and 2?

Business Analysis Case 3   *Grumman Corporation*

Grumman Corporation current asset balances (in thousands) for two recent years were as follows:

	Year 2	Year 1
Cash	$ 19,812	$ 29,021
Marketable securities	82,905	245,773
Accounts receivable	377,763	271,403
Inventories	550,463	447,000
Prepaid expenses	11,296	10,105
	$1,042,239	$1,003,302

Required: On the basis of these data, answer the following questions:

1. Which current assets decreased from year 1 to year 2?
2. On the basis of current assets only, was Grumman Corporation more liquid in year 1 or year 2? Why?

Ethics Case   *FishCreek Investments*

You work as a manager for FishCreek Investments, a company that realizes that good cash management is critical and has devised a plan to save millions of dollars per year. Every manager has been instructed to use banks in other cities to deposit money in checking accounts two to three days after checks have been written against those accounts. By opening bank accounts in separate cities, the time it takes checks to clear the banking system is extended another day or so. The officers of the company are convinced that it will now take four to five days for checks to clear and that using the bank's money during the "float" period will allow the company to earn an additional two to three days' interest on investments or save two to three days' interest on loans.

You wonder whether it is ethical or even legal to write checks knowing there are insufficient current balances to cover them. The officers insist that it is legal, creative, and very profitable, and that the company is simply taking advantage of what the law and the bankers' tolerance permit. You do recall several occasions when you wrote personal checks on the last two or three days of a month to be covered by your salary deposit on the first of the following month. Nevertheless, the systematic, company-wide, nature of this program bothers you.

Required:
1. Is the company's policy to use the "float" for two or three days ethical? Is it legal?
2. If you believe it is unethical, what should you, as a manager, do?

Chapter 9

Property, Plant, and Equipment; Intangible Assets; and Natural Resources

Learning Objectives

After studying this chapter, you should be able to:
1. Record the acquisition of property, plant, and equipment.
2. Compute depreciation expense for plant and equipment.
3. Account for repairs and improvements of property, plant, and equipment.
4. Record the disposal of property, plant, and equipment.
5. Account for the acquisition and amortization of intangible assets.
6. Account for the acquisition and depletion of natural resources.

SETTING THE STAGE

A number of years ago, the New York Central Railway Company merged with the Pennsylvania Railroad Corporation to form Penn Central. One of the "Big 6" CPA firms was chosen to serve as independent auditors for the merged railroad company. A few years later, Penn Central was the defendant in a major lawsuit that alleged the company, among other things, had significantly overstated its assets. Along with Penn Central, the CPA firm was named as a defendant in the lawsuit for negligent auditing.

One of the principal issues involved in the lawsuit was the alleged overstatement of long-term assets. Plaintiffs charged that many of Penn Central's assets, including much of its equipment, were totally worthless and should not have been reported on the balance sheet. In particular, plaintiffs alleged that railroad cars, reported to be worth millions of dollars, were abandoned in old mines and could not be retrieved or used. They argued that since these cars did not have future value to the company, they should not have been reported as assets, but instead, their recorded values should have been written off as losses. Plaintiffs charged that this flagrant overstatement of equipment caused total assets and net income to be overstated and that this overstatement caused them to make faulty investment and credit decisions, thus resulting in personal losses.

In recent years, similar allegations have been made against many real estate companies, especially in Texas and other Southwestern states. In these cases, instead of worthless railroad cars, the overstated asset being reported on balance sheets was land. In numerous lawsuits, plaintiffs have charged companies with overvaluing land and thus overstating assets and net income. One particularly notable abuse has been "land flipping," where land was sold and purchased by related companies and individuals several times, each time resulting in an inflated price. For example, in one company, land was sold and purchased 15 times with its reported amount increasing from $2,000 per acre to over $40,000 per acre. All these increases were reported as income, and assets were significantly overstated.

In Chapters 7 and 8, we focused on current assets. In this chapter, you will be studying the accounting for long-term, or noncurrent, assets that are used in operating a business. We will refer to them collectively as **operating assets.** They include (1) property, plant, and equipment; (2) intangible assets; and (3) natural resources. Unlike inventories, operating assets are not acquired for resale to customers but are held and used by a business to generate revenues.

As indicated by the Penn Central case, the accounting for these assets can have a substantial impact on the financial statements. If operating assets are overstated on the balance sheet, net income is usually overstated. And because these assets are long term, the accounting for them can affect the income statement and balance sheet for several periods.

> **operating assets** *long-term, or noncurrent, assets acquired for use in the business rather than for resale; includes property, plant, and equipment; intangible assets; and natural resources*

NATURE OF OPERATING ASSETS

The same basic accounting concepts apply to all long-term operating assets. When an asset is acquired, its cost is recorded as an asset. Then, as the asset is used up, or the benefits expire, the cost is transferred to an expense account. Thus, the cost is allocated systematically over the asset's useful life. Though these basic concepts are the same for all operating assets, the procedures applied in accounting for the three major categories vary somewhat because of the nature of the assets in each category.

Property, plant, and equipment refers to tangible, long-lived assets acquired for use in business operations. This category includes land, buildings, machinery, equipment, and furniture. The process of allocating the costs of these assets over their estimated useful lives is called *depreciation*. The concept of depreciation applies to all these assets except land, which has an unlimited life.

Intangible assets are long-lived assets that are used in the operation of a business but do not have physical substance. In most cases, they provide their owners with competitive advantages over other firms. Typical intangible assets are patents, licenses, franchises, and goodwill. The process of allocating the costs of intangible assets over their estimated useful lives is called *amortization*. All intangible assets are eventually fully amortized, that is, are written down to a zero balance.

Natural resources, such as oil wells, mineral deposits, gravel deposits, and timber tracts, are assets that are physically consumed or that waste away. The process of allocating the costs of natural resources over their estimated useful lives is called *depletion*. All natural resources are depleted.

The same basic accounting concepts apply to all long-term operating assets. The procedures applied in accounting for the three major categories are somewhat different, however, because of the nature of the assets in each category. First, we will consider accounting for property, plant, and equipment, followed by intangible assets and natural resources.

> **useful life** *the period of time over which an asset is expected to be useful to the company; cost is assigned to the periods benefited from using the asset*
>
> **property, plant, and equipment** *tangible, long-lived assets acquired for use in business operations; includes land, buildings, machinery, equipment, and furniture*
>
> **intangible assets** *long-lived assets without physical substance that are used in business, such as licenses, patents, franchises, and goodwill*
>
> **natural resources** *assets that are physically consumed or waste away, such as oil, minerals, gravel, and timber*

ACCOUNTING FOR PROPERTY, PLANT, AND EQUIPMENT

The major elements in accounting for property, plant, and equipment are:

1. Recording asset acquisitions.
2. Allocating the cost of an asset over its useful life.

Chapter 9 *Property, Plant, and Equipment; Intangible Assets; and Natural Resources*   359

3. Accounting for maintenance, repairs, and improvements (for example, overhauling the engine of a truck).
4. Accounting for the sale or disposal of an asset.

Acquisitions of Property, Plant, and Equipment

Objective 1
Record the acquisition of property, plant, and equipment.

Like all other assets, property, plant, and equipment are initially recorded at cost. The cost of an asset includes not only the purchase price but also any other costs incurred in acquiring the asset and getting it ready for its intended use. Examples of these other costs include shipping, installation, and sales taxes.

Property, plant, and equipment are usually acquired by purchase. In some cases, assets are acquired by leasing but are accounted for in essentially the same way as purchased assets.

ASSETS ACQUIRED BY PURCHASE. A company can purchase an asset by paying cash, incurring a liability, or trading in another asset, or by a combination of these. If a single asset is purchased for cash, the accounting is relatively simple. To illustrate, we assume that Wheeler Resorts, Inc. purchased a new delivery truck for $15,096 (purchase price, $15,000, less 2% discount for paying cash, plus sales tax of $396). The entry to record this purchase would be:

Delivery Truck	15,096	
Cash		15,096

Purchased a delivery truck for $15,096 ($15,000 − $300 cash discount + $396 sales tax).

In this instance, cash was paid for a single asset, the truck. An alternative would have been to borrow part of the purchase price. If the company had borrowed $12,000 of the $15,096 from a bank, the entry would have been:

Delivery Truck	15,096	
Cash		3,096
Notes Payable		12,000

Purchased a delivery truck for $15,096; paid $3,096 cash and issued a note for $12,000 to Chemical Bank.

The $12,000 represents the principal of the note; it does not include any interest charged by the lending institution. (The interest is recognized later as interest expense.)

Another type of transaction, a basket purchase, involves two or more assets acquired at a single price. A common basket purchase is land and the building on it. Since the building is subject to depreciation while the land is not, the purchase price must be allocated between the two assets on some reasonable basis. The **relative fair market value method** is used to determine the respective costs to be assigned to the land and the building.

To illustrate, we will assume that Wheeler Resorts purchased a 40,000-square-foot building on 2.6 acres of land for $360,000. How much of the total cost should be assigned to the land and how much to the building? If the fair

relative fair market value method a way of allocating a lump-sum or "basket" purchase price to the individual assets acquired based on their respective market values

market values of the land and the building are $100,000 and $300,000, respectively, the resulting individual costs would be $90,000 and $270,000, as calculated here.

Asset	Fair Market Value	Percentage of Total Value	Apportionment of Lump-Sum Cost
Land	$100,000	25	0.25 × $360,000 = $ 90,000
Building	300,000	75	0.75 × 360,000 = 270,000
Total	$400,000	100	$360,000

The total of the fair market values of the individual assets is often more than the basket-purchase price, either because the seller is willing to offer the group of assets at a discount to obtain a quick sale or because one of the assets, such as the land, is undervalued by the seller. However, regardless of whether the lump-sum cost is more or less than the fair market values of the assets acquired, the lump-sum cost is apportioned among the assets based on their relative fair market values. The journal entry to record this basket purchase would be:

```
Land .................................................... 90,000
Building................................................. 270,000
    Cash ................................................ 360,000
Purchased 2.6 acres of land and a 40,000-square-foot building.
```

If part of the purchase price were financed by a bank, an additional credit to Notes or Mortgage Payable would have been included in the entry.

Assets are usually purchased with cash or debt (notes payable), as illustrated in the preceding examples. Sometimes, however, the buyer transfers assets other than cash to the seller. The most common example would be the trade-in of a used asset, such as a truck, as partial payment for the purchase of a new asset. There are different accounting treatments for exchanges of similar assets than for exchanges of dissimilar assets. Accounting for both types of exchange transactions is explained later in the chapter.

ASSETS ACQUIRED BY LEASING. Leases are often short-term rental agreements in which one party, the **lessee,** is granted the right to use property owned by another party, the **lessor.** For example, as a student, you may decide to lease (rent) an apartment to live in while you are attending college. The owner of the apartment (lessor) would probably require you to sign a lease specifying the terms of the arrangement. The lease would state the period of time in which you would live in the apartment, the amount of rent you would pay, and when each rent payment is due. When the lease expires, you would either sign a new lease or move out of the apartment, which would then be rented to someone else.

Companies enter into similar types of lease arrangements. For example, Wheeler Resorts might decide to lease a building because of a need for additional office space. Assume Wheeler signs a two-year lease requiring monthly

---

lessee *the party that is granted the right to use property under the terms of a lease*

lessor *the owner of property that is rented (leased) to another party*

Chapter 9 *Property, Plant, and Equipment; Intangible Assets; and Natural Resources*   361

operating lease *a simple rental agreement*

rental payments of $1,000. When the lease expires, Wheeler will either move out of the building or negotiate a new lease with the owner. Accounting for this type of rental agreement, called an **operating lease,** is straightforward. When rent is paid each month, Wheeler would record the following journal entry:

```
Rent (or Lease) Expense..........................................  1,000
    Cash ........................................................          1,000
To record monthly rent on office building.
```

Some lease agreements, however, are not so simple. Suppose Wheeler has decided to expand its operations and wants to acquire a hotel in the Phoenix area. Wheeler's alternatives would be to buy land and build a new hotel, purchase an existing hotel, or lease a hotel. Assume Wheeler locates a desirable piece of land, and the owner of the land agrees to build a hotel and lease the property to Wheeler. The lease agreement is noncancellable and requires Wheeler to make annual lease payments of $100,000 for 20 years. At the end of 20 years, Wheeler will become the owner of the property. Clearly, this is not a simple rental agreement, even though the transaction is called a lease by the parties involved. In reality, this transaction is an installment purchase of property. The result is the same as if Wheeler had borrowed money on a 20-year mortgage and purchased the property.

Generally accepted accounting principles require that the recording of the transaction reflect the true economic nature, not the form of, the transaction. Wheeler would record the property as an asset and would also record a liability reflecting the obligation to the lessor. The amount to be recorded is the present value of the lease payments (in the Wheeler example, the present value of 20 annual payments of $100,000). The concept of present value will be explained in Chapter 10, but generally the present value is the value today of payments to be made in the future, given a specified interest rate.

Continuing the example, assume that, at the beginning of the lease term, the present value of the future lease payments is $851,360. Wheeler would make the following journal entry to record the lease:

```
Leased Property ..............................................  851,360
    Lease Liability ............................................          851,360
To record hotel acquired under a 20-year noncancellable lease.
```

capital lease *a leasing transaction that is recorded as a purchase by the lessee*

This type of lease is called a **capital lease** because the lessee records (capitalizes) the leased asset. The asset will be reported with Property, Plant, and Equipment on the lessee's balance sheet. In addition, the lessee (Wheeler) will allocate the $851,360 cost over the asset's useful life by recording depreciation expense each year using one of the methods discussed in the next section of this chapter.

When annual lease payments are made, Wheeler will not record rent expense. Part of each payment will be interest expense, and the remainder will reduce the liability. The difference between the total lease payments (20 years × $100,000, or $2 million) and the "cost" or present value of the property is the amount of interest that will be paid over the term of the lease. To illustrate, assume that the first payment is made one year after the lease term begins and includes interest of $85,136 and a $14,864 reduction in the liability. The payment would be recorded as follows:

Lease Liability...	14,864	
Interest Expense..	85,136	
Cash...		100,000
To record annual lease payment under capital lease.		

CLASSIFYING LEASES. Leasing is a widely used method of acquiring assets, and as indicated in the Business Environment Essay on page 364, it can be an attractive alternative to purchasing assets. Because the treatment of a lease can have a major impact on the financial statements, the accounting profession has established criteria for determining whether a lease should be classified as an operating or a capital lease.[1] If a lease is **noncancellable** and meets any one of the following four criteria, it is recorded as a capital lease:

1. The lease transfers ownership of the leased asset to the lessee by the end of the lease term (as in the Wheeler example).
2. The lease contains an option allowing the lessee to purchase the asset at the end of the lease term at a bargain price (a price that is substantially lower than the expected fair value of the property at the end of the lease term).
3. The lease term is equal to 75 percent or more of the estimated economic life of the asset.
4. The present value of the lease payments at the beginning of the lease is 90 percent or more of the fair market value of the leased asset.

If at least one of these criteria is met, the lease is considered to be, in substance, a purchase of property by the lessee. Thus, the lessee records the leased property as an asset and recognizes a liability to the lessor. Applying the same criteria, the lessor will account for the lease as a sale of property and recognize a receivable from the lessee.[2]

Leases are often very complex documents, and careful analysis is required in applying the classification criteria. These criteria and other considerations in accounting for leases are discussed in detail in intermediate accounting textbooks.

> **To Summarize** *Long-term operating assets (property, plant, and equipment, intangible assets, and natural resources) are used in a business to generate revenues. The property, plant, and equipment category includes tangible, long-lived assets such as land, buildings, machinery, and equipment. When these assets are purchased, they are*

---

[1] *FASB Statement No. 13,* "Accounting for Leases" (Norwalk, Conn.: Financial Accounting Standards Board, 1976).

[2] In some cases, a lease may be classified differently by the lessor and lessee as a result of considerations that are beyond the scope of our introductory discussion of leases.

Chapter 9   *Property, Plant, and Equipment; Intangible Assets; and Natural Resources* 363

> *recorded at cost, which includes all expenditures associated with acquiring them and getting them ready for their intended use, such as sales tax, shipping, and installation. When two or more assets are acquired for a single price in a basket purchase, the relative fair market value method is used to determine their respective costs. Sometimes assets are acquired by lease rather than purchase. A lease may be a simple short-term rental agreement, called an operating lease, or it may be substantially the same as a purchase transaction. In the latter case, called a capital lease, the party acquiring the asset (the lessee) records the asset and related liability as if the property had been purchased and financed with long-term debt. Similarly, the owner of the property (lessor) treats the lease as the sale of an asset. Classification criteria have been established to distinguish operating leases from capital leases.*

Allocating the Cost of Plant and Equipment to Expense

Objective 2

Compute depreciation expense for plant and equipment.

depreciation *the process of cost allocation that assigns the original cost of plant and equipment to the periods benefited*

The second element in accounting for plant and equipment is the allocation of the asset's cost over its useful life. The matching principle requires that this cost be assigned to expense in the periods benefited from the use of the asset. The allocation procedure is called **depreciation,** and the allocated amount is an expense that is deducted from revenues in order to determine income. It should be noted that the asset "plant" normally refers to the building only. Land is recorded as a separate asset. It is not depreciated because it has an unlimited useful life.

Accounting for depreciation is often confusing because students tend to think that depreciation expense reflects the decline in an asset's "value." The concept of depreciation is nothing more than a systematic write-off of the original cost assigned to an asset. The undepreciated cost is referred to as "book value," which represents that portion of the original cost not yet assigned to the income statement as an expense. A company never claims that an asset's recorded book value is equal to its market value. In fact, market values of assets could increase at the same time that depreciation expense is being recorded.

salvage, or residual, value *estimated value or actual price of an asset at the conclusion of its useful life, net of disposal costs*

To calculate depreciation expense for an asset, you need to know (1) its original cost, (2) its estimated useful life (number of periods benefited), and (3) its estimated **salvage, or residual, value** (the amount of an asset's cost that will be recovered when the asset is sold or disposed of). When an asset is purchased, its actual useful life and salvage value are obviously unknown; they must be estimated as realistically as is feasible, usually on the basis of experience with similar assets. In some cases, an asset will have little or no salvage value. If the salvage value is not material, it is usually ignored in computing depreciation.

Any one of several methods may be used for depreciating the costs of assets for financial reporting. The four methods most commonly used in practice are:

1. Straight-line.
2. Declining-balance.
3. Sum-of-the-years'-digits.
4. Units-of-production.

Each method assumes a different pattern of benefits for allocating the cost of an asset over its estimated life. For example, if an asset is expected to benefit all periods equally, a straight-line method of depreciation probably should be

> **BUSINESS ENVIRONMENT ESSAY**
> *Lease or Buy?*
>
> Virtually any type of operating asset can be acquired by leasing. Companies often lease such assets as computers, automobiles and trucks, airplanes, and various other types of equipment, as well as real estate. There are several reasons why a company might choose to lease, rather than purchase, an asset. A purchase transaction often requires a significant cash outlay in the form of a down payment at the date of purchase; leasing, therefore, can be used to minimize the amount of cash paid initially to acquire the asset. For some types of assets, such as computers, leasing enables the lessee to avoid risks of obsolescence.
>
> Another potential advantage of leasing is that if the agreement can be recorded as an operating lease, the lessee does not have to report any related liability. This is an important consideration if a company is concerned about the effect of reporting additional debt on the balance sheet. Before criteria were established for classifying leases as operating or capital, almost all leases were treated as operating leases. Often the primary purpose of a leasing arrangement was to acquire property without reporting any related liability. Some companies are still using leasing for this purpose. They do so by writing the terms of a lease agreement in a manner that circumvents the capitalization criteria. The result is that some leasing transactions are reported as simple rental agreements (operating leases) when in fact they have many characteristics of a purchase transaction. Leasing and other forms of "off-balance-sheet financing" are of major concern to the accounting profession and financial statement users.

used. If, on the other hand, most of the benefits will be realized in the earlier periods of the asset's life, the method used should assign more depreciation to the earlier years and less to the later years. Examples of these "accelerated" depreciation methods are the declining-balance and the sum-of-the-years'-digits methods. If an asset's benefits are thought to be related to its productive output (miles driven, for example), the units-of-production method would be appropriate. Exhibit 9-1 compares the first three depreciation methods with regard to the relative amount of depreciation expense incurred in each year of a 5-year useful life. The units-of-production method is not illustrated since there would be no standard pattern of cost allocation.

To illustrate the four common depreciation methods, we assume that Wheeler Resorts purchased a van for transporting hotel guests to and from the airport. The following facts apply:

Acquisition cost	$24,000
Estimated salvage value	$ 2,000
Estimated life:	
In years	4 years
In miles driven	60,000 miles

straight-line depreciation method *the depreciation method in which the cost of an asset is allocated equally over the periods of the asset's estimated useful life*

STRAIGHT-LINE METHOD OF DEPRECIATION. The **straight-line depreciation method** is the simplest depreciation method. It assumes that an asset's cost should be assigned equally to all periods benefited. The formula for calculating annual straight-line depreciation is:

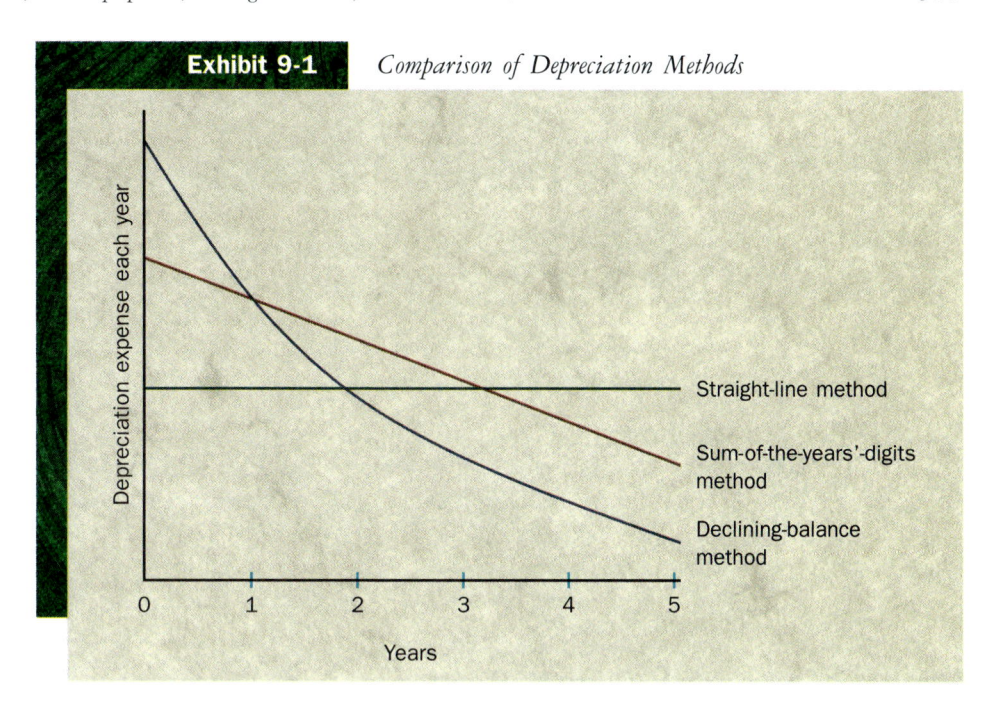

Exhibit 9-1 *Comparison of Depreciation Methods*

[Graph showing three curves of Depreciation expense each year vs Years (0 to 5):
- Straight-line method (horizontal line)
- Sum-of-the-years'-digits method (linearly decreasing)
- Declining-balance method (curved, steeply decreasing)]

$$\frac{\text{cost} - \text{salvage value}}{\text{estimated useful life (years)}} = \text{annual depreciation expense}$$

With this formula, the annual depreciation expense for the van would be calculated as:

$$\frac{\$24{,}000 - \$2{,}000}{4 \text{ years}} = \$5{,}500 \text{ depreciation expense per year}$$

The annual expense can also be computed using a depreciation rate or percentage. The straight-line rate is calculated as 1 ÷ estimated life. In this example, the rate would be 1 ÷ 4, or 25%, and the annual expense would be determined as follows:

($24,000 − $2,000) × .25 = $5,500

When the depreciation expense for an asset has been calculated, a schedule showing the annual depreciation expense, the total **accumulated depreciation,** and the asset's **book value** (undepreciated cost) for each year can be prepared. The depreciation schedule for the van (using straight-line depreciation) is shown in Exhibit 9-2.

The entry to record straight-line depreciation each year would be:

accumulated depreciation *the total depreciation recorded on an asset since its acquisition; a contra account deducted from the original cost of an asset on the balance sheet*

book value *the undepreciated portion of an asset's cost*

Depreciation Expense	5,500	
Accumulated Depreciation, Hotel Van..........................		5,500
To record annual depreciation for the hotel van.		

Exhibit 9-2 — Depreciation Schedule with Straight-Line Depreciation

	Annual Depreciation Expense	Accumulated Depreciation	Book Value
Acquisition date	—	—	$24,000
End of year 1	$5,500	$ 5,500	18,500
End of year 2	5,500	11,000	13,000
End of year 3	5,500	16,500	7,500
End of year 4	5,500	22,000	2,000

Depreciation Expense is reported on the income statement. Accumulated Depreciation is a contra-asset account that is offset against the cost of the asset on the balance sheet.

At the end of the first year, the acquisition cost, accumulated depreciation, and book value of the van would be presented on the balance sheet as follows:

Property, Plant, and Equipment:
Hotel van $24,000
Less accumulated depreciation .... 5,500 $18,500 (book value)

declining-balance depreciation method *an accelerated depreciation method in which an asset's book value is multiplied by a constant depreciation rate (such as double the straight-line percentage, in the case of double-declining-balance)*

DECLINING-BALANCE METHOD OF DEPRECIATION. The **declining-balance depreciation method** provides for higher depreciation charges in the earlier years of an asset's life than does the straight-line method. The declining-balance method involves multiplying a fixed rate, or percentage, by a decreasing book value. This rate is a multiple of the straight-line rate. Typically, it is twice the straight-line rate, but it also can be 175%, 150%, or 125% of the straight-line rate. Our depreciation of Wheeler's hotel van will illustrate the declining-balance method using a fixed rate equal to twice the straight-line rate. This rate is often referred to as the *double-declining-balance* rate.

Declining-balance depreciation is different in two respects from the other depreciation methods: (1) the *initial computation* ignores the asset's salvage value, and (2) a constant depreciation rate is multiplied by a decreasing book value. The salvage value is not ignored completely because the depreciation taken during the asset's life cannot reduce the asset's book value below the salvage value.

The double-declining-balance rate is twice the straight-line rate, computed as follows:

$$\frac{1}{\text{estimated life (years)}} \times 2 = \text{DDB rate}$$

This rate is applied to the book value at the end of each year (cost − accumulated depreciation) to compute the annual depreciation expense. If the 150% declining balance were being used instead, the 2 in the rate formula would be replaced by 1.5, and so on for any other percentages.

To illustrate, the depreciation calculation for the van using the 200% declining-balance method would be:

Chapter 9 *Property, Plant, and Equipment; Intangible Assets; and Natural Resources* 367

Straight-line rate	4 years = 1 ÷ 4 = 25 percent
Double the straight-line rate	25 percent × 2 = 50 percent
Annual depreciation	50 percent × undepreciated cost (book value)

Based on this information, the formula for double-declining-balance depreciation could be expressed as (straight-line rate × 2) × (cost − accumulated depreciation) = current year's depreciation expense. The double-declining-balance depreciation for the 4 years is shown in Exhibit 9-3. As you review this exhibit, note that the book value of the van at the end of year 4 is $2,000, its salvage value. *Although salvage value is ignored in the initial computations, the asset is not depreciated below its salvage value*—an important point to remember.

Exhibit 9-3 *Depreciation Schedule with Double-Declining-Balance Depreciation*

	Computation	Annual Depreciation Expense	Accumulated Depreciation	Book Value
Acquisition date	—	—	—	$24,000
End of year 1	$24,000 × 0.50	$12,000	$12,000	12,000
End of year 2	12,000 × 0.50	6,000	18,000	6,000
End of year 3	6,000 × 0.50	3,000	21,000	3,000
End of year 4	*	1,000	22,000	2,000

* In year 4, depreciation expense cannot exceed $1,000 since the book value cannot be reduced below salvage value.

If Wheeler had applied the declining-balance method to depreciate the hotel van on the basis of 150% of the straight-line rate, the fixed rate would have been 37.5% computed as follows: 25% × 1.50 = 37.5%. Using the 37.5% fixed rate, the annual depreciation of the hotel van would have been as follows:

First year: $24,000 × 37.5% = $9,000
Second year: $24,000 − $9,000 = $15,000 × 37.5% = $5,625
Third year: $15,000 − $5,625 = $9,375 × 37.5% = $3,516
Fourth year: $ 9,375 − $3,516 = $5,859 − $2,000 salvage value = $3,859

Since a total book value of $5,859 remains at the end of year 3, the remaining book value less the estimated salvage value was written off in year 4.

SUM-OF-THE-YEARS'-DIGITS METHOD OF DEPRECIATION. Like the declining-balance method, the **sum-of-the-years'-digits (SYD) method** provides for a proportionately higher depreciation expense in the early years of an asset's life. It is therefore appropriate for assets that provide greater benefits in their earlier years (such as trucks, machinery, and equipment) as opposed to assets that benefit all years equally (as buildings do). The formula for calculating SYD is:

sum-of-the-years'-digits (SYD) depreciation method *the accelerated depreciation method in which a constant balance (cost minus salvage value) is multiplied by a declining depreciation rate*

$$\frac{\text{number of years of life remaining at beginning of year}}{\text{sum-of-the-years'-digits}} \times (\text{cost} - \text{salvage value}) = \text{depreciation expense}$$

The numerator is the number of years of estimated life remaining at the beginning of the current year. The van, with a 4-year life, would have 4 years remaining at the beginning of the first year, 3 at the beginning of the second, and so on. The denominator is the sum of the years of the asset's life. The sum-of-the-years'-digits for the van is 10 (4 + 3 + 2 + 1). In other words, the numerator decreases by 1 year each year, whereas the denominator remains the same for each year's calculation of depreciation.

Also note that the asset's cost is reduced by the salvage value in computing the annual depreciation expense as is done for the straight-line method but not for the declining-balance method.

The depreciation on the van for the first 2 years would be:

First year: $\frac{4}{10} \times (\$24{,}000 - \$2{,}000) = \$8{,}800$

Second year: $\frac{3}{10} \times (\$24{,}000 - \$2{,}000) = \$6{,}600$

The depreciation schedule for 4 years is shown in Exhibit 9-4.

Exhibit 9-4 *Depreciation Schedule with Sum-of-the-Years'-Digits Depreciation*

	Annual Depreciation Expense	Accumulated Depreciation	Book Value
Acquisition date	—	—	$24,000
End of year 1	$8,800	$ 8,800	15,200
End of year 2	6,600	15,400	8,600
End of year 3	4,400	19,800	4,200
End of year 4	2,200	22,000	2,000

The entry to record the sum-of-the-years'-digits depreciation for the first year would be:

```
Depreciation Expense ................................................ 8,800
    Accumulated Depreciation, Hotel Van........................         8,800
To record the first year's depreciation for the van.
```

Subsequent years' depreciation entries would show depreciation expense of $6,600, $4,400, and $2,200.

When an asset has a long life, the computation of the denominator (the sum-of-the-years'-digits) can become quite involved. There is, however, a simple formula for determining the denominator. It is:

$\frac{n(n + 1)}{2}$, where n is the life (in years) of the asset

Given that the van has a useful life of 4 years, the formula would work as follows:

$$\frac{4(5)}{2} = 10$$

As you can see, the answer is the same as if you had added the years' digits (4 + 3 + 2 + 1). If an asset has a 10-year life, the sum of the years' digits is:

$$\frac{10(11)}{2} = 55$$

The depreciation fraction in year 1 would be 10/55, in year 2, 9/55, and so on.

UNITS-OF-PRODUCTION METHOD OF DEPRECIATION. The **units-of-production method** allocates an asset's cost on the basis of use rather than time. This method is used primarily when a company expects that asset usage will vary significantly from year to year. If the asset's usage pattern is uniform from year to year, the units-of-production method would produce the same depreciation pattern as the straight-line method. Assets with varying usage patterns, for which this method of depreciation may be appropriate, are airplanes, where life is estimated in terms of number of hours flown; automobiles and other vehicles, where life is estimated in terms of numbers of miles driven; and certain machines, where life is estimated in terms of number of units produced or number of hours of operating life. The formula for calculating the units-of-production depreciation for the year is:

units-of-production depreciation method the depreciation method in which the cost of an asset is allocated to each period on the basis of the productive output or use of the asset during the period

$$\text{cost} - \text{salvage value} \times \frac{\text{number of units (hours) produced during the year}}{\text{total estimated life in units (hours)}} = \text{current year's depreciation expense}$$

To illustrate, we again consider Wheeler's van, which has an expected life of 60,000 miles. With the units-of-production method, if the van were driven 12,000 miles during the first year, the depreciation expense for that year would be calculated as follows:

$$(\$24{,}000 - \$2{,}000) \times \frac{12{,}000 \text{ hours}}{60{,}000 \text{ hours}} = \$4{,}400 \text{ depreciation expense}$$

19,600 − 2000 × 1800

The entry to record units-of-production depreciation at the end of the first year of the van's life would be:

Depreciation Expense	4,400	
Accumulated Depreciation, Hotel Van		4,400
To record depreciation for the first year of the van's life.		

The depreciation schedule for the 4 years is shown in Exhibit 9-5. This exhibit assumes that 18,000 miles were driven the second year, 21,000 the third year, and 9,000 the fourth year.

Exhibit 9-5 *Depreciation Schedule with Units-of-Production Depreciation*

	Miles Driven	Depreciation Expense	Accumulated Depreciation	Book Value
Acquisition date	—	—	—	$24,000
End of year 1	12,000	$4,400	$ 4,400	19,600
End of year 2	18,000	6,600	11,000	13,000
End of year 3	21,000	7,700	18,700	5,300
End of year 4	9,000	3,300	22,000	2,000

A COMPARISON OF DEPRECIATION METHODS. The amount of depreciation expense will vary according to the depreciation method used by a company. Exhibit 9-6 compares the annual depreciation expense on Wheeler's van under the straight-line, double-declining-balance, sum-of-the-years'-digits, and units-of-production depreciation methods.

This schedule makes it clear that the total amount of depreciation is the same regardless of which method is used. It also shows that the double-declining-balance method provides the highest amounts of depreciation in the early years of an asset's life, whereas the straight-line rate provides the lowest amounts of depreciation in these early years. (The units-of-production method cannot be compared for this particular feature since units-of-production calculations do not depend on time periods.)

A survey of companies' annual reports indicates that, in a recent year, 559 of the companies surveyed used straight-line depreciation, 132 used an accelerated method (sum-of-the-years'-digits or declining balance), and 51 used the units of production method.[3] As these data indicate, straight-line is by far the most commonly used depreciation method, probably because it is the simplest method to apply.

Exhibit 9-6 *Comparison of Depreciation Expense Using Different Depreciation Methods*

	Straight-Line Depreciation	DDB Depreciation	SYD Depreciation	Units-of-Production Depreciation
End of year 1	$ 5,500	$12,000	$ 8,800	$ 4,400
End of year 2	5,500	6,000	6,600	6,600
End of year 3	5,500	3,000	4,400	7,700
End of year 4	5,500	1,000	2,200	3,300
Totals	$22,000	$22,000	$22,000	$22,000

---

[3] *Accounting Trends & Techniques*—1988 (New York: American Institute of Certified Public Accountants, 1988), p. 261.

PARTIAL-YEAR DEPRECIATION CALCULATIONS. Thus far, depreciation expense has been calculated on the basis of a full year. However, businesses purchase assets at all times during the year, so partial-year depreciation calculations are often required. To compute depreciation expense for less than a full year with any of the methods discussed, first calculate the depreciation expense for the year and then prorate it (distribute it evenly) over the number of months the asset is held during the year. This is equivalent to saying that any one of the depreciation methods can be used for calculating depreciation expense for full years, but a straight-line proportion is always used when computing depreciation expense within a year.

To illustrate, we will assume that Wheeler purchased its $24,000 van on July 1 instead of January 1. The depreciation calculations for the first 1½ years are shown in Exhibit 9-7. (You may find it helpful to refer also to Exhibit 9-6, which shows the full-year calculations.) The units-of-production method has been omitted from the exhibit; midyear purchases do not complicate the calculations with this method since it involves numbers of miles driven, hours flown, and so on, rather than time periods.

Exhibit 9-7 *Partial-Year Depreciation*

Method	Full-Year Depreciation	Depreciation 1st Year (6 Months)	Depreciation 2nd Year (12 Months)
Straight-line	$ 5,500	$2,750 ($5,500 × ½)	$5,500
Double-declining-balance	$12,000	$6,000 ($12,000 × ½)	$9,000*
Sum-of-the-years'-digits	$ 8,800	$4,400 ($8,800 × ½)	$7,700**

* ($24,000 − $6,000) × 50% = $9,000.
**($8,800 × ½) + ($6,600 × ½) = $7,700. An alternative is to use (3.5/10) × ($24,000 − $2,000) = $7,700, since one-half year was taken in the first year.

Note that in Exhibit 9-7, when sum-of-the-years'-digits depreciation is used, the partial-year calculation affects not only the year of purchase but succeeding years as well. This is because a full year of depreciation is recorded at each rate before the rate changes.

In practice, many companies simplify their depreciation computations by taking a full year of depreciation in the year an asset is purchased and none in the year the asset is sold, or vice versa. This is allowed because depreciation is based on estimates and, in the long run, the difference in the amounts is immaterial.

CHANGES IN DEPRECIATION ESTIMATES. As mentioned earlier, useful lives and salvage values are only estimates. Wheeler's van, for example, was assumed to have a useful life of 4 years and a salvage value of $2,000. In reality, the van's life and salvage value may be different from the original estimates. If after 3 years, Wheeler realizes that the van will last another 3 years and that the salvage value will be $3,000 instead of $2,000, the accountant would need to calculate a new depreciation expense for the remaining 3 years. Using straight-line depreciation, the calculations would be as follows:

	Formula	Calculation	Total Depreciation
Annual depreciation for first 3 years....	$\dfrac{\text{cost} - \text{salvage value}}{\text{estimated useful life}} = \dfrac{\text{depreciation}}{\text{expense}}$	$\dfrac{\$24{,}000 - \$2{,}000}{4 \text{ years}} = \$5{,}500$	$16,500
Book value after 3 years.............	cost − accumulated depreciation to date = book value	$24,000 − $16,500 = $7,500	
Annual depreciation for last 3 years (based on new life of 6 years and new salvage value of $3,000)........	$\dfrac{\text{book value} - \text{salvage value}}{\text{remaining useful life}} = \dfrac{\text{depreciation}}{\text{expense}}$	$\dfrac{\$7{,}500 - \$3{,}000}{3 \text{ years}} = \$1{,}500$	4,500
Total depreciation.................			$21,000

The example shows that a change in the estimate of useful life or salvage value does not require a modification of the depreciation expense already taken. New information affects depreciation only in future years. Exhibit 9-8 shows the revised depreciation expense. Similar calculations, although more complex, would apply if either the sum-of-the-years'-digits or the double-declining-balance depreciation method had been used.

DEPRECIATION FOR INCOME TAX PURPOSES. Amounts reported in the financial statements prepared for stockholders, creditors, and other external users often differ from amounts reported in income tax returns. The most common cause of differences between financial reporting and tax returns is the computation of depreciation. Thus far in this chapter, the discussion has focused on the depreciation concepts and methods used for financial accounting and reporting. The annual depreciation expense reported in the income statement reflects a company's estimates of useful lives and residual values and the method selected for computing depreciation. A company may select any of the methods presented in the preceding sections for financial reporting purposes.

In contrast, depreciation for tax purposes must be computed in accordance with federal income tax law, which specifies rules to be applied in computing tax depreciation for various categories of assets. Income tax rules are designed to achieve economic objectives, such as stimulating investment in productive assets, and are not guided by the concepts of depreciation for financial statement purposes. Income tax rules change over time as economic conditions and

Exhibit 9-8 *Depreciation Schedule When There Is a Change in Estimate*

	Annual Depreciation Expense	Accumulated Depreciation	Book Value
Acquisition date......................	—	—	$24,000
Year 1...............................	$5,500	$ 5,500	18,500
Year 2...............................	5,500	11,000	13,000
Year 3...............................	5,500	16,500	7,500
Change			
Year 4...............................	1,500	18,000	6,000
Year 5...............................	1,500	19,500	4,500
Year 6...............................	1,500	21,000	3,000

The journal entry to record the $8,000 capitalized expenditure would be:

Delivery Truck[4]	8,000	
Cash		8,000
Spent $8,000 to overhaul the engine of the $42,000 delivery truck.		

Another example of capital expenditures is the cost of land improvements. Certain improvements are considered permanent, such as moving earth to change the land contour. Such an expenditure would be capitalized as part of the Land account. Other expenditures may have a limited life, such as incurred in building a road, a sidewalk, or a fence. These expenditures would be capitalized in a separate Land Improvements account and be depreciated over their useful lives.

It is often difficult to determine whether a given expenditure should be capitalized or expensed. However, because the two procedures produce a different net income, it is extremely important that such expenditures be properly classified. In practice, if there is any doubt, a firm usually expenses rather than capitalizes because this results in the paying of lower taxes in the immediate year and because it does not allow assets to be carried at amounts that exceed their future benefits.

> **To Summarize** *There are two types of expenditures for existing long-term operational assets: ordinary and capital. In general, for an expenditure to be capitalized, it must (1) be significant in amount, (2) provide benefits for more than one period, and (3) increase the productive life or capacity of an asset. Ordinary expenditures merely maintain an asset's productive capacity at the level originally projected. Capital expenditures are added to the cost of an asset and thus affect future depreciation, whereas ordinary expenditures are expenses of the current period.*

DISPOSAL OF PROPERTY, PLANT, AND EQUIPMENT

Objective 4
Record the disposal of property, plant, and equipment.

Plant and equipment eventually become worthless or are sold. When a company removes one of these assets from service, it has to eliminate the asset's cost and accumulated depreciation from the accounting records. There are basically three ways to dispose of an asset: (1) discard or scrap it, (2) sell it, or (3) trade it in for another asset.

Discarding Property, Plant, and Equipment

When an asset becomes worthless and must be scrapped, its cost and its accumulated depreciation balance should be removed from the accounting records.

---

[4] An alternative treatment would be to debit Accumulated Depreciation instead of Delivery Truck and recalculate the net book value on the remaining life of the truck. The effect would be the same, in that the book value would be $18,000 and the depreciation expense would still be $4,500 in each of the last 4 years.

If the asset's total cost has been depreciated, there is no loss on the disposal. If, on the other hand, the cost is not completely depreciated, the undepreciated cost represents a loss on disposal.

To illustrate, we assume that Wheeler Resorts, Inc. purchased a computer for $15,000. The computer had a 5-year life and no estimated salvage value, and was depreciated on a straight-line basis. If the computer were scrapped after 5 full years, the entry to record the disposal would be as follows:

Accumulated Depreciation, Computer..........................	15,000	
Computer		15,000
Scrapped $15,000 computer.		

If it cost Wheeler $300 to have the computer dismantled and removed, the entry to record the disposal would be:

Accumulated Depreciation, Computer..........................	15,000	
Loss on Disposal of Computer	300	
Computer		15,000
Cash		300
Scrapped $15,000 computer and paid disposal costs of $300.		

If the computer had been scrapped after only 4 years of service (and after $12,000 of the original cost had been depreciated), there would have been a loss on disposal of $3,300 (including the disposal cost), and the entry would have been:

Accumulated Depreciation, Computer..........................	12,000	
Loss on Disposal of Computer	3,300	
Computer		15,000
Cash		300
Scrapped $15,000 computer and recognized loss of $3,300 (including $300 disposal costs).		

Selling Property, Plant, and Equipment

A second way of disposing of property, plant, or equipment is to sell it. If the net sales price of the asset exceeds its book value (the original cost less accumulated depreciation), there is a gain on the sale. Conversely, if the sales price is less than the book value, there is a loss.

To illustrate, we refer again to Wheeler's $15,000 computer. If the asset were sold for $600 after 5 full years of service, assuming no disposal costs, the entry to record the sale would be:

Cash	600	
Accumulated Depreciation, Computer..........................	15,000	
Computer		15,000
Gain on Sale of Computer		600
Sold $15,000 computer at a gain of $600.		

Since the asset was fully depreciated, its book value was zero and the $600 cash received represents a gain. If the computer had been sold for $600 after only 4 years of service, there would have been a loss of $2,400 on the sale, and the entry to record the sale would have been:

Cash	600	
Accumulated Depreciation, Computer...........................	12,000	
Loss on Sale of Computer	2,400	
Computer		15,000

Sold $15,000 computer at a loss of $2,400.

The $2,400 loss is the difference between the sales price of $600 and the book value of $3,000 ($15,000 − $12,000). The amount of a gain or loss is thus a function of two factors: (1) the amount of cash received from the sale, and (2) the book value of the asset at the date of sale.

Exchanging Property, Plant, and Equipment

A third way of disposing of property, plant, or equipment is to exchange it for another asset. Such exchanges occur regularly with cars, trucks, machines, and other types of large equipment. When a company acquires an asset by giving up another tangible asset, the transaction is referred to as an exchange of nonmonetary assets. For accounting purposes, an exchange of nonmonetary assets is classified as either a similar exchange or a dissimilar exchange. We will discuss the most common exchanges of each type from the point of view of the buyer (the customer), not the seller (the dealer).

GAIN ON THE EXCHANGE OF SIMILAR OPERATING ASSETS. The most common type of exchange involves a buyer giving up a used operating asset, such as a truck or machinery, *plus cash,* for a *similar* new operating asset. This transaction may result in a gain or a loss. Since the accounting for gains and losses is different, we will illustrate the two situations separately.

When there is a *gain* on the exchange of similar operating assets (and the buyer pays out cash), the accounting rules specify that the gain should not be recognized. This is because it is assumed that no gain results from the substitution of one asset for another performing the same function. The new asset acquired is therefore recorded at an amount equal to the book value of the used asset given up plus the cash paid.

To illustrate the accounting for an exchange of similar assets resulting in a gain, we assume that Wheeler is acquiring a new hotel van in exchange for a used van. The used van had cost $14,000 and had accumulated depreciation of $11,000, so the van's current book value is $3,000. The new van has a list or "sticker" price of $20,400 but can be purchased for $18,900 cash. The cash price is the actual fair market value of the asset, which is in many cases lower than the list price. Since the seller is willing to accept $15,000 plus the used van, the fair market value of the used van is $3,900, and there is a gain on the exchange of $900 ($3,900 FMV − $3,000 book value). The gain can also be computed as follows:

> **BUSINESS ENVIRONMENT ESSAY**
> *Disposing of Old Airplanes*
>
> Although many operating assets have little or no value by the time they are disposed of, that is not the case with airplanes. Each year, major U.S. airlines retire about 100 planes, replacing them with new ones that are more fuel efficient and less noisy at takeoff, as required by federal noise standards. As a result of this upgrading of airline fleets, business is booming for International Airline Support Group (IASG), a Miami-based company.
>
> IASG buys the old planes and disposes of them at a substantial profit. In some cases, a plane is sold or leased intact to a customer. More often, however, the planes are dismantled and sold piece by piece. For example, a Boeing 727 might be purchased from Delta for $750,000. Then, the three engines are sold for $200,000 apiece, and the landing gear for another $200,000. Other parts are inspected at an FAA-certified repair station and then entered into a computer database that can be accessed by airlines and airplane mechanics around the world as they search for needed parts. The remaining scrap from the plane is sold to an aluminum smelter.
>
> According to IASG's top executive, the company usually realizes a 200 percent gross margin from the sale of a plane's parts. The demand for parts from used airplanes is significant because many new planes use the same parts as old planes. A major portion of IASG's sales have been to cargo companies, such as UPS and Federal Express, but the customer base is expanding to include some major airlines, such as American and Northwest.
>
> While earning huge profits, IASG has also created market efficiencies that benefit all the parties. The airlines benefit by having a ready buyer for the planes they retire, and companies looking for spare parts have a dependable supplier to fill their requests.
>
> *Source:* Adapted from Shelley Neumeier, "Companies to Watch," *Fortune,* December 16, 1991, p. 106.

Fair market value of new van..		$18,900
Book value of used van	$ 3,000	
Cash paid..	15,000	
Total book value given up		18,000
Gain to Wheeler on the exchange		$ 900

Because the used van is being exchanged for a similar asset, the gain is not recognized. The new van will be recorded at $18,000, which is the used van's book value ($3,000) plus the $15,000 cash paid. The entry to record this transaction would be:

Hotel Van (new)	18,000	
Accumulated Depreciation, Hotel Van (old)	11,000	
Hotel Van (old)		14,000
Cash		15,000
Exchanged used asset plus $15,000 cash in return for new asset.		

LOSS ON THE EXCHANGE OF SIMILAR OPERATING ASSETS. Assume now that the transaction to buy the new hotel van resulted in an accounting loss to Wheeler. All the data presented earlier apply, except that Wheeler had to pay $16,500 instead of $15,000. The result would be a loss of $600, computed as follows:

Fair market value of new van		$18,900
Book value of used van	$ 3,000	
Cash paid	16,500	
Total book value given up		19,500
Loss to Wheeler on the exchange		$ (600)

Current accounting principles stipulate that this loss must be recognized in the period of the exchange. The entry to record the exchange, and the resulting loss, would be:

Hotel Van (new)	18,900	
Accumulated Depreciation, Hotel Van (old)	11,000	
Loss on Exchange	600	
Hotel Van (old)		14,000
Cash		16,500

Exchanged used asset plus $16,500 cash in return for new asset costing $18,900.

EXCHANGES OF DISSIMILAR ASSETS. As we have explained, the majority of exchanges involve similar assets—an old truck for a new one, old equipment for new equipment performing a similar function. Sometimes, however, the exchange involves assets with unrelated functions, such as exchanging securities for land and a building, or exchanging inventories for equipment. When dissimilar assets are exchanged, the general rule is that the new asset is recorded either at its fair market value or at the fair market value of the assets given up, whichever amount may be more accurately determined. The difference between the total value of the assets given up (the additional cash paid plus the book value of the old asset) and the amount received (the fair market value of the new asset) should be recognized as a gain or a loss on the exchange. Unlike the exchange of similar assets, where only losses are recognized, the exchange of dissimilar assets results in the recognition of both gains and losses.

The financial reporting rules for exchanges of similar and dissimilar assets are presented in Exhibit 9-9.

Exhibit 9-9   *A Summary of Exchanges of Assets by a Buyer**

	Accounting Treatment of Gain or Loss	Recording of the New Asset
Exchanges of similar, productive assets:		
Accounting for gains	Not Recognized	Book value of old asset plus cash paid
Accounting for losses	Recognized	Fair market value of new asset
Exchanges of dissimilar assets:		
Accounting for gains	Recognized	Fair market value of new asset
Accounting for losses	Recognized	Fair market value of new asset

* Assuming that cash is *paid* by the buyer as part of the exchange.

> **To Summarize** *There are three ways of disposing of assets: (1) scrapping, (2) selling, and (3) exchanging. If a scrapped asset has not been fully depreciated, a loss equal to the undepreciated cost or book value is recognized. When an asset is sold, there is a gain if the sales price exceeds the book value, and a loss if the sales price is less than the book value. When assets are exchanged, there is a gain if the cash-equivalent price of the asset received exceeds the sum of the book value of the old asset and the cash paid, and a loss if the opposite is true. If the buyer pays cash in the exchange of similar operating assets, losses are recognized and gains are not. When there is a gain, the acquired asset should be recorded at the sum of the book value of the asset given up and the cash paid. When there is a loss, the asset acquired through the exchange should be recorded at its fair market value. When dissimilar assets are exchanged, both gains and losses are recognized; the asset acquired in the exchange is recorded at its fair market value.*

ACCOUNTING FOR INTANGIBLE ASSETS

Objective 5
Account for the acquisition and amortization of intangible assets.

Intangible assets are rights and privileges that are long-lived, are not held for resale, have no physical substance, and usually provide their owner with competitive advantages over other firms. Familiar examples are patents, franchises, licenses, and goodwill. Although intangible assets have no physical substance, they are accounted for in the same way as other long-term operational assets. That is, they are originally recorded at cost and the cost is allocated over the useful or legal life, whichever is shorter. The periodic allocation to expense of an intangible asset's cost is called **amortization**. Straight-line amortization is generally used for intangible assets.

amortization *the process of cost allocation that assigns the original cost of an intangible asset to the periods benefited*

Patents

patent *an exclusive right granted for 17 years by the federal government to manufacture and sell an invention*

A **patent** is an exclusive right to produce and sell a commodity that has one or more unique features. Issued to inventors by the federal government, patents have a legal life of 17 years. They may be obtained on new products developed in a company's own research laboratories, or they may be purchased from others. If a patent is purchased from others, its cost is simply the purchase price, and it is recorded as an asset (patent). The cost of the patent is amortized over the useful life of the patent, which may or may not coincide with the patent's legal life.

The cost of a patent for a product developed within a firm is difficult to determine. Should it include research and development costs as well as legal fees to obtain the patent? Should other company expenses be included? Prior to 1974, there were no real accounting guidelines specifying which expenditures should be capitalized as part of the cost of a patent. In 1974, however, the Financial Accounting Standards Board determined that because of the high degree of uncertainty about their future benefits, research and development costs must be expensed in the period in which they are incurred. Therefore, all research and development costs of internally developed patents are expensed as they are incurred.

To illustrate the accounting for patents, we assume that Wheeler Resorts, Inc., acquires, for $200,000, a patent granted 7 years earlier to another firm. The entry to record the purchase of the patent would be:

```
Patent ..................................................  200,000
    Cash ..................................................          200,000
Purchased patent for $200,000.
```

Because 7 years of its 17-year legal life have already elapsed, the patent now has a legal life of only 10 years although it may have a shorter useful life. If its useful life is assumed to be 8 years, one-eighth of the $200,000 cost should be amortized each year for the next 8 years. The entry each year to record the patent amortization expense would be:

```
Amortization Expense, Patent .................................  25,000
    Patent ..................................................          25,000
To amortize one-eighth of the cost of the patent.
```

Alternatively, a contra-asset account, such as Accumulated Amortization, could have been credited. In practice, however, crediting the intangible asset account directly is more common.

Franchises and Licenses

franchise *an exclusive right to sell a product or offer a service in a certain geographical area*

Issued either by companies or by government agencies, **franchises** and licenses are exclusive rights to perform services in certain geographical areas. For example, McDonald's Corporation sells franchises to individuals to operate its hamburger outlets in specific locations. Similarly, the Interstate Commerce Commission issues licenses to trucking firms, allowing them to transport certain types of goods in specific geographical areas. The cost of a franchise or license is amortized over its useful or legal life, whichever is shorter.

Goodwill

goodwill *an intangible asset showing that a business is worth more than the value of its net assets because of strategic location, reputation, good customer relations, or similar factors; equal to the excess of cost over the fair market value of the net assets purchased*

When businesses are purchased, the negotiated price often exceeds the total value of the identifiable assets minus the outstanding liabilities assumed by the buyer. This excess in purchase price that cannot be allocated to specific assets is called **goodwill** and is an intangible asset. The emergence of goodwill in such a transaction is considered an indication that the purchased business is worth more than its net assets, due to such favorable characteristics as a good reputation, a strategic location, product superiority, or management skill.

Goodwill should be recorded only if its value can be objectively determined by a transaction. Therefore, even though two businesses may enjoy the same favorable characteristics, goodwill will be recognized only when it is purchased—that is, when one company buys another company. This disparity in accounting exists because the action of a buyer in paying a premium for a firm is objective evidence that goodwill exists and has a specific value.

Unlike other intangible assets that decrease in value with time, goodwill often increases in value. However, like those assets that do increase in value, goodwill is not written up above its original cost. Regardless of whether goodwill increases in value, accounting practice dictates that goodwill must be amortized over its expected life, not to exceed 40 years, in order to ensure that all firms with purchased goodwill account for it in similar ways.

To illustrate the accounting for goodwill, we assume that Wheeler Corporation purchased Valley Drug Store for $400,000. At that time, the recorded assets and liabilities of Valley Drug had the following fair market values:

Inventory.	$220,000
Long-term operating assets	110,000
Other assets (prepaid expenses, etc.).	10,000
Liabilities	(20,000)
Total net assets	$320,000

Note that fair market values (the current prices of items) will generally differ from book values (the historical costs paid for items less any depreciation, amortization, or depletion).

Because Wheeler was willing to pay $400,000 for Valley Drug, there must have been other favorable, intangible factors worth approximately $80,000. These factors are called goodwill, and the entry to record the purchase of the drug store would be:

Inventory.	220,000	
Long-Term Operating Assets	110,000	
Other Assets	10,000	
Goodwill	80,000	
Liabilities		20,000
Cash		400,000
Purchased Valley Drug Store for $400,000.		

If Wheeler decides to use 40 years as the useful life of the goodwill, each year the amortization entry will be:

Amortization Expense, Goodwill	2,000	
Goodwill		2,000
To record annual straight-line amortization of goodwill ($80,000 ÷ 40 years).		

ACCOUNTING FOR NATURAL RESOURCES

Objective 6

Account for the acquisition and depletion of natural resources.

As noted at the beginning of this chapter, natural resources include such assets as oil wells, timber tracts, coal mines, and gravel deposits. Like all other assets, newly purchased or developed natural resources are recorded at cost. This cost must be written off as the assets are extracted or otherwise depleted. This process of writing off the cost of natural resources is called **depletion** and involves the calculation of a depletion rate for each unit of the natural resource.

depletion *the process of cost allocation that assigns the original cost of a natural resource to the periods benefited*

To illustrate, we will assume that Power-T Company, which manufactures heavy tractor equipment, decides to diversify (invest in another type of business) and purchases a coal mine for $1,200,000 cash. The entry to record the purchase would be:

Coal Mine...	1,200,000	
Cash		1,200,000
Purchased a coal mine for $1,200,000.		

If the mine has an estimated 200,000 tons of coal deposits, the depletion expense for each ton of coal extracted will be $6 ($1,200,000/200,000 tons). If 12,000 tons of coal were mined in the current year, the depletion entry would be:

Depletion Expense	72,000	
Coal Mine...		72,000
To record depletion for the year: 12,000 tons at $6.00 per ton.		

A contra-asset account, such as Accumulated Depletion, could have been credited instead of the asset account, Coal Mine. As with intangible assets, we have credited the asset directly. This is the procedure used most commonly in practice since the asset actually is physically depleted or used up.

After the first year's depletion expense has been recorded, the coal mine will be shown on the balance sheet as follows:

Natural Resources:
Coal Mine (cost $1,200,000) $1,128,000

But how do you determine the number of tons of coal in a mine? Since most natural resources cannot be counted, the amount of the resource owned is an estimate. The depletion calculation is therefore likely to be revised as new information becomes available. When an estimate is changed, a new depletion rate per unit is calculated and used to compute depletion during the remaining life of the natural resource or until another new estimate is made.

To Summarize *Intangible assets are long-term rights and privileges that have no physical substance but that provide competitive advantages to owners. Common intangible assets are patents, franchises, licenses, and goodwill. Natural resources are assets, such as gravel deposits or coal mines, that are consumed or that waste away. The costs of intangible assets are amortized, whereas the costs of natural resources are depleted.*

Review of Learning Objectives

Objective 1

Record the acquisition of property, plant, and equipment. Property, plant, and equipment includes tangible, long-lived assets such as land, buildings, machinery, furniture, and equipment. These assets may be acquired by purchase or lease. When purchased, they are recorded at cost, which includes all expenditures associated with acquiring them and getting them ready for their intended use. If two or more assets are acquired in a "basket" purchase, the relative fair market value method is used to assign costs to individual assets. When these types of assets are leased, the lease agreement may be classified as an operating lease or as a capital lease. An operating lease results in a short-term use of the asset without recording the asset on the books of the user, the lessee. Instead, the lessee only records the rental expense paid each month. If the lease is for a longer term and meets the conditions of a capital lease, the lessee records the leased property as an asset and a related liability as if the property had been purchased and financed with long-term debt. The asset is recorded at the present value of the lease rental payments, which usually is equivalent to the current market value or the cash equivalent price.

Objective 2

Compute depreciation expense for plant and equipment. Depreciation is the process of allocating the cost of plant and equipment to expense in the periods that are benefited from the use of the asset. Four methods commonly used to compute depreciation for financial reporting include straight-line, declining-balance, sum-of-the-years'-digits, and units-of-production.

The straight-line method is the only method that results in the same amount of depreciation for each full year. The declining-balance and SYD methods allow for accelerated cost allocation in the early years of an asset's life. The units-of-production method allocates cost over the useful life measured in units of output or usage. All the methods require salvage value to be subtracted from the original cost in computing depreciation expense except for the declining-balance method. The salvage value is ignored in the declining-balance method in the annual computation, but the book value of the asset cannot be less than the salvage value at the end of any reporting year.

For income tax purposes, depreciation expense is computed according to the federal income tax law and frequently differs from the depreciation computed for financial recording purposes.

Objective 3

Account for repairs and improvement of property, plant, and equipment. Expenditures incurred for property, plant, and equipment after acquisition may be classified as either ordinary expenditures or capital expenditures. Since ordinary expenditures merely maintain an asset's productive capacity at the level originally projected, they are reported as repairs and maintenance expense and do not affect the asset's reported cost. For an expenditure to be classified as a capital expenditure, it must (1) increase the productive life or annual capacity of the asset, (2) increase the quality of the output, or (3) significantly reduce the cost of producing the output. Since capital expenditures are added to the cost of an asset, they affect future depreciation, whereas ordinary expenditures are expenses of the current period.

Objective 4

Record the disposal of property, plant, and equipment. Property, plant, and equipment may be disposed of by selling, exchanging, or scrapping. When an asset is sold, a gain is reported if the sales price exceeds the book value, or a loss is reported if the book value exceeds the sales price. When assets are exchanged, recognition of gains and losses depends on whether it is an exchange of similar assets or dissimilar assets. For similar assets, a gain is reported if the buyer receives cash and the total value of the cash, cash equivalents, and the asset received exceeds the book value of the old asset. There is a loss if the opposite is true. If the buyer pays cash in the exchange of similar operating assets, losses are recognized but gains are not. The asset acquired through the exchange should be recorded at its fair market value when losses are recognized. When dissimilar assets are exchanged, both gains and losses are recognized, with the asset acquired being recorded at its fair market value.

Objective 5

Account for the acquisition and amortization of intangible assets. Intangible assets are rights and privileges that are long-lived, are not held for resale, have no physical substance, and usually provide competitive advantages for the owner. Common examples are patents, franchises, licenses, and goodwill. Patents acquired by purchase are recorded at cost and amortized over the shorter of their economic life or their 17-year legal life. Research and development costs incurred internally in a firm are expensed as incurred even if they result in the development of a legal patent. Franchises and licenses are exclusive

Chapter 9 *Property, Plant, and Equipment; Intangible Assets; and Natural Resources*   385

rights to perform services in certain geographical areas. The cost of acquiring a franchise or license is recorded as an asset, which is then amortized over its useful or legal life, whichever is shorter. Goodwill occurs when a business is purchased and the purchase price exceeds the total value of the identifiable assets less outstanding liabilities assumed. The excess purchase price that cannot be allocated to specific assets is called goodwill and is recorded as an intangible asset. Goodwill is amortized to expense over its expected life, not to exceed 40 years.

Objective 6

Account for the acquisition and depletion of natural resources. Natural resources acquired for a firm at a cost are recorded as assets. They include oil wells, timber tracts, coal mines, and various types of deposits, such as gold, gravel, and stone. The cost of these assets are written off as the assets are extracted or otherwise depleted. The process of writing off the cost of extracted natural resources is called depletion. Depletion expense for a year is computed by first computing a depletion rate by dividing the cost assigned to the natural resource by the estimated number of remaining units to be extracted. This depletion rate is multiplied by the number of units extracted for the year to arrive at the dollar amount of depletion for the year. The total depletion for the year becomes an expense on the income statement to the extent that units extracted that year have been sold. The amount of calculated depletion that is not assigned to units sold would be included in the inventory cost of extracted units that have not been sold.

Key Terms and Concepts

accumulated depreciation *(365)*
amortization *(380)*
book value *(365)*
capital expenditure *(374)*
capital lease *(361)*
declining-balance depreciation method *(366)*
depletion *(383)*
depreciation *(363)*
franchise *(381)*

goodwill *(381)*
intangible assets *(358)*
lessee *(360)*
lessor *(360)*
natural resources *(358)*
operating assets *(358)*
operating lease *(361)*
patent *(380)*
property, plant, and equipment *(358)*

relative fair market value method *(359)*
salvage, or residual, value *(363)*
straight-line depreciation method *(364)*
sum-of-the-years'-digits (SYD) depreciation method *(367)*
units-of-production depreciation method *(369)*
useful life *(358)*

Review Problem

Property, Plant, and Equipment

Barton Motor Lines is a trucking company that hauls crude oil in the Rocky Mountain states. It presently has 20 trucks. The following information relates to a single truck:

1. Date truck was purchased, July 1, 1991
2. Cost of truck:

Truck..................	$125,000
Paint job	3,000
Sales tax...............	7,000

3. Estimated useful life of truck, 120,000 miles.
4. Estimated salvage value of truck, $27,000.
5. 1993 expenditures on truck:
   (a) $6,000 on new tires and regular maintenance.
   (b) $44,440 to completely rework the truck's engine; increased life by 80,000 miles but left expected salvage value unchanged.

6. Miles driven:

1991	11,000
1992	24,000
1993 (before reworking of engine)	13,000
1993 (after reworking of engine)	7,000
1994 (to date of trade-in)	14,000

7. During 1994, the truck was traded in for a new one with a list price of $142,000. Barton determined that the new truck could have been purchased for $130,000 cash. Cash of $50,000 was paid on the trade-in.

Required: Record journal entries to account for the following. (Use the units-of-production depreciation method.)

1. The purchase of the truck.
2. Depreciation expense for:
   (a) 1991.
   (b) 1992.
   (c) 1993.
   (d) 1994 (to date of trade-in).
3. The expenditures on the truck during 1993.
4. The exchange of the truck for the new one during 1994.

Solution

1. Truck Purchase

The cost of the truck includes both the amount paid for it and all costs incurred to get it in working condition. In this case, the cost includes both the paint job and the sales tax. Thus, the entry to record the purchase is:

Truck	135,000	
Cash		135,000

2. Depreciation Expense

The formula for units-of-production depreciation on the truck is:

$$\frac{\text{cost} - \text{salvage value}}{\text{total miles expected to be driven}} \times \begin{array}{c}\text{number of miles}\\ \text{driven in any}\\ \text{year}\end{array} = \begin{array}{c}\text{depreciation}\\ \text{expense}\end{array}$$

Depreciation for the 4 years is calculated as follows:

1991:

$$\frac{\$135,000 - \$27,000}{120,000 \text{ miles}} \times 11,000 \text{ miles} = \$9,900 \text{ or } \$0.90 \text{ per mile} \times 11,000 \text{ miles}$$

1992:

$$\frac{\$135,000 - \$27,000}{120,000 \text{ miles}} \times 24,000 \text{ miles} = \$21,600 \text{ or } \$0.90 \text{ per mile} \times 24,000 \text{ miles}$$

1993 (before reworking engine):

$$\frac{\$135,000 - \$27,000}{120,000 \text{ miles}} \times 13,000 \text{ miles} = \$11,700 \text{ or } \$0.90 \text{ per mile} \times 13,000 \text{ miles}$$

1993 (after reworking engine):
Depreciation already taken: $43,200
Left to depreciate: $64,800 ($135,000 − $43,200 − $27,000)
New amount to depreciate: $109,240 ($64,800 + $44,440)
Remaining life in miles: 152,000 (120,000 + 80,000 − 48,000)
New depreciation per mile: $0.719 ($109,240 ÷ 152,000 miles)
Depreciation for remainder of 1993:

$0.719 per mile × 7,000 miles = $5,033

1994 (to date of trade-in):

$0.719 per mile × 14,000 miles = $10,066

The depreciation entries are:

(a)	1991	Depreciation Expense	9,900	
		Accumulated Depreciation		9,900
(b)	1992	Depreciation Expense	21,600	
		Accumulated Depreciation		21,600
(c)	1993	Depreciation Expense	16,733	
		Accumulated Depreciation ($11,700 + $5,033)		16,733
(d)	1994	Depreciation Expense	10,066	
		Accumulated Depreciation		10,066

3. Expenditures

The first expenditure of $6,000 is an ordinary expenditure and is expensed in the current year. The $44,440 expenditure is capitalized because it lengthens the truck's life. The entries are:

Repairs and Maintenance Expense	6,000	
Cash		6,000
Truck	44,440	
Cash		44,440

4. Exchange

This is a trade of similar, productive assets involving a loss, so the new asset is recorded at its fair market value (its cash-equivalent price of $130,000). The loss is the difference between the value received ($130,000) and the amount given up (cash plus the book value of the old truck). The calculation of the loss is as follows:

Cost of old truck ($135,000 + $44,440)		$179,440
Depreciation to date of trade:		
1991	$ 9,900	
1992	21,600	
1993	16,733	
1994	10,066	58,299
Book value of old truck		$121,141
Cash paid		50,000
Total assets given up		$171,141
Fair market value of new truck		130,000
Loss on trade-in		$ 41,141

Given these calculations, the journal entry is:

New Truck	130,000	
Accumulated Depreciation	58,299	
Loss on Trade-in	41,141	
Cash		50,000
Old Truck		179,440

Discussion Questions

1. What are the major characteristics of property, plant, and equipment?
2. Why are expenditures other than the net purchase price included in the cost of an asset?
3. Why are fair market values used to determine the cost of operating assets acquired in a basket purchase?
4. Why would a company include leased assets in the property, plant, and equipment section of its balance sheet when the assets are owned by another entity?
5. It is sometimes said that the depreciation expense reported in the income statement does not necessarily measure the amount of an asset's service potential that was used up during the period. Under what circumstances would the reported depreciation expense not measure the used-up service potential?
6. Which of the depreciation methods discussed in this chapter will usually result in the highest net income in the early years of an asset's life?
7. It is said that no matter which depreciation method is being used to allocate costs over a period of years, a straight-line method of apportionment is always made when an asset is acquired or disposed of during a year. What does this statement mean?
8. When changing the estimate of the useful life of an asset, should depreciation expense for all the previous years be recalculated? If not, how do you account for a change in this estimate?
9. How does the company accountant decide whether an expenditure should be capitalized or expensed?
10. If it is uncertain whether an expenditure will benefit one or more than one accounting period, or whether it will increase the capacity or useful life of an operational asset, most firms will expense rather than capitalize the expenditure. Why?
11. Why is it common to have a gain or loss on the disposal of a long-term operating asset? Is it true that if the useful life and salvage value of an asset are known with certainty and are realized, there will never be such a gain or loss?
12. When recording the disposal of a long-term operating asset, why is it necessary to debit the accumulated depreciation of the old asset?
13. Why is the list price of a new asset often ignored in accounting for the purchase of long-term operating assets?
14. Why are intangible assets considered assets if they have no physical substance?
15. Goodwill can only be recorded when a business is purchased. Does this result in similar businesses having incomparable financial statements?
16. Why is it often necessary to recalculate the depletion rate for natural resources?

Exercises

E9-1
Computing Asset Cost and Depreciation Expense

Crown Furniture Company decided to purchase a new furniture-polishing machine for its store in New York City. After a long search, it found the appropriate polisher in Chicago. The machine cost $75,000, and had an estimated 10-year life and no salvage value. Crown Company had the following additional expenditures with respect to this purchase:

Sales tax	$4,000
Delivery costs (FOB shipping point)	1,500
Installation costs	2,200
Painting of machine to match the decor	300

Chapter 9 *Property, Plant, and Equipment; Intangible Assets; and Natural Resources*   389

1. What is the cost of the machine to Crown Furniture Company?
2. What is the amount of the first full year's depreciation if Crown uses (a) the straight-line method? (b) the double-declining-balance method? (c) sum-of-the-years'-digits method?

E9-2
Accounting for the Acquisition of Assets—Basket Purchase

Seaport Corporation purchased land, a building, and equipment for a total cost of $450,000. After the purchase, the property was appraised. Fair market values were determined to be $120,000 for the land, $280,000 for the building, and $80,000 for the equipment. Given these appraisals, record the purchase of the property by Seaport Corporation.

E9-3
Accounting for Leased Assets

On January 1, 1994, Hartmeyer Co. leased a fax machine with a laser printer from Teleproducts, Inc. The 5-year lease is noncancellable and requires monthly payments of $150 at the end of each month, with the first payment due on January 31, 1994. At the end of five years, Hartmeyer will own the equipment. The present value of the lease payment at the beginning of the lease is determined to be $6,740.

1. Prepare journal entries to record:
   (a) The lease agreement on January 1, 1994.
   (b) The first lease payment on January 31, 1994, assuming that $68 of the $150 payment is interest.
2. Assume the lease expires after one year at which time a new lease can be negotiated or Hartmeyer can return the equipment to Teleproducts. Prepare any journal entries relating to the lease that would be required on January 1 and January 31, 1994.

E9-4
Lease Classification

Malone Corporation leased a computer from Chambers Company. The lease term is five years, and the lease cannot be canceled by either the lessee or the lessor.

1. What additional information would you need in order to determine whether this is an operating lease or a capital lease?
2. Explain how this information would be used in classifying the lease.

E9-5
Acquisition and Depreciation of Assets

Western Oil Company, which prepares financial statements on a calendar-year basis, purchased new drilling equipment on July 1, 1994, using checks #1015 and #1016 to do so. The check totals are shown here, along with a breakdown of the charges.

1015 (Payee—Oil Equipment, Inc.):
Cost of drilling equipment	$ 75,000
Cost of cement platform	25,000
Installation charges	13,000
Total	$113,000

1016 (Payee—Red Ball Freight):
Freight-In on drilling equipment	$ 2,000

Assuming that the estimated life of the drilling equipment is 10 years and its salvage value is $5,000:

1. Record the disbursements on 7/1/94, assuming that no entry had been recorded for the drilling equipment.

2. Disregarding the information given about the two checks, assume that the drilling equipment was capitalized at a total cost of $95,000. Calculate the depreciation expense for 1994 using the following methods:
   (a) Sum-of-the-years'-digits.
   (b) Double-declining-balance.
   (c) 150 percent declining-balance.
   (d) Straight-line.
3. Prepare the journal entry to record the depreciation for 1994 in accordance with 2(a).

E9-6
Acquisition, Depreciation, and Disposal of Assets

On January 2, 1994, Sampson Company purchased a building and land for $440,000. The most recent appraisal values for the building and the land were $360,000 and $120,000, respectively. The building has an estimated useful life of 20 years and a salvage value of $10,000.

1. Assuming cash transactions and straight-line depreciation, prepare journal entries to record:
   (a) Purchase of the building and land on January 2, 1994.
   (b) Depreciation expense on December 31, 1994.
2. Assume that after 3 years the property (land and building) was sold for $350,000. Prepare the journal entry to record the sale.

E9-7
Acquisition and Trade-In of Assets

Prepare entries in the books of Sanmara, Inc. to reflect the following. (Assume cash transactions.)

1. Purchased a lathing machine to be used by the firm in its production process.

Invoice price	$45,000
Cash discount taken	900
Installation costs	1,200
Sales tax on machine	1,800

2. Performed normal periodic maintenance on the lathing machine at a cost of $500.
3. Added to the lathing machine a governor costing $400, which is expected to increase the machine's useful life.
4. On January 1, traded a cleaning machine that originally cost $5,000 for a new cleaning machine with a cash purchase price of $6,000. At the time of the trade, the old machine had an accumulated depreciation balance of $3,000. The company received a trade-in allowance of $2,100 and paid $3,900 in cash.

E9-8
Depreciation Calculations

Luric Company purchased a new car on July 1, 1993, for $15,000. The estimated life of the car was 4 years or 104,000 miles, and its salvage value was estimated to be $2,000. The car was driven 9,000 miles in 1993 and 27,000 miles in 1994.

1. Compute the amount of depreciation expense for 1993 and 1994 using the following methods:
   (a) Straight-line.
   (b) Sum-of-the-years'-digits.
   (c) Double-declining-balance.
   (d) Units-of-production.

2. Which depreciation method reflects most closely the used-up service potential of the car? Explain.

E9-9
Depreciation Calculations

On January 2, 1993, a machine was purchased for $50,000. The installation cost was $2,000. It was estimated that the salvage value of the machine would be $4,000. The machine has a useful life of 5 years. Compute the depreciation expense for 1993 and 1994 using the following methods:

1. Straight-line.
2. 150% declining-balance.
3. Sum-of-the-years'-digits.

E9-10
Depreciation Computations with Change in Estimate

Laser Company purchases a $400,000 piece of equipment on January 2, 1992, for use in its manufacturing process. The equipment's estimated useful life is 10 years with no salvage value. Laser uses 150% declining-balance depreciation for all its equipment.

1. Compute the depreciation expense for 1992, 1993, and 1994.
2. Compute the book value of the equipment on December 31, 1994.
3. Assume that the company reviews its operating assets at the beginning of 1995 and determines that this piece of equipment will have a remaining useful life of only 3 more years. What will be the depreciation expense for the years 1996–1997 based on the new estimated life?

E9-11
Disposal of Assets by Sale and Exchange

Sleepease Mattress Company purchased a delivery truck 5 years ago for $20,000. Presently, accumulated depreciation on the truck is $12,000.

Prepare journal entries to record the sale or exchange of the truck, assuming that:

1. The truck is sold for $9,500 cash.
2. The truck is exchanged for $6,000 of supplies.
3. The truck is exchanged for a new truck with a fair market value of $16,000. In addition to the old truck, $9,000 cash is paid in the exchange.
4. The truck is exchanged for a $10,000 note receivable.
5. The truck, plus a cash payment of $4,000, is exchanged for a new truck having a fair market value of $14,000.

E9-12
Accounting for the Exchange of Assets

Johnson Company decided to purchase a new machine that had a list price of $19,000 and a cash price without trade-in of $17,500. The dealer required a cash payment of $16,600 in addition to the trade-in of an old, similar machine that had a $1,400 book value. The cost of the old machine was $8,000.

1. Give the entry to record the exchange.
2. Record the exchange, assuming now that $16,000 cash plus the old machine were given for the new one.

E9-13
Accounting for the Disposal of Assets

Zimer Concrete Company has a truck that it wants to either sell or trade. The truck had an original cost of $60,000, was purchased 3 years ago, and was expected to have a useful life of 5 years with no salvage value.

Using straight-line depreciation, and assuming that depreciation expense for 3 full years has been recorded, prepare journal entries to record the disposal of the truck under each of the following independent conditions:

1. Zimer Company sells the truck for $25,000 cash.
2. Zimer Company sells the truck for $20,000 cash.
3. Zimer Company trades the truck for a new one with a fair market value of $80,000 and is given a trade-in allowance of $30,000 on the old truck.
4. Zimer Company trades the truck for a piece of land that is valued at $60,000, and pays $32,000 in addition to the old truck.
5. The old truck is wrecked and Zimer Company hauls it to the junkyard.

E9-14
Accounting for Intangible Assets

During 1994, Graham Research, Inc. had the following intangible assets:

Asset	Cost	Date Purchased	Expected Useful or Legal Life
Goodwill	$ 16,000	January 1, 1985	40 years
Patent	136,000	January 1, 1987	17 years
Franchise	180,000	January 1, 1988	10 years

1. Record the amortization expense for each of these intangible assets for 1994.
2. Prepare an intangible asset section of the balance sheet for Graham Research, Inc. as of December 31, 1994.

E9-15
Accounting for Natural Resources

On January 1, 1993, Castle Investment Corporation purchased a coal mine for cash, having taken into consideration the favorable tax consequences and the inevitable energy crunch in the future. Castle paid $800,000 for the mine. Shortly before the purchase, an engineer estimated that there were 80,000 tons of coal in the mine.

1. Record the purchase of the mine on January 1, 1993.
2. Record the depletion expense for 1993, assuming that 20,000 tons of coal were mined during the year.
3. Assume that on January 1, 1994, the company received a new estimate that the mine contained 120,000 tons of coal. Record the entry (if any) to show the change in estimate.
4. Record the depletion expense for 1994, assuming that another 20,000 tons of coal were mined.

Problem Set A

P9A-1
Classification of Asset Expenditures

Pioneer Company made the following expenditures in connection with starting a new consulting business:

(a) Purchase price of land, $75,000.
(b) Attorney's fees and title transfer costs incurred in purchasing land, $500.
(c) Cost of clearing and grading land, $24,000.
(d) Cost of fence, $9,000, including $1,500 for installation.
(e) Architect's fees for designing office building, $8,000.

Chapter 9 *Property, Plant, and Equipment; Intangible Assets; and Natural Resources* 393

    (f) Contractor's price for construction of office building, $153,000.
    (g) Cost of parking lot and sidewalks, $22,000.
    (h) Purchase price of equipment, $45,000 plus $2,000 sales tax.
    (i) Freight cost for equipment, $3,500.
    (j) Installation cost for equipment, $6,000.

  Required: Classify the expenditures by designating how much should be included in each of the following accounts: Land, Land Improvements, Office Building, and Equipment.

P9A-2
Acquisition of an Asset

Pacific Printing Company purchased a new printing press. The invoice price was $158,500. The company paid for the press within 30 days, so they were allowed a 3 percent discount. The freight to have the press delivered cost $2,500. A premium of $900 was paid for a special insurance policy to cover the transportation of the press. The company spent $2,800 to install the press, and an additional $400 in start-up costs to get the press ready for regular production.

  Required:
1. At what amount should the press be recorded as an asset?
2. What additional information must be known before the depreciation expense for the first year of operation of the new press can be computed?
3. **Interpretive Question** What criterion is used to determine whether the start-up costs of $400 are included in the cost of the asset? Explain.

P9A-3
Accounting for Leased Assets

On January 2, 1994, Allied Company contracted to lease a computer on a noncancellable basis for 5 years at an annual rental of $63,000, payable at the end of each year. The computer has an estimated economic life of 6 years. There is no bargain purchase option and the computer will be returned to the lessor at the end of the 5-year term of the lease. At the beginning of the lease, the computer has a fair market value of $240,000, and the present value of the lease payments equals $238,820.

  Required:
1. Is this a capital lease or an operating lease? Explain.
2. Assuming that the lease is an operating lease, prepare the journal entries for the Allied Company for 1994.
3. Assuming that the lease is a capital lease, prepare the journal entries for the Allied Company for 1994. Assume the lease payment at the end of 1994 includes interest of $23,882.

P9A-4
Depreciation Calculations

Denver Hardware Company has a giant paint mixer that cost $31,500 plus $400 to install. The estimated salvage value of the paint mixer at the end of its useful life in 15 years is estimated to be $1,900. Denver estimates that the machine can mix 850,000 cans of paint during its lifetime.

  Required: Compute the second full year's depreciation expense, using the following methods:

1. Straight-line.
2. Double-declining-balance.
3. Sum-of-the-years'-digits.
4. Units-of-production, assuming that the machine mixes 51,000 cans of paint during the second year.

P9A-5
Depreciation Calculations

On January 1, VICOM Company purchased a $68,000 machine. The estimated life of the machine was 5 years and the estimated salvage value was $5,000. The machine had an estimated useful life in productive output of 75,000 units. Actual output for the first 2 years was: year 1, 20,000 units; year 2, 15,000 units.

Required:
1. Compute the amount of depreciation expense for the first year, using each of the following methods:
   (a) Straight-line.
   (b) Units-of-production.
   (c) Sum-of-the-years'-digits.
   (d) Double-declining-balance.
2. What was the book value of the machine at the end of the first year, assuming that straight-line depreciation was used?
3. If the machine is sold at the end of the fourth year for $15,000, how much should the company report as a gain or loss (assume straight-line depreciation)?

P9A-6
Acquisition, Depreciation, and Sale of an Asset

On January 2, 1992, Hamilton Oil Company purchased a new airplane. The following costs are related to the purchase:

Airplane, base price	$112,000
Cash discount	3,000
Sales tax	4,000
Delivery charges	1,000

Required:
1. Prepare the journal entry to record the payment of these items on January 2, 1992.
2. Ignore your answer to (1) and assume that the airplane cost $90,000 and has an expected useful life of 5 years or 1,500 hours. The estimated salvage value is $3,000. Using each of the following methods, calculate the amount of depreciation expense to be recorded for the second year:
   (a) Units-of-production, assuming that 300 hours are flown in 1993.
   (b) Sum-of-the-years'-digits.
   (c) Double-declining-balance.
3. Ignore the information in (1) and (2) and assume that the airplane costs $90,000, that its expected useful life is 5 years, and that its estimated salvage value is $5,000. The company now uses the straight-line depreciation method. On July 1, 1995 the following balances are in the related accounts:

Airplane	$90,000
Accumulated Depreciation, Airplane	51,000

Prepare the necessary journal entries to record the trade-in of this airplane on July 1, 1995, for a smaller airplane with a list price of $35,000. (The cash price was determined to be $32,000.) No additional cash is paid for the new airplane.
4. **Interpretive Question** In (3), why is the new airplane not recorded at $35,000?

P9A-7
Basket Purchase and Partial Year Depreciation

On April 1, 1994, Chapman Company purchased for $200,000 a tract of land on which was located a fully-equipped factory. The following information was compiled regarding this purchase:

	Market Value	Seller's Book Value
Land	$ 75,000	$ 30,000
Building	100,000	75,000
Equipment	50,000	60,000
Totals	$225,000	$165,000

Required:
1. Prepare the journal entry to record the purchase of these assets.
2. Assume that the building is depreciated on a straight-line basis over a remaining life of 20 years and the equipment is depreciated on a double-declining-balance basis over 5 years. Neither the building nor the equipment is expected to have any salvage value. Compute the depreciation expense for 1994 assuming the assets were placed in service immediately upon acquisition.

P9A-8
Changes in Depreciation Estimates and Capitalization of Expenditures

Ironic Metal Products, Inc. acquired a machine on January 2, 1992, for $76,600. The useful life of the machine was estimated to be 8 years with a residual value of $4,600. Depreciation is recorded on December 31 of each year using the sum-of-the-years'-digits method.

At the beginning of 1994, the company estimated the remaining useful life of the machine to be 4 years and changed the estimate of scrap value from $4,600 to $2,600. On January 2, 1995, major repairs on the machine cost the company $34,000. The repairs added 2 years to the machine's useful life and increased the salvage value to $3,000.

Required:
1. Prepare journal entries to record:
   (a) The purchase of the machine.
   (b) Annual depreciation expense for the years 1992 and 1993.
   (c) Depreciation in 1994 under the revised estimates of useful life and salvage value.
   (d) The expenditure for major repairs in 1995.
   (e) To record depreciation expense for 1995.
2. Compute the book value of the machine at the end of 1995.

P9A-9
Accounting for the Exchange of Assets

On June 30, 1994, Cross Corporation exchanged a used machine for a new one with a list price of $80,000. (The cash price of the new machine was determined to be $77,000.) The old machine was originally purchased for $60,000 on January 1, 1991, and had a 4-year estimated life with no salvage value. In making the exchange, the company received a trade-in allowance of $6,000 on the old machine. Cross Corporation uses sum-of-the-years'-digits depreciation.

Required: Assuming that Cross is a calendar-year corporation:

1. Record depreciation on the old machine to the date of the trade. (Depreciation was last recorded on December 31, 1993.)
2. Compute the book value of the old machine at the date of trade.
3. Prepare the journal entry to record the exchange.

P9A-10
Unifying Concepts: Property, Plant, and Equipment

Smithfield Corporation owns and operates three sawmills that make lumber for building homes. The operations consist of cutting logs in the forest, hauling them to the various sawmills, sawing the lumber, and shipping it to building supply warehouses throughout the western part of the United States. To haul the logs, Smithfield has several trucks. Relevant data pertaining to one truck are:

1. Date of purchase, July 1, 1992
2. Cost:

Truck	$60,000
Trailer	20,000
Paint job (to match company colors)	1,500
Sales tax	3,500

3. Estimated useful life of the truck, 150,000 miles
4. Estimated salvage value, zero
5. 1993 expenditures on truck:
    (a) Spent $5,000 on tires, oil changes, greasing, and other miscellaneous items.
    (b) Spent $22,000 to overhaul the engine and replace the transmission on January 1, 1993. This expenditure increased the life of the truck by 135,000 miles.
6. Exchanged the truck on April 1, 1994, for a new truck with a fair market value of $90,000. The old truck was driven 20,000 miles in 1994. A payment of $30,000 was made on the exchange.

Required: Record journal entries to account for:

1. The purchase of the truck.
2. The 1992 depreciation expense using units-of-production depreciation and assuming the truck was driven 45,000 miles.
3. The expenditures relating to the truck during 1993.
4. The 1993 depreciation expense using the units-of-production method and assuming the truck was driven 60,000 miles.
5. The exchange of the truck on April 1, 1994.

P9A-11
Accounting for Natural Resources

On April 30, 1992, Shale Oil Company purchased an oil well, with reserves of an estimated 100,000 barrels of oil, for $1,000,000 cash.

Required: Prepare journal entries for the following:

1. Record the purchase of the oil well.
2. During 1992, 10,000 barrels of oil were extracted from the well. Record the depletion expense for 1992.
3. During 1993, 18,000 barrels of oil were extracted from the well. Record the depletion expense for 1993.
4. At the beginning of 1994, it was determined that only 60,000 barrels of oil remained in the well. During that year, 15,000 barrels of oil were extracted from the well. Record the depletion expense for 1994.

Problem Set B

P9B-1
Acquisition of Assets

Salem Company acquired the assets listed here in separate, unrelated transactions.

1. New office equipment was purchased at a list price of $32,000, with payment terms of 2/15, n/40. To take advantage of the discount, the company borrowed $24,000 from its bank, agreeing to repay the loan at the end of one year plus 10% interest.
2. Salem purchased a tract of land as a site for a warehouse for $77,000. An old building on the site was immediately razed at a cost of $15,000. The materials salvaged from the razed building were sold for $3,400. Legal fees, title insurance, and recording fees for the purchase totaled $3,700.
3. Salem acquired a used semi-trailer in exchange for some used office equipment owned by Salem. The trailer and the office equipment were both appraised at $12,000. The office equipment was carried on Salem's books at $8,500 (cost, $28,000; accumulated depreciation, $19,500).

Required: Prepare journal entries for the acquisition of each of the assets described.

P9B-2
Depreciation Calculations

Curtis, Inc., a firm that makes oversized boots, purchased a machine for its factory. The following data relate to the machine:

Price	$16,000
Delivery charges	$ 200
Installation charges	$ 600
Date purchased	May 1, 1993
Estimated useful life:	
In years	8 years
In hours of production	30,000 hours of operating time
Salvage value	$ 1,800

During 1993, the machine was used 4,400 hours. During 1994, the machine was used 3,200 hours.

Required: Determine the depreciation expense and the year-end book values for the machine for the years 1993 and 1994, assuming that:

1. The straight-line method is used.
2. The double-declining-balance method is used.
3. The units-of-production method is used.
4. The sum-of-the-years'-digits method is used.
5. **Interpretive Question** If you were Curtis, which method would you use in order to report the highest profits in 1993 and 1994?

P9B-3
Accounting for Leased Assets

The Board of Directors of Swift Company authorized the president to lease a corporate jet to facilitate his travels to domestic and international subsidiaries of the company. After extensive investigation of the alternatives, the company agreed to lease a jet for $300,548 for five years, payable at the end of each year. Title to the jet will pass to Swift Company at the end of five years with no further payments required. The lease agreement starts on January 2, 1994. The jet has an economic life of 8 years. The lease contract is noncancellable and contains an interest rate of 8%, resulting in a present value of the lease payments of $1,200,000 as of January 2, 1994.

Required:
1. Does this lease contract meet the requirements to be accounted for as a capital lease? Why or why not?
2. Assuming that the lease contract is to be accounted for as a capital lease, prepare the journal entries for the Swift Company for 1994. Interest included in the first payment is $96,000.

P9B-4
Depreciation Calculations

Markham Company acquired a trailer with an estimated life of 12 years on January 1, 1993, for $15,900. The estimated salvage value is $1,500 and the service life is estimated to be 150,000 miles. The company's accounting year ends December 31.

Required:
1. Compute the depreciation expense for 1993 and 1994 using each of the following four methods:
    (a) Straight-line.
    (b) 150% declining-balance.
    (c) Sum-of-the-years'-digits.
    (d) Units-of-production, given 25,000 miles in 1993 and 30,000 in 1994.
2. What would be the basis for the company accountant to choose between 200% and 150% for the declining-balance method?

P9B-5
Purchase of Multiple Assets for a Lump Sum

On April 1, 1994, Leisure Company paid $360,000 in cash to purchase land, a building, and equipment. The appraised fair market values of the assets were as follows: land, $90,000; building, $260,000; and equipment, $50,000. The company incurred legal fees of $3,000 to determine they would have a clear title to the land. Before the facilities could be used, Leisure had to spend $2,500 to grade and landscape the land, $4,000 to put the equipment in working order, and $15,000 to renovate the building. The equipment was then estimated to have a useful life of 6 years with no salvage value, and the building would have a useful life of 20 years with a net salvage value of $15,000. Both the equipment and the building are to be depreciated on a straight-line basis. The company is on a calendar-year reporting basis.

Required:
1. Allocate the lump-sum purchase price to the individual assets acquired.
2. Prepare the journal entry to acquire the land, building, and equipment.
3. Prepare the journal entry to record the title search, put the equipment in working order, and renovate the building.
4. Prepare the journal entries on December 31, 1994, to record the depreciation on the building and the equipment.

P9B-6
Exchange and Depreciation of Assets

Equipment belonging to Peerless Manufacturing Company was traded for new equipment that had a fair market value of $120,000 on March 31, 1994. A trade-in allowance of $90,000 was given, and the balance was paid in cash. Accounts relating to the old equipment had the following balances on December 31, 1993:

Equipment	$100,000
Accumulated Depreciation, Equipment	24,950

Depreciation expense is calculated using the units-of-production method, with the machine's estimated useful life being 100,000 units. Salvage value is expected to be $1,000. Two thousand units were produced in the first quarter of 1994.

Required: 1. Provide the journal entries necessary on March 31, 1994, to update the depreciation expense and record the exchange.
2. Now assume that the March 31, 1994, exchange did not take place. If the cost of the old machine is still $100,000, record its depreciation expense for 1994 if a salvage value of $5,000 is now expected. Its remaining useful life is estimated to be 23,750 units, and 3,500 units were produced in 1994.

P9B-7
Acquisition, Depreciation, and Sale of an Asset

On July 1, 1994, Philip Ward bought a used pickup truck at a cost of $5,300 for use in his business. On the same day, Ward had the truck painted blue and white (his company's colors) at a cost of $800. Mr. Ward estimates the life of the truck to be 3 years or 40,000 miles. He further estimates that the truck will have a $450 scrap value at the end of its life, but that it will also cost him $50 to transfer the truck to the junkyard.

Required: 1. Record the following in General Journal form:
(a) July 1, 1994   Paid all bills pertaining to the truck. (No previous entries have been recorded concerning these bills.)
(b) Dec. 31, 1994 The depreciation expense for the year, using the straight-line method.
(c) Dec. 31, 1995 The depreciation expense for 1995, again using the straight-line method.
(d) Jan. 2, 1996   Sold the truck for $2,600 cash.
2. What would the depreciation expense for 1994 have been if the truck had been driven 8,000 miles and the units-of-production method of depreciation had been used?
3. **Interpretive Question** In 1(d), there is a loss of $650. Why did this loss occur?

P9B-8
Disposal of an Asset

Honey Bee Company purchased a machine for $91,000. The machine has an estimated useful life of 7 years and a salvage value of $7,000.

Required: 1. Journalize the disposal of the machine under each of the following conditions. (Assume straight-line depreciation.)
(a) Sold the machine for $72,000 cash after 2 years.
(b) Sold the machine for $28,000 cash after 5 years.
(c) After 3 years, traded the machine for a similar new one that had a fair market value of $87,000. A trade-in allowance of $40,000 was received.
2. **Interpretive Question** Why is the loss on the trade-in in 1(c) recognized?

P9B-9
Financial Statement Effects of Depreciation Methods

SPREADSHEET PROBLEM   SOLUTIONS SOFTWARE

On July 1, 1993, the consulting firm of Little, Smart, and Quick bought a new computer for $120,000 to help them service their clients more efficiently. The new computer was estimated to have a useful life of five years with an estimated salvage value of $20,000 at the end of five years. It was further estimated that the computer would be in operation about 1,500 hours in each of the five years with some variation of use from year to year. Janet Little, who manages the firm's internal operations, has asked you to help her decide which depreciation method should be selected for the new computer. The methods being considered are straight-line, double-declining balance, and sum-of-the-years'-digits.

Required:
1. Prepare a schedule showing depreciation for 1993, 1994, and 1995 for each of the three methods being considered.
2. For each of the three methods, compute the asset book value that would be reported on the balance sheet at December 31, 1995.
3. **Interpretive Question** Which method would maximize income for the three years (1993–1995), and which would minimize income for the same period?

P9B-10
Accounting for Intangible Assets (Goodwill)

On January 1, 1994, Universal Company purchased the following assets and liabilities from Grand Company for $250,000:

	Book Value	Fair Market Value
Inventory	$40,000	$50,000
Building	80,000	100,000
Land	50,000	60,000
Accounts receivable	20,000	20,000
Accounts payable	(10,000)	(10,000)

Required:
1. Prepare a journal entry to record the purchase of Grand by Universal.
2. Record amortization of goodwill as of December 31, 1994. (Assume a 40-year amortization period for the goodwill.)

P9B-11
Unifying Concepts: Accounting for Natural Resources

Forest Products, Inc. buys and develops natural resources for profit. Since 1991 it has had the following activities:

1/1/91 Purchased for $800,000 a tract of timber estimated to contain 1,600,000 board feet of lumber.
1/1/92 Purchased for $600,000 a silver mine estimated to contain 30,000 tons of silver.
7/1/92 Purchased for $60,000 a uranium mine estimated to contain 5,000 tons of uranium.
1/1/93 Purchased for $500,000 an oil well estimated to contain 100,000 barrels of oil.

Required:
1. Provide the necessary journal entries to account for the following:
   (a) The purchase of these assets.
   (b) The depletion expense for 1993 on all four assets, assuming that the following were extracted:
      (1) 200,000 board feet of lumber.
      (2) 5,000 tons of silver.
      (3) 1,000 tons of uranium.
      (4) 10,000 barrels of oil.
2. Assume that on January 1, 1994, after 20,000 tons of silver had been mined, engineers' estimates revealed that only 4,000 tons of silver remained. Record the depletion expense for 1994, assuming that 2,000 tons were mined.

3. Compute the book values of all four assets as of December 31, 1994, assuming that the total extracted to date is:
   (a) Timber tract, 800,000 board feet.
   (b) Silver mine, 22,000 tons [only 2,000 tons are left per (2)].
   (c) Uranium mine, 3,000 tons.
   (d) Oil well, 80,000 barrels.

Business Analysis Case 1 *Gould Company*

Gould Company produces custom-made packaging and product identification materials requiring superior printing and production. The majority of the company's output is sold to manufacturers of consumer products that are packaged in a variety of materials, including flexible films, specialty papers and paperboard, and rigid vinyl.

Gould recently acquired a specialized machine to produce rigid vinyl for use in packaging its customers' products. The machine, which was custom-made for the company, cost $180,000 delivered and installed. As an accounting staff employee in the controller's office, you have been asked to study the use, maintenance, and obsolescence related to this machine and recommend a useful life, a depreciation method, and a salvage value to use for financial-reporting purposes.

Required:
1. What sources of information would you use in determining the probable use, level of maintenance, and the likelihood of obsolescence for this machine?
2. What factors should be considered in selecting a depreciation method?

Business Analysis Case 2 *NXS Corporation*

The following balance sheet information and related note disclosures were reported by NXS Corporation in its 1994 annual report to shareholders:

NXS Corporation
Partial Balance Sheet
December 31, 1994

Assets (in millions)	December 31, 1994	1993
Property, plant, and equipment:		
Land	$ 246	$ 237
Building and improvements	1,324	1,026
Machinery and equipment	976	802
Total cost	$2,546	$2,065
Less: accumulated depreciation	784	662
Net property, plant, and equipment	$1,762	$1,403

Note 1 (in part):
Property, plant, and equipment is stated at cost. Depreciation is computed using the straight-line method for financial statement purposes and accelerated methods for tax purposes. Estimated useful lives are buildings and improvements, 10 to 40 years;

machinery and equipment, 3 to 20 years. Effective January 1, 1994, the company lengthened the depreciable lives of certain properties. The change increased earnings before income taxes by $10 million.

Required:
1. Why would the company lengthen the depreciable (useful) lives of some of its assets?
2. What effect does the lengthening of asset lives have on current and future financial statements?
3. Why would the company use a different depreciation method for its tax return than for its financial statements?

Ethics Case *Dawson Manufacturing Company*[5]

Dawson Manufacturing Company has two operating divisions, each producing different products. Company policy requires that capital expenditures of each division be approved by the company's budget committee if an expenditure exceeds $50,000. The manager of Division A, Joe Beaver, received a memo from the Budget committee in mid-September which stated that no further requests for capital expenditures above $50,000 would be considered for the remainder of this year because of the company's overall financial situation. After reading the memo, Joe called the chairman of the budget committee to see if an exception could be made since the division needed a new machine that would cost $115,000 in order to complete a large order from one of the division's best customers by December 31. Otherwise, Division A would not be able to meet its profit projections for the year and Joe could be on the hotseat with management, as well as the customer. The chairman responded that there would be no exceptions to the budget committee's decision as stated in the memo and suggested that Joe submit a request for the new machine after the end of the year.

After mulling over the situation for a while, Joe decided to call in the division controller, Jill Wright, to explore ways to solve this problem. During their discussion, Joe came up with what he thought was a brilliant idea. He told Jill to order the new machine for delivery and installation by November 1. He further instructed Jill to insist that the machine manufacturer bill the division for three separate components of the machine by means of three separate invoices, which should be written as if each invoice were for a different machine. He suggested that Jill tell the machine manufacturer that they would take their business elsewhere if the manufacturer is not willing to bill with three separate invoices in the amounts of $39,000, $27,500 and $48,500. On this basis, Joe reasoned that no one invoice would exceed $50,000, so the policy stated in the budget committee's memo would not be violated.

As they discussed this proposal, Jill indicated her reluctance to go along with it, pointing out that both she and Joe would have some serious explaining to do if the intentional deviation from company policy were discovered. As Division A's controller, Jill was responsible to both Joe, the division manager, and the company controller. She realized that she could be in an awkward position if she did what Joe asked and later it was discovered that she was not forthright with the company controller about the situation. Despite Jill's concerns, Joe insisted that his plan was the only solution to the division's dilemma. He told Jill to call in the order the next day and request the

---

[5] Adapted from a case developed for the American Accounting Association's project on professionalism and ethics.

Chapter 9 *Property, Plant, and Equipment; Intangible Assets; and Natural Resources* 403

separate invoices for the three components of the machine. Jill left Joe's office in a state of deep concern, wondering how she got into this situation and worried as to how it would turn out.

Required:
1. What are the issues in this case?
2. Who are the parties directly or indirectly affected by the decision made in this situation?
3. What are Jill's alternative courses of action?
4. What should Jill do?

Chapter 10

Liabilities

Learning Objectives

After studying this chapter, you should be able to:
1. Understand the nature of current liabilities and how to account for them.
2. Use present value concepts in measuring long-term liabilities.
3. Account for long-term liabilities, including notes payable, mortgages payable, and lease obligations.
4. Describe the general nature of long-term liabilities for deferred taxes and pensions.
5. Describe the types of contingent liabilities and how they are reported.

SETTING THE STAGE

Some of the most important decisions you will make will be when and how much money to borrow. Very few individuals go through life without borrowing money for one reason or another. People borrow money to purchase homes, automobiles, and other assets and to cover major expenses, such as college tuition. Incurring liabilities to acquire assets or pay expenses can be a two-edged sword. When used wisely, borrowed money can help you finance a home, enjoy a better life, or even become wealthy through ownership of profitable assets. When abused or used excessively, interest and the requirement to repay debt can result in financial disaster. Nevertheless, debt is becoming an increasingly important part of our lives. In fact, it is estimated that out of every 100 people in the United States, only 5 are "net savers," whereas 95 are "net borrowers." Each year, the number of personal bankruptcies increases. Each year, the federal deficit and amount of government borrowing also increase.

Excessive borrowing is a problem for businesses as well as individuals. Every day seems to bring another news release announcing a company that can no longer meet its debt obligations. In January 1992, for example, TWA, one of the oldest airline companies, announced that because of high debt, it was declaring bankruptcy. Its chairman stated that TWA's liabilities had become too great and that the company could no longer afford to pay interest. The same month, Macy's, one of the oldest and most respected retail stores, announced that it, too, was overburdened with debt and was declaring bankruptcy.[1] Other companies, though not yet forced into bankruptcy, have found debt to be an unwelcome companion. Boise Cascade Corporation, for example, borrowed nearly $1 billion to modernize its paper manufacturing plants during the late 1980s and early 1990s. Because of high interest expense on this debt and falling paper prices, it reported a net loss of approximately $100 million in 1991.

In business, debt can take many forms. On a day-to-day basis, inventory is usually purchased on credit from suppliers, resulting in accounts payable. Macy's, for example, owed $5.3 billion to suppliers when it declared bankruptcy. Short-term financial needs to increase inventories for seasonal sales are often met by signing notes payable with banks and other financial institutions. Money needed for expansion or making long-term investments usually results in long-term debt such as mortgages payable. At the time of its bankruptcy filing, Macy's was weighed down by $3.4 billion in long-term debt.

[1] Adapted from "Macy's Second Chance," *USA Today,* February 3, 1992, p. B1.

liabilities *obligations measurable in monetary terms that represent amounts owed to creditors, governments, employees, and other parties*

In this chapter, we will discuss the accounting for various types of **liabilities.** Our focus will be on accounting procedures, but you should realize that learning to properly manage debt is one of the most important lessons you can learn.

As you will recall from Chapter 2, a liability is an obligation of an enterprise that is measurable in monetary terms. Some liabilities represent amounts owed to creditors, such as suppliers and banks, whereas others reflect obligations to other parties, such as government agencies and employees. All recorded liabilities represent obligations that arose from past transactions or events and will be settled by a future transfer of cash or other resources. Liabilities appear on the balance sheet as one of two major sources of assets. Liabilities represent a company's obligations to creditors; owners' equity represents owners' contributed capital and retained earnings, which are residual claims on assets after obligations to creditors have been satisfied.

A typical balance sheet includes two categories of liabilities: current liabilities, which are expected to be paid or satisfied within one year, and long-term liabilities, which cover periods longer than one year. In this chapter, we first discuss current (short-term) liabilities; then we describe long-term liabilities. Bonds payable, a particularly complex long-term liability, will be covered separately in Chapter 11.

CURRENT LIABILITIES

Objective 1
Understand the nature of current liabilities and how to account for them.

current liabilities *debts and other obligations that will be paid in cash or satisfied with other assets or services within one year*

Current liabilities are debts and other obligations that can reasonably be expected to be paid in cash or satisfied with other assets or services within one year.

In this chapter, we will discuss the following types of current liabilities: (1) short-term obligations to creditors, (2) payroll liabilities, (3) tax liabilities, and (4) obligations to provide goods or services. Examples of obligations to creditors include accounts payable to suppliers and notes payable to banks. Examples of payroll liabilities include salaries and wages payable and payroll taxes payable. Examples of tax liabilities (in addition to payroll taxes) include sales taxes, property taxes, and income taxes. Obligations to provide goods or services include unearned revenues (advance payments from customers) and liabilities under warranty agreements.

Current liabilities are generally valued at the amount of money needed to pay the obligation or at the fair market value of the goods or services to be delivered. Most current liabilities have preestablished values; a few, such as liabilities to honor warranty contracts, involve estimated amounts.

Short-Term Obligations to Creditors

Obligations that arise from business transactions are the most common current liabilities. They reflect the day-to-day operating activities of a business. For example, a retail shoe store will purchase its shoe inventory on credit, creating an account payable with each purchase. Use of credit allows the company time to accumulate enough cash inflow from sales to pay for the shoes. If all purchases had to be paid for on receipt of the merchandise, the company might have to limit its inventory and, hence, lose sales because of an inadequate inventory of shoes. In this section, we will discuss accounts payable, notes payable, and the current portion of long-term debt.

Chapter 10 *Liabilities*

account payable *an amount owed to a supplier for goods or services purchased on credit; payment is due within a short time period, usually 30 days or less*

ACCOUNTS PAYABLE. An account payable is a short-term obligation to a supplier for goods or services purchased on credit. Accounts payable (sometimes referred to as *trade payables*) represent informal credit arrangements with suppliers and frequently involve an ongoing relationship between the buyer and seller. Amounts owed on account are due within a short period of time, usually 30 days or less, and normally do not involve any interest charges if paid by the due date.

The accounting for accounts payable is fairly simple: Accounts Payable is increased, or credited, when inventory, supplies, or other items are purchased on credit, and decreased, or debited, when cash is paid to vendors. For example:

```
1994
Sept. 1   Inventory (or Purchases)..........................  1,500
             Accounts Payable..............................          1,500
          Purchased inventory on account.

Nov. 1    Accounts Payable ................................  1,500
             Cash..........................................          1,500
          Paid for inventory purchased September 1, 1994.
```

These recorded transactions are posted to Accounts Payable in the General Ledger, which is usually supported by an individual account for each creditor. The total of all the individual creditors' account balances must equal the balance in Accounts Payable in the General Ledger.

Creditors expect those who owe accounts payable to pay within a reasonable time period, such as within 30 days, and often encourage an even earlier payment by granting a discount if obligations are paid within a specified period. For example, a common set of payment terms on an account payable might be 2/10, net 30, which means that the debtor gets a discount of 2% if payment is made within 10 days and that the debtor is required to pay the full amount by the end of 30 days. For the purchase of inventory described here, if the purchaser decided to pay the account payable by the 10th day to take advantage of a 2% discount, the entry on September 11, 1994 would have been:

```
1994
Sept. 11  Accounts Payable .................................  1,500
             Cash..........................................          1,470
             Inventory*....................................             30
          Paid for inventory purchased September 1 within 10-day discount period
          ($1,500 × 2% = $30 discount).
```
*Assumes perpetual inventory method; with periodic method, Purchase Discounts would be credited.

A savings of $30 on a $1,500 order might not seem to be of significant benefit to the debtor, but in most cases, waiting to pay at the end of 30 days would constitute a high rate of interest to the debtor. To illustrate, if the debtor does not take the 2% discount, the entity is paying 2% for the use of

$1,500 for an additional 20 days (30 days − 10 days). A rate of 2% for the use of money for 20 days is equivalent to an annual interest rate of 36.5% (365 days/20 days = 18.25 times; 2% × 18.25 times = 36.5%). Most enterprises would not think of paying 36% interest per year on a loan, yet discounts are sometimes not taken because of carelessness, shortages of cash, or not understanding the cost of delaying payment. Thus, even though accounts payable do not stipulate an interest charge, the debtor is paying the equivalent of an interest charge if the discount is not taken.

NOTES PAYABLE. A **note payable** differs from an account payable in that it represents a formal written promise to pay a certain amount of money on or before a specified future date. Since the term of a note payable is usually longer than for an account payable, the provisions of a note usually specify that interest, in addition to the face value of the note, will be paid at the end of the note term. If a note is short term, that is, if the business signs a note in order to borrow money from a bank or other financial institution for less than a year, it is considered to be a current liability. If a note has a term that extends beyond one year, it is classified as a long-term liability. When the remaining life of a long-term note becomes one year or less, the note falls into the short-term category and is reclassified on the balance sheet as a current liability.

When a note stipulates that interest is to be paid, the amount of interest is computed in the same way it is for notes receivable:

> **note payable** *a debt owed to a creditor, evidenced by an unconditional written promise to pay a sum of money on or before a specified future date, including a charge for interest*

principal × interest rate × time (in terms of a year) = interest

For example, if Farr Company borrows $2,000 from the First Security Bank on May 1, 1994, for 2 months at 12 percent interest, the calculation would be:

$2,000 × 0.12 × 2/12 = $40

The entries to record Farr's borrowing of $2,000 and repayment 2 months later would be:

```
1994
May 1    Cash..................................................  2,000
              Notes Payable.....................................          2,000
         Borrowed $2,000 from First Security Bank for two months at a 12% annual rate of
         interest.

July 1   Notes Payable ........................................  2,000
         Interest Expense ......................................     40
              Cash..............................................          2,040
         Repaid a $2,000, 12% note to First Security Bank with interest.
```

If the note had specified that it was due in 60 days rather than in two months, the interest would have been computed as follows: $2,000 × 12% × 60/365 = $39.45. The $39.45 would be substituted for the $40 in the entry, and the cash paid would have been $2,039.45.

In the previous example, Farr Company borrowed money in 1994 and repaid it in the same year. Assume now that Farr borrowed the money on

December 1, 1994, and will repay it in 60 days from that date, which would be January 30, 1995. Further assume that the Farr Company closes its books and prepares its financial statements on December 31 of each year. When a note is outstanding at the end of an accounting period, the amount of interest that has accumulated or *accrued* as of the end of the period is recognized in the adjusting process. Since the company has used the $2,000 for the month of December 1994, it has incurred 30 days of interest which will not be paid until it is due on January 30, 1995. Therefore, to properly reflect its accrued interest expense and interest liability on its financial statements, Farr must make the following adjusting entry on December 31, 1994:

```
1994
Dec. 31   Interest Expense....................................   19.73
              Interest Payable ...............................           19.73
          To record accrued interest for 30 days on a 12% note due to the First Security
          Bank on January 30, 1995 ($2,000 × 12% × 30/365 = $19.73).
```

The account Interest Payable will be classified as a current liability on the balance sheet of Farr Company.

Sometimes a company borrowing money will sign a *noninterest-bearing note*. A noninterest-bearing note has no interest specified on its face, but there is an effective interest charge because the lender sets the face value of the note at a higher amount than the actual cash loaned. The difference between the cash loaned and the amount to be repaid at maturity constitutes the interest on the note. Thus, the real difference between a note with interest specified on its face and a noninterest-bearing note is the form in which they are written, not the substance of the transaction. The business documents that support a noninterest-bearing note would normally indicate the effective rate of interest on the contract to meet the truth-in-lending requirements. Nevertheless, the face of the note would not indicate an interest rate.

As an example of this type of note, assume that Jorgensen Company signs a 3-month, $1,000 note with the Crescent Life Insurance Company. Further assume that the insurance company actually lends Jorgensen Company $960 with the note specifying that Jorgensen will pay $1,000 at maturity. The entries for this loan are:

```
Upon Signing:
Cash ....................................................................    960
Discount on Note Payable ...........................................     40
    Note Payable .....................................................           1,000
Borrowed $960 from Crescent Life Insurance Company, signing a 3-month, noninterest-
bearing note for $1,000.

At Maturity:
Interest Expense........................................................     40
Note Payable ..........................................................   1,000
    Cash .............................................................           1,000
    Discount on Note Payable.......................................              40
Paid $1,000, 3-month, noninterest-bearing note to Crescent Life Insurance Company.
```

The Discount on Notes Payable is a contra-liability account that is subtracted from Notes Payable on the balance sheet. As indicated by the title of the contra account, noninterest-bearing notes are sometimes called discounted notes. In this example, a naive borrower might assume that the rate of interest on the $1,000 note is 16 percent ($1,000 × .016 × 3/12 = $40). In fact, the effective annual rate of interest is 16.67 percent ($40/$960 = 4.167% per quarter × 4 quarters = 16.67%) because Jorgensen Company borrowed and had the use of only $960, not the full $1,000, during the three months. Under the present truth-in-lending laws, the effective interest rate would need to be spelled out to the borrower.

THE CURRENT PORTION OF LONG-TERM DEBT. If a portion of a long-term debt (a note payable or mortgage payable, for example) is due within the coming year and is to be paid with cash or other current assets, that amount is considered current and must be classified as a current liability (called the *current portion of long-term debt* or *current maturities of long-term debt*). Transferring the liability from the long-term category to the short-term category does not affect the recording or accounting for the debt. It merely changes the classification on the balance sheet to a current liability from a long-term liability.

Payroll Liabilities

Accounting for salaries and related payroll taxes is somewhat more complex than accounting for other current liabilities. This is primarily because every business is legally required to withhold certain taxes from employees' salaries and wages.

Very few people receive their full salary as take-home pay. For example, an employee who earns $30,000 a year probably takes home between $20,000 and $25,000. The balance is withheld by the employer to pay the employee's federal and state income taxes, **social security (FICA) taxes,** and any voluntary or contractual withholdings that the employee has authorized (such as union dues, medical insurance premiums, and charitable contributions). Thus, the accounting entry to record the liability for an employee's monthly salary (computed as one-twelfth of $30,000) might be:

> **social security (FICA) taxes** *Federal Insurance Contributions Act taxes imposed on employee and employer; used mainly to provide retirement benefits*

Salary and Wages Expense	2,500	
FICA Taxes Payable, Mary Perrico		167
State Withholding Taxes Payable		200
Federal Withholding Taxes Payable		400
Union Dues Payable		50
Salary and Wages Payable		1,683
To record Mary Perrico's salary for July.		

All the credit amounts (which are arbitrary in this example) are liabilities that must be paid by the employer to the federal and state governments, the union, and the employee. It should be noted that these withholdings do not represent an additional expense to the employer since they are a component of the total salary and wage expense. The employer merely serves as an agent for the governments and the union for collecting and paying these withheld amounts.

In addition to serving as agents for the government by remitting employees' income and FICA taxes, companies must also pay certain payroll-related taxes, such as the employer's portion of the FICA tax (an amount equal to the employee's portion) and state and federal unemployment taxes. The payroll-related taxes paid by employers are expenses to the company and are included in operating expenses on the income statement. An entry to record the company's share of payroll taxes relating to Mary Perrico's employment (again using arbitrary amounts) would be:

Payroll Tax Expense	255	
FICA Taxes Payable, Employer		167
Federal Unemployment Taxes Payable		18
State Unemployment Taxes Payable		70

To record employer payroll tax liabilities associated with Mary Perrico for July.

The eight different liabilities recorded in the preceding two entries for payroll would be eliminated as payments are made. The entries to account for the payments would be:

FICA Taxes Payable	334	
Federal Withholding Taxes Payable	400	
Federal Unemployment Taxes Payable	18	
Cash		752

Paid July withholdings and payroll taxes to federal government.

State Withholding Taxes Payable	200	
State Unemployment Taxes Payable	70	
Cash		270

Paid July withholdings and payroll taxes to state government.

Union Dues Payable	50	
Cash		50

Paid July union dues for Mary Perrico.

Salary and Wages Payable	1,683	
Cash		1,683

Paid July salary to Mary Perrico.

As these entries show, four checks are written for payroll-related expenses: one to the federal government, one to the state, one to the union, and one to the employee.

One further point about salaries and wages should be noted. The period of time covered by the payroll may not coincide with the last day of the year for financial reporting. Thus, if the reporting year ends on a Wednesday, December 31, and the salaries and wages for that week will be paid Monday, January 5 of the following year, then the company must show the salaries and wages earned from Monday through Wednesday (December 29, 30, and 31) as a liability on the December 31 balance sheet. To accomplish this, the company would record an end-of-year adjusting entry to record the salaries and wages earned for those three days.

Tax Liabilities

In addition to the payroll taxes described in the previous section, companies are responsible for other taxes to federal, state, and local governments, including sales taxes, property taxes, and income taxes. The accounting for each of these types of taxes is described next.

SALES TAXES PAYABLE. Most states and some cities charge a sales tax on retail transactions. The taxes are paid by customers to the seller, who in turn forwards them to the state or city. Taxes collected from customers represent a current liability until remitted to the appropriate governmental agency. For example, assume that a sporting goods store in Denver prices a pair of skis at $200 and that the state of Colorado charges a 5 percent sales tax. When the store sells the skis, it collects $210 and records the transaction as follows:

Cash	210	
Sales Revenue		200
Sales Tax Payable		10
Sold a pair of skis for $200. Collected $210, including 5% sales tax.		

sales tax payable money collected from customers for sales taxes, which must be remitted to local governments and other taxing authorities

The sales revenue is properly recorded at $200, and the $10 is recorded as **Sales Tax Payable,** a liability. Then, on a regular basis, a sales tax return is completed and filed with the state tax commission, and all sales taxes collected are paid to the state. Note that the collection of the sales tax from customers creates a liability to the state but does not result in the recognition of revenue when collected or an expense when paid to the state. The company collects the tax as an agent of the state and reflects a liability only until the collected amount is remitted to the state.

PROPERTY TAXES PAYABLE. Property taxes are usually assessed by county or city governments. The period covered by the assessment of property taxes is usually from July 1 of one year to June 30 of the next year. If a property tax payer is on a calendar-year financial reporting basis (or on a fiscal year basis ending on a day other than June 30), the property tax assessment year and the company's financial reporting year will not coincide. Therefore, when the company prepares its financial statements at calendar-year end, it must report a property tax liability for taxes owed for the first portion of the assessment year. To illustrate, assume that Yokum Company pays its property taxes of $3,600 on June 30, 1994, for the period July 1, 1993 to June 30, 1994. If the company reports on a calendar-year basis, the estimated property tax expense and liability must be recorded for the 6 months beginning July 1, 1993. The adjusting entry at December 31, 1993, would be:

1993			
Dec. 31	Property Tax Expense	1,800	
	Property Taxes Payable		1,800
	To record property tax expense and liability for 6 months.		

The property taxes payable account balance of $1,800 would be shown on Yokum's balance sheet at December 31, 1993, as a current liability since the taxes for the 1993–1994 assessment year are due on June 30, 1994.

Then, on June 30, 1994, property tax expense would be recognized for the period January 1, 1994–June 30, 1994 and the entire year's tax assessment would be paid, as reflected in the following entries:

1994			
June 30	Property Tax Expense	1,800	
	Property Taxes Payable		1,800
	To record property tax expense and liability for the property assessment period January 1–June 30, 1994.		
June 30	Property Taxes Payable	3,600	
	Cash		3,600
	Paid property taxes for the property assessment period July 1, 1993 to June 30, 1994.		

INCOME TAXES PAYABLE. Another current liability reflected on a company's balance sheet is **Income Taxes Payable**. This liability reflects the amount expected to be paid to the federal and state governments based on the income before taxes reported on the current year's income statement. To illustrate, assume that Salem Company's 1994 income before taxes was computed at $186,000 and that the company's effective tax rate for the reporting year (for both federal and state income taxes) will be 40%. Based on these facts, an adjusting entry would be prepared at year-end showing a tax liability of $74,400:

income taxes payable *the amount expected to be paid to the federal and state governments based on the income before taxes reported on the income statement*

1994			
Dec. 31	Income Tax Expense	74,400	
	Income Taxes Payable		74,400
	To record the income tax expense and tax liability on $186,000 of income before taxes for the year 1994 using a 40% effective tax rate.		

As shown on the partial income statement that follows, the income tax expense would be subtracted from income before taxes to arrive at net income of $111,600:

Income before income taxes	$186,000
Income taxes	74,400
Net income	$111,600

The Income Taxes Payable account would be shown on the year-end balance sheet as a current liability. In addition to the income taxes payable for the current year, many companies report liabilities for deferred income taxes payable. The concept of deferred taxes is discussed briefly later in this chapter.

Obligations to Provide Goods or Services

unearned revenues
amounts received before they have been earned

The most common obligations to deliver goods or perform services arise when customers pay in advance (the amounts are called **unearned revenues**) and when a company issues warranties or guarantees on its products. With unearned revenues, the company has an obligation to ship a product or perform a service. If the goods are not shipped or the service is not performed, the amount of cash received in advance must be repaid to the customer. With warranties, the company has an obligation to repair or replace defective merchandise sold.

To illustrate advance payments by customers, we assume that MacBeth Company pays Berry Company $300 for goods to be shipped in the future. Berry thus has a liability until the time of shipment. The entry to record this advance from MacBeth would be:

```
Cash ..................................................... 300
    Unearned Sales Revenue ............................         300
Received an advance from MacBeth Company.
```

When the goods are shipped, revenue is earned, and Berry's liability is eliminated. The entry to eliminate this liability would be:

```
Unearned Sales Revenue .................................. 300
    Sales Revenue ......................................         300
To recognize revenue on the shipment of goods to MacBeth Company.
```

The performance liability created when a firm offers a warranty or guarantee involves a similar recording process. For example, some major automobile manufacturers offer a 36,000-mile, 36-month warranty on new cars. Because warranties create obligations to perform repair services free of charge, they must be recognized as current liabilities at the time of sale. Obviously, the amount of a warranty liability can only be estimated since the actual repair expenditures will not be known until the services have been performed. Generally accepted accounting principles require that a period's expenses be matched with its revenues, so it is better to make a timely, although inexact, estimate than to record no expense at all. A typical warranty liability entry would be:

```
Warranty Expense ........................................ 15,000
    Estimated Liability for Warranties .................         15,000
Estimated warranty costs on 1994 sales.
```

The credit entry, Estimated Liability for Warranties, is a current liability. When actual expenses are incurred in servicing the warranties, the liability is eliminated with the type of entry shown at the top of the next page.

Chapter 10 *Liabilities* 415

Estimated Liability for Warranties	15,000	
Wages Payable (to service employees)		4,000
Supplies		11,000
Paid service costs of the warranties.		

This entry shows that supplies and labor were required to honor the warranty agreements. Note that if the entire amount of Estimated Liability for Warranties is not used, a lower estimate is made in a subsequent period; if Estimated Liability for Warranties is inadequate, a higher estimate is made.

> **To Summarize** *Current liabilities are debts or other obligations that can reasonably be expected to be paid or satisfied within one year. The four categories of current liabilities are (1) short-term obligations to creditors, such as accounts payable, notes payable, and the current portion of long-term debt; (2) payroll liabilities, such as salaries and wages and unemployment and FICA taxes; (3) other tax liabilities, such as sales taxes, property taxes, and income taxes; and (4) obligations to provide goods and services, such as unearned revenues for cash received in advance and estimated liabilities under warranties. In most cases, current liabilities are recorded and paid within one financial reporting year. However, if the liability exists at year-end, but has not been paid or recognized, an adjusting entry is necessary to record the expense and related liability. Typical liabilities that are recognized through adjusting entries include salaries and wages earned but not yet paid, property taxes assessed but not due to be paid until the following year, and income tax expenses that are determined at year-end based on reported income before taxes.*

LONG-TERM LIABILITIES

long-term liabilities *debts or other obligations that will not be paid within 1 year*

Debts or other obligations that will not be paid or otherwise satisfied within 1 year are classified on the balance sheet as **long-term liabilities.** The most common long-term liabilities are notes payable, bonds payable, mortgages payable, deferred income taxes payable, lease obligations, and pensions. All these are considered here, except bonds payable, which are discussed in Chapter 11.

Measuring Long-Term Liabilities

Objective 2
Use present value concepts in measuring long-term liabilities.

Conceptually, the amount of any liability at a particular time is the cash that would be required to pay the liability in full today. Since money has a time value, most people are willing to accept less money today than they would if it were paid in the future. Therefore, with the exception of Accounts Payable, liabilities to be paid in the future usually involve interest.

Earlier in the chapter, we illustrated the recording of interest on short-term notes payable. The examples involved a single payment of both principal (the amount borrowed) and interest on the maturity date of the note. Accounting for long-term obligations is more complex because usually payments of interest, or in some cases principal and interest, are made periodically over the period in which the liability is outstanding. Further, in some cases the amount of the liability in a noncash transaction may not be readily apparent. An example would be issuing a noninterest-bearing note to purchase equipment. Measurement and recording of these liabilities is based on the time value of money concept.

PRESENT VALUE AND FUTURE VALUE CONCEPTS. The concepts of present value and future value are used to measure the effect of time on the value of money. The **present value of $1** is the value today of $1 to be received or paid in the future, given a specified interest rate. Obviously, money that will be received in the future cannot be invested now to earn interest, so it is worth less than money that is now on hand, which can earn interest. To determine the value today of money to be received in the future, we must "discount" the future amount (reduce the amount to its present value) by an appropriate interest rate. For example, if money can earn 10% per year, $100 to be received 1 year from now is approximately equal to $90.91 received today.

Putting it another way, if $90.91 were invested today in an account that earned 10 percent interest for one year, the interest earned would be $9.09 ($90.91 × 10 percent × 1 year = $9.09). The sum of the $90.91 principal plus $9.09 interest would equal $100 at the end of one year. Thus, the present value of $100 to be received (or paid) in one year with 10 percent interest is $90.91. This present value relationship can be diagrammed as follows:

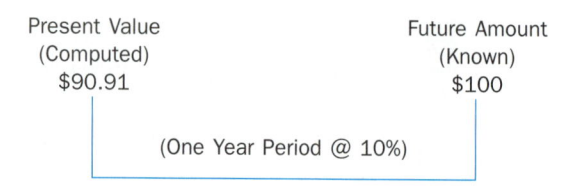

> **present value of $1** *the value today of $1 to be received or paid at some future date, given a specified interest rate*

```
Present Value              Future Amount
(Computed)                 (Known)
$90.91                     $100
     └──── (One Year Period @ 10%) ────┘
```

$90.91 is the present value of the $100 future amount

The relationships in this diagram can be described in two ways. We have just looked at the relationship by recognizing that the $90.91 is the present value of $100 to be received one year from now when interest is 10 percent. In this example, the $100 to be received one year from now is known, and the present value of $90.91 must be computed. We are computing a present value amount from a known future value amount.

Another way to look at the relationship is on a future value basis. Future values apply when the amount today ($90.91) is known, and the future amount must be calculated. Future values are exactly the opposite of present values. Thinking in terms of future values, $100 is the future amount we can expect to receive in one year, given a present known amount of $90.91 when the interest rate is 10 percent. We can diagram this relationship as follows:

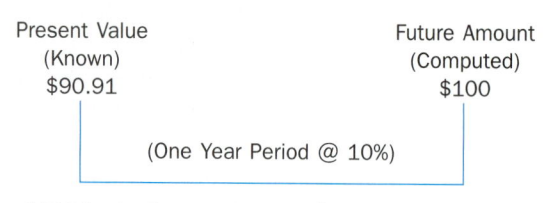

```
Present Value              Future Amount
(Known)                    (Computed)
$90.91                     $100
     └──── (One Year Period @ 10%) ────┘
```

$100 is the future value of a $90.91 present value

Present and future values can be calculated using formulas. However, if more than one period is involved, the calculations become rather complicated. Therefore, it is more convenient to use either a present value table or calculator that gives the present value of $1 for various numbers of periods and interest rates (see Table I, page 446) or a future value table that gives the future value of $1 for various numbers of periods and interest rates (see Table III, page 448). We will illustrate the use of both a present value table and a future value table.

Present Value Table. To use a present value table, you simply locate the appropriate number of periods in the leftmost column and the interest rate in the row at the top of the table. The intersection of the row and column is the factor representing the present value of $1 for the number of periods and the relevant interest rate. To find the present value of an amount other than $1, multiply the factor in the table by that amount.

To illustrate the use of a present value table (Table I) to find the present value of a known future amount, assume that $10,000 is to be paid 4 years from today when the interest rate is 10 percent. What is the present value of that $10,000 payment? The present value of $1 received or paid in four periods at 10 percent is 0.6830. Multiplying this factor by $10,000 results in a present value of $6,830, the amount that could be paid today to satisfy the obligation that is due four years from now. As indicated, this procedure is sometimes referred to as "discounting." Thus, we say that $10,000 discounted for four periods at 10 percent is $6,830. Stated another way, if $6,830 were invested today in an account that paid 10 percent interest, in four years, the balance in that account would be $10,000.

Future Value Table. To find the future value of an amount that is known today, you use a future value table. When using a future value table, you simply locate the appropriate number of periods in the leftmost column and the interest rate in the row at the top of the table. The intersection of the row and column is the factor representing the future value of $1 for the number of periods and the relevant interest rate. To find the future value of an amount other than $1, multiply the factor in the table by that amount.

To illustrate the use of a future value table (Table III), we will use the same information that was presented before, except that we will now assume that the present value of $6,830 is known, not the future amount of $10,000. Assume that we have a savings account with a current balance of $6,830 that earns interest of 10 percent. What will be the balance in that account in four years? The future value of $1 in four years at 10 percent is 1.4641. Multiplying this factor by the current value of $6,830 results in a future value of $10,000. When computing future values, we often use the term *compounding* to mean the frequency with which interest is added to the principal. Thus, we say that interest of 10 percent has been compounded once a year (annually) to arrive at a future value at the end of four years of $10,000. If the interest were added more or less frequently than once a year, the future amount would be different.

compounding period *the period of time for which interest is computed*

The preceding example assumed an annual **compounding period** for interest. If the 10 percent interest had been compounded semiannually (twice a year) for four years, the calculation would have involved using a 5% (one half of the 10%) rate for 8 (4 years times 2 periods per year) periods instead of 10% for four periods. The present value (Table I) factor for 8 periods at 5% interest is .6768. Thus, the present value of $10,000 to be received or paid in four years is $6,768 ($10,000 × .6768) if interest is compounded semiannually. Likewise, if semiannual compounding were used to determine the future value of $6,768 in four years at 5 percent, the future value factor from Table III would be 1.4775. Accordingly, the future amount at the end of 8 periods would be $10,000 ($6,768 × 1.4775). Note that the present value ($6,768) is lower with semiannual compounding than with annual compounding ($6,830). The more frequently that interest is compounded, the greater the total amount of interest deducted (in computing present values) or added (in computing future values).

Since interest may also be compounded quarterly, monthly, or for some other period, you should learn the relationship of interest to the compounding period. Semiannual interest means that you double the interest periods and halve the annual interest rate; with quarterly interest you quadruple the periods and take one-fourth of the annual interest rate. The formula for interest rate is:

$$\frac{\text{yearly interest rate}}{\text{compounding periods per year}} = \frac{\text{interest rate per}}{\text{compounding period}}$$

The number of interest periods is simply the number of periods per year times the number of years.

THE PRESENT VALUE OF AN ANNUITY. In discussing present values and future values, we have assumed only a single present value or future value with one of the amounts known and the other to be computed. With liabilities, we generally know the future amount that must be paid and would like to compute the present value of that future payment. Since this chapter focuses on liabilities, we will concentrate on present value calculations. Future value calculations will be discussed more fully in later chapters.

Many long-term liabilities involve a series of payments rather than one lump-sum payment. For example, a company might purchase equipment under an installment agreement requiring payments of $5,000 each year for five years. Determining the value today (present value) of a series of equally spaced, equal-amount payments (called an **annuity**) is more complicated than determining the present value of a single future payment. If you were to try to calculate the **present value of an annuity** by hand, you would have to discount the first payment for 1 period, the second payment for 2 periods, and so on, and then add all the present values together. Because such calculations are time-consuming, a table is generally used (see Table II, page 447). The factors in the table are the sums of the individual present values of all future payments. Based on the present value of an annuity of $1, the table provides factors for various interest rates and periods.

To illustrate the use of a present value of an annuity table (Table II), we will assume that $10,000 is to be paid at the end of each of the next 10 years. If the interest rate is 12% compounded annually, Table II shows a present value factor of 5.6502. This factor means that the present value of $1 paid each year for 10 years discounted at 12 percent is approximately $5.65. Multiplying that factor by the annual payment (annuity) of $10,000, we find that the present value of the 10 payments is $56,502 ($10,000 × 5.6502). This is the amount (present value) that could be paid today to satisfy the obligation if interest is 12%.

annuity a series of equal amounts to be received or paid at the end of equal time intervals

present value of an annuity the value today of a series of equally spaced, equal-amount payments to be made or received in the future given a specified interest rate

Chapter 10 *Liabilities*

> **To Summarize** *Long-term liabilities are debts or other obligations that will not be paid or satisfied within one year. Present value concepts, which equate the value of money received or paid in different periods, are used to measure long-term liabilities. Although present values can be computed using formulas, it is usually more convenient to use a table, such as Table I or II on pages 446–447. If a future lump-sum payment is involved, Table I can be used to determine the present value. Table II is used to compute the present value of an annuity, which is a series of equally spaced, equal-amount payments. In calculating present values, you must consider the compounding period and the interest rate. For other than annual payments, the number of periods is the number of periods per year times the number of years; the interest rate is the annual rate divided by the number of periods per year.*

Accounting for Long-Term Liabilities

Objective 3
Account for long-term liabilities, including notes payable, mortgages payable, and lease obligations.

Now that we have explained how present value concepts are applied in measuring long-term liabilities, we are ready to discuss the accounting for those liabilities. In this section, we will discuss the recording of long-term debt, including notes payable, mortgages payable, and obligations under capital leases. Long-term notes payable, like short-term notes payable, may be written in either an interest-bearing or noninterest-bearing form. We will illustrate the accounting for each type of note, beginning with the more common interest-bearing form.

INTEREST-BEARING NOTES. To illustrate the accounting for a long-term interest-bearing note payable, assume that on January 1, 1993, Giraffe Company borrowed $10,000 from City Bank for 3 years at 10 percent interest. Assume also that interest is payable annually on December 31. The entries to account for the note would be:

```
1993
Jan. 1    Cash ............................................. 10,000
             Note Payable ...............................            10,000
          Borrowed $10,000 from City Bank for 3 years.

Dec. 31   Interest Expense............................. 1,000
             Cash ..........................................             1,000
          Made first annual interest payment on City Bank note ($10,000 × 0.10).

1994
Dec. 31   Interest Expense............................. 1,000
             Cash ..........................................             1,000
          Made second annual interest payment on City Bank note ($10,000 × 0.10).

1995
Dec. 31   Interest Expense.............................  1,000
          Note Payable ................................. 10,000
             Cash ..........................................            11,000
          Made final interest payment ($10,000 × 0.10) and repaid principal on City Bank note.
```

When a note is issued for cash, present value computations are not necessary because the amount of cash received is always equal to the present value. However, to show that the present value of the note in the example is $10,000, we can compute the present value as shown here:

Present value of interest payments:		
Amount of each interest payment	$ 1,000	
Table II factor for 3 periods at 10%	×2.4869	
Present value of annuity		$ 2,487
Present value of principal payment:		
Amount of principal payment	$10,000	
Table I factor for 3 periods at 10%	×0.7513	
Present value of lump-sum payment		7,513
Present value of interest and principal		$10,000

The total present value is the sum of the present values of the interest payments (an annuity) and the lump-sum principal payment due in three years.

NONINTEREST-BEARING NOTES. To illustrate the accounting for a noninterest-bearing note, assume that on January 1, 1993, Claven Company purchased a machine for $10,000 from Peterson Company. A note is written for the full amount ($10,000) to be paid in 3 years. Although the loan appears to be interest free, can we really say the liability is $10,000? Given the value of money over time, it is highly unlikely that Peterson or any other company would extend a 3-year interest-free loan. The $10,000 must therefore include a finance charge, and the real liability (the cash price for which the machine could have been purchased today) must be less than $10,000. If we assume that the market rate of interest is 10 percent, with annual compounding, then the $10,000 should be discounted to a present value of $7,513 ($10,000 × 0.7513; see Table I, 3 periods at 10 percent). The purchase would be recorded as follows:

1993			
Jan. 1	Machine	7,513	
	Discount on Note Payable	2,487	
	Note Payable		10,000
	Purchased machine by issuing a 3-year, noninterest-bearing $10,000 note.		

The discount represents the interest included in the face amount of the note and is a contra-liability account. As such, it must be subtracted from Notes Payable on the balance sheet and amortized, or written off, as interest expense over the life of the loan. Assuming Claven Company reports on a calendar-year basis, the journal entries to recognize the interest expense and discount amortization for the note would be:

```
1993
Dec. 31   Interest Expense..........................................    751
              Discount on Note Payable.........................              751
          To recognize the first year's interest expense on the 3-year, $10,000 note
          ($7,513 × 0.10 ≈ $751).

1994
Dec. 31   Interest Expense..........................................    826
              Discount on Note Payable.........................              826
          To recognize the second year's interest expense on the 3-year, $10,000 note
          ($7,513 + $751 = $8,264; $8,264 × 0.10 ≈ $826).

1995
Dec. 31   Interest Expense..........................................    910
              Discount on Note Payable.........................              910
          To recognize the third year's interest expense on the 3-year, $10,000 note.
          ($7,513 + $751 + $826 = $9,090; $9,090 × 0.10 = $909, adjusted for $1
          rounding difference to write off remaining discount of $910).
```

Each year, the discount is amortized by the amount of that year's interest expense, until at the end of 3 years, the Discount on Note Payable account has a zero balance ($2,487 − $751 − $826 − $910). The interest expense is calculated by multiplying the effective rate of interest, 10 percent, by the increasing loan balance (the difference between the Note Payable and the Discount on Note Payable accounts). The amortization of the discount over the 3-year period is summarized as follows:

Date	Interest Expense and Discount Amortization	Loan Balance
Beginning balance		$ 7,513
December 31, 1993	(0.10 × $7,513) ≈ $751	8,264
December 31, 1994	(0.10 × 8,264) ≈ 826	9,090
December 31, 1995	(0.10 × 9,090) ≈ 910	10,000

The final journal entry will be to record the payment of the note, as follows:

```
1995
Dec. 31   Note Payable.............................................. 10,000
              Cash ............................................................        10,000
          Paid 3-year, noninterest-bearing $10,000 note at maturity.
```

Although this type of note may be called noninterest-bearing, it is really interest-bearing because when the note is issued, the present value is less than the face value.

> **To Summarize** *Like short-term notes, a long-term note payable may be written in either an interest-bearing or noninterest-bearing form. Regardless of its form, a note payable is recorded at the present value of all future interest and principal payments. Interest-bearing notes are recorded at face value; whereas noninterest-bearing notes must be discounted to their present value because the face amount includes both principal and interest. With noninterest-bearing notes, Note Payable is credited for the face value of the note, and the discount is recorded in a contra-liability account, Discount on Note Payable. The discount is amortized by the amount of interest expense each period, determined by applying a constant interest rate to the loan balance.*

MORTGAGES PAYABLE. A **mortgage payable** is similar to a note payable in that it is a written promise to pay a stated sum of money at one or more specified future dates. It is different from a note in the way it is applied. Whereas money borrowed with a note can often be used for *any* business purpose, mortgage money is usually related to a specific asset, typically real estate. Assets purchased with a mortgage are usually pledged as security or collateral on the loan. For individuals, home mortgages are common, and for companies, plant mortgages are frequent. In either case, mortgages generally require periodic (usually monthly) payments of principal plus interest.

mortgage payable *a written promise to pay a stated amount of money at one or more specified future dates; a mortgage is secured by the pledging of certain assets—usually real estate—as collateral*

To illustrate the accounting for a mortgage, we will assume that McGiven Automobile Company borrows $100,000 on January 1 to purchase a new showroom and signs a mortgage agreement pledging the showroom as collateral on the loan. If the mortgage is at 8 percent for 30 years, and the monthly payment is $733.76 payable on January 31, with subsequent payments due at the end of each month thereafter, the entries to record the acquisition of the mortgage and the first monthly payment will be:

```
Cash .....................................................  100,000
    Mortgage Payable ....................................             100,000
Borrowed $100,000 to purchase the automobile showroom.

Mortgage Payable ..........................................   67.09
Interest Expense ..........................................  666.67
    Cash .................................................              733.76
Made first month's mortgage payment.
```

As this entry shows, only $67.09 of the $733.76 payment is applied to reducing the mortgage; the remainder is interest ($100,000 × 0.08 × 1/12). In each successive month, the amount applied to reducing the mortgage will increase slightly until, toward the end of the 30-year mortgage, almost all the payment will be for principal. A **mortgage amortization schedule** identifies how much of each mortgage payment is interest and how much is principal reduction, as shown in Exhibit 10-1. Note that during the first 20 years of McGiven's $100,000, 8 percent, 30-year mortgage, more of each mortgage payment is for interest than for principal.

mortgage amortization schedule *a schedule that shows the breakdown between interest and principal for each payment over the life of a mortgage*

Exhibit 10-1 — Mortgage Amortization Schedule ($100,000, 30-Year Mortgage at 8%)

Year	Monthly Payment	Principal Paid	Interest Paid	Outstanding Mortgage Balance
1	$733.76	$ 835	$7,970	$99,165
2	733.76	905	7,900	98,260
3	733.76	980	7,825	97,280
4	733.76	1,061	7,744	96,219
5	733.76	1,149	7,656	95,070
10	733.76	1,712	7,093	87,725
15	733.76	2,551	6,254	76,783
20	733.76	3,800	5,005	60,080
25	733.76	5,661	3,144	36,793
30	733.76	8,434	371	0

Total payments over life of mortgage: $264,154*

*$733.76 × 360 payments = $264,154.

At the end of each year, a mortgage is reported on the balance sheet in two places: (1) the principal to be paid during the next year is shown as a current liability, and (2) the balance of the mortgage payable is shown as a long-term liability. Further, any accrued interest on the mortgage is reported as a current liability, and the interest expense for the year is included with other expenses on the income statement.

> **To Summarize** *Mortgages payable are long-term liabilities that arise because companies borrow money to buy land, construct buildings, or purchase additional operating assets. Mortgages are tied to specific assets. They are amortized over a period of time and involve periodic, usually monthly, payments that include both principal and interest.*

lease *a contract that specifies the terms under which the owner of an asset (the lessor) agrees to transfer the right to use the asset to another party (the lessee)*

operating lease *a simple rental agreement*

lessee *the party that is granted the right to use property under the terms of a lease*

lessor *the owner of property that is rented (leased) to another party*

capital lease *a leasing transaction that is recorded as a purchase by the lessee*

LEASE OBLIGATIONS. As discussed in Chapter 9, a company might choose to lease rather than purchase an asset. If a lease is a simple, short-term rental agreement, called an **operating lease,** lease payments are recorded as Rent Expense by the **lessee** and as Rent Revenue by the **lessor.** However, if the terms of a lease agreement meet specific criteria (see Chapter 9, page 362), the transaction is classified as a **capital lease** and is accounted for as if the asset had been purchased with long-term debt. The lessee records the leased property as an asset and recognizes a liability to the lessor.

In Chapter 9, we focused on the recording of assets acquired under capital leases, using assumed amounts for the present value. Here we will explain how the present value of a capital lease is determined. To illustrate the measurement and recording of a capital lease, we will assume that Malone Corporation leases a mainframe computer from Macro Data, Inc. on December 31, 1993. The lease

BUSINESS ENVIRONMENT ESSAY
How Interest Rates Affect Mortgage Payments

The interest rate on a mortgage is as important as the amount of the loan in determining whether a person can afford a mortgage. This is because the amount of interest paid over an extended period of time will be at least equal to, or even two or three times, the amount of the loan. The table below shows the monthly payments on a $100,000, 25-year mortgage at interest rates from 7 to 14 percent, as well as the qualifying annual income.

To calculate monthly payments on smaller or larger mortgages, divide the amount by $100,000, then multiply that percentage by the figure in the table. For example, the monthly payment on a $60,000 mortgage at 9 percent would be $503.40 [($60,000 ÷ $100,000) × $839].

The qualifying annual income is the minimum amount a person can earn in order to afford payments at each interest rate. The Federal Home Loan Mortgage Corporation, and most lending institutions, recommend that the monthly payments not exceed 28 percent of a person's monthly gross income. If, for example, you earn $30,000 a year, you should pay no more than $700 a month on a mortgage, which would be a $100,000 mortgage at 7 percent, or $55,000 at 14 percent. For this reason, most people "shop around" for the lowest mortgage rates—and even then, many will not qualify for a loan.

$100,000, 25-Year Mortgage

Interest Rate	Monthly Payment	Total Amount Paid	Qualifying Annual Income
7%	$ 707	$212,100	$30,300
8%	772	231,600	33,084
9%	839	251,700	35,957
10%	909	272,700	38,957
11%	980	294,000	42,000
12%	1,053	315,900	45,129
13%	1,128	338,400	48,348
14%	1,204	361,200	51,600

requires annual payments of $10,000 for 10 years, with the first payment due on December 31, 1994.[2] The rate of interest applicable to the lease is 14 percent compounded annually. Assuming the lease meets criteria for a capital lease, the computer and the related liability will be recorded by Malone Corporation at the present value of the future lease payments. From Table II, on page 447, the factor for the present value of an annuity for 10 periods at 14 percent is 5.2161. This factor is multiplied by the annual lease payment to determine the present value. The entry to record the lease on Malone's books would be:

---

[2] Readers should be aware that the illustration of a capital lease presented here assumes that lease payments are made at the end of each year, with the present values based on an ordinary annuity. Usually lease payments are made at the beginning of each lease period, which requires present value calculations using the concept of an annuity in advance or "annuity due." These calculations are explained in intermediate accounting texts.

Chapter 10 *Liabilities*

```
1993
Dec. 31   Leased Computer.................................  52,161
              Lease Obligation............................           52,161
          Leased a computer from Macro Data, Inc. for $10,000 a year for 10 years
          discounted at 14% ($10,000 × 5.2161 = $52,161).
```

If Malone Corporation uses a calendar year for financial reporting, the December 31, 1993, balance sheet would report the leased asset in the property, plant, and equipment section and the lease obligation in the liabilities section.

A schedule of the computer lease payments is presented in Exhibit 10-2. Each year the Lease Obligation account balance is multiplied by 14 percent to determine the amount of interest included in each of the annual $10,000 lease payments.

The remainder is a reduction in the liability. For example, the first lease payment would be recorded as follows:

```
1994
Dec. 31   Interest Expense..................................  7,303
          Lease Obligation..................................  2,697
              Cash ........................................          10,000
          Paid annual lease payment for computer ($52,161 × 0.14 = $7,303; $10,000 −
          $7,303 = $2,697).
```

Similar entries would be made in each of the remaining 9 years of the lease, except that the principal payment (reduction in Lease Obligation) would increase while the Interest Expense would decrease. Interest decreases over the lease term because a constant rate (14 percent) is applied to a decreasing principal balance.

Although the asset and liability accounts have the same balance at the beginning of the lease term, they seldom remain the same during the lease

Exhibit 10-2 *Schedule of Computer Lease Payments*

Year	Total Payments	Interest Expense (0.14 × Lease Obligation)	Principal	Lease Obligation
				$52,161
1	$10,000	(0.14 × $52,161) = $7,303	$2,697	49,464
2	10,000	(0.14 × 49,464) = 6,925	3,075	46,389
3	10,000	(0.14 × 46,389) = 6,494	3,506	42,883
4	10,000	(0.14 × 42,883) = 6,004	3,996	38,887
5	10,000	(0.14 × 38,887) = 5,444	4,556	34,331
6	10,000	(0.14 × 34,331) = 4,806	5,194	29,137
7	10,000	(0.14 × 29,137) = 4,079	5,921	23,216
8	10,000	(0.14 × 23,216) = 3,250	6,750	16,466
9	10,000	(0.14 × 16,466) = 2,305	7,695	8,771
10	10,000	(0.14 × 8,771) = 1,229	8,771	-0-

period. The asset and the liability are accounted for separately, with the asset being depreciated using one of the methods discussed in Chapter 9.

> **To Summarize** *A lease is a contract whereby the lessee makes periodic payments to the lessor for the use of an asset. A simple short-term rental agreement, or operating lease, involves only the recording of rent expense by the lessee and rent revenue by the lessor. A capital lease is accounted for as a debt-financed purchase of the leased asset. Both the asset and liability are initially recorded by the lessee at the present value of the future lease payments discounted at the applicable interest rate. Subsequently, the asset is depreciated and the lease obligation is written off as periodic payments are made. Part of each lease payment is interest expense, computed at a constant interest rate, and the remainder is a reduction of the principal amount of the liability.*

Other Long-Term Liabilities

Objective 4

Describe the general nature of long-term liabilities for deferred taxes and pensions.

Thus far, we have discussed long-term liabilities for notes payable, mortgages, and leases. Each of these obligations is a form of long-term debt. Other long-term liabilities that you should be aware of include deferred income taxes and pensions. Because these obligations are frequently reported and often involve significant amounts, they are introduced briefly here to provide a general understanding of their nature. The accounting for deferred taxes and pensions is quite complex and is covered in more advanced accounting texts.

DEFERRED INCOME TAXES. Often, the income tax expense reported on a corporation's income statement for the year differs considerably from the amount of income taxes paid for that year to federal and state governments. These differences are temporary and relate to the timing of revenue and expense recognition. Whereas income tax expense on the income statement is obtained by accounting for revenues and expenses on the basis of generally accepted accounting principles, income taxes payable to governments are calculated on the basis of taxable income as defined by the Internal Revenue Service and by state tax laws.

Differences in measuring accounting income and taxable income can be attributed to using different methods to measure such amounts as depreciation expense, warranty expense, lease expense, and cost of goods sold. For example, companies frequently use straight-line depreciation for financial reporting purposes and an accelerated method, such as double-declining balance, for tax purposes. By deducting more depreciation expense in the early years of asset life on the tax return, taxable income is less than accounting income. As a result, the taxes payable currently are less than the tax expense computed based on accounting income. That is, a portion of the income tax expense on the income statement will be paid in future years.

deferred income taxes *an account used to record the difference between income tax expense on the income statement and income taxes payable for the year to federal and state governments*

The difference between income tax expense and the income taxes payable currently must be accounted for. An account called **Deferred Income Taxes** is used to record the difference each year. When this account has a credit balance, as is usually the case, it is reported in the liabilities section of the balance sheet and represents income taxes that have been deferred to future years. Calculating and reporting deferred taxes are complex issues involving the application of accounting standards which, at the present time, are quite controversial.

PENSION LIABILITIES. The employees of most medium-sized and large companies are covered by some kind of pension plan. A **pension plan** is a contract between a company and its employees whereby the company agrees to pay retirement benefits to employees. There are many types of pension plans, and each has its own unique features. In some cases, the company pays the entire cost of the pension plan, whereas in other cases, the employees contribute part of their earnings toward the cost of the plan. In either case, all contributions are paid to a pension fund from which benefits are paid to retired or disabled employees. Amounts paid into the fund, which usually is managed by an independent trustee, are invested in stocks, bonds, and other assets to earn income.

Estimating the company's obligations for future retirement benefits is not an easy task. It requires consideration of several factors: the life expectancy of the employees, the number of employees that will remain with the company and be eligible for pension benefits, the number of years each employee will work, retirement ages, future salary levels, pension fund earnings, and future interest rates. Generally, these estimates are made by specialists, called actuaries, who work with complex tables and formulas in deriving an estimate of future benefits. The present value of these estimated future benefits is used as the basis for determining the amount of pension liability, if any, to be reported on the company's balance sheet. The reporting of pension liabilities and other pension information is governed by a complex set of accounting standards that are beyond the scope of this text.

pension plan a contract between a company and its employees whereby the company agrees to pay benefits to employees after their retirement

CONTINGENT LIABILITIES

Objective 5
Describe the types of contingent liabilities and how they are reported.

contingent liability a potential obligation, dependent upon the occurrence of future events

In addition to actual obligations to pay cash or perform services, a company often has potential obligations to do so. These **contingent liabilities** are usually tied to the occurrence of some future event and so are paid only when that event takes place (if it does). Examples of contingent liabilities are notes receivable that have been discounted with recourse (for which the payee is obligated to pay if the maker of the note defaults), lawsuits (in which the company is obligated to pay if the lawsuit is lost), and cosigned notes (for which the cosigner is obligated to pay if the signer does not). Potential obligations that qualify as contingent liabilities can be recorded as actual liabilities, ignored, or disclosed in the notes to the financial statements, depending on the materiality of these obligations and their probability of occurrence. Generally, if payment is determined to be likely or probable, an actual liability is recorded; if payment is reasonably possible, note disclosure is necessary; and if the probability of payment is determined to be remote, the contingent liability is not disclosed in the financial statements.

There are numerous examples of events that could give rise to the question of whether or how a company should report the extent of the potential liability for damages to injured parties. These events include plant explosions, nuclear power accidents, earthquakes, tornados and hurricanes, oil spills, and health problems due to the side effects of using prescribed drugs. An assessment of the degree of liability will dictate how these events would be reported on the financial statements.

BUSINESS ENVIRONMENT ESSAY
Frequent Flier Liabilities

Obligations to creditors, such as notes and mortgages payable, are readily identifiable liabilities with definite amounts. Some obligations, however, are not so easy to identify and measure. One example is the liability for frequent flier coupons issued by airlines. In recent years, the accounting profession has challenged the way in which airlines have measured and reported frequent flier obligations. Accounting rules have been proposed that could significantly increase reported liabilities. Generally, the airline industry has disagreed with the accounting profession on how to measure the liability under their frequent flier obligation. Since the adoption of such programs in 1981, the airline industry has been accounting for these obligations using the incremental cost method.

Measuring the actual liability under the incremental cost method is quite complicated. The most often considered incremental costs are food and beverages, additional fuel, making reservations and issuing tickets, passenger liability insurance, and baggage handling. The calculations also must consider the number of unused awards, the route segments to be used by the frequent fliers, and the number of miles that will be redeemed. A survey indicated that the average incremental cost of providing free air transportation was $8 per trip.

An alternative to using the incremental cost method to account for the frequent flier liability is the deferred revenue method. Under this method, the airline would defer a portion of the sales price of a ticket purchased by a program member by creating a liability account, such as Air Traffic Liability, which would remain as a liability until a free travel award is used. The deferred revenue under this method would represent the equivalent of a discounted fare, which would be recognized when the passenger used the travel award. The calculation of the liability under this method is very complicated and includes an estimate of the average amount paid by a passenger flying one mile.

The difference in philosophy of the two methods is this: The incremental cost method is considered appropriate when the program is a promotional or premium program. The deferred revenue method is considered appropriate when the program is really providing discounted tickets. The key question in determining which method to use is the issue of when is the earnings process substantially completed.

Recently, a conflict has developed within the accounting profession between the AICPA and the FASB regarding the proper accounting treatment of these awards. The FASB feels strongly that all free travel awards, without exception, should be accounted for under the deferred revenue method. The AICPA believes that the incremental cost method should be used to account for the liability if the free travel award programs are incidental in nature. If a program failed the incidental-in-nature test, the deferred revenue method would have to be used. In late 1990, the AICPA decided not to issue a guideline that was scheduled to take effect January 1, 1991, and encouraged the FASB or the SEC to pursue the project. The FASB encouraged the AICPA not to abandon the project, but the AICPA declined to study the issue further. In the meantime, until some accounting body takes a position on this issue, the airlines are free to use the incremental cost method to account for their free travel awards. Thus, the question of what the real liability should be in reporting frequent flier award programs remains unsettled.

Source: Adapted from *Forbes,* June 13, 1988, p. 62, and *The CPA Journal,* December, 1991, pp. 60–61.

Review of Learning Objectives

Objective 1

Understand the nature of current liabilities and how to account for them. Liabilities represent a company's obligations to nonowners. The two major classes of liabilities are current liabilities, which are expected to be paid or satisfied within one year, and long-term liabilities, which are debts or other obligations that will not be paid or otherwise satisfied within one year. The four major types of current liabilities are (1) short-term obligations to creditors, such as accounts payable, notes payable, and the current portion of long-term debt; (2) payroll liabilities, such as salaries and wages, withheld taxes, and employer's payroll taxes; (3) tax liabilities, such as sales taxes payable, property taxes payable, and income taxes payable; and (4) obligations to provide goods and services, such as unearned sales revenue and estimated liabilities for warranties.

Objective 2

Use present value concepts in measuring long-term liabilities. Obligations that will not be paid or otherwise satisfied within one year are classified on the balance sheet as long-term liabilities. Some common types of long-term liabilities are notes payable, mortgages payable, lease obligations, deferred income taxes, and pension liabilities. The present value of a long-term liability is the current value (representing only principal), which is computed by discounting the known future amount using the current interest rate. If the present value amounts of assets or liabilities are known and a future amount is desired, then the present value must be compounded to arrive at a future amount that includes both principal and interest.

Objective 3

Account for long-term liabilities, including notes payable, mortgages payable, and lease obligations. Long-term notes payable can be interest bearing or noninterest bearing. Noninterest-bearing notes must be accounted for based on an assumed market rate of interest. Thus, the present value of a noninterest-bearing note is computed by discounting the maturity value of the note by the market rate of interest. The difference between the maturity value and the present value represents the amount by which the note has been discounted. The discount is amortized over the life of the note in computing the periodic interest expense.

Mortgage liabilities are paid by a series of regular payments that include interest expense and a reduction of the principle of the mortgage note. The balance sheet liability at any given time is the present value of the remaining mortgage payments.

A lease is treated as an operating lease if it is short term and does not meet any of the criteria of a capital lease.

A firm can acquire new assets by either purchasing or leasing them. Leasing involves periodic payments over the life of the lease. A lease is treated as a purchase if it meets specified criteria. A lease treated as a purchase is referred to as a capital lease. As such, it is recorded as both an asset and a long-term liability. The asset is amortized and the liability is reduced as lease payments are made.

Objective 4

Describe the general nature of long-term liabilities for deferred taxes and pensions. Deferred income taxes arise because different methods are used on the income statement for computing accounting income than are used on the tax return for computing taxable income. The difference between income tax expense on the income statement and the income taxes payable to the government based on taxable income is recorded in the Deferred Income Taxes account. Many items give rise to deferred income taxes, such as depreciation, warranty expenses, and inventory valuation methods. Pension liabilities are a company's obligation to pay retirement benefits to its employees.

Objective 5

Describe the types of contingent liabilities and how they are reported. Contingent liabilities are potential obligations tied to the occurrence of some future event. They are included with other liabilities on the balance sheet if their probability of occurrence is high; they are presented as a footnote if their probability of occurrence is reasonably possible; or they are ignored in the financial statements if their probability of occurrence is remote.

Key Terms and Concepts

account payable *(407)*
annuity *(418)*
capital lease *(423)*
compounding period *(417)*
contingent liability *(427)*
current liabilities *(406)*
deferred income taxes *(426)*
income taxes payable *(413)*
lease *(423)*

lessee *(423)*
lessor *(423)*
liabilities *(406)*
long-term liabilities *(415)*
mortgage amortization schedule *(422)*
mortgage payable *(422)*
note payable *(408)*
operating lease *(423)*

pension plan *(427)*
present value of $1 *(416)*
present value of an annuity *(418)*
sales taxes payable *(412)*
social security (FICA) taxes *(410)*
unearned revenues *(414)*

Review Problem

Accounting for Current and Long-Term Liabilities

Energy Corporation has four notes payable on its books.

1. A $2,000, 90-day, 12% note for money borrowed from the Second National Bank on December 1, 1993. Interest is payable at maturity.
2. A $4,000, one-year noninterest-bearing note for money borrowed from Howden City Bank on January 2, 1994. The $4,000 is to be paid on December 31, 1994. The note was issued when the market rate of interest was 10%.
3. A $5,000, 3-year, noninterest-bearing note owed to Amerind Corporation for a machine purchased on January 2, 1993. The $5,000 is to be paid on December 31, 1995. The interest rate was 12% when the note was issued.
4. A $30,000, 3-year, 8% note payable to White Corporation for a truck purchased on December 31, 1992. Interest is payable annually on December 31 of each year and the note matures on December 31, 1995.

Required: Make all journal entries required to account for the four notes. Energy Corporation reports on a calendar-year basis.

Solution

1. Note 1

The journal entries to account for the note are:

1993
Dec. 1   Cash 2,000
            Notes Payable 2,000
Borrowed $2,000 for 90 days from Second National Bank.

Dec. 31 Interest Expense 19.73
            Interest Payable 19.73
To record 30 days' interest on the 90-day note to Second National Bank ($2,000 × 30/365 × 0.12 = $19.73). This is an adjusting entry.

1994
Mar. 1   Interest Expense 39.45
         Interest Payable 19.73
         Notes Payable 2,000.00
            Cash 2,059.18
Paid off $2,000, 90-day note at Second National Bank. Interest of $19.73 was recognized as an expense in 1993. Interest this year is $39.45 ($2,000 × 60/365 × 0.12).

2. Note 2

The journal entries for this note are:

1994
Jan. 2 Cash 3,636.40
        Discount on Note Payable 363.60
          Note Payable 4,000.00

Borrowed money from Howden City Bank on a one-year, noninterest-bearing note discounted at 10%: $4,000 × .9091 (Table I) = $3,636.40 (present value of note).

1994
Dec. 31 Interest Expense 363.60
          Discount on Note Payable 363.60

To record the interest incurred on a one-year, noninterest-bearing note.

Dec. 31 Note Payable 4,000.00
          Cash 4,000.00

Paid off a one-year, noninterest-bearing note.

3. Note 3

This long-term, noninterest-bearing note must be discounted at the market rate of interest of 12 percent. The discounted amount is $3,559 ($5,000 × present value factor of 0.7118). The amortization schedule is as follows:

Date	Interest Expense	Loan Balance
Beginning Balance		$3,559.00
December 31, 1993	(0.12 × $3,559) = $427.08	3,986.08
December 31, 1994	(0.12 × $3,986.08) = $478.33	4,464.41
December 31, 1995	(0.12 × $4,464.41) = $535.59*	5,000.00

* Rounded

Based on this amortization schedule, entries for the note would be as follows:

1993
Jan. 1 Machine 3,559
        Discount on Note Payable 1,441
          Note Payable 5,000

Purchased a machine for $5,000 from Amerind Corporation. The full amount is to be paid in 3 years with no stated interest.

Dec. 31 Interest Expense 427.08
          Discount on Note Payable 427.08

To recognize the first year's interest on the Amerind Corporation note.

1994
Dec. 31 Interest Expense 478.33
          Discount on Note Payable 478.33

To recognize the second year's interest on the Amerind Corporation note.

1995
Dec. 31 Interest Expense 535.59
          Discount on Note Payable 535.59

To recognize the third year's interest on the Amerind Corporation note.

The interest expense increases each year because it is calculated on the basis of an increasing loan balance.

Dec. 31	Note Payable	5,000	
	Cash		5,000

To pay off note payable to Amerind Corporation at maturity.

4. Note 4

The journal entries for this note are:

1992
Dec. 31	Truck	30,000	
	Note Payable		30,000

Issued a 3-year, 8% note to purchase a truck.

1993
Dec. 31	Interest Expense	2,400	
	Cash		2,400

Paid interest on $30,000 note for one year at 8%.

1994
Dec. 31	Interest Expense	2,400	
	Cash		2,400

Paid interest on $30,000 note for one year at 8%.

1995
Dec. 31	Note Payable	30,000	
	Interest Expense	2,400	
	Cash		32,400

Paid interest for one year on a $30,000 note at 8% and paid off the face value of the note at maturity.

Discussion Questions

1. What is a liability?
2. What is a current liability, and how does it differ from a long-term liability?
3. What type of business transaction gives rise to an account payable?
4. If a company has an account payable with terms of 2/10, net 30, explain what these terms mean and whether the company should be concerned if it does not utilize these terms to its advantage.
5. If a company that uses the calendar year for financial reporting borrows money on December 1 by issuing an interest-bearing note for 60 days, is any accounting necessary for this note before it is paid off 60 days later? Explain.
6. If a company issues a noninterest-bearing note, does that indicate that the company is borrowing money without paying any interest for the use of the money? Explain.
7. Describe what the term *current portion of long-term debt* means.
8. Why is the accounting for payroll-related liabilities more complicated than the accounting for other current liabilities?
9. If the period of time covered by a company's payroll does not coincide with the last day of the year for financial reporting, how is accounting for the payroll affected by this situation?
10. The higher the interest rate, the lower the present value of a future amount. Why?
11. What is the difference between a note and a mortgage payable?
12. Why is an end-of-year adjusting entry often neces-

Chapter 10 *Liabilities*

sary in connection with property taxes owed to city or county governments?

13. When and how does a company record the amount owed to the government for income taxes for a given year?

14. Which table and what factor in that table would be used to discount a 5-year, noninterest-bearing note, if the applicable interest rate is 12% compounded semiannually?

15. If a lease is recorded as a capital lease, what is the relationship of the lease payments and the lease liability?

16. What types of financial disclosures are required for contingent liabilities?

Exercises

E10-1
Short-Term Obligations to Suppliers

Bach Company purchased $2,000 of inventory from a supplier with credit terms of 3/10, n/60.

1. Prepare the journal entries to record:
    (a) The purchase of inventory, assuming the perpetual inventory method is used.
    (b) Payment of the invoice within 10 days of purchase.
    (c) Payment of the invoice 60 days from the date of purchase.
2. Compute the interest rate that Bach Company is paying for the use of $2,000 if payment is not made within the discount period.

E10-2
Accounting for Short-Term Notes Payable

Rogers Inc., a calendar-year corporation, borrowed $40,000 on a 10 percent, 9-month note dated June 1, 1994. All the interest on the note will be paid at maturity.

1. Prepare the journal entries to account for the note on each of the following dates: June 1, 1994, December 31, 1994, and the maturity date, assuming the note is paid at maturity. (Round amounts to the nearest dollar.)
2. Explain why a corporation might borrow funds on a short-term basis.

E10-3
Accounting for Short-Term Notes Payable

Upchurch Company borrowed $10,000 for 90 days and signed a note promising to pay the principal plus interest on the note at an annual rate of 12 percent. The note was dated November 30, 1993.

1. What type of note is this, and what is the maturity date?
2. Prepare the journal entry to record the note on the date it was issued.
3. If the company's financial reporting period ends on December 31, prepare any necessary adjusting entry for the note on December 31, 1993.
4. Prepare the entry to record the payment of the note on the date it matures.

E10-4
Adjusting Entries for Current Liabilities

Assume that December 31, 1993, is a Wednesday. As the accountant for Pilgrim Industries, a calendar-year corporation, you are to make all necessary adjusting journal entries on that date. The following information is available:

1. Pilgrim Industries pays weekly salaries to its employees, with the payroll for each five-day workweek distributed on the following Monday. The payroll for the preceding week (ending Friday, December 26) included the following items, and there have been no changes in salaries or withholdings. (Assume that none of the employees' salaries is subject to unemployment taxes.)

Salaries Expense	$80,000
Income Taxes Withheld from Employees	16,000
FICA Taxes Withheld from Employees	4,800
Union Dues Withheld from Employees	300
Cash Paid to Employees	58,900

2. On November 1, 1993, rent revenue of $6,000 was collected in advance. The payment was for the period November 1, 1993, to October 31, 1994. The original entry included a credit to Unearned Rent Revenue for the full amount of the cash received.
3. Assume the same facts as in (2), except that the credit in the original entry was to Rent Revenue instead of Unearned Rent Revenue.

E10-5
Accounting for Warranties

Rick Procter, president of Sharp Television Stores, has been concerned recently with declining sales due to increased competition in the area. Rick has noticed that many of the national stores selling television sets and appliances have been placing heavy emphasis in their marketing programs on warranties. In an effort to revitalize sales, Rick has decided to offer free service and repairs for 1 year as a warranty on his television sets. Based on experience, Rick believes that first-year service and repair costs on the television sets will be approximately 5 percent of sales. The first month of operations following the initiation of Rick's new marketing plan showed significant increases in sales of TV sets. Total sales of TV sets for the first 3 months under the warranty plan were $10,000, $8,000, and $12,000, respectively.

1. Assuming that Rick prepares adjusting entries and financial statements for his own use at the end of each month, prepare the appropriate entry to recognize warranty expense for each of these first 3 months.
2. Prepare the appropriate entry to record services provided to repair sets under warranty in the second month, assuming that the following costs were incurred: labor (paid in cash), $550; supplies, $330.

E10-6
Accounting for Long-Term Note Payable

Craft Company borrowed $25,000 on a 2-year, 12 percent note dated October 1, 1993. Interest is payable annually on October 1, 1994, and October 1, 1995, the maturity date of the note. The company prepares its financial statements on a calendar-year basis. Prepare all journal entries relating to the note for 1993, 1994, and 1995.

E10-7
Accounting for a Non-interest-Bearing Note

On July 1, 1993, Bright Corporation, a calendar-year company, borrowed money from its bank on a one-year, noninterest-bearing note with a face amount of $20,000. The bank discounted the note at a 12 percent annual rate of interest, compounded semiannually.

1. Prepare journal entries for the note on the following dates: July 1, 1993, December 31, 1993, and July 1, 1994 (maturity date).
2. Show how the note would be presented on the December 31, 1993, balance sheet for Bright Corporation.

E10-8
Accounting for Property Taxes

Reynolds Company received a bill from the county government for property taxes on its land and buildings for the period July 1, 1993, through June 30, 1994. The amount of the tax bill is $7,600, and payment is due August 1, 1994. The tax rate for the period July 1, 1994, to June 30, 1995, will not change, and the company does not

Chapter 10 *Liabilities*

plan to acquire any additional taxable assets during that period. Reynolds Company uses the calendar year for financial reporting purposes.

1. Prepare the journal entry to record payment of the property taxes on August 1, 1994, assuming no entry has been made to record a liability for the property taxes.
2. Prepare the adjusting entry for property taxes on December 31, 1994.

E10-9
Computing the Present Value of a Lump-Sum

Find the present value (rounded to the nearest dollar) of:

1. $15,000 due in 5 years at 8 percent compounded annually.
2. $25,000 due in 8 1/2 years at 10 percent compounded semiannually.
3. $9,500 due in 4 years at 12 percent compounded quarterly.
4. $20,000 due in 20 years at 8 percent compounded semiannually.

E10-10
Computing the Future Value of a Lump-Sum

Compute the future value (rounded to the nearest dollar) of the following investments.

1. $10,209 invested to earn interest at 8% compounded annually for 5 years.
2. $10,908 invested to earn interest at 10% compounded semiannually for 8 1/2 years.
3. $5,920 invested to earn interest at 12% compounded quarterly for 4 years.
4. $4,166 invested to earn interest at 8% compounded semiannually for 20 years.

E10-11
Computing the Present Value of an Annuity

What is the present value (rounded to the nearest dollar) of an annuity of $8,000 per year for 5 years if the interest rate is:

1. 8 percent compounded annually.
2. 10 percent compounded annually.

E10-12
Lease Accounting

Temple Corporation signed a lease to use a machine for 4 years. The annual lease payment is $10,500 payable at the end of each year.

1. Record the lease, assuming that the lease should be accounted for as a capital lease and the applicable interest rate is 10 percent. (Round to the nearest dollar.)
2. For the initial year, record the annual lease payment.

Problem Set A

P10A-1
Accounts and Notes Payable

SOLUTIONS SOFTWARE

Mason Industries purchases raw materials on credit with terms of 2/10, n/30. Occasionally, a short-term note payable is issued to obtain cash for current operations. The following two transactions were selected from the many 1994 transactions for your analysis:

June 1, 1994 Purchased materials on credit for $7,000; terms, 2/10, n/30. (Assume the company uses the perpetual inventory method.)
June 30, 1994 Borrowed $15,000 cash from a local bank and signed a 9-month, 10 percent note. All interest is payable at maturity.

Required:
1. Prepare the original journal entry for each of the foregoing transactions.
2. Prepare the entry to record payment for the June 1 purchase on June 10.

3. Prepare the entry to record payment for the June 1 purchase assuming payment is not made until July 9.
4. Prepare the entry to record interest on the $15,000 note as of December 31, 1994.
5. Prepare the entry to record payment of the note plus interest at maturity (March 31, 1995).

P10A-2
Accounting for Notes Payable

Murdoch Corporation has the following long-term notes payable as of December 31, 1993:

(a) A $200,000, 3-year, 10 percent note payable to Mountain States Bank. The note was dated January 1, 1993, and interest is due each year on December 31. The note is to be paid off on December 31, 1995.
(b) A 3-year, $100,000, noninterest-bearing note payable to Amanda Jacobs. This note is dated January 1, 1993, for equipment purchased from Jacobs. The note matures on December 31, 1995.

Required: Assuming that the market rate of interest on January 1, 1993, is 10%, provide all journal entries necessary to account for the two notes for the years 1993 (including issuance of the notes on January 1), 1994, and 1995. (Round amounts to the nearest dollar.)

P10A-3
Accounting for Notes Payable

During 1994, Craig Corporation, a calendar-year reporting entity, had the following transactions:

Aug. 9	Borrowed $30,000 from Barton Company and issued a 60-day, 12 percent note payable.
Sept. 12	Purchased a machine from Wakichi Corporation. Issued a 2-year, noninterest-bearing note for $120,000 to be paid in full on September 12, 1996. The market rate of interest is 10%.
Sept. 23	Paid the note issued to Barton Company plus interest accrued to date.
Nov. 1	Purchased a building for $300,000 from Blue Corporation, issuing a 2-year, 12%, $300,000 note. Interest is payable annually on October 31.
Nov. 30	Purchased $25,000 worth of merchandise from Texas Corporation. Issued a 90-day note bearing 16 percent interest annually. Craig Corporation uses the periodic inventory method.

Required: Prepare the journal entries to record these transactions and any adjusting entries needed on December 31. (Round all calculations to the nearest dollar.)

P10A-4
Payroll Accounting

Stockbridge Stores, Inc. has three employees, Frank Wall, Mary Jones, and Susan Wright. Summaries of their 1994 salaries and withholdings are as follows:

Employee	Gross Salaries	Federal Income Taxes Withheld	State Income Taxes Withheld	FICA Taxes Withheld
Frank Wall	$54,000	$6,500	$2,500	$3,825
Mary Jones	39,000	4,800	1,900	2,984
Susan Wright	34,000	4,250	1,500	2,601

Required:
1. Prepare the summary entry for salaries paid to the employees for the year 1994.
2. Assume that, in addition to FICA taxes, the employer has incurred $192 for federal unemployment taxes and $720 for state unemployment taxes. Prepare the

summary journal entry to record the payroll tax liability for 1994, assuming no taxes have yet been paid.
3. **Interpretative Question** What other types of charges are frequently withheld from employees' paychecks in addition to income taxes and FICA taxes?

P10A-5

Operating Transactions and Adjusting Entries

Frazier Corporation was organized in September 1994 and began business operations on October 1, 1994. Following is a summary of transactions for the first month.

Oct. 1   Signed a one-year lease on a building, paying $4,500 for six months rent in advance. The Prepaid Rent account was debited for the amount paid.
Oct. 8   Purchased inventory costing $35,000 on account from Crane Wholesale Company, terms 3/10, n/30. Frazier Corporation uses the perpetual inventory method.
Oct. 17   Paid Crane Wholesale Company in full for the October purchase of inventory.
Oct. 25   Sold merchandise on account, terms n/30. The selling price of the merchandise was $24,000. All sales are subject to a 5 percent sales tax. Cost of the merchandise sold was $13,500.

Required: Assuming that there were no other transactions for October and that Frazier is subject to a 20 percent income tax rate:

1. Prepare entries to record the transactions for the month.
2. Prepare adjusting entries at October 31, and determine the net income or loss for the month.

P10A-6

Present and Future Value Computations

Required:
1. Compute the present value for each of the following situations, assuming a rate of interest of 10 percent compounded annually. (Round amount to the nearest dollar.)
   (a) A lump-sum payment of $30,000 due on a mortgage five years from now.
   (b) A 3-year, noninterest-bearing note for $7,500.
   (c) A series of payments of $5,000 each, due at the end of each year for five years.
   (d) A 5-year, 10% loan of $25,000, with interest payable annually, and the principal due in five years.
2. Compute the future value amounts (rounded to the nearest dollar) in each of the following situations:
   (a) A $20,000 lump-sum investment today that will earn interest at 10% compounded annually over 5 years.
   (b) A $5,000 lump-sum investment today that will earn interest at 8%, compounded quarterly to provide money for a child's college education 15 years from now.

P10A-7

Accounting for a Non-interest-Bearing Note

SPREADSHEET PROBLEM

On January 1, 1993, Switzer, Inc., makers of quality applesauce, purchased two new delivery trucks by issuing a 4-year, noninterest-bearing note for $54,000. The note is payable in full on December 31, 1996. The market rate of interest was 9 percent when the note was issued. Switzer uses the calendar year for financial reporting. (Round amounts to the nearest dollar.)

438 Part 3 Reporting Assets, Liabilities, and Owners' Equity

Required:
1. Determine the cost of the two trucks, and prepare a schedule of interest and discount amortization over the four-year term of the note.
2. Prepare the journal entry to record the purchase of the trucks and any adjusting entry related to the note on December 31, 1993.
3. Show how the note would be presented on the December 31, 1993, balance sheet.
4. Prepare journal entries relating to the note on December 31, 1996, assuming the note is paid on the due date.
5. **Interpretative Question** Would the balance sheet presentation of the note on December 31, 1995, be different from the presentation you prepared for item (3)? Explain.

P10A-8
Lease Accounting

On January 1, 1993, Linda Lou Foods, Inc. leased a tractor. The lease agreement calls for payments of $7,000 per year (payable each year on January 1, starting in 1994) for 8 years. The annual interest rate on the lease is 8%. Linda Lou Foods uses a calendar-year reporting period.

Required:
1. Prepare the journal entries for the following dates:
   (a) January 1, 1993, to record the leasing of the tractor.
   (b) December 31, 1993, to recognize the interest expense for the year 1993.
   (c) January 1, 1994, to record the first lease payment.
2. Prepare the appropriate journal entries at December 31, 1994, and January 1, 1995.
3. **Interpretative Question** Explain briefly how the leased asset is accounted for annually.

P10A-9
Reporting Liabilities on the Balance Sheet

Required: Using the appropriate accounts from the following list of accounts taken from the adjusted trial balance of Goforth Company, prepare the liabilities section of the company's balance sheet:

Accounts Payable	$45,000
Note Payable (Due in 6 months)	24,000
Income Taxes Payable	18,000
Unearned Sales Revenue	27,500
Note Payable (Due in 2 years)	40,000
Prepaid Insurance	6,200
Accounts Receivable	53,000
Current Portion of Mortgage Payable	12,300
Mortgage Payable (Due beyond 1 year)	93,000
Retained Earnings	91,400
Property Taxes Payable	8,700
Salaries & Wages Payable	15,200
Federal & State Withholding Taxes Payable	3,400
Union Dues Payable	1,500
Sales Tax Payable	3,100

Chapter 10 *Liabilities* 439

P10A-10
Unifying Concepts: Accounting for and Reporting Liabilities

As part of its application for a loan at Ohio National Bank, Hampton Company provided the following balance sheet:

Hampton Company
Balance Sheet
December 31, 1994

Assets

Current assets:
Cash		$ 16,000
Accounts receivable		38,000
Note receivable		24,000
Inventory		86,000
Total current assets		$164,000
Property, plant, and equipment (net)		200,000
Total assets		$364,000

Liabilities and Stockholders' Equity

Current liabilities:
Accounts payable		$ 18,000
Note payable		22,000
Income taxes payable		25,000
Total current liabilities		$ 65,000
Long-term liabilities:		
Mortgage payable		169,000
Total liabilities		$234,000
Stockholders' equity:		
Capital stock	$50,000	
Retained earnings	80,000	130,000
Total liabilities and stockholders' equity		$364,000

After reviewing the balance sheet, the loan officer for the bank had some reservations about the accuracy of the information presented. Since this was the first application for a loan by this company, the loan officer decided to request that the financial statements be audited by an independent CPA. During the audit, the following information was discovered.

(a) The note receivable of $24,000 is for 1 year and has been outstanding for 1 month. Interest revenue at an annual rate of 10 percent has not been recorded.
(b) No interest expense has been accrued on either the short-term note payable or the mortgage payable. The short-term note is for 1 year at 12 percent and has been outstanding for 4 months. Interest for 1 full year at 10 percent has accrued on the mortgage. The mortgage is paid in annual installments of $18,000 (including both interest and principal) due on January 1 of each year.
(c) Accrued property tax expense of $3,000 should have been recorded at the end of 1994.
(d) Accrued wages and salaries totaling $3,600 have not been recorded. (Ignore payroll taxes and withholdings.)
(e) Sales taxes of $5,800 are owed to the state as of December 31, 1994. All sales tax was credited to the Sales Revenue account.

Required: 1. Prepare journal entries to account for the information discovered during the audit.
2. Prepare a corrected balance sheet for Hampton Company as of December 31, 1994.

Problem Set B

P10B-1
Accounts and Notes Payable

Randolph Company purchases raw materials on credit with terms of 2/10, n/30. Occasionally a short-term note payable is executed to obtain cash for current operations. The following two transactions were selected from the many 1994 transactions for your analysis.

Aug. 10, 1994 Purchased materials on credit, $9,000; terms, 2/10, n/30. (Assume that the company uses the periodic inventory method.)
Aug. 31, 1994 Borrowed $20,000 cash from a local bank signing a 6-month note with 12 percent annual interest payable at maturity.

Required: 1. Prepare the original journal entry for each of the foregoing transactions.
2. Prepare an entry to record the payment of the August 10 account payable on August 18.
3. Prepare the same entry as in (2), but assume that the payment was not made until September 9.
4. Prepare the entry to record the accrued interest on the $20,000 note as of December 31, 1994.
5. Prepare the entry to record the payment of the $20,000 note plus interest at maturity (February 28, 1995).

P10B-2
Accounting for Notes Payable

Sweet's Candy Company needed cash for its current business operations. On March 1, 1993, the company borrowed $8,000 on a 2-year interest-bearing note from Peterson Bank at an annual interest rate of 10%. Interest is payable annually on March 1, and the note matures March 1, 1995. Sweet's Candy Company also borrowed $4,500 from Laurence National Bank on March 1, 1993, signing a one-year noninterest-bearing note for $5,000. The note is due March 1, 1994.

Required: 1. Compute the effective rate of interest on the Laurence National Bank note.
2. Prepare all journal entries relating to the two notes for 1993, 1994, and 1995. Assume that Sweet's Candy Company uses the calendar year for financial reporting. (Round all amounts to the nearest dollar.)

P10B-3
Accounting for Notes Payable

During 1994 Kenan Corp. had these transactions.

July 20   Purchased a machine costing $200,000 from Perry Corporation. Issued a 1-year, noninterest-bearing note to be paid in full on July 20, 1995. The market rate of interest is 14 percent.
Aug. 9   Borrowed $15,000 from Little Corporation and issued a 45-day, 12 percent note payable.
Sept. 23 Paid the note due today to Little plus accrued interest.
Nov. 1   Purchased $17,000 of merchandise from Dowd Corporation. Issued a 90-day note bearing interest of 12 percent annually. Kenan Corporation uses the perpetual inventory method.

Chapter 10 *Liabilities*

Required: Prepare the journal entries to record these transactions, and then make the entries needed on December 31. (Round all calculations to the nearest dollar.)

P10B-4
Payroll Accounting

Orange County Bank has three employees, Albert Myers, Juan Moreno, and Michi Endo. During January 1994, these three employees earned $6,000, $4,200, and $4,000 respectively. The following table summarizes the required withholding rates on their income for the month of January:

Employee	Federal Income Tax Withholdings	State Income Tax Withholdings	FICA Tax
Albert Myers	33%	3%	7.65%
Juan Moreno	28	4	7.65%
Michi Endo	28	5	7.65%

You are also informed that the bank is subject to the following unemployment tax rates on the salaries earned by the employees during January 1994:

Federal Unemployment Tax .... .8 percent
State Unemployment Tax .... 3.0 percent

Required:
1. Prepare the journal entry to record salaries payable for the month of January.
2. Prepare the journal entry to record payment of the January salaries to employees.
3. Prepare the journal entry to record the bank's payroll taxes for the month of January.

P10B-5
Accounting for Tax Liabilities

The new controller for Whitely Corporation is in the process of preparing the company's financial statements at year-end. In reviewing the year's transactions, she discovers the following information and asks you to make the appropriate entries to incorporate this information into the accounting records as of December 31, 1994.

1. The company's sales for the year were $120,000 on which the company collected $3,600 of sales tax, none of which has yet been paid to the state. The following entry summarizes the way the company has recorded sales and sales tax:

   Cash 123,600
       Sales Revenue 123,600
   To record sales of merchandise and the collection of $3,600 of sales taxes.

2. Property taxes are payable on October 31 of each year for the tax period July 1 of the previous year to June 30 of the current year. The property taxes for the period July 1, 1993, to June 30, 1994, amounted to $7,600. The company anticipates that the property taxes for the period July 1, 1994, to June 30, 1995, will be $8,200.

3. Before making the adjustments for the two situations described above, the controller computed the income before income taxes for the year 1994 to be $32,000. She would like you to compute the correct income tax expense to be reported on the income statement for the year 1994 after you have made the appropriate entries for situations 1 and 2. You are informed that the correct tax rate to use in calculating the income tax expense is 20%.

Required: Prepare the appropriate journal entries at December 31, 1994, to properly reflect liabilities on the balance sheet at December 31, 1994, and expenses on the income statement for the year 1994.

P10B-6
Present and Future Value Computations

Required:
1. Determine the present value in each of the following situations.
   (a) A 6-month, noninterest-bearing note with a face amount of $3,600. The note was issued when the market rate of interest was 10 percent.
   (b) A loan to be repaid in full at the end of 3 years. All interest on the loan is also payable at the end of 3 years. Total principal and interest at maturity is $5,000, and the interest rate is 12 percent compounded quarterly.
   (c) A 2-year note for $8,000 bearing interest at an annual rate of 10 percent, compounded semiannually. Interest is payable semiannually.
   (d) A 5-year mortgage to be paid in monthly installments of $1,000. The interest rate is 12 percent compounded monthly.
2. Determine the future value in each of the following situations:
   (a) An investment of $10,000 today to earn interest at 6% compounded semiannually to provide for a downpayment on a house 5 years from now.
   (b) An investment of $25,000 today to earn interest at 8% compounded quarterly that is designated for a charitable contribution 10 years from now when the donor retires.

P10B-7
Accounting for a Mortgage

On November 1, 1994, Hill Company arranges with an insurance company to borrow $200,000 on a 20-year mortgage to purchase land and a building to be used in its operations. The land and the building are pledged as collateral for the loan, which has an annual interest rate of 12% compounded monthly. The monthly payments of $2,200 are made at the end of each month beginning on November 30, 1994.

Required:
1. Prepare the journal entry to record the purchase of the land and building, assuming that $40,000 of the purchase price is assignable to the land.
2. Prepare the journal entries on November 30 and December 31 for the monthly payments on the mortgage.
3. **Interpretative Question** Explain generally how the remaining liability at December 31, 1994, will be reported on the company's balance sheet dated December 31, 1994.

P10B-8
Lease Accounting

On January 1, 1994, Holley Trucking Company leased a truck from Spangler, Inc. The lease terms call for payments of $6,000 per year for 5 years. Assume that the first payment is made on December 31, 1994.

Required: Assuming that the lease is a capital lease, and that the market rate of interest is 12 percent, complete the following:

1. Compute the present value of the lease payments.
2. Record the lease in Holley's accounting records at January 1, 1994.
3. Complete a lease amortization schedule. (Round to the nearest dollar.)
4. Prepare Holley's journal entry on December 31, 1994, when the first lease payment is made.

Chapter 10 *Liabilities* 443

P10B-9

Reporting Liabilities on the Balance Sheet

The following amounts are shown on the Plymouth Company's adjusted trial balance for the year 1994:

Accounts Payable	$ 36,000
Property Taxes Payable	6,300
Short-Term Notes Payable	44,000
Mortgage Payable (Due within one year)	28,000
Mortgage Payable (Due after one year)	300,000
Accrued Interest on Mortgage Payable	3,000
Lease Obligations (Current Portion)	58,000
Lease Obligations (Long Term)	414,000
Rent Payable	70,000
Income Taxes Payable	50,000
Federal & State Unemployment Taxes Payable	16,000

Required: Prepare the liabilities section of Plymouth Company's balance sheet at December 31, 1994.

P10B-10

Unifying Concepts: Accounting for and Reporting Liabilities

SOLUTIONS SOFTWARE

Madison Corporation is applying to the Second National Bank for a $200,000 loan for a planned expansion of its operating facilities. As part of the application, Madison provided the balance sheet shown here.

After reviewing Madison Corporation's balance sheet, the loan officer for Second National Bank decided that, because of the large amount of the loan request, the company's financial statements would have to be audited by an independent CPA before the bank could approve the application. During the audit, the following information was discovered:

(a) No interest has been recorded on either the short-term or the long-term note payable. The short-term note is an 8 percent note that has been outstanding for 6 months, and 3 months' interest has accrued on the long-term note, which bears interest at an annual rate of 10 percent.
(b) Accrued wages totaling $2,000 should have been recorded at year-end. (Ignore payroll taxes and withholdings.)
(c) The balance in the Sales Revenue account at year-end included a $3,600 advance payment from a customer for merchandise to be delivered in 1995.
(d) No entry was made to record income taxes for 1994. The auditor determines that Madison is subject to a 20% tax rate for 1994. The company had originally computed net income of $48,000, which was added to the Retained Earnings account balance.

**Madison Corporation
Balance Sheet
December 31, 1994**

Assets

Current assets:	
Cash	$ 26,000
Accounts receivable	34,000
Inventory	45,000
Prepaid insurance	6,000
Total current assets	$111,000
Property, plant, and equipment (net)	179,000
Total assets	$290,000

Liabilities and Stockholders' Equity

Current liabilities:		
Accounts payable		$ 19,000
Note payable		8,000
Total current liabilities		$ 27,000
Long-term liabilities:		
Long-term note payable		100,000
Total liabilities		$127,000
Stockholders' equity:		
Common stock	$90,000	
Retained earnings	73,000	163,000
Total liabilities and stockholders' equity		$290,000

Required:
1. Prepare journal entries to account for the information discovered during the audit.
2. Prepare a revised balance sheet for Madison Corporation as of December 31, 1994.

Business Analysis Case *Plymouth Company*

On January 2, 1994, Henry King, the president of Plymouth Company, decides that the firm needs a minicomputer to make its sales and marketing systems more efficient and more effective. The company can either lease or buy a computer. If they lease a computer, they will pay $45,000 each December 31 for 5 years. At the end of the lease term, the computer will be owned by Plymouth Company. Alternatively, the company can buy a similar computer. Terms of the purchase would be $50,000 down and $30,000 per year (payable at the end of each year) for 5 years, including interest at 12 percent.

Required:
1. Should Plymouth Company lease or buy the computer, assuming the market rate of interest is 12 percent?
2. Assuming that Plymouth Company leases the computer, prepare the entries to record the lease and the first annual payment on December 31, 1994.
3. Assuming that Plymouth Company purchases the computer, prepare the entries to record the purchase and the first annual payment on December 31, 1994.
4. What factors should Plymouth Company consider in deciding whether to lease or purchase the computer?

Ethics Case 1 *Sanders Company*

Sanders Company has not performed up to expectations for the current year. The president has been encouraging the controller to make the "bottom line" look as good as possible in order to at least partially mollify the company's stockholders. Not only has business slowed down generally, but the company's products have had a larger percentage of defects than had been anticipated. The controller has estimated that the company will need to establish an estimated liability to meet its product warranty responsibilities in the amount of $480,000, which is triple what it has been in prior years. With such a large liability, the company will show a loss for the year, which is the first time ever that the company has not reported a profit.

The president calls the controller to his office to discuss the situation. He is very distraught over the prospects of a loss and has determined that if the warranty liability is established at $200,000 or less, the company can show a modest profit. Accordingly, he orders the controller to establish the estimated warranty liability at $195,000, which is higher than last year even with a sales slowdown. The president notes that this amount of liability will not only result in a modest profit, but will be within the limitations of their bank debt limits. He indicates to the controller that the entire financial situation can be improved in the coming year by diligent efforts to control costs and reduce the number of defective products. The controller seems reluctant to go along with the president's order, but he is not in a personal financial position to argue with the president and perhaps lose his job. At this point, he figures that he doesn't have much choice except to go along with the president's suggestion to estimate the warranty liability at less than one-half of what he thinks it ought to be.

Required:
1. Identify the stakeholders who are directly or indirectly affected by a decision in this issue.
2. What are the ethical issues in this case?
3. What are the controller's alternative courses of action?
4. What should the controller do?

Ethics Case 2 *Medfirst Company*

Jill Nurango is the chief financial officer for Medfirst Company, a manufacturer of several types of medicines and orthopedic devices. Because Jill is one of the top officers in the company, her compensation package includes a salary plus a yearly bonus based on the reported pretax income of Medfirst. The controller has just brought a serious accounting issue to Jill. After closing the books for the year, the controller reports to Jill that Medfirst's pretax income will be $8,000,000. Jill is thrilled because with that level of income, her bonus for the year will be $50,000. However, the accountant informs Jill that Medfirst is involved as the defendant in a lawsuit over one of its medicines, Projac. The class-action suit against the company was filed two years ago complaining that Projac has serious side-effects that cause depression. In fact, Projac is even being blamed for one death where a user became depressed and committed suicide.

The controller tells Jill that the lawsuit is now in its final stages and that even their own attorney believes Medfirst will lose the case. The best estimate of the amount that Medfirst will have to pay is $6,000,000. The controller thinks the following journal entry should be made:

Losses from Lawsuit	6,000,000	
Payable to Plaintiffs		6,000,000

Jill knows that if this entry is booked, the company's income before taxes will be reduced to $2,000,000, and she will lose most of her bonus. Besides, she rationalizes, the final amount of the damages hasn't yet been determined by the court. Finally, she tells the controller, "Booking the loss now will be an admission of guilt—it will tell the world that we know Medfirst is guilty, which will cause Medfirst to lose the lawsuit." Therefore, she informs the controller to wait until next year to book the liability from the lawsuit.

Required:
1. Is Jill's advice to the controller appropriate?
2. Is Jill's action ethical or is she motivated only by her desire to keep her bonus? Does she have an ethical obligation to book the liability?

Table I — The Present Value of $1 Due in n Periods*

Period	1%	2%	3%	4%	5%	6%	7%	8%	9%	10%	12%	14%	15%	16%	18%	20%
1	.9901	.9804	.9709	.9615	.9524	.9434	.9346	.9259	.9174	.9091	.8929	.8772	.8696	.8621	.8475	.8333
2	.9803	.9612	.9426	.9246	.9070	.8900	.8734	.8573	.8417	.8264	.7972	.7695	.7561	.7432	.7182	.6944
3	.9706	.9423	.9151	.8890	.8638	.8396	.8163	.7938	.7722	.7513	.7118	.6750	.6575	.6407	.6086	.5787
4	.9610	.9238	.8885	.8548	.8227	.7921	.7629	.7350	.7084	.6830	.6355	.5921	.5718	.5523	.5158	.4823
5	.9515	.9057	.8626	.8219	.7835	.7473	.7130	.6806	.6499	.6209	.5674	.5194	.4972	.4761	.4371	.4019
6	.9420	.8880	.8375	.7903	.7462	.7050	.6663	.6302	.5963	.5645	.5066	.4556	.4323	.4104	.3704	.3349
7	.9327	.8706	.8131	.7599	.7107	.6651	.6227	.5835	.5470	.5132	.4523	.3996	.3759	.3538	.3139	.2791
8	.9235	.8535	.7894	.7307	.6768	.6274	.5820	.5403	.5019	.4665	.4039	.3506	.3269	.3050	.2660	.2326
9	.9143	.8368	.7664	.7026	.6446	.5919	.5439	.5002	.4604	.4241	.3606	.3075	.2843	.2630	.2255	.1938
10	.9053	.8203	.7441	.6756	.6139	.5584	.5083	.4632	.4224	.3855	.3220	.2697	.2472	.2267	.1911	.1615
11	.8963	.8043	.7224	.6496	.5847	.5268	.4751	.4289	.3875	.3503	.2875	.2366	.2149	.1954	.1619	.1346
12	.8874	.7885	.7014	.6246	.5568	.4970	.4440	.3971	.3555	.3186	.2567	.2076	.1869	.1685	.1372	.1122
13	.8787	.7730	.6810	.6006	.5303	.4688	.4150	.3677	.3262	.2897	.2292	.1821	.1625	.1452	.1163	.0935
14	.8700	.7579	.6611	.5775	.5051	.4423	.3878	.3405	.2992	.2633	.2046	.1597	.1413	.1252	.0985	.0779
15	.8613	.7430	.6419	.5553	.4810	.4173	.3624	.3152	.2745	.2394	.1827	.1401	.1229	.1079	.0835	.0649
16	.8528	.7284	.6232	.5339	.4581	.3936	.3387	.2919	.2519	.2176	.1631	.1229	.1069	.0930	.0708	.0541
17	.8444	.7142	.6050	.5134	.4363	.3714	.3166	.2703	.2311	.1978	.1456	.1078	.0929	.0802	.0600	.0451
18	.8360	.7002	.5874	.4936	.4155	.3503	.2959	.2502	.2120	.1799	.1300	.0946	.0808	.0691	.0508	.0376
19	.8277	.6864	.5703	.4746	.3957	.3305	.2765	.2317	.1945	.1635	.1161	.0829	.0703	.0596	.0431	.0313
20	.8195	.6730	.5537	.4564	.3769	.3118	.2584	.2145	.1784	.1486	.1037	.0728	.0611	.0514	.0365	.0261
25	.7798	.6095	.4776	.3751	.2953	.2330	.1842	.1460	.1160	.0923	.0588	.0378	.0304	.0245	.0160	.0105
30	.7419	.5521	.4120	.3083	.2314	.1741	.1314	.0994	.0754	.0573	.0334	.0196	.0151	.0116	.0070	.0042
40	.6717	.4529	.3066	.2083	.1420	.0972	.0668	.0460	.0318	.0221	.0107	.0053	.0037	.0026	.0013	.0007
50	.6080	.3715	.2281	.1407	.0872	.0543	.0339	.0213	.0134	.0085	.0035	.0014	.0009	.0006	.0003	.0001
60	.5504	.3048	.1697	.0951	.0535	.0303	.0173	.0099	.0057	.0033	.0011	.0004	.0002	.0001	†	†

*The formula used to derive the values in this table was $PV = F \frac{1}{(1+i)^n}$ where PV = present value, F = future amount to be discounted, i = interest rate, and n = number of periods.

†The value of 0 to four decimal places.

Chapter 10 *Liabilities*

Table II The Present Value of an Annuity of $1 per Period*

Number of Payments	1%	2%	3%	4%	5%	6%	7%	8%	9%	10%	12%	14%	15%	16%	18%	20%
1	0.9901	0.9804	0.9709	0.9615	0.9524	0.9434	0.9346	0.9259	0.9174	0.9091	0.8929	0.8772	0.8696	0.8621	0.8475	0.8333
2	1.9704	1.9416	1.9135	1.8861	1.8594	1.8334	1.8080	1.7833	1.7591	1.7355	1.6901	1.6467	1.6257	1.6052	1.5656	1.5278
3	2.9410	2.8839	2.8286	2.7751	2.7232	2.6730	2.6243	2.5771	2.5313	2.4869	2.4018	2.3216	2.2832	2.2459	2.1743	2.1065
4	3.9020	3.8077	3.7171	3.6299	3.5460	3.4651	3.3872	3.3121	3.2397	3.1699	3.0373	2.9137	2.8550	2.7982	2.6901	2.5887
5	4.8834	4.7135	4.5797	4.4518	4.3295	4.2124	4.1002	3.9927	3.8897	3.7908	3.6048	3.4331	3.3522	3.2743	3.1272	2.9906
6	5.7955	5.6014	5.4172	5.2421	5.0757	4.9173	4.7665	4.6229	4.4859	4.3553	4.1114	3.8887	3.7845	3.6847	3.4976	3.3255
7	6.7282	6.4720	6.2303	6.0021	5.7864	5.5824	5.3893	5.2064	5.0330	4.8684	4.5638	4.2883	4.1604	4.0386	3.8115	3.6046
8	7.6517	7.3255	7.0197	6.7327	6.4632	6.2098	5.9713	5.7466	5.5348	5.3349	4.9676	4.6389	4.4873	4.3436	4.0776	3.8372
9	8.5660	8.1622	7.7861	7.4353	7.1078	6.8017	6.5152	6.2469	5.9952	5.7590	5.3282	4.9464	4.7716	4.6065	4.3030	4.0310
10	9.4713	8.9826	8.5302	8.1109	7.7217	7.3601	7.0236	6.7101	6.4177	6.1446	5.6502	5.2161	5.0188	4.8332	4.4941	4.1925
11	10.3676	9.7868	9.2526	8.7605	8.3064	7.8869	7.4987	7.1390	6.8052	6.4951	5.9377	5.4527	5.2337	5.0286	4.6560	4.3271
12	11.2551	10.5733	9.9540	9.3851	8.8633	8.3838	7.9427	7.5361	7.1607	6.8137	6.1944	5.6603	5.4206	5.1971	4.7932	4.4392
13	12.1337	11.3484	10.6350	9.9856	9.3936	8.8527	8.3577	7.9038	7.4869	7.1034	6.4235	5.8424	5.5831	5.3423	4.9095	4.5327
14	13.0037	12.1062	11.2961	10.5631	9.8986	9.2950	8.7455	8.2442	7.7862	7.3667	6.6282	6.0021	5.7245	5.4675	5.0081	4.6106
15	13.8651	12.8493	11.9379	11.1184	10.3797	9.7122	9.1079	8.5595	8.0607	7.6061	6.8109	6.1422	5.8474	5.5755	5.0916	4.6755
16	14.7179	13.5777	12.5611	11.6523	10.8378	10.1059	9.4466	8.8514	8.3126	7.8237	6.9740	6.2651	5.9542	5.6685	5.1624	4.7296
17	15.5623	14.2919	13.1661	12.1657	11.2741	10.4773	9.7632	9.1216	8.5436	8.0216	7.1196	6.3729	6.0472	5.7487	5.2223	4.7746
18	16.3983	14.9920	13.7535	12.6593	11.6896	10.8276	10.0591	9.3719	8.7556	8.2014	7.2497	6.4674	6.1280	5.8178	5.2732	4.8122
19	17.2260	15.6785	14.3238	13.1339	12.0853	11.1581	10.3356	9.6036	8.9501	8.3649	7.3658	6.5504	6.1982	5.8775	5.3162	4.8435
20	18.0456	16.3514	14.8775	13.5903	12.4622	11.4699	10.5940	9.8181	9.1285	8.5136	7.4694	6.6231	6.2593	5.9288	5.3527	4.8696
25	22.0232	19.5235	17.4131	15.6221	14.0939	12.7834	11.6536	10.6748	9.8226	9.0770	7.8431	6.8729	6.4641	6.0971	5.4669	4.9476
30	25.8077	22.3965	19.6004	17.2920	15.3725	13.7648	12.4090	11.2578	10.2737	9.4269	8.0552	7.0027	6.5660	6.1772	5.5168	4.9789
40	32.8347	27.3555	23.1148	19.7928	17.1591	15.0463	13.3317	11.9246	10.7574	9.7791	8.2438	7.1050	6.6418	6.2335	5.5482	4.9966
50	39.1961	31.4236	25.7298	21.4822	18.2559	15.7619	13.8007	12.2335	10.9617	9.9148	8.3045	7.1327	6.6605	6.2463	5.5641	4.9995
60	44.9550	34.7609	27.6756	22.6235	18.9293	16.1614	14.0392	12.3766	11.0480	9.9672	8.3240	7.1401	6.6651	6.2482	5.5553	4.9999

*The formula used to derive the values in this table was $PV = R\left(\dfrac{1 - \dfrac{1}{(1+i)^n}}{i}\right)$ where PV = present value, R = periodic payment to be discounted, i = interest rate, and n = number of payments.

Table III — Amount of $1 Due in n Periods

Period	1%	2%	3%	4%	5%	6%	7%	8%	9%	10%	12%	14%	15%	16%	18%	20%
1	1.0100	1.0200	1.0300	1.0400	1.0500	1.0600	1.0700	1.0800	1.0900	1.1000	1.1200	1.1400	1.1500	1.1600	1.1800	1.2000
2	1.0201	1.0404	1.0609	1.0816	1.1025	1.1236	1.1449	1.1664	1.1881	1.2100	1.2544	1.2996	1.3225	1.3456	1.3924	1.4400
3	1.0303	1.0612	1.0927	1.1249	1.1576	1.1910	1.2250	1.2597	1.2950	1.3310	1.4049	1.4815	1.5209	1.5609	1.6430	1.7280
4	1.0406	1.0824	1.1255	1.1699	1.2155	1.2625	1.3108	1.3605	1.4116	1.4641	1.5735	1.6890	1.7490	1.8106	1.9388	2.0736
5	1.0510	1.1041	1.1593	1.2167	1.2763	1.3382	1.4026	1.4693	1.5386	1.6105	1.7623	1.9254	2.0114	2.1003	2.2878	2.4883
6	1.0615	1.1262	1.1941	1.2653	1.3401	1.4185	1.5007	1.5869	1.6771	1.7716	1.9738	2.1950	2.3131	2.4364	2.6996	2.9860
7	1.0721	1.1487	1.2299	1.3159	1.4071	1.5036	1.6058	1.7138	1.8280	1.9487	2.2107	2.5023	2.6600	2.8262	3.1855	3.5832
8	1.0829	1.1717	1.2668	1.3686	1.4775	1.5938	1.7182	1.8509	1.9926	2.1436	2.4760	2.8526	3.0590	3.2784	3.7589	4.2998
9	1.0937	1.1951	1.3048	1.4233	1.5513	1.6895	1.8385	1.9990	2.1719	2.3579	2.7731	3.2519	3.5179	3.8030	4.4355	5.1598
10	1.1046	1.2190	1.3439	1.4802	1.6289	1.7908	1.9672	2.1589	2.3674	2.5937	3.1058	3.7072	4.0456	4.4114	5.2338	6.1917
11	1.1157	1.2434	1.3842	1.5395	1.7103	1.8983	2.1049	2.3316	2.5804	2.8531	3.4785	4.2262	4.6524	5.1173	6.1759	7.4031
12	1.1268	1.2682	1.4258	1.6010	1.7959	2.0122	2.2522	2.5182	2.8127	3.1384	3.8960	4.8179	5.3502	5.9360	7.2876	8.9161
13	1.1381	1.2936	1.4685	1.6651	1.8856	2.1329	2.4098	2.7196	3.0658	3.4523	4.3635	5.4924	6.1528	6.8858	8.5994	10.699
14	1.1495	1.3195	1.5126	1.7317	1.9799	2.2609	2.5785	2.9372	3.3417	3.7975	4.8871	6.2613	7.0757	7.9875	10.147	12.839
15	1.1610	1.3459	1.5580	1.8009	2.0789	2.3966	2.7590	3.1722	3.6425	4.1772	5.4736	7.1379	8.1371	9.2655	11.973	15.407
16	1.1726	1.3728	1.6047	1.8730	2.1829	2.5404	2.9522	3.4259	3.9703	4.5950	6.1304	8.1372	9.3576	10.748	14.129	18.488
17	1.1843	1.4002	1.6528	1.9479	2.2920	2.6928	3.1588	3.7000	4.3276	5.0545	6.8660	9.2765	10.761	12.467	16.672	22.186
18	1.1961	1.4282	1.7024	2.0258	2.4066	2.8543	3.3799	3.9960	4.7171	5.5599	7.6900	10.575	12.375	14.462	19.673	26.623
19	1.2081	1.4568	1.7535	2.1068	2.5270	3.0256	3.6165	4.3157	5.1417	6.1159	8.6128	12.055	14.231	16.776	23.214	31.948
20	1.2202	1.4859	1.8061	2.1911	2.6533	3.2071	3.8697	4.6610	5.6044	6.7275	9.6463	13.743	16.366	19.460	27.393	38.337
30	1.3478	1.8114	2.4273	3.2434	4.3219	5.7435	7.6123	10.062	13.267	17.449	29.959	50.950	66.211	85.849	143.37	237.37
40	1.4889	2.2080	3.2620	4.8010	7.0400	10.285	14.974	21.724	31.409	45.259	93.050	188.88	267.86	378.72	750.37	1469.7
50	1.6446	2.6916	4.3839	7.1067	11.467	18.420	29.457	46.901	74.357	117.39	289.00	700.23	1083.6	1670.7	3927.3	9100.4
60	1.8167	3.2810	5.8916	10.519	18.679	32.987	57.946	101.25	176.03	304.48	897.59	2595.9	4383.9	7370.1	20555.	56347.

Chapter 10 Liabilities

Table IV — Amount of an Annuity of $1 per Period

Period	1%	2%	3%	4%	5%	6%	7%	8%	9%	10%	12%	14%	15%	16%	18%	20%
1	1.0000	1.0000	1.0000	1.0000	1.0000	1.0000	1.0000	1.0000	1.0000	1.0000	1.0000	1.0000	1.0000	1.0000	1.0000	1.0000
2	2.0100	2.0200	2.0300	2.0400	2.0500	2.0600	2.0700	2.0800	2.0900	2.1000	2.1200	2.1400	2.1500	2.1600	2.1800	2.2000
3	3.0301	3.0604	3.0909	3.1216	3.1525	3.1836	3.2149	3.2464	3.2781	3.3100	3.3744	3.4396	3.4725	3.5056	3.5724	3.6400
4	4.0604	4.1216	4.1836	4.2465	4.3101	4.3746	4.4399	4.5061	4.5731	4.6410	4.7793	4.9211	4.9934	5.0665	5.2154	5.3680
5	5.1010	5.2040	5.3091	5.4163	5.5256	5.6371	5.7507	5.8666	5.9847	6.1051	6.3528	6.6101	6.7424	6.8771	7.1542	7.4416
6	6.1520	6.3081	6.4684	6.6330	6.8019	6.9753	7.1533	7.3359	7.5233	7.7156	8.1152	8.5355	8.7537	8.9775	9.4420	9.9299
7	7.2135	7.4343	7.6625	7.8983	8.1420	8.3938	8.6540	8.9228	9.2004	9.4872	10.0890	10.7305	11.0668	11.4139	12.1415	12.9159
8	8.2857	8.5830	8.8923	9.2142	9.5491	9.8975	10.2598	10.6366	11.0285	11.4359	12.2997	13.2328	13.7268	14.2401	15.3270	16.4991
9	9.3685	9.7546	10.1591	10.5828	11.0266	11.4913	11.9780	12.4876	13.0210	13.5795	14.7757	16.0853	16.7858	17.5185	19.0859	20.7989
10	10.4622	10.9497	11.4639	12.0061	12.5779	13.1808	13.8164	14.4866	15.1929	15.9374	17.5487	19.3373	20.3037	21.3215	23.5213	25.9587
11	11.5668	12.1687	12.8078	13.4864	14.2068	14.9716	15.7836	16.6455	17.5603	18.5312	20.6546	23.0445	24.3493	25.7329	28.7551	32.1504
12	12.6825	13.4121	14.1920	15.0258	15.9171	16.8699	17.8885	18.9771	20.1407	21.3843	24.1331	27.2707	29.0017	30.8502	34.9311	39.5805
13	13.8093	14.6803	15.6178	16.6268	17.7130	18.8821	20.1406	21.4953	22.9534	24.5227	28.0291	32.0887	34.3519	36.7862	42.2187	48.4966
14	14.9474	15.9739	17.0863	18.2919	19.5986	21.0151	22.5505	24.2149	26.0192	27.9750	32.3926	37.5811	40.5047	43.6720	50.8180	59.1959
15	16.0969	17.2934	18.5989	20.0236	21.5786	23.2760	25.1290	27.1521	29.3609	31.7725	37.2797	43.8424	47.5804	51.6595	60.9653	72.0351
16	17.2579	18.6393	20.1569	21.8245	23.6575	25.6725	27.8881	30.3243	33.0034	35.9497	42.7533	50.9804	55.7175	60.9250	72.9390	87.4421
17	18.4304	20.0121	21.7616	23.6975	25.8404	28.2129	30.8402	33.7502	36.9737	40.5447	48.8837	59.1176	65.0751	71.6730	87.0680	105.9306
18	19.6147	21.4123	23.4144	25.6454	28.1324	30.9057	33.9990	37.4502	41.3013	45.5992	55.7497	68.3941	75.8364	84.1407	103.7403	128.1167
19	20.8190	22.8406	25.1169	27.6712	30.5390	33.7600	37.3790	41.4463	46.0185	51.1591	63.4397	78.9692	88.2118	98.6032	123.4135	154.7400
20	22.0190	24.2974	26.8704	29.7781	33.0660	36.7856	40.9955	45.7620	51.1601	57.2750	72.0524	91.0249	102.4436	115.3797	146.6280	186.6880
30	34.7849	40.5681	47.5754	56.0849	66.4388	79.0582	94.4608	113.2832	136.3075	164.4940	241.3327	356.7868	434.7451	530.3117	790.9480	1181.8816
40	48.8864	60.4020	75.4013	95.0255	120.7998	154.7620	199.6351	259.0565	337.8824	442.5926	767.0914	1342.0251	1779.0903	2360.7572	4163.2130	7343.8578
50	64.4632	84.5794	112.7969	152.6671	209.3480	290.3359	406.5289	573.7702	815.0836	1163.9085	2400.0182	4994.5213	7217.7163	10435.6488	21813.0937	45497.1908
60	81.6697	114.0515	163.0534	237.9907	353.5837	533.1282	813.5204	1253.2133	1944.7921	3034.8164	7471.6411	18535.1333	29219.9916	46057.5085	114189.6665	281732.5718

Chapter 11

Bonds Payable

Learning Objectives

After studying this chapter, you should be able to:
1. Understand the types and characteristics of bonds.
2. Determine the issuance price of a bond.
3. Account for bonds sold at face value, at a discount, and at a premium.
4. Amortize bond discount and bond premium using either the straight-line or the effective-interest method.
5. Account for the retirement of bonds.

SETTING THE STAGE

Several years ago, United Brands (the company that markets Chiquita bananas) completed a financial transaction that fooled investors, allowed the company to report high income, and caused the company's stock price to increase substantially. Because Eli Black, the company's president, owned thousands of shares of stock, his personal net worth soared.

United Brands had borrowed millions of dollars from investors through offering bonds. Those bonds were a form of long-term debt that promised investors semiannual interest payments and return of the borrowed amount (principal) at some future date, usually 30 years later. United Brands reported this debt as "bonds payable" on its balance sheet.

When the company originally issued the bonds, interest rates were low, averaging approximately 5 percent.[1] Because United Brands was reporting annual losses, Eli Black, an accountant by training, conceived a plan to increase reported earnings. He reasoned that because the principal, or face amount of the bonds, would not be repaid for many years, investors were more interested in the semiannual interest payments. For example, with 5 percent bonds with a total face amount of $100 million, investors would not get the $100 million back for 30 years but were getting $2.5 million ($100,000,000 × .05 × ½ year) in interest every six months. Therefore, he decided to offer the bondholders a deal. He would trade them $60 million of 10 percent, 30-year bonds for the $100 million of 5 percent bonds. Thus, though investors would get only $60 million back in 30 years instead of $100 million, they would receive $3 million ($60,000,000 × .10 × ½ year) in interest every six months instead of only $2.5 million.

As it turned out, investors jumped at the opportunity to trade their lower-interest-rate bond investments for the higher-interest-rate bonds. Because of the time value of money, receiving $3 million every 6 months for 30 years and a $60 million payment at the end of the bonds' life has a greater value than receiving $2.5 million every 6 months and getting $100 million in 30 years.

Eli Black was ecstatic. Although United Brands would actually be worse off because of the higher interest payments and the several million dollars in brokerage fees to issue the new bonds, at last the company would be able to report a positive net income. The increase in income resulted from accounting for the bond transaction as follows:

Bonds Payable (old bonds)..........................	100,000,000	
Bonds Payable (new bonds)........................		60,000,000
Gain from Refinancing		40,000,000

---

[1] The numbers used in this example are not exact but have been simplified for illustrative purposes. The substance of the transaction is described accurately.

The $40 million gain was included with revenue from operations resulting in net income being increased by $40 million.[2] Investors, unaware that the increased profits were of a one-time nature and would actually hurt the company in the long run, increased their purchases of the company's stock, resulting in a significant increase in stock price. Eli Black's personal worth increased substantially, and he sold several thousand shares of stock, making huge profits.

Several weeks later, when investors and regulators discovered that the increased earnings resulted from the refinancing of bonds payable and that both income and stock price had been manipulated, Eli Black was heavily criticized, and several lawsuits were filed against him and the company. Unable to deal with the pressure, Eli Black penned a suicide note and jumped to his death from a window in his New York apartment.

[2] Because of this transaction and other similar abuses, the FASB established new accounting standards for debt refinancing transactions. Gains from refinancing long-term debt can no longer be included with operating revenues but instead have to be reported separately as an extraordinary item on the income statement. Separate disclosure alerts financial statement readers to the nature and source of the gain.

debt financing acquiring funds by borrowing money from creditors in the form of long-term notes, mortgages, leases, or bonds

equity financing acquiring funds in the form of investments by owners (proprietor, partner, or stockholder)

Long-term financing through notes payable, mortgages, and leases was explained in Chapter 10. In this chapter, we will focus on long-term financing with corporate bonds, such as those described in the United Brands scenario. This will complete our discussion of long-term **debt financing,** the generation of financial resources by borrowing money. In Chapters 13 and 14, we will cover **equity financing,** whereby financial resources are acquired through the issuance of stock (by a corporation) or through additional owner contributions (in a partnership or a proprietorship).

THE NATURE OF BONDS

Objective 1
Understand the types and characteristics of bonds.

bond a contract between a borrower and a lender in which the borrower promises to pay a specified amount of interest for each period the bond is outstanding and repay the principal at the maturity date

debentures (unsecured bonds) bonds for which no collateral has been pledged

secured bonds bonds for which assets have been pledged in order to guarantee repayment

A **bond** is a contract between the borrowing company (issuer) and the lender (investor) in which the borrower promises to pay a specified amount of interest at the end of each period the bond is outstanding and repay the principal at the maturity date of the bond contract.

Types of Bonds

Bonds can be categorized on the basis of certain characteristics. A three-way classification system is:

1. The extent to which bondholders are protected.
    (a) **Debentures (or unsecured bonds).** Bonds that have no underlying assets pledged as security, or collateral, to guarantee their repayment.
    (b) **Secured bonds.** Secured bonds are bonds that have a pledge of company assets, such as land or buildings, as a protection for lenders. If the company fails to meet its bond obligations, the pledged assets can be sold and used to pay the bondholders. Bonds that are secured with the issuer's assets are often referred to as "mortgage bonds."

Chapter 11 *Bonds Payable* 453

sinking fund bonds *bonds for which the borrowing company agrees to accumulate cash to retire the bonds*

(c) **Sinking fund bonds.** Sinking fund bonds include a provision that the borrowing company agrees to accumulate cash in a fund (called a bond sinking fund) to be used to retire the bonds at maturity. Periodic cash payments are made to the sinking fund trustee (often a bank or a trust company) who invests the funds in securities that are sold at the maturity of the bonds to pay off the bondholders. Alternatively, the trustee may use the funds to buy back the bonds at favorable prices in the open bond market. Because of the requirement to accumulate funds to retire the bonds, sinking fund bonds are sometimes thought to be secured bonds. However, since the funds are managed by a trustee who has options on how to invest the funds and when to retire the bonds, the sinking fund bonds are not secured by specific assets and therefore are not considered to be secured in the same sense that mortgage bonds are secured.

2. How the bond interest is paid.

registered bonds *bonds for which the names and addresses of the bondholders are kept on file by the issuing company*

(a) **Registered bonds.** Bonds for which the issuing company keeps a record of the names and addresses of all bondholders and pays interest only to those individuals whose names are on file.

coupon bonds *unregistered bonds for which owners receive periodic interest payments by clipping a coupon from the bond and sending it to the issuer as evidence of ownership*

(b) **Coupon bonds.** Unregistered bonds for which the issuer has no record of current bondholders but instead pays interest to anyone who can show evidence of ownership. Usually these bonds contain a printed coupon for each interest payment. When a payment is due, the bondholder clips the coupon from the certificate and sends it to the issuer as evidence of bond ownership. The issuer then sends an interest payment to the bondholder.

term bonds *bonds that mature in one lump sum at a specified future date*

3. How the bonds mature.

(a) **Term bonds.** Bonds that mature in one lump sum on a specified future date.

serial bonds *bonds that mature in a series of installments at specified future dates*

(b) **Serial bonds.** Bonds that mature in a series of installments.

callable bonds *bonds for which the issuer reserves the right to pay the obligation before its maturity date*

(c) **Callable bonds.** Term or serial bonds that the issuer can redeem at any time at a specified price.

convertible bonds *bonds that can be traded for or converted to other securities after a specified period of time*

(d) **Convertible bonds.** Term or serial bonds that can be converted to other securities, such as stocks, after a specified period, at the option of the bondholder. (The accounting for this type of bond is discussed in advanced accounting texts.)

bond indenture *a contract between a bond issuer and a bond purchaser that specifies the terms of a bond*

Characteristics of Bonds

principal (face value or maturity value) *the amount that will be paid on a bond at the maturity date*

bond maturity date *the date at which a bond principal or face amount becomes payable*

When an organization issues bonds, it usually sells them to underwriters (brokers and investment bankers), who in turn sell them to various institutions and to the public. At the time of the original sale, the company issuing the bonds chooses a trustee to represent the bondholders. In most cases, the trustee is a large bank or trust company to which the company issuing bonds delivers a contract called a **bond indenture,** deed of trust, or trust indenture. The bond indenture specifies that in return for an investment of cash by investors, the company promises to pay a specific amount of interest each period the bonds are outstanding and to repay the **principal** (also called face value, or maturity value) of the bonds at a specified future date (the **maturity date**). It is the duty of the trustee to protect investors and to make sure that the bond issuer fulfills its responsibilities.

The total value of a single "bond issue" often exceeds several million dollars. A bond issue is generally divided into a number of individual bonds, which may be of varying denominations. The principal or face value of each bond is usually $1,000, or a multiple thereof. Note that the price of bonds is quoted as a percentage of $1,000 face value. Thus, a bond quoted at 98 is selling for $980 (98% × $1,000), and a bond quoted at 103 is selling for $1,030 (103% × $1,000). By issuing bonds in small denominations, a company increases the chances that a broad range of investors will be able to compete for the purchase of the bonds. This increased demand usually results in the bonds selling for higher prices.

In most cases, the market price of bonds is influenced by (1) the riskiness of the bonds and (2) the interest rate at which the bonds are issued. The first factor, riskiness of the bonds, is determined by general economic conditions and the financial status of the company selling the bonds, as measured by organizations (Moody's or Standard and Poor's, for instance) that regularly assign a rating, or a grade, to all corporate bonds.

Companies strive to earn as high a bond rating as possible because the higher the rating, the lower the interest rate they will have to pay to attract buyers. A high-risk bond, on the other hand, will have a low rating, which means the company will have to offer a higher rate of interest to attract buyers.

> **To Summarize** *Bonds are certificates of debt issued by companies or government agencies, guaranteeing a stated interest rate and repayment of the principal at a specified maturity date. Corporations issue bonds as a form of long-term borrowing to finance the acquisition of operating assets, such as land, buildings, and equipment. Bonds can be classified by their level of security (debentures versus secured bonds), by the way interest is paid (registered versus coupon bonds), and by the way they mature (term bonds, serial bonds, callable bonds, and convertible bonds).*

DETERMINING A BOND'S ISSUANCE PRICE

Objective 2
Determine the issuance price of a bond.

When a company issues bonds, it is promising to make two types of payments: (1) a payment of interest of a fixed amount at equal intervals (usually semiannually but sometimes quarterly or annually) over the life of the bond and (2) a lump-sum payment—the principal, or face value, of the bond—at the maturity date. For example, assume that Denver Company issues 10 percent, 5-year bonds with a total face value of $800,000. Interest is to be paid semiannually. This information tells us that Denver agrees to pay $40,000 ($800,000 × 0.10 × ½ year) in interest every 6 months and also agrees to return to the investors the principal amount of $800,000 at the end of 5 years. The following diagram reflects this agreement between Denver and the bond investors:

Chapter 11 *Bonds Payable*

```
Issued bonds                                                                                    $800,000
face value                                                                                      principal
$800,000                                                                                        repayment
        Interest payments
        $40,000   $40,000   $40,000   $40,000   $40,000   $40,000   $40,000   $40,000   $40,000   $40,000

0         ½         1         1½        2         2½        3         3½        4         4½        5
Years
```

In this example, it was assumed that the bonds were issued at their face value of $800,000. However, bonds are frequently issued at a price that is more or less than their face value. The actual price at which bonds are issued is affected by what interest rate investors are seeking at the time the bonds are sold in relation to the interest rate specified by the borrower in the bond indenture. How, then, is the issuance price of bonds determined?

Essentially, present value concepts are used, which, as you learned in Chapter 10, measure the effect of time on the value of money. The price should equal the present value of the interest payments (an annuity) plus the present value of the bond's lump-sum face value at maturity. These present values are computed using the market rate of interest, which is the rate investors expect to earn on their investment. This rate is called the **effective rate,** the **yield rate,** or the **market rate** of interest. It is contrasted with the **stated rate,** which is the rate printed on the bond (10 percent in the Denver Company example).

effective (yield, or market) rate of interest *the actual interest rate earned or paid on a bond investment*

stated rate of interest *the rate of interest printed on the bond*

bond discount *the difference between the face value and the sales price when bonds are sold below their face value*

bond premium *the difference between the face value and the sales price when bonds are sold above their face value*

If the effective rate is equal to the stated rate, the bonds will sell at face value (that is, at $800,000). If the effective rate is higher than the stated rate, the bonds will sell at a **discount** (at less than the face value) because the investors desire a higher rate than the company is promising to pay. Likewise, if the effective rate is lower than the stated rate, the bonds will sell at a **premium** (at more than face value) because the company is promising to pay a higher rate than the investors are seeking at that time. We will use the Denver bonds to explain how the price is computed in each situation.

Bonds Issued at Face Value

Denver Company has agreed to issue $800,000 bonds and pay 10 percent interest, compounded semiannually. Assume that the effective interest rate demanded by investors for bonds of this level of risk is also 10 percent. Using the effective interest rate, which happens to be the same as the stated rate, the calculation to determine the price at which the bonds will be issued is as shown at the top of the next page. (Note that since the interest is compounded semiannually, the interest rate is halved and the 5-year bond life is treated as ten 6-month periods.)

The calculation shows why the bonds sell at face value. At the effective rate, the sum of the present value of the interest payments and the payment at maturity is $800,000, which is the issuance price at the stated rate. This equality of present values will occur only when the effective rate and the stated rate are the same.

1.	Semiannual interest payments	$ 40,000	
	Present value of an annuity of 10 payments of $1 at 5% (Table II).......................................	× 7.7217	
	Present value of interest payments		$308,868*
2.	Maturity value of bonds	$800,000	
	Present value of $1 received 10 periods in the future discounted at 5% (Table I)	× 0.6139	
	Present value of principal amount		490,112
3.	Issuance price of bonds (total present value)		$800,000

* Difference is due to the rounding of the present value factor.

Bonds Issued at a Discount

The Denver Company will sell its bonds at less than the face value of $800,000 (at a discount) if the stated rate of interest is less than the effective rate that investors are seeking. To illustrate the issuance of bonds at a discount, assume that the effective rate is 12 percent compounded semiannually; the stated rate remains 10 percent compounded semiannually. In this case, the bonds will be issued at a price of $741,124, as shown here.

1.	Semiannual interest payments	$ 40,000	
	Present value of an annuity of 10 payments of $1 at 6% (Table II).......................................	× 7.3601	
	Present value of interest payments		$294,404
2.	Maturity value of bonds	$800,000	
	Present value of $1 received 10 periods in the future discounted at 6% (Table I)	× 0.5584	
	Present value of principal amount		446,720
3.	Issuance Price of Bonds (total present value)............		$741,124

Denver Company will receive less than the $800,000 face value because the stated rate of interest is lower than the effective rate. In this case, there is a discount of $58,876 ($800,000 − $741,124).

Bonds Issued at a Premium

The Denver bonds will be issued for more than $800,000 (at a premium) when the stated interest rate is higher than the effective rate. Let us now assume that the effective rate is 8 percent compounded semiannually and that the stated rate is still 10 percent compounded semiannually. In this case, the bonds will be issued at $864,916, as shown here.

1.	Interest payments	$ 40,000	
	Present value of an annuity of 10 payments of $1 at 4% (Table II).......................................	× 8.1109	
	Present value of interest payments		$324,436
2.	Maturity value of bonds	$800,000	
	Present value of $1 received 10 periods in the future discounted at 4% (Table I)	× 0.6756	
	Present value of principal amount		540,480
3.	Issuance price of bonds (total present value)		$864,916

BUSINESS ENVIRONMENT ESSAY
Underwriting Bond Issues

When a company wants to raise money by issuing bonds, the marketing of those bonds is often handled by an investment banking group, referred to as the underwriters. The underwriters establish the price to be quoted to investors and are compensated for their efforts by taking the risk that the amount received from investors will exceed the amount they have agreed to pay to the borrowing (issuing) company. The following advertisement in *The Wall Street Journal* illustrates the announcement of a first mortgage bond issue of Gulf States Utilities Company, which is being marketed by four investment banking firms that are operating as the underwriting group to market this issue. The stated rate of interest is 8.21% on a first mortgage bond series due January 1, 2002, and 8.94% on a series due January 1, 2022, with the effective rate equal to the stated rate because the bonds are being offered at face value.

$300,000,000

GULF STATES UTILITIES COMPANY

$150,000,000

First Mortgage Bonds, 8.21% Series Due January 1, 2002

Price 100%
Plus accrued interest, if any, from January 1, 1992

$150,000,000

First Mortgage Bonds, 8.94% Series Due January 1, 2022

Price 100%
Plus accrued interest, if any, from January 1, 1992

Upon request, a copy of the Prospectus describing these securities and the business of the Company may be obtained within any State from any Underwriter who may legally distribute it within such State. The securities are offered only by means of the Prospectus, and this announcement is neither an offer to sell nor a solicitation of any offer to buy.

Goldman, Sachs & Co.
    The First Boston Corporation
        Kidder, Peabody & Co.
          Incorporated
            J.P. Morgan Securities Inc.

January 23, 1992

Denver will receive more than the $800,000 face value when the bonds are issued because the company has agreed to pay the investors a higher rate of interest than the market rate.

In all three situations, the 10 percent stated rate determined the amount of each interest payment, but the price of the bonds was determined by discounting the $40,000 of interest payments and the $800,000 lump sum at maturity by the effective rate of interest, which may vary from day to day, depending on market conditions. In essence, then, the issuance price depends on four factors: (1) the face value of the bonds, (2) the periodic interest payments (face value × stated interest rate), (3) the time period, and (4) the effective interest rate. Although the bond price is the exact amount that allows investors to earn the interest rate they are seeking, it also reflects the real cost of money to the borrowing company.

> **To Summarize** *The price at which bonds are issued is a function of the interest rate investors are seeking when the bonds are issued in relation to the interest rate the borrowing company is promising to pay. The bond's face value, or principal, and future interest payments (face value × stated interest rate) are discounted by the interest rate desired by investors (the effective, yield, or market rate) to arrive at the issuance price of the bonds. Bonds will sell at their face value if the stated interest rate is equal to the effective rate. If the effective rate is higher than the stated rate, the bonds will sell at a discount. If the effective rate is lower than the stated rate, the bonds will sell at a premium. The effective rate used to discount the payments promised by the borrower reflects the real cost of the money borrowed.*

ACCOUNTING FOR BONDS PAYABLE

Objective 3
Account for bonds sold at face value, at a discount, and at a premium.

When a company issues bonds, it must account for the issuance (sale) of the bonds, for the interest payments, and for the amortization of any bond premium or discount. Then, at or before maturity, the company must account for the bond's retirement.

The accounting for these four elements depends on the issuance price of the bonds and on the date of issuance in relation to the date on which interest is paid. In the following sections, we explain the accounting for bonds when the issue price is equal to face value, below face value, or above face value. In each case, we assume that the bonds are issued on an interest-paying date. Accounting for bonds issued between interest dates is discussed later in the chapter. For most of this discussion, we will use the following data:

Issuing company	Central Trucking Company
Accounting year	Calendar year ending December 31
Face value of bonds issued	$100,000
Stated interest rate	12 percent
Effective interest rate assumed in different situations:	
When issued at face value	12 percent
When issued at a discount	12.45 percent
When issued at a premium	11.36 percent

Initial date of issuance	January 1, 1994
Date of maturity	January 1, 2004
Interest-payment dates	January 1 and July 1

Accounting for Bonds Issued at Face Value

We first assume that Central Trucking Company issued $100,000 bonds with a stated interest rate of 12 percent on January 1, 1994. The bonds were issued at face value, apparently because Central Trucking is no more or less risky than other firms in the same industry and 12 percent is the effective, or market, rate of interest for similar bonds. The journal entry to record their issuance on January 1, 1994, would be as follows:

Cash	100,000	
Bonds Payable		100,000

Issued $100,000, 12%, 10-year bonds at face value.

The entry to record the first payment of interest on July 1, 1994, would be:

Bond Interest Expense	6,000	
Cash		6,000

Paid semiannual interest on the $100,000, 12%, 10-year bonds ($100,000 × 0.12 × ½ year).

Since Central Trucking operates on a calendar-year basis, it will need to make the following adjusting entry on December 31, 1994, to account for the interest expense between July 1 and December 31, 1994:

Bond Interest Expense	6,000	
Bond Interest Payable		6,000

To recognize expense for the 6 months July 1 to December 31, 1994 ($100,000 × 0.12 × ½ year).

At the end of the accounting period (December 31, 1994), the financial statements would report the following:

Income Statement

Bond interest expense ($6,000 × 2)	$ 12,000

Balance Sheet

Current liabilities:

Bond interest payable	$ 6,000

Long-term liabilities:

Bonds payable (12%, due January 1, 2004)	$100,000

Then, on January 1, 1995, when the semiannual interest is paid, the Bond Interest Payable account is eliminated. The January 1 entry would be:

```
Bond Interest Payable ............................................. 6,000
    Cash ......................................................            6,000
Paid semiannual bond interest.
```

The entries to record the interest expense payments during the remaining nine years would be the same as those made during 1994 and on January 1, 1995. The only other entry required in accounting for these bonds is the recording of their retirement on January 1, 2004. That entry, assuming that all interest has been accounted for, would be:

```
Bonds Payable ....................................................... 100,000
    Cash ......................................................         100,000
Retired the $100,000, 10-year, 12% bonds.
```

As the preceding entries illustrate, accounting for the issuance of bonds, the payment of the interest, and the retirement of the bonds is relatively simple when the bonds are issued at face value. As we will see in the following pages, the accounting for bonds becomes more complicated when bonds are issued at a discount or a premium.

Accounting for Bonds Issued at a Discount or at a Premium

Objective 4
Amortize bond discount and bond premium using either the straight-line or the effective-interest method.

As we have explained, bonds may be issued at a discount or a premium because their stated interest rate may be (and often is) lower or higher than the effective rate. The two rates often differ because economic conditions in the marketplace have changed between the date the stated interest rate was set and the date the bonds were actually sold. Various factors determine this second date—for example, the time it takes to print the bonds and the investment banker's decision regarding the best time to offer the bonds. Since the cost to the company for the use of the bond money is really the effective interest rate rather than the stated rate, the discount or premium must be written off (amortized) over the period the bonds are outstanding, and the amortization is treated as an adjustment to interest expense.

straight-line amortization *a method of systematically writing off a bond premium or discount, resulting in equal amounts being amortized each period*

effective-interest amortization *a method of systematically writing off a bond premium or discount, taking into consideration the time value of money and resulting in an equal rate of amortization for each period*

There are two methods of amortizing bond discounts and bond premiums: **straight-line amortization** and **effective-interest amortization**. With straight-line amortization, a company writes off the same amount of discount or premium each period the bonds are held—for example, with a $4,000 discount on a 10-year bond, $400 is amortized each year. Effective-interest amortization takes the time value of money into consideration. The amount of discount or premium amortized is the difference between the interest actually incurred (based on the effective rate) and the interest actually paid (based on the stated rate). The straight-line amortization method will be used to explain the accounting for the amortization of discounts and premiums; then the effective-interest method will be explained and illustrated.

Chapter 11 *Bonds Payable*

ACCOUNTING FOR BONDS ISSUED AT A DISCOUNT. When bonds are issued at a discount, the accounting involves the use of a contra-liability account to keep a separate record of the discounted amount. To illustrate, we will assume that the $100,000, 10-year, 12 percent bonds issued by Central Trucking on January 1, 1994, sold for $98,000. The entry to record the issuance of the bonds would be:

```
Cash .....................................................   98,000
Discount on Bonds ........................................    2,000
    Bonds Payable ........................................           100,000
Issued $100,000, 12%, 10-year bonds at 98.
```

The Discount on Bonds account represents the difference between the face value of the bonds and the issuance price. This discount is accounted for as additional interest expense over the life of the bonds. In other words, if the company receives only $98,000 when the bonds are issued and is required to pay $100,000 at maturity, the $2,000 difference is additional interest. The following analysis shows that total interest on the bonds is $122,000, comprised of the periodic interest payments ($120,000) plus the $2,000 discount.

Amount to be paid to bondholders:	
Interest paid each year for 10 years ($100,000 × 0.12 × 10)	$120,000
Face value to be paid at maturity	100,000
Total amount to be paid to bondholders	$220,000
Proceeds received from sale of bonds ($100,000 × .98)	98,000
Total interest expense	$122,000

Average annual interest expense: $122,000 ÷ 10 years = $12,200

Although the $2,000 of additional interest arising from the discount will not be paid until the bonds mature, interest accrues, or accumulates, over time. Thus, each year that the bonds are outstanding, Central will record interest expense for the amount paid at the stated rate ($100,000 × 0.12 = $12,000) and will also recognize a portion of the discount as interest expense. In recording the additional interest expense, the contra account, Discount on Bonds, is amortized or written off over the life of the bonds. Using straight-line amortization, an even amount is amortized each period. In the Central Trucking Company example, the semiannual amortization would be $100 ($2,000 discount ÷ 10 years × ½). Bond amortization is recorded when interest payments are made, and the entry on July 1, 1994, would be:

```
Bond Interest Expense ....................................   6,100
    Discount on Bonds ....................................             100
    Cash .................................................           6,000
Paid semiannual interest on the $100,000, 12%, 10-year bonds ($100,000 × 0.12 × ½
year) and amortized the bond discount ($2,000 ÷ 10 years × ½ year).
```

As illustrated, amortization of a discount increases bond interest expense. In this case, the interest expense is $6,100, or the sum of the semiannual interest payment and the semiannual amortization of the bond discount. Over the 10-year life of the bonds, the interest expense will be increased by $2,000 (20 periods × $100), the amount of the discount. Thus these bonds pay an effective interest rate of approximately 12.45 percent[3] per year ($12,200 interest ÷ $98,000 received on the bonds).

The adjusting entry to record the interest expense on December 31, 1994, would be:

Bond Interest Expense	6,100	
Discount on Bonds		100
Bond Interest Payable		6,000

To recognize interest expense for the 6 months July 1 to December 31, 1994.

The financial statements, prepared at December 31, 1994, would report the following:

Income Statement

Bond interest expense ($6,100 × 2)	$12,200

Balance Sheet

Current liabilities:

Bond interest payable	$ 6,000

Long-term liabilities:

Bonds payable (12%, due January 1, 2004)	$100,000	
Less unamortized discount ($2,000 − $200)	1,800	$98,200

The entries to account for the interest expense and bond discount amortization during the remaining 9 years would be the same as those illustrated. And since the bond discount would be completely amortized at the end of the 10 years, the entry to record the retirement of the bonds would be the same as that for bonds issued at face value. That entry would be:

Bonds Payable	100,000	
Cash		100,000

Retired the $100,000, 12%, 10-year bonds.

ACCOUNTING FOR BONDS ISSUED AT A PREMIUM. Like discounts, premiums must be amortized over the life of the bonds. To illustrate the accounting for bonds sold at a premium, we will assume that Central Trucking was able to sell its $100,000, 12 percent, 10-year bonds at 103 (that is, at 103 percent of face value). The entry to record the issuance of these bonds on January 1, 1994, would be:

---

[3] Because straight-line amortization was used, this effective rate of 12.45 percent is only an approximation that will change slightly each period. An accurate effective rate can be calculated only if the effective-interest method of amortization is used.

```
Cash ..................................................  103,000
   Premium on Bonds ..................................           3,000
   Bonds Payable ......................................         100,000
Sold $100,000, 12%, 10-year bonds at 103.
```

Premium on Bonds is added to Bonds Payable on the balance sheet and, like Discounts on Bonds, is amortized using either the straight-line or the effective-interest method. Thus, if Central were to use the straight-line method, the annual amortization of the premium would be $300 ($3,000 ÷ 10 years), or $150 every 6 months. The entry to record the first semiannual interest payment and the premium amortization on July 1, 1994, would be:

```
Bond Interest Expense ..................................  5,850
Premium on Bonds ......................................    150
   Cash ..............................................           6,000
Paid semiannual interest on the $100,000, 12%, 10-year bonds ($100,000 × 0.12 × ½
year), and amortized the bond premium ($3,000 ÷ 10 years × ½).
```

The amortization of a premium on bonds reduces the actual interest expense on the bonds. The following analysis shows why interest expense is reduced when bonds are sold at a premium:

Amount to be paid to bondholders	
[($12,000 interest × 10 years) + $100,000 face value]	$220,000
Proceeds received from sale of bonds	103,000
Total interest to be paid	$117,000
Average interest expense each year ($117,000 ÷ 10 years)	$11,700

In this case, the annual payments of $12,000 include interest of $11,700 and $300, which represents a partial repayment (one-tenth) of the bond premium. Thus, the effective interest rate is approximately 11.36 percent ($11,700 ÷ $103,000), which is less than the stated rate of 12 percent.

The adjusting entry to record the accrual of the interest expense on December 31, 1994, would be:

```
Bond Interest Expense ..................................  5,850
Premium on Bonds ......................................    150
   Bond Interest Payable ..............................           6,000
To recognize interest expense on the bonds for the 6 months July 1 to December 31, 1994.
```

The financial statements prepared at December 31, 1994, would report the following:

Income Statement

Bond interest expense ($5,850 × 2) .... $ 11,700

Balance Sheet

Current liabilities:
Bond interest payable .... $ 6,000

Long-term liabilities:
Bonds payable (12%, due January 1, 2004) $100,000
Plus unamortized premium ($3,000 − $300).................... 2,700 $102,700

Effective-Interest Amortization

Companies can often justify use of the straight-line method of amortizing bond premiums and discounts on the grounds that its results are not significantly different from those of the theoretically more accurate effective-interest method. However, because the effective-interest method considers the time value of money, it is required by generally accepted accounting principles if it leads to results that differ significantly from those obtained by the straight-line method.

bond carrying value the face value of bonds minus the unamortized discount or plus the unamortized premium

The effective-interest method amortizes a varying amount each period, which is the difference between the interest actually incurred and the cash actually paid. The amount actually incurred is the changing **bond carrying value** (the face value of the bond minus the unamortized discount or plus the unamortized premium) multiplied by a constant rate, the effective-interest rate.

To illustrate the effective-interest method, we assume that on January 1, 1994, Johnson Wholesale Company issued $40,000 of 10 percent, 5-year bonds for $43,246. If the bonds pay interest semiannually on January 1 and July 1, their effective interest rate is approximately 8 percent[4] a year, or 4 percent every 6 months. Since the actual interest expense for each interest period is equal to the effective rate of 4 percent multiplied by the bond carrying value, the amortization (rounded to the nearest $1) for the 5 years would be as follows:

Period	(1) Cash Paid for Interest	(2) Semiannual Interest Expense (0.04 × Bond Carrying Value)	(3) Premium Amortization (1)−(2)	(4) Carrying Value
Issuance date				$43,246
Year 1, first 6 months.....................	$2,000	(0.04 × $43,246) = $1,730	$270	42,976
Year 1, second 6 months...................	2,000	(0.04 × 42,976) = $1,719	281	42,695
Year 2, first 6 months.....................	2,000	(0.04 × 42,695) = $1,708	292	42,403
Year 2, second 6 months...................	2,000	(0.04 × 42,403) = $1,696	304	42,099
Year 3, first 6 months.....................	2,000	(0.04 × 42,099) = $1,684	316	41,783
Year 3, second 6 months...................	2,000	(0.04 × 41,783) = $1,671	329	41,454
Year 4, first 6 months.....................	2,000	(0.04 × 41,454) = $1,658	342	41,112
Year 4, second 6 months...................	2,000	(0.04 × 41,112) = $1,644	356	40,756
Year 5, first 6 months.....................	2,000	(0.04 × 40,756) = $1,630	370	40,386
Year 5, second 6 months...................	2,000	(0.04 × 40,386) = $1,614	386	40,000

[4] The 8 percent rate is the rate that will discount the face value of the bonds and the semiannual interest payments to a present value that equals the issuance price of the bonds, computed as follows:

Present value of $40,000 at 4% for 10 periods .... $40,000 × 0.6756 = $27,024
Present value of $2,000 at 4% for 10 periods ....   2,000 × 8.1109 = 16,222
Total present value = issuance price of the bonds $43,246

In this computation, the $2,000 in column (1) is the actual interest paid each 6 months; column (2) shows the interest expense for each 6 months, which is the amount that will be reported on the income statement; column (3), which is the difference between columns (1) and (2), represents the amortization of the premium; and column (4) shows the carrying, or book, value of the bonds (that is, the total of the bond payable and the unamortized bond premium), which is the amount that will be reported on the balance sheet each period. Using the effective-interest method, the bond carrying value is always equal to the present value of the bond obligation. As the carrying value decreases, while the effective rate of interest remains constant, the interest expense also decreases from one period to the next, as illustrated in column (2) of the amortization schedule.

To help you translate this table into the entries for the interest payments and premium amortization at the end of each 6-month period, we have provided the semiannual journal entries for year 3.

Year 3, End of First 6 Months

Interest Expense..	1,684	
Bond Premium...	316	
Cash		2,000

To record effective-interest expense on Johnson Wholesale bonds for the first 6 months of year 3.

Year 3, End of Second 6 Months

Interest Expense..	1,671	
Bond Premium...	329	
Bond Interest Payable		2,000

To record effective-interest expense on Johnson Wholesale bonds for the second 6 months of year 3.

Because the straight-line method would show a constant amortization ($3,246 ÷ 10 = $324.60 per 6-month period) on a decreasing bond balance, the straight-line interest rate cannot be constant. It is for this reason that when the straight-line results differ significantly from the effective-interest results, generally accepted accounting principles require use of the effective-interest method.

The effective-interest method of amortizing a bond discount is essentially the same as amortizing a bond premium. The main difference is that the bond carrying value is increasing instead of decreasing.

Accounting for Bonds Issued Between Interest Dates

To this point, we have assumed in every example that bonds were issued on an interest-payment date. In reality, however, bonds are often issued between interest dates. When this occurs, accounting for interest and premium or discount amortization becomes somewhat more complicated.

With regard to the first interest payment, the complication rises because interest is usually paid for a full period regardless of how long the bonds have been held. Therefore if interest is to be paid semiannually and the bonds are sold between interest dates, it is customary for the bond investor to pay the seller (the previous owner or the original issuer) for the interest between the last payment date and the date of sale. (This is often referred to as accrued interest because it is the amount of interest accumulated since the last interest payment date.)

To illustrate, we will assume that on January 1, 1994, Higgins Corporation received authorization to issue $200,000 of 12 percent, 7-year bonds with interest payments to be made on January 1 and July 1 of each year. Since the bonds mature in 7 years, they will have an authorized life of 84 months and pay interest of $12,000 ($200,000 × 0.12 × ½ year) every January 1 and July 1. However, if Higgins Corporation did not actually sell the bonds until May 1, 1994, then on July 1 the investors would have held the bonds for only 2 months and would have earned only $4,000 in interest ($200,000 × 0.12 × ⅙ year). Since the investors would receive $12,000 on July 1, Higgins Corporation would add $8,000 in unearned accrued interest to the selling price of the bonds. This accrued interest complication can be diagrammed as shown in Exhibit 11-1.

If the bonds were sold on May 1, 1994, at face value, the entry to record the sale of the bonds and the payment of $8,000 accrued interest by investors would be:

Cash ($200,000 + $8,000 accrued interest)	208,000	
Bonds Payable		200,000
Bond Interest Payable		8,000

Sold $200,000, 12%, 7-year bonds at face value plus four months' accrued interest.

The $8,000 accrued interest is credited to Bond Interest Payable. On July 1, 1994, when the full $12,000 of semiannual interest is paid to bondholders, only $4,000 will be recognized as interest expense; the $8,000 debit will eliminate the payable previously established. The journal entry to record the July 1, 1994, interest payment would be:

Bond Interest Payable	8,000	
Bond Interest Expense	4,000	
Cash		12,000

Made semiannual interest payment (including 4 months' interest accrued at date of issuance) on $200,000, 12%, 7-year bonds.

At this point, you are probably wondering why the issuer does not simply keep track of bonds as they are sold, and pay only the amount of interest earned by investors instead of the full amount for six months. Such a system would be much more complicated than the one just presented. One reason is that bonds might be issued to many different investors over a period of days or weeks, and the amount of accrued interest would change daily. Further, after bonds are issued, they are traded daily among investors. Thus, it would be an impossible task for bond issuers to keep track of which investors own how many bonds and on what dates the different bonds were purchased. It is actually easier for issuers to pay specified amounts of interest every period and require investors who buy between interest dates to pay in advance for any unearned interest.

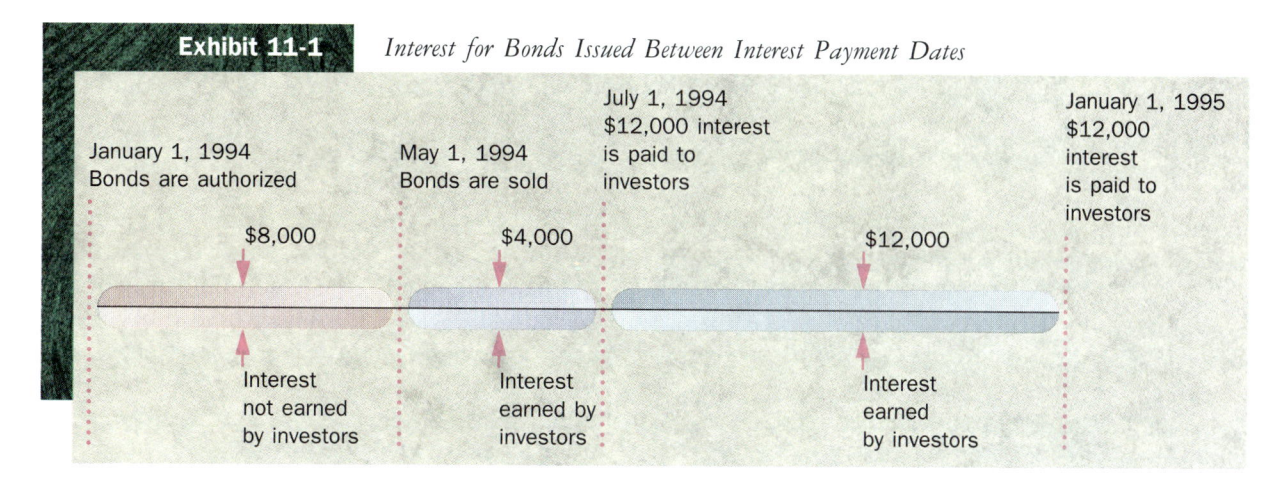

Exhibit 11-1 Interest for Bonds Issued Between Interest Payment Dates

| January 1, 1994 Bonds are authorized | May 1, 1994 Bonds are sold | July 1, 1994 $12,000 interest is paid to investors | January 1, 1995 $12,000 interest is paid to investors |

$8,000 — Interest not earned by investors

$4,000 — Interest earned by investors

$12,000 — Interest earned by investors

When bonds are sold between interest dates at a premium or discount, an additional complication arises because the premium or discount must be amortized over the actual time the bonds are outstanding, not over their entire authorized life. For example, assume the Higgins Corporation bonds, authorized on January 1, 1994, and issued on May 1, 1994, were sold at 103. The selling price of $206,000 ($200,000 × 1.03) includes a premium of $6,000. The journal entry to record the issuance on May 1 would be:

```
Cash [($200,000 × 1.03) + $8,000 accrued interest] .........   214,000
    Bonds Payable.............................................              200,000
    Premium on Bonds.........................................                6,000
    Bond Interest Payable ...................................                8,000
Sold $200,000, 12%, 7-year bonds at 103 plus accrued interest.
```

In this case, since the bonds were authorized on January 1, 1994, but were not issued until May 1, 1994, the amortization period would be 6 years and 8 months (80 months), not the full 7 years. The monthly amortization of the premium (assuming straight-line amortization) would therefore be $75 per month ($6,000 ÷ 80 months). On July 1, 1994, with the bonds outstanding for only 2 months, the entry to record the interest payment and premium amortization would be:

```
Bond Interest Payable ..........................................   8,000
Bond Interest Expense .........................................   3,850
Premium on Bonds ($75 × 2 months)..........................     150
    Cash ......................................................              12,000
Made semiannual interest payment on the $200,000, 12%, 7-year bonds and amortized the bond premium.
```

Note that on all succeeding interest payment dates, the amount of the premium amortization will be $450 ($75 per month × 6 months).

Objective 5

Account for the retirement of bonds.

Bond Retirements at Maturity

The maturity date of a bond should also be the last interest payment date. The entry to record that last interest payment and the amortization of the premium or discount results in a zero balance in the Premium or Discount on Bonds account. The only remaining bond account should be Bonds Payable with a credit balance equal to the face value of the bonds. This account is eliminated when the face value, or principal amount, of the bonds is paid to the bondholders. For example, suppose that Teltrex Manufacturing Company had issued at 98 a $200,000, 10 percent, 10-year bond, with semiannual interest payments, due to mature on July 1, 1994. Teltrex uses straight-line amortization, and so on that date, the Discount on Bonds account shows a balance of $200 (the final amount of the discount to be amortized for the last 6-month period). The entries to make the last interest payment and to retire the bonds would be:

Bond Interest Expense	10,200	
Discount on Bonds		200
Cash		10,000

Paid 6 months' interest on bonds payable (5% × $200,000) and amortized the remaining bond discount.

Bonds Payable	200,000	
Cash		200,000

Retired the 10%, $200,000 issue of bonds that matured on July 1, 1994.

There is no gain or loss when bonds are retired at maturity since the amount paid to bondholders is exactly equal to the face value of the bonds.

Bond Retirements Before Maturity

Bond issues are, by definition, an inflexible form of long-term debt. The issuing company has a set schedule of interest payments and a specified maturity date, usually at least 5 or 10 years from the issuance date. In many cases, however, a company may want to pay off (redeem) and retire its bonds before maturity. This situation might occur when interest rates fall; a company uses the money obtained by issuing new bonds at a lower interest rate to retire the older, higher interest bonds. As a result, the company retains the money it needs for expansion or other long-range projects but pays less interest for using that money.

As noted earlier, callable bonds are issued with an early redemption provision. Although the company usually has to pay a premium (penalty) for the privilege of redeeming (calling) the bonds, the amount of the premium will probably be less than the amount gained in paying a lower interest rate. With bonds that are not callable, the company simply purchases the bonds in the open market, as available, at the going price.

To illustrate the retirement of bonds before maturity, assume that Wright Company had issued $150,000, 14 percent bonds, which are now selling in the bond market at 109 and are callable at 110. The company decides to take advantage of lower interest rates (12 percent) by issuing new bonds and using the proceeds to pay off the outstanding bonds. The amount of unamortized discount still on the books for the original bonds is $8,000, and the penalty (the call premium) is $15,000. The entry to record the retirement of the bonds at 110 is:

Bonds Payable	150,000	
Loss on Bond Retirement	23,000	
Discount on Bonds		8,000
Cash ($150,000 × 110)		165,000

To retire $150,000 of bonds at a call price of 110.

In this case, the bonds were retired at a loss of $23,000 ($15,000 call premium + $8,000 unamortized discount). The loss is probably tolerable because the company expects to pay significantly less interest over the life of the new bond issue than it would have had to continue to pay on the old bonds. Gains and losses on the early retirement of bonds are reported on the income statement as extraordinary gains and losses.

> **To Summarize** *Accounting for bonds involves four steps: (1) accounting for their issuance, (2) accounting for the periodic interest payments, (3) accounting for the amortization of discounts and premiums, and (4) accounting for their retirement. When bonds are sold at a premium or at a discount, the effective-interest method of amortization reflects a constant effective interest rate, whereas the straight-line method only approximates an effective rate. Bonds are often issued between interest dates, requiring investors to pay in advance for unearned interest they will receive in the first interest payment. When bonds are retired at maturity, there is no gain or loss since the amount paid is equal to the face value of the bonds. The remaining premium or discount would have been amortized when the last interest payment was made and recorded. When bonds are retired before maturity, a gain or loss often results since the price paid to retire the bonds can be different from the carrying value of the bonds. The gain or loss on retirement of bonds is reported on the income statement as an extraordinary item.*

Review of Learning Objectives

Objective 1

Understand the types and characteristics of bonds. A bond is a contract in which the issuing company promises to pay a specified amount of interest at regular intervals (usually every 6 months) and to return the face value of the bonds to the bondholders at maturity. A bond contract is a common form of long-term debt financing by corporations and government agencies. The characteristics of a bond depend on whether any security underlies the debt (secured or debentured bonds), how interest is paid (registered or coupon bonds), and the manner in which the bonds mature (term, serial, callable, or convertible bonds).

Objective 2

Determine the issuance price of a bond. Present value concepts are used to determine the issuance price of a bond. The price of the bond is thus (1) the present value of the periodic interest payments (an annuity) plus (2) the present value of the principal (a lump sum) to be repaid at maturity. These amounts are computed by discounting the periodic interest payments and the maturity value by the effective interest rate, which is the yield or market rate that investors are seeking on the day the bonds are issued. Bonds can be issued at face value, below face value (at a discount), or above face value (at a premium). Bonds sell at face value when the stated and effective (market) interest rates are the same. Bonds sell at a discount when the company's stated rate is lower than the effective rate. Bonds sell at a premium when the stated rate is higher than the effective rate.

Objective 3

Account for bonds sold at face value, at a discount, and at a premium. Accounting for bonds by the borrowing company (the issuer) includes four elements: accounting for their issuance, for interest payments, for the amortization of premium or discount, and for their retirement. If bonds are sold at face value, Cash is debited and Bonds Payable is credited. However, bonds are more often sold at a premium or at a discount. The bond liability is recorded at face value in the Bonds Payable account, whereas the premium or discount is recorded in a separate account. A bond discount is a contra-liability account that is deducted from Bonds Payable on the balance sheet; a bond premium is added to Bonds Payable on the balance sheet. The premium or discount is amortized on each interest-paying date as an adjustment in arriving at the interest expense.

Objective 4

Amortize bond discount and bond premium using either the straight-line or the effective-interest method. If bonds are issued at a discount, the interest expense for the year is the interest paid plus the bond discount amortized that year. If the bonds are sold at a premium, the interest expense for the year is the interest paid minus the bond premium amortized that year. Bond premiums and discounts may be amortized using either the straight-line or the effective-interest method, provided that the two methods produce similar results. Otherwise, GAAP requires the effective-interest method. When bonds are sold between interest dates, the bond premium or bond discount is amortized over the actual period that the bonds are outstanding. Accounting for the first interest payment when bonds are sold between interest dates is complicated by the payment of accrued interest by the bond buyer for the fractional period between the last interest date and the date of sale of the bonds. Premiums or discounts must be properly related to the fractional period in order to accurately show the interest expense for that year.

Objective 5

Account for the retirement of bonds. At the date a bond matures, the bond premium or discount should have been fully amortized so that the Bonds Payable account at face value is the only bond account remaining on the books. At the maturity date, the borrowing company pays the face value to the investors, and the bonds are canceled. If bonds are retired before maturity, a gain or loss will be recognized when the carrying value of the bonds differs from the amount paid to retire the bonds.

Key Terms and Concepts

bond *(452)*
bond carrying value *(464)*
bond discount *(455)*
bond indenture *(453)*
bond maturity date *(453)*
bond premium *(455)*
callable bonds *(453)*
convertible bonds *(453)*
coupon bonds *(453)*

debentures (unsecured bonds) *(452)*
debt financing *(452)*
effective-interest amortization *(460)*
effective (yield, or market) rate of interest *(455)*
equity financing *(452)*

principal (face value or maturity value) *(453)*
registered bonds *(453)*
secured bonds *(452)*
serial bonds *(453)*
sinking fund bonds *(453)*
stated rate of interest *(455)*
straight-line amortization *(460)*
term bonds *(453)*

Review Problem

Bonds Payable

Scientific Engineering Company received authorization on July 1, 1993, to issue $300,000 of 12 percent bonds. The maturity date of the bonds is July 1, 2013. Interest is payable on January 1 and July 1 of each year. The bonds were sold for $289,200 on July 1, 1993 (the same day as authorized). Scientific Engineering uses straight-line amortization.

Required:
1. Compute the approximate effective interest rate for the bonds.
2. Record the journal entries on:
   (a) July 1, 1993.
   (b) December 31, 1993.
   (c) January 1, 1994.
   (d) July 1, 1994.
   (e) December 31, 1994.
3. Record the journal entries on July 1, 2013, for the final interest payment and the retirement of the bonds.

Solution

1. Effective Interest Rate

Since the bonds sold at a discount, the actual or effective rate of interest is higher than the stated interest rate of 12 percent. The effective interest rate can be approximated as follows:

Bond discount amortized per year = $10,800/20 periods = $540
Annual interest expense = ($300,000 × 12%) + $540 = $36,540
Effective interest rate = $36,540/$289,200 = 12.63%

2. Journal Entries

(a) 1993
July 1   Cash 289,200
         Discount on Bonds 10,800
              Bonds Payable   300,000
         To record the sale of $300,000 of 12% bonds due on July 1, 2013.

(b) 1993
Dec. 31 Bond Interest Expense 18,270
              Discount on Bonds   270
              Bond Interest Payable   18,000
         To record semiannual interest expense on $300,000, 12%, 20-year bonds ($300,000 × .12 × ½ year) and amortize bond discount ($10,800 ÷ 20 years × ½ year).

(c) 1994
Jan. 1   Bond Interest Payable 18,000
              Cash   18,000
         Paid semiannual interest on $300,000 bonds.

(d) 1994
July 1   Bond Interest Expense 18,270
              Discount on Bonds   270
              Cash   18,000
         Paid semiannual interest on $300,000 bonds and amortized bond discount.

(e) 1994
Dec. 31   Bond Interest Expense 18,270
             Discount on Bonds   270
             Bond Interest Payable   18,000

To record semiannual interest expense on $300,000 bonds and amortize bond discount.

3. Retirement of the Bonds

2013
July 1   Bond Interest Expense 18,270
             Discount on Bonds   270
             Bond Interest Payable   18,000

To record the bond interest expense and discount amortization up to the date of maturity.

          Bonds Payable 300,000
          Bond Interest Payable   18,000
             Cash   318,000

To record the payment of interest for 6 months and retire the bonds at maturity.

The first entry on July 1, 2013, updates the amortization of the bond discount to the retirement date and reflects the cash owed for interest for the period January 1–July 1, 2013. The second entry reflects payment for retiring the bonds plus payment of the interest owed.

Discussion Questions

1. What is the difference between debt and equity financing?
2. For a profitable company, why is the effective cost of borrowing usually lower than the stated interest rates on loans?
3. What are two important features that determine the issuance price of a bond?
4. When does the stated amount of a liability equal its present value?
5. To whom do companies usually sell bonds?
6. If the effective rate of interest for a bond is greater than its stated rate of interest, explain why the annual interest expense will be different from the periodic cash interest payments to the bondholders.
7. What is the carrying value of a bond, and how does the carrying value affect the accounting for bonds payable under the effective-interest method?
8. If a bond's stated interest rate is below the market interest rate, will the bond sell at a premium or at a discount?
9. If you think the market interest rate is going to drop in the near future, should you invest in bonds?
10. When do you think bonds would sell at or near face value?
11. What type of account is Discount on Bonds?
12. Why does the amortization of a bond discount increase the effective interest rate of bonds?
13. Why is the effective-interest amortization method more theoretically appropriate than the straight-line amortization method?
14. Why must investors pay for unearned interest when purchasing bonds between interest dates?
15. Explain why bonds retired before maturity may result in a gain or loss to the issuing company.

Exercises

E11-1

Accounting for Bonds Issued at Face Value

Oakland Company issued $500,000 of 12 percent, 10-year bonds at face value on July 1, 1993. Interest is payable semiannually on July 1 and January 1. Oakland uses the calendar year for financial reporting.

1. Record the journal entries to account for these bonds on July 1 and December 31, 1993.
2. Record the entries on July 1, 2003, when the bonds are retired.

E11-2
Accounting for Bonds Issued at a Premium

Sealon Corporation issued $100,000 of 10 percent, 10-year bonds at 102 on April 1, 1994. Interest is payable semiannually on April 1 and October 1. Sealon Corporation uses the calendar year for financial reporting.

1. Record the necessary entries to account for these bonds on the following three dates. (Use the straight-line method to amortize the bond premium.)
   (a) April 1, 1994.
   (b) October 1, 1994.
   (c) December 31, 1994.
2. Show how the bonds would be reported on the balance sheet of Sealon Corporation on December 31, 1994.

E11-3
Accounting for Bonds Issued at a Discount

Pacific Equipment Company issued $300,000 of 8 percent, 5-year bonds at 97 on June 30, 1993. Interest is payable on June 30 and December 31. The company uses the straight-line method to amortize bond premiums and discounts. The company's fiscal year is from February 1 through January 31.

Prepare all necessary journal entries to account for the bonds from the date of issuance through June 30, 1994. Also record the retirement of the bonds on June 30, 1998, assuming that all interest has been paid and that the discount has been fully amortized.

E11-4
Effective-Interest Calculation

Determine the *approximate* effective rate of interest for $300,000, 8 percent, 5-year bonds issued at 95. (Assume straight-line amortization.)

E11-5
Effective-Interest Amortization

Determine the effective interest rate for $100,000, 12 percent, 10-year bonds issued at a price of $89,404. Interest is payable semiannually. Assume the effective-interest amortization method is used for the bonds.

E11-6
Bond Amortization Schedule

The following is a partially completed amortization schedule prepared for the Liggett Company to account for its 3-year bond issue with a face value of $50,000. The schedule covers the first three semiannual interest payment dates. Amounts are rounded to the nearest dollar. Compute the missing numbers.

Year	Interest Paid	Interest Expense	Premium Amortized	Bonds Payable Carrying Value
0				$52,537
½	(1)	$2,627	(2)	52,164
1	$3,000	(3)	$392	(4)
1½	(5)	(6)	(7)	(8)

E11-7
Accounting for Bonds

Parker Corporation, a calendar-year firm, is authorized to issue $400,000 of 12 percent, 10-year bonds dated May 1, 1993, with interest payable semiannually on May 1 and November 1.

Amortization of bond premiums or discounts is recorded using the straight-line amortization method. Prepare journal entries to record the following events, assuming that the bonds are sold at 96 on May 1, 1993.

1. The bond issuance on May 1, 1993.
2. Payment of interest on November 1, 1993.
3. Adjusting entry on December 31, 1993.
4. Payment of the interest on May 1, 1994.

E11-8
Bonds Issued Between Interest Dates

Quaker Company issued $480,000 of 10 percent, 10-year bonds on June 1, 1994, for $494,375 plus accrued interest. The bonds were dated January 1, 1994, and interest is payable on January 1 and July 1 of each year. Make the following journal entries. (Round to the nearest dollar.)

1. Record the issuance of the bonds on June 1, 1994.
2. Record the interest payment on July 1, 1994, using straight-line amortization.
3. Record the interest accrual on December 31, 1994, including amortization.

E11-9
Retirement of Bonds Before Maturity

The balance sheet of Zennex Corporation shows the following long-term liabilities at December 31, 1993:

Long-Term Liabilities:
Bonds Payable (10%, due 12/31/98)	$600,000	
Unamortized Bond Premium	19,200	$619,200

On April 30, 1994, Zennex Corporation retired the bonds at 101.75, plus four months' accrued interest.

1. Record the interest payment and bond amortization on April 30, 1994. (Use straight-line amortization.)
2. Record the payment to retire the bonds at April 30, 1994.
3. Explain why the corporation was able to retire the bonds at less than their carrying value.

Problem Set A

P11A-1
Accounting for Bonds

On July 1, 1993, Worcester Corporation issued $100,000, 10-year, 12 percent bonds at 96. The bonds pay interest each June 30 and December 31.

Required:
1. Give the journal entry to record:
   (a) The issuance of the bonds.
   (b) The December 31, 1993, interest payment. Assume straight-line amortization of bond discount.
2. Assume that on May 1, 1994, Worcester Corporation issued additional bonds. These 5-year, 8 percent bonds had a face value of $50,000, and were sold at 116. Interest is payable each May 1 and November 1. Record the issuance of the bonds.
3. **Interpretative Question** With regard to (2), why are investors sometimes required to pay more than the face value of the bonds in order to acquire them?

P11A-2
Accounting for Bonds

Nemo Company authorized and sold $90,000 of 10 percent, 15-year bonds on April 1, 1994. The bonds pay interest each April 1, and Nemo's year-end is December 31.

Required:
1. Prepare journal entries to record the issuance of Nemo Company's bonds under each of the following three assumptions:
   (a) Sold at 97.

Chapter 11 Bonds Payable

(b) Sold at face value.
(c) Sold at 105.

2. Prepare adjusting entries for the bonds on December 31, 1994, under all three assumptions. (Use the straight-line amortization method.)
3. Show how the bond liabilities would appear on the December 31, 1994, balance sheet under each of the three assumptions.
4. **Interpretive Question** What condition would cause the bonds to sell at 97? At 105?

P11A-3
Bonds Retired at Maturity

Stottard Company issued $450,000 of 10 percent, 10-year bonds on June 1, 1993, at 103. The bonds were dated June 1, and interest is payable on June 1 and December 1 of each year.

Required:
1. Record the issuance of the bonds on June 1, 1993. (Round to the nearest dollar.)
2. Record the interest payment on December 1, 1993. Stottard uses the straight-line method of amortization.
3. Record the interest accrual on December 31, 1993, including amortization.
4. Record the journal entries required on June 1, 2003, when the bonds mature.

P11A-4
Straight-Line Versus Effective-Interest Amortization

Cyprus Corporation issued $150,000 face value of bonds on January 1, 1993, to raise funds to buy some special machinery. The maturity date of the bonds is January 1, 1998, with interest payable each January 1 and July 1. The stated rate of interest is 10 percent. When the bonds were sold, the effective rate of interest was 12 percent. The company's financial reporting year ends December 31.

Required:
1. Determine the price at which the bonds would be sold.
2. Prepare the amortization schedule using the effective-interest method.
3. Prepare a comparative schedule of interest expense for each year (1993–1997) for the effective-interest and straight-line methods of amortization.
4. Record the journal entry for the last interest payment in 1998 using the amortization schedule in (2).
5. Record the journal entry for the retirement of the bonds.
6. **Interpretive Question** Is the difference between the interest expense each year between the straight-line and effective-interest methods sufficient to require the use of the effective-interest method? How do you think this question would be answered in practice?

P11A-5
Analysis of Bonds

Bonds with a face value of $200,000 and a stated interest rate of 12 percent were issued on March 1, 1994. The bonds pay interest each February 28 and August 31 and mature on March 1, 2004. The issuing company uses the calendar year for financial reporting.

Required:
Using these data, complete the following tables for each of the conditions listed. (Show computations and assume straight-line amortization.)

1. The bonds sold at face value.
2. The bond sold at 97.
3. The bonds sold at 103.

	Case 1	Case 2	Case 3
Cash received at issuance date	___	___	___
Total cash paid to bondholders through maturity	___	___	___
Income Statement for 1994			
Bond interest expense	___	___	___

	Case 1	Case 2	Case 3
Balance Sheet at December 31, 1994			
Long-term liabilities:			
Bonds payable, 12%	___	___	___
Unamortized discount	___	___	___
Unamortized premium	___	___	___
Bond carrying value	___	___	___
Approximate effective interest rate*	___	___	___

*Round to the nearest tenth of a percent.

P11A-6
Interpreting a Bond Amortization Schedule

The following amortization schedule of the Krueger Company presents information for the issuance of 5-year bonds on January 1, 1993, and the interest payments each six months over a 5-year period. The company closes its books on December 31, and financial statements are prepared at that time.

Amortization Schedule

Date	Cash Paid	Interest	Amount Amortized	Bond Carrying Value
Jan. 1, 1993				$ 92,278
Jul. 1, 1993	$ 4,000	$ 4,614	$ 614	$ 92,892
Jan. 1, 1994	4,000	4,645	645	93,537
Jul. 1, 1994	4,000	4,677	677	94,214
Jan. 1, 1995	4,000	4,711	711	94,925
Jul. 1, 1995	4,000	4,746	746	95,671
Jan. 1, 1996	4,000	4,783	783	96,454
Jul. 1, 1996	4,000	4,823	823	97,277
Jan. 1, 1997	4,000	4,864	864	98,141
Jul. 1, 1997	4,000	4,907	907	99,048
Jan. 1, 1998	4,000	4,952	952	100,000
	$40,000	$47,722	$7,722	

Required:
1. Were the bonds issued at a premium or a discount? How did you determine this information?
2. What was the face amount of the bonds, and what was the stated rate of interest?
3. Is the amortization schedule based on the straight-line method or the effective-interest method? How did you determine which method was used?
4. Using the amortization schedule, prepare the journal entry to record the issuance of the bonds on January 1, 1993.
5. Using the amortization schedule, prepare the journal entries to reflect interest and amortization for the year 1996.
6. How much interest expense will be shown on the company's income statement for 1996?

P11A-7
Bonds Sold Between Interest Dates

Kaiser Company sold $200,000 of 12 percent, 10-year bonds dated January 1, 1994, for $188,200 plus accrued interest on March 1, 1994. Interest is payable on January 1 and July 1.

Required:
1. Over how many months is the bond discount amortized?
2. Record the issuance of the bonds, including the collection of accrued interest.
3. Record the first interest payment on July 1, 1994, including amortization of the bond discount using the straight-line method.

Chapter 11 Bonds Payable

4. Record the adjusting entry for the interest accrual on December 31, 1994, including the amortization of bond discount.

P11A-8
Bonds Retired Before Maturity

Amity Construction Company issued $100,000 of 10 percent bonds on January 1, 1994. The maturity date of the bonds is January 1, 2004. Interest is payable January 1 and July 1. The bonds were sold at 111.3 plus accrued interest on August 1, 1994. The company uses the straight-line method of amortizing bond premiums and discounts.

Required:
1. Make the required journal entries for each of the following dates:
   (a) August 1, 1994.
   (b) December 31, 1994.
   (c) January 1, 1995.
   (d) July 1, 1995.
2. Because of a substantial decline in the market rate of interest, Amity Company purchased all the bonds on the open market at face value (100) on July 1, 1997. The following entry had just been made on that day:

Bond Interest Expense	4,400	
Bond Premium	600	
Cash		5,000

   Made semiannual interest payment on the bonds and amortized bond premium for 6 months.

   Prepare the journal entry to record the retirement of the bonds on July 1, 1997.

Problem Set B

P11B-1
Accounting for Bonds Issued at a Premium

On March 1, 1993, Devone Corporation issued $50,000 of 10 percent, 5-year bonds at 118. The bonds were dated March 1, 1993, and interest is payable on March 1 and September 1. Devone records amortization using the straight-line method. Devone's financial reporting year ends on December 31.

SOLUTIONS SOFTWARE

Required: Provide all necessary journal entries on each of the following dates:

1. March 1, 1993.
2. September 1, 1993.
3. December 31, 1993.
4. March 1, 1998.

P11B-2
Straight-Line Versus Effective-Interest Amortization

On January 1, 1993, Charon Company issued 12 percent, 10-year bonds with a face amount of $100,000. The effective rate of interest was 10% at the time of issuance. Interest is paid semiannually on January 1 and July 1.

Required:
1. Calculate the issuance price of the bonds on January 1, 1993.
2. Assume Charon Company has been using the straight-line method of amortizing the bond premium. On January 1, 1997, the company decides to change to the effective-interest method. How much has the interest expense been overstated or understated for the past 4 years in total?

P11B-3
Effective-Interest Amortization

Lancell Corporation issued $100,000 of 3-year, 10 percent bonds on January 1, 1993. The bonds pay interest on January 1 and July 1 each year. The bonds were sold to yield an 8 percent return, compounded semiannually.

Required:
1. At what price were the bonds issued?
2. Prepare a schedule to amortize the premium or discount on the bonds using the effective-interest amortization method.
3. Use the information in the amortization schedule prepared for (2) to record the interest payment on July 1, 1995, including the appropriate amortization of the premium or discount.
4. **Interpretive Question** Explain why these bonds sold for more or less than face value.

P11B-4
Accounting for Bonds

Bell Company sold $200,000 of 10-year bonds on January 1, 1993, to Brown Corporation. The bond indenture included the following information:

Face value	$200,000
Date of bonds	January 1, 1993
Maturity date	January 1, 2003
Stated rate of interest	14 percent*
Effective (market) rate of interest	12 percent*

*Compounded semiannually

Required:
1. Prepare the journal entry to record the issuance of the bonds.
2. What is the interest expense on the Bell Company books for the years ending December 31, 1993, and December 31, 1994, using straight-line amortization?
3. Explain how the bonds would be presented on Bell's balance sheet at December 31, 1994.

P11B-5
Effective-Interest Amortization

Justin Company issued a 12 percent, 4-year, $1,000 bond on January 1, 1993. The interest is payable each year on December 31. The bond was sold at an effective rate of interest of 10 percent. With respect to the bond, the following computations have been made:

Date	Cash	Interest	Principal	Balance
January 1, 1993				$1,063
End of Year 1	$120	$106	$14	1,049
End of Year 2	120	105	15	1,034
End of Year 3	120	104	16	1,018
End of Year 4	120	102	18	1,000

Required:
1. At what price was the bond issued?
2. Did the bond sell at a premium or a discount? How much?
3. How much interest expense would be shown on the income statement each year?
4. What long-term liability amount would be shown on the balance sheet at the end of year 3?
5. How were the following amounts calculated for year 3? (a) $120 (b) $104 (c) $16 (d) $1,018

Chapter 11 Bonds Payable

P11B-6

Straight-Line Versus Effective-Interest Amortization

SPREADSHEET PROBLEM

Foster Corporation issued 3-year bonds with a $180,000 face value on March 1, 1993, in order to pay for a new computer system. The bonds mature on March 1, 1996, with interest payable on March 1 and September 1. The contract rate of interest is 10 percent. (Interest is earned semiannually.) When the bonds were sold, the effective rate of interest was 12%. The company's fiscal year ends on February 28.

Required:
1. At what price were the bonds issued based on the information presented?
2. Prepare an amortization schedule using the effective-interest method.
3. Prepare a schedule of interest expense for each year (1993–1996) comparing the annual interest expense for straight-line and effective-interest amortization.
4. Using the amortization schedule prepared in (2), prepare the journal entry to record the interest payment on September 1, 1993.
5. Prepare the adjusting journal entry to record accrued interest on February 28, 1994.
6. Prepare the journal entry to retire the bonds on March 1, 1996.

P11B-7

Unifying Concepts: Accounting for Bonds Payable

Bull Durham Corporation was authorized to issue $500,000 of 8 percent, 4-year bonds, dated May 1, 1993. All the bonds were sold on that date when the effective interest rate was 10 percent. Interest is payable on May 1 and November 1 each year. The company follows a policy of amortizing premium or discount using the effective-interest method. The company closes its books on December 31 of each year.

Required:
1. Calculate the issuance price of the bonds.
2. Prepare an amortization schedule that covers the life of the bond.
3. Prepare journal entries at the following dates based on the information shown in the amortization schedule prepared for requirement (2).
   (a) December 31, 1993.
   (b) May 1, 1994.
   (c) November 1, 1994.
   (d) December 31, 1994.
4. How much interest expense did the company report on its income statement for the year 1994 related to this bond issue based on the journal entries prepared for requirement (3)?
5. What was the carrying value of this bond issue on the balance sheet of the company at December 31, 1994?
6. **Interpretive Question** Explain why another company in the same industry, which issued bonds with the same amount of face value, the same date of issuance, and the same stated rate of interest, might have had an issuance price of more or less than the price you computed for issuance of the Bull Durham Corporation bonds.

Business Analysis Case *GTE Florida Incorporated*

The following advertisement by a group of investment underwriters appeared in *The Wall Street Journal* offering to sell first mortgage bonds of GTE Florida Incorporated.

Required:
1. If the total $75,000,000 face value of bonds were sold, how much would the investment banking group collect from the purchasers, ignoring any accrued interest?

> *This announcement is neither an offer to sell nor a solicitation of an offer to buy these securities. The offer is made only by the Prospectus and the related Prospectus Supplement.*
>
> April 6, 1990
>
> # $75,000,000
>
> # GTE GTE Florida Incorporated
>
> ### First Mortgage 9⅝% Bonds, Series DD Due 2030
>
> ### Price 97.273%
> (Plus accrued interest from April 1, 1990)
>
> *Copies of the Prospectus and the related Prospectus Supplement may be obtained in any State in which this announcement is circulated only from such of the undersigned as may legally offer these securities in such State.*
>
> ### Shearson Lehman Hutton Inc.
> ### Paine Webber Incorporated
> ### Salomon Brothers, Inc

2. What is the maturity date of the bonds?
3. What is the stated rate of interest on the bonds?
4. Are the bonds being issued at a premium or a discount? Explain.
5. Is the effective rate of interest to be paid by the issuer more or less than the stated rate of interest?
6. What type of assurance is the issuer offering to purchasers, if any, regarding the issuer's capability of retiring the bonds at maturity?

Ethics Case *Leverage Company*

Below is the lead paragraph of an article that appeared in *The Wall Street Journal* on March 1, 1990:

> **FRAUD IS COMMON and tied to company supervision, studies find.**
> Some 87% of managers in a National Association of Accountants study were willing to commit fraud in one or more of the cases presented to them. More than half were willing to overstate assets, while 48% said they would establish insufficient return reserves for defective products and 38% said they would pad a government contract. "I was just so surprised that that many people would operate in a fraudulent way," says Paul Brown of New York University, co-author of the study. Those most likely to commit fraud valued pleasure and a comfortable life rather than self-respect, he says.

Keeping this article in mind, assume that Leverage Company has issued long-term debt in the form of bonds that have a clause in the bond contract stipulating that the company is in violation of the bond contract if long-term debt at year-end is more than 50% of total debt and equity. A violation of the bond contract means that the bonds are subject to redemption at any time by the bondholders. Further assume that just before the financial statements at year-end are to be finalized, it comes to the company's attention that there is a serious defect in one of their major products, which could lead to significant lawsuits by customers. Assume further that the president has just learned this information from the engineering department, but it is not general knowledge in the company. The president instructs the head of the engineering department not to tell a soul about this product defect, especially the auditors. The president is concerned that, if a substantial liability has to be included among the long-term liabilities, the company will be in violation of its bond indenture, and it is not in a financial position to honor requests for bond redemptions.

Required:
1. What are the ethical issues in this situation?
2. If company fraud in financial reporting is as common as *The Wall Street Journal* article suggests, what ramifications does this have for the ability of companies to raise money in the bond market and the stock market?
3. Who are the stakeholders that will be affected by the company president's decision not to establish a reserve for a significant product defect?
4. Discuss in a general way what actions can be taken in our society to overcome the problem of managers who commit fraud in financial reporting.

Chapter 12

Long-Term Investments

Learning Objectives

After studying this chapter, you should be able to:
1. Record the acquisition of long-term investments in bonds.
2. Amortize discounts and premiums on investments in bonds.
3. Account for the sale or maturity of bond investments.
4. Account for long-term stock investments using either the cost method or the equity method.

SETTING THE STAGE

There are many reasons why one company purchases another. Sometimes the motivation for an acquisition is to gain control of a key supplier. Other times, the purpose may be to increase profitability, reduce competition, or increase market share. Now comes another reason to acquire a company.

Earl Braxton owned at least two related businesses—Porta-John, which rented portable toilets to construction sites and special events, and Enzymes of America, a business that extracted proteins from urine collected in collapsible toilets.[1] In 1983, the companies retained Deloitte and Touche, a big-six CPA firm, to be their auditor. Deloitte partners reasoned that Braxton's companies offered a promising little account that could easily become a big account. However, after a bitter dispute over how the company's revenues should be accounted for, Porta-John reported losses of $870,000 for 1984 and $570,000 for 1985. The losses wiped out owners' equity, leaving the firm with a negative equity of $245,000. Even with these losses, the company continued to struggle along until 1990, when it filed bankruptcy with a staggering $4 million in liabilities and assets of merely $57,000.

Even before declaring bankruptcy, Braxton hired a lawyer and sued Deloitte for negligence, largely blaming the company's problems on Deloitte's recommended accounting methods. Deloitte fought back, claiming Braxton and his companies owed $157,000 in unpaid audit fees. And then Deloitte made a surprise move: In July 1991, it bought Porta-John out of bankruptcy for $70,000.

Why would Deloitte buy a company whose owner was suing the CPA firm? Was Deloitte going into the toilet business? Not a chance. By buying Porta-John, Deloitte was ridding itself of a plaintiff and also acquired the bankruptcy trustee's rights to sue Braxton. Evidently, that ability to sue Braxton is the leverage Deloitte thinks it will need to keep Braxton from pursuing the lawsuit against Deloitte and Touche. With this clever maneuver, we now have another reason why one company purchases another—as a new weapon in the growing legal wars.

Braxton doesn't appear scared, though. He vows to take his case to court. "They got to kill me to stop me," he threatens. "Ho ho, they're going to be sorry they sued me," he claims. Whether or not Deloitte will be sorry it sued Braxton or purchased Porta-John will be for the courts to decide. One thing is certain, however—Deloitte is sorry it took on Braxton and his companies as an audit client.

---

[1] This scenario is adapted from Weisman, Katherine and Roula Khalaf, "Number Pumpers," *Forbes,* November 11, 1991, pp. 110–111.

In most cases, one company purchases another company by buying the acquired company's stock from its stockholders. In this chapter, you will learn about such long-term investments in stock as well as long-term bond investments.

long-term investment *an expenditure to acquire a non-operating asset that is expected to increase in value or generate income for longer than 1 year*

A **long-term investment** is an expenditure to acquire a nonoperating asset that is expected to appreciate in value or generate income for longer than 1 year. Typical long-term investments include real estate, annuities (investments that yield fixed payments in the future, such as insurance), art works, and corporate stocks and bonds. Real estate, annuities, and art works are initially recorded at cost, and gains and losses are recognized at the time of sale or at maturity. The accounting for long-term investments in corporate stocks and bonds is more complex and is therefore the focus of this chapter.

This chapter is presented out of balance-sheet sequence—most assets were covered in Chapters 8 and 9—but there is a good reason for this. The accounting for long-term investments in bonds is best explained after present value concepts and the nature of bonds have been introduced (see Chapters 10 and 11). We will discuss long-term investments in bonds first and then long-term investments in stocks.

ACCOUNTING FOR LONG-TERM INVESTMENTS IN BONDS

A bond is a common type of long-term investment. As explained in Chapter 11, bonds are issued by corporations and government agencies as a means of long-term borrowing. Investors often prefer to invest in bonds rather than in stock because of the certainty of the income stream (interest) and because of the relative safety of bonds as an investment. Investors in corporate bonds have priority over investors in stock both for the interest payments each year and for the return of principal if the issuing corporation gets into financial difficulty.

In accounting for bonds as a long-term investment, there are four recording stages in the life of the investment, beginning with the acquisition of the bonds and ending with their disposal at or before maturity. These stages are the mirror image of those presented in Chapter 11 for bond liabilities.

Investments in Bonds (Chapter 12)	**Bond Liabilities (Chapter 11)**
1. Accounting for the purchase of bonds	1. Accounting for the issuance of bonds
2. Accounting for interest receipts	2. Accounting for interest payments
3. Amortizing the difference between the investment cost and the face value of the bonds	3. Amortizing bond premiums and discounts
4. Accounting for bond investments at maturity or when sold	4. Accounting for the retirement of bonds

In accounting for these four stages, the issuer and the investor record the same amounts but in a different way. With bond liabilities, the face value of the bonds issued is recorded in the Bonds Payable account, and a separate contra account is maintained for any discount or premium. Amortization of the discount or premium is then recorded in these contra accounts. With bond investments, the actual amount paid for the bonds (the cost of the asset), not the face value, is originally debited to the Investment account. The amortization of any bond premium or discount is then recorded directly in the Investment account. We now examine the accounting for each of these four stages in the life of a bond investment.

Accounting for the Acquisition of Bonds

Objective 1
Record the acquisition of long-term investments in bonds.

Bonds can be purchased at amounts either above face value (at a premium), below face value (at a discount), or at face value. Regardless of the purchase price, like all other assets, bonds are initially recorded at cost. The cost is the total amount paid to acquire the bonds, which includes the actual price paid for the bonds and any other purchasing expenditures, such as commissions or broker's fees.

To illustrate, assume that Burton Company is considering the purchase of twenty $1,000 bonds of Chicago Company. The bonds will be issued on January 1, 1994, and will mature five years from the date of issue. The bonds will pay interest at a stated annual rate of 12 percent, with payments to be made semiannually on January 1 and July 1. In calculating how much to pay for these bonds, Burton must decide what rate of return it wants to earn. For example, let us assume that Burton needs an annual interest rate of 16 percent to justify the investment. The purchase price Burton should pay may be obtained by adding the present value of $20,000 (received 10 periods in the future and discounted at 8 percent) to the present value of the annuity of the 10 interest payments of $1,200 each (discounted at 8 percent). The reason for the use of 8 percent is that interest is received semiannually; recall that in calculating present value, you must halve the interest rate (16 percent ÷ 2) for semiannual compounding periods. Likewise, you must double the number of years to determine the number of periods (5 years × 2 periods per year = 10 periods). The calculations are:

1.	Semiannual interest payment	$1,200	
	Present value of an annuity of 10 payments of $1 at 8% (Table II, page 447)	× 6.7101	
	Present value of interest payments		$ 8,052
2.	Principal (face value) of bonds	$20,000	
	Present value of $1 received 10 periods in the future discounted at 8% (Table I, page 446)	× 0.4632	
	Present value of principal...............................		9,264
3.	Total present value of investment		$17,316

In this example, 16 percent is the effective rate of interest because that is the amount of interest actually earned; 12 percent is the stated, or nominal, rate of interest on Chicago Company's bonds. Note that the 12 percent stated rate determines the size of the annuity payments ($20,000 × 0.12 × ½ year) but not the purchase price of the bond; the purchase price varies according to market conditions. The 16 percent effective rate depends on three amounts: the purchase price, the interest payments, and the face value of the bonds. The $17,316 bond price is the amount that earns Burton exactly 16 percent. Thus Burton would invest in the bonds only if they can be purchased for $17,316 or less.

Assume that on January 1, 1994, Burton Company acquires the bonds at a cost of $17,316. The entry to record the investment would be:

> 1994
> Jan. 1 Investment in Bonds, Chicago Company................. 17,316
>   Cash.. 17,316
>   *Purchased 12% Chicago Company bonds with face value of $20,000 for $17,316.*

Note that the Investment account is debited for the cost of the bonds with no separate amount shown for the discount of $2,684 ($20,000 − $17,316). Although the discount could be recorded in a separate contra-asset account, in practice it is more common for investors to record the asset cost in the Investment account as shown.

Accounting for Bonds Purchased Between Interest Dates

The preceding entry assumes that the investing company purchased the bonds on the issuance date, which was also the beginning date for the first interest period. In many cases, however, the date bonds are actually issued does not coincide with an interest date. Further, investors often acquire bonds in the "secondary market," that is, they purchase bonds from other investors rather than from the issuing company. The secondary market for bonds includes the New York Bond Exchange and the over-the-counter bond market as described in the Business Environment Essay on page 489. Since bonds are traded actively in this market each weekday, investors are often acquiring bonds between interest dates.

An investor who buys bonds between interest dates, either from the issuing company or in the secondary market, has to pay for the interest that has accrued since the last interest payment date. As explained in Chapter 11, this is necessary because whoever owns bonds at the time interest is paid receives interest for one full interest period, usually six months, regardless of how long the bonds have been held.

To illustrate, we will assume that Burton purchased the Chicago bonds in the secondary market for $17,316 on May 1, 1994. Semiannual interest of $1,200 ($20,000 × .12 × ½) is paid on the bonds each January 1 and July 1. On July 1, 1994, Burton will receive $1,200 even though the bonds were purchased only 2 months before. Since the previous owner is entitled to 4 months' interest on May 1, Burton will have to pay that individual or company the interest for the period January 1 to May 1. This is illustrated in Exhibit 12-1.

Chapter 12 *Long-Term Investments*

Exhibit 12-1 *Investing Between Interest Dates*

```
January 1          May 1              July 1              January 1
                   purchase           $1,200              $1,200
                   date               interest            interest
                                      received by         received by
                                      Burton              Burton

         $800 interest earned    $400 interest         $1,200 interest earned
         by previous investor    earned by             by Burton
                                 Burton
```

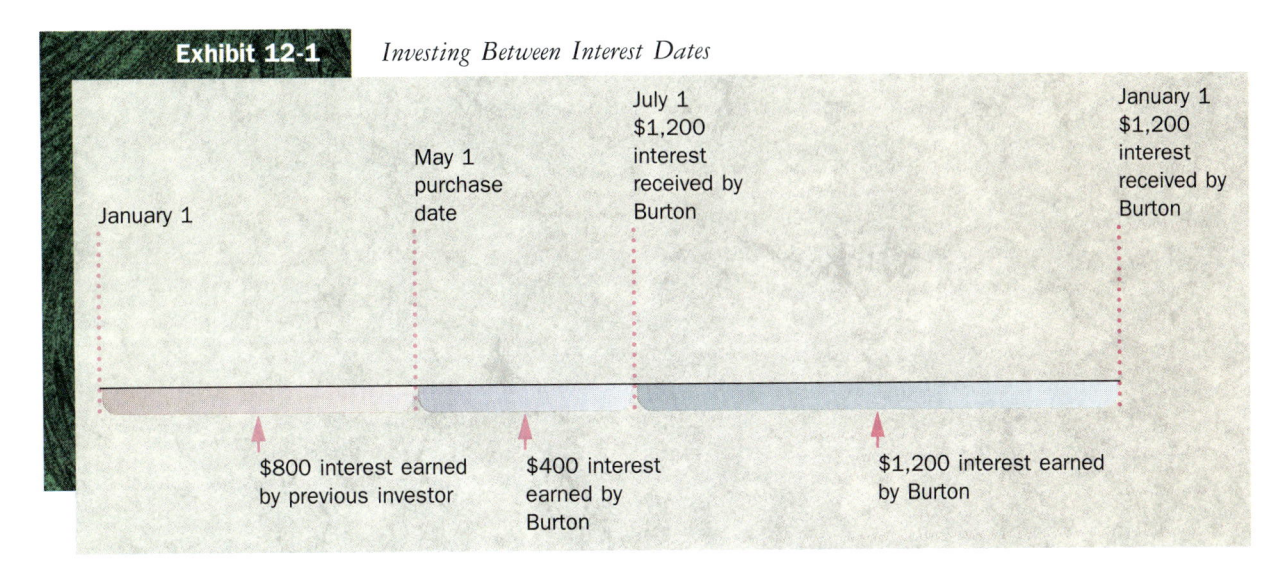

The entry to record the investment in bonds on May 1 (between interest dates) would be:

1994			
May 1	Investment in Bonds, Chicago Company..............	17,316	
	Bond Interest Receivable	800	
	Cash...		18,116
	Purchased $20,000 of Chicago bonds for $17,316 and paid four months' accrued interest.		

When Burton receives $1,200 in interest on July 1, it would make the following entry:

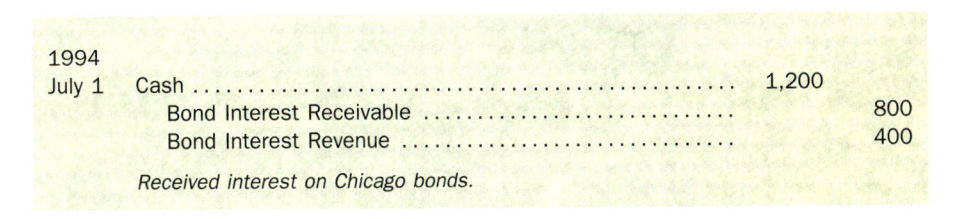

1994			
July 1	Cash	1,200	
	Bond Interest Receivable		800
	Bond Interest Revenue		400
	Received interest on Chicago bonds.		

Accounting for the Amortization of Bond Discounts and Premiums

Objective 2

Amortize discounts and premiums on investments in bonds.

Only in those rare instances when the stated interest rate of a bond is exactly equivalent to the prevailing market, or yield, rate for similar investments is a bond purchased at face value. At all other times, bonds are purchased either at a discount (below face value) or at a premium (above face value). Because the face amount of a bond is received at maturity, discounts and premiums must be written off (amortized) over the period that a bond is held.

straight-line amortization *a method of systematically writing off a bond discount or premium, in equal amounts each period until maturity*

As you learned in Chapter 11, there are two common methods of amortizing bond discounts and premiums: the straight-line method and the effective-interest method. Since **straight-line amortization** is simpler, it will be used to illustrate the amortization process; then the effective-interest method will be described.

STRAIGHT-LINE AMORTIZATION. To illustrate the straight-line method of amortizing a bond discount, we will assume again that Burton purchased the Chicago $20,000, 12 percent, 5-year bonds for $17,316 on the issuance date, January 1, 1994. The entry to record this investment was given on page 486. Burton would record amortization of $268.40 ($2,684 ÷ 5 years × ½) on each interest date. Thus, every 6 months, beginning on July 1, 1984, Burton would make the following entry:

Cash	1,200.00	
Investment in Bonds, Chicago Company	268.40	
Bond Interest Revenue		1,468.40
Received semiannual bond interest and amortized bond discount.		

At the end of 5 years, the Investment in Bonds, Chicago Company account would have a balance of $20,000.

The discount amortization is revenue earned on the bonds because when they mature, Burton will receive $20,000, or the face value, in return for an original investment of $17,316. It is this additional revenue of $2,684 that increases the return the investor actually earns from the 12 percent stated interest rate to the effective interest rate of 16 percent. The following analysis shows how this works:

Maturity value to be received................................		$20,000
Interest to be received ($1,200 × 10 payments)		12,000
Total amount to be received...............................		$32,000
Investment		17,316
Total interest revenue to be earned		$14,684
Interest earned per year:		
Stated amount of interest ($20,000 × 0.12)..................	$2,400.00	12%
Additional interest from discount ($2,684 ÷ 5 years)	536.80	4%*
Total	$2,936.80	16%

*This is an approximation because, with the straight-line method, the actual interest earned each year changes.

When accounting for the amortization of a bond discount, a company must be careful to amortize the discount only over the period the bonds are actually held. For example, if Burton had purchased the Chicago bonds 4 months after the issuance date, the discount would have been amortized over a period of 56

BUSINESS ENVIRONMENT ESSAY
Following the Bond Market

Bonds are sold in a variety of markets. Original issues of bonds, both industrial and governmental, are usually sold by an investment banking group referred to as the underwriters. The bonds are then traded in the market place, either on the New York Bond exchange or over-the-counter through brokers who make a market for a particular company's bonds. Following is an excerpt from *The Wall Street Journal* showing some composite information regarding bond transactions as well as price quotations involving specific bond issues. The composite information gives investors a sense of the overall activity level of the bond market in relation to previous years. In this case, it shows that sales through June 5, 1992, were higher than in either 1990 or 1991 for comparable periods. Using a representative sample of bonds trading in the marketplace, it also gives the high and low prices for 1991 and 1992.

The listings for specific bonds give the stated interest rate; the year of maturity; the current yield (effective rate); the sales volume for that trading date (with 000s omitted); the closing price for the day; and the net change from the closing price on the previous day that the bond market was open. For example, The Procter & Gamble Company (abbreviated ProcG) bonds listed have a stated interest rate of 7% and mature in 2002. The current yield (effective interest) on the bonds is 7.1 percent. Trading volume for the day was $50,000 face value, and the market price of the bonds at the end of the day was 98 3/8 or 98.375, a decline of 1/4 point from the previous day's closing price. Thus, each $1,000 bond was selling for $983.75.

months (4 full years plus 8 months of the first year). The amortization for the first year would then have been approximately $383.43 ($2,684 × 8/56), and the amortization for each of the succeeding 4 years would be approximately $575.14 ($2,684 × 12/56).

Accounting for the amortization of a premium on investments is essentially the opposite of accounting for a discount. Amortization of a premium decreases revenue earned, and the effect of the amortization entry is to reduce Investment in Bonds to the face value of the bonds by the maturity date.

To illustrate the amortization of bond premium by the investor, assume that Burton acquired the $20,000, 12%, 5-year Chicago Company bonds for $21,540 on January 1, 1994, the date of issuance. The entry to record the purchase would be:

Investment in Bonds, Chicago Company 21,540
   Cash 21,540
Purchased $20,000 of Chicago Company bonds for $21,540.

At each interest payment date, beginning July 1, 1994, Burton would make the following entry:

Cash 1,200
   Investment in Bonds, Chicago Company 154
   Bond Interest Revenue 1,046
Received semiannual bond interest and amortized bond premium (1,540 ÷ 5 × ½).

The effect of the amortization entries is to reduce the return earned on the bonds from the stated annual interest rate of 12 percent to the rate actually earned on the investment (approximately 10 percent).

EFFECTIVE-INTEREST AMORTIZATION. To illustrate the computations involved in using the **effective-interest amortization** method, we will again consider Burton's purchase of 12 percent, 5-year, $20,000 bonds of Chicago Company for $17,316 on the issuance date. The amount of discount amortized in each of the 5 years using the effective-interest method is computed as shown in the table at the top of the next page.

In the computation, column (2) represents the cash received at the end of each interest period; column (3) shows the amount of effective interest earned, which is the amount that will be reported on the income statement each period; column (4) is the difference between columns (3) and (2) and so represents the amortization; and column (5) shows the investment balance that will be reported on the balance sheet at the end of each period. Note that the interest rate used to compute the actual interest earned is the effective rate of 8 percent (16 percent ÷ 2) and not the stated rate of 12 percent. Also note that the total discount is the same as it was when the straight-line method was used, namely, $2,684.

---

effective-interest amortization *a method of systematically writing off a bond premium or discount that takes into consideration the time value of money and results in an equal rate of amortization for each period*

(1) Time Period	(2) Cash Received	(3) Interest Actually Earned (0.16 × 1/2 × Investment Balance)	(4) Amount of Amortization (3) − (2)	(5) Investment Balance
Acquisition date				$17,316
Year 1, first 6 months	$1,200	(0.08 × $17,316) = $1,385	$ 185	17,501
Year 1, second 6 months	1,200	(0.08 × 17,501) = 1,400	200	17,701
Year 2, first 6 months	1,200	(0.08 × 17,701) = 1,416	216	17,917
Year 2, second 6 months	1,200	(0.08 × 17,917) = 1,433	233	18,150
Year 3, first 6 months	1,200	(0.08 × 18,150) = 1,452	252	18,402
Year 3, second 6 months	1,200	(0.08 × 18,402) = 1,472	272	18,674
Year 4, first 6 months	1,200	(0.08 × 18,674) = 1,494	294	18,968
Year 4, second 6 months	1,200	(0.08 × 18,968) = 1,517	317	19,285
Year 5, first 6 months	1,200	(0.08 × 19,285) = 1,543	343	19,628
Year 5, second 6 months	1,200	(0.08 × 19,628) = 1,572	372	20,000
			$2,684	

When bonds are purchased at a discount, the amount of amortization increases each successive period. This is so because the investment balance of the bonds increases, and a constant interest rate times an increasing balance results in an increasing amount of interest income. If the bonds had been purchased at a premium, the effective-interest amortization method would involve a constant interest rate being multiplied by a declining investment balance each period. The result would be a decline in actual interest earned each period.

Since the effective-interest amortization method takes into account the time value of money and thus shows the true revenue earned each period (whereas the straight-line method represents only approximations), companies normally should use the effective-interest amortization method. As an exception to this rule, however, companies are allowed to use the straight-line method when the two methods produce amortization amounts that are not significantly different. Because that is often the case, both methods continue to be used.

Accounting for the Sale or Maturity of Bond Investments

Objective 3
Account for the sale or maturity of bond investments.

If bonds are held until their maturity date, the accounting for the proceeds at maturity includes a debit to Cash and a credit to the investment account for the principal amount. For example, if Burton Company were to hold the $20,000, 12 percent bonds from Chicago until they mature, the entry to record the receipt of the bond principal on the maturity date would be:

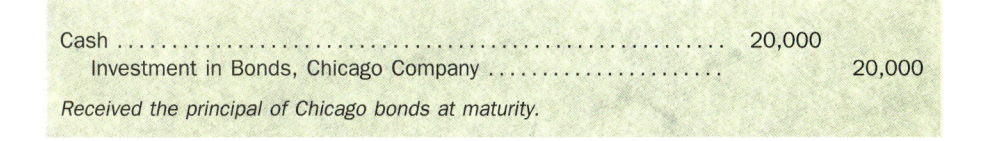

```
Cash ............................................................ 20,000
     Investment in Bonds, Chicago Company ................       20,000
Received the principal of Chicago bonds at maturity.
```

This entry assumes, of course, that all previous receipts of interest and bond amortizations have been properly recorded.

Bonds are accounted for as though they will be held until maturity. However, because they are usually traded on major exchanges, which provide a continuous and ready market, they are often sold to other investors prior to that time. When bonds are sold prior to their maturity, the difference between the sales price and the investment balance is recognized as a gain or loss on the sale of the investment.

To illustrate, we will assume that Sawyer Company purchased ten $1,000, 8 percent, 5-year bonds of REX Company. We will also assume that the bonds were originally purchased on January 1, 1991, at 101 percent of their face value and that on January 1, 1994, Sawyer showed a balance of $10,040 for these bonds. If the bonds were sold on that day for $10,300, the entry to record the sale and recognize the gain would be (assuming no sales commission):

```
Cash ..................................................... 10,300
    Gain on Sale of Bonds ......................................   260
    Investment in Bonds, REX Company .........................  10,040
Sold the REX bonds for $10,300.
```

When bonds are sold prior to their maturity date, it is important that the amortization of the bond premium or discount be recorded up to the date of sale. If the amortization of the discount or premium is not updated, the gain or loss recognized on the sale will be incorrect.

Valuation of Long-Term Investments in Bonds

As discussed in Chapter 8, marketable equity securities (stocks) held as short-term investments are valued at the lower of cost or market. If the market value at the end of the year is less than cost, the securities are written down to market. Later in this chapter, you will learn that, in some cases, long-term investments in stocks also are valued at the lower of cost or market. You might expect that the same valuation procedures would apply to investments in bonds, but that is not the case. Generally, companies report investments in bonds and other debt securities at their carrying value (original cost adjusted for premium or discount amortization) regardless of whether the carrying value is greater than or less than market value. However, companies are required to disclose the fair value of bond investments, either in the financial statements or in the accompanying notes, under a new standard issued by the Financial Accounting Standards Board in 1991.[2]

> **To Summarize** *Accounting for investments in bonds involves four steps: (1) accounting for the purchase of bonds, (2) accounting for interest received on bonds, (3) accounting for amortization of the premium or discount, and (4) accounting for the sale or maturity of the bonds. Amortization of premiums and discounts is usually accounted*

---

[2] *FASB Statement No. 107,* "Disclosures About Fair Value of Financial Instruments" (Norwalk, CT: Financial Accounting Standards Board, 1991).

for by (1) the simple straight-line amortization method or (2) the theoretically more correct effective-interest method. The amortization adjusts the interest earned on the bonds from the stated to the effective rate. Investments in bonds are generally reported at cost (adjusted for premium or discount amortization) regardless of whether market value is less than or greater than cost. When bonds are sold before maturity, the premium or discount must be amortized to the date of sale and a gain or loss would be reflected in the income statement for the difference between the selling price and the carrying value on the date of sale. Bonds held until maturity result in no gain or loss on retirement since the carrying value after amortization of premium or discount should be equal to the face value of the bonds.

ACCOUNTING FOR LONG-TERM INVESTMENTS IN STOCKS

Objective 4

Account for long-term stock investments using either the cost method or the equity method.

In Chapter 8, we discussed the accounting for a company's short-term investments in marketable equity securities (stocks). Short-term investments in marketable equity securities are reported in the current asset section of the balance sheet and are valued at the lower of aggregate cost or market. In the remainder of this chapter, we will discuss long-term investments in equity securities. The discussion will cover two methods of accounting for long-term investments in stock: the cost method and the equity method. We will begin the discussion with how to account for the initial acquisition of stocks.

Acquisition of Stocks

Like short-term investments, long-term investments in stock are initially accounted for on a cost basis; that is, the total amount paid to acquire the stock (market price plus commission) is recognized as the cost of the long-term investment.

To illustrate, we assume that Boynton, Inc. purchased 300 shares of Bell Company stock on September 12, 1993, at $80 per share as a long-term investment. In addition to the purchase price, Boynton paid $1,250 in commissions. The initial entry to record the long-term investment would be as follows:

```
1993
Sept. 12   Long-Term Investment, Bell Company Stock ..........   25,250
               Cash........................................................          25,250
           Purchased 300 shares of Bell Company stock at $80 per share [(300 × $80) +
           $1,250 commission].
```

Whether the investment will be carried on a cost basis indefinitely depends on the size of the investment to the total outstanding voting stock of the investee. Generally, stock investments fall into one of three categories:

1. A purchase of a relatively small interest (usually less than 20 percent of the outstanding voting stock) in order to receive dividend income or to realize gains on the sale of the stock through increases in its purchase price.

cost method of accounting for investments in stocks *accounting for an investment in another company when less than 20 percent of the outstanding voting stock is owned*

equity method of accounting for investments in stocks *accounting for an investment in another company, where significant influence can be imposed (presumed to exist when 20 to 50 percent of the outstanding voting stock is owned)*

parent company *a company that owns or controls other companies, known as subsidiaries, which are themselves separate legal entities*

subsidiary company *a company owned or controlled by another company, known as the parent company*

consolidated financial statements *statements that show the operating results, financial position, and cash flows of two or more legally separate but affiliated companies as if they were one economic entity*

2. A purchase of a significant interest in another company (usually at least 20 percent but no more than 50 percent of the outstanding voting stock) in order to exert some influence over the company's operations in the expectation of achieving gains through both dividends and stock appreciation.
3. A purchase of a controlling interest in another company (more than 50 percent of the outstanding voting stock), often in order to integrate that company's operations into the investing company's overall finance, production, and marketing functions.

In this chapter, we will discuss the accounting for situations 1 and 2. In situation 1, where the company acquiring the stock exercises no significant influence (usually because it has less than 20 percent interest), the **cost method** is used. This is because less than 20 percent is presumed to be too small an amount to provide significant influence, unless the actual operating relationship between the two companies suggests that significant influence is exerted even with less than 20 percent ownership.

In situation 2, where the acquiring company actually exercises significant influence (usually owning 20 to 50 percent of the acquired company's stock), the **equity method** is used. Having at least 20 percent but no more than 50 percent ownership interest is presumed to provide significant influence unless the operating relationship between the two companies suggests that no significant influence is exerted. Exhibit 12-2 outlines the circumstances that determine when the cost and equity methods of accounting for long-term investments should be used.

In situation 3, involving a controlling interest, the accounting is far more complex than it is for investments under situations 1 and 2. Generally, the **parent company** (the acquiring company) and the **subsidiary company** (the acquired company) are required to combine their financial statements into one set of statements as if they were one economic entity. Such combined statements are called **consolidated financial statements.** The preparation of consolidated statements is discussed in the appendix to Chapter 13.

Exhibit 12-2 *The Cost and Equity Methods of Accounting for Long-Term Investments in Stocks*

Accounting Method	Circumstances
Cost	The cost method is to be used when the number of shares of stock is so small that the investor can exercise *no significant influence on, or control over,* the company. The ability to exercise influence or control is presumed not to exist if an investor owns less than 20 percent of the outstanding voting stock. The 20 percent test is only a guide that can be overturned by the weight of contrary evidence.
Equity	The equity method is to be used when one company's investment in the stock of another company is large enough that the investor can and does exercise a *significant influence* over the operations of the investee company. The ability to exercise significant influence is presumed to exist if an investor owns at least 20 percent but no more than 50 percent of the outstanding voting stock of another company. (A controlling interest exists if over 50 percent is owned; this generally requires the use of consolidated financial statements.)

The Cost Method

The cost method of accounting for long-term investments in the stock of other companies is applied in essentially the same way as it is for accounting for short-term equity investments. That is, the original investment is recorded at cost, dividends received are recognized as earned revenues, and the investment is carried on a lower-of-cost-or-market basis (see Exhibit 12-3 on page 498 for illustrative entries). Generally, if the market value of a company's portfolio of long-term equity investments falls below its original cost, the long-term investments are written down at year-end to the portfolio's aggregate market value. The entry to recognize the lower market value, however, is different from the one used to write down short-term investments in stock. To illustrate, assume that the Bell Company stock acquired by Boynton, Inc. on September 12, 1993, for $25,250 had declined in value to $24,080 on December 31, 1993. The following adjusting entry would be made on December 31, 1993, to reflect this decline in value:

```
1993
Dec. 31   Unrealized Loss on Long-Term Investments ............   1,170
              Allowance to Reduce Long-Term
                 Investments to Market ...........................          1,170
          To write down long-term investments to lower of cost or market.
```

The account debited, Unrealized Loss on Long-Term Investments, is a contra-owners' equity account (balance sheet), and the account credited, Allowance to Reduce Long-Term Investments to Market, is a contra-asset account (balance sheet). Since neither account appears on the income statement (unlike Loss on Short-Term Investments), no loss is recognized when the market price of long-term investments drops below cost.[3] The rationale for not including these declines in current income is that the investments will be held for a long time, and the price may rise and fall several times before the stock is sold.

These two accounts—Unrealized Loss on Long-Term Investments and Allowance to Reduce Long-Term Investments to Market—would appear on the December 31, 1993, balance sheet of Boynton, Inc. as follows:

Long-term investments:
Long-term investments in stocks	$ 25,250
Less allowance to reduce long-term investments to market	(1,170)
Long-term investments at market value	$ 24,080

Stockholders' equity:
Common stock	$ 80,000
Retained earnings	36,700
Less unrealized loss on long-term investments	(1,170)
Total stockholders' equity	$115,530

---

[3] However, if the decline in the market value of a long-term equity security is judged to be other than temporary, the cost basis should be written down, and the write-down should be recorded as a loss on the income statement. In such cases, the new cost basis is not to be changed for subsequent increases in market value. As with short-term equity securities, such losses are not deductible for tax purposes.

Using assumed amounts for Common Stock and Retained Earnings, the illustration shows how a decline in the market value of long-term investments in stock reduces total stockholders' equity. If the Bell Company stock had been acquired as a short-term investment, the $1,170 would have been reported as a loss in the 1993 income statement rather than as a reduction in stockholders' equity.

As was the case with short-term investments, if the market price of a written-down portfolio of long-term investments subsequently rises, it should be written up to the new market price, as long as that price does not exceed the original cost. The entry to recognize a subsequent recovery in the market price of long-term investments that have previously been written down is the reverse of the previous entry. To illustrate, assume that the Bell Company stock had a market value of $24,800 at December 31, 1994. The adjusting entry to recognize the partial recovery in market value ($24,800 − $24,080 = $720) would be:

```
1994
Dec. 31   Allowance to Reduce Long-Term Investments
            to Market .................................................  720
              Unrealized Loss on Long-Term Investments ...............         720
          To recognize partial recovery in the market price of long-term investments.
```

Under current generally accepted accounting principles, investments usually are not written up to a market price that exceeds cost.[4] However, FASB Statement No. 107, discussed on page 492, requires companies to disclose the market value of stock investments as well as bonds and other financial instruments. Thus, when market value of stock is greater than cost, the market value could be shown either parenthetically in the balance sheet or in a note to the financial statements.

To determine whether market values of stocks have declined or risen, investors refer to stock price quotations published in *The Wall Street Journal* and most large daily newspapers. Illustrative stock quotations are included in the Business Environment Essay on page 499.

The Equity Method

In the preceding discussion of Boynton's investment in Bell Company stock, it was assumed that Boynton did not own a sufficient number of Bell Company shares to exercise significant influence over Bell's operating policies. However, if a stock investment is large enough to give the investor significant influence over the *investee* (the company whose stock is owned), it is presumed that the investor can affect the investee's operating performance and the timing and amount of its dividend payments. In such cases, the equity method of accounting for the investment must be used. The equity method is generally used when the investee owns 20 to 50 percent of the investee's outstanding stock. In

---

[4] An exception applies to companies such as brokerage firms that follow specialized accounting practices for stocks and other securities. These firms carry securities at market value even when market exceeds cost.

some cases, however, the investor can exercise significant influence with less than 20 percent ownership and would therefore use the equity method.

Under the equity method, dividend payments represent a return of investment; they do not represent revenue, as they do with the cost method. Revenue *is* recognized when the investee company has earnings. When earnings are announced, the carrying (book) value of the investment is increased because the investor owns a fixed percentage of a company that is worth more now than it was when the investment was originally made.

In accounting for investments with the equity method, the original investment is first recorded on the books at cost and is subsequently modified to reflect the investor's share of the investee's reported income, losses, and dividends. In this way, book value is increased to recognize the investor's share of earnings and decreased by the dividends received or to recognize the investor's share of losses. Unless a permanent decline in the value of an investment is considered to have occurred, the lower-of-cost-or-market rule is not applied under the equity method.

There are two reasons why the equity method is preferred over the cost method when significant influence can be exerted. First, it prevents the investing company from manipulating its earnings by dictating the dividend policies of the investee. Under the cost method, where dividend payments are reported as revenue, an influential investor could increase its income by putting pressure on the investee to pay larger and more frequent dividends. With the equity method, dividends do not affect earnings. Second, the equity method provides more timely recognition of the investee's earnings and losses than does the cost method.

There is one exception to the general rule that the equity method must be used by an investing company that owns 20 to 50 percent of an investee's stock. This occurs when the investing company does not or cannot exercise significant influence on the operating and dividend policies of the investee.

The investor may lack influence by choice or because the purchased stock does not carry with it any voting rights. No matter what the reason for a lack of significant influence, and regardless of the ownership percentage, the cost method is used in accounting for such investments.

The Cost and Equity Methods Illustrated

The accounting for the purchase and holding of long-term investments in stock under both the cost and the equity methods is illustrated in Exhibit 12-3. First we will assume that Mott Corporation purchases 15 percent of Castleford Company's 1,000 shares of outstanding stock for $10 per share. Later in the year, Mott receives a dividend of $0.80 per share; at year-end Mott receives Castleford's income statement showing that the company earned $6,000 for the year. The accounting for this purchase of stock and the subsequent events, using the cost method, is shown in the first column of Exhibit 12-3. It is assumed that Castleford stock is selling for $9 per share at year-end.

Next, we assume that Mott Corporation purchased 40 percent (instead of 15 percent) of the outstanding stock of Castleford Company, that Mott will exert significant influence over Castleford, and that Castleford has the same dividends and earnings as before ($0.80 and $6,000, respectively). The ac-

Exhibit 12-3 — Long-Term Investments in Stock

Event	Cost Method	Equity Method
	Mott purchases 150 shares of Castleford Company stock (15% ownership):	Mott purchases 400 shares of Castleford Company stock (40% ownership):

The Initial Purchase	Investment in Castleford Stock 1,500
	    Cash 1,500
	Purchased 150 shares of Castleford Company stock at $10 per share (15% ownership).
		Investment in Castleford Stock 4,000
		    Cash 4,000
		Purchased 400 shares of Castleford Company stock at $10 per share (40% ownership).

Payment of an 80¢-per-Share Dividend by Castleford Company	Cash 120
	    Dividend Revenue, Castleford Stock 120
	Received 80¢-per-share dividend from Castleford Company.
		Cash 320
		    Investment in Castleford Stock 320
		Received 80¢-per-share dividend from Castleford Company.

Announcement by Castleford Company of Net Income of $6,000 for the Year	No entry.	Investment in Castleford Stock .... 2,400 Revenue from Investments .... 2,400 *To recognize share of Castleford Company earnings for the year (40% of $6,000).*
Castleford Stock is Selling at $9 per Share at Year-End	Unrealized Loss on Long-Term Investments .... 150 Allowance to Reduce Long-Term Investments to Market .... 150 *To write down long-term investments to lower of cost or market.*	No entry.

counting for the stock purchase and the subsequent events using the equity method is shown in the second column of Exhibit 12-3.

Although accounting for the holding of long-term investments is different under the cost and equity methods, accounting for the sale of a stock investment is the same under both methods. If the selling price exceeds the balance in the Investment account, the difference is recognized as a gain. If the selling price is less than the recorded Investment balance, the difference is recognized as a loss. To illustrate the recording of a sale of stock held as an investment, assume that Mott sells the 400 shares of Castleford stock (see the Equity Method example in Exhibit 12-3) for $7,500 shortly after the year-end recognition of its $2,400 share of Castleford's earnings. The entry to record the sale would be:

```
Cash ................................................................. 7,500
    Investment in Castleford Stock ............................. 6,080
    Gain on Sale of Investment ................................. 1,420
```
Sold long-term investment in Castleford stock for $7,500 (book value = $4,000 − $320 + $2,400 = $6,080; $7,500 − $6,080 = $1,420 gain).

Chapter 12 *Long-Term Investments* 499

A gain or loss on the sale of stock under the cost method is computed in the same way as under the equity method; that is, the gain or loss is the difference between selling price and the balance in the Investment account. Note, however, that in recording the sale under the cost method, the entry

BUSINESS ENVIRONMENT ESSAY
Following the Stock Market

Stocks are sold in a variety of markets in the same way that bonds are sold. Original issues of stocks are usually sold by an investment banking group, referred to as the underwriters. After stocks are originally sold, they are traded in the market place, either on the New York Stock Exchange, the American Stock Exchange, regional market exchanges, or in the over-the-counter market. A selected portion of stocks traded on the New York Stock Exchange on Wednesday, January 22, 1992, are listed here as they were reported in *The Wall Street Journal* of Thursday, January 23, 1992. The quotations show the following information for each stock: (1) 52-week high and low, (2) name of company, (3) the trading symbol for that company, (4) the current dividend, (5) the yield percentage in relation to the current price, (6) the price-earnings ratio, (7) the volume of sales for that day, (8) the high, low and closing prices for the day, and (9) the net change from the closing price of the previous day's trading. To illustrate how to read the quotation, the information for the Campbell Soup Company is as follows: The 52-week high was 43⅞ and the low was 28¾. The annual dividend rate is $.70 with a current yield of 1.8%. The current price is 23 times the annual earnings. A total of 690,400 shares were traded on Wednesday, January 22, 1992, with the high price for the day being 39 and the low price being 38⅛. The stock closed for the day at 39, which was 2¼ higher than the close on Tuesday, January 21, 1992.

NEW YORK STOCK EXCHANGE COMPOSITE TRANSACTIONS

Quotations as of 5 p.m. Eastern Time
Wednesday, January 22, 1992

ignores any balance in the Allowance to Reduce Long-Term Investments to Market account. This account will be adjusted at year-end on the basis of any other long-term investments still held by the company. Thus, the gain or loss equals the difference between selling price and the original cost of the stock.

> **To Summarize** *All long-term investments in stock are initially accounted for on a cost basis. However, because different levels of investment provide different degrees of influence over investee companies, two methods of accounting for long-term stock invest- ments are used. If an investor company exercises no significant influence (usually owning less than 20 percent of the voting stock of another company), the cost method is generally used. With the cost method, revenue is recognized when dividends are received, and the investment is accounted for at the lower of cost or market. (Note that when long-term investments are written down to the lower of cost or market, the adjustment reduces owners' equity and investments; it does not affect the income statement. This is not true of short-term investments.) When the percentage of outstanding voting stock owned is sufficient to exercise significant influence (as is usually true with ownership of 20 to 50 percent), the equity method is used. This method involves increasing the book value of the investment for earnings and decreasing it for dividends and losses.*

Review of Learning Objectives

Objective 1

Record the acquisition of long-term investments in bonds. Long-term investments in bonds are initially recorded at cost. Present value concepts are used to determine the purchase price (cost) of long-term bond investments, which is consistent with the time-value of money concept that you learned in Chapter 11. If bonds are purchased between interest dates, the investor has to pay the interest that has accrued since the last interest payment date. This is necessary because whoever owns the bonds at the time interest is paid receives interest for one full interest period, regardless of how long the bonds have been held. The amount that the investor pays for accrued interest is debited to Bond Interest Receivable since that account will be credited for the same amount when the first interest payment is received.

Objective 2

Amortize discounts and premiums on investments in bonds. The purchase price of a bond investment is usually less than face value, resulting in a discount, or more than face value, resulting in a premium. The discount or premium is amortized over the life of the bond by adjusting the cost upward if purchased at a discount and downward if purchased at a premium. Adjusting the cost of the bond up or down assures that the cost of the bond will be equal to the face value of the bond at the maturity date. This adjustment is accomplished through the amortization of the premiums and discounts, which adjusts the interest earned on bonds from the stated to the effective rate. Bond discounts and premiums can be amortized using either the straight-line or the effective-interest method. The latter is theoretically more correct, but since the differences between the two are usually insignificant, both are widely used. The carrying value of the bonds usually is not reduced to reflect declines in market value, but the market value should be disclosed.

Objective 3

Account for the sale or maturity of bond investments. If bonds are held until maturity, the bond will be returned to the issuing company in exchange for the principal (face) amount of the bond. The entry to collect the face value would be a debit to Cash and a credit to Investment in

Bonds. A separate entry would be made to record the receipt of the last interest payment, which would include the final portion of the amortization of the bond premium or discount that would bring the Investment in Bonds account up or down to face value. If the bond investment were sold before maturity, the difference between the selling price and the carrying value at the date of sale would be recorded as a gain or loss on sale. When bonds are sold prior to their maturity date, it is important that the amortization of the bond premium or discount be recorded up to the date of the sale in order to recognize the correct amount of gain or loss on the sale.

Objective 4

Account for long-term stock investments using either the cost method or the equity method. Long-term investments in stocks can be accounted for by using either the cost or the equity method, depending on the degree of ownership in the investee company. If ownership of the outstanding stock of another company does not give the investor significant influence over the investee's operating policies (as is usually the case with less than 20 percent ownership), the cost method is used. If the level of ownership results in significant influence (as generally happens with 20 to 50 percent ownership), the equity method is used. With the cost method, dividends received from investee companies are recorded as revenue. With the equity method, the investment balance (its book value) is decreased by dividends or losses and increased by the investor's share of the investee company's earnings. If the ownership is more than 50 percent, consolidated financial statements are prepared.

Key Terms and Concepts

consolidated financial statements *(494)*
cost method of accounting for investments in stocks *(494)*
effective-interest amortization *(490)*
equity method of accounting for investments in stocks *(494)*
long-term investment *(484)*
parent company *(494)*
straight-line amortization *(488)*
subsidiary company *(494)*

Review Problem

Long-Term Investments in Stocks and Bonds

On January 1, 1994, Kirby Manufacturing purchased $100,000 of 12 percent, 20-year bonds of Pioneer Corporation as a long-term investment for $96,460 plus accrued interest. The bonds mature on September 1, 2013, and interest is payable semiannually on March 1 and September 1. Kirby Manufacturing uses the straight-line method of amortizing bond premiums and discounts.

On January 2, 1994, Kirby also purchased 35 percent of the 60,000 shares of outstanding stock of Mariner Company at $36 per share, plus broker's fees of $1,300. On December 31, 1994, Mariner announced that its net income for 1994 was $94,000, and it paid an annual dividend of $1 per share. The closing price of Mariner Company stock on December 31 was $34 per share.

Required: Record all necessary transactions to account for these investments during 1994.

Solution To account for the two investments, seven transactions must be recorded.

Investment in Bonds:

1. Original investment .... (Jan. 1)
2. Interest receipt and amortization of discount .... (Mar. 1)
3. Interest receipt and amortization of discount .... (Sept. 1)
4. Interest accrual and amortization of discount .... (Dec. 31)

Investment in Stock:

5	Original investment	(Jan. 2)
6	Recognition of investee's income	(Dec. 31)
7	Dividend receipt	(Dec. 31)

The entries to record these events are:

1	Investment in Bonds	96,460	
	Interest Receivable	4,000	
	Cash		100,460

Purchased $100,000 of Pioneer Corporation's 12 percent bonds for $96,460 plus accrued interest.

The interest is $100,000 \times 0.12 \times 4/12$ year $= \$4,000$. Interest Receivable is debited so that when it is credited in step 2, the result is a net interest revenue of $2,000 ($6,000 - $4,000), which is the amount earned during January and February.

2	Cash	6,000	
	Investment in Bonds	30	
	Interest Revenue		2,030
	Interest Receivable		4,000

Received semiannual interest payment on Pioneer Corporation's bonds and amortized the discount for 2 months.

The amortization of the discount is $100,000 - $96,460 = $3,540; $3,540 ÷ 236 months = $15 per month. The discount is amortized over 236 months instead of 20 years because only 236 months remain from the date of investment until the date of the bond's maturity.

3	Cash	6,000	
	Investment in Bonds	90	
	Interest Revenue		6,090

Received semiannual interest payment on Pioneer Corporation's bonds and amortized the discount for 6 months.

The amortization is 6 months $\times$ $15.

4	Interest Receivable	4,000	
	Investment in Bonds	60	
	Interest Revenue		4,060

To record accrued interest for period September 1–December 31, and amortization of discount for 4 months.

The amortization in step 4 is 4 months $\times$ $15. Further, 4 months of interest have been earned although payment will not be received until the following year.

5	Investment in Stock	757,300	
	Cash		757,300

Purchased 35 percent of the outstanding stock of Mariner Company at $36 per share plus brokerage fees of $1,300.

60,000 shares $\times$ 0.35 $\times$ $36 = $756,000; $756,000 + $1,300 = $757,300.

6	Investment in Stock	32,900	
	Revenue from Investments		32,900

To recognize 35 percent of Mariner Company's 1994 earnings.

$94,000 \times 0.35 = $32,900. (The equity method is used to account for this investment since more than 20 percent is owned. With the equity method, the investments account increases when the investee has earnings.)

7	Cash	21,000	
	Investment in Stock		21,000

Received $1-per-share dividend on Mariner Company's stock.

60,000 shares $\times$ 0.35 $\times$ $1 = $21,000. (With the equity method, receipt of dividends is accounted for by reducing the investments account. Under the equity method, declines in market price are ignored.)

Discussion Questions

1. Why do firms invest in assets that are not directly related to their primary business operations?
2. Describe the risk and return tradeoff of investments.
3. What is the primary basis for classifying investments as short- or long-term?
4. What future cash inflows is a company buying when it purchases a bond?
5. When would a company be willing to pay more than the face amount (that is, a premium) for a bond?
6. Why does the amortization of a bond discount increase the amount of interest revenue earned on a bond?
7. Why is the effective-interest amortization method theoretically superior to the straight-line method?
8. Why must an investor purchasing bonds between interest payment dates pay the previous owner for accrued interest on those bonds?
9. In which direction would the market interest rate have to move in order for an investor in bonds to be able to sell the bonds at a price that is higher than the acquisition cost?
10. Why are long-term investments in stocks where there is less than 20 percent ownership usually written down if cost exceeds market price but not written up if the market price exceeds cost?
11. What is meant by a portfolio of stocks?
12. Are losses resulting from the write-down of long-term investments to market treated the same as write-downs of short-term investments? If not, how does the accounting differ?
13. Define a subsidiary and a parent company.
14. Why is the equity method usually required when accounting for investments in which an investor has between 20 and 50 percent ownership of all outstanding voting stock?

Exercises

E12-1
Bond Price Determination

1. How much should an investor pay for $100,000 of debenture bonds that pay interest every six months at an annual rate of 8%, assuming that the bonds mature in 10 years and that the effective interest rate at the date of purchase is also 8%?
2. How much should an investor pay for $100,000 of debenture bonds that pay $5,000 of interest every six months, have a maturity date in 10 years, and are sold to yield 8% interest, compounded semiannually?

E12-2
Bond Price Determination

Flat Rock Corporation has decided to purchase bonds of Vicon Corporation as a long-term investment. The 8-year bonds have a stated rate of interest of 10%, with interest payments being made semiannually. How much should Flat Rock be willing to pay for $35,000 of the bonds if:

1. A rate of return of 12% is deemed necessary to justify the investment?
2. A return of return of 8% is considered to be an adequate return?

E12-3
Long-Term Investments in Bonds

Control Group purchased thirty $1,000, 10%, 20-year bonds of Natchez Corporation on January 1, 1994, as a long-term investment. The bonds mature on January 1, 2014, and interest is payable every January 1 and July 1. Control Group's reporting year ends December 31, and the company uses the straight-line method of amortizing bond premiums and discounts.

Make all necessary journal entries relating to the bonds for 1994, assuming:

1. The purchase price is 104 percent of face value.
2. The purchase price is 94 percent of face value.

E12-4
Straight-Line Amortization of Bond Premium

On their issuance date, Blue Company purchased twenty $1,000, 8%, 5-year bonds of Glaxon Company as a long-term investment for $21,706. Interest payments are made semiannually. Prepare a schedule showing the amortization of the bond premium over the 5-year life of the bonds. Use the straight-line method of amortization.

E12-5
Effective-Interest Amortization of Bond Premium

Assume the same facts as in E12-4. Prepare a schedule showing the amortization of the bond premium over the 5-year life of the bonds, using the effective-interest method of amortization. (Hint: The effective rate of interest earned on the bonds is 6 percent compounded semiannually.)

E12-6
Recording Long-Term Investments

Prepare journal entries to record the following long-term investment transactions. (Assume that the cost method is used.)

1. Purchased 2,000 shares of Clarke Company common stock at $31.60 per share and paid brokerage fees of $675.
2. Received a cash dividend of 30 cents per share on Clarke Corporation stock.
3. Sold 800 shares of Clarke Corporation stock at $37.50 per share, paying $480 in brokerage fees.

E12-7
Long-Term Investments in Stocks—The Cost Method

In December, 1992, the treasurer of Solitron Corporation discovered that the company had excess cash on hand and decided to invest in Horner Company stock. The company intends to hold the stock for a period of 3 to 5 years. The following transactions took place in 1993, 1994, and 1995:

1993
Jan. 1   Purchased 2,750 shares of Horner Company stock for $89,500, including brokerage fees.
May 10   Received a cash dividend of $1.30 per share on Horner Company stock.

1994
May 22   Purchased 750 shares of Horner Company stock at $40 per share for cash, including brokerage fees.
July 18 Received a cash dividend of 90 cents per share on the Horner Company stock.

1995
Oct. 5   Sold the Horner Company stock at $27 per share for cash.

Prepare the journal entries needed to record each of the above transactions, assuming that the cost method is used.

E12-8
Long-Term Investments in Stock—The Equity Method

During 1994 Genco Corporation purchased 10,000 shares of Wiener Company stock for $85 per share. Wiener had a total of 40,000 shares of stock outstanding.

1. Prepare journal entries for the following transactions:

   Jan. 1   Purchased 10,000 shares of common stock at $85.
   Dec. 31 Wiener Company declared and paid a $4.60 per share dividend.
   Dec. 31 Wiener Company reported a net income for 1994 of $360,000.

2. On December 31, 1994, the market price of Wiener's stock was $79 per share. Show how this investment would be reported on Genco's balance sheet at December 31, 1994, assuming that this is the only stock investment owned by Genco.

E12-9
Investment Decisions

Indiana Power Company accumulated $200,000 of excess cash during a recent profitable year. Management has determined that it needs to invest enough of the excess cash in marketable securities to provide a cash flow of $25,000 per year for the next 5 years. The remainder will then be spent on research and development activities.

1. How much cash must Indiana Power Company invest in marketable securities to provide the necessary cash flow if the investment opportunities that are available will earn 8%?
2. If the minimum effective investment in research and development activities is $80,000, will the company have sufficient funds to make the research and development investment?

Problem Set A

P12A-1
Long-Term Investments in Bonds

SOLUTIONS SOFTWARE

Cyril Corporation purchased $25,000 of Baker Construction Company's 12 percent bonds at 102½ plus accrued interest on February 1, 1993. The bonds mature on April 1, 2000, and interest is payable on April 1 and October 1.

On June 1, 1995, Cyril Corporation sold the Baker Construction Company bonds at 97 plus accrued interest. Cyril Corporation uses the straight-line method of amortizing bond premiums and discounts.

Required:
1. Record all journal entries to account for this investment during the years 1993, 1994, and 1995 assuming that Cyril closes it books annually on December 31.
2. **Interpretive Question** At the time these bonds were purchased (February 1, 1993), was the market rate of interest above or below 10 percent? Explain.

P12A-2
Determining the Purchase Price of Bonds and Effective-Interest Amortization

SPREADSHEET PROBLEM

Corbett Corporation decided to purchase twenty $1,000, 10 percent, 6-year bonds of Texas Manufacturing Company as a long-term investment on February 1, 1993. The bonds mature on February 1, 2000, and interest payments are made semiannually on February 1 and August 1.

Required:
1. How much should Corbett Corporation be willing to pay for the bonds if the current interest rate on similar bonds is 8%?
2. Prepare a schedule showing the amortization of the bond premium or discount over the remaining life of the bonds, assuming that Corbett Corporation uses the effective-interest method of amortization.

3. How much interest revenue would be recorded each year if the straight-line method of amortization were used? Show how these amounts differ from the annual interest recognized using the effective-interest method. (Assume a fiscal year ending July 31.)
4. **Interpretive Question** Which of the two amortization methods is preferable? Why?

P12A-3

Long-Term Investments in Bonds

Sterling Equipment Company made the following purchases of bonds during 1994. All are long-term investments and all pay interest semiannually.

Purchase Date	Corp.	Face Amount	Cost	Interest Rate, %	Maturity Date	Last Interest Payment Date
10/15/94	A	$ 5,000	102	9	1/1/99	7/1/94
11/30/94	B	10,000	96	12	4/1/97	10/1/94
12/15/94	C	15,000	98	14	6/1/98	12/1/94
12/31/94	D	12,000	105	10¼	5/1/95	11/1/94

Required:
1. Record the purchases in General Journal entry form.
2. Show all adjusting entries relating to the bonds on December 31, 1994, assuming that Sterling Equipment closes its books on that date and uses the straight-line amortization method.
3. **Interpretive Question** On the basis of these data, which of these four investments do you think has the highest rating? Is the least risky?

P12A-4

Recording Investment Transactions

The following data pertain to the marketable securities of Mark Company during 1994 the company's first year of operations.

(a) Purchased 200 shares of Corporation A stock at $40 per share, plus brokerage fees of $100. No significant influence is exercised.
(b) Purchased $10,000 of Corporation B bonds at face value, plus accrued interest of $500.
(c) Received a cash dividend of 50 cents per share on the Corporation A stock.
(d) Received interest of $600 on the Corporation B bonds.
(e) Purchased 50 shares of Corporation C stock for $3,500. No significant influence is exercised.
(f) Received interest of $600 on the Corporation B bonds.
(g) Sold 80 shares of Corporation A stock for $32 per share due to a significant decline in the market.
(h) Received a cash dividend of $1.40 per share on the Corporation C stock.
(i) Interest receivable at year-end on the Corporation B bonds amounts to $200.

Required: Enter these transactions in T-accounts, and determine each of the following for the year:

1. Dividend revenue.
2. Bond interest revenue.
3. Net gain or loss from selling securities.

Chapter 12 *Long-Term Investments*

12A-5
Long-Term Investments in Stocks

Durham Company often purchases common stocks of other companies as long-term investments. At the end of 1993, Durham held the common stocks listed. (Assume that Durham Company exercises no significant influence over these companies.)

Corporation	Number of Shares	Total Cost per Share
A	2,000	$ 70
B	3,000	50
C	1,500	148
D	1,000	82

Additional information for 1993:
Sept. 30   Durham received a cash dividend of $2.50 per share on Corporation A stock.
Dec. 31   The market prices were quoted as follows:
           Corporation A stock, $64; Corporation B stock, $48;
           Corporation C stock, $150; Corporation D stock, $78.

Required:
1. Illustrate how these investments would be reported on the balance sheet at December 31, 1993, and prepare the adjusting entry at that date.
2. What items and amounts would be reported on the income statement for 1993?
3. Prepare the journal entry for the sale of Corporation D stock for $74 per share in 1994.
4. **Interpretive Question** Why are losses from the write-down of long-term investments in stock to the lower of cost or market not included in the current year's income, whereas most similar losses for short-term investments in stock are?

P12A-6
Long-Term Investments in Stocks

On April 20, 1994, Samson Company acquired 20,000 shares of Salem Industries common stock at $38 per share as a long-term investment. Salem has 50,000 shares of outstanding voting common stock. The following additional information is presented for the calendar year ending December 31, 1994.

Nov. 20   Samson received a cash dividend of $2.00 per share from Salem Industries.
Dec. 31   Salem announced earnings for the year of $135,000.
     31   Salem Industries common stock had a closing market price of $35 per share.

Required:
1. **Interpretive Question** What accounting method should be used by Samson Company to account for this investment? Why?
2. Prepare journal entries for the transactions and events described.
3. Prepare a partial income statement and balance sheet to show how the investments and related accounts would be shown on the financial statements.

P12A-7
Long-Term Investments in Stock—The Cost and Equity Methods

During January 1994, Danbury, Inc. acquired 40,000 shares of Corporation A common stock for $24 per share. In addition, it purchased 5,000 shares of Corporation B preferred (nonvoting) stock for $112 per share. Corporation A has 160,000 shares of common stock outstanding, and Corporation B has 12,000 shares of nonvoting stock outstanding.

The following data were obtained from operations during 1994:

	1994
Net income:	
Corporation A	$190,000
Corporation B	80,000
Dividends paid (per share):	
Corporation A	$ 0.60
Corporation B	2.50
Market value per share at Dec. 31:	
Corporation A	$ 25
Corporation B	109

Required:
1. **Interpretive Question** What method should Danbury, Inc. use in accounting for the investment in Corporation A stock? Why? What accounting method should be used in accounting for Corporation B nonvoting stock? Why?
2. Give the General Journal entries necessary to record the transactions for 1994.

P12A-8
Unifying Concepts: Long-Term Investments in Stocks and Bonds

On January 1, Copley Company had surplus cash and decided to make some long-term investments. The following transactions occurred during the year:

Jan. 1	Purchased twenty $1,000, 12 percent bonds of Sifco Corporation at face value, plus accrued interest. Semiannual interest payment dates are November 1 and May 1 each year.
Feb. 15	Purchased 4,000 shares of Porto Corporation stock at $35 per share, plus brokerage fees of $1,500.
May 1	Received a semiannual interest payment on the Sifco Corporation bonds.
Sept. 30	Received an annual cash dividend of $1.50 per share on Porto stock.
Oct. 15	Sold 1,000 shares of the Porto Corporation stock at $42 per share.
Nov. 1	Received a semiannual interest payment on the Sifco Corporation bonds.
Dec. 31	Adjusted the accounts to accrue interest on the Sifco Corporation bonds.

Required:
1. Record the transactions in General Journal entry form.
2. The market quote for Sifco Corporation's bonds at closing on December 31 was 104. The Porto stock closed at $40 per share. Prepare a partial balance sheet showing all the necessary data for these securities. Assume that Copley exercises no significant influence over its investees.

P12A-9
Long-Term Investment in Stocks—Cost Versus Equity Method

SPREADSHEET PROBLEM

Nevada Company owned 10,000 shares (40 percent) of the voting stock of Vegas Company and exercised significant influence over Vegas through positions held on its board of directors. In studying the financial situation of the two companies in December, 1994, the president of Nevada Company estimated that his company's earnings would be $240,000 in 1994 and that Vegas Company's earnings would be about $300,000.

Chapter 12 Long-Term Investments

Required:
1. If Vegas Company declares its normal annual dividend of $2 per share in 1994, how much will Nevada Company's total income be for 1994 using the equity method?
2. If Nevada Company were allowed to account for its investment in Vegas Company on a cost basis, how much would Nevada Company's total income be for 1994, assuming that Vegas Company pays its normal $2 per share dividend?
3. What would be Nevada Company's total income for 1994, assuming that Vegas Company is directed to pay a dividend of $8 per share, assuming that Nevada Company uses:
    (a) The cost method?
    (b) The equity method?
4. **Interpretive Question** Why would investors in Nevada Company prefer that it use the equity method for reporting its investment in Vegas Company if Nevada exerts significant influence over the investee?

Problem Set B

P12B-1
Long-Term Investments in Bonds

On January 1, 1994, Poland Company purchased a $25,000, 12 percent bond at 104 as a long-term investment. The bond pays interest annually on each December 31 and matures on December 31, 1996.

Required: Assuming straight-line amortization, answer the following questions:

1. What will be the net amount of cash received (total inflows minus total outflows) from this investment over its life?
2. How much cash will be collected each year?
3. How much premium will be amortized each year (using straight-line amortization)?
4. By how much will the Long-Term Investments account decrease each year?
5. How much investment revenue will be reported on the income statement each year?

P12B-2
Determining the Purchase Price of Bonds and Effective-Interest Amortization

Brown Corporation is selling $300,000, 4-year, 8 percent bonds at a time when the market rate of interest for similar investments is 10 percent. These bonds pay semiannual interest.

Required:
1. Would these bonds be issued at a premium or at a discount?
2. Compute the total selling price of the bonds. (Hint: Determine the price that would result in an effective rate of interest of 10 percent compounded semiannually.)
3. Ignore your solutions to (1) and (2), and assume that your calculations in (2) yielded a selling price of $282,000. Using this amount, compute the bond premium to be amortized the first year using the effective-interest method. Assume that all bonds were sold on the first day of the year in which they were authorized.

P12B-3
Long-Term Investments in Stock

On March 15, 1994, Boston Company acquired 5,000 shares of Richfield Corporation common stock at $45 per share as a long-term investment. Richfield has 50,000 shares of outstanding voting common stock. Boston does not own any other stocks. The following additional events occurred during the fiscal year ending December 31, 1994:

Dec. 1 Boston received a cash dividend of $2.50 per share from Richfield Corporation.
31 Richfield Corporation announced earnings for the year of $150,000.
31 Richfield common stock had a closing market price of $42 per share.

Required:
1. What accounting method should be used to account for this investment? Why?
2. Record the events in General Journal form.
3. Prepare a partial income statement and balance sheet to show how the Investments accounts would be shown on the financial statements.

P12B-4
Long-Term Investment Portfolio

General Corporation has the following investments in long-term marketable equity securities at December 31, 1993:

Company	Shares	Percentage of Shares Owned	Cost	Market Price at 12/31/1993
Marlin Company	4,000	15%	$34	$32
Clarke Corporation	1,000	2	75	78
Air Products, Inc.	3,000	10	46	43

Required:
1. Prepare any adjusting entry required at December 31, 1993.
2. Illustrate how these investments would be presented on General Corporation's balance sheet at December 31, 1993.
3. Prepare the journal entry on April 10, 1994, when General Corporation sold Air Products, Inc. for $41 per share.
4. Assume that General Corporation still owns its investment in Marlin Company and Clarke Corporation at December 31, 1994, and that their market prices are $37 for Marlin and $74 for Clarke on that date. Prepare the adjusting journal entry at December 31, 1994.

P12B-5
Long-Term Investments in Stock

Century Corporation acquired 8,400 common shares of Fidelity Company on January 10, 1994, for $12 per share and acquired 15,000 common shares of Essem Corporation on January 25, 1994, for $22 per share. Fidelity has 60,000 shares of common stock outstanding, and Essem has 50,000 shares outstanding. At December 31, 1994, the following information was obtained about the operations of Fidelity and Essem:

	Fidelity	Essem
Net income	$36,000	$100,000
Dividends paid per share	$ 0.40	$ 1.00
Market value at December 31, 1994	$ 10.00	$ 20.00

Assume that Century Corporation exerted significant influence over the policies of Essem Corporation but only influenced the policies of Fidelity Corporation to a very limited extent.

Required:
1. How should Century account for its investments in Fidelity Company and Essem Corporation?
2. Prepare the journal entries for each investment for the year 1994 using the method or methods you selected in (1).

P12B-6

Long-Term Investments in Stock—The Cost and Equity Methods

SOLUTIONS SOFTWARE

The following activities relate to the Hilton Company during the years 1993 and 1994:

1993
Feb. 15 Hilton purchased 5,000 shares of Brock Equipment stock for $35 per share.
Dec. 1   Hilton received payment of $1.25 per share cash dividend from Brock Equipment.
Dec. 31 Brock Equipment common stock had a closing market price of $32 per share. Brock's 1991 net income was $60,000.

1994
July 1   Hilton sold all 5,000 shares of Brock Equipment stock for $37 per share.

Additional Information: Brock Equipment had 25,000 shares of common stock outstanding on January 1, 1993.

Required:
1. Record the transactions in General Journal entry form using:
   (a) The cost method.
   (b) The equity method.
2. Show the amounts that would be reported on the financial statements of Hilton Company at December 31, 1993, under each assumption.
3. **Interpretive Question** What is the minimum number of shares of stock that Brock could have outstanding in order for Hilton to use the cost method?

P12B-7

Unifying Concepts: Long-Term Investments in Stocks & Bonds

On January 2, 1994, Drexello, Inc. purchased $75,000 of 10 percent, 5-year bonds of Greasy Trucking as a long-term investment at a price of $77,610 plus accrued interest. The bonds mature on November 1, 1998, and interest is payable semiannually on May 1 and November 1. Drexello uses the straight-line method of amortizing bond premiums and discounts.

In addition to the bonds, Drexello purchased 30 percent of the 50,000 shares of outstanding common stock of Mellon Company at $42 per share, plus brokerage fees of $450, on January 10, 1994. On December 31, 1994, Mellon announced that its net income for the year was $150,000 and paid an annual dividend of $2 per share as advised by the board of directors of Drexello. The closing market price of Mellon common stock on December 31 was $38 per share.

Required:
1. Record all the 1994 transactions relating to these two investments in general journal form.
2. Show how the long-term investments and the related revenues would be reported on the financial statements of Drexello at December 31, 1994.

P12B-8
Valuation of Long-Term Investments in Stocks

Perry Company's comparative balance sheets for 1994 and 1993 including the following:

Investments	1994	1993
Investment in Berkey Company	$210,000	$140,000

Additional information concerning this asset is revealed in other financial statements or in footnotes as follows:

(a) On January 2, 1994, Perry spent $50,000 in cash to purchase additional shares of Berkey Company stock.
(b) Berkey Company reported that net income for 1994 was $200,000, and dividends paid by the company in 1994 were $150,000.
(c) Perry's share of Berkey Company's income during 1994 was $80,000.
(d) Dividends received from Berkey Company during 1994 were $60,000.

Required:
1. What percentage of Berkey Company did Perry own at December 31, 1994? How did you determine this percentage?
2. What valuation method did Perry Company use to account for its investment in Berkey Company? Why?
3. Explain the change in the investment balance in Perry's balance sheets from $140,000 to $210,000.
4. **Interpretive Question** What effect did the ownership of Berkey Company stock have on Perry's working capital for 1994?

P12B-9
Long-Term Investments in Stocks—Cost Versus Equity Method

On January 2, 1993, Groller Company acquired 20 percent of the 20,000 shares outstanding of Becker Company's common stock for $40 per share. This price is equal to Becker's book value per share. Groller planned to hold its investment in Becker for more than one year. Becker earned $70,000 in 1993 and paid $20,000 in dividends. Becker's shares were selling at $37 per share on December 31, 1993.

During 1994, Becker Company earned $80,000 and paid $24,000 in dividends. Its common stock was selling at $39 per share on December 31, 1994.

On June 5, 1995, Groller sold 1,000 shares of Becker stock for $41 per share. During 1995, Becker earned $60,000, and in October 1995, the company paid $10,000 in dividends. Becker's stock was selling for $42 per share on December 31, 1995. After selling the 1,000 shares of Becker's stock in June, Groller no longer expects to exercise significant influence over Becker.

Required:
1. Prepare the journal entry to account for Groller Company's acquisition of Becker Company's stock.
2. If Groller Company still owns the Becker Company stock at December 31, 1993, and plans to keep it for more than one more year, what choices does Groller management have as to how the Becker investment will be reported on the financial statements?
3. Prepare the journal entries on Groller Company's books at December 31, 1993, for each of the choices identified in (2).

Chapter 12 Long-Term Investments

4. Show how the investment in Becker would be presented on Groller's 1993 balance sheet for each of the two methods noted in (2).
5. Prepare the journal entries that Groller needs to make to reflect the results of Becker's operations in 1994 using both methods identified in your answer to (2).
6. Show how the investment in Becker would be presented on Groller's balance sheet as of December 31, 1994, using both methods identified in (2).
7. Prepare the journal entry for Groller to account for the sale of 1,000 shares of Becker's stock using both methods.
8. Prepare any journal entries that Groller needs to make between June 5 and December 31, 1995, regarding its investment in Becker.
9. Show how the remaining investment in Becker would be presented on Groller's balance sheet at December 31, 1995.

Business Analysis Case 1 *The Bond Market*

On Friday, January 24, 1992, *The Wall Street Journal* presented the following selected quotations as of 4 P.M., Thursday, January 23, 1992, for corporate bonds traded on the New York Bond Exchange for that day.

Bonds	Curr. Yld.	Volume	Close	Net Change
AlaP 8⅞ 03	8.6	25	102.875	+⅛
ATT 8.80s 05	8.5	113	103.0	—
ProcG 8.25 05	8.1	90	102.0	−¾

Required:
1. For each company's bonds listed (Alabama Power, American Telephone, and Proctor & Gamble), explain the information presented.
2. What was the actual closing price for one $1,000 bond for each company at 4 P.M. on Thursday, January 23, 1992?
3. If the ATT bond had been purchased near the close of January 23, 1992, would the purchaser have acquired the bond at a premium or discount?
4. What time period is covered by the information in the Net Change column?
5. Why would the price of certain bonds increase from one day to the next and decrease for other bonds?
6. If you were comparing the three bonds listed as investment alternatives, what factors would you consider in making an investment decision?

Business Analysis Case 2 *Pentron Data Corporation*

Pentron Data Corporation has a significant amount of excess cash on hand and has decided to use it to make a long-term investment in either marketable debt or marketable equity securities. After a careful analysis, the investment committee has recommended either one of the following two investments to the company treasurer. The first investment involves purchasing sixty $1,000, 8% bonds issued by the Andrea Company. The bonds mature in 4 years, pay interest semiannually, and are currently selling at 92. The second investment alternative involves purchasing 3,000 shares of Franklin Corporation common stock at $30 per share (including brokerage fees). The investment committee believes that the Franklin stock will pay an annual dividend of $3.50 per share and is likely to be saleable at the end of 4 years for $36 per share.

Required:
1. If Pentron wants to earn 12% per year, should it make either investment?
2. Which of the two investments would you advise the treasurer to invest in assuming the inherent risk is approximately equal? Your decision should be based on which investment provides the more attractive return ignoring income tax effects.

Ethics Case *Manley's Dilemma*

A large accounting firm has granted permission for the partner in charge of financial reporting, Raymond Manley, to serve on the accounting policy committee of the national organization representing professional accountants. At the next meeting of the policy committee, a vote is to be taken to determine what stance the committee should take regarding the valuation of certain assets held by banks and other financial institutions. The existing policy allows these financial institutions to value bonds and other debt securities held as long-term investments at their cost on year-end balance sheets. The policy committee has discussed the issue at length and appears to be favoring the position that these debt securities should be valued at the lower of cost or market in order to provide investors and depositors better information to assess the financial strength of institutions holding such debt securities. The policy committee has determined that banks and other financial institutions that have significant investments in such securities were valuing these securities at cost even though their market value was considerably less because of various economic factors. By continuing to report debt securities at original cost, the financial institutions were showing higher profits than would be the case if these investments were written down to market.

The day before going to the policy committee meeting, Manley expressed his concern about how he should vote on the debt security valuation issue since his firm has a number of banks and other financial institutions as audit clients and realizes that valuing these debt securities at the lower of cost or market will cause a significant decline in the earnings of some of the financial institutions that are his firm's clients. In fact, he had a call a few days ago from the audit engagement partner for one of the banks that would be adversely affected by a change in valuation policy. The audit partner indicated that this particular client would surely change auditors if it learned that Manley voted in favor of changing the valuation policy.

Following his conversation with the audit partner, Manley is very concerned. After studying the valuation issue carefully, he feels strongly that the accounting profession should revise its standards to require that investments in debt securities be valued the same way as investments in long-term equity securities, namely at the lower of cost or market. Yet, his loyalty to his firm suggests that he should not push this position in tomorrow's policy committee discussion that will take place just prior to the vote.

Required:
1. What are the ethical issues in this case?
2. Who are the parties that will be affected by the reporting policy adopted?
3. What should Manley do?

Chapter 13

Owners' Equity – The Corporation

Learning Objectives

After studying this chapter, you should be able to:
1. Describe the basic characteristics of a corporation and the various types of stock that corporations sell to investors.
2. Account for the issuance of common and preferred stock.
3. Explain and record the effects of treasury stock transactions.
4. Account for cash dividends on common and preferred stock.
5. Account for stock dividends and distinguish them from stock splits.
6. Account for, and prepare a statement of, retained earnings.
7. Understand the information reported in a statement of stockholders' equity.

SETTING THE STAGE

In December 1991, the world saw the once-powerful Soviet Union come to an abrupt end. The totalitarian government that had been led by such men as Lenin, Stalin, Khrushchev, and Gorbachev was dismantled, and the many republics that composed the Soviet Union, such as Russia, Ukraine, and Georgia, went their own separate ways, united only in a loose alliance for trade and military purposes. For over 70 years, the Communist Party had controlled the Soviet Union, running all state-owned businesses and quelling any resistance by force. In many ways, the Communist-controlled Soviet Union was a 70-year experiment in economics. Their imposed socialistic policies with very little private ownership stood in stark contrast to the democratic societies of the United States, Japan, and other countries where capitalism prevails. Only recently has the world discovered that the once-thought-to-be-strong Soviet Union has been in economic chaos for several years. Even getting sufficient food to eat has been and is a major undertaking in the Soviet Union.

Indeed, capitalism appears to have prevailed over communism. The new Russian president, Boris Yeltsin, as well as the leaders of the other republics that formerly made up the Soviet Union, are moving their countries to capitalistic, market-driven economies as rapidly as possible.

One of the major elements of a capitalistic, market-driven economy is private ownership of business organizations. In the United States and other capitalistic countries, individuals can become owners of corporations merely by purchasing stock, or ownership interests. Each share of stock usually entitles the investor to vote in corporate matters and assume other rights enjoyed by someone who owns a business. In the United States, there are hundreds of thousands of small and large corporations, partnerships, and proprietorships that are privately owned. Accounting for ownership interests in these organizations is the focus of this and the next chapter. As you study these pages, keep in mind that the concepts discussed here have been nonexistent in countries such as the Soviet Union, Cuba, and China for many decades.

Assets and liabilities were discussed in Chapters 8 through 12. In this chapter and the next, the focus is on owners' equity. This will complete our coverage of the balance sheet. Although accounting for the asset and liability accounts is generally the same in all businesses (corporations, partnerships, and proprietorships), accounting for equity is different for each of the three forms of business. Here owners' equity is discussed in the context of corporations; in Chapter 14, equity considerations for partnerships and proprietorships are covered.

Certain basic characteristics are common to all owners' equity accounts, no matter what the type of business. The first is that they represent the owners' interests in a firm, revealing how much the owners have contributed and how much of the firm's earnings have been retained in the business. Owners' equity accounts can therefore be thought of as identifying some of the sources of a firm's assets. Second, if all three types of businesses entered into the same transactions over their lifetimes, the total amounts in their owners' equity sections (ignoring tax differences) would be approximately the same. These totals are determined by the types of transactions entered into and the amounts involved, not by the form of organization. In other words, though owners' equity accounts differ in ways that will be illustrated for the three types of businesses, their purposes and functions are the same.

CORPORATIONS AND CORPORATE STOCK

Objective 1
Describe the basic characteristics of a corporation and the various types of stock that corporations sell to investors.

corporation *a legal entity chartered by a state; ownership is represented by transferable shares of stock*

charter (articles of incorporation) *a document issued by a state that gives legal status to a corporation and details its specific rights, including the authority to issue a certain maximum number of shares of stock*

limited liability *the legal protection given stockholders whereby they are responsible for the debts and obligations of a corporation only to the extent of their capital contributions*

Corporations are the dominant form of business enterprise in the United States. Established as separate legal entities, corporations are legally distinct from the persons responsible for their creation. In many respects, they are accorded the same rights as individuals; they can conduct business, be sued, enter into contracts, and own property. Firms are incorporated by the state in which they are organized and are subject to that state's laws and requirements.

Suppose that you wanted to start a corporation. First, you would study your state's corporate laws (usually with the aid of an attorney). Then you would apply for a charter with the appropriate state official. In the application, you would give the intended name of your corporation, its purpose (that is, the type of activity it will engage in), the type and amount of stock you plan to have authorized for your corporation, and in some cases, the names and addresses of the potential stockholders. Finally, if the state approves your application, you will be issued a **charter** (also called **articles of incorporation**), giving legal status to your corporation.

Characteristics of a Corporation

Corporations have several characteristics that distinguish them from other types of business entities. Probably the most significant is the **limited liability** of stockholders. This means that in the event of corporate bankruptcy, the maximum financial loss any stockholder can sustain is his or her investment in the corporation (unless fraud can be proven). Since a corporation is a separate legal entity and is responsible for its own acts and obligations, creditors cannot usually look beyond the corporation's assets for satisfaction of their claims. This is not true of other forms of business organizations. In a partnership, for example, the partners can usually be held liable for the debts of the partnership, even to the extent of their personal assets. This limited liability feature has probably

CHAPTER 13 Owners' Equity—The Corporation 519

been most responsible for the phenomenal growth of the corporate form of business because it protects investors from sustaining losses beyond their investments. In most cases of bankruptcy, however, stockholders will lose most of their investment since the claims of creditors must be satisfied before stockholders receive anything.

A second characteristic of a corporation is its continuous existence because of the easy transferability of ownership interests. Shares of stock in a corporation can be bought, sold, passed from one generation to another, or otherwise transferred, without affecting the legal or economic status of the corporation. In other words, most corporations have perpetual existence—the life of the corporation continues by the transfer of shares of stock to new owners.

stock certificate *a document issued by a corporation to stockholders evidencing ownership in the corporation*

stockholders *individuals or organizations that own a portion (shares of stock) of a corporation*

board of directors *individuals elected by the stockholders to govern a corporation*

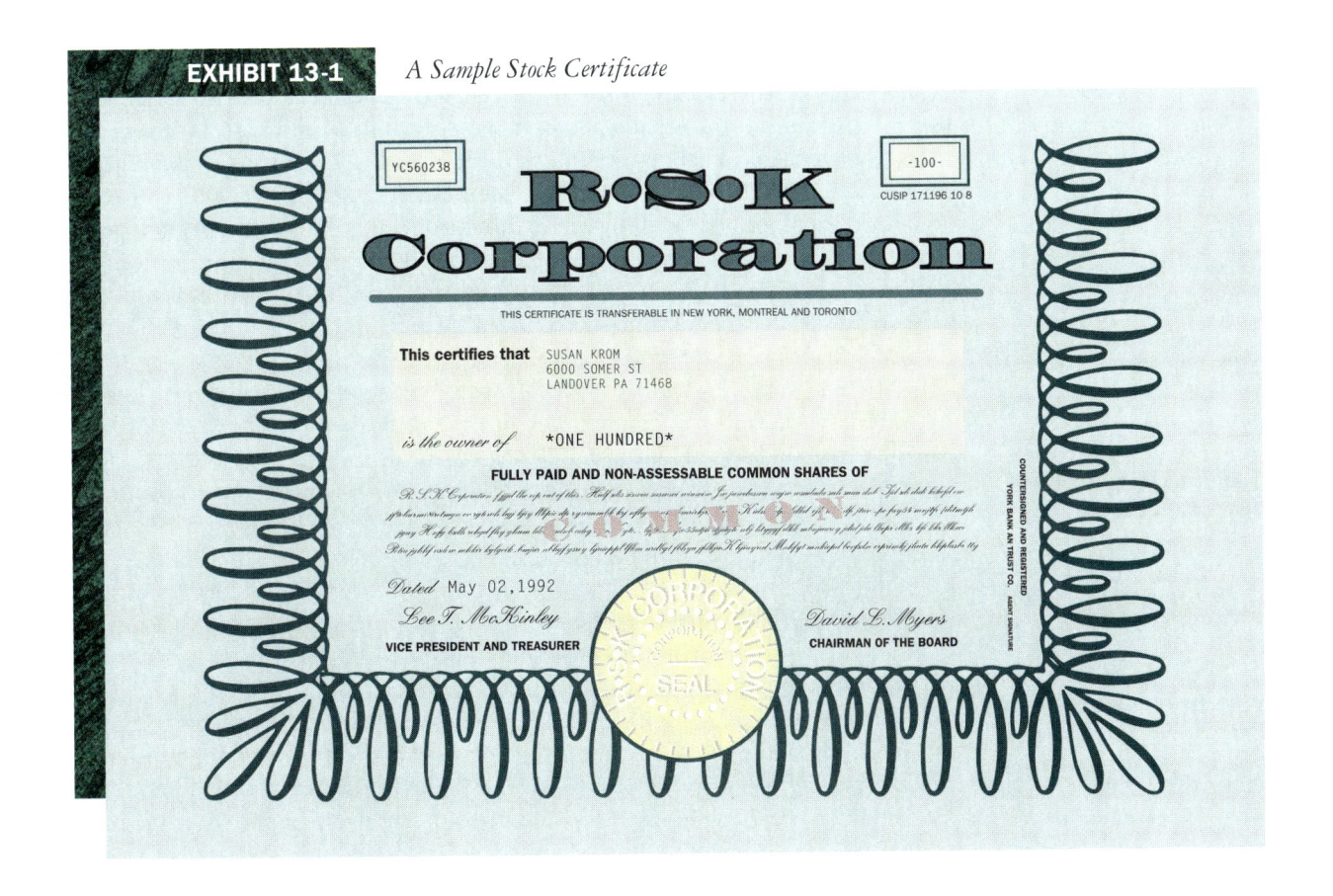

When you buy stock in a corporation, you receive a **stock certificate** as evidence of ownership. (See Exhibit 13-1 for a sample stock certificate.) The owners are called **stockholders,** and they govern the corporation through an elected **board of directors.** (In most corporations, the board of directors then chooses a management team to direct the daily affairs of the corporation. In smaller companies, the board of directors is made up of members of that management team.)

A third characteristic of corporations is their ability to raise larger amounts of capital than is possible with other forms of business organizations. The sale of shares of stock permits many investors, both large and small, to participate in ownership of the business. Some corporations actually have thousands of

EXHIBIT 13-1 *A Sample Stock Certificate*

individual stockholders. Because of this widespread ownership, large corporations are said to be publicly owned.

A fourth characteristic of corporations is that they are separately taxed. Because corporations are separate legal entities, they are taxed independently of their owners. This often results in a disadvantage, however, because the portion of corporate profits that is paid out in dividends is taxed twice. First, the profits are taxed to the corporation; second, the owners, or stockholders, are taxed on their dividend income. (Small corporations can avoid this double taxation by forming an **S corporation**.)

A fifth characteristic of very large corporations is that they are closely regulated by the government. Because large corporations may have thousands of stockholders, each with only small ownership interests, the government has assumed the task of monitoring certain corporate activities. Examples of government regulations are the requirements that all major corporations be audited and that they issue periodic financial statements. As a result, in certain respects major corporations often enjoy less freedom than do partnerships and proprietorships.

The Stock of a Corporation

The owners' equity section of a corporate balance sheet is usually divided into two parts: (1) **contributed capital,** which identifies the amount of capital contributed by the owners of a firm, and (2) retained earnings, which shows the amount of undistributed earnings of a firm since incorporation. In this section, we focus on the contributed capital accounts.

When a corporation is given its charter by a state, it can sell shares of stock to raise capital. These shares, which are generally referred to as **capital stock,** may be sold publicly to many investors or privately to only a few investors.

Corporate stock that has been approved for sale by a state is known as **authorized stock.** When the stock is sold, it becomes **issued stock.** If it is issued and not bought back by the corporation, it is said to be **issued and outstanding,** but if it has been reacquired by the corporation, it is known as **treasury stock** and is no longer considered outstanding. These stages in the status of stock are diagrammed in Exhibit 13-2.

In addition, several types of stock can be authorized by the charter and issued by the corporation. The most familiar types are **common stock** and **preferred stock,** and the major difference between them concerns the degree to which their holders are allowed to participate in the rights of ownership of the corporation. The three basic rights inherent in the ownership of common stock are (1) the right to vote in corporate matters, (2) the right to share in distributed corporate earnings, and (3) the right to share in corporate assets upon liquidation. Usually, preferred stock takes precedence over common stock in rights (2) and (3), whereas common stock is often the only type of stock that provides voting rights. Another right granted to stockholders in some states is the **preemptive right,** which permits existing stockholders to purchase additional shares whenever stock is issued by the corporation. This allows stockholders to maintain the same percentage of ownership in the company if they choose to do so.

In addition to dividend and liquidation preferences, preferred stock may include other types of privileges, the most common of which is convertibility.

S corporation *a corporation legally organized in such a way that income or loss is passed through to individual stockholders without being taxed at the corporate level*

contributed capital *the portion of owners' equity contributed by investors (the owners) in exchange for shares of stock*

capital stock *the general term applied to all shares of ownership in a corporation*

authorized stock *the amount and type of stock that may be issued by a company, as specified in its articles of incorporation*

issued stock *authorized stock originally issued to stockholders; it may or may not still be outstanding*

outstanding stock *issued stock that is still being held by investors*

treasury stock *issued stock that has subsequently been reacquired by the corporation*

common stock *the most frequently issued class of stock; usually it provides a voting right, but is secondary to preferred stock in dividend and liquidation rights*

preferred stock *a class of stock that usually provides dividend and liquidation preferences over common stock*

preemptive right *the right of current stockholders to purchase additional shares of stock in order to maintain their same percentage of ownership if new shares are issued*

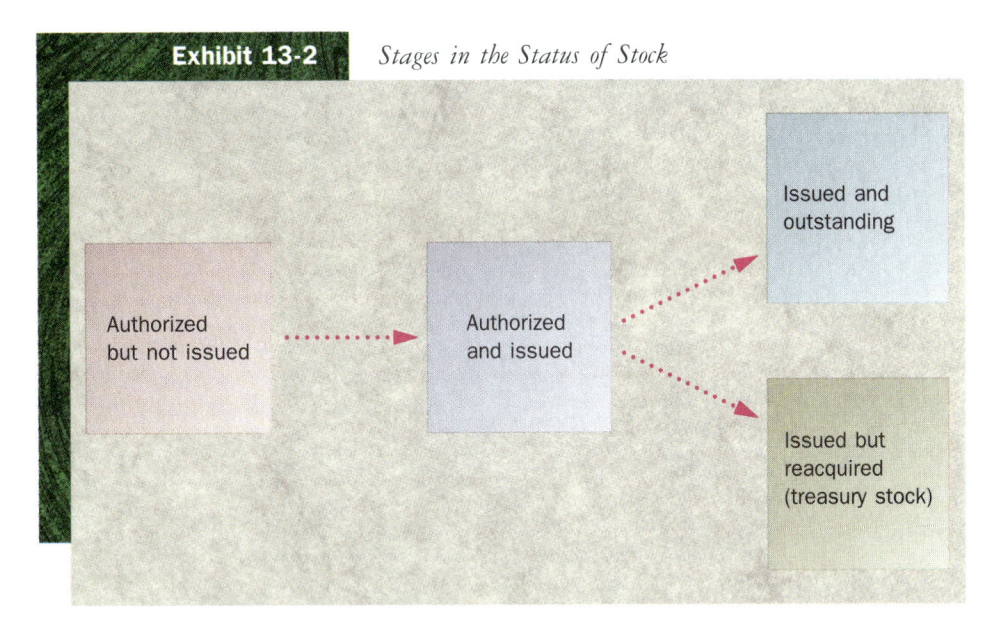

Exhibit 13-2 Stages in the Status of Stock

Authorized but not issued → Authorized and issued → Issued and outstanding / Issued but reacquired (treasury stock)

convertible preferred stock *preferred stock that can be converted to common stock at a specified conversion rate*

Convertible preferred stock is preferred stock that can be converted to common stock at a specified conversion rate. For example, the preferred stock of Bristol-Myers Company can be converted at a rate of 4.24 shares of common for each share of preferred stock. Convertible preferred stock can be very appealing to investors. They can enjoy the dividend privileges of the preferred stock while having the option to convert to common stock if the market value of the common stock increases significantly. By issuing stocks with varying rights and privileges, companies can appeal to a wider range of investors.

When only one type of stock is issued by a corporation, it is common stock. There are several different types of common stock, the most popular of which is **par-value stock.** Basically, this stock has a par, or nominal, value provided for in the corporate charter and printed on the face of each stock certificate. When par-value stock sells for a price above par, it is said to sell at a **premium;** in most states, it is illegal to issue stock for a price below par value. The par value multiplied by the total number of shares outstanding is usually equal to a company's **legal capital,** and it represents the amount of contributed capital that is not available for dividends. This legal capital requirement was intended to provide a means of protecting a company's creditors; without it, excessive dividends could be paid, leaving nothing for creditors. Because the assignment of a par value to stock has proved to be an ineffective way of protecting creditors, most states now allow the sale of **no-par stock.** Many states require, however, that no-par stock have a **stated value,** which is designated by the board of directors of a corporation and has the same purpose as par value. For no-par stock without a stated value, the legal capital is usually the total amount for which the stock was initially issued.

par-value stock *stock that has a nominal value assigned to it in the corporation's charter and printed on the face of each share of stock*

premium on stock *the excess of the issuance (market) price of stock over its par or stated value*

legal capital *the amount of contributed capital not available for dividends; usually equal to the par or stated value of outstanding capital stock*

no-par stock *stock that does not have a par value printed on the face of the stock certificate*

stated value *a nominal value assigned to no-par stock by the board of directors of a corporation*

A final note about par value and stated value: Stock often sells for a much higher price than its par or stated value. Indeed, the trend has been for companies to establish a very low par value, say, $1 or $2 per share, and then sell the stock for a much higher amount, say $10 per share. This strategy usually eliminates the possibility of stock ever selling below par value. If stock were to be issued at a discount (below par), stockholders could be liable for legal capital in excess of their investments in the corporation.

> **To Summarize** *Unlike the asset and liability accounts, owners' equity accounts vary depending on whether the business is a corporation, a partnership, or a proprietorship. A corporation is a business entity that has a legal existence separate from that of its owners; it can conduct business, own property, and enter into contracts. The five major features of a corporation are (1) limited liability for stockholders, (2) easy transferability of ownership, (3) the ability to raise large amounts of capital, (4) separate taxation, and (5) (for major corporations) closer regulation by government. The owners' equity section of a corporation's balance sheet is divided into two parts: (1) contributed capital and (2) retained earnings. A corporation's stock can be authorized but unsold, issued and outstanding, or repurchased by the company and held as treasury stock. Common stock confers three rights upon its owners: (1) the right to vote in corporate matters, (2) the right to share in company earnings, and (3) the right to share in the assets upon liquidation of a corporation. Preferred stock typically carries preferential claims to dividend and liquidation privileges but has no voting rights. Stock can be par value, no par with a stated value, or no par with no stated value. If par value, it usually sells above par (at a premium). The minimum amount of contributed capital a firm must maintain is called its legal capital.*

ACCOUNTING FOR STOCK

Objective 2
Account for the issuance of common and preferred stock.

In the previous section, we described the basic characteristics of the different types of stocks most frequently issued by corporations. Now we will focus on recording the issuance of stock and accounting for treasury stock, that is, shares that have been reacquired by the issuing corporation.

Issuance of Par-Value Stock and No-Par Stock with Stated Value

When par-value stock is issued by a corporation, usually Cash is debited, and the appropriate stockholders' equity accounts are credited. For par-value common stock, the equity accounts credited are Common Stock, for an amount equal to the par value, and Paid-In Capital in Excess of Par, Common Stock, for the premium on common stock.

To illustrate, we will assume that the Boston Lakers Basketball Team (a corporation) issued 1,000 shares of $10 par common stock for $50 per share. (Note that an accounting entry is not required at the time the stock is authorized, only when it is issued.) The entry to record the stock issuance would be:

Cash (1,000 shares × $50)........................	50,000	
Common Stock (1,000 shares × $10 par value).............		10,000
Paid-In Capital in Excess of Par, Common Stock		
(1,000 shares × $40).......................		40,000
Issued 1,000 shares of $10 par-value common stock at $50 per share.		

BUSINESS ENVIRONMENT ESSAY
Investing in the Stock Market

"October," said Mark Twain, "is one of the peculiarly dangerous months to speculate in stocks. Others are July, January, September, April, November, May, March, June, December, August, and February." Despite Mark Twain's warning, stocks have always been one of the most prestigious and desired investments. They have also been the source of tremendous riches. For example, if your great grandparents had purchased 100 shares of IBM stock in 1914 at a total cost of $2,750, their stock would now be worth over $18.8 million, and you would be receiving over $1.6 million each year in dividends. Likewise, a $300 investment in Minnesota Mining and Manufacturing (3M Company) in 1914 would now be worth close to $6 million, and you would be receiving over $100,000 in yearly dividends.

Obviously, some stock investments provide a better return than others. In recent years, the stock market has had extreme highs and lows, particularly in the computer and computer-related industries. For example, if you had purchased shares of Commodore International in 1984, at $49.75 per share (its high), your investment would have been worth $8.75 per share in 1985.

Here are some guidelines to consider when deciding to buy stock.

1. Do not make hasty, emotional decisions about buying and selling stocks.
2. Do not "fall in love" with stocks so that you are no longer objective in your appraisal of them.
3. Remember, you will seldom—if ever—buy stocks at their lowest price and sell them at their highest price.
4. There are stock market "fads," so when you buy at the height of a stock's popularity, you almost always pay too much.
5. Don't invest in stocks unless you can afford to lose the money you invest, or at least have no access to it for a long time.
6. Plan to hold your stock investments for a long time. Most stock-market millionaires were not speculators, and commissions on frequent sales and purchases will eat up your short-term gains.

Source: W. S. Albrecht, *Money Wise* (Salt Lake City, Utah: Deseret Book Company, 1983), pp. 134–139.

If the par-value stock being issued were preferred stock, the entry would be:

Cash (1,000 shares × $50)...........................	50,000	
Preferred Stock (1,000 shares × $10 par value)		10,000
Paid-In Capital in Excess of Par, Preferred Stock		
(1,000 shares × $40)		40,000
Issued 1,000 shares of $10 par-value preferred stock at $50 per share.		

This illustration points out two important elements in accounting for the issuance of stock: (1) the equity accounts identify the type of stock being issued (common or preferred), and (2) the proceeds from the sale of the stock are divided into the portion attributable to its par value and the portion paid in excess of par value. These distinctions are important because the owners' equity section of the balance sheet should correctly identify the specific sources of capital so that the respective rights of the various stockholders can be known.

If issued stock is no-par with a stated value, the entries are virtually the same as those just illustrated. For example, we now assume that the Boston Lakers' authorized stock was no-par stock with a stated value of $1 per share, and that 4,000 shares were issued for $5 per share. The entry would be:

```
Cash (4,000 shares × $5)..................................   20,000
     Common Stock (4,000 shares × $1 stated value) ............          4,000
     Paid-In Capital in Excess of Stated Value, Common
     Stock (4,000 shares × $4) ..................................        16,000
Issued 4,000 shares of no-par common stock with a $1 stated value at $5 per share.
```

Again, if the stock issued were preferred stock, the only change in this entry would be to identify the stock as preferred stock.

Although stock is usually issued for cash, other considerations may be involved. When a corporation is being organized, for example, attorneys and accountants may be paid with stock. The only difference between stock issued for noncash considerations and stock issued for cash is in the debit entry. In the case of stock being given to an attorney for help in organizing a corporation, the debit entry is usually to Organization Costs rather than to Legal Expense. The Organization Costs account is an intangible asset that is usually amortized over the first 5 years of a corporation's existence.

To illustrate the kinds of entries made when stock is issued for noncash considerations, we will assume that a prospective stockholder exchanged a piece of land for 5,000 shares of the Boston Lakers' $1-per-share stated-value common stock. Assuming the market value of the stock at the date of the exchange was $5 per share, the entry would be:

```
Land .....................................................   25,000
     Common Stock (5,000 shares × $1) ........................          5,000
     Paid-In Capital in Excess of Stated Value, Common
     Stock.................................................            20,000
Issued 5,000 shares of no-par common stock, $1 stated value, for land (5,000 shares × $5
per share = $25,000).
```

When noncash considerations are received in payment for stock, the assets or services received should be recorded at the current market value of the stock issued. If the market value of the stock cannot be determined, the market value of the assets or services received should be used as the basis for recording the transaction.

Issuance of No-Par Stock Without a Stated Value

If the stock being issued is no par without a stated value, only one credit is included in the entry. To illustrate, we assume that the Lakers' stock does not have a par or stated value and that the corporation issued 2,000 shares for $14 per share. The entry to record this stock issuance would be:

Cash	28,000	
Common Stock		28,000

Issued 2,000 shares of no-par stock at $14 per share.

Since most stock issued is either par-value stock or no-par stock with a stated value, only these two categories will be discussed in the remainder of this chapter.

Accounting for Treasury Stock

Objective 3
Explain and record the effects of treasury stock transactions.

As noted earlier, a corporation may acquire some of its own outstanding stock. This reacquired stock is called treasury stock and is much like unissued stock in that it usually has no voting, dividend, or other rights. Because the acquisition of treasury stock effectively reduces the amount of stock outstanding and thereby allows a corporation to reduce its legal capital, most states restrict the amount of treasury stock a firm can have.

There are many reasons for a firm to buy back its own stock. Five of the most common are that management (1) may want the stock for a profit-sharing, bonus, or stock-option plan for employees, (2) may feel that the stock is selling for an unusually low price and is a good buy, (3) may want to stimulate trading in the company's stock, (4) may want the stock for use in purchasing another company, and (5) may want to increase reported earnings per share by reducing the number of shares of stock outstanding. As an example, a few years ago American Telephone & Telegraph (AT&T) announced plans to spend $809 million to buy back 15.5 million shares of its own stock. The purpose of the buyback was to reduce the amount the company would have to pay each year in dividends by $50 million. AT&T estimated that the stock repurchase would boost company earnings by about 2½ cents per share annually since fewer shares would be outstanding. This amount is significant given that AT&T had reported total earnings per share of only 5 cents in the previous year.

When a firm purchases stock of another company, the investment is included as an asset on the balance sheet. However, a corporation cannot own part of itself, so treasury stock is not considered an asset. Instead, it is a contra-equity account and is included on the balance sheet as a deduction from stockholders' equity. The reporting of treasury stock is illustrated in the following partial balance sheet for Markos Company.

Markos Company
Partial Balance Sheet
December 31, 1994

Stockholders' Equity		
Contributed capital:		
Preferred stock (7%, par $10, 10,000 shares authorized, 5,000 shares issued and outstanding)	$ 50,000	
Common stock (par $2, 100,000 shares authorized, 50,000 shares issued, 45,000 shares outstanding)	100,000	
Paid-in capital in excess of par, common stock	10,000	
Total contributed capital		$160,000
Retained earnings		42,000
Less treasury stock (5,000 common shares at cost of $2.80 per share)		(14,000)
Total stockholders' equity		$188,000

In this example, Markos Company has issued 50,000 shares of common stock. Because 5,000 shares have been reacquired and are held as treasury stock, the number of shares outstanding is 45,000.

Treasury stock is usually accounted for on a cost basis; that is, the stock is debited at its cost (market value) on the date of repurchase, not at its par or stated value. To illustrate, we assume that 100 shares of the $10 par common stock were reacquired by the Boston Lakers for $60 per share. The entry to record the acquisition would be:

Treasury Stock, Common	6,000	
Cash		6,000
Purchased 100 shares of treasury stock at $60 per share.		

The effect of this entry is to reduce both total assets (cash) and total stockholders' equity by $6,000.

When treasury stock is reissued, the Treasury Stock account must be credited for the amount paid to reacquire the stock. If the treasury stock's reissuance price is greater than its cost, an additional credit must be made to an account called Paid-In Capital, Treasury Stock. Together, these credits show the net increase in total stockholders' equity. At the same time, the Cash account is increased by the total amount received upon reissuance of the treasury stock. Be careful when accounting for treasury stock that is reissued at a price greater than its cost. Many students are tempted to credit the excess received as a gain instead of additional paid-in capital. The excess is not considered a gain because a company cannot recognize a gain or revenue on the purchase or sale of its own stock.

To illustrate, we assume that 40 of the 100 shares of treasury stock are reissued at $80 per share. The entry to record this reissuance would be:

Cash (40 shares × $80)	3,200	
Treasury Stock, Common (40 shares × $60 cost)		2,400
Paid-In Capital, Treasury Stock [($80 − $60) × 40]		800
Reissued 40 shares of treasury stock at $80 per share.		

The company now has a balance of $3,600 in the Treasury Stock account (60 shares at $60 per share). Note that Retained Earnings is never credited for the excess of selling price over cost. Although Retained Earnings may be reduced by treasury stock transactions, as you will soon see, it cannot be increased by such transactions.

Sometimes the reissuance price of treasury stock is less than its cost. As before, the entry involves a debit to Cash for the amount received and a credit to Treasury Stock for the cost of the stock. However, since less than cost has been received, an additional debit is required. The debit is to Paid-In Capital, Treasury Stock if there is a balance in that account from previous transactions, or to Retained Earnings if there is no balance in the Paid-In Capital, Treasury Stock account. Alternatively, Retained Earnings may be reduced for the entire amount even if the Paid-In Capital, Treasury Stock account has a balance. (In

Chapter 13 Owners' Equity—The Corporation

BUSINESS ENVIRONMENT ESSAY
Does Treasury Stock Hide Corporate Losses?

In September, 1987, Hospital Corp. of America (HCA) purchased 12 million shares of its own stock in the marketplace at $47 per share. On Monday, October 19, 1987, what is commonly referred to as "Black Monday," the stock market suffered its worst one-day drop in history. By December 31, 1987, HCA's stock was selling at approximately $31 per share. Did HCA have to report a loss of $16 per share, or $190 million, on its income statement? According to some, common sense would answer with a resounding yes. But like many other corporations with similar transactions, HCA's 1987 annual report showed no such loss.

The reason for reporting no loss is a 1938 securities rule that prevents firms from speculating in their own stock, requiring repurchased shares to be held as Treasury Stock and shown in the stockholders' equity section. Companies cannot report profits and losses on treasury stock transactions. It's a far different story when a company buys stock in another firm. Then, the corporation counts its stock holdings as a long-term investment. If the value of that investment goes down, those assets are written down to market, and the losses are reported. The following table shows seven companies that suffered huge losses from buying their own stock in 1987. Since the stock was all reported as treasury stock, none of these losses were reported.

Company	Price When Purchased	Number of Shares Purchased in 1987	December 31, 1987 Price	Unrecognized Losses
Allied-Signal	$44.50	27.4 million	$28.75	$289.3 million
ITT	$63.00	8.0 million	$45.00	$40.0 million
Hospital Corp. of America	$47.00	12.0 million	$31.25	$190.5 million
Kraft	$57.25	2.8 million	$48.00	$26.0 million
IBM	$144.12	19.0 million	$116.37	$288.9 million
GenCorp	$130.00	12.5 million	$22.50	$1,118.8 million
Merck	$184.50	5.7 million	$158.87	$94.4 million

Some people contend that losses such as these should be reported. Their argument is that, "Anytime you make an investment with corporate assets and lose money, it's a loss to shareholders and a poor use of corporate capital." They believe that accounting rules should reveal this important truth, rather than help obscure it.

Source: Adapted from "Losses? What Losses?", *Forbes*, February 8, 1988, p. 118.

---

this book, we will always assume that if Paid-In Capital, Treasury Stock has a balance, it will be reduced first and any excess will then reduce Retained Earnings.)

To illustrate, we will consider two more treasury stock transactions. First, we assume that another 30 shares of treasury stock are reissued for $40 per share, $20 less than their cost. Since Paid-In Capital, Treasury Stock has a balance of $800, the entry to record this transaction would be:

Cash (30 shares × $40)	1,200	
Paid-In Capital, Treasury Stock	600	
Treasury Stock, Common (30 shares × $60 cost)		1,800

Reissued 30 shares of treasury stock at $40 per share; original cost was $60 per share.

Note that after this transaction is recorded, the balance in Paid-In Capital, Treasury Stock is $200 ($800 − $600).

Next, we assume the company reissues 20 additional shares at $45 per share. The entry to record this transaction would be:

Cash (20 shares × $45)	900	
Paid-In Capital, Treasury Stock	200	
Retained Earnings	100	
Treasury Stock (20 shares × $60 cost)		1,200

Reissued 20 shares of treasury stock at $45 per share; original cost was $60 per share.

In this transaction, the selling price was $300 less than the cost of the treasury stock. Since the Paid-In Capital, Treasury Stock account had a balance of only $200, Retained Earnings was debited for the remaining $100.

Reporting Stock on the Balance Sheet

We have discussed the ways in which stock transactions affect owners' equity accounts. We will now show how these accounts are summarized and presented on the balance sheet. The following data, which summarize the stock transactions of the Boston Lakers, will be used to illustrate our points:

1. $10 par-value preferred stock: issued 1,000 shares at $50 per share.
2. $10 par-value common stock: issued 1,000 shares at $50 per share.
3. No-par common stock with a $1 stated value: issued 4,000 shares at $5 per share.
4. No-par common stock with a $1 stated value: issued 5,000 shares for land with a fair market value of $25,000.
5. No-par, no-stated-value common stock: issued 2,000 shares at $14 per share.
6. Treasury stock, common: purchased 100 shares at $60; reissued 40 shares at $80; reissued 30 shares at $40; reissued 20 shares at $45.

With these data, and assuming a Retained Earnings balance of $100,000, the stockholders' equity section would be as shown on the top of the next page.

Although this presentation of stockholders' equity is not realistic (companies rarely issue more than one type of common stock), it does summarize the information discussed thus far, and it illustrates that the various types of stock, as well as their par or stated values, must be separately identified in the stockholders' equity section.

Boston Lakers Basketball Team
Stockholders' Equity Section of Balance Sheet*

Preferred stock ($10 par value, 1,000 shares issued and outstanding)	$10,000	
Common stock ($10 par value, 1,000 shares issued, 990 shares outstanding)	10,000	
Common stock (no par, $1 stated value, 9,000 shares issued and outstanding)	9,000	
Common stock (no par, no stated value, 2,000 shares issued and outstanding)	28,000	
Paid-in capital in excess of par, preferred stock	40,000	
Paid-in capital in excess of par, common stock	40,000	
Paid-in capital in excess of stated value, common stock	36,000	
Total contributed capital		$173,000
Retained earnings (to be discussed)		100,000
Total contributed capital and retained earnings		$273,000
Less treasury stock (10 shares of $10 par common at cost of $60 per share)		(600)
Total stockholders' equity		$272,400

* Note: The number of shares authorized is deleted in this illustration.

> **To Summarize** *When a company issues stock, it debits Cash or a noncash account (property, for example) and credits various stockholders' equity accounts. The credit entries depend on the type of stock issued (common or preferred), its features (par value, no par with stated value, or no par without stated value), and the per-share amounts the stock is issued for (above par and at par). A company's own stock that is reacquired in the marketplace is known as treasury stock and is included in the financial statements as a contra-stockholders' equity account. Treasury stock is usually accounted for on a cost basis. The stockholders' equity section of a balance sheet contains separate accounts for each type of stock issued, amounts paid in excess of par or stated values, treasury stock, and retained earnings.*

DISTRIBUTIONS TO STOCKHOLDERS

Objective 4
Account for cash dividends on common and preferred stock.

pro rata *a term describing an allocation that is based on a proportionate distribution of the total*

dividends *periodic distributions of earnings in the form of cash, stock, or other property to the owners (stockholders) of a corporation*

If you had your own business and wanted to withdraw money for personal use, you would simply withdraw it from the company's checking account or cash register. In a corporation, a formal action by the board of directors is required before money can be distributed to the owners. In addition, such payments must be made on a **pro rata** basis. (That is, each owner must receive a proportionate amount on the basis of ownership percentage.) These pro rata distributions to owners are called **dividends** and are usually paid on a per-share basis. Thus, the amount of dividends a shareholder receives depends on the number of shares owned and on the per-share amount of the dividend.

Note that a company does not have to pay dividends. Theoretically, a company that does not pay dividends should be able to reinvest its earnings in

BUSINESS ENVIRONMENT ESSAY
Inequitable Equity

If you were to look at the balance sheet for King World Productions, Inc., the $285-million-a-year syndicator of such shows as *Jeopardy, Wheel of Fortune,* and *Oprah Winfrey,* you would see a puzzling stockholders' equity section. Because the company has borrowed so much money that debt exceeds the book value of the assets, you would see a $30 million negative stockholders' equity balance. Yet, the company is nowhere close to being bankrupt, as are many companies with negative equity. The company has revenues of hundreds of millions of dollars and profits of 20 cents per every dollar of revenue. Why then, does its balance sheet look so bad?

The answer is in the way traditional accounting rules require assets to be accounted for. King World's television programs are its assets and are reported at a book value of only $3 million with a zero value for *Wheel of Fortune.* Yet, these same programs have contracts that will bring in over $700 million in licensing fees in the next two years alone. Banks are willing to loan money on these contractual "assets," but traditional accounting rules prohibit them from being reported.

Contracts such as King World's are not the only assets that accounting rules don't allow to be reported. Patents, advertising, research and development, and many other intangible assets, which make up a great deal of the worth of many giant firms, fall into this same category. Instead of being reported as assets, such expenditures are charged against income as expenses when incurred. The CocaCola logo, for example, is one of the best-recognized trademarks in the world, but it is not reported as an asset on the company's balance sheet. All the money spent in advertising to create its recognition was charged as expense when incurred.

King World Productions, Inc., is not happy with its reported negative stockholders' equity. It does not want the appearance of having had losses in the past. Until there is a fundamental change in historical cost accounting, however, it and many other companies will have to be content with negative equity if they want to borrow such large amounts.

Source: Adapted from "Inequitable Equity," *Forbes,* July 11, 1988, p. 83.

---

assets that will enable it to grow more rapidly than its dividend-paying competitors. This added growth will presumably be reflected in increases in the per-share price of the stock. In practice, most public companies pay regular cash dividends because investors expect them to.

Types of Dividends

cash dividend *a cash distribution of earnings to shareholders*

stock dividend *a pro rata distribution of additional shares of stock to shareholders*

property dividend *the distribution to shareholders of assets other than cash*

Corporations can distribute any one of several types of dividends. The most common is a **cash dividend,** which is a payment of some of the cash generated by corporate earnings. A second type is a **stock dividend,** which is a distribution of additional shares of stock to stockholders. Stock dividends will be discussed later in the chapter. Finally, there is a **property dividend,** a distribution of corporate assets (for example, the stock of another firm) to stockholders. Property dividends are quite rare. In the following sections, the most common types of dividends, cash and stock, will be discussed and illustrated.

Accounting for Cash Dividends

declaration date *the date on which a corporation's board of directors formally decides to pay a dividend to shareholders*

Three important dates are associated with dividends. The first is when the board of directors formally declares its intent to pay a dividend. On this **declaration date,** the company becomes legally obligated to pay the dividends. This liability may be recorded as follows:

```
Dividends, Common Stock .......................................   8,000
    Dividends Payable ..........................................          8,000
Declared a 50-cent-per-share dividend to stockholders of record on December 15, 1994.
```

At the end of the year, the account Dividends, Common Stock is closed to Retained Earnings by the following entry:

```
Retained Earnings .............................................   8,000
    Dividends, Common Stock ....................................          8,000
To close Dividends to Retained Earnings.
```

From this entry, you can see that a declaration of dividends reduces Retained Earnings and, eventually, the amount of cash on hand. Thus, although not considered to be expenses, dividends do reduce the amount a company could otherwise invest in productive assets.

An alternative way of recording the declaration of dividends involves debiting Retained Earnings directly. However, using the Dividends account instead of Retained Earnings allows a company to keep separate records of dividends paid to preferred and common stockholders. Whichever method is used, the result is the same: a decrease in Retained Earnings.

date of record *the date selected by a corporation's board of directors on which the shareholders of record are identified as those who will receive dividends*

The second important dividend date is the **date of record.** Falling somewhere between the declaration date and the payment date, this is the date selected by the board of directors on which the stockholders of record are identified as those who will receive dividends. Since many corporate stocks are in flux—being bought and sold daily—it is important that the stockholders who will receive the dividends be identified. No journal entry is required on the date of record; the date of record is simply noted in the minutes of the directors meeting and in a letter to stockholders.

dividend payment date *the date on which a corporation pays dividends to its shareholders*

As you might expect, the third important date is the **dividend payment date.** This is the date on which, by order of the board of directors, dividends will be paid. The entry to record a dividend payment would typically be:

```
Dividends Payable .............................................   8,000
    Cash .......................................................          8,000
Paid a 50-cent-per-share dividend.
```

Once a dividend-paying pattern has been established, the expectation of dividends is built into the per-share price of the stock. A reduction in the dividend pattern usually produces a sharp drop in the price. Similarly, an increased dividend is a sign of growth and usually triggers a stock price increase. Dividend increases are usually considered to set a precedent, indicating that future dividends will be at this per-share amount or more. With this in mind, boards of directors are careful about increasing or decreasing dividends.

DIVIDEND PREFERENCES. The declaration and payment of a cash dividend requires (1) a sufficient amount of uncommitted retained earnings, (2) cash to pay the dividend, and (3) a formal written action (referred to as a dividend declaration) by the board of directors. Cash dividends are by far the most common types of dividends. They can be paid on any kind of stock, except, of course, unissued or treasury stock. If cash dividends were paid on treasury stock, the corporation would be paying a dividend to itself.

When cash dividends are declared by a corporation that has preferred stock outstanding, allocation of the dividends depends on the rights of the preferred stockholders. These rights are identified when the stock is approved by the state. Three "dividend preferences," as they are called, are (1) current-dividend preference, (2) cumulative-dividend preference, and (3) participating-dividend preference. Preferred stockholders often have current- and cumulative-dividend preferences, but the participating feature is rare and thus will not be illustrated in this text.

Current-Dividend Preference. Preferred stock has a dividend percentage associated with it and is typically described as follows: "5 percent preferred, par $10 per share, 6,000 shares outstanding." The first figure—"5 percent" in this example—is a percentage of the par value, and can be any amount, depending on the particular stock. So, 50 cents per share (0.05 × $10 = $0.50) is the amount that will be paid in dividends to preferred stockholders each year that dividends are declared. The fact that preferred stock dividends are fixed at a specific percentage of their par value makes them somewhat similar to the interest paid to bondholders. The **current-dividend preference** requires that when dividends are paid, this percentage of the preferred stock's par value be paid to preferred stockholders before common stockholders receive any dividends.

current-dividend preference the right of preferred shareholders to receive current dividends before common shareholders receive dividends

To illustrate the payment of different types of dividends, the following data from the Boston Lakers Basketball Team will be used throughout this section. (The various combinations of dividend preferences illustrated over the next few pages are summarized as Cases 1 to 4 in Exhibit 13-3.) Assume that outstanding stock includes:

Preferred stock (5%, $10 par value, 6,000 shares issued and outstanding)...	$60,000
Common stock ($5 par value, 8,000 shares issued and outstanding)...	40,000
Total	$100,000

To begin, assume that the Lakers' 5 percent preferred stock has a current-dividend preference: Before any dividends can be paid to common stockholders, preferred stockholders must be paid a total of $3,000 ($60,000 × 0.05). Thus, if only $2,000 of dividends were declared (case 1), preferred stockholders would

Exhibit 13-3   Dividend Preferences: Summary of Cases 1 to 4

Case	Preferred Dividend Feature	Years in Arrears	Total Dividend	Preferred Dividend	Common Dividend
1	5%, Noncumulative	Not applicable	$ 2,000	$2,000	-0-
2	5%, Noncumulative	Not applicable	4,000	3,000	$1,000
3	5%, Cumulative	2	7,000	7,000	-0-
4	5%, Cumulative	2	11,000	9,000	2,000

receive the entire dividend payment. If $4,000 were declared (case 2), preferred stockholders would receive $3,000 and common stockholders, $1,000.

Cumulative-Dividend Preference. The cumulative-dividend preference can be quite costly for common stockholders because it requires that preferred stockholders be paid current dividends plus all unpaid dividends from past years before common stockholders receive anything. If dividends have been paid in all previous years, then only the current 5 percent must be paid to preferred stockholders. But if dividends on preferred stock were not paid in full in prior years, the cumulative deficiency must be paid before common stockholders receive anything.

With respect to the cumulative feature, it is important to repeat that companies are not required to pay dividends. Such past unpaid dividends are called **dividends in arrears.** Since they do not have to be paid unless dividends are declared in the future, dividends in arrears do not represent actual liabilities and thus are not recorded in the accounts. Instead, they are reported in the notes to the financial statements.

To illustrate the distribution of dividends for cumulative preferred stock, we will assume that the Boston Lakers Basketball Team has not paid any dividends for the last 2 years but has declared a dividend in the current year. The Lakers must pay $9,000 in dividends to preferred stockholders before they can give anything to the common stockholders. The calculation is as follows:

cumulative-dividend preference *the right of preferred stockholders to receive current dividends plus all dividends in arrears before common stockholders receive any dividends*

dividends in arrears *missed dividends for past years that preferred stockholders have a right to receive under the cumulative-dividend preference if and when dividends are declared*

Dividends in arrears, 2 years (0.05 × $60,000 × 2)	$6,000
Current dividend preference (0.05 × $60,000)	3,000
Total	$9,000

Therefore, if the Lakers paid only $7,000 in dividends (case 3), preferred stockholders would receive all the dividends, common stockholders would receive nothing, and there would still be dividends in arrears of $2,000 the next year. If $11,000 in dividends were paid (case 4), preferred stockholders would receive $9,000, and common stockholders would receive $2,000.

Whether or not preferred stock is cumulative, the entries to record the declaration and payment of dividends are similar to those illustrated on page 531. For example, the entries to account for the transactions in case 4 would be:

Date of Declaration

Dividends, Preferred Stock	9,000	
Dividends, Common Stock	2,000	
Dividends Payable		11,000
Declared dividends on preferred and common stock.		

Date of Payment

Dividends Payable	11,000	
Cash		11,000
Paid dividends on preferred and common stock.		

Accounting for Stock Dividends

Objective 5
Account for stock dividends and distinguish them from stock splits.

Corporations sometimes distribute additional shares of their own stock to stockholders instead of paying a cash dividend. These stock dividends must be distributed to each stockholder in proportion to the number of shares held. For example, if a company issued a 10 percent stock dividend, each stockholder would receive 1 additional share for every 10 shares owned.

There is considerable disagreement as to whether stockholders receive anything of value from a stock dividend. Certainly, they do not receive corporate assets, as with a cash or property dividend. Nor does any stockholder own a larger percentage of the corporation after the stock dividend than before since each stockholder receives a pro rata share of the stock issued. Those who argue that stock dividends have value to stockholders give two reasons for their views.

1. If a company maintains the same level of cash dividends per share after the stock dividend as before, then an investor's long-run cash dividends will be increased by a stock dividend. Clearly, the issuance of a stock dividend in such a case represents a firm's decision to increase the total amount of cash dividends it will pay in the future.
2. If the stock dividend is small, say 10 percent, then the market will probably not discount the company's stock to a price that reflects the new total number of shares outstanding. In other words, the stock's market price will usually not drop by a percentage equivalent to that of the stock dividend. The investor's increased number of shares would, if this view is correct, have an increased value. (In fact, if the price of the stock does not drop proportionately, the reason may be the anticipation of increased future dividends, as described earlier.)

Stock dividends play an important role for the issuing corporation by maintaining dividend consistency. Corporations that issue dividends each year do not want to miss a year, so for them a stock dividend can be a useful substitute for cash. Because of the expectation of increased future dividends, most investors are happy to receive stock dividends.

To illustrate the accounting for a stock dividend, we will assume that stockholders' equity of the Boston Lakers Basketball Team was:

Common stock ($10 par value, 1,000 shares issued and outstanding)	$10,000
Paid-in capital in excess of par, common stock	40,000
Retained earnings	50,000
Total stockholders' equity	$100,000

If a 10 percent stock dividend is declared and issued when the stock's current market price is $70, the entry to record the stock dividend would be:

Retained Earnings (100 shares × $70)	7,000	
Common Stock (100 shares × $10 par)		1,000
Paid-In Capital, Stock Dividend		6,000

Declared and issued a 10% stock dividend.

Since the dividend was 10 percent, and since there were previously 1,000 shares outstanding, 100 additional shares were issued for the dividend. The market value of the stock ($70) was used as the basis for converting retained earnings to contributed capital because this was a relatively small stock dividend and presumably would not have a significant effect on the existing market price of the stock. Debiting the Retained Earnings account only for the par value of $10 would not have been realistic since the market value of the stock was much greater than $10.

If a stock dividend is relatively large, the market price of the outstanding stock is likely to be significantly affected, so the market price at the time the dividend is issued becomes irrelevant. For this reason, the accounting profession has required that par value be used for reporting large stock dividends.

Where does one draw the line between a large and a small stock dividend? The Securities and Exchange Commission (SEC) draws the line at 25 percent of total outstanding stock. Thus, for a stock dividend of 25 percent or larger, Retained Earnings is generally debited at par value; for smaller stock dividends, the market value of the stock is used.

To illustrate the accounting for a large stock dividend, we assume the same stockholders' equity for the Boston Lakers Basketball Team, except that the stock dividend is now 30 percent. The entry would be:

Retained Earnings	3,000	
Common Stock		3,000

Declared and issued a 30% stock dividend (1,000 shares × 0.30 = 300 shares; 300 shares × $10 = $3,000).

Note that stock dividends do not change the total amount of stockholders' equity, regardless of the size of the dividend. The only effect is to reallocate some of the stockholders' equity from retained earnings to common or preferred stock.

Stock Splits

Many investors, particularly individuals with limited amounts to invest, will not purchase stocks with very high market prices per share. To encourage more investors to buy their stocks, companies sometimes enact a **stock split,** replacing the shares outstanding with a larger number of new shares that sell at a lower price per share. IBM, for example, has split its stock numerous times in order to bring down the price. Because of these splits, an original share of IBM stock is now the equivalent of several hundred shares.

A stock split increases the shares of outstanding stock more dramatically than a stock dividend does. With a stock split, a company reduces the par or stated value of its stock by a certain amount and at the same time increases the number of shares outstanding by the reciprocal amount; if par value is halved, the number of shares is doubled. Thus, the total par or stated value of stock outstanding is unchanged. For example, a firm with 20,000 shares of $10 par-value stock outstanding may reduce the par value to $5 and increase the number of shares outstanding to 40,000. In this case—involving a 2-for-1 stock split—an investor who had one share of stock will instead own two shares of the new $5 par-value stock. (Other ratio splits, such as 3-for-1 and 4-for-1, are also common.)

In contrast to a stock dividend, a stock split does not require an accounting entry or involve a transfer of retained earnings to contributed capital. Rather, the company simply notes in the records that both the par value and the number of shares of stock outstanding have changed. If any shares are being held as treasury stock, those shares are affected by a stock split in the same manner as outstanding shares.

stock split the replacement of outstanding shares of stock with a greater number of new shares that have a proportionately lower par or stated value

> **To Summarize** *Three types of dividends are cash dividends, stock dividends, and property dividends, with cash and stock dividends being the most common. The important dividend dates are the date of declaration, the date of record, and the payment date. Preferred stockholders can be granted a current and a cumulative preference. Stock dividends are distributions of additional stock to shareholders. Although a stock dividend does not increase percentage ownership in a corporation, the additional stock provides the expectation of increased future cash dividends. With small stock dividends, Retained Earnings is debited at the stock's market value; with large stock dividends (25 percent or more), Retained Earnings is debited at the stock's par value.*
>
> *A stock split is an increase in the number of shares outstanding corresponding to a reduction in the par or stated value of the stock. Generally, stock splits are authorized so that companies can attract more investors with a lower market price per share.*

ACCOUNTING FOR RETAINED EARNINGS

Objective 6
Account for, and prepare a statement of, retained earnings.

Retained Earnings is the account that represents the owners' claims on assets due to the profitability of the firm in prior years. It is increased each year by net income and decreased by losses, dividends declared, and some treasury stock transactions. As you saw in Chapter 5, the entries to close net income and dividends to Retained Earnings, when an Income Summary account is used, are:

Income Summary	xxx	
Retained Earnings		xxx
To close net income to Retained Earnings.		
Retained Earnings	xxx	
Dividends		xxx
To close the Dividends account to Retained Earnings.		

Remember, retained earnings is not the same as cash. In fact, a company can have a large retained earnings balance and be without cash, or it can have a lot of cash and a very small retained earnings balance. Although both cash and retained earnings are usually increased when a company has earnings, the amounts by which they are increased are usually different. This occurs for two reasons: (1) the company's net income, which increases retained earnings, is accrual based, not cash based; and (2) cash from earnings may be invested in productive assets, such as inventories, used to pay off loans, or spent in any number of ways, many of which do not affect net income or retained earnings. In other words, Retained Earnings represents a portion of the owners' claims on assets; the Cash account represents an asset that can be spent.

Prior-Period Adjustments

Besides profits and losses, dividends, and certain treasury stock transactions, there is one other type of event that affects retained earnings directly. This category includes adjustments to restate the net income of prior periods; these are called, appropriately, **prior-period adjustments.** Prior-period adjustments are relatively infrequent. In addition to some technical adjustments involving taxes and bonds, which are beyond the scope of this book, the main event that qualifies as a prior-period adjustment is the correction of a material error in previous financial statements—for example, an error in accounting for revenues or expenses of a previous period. In accounting for prior-period adjustments, retained earnings is increased or decreased directly because the net income for the years affected by the adjustments has already been closed to the Retained Earnings account.

prior-period adjustments adjustments made directly to Retained Earnings in order to correct errors in the financial statements of prior periods

The Statement of Retained Earnings

Prior-period adjustments (if there are any) and dividends are usually disclosed in a **statement of retained earnings.** Exhibit 13-4 shows how the Boston Lakers Basketball Team might present a statement of retained earnings, using arbitrary numbers.

statement of retained earnings a report that shows the changes in the Retained Earnings account during a period of time

Retained Earnings Restrictions

Corporations frequently restrict the use of part of retained earnings. These restrictions may be imposed as a result of (1) debt requirements, such as a requirement to restrict dividends in order to retire bonds at a future date, or (2) action by the board of directors to earmark earnings for special purposes, such as plant expansion or the purchase of treasury stock. When retained earnings are restricted, they are removed from dividend-availability status.

Exhibit 13-4

Boston Lakers Basketball Team
Statement of Retained Earnings
For the Year Ended December 31, 1994

Retained earnings, January 1, 1994		$300,000
Prior-period adjustment:		
Deduct adjustment for 1993 inventory correction		(25,000)
Balance as restated..		$275,000
Net income for 1994.......................................		50,000
Less dividends declared in 1994:		
Preferred stock	$10,000	
Common stock	12,000	(22,000)
Retained earnings, December 31, 1994		$303,000

Although restrictions on retained earnings do not actually create cash funds, they do serve to alert stockholders and others of management's intentions and requirements. Such restrictions are usually disclosed in the financial statements.

To illustrate, we will assume the Mountain View Corporation has a $160,000 balance in Retained Earnings. If $40,000 of that amount were appropriated to retire preferred stock, the entry would be:

Retained Earnings	40,000	
Retained Earnings Appropriated for Retirement of		
Preferred Stock		40,000
Appropriated $40,000 of retained earnings for the retirement of preferred stock.		

Note that the same effect can be produced by a note disclosure, which is becoming a more common way of identifying a restriction on retained earnings.

Exhibit 13-5 is the stockholders' equity section of Mountain View's balance sheet. (Note that the entries under Contributed Capital are arbitrary.) In the absence of any restrictions, the balance in Retained Earnings (unappropriated) usually represents the maximum amount of dividends that can be declared and paid.

To Summarize *The Retained Earnings account reflects the total undistributed earnings of a business since incorporation. It is increased by net income and decreased by dividends, net losses, and some treasury stock transactions. Retained earnings can also be either increased or decreased by prior-period adjustments, which do not occur often. Prior-period adjustments usually involve corrections of errors in previous financial statements. Retained earnings can be appropriated or restricted for special purposes, such as the retirement of preferred stock or debt. Such appropriations do not provide cash, but they do remove a portion of retained earnings from dividend-availability status and alert financial statement users to management's plans.*

Exhibit 13-5

Mountain View Corporation
Partial Balance Sheet
December 31, 1994

Stockholders' Equity

Contributed capital:
Preferred stock (10%, $30 par, 4,000 shares authorized, 2,000 shares issued and outstanding)...	$ 60,000	
Common stock ($10 par, 10,000 shares authorized, 5,000 shares issued and outstanding)....................	50,000	
Paid-in capital in excess of par, preferred stock.............	10,000	
Paid-in capital in excess of par, common stock..............	20,000	
Total contributed capital...............................		$140,000

Retained earnings:
Retained earnings appropriated for the retirement of preferred stock......................................	$ 40,000	
Unappropriated retained earnings.........................	120,000	
Total retained earnings.................................		160,000
Total stockholders' equity..............................		$300,000

STATEMENT OF STOCKHOLDERS' EQUITY

Objective 7
Understand the information reported in a statement of stockholders' equity.

statement of stockholders' equity *a financial statement that reports all changes in stockholders' equity*

Companies that have numerous changes in their stockholders' equity accounts during the year usually present a **statement of stockholders' equity** with their financial statements instead of a statement of retained earnings. This statement reconciles the beginning and ending balances for all stockholders' equity accounts reported on the balance sheet.

An illustrative Statement of Stockholders' Equity from the 1989 Annual Report of Circus Circus Enterprises, Inc. is presented in Exhibit 13-6, along with the stockholders' equity section of the balance sheet. The comparative balance sheet reports stockholders' equity as of January 31, 1989, and 1988. The statement of stockholders' equity begins with the balance of each account at January 31, 1986, and presents all increases and decreases for the three-year period ending January 31, 1989.

The Common Stock and Additional Paid-In Capital accounts were increased each year by the sale of stock to employees who exercised their options to purchase shares. Stock options give employees the right to purchase shares of stock, usually at favorable prices. Retained Earnings was increased each year by net income. You can see from the statement that the company did not pay any dividends during the three-year period since there are no decreases to Retained Earnings for dividends. This is typical of "growth companies," such as Circus Circus, that reinvest earnings to expand operations rather than distributing dividends to stockholders.

The Treasury Stock account was increased for purchases of treasury stock and decreased by the retirement, or permanent cancellation, of 6,950 treasury shares. Retained Earnings was decreased by the cost of treasury stock retired and also by the cost of stock warrants purchased. (Accounting for stock retirements and warrants is covered in more advanced accounting texts.) Note that increases in Treasury Stock are shown in parentheses because, unlike the other

Exhibit 13-6 Reporting Changes in Stockholders' Equity

Circus Circus Enterprises, Inc. and Subsidiaries
Consolidated Balance Sheets (Partial)
January 31, 1988 and 1989

January 31, (in thousands, except share data)	1989	1988
**		
Stockholders' equity (Notes 8, 9, 10 and 12)		
Common stock $.05 par value		
Authorized—150,000,000 shares		
Issued—31,180,508 and 38,065,046 shares, respectively	$ 1,907	$ 1,903
Additional paid-in capital	43,273	42,035
Retained earnings	130,370	237,290
Treasury stock (1,005,000 and 157,700 shares), at cost	(30,638)	(3,170)
Total stockholders' equity	$144,912	$278,058
Total liabilities and stockholders' equity	$524,112	$529,057

**Assets and liabilities omitted

Circus Circus Enterprises, Inc. and Subsidiaries
Consolidated Statements of Stockholders' Equity
For the Years Ended January 31, 1987 Through January 31, 1989

(In thousands)	Common Stock Issued Shares	Amount	Additional Paid-In Capital	Retained Earnings	Treasury Stock	Total Stockholders' Equity
Balance, January 31, 1986	37,588	$1,879	$36,821	$153,191	$ —	$191,891
Net income	—	—	—	28,199	—	28,199
Exercise of stock options	166	9	1,565	—	—	1,574
Balance, January 31, 1987	37,754	$1,888	$38,386	$181,390	$ —	$221,664
Net income	—	—	—	55,900	—	55,900
Exercise of stock options	311	15	3,649	—	—	3,664
Treasury stock purchased (158 shares), at cost	—	—	—	—	(3,170)	(3,170)
Balance, January 31, 1988	38,065	$1,903	$42,035	$237,290	$ (3,170)	$278,058
Net income	—	—	—	81,714	—	81,714
Exercise of stock options	66	4	1,238	—	—	1,242
Treasury stock purchased (7,797 shares), at cost	—	—	—	—	(211,601)	(211,601)
Treasury stock retired	(6,950)	—	—	(184,133)	184,133	—
Purchase of stock warrants	—	—	—	(4,501)	—	(4,501)
Balance, January 31, 1989	31,181	$1,907	$43,273	$130,370	$ (30,638)	$144,912

equity accounts, Treasury Stock is increased by a debit, and its balance reduces stockholders' equity.

The last column in the statement reflects the total beginning and ending stockholders' equity account balances and all increases and decreases. Both the individual account balances and total Stockholders' Equity at January 31, 1988, and January 31, 1989, are reported on the balance sheet for Circus Circus.

Appendix
Consolidated Financial Statements

consolidated financial statements *statements that show the operating results and the financial position of two or more legally separate but affiliated companies as if they were one economic entity*

subsidiary company *a company owned or controlled by another company, known as the parent company*

parent company *a company that owns or controls other companies, known as subsidiaries, which are themselves separate legal entities; control generally refers to more than 50 percent ownership of stock of another company*

You have learned how to account for the transactions of a single company and how to prepare financial statements based on that accounting. Many large corporations, however, own, or have ownership interests in, other companies, and it is important for you to understand the relevant accounting principles and procedures. As we explained in Chapter 12, the cost and equity methods are used to account for investments involving ownership interests of 50 percent or less. For larger ownership interests, where control exists, **consolidated financial statements** should be prepared. This means that the financial statements of the **subsidiary company** (the investee) should be combined with those of the **parent company** (the investing company). In this way, the financial statements reflect the operating results and the financial position of the total economic entity, the main concern of stockholders, creditors, and prospective investors.

Consolidated financial statements are prepared by combining the individual statements of the entities, item by item, except for intercompany transactions, that is, transactions between the parent company and its subsidiaries or between subsidiaries. Thus, if a parent company sells materials to its subsidiary, that transaction would not be included in the combined sales, purchases, or inventory figures in the consolidated financial statements for the two companies.

THE NEED FOR CONSOLIDATED FINANCIAL STATEMENTS

merger *the acquisition of one company by another company, whereby the companies combine as one legal entity, with the acquired company going out of existence*

consolidation *the combining of two or more companies into a new legal corporation, with the original companies going out of existence*

As you will recall, when a company acquires over 50 percent of the outstanding voting stock of another company, a controlling interest exists. When this happens, the two companies sometimes become one. Companies can legally combine into one company by means of either a merger or a consolidation. A **merger** occurs when one company, A, acquires another company, B, and Company B goes out of existence. A **consolidation** occurs when Company A and Company B are combined into Company C, and both companies A and B go out of existence. Alternatively, the combining companies may remain as separate legal entities, but may prepare consolidated financial statements as if they were one economic entity. Consolidated statements are necessary in such cases because they provide a more informative picture of the combined companies.

PREPARATION OF CONSOLIDATED FINANCIAL STATEMENTS

A parent company can acquire a controlling interest in a subsidiary by exchanging cash, other assets, or some of its own stock for over 50 percent of the subsidiary's outstanding voting stock. When control is achieved in this way,

purchase *the acquisition of one company by another, whereby the acquiring company exchanges cash or other assets for more than 50 percent of the acquired company's outstanding voting stock*

pooling of interests *the acquisition of one company by another, whereby the acquiring company issues voting stock to the acquired company's stockholders in exchange for at least 90 percent of the acquired company's outstanding voting stock*

minority interest *the interest owned in a subsidiary by stockholders other than those of the parent company; occurs when the acquiring company has less than a 100 percent ownership interest*

the acquisition is called a **purchase.** When a company acquires another company by exchanging its stock for at least 90 percent of the acquired company's outstanding voting stock (and when 11 other specific conditions are met), the acquisition is referred to as a **pooling of interests.** If the acquiring company does not acquire 100 percent of the outstanding voting shares of the subsidiary, the shares not acquired by the parent are referred to as the **minority interest** in the combined companies. Since we are concerned here with helping you understand the general concepts and procedures involved in preparing consolidated financial statements, we will assume that the parent company acquires 100 percent of the outstanding voting stock of the subsidiary. We will use relatively simple transactions between the parent company and its subsidiaries. First, we will discuss the purchase method, then the pooling-of-interests method.

The Purchase Method—Consolidated Balance Sheets

When the stock of the acquired company is purchased with cash, other assets, or debt (such as bonds or notes), the purchase method is used to prepare the consolidated financial statements. To illustrate, we will assume that Reece Corporation is acquiring Bahr Corporation and that the two companies had the balance sheets shown in Exhibit 13-7 just prior to the acquisition. When the Bahr stock is acquired, the investment in Bahr is recorded on the books of Reece Corporation by debiting an Investment in Subsidiary account and crediting Cash, Other Assets, or an account for the debt issued. If we assume that Reece Corporation acquired all the common stock of Bahr Corporation on December 31, 1993, by making a cash payment of $250,000 (which is equal to the book value of Bahr's equity and likewise to the book value of its net

Exhibit 13-7

Reece and Bahr Corporations
Condensed Balance Sheets
December 31, 1993

Assets	Reece	Bahr
Cash	$ 450,000	$ 50,000
Accounts receivable (net)	650,000	200,000
Note receivable (owed by Bahr)	200,000	—
Inventory	700,000	150,000
Plant equipment (net)	600,000	300,000
Total assets	$2,600,000	$700,000

Liabilities and Stockholders' Equity		
Accounts payable	$ 400,000	$250,000
Note payable (owed to Reece)	—	200,000
Bonds payable	800,000	—
Common stock ($100 par)	600,000	100,000
Paid-in capital in excess of par	350,000	40,000
Retained earnings	450,000	110,000
Total liabilities and stockholders' equity	$2,600,000	$700,000

Chapter 13 Owners' Equity—The Corporation

assets, $700,000 − $450,000), the entry on the books of Reece Corporation would be:

Investment in Bahr Corporation............................	250,000	
Cash		250,000

Acquired 100% (1,000 shares) of the stock of Bahr Corporation at book value.

Immediately after the acquisition, the balance sheet of Bahr Corporation would not change because the cash is paid directly to the stockholders of Bahr. In other words, because Reece is purchasing the stock from the stockholders, not from Bahr Corporation, the stock is still outstanding, with Reece being the only stockholder. The balance sheet of Reece would then reflect a decrease in cash of $250,000 and an increase in the corresponding investment in Bahr.

PREPARING A CONSOLIDATED WORK SHEET. The consolidation is accounted for by setting up and completing a consolidated work sheet, as in Exhibit 13-8.

Exhibit 13-8

Reece Corporation and Subsidiary
Consolidated Work Sheet
December 31, 1993

Accounts	Reece Corporation	Bahr Corporation	Adjustments and Eliminations Debits	Adjustments and Eliminations Credits	Consolidated Balance Sheet
Assets					
Cash	200,000	50,000			250,000
Accounts receivable	650,000	200,000			850,000
Note receivable, Bahr	200,000			(1) 200,000	
Inventory	700,000	150,000			850,000
Plant and equipment	600,000	300,000			900,000
Investment in Bahr Corporation	250,000			(2) 250,000	
Total assets	2,600,000	700,000			2,850,000
Liabilities and Stockholders' Equity					
Accounts payable	400,000	250,000			650,000
Note payable, Reece		200,000	(1) 200,000		
Bonds payable	800,000				800,000
Common stock ($100 par)	600,000	100,000	(2) 100,000		600,000
Paid-in capital in excess of par	350,000	40,000	(2) 40,000		350,000
Retained earnings	450,000	110,000	(2) 110,000		450,000
Total liabilities and stockholders' equity	2,600,000	700,000	450,000	450,000	2,850,000

Note that the work sheet has five columns, two for the account balances of the two companies at the date of consolidation, two for the "adjustment and elimination" entries, and one for the consolidated balance sheet. The column for Reece Corporation's accounts reflects the account balances immediately after the acquisition of the common stock of Bahr Corporation. The columns for adjustments and eliminations contain entries required to correctly state the account balances for the two companies.

When the balance sheet accounts of the two companies are consolidated as a purchase, the individual asset and liability accounts are added together, except for items that are internal to the two companies, such as the $200,000 that Bahr owed to Reece. This is an **intercompany transaction** and requires an adjustment and elimination entry on the work sheet [entry (1)], as shown.

intercompany transaction a transaction between a parent company and a subsidiary company

Note Payable, Reece	200,000	
Note Receivable, Bahr		200,000
To eliminate Bahr's obligation to Reece.		

Other types of intercompany transactions might involve one company selling inventory or equipment to the other.

A second type of adjustment and elimination entry is made to avoid a double counting of assets and equities [see entry (2)]. The entry involves the elimination of Reece Corporation's Investment in Bahr Corporation account against all the equity accounts of Bahr Corporation. This is done because the asset account of the parent—Investment in Bahr Corporation—and the equity accounts of the subsidiary both represent the net assets of the subsidiary, and these net assets are already included in the consolidated asset and liability accounts. To include these accounts as well as the net assets would result in a double counting. That is, if Investment in Bahr Corporation and Bahr's equity accounts were not eliminated, the consolidated entity would be overvalued. Elimination of these accounts is accomplished by the following entry:

Common Stock, Bahr	100,000	
Paid-In Capital in Excess of Par, Bahr	40,000	
Retained Earnings, Bahr	110,000	
Investment in Bahr Corporation		250,000
To eliminate the cost of Reece Corporation's investment against Bahr Corporation's equity accounts.		

It might help you to understand the reason for these adjustment and elimination entries if you were to consider how the consolidated balance sheet would look without them:

Chapter 13 *Owners' Equity—The Corporation*

Assets			Liabilities and Stockholders' Equity		
Cash		$ 250,000	Accounts payable		$ 650,000
Accounts receivable		850,000	Note payable, Reece		200,000
Note receivable, Bahr		200,000	Bonds payable		800,000
Inventory		850,000	Common stock, Reece		600,000
Plant and equipment (net)		900,000	Common stock, Bahr		100,000
Investment in Bahr Corporation		250,000	Paid-in capital in excess of par		390,000
			Retained earnings		560,000
Total assets		$3,300,000	Total liabilities and stockholders' equity		$3,300,000

Clearly, this does not work. First, the same note (the Note Receivable, Bahr and the Note Payable, Reece) is counted as both an asset and a liability. Second, the purchase price of Bahr Corporation (the amount in Investment in Bahr Corporation) cannot be an asset of the consolidated statement since the net assets it represents are reflected individually in the balance sheet as the assets and liabilities of the subsidiary. Third, the stockholders' equity portion of Reece Corporation already reflects the equity claim on Bahr's assets. Including Bahr's equity accounts would result in a double counting of the claims on those assets. It is also inappropriate to treat the subsidiary's stock as outstanding since it is now held by Reece Corporation. Thus, the two Notes accounts, the Investment in Bahr's account and all of Bahr's subsidiary equity accounts (all stock accounts and Retained Earnings), must be eliminated on the consolidated work sheet to produce a consolidated balance sheet that fairly represents the two entities as a single economic unit.

PREPARING A CONSOLIDATED BALANCE SHEET. After all necessary adjustment and elimination entries have been made on the work sheet, all asset, liability, and equity accounts can be added across to the consolidated balance sheet columns to complete the work sheet. Bear in mind that the entries in the adjustment and elimination columns are *work sheet* entries only. They merely facilitate the elimination process; they are not recorded in the journals or the accounts of the respective companies. Only when an adjustment is made to correct an error on the books of one of the companies is an entry recorded in that company's accounts. The completed work sheet now serves as a basis for preparing the consolidated balance sheet of the parent company and its subsidiary, shown in Exhibit 13-9. Note that the consolidated balance sheet shows the assets and liabilities of the two companies in combined form. The two Notes accounts have been eliminated and so has the Investment in Subsidiary account on the parent's books. Further, the equity accounts are those of the parent only.

CONSOLIDATIONS INVOLVING PAYMENTS IN EXCESS OF BOOK VALUE. The consolidated balance sheet in Exhibit 13-9 involved a fairly straightforward combination of assets and liabilities because the purchase price paid by the parent was equal to the book value of the subsidiary's net assets. However, in many cases, a company will pay more than the book value of the subsidiary.

Exhibit 13-9

Reece Corporation and Subsidiary
Consolidated Balance Sheet (Purchase Method)
December 31, 1993

Assets			Liabilities and Stockholders' Equity		
Current assets:			*Current liabilities:*		
Cash	$250,000		Accounts payable	$650,000	
Accounts receivable	850,000		*Long-term liabilities:*		
Inventory	850,000		Bonds payable	800,000	
Total current assets		$1,950,000	Total liabilities		$1,450,000
Long-term assets:			*Stockholders' equity:*		
Plant and equipment		900,000	Common stock ($100 par)	$600,000	
			Paid-in capital in excess of par	350,000	
			Retained earnings	450,000	
			Total stockholders' equity		1,400,000
Total assets		$2,850,000	Total liabilites and stockholders' equity		$2,850,000

To illustrate, we will assume that Reece Corporation paid $300,000 cash for the common stock of Bahr Corporation even though the book value of the net assets (equity) of Bahr Corporation amounted to $250,000 ($700,000 − $450,000). This $50,000 payment in excess of the book value of the net assets acquired must be accounted for as additional assets of the consolidated entity. The current theoretical assumption is that Reece Corporation would be willing to pay more than the book value of the net assets for either of two reasons: (1) specific assets of Bahr Corporation were undervalued, or (2) Bahr Corporation owns intangible values not reflected in assets on its balance sheet. For this example, we will assume that the $50,000 excess paid by Reece over the book value of Bahr's net assets is partly accounted for by the fact that the fair market value of the plant and equipment exceeds the net book value by $30,000 but that the fair market values of all other assets of Bahr Corporation are equal to the book values. Based on these assumptions, we must still account for the other $20,000 of remaining excess cost ($50,000 − $30,000). Because no other assets require adjustment to fair market value, the $20,000 must be attributed to an intangible asset called **goodwill**. Goodwill reflects the benefits the subsidiary enjoys in the form of good customer and employee relations, a reputation for product quality, or other intangible qualities that contribute to additional earnings. The excess cost can be accounted for as shown.

goodwill *an intangible asset showing that a business is worth more than the fair market value of its net assets because of strategic location, reputation, good customer relations, or similar factors; equal to the excess of cost over the fair market value of the net assets purchased*

Purchase price	$300,000
Net assets (book value) acquired	250,000
Excess cost	$ 50,000
Additional fair market value of plant and equipment	30,000
Goodwill	$ 20,000

This excess payment must appear in the consolidated balance sheet. To include it, we insert in the adjustment and elimination columns debits of $30,000 for plant and equipment and $20,000 for goodwill. This brings the net assets up to $300,000 paid for Bahr Corporation. As before, the Investment in Bahr Corporation account on Reece Corporation's books and the equity accounts of Bahr are eliminated. The result is the work sheet shown in Exhibit 13-10. The consolidated balance sheet would show the account totals in the final column.

Exhibit 13-10

Reece Corporation and Subsidiary
Consolidated Work Sheet
December 31, 1993

Accounts	Reece Corporation	Bahr Corporation	Adjustments and Eliminations Debits	Adjustments and Eliminations Credits	Consolidated Balance Sheet
Assets					
Cash	150,000	50,000			200,000
Accounts receivable	650,000	200,000			850,000
Note receivable, Bahr	200,000			(1) 200,000	
Inventory	700,000	150,000			850,000
Plant and equipment (net)	600,000	300,000	(2) 30,000		930,000
Goodwill			(2) 20,000		20,000
Investment in Bahr Corporation	300,000			(2) 300,000	
Total assets	2,600,000	700,000			2,850,000
Liabilities and Stockholders' Equity					
Accounts payable	400,000	250,000			650,000
Note payable, Reece		200,000	(1) 200,000		
Bonds payable	800,000				800,000
Common stock ($100 par)	600,000	100,000	(2) 100,000		600,000
Paid-in capital in excess of par	350,000	40,000	(2) 40,000		350,000
Retained earnings	450,000	110,000	(2) 110,000		450,000
Total liabilities and stockholders' equity	2,600,000	700,000	500,000	500,000	2,850,000

To Summarize *When one company acquires a controlling interest in another company (that is, acquires more than 50 percent of its stock), and the two companies have substantially similar business objectives, the financial statements of the companies are combined as consolidated statements. The acquiring company is called the parent company and the acquired company is called the subsidiary company. If the parent obtains the controlling interest by giving up cash or other assets in exchange for the* *common stock of the subsidiary, the combination is accounted for as a purchase. This means that the assets of the subsidiary are included in the consolidated balance sheet at their fair market values and that any excess cost of acquisition over the fair market values of the subsidiary's assets is called goodwill. The key characteristics of a consolidated balance sheet for two companies, assuming that one has purchased 100 percent ownership of the other, are as follows:*

1. *Any amount paid in excess of book value of the subsidiary's assets must be accounted for as additional assets on the consolidated balance sheet. If the book value of assets such as inventory or plant and equipment is less than fair market value, the appropriate amount of the cost is assigned to the asset, and the rest is used to create a Goodwill account. Note that only the subsidiary's assets are adjusted to fair market value.*
2. *The Common Stock account comprises entirely the outstanding stock of the parent company.*
3. *The Retained Earnings account of the consolidated entity at the date of acquisition shows the retained earnings of the parent company only.*
4. *Assets and liabilities created in intercompany transactions are eliminated.*
5. *The Investment in Subsidiary asset account on the parent's books is eliminated against the Common Stock, Paid-In Capital in Excess of Par and Retained Earnings accounts of the subsidiary since including these accounts would duplicate the net assets and equity accounts in the consolidated balance sheet.*

The Purchase Method—Consolidated Income Statements

At the end of the consolidated entity's first year of operations, a consolidated income statement is prepared. To illustrate this process, we use the income statements shown in Exhibit 13-11.

If there are no intercompany transactions in the first year after Reece acquires Bahr, the combination of their income statements into a consolidated income statement is primarily a matter of combining the accounts on the two statements. However, if we return to our example in which Reece paid $300,000 cash for Bahr Corporation's stock, two adjustments will be necessary.

Exhibit 13-11

Reece and Bahr Corporations
Condensed Income Statements
For the Year Ended December 31, 1993

	Reece	Bahr
Sales revenue	$4,000,000	$1,200,000
Cost of goods sold	2,400,000	780,000
Gross margin	$1,600,000	$ 420,000
Operating expenses (including depreciation)	1,300,000	350,000
Income before taxes	$ 300,000	$ 70,000
Income taxes	130,000	30,000
Net income	$ 170,000	$ 40,000

	Reece	Bahr
Sales revenue	$4,000,000	$1,200,000
Cost of goods sold	2,400,000	780,000
Gross margin	$1,600,000	$ 420,000
Operating expenses	1,300,000	350,000
Income before taxes	$ 300,000	$ 70,000
Income taxes	130,000	30,000
Net income	$ 170,000	$ 40,000

Based on these income statements for the year 1993, the consolidated income statement under the pooling method would be as shown in Exhibit 13-16. As you can see, this consolidated income statement results from simply combining the accounts of the two companies. The statement has been simplified by the assumption that there were no intercompany transactions involving inventories, operational assets, or securities. Such transactions are beyond the scope of this text.

Exhibit 13-16

Reece Corporation and Subsidiary
Consolidated Income Statement
For the Year Ended December 31, 1993

Sales revenue	$5,200,000
Cost of goods sold	3,180,000
Gross margin	$2,020,000
Operating expenses	1,650,000
Income before taxes	$ 370,000
Income taxes	160,000
Net income	$ 210,000

To Summarize *Under the pooling-of-interests method, income statements are consolidated by simply combining the balances in each account, assuming that there are no complicating factors.*

Review of Learning Objectives

Objective 1

Describe the basic characteristics of a corporation and the various types of stock that corporations sell to investors. The accounting for all three types of business entities—corporations, proprietorships, and partnerships—is identical except for owners' equity.

A corporation is a business equity that is legally separate from its owners and chartered by a state. It is independently taxed, and it can incur debts, conduct business, own property, and enter into contracts. The owners' equity section of a corporation's balance sheet is generally divided into two sections: contributed capital and retained earnings. Contributed capital identifies the resources contributed by owners and the stock that has been issued by the corporation.

Objective 2

Account for the issuance of common and preferred stock. The two major types of stock are common and preferred. Common stock is usually voting stock. Preferred stock may have current- and cumulative-dividend privileges, and it is usually nonvoting. Stock can be authorized but not yet issued; authorized, issued, and outstanding; or authorized, issued, and reacquired by the corporation. Stock can have a par value, be no par with a stated value, or be no par with no stated value. The accounting is different for each case.

Objective 3

Explain and record the effects of treasury stock transactions. Reacquired stock is called treasury stock. When treasury stock is purchased by a corporation, it is usually accounted for at cost and deducted from total stockholders' equity as a contra-equity account.

Objective 4

Account for cash dividends on common and preferred stock. Corporations usually distribute dividends to their owners. These distributions to owners can be in the form of cash, additional stock, or property. The three important dates in accounting for dividends are the declaration date, the date of record, and the payment date. Dividends are not a liability until they are declared. If a company has common and preferred stock, the allocation of dividends between the two types of stock depends on the dividend preferences of the preferred stock.

Objective 5

Account for stock dividends and distinguish them from stock splits. When a company distributes stock to its shareholders, it can be in the form of a stock dividend or a stock split. Stock dividends involve cases where additional shares of the same par value are distributed. Stock splits, such as a 2-for-1 split, increase the number of shares outstanding and decrease proportionately the par or stated value of the stock.

Objective 6

Account for, and prepare a statement of, retained earnings. Owners' equity also includes retained earnings, which shows the cumulative undistributed earnings of a company since incorporation. Retained earnings is decreased by (1) the declaration of dividends, (2) operating losses, (3) some treasury stock transactions, and (4) certain prior-period adjustments. Retained earnings is increased by net income and some prior-period adjustments. Retained earnings may be restricted or appropriated for specific uses. Companies often include a statement of retained earnings as part of their financial statements, showing the beginning balance, increases and decreases for the period, and the ending Retained Earnings balance.

Objective 7

Understand the information reported in a statement of stockholders' equity. When changes occur in other stockholders' equity accounts, the retained earnings statement is usually replaced by a statement of stockholders' equity, which reconciles changes in all stockholders' equity accounts.

Key Terms and Concepts

authorized stock *(520)*
board of directors *(519)*
capital stock *(520)*
cash dividend *(530)*
charter (articles of incorporation) *(518)*
common stock *(520)*
consolidated financial statements *(541)**
consolidation *(541)**
contributed capital *(520)*
convertible preferred stock *(521)*
corporation *(518)*
cumulative-dividend preference *(533)*
current-dividend preference *(532)*
date of record *(531)*

Chapter 13 Owners' Equity—The Corporation

declaration date *(531)*	outstanding stock *(520)*	stated value *(521)*
dividends *(529)*	parent company *(541)**	statement of retained earnings *(537)*
dividends in arrears *(533)*	par-value stock *(521)*	statement of stockholders' equity *(539)*
dividend payment date *(531)*	pooling of interests *(542)**	
goodwill *(546)**	preemptive right *(520)*	stock certificate *(519)*
intercompany transaction *(544)**	preferred stock *(520)*	stock dividend *(530)*
issued stock *(520)*	premium on stock *(521)*	stock split *(536)*
legal capital *(521)*	prior-period adjustments *(537)*	stockholders *(519)*
limited liability *(518)*	pro rata *(529)*	subsidiary company *(541)**
merger *(541)**	property dividend *(530)*	treasury stock *(520)*
minority interest *(542)**	purchase *(542)**	
no-par stock *(521)*	S corporation *(520)*	

* Relates to Appendix

Review Problem

Stockholders' Equity

Parker Corporation was organized during 1967. At the end of 1993 the equity section of the balance sheet was:

Contributed capital:
Preferred stock (8%, $30 par, 6,000 shares authorized, 5,000
   shares issued and outstanding) $150,000
Common stock ($5 par, 50,000 shares authorized, 20,000 shares
   issued, 17,000 shares outstanding) 100,000
Paid-in capital in excess of par, common stock.........................   80,000
   Total contributed capital $330,000
Retained earnings 140,000
   Total contributed capital plus retained earnings $470,000
Less treasury stock (3,000 shares of common stock at cost, $10
   per share) .... (30,000)
   Total stockholders' equity $440,000

During 1994, the following stockholders' equity transactions occurred in chronological sequence:

(a) Issued 800 shares of common stock at $11 per share.
(b) Reissued 1,200 shares of treasury stock at $12 per share.
(c) Issued 300 shares of preferred stock at $33 per share.
(d) Reissued 400 shares of treasury stock at $9 per share.
(e) Declared and paid a dividend large enough to meet the current-dividend preference on the preferred stock and to pay the common stockholders $1.50 per share.
(f) Appropriated $25,000 of retained earnings for the retirement of debt.
(g) Declared a 2-for-1 stock split on common stock.
(h) Net income for 1994 was $70,000.
(i) Closed the Dividends accounts for 1994.

Required:
1. Journalize the transactions.
2. Set up T-accounts with beginning balances and post the journal entries to the T-accounts, adding any necessary new accounts. (Assume a beginning balance of $20,000 for the Cash account.)

3. Prepare the stockholders' equity section of the balance sheet as of December 31, 1994.

Solution **1. Journalize the Transactions**

(a) Cash 8,800
    Common Stock 4,000
    Paid-In Capital in Excess of Par, Common Stock 4,800
Issued 800 shares of common stock at $11 per share.

Cash received is $11 × 800 shares; common stock is par value times the number of shares ($5 × 800); and paid-in capital is the excess.

(b) Cash 14,400
    Treasury Stock 12,000
    Paid-In Capital, Treasury Stock 2,400
Reissued 1,200 shares of treasury stock at $12 per share.

Cash is $12 × 1,200 shares; treasury stock is the cost times the number of shares sold ($10 × 1,200 shares); and paid-in capital is the excess.

(c) Cash 9,900
    Preferred Stock 9,000
    Paid-In Capital in Excess of Par, Preferred Stock 900
Issued 300 shares of preferred stock at $33 per share.

Cash is $33 × 300 shares; preferred stock is par value times the number of shares issued ($30 × 300); and paid-in capital is the excess.

(d) Cash 3,600
    Paid-In Capital, Treasury Stock 400
    Treasury Stock 4,000
Reissued 400 shares of treasury stock at $9 per share.

Cash is $9 × 400 shares; treasury stock is the cost times the number of shares sold ($10 × 400); and paid-in capital is decreased for the difference. If no Paid-In Capital, Treasury Stock account had existed, Retained Earnings would have been debited.

(e) Dividends, Preferred Stock 12,720
    Dividends, Common Stock 29,100
    Cash 41,820
Declared and paid cash dividend.

Calculations:

Preferred Stock	Number of Shares	Par-Value Amount
Original balance	5,000	$150,000
Entry (c)	300	9,000
Total	5,300	$159,000
		× 0.08
		$ 12,720

Common Stock	Number of Shares
Original balance	17,000 (excludes treasury stock)
Entry (**a**)	800
Entry (**b**)	1,200
Entry (**d**)	400
Total	19,400 shares
	× $1.50
	$29,100

Total preferred stock dividend	$12,720
Total common stock dividend	29,100
Total dividend	$41,820

(f) Retained Earnings 25,000
    Retained Earnings Appropriated for Debt Retirement 25,000

Appropriated $25,000 of retained earnings for debt retirement.

(g) No journal entry. There is no journal entry with a stock split. The accountant generally notes in the records that the par value of the common stock is divided in half, and so the number of shares is doubled.

(h) Income Summary 70,000
    Retained Earnings 70,000

To close net income to Retained Earnings.

(i) Retained Earnings 41,820
    Dividends, Preferred Stock 12,720
    Dividends, Common Stock 29,100

To close the Dividends accounts for 1994.

2. Set Up T-Accounts and Post to the Accounts

Cash

Beg. Bal.	20,000	(e)	41,820
(a)	8,800		
(b)	14,400		
(c)	9,900		
(d)	3,600		

Preferred Stock

		Beg. Bal.	150,000
		(c)	9,000
			159,000

Paid-In Capital in Excess of Par, Preferred Stock

		(c)	900

Common Stock

		Beg. Bal.	100,000
		(a)	4,000
			104,000

Paid-In Capital in Excess of Par, Common Stock

		Beg. Bal.	80,000
		(a)	4,800
			84,800

Treasury Stock

Beg. Bal.	30,000	(b)	12,000
		(d)	4,000
	14,000		

Paid-In Capital, Treasury Stock		Income Summary		Retained Earnings
(d) 400	(b) 2,400 2,000	(h) 70,000	Net Inc. 70,000	(f) 25,000 Beg. Bal. 140,000 (i) 41,820 (h) 70,000 143,180

Retained Earnings Appropriated for Debt Retirement	Dividends, Preferred Stock	Dividends, Common Stock
(f) 25,000	(e) 12,720 (i) 12,720	(e) 29,100 (i) 29,100

3. Prepare Stockholders' Equity Section of the Balance Sheet

Parker Corporation
Partial Balance Sheet
December 31, 1994

Stockholders' Equity

Contributed Capital:
Preferred stock (8%, $30 par, 6,000 shares authorized, 5,300 shares issued and outstanding)	$159,000
Common stock ($2.50 par, 100,000 shares authorized, 41,600 shares issued, 38,800 shares outstanding)	104,000
Paid-in capital in excess of par, preferred stock	900
Paid-in capital in excess of par, common stock	84,800
Paid-in capital, treasury stock	2,000
Total contributed capital	$350,700

Retained Earnings:
Unrestricted retained earnings	$143,180	
Retained earnings appropriated for debt retirement	25,000	168,180
Total contributed capital plus retained earnings		$518,880
Less treasury stock (2,800* shares of common stock at cost, $5 per share)		(14,000)
Total stockholders' equity		$504,880

*The number of common shares, including treasury stock, has been doubled to account for the stock split. Further, the par value has been divided in half, and the cost per share of treasury stock has been reduced by half. The following table summarizes the calculations:

Transaction	Common Stock Issued	Common Stock Authorized	Treasury Stock
Number of shares originally issued	20,000	50,000	3,000
Entry (a)	800		
Entry (b)			(1,200)
Entry (d)			(400)
Total	20,800	50,000	1,400
Stock split	× 2	× 2	× 2
Number of shares as of December 31, 1994	41,600	100,000	2,800

Discussion Questions

1. In what way is the balance sheet of a corporation different from that of a partnership or proprietorship?
2. In what way does the owners' equity section of a balance sheet identify the sources of the assets?
3. In which type of business entity do owners have limited liability?
4. In what way is there a double taxation of corporate profits?
5. Many people, including some legislators, think that corporations should not be taxed. What do you think is the basis of their arguments?
6. How are common and preferred stock different from each other?
7. How is treasury stock different from unissued stock?
8. Is treasury stock an asset? If not, why not?
9. What is the purpose of having a par or stated value for stock?
10. Does treasury stock possess the same voting, dividend, and other rights that outstanding stock does?
11. How is treasury stock usually accounted for?
12. When does a corporation have a legal obligation to pay dividends to its stockholders?
13. Based on what you've read in this chapter, what do you suppose is the difference between a "growth company" and a "dividend company"?
14. Why should a potential common stockholder carefully examine the dividend preferences of a company's preferred stock?
15. Are dividends in arrears a liability? If not, why not?
16. Does a stock dividend have value to stockholders? Explain.
17. What is the difference between a stock dividend and a stock split? Why would a company split its stock?
18. Is it possible for a firm to have a large Retained Earnings balance and no cash? Explain.
19. Why are prior-period adjustments entered directly into Retained Earnings instead of being reflected on the income statement?

Exercises

E13-1
Issuance of Stock

Brockbank Corporation was organized on July 15, 1994. Record the journal entries for Brockbank to account for the following.

1. The state authorized 30,000 shares of 7 percent preferred stock ($20 par) and 100,000 shares of no-par common stock.
2. Peter Brockbank gave 6,000 shares of common stock to his attorney in return for her help in incorporating the business. Fees for this work are normally about $18,000.
3. Brockbank gave 15,000 shares of common stock to a friend who contributed a building worth $50,000.
4. Brockbank issued 5,000 shares of preferred stock at $25 per share.
5. Brockbank paid $70,000 cash for 30,000 shares of common stock.
6. Another friend donated a $15,000 machine and received 4,000 shares of common stock.
7. The attorney sold all of her shares to her brother-in-law for $18,000.

E13-2
No-Par Stock Transactions

Clark Maintenance Corporation was organized in early 1994 with 40,000 shares of no-par common stock authorized. During 1994, the following transactions occurred:

(a) Issued 17,000 shares of stock at $36 per share.
(b) Issued another 2,400 shares of stock at $38 per share.
(c) Issued 2,000 shares for a building appraised at $40,000.
(d) Declared dividends of $1 per share.
(e) Earned net income of $99,000 for the year.

Given this information:

1. Journalize the transactions.
2. Present the stockholders' equity section of the balance sheet as it would appear on December 31, 1994.

E13-3
Stock Issuance and Dividends

Atlanta Corporation was organized in January 1994. The state authorized 100,000 shares of no-par common stock and 50,000 shares of 10%, $20 par, preferred stock. Record the following transactions that occurred in 1994.

(a) Issued 10,000 shares of common stock at $30 per share.
(b) Issued 2,000 shares of preferred stock for a building appraised at $60,000.
(c) Declared a cash dividend sufficient to meet the current dividend preference on preferred stock and pay common shareholders $2 per share.

E13-4
Stock Issuance, Treasury Stock, and Dividends

On January 1, 1994, Abbott Corporation was granted a charter authorizing the following capital stock: common stock, $20 par, 100,000 shares; preferred stock, $10 par, 6 percent, 30,000 shares.

Record the following 1994 transactions:

1. Issued 80,000 shares of common stock at $30 per share.
2. Issued 14,000 shares of preferred stock at $12 per share.
3. Brought back 5,000 shares of common stock at $40 per share.
4. Reissued 500 shares of treasury stock at $25 per share.
5. Declared cash dividends of $38,600 to be allocated between common and preferred stockholders. (The preferred stock, which has a current-dividend preference, is noncumulative.)
6. Paid dividends of $38,600.

E13-5
Stock Issuance, Treasury Stock, and Dividends

On January 1, 1994, Baker Company was authorized to issue 100,000 shares of common stock, par value $10 per share and 10,000 shares of 8% preferred stock, par value $20 per share. Record the following transactions for 1994:

(a) Issued 70,000 shares of common stock at $25 per share.
(b) Issued 8,000 shares of preferred stock at $30 per share.
(c) Reacquired 5,000 shares of common stock at $20 per share.
(d) Reissued 2,000 shares of treasury stock for $46,000.
(e) Declared a cash dividend sufficient to meet the current dividend preference on preferred stock and pay common shareholders $1 per share.

E13-6
Treasury Stock Transactions

Provide the necessary journal entries to record the following:

1. Fayette Corporation was granted a charter authorizing the issuance of 100,000 shares of no-par common stock. Management established a stated value of $16 per share.
2. The company issued 40,000 shares of common stock at $20 per share.
3. The company reacquired 2,000 shares of its own stock at $22 per share, to be held in treasury.
4. Another 2,000 shares of stock were reacquired at $24 per share.
5. Of the shares reacquired in part (3), 800 were reissued for $26 per share.
6. Of the shares reacquired in part (4), 1,400 were reissued for $18 per share.
7. Given the preceding transactions, what is the balance in the Treasury Stock account?

E13-7
Analysis of Stockholders' Equity

The stockholders' equity section of Nina Corporation at the end of the current year showed:

Preferred stock (6%, $40 par value, 10,000 shares authorized, 6,000 shares issued and outstanding)	$?
Common stock ($6 par value, 80,000 shares authorized, 53,000 issued, 52,650 shares outstanding)	318,000
Paid-in capital in excess of par, preferred stock	?
Paid-in capital in excess of par, common stock	129,000
Retained earnings	86,000
Less treasury stock (350 shares at cost)	(2,000)
Total stockholders' equity	$?

1. What is the dollar amount to be reported for Preferred Stock?
2. What is the average price for which common stock was issued? (Round to the nearest penny.)
3. If preferred stock was issued at an average price of $43 per share, what amount should appear in the Paid-In Capital in Excess of Par, Preferred Stock account?
4. What is the average cost per share of treasury stock? (Round to the nearest penny.)
5. Assuming that the preferred stock was issued for an average price of $43 per share, what is total stockholders' equity?
6. If net income for the year were $67,000 and if only dividends on preferred stock were paid, by how much would retained earnings increase?

E13-8
Preparing the Stockholders' Equity Section

The following account balances, before any closing entries, appear on the books of Wood Company as of December 31, 1994:

Retained Earnings (balance at Jan. 1, 1994)	$240,000
Dividends, Preferred Stock	15,000
Dividends, Common Stock	35,000
Common Stock ($5 par, 100,000 shares authorized, 70,000 issued and outstanding)	350,000
Paid-In Capital in Excess of Par, Common Stock	350,000
Preferred Stock (6%, $50 par, 50,000 shares authorized, 5,000 issued and outstanding)	250,000
Paid-In Capital in Excess of Par, Preferred Stock	25,000

Based on these account balances, and assuming net income for 1994 of $80,000, prepare the stockholders' equity section of the December 31, 1994, balance sheet for Wood Company.

E13-9
Preparing a Statement of Retained Earnings

Using the information presented in the preceding exercise (E13-8), prepare a statement of retained earnings for Wood Company for the year ending December 31, 1994.

E13-10
Dividend Calculations

On January 1, 1994, Oldroyd Corporation had 130,000 shares of common stock issued and outstanding. During 1994, the following transactions occurred (in chronological order).

(a) 10,000 new shares of common stock were issued.
(b) 2,000 shares of stock were reacquired for use in the company's employee stock-option plan.
(c) At the end of the option period, 1,200 shares had been purchased by corporate officials.

Given this information, compute the following:

1. After the foregoing three transactions have occurred, what amount of dividends must Oldroyd Corporation declare in order to pay 50 cents per share? To pay $1 per share?
2. What is the dividend per share if $236,640 is paid?
3. If all 2,000 treasury shares had been purchased by corporate officials through the stock-option plan, what would the dividends per share have been, again assuming $236,640 in dividends were paid? (Round to the nearest penny.)

E13-11
Dividend Calculations

Marrion Corporation has the following stock outstanding:

Preferred stock (5%, $20 par, 20,000 shares)	$400,000
Common stock ($5 par, 80,000 shares)	400,000

For the two independent cases that follow, compute the amount of dividends that would be paid to preferred and common shareholders. Assume that total dividends paid are $86,000. No dividends have been paid for the past 2 years.

Case A, Preferred is noncumulative.
Case B, Preferred is cumulative.

E13-12
Stock Issuance, Treasury Stock, and Dividends

During 1994, Doxey Corporation had the following transactions and related events:

Jan.	15	Issued 6,500 shares of common stock at par ($16 per share), bringing the total number of shares outstanding to 121,300.
Feb.	6	Declared a 50-cent-per-share dividend on common stock for stockholders of record on March 6.
Mar.	6	Date of record.
Mar.	8	Pedro Garcia, a prominent banker, purchased 20,000 shares of Doxey Corporation common stock from the company for $346,000.
Apr.	6	Paid dividends declared on February 6.
Jun.	19	Reacquired 800 shares of common stock as treasury stock at a total cost of $9,350.
Sept.	6	Declared dividends of 55 cents per share to be paid to common stockholders of record on October 15, 1994.
Oct.	6	The Dow Jones Industrial Average plummeted 24 points and Doxey's stock price fell $3 per share.
Oct.	15	Date of record.
Nov.	6	Paid dividends that were declared on September 6.
Dec.	15	Declared and paid a 6 percent cash dividend on 18,000 outstanding shares of preferred stock (par value $32).

Given this information:

1. Prepare the journal entries for these transactions.
2. What is the total amount of dividends paid to common and preferred stockholders during 1994?

Chapter 13 Owners' Equity—The Corporation

E13-13
Stock Dividends and Stock Splits

The stockholders' equity section of Ardvark Corporation's December 31, 1993, balance sheet included the following items:

Common stock ($20 par, 250,000 shares authorized, 50,000 shares issued and outstanding)	1,000,000
Paid-in capital in excess of par, common stock	150,000
Retained earnings	2,000,000

Record the following transactions for 1994:

1. On March 1, Ardvark declared and issued a 25 percent stock dividend on common stock. The market price of the stock was $40 per share on that date.
2. On June 30, a 4-for-1 stock split was declared.
3. On September 15, a 10% stock dividend on common stock was declared and distributed. The market price of the stock was $30 per share on the dividend date.

E13-14
Recording an Investment *(Appendix)*

Hillman Company acquired 100 percent of the 8,000 shares ($10 par) of the voting common stock of Sloan Corporation on January 2, 1993. Prepare the journal entry to record Hillman's investment in Sloan under each of the following independent situations:

1. Hillman Company paid cash to Sloan's stockholders at $15 per share. The acquisition was accounted for as a purchase.
2. Hillman issued 3,000 shares of its voting common stock in exchange for the 8,000 shares of Sloan Corporation stock. The acquisition was accounted for as a pooling of interests. The fair market value of Hillman's stock at the time of the exchange was $46 per share ($30 par), and the book value of Sloan's net assets was $145,000.

E13-15
Elimination Entries *(Appendix)*

Smart Company acquired 100 percent of the common stock of Dull Company when the stockholders' equity of Dull Company was as follows:

Common stock ($100 par, 2,000 shares outstanding)	$200,000
Paid-in capital in excess of par	40,000
Retained earnings	100,000
Total stockholders' equity	$340,000

1. If Smart Company purchased all of Dull Company's stock at $228 per share, give the elimination entry that would be made on the consolidated work sheet. Assume that the fair market values of Dull Company's assets are equal to their book values, except that land is undervalued by $45,000.
2. If Smart Company acquired all of Dull Company's common stock by issuing its own common stock in exchange, what would the entry on the consolidated work sheet be under the pooling method? Assume that Smart Company issued 800 shares of its voting common stock ($100 par) and recorded the investment in Dull Company at $456,000.

E13-16
Elimination Entries *(Appendix)*

Just prior to acquisition by National Company, the balance sheet of Missouri Company had the following balances.

Common stock ($10 par, 10,000 shares outstanding)	$100,000
Paid-in capital in excess of par	27,000
Retained earnings	63,000
Total stockholders' equity	$190,000

Prepare the elimination entry on the consolidated work sheet if National Company purchased all the shares of Missouri Company under each of the following independent situations.

1. Paid $19 per share. The fair market value of the net assets of Missouri Company equaled the book value.
2. Paid $23 per share. The price paid was greater than the book value of Missouri's net assets because land was undervalued by $40,000.
3. Paid $25 per share. Plant and equipment on the books of Missouri Company was undervalued by $35,000. The fair market values of all other recorded assets, including land, of Missouri Company were equal to their book values.

E13-17
Accounting for Cost over Book Value with the Purchase Method *(Appendix)*

Referring to E13-16, assume that National Company paid an excess of $70,000 over book value for its interest in Missouri Company. Of the excess cost, $50,000 was assigned to depreciable equipment and $20,000 to goodwill. The equipment has a remaining life of 8 years and the goodwill is to be amortized over 10 years. (Straight-line methods are used for depreciation and amortization.) A full year's depreciation and amortization are taken in the year of acquisition. Under the purchase method, how much additional expense will be included in the consolidated income statement as a result of the excess cost paid for the Missouri Company?

Problem Set A

P13A-1
Stock Transactions and Analysis

The following selected items and amounts were taken from the balance sheet of Peterson Lighting Company as of December 31, 1993:

Cash	$ 93,000
Property, plant, and equipment	850,000
Accumulated depreciation	150,000
Liabilities	50,000
Preferred stock (7%, $100 par, noncumulative, 10,000 shares authorized, 5,000 shares issued and outstanding)	500,000
Common stock ($10 par, 100,000 shares authorized, 80,000 shares issued and outstanding)	800,000
Paid-in capital in excess of par, preferred stock	1,000
Paid-in capital in excess of par, common stock	125,000
Paid-in capital, treasury stock	1,000
Retained earnings:	
Appropriated for plant expansion	84,000
Unappropriated	226,000

Chapter 13 Owners' Equity—The Corporation

Required: For each of parts (1) to (7), (a) prepare the necessary journal entry (or entries) to record each transaction, and (b) calculate the amount that would appear on the December 31, 1994, balance sheet as a consequence of this transaction only. (Note: In your answer to each part of this problem, consider this to be the *only* transaction that took place during 1994.)

1. Two hundred shares of common stock are issued in exchange for cash of $4,000.
   (a) Entry
   (b) Paid-in capital in excess of par, common stock
2. Two hundred shares of preferred stock are issued at a price of $102 per share.
   (a) Entry
   (b) Paid-in capital in excess of par, preferred stock
3. Five hundred shares of common stock are issued in exchange for a building. The common stock is not actively traded, but the building was recently appraised at $11,000.
   (a) Entry
   (b) Property, plant, and equipment
4. One thousand shares of common stock were reacquired from a stockholder for $23,000 and subsequently reissued for $21,500 to a different investor. (Note: Make two entries.)
   (a) Entries
   (b) Paid-in capital, treasury stock
5. The board of directors declared dividends of $75,000. This amount includes the current-year dividend preference on preferred stock, with the remainder to be paid to common shareholders.
   (a) Entry
   (b) Retained earnings, unappropriated
6. The board of directors declared and the stockholders approved a 5-for-4 stock split on common stock.
   (a) Entry
   (b) Retained earnings, unappropriated
7. The planned plant expansion is now expected to cost $100,000, and the additional appropriation has been authorized.
   (a) Entry
   (b) Total retained earnings

P13A-2

Stock Transactions and the Stockholders' Equity Section

The following is Orchard Company's stockholders' equity section of the balance sheet on December 31, 1993:

Preferred stock (8%, $60 par, noncumulative, 16,000 shares authorized, 8,000 shares issued and outstanding)	$480,000
Common stock ($10 par, 120,000 shares authorized, 80,000 shares issued and outstanding)	800,000
Paid-in capital in excess of par, preferred stock	130,000
Paid-in capital in excess of par, common stock	252,000
Retained earnings	330,000

Required:
1. Journalize the following 1994 transactions:
   (a) Issued 2,000 preferred shares at $70 per share.
   (b) Reacquired 1,000 common shares for the treasury at $13 per share.

(c) Declared and paid a $2-per-share dividend on common stock in addition to paying the required preferred dividends. (Note: Debit Retained Earnings directly.)
(d) Reissued 600 treasury shares at $14 per share.
(e) Reissued the remaining treasury shares at $12 per share.
(f) Earnings for the year were $92,000.

2. Prepare the stockholders' equity section of the balance sheet for the company at December 31, 1994.

P13A-3
Recording Stockholders' Equity Transactions

ABC Corporation was organized during 1993. At the end of 1993, the stockholders' equity section of the balance sheet appeared as follows:

Contributed capital:	
Preferred stock (8%, $40 par, 10,000 shares authorized, 5,000 shares issued and outstanding)	$200,000
Common stock ($20 par, 30,000 shares authorized, 12,000 issued, 10,000 outstanding)	240,000
Paid-in capital in excess of par, preferred stock	50,000
Total contributed capital	$490,000
Retained earnings	110,000
Total contributed capital plus retained earnings	$600,000
Less treasury stock (2,000 shares at cost of $25 per share)	(50,000)
Total stockholders' equity	$550,000

During 1994, the following transactions occurred in the order given:

(a) Issued 1,000 shares of common stock at $24 per share.
(b) Reissued 1,000 shares of treasury stock at $27 per share.
(c) Reissued 500 shares of treasury stock at $20 per share.
(d) Declared and issued a 16 percent stock dividend on common stock. Market value was $25 per share.

Required: Record the transactions.

P13A-4
Dividend Calculations

SLC Corporation was organized in January, 1991, and issued shares of preferred and common stock as shown. As of December 31, 1994, there have been no changes in outstanding stock.

Preferred stock (8%, $10 par, 20,000 shares issued and outstanding)	$200,000
Common stock ($40 par, 10,000 shares issued and outstanding)	400,000

Required: For each of the following independent situations, compute the amount of dividends that would be paid for each class of stock in 1993 and 1994. Assume that total dividends of $10,000 and $80,000 are paid in 1993 and 1994, respectively.

(a) Preferred stock is noncumulative.
(b) Preferred stock is cumulative, and no dividends are in arrears in 1993.
(c) Preferred stock is cumulative, and no dividends have been paid during 1991 and 1992.

P13A-5
Dividend Transactions and Calculations

As of December 31, 1993, Monson Corporation has 200,000 shares of $10 par-value common stock authorized, with 100,000 of these shares issued and outstanding.

Required:
1. Prepare journal entries to record the following 1994 transactions:

   Jan. 1 Received authorization for 200,000 shares of 7 percent, cumulative preferred stock with a par value of $10.
   Jan. 2 Issued 10,000 shares of the preferred stock at $15 per share.
   Feb. 1 Declared a 2-for-1 common stock split to be effective on February 15.
   Feb. 15 The date of the common stock split.
   June 1 Reacquired 20 percent of the common stock outstanding for $18 per share.
   June 2 Declared a cash dividend of $10,000. The date of record is June 15.
   June 30 Paid the previously declared cash dividend of $10,000.
   Oct. 10 Declared and issued a 40 percent common stock dividend to common stockholders. (The market price of common stock is $16 per share.)

2. Determine the proper allocation to preferred and common stockholders of a $100,000 cash dividend declared on December 31, 1994. (This dividend is in addition to the June 2 dividend.)
3. **Interpretive Question** Why didn't the preferred stockholders receive their current-dividend preference of $7,000 in part (2)?

P13A-6
Stock Calculations and the Stockholders' Equity Section

The following account balances appear on the books of Atlas Corporation as of December 31, 1994:

Preferred stock (7%, $40 par value, 70,000 shares authorized, 50,000 shares issued and outstanding)	$2,000,000
Common stock ($3 par value, 500,000 shares authorized, 300,000 shares issued and outstanding)	900,000
Paid-in capital in excess of par, preferred stock	310,000
Paid-in capital in excess of par, common stock	490,000
Net income for 1994	130,000
Dividends paid during 1994	70,000
Retained earnings, January 1, 1994	1,360,000

Required:
1. If the preferred stock is selling at $45 per share, what is the maximum amount of cash that Atlas Corporation can obtain by issuing additional preferred stock given the present number of authorized shares?
2. If common stock is selling for $12 per share, what is the maximum amount of cash that can be obtained by issuing additional common stock given the present number of authorized shares?
3. Given the account balances at December 31, 1994, and ignoring parts (1) and (2), prepare, in good form, the stockholders' equity section of the balance sheet.

P13A-7
The Retained Earnings Statement and Stockholders' Equity

The following balances appear in the accounts of Steele Corporation as of December 31, 1994:

Retained Earnings, January 1, 1994	$128,000
Prior-Period Adjustment (tax adjustment for 1992)	(57,000)

Net Income for 1994	60,000
Preferred Stock (7%, $12 par, 20,000 shares authorized, 5,000 shares issued and outstanding)	60,000
Common Stock ($5 par, 100,000 shares authorized, 16,000 shares issued, 200 held as treasury stock)	80,000
Paid-In Capital in Excess of Par, Preferred Stock	13,400
Paid-In Capital in Excess of Par, Common Stock	42,800
Treasury Stock	3,600
Cash Dividends (paid during 1994)	10,000

Required:
1. Prepare the retained earnings statement for Steele Corporation as of December 31, 1994.
2. Prepare the stockholders' equity section of Steele Corporation's balance sheet as of December 31, 1994.

P13A-8

Unifying Concepts: Stock Transactions and the Stockholders' Equity Section

Richard Corporation was founded on January 1, 1994, and entered into the following stock transactions during 1994.

(a) Received authorization for 100,000 shares of $20 par-value common stock, 50,000 shares of 6 percent preferred stock with a stated value of $5, and 50,000 shares of no-par common stock.
(b) Issued 25,000 shares of the $20 par-value common stock at $24 per share.
(c) Issued 10,000 shares of the preferred stock at $8 per share.
(d) Issued 5,000 shares of the no-par common stock at $22 per share.
(e) Reacquired 1,000 shares of the $20 par-value common stock at $25 per share.
(f) Reacquired 500 shares of the no-par common stock at $20 per share.
(g) Reissued 250 of the 1,000 reacquired shares of $20 par-value common stock at $23 per share.
(h) Reissued all the 500 reacquired shares of no-par common stock at $23 per share.
(i) Closed the $14,000 credit balance in Income Summary to Retained Earnings. This amount is net income for 1994.

Required:
1. Prepare journal entries to record the 1994 transactions in Richard Corporation's books.
2. Prepare the stockholders' equity section of Richard Corporation's balance sheet at December 31, 1994. Assume that the transactions represent all the events involving equity accounts during 1994.

P13A-9

Unifying Concepts: Stock Transactions, the Stockholders' Equity Section, and Statement of Stockholders' Equity

The condensed balance sheet of Med-First Corporation at December 31, 1993, is shown.

Med-First Corporation
Balance Sheet
December 31, 1993

Assets

Cash	$ 400,000
All other assets	1,042,000
	$1,442,000

Chapter 13 Owners' Equity—The Corporation

Liabilities and Stockholders' Equity

Current liabilities	$ 164,000
Long-term liabilities	230,000
	$ 394,000
Contributed capital:	
Common stock ($10 par, 100,000 shares authorized, 80,000 shares outstanding)	800,000
Paid-in capital in excess of par	80,000
Retained earnings	168,000
	$1,442,000

During 1994, the following transactions affected stockholders' equity:

Feb. 15	Purchased 2,000 shares of Med-First common stock at $15 per share.	
May 21	Sold 1,200 of the shares purchased on February 15 at $19 per share.	
Sept. 15	Issued 8,000 shares of previously unissued common stock at $21 per share.	
Dec. 21	Sold the remaining 800 shares of treasury stock at $22 per share.	
Dec. 31	Closed net income of $85,360 to Retained Earnings.	

Required:
1. Prepare the journal entries to record the 1994 transactions.
2. Prepare the stockholders' equity section of the balance sheet at December 31, 1994.
3. Prepare a statement of stockholders' equity for the year ending December 31, 1994.

P13A-10
The Purchase Method
(Appendix)

On January 1, 1993, Acme Company acquired 100 percent of the common stock of Sawyer Company for a cash payment of $250,000. The balance sheets of the two companies just prior to the acquisition were as follows:

Assets	Acme	Sawyer
Current assets	$475,000	$ 75,000
Plant and equipment	220,000	185,000
Land	50,000	30,000
Total assets	$745,000	$290,000

Liabilities and Stockholders' Equity		
Current liabilities	$190,000	$ 40,000
Common stock ($100 par)	350,000	120,000
Paid-in capital in excess of par	30,000	32,000
Retained earnings	175,000	98,000
Total liabilities and stockholders' equity	$745,000	$290,000

The fair market values of Sawyer Company's assets were equal to their book values.

Required:
1. Prepare the Acme Company journal entry to account for the acquisition of Sawyer Company stock for $250,000 in cash.
2. Prepare the entry made on the consolidated work sheet to eliminate the appropriate asset and equity accounts.
3. Assume instead that Acme Company acquired Sawyer Company's stock for a cash payment of $280,000. Also assume that the fair market value of Sawyer Company's land was $38,000, whereas the fair market values of all its other assets were equal to their book values. Prepare a consolidated work sheet as of January 1, 1993.

P13A-11
The Pooling-of-Interests Method *(Appendix)*

On April 1, 1993, Gable Corporation exchanged 8,000 shares of its $10-par-value common stock with a fair market value of $16 per share for all the common stock shares of Emerson Corporation. As of March 31, 1993, the balance sheets of the two companies were as follows:

Assets	Gable	Emerson
Current assets	$ 75,000	$ 30,000
Property and equipment	180,000	85,000
Land	65,000	15,000
Total assets	$320,000	$130,000

Liabilities and Stockholders' Equity		
Current liabilities	$ 40,000	$ 20,000
Common stock ($10 par)	200,000	60,000
Paid-in capital in excess of par	25,000	10,000
Retained earnings	55,000	40,000
Total liabilities and stockholders' equity	$320,000	$130,000

On April 1, the fair market values of Emerson Corporation's assets were equal to their book values, except that the land's fair market value was $35,000. The current assets on Gable Corporation's books included an account receivable of $15,000 from Emerson Corporation. Likewise, the current liabilities on Emerson Corporation's books include an account payable of $15,000 to Gable Corporation.

Required:
1. Prepare the entry in the books of Gable Corporation for the acquisition of Emerson Corporation's common stock under the pooling-of-interests method.
2. Prepare a consolidated work sheet for the acquisition of Emerson Corporation by Gable Corporation under the pooling-of-interests method.

Problem Set B

P13B-1
Stock Transactions and Stockholders' Equity Section

SOLUTIONS SOFTWARE

The balance sheet for Ashley Corporation as of December 31, 1993, is as follows:

Assets		$750,000
Liabilities		$410,000
Stockholders' Equity:		
Convertible preferred stock (5%, $20 par)	$ 50,000	
Common stock ($10 par)	150,000	
Paid-in capital in excess of par, common stock	30,000	
Retained earnings	116,000	
	$346,000	
Less treasury stock, common (500 shares at cost)	(6,000)	340,000
Total liabilities and stockholders' equity		$750,000

During 1994, the following transactions were completed in the order given:

(a) 750 shares of outstanding common stock were reacquired by the company at $7 per share.

Chapter 13 Owners' Equity—The Corporation

(b) 150 shares of common stock were reacquired in settlement of an account receivable of $1,500.
(c) Semiannual cash dividends of 75 cents per share on common stock and 50 cents per share on preferred stock were declared and paid.
(d) Each share of preferred stock is convertible into three shares of common stock. Five hundred shares of preferred stock were converted into common stock. (Hint: Shares are converted at par values, and any excess reduces Retained Earnings.)
(e) The 900 shares of common treasury stock acquired during 1994 were sold at $13. The remaining treasury shares were exchanged for a machine with a fair market value of $6,300.
(f) 3,000 shares of common stock were issued in exchange for land appraised at $39,000.
(g) Semiannual cash dividends of 75 cents per share on common stock and 50 cents per share on preferred stock were declared and paid.
(h) Closed net income of $35,000 to Retained Earnings.
(i) Closed Dividends accounts to Retained Earnings.

Required:
1. Give the necessary journal entries to record the transactions listed.
2. Prepare the stockholders' equity section of the balance sheet as of December 31, 1994.

P13B-2

Stockholders' Equity, Dividends, and Treasury Stock

The stockholders' equity section of Nielsen Corporation's December 31, 1993, balance sheet is as follows:

Stockholders' equity:

Preferred stock (10%, $50 par, 10,000 shares authorized, 1,000 shares issued and outstanding)	$ 50,000
Common stock ($15 par, 100,000 shares authorized, 5,000 shares issued and outstanding)	75,000
Paid-in capital in excess of par, preferred stock	2,000
Paid-in capital in excess of par, common stock	25,000
Total contributed capital	$152,000
Retained earnings	102,000
Total stockholders' equity	$254,000

During 1994, Nielsen Corporation had the following transactions affecting stockholders' equity:

Jan. 20	Paid a cash dividend of $2 per share on common stock. The dividend was declared on December 15, 1993.
May 15	Declared a 10 percent common stock dividend. The market price on this date was $24 per share.
June 1	Issued the stock dividend declared on May 15.
Aug. 15	Reacquired 1,000 shares of common stock at $20 per share.
Sept. 30	Reissued 500 shares of the treasury stock at $21 per share.
Oct. 15	Declared and paid cash dividends of $3 per share on the common stock.
Nov. 1	Reissued 200 shares of treasury stock at $18 per share.
Dec. 15	Declared and paid the 10 percent preferred cash dividend.
Dec. 31	Closed net income of $40,000 to Retained Earnings. Also closed the Dividends account to Retained Earnings.

Required:
1. Journalize the transactions.
2. Prepare the stockholders' equity section of Nielsen Corporation's December 31, 1994, balance sheet.
3. **Interpretive Question** What is the effect on earnings per share when a company purchases treasury stock?

P13B-3
Recording Stockholders' Equity Transactions

The stockholders' equity section of Hathaway Corporation's December 31, 1993, balance sheet is as follows:

Stockholders' Equity

Contributed capital:
Preferred stock (5%, $25 par, 2,000 shares issued and outstanding)	$ 50,000
Common stock ($30 par, 10,000 shares issued and outstanding)	300,000
Paid-in capital in excess of par, preferred stock	10,000
Paid-in capital in excess of par, common stock	100,000
Total contributed capital	$460,000
Retained earnings	340,000
Total stockholders' equity	$800,000

During 1994 Hathaway Corporation had the following transactions:

Feb. 1   Paid a cash dividend of $3 per share on common stock. The dividend was declared December 31, 1993.
Mar. 15   Declared and issued a 19% common stock dividend. The market price of the stock on this date was $40 per share.
June 1   Reacquired 3,000 shares of common stock at $35 per share.
Sept. 1   Reissued 500 shares of treasury stock at $40 per share.
Nov. 15   Reissued 500 shares of treasury stock at $32 per share.

Required: Record the transactions.

P13B-4
Dividend Calculations

Rasmussen Corporation has authorization for 40,000 shares of 6 percent preferred stock, par value $10 per share, and 8,000 shares of common stock, par value $100 per share, all of which are issued and outstanding. During the years beginning in 1993, Rasmussen Corporation maintained a policy of paying out 50 percent of net income in cash dividends. One-half the net income for the 3 years beginning in 1993 was $16,000, $160,000, and $128,000. There are no dividends in arrears for years prior to 1993.

Required: Compute the amount of dividends paid to each class of stock for each year under the following separate cases:

1. Preferred stock is noncumulative.
2. Preferred stock is cumulative.
3. **Interpretive Question** Why is it important that a common stockholder know about the dividend privileges of the preferred stock?

Chapter 13 Owners' Equity—The Corporation 575

P13B-5

Recording Dividend Transactions and Reporting Stockholders' Equity

Murtry, Inc. reported the following stockholders' equity balances in its June 30, 1993, balance sheet:

Preferred stock (6%, $100 par, cumulative; 20,000 shares authorized, 6,000 shares issued and outstanding)	$ 600,000
Common stock ($20 par; 250,000 shares authorized, 60,000 shares issued and outstanding)	1,200,000
Retained earnings	950,000

Required:
1. The following stockholders' equity transactions occurred (in the order presented) during the fiscal year ending June 30, 1994. Prepare the necessary journal entries to record the transactions.
   (a) Murtry declared and issued a 5 percent dividend on common stock; the market value of the stock was $30 per share on the date of the dividend.
   (b) A 50 percent dividend on common stock was declared and issued when the stock was trading at a market price of $40 per share.
   (c) The board of directors declared a 2-for-1 split of the common stock.
   (d) A cash dividend was declared at the end of the fiscal year. The common stockholders will receive 50 cents per share after the current and cumulative preference on the preferred stock is satisfied. Preferred stock dividends are one year in arrears.
2. Assuming Murtry's net income for the year ending June 30, 1994, is $310,000, prepare the stockholders' equity section of the June 30, 1994, balance sheet and a statement of stockholders' equity for the 1993–1994 fiscal year.
3. **Interpretive Question** What is the effect on earnings per share when a company has a stock dividend or stock split?

P13B-6

Preparing the Stockholders' Equity Section and Recording Dividends

In 1992, Le Ann Adams and some college friends organized The Candy Jar, a gourmet candy company. In 1992, The Candy Jar issued 150,000 of the 300,000 authorized shares of common stock, par value $15, for $3,000,000 and all the 50,000 authorized shares of 10 percent, $20 par, cumulative preferred stock for $1,100,000. Combined earnings for 1992, 1993, 1994, and 1995 amounted to $1,250,000. Dividends paid in the 4 years were as follows: 1992—$100,000, 1993—$300,000, 1994—$0, 1995—$150,000.

Required:
1. Prepare the stockholders' equity section of the balance sheet as of December 31, 1995, for The Candy Jar.
2. Prepare the journal entry that would be necessary to record the dividends paid in 1995.

P13B-7

The Statement of Retained Earnings

Marsh Corporation records show the following at December 31, 1994:

Extraordinary loss (net of tax)	$(50,000)
Current year retained earnings appropriation for bond retirement	20,000
January 1, 1994, retained earnings appropriation balance for bond retirement	180,000
Cash dividends paid during 1994	30,000
Stock dividends issued during 1994	14,000
January 1, 1994, unappropriated retained earnings balance	510,000
Prior-period adjustment (net of tax)	(36,000)
Net income before extraordinary items and taxes (assume a 40% tax rate)	160,000

Required: 1. Prepare a 1994 statement of retained earnings.
2. **Interpretive Question** Why would a firm appropriate retained earnings if such action does not provide any cash?

P13B-8

Unifying Concepts: Stockholders' Equity

Lee Corporation was organized during 1992. At the end of 1993, the equity section of its balance sheet appeared as follows:

Contributed capital:
Preferred stock (6%, $20 par, 10,000 shares authorized, 5,000 shares issued and outstanding)...........	$100,000	
Common stock ($10 par, 50,000 shares authorized, 11,000 shares issued, 10,000 outstanding)...............	110,000	
Paid-in capital in excess of par, preferred stock	20,000	
Total contributed capital		$230,000
Retained earnings		100,000
Total contributed capital plus retained earnings		$330,000
Less treasury stock (1,000 shares of common at cost)		(12,000)
Total owners' equity.....................................		$318,000

During 1994, the following stockholders' equity transactions occurred (in chronological sequence):

(a) Issued 500 shares of common stock at $13 per share.
(b) Reissued 500 shares of treasury stock at $13 per share.
(c) Issued 1,000 shares of preferred stock at $25 per share.
(d) Reissued 500 shares of treasury stock at $10 per share.
(e) Declared a dividend large enough to meet the current-dividend preference of the preferred stock and to pay the common stockholders $2 per share. Dividends are recorded directly in the Retained Earnings account.
(f) Appropriated $15,000 of retained earnings for the retirement of debt.
(g) Declared a 2-for-1 stock split on the common stock.
(h) Closed net income of $65,000 to Retained Earnings.

Required: 1. Journalize the transactions.
2. Prepare the stockholders' equity section at December 31, 1994.
3. **Interpretive Question** Does the appropriated retained earnings mean that $15,000 cash is available to retire the debt? If not, what is the purpose of such an account?

P13B-9

Unifying Concepts: Stockholders' Equity

In January 1994, Smith Dry Cleaning obtained a charter from the state. The charter authorized 120,000 shares of common stock, par value $2. During 1994, the following selected transactions occurred in the order given:

(a) Sold 8,000 shares of common stock at $6 per share.
(b) Reacquired 800 shares of common stock at $7 per share.
(c) Sold 400 of the reacquired shares for $8 per share.
(d) Sold the remaining 400 shares of treasury stock for $6.50 per share.

(e) Declared a 50¢-per-share cash dividend on shares outstanding.
(f) Declared a 2-for-1 stock split.
(g) Closed net income of $51,200 to Retained Earnings.
(h) Closed the Dividends account.

Required:
1. Prepare journal entries to record the 1994 transactions.
2. Prepare the stockholders' equity section of the balance sheet at December 31, 1994.

P13B-10
The Purchase and Pooling-of-Interests Methods *(Appendix)*

The operating results of Rome Corporation and its wholly owned subsidiary, Westin Corporation, for the year ended December 31, 1993, are presented here.

	Rome	Westin
Sales revenue	$700,000	$480,000
Cost of goods sold	480,000	320,000
Gross margin	$220,000	$160,000
Selling and general expenses	125,000	85,000
Income before taxes	$ 95,000	$ 75,000
Income taxes	22,000	21,000
Net income	$ 73,000	$ 54,000

Required:
1. Prepare a consolidated income statement if the combination is accounted for as a purchase. When Rome Corporation acquired Westin on January 1, 1993, plant and equipment on Westin's books had a remaining life of 8 years and a fair market value $16,000 in excess of book value. Consolidated goodwill amounted to $38,000. Goodwill is amortized over a 20-year period.
2. Assuming the same facts regarding the valuation of plant and equipment as in part (1), prepare a consolidated income statement if the combination is accounted for as a pooling of interests.

P13B-11
Analysis of Consolidated Balance Sheet *(Appendix)*

The comparative consolidated balance sheets for Kelly Company for the years 1992 and 1993 are presented at the top of the next page. Kelly Company owns a controlling interest (over 50 percent) in one other company and exerts significant influence over several other companies.

Required:
1. **Interpretive Question** Why is this statement called a "consolidated" balance sheet?
2. If the company has a controlling interest over only one subsidiary, in what year was the subsidiary acquired? Explain.
3. Is there any evidence to indicate whether the subsidiary was accounted for as a purchase or as a pooling of interests? Explain.
4. In general, can you explain how Curtis Company paid for the acquisition of the subsidiary?
5. Assuming that Curtis Company did not acquire any new holdings in affiliated companies during either 1992 or 1993, why did the asset Investments in Affiliated Companies increase from 1992 to 1993?

Kelly Company
Consolidated Balance Sheets
December 31, 1992 and 1993

Assets	1993	1992
Current assets:		
Cash	$ 232,000	$ 295,000
Short-term investments	451,000	3,131,000
Accounts receivable	855,000	187,000
Inventories	623,000	47,000
Prepaid expenses	119,000	20,000
Total current assets	$2,280,000	$3,680,000
Property, plant, and equipment:		
Land	$ 358,000	$ 105,000
Equipment (net)	1,397,000	384,000
Buildings (net)	3,015,000	2,751,000
Total property, plant, and equipment	$4,770,000	$3,240,000
Other assets:		
Investments in affiliated companies	$ 249,000	$ 230,000
Excess of cost over fair value of assets acquired	501,000	—
Total other assets	$ 750,000	$ 230,000
Total assets	$7,800,000	$7,150,000
Liabilities and Stockholders' Equity		
Liabilities:		
Current liabilities	$1,714,000	$1,326,000
Long-term debt	2,455,000	2,565,000
Deferred income taxes	411,000	229,000
Total liabilities	$4,580,000	$4,120,000
Stockholders' equity:		
Common stock (par $1)	$ 45,000	$ 44,000
Paid-in capital in excess of par	2,025,000	2,017,000
Retained earnings	1,150,000	969,000
Total stockholders' equity	$3,220,000	$3,030,000
Total liabilities and stockholders' equity	$7,800,000	$7,150,000

Business Analysis Case 1   *Urton Corporation*

During the first week of October, the board of directors of Urton Corporation was presented with the following stockholders' equity section of the balance sheet:

Common stock (80,000 shares issued and outstanding)	$1,600,000
Paid-in capital in excess of par	825,000
Retained earnings	1,360,000
Total stockholders' equity	$3,785,000

Urton Corporation has paid dividends of $4 per share in each of the last 3 years. On September 30, the board of directors declared and distributed a stock dividend of 16,000 shares. Three months later, on December 31, they declared a cash dividend of $3.40 per share.

Pastor David Thompson's Little Dell Church owns 8,000 shares of Urton stock, which it received from John Urton, the founder of the company and a faithful member of the church until he passed away 4 years ago. The market price of the stock before the stock dividend was $70 per share.

Required:
1. What was Little Dell's share (in dollars) of total stockholders' equity before the stock dividend? What was Little Dell's share after the stock dividend? Is there any change in Little Dell's ownership share as a result of the 20 percent stock dividend? Explain.
2. What was the amount of stockholders' equity per share before the stock dividend? Why do you think the market value of Urton stock differed from this amount?
3. How much more or less did the Little Dell Church receive in cash dividends this year as compared with the previous 3 years?
4. Immediately after the stock dividend was announced and distributed, the stock's market price dropped from $70 to $60 per share. Is this a loss to Little Dell Church? Explain.
5. If Urton had announced that it would continue its regular cash dividend of $4 per share after the stock dividend, how would you expect the market price of the stock to change?

Business Analysis Case 2   *Exxon Corporation*

Exxon Corporation is one of the largest companies in the world. The statement of shareholders' equity for three recent years is shown on the next page.

Required: On the basis of the information provided, answer the following questions:
1. How many shares of capital stock did Exxon have outstanding at the end of each of the three years?
2. For how much per share was the capital stock originally issued? (Round to the nearest cent.)
3. How much was the average price per share paid for the Treasury Stock in each of the three years? (Round to the nearest cent.)
4. On how many shares of stock were the dividends paid in each of the three years? (Round to the nearest share.) Why doesn't your answer agree with the number of shares issued?
5. Why is total shareholders' equity in each of the three years less than the amount of Retained Earnings at the end of each year?

Exxon Corporation
Statement of Shareholders' Equity
(In Millions)

	Year 1 Shares	Year 1 Dollars	Year 2 Shares	Year 2 Dollars	Year 3 Shares	Year 3 Dollars
Capital stock (authorized—1 billion shares without par value)						
Issued at end of year	906	$ 2,822	906	$ 2,822	906	$ 2,822
Retained earnings						
At beginning of year		$27,211		$29,515		$32,302
Net income for year		4,978		5,528		4,870
Dividends ($3.10 per share in year 1, $3.35 in year 2, and $3.45 in year 3)		(2,674)		(2,741)		(2,607)
At end of year		$29,515		$32,302		$34,565
Cumulative foreign exchange translation adjustment						
At beginning of year		$ (531)		$ (1,070)		$ (1,818)
Change during the year		(539)		(748)		669
At end of year		$ (1,070)		$ (1,818)		$ (1,149)
Capital stock held in treasury, at cost						
At beginning of year	(40)	$ (1,062)	(60)	$ (1,824)	(123)	$ (4,455)
Acquisitions	(21)	(784)	(64)	(2,672)	(54)	(2,748)
Dispositions	1	22	1	41	2	61
At end of year	(60)	$ (1,824)	(123)	$ (4,455)	(175)	$ (7,142)
Shareholders' equity at end of year		$29,443		$28,851		$29,096

Ethics Case *Johnson Company*

Johnson Company is a large, publicly held manufacturer of automobile parts located in the Southeastern part of the United States. Its managers are paid respectable salaries, but a significant portion of their compensation is in the form of bonuses based on company earnings. Presently, the company has a significant amount of excess cash that it needs to invest. Management is considering two alternative investments: buying the stock of Donner Company, a young company with high profit potential because of its advanced technology and patents, or buying shares of its own company's stock. Of the two, the return on the Donner Company stock will probably be greater. However, management does not want to risk impairing reported profits and bonuses with losses from either investment, should the stocks go down in value.

Management knows that if the Donner stock is purchased, it must be reported as an investment at the lower-of-cost-or-market, and all losses must be recognized on the income statement. On the other hand, if Johnson Company stock is purchased, it will be accounted for as treasury stock, and losses will not be reported.

Required:
1. Is it in the best interest of the shareholders for management to buy the company's own stock so that reported earnings will not be impaired even though the anticipated return is greater on the Donner Company stock?
2. Should accounting rules affect business decisions or just the reported results of those decisions?
3. Do you think it is ethical for management to buy Johnson Company stock in this case even though the return on the Donner Company stock is expected to be higher?

Chapter 14

Owners' Equity—Proprietorships and Partnerships

Learning Objectives

After studying this chapter, you should be able to:
1. Identify the major characteristics shared by proprietorships and partnerships.
2. Record and report changes in the owner's equity of a proprietorship.
3. Identify the major characteristics unique to partnerships.
4. Describe and apply basic partnership accounting and reporting procedures.
5. Explain and apply various methods of allocating partnership profits and losses.
6. Account for the admission of a new partner and withdrawal of an existing partner.

SETTING THE STAGE

Howard Cougar lives in a rural county of Southern Maine. He is contemplating starting a dealership to sell Yamaha snowmobiles and motorcycles. He rationalizes that motorcycles will sell well to farmers and outdoorsmen during the summer, and snowmobiles will sell well to the same groups during the winter. Though Howard is a good mechanic and is well liked in the community, he knows very little about business. He has been told by one friend that he should organize the dealership as a proprietorship, by another friend that it should be a partnership, and by a third friend that he is stupid not to incorporate. Howard is confused. He understands that corporations are taxed separately but has heard that the corporate form of organization will limit his liability. Anyway, his third friend says, "A small corporation should never pay any income tax because the business can deduct a salary expense for the owner equal to the 'income,' and therefore, the taxable income should always be zero." The friend who argues for the proprietorship form of business tells Howard that he will maintain flexibility if he doesn't incorporate. Besides, he argues, "Personal income tax rates are lower than corporate tax rates, and you can have complete control of the business." His second friend agrees that he should not incorporate but tells Howard that with a partnership, he and his partner will have more capital and can have a better stock and selection of snowmobiles and motorcycles on hand and will therefore get more customers.

Howard is facing the same kind of decision that is faced by thousands of people every day as they start businesses. Every doctor, dentist, lawyer, or business owner must ultimately decide the form of his or her business organization. Depending on the nature and profitability of their businesses, organizational form can make a tremendous difference financially for such things as pension plans, loans to the business, insurance, legal liability, tax liabilities, and accounting and legal costs. In the preceding chapter, we discussed the corporate form of business organization. In this chapter, we cover proprietorships and partnerships.

Because of their size, corporations dominate economic activity in the United States. However, proprietorships and partnerships are by far the most common types of businesses. They are most numerous in the professions and businesses that stress personal services. For example, many doctors, lawyers, dentists, accountants, and small retail businesses (repair shops, real estate agencies, and other service businesses) operate as proprietorships or partnerships.

A partnership allows two or more people to combine their capital and skills in order to operate on a larger scale and perhaps more efficiently than they could individually, as proprietors. For example, a realtor and a building contractor may combine their talents in a construction partnership. The flexibility of a partnership allows the partners to withdraw funds and make business decisions without consulting many other owners or adhering to complex legal procedures. In this chapter, we discuss the principles and procedures used in accounting for proprietorships and partnerships. As noted in Chapter 13, accounting for assets and liabilities is the same in proprietorships, partnerships, and corporations; only the equity sections differ. In all cases, the equity sections represent owners' claims on the firm's assets. Corporations, however, separate the ownership interests (in the various stock accounts) from residual earnings (in Retained Earnings), whereas proprietorships and partnerships put all earnings and owner contributions into the owners' capital accounts.

The discussion of owners' equity of proprietorships and partnerships will be divided into seven parts: (1) characteristics shared by proprietorships and partnerships, (2) accounting for proprietorships, (3) characteristics unique to partnerships, (4) basic accounting for partnerships, (5) accounting for partnership profits and losses, (6) accounting for changing partnership members, and (7) a brief introduction to liquidating a partnership.

CHARACTERISTICS SHARED BY PROPRIETORSHIPS AND PARTNERSHIPS

Objective 1

Identify the major characteristics shared by proprietorships and partnerships.

proprietorship *a business owned by one person*

partnership *a business owned by two or more persons or entities*

A **proprietorship** is a business owned by one person. A **partnership** is a business owned by two or more persons or entities. In most respects, proprietorships and partnerships are similar to each other but very different from corporations. As discussed in Chapter 13, corporations are legal entities authorized by states; they are separately taxed and offer limited liability to their stockholders. Proprietorships and partnerships are unincorporated businesses that are not legally separate from their owners, nor are they taxed separately. Both proprietorships and partnerships are less subject to government regulation than are corporations. Some of their common characteristics are their ease of formation, limited life, and unlimited liability.

Ease of Formation

Proprietorships and partnerships can be formed with few legal formalities. When a person decides to establish a proprietorship, he or she merely acquires the necessary cash, inventory, equipment, and other assets; obtains a business license; and begins providing goods or services to customers. The same is true for a partnership, except that since two or more persons are involved, they must decide together which assets will be acquired and how business will be conducted.

Chapter 14 Owners' Equity—Proprietorships and Partnerships

partnership agreement a legal agreement between partners; it usually specifies, among other things, the capital contributions to be made by each partner, the ratios in which partnership earnings and losses will be distributed, the management responsibilities of the partners, and the partners' rights to transfer or sell their individual interests

When two or more persons voluntarily agree to be partners, the agreement between them becomes a contract. A **partnership agreement** can be oral or written, but because each partner is legally responsible for the actions of the other partner(s), the agreement should be written to avoid misunderstandings. A partnership agreement should specify the following:

1. The name, location, and purpose of the business.
2. The names of the parties and their respective duties, obligations, and rights.
3. The investments in the partnership to be made by each partner.
4. The arrangement agreed upon for sharing business profits and losses.
5. The amount of assets the partners are allowed to withdraw and the timing of withdrawals.
6. The partners' rights to transfer or sell their interests and the procedures to be followed when new partners are admitted and when partners withdraw.
7. The procedures for dissolving the partnership.

Limited Life

Because proprietorships and partnerships are not legal entities that are separate and distinct from their owners, they are easily terminated. In the case of a proprietorship, the owner can decide to dissolve the business at any time. For a partnership, anything that terminates or changes the contract between the partners legally dissolves the partnership. Among the events that dissolve a partnership are (1) the death or withdrawal of a partner, (2) the bankruptcy of a partner, (3) the admission of a new partner, (4) the retirement of a partner, or (5) the completion of the project for which the partnership was formed. The occurrence of any of these events does not necessarily mean that a partnership must cease business; rather, the existing partnership is legally terminated, and another partnership must be formed.

Unlimited Liability

unlimited liability the lack of a ceiling on the amount of liability a proprietor or partner must assume; meaning that if business assets are not sufficient to settle creditor claims, the personal assets of the proprietor or partners may be used to settle the claims

Proprietorships and partnerships have **unlimited liability,** which means that the proprietor or partners are personally responsible for all debts of the business. If a partnership is in poor financial condition, creditors first attempt to satisfy their claims from the assets of the partnership. After those assets are exhausted, creditors may seek payment from the personal assets of the partners. In addition, since partners are responsible for one another's actions (within the scope of the partnership), creditors may seek payment for claims authorized by a departed partner from the personal assets of the remaining partners.

There are two exceptions to this unlimited liability rule. First, a person joining an existing partnership does not have to assume liability for debts incurred prior to his or her admission. Second, if a partner decides to withdraw from a partnership and gives adequate public notice of withdrawal, he or she cannot be held liable for debts subsequently incurred by the partnership.

This unlimited liability feature is probably the single most significant disadvantage of a proprietorship or partnership. It can deter a wealthy person from joining a partnership for fear of losing personal assets.

> **To Summarize** A *proprietorship* is a business owned by one person. A *partnership* is a business owned by two or more persons. Both types of businesses are easy to start and easy to terminate, and they are not separately taxed. Most partnerships are based on a partnership agreement that specifies how business will be conducted, how profits will be divided, and other important elements of the partnership. Anything that changes the partnership agreement, such as the death or retirement of a partner, legally terminates the partnership but does not necessarily terminate the business. A major disadvantage of proprietorships and partnerships is the unlimited liability of the owner or partners.

PROPRIETORSHIP ACCOUNTING

Objective 2
Record and report changes in the owner's equity of a proprietorship.

Capital account *an account in which a proprietor's or partner's interest in a firm is recorded; it is increased by owner investments and net income and decreased by owner withdrawals and net losses*

Drawings account *a temporary account in which an owner's withdrawals of cash or other assets from proprietorships or partnerships are recorded*

As indicated earlier, the difference between accounting for a proprietorship and accounting for a corporation is the owners' equity accounts. In a corporation, owners' equity is divided into contributed capital and retained earnings, with each of these categories possibly having several different accounts. In a proprietorship, all owner's equity transactions are recorded in only two accounts, **Capital** and **Drawings**.

To illustrate the accounting for the owner's equity of a proprietorship, we will assume that Megan Wilkes decides to start a small, independent real estate brokerage business. On January 1, 1994, she deposits $40,000 into a bank account to finance the business. The entry to record the $40,000 deposit would be:

Cash	40,000	
Megan Wilkes, Capital		40,000
Invested $40,000 to start a real estate business.		

Once the business is established, the entries to account for the purchase of assets, the payment of business expenses, and the receipt of revenues are similar to those for corporations. There is one exception, however. Whereas in a corporation salaries to management are accounted for as expenses, in a proprietorship the salary paid to the owner is a distribution of earnings. The managers of a corporation are considered to be employees, even if they are also stockholders in the company. The owners of a corporation receive dividends, which are deducted directly from Retained Earnings. In a proprietorship, the owner receives no dividends, so any "drawing out" of funds is considered to be a distribution to the owner. Hence, the name "Drawings" account. If Megan Wilkes decided to withdraw $650 cash for personal use or as salary, the entry would be:

Megan Wilkes, Drawings	650	
Cash		650
Withdrew $650 for personal use.		

Chapter 14 Owners' Equity—Proprietorships and Partnerships

> **BUSINESS ENVIRONMENT ESSAY**
> *The Dangers of Unlimited Liability*
>
> One of the strong disadvantages of proprietorships and most partnerships is their unlimited liability, which holds the owners personally responsible for the debts of the business. This unlimited liability provision is especially worrisome for doctors, lawyers, engineers, certified public accountants (CPAs), dentists, and other professionals who are more and more frequently being sued for malpractice. A good example of the degree of liability is a lawsuit that was brought against Alexander Grant & Co., an international CPA firm, during the mid-1980s for its role in auditing ESM Government Securities. The following article describes the lawsuit.
>
> > FORT LAUDERDALE, Fla. (UPI)—Financier Marvin Warner, saying he suffered massive losses and damage to his reputation, has filed a $1.15 billion suit against the auditors of collapsed ESM Government Securities.
> >
> > The 144-page civil suit was filed in federal court by the Cincinnati financier's lawyers against the accounting firm of Alexander Grant & Co. and Grant's 100 partners.
> >
> > It charges that Home State Savings Bank of Ohio and American Savings and Loan of Miami, both controlled by Warner, never would have invested with ESM if they had known the financial statements were false.
> >
> > The suit, which asks for a jury trial, charges the Grant firm and the managing partner of its South Florida office with fraud, negligence, theft and racketeering.
> >
> > In a statement issued along with filing of the lawsuit, Warner said, "I intend to seek legal redress against everyone who has injured me or my family."
> >
> > The suit charges that Warner suffered "large financial losses, emotional trauma and distress, and damage to his reputation" as a result of the ESM failure.
> >
> > Warner-owned Home State collapsed after the March 4 failure of ESM. That set off the closing of 70 other Ohio savings and loan firms. Home State lost about $144 million through its ESM investments. American Savings has set aside $68.7 million to guard against ESM losses. In January, Warner sold his co-controlling interest in American Savings.
> >
> > Warner said last week he lost about $30 million personally in the collapse of ESM.
> >
> > Source: *Daily Herald,* Provo, Utah, May 15, 1985.
>
> Had Alexander Grant lost this lawsuit, each of its 100 partners would have been liable for $11.5 million ($1.5 billion ÷ 100 partners), or more than their entire career earnings. And if insurance and partnership assets were insufficient to cover losses, the partners' personal assets (homes, savings, and so on) could have been used to satisfy the claims.

The account Megan Wilkes, Drawings is similar to a dividends account in a corporation: at year-end, it is closed to the owner's equity account, Megan Wilkes, Capital.

Assuming that Megan Wilkes withdrew only $650 during the year, the closing entry to eliminate the balance in the Drawings account would be:

Megan Wilkes, Capital...	650	
Megan Wilkes, Drawings		650
To close the Drawings account for the year.		

If we also assume that an Income Summary account is used and that it has a $14,000 credit balance (profit) after closing revenues and expenses, Megan Wilkes's closing entry for net income will be:

Income Summary	14,000	
Megan Wilkes, Capital		14,000

To close net income for the year to the owner's Capital account.

From the preceding two entries, we see that Megan Wilkes's capital account has increased by $13,350 since January 1. Adding this amount to her original contribution results in a $53,350 balance at year-end, as the following statement of owner's capital shows:

Megan Wilkes
Statement of Owner's Capital
For the Year Ending December 31, 1994

Megan Wilkes, capital, January 1, 1994	$40,000
Add net income	14,000
Total	$54,000
Less withdrawals	(650)
Megan Wilkes, capital, December 31, 1994	$53,350

The owner's equity section of Megan Wilkes's balance sheet would have only one entry.

Megan Wilkes, capital	$53,350

> **To Summarize** *The assets and liabilities of a proprietorship are accounted for in the same way as they are in a corporation. Equity is handled differently. Whereas the accounting for corporate equity may involve several accounts, the accounting for proprietorship equity requires only two accounts, Drawings and Capital. The Drawings account is used for recording withdrawals of funds by the owner. It is closed to the Capital account at year-end. The Capital account is increased when capital is invested in the business and when profits are earned; it is decreased when cash or other assets are withdrawn from the business or when losses occur.*

CHARACTERISTICS UNIQUE TO PARTNERSHIPS

Objective 3
Identify the major characteristics unique to partnerships.

Earlier in this chapter we discussed some of the characteristics shared by proprietorships and partnerships: ease of formation, limited life, and unlimited liability. We now discuss the characteristics that are unique to partnerships: (1) mutual agency, (2) co-ownership of all partnership property, and (3) sharing of partnership profits.

Mutual Agency

Each partner is an agent of the partnership and can enter into contracts, incur debts, buy merchandise, or conduct other business on behalf of the partnership. This **mutual agency** feature allows any partner to bind the partnership to agreements that relate to normal business operations. For example, suppose Tim Thompson and Joann Johnson have a building construction company. If Tim Thompson contracts to purchase lumber, bricks, or other building materials for the partnership, the partnership is obligated to pay for these items. Of course, if Tim Thompson decides to buy himself a sports car or anything else not intended for the business, the partnership has no such obligation, unless he uses partnership credit cards or money to pay for the car. The mutual agency aspect of partnerships makes it important to select partners who are responsible and honest.

mutual agency the right of all partners in a partnership to act as agents for the normal business operations of the partnership, with the authority to bind it to business agreements

Co-Ownership of Partnership Property

Property invested in a partnership becomes an asset of the business and is jointly owned by all partners, not just by the partner transferring the property. Thus, if a partner transfers a building, land, inventory, or other assets to a partnership, he or she gives up the right to separate use of the property. And when the property is sold, all partners benefit from the gain, or share in the loss, from the sale.

Sharing of Partnership Profits

All members of a partnership have the right to share in the partnership's profits, and the obligation to share in its losses. The arrangement for dividing the profits and losses should be spelled out in the partnership agreement. If the partnership agreement refers only to the ratio for the distribution of profits, losses must be shared in the same ratio. If the agreement does not specify how earnings are to be divided, or if no formal partnership agreement exists, the law requires that profits and losses be shared equally.

> **To Summarize** *Three important characteristics of a partnership are mutual agency, co-ownership of partnership property, and the sharing of partnership profits and losses. Mutual agency means that each partner is an agent of the partnership and can bind it to business agreements that relate to normal operations. Co-ownership of property means that property transferred to a partnership is jointly owned by all partners. Sharing of partnership profits and losses means that all partners have a right to receive predetermined portions of the profits and an obligation to share in any losses.*

BASIC PARTNERSHIP ACCOUNTING

Objective 4
Describe and apply basic partnership accounting and reporting procedures.

Like a proprietorship, a partnership differs from a corporation primarily in accounting for owners' equity. That is, a partnership has only two types of owners' equity accounts, Capital and Drawings. Whereas a proprietorship has only one of each type of account, a partnership maintains separate Capital and Drawings accounts for each partner.

Forming a Partnership

To illustrate the accounting for the formation of a partnership, assume that Dr. Mary Adams and Dr. Jim Bell decide to form a partnership on January 1, 1994. Their partnership agreement specifies that Dr. Adams will contribute land valued at $30,000, a building valued at $50,000, and $10,000 cash to the business, and that Dr. Bell will contribute medical equipment valued at $40,000 plus $50,000 cash. The entry to record the capital contributions of the two partners would be:

Cash	60,000	
Equipment	40,000	
Land	30,000	
Building	50,000	
Adams, Capital		90,000
Bell, Capital		90,000

To record the investments of Adams and Bell in a partnership.

The valuation of noncash assets invested in a business is one of the most difficult tasks in accounting for the formation of a partnership. Generally, the fair market values on the date of transfer should be used, but these values must be agreed upon by all partners. For example, if the assets contributed by either Bell or Adams had been used in another business prior to the partnership, the values assigned to them for the partnership might be quite different from the amounts they were being carried at on the previous business's books. Although the equipment invested by Bell may have had a book value of only $30,000, or the land and building invested by Adams may have cost only $15,000 several years ago, it is only fair to give each partner credit for the current market values of the assets at the time they are transferred to the partnership.

Partners' Drawings Accounts

As mentioned previously, in a corporation, the managers are employees, so their salaries are accounted for as expenses; the stockholders are the owners, and distributions to them are in the form of dividends. In a partnership, the managers are usually the owners, and any amounts they withdraw, either as salary or as a distribution of profits, are debited to their Drawings accounts, which eventually reduces the Capital accounts. Each partner has a Drawings account in which his or her withdrawals are recorded for the year. For example, assume that sufficient income was earned during the year and that Adams and Bell each withdrew $55,000 as salary for the year. The entry would be:

Adams, Drawings	55,000	
Bell, Drawings	55,000	
Cash		110,000

To record cash taken from the partnership as salary.

Note that any salaries paid to employees who are not partners are expenses of the business.

If Adams or Bell had withdrawn funds, say to repay a personal loan, that amount would also be debited to the Drawings account. At year-end, the debits in the Drawings accounts would be totaled, and the accounts would be closed to the partners' Capital accounts. Assuming that the total in each Drawings account was the $55,000 salary, the entry to close the Drawings accounts for the year would be:

```
Adams, Capital ...............................................   55,000
Bell, Capital .................................................   55,000
    Adams, Drawings .........................................              55,000
    Bell, Drawings ...........................................              55,000
To close the Drawings accounts for the year.
```

The Statement of Partners' Capital

statement of partners' capital *a partnership report showing the changes in the capital balances; similar to a statement of changes in retained earnings for a corporation*

Because most partners want an explanation of how their capital accounts change from year to year, a **statement of partners' capital** is usually prepared. This statement, which is similar to a retained earnings statement for a corporation, lists the beginning capital balances, additional investments, profits or losses from operations, withdrawals, and each partner's ending capital balance. For example, given the preceding information and assuming that the Adams and Bell partnership had a 1994 profit of $140,000, which was shared equally, the statement of partners' capital as of December 31, 1994, would be as shown in Exhibit 14-1.

In addition, a partnership will prepare an income statement and a balance sheet as illustrated in Exhibits 14-2 and 14-3. The format of the income statement will be the same as for a corporation, with two exceptions: (1) no income taxes are reported since profits are taxed directly to the individual owners, and (2) the allocation of net income (or loss) is usually noted at the bottom of the statement. The balance sheet resembles that of a corporation with the exception of the owners' equity section.

Exhibit 14-1

Adams and Bell Partnership
Statement of Partners' Capital
For the Year Ended December 31, 1994

	Dr. Adams	Dr. Bell	Total
Investments, January 1, 1994	$ 90,000	$ 90,000	$180,000
Add net income for 1994	70,000	70,000	140,000
Subtotal	$160,000	$160,000	$320,000
Less withdrawals during 1994	(55,000)	(55,000)	(110,000)
Capital balances, December 31, 1994	$105,000	$105,000	$210,000

Exhibit 14-2

Adams and Bell Partnership
Income Statement
For the Year Ended December 31, 1994

Fee revenues...		$240,000
Expenses:		
Salary expense	$20,000	
Utilities expense	10,000	
Other expenses..	70,000	
Total expenses		100,000
Net income		$140,000
Allocation to Partners:		
To Adams...		$ 70,000
To Bell		70,000
Net income allocated.....................................		$140,000

Note: Revenue and expense amounts are arbitrary, and we assume that the partners share profits equally.

Exhibit 14-3

Adams and Bell Partnership
Balance Sheet
December 31, 1994

Assets

Cash	$ 60,000	
Accounts receivable	23,000	
Supplies	26,000	
Land	30,000	
Equipment (net)	38,000	
Building (net)...	48,000	
Total assets...		$225,000

Liabilities and partners' equity

Liabilities:		
Accounts payable	$ 5,000	
Notes payable	10,000	
Total liabilities..		$ 15,000
Partners' equity:		
Adams, capital	$105,000	
Bell, capital	105,000	
Total partners' equity..................................		210,000
Total liabilities and partners' equity		$225,000

Note: Many of the figures are arbitrary, and we assume that the partners share all profits equally.

To Summarize *The basic elements in accounting for the owners' equity of a partnership are (1) accounting for investments by the partners, (2) recording withdrawals of assets by the partners, (3) closing the Drawings accounts, and (4) preparing a* *statement of partners' capital. Investments by owners are usually recorded at the fair market value and are credited to the owners' capital balances. Owners' withdrawals of cash, inventory, and other business assets are recorded in Drawings accounts, which are closed to the Capital accounts at year-end. There is one Capital and one Drawings account for each partner. A statement of partners' capital reconciles the beginning and the ending capital balances by adding any profits and additional investments to the beginning capital balances and subtracting any losses and withdrawals. The income statement and balance sheet for a partnership resemble those for a corporation. The major differences are that no income taxes are reported on the partnership income statement, and the owners' equity section of the balance sheet shows a capital account for each partner rather than capital stock and retained earnings.*

ACCOUNTING FOR PARTNERSHIP PROFITS AND LOSSES

Objective 5
Explain and apply various methods of allocating partnership profits and losses.

In the preceding section, we assumed that Adams and Bell distributed the profits equally. Partnership profits (or losses) may be divided in any way the partners see fit—60%/40%, 70%/30%, and so forth. This profit-and-loss-sharing ratio is usually specified in the partnership agreement. If it is not, the partners are legally bound to divide the profits (or losses) equally.

To determine an equitable distribution of profits, partners normally consider three factors: (1) how much cash and other property each partner contributed, (2) how much time and energy each partner puts into the business and the value of the respective partners' talents, and (3) the risks each partner is taking (for example, by foregoing other opportunities or by tying his or her reputation to the other partners). For example, Dr. Adams and Dr. Bell each contributed $90,000 of assets to the partnership. Assuming that they also devote equal time to the business, a 50/50 division of profits would probably be fair. If, however, Dr. Adams works five days a week and Dr. Bell spends only two days working for the partnership, then Dr. Adams probably should be assigned a larger percentage of the profits. Note that their $55,000 salaries are paid in anticipation of profits and are actually advances against those profits. If a partner whose share of net income is $40,000, for example, has already withdrawn $35,000 (as an advance), that partner's capital balance would increase by $5,000.

Because profits and losses may be allocated in any manner agreed upon by the partners, there are many ways of sharing profits. We will discuss three of the most common types of profit-sharing arrangements.

Stated Ratio

Partnership profits are frequently allocated on the basis of a predetermined fixed ratio, such as an equal percentage to each partner, or 60 percent to one partner and 40 percent to the other. To illustrate the allocation of profits at a stated ratio, we will assume that although Adams and Bell invested equally in the business, Bell manages all the daily operations, whereas Adams spends considerably less time in the business. Therefore, they agree that Adams will receive only 40 percent of the profits and Bell 60 percent. (Note that the total of all partners' shares must always equal 100 percent.) The $140,000 of partnership net income would then be divided as follows:

Adams ($140,000 × 0.40)	$ 56,000
Bell ($140,000 × 0.60)	84,000
Total	$140,000

The entry to close net income to the partners' Capital accounts would be:

Income Summary	140,000	
Adams, Capital		56,000
Bell, Capital		84,000

To close 1994 earnings to the partners' Capital accounts.

Capital Investment Ratio

In the previous example, Adams and Bell contributed the same amount of capital but different amounts of time. If they had contributed different amounts of capital, they might decide to divide profits on the basis of their respective investments. That is, each partner's share of the profits would be calculated as a percentage of the total capital balance.

To illustrate this approach, we assume that at the end of 1994, Adams and Bell had the following balances in their Capital accounts and that each had withdrawn $55,000 during the year:

Adams, Capital			Adams, Drawings	
	1/1/94	90,000	55,000	

Bell, Capital			Bell, Drawings	
	1/1/94	110,000	55,000	

Since Adams has a capital balance of $90,000, she receives 45 percent ($90,000 ÷ $200,000) of the $140,000 profit. The complete calculation is as follows:

Adams ($90,000/$200,000 × $140,000)	$ 63,000
Bell ($110,000/$200,000 × $140,000)	77,000
	$140,000

The entry to close net income to the partners' Capital accounts would then be:

```
Income Summary ..........................................    140,000
    Adams, Capital ......................................              63,000
    Bell, Capital .......................................              77,000
To close 1994 earnings to the partners' Capital accounts.
```

If a partner's capital balance changes during the year because of either additional investments or withdrawals, the weighted-average capital balance is usually used to allocate profits.

Allowance for Salaries with the Remainder at Stated Ratio

Individual partners may take on greater responsibilities or, by their special initiative or talent, may contribute more to the partnership than others. In such cases, salaries that reflect the partners' different responsibilities can be made part of the profit-sharing arrangement.

To illustrate the calculation for this type of arrangement, assume that the Adams and Bell partnership agreement specifies that Adams is to work 5 days a week, whereas Bell will work only 3. For this reason, Adams will receive a salary of $70,000; Bell will receive $40,000. The rest of the net income (or loss) is divided equally. As calculated here, Adams receives a total of $85,000 in 1994, and Bell receives $55,000.

	Adams	Bell	Total
Net income			$ 140,000
Salaries to partners	$70,000	$40,000	(110,000)
Remainder to be divided equally:			$ 30,000
Adams (50%)	15,000		
Bell (50%)		15,000	(30,000)
Total to each partner	$85,000	$55,000	$ -0-

The entry to close net income to the partners' Capital accounts would then be:

```
Income Summary ..........................................    140,000
    Adams, Capital ......................................              85,000
    Bell, Capital .......................................              55,000
To close 1994 earnings to the partners' Capital accounts.
```

If total partnership income is inadequate to cover the agreed-upon salaries, both partners still receive their salaries, and the deficiency is then allocated to the partners. For example, if total income had been only $90,000, it would have been allocated as follows:

	Adams	Bell	Net Income
Net income			$ 90,000
Salaries to partners	$ 70,000	$ 40,000	(110,000)
Deficit to be divided equally:			$ (20,000)
Adams (50%)	(10,000)		
Bell (50%)		(10,000)	20,000
Total to each partner	$ 60,000	$ 30,000	$ -0-

The entry to close net income to the partners' capital accounts would then be:

```
Income Summary ..................................... 90,000
    Adams, Capital ..................................       60,000
    Bell, Capital ...................................       30,000
To close 1994 earnings to the partners' Capital accounts.
```

The three profit-allocation methods we have described involved fairly simple calculations. In some cases, salary, capital investment ratios, and stated ratios are combined with other factors, making the calculation far more complex. This added complexity is often necessary to achieve equity among partners when they contribute differing amounts of assets, time, and talent to the business.

As stated earlier, partnerships do not pay taxes on profits earned. Although they do file a tax return that shows how profits (or losses) are divided among the partners, it is for information purposes only. Taxes are paid by the individual partners, who include their portion of the partnership's profit (or deduct their share of the partnership's loss) on their personal tax returns. The income tax rules pertaining to partnerships are too complex to be discussed here, but you do need to know that all partnership income is taxable to the respective partners in the year it is earned, regardless of whether cash is distributed to them. In the Adams and Bell partnership, the partners would be taxed on their shares of the $140,000 net income, not on their withdrawals of $55,000 each. This principle is also true of proprietorships.

To Summarize *Partnership profits and losses can be shared in a variety of ways. Allocation arrangements are usually specified in the partnership agreement. If they are not, profits and losses must be shared equally. Losses must be shared in the same ratio as profits. Factors that are often considered in determining how to allocate profits are (1) the personal services provided by the partners, (2) the amounts of capital invested in the business by the partners, and (3) the risks being taken by the partners. Three common methods of distributing profits are (1) stated ratio, (2) capital investment ratio, and (3) allowance for salaries with the remainder at some stated ratio.*

> **BUSINESS ENVIRONMENT ESSAY**
> *Master Limited Partnerships*
>
> When Congress rewrote the tax law in 1986, it set the top rate on high income taxpayers at 28 percent. That's less than the 34 percent maximum for corporations, and marks the first time in memory that individuals have been taxed at lower rates than corporations. Since partnerships pay no income tax, a new type of partnership has emerged that avoids the higher corporate rate but still allows for large businesses whose shares trade on stock exchanges. This new entity is called the Master Limited Partnership (MLP). MLPs are partnerships with a general partner who retains full control and many limited partners who share in the profits, make no decisions, and whose liability is limited to their investments, much like that of corporate shareholders. Individuals can buy limited partnership interests for as little as $1,000 and they are usually meant to be held for 7 to 10 years.
>
> If an MLP were a corporation, it would pay 34 cents of each $1 in profits as taxes, leaving 66 cents in after-tax earnings. Assuming all profits are distributed as dividends, the shareholders, taxed at a 28 percent rate, would owe 18 cents on the 66 cents dividend, for a total tax bite of 52 cents on the original $1. But with an MLP, $1 in earnings produces no more than 28 cents in federal income taxes, based on the limited partner's individual rate. Is it any wonder that the Boston Celtics, Merrill Lynch (real-estate division), Houston Commonwealth Savings Association, and numerous other businesses are electing MLP status?
>
> Because MLPs are so attractive, it is inevitable that Congress will review them and maybe even revoke their special tax status. One possible result is that they could be treated as corporations for tax purposes.
>
> Source: Adapted from *Business Week,* December 19, 1986, p. 124, and *U.S. News & World Report,* March 30, 1987, p. 63.

ACCOUNTING FOR CHANGING PARTNERSHIP MEMBERS

Objective 6
Account for the admission of a new partner and withdrawal of an existing partner.

Partnership agreements specify the names of the partners and their respective duties, obligations, and rights. If a new partner is admitted or an original partner withdraws, the agreement is legally terminated, and a new one must be written. Note, however, that this does not necessarily end the business itself; it may continue to function, except that it will be a new legal entity with a new partner. In this section, we discuss the accounting for changes in partners' interests.

Either of two methods can be used to account for changes in a partnership: the book-value or the market-value approach. Because the admission of a new partner or the withdrawal of an existing partner makes necessary the creation of a new legal entity, the assets of the old partnership can be transferred to the new entity at their recorded book values or at their current market values. Transferring assets at book value is straightforward; transferring them at market value usually involves revaluing each asset and often recognizing **goodwill**. Proponents of the market-value approach argue that market values should be used whenever a new partnership is formed because they were used when the original partnership was created. If a new partner, for example, is willing to pay the withdrawing partner more than the book value of the withdrawing partner's Capital account to join the business, then it can be argued that the assets of the partnership are understated and should be written up. Proponents of the

goodwill *an intangible asset that exists when a business is valued at more than the fair market value of its net assets, usually due to strategic location, reputation, good customer relations, or similar factors; equal to the excess of the purchase price over the fair market value of the net assets purchased*

book-value approach argue that although a change in partners legally creates an entity, in substance the business is not changed.

In practice, although both alternatives are used, the book-value approach is more common, especially in large partnerships. It is even required in some cases. In this book, we will illustrate only the book-value alternative.

Admitting a New Partner

Sometimes a partnership will need additional capital or a person who will bring in new skills. Alternatively, a partnership may be so successful that individuals will ask to be admitted. If the partners are unable to invest more of their own capital or borrow the necessary funds, or if they find the idea of a new partner attractive, they may decide to admit someone who will contribute assets or needed skills. Of course, the new partner must be someone approved by all the existing partners.

A person may be admitted to a partnership in either of two ways: (1) by purchasing an ownership interest directly from one or more of the present partners or (2) by investing cash or other assets in the partnership. In the first case, where the interest is bought outright, payment is made directly to the original partner or partners, and the assets of the partnership are not affected. In the second case, where the interest is purchased through a direct investment in the partnership, the new partner's contribution increases the partnership's total assets and total partners' equity.

PURCHASING AN INTEREST. To illustrate the accounting for purchasing an interest from a partner, we will assume that at the end of 1994, Adams and Bell had capital balances of $110,000 each, as calculated here.

	Adams	Bell	Total
Initial investments	$ 90,000	$ 90,000	$180,000
Profits (shared equally)	70,000	70,000	140,000
Total	$160,000	$160,000	$320,000
Less withdrawals	(50,000)	(50,000)	(100,000)
Balance at 12/31/94	$110,000	$110,000	$220,000

Now assume that Dr. Adams decides to sell her interest in the partnership to Dr. Dick Rowe for $180,000. Since the transaction is between Adams and Rowe, it does not matter how much Rowe actually pays Adams for her interest: The amount recorded is the book value of the withdrawing partner's equity. So $110,000 is recorded, and Dr. Adams keeps the extra $70,000 as a bonus. The entry on the partnership books to record the sale to Dr. Rowe would be:

```
Adams, Capital .................................................. 110,000
    Rowe, Capital .............................................          110,000
To record the transfer of Dr. Adams's equity in the partnership to Dr. Rowe.
```

In the preceding example, Rowe purchased Adams's entire interest in the partnership. Assume now that Adams wants to remain a partner, but both she and Bell feel that the partnership needs another person. They decide to admit Dr. Dick Rowe, who agrees to pay $147,000 to Adams and Bell (not to the partnership). Of that sum, $63,000 is to go for a 30 percent interest in Dr. Adams's equity, and $84,000 is to go to Dr. Bell for a 40 percent interest in his equity. As the following calculations show, Adams and Bell now have capital balances of $77,000 and $66,000, respectively, and Rowe has a capital balance of $77,000:

		Sold		
Partner	Beginning Balance ×	Percentage =	Amount	Ending Balance
Adams...............	$110,000 ×	0.30 =	$33,000	$ 77,000
Bell	110,000 ×	0.40 =	44,000	66,000
Rowe	–0–		$77,000	77,000
Totals	$220,000			$220,000

The entry to record the transfer would be:

Adams, Capital	33,000	
Bell, Capital	44,000	
Rowe, Capital		77,000

To record the transfer of 30% of Adams's interest and 40% of Bell's interest to a new partner, Dr. Rowe.

Although Rowe paid more than the $77,000 book value assigned to his Capital account, only the book value of the purchased ownership interest is transferred. The excess amount does not show up on the partnership's records. The payments were made to Adams and Bell, not the partnership.

INVESTING DIRECTLY IN THE PARTNERSHIP. The second way to be admitted into a partnership is to buy an interest through a direct investment in the firm. This investment can be for an amount that is equal to, greater than, or less than the book value of the amount to be credited to the new partner's capital account. For example, if a new partner invests $90,000 when the book value is only $70,000, his or her Capital account is credited for $70,000, and the $20,000 above book value is a bonus to the original partners. We will illustrate all three situations using independent examples.

To illustrate the investment of an amount equal to book value, we assume that on December 31, 1994, Adams and Bell decide to admit Dr. Jonathan Dole, a noted orthopedic surgeon, to the partnership. Dr. Dole agrees to invest $85,000 for a one-third interest. Assuming that the Capital accounts of Drs. Adams and Bell are $70,000 and $100,000, respectively, on December 31, 1994, Dr. Dole's payment of $85,000 is exactly one-third of the new total capital.

Adams's capital	$ 70,000
Bell's capital	100,000
Dole's investment	85,000
Total capital of new partnership	$255,000
One-third interest ($255,000 ÷ 3)	$ 85,000

The entry to record the admission of Dole would be:

Cash	85,000	
Dole, Capital		85,000

To record the admission of Dole in to the partnership for a one-third interest.

You should note, however, that a one-third interest in the partnership does not automatically entitle Dole to one-third of the profits. The profit-sharing arrangement, which would be specified in the new partnership agreement, might depend on other factors, such as the services Dole will provide.

In some cases, a person may be willing to pay an amount greater than the book value to join the partnership. Such a situation may exist because the business has exceptionally high earnings, a good location, an excellent clientele, or other attributes. Under the book-value approach, when a new partner invests an amount greater than the book value, the excess is said to be a bonus to the existing partners and is credited to their Capital accounts.

To illustrate, we assume again that Adams's and Bell's capital balances are $70,000 and $100,000, respectively, and that Dr. Dole is willing to pay $130,000 for a one-third interest in the partnership. The following calculation is made to determine how much Dole's Capital account should be:

Adams's capital	$ 70,000
Bell's capital	100,000
Dole's investment	130,000
Total capital of new partnership	$300,000
One-third interest ($300,000 ÷ 3)	$100,000

Based on these calculations, Dole's Capital account should be $100,000. The excess $30,000 would then be allocated to Adams's and Bell's Capital accounts according to their original profit-sharing ratio. Assuming that they share profits equally, each gets $15,000. The entry to record the admission of Dole at a $130,000 investment is:

Cash	130,000	
Dole, Capital		100,000
Adams, Capital		15,000
Bell, Capital		15,000

To record the admission of Dole into the partnership at a one-third interest.

If a partnership is short of cash or needs someone with a special skill or other characteristic, a new partner might be admitted for an amount less than book value.

To illustrate, we assume that Drs. Adams and Bell are anxious to have Dr. Dole join their partnership because they believe that his presence will enhance their reputations and increase their clientele. So on December 31, 1994, they agree to allow Dole to pay only $70,000 for a one-third interest in the partnership. As the following calculations show, Dole is receiving an interest worth $80,000 for only $70,000:

Adams's capital	$ 70,000
Bell's capital	100,000
Dole's investment	70,000
Total capital of new partnership	$240,000
One-third interest ($240,000 ÷ 3)	$ 80,000

With the book-value approach, the new partner is said to receive a bonus, and the old partners' capital balances are reduced accordingly. The amount that each partner's capital balance is reduced depends on the profit-sharing arrangement. If we again assume that Adams and Bell split profits and losses equally, each partner's capital would be reduced by $5,000, and the entry to record the admission of Dole for a $70,000 investment would be:

Cash	70,000	
Adams, Capital	5,000	
Bell, Capital	5,000	
Dole, Capital		80,000

To record the admission of Dole to the partnership for a one-third interest.

To Summarize *A new partner may gain admission into a partnership either by purchasing an interest directly from an existing partner (or partners) or by investing in the partnership. If the interest is purchased from another partner, the transaction is a personal one between the buyer and the seller, and regardless of the purchase price, the only entry on the books of the partnership is the transfer of the capital from the old partner to the new partner at book value. Admission by direct investment in the partnership can result in a bonus to the old partners, no bonus to anyone, or a bonus to the new partner, depending on the amount of the investment.*

Exhibit 14-4 summarizes the various ways a new partner can be admitted into a partnership and the effect each way has on partnership assets and the individual partners' Capital accounts, assuming that assets are transferred to the new partnership at book value rather than at market value.

The Withdrawal of a Partner

A partner may withdraw from a partnership for a variety of reasons—reaching retirement age or a desire to start a new company, for example. Because assets are divided upon the withdrawal of a partner, to avoid misunderstandings, most partnership agreements specify whether or not an audit must be performed when a partner withdraws, how values will be assigned to company assets, whether a bonus will be given to the departing partner, how that partner will be paid, and other procedures to be followed.

Exhibit 14-4 *Admission of a New Partner*

```
                            Partner is admitted.
                   ┌─────────────────┴─────────────────┐
         New partner buys                    New partner
         old partner's                       invests directly in
         interest.                           the partnership.
```

New partner buys all of old partner's interest.	New partner buys a portion of old partner's interest.	New partner pays an amount greater than book value of the ownership interest.	New partner pays an amount equal to book value of the ownership interest.	New partner pays an amount less than book value of the ownership interest.
Total assets and owners' equity of the partnership do not change because the transaction is a personal one. Old partner's capital balance is transferred to new partner.	Total assets and owners' equity of the partnership do not change because the transaction is a personal one. Old partner's capital balance is reduced to book value of the ownership interest, and new partner's Capital account is opened at book value of the ownership interest.	Total assets and owners' equity of the partnership increase. A bonus is given to old partners. Their capital balances are increased in accordance with their profit-sharing ratios, and new partner's Capital account is opened at book value of the ownership interest.	Total assets and owners' equity of the partnership increase. No bonus is involved. New partner's Capital account is opened at the amount paid, which is the book value of the ownership interest.	Total assets and owners' equity of the partnership increase. A bonus is given to the new partner. Old partner's capital balances are reduced in accordance with their profit-sharing ratios, and new partner's Capital account is opened at book value of the ownership interest.

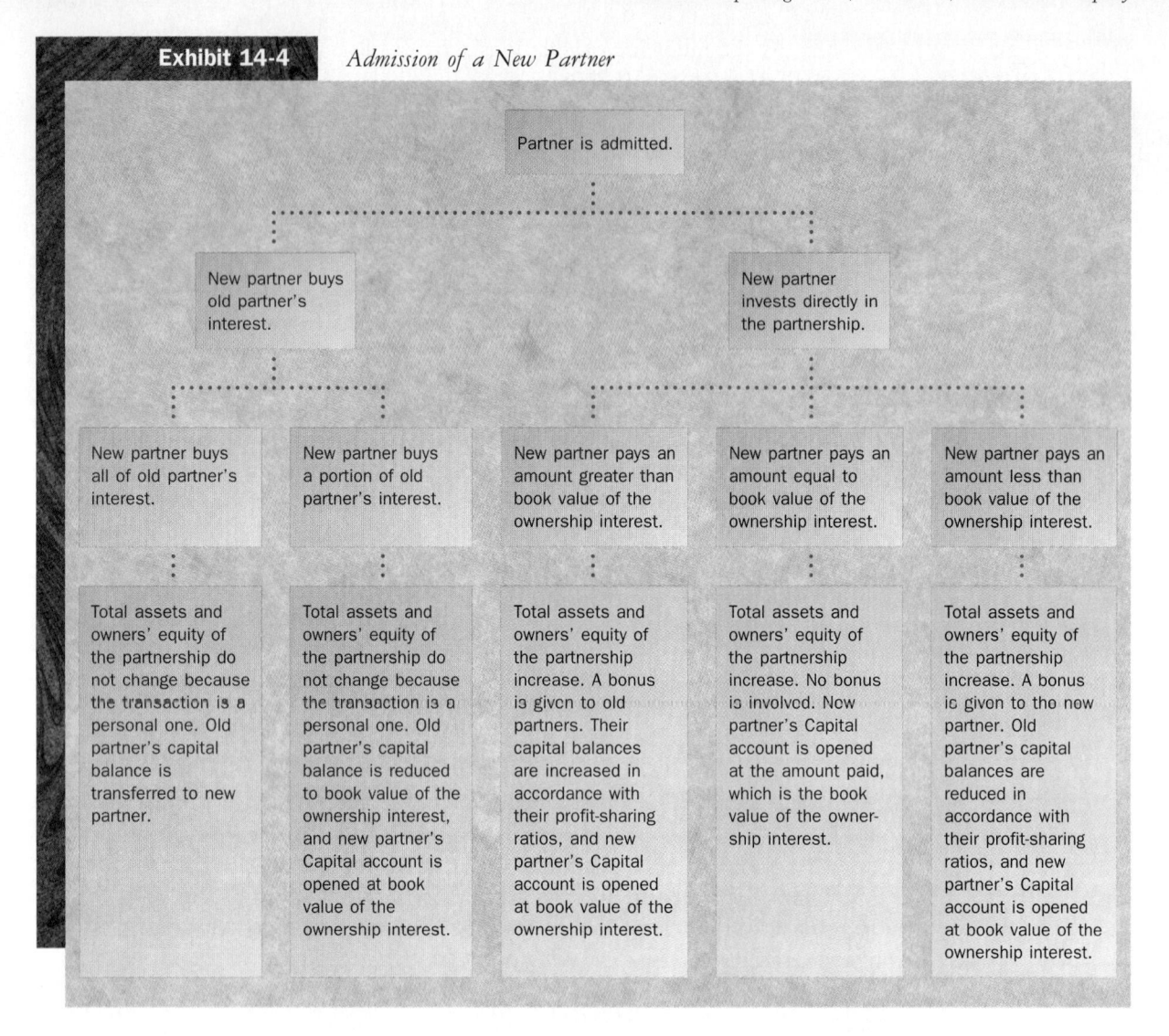

Because the withdrawal of a partner is the reciprocal of admitting a partner, the transactions and accounting are quite similar. Just as there are several ways to admit a new partner, there are several ways a partner can withdraw from a partnership. Common alternatives are (1) selling his or her interest to an outsider, (2) selling his or her interest to the other partners, or (3) being paid with partnership assets. If the partner is paid with partnership assets, the amount may be equal to, greater than, or less than the departing partner's capital balance, depending on the market values of the partnership's assets, the existing agreement, and other factors.

SELLING AN INTEREST TO AN OUTSIDER. A partner can sell his or her interest to an outsider only with the consent of the other partner or partners. The price of the interest is a personal matter between the existing partner and the new partner. Therefore, regardless of the amount paid to the departing partner, the entry made in the partnership records is simply to replace the old partner's capital balance with the new partner's capital balance for the same amount.

To illustrate the selling of an interest to an outsider, we will assume that Drs. Adams, Bell, and Dole now work together in a partnership and have capital balances of $70,000, $100,000, and $60,000, respectively, on December 31, 1994. If, on that date, Adams sold her interest to Dr. Gates for $90,000, the entry to record the transfer of capital balances in the company's books would be:

Adams, Capital	70,000	
Gates, Capital		70,000
To record the sale of Adams's interest in the partnership to Dr. Gates.		

The $20,000 above book value is a bonus to the departing partner, but is not accounted for on the books of the partnership.

SELLING AN INTEREST TO THE OTHER PARTNERS. A partner will sometimes withdraw from a partnership by selling his or her interest to the other partners. If the remaining partners pay for the departing partner's interest with their personal assets, the transaction is again considered to be outside the business. The only entry made in the partnership records is the transfer of the capital balances. Therefore, no matter what price is paid, if Adams sells Bell and Dole each $35,000 of her $70,000 interest in the partnership, the entry to record the withdrawal of Adams would be as follows:

Adams, Capital	70,000	
Bell, Capital		35,000
Dole, Capital		35,000
To record the transfer of Adams's partnership interest to Bell and Dole.		

PAYMENT TO A DEPARTING PARTNER FROM THE PARTNERSHIP'S ASSETS. The partnership agreement may specify that the assets of the business be used to pay the departing partner. In such cases, the agreement would probably also specify how assets are to be valued in order to determine how much the exiting partner is to be paid. The agreement might stipulate that a withdrawing partner would receive an amount equal to the book value of his or her interest in the business. More often, however, a partnership agreement will provide for valuation of the withdrawing partner's interest at market value rather than book value. Because of inflation, goodwill, and other factors, it is very unlikely that the market value of the firm's assets would be equal to its book value. If the amount paid is more than the book value of the withdrawing partner's capital balance, the excess reduces the remaining partners' capital balances. Conversely, if the amount paid the exiting partner is less than the book value of his or her equity, the remaining partners' capital balances are increased.

To illustrate, we again assume that Adams, Bell, and Dole have capital balances of $70,000, $100,000, and $60,000 on December 31, 1994. The following three entries show how Adams's withdrawal would be recorded if she were paid $50,000, $70,000, or $100,000, respectively, from partnership assets and if Bell and Dole split profits and losses equally.

Amount Less than Book Value: $50,000

Adams, Capital	70,000	
Cash		50,000
Bell, Capital		10,000
Dole, Capital		10,000

To record the payment of $50,000 to Adams on her withdrawal from the partnership.

Amount Equal to Book Value: $70,000

Adams, Capital	70,000	
Cash		70,000

To record the payment of $70,000 to Adams on her withdrawal from the partnership.

Amount Greater than Book Value: $100,000

Adams, Capital	70,000	
Bell, Capital	15,000	
Dole, Capital	15,000	
Cash		100,000

To record the payment of $100,000 to Adams on her withdrawal from the partnership.

Note that when the departing partner is paid more or less than book value, the remaining partners' capital balances are increased or decreased in accordance with their profit-sharing ratios, not their capital balance ratios.

The Death of a Partner

The death of a partner has basically the same effect on a partnership as the withdrawal of a partner. In all cases, the partnership agreement is terminated, and a new one must be written if the partnership is to continue. Because assets often have to be valued to determine how much to pay the partner's estate, an audit may be conducted. The original partnership agreement should specify how this and other matters are to be handled.

Two aspects of the accounting required upon the death of a partner are somewhat different from accounting for the withdrawal of a partner. First, the payment is made to an estate. Second, when a partner dies, interim financial statements are usually prepared so that the capital balances can be updated to the date of death.

Because the success of many partnerships is so dependent upon the contribution of the individual partners, partnerships often obtain life insurance on key partners, with the partnership named as the beneficiary. Then, upon the death of a partner, the proceeds are used to pay the estate of the deceased. Having life insurance policies ensures that sufficient cash will be available to pay the estate of the deceased partner.

Chapter 14 *Owners' Equity—Proprietorships and Partnerships*

> **To Summarize** A *partner can withdraw from a partnership any time he or she chooses, provided that an agreement can be reached with the remaining partners. To avoid misunderstandings, the partnership agreement should specify procedures to be followed if a partner exercises this right of withdrawal. Withdrawal can be handled in one of three ways. The departing partner can sell his or her interest to (1) an outsider, (2) the remaining partners, or (3) the partnership. If partnership assets are used, the remaining partners' capital balances increase, stay the same, or decrease, depending on the amount paid.*
>
> *Exhibit 14-5 summarizes the various ways a member may withdraw from a partnership, and the effect each way has on the assets and liabilities of the partnership and the remaining partners' capital balances, assuming that assets are transferred to the new partnership at book value.*

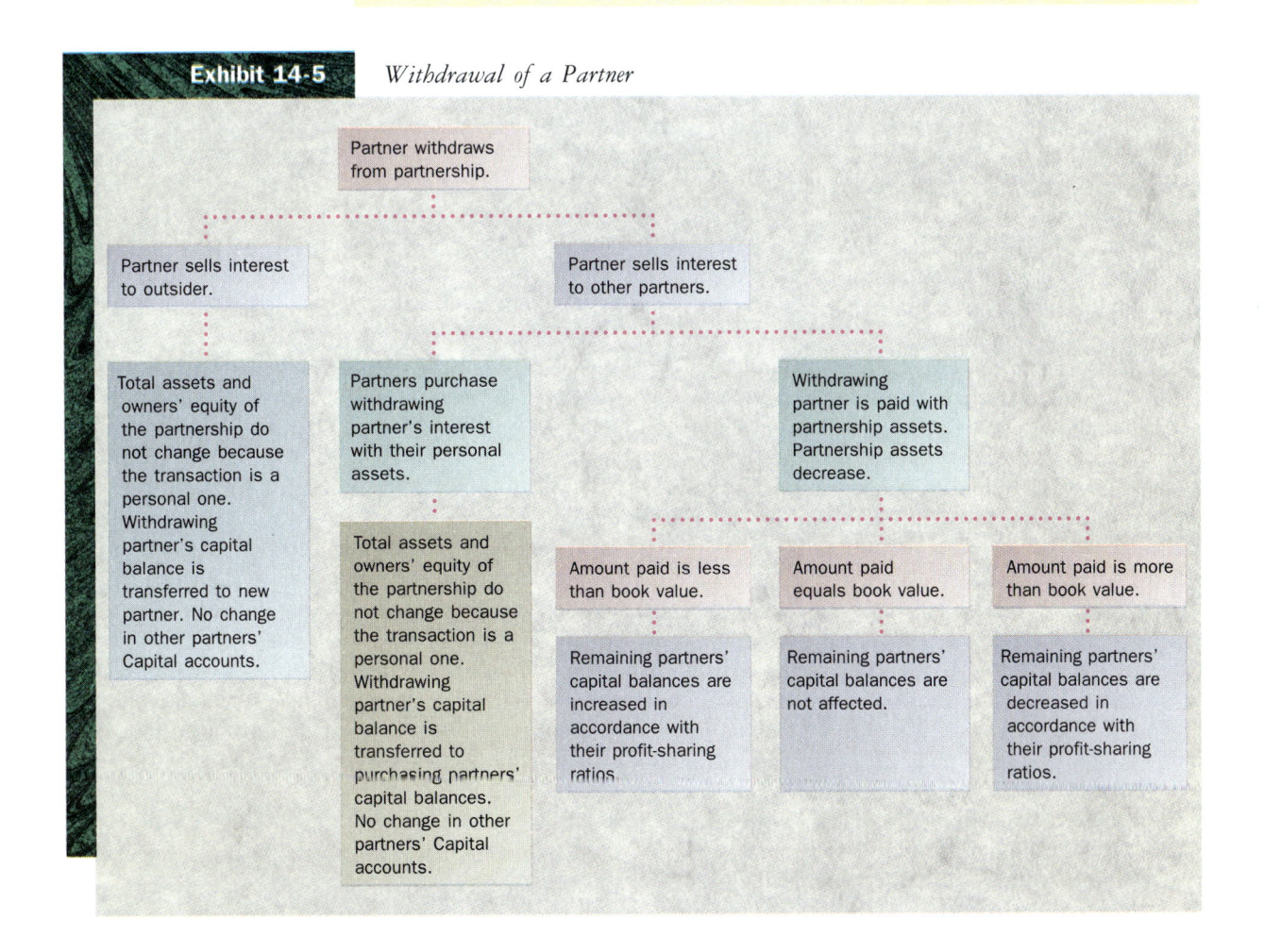

Exhibit 14-5 *Withdrawal of a Partner*

```
                        Partner withdraws
                        from partnership.
           ┌───────────────────┼───────────────────┐
Partner sells interest                    Partner sells interest
to outsider.                              to other partners.
```

Partner sells interest to outsider	Partners purchase withdrawing partner's interest with their personal assets	Withdrawing partner is paid with partnership assets. Partnership assets decrease.
Total assets and owners' equity of the partnership do not change because the transaction is a personal one. Withdrawing partner's capital balance is transferred to new partner. No change in other partners' Capital accounts.	Total assets and owners' equity of the partnership do not change because the transaction is a personal one. Withdrawing partner's capital balance is transferred to purchasing partners' capital balances. No change in other partners' Capital accounts.	**Amount paid is less than book value.** Remaining partners' capital balances are increased in accordance with their profit-sharing ratios. / **Amount paid equals book value.** Remaining partners' capital balances are not affected. / **Amount paid is more than book value.** Remaining partners' capital balances are decreased in accordance with their profit-sharing ratios.

THE LIQUIDATION OF A PARTNERSHIP

Any time a new partner is admitted or an existing partner withdraws or dies, a partnership is legally terminated. This does not mean that the *business* has to be terminated. Usually, partnership agreements define admission and withdrawal procedures in such a way that there is no outward appearance that any change has taken place.

Sometimes, however, a business is terminated. The process of dissolving a business is called **liquidation**. Liquidation means that all assets except cash are sold or disposed of, liabilities are paid, and the remaining cash is divided among the partners. Three steps are usually involved in a partnership liquidation: (1) noncash assets of the business are sold, (2) the profit or loss from the sale of assets is allocated to the partners in accordance with their profit-sharing ratio, and (3) the liabilities are paid and the remaining cash is distributed to the partners. Because liquidation of a partnership is an advanced accounting topic, we will not discuss it further in this text.

liquidation *the process of dissolving a business by selling the assets, paying the debts, and distributing the remaining equity to the owners*

Review of Learning Objectives

Objective 1

Identify the major characteristics shared by proprietorships and partnerships. Proprietorships and partnerships are unincorporated businesses. Proprietorships are owned by one person; partnerships are owned by two or more persons or entities. Partnerships and proprietorships share three characteristics: (1) ease of formation, (2) limited life, and (3) unlimited liability.

Objective 2

Record and report changes in the owner's equity of a proprietorship. There are two owner's equity accounts in a proprietorship: a Capital and a Drawings account. The Capital account is increased by owner contributions and profits and decreased by owner withdrawals and losses.

Objective 3

Identify the major characteristics unique to partnerships. Three additional characteristics unique to partnerships are (1) mutual agency, which means that each partner is an agent and can bind the partnership to business agreements; (2) co-ownership of partnership property, which means that property transferred to the partnership is jointly owned by all partners; and (3) sharing of partnership profits, meaning that all partners have a right to share in partnership profits and an obligation to share in partnership losses.

Objective 4

Describe and apply basic partnership accounting and reporting procedures. There are several aspects of partnership accounting. Events commonly accounted for are investments by owners, withdrawals by partners, partnership profits and losses, admission of new partners, withdrawal of old partners, the death of a partner, and partnership liquidation.

Investments and withdrawals by partners are treated in the same way as they are in a proprietorship. That is, investments increase the partners' capital balances, and withdrawals decrease the capital balances.

In addition to the balance sheet and income statement, a statement of partners' capital is usually prepared at year-end. This statement reconciles the ending capital balances with the beginning capital balances by adding profits and additional investments and deducting losses and partner withdrawals.

Objective 5

Explain and apply various methods of allocating partnership profits and losses. Partnership profits and losses can be shared in any way the partners specify. Factors considered in determining the allocation of profits and losses include amounts invested by owners, time and energy spent by each partner, and risks taken by the respective partners. Three common methods of allocating profits and losses are stated ratio, capital investment ratio, and allowance for salaries with the remainder at stated ratio.

Objective 6

Account for the admission of a new partner and withdrawal of an existing partner. New partners can be admitted only with the consent of all existing partners. A new partner may gain admission by purchasing the interest of an existing partner (or partners) or by investing directly in the partnership. When a partner's interest is purchased by an outsider, the price paid in the transaction is extraneous to the partnership; only the book value of the departing partner's capital balance is transferred to the new partner. With regard to investing in the partnership, since there is a legal obligation to form a new partnership because of a change in partners, the partnership can choose to restate the assets of the old partnership at their market values or transfer them to the new partnership at their book values. With the book-value approach, if the amount invested is greater or less than the book value of the equity received, the investment is still recorded at book value. (If the investment is greater than the book value, the original partners receive bonuses; if the investment is less, the new partner receives a bonus.)

A partner can withdraw from a partnership any time he or she desires. If a partner withdraws, the departing partner's interest can be purchased by an outsider or by the other partners, either with their personal assets or with partnership assets. Purchase of one partner's equity by an outsider or by other partners does not involve a change in the partners' asset or liability accounts. The other alternative, payment of partnership assets, results in an increase, no change, or a decrease in the remaining partners' capital balances, depending on the amount paid.

Any time a partner is admitted, withdraws, or dies, the old partnership is legally terminated, and a new one is created. When this occurs, a new partnership agreement should be executed. Such changes often go unnoticed by outsiders because the business of the partnership continues without interruption. However, sometimes a partnership's business is terminated. The process of dissolving a business is referred to as liquidation.

Key Terms and Concepts

Capital account *(586)*
Drawings account *(586)*
goodwill *(597)*
liquidation *(606)*

mutual agency *(589)*
partnership *(584)*
partnership agreement *(585)*
proprietorship *(584)*

statement of partners' capital *(591)*
unlimited liability *(585)*

Review Problem

Distribution of Income and Admission of a Partner

On January 1, 1993, Jackie Truman and Beth Palmer, both certified public accountants (CPAs), entered into a partnership agreement to start a public accounting firm. In forming the partnership, Truman and Palmer contributed $40,000 and $60,000, respectively. Their partnership agreement specified the following: Truman was to be the full-time manager of the firm, and she would receive a salary of $18,000 per year. All remaining profits (or losses) were to be shared equally.

Required:
1. Compute the amount of profit allocated to Truman and Palmer in 1993, 1994, and 1995, if total profits during those 3 years were $44,000, $56,000, and $70,000, respectively. Make the necessary journal entries to close net income to the partners' respective Capital accounts in each year.
2. Assume that on January 1, 1996, Mark Hernandez, CPA, offers to pay $50,000 to Truman and Palmer for a 20 percent interest in the partnership. Truman and Palmer agree to admit Hernandez on these terms because the business is growing rapidly, and Hernandez is a respected and experienced professional accountant. The capital balances of Truman and Palmer on January 1, 1996, are $48,000 and $72,000, respectively. Record the admission of Hernandez to the partnership, assuming that his investment is to represent a 20 percent interest in the total partners' capital and that any bonus is to be divided equally between Truman and Palmer.

Solution **1. Allocation of Profits**

	Truman	Palmer	Net Income
1993:			
Net income			$44,000
Salary to Truman	$18,000		(18,000)
Remainder to be divided equally:			$ 26,000
Truman	13,000		
Palmer		$13,000	(26,000)
Total to each partner	$31,000	$13,000	$ -0-
1994:			
Net income			$56,000
Salary to Truman	$18,000		(18,000)
Remainder to be divided equally:			$ 38,000
Truman	19,000		
Palmer		$19,000	(38,000)
Total to each partner	$37,000	$19,000	$ -0-
1995:			
Net income			$ 70,000
Salary to Truman	$18,000		(18,000)
Remainder to be divided equally:			$ 52,000
Truman	26,000		
Palmer		$26,000	(52,000)
Total to each partner	$44,000	$26,000	$ -0-

1993 Entry:

Income Summary	44,000	
Truman, Capital		31,000
Palmer, Capital		13,000

To close 1993 earnings to the partners' Capital accounts.

1994 Entry:

Income Summary	56,000	
Truman, Capital		37,000
Palmer, Capital		19,000

To close 1994 earnings to the partners' Capital accounts.

1995 Entry:

Income Summary	70,000	
Truman, Capital		44,000
Palmer, Capital		26,000

To close 1995 earnings to the partners' Capital accounts.

2. Admission of Mark Hernandez

Capital balance before investment ($48,000 + $72,000)	$120,000
Investment by Hernandez	50,000
Total capital of new partnership	$170,000
Hernandez's 20% interest ($170,000 × 0.20)	$ 34,000
Hernandez's investment	$ 50,000
Hernandez's capital	34,000
Bonus to be divided equally	$ 16,000

Jan. 1, 1996 Entry:

Cash	50,000	
Truman, Capital		8,000
Palmer, Capital		8,000
Hernandez, Capital		34,000

To record the admission of Mark Hernandez to the partnership at a 20 percent interest.

Discussion Questions

1. What are the major differences between a partnership and a corporation?
2. How is a proprietorship or partnership established?
3. Identify some of the elements that should be spelled out in a partnership agreement.
4. Does the death of a partner legally terminate a partnership? If so, does it mean that the partnership must cease operating?
5. Are partners legally liable for the actions of other partners? Explain.
6. Is the payment of salary to a proprietor an expense that would be deducted on a proprietorship's income statement? Explain.
7. In a corporation, contributions by owners and accumulated earnings of the business are separated into Contributed Capital and Retained Earnings accounts. Are earnings and contributions separated into different accounts in a partnership? Explain.
8. If a partnership agreement does not specify how profits are to be shared by the partners, how much does each partner receive?
9. What factors are usually considered in determining how much profit each partner should receive?
10. Are partnerships taxed on their profits?
11. When a new partner is admitted, can the partnership increase the recorded amounts of its assets up to their current market values?
12. What are the two ways a new partner can be admitted to a partnership?
13. What steps are usually involved in liquidating a partnership?

Exercises

E14-1
Accounting for a Proprietorship

At the beginning of 1994, Marena Sanchez decided to go into the business of making and selling decorative artificial plants. During the year ending December 31, 1994, Sanchez had the following transactions:

(a) Withdrew $20,000 from a personal savings account and deposited that amount in a new checking account to be used solely for the business.
(b) Paid cash to purchase $12,000 of materials needed to make plants.
(c) Invested another $24,000 in the business.
(d) Sold 450 plants during the year at $60 each for cash.
(e) Incurred and paid operating expenses for the year of $10,500.
(f) At the end of the year, $4,000 of materials remained on hand. The cost of materials used was transferred to a Cost of Goods Sold account.
(g) Withdrew $5,000 for personal use.

Prepare journal entries to record the transactions and a statement of owner's equity for the year.

E14-2
Partnership Accounting

Jill Emerson owned a pet shop. On August 1, 1994, Emerson accepted Allan Jacobs as a partner. At that time, Emerson's Capital account showed a balance of $135,000. Jacobs contributed $90,000 cash for a 40 percent share in both capital and earnings.

During the rest of 1994, the following transactions took place:

(a) Emerson withdrew $12,000, and Jacobs withdrew $4,000.
(b) Emerson invested another $4,500 cash, and Jacobs contributed a truck valued at $6,000.
(c) Net income from August 1, 1994, through December 31, 1994, was $26,700.

Given this information:

1. Prepare the journal entries (including closing entries) for the transactions.
2. Prepare a statement of partners' capital for the period ending December 31, 1994, for the Emerson and Jacobs partnership.

E14-3
Starting a Partnership

On July 1, 1994, Dr. Wright and Dr. O'Flaherty decided to form a partnership by combining all the assets and liabilities of their respective dental practices. The partnership will have a new and separate set of books. Dr. Wright's balance sheet at June 30, 1994, was as follows:

Assets

Cash		$ 27,000
Accounts receivable	$116,000	
Less allowance for uncollectible accounts	6,600	109,400
Dental equipment	$ 52,900	
Less accumulated depreciation	24,200	28,700
Building	$169,400	
Less accumulated depreciation	13,500	155,900
Total assets		$321,000

Liabilities and Proprietor's Equity

Accounts payable	$ 22,700
Mortgage payable	150,000
Dr. Wright, capital	148,300
Total liabilities and proprietor's equity	$321,000

The partners agreed that $5,600 of the accounts receivable were uncollectible and that $2,400 was a reasonable allowance for the uncollectibility of the remaining receivables. They also agreed that the dental equipment and the building should be recorded at their respective fair market values of $46,000 and $182,000.

Prepare the journal entry to record Dr. Wright's investment in the partnership.

E14-4
Allocation of Partnership Income

On January 1, 1994, Johnson & Smith formed a partnership by investing $35,000 and $50,000, respectively. The partners agreed that the most equitable plan of income sharing was to allow monthly salaries of $1,500 for Johnson and $1,250 for Smith. The partnership agreement makes no other mention of the sharing of profits and losses. For the year ended December 31, 1994, the partnership had net income of $75,000. Compute each partner's share of 1994 income.

E14-5
Allocation of Partnership Income

On January 1, 1994, Stone and Pound formed a partnership by investing $500,000 and $250,000, respectively. The partnership agreement specified that partners would first be paid salaries of $50,000 and $25,000, respectively; that remaining profits would be shared equally; and that losses and deficiencies would be allocated propor-

Chapter 14 *Owners' Equity—Proprietorships and Partnerships* 611

tionally based on the beginning-of-the-year capital account balances. Net income for 1994 was $50,000. Compute each partner's share of the 1994 net income.

E14-6
Admitting a New Partner

Eldon Thomas and Don McKinley have agreed to admit Kim Griffin to their law partnership on January 1, 1995. Griffin will be given a one-third interest in the partnership for an investment of $20,000 cash plus a library of law books that had cost Griffin $5,000. The current fair market value of the library is $10,000.

The balance sheet of Thomas & McKinley on December 31, 1994, was as follows:

Thomas & McKinley
Balance Sheet
December 31, 1994

Assets

Cash	$ 5,000
Accounts receivable	25,000
Equipment	51,000
Accumulated depreciation	(9,000)
Total assets	$72,000

Liabilities and Partners' Equity

Accounts payable	$ 6,000
Notes payable	15,000
Thomas, capital	28,500
McKinley, capital	22,500
Total liabilities and partners' equity	$72,000

Thomas and McKinley currently share profits and losses in a ratio of 60%/40%.

1. Prepare the journal entry to record the admission of Griffin to the partnership.
2. Compute the partners' capital balances as of January 1, 1995.

E14-7
Admitting a New Partner

Prior to the admission of Danielle Harrison to the partnership of Brown & Jacobsen, the capital accounts showed balances of $68,000 for Brown and $42,000 for Jacobsen. The partners have always shared partnership profits and losses in a ratio of 67%/33%. On July 1, 1994, Harrison, a well-known salesperson, was to be given a 40 percent share of the partnership for an investment of $30,000 cash and a personal computer that originally cost $6,000 (fair market value, $4,000).

1. Prepare the journal entry to record Danielle Harrison's investment in the new partnership.
2. Compute the partners' capital balances as of July 1, 1994.

E14-8
Withdrawal of a Partner

On June 30, 1994, Stacey Lyman decided to sell her interest in the partnership of Lyman, Frost, & James. The partners' capital accounts at that date were $80,000, $90,000, and $100,000, respectively.

1. Given this information, prepare the journal entry to record the sale of Lyman's partnership for each of the following independent cases:
    (a) With the approval of the other partners, Lyman sold her interest to Roger Trump for $124,000 cash.

(b) Lyman sold half of her partnership interest to Frost and the other half to James for $26,000 each.

2. Would the journal entry in item (a) differ if Lyman were to accept $24,000 cash and a $80,000 note from Trump? If so, how?

E14-9
Withdrawal of a Partner

On August 30, 1994, Blake Watson retired from the partnership of Watson, Whyte, & Rigg. At that time, the partners' capital balances were $120,000, $100,000, and $80,000, respectively. Watson, Whyte, and Rigg share profits and losses in the ratio of 40%/30%/30%. Assuming Whyte & Rigg plan to continue business under a new partnership agreement, prepare the journal entries to record the retirement of Watson, given the following situations:

1. Watson sells 1/3 of his partnership interest to Whyte for $50,000 and 2/3 of his interest to Rigg for $100,000.
2. Watson is given $40,000 cash, equipment that cost $80,000 and has accumulated depreciation of $32,000, and a note for $80,000. All payments are made from partnership assets, and the note is a partnership liability. Whyte and Rigg will share profits and losses equally.

Problem Set A

P14A-1
Accounting for a Proprietorship

On January 1, 1994, Pat Larsen decided to open the Donut Shop. Pat deposited $40,000 of her own money in a company bank account and obtained a $30,000 loan from a local bank. During its first year of operation, the shop had net income of $84,000. Pat withdrew a lump sum of $48,000 from the business that year to cover personal living expenses.

Required:
1. Prepare journal entries to record:
   (a) Pat's original contribution to the firm.
   (b) The bank loan.
   (c) Pat's withdrawal for her living expenses.
   (d) Any closing entries required at year-end.
2. Prepare a statement of owner's equity for 1994.
3. **Interpretive Question** How would the accounting for the transactions in part (1) be different if Pat's business were a corporation?

P14A-2
Partnership Accounting

On January 1, 1994, Reed and Bailey established a partnership to sell fruit.

(a) Reed invested $42,000 cash in the partnership, and Bailey invested $20,000 cash and a building valued at $25,000.
(b) Reed invested another $6,000 cash. Bailey donated a truck valued at $7,000.
(c) Reed withdrew $11,000 cash, and Bailey withdrew $6,300 of inventory.
(d) A fire destroyed half of the building donated by Bailey. There was no insurance on the building.
(e) Reed and Bailey agree to admit a third partner on March 1 of the next year. This partner, Kiefer, promises to invest $50,000 cash.

Required: Assuming net income for 1994 was $19,000 and the partners share profits equally:

1. Journalize the transactions.
2. Journalize the closing entries.

Chapter 14 Owners' Equity—Proprietorships and Partnerships

3. Compute each partner's capital balance at the end of 1994.
4. What is the relationship between the amount of capital contributed by each owner and the way profits are to be allocated?

P14A-3
Allocation of Partnership Profits and Losses

SPREADSHEET PROBLEM

Dara Muley and Richard Whitetail are in the process of forming a real estate partnership. In order to complete their partnership agreement, they need to determine an equitable method of allocating partnership profits and losses. Muley is investing $25,000 in the partnership; Whitetail is investing $48,000. Based on the amount of time each partner expects to devote to the business, they have agreed that Muley's services would be worth $25,000 annually and that Whitetail's services would be worth $18,000 annually. Estimated net income for the partnership is $18,000 for 1993 and $55,000 for 1994.

Required:
1. Compute each partner's share of the partnership's net income for 1993 and 1994 under each of the following proposed allocation methods:
   (a) The partners do not agree on any method.
   (b) Muley and Whitetail share profits in a ratio of 60%/40%.
   (c) The partners agree to share profits in the ratio of their original investments.
   (d) The partners agree to share profits by making salary allowances to each partner according to the value of their services, with any balance (or deficiency) being shared equally by the partners.
2. Prepare a schedule of estimated income under the four alternatives using the following format:

	1993		1994	
Plan	Muley	Whitetail	Muley	Whitetail

3. **Interpretive Question** Which allocation method is the most fair? Explain.

P14A-4
Admitting a New Partner

Prior to the admission of Carson to the partnership of Abbott and Becker, the capital accounts showed $80,000 for Abbott and $40,000 for Becker. The partners share profits and losses in the ratio of ⅔/⅓, respectively. The partners are considering the following two scenarios for Carson's admission:

1. Carson will pay $30,000 for a 25% interest in the partnership.
2. Carson will contribute $25,000 cash, land with a fair market value of $17,000 and a book value of $15,000, and a warehouse with a fair market value of $24,000 and a book value of $20,000 for a ⅓ interest.

Required: Prepare the necessary journal entry to admit Carson under each scenario, and show the Capital account balances after admission.

P14A-5
Preparation of Partnership Financial Statements and Admission of a Partner

On January 1, 1994, Hanna Oldroyd, Don Blake, and Myrna Skinner formed the partnership of Oldroyd, Blake, and Skinner with investments of $50,000, $30,000, and $20,000, respectively. They agreed to share profits in a ratio of 3:2:1. During 1994, the partnership had a net income of $240,000. There were no withdrawals during 1994. On January 1, 1995, Mitch Long purchased one-fifth of Oldroyd's interest, one-third of Blake's interest, and one-third of Skinner's interest for $110,000. The partnership agreement of Oldroyd, Blake, Skinner, & Long called for the allocation of profits and losses in a stated ratio of 40%/20%/10%/30%.

Required:
1. Prepare a statement of partners' capital at December 31, 1994.
2. Prepare the journal entries to record the admission of Mitch Long to the partnership.
3. What are the partners' capital balances on January 1, 1995?

P14A-6
Withdrawal of a Partner

On March 31, 1994, Will Ekker retired from the partnership of Ekker, Maybe, & Brown. At that time, the partners' capital balances were $120,000, $100,000, and $80,000, respectively. The partners share partnership profits and losses in the ratio 50%/30%/20%.

Required: Assuming that Maybe and Brown plan to continue business under a new partnership agreement, prepare the journal entries to record the retirement of Ekker, given the following independent situations:

1. With the approval of the other partners, Ekker sells his partnership interest to Don Dawson for $140,000 cash.
2. With the approval of the other partners, Ekker sells his partnership interest to Dawson for $60,000 cash and a $100,000 note.
3. Ekker sells one-third of his partnership interest to Maybe for $60,000 and two-thirds of his interest to Brown for $120,000.
4. Ekker's interest in the partnership is settled with a cash payment of $40,000 from the partnership assets and a note for $80,000.
5. Ekker is given $60,000 cash and equipment that cost $40,000 and that has accumulated depreciation of $12,000 for his equity in the partnership. (All payments are made from partnership assets.)
6. Ekker is given $40,000 cash, equipment that cost $80,000 and that has accumulated depreciation of $32,000, and an $80,000 note for his interest in the partnership. (All payments are made from partnership assets.)

P14A-7
Partnership Financial Statements and Admission of a New Partner

On June 30, 1994, the adjusted trial balance of Martin & Seggars, attorneys-at-law, was as follows:

	Debits	Credits
Cash	$ 8,550	
Accounts Receivable	15,800	
Allowance for Uncollectible Accounts		$ 1,300
Office Equipment (new)	13,800	
Office Furniture	6,400	
Accumulated Depreciation, Office Furniture		4,800
Accounts Payable		2,300
Notes Payable		3,000
Martin, Capital		10,000
Seggars, Capital		10,150
Martin, Drawings	18,000	
Seggars, Drawings	19,500	
Professional Fees		78,500
Salary Expense	14,400	
Rent Expense	5,400	
Interest Expense	450	
Office Supplies Expense	1,250	
Depreciation Expense	2,200	
Miscellaneous Expenses	4,300	
Totals	$110,050	$110,050

Chapter 14 Owners' Equity—Proprietorships and Partnerships

On July 1, 1994, Linda Donovan is to be admitted to the partnership by contributing $8,000 cash and library assets that cost $3,000 but have a fair market value of $4,500. Because Donovan is considered an expert in the field of tax law, the other partners have agreed that she will receive a one-third interest in the partnership for her investment.

Required:
1. Prepare a balance sheet as of June 30, 1994, and an income statement and statement of partners' capital for Martin & Seggars for the year ending June 30, 1994. (Assume that profits and losses were shared equally in the old partnership.)
2. Give the necessary journal entry to record Linda Donovan's admission to the partnership. (Assume that the new partnership of Martin, Seggars, & Donovan will share profits and losses in the ratio of 30%/30%/40%.)
3. Prepare the balance sheet of Martin, Seggars, & Donovan as of July 1, 1994.

P14A-8

Unifying Concepts: Preparing a Statement of Partners' Capital and Admitting a New Partner

On January 1, 1994, Little and Smith admitted Jody Threat into their partnership. Before the allocation of 1993 net income, the partners' capital balances were $39,000 and $15,000, respectively. Little and Smith, who share profits and losses equally, had a net income of $30,000 in 1993. On January 1, 1994, Threat purchased one-third of Little's interest for $20,000, and one-fifth of Smith's interest for $9,000. The partnership of Little, Smith, & Threat had net income of $45,000 in 1994. The partners' Drawings accounts for 1994 showed balances of $12,000, $10,000, and $15,000, respectively.

On January 1, 1995, Richard Meeks obtained a 25 percent interest in the partnership with an investment of $20,000.

Required:
1. Compute the capital balances of Little and Smith as of December 31, 1993.
2. Prepare the journal entry to record the admission of Jody Threat to the partnership.
3. Prepare a statement of partners' capital for the partnership of Little, Smith, & Threat as of December 31, 1994. (Assume that partnership profits and losses are allocated in the ratio 50%/30%/20%.)
4. Prepare the journal entry to record the admission of Richard Meeks to the partnership.
5. Compute the partners' capital balances as of January 1, 1995.

Problem Set B

P14B-1

Accounting for a Proprietorship

Tom Jameson is sole proprietor of a grocery store he opened on June 1, 1994. During the year, he had the following transactions:

(a) Contributed a building worth $100,000, furniture and fixtures valued at $40,000, and $20,000 cash to establish the business.
(b) Withdrew $12,000 for personal use from the interim earnings of the proprietorship.
(c) Contributed a new set of shelves to the business. The cost of the shelves was $9,000.
(d) Contributed another $6,000 in cash to the business.
(e) During 1994, Jameson's income from the business was $28,600. (Show only the entry to close the Income Summary account.)
(f) Withdrew all remaining earnings except $4,000, which he left in the business.

Required: 1. Prepare the journal entries (including closing entries) for the transactions.
2. Prepare a statement of owner's equity for Jameson's Corner Grocery Store for the period ending December 31, 1994.

P14B-2
Unifying Concepts: Partnership Financial Statements

On January 1, 1994, Mary Roberts and Jane Wiseman formed a partnership with investments of $18,000 and $14,000, respectively. Their partnership agreement called for annual salary allowances of $20,000 for Roberts and $18,000 for Wiseman with the remainder of the profit or loss to be divided equally. During the year, Wiseman made an additional investment of $3,000 of office equipment.

The adjusted trial balance of Roberts and Wiseman at December 31, 1994, was as follows:

	Debits	Credits
Cash	$ 5,650	
Accounts Receivable	19,800	
Allowance for Uncollectible Accounts		$ 850
Office Furniture (new)	8,500	
Office Equipment	11,400	
Accumulated Depreciation, Office Equipment		1,980
Accounts Payable		2,650
Mary Roberts, Capital		18,000
Mary Roberts, Drawings	13,800	
Jane Wiseman, Capital		17,000
Jane Wiseman, Drawings	19,350	
Service Fees		69,850
Salary Expense	18,900*	
Rent Expense	3,960	
Office Supplies Expense	1,540	
Depreciation Expense	1,980	
Miscellaneous Expenses	5,450	
Totals	$110,330	$110,330

* Salary Expense does not include any payments to the partners.

Required: 1. Prepare an income statement, including a schedule showing the allocation of the partnership's net income, for the year ended December 31, 1994.
2. Prepare a statement of partners' capital for the year ending December 31, 1994.
3. Prepare a balance sheet as of December 31, 1994.

P14B-3
Sharing of Profits—the Capital Investment Ratio (Using Weighted Average)

On January 1, 1994, the capital balances of Kawakami and Ishi were $90,000 and $74,000, respectively. On June 30, Kawakami made an additional contribution of $10,000. Kawakami made a withdrawal of $40,000 on June 30, and Ishi made a withdrawal of $30,000 on June 30. Partnership profits for 1994 were $138,000.

Required: 1. Compute each partner's share of the partnership's 1994 profits, assuming that profits are to be shared in the ratio of the partners' weighted-average capital balances.
2. Prepare the journal entry to close net income for 1994.
3. Prepare a statement of partners' capital as of December 31, 1994.

P14B-4
Admission of a Partner

The following information was available for the Ringo-Ferris partnership:

Net income, January 1 through June 30, 1994	$ 50,000
Ringo, drawings, January 1 through June 30, 1994	5,000
Ferris, drawings, January 1 through June 30, 1994	3,000
Ringo, capital, January 1, 1994	25,000
Ferris, capital, January 1, 1994	30,000
Income, July 1 through December 31, 1994	100,000

On July 1, 1994, Julie Weeble was admitted to the partnership by contributing cash of $25,000 and furniture with a cost of $5,000 and fair market value of $10,000. Weeble, considered invaluable in her profession, received a ⅓ interest in the partnership for her investment.

Assume profits and losses were shared equally in the Ringo-Ferris partnership and that profits are shared 20%/40%/40% in the new Ringo, Ferris, & Weeble partnership.

Required:
1. Give the necessary journal entry for the admission of Weeble.
2. Show the income allocation from July 1 through December 31, 1994.
3. Show the capital account balances at December 31, 1994.

P14B-5
Withdrawal of a Partner

On June 30, 1994, David Easton will retire from the partnership of Easton, North, & Shyam. In planning for this retirement, the partners want to determine how various methods of handling the retirement would affect the partnership assets and financial statements. It is estimated that on June 30 the partners' capital accounts will be $45,000, $50,000, and $55,000, respectively.

Required:
1. Prepare journal entries for each of the following independent proposals to handle the retirement of David Easton:
   (a) Tom Easton (David's son) purchases his father's interest in the partnership for $20,000 cash and a $100,000 note, payable to David in five equal annual installments with 10 percent interest on the unpaid balance.
   (b) North and Shyam agree to personally purchase Easton's interest in the partnership. North will purchase one-third of his interest for $10,000 cash and a $40,000 noninterest-bearing note due in 3 years. Shyam will purchase two-thirds of David's interest for $60,000 cash and a $24,000 note due in 1 year.
   (c) North, Shyam, and Tom Easton each agree to purchase one-third of David Easton's partnership interest for $40,000.
   (d) North and Shyam agree to make payments to David Easton for his partnership interest from the partnership assets. The partners agree that Easton's interest in the partnership, based on current market values, is $124,000. He will be paid $24,000 cash and be given a $100,000 note to be paid in five equal annual installments with 10 percent interest on the unpaid balance. Assume that profits are shared equally among the partners.
2. What effect will each of the proposals have on the partnership assets and the continuity of the business?
3. What effect will each of the proposals have on the sharing of future profits and losses by the partners?

P14B-6
Computation of Partner Capital Balances and Admission of a New Partner

On January 1, 1994, Jones & Smith admitted Steve Johnson to their partnership. Before the allocation of 1993 net income, the partners capital balances were $51,000 and $26,000, respectively. The partners shared profits and losses equally. Jones & Smith had a net income of $40,000 in 1993. On January 1, 1994, Johnson purchased ¼ of Jones' interest for $17,750 and ¼ of Smith's interest for $11,500. The partnership of Jones, Smith, & Johnson had net income of $50,000 for 1994. The partners' drawing accounts for 1994 showed balances of $10,000, $15,000, and $12,500, respectively. Profits and losses for the partnership of Jones, Smith, & Johnson are allocated in the ratio of 40%/40%/20%, respectively.

Required:
1. Compute the capital balances of Jones and Smith as of December 31, 1993.
2. Prepare the journal entry to record the admission of Johnson to the partnership.
3. Prepare a statement of partners' capital for the partnership of Jones, Smith, & Johnson as of December 31, 1994.

P14B-7
Preparation of Partnership Financial Statements

Raditch Pet Shop is a partnership owned and operated by Dennis Raditch and Brad Raditch. On December 31, 1994, the partnership's adjusted trial balance was as follows:

Raditch Pet Shop
Adjusted Trial Balance
December 31, 1994

	Debits	Credits
Cash	$ 7,000	
Accounts Receivable	14,000	
Allowance for Uncollectible Accounts		$ 400
Furniture and Fixtures	25,000	
Accumulated Depreciation—Furniture and Fixtures		5,000
Land	22,000	
Building	88,000	
Accumulated Depreciation—Building		8,000
Accounts Payable		10,000
Mortgage Payable		40,000
Dennis Raditch, Capital		17,600
Dennis Raditch, Drawings	18,000	
Brad Raditch, Capital		20,000
Brad Raditch, Drawings	16,000	
Sales Revenue		180,000
Cost of Goods Sold	42,000	
Salary Expense (to employees)	31,000	
Supplies Expense	4,500	
Utility Expense	5,300	
Miscellaneous Expenses	1,700	
Depreciation Expense—Furniture and Fixtures	2,500	
Depreciation Expense—Building	4,000	
	$281,000	$281,000

Required:
1. Prepare an income statement, including a schedule showing the allocation of the partnership's net income for the year ended December 31, 1994. Assume that Dennis and Brad share profits 40%/60%.
2. Prepare a statement of partners' capital as of December 31, 1994.
3. Prepare a balance sheet for the partnership as of December 31, 1994.

P14B-8

Admitting a New Partner

Eiko Uno, Ursula Anders, and Gupta Steinberg own and operate the Quality Jewelry Store, a partnership. They opened the store 10 years ago in Denver, Colorado, and on January 1, 1994, their capital balances are $130,000, $106,000, and $97,000, respectively. Because the store has been so successful, they decide to open a second store in Salt Lake City, Utah. They ask Sam Smith, a long-time resident of that city, to buy into the partnership and operate the store. These options are being considered:

(a) Smith will invest $111,000 for a one-fourth interest in the partnership.
(b) Smith will invest $77,000 for a one-fifth interest in the partnership.
(c) Smith will invest $67,500 for a one-sixth interest in the partnership.
(d) Smith will buy one-fourth of Uno's interest for $50,000, one-fifth of Anders's interest for $35,000, and 30 percent of Steinberg's interest for $42,000.

Required:
1. Prepare the journal entry that would be required in each independent case, assuming that Uno, Anders, and Steinberg share profits and losses equally.
2. Which of the alternatives would give Smith the greatest ownership interest for the least amount of money?

Business Analysis Case 1 *Romero and Salazar Partnership*

Mike Romero and Rich Salazar are partners in a real estate development firm. During the last 3 years, Mike's share of partnership profits have been $35,000, $40,000, and $50,000. Tom Tuke wants to pay Mike $230,000 to purchase his share of the partnership, and Mike is considering the offer. He has decided that if his share of the profits over the next 5 years is less than the sales price, he will sell. Mike prepares the following schedule of estimated profits:

Total Partnership Profits

	Year 1	Year 2	Year 3	Year 4	Year 5
Optimistic estimate	$80,000	$90,000	$100,000	$110,000	$120,000
Most probable estimate	70,000	75,000	80,000	85,000	90,000
Pessimistic estimate	65,000	65,000	70,000	70,000	70,000

Mike and Rich currently share profits as follows: Mike receives a salary of $18,000, Rich's salary is $16,000, and the remainder is split in a 60%/40% ratio, with Mike getting 60%.

Required:
1. Compute Mike's share of the profits over the next 5 years if his optimistic estimate is realized.
2. Compute Mike's share of the profits over the next 5 years if his most probable estimate is realized.
3. Compute Mike's share of the profits over the next 5 years if his pessimistic estimate is realized.
4. If the probabilities are 20 percent that the optimistic estimate will be realized, 60 percent that the most probable estimate will be realized, and 20 percent that the pessimistic estimate will be realized, should Mike sell for $230,000?
5. What other factors should Mike consider in deciding whether or not to sell?

Business Analysis Case 2 *Sutherland and Stroble Medical Practice*

Ron Sutherland and Sally Stroble graduated from medical school together and have just completed their internship and residency programs. They want to practice medicine together and are trying to decide whether to incorporate or form a partnership. Regardless of which form of organization they choose, profits and losses will be shared equally.

Assume that all individual income is taxed at a rate of 28 percent and that corporate income is taxed at a rate of 34 percent.

Required:
1. Determine the total income taxes for the first year under each type of business organization assuming income before any taxes of $280,000. Assume also that all corporate profits, after taxes, will be paid out as dividends. What is the effective tax rate in each case?
2. If the corporate form is chosen and income before any salaries or taxes is $280,000, how much would total taxes be under each of the following scenarios?
   (a) They each receive a salary of $100,000, and no dividends are paid.
   (b) They each receive a salary of $100,000, and the remaining profits are paid out in dividends.
3. What other factors besides income taxes should the two doctors consider in deciding which form of business organization to use?

Ethics Case *John Jones Family Partnership*

John Jones was a farmer who had three children—two boys and one girl. He was quite mechanically inclined and invented a hay rake that was efficient and effective. He sold the rights to the rake to a large farm implement company for $2,000,000 plus 5 percent of all future sales. On the recommendation of his tax advisor, John formed a partnership with himself and his three children as partners. Each partner was to receive ¼ of the future royalties.

For the first few years, royalties were excellent, and the partnership invested in various real estate and other projects. Eventually, the children left home and got married and John retired. John's older son, Dave, became the manager of the partnership.

Dave was not as good a manager as his father. Over a period of 5 years, he proceeded to lose most of the assets and incurred partnership debts of $3 million. Dave's father, brother, and sister were not informed of the partnership financial problems until Dave could not meet the debt obligations.

Required:
1. Are the other three partners responsible for the partnership debts even though they had nothing to do with their incurrence?
2. Was Dave merely a poor manager or were his managerial actions unethical?

Part 4

Other Dimensions of Financial Reporting

CHAPTERS

15 The Statement of Cash Flows
16 Financial Statement Analysis
    Appendix—International Aspects of Financial Reporting

Chapter 15

The Statement of Cash Flows

Learning Objectives

After studying this chapter, you should be able to:
1. Explain the purposes of a statement of cash flows.
2. Describe the information reported in the statement of cash flows, including the major classifications of cash into operating, investing, and financing activities.
3. Understand the indirect and direct methods of reporting operating cash flows.
4. Prepare a statement of cash flows.
5. Understand the usefulness of cash flow statements.

SETTING THE STAGE

Intellicall, Inc. of Dallas was founded in 1984, right after AT&T lost its monopoly. Intellicall was the first company to make and sell so-called smart phones for the pay telephone market. Inside these phones are computer chips that perform such tasks as calculating calling rates and processing collect calls using a simulated human voice.

Intellicall rapidly became a profitable company. By 1990, revenues had reached $207 million, with profits of $7.6 million. The company's stock climbed from $3\frac{1}{4}$ to its peak of $18\frac{1}{4}$ in late 1989. To quote a *Forbes* reporter, "Intellicall was a hot little company."

In December 1990, however, questions about the company's actual profitability began to surface when Intellicall's auditors, Ernst & Young, received a surprise phone call from an Intellicall customer. The auditors were shaken when the caller said that at the end of two quarters in 1990, he had agreed to take hundreds more phones than he needed in order to help Intellicall meet its quarterly revenue goals. The company promised him that, except for a small deposit, he would not have to pay for the phones until he actually had customers for them, which might take about a year. In the meantime, the phones would be stored in a New Jersey warehouse, in a space Intellicall rented that was roughly the size of a two-car garage. Intellicall would keep the key to the warehouse.

Soon there were rumors of other similar deals and special payment arrangements. To counter the rumors, Intellicall's audit committee brought in a high-powered securities lawyer who gave the company a "clean bill of health" after conducting a two-week investigation. In March of 1991, the company announced that both the securities lawyer and Ernst & Young considered the allegations of accounting improprieties "unfounded."

Even before the rumors, however, at least one financial analyst suspected something was amiss and advised her clients to sell short the company's stock. She reasoned that, with accounts receivable of $91 million and revenues of $60 million in the second quarter of 1990, the average collection period for Intellicall's receivables was 136 days—much longer than the 60 to 90 days customers usually have to pay. The inability to collect receivables places the company in a cash crunch and jeopardizes its ability to pay off debts.

Although this analyst made her sell decision without the knowledge that Intellicall had been "stuffing" its dealers with equipment, her decision appears to have been a correct one. In fact, it now appears that several dealers have stopped paying the license fees, claiming Intellicall misled them on the economics of owning smart phones. To *Forbes,* "this hot little company begins to look more than a little warmed over."

Adapted from Dana Wechsler Linden, "Dial F for Fishy," *Forbes,* November 25, 1991, pp. 158–160.

In this chapter, you will study the cash flow statement. You will learn that this statement provides one of the earliest warning signs of cash concerns and receivable collection problems of the type experienced by Intellicall. The cash flow statement alerts financial statement readers to increases and decreases in cash as well as to the reasons and trends for the changes. In 1991, for example, there were a record number of bankruptcies in the United States. In many instances, the cause of these business failures was poor cash management, a problem that would have been revealed by the statement of cash flows.

It is not enough in today's business environment to just monitor earnings and earnings per share measurements. The financial position of an entity and especially the inflows and outflows of cash are critical elements that determine the financial success of an organization.

Each of the three primary financial statements was introduced and illustrated in Chapter 2. In subsequent chapters, we examined in detail the components of the balance sheet and income statement. In this chapter, we discuss the statement of cash flows, which is based on analysis of the balance sheet and income statement accounts. We first describe the purposes and general format of a statement of cash flows. We then illustrate the preparation of a cash flow statement.

PURPOSES OF A STATEMENT OF CASH FLOWS

Objective 1

Explain the purposes of a statement of cash flows.

statement of cash flows
the general-purpose financial statement that summarizes an entity's cash receipts and payments during a period

The income statement, as you know, measures the results of operations for a period of time and ties together the owners' equity sections of comparative balance sheets. For a corporation, this means that the net income (or net loss) for the period is added to (or subtracted from) the beginning retained earnings balance in determining retained earnings at the end of the period. The net income or loss for the period, however, often does not explain the total change in the retained earnings balance. Other events that are not reported in the income statement, such as dividends and some treasury stock transactions, also affect retained earnings. Further, the income statement does not reflect changes in other owners' equity accounts, for example an increase in the Common Stock account as a result of issuing new shares of stock during the period. All these changes in owners' equity, however, are included in the **statement of cash flows**. In addition, the statement explains changes in the individual asset and liability accounts.

The statement of cash flows provides information about the cash receipts and payments of an entity during a period of time. It does not include any transactions or accounts that are not reflected in the balance sheet or the income statement. Rather, the statement of cash flows reports the period's transactions and events in terms of their impact on cash. In Chapter 6, we compared the cash-basis and accrual-basis methods of measuring income and explained why accrual-basis income is considered a better measure of periodic income. The statement of cash flows provides important information from a cash-basis perspective that complements the income statement and balance sheet and thus provides a more complete picture of a company's operations and financial position.

Users of financial statements, particularly investors and creditors, need information about a company's cash flows in order to evaluate the company's ability to generate positive net cash flows in the future to meet its obligations and to pay dividends. As indicated in the Business Environment Essay on page 628, financial statement analysts are placing more and more emphasis on the statement of cash flows. In some cases, careful analysis of cash flows can provide early warning of impending financial problems.

The statement of cash flows is a relatively new financial statement. In 1987, the Financial Accounting Standards Board (FASB) issued a new accounting standard, *FASB Statement No. 95*, requiring that the statement of cash flows be presented as one of the primary financial statements. Previously companies had been required to present a *statement of changes in financial position*, often called the *funds statement*. Later in the chapter, we will explain some of the limitations of the funds statement that led the FASB to conclude that the statement of cash flows would provide more useful information for investors, creditors, and others who rely on financial statements as a basis for making economic decisions.

INFORMATION REPORTED IN THE STATEMENT OF CASH FLOWS

Objective 2

Describe the information reported in the statement of cash flows, including the major classifications of cash into operating, investing, and financing activities.

cash equivalents short-term, highly liquid investments that can be converted easily into cash

FASB Statement No. 95 includes specific requirements for the reporting of cash flows. The general format for a statement of cash flows, with details and dollar amounts omitted, is presented in Exhibit 15-1. As illustrated, the inflows and outflows of cash must be divided into three main categories: operating activities, investing activities, and financing activities. Further, the statement of cash flows is to be presented in a manner that reconciles the beginning and ending balances of cash and cash equivalents. **Cash equivalents** are short-term, highly liquid investments that can be converted easily to cash. Generally, only investments with maturities of three months or less qualify as cash equivalents. Examples are U.S. Treasury bills, money market funds, and commercial paper (short-term debt issued by corporations). In this chapter, as in practice, the term *cash* will be used to include cash and cash equivalents.

Major Classifications of Cash Flows

Exhibit 15-2 shows the three main categories of cash inflows and outflows—operating, investing, and financing. Exhibit 15-3 summarizes the specific activities included in each category. Beginning with operating activities, each of the cash flow categories will be explained. We will also discuss the reporting of significant noncash transactions and events.

Exhibit 15-1 *General Format for a Statement of Cash Flows*

Cash provided by (used in):	
Operating activities	$XXX
Investing activities	XXX
Financing activities	XXX
Net increase (decrease) in cash and cash equivalents	$XXX
Cash and cash equivalents at beginning of year	XXX
Cash and cash equivalents at end of year	$XXX

Exhibit 15-2 *The Flow of Cash*

```
Cash received          Cash received          Cash received
from operating         from investing         from financing
activities             activities             activities
                           │
                        Inflows
                           ▼
                   Cash and cash
                    equivalents
                           │
                       Outflows
                           ▼
Cash paid              Cash paid              Cash paid
for operating          for investing          for financing
activities             activities             activities
```

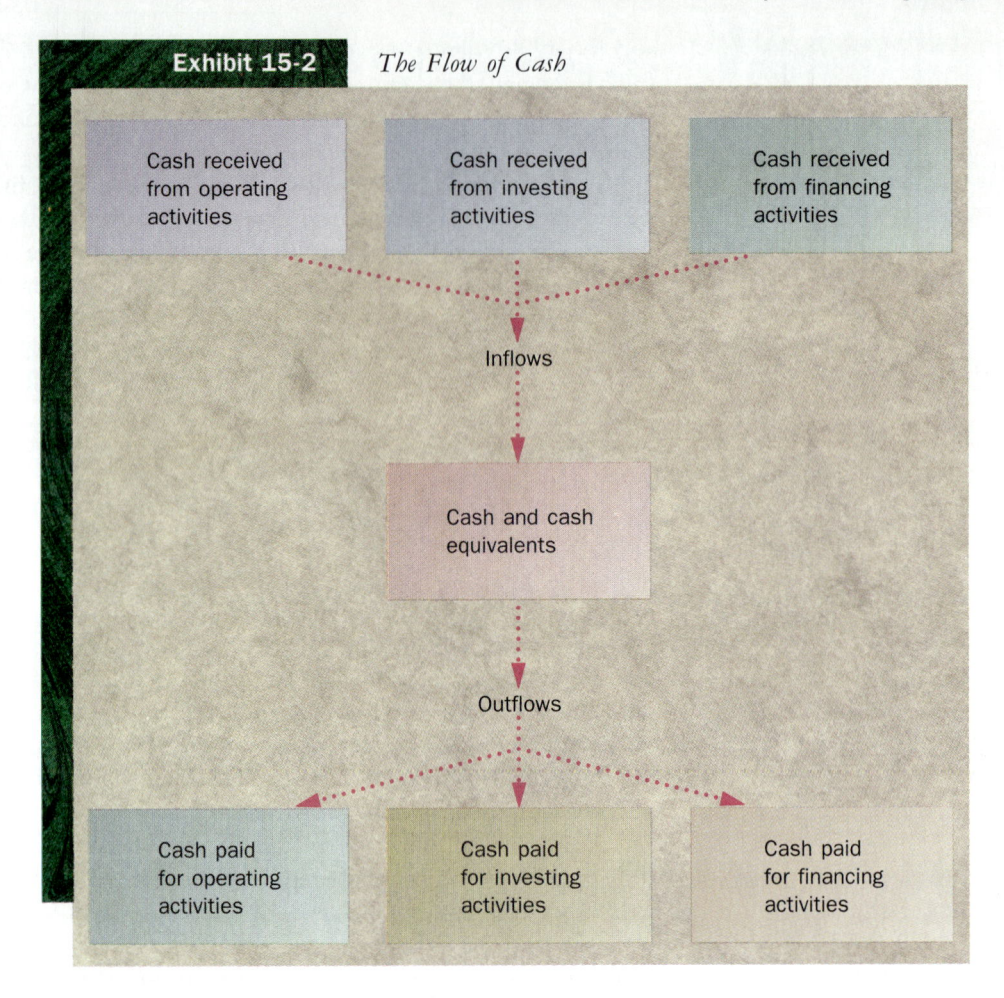

operating activities *transactions and events that enter into the determination of net income*

OPERATING ACTIVITIES. Operating activities include those transactions and events that enter into the determination of net income. Cash receipts from the sale of goods or services would be the major cash inflow for most businesses. Others would be receipts for interest revenue, dividend revenue, and similar items. Major outflows of cash would be the purchase of inventory and the payment of wages, taxes, interest, utilities, rent, and similar expenses. As we will explain later, the amount of cash provided by (or used in) operating activities is a key figure and should be highlighted on a statement of cash flows.

Although cash inflows from interest and dividends logically might be classified as investing or financing activities, the FASB has decided to classify them as operating activities, which conforms to their presentation on the income statement. Furthermore, interest and dividends are the major operating items of financial institutions (banks, loan companies, and so on).

investing activities *transactions and events that involve the purchase and sale of securities (excluding cash equivalents), property, plant, equipment, and other assets not generally held for resale, and the making and collecting of loans*

INVESTING ACTIVITIES. Transactions and events that involve the purchase and sale of securities (excluding cash equivalents), property, buildings, equipment, and other assets not generally held for resale, and the making and collecting of loans are classified as **investing activities**. These activities occur regularly and result in cash inflows and outflows. They are not classified under operating activities since they relate only indirectly to the central, ongoing operations of the entity, which is usually the sale of goods or services.

Exhibit 15-3 Major Classifications of Cash Flows

Operating Activities
Cash receipts from:
  Sale of goods or services
  Interest revenue
  Dividend revenue
Cash payments to:
  Suppliers for inventory purchases
  Employees for services
  Governments for taxes
  Lenders for interest expense
  Others for other expenses (e.g., utilities, rent)

Investing Activities
Cash receipts from:
  Sale of property, plant, and equipment
  Sale of a business segment
  Sale of investments in debt or equity securities (other than cash equivalents)
  Collection of principal on loans made to other entities
Cash payments to:
  Purchase property, plant, and equipment
  Purchase debt or equity securities of other entities (other than cash equivalents)
  Make loans to other entities

Financing Activities
Cash receipts from:
  Issuance of own stock
  Borrowing (e.g., bonds, notes, mortgages)
Cash payments to:
  Stockholders as dividends
  Repay principal amounts borrowed
  Repurchase an entity's own stock (treasury stock)

---

financing activities transactions and events whereby resources are obtained from or repaid to owners (equity financing) and creditors (debt financing)

FINANCING ACTIVITIES. **Financing activities** include transactions and events whereby resources are obtained from or paid to owners (equity financing) and creditors (debt financing). Dividend payments, for example, fit this definition. As noted earlier, the receipt of dividends and interest and the payment of interest are classified under operating activities simply because they are reported as a part of income from operations on the income statement and are therefore classified as operating activities by the FASB. The receipt or payment of the principal amount borrowed or repaid is considered a financing activity.

Noncash Investing and Financing Activities

noncash transactions investing and financing activities that do not affect cash; if significant, they are disclosed below the statement of cash flows or in the notes to the financial statements

Some investing and financing activities do not affect cash. For example, equipment may be purchased with a note payable, or land may be acquired by issuing stock. These **noncash transactions** are not reported in the statement of cash flows. However, if a company has any significant noncash financing and investing activities, they must be disclosed in a separate schedule or in a narrative explanation. The disclosure may be presented below the statement of cash flows or in the notes to the financial statements.

BUSINESS ENVIRONMENT ESSAY
Focus on Cash Flows

As reported in an article in *The Wall Street Journal,* an increasing number of stock analysts are focusing on the cash flows of companies. These analysts point out that reported earnings, which are based on accrual accounting instead of a cash-flow basis, are sometimes misleading. By analyzing cash flows, that is, the money flowing into and out of a business, important developments and events are highlighted.

For example, take a company that spent $150 million on new machinery last year and assume that this company depreciates the machinery evenly over its estimated useful life of five years. In other words, the company will report $30 million of depreciation expense in its income statement each year, which will reduce reported earnings in each of those years. Thus, the reported earnings may understate the true strength of the company since the depreciation expense does not represent a cash outflow but simply an allocation of the cost of the equipment. On that basis, some analysts are attracted to a company, such as Burlington Industries or Chrysler Corporation, that reports large amounts of depreciation expense that, in effect, shelter income through lower income taxes.

On the other hand, take a company that has neglected capital spending on new plant assets. That company's reported income may look good because of low amounts for depreciation, but on a cash-flow basis, the picture might not be as rosy. A company with cash flow problems can report better earnings in the short run by postponing the replacement of aging or obsolete plant assets at the sacrifice of long-term operating performance and efficiency.

As a specific example of the value of cash flow analysis, an analyst for Gruntal & Co. in New York maintains that cash flow trends gave alert investors an early warning of the U.S. auto industry's problems in the 1970s. By the end of the decade, poor earnings made those problems apparent to everyone.

Source: Adapted from John R. Dorfman, "Stock Analysts Increase Focus on Cash Flow," *The Wall Street Journal,* February 17, 1987.

To Summarize *The statement of cash flows, one of the three primary financial statements, provides information about the cash receipts and payments of an entity during a period. It provides important information that complements the income statement and balance sheet. The statement of cash flows is required by* **FASB** *Statement No. 95 and replaced the previously required statement of changes in financial position. FASB Statement No. 95 requires that the statement of cash flows be presented in a manner that highlights three major categories of cash flows: operating activities, investing activities, and financing activities. In addition, the format of the statement should provide a reconciliation of the beginning and ending balances of cash and cash equivalents (short-term, highly liquid investments). Any significant noncash investing and financing activities should be disclosed separately, either below the statement of cash flows or in the notes to the financial statements.*

THE DIRECT AND INDIRECT METHODS OF REPORTING OPERATING CASH FLOWS

Objective 3

Understand the indirect and direct methods of reporting operating cash flows.

One of the most important items of information reported on the statement of cash flows is the net cash provided by (or used in) operating activities. It is this amount that determines whether or not an organization will continue to exist in the long run. Cash flows from investing and financing activities also are important, but the net cash flow from the major, ongoing operating activity of the organization is the critical element.

There are two ways of calculating and reporting the amount of net cash flow from operating activities on a statement of cash flows: the direct method and the indirect method. The direct method shows the major classes of operating cash receipts (cash collected from customers and cash received from interest or dividends, for example) and cash payments (cash paid to suppliers for goods and services, to employees for services, to creditors for interest, to government agencies for taxes, and so on). The difference between cash receipts and payments is the net cash flow provided by (used in) operating activities. The direct method is favored by many financial statement users because it is straightforward and is not likely to be misunderstood. Some accountants are concerned, however, that use of the direct method might inappropriately imply that cash-basis income is a better measure of performance than accrual-basis income, which is contrary to generally accepted accounting principles.

The indirect method involves a reconciliation between net income, as reported on the income statement, and net cash flow from operating activities, as calculated on the statement of cash flows. Essentially, this requires adjusting net income for any items that do not affect cash, such as depreciation or amortization, and then adjusting accrual-based account balances to a cash basis.

The indirect method produces the same result as the direct method. It is favored and used by most accountants because it is the easier method to apply and because it helps explain the reasons for the difference between net income and net cash flow provided by (used in) operating activities. Because the indirect method is used by over 95 percent of the companies in the United States, it will be described first and emphasized in this chapter.

The Indirect Method

indirect method a method of reporting net cash flow from operations that involves converting accrual-basis net income to a cash basis

The **indirect method** begins with net income as reported on the income statement. Several adjustments must then be made on the cash flow statement to convert accrual net income to cash flow from operations.

ADJUSTMENTS FOR RECEIVABLES AND OTHER CURRENT OPERATING ASSETS.

When a receivable account balance decreases during a period, this means that cash collections exceed revenues recorded on an accrual basis. The decrease has to be added to net income to reflect the cash provided for the period. If the balance had increased, the opposite would be true: The increase would be deducted from net income. As an example, suppose that Accounts Receivable was $34,000 at the beginning of the year and $30,000 at the end. The $4,000 decrease would be added to net income. Conversely, an increase of $18,000 for inventory would mean that more cash had been used than had been reflected in

Cost of Goods Sold, so this amount would have to be subtracted from net income.

ADJUSTMENTS FOR PAYABLES AND OTHER CURRENT LIABILITIES. Changes in payable and other current operating liability account balances mean the reverse of changes in current operating asset accounts. Decreases mean that more cash was paid than was recorded on an accrual basis, and the decreases would have to be deducted from net income. Increases would be added to net income.

ADJUSTMENTS FOR DEPRECIATION AND OTHER NONCASH ITEMS. Depreciation and similar **noncash items** do not affect cash and should not be reported on a statement of cash flows. When using the indirect method, we start with net income, which already includes the effects of these items. To isolate actual cash flows, therefore, we must add or subtract these noncash items.

To illustrate, assume an annual depreciation expense of $12,000. The journal entry would be:

> **Noncash items** *items included in the determination of net income on an accrual basis that do not affect cash; examples are depreciation and amortization*

```
Depreciation Expense .........................................    12,000
    Accumulated Depreciation.................................              12,000
To record depreciation expense.
```

Note that the Cash account is not affected by this journal entry. The expense was included on the income statement, however, and reduced net income by $12,000. Thus, to convert net income to cash flow, we have to add back depreciation expense. Similarly, any noncash item, such as amortization of a bond premium, that had increased net income would have to be deducted on a statement of cash flows prepared with the indirect method.

ADJUSTMENTS FOR GAINS AND LOSSES. When a company sells assets other than inventory, a gain or loss is reported in the income statement if the selling price is greater or less than the book value of the asset. For example, assume that a company sells its investment in the stock of another company for $25,000 and the book value of the investment is $26,500. The entry to record the sale would be:

```
Cash ........................................................    25,000
Loss on Sale of Investment ..................................     1,500
    Investment in Stock .....................................              26,500
```

The loss of $1,500 is the excess of book value over selling price and does not represent the cash effect of the transaction. The cash effect is an inflow of $25,000 from investing activities and would be reported as such on the statement of cash flows. In addition, the $1,500 needs to be added as an adjustment to net income in computing cash flows from operations since that amount was deducted in determining net income on the income statement.

If the investment had been sold at a gain, the gain would be subtracted from net income in computing net cash flow from operating activities. To illustrate, assume the investment was sold for $28,500, or at a gain of $2,000. The entry to record the sale would be:

```
Cash ...................................................... 28,500
    Investment in Stock ..................................         26,500
    Gain on Sale of Investment ...........................          2,000
```

In this example, $28,500 would be reported in the statement of cash flows as cash received from investing activities and the $2,000 gain would be deducted as an adjustment to net income in the operating activities section of the statement.

Exhibit 15-4 summarizes the adjustments required to convert net income to cash flow from operations when using the indirect method.

Exhibit 15-4 *Cash Flows from Operating Activities—Indirect Method*

Net income reported on the income statement		$XXX
Adjustments for changes in current operating accounts:		
− Increases in current operating asset accounts (except cash and cash equivalents)	$XXX	
+ Decreases in current operating asset accounts (except cash and cash equivalents)	XXX	
+ Increases in current operating liability accounts	XXX	
− Decreases in current operating liability accounts	XXX	XXX
Adjustments for noncash items:		
+ Depreciation	$XXX	
+ Amortization of intangible assets	XXX	
+/− Other noncash items included in net income	XXX	XXX
Adjustments for gains and losses:		
− Gains on sales of assets	$XXX	
+ Losses on sales of assets	XXX	XXX
Net cash provided by (used in) operating activities		$XXX

The Direct Method

direct method *a method of reporting net cash flow from operations that shows the major classes of cash receipts and payments for a period of time*

A statement of cash flows prepared using the direct method is, in effect, a cash-basis income statement. Unlike the indirect method, however, the **direct method** does not start with net income. Instead, this method reports directly the major classes of operating cash receipts and payments of an entity during a period.

To prepare a statement of cash flows using the direct method, we could analyze each cash transaction separately and derive the total cash receipts and payments for the period. Alternatively, we could use the summarized data provided in the financial statements along with additional information, such as the amount of uncollected revenues (receivables), and convert accrual-basis revenues and expenses to equivalent cash receipts and payments.

To convert from an accrual to a cash basis, we use a similar calculation for each account. This is because the reasoning applies equally to all situations. Beginning receivable balances, for example, represent transactions from a previous period and so are assumed to have been collected in cash during the current period. Ending receivable balances represent uncollected revenues from transactions during the current period. By adding a beginning receivable or payable balance to a revenue or an expense amount and then subtracting the appropriate ending balance, we determine the amount of cash actually collected or paid during the period. (Alternatively, you can use the net increase or decrease in the account balance and add or subtract the net change as was illustrated under the indirect method for adjusting current operating accounts.)

Following are representative calculations for converting revenues (Sales Revenue) and expenses (Wages Expense) from an accrual to a cash basis (using arbitrary numbers). We will also discuss two items—Insurance Expense and Cost of Goods Sold—separately since they involve slightly different calculations.

From accrual revenues to cash receipts:

Sales revenue	$200,000
+ Beginning accounts receivable	34,000
− Ending accounts receivable	(30,000)
= Cash receipts from customers	$204,000

From accrual expenses to cash payments:

Wages expense	$24,000
+ Beginning wages payable	5,000
− Ending wages payable	(2,000)
= Cash paid for wages	$27,000

As shown here, in converting expenses such as wages, interest, and income taxes to the amount of cash paid, beginning payables are added, and ending payables are subtracted. These calculations are necessary because these expenses are incurred (and become liabilities) prior to being paid. Because insurance is usually purchased (and recorded as an asset) before it is an expense, the opposite calculation is needed, as follows:

From insurance expense to cash payments for insurance:

Insurance expense	$ 3,140
+ Ending prepaid insurance	4,000
− Beginning prepaid insurance	(2,800)
= Cash paid for insurance	$ 4,340

The calculation for Cost of Goods Sold is also different because a company must first determine the amount of purchases during the period. As you recall from Chapter 6, under the periodic inventory method, Cost of Goods Sold is calculated by adding beginning inventory to purchases, then subtracting ending inventory. Since we know Cost of Goods Sold, we reverse the calculation to determine purchases, as follows:

Cost of goods sold	$120,000
+ Ending inventory	65,000
− Beginning inventory	(47,000)
= Purchases	$138,000

To convert the accrual-based amount of purchases to a cash basis, we add the beginning Accounts Payable balance and subtract the ending balance.

Purchases	$138,000
+ Beginning accounts payable	17,000
− Ending accounts payable	(7,500)
= Cash paid for inventory	$147,500

As noted earlier, some items that are included in the determination of net income on an accrual basis do not affect cash. Examples are depreciation of buildings and equipment and amortization of intangible assets or of bond discounts or premiums. Because the direct method analyzes and includes only cash transactions, these noncash items are omitted from the statement of cash flows and may be ignored when using the direct method.

Note also that when the direct method is used to compute net cash flow from operating activities, no adjustment for a gain or loss on the sale of assets is needed since operating cash receipts and payments are reported "directly" in the statement of cash flows rather than determined by adjusting net income. The cash received from investing activities is reported in the same manner regardless of whether the direct or indirect method is used to determine operating cash flows.

Exhibit 15-5 summarizes the procedures for converting accounts from an accrual to a cash basis.

Recommendation of FASB Statement No. 95

FASB Statement No. 95 encourages use of the direct method for preparing a statement of cash flows, with a separate schedule to reconcile net income and net cash flow from operating activities. A company may choose, however, to use the indirect method, which already includes the required reconciliation. If the indirect method is used, the company should disclose the amounts of interest and income taxes paid during the period since these items are considered significant by the FASB.

Regardless of which method is used, the amount reported as net cash flow provided by (used in) operating activities will be the same. The cash flows from investing and financing activities also will be the same. As we will show shortly, only the format and extent of detail on the statement of cash flows will differ for the two methods. Since most accounting systems are set up to report revenues and expenses on an accrual basis for the income statement, most companies start with net income, make the necessary conversions, and report cash flows from operating activities using the indirect method.

Exhibit 15-5   *Guidelines for Converting from Accrual to Cash Basis*

Accrual Basis	± Adjustments Required	= Cash Basis
Net sales	+ Beginning accounts receivable* − Ending accounts receivable*	= Cash receipts from customers
Other revenues (e.g., rent and interest):		
Rent revenue	+ Ending unearned rent − Beginning unearned rent	= Cash received for rent
Interest revenue	+ Beginning interest receivable − Ending interest receivable	= Cash received for interest
Cost of goods sold	+ Ending inventory − Beginning inventory + Beginning accounts payable − Ending accounts payable	= Cash paid for inventory
Operating expenses** (e.g., insurance and wages)		
Insurance expense	+ Ending prepaid insurance − Beginning prepaid insurance	= Cash paid for insurance
Wages expense	+ Beginning wages payable − Ending wages payable	= Cash paid for wages
Income tax expense	+ Beginning income taxes payable − Ending income taxes payable	= Cash paid for income taxes
		Net cash flow provided by (used in) operating activities

* Net of allowance for uncollectible accounts
** Excluding depreciation and other noncash items

To Summarize *In preparing a statement of cash flows, the direct or the indirect method may be used to show the net cash flow provided by (used in) operating activities. The indirect method starts with net income, as reported on the income statement, and adds or subtracts adjustments to convert accrual net income to net cash flow from operations. Adjustments to net income are made for increases and decreases in operating account balances, noncash items such as depreciation, and gains and losses from the sale of assets. The direct method shows the major classes of operating cash receipts and payments. The difference is net cash flow from operations. The direct method requires analysis of each cash transaction or an analysis of accrual revenues and expenses in order to convert them to cash receipts and payments. Both methods produce the same results, and either method is allowed under generally accepted accounting principles.*

PREPARING A STATEMENT OF CASH FLOWS

Objective 4
Prepare a statement of cash flows.

We now direct our attention to the actual preparation of a statement of cash flows. A five-step procedure may be used.

Step 1 Compute the change in the Cash and cash-equivalent accounts for the period of the statement (month, year, and so on). This is the "target figure"—the amount you are trying to explain with the statement of cash flows. The results will be the cash receipts and payments during the period that caused the Cash and cash-equivalent accounts to increase or decrease, thus reconciling the beginning and ending Cash balances for the period.

Step 2 Analyze all accounts other than Cash (and cash equivalents) to see if cash receipts or payments were involved in the changes of these account balances between periods. With the indirect method, net income is converted from an accrual to a cash basis. The result is net cash flow from operating activities. Other cash inflows and outflows are reported under investing and financing activities. With the direct method, each cash transaction is analyzed and the cash receipts and payments are reported directly on the statement, classified as operating, investing, or financing activities.

Step 3 Make sure that the total net cash flow from the statement (the sum of net cash flows from operating, investing, and financing activities) is equal to the net increase (decrease) in cash as computed in Step 1.

Step 4 Prepare a formal statement of cash flows by classifying all cash inflows and outflows according to operating, investing, and financing activities. The net cash flow provided by (used in) each of the three main activities of an entity should be highlighted.

Step 5 Report any significant investing or financing transactions that did not involve cash in a narrative explanation or in a separate schedule to the statement of cash flows. This would include such transactions as the purchase of land by issuing stock or the retirement of bonds by issuing stock.

In following these steps, it is often helpful to use T-accounts to explain changes in account balances. The data for our explanations come from Exhibits 15-6 and 15-7, comparative balance sheets and an income statement and statement of retained earnings for Pioneer Stores, Inc. Because the indirect method is more commonly used in practice, we will illustrate this method first. We will then illustrate the direct method, using the same data.

The Indirect Method Illustrated

Following our five-step approach, we begin by computing the change in the Cash and cash-equivalent accounts. From the balance sheets in Exhibit 15-6, we determine that there has been an increase in cash and cash equivalents of $9,700 ($17,600 − $7,900). Our next step is to analyze the other accounts in order to explain that change.

ANALYSIS OF RETAINED EARNINGS. Since the indirect method begins with net income, we will first explain the change in Retained Earnings. Net income, as

Exhibit 15-6

Pioneer Stores, Inc.
Comparative Balance Sheets
December 31, 1994 and 1993

Assets	1994	1993
Current assets:		
Cash and cash equivalents	$ 17,600	$ 7,900
Accounts receivable (net of allowance for doubtful accounts)	106,700	104,900
Inventory	187,300	197,500
Prepaid expenses	7,000	9,200
Total current assets	$318,600	$319,500
Property, plant, and equipment:		
Land (note 1)	$ 90,000	$ 10,000
Buildings and equipment (at cost)	623,200	577,200
Less accumulated depreciation	(243,900)	(223,600)
Total property, plant, and equipment	$469,300	$363,600
Total assets	$787,900	$683,100
Liabilities and Stockholders' Equity		
Current liabilities:		
Accounts payable	$ 72,200	$ 71,700
Income taxes payable	7,000	1,500
Total current liabilities	$ 79,200	$ 73,200
Long-term liabilities:		
Notes payable	$ 20,000	$ -0-
Mortgage payable	72,100	85,000
Total long-term liabilities	$ 92,100	$ 85,000
Total liabilities	$171,300	$158,200
Stockholders' equity:		
Common stock, no par (note 1)	$269,400	$189,400
Retained earnings	347,200	335,500
Total stockholders' equity	$616,600	$524,900
Total liabilities and stockholders' equity	$787,900	$683,100

Note 1 Land with a fair market value of $80,000 was acquired through the issuance of 40,000 shares of common stock.

you know, contributes to the amount of Retained Earnings; in this case, it increases Retained Earnings by $36,600 for the period. Retained earnings and cash flows are also affected by cash dividends paid. The total change in Retained Earnings is shown in the T-account.

Retained Earnings

Cash Outflow: Dividends	24,900	12/31/93 Balance	335,500
		Cash Inflow: Net Income	36,600
		12/31/94 Balance	347,200

Exhibit 15-7

Pioneer Stores, Inc.
Income Statement
For the Year Ended December 31, 1994

Net sales revenue	$859,400	
Other revenues (note 2)	7,800	
Total revenues		$867,200
Expenses:		
Cost of goods sold	$610,100	
Selling and administrative expenses	147,000	
Depreciation expense	32,100	
Interest expense	14,200	
Total expenses		803,400
Income before taxes		$ 63,800
Income taxes		27,200
Net income		$ 36,600

Note 2 Gain on the sale of equipment (cost, $12,300; book value, $500; sale price, $8,300 cash).

Pioneer Stores, Inc.
Statement of Retained Earnings
For the Year Ended December 31, 1994

Retained earnings, January 1, 1994	$335,500
Add net income	36,600
	$372,100
Dividends declared and paid	24,900
Retained earnings, December 31, 1994	$347,200

Based on this analysis, the $36,600 of net income, prior to any adjustments, would be shown as an operating source of cash and the $24,900 of dividends as a use of cash for financing activities. These items would appear on a partially completed statement of cash flows as follows:

Cash Flow from Operating Activities

Net income	$ 36,600

Cash Flow from Financing Activities

Cash payment for dividends	$(24,900)

ANALYSIS OF CURRENT ASSETS. We next analyze Accounts Receivable, which has increased $1,800 during the period (from $104,900 to $106,700). As with most current asset and current liability accounts, this change affects net income; that is, as Accounts Receivable is increased, so is Sales Revenue, which increases net income. This is in accordance with accrual-basis accounting, whereby revenues are recognized when they are earned whether or not cash has been received, and expenses are reported when they are incurred, whether or not cash has been paid. Since the increase in Accounts Receivable produced an increase in accrual-basis income, but not in cash-basis income, the $1,800 must be subtracted from the reported net income of $36,600. If Accounts Receivable had decreased, the amount of the change would have been added to net income since more cash would have been generated during the period than was reported as income on an accrual basis.

Continuing with the Pioneer Stores illustration, Inventory decreased by $10,200. Instead of using cash to purchase new inventory, Pioneer Stores allowed inventory to decline. The cash-basis income, therefore, would be greater than the accrual-basis net income figure. Similar reasoning can be used to explain the change in Prepaid Expenses. The decrease in prepaid expenses means that the amount of cash paid for selling and administrative expenses was $2,200 less than the expenses reported on the income statement.

These adjustments would be added to the operating activities section of the developing cash flow statement as shown.

Cash Flow from Operating Activities

Net income	$36,600
Add (deduct) adjustments to cash basis:	
Increase in accounts receivable	(1,800)
Decrease in inventory	10,200
Decrease in prepaid expenses	2,200

ANALYSIS OF LAND, BUILDINGS, AND EQUIPMENT. The next account to be analyzed, Land, shows a significant change ($80,000). However, as Note 1 in Exhibit 15-6 explains, this change resulted from the purchase of land by issuing 40,000 shares of stock. Though this is a significant transaction and therefore should be disclosed, it did not involve cash and should not be reported on the statement of cash flows. Instead, it would be reported in a narrative or in a separate schedule accompanying the financial statements.

The next two accounts, Buildings and Equipment and the related Accumulated Depreciation, must be considered together. In analyzing the changes in these accounts, you must be certain to recognize all transactions affecting them. You cannot assume that the net change in account balances represents cash flows.

To illustrate, we know from Note 2 on the income statement (Exhibit 15-7) that equipment purchased for $12,300 in a previous year was sold for $8,300 in 1994 and a gain of $7,800 was recognized. This transaction reduces both the Buildings and Equipment and Accumulated Depreciation accounts. During 1994, the cost of the equipment ($12,300) was written off along with the related portion of the accumulated depreciation. Since the book value is $500 and the cost of the equipment is $12,300, the amount of accumulated depreciation written off was $11,800 ($12,300 − $500 book value). The cash proceeds from the sale were $8,300, which produced the gain of $7,800 ($8,300 proceeds − $500 book value), as shown in the following journal entry.

Cash	8,300	
Accumulated Depreciation	11,800	
Equipment		12,300
Gain on Sale of Equipment		7,800
Sold used equipment with a book value of $500 for $8,300.		

This transaction is different from those explained so far. The $12,300 credit to Buildings and Equipment and the $11,800 debit to Accumulated Depreciation are required to eliminate those amounts from the accounts upon the sale of the assets. However, these amounts relate to earlier accounting periods, dating from the time the equipment was first purchased. They do not affect cash flows in the current period. Only the proceeds from the sale is a cash flow during the current period, and so it is shown in the investing activities section. However, the $36,600 of net income already includes the $7,800 gain. If net income is reported at $36,600 and the $8,300 is listed separately as a cash inflow, the $7,800 gain would be counted twice. Therefore, to correctly show the total amount of the proceeds from the sale as a separate cash inflow requires that we adjust the net income amount by subtracting the $7,800 gain. After this adjustment is made, the accrual-basis gain will be eliminated from net income and the cash proceeds from the sale of equipment ($8,300) will be shown under investing activities.

The remaining changes in the Buildings and Equipment account ($58,300) must have resulted from the use of cash to purchase buildings and equipment, as shown in the following T-account.

Buildings and Equipment

12/31/93 Balance	577,200		
1994 Purchases	58,300	1994 Sales	12,300
12/31/94 Balance	623,200		

Similarly, after the write-off of accumulated depreciation on the sale of the equipment, the depreciation expense for the period ($32,100, as reported on the income statement in Exhibit 15-7) explains the remaining difference in Accumulated Depreciation as shown in the following T-account:

Accumulated Depreciation

		12/31/93 Balance	223,600
1994 Sale of Equipment	11,800	1994 Depreciation	32,100
		12/31/94 Balance	243,900

Depreciation expense is only a bookkeeping entry; it does not involve cash. Although net income has been reduced by the amount of the depreciation expense, no cash has actually flowed out of the company. (Cash is reduced when the equipment is purchased, not when it is depreciated.) Thus, the amount of depreciation expense must be added back to net income to correctly report the cash from operations.

It is important to note that other noncash expenses would be treated as adjustments to net income in the same way as depreciation. For example, amortization expense for intangible assets such as patents or goodwill, amortization of bond discounts or premiums, or any other expense that decreases (or increases) net income but not cash must be added to (or subtracted from) net income to arrive at the amount of cash from operations.

The partially completed statement of cash flows for Pioneer Stores would now appear as follows:

Cash Flow from Operating Activities

Net income	$ 36,600
Add (deduct) adjustments to cash basis:	
Increase in accounts receivable	(1,800)
Decrease in inventory	10,200
Decrease in prepaid expenses	2,200
Gain on sale of equipment	(7,800)
Depreciation	32,100

Cash Flow from Investing Activities

Sale of equipment	$ 8,300
Purchase of equipment	(58,300)

Cash Flow from Financing Activities

Cash payments for dividends	$(24,900)

ANALYSIS OF CURRENT LIABILITIES. As explained earlier in the chapter, an increase in a payable account means that the accrual-basis expenses reported in the income statement exceed the amount of cash paid during the period. Thus, the $500 increase in Accounts Payable and the $5,500 increase in Income Taxes Payable would be added to net income. If there had been a decrease in a payable account, that amount would be deducted from net income since the amount of cash paid would have been greater than accrual-basis expenses reported.

Note that some current accounts do not affect operations, so they do not require adjustments to net income. For example, suppose a company has an increase in Short-Term Notes Payable. This change would involve a cash inflow—the proceeds from borrowing—but not an adjustment to net income since this transaction does not generate revenue and is not included in the income statement. The cash inflow from short-term borrowing would be reported in the financing activities section of a statement of cash flows.

ANALYSIS OF LONG-TERM LIABILITIES. Only two additional accounts need to be analyzed. The Long-Term Notes Payable account increased by $20,000, indicating that cash was provided by borrowing, a financing activity. The Mortgage Payable account decreased by $12,900, indicating that cash was used to pay a portion of the mortgage. The payment of the mortgage principal is classified as a financing activity.

NET INCREASE IN CASH AND CASH EQUIVALENTS. Since the stockholders' equity accounts have already been analyzed, all changes in account balances have now been explained, and we are ready to complete the cash flow statement. Recall that the first step in preparing the statement of cash flows was to determine that Pioneer had a $9,700 increase in cash and cash equivalents. Therefore, the net total of cash flows from operating, investing, and financing activities should equal $9,700.

Chapter 15 *Statement of Cash Flows*

THE STATEMENT OF CASH FLOWS AND SUPPLEMENTAL DISCLOSURES. The formal statement of cash flows can now be prepared and is presented as Exhibit 15-8. As explained earlier in the chapter, the disclosure of noncash transactions can be presented below the statement of cash flows or in the notes to the financial statements. In our example, we have presented the information below the statement of cash flows.

Other disclosures required by FASB Statement No. 95 include the amounts paid for interest and income taxes. When the indirect method is used to report cash flows from operating activities, cash paid for interest and income taxes does not appear in the statement of cash flows and is disclosed as supplemental information as illustrated in Exhibit 15-8. For Pioneer Stores, the amount of interest paid was $14,200, which is the Interest Expense shown on

Exhibit 15-8

Pioneer Stores, Inc.
Statement of Cash Flows (Indirect Method)
For the Year Ended December 31, 1994

Cash Flow from Operating Activities

Net income		$ 36,600
Add (deduct) adjustments to cash basis:		
Increase in accounts receivable	(1,800)	
Decrease in inventory	10,200	
Decrease in prepaid expenses	2,200	
Gain on sale of equipment	(7,800)	
Depreciation	32,100	
Increase in accounts payable	500	
Increase in income taxes payable	5,500	
Net cash flow provided by operating activities		$ 77,500

Cash Flow from Investing Activities

Sale of equipment	$ 8,300	
Purchase of equipment	(58,300)	
Net cash flow used in investing activities		(50,000)

Cash Flow from Financing Activities

Cash payments for dividends	$(24,900)	
Cash receipt from long-term notes payable	20,000	
Cash payment of mortgage payable	(12,900)	
Net cash flow used in financing activities		(17,800)
Net increase in cash and cash equivalents		$ 9,700
Cash and cash equivalents at beginning of year		7,900
Cash and cash equivalents at end of year		$ 17,600

Supplemental Disclosures

Cash payments for:	
Interest	$ 14,200
Income taxes	21,700

Noncash transactions:
 Land with a fair market value of $80,000 was acquired through the issuance of 40,000 shares of no-par common stock.

the income statement since there is no Interest Payable account. The amount of cash paid for income taxes is $21,700 ($27,200 Income Tax Expense less the $5,500 increase in Income Taxes Payable). When the direct method is used to report cash flows from operating activities, these amounts are included in the statement of cash flows, as will be illustrated in the following section.

The Direct Method Illustrated

As indicated earlier, the net cash flow provided by (used in) operating activities is an important number for investors and creditors to know. For Pioneer Stores, the $9,700 net cash flow provided by operating activities may be determined using the direct method, either by analyzing all cash transactions individually or by converting revenues and expenses from an accrual-basis income statement to a cash-basis one, as shown in Exhibit 15-9. The statement of cash flows prepared from the work sheet is shown in Exhibit 15-10.

Exhibit 15-9

Pioneer Stores, Inc.
Work Sheet for Statement of Cash Flows (Direct Method)
For the Year Ended December 31, 1994

	Accrual Basis	Adjustments Debits	Adjustments Credits	Cash Basis
Net sales revenue	$859,400	(1) $1,800		$857,600
Other revenues	7,800	(2) $7,800		–0–
Total revenues	$867,200			$857,600
Expenses:				
Cost of goods sold	$610,100		(3) 10,200	
			(4) 500	$599,400
Selling and administrative expenses	147,000		(5) 2,200	144,800
Depreciation expense	32,100		(6) 32,100	–0–
Interest expense	14,200			14,200
Total expenses	$803,400			$758,400
Income before taxes	$ 63,800			$ 99,200
Income taxes	27,200		(7) 5,500	21,700
Net income	$ 36,600			$ 77,500

Key:

(1) Increase in Accounts Receivable (sales not yet collected).
(2) Gain on sale of equipment.
(3) Decrease in Inventory (inventory sold this period but purchased last period).
(4) Increase in Accounts Payable (purchases made this period but not yet paid for).
(5) Decrease in Prepaid Expenses (prepaid expenses used this period but paid for last period).
(6) Depreciation (noncash item).
(7) Increase in Income Taxes Payable (income taxes of this period but not yet paid).

Exhibit 15-10

Pioneer Stores, Inc.
Statement of Cash Flows (Direct Method)
For the Year Ended December 31, 1994

Cash Flow from Operating Activities

Cash receipts from:
Customers		$857,600
Cash payments for:		
Inventory	$599,400	
Selling and administrative expenses	144,800	
Interest expense	14,200	
Income tax expense	21,700	780,100
Net cash flow provided by operating activities		$ 77,500

Cash Flow from Investing Activities

Cash receipts from sale of equipment	$ 8,300	
Cash payments for equipment	(58,300)	
Net cash flow used in investing activities		(50,000)

Cash Flow from Financing Activities

Cash payments for dividends	$ (24,900)	
Cash receipts from borrowing (long-term note payable)	20,000	
Cash payments for mortgage payable	(12,900)	
Net cash flow used in financing activities		(17,800)
Net increase in cash		$ 9,700
Cash and cash equivalents at beginning of year		7,900
Cash and cash equivalents at end of year		$ 17,600

Supplemental Disclosures

Noncash transaction: Land with a fair market value of $80,000 was acquired through the issuance of 40,000 shares of no-par common stock.

Reconciliation of net income to net cash flow provided by operations:

Net income	$36,600
Add (deduct) adjustments to cash basis:	
Increase in accounts receivable	(1,800)
Decrease in inventory	10,200
Decrease in prepaid expenses	2,200
Gain on sale of equipment	(7,800)
Depreciation	32,100
Increase in accounts payable	500
Increase in income taxes payable	5,500
Net cash flow provided by operating activities	$77,500

Exhibit 15-9 uses the same analysis described earlier, whereby sales and other revenues as well as cost of goods sold and other expenses are converted to a cash basis, and noncash items are eliminated. Once the net cash flow provided by (used in) operating activities is determined, the nonoperating balance sheet accounts are analyzed to determine cash flows from investing and financing activities. The reporting for these activities is the same regardless of the method used for operating activities. (Compare Exhibits 15-8 and 15-10.)

As explained previously, FASB Statement No. 95 requires disclosure of amounts paid for interest and income taxes. With the direct method, these amounts are included in the statement of cash flows, as shown in Exhibit 15-10. The disclosure of noncash transactions is presented separately as it was in the illustration of the statement of cash flows prepared using the indirect method. An additional disclosure required when the direct method is used is a schedule reconciling net income with net cash flow provided by (used in) operating activities. This schedule is, in effect, the same as the operating activities section of a cash flow statement prepared using the indirect method.

> **To Summarize** *In preparing a statement of cash flows, the following steps may be used: (1) compute the change in the Cash and cash-equivalent accounts for the period; (2) analyze all accounts other than Cash to see if cash receipts or payments were involved, using either the direct or the indirect method; (3) check to see that the total net cash flow from the statement is equal to the net increase (decrease) in cash as computed in (1); (4) prepare a formal statement of cash flows, classifying all cash inflows and outflows as operating, investing, or financing activities; and (5) report any significant noncash investing and financing transactions in a narrative or in a separate schedule to the financial statements.*

USEFULNESS OF CASH FLOW STATEMENTS

Objective 5
Understand the usefulness of cash flow statements.

The overriding objective of financial reporting is to provide information that is useful in making economic decisions. As mentioned briefly at the beginning of the chapter, the Financial Accounting Standards Board determined that a statement of cash flows would be more useful than the previously required statement of changes in financial position or funds statement. Now that you are familiar with the statement of cash flows, we will explain how and why this statement became one of the three primary financial statements.

Historical Perspective

In 1971, APB Opinion No. 19 made the funds statement a required financial statement although many companies had begun reporting funds flow information several years earlier. The funds statement provided useful information, but it had several limitations. First, APB Opinion No. 19 allowed considerable flexibility in how funds could be defined and how they were reported on the statement. As a result, many companies reported on a working-capital basis (current assets minus current liabilities), whereas others reported on a cash basis or some other basis. Further, in each case, the individual company selected its own format. This inconsistency across companies made comparisons difficult.

Second, the funds statement, even when prepared on a cash basis, did not provide a complete and clear picture of a company's ability to generate positive cash flows. One reason is that APB Opinion No. 19 required that all investing and financing activities be reported in the statement, even those that did not affect cash or working capital. Another problem was that the funds statement usually included two sections—sources (inflows) and uses (outflows) of funds. Thus, the amount of working capital or cash provided or used by each major type of activity (operating, financing, and investing) was not identified.

Importance of Cash Flow Analysis

The limitations of the funds statement often made it difficult to assess a company's ability to generate sufficient cash. Some companies were able to report favorable earnings in the income statement, even while experiencing serious cash flow problems that were not readily apparent from the information reported in the funds statement. For example, Endo-Lase, a distributor of medical lasers, reported a 200 percent increase in sales in one year. Unfortunately, because receivables increased at an even faster rate than sales due to poor collection performance, much of the reported increase in revenues took the form of IOUs. When many of these receivables were determined to be uncollectible, Endo-Lase had to restate its previously reported earnings. So, though reported earnings appeared strong, Endo-Lase's cash flow was actually negative, and eventually the company had to file for bankruptcy protection. The Business Environment Essay on page 646 provides another example of the value of cash flow analysis in predicting a company's ability to survive.

Although the statement of cash flows, like the other financial statements, reports information about the past, careful analysis of this information can help investors, creditors, and others assess the amounts, timing, and uncertainty of future cash flows. Specifically, the statement helps users answer questions such as, How is a company able to pay dividends when it had a net loss? or Why is a company short of cash despite increased earnings? A statement of cash flows may show, for example, that external borrowing or the issuance of capital stock provided the cash from which dividends were paid even though a net loss was reported for that year. Similarly, a company may be short on cash, even with increased earnings, because of increased inventory purchases, plant expansion, or debt retirement.

Because companies are required to highlight cash flows from operating, investing, and financing activities, a company's operating cash flows and investing and financing policies can be compared with those of other companies. Furthermore, statements of cash flows are usually presented on a comparative basis, which enables users to identify important trends in a company's cash flows over time. A comparative cash flow statement for General Mills is presented in the Illustrative Financial Statements at the end of the book.

BUSINESS ENVIRONMENT ESSAY
The W. T. Grant Company Bankruptcy

The W. T. Grant Company was the nation's largest retailer when it filed for protection under Chapter XI of the National Bankruptcy Act on October 2, 1975. Only 4 months later, the creditors committee voted for liquidation, and Grant ceased to exist. As late as 1973, Grant stock was selling at nearly 20 times earnings, and as late as September 1974, a group of banks extended loans totaling $600 million to the company. Why couldn't creditors and stockholders see Grant's impending problems any sooner? As the following chart shows, net income and working capital provided by operations was of little help in predicting Grant's problems before 1973, but a careful analysis of the company's cash flows would have revealed the problems as much as a decade before the collapse.

W. T. Grant Company
Net Income, Working Capital, and Cash Flow from Operations
For Fiscal Years Ending January 31, 1966 to 1975

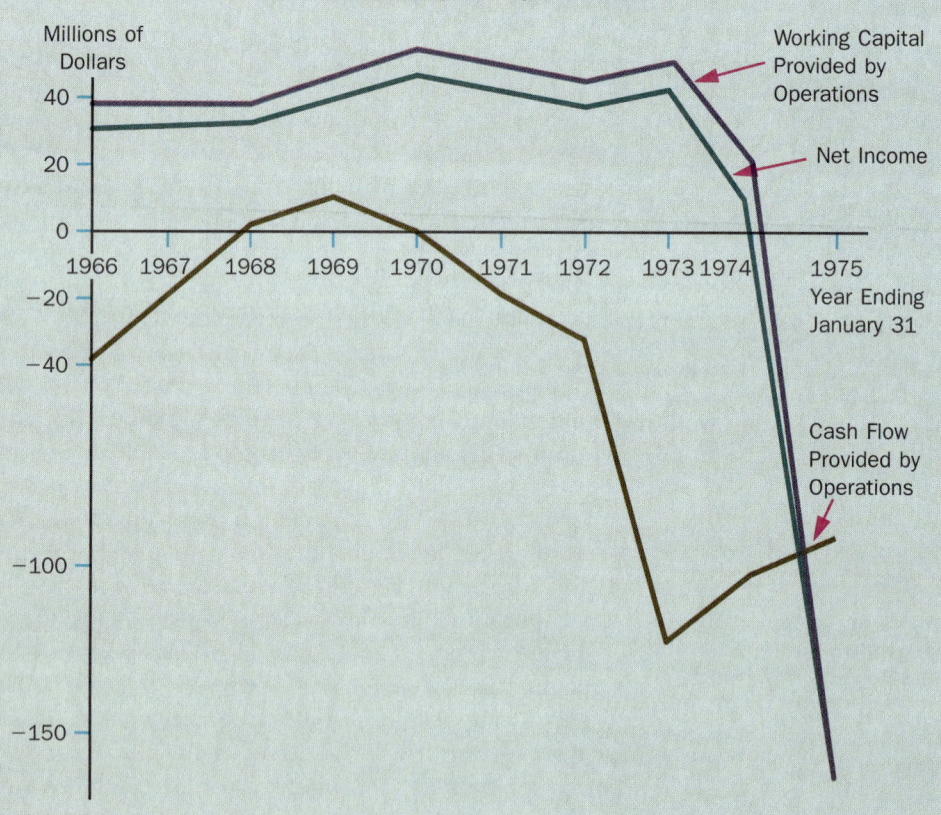

This chart shows that although both working capital and net income remained positive through 1974, cash flow provided by operations was almost consistently negative from 1966 to 1975. During this period, the company simply lost its ability to derive cash from operations. And after exhausting the possibilities of its liquid resources, it had to tap external markets for funds. As the failure to generate cash internally continued, the need for external financing snowballed.

Selected Events in the Life of W. T. Grant
12/6/06 William T. Grant opened $.25 cent store in Lynn, Massachusetts.
   1928 Stock was offered to the public.

1953	Had 500 stores.
1963	William T. Grant retired.
1969	Opened 410 new stores.
9/26/74	Banks loaned $600 million to the company.
11/7/74	Signed agreement to accept MasterCard and Bank Americard.
12/9/74	Stock price was at $2 per share from a high of $70⅝.
4/23/74	Hired new president.
8/1/75	Opened 6 new stores.
9/11/75	Closed 107 stores and laid off 7,000 employees.
10/2/75	Chairman, Senior Vice President and all outside directors resign.
2/13/76	Judge orders liquidation in 60 days.
4/15/76	Company adjudicated as a bankrupt.

Source: Adapted from "Cash Flows, Ratio Analysis and the W. T. Grant Company Bankruptcy," James A. Largay, III, and Clyde P. Stickney, *Financial Analysis Journal,* July–August 1980, pp. 51–54.

Review of Learning Objectives

Objective 1

Explain the purposes of a statement of cash flows. The statement of cash flows is one of the three primary financial statements presented by companies in their annual reports. Its primary purpose is to provide information about the cash receipts and payments of an entity during a period. The statement of cash flows also explains the changes in the balance sheet accounts and the cash effects of the accrual-basis amounts reported in the income statement. It has replaced the statement of changes in financial position or funds statement.

Objective 2

Describe the information reported in the statement of cash flows, including the major classifications of cash into operating, investing, and financing activities. The statement of cash flows reports an entity's inflows and outflows of cash for a period of time and reconciles the beginning and ending balances of cash and cash equivalents.

The inflows and outflows of cash should be classified and reported for three main categories: operating activities, investing activities, and financing activities. Cash receipts and payments classified under operating activities generally include all items that enter into the determination of net income. Examples include receipts from the sale of goods or services and from interest and the payments for inventory, wages, utilities, taxes, and interest. Investing activities include the purchase and sale of securities (other than cash equivalents, which are included with cash), buildings and equipment, and other assets that are not generally purchased for resale by the entity. Also included are the making and collecting of loans.

Financing activities include obtaining and repaying cash from owners (equity financing) and from creditors (debt financing). Selling stock, paying cash dividends, and borrowing money, for example, are included under this category.

Significant noncash transactions involving investing and financing activities should be reported in a narrative or in a separate schedule to the financial statements. Since they do not involve cash flows, they should not be reported in the statement of cash flows. An example would be the purchase of land by the issuance of stock.

Objective 3

Understand the indirect and direct methods of reporting operating cash flows. The net cash flow provided by (used in) operating activities is an important item that should be highlighted on a statement of cash flows. There are two methods of computing this amount: the indirect and the direct methods. The indirect method reconciles net income, as reported on the income statement, with the net cash flow provided by (used in) operating activities by converting accrual-basis net income to a cash basis. The direct method shows the major classes of operating cash receipts and payments, the difference being net cash flow provided by (used in) operating activities. Preparers of financial statements tend to favor the indirect method, whereas users often prefer the direct method. Both methods produce the same results, and both are acceptable accounting methods. The indirect method is by far the most commonly used method in practice.

Objective 4

Prepare a statement of cash flows. A statement of cash flows may be prepared by following a five-step approach. First, compute the change in the Cash and cash-equivalent accounts for the period of the statement. Second, analyze all accounts other than Cash to see if cash receipts or payments were involved in the changes in account balances between periods. Third, make sure the total net cash flow is equal to the net increase or decrease in Cash, as computed in the first step. Fourth, prepare a formal statement of cash flows by classifying all cash inflows and outflows according to operating, investing, and financing activities. Fifth, report separately any significant investing or financing transactions that did not involve cash.

Objective 5

Understand the usefulness of cash flow statements. A careful analysis of the statement of cash flows will indicate shifts in a company's operating, investing, and financing policies. The statement explains the change in the cash balance during the period by identifying the inflows and outflows of cash. This helps investors and creditors observe trends related to a company's use of operating income and to its use of external sources of capital such as the issuance of stock or bonds. Used with the income statement and the balance sheet, the statement of cash flows is a valuable source of information.

Key Terms and Concepts

cash equivalents *(625)*
direct method *(631)*
financing activities *(627)*

indirect method *(629)*
investing activities *(626)*
noncash items *(630)*

noncash transactions *(627)*
operating activities *(626)*
statement of cash flows *(624)*

Review Problem

Preparing a Statement of Cash Flows

Cougar Corporation produces clock radios. Comparative income statements and balance sheets for the years ended December 31, 1994 and 1993, are presented.

Cougar Corporation
Income Statements
For the Years Ended December 31, 1994 and 1993

	1994	1993
Net sales revenue	$600,000	$575,000
Cost of goods sold	500,000	460,000
Gross margin	$100,000	$115,000
Operating expenses	66,000	60,000
Operating income	$ 34,000	$ 55,000
Interest expense	4,000	3,000
Income before taxes	$ 30,000	$ 52,000
Income taxes	12,000	21,000
Net income	$ 18,000	$ 31,000

Cougar Corporation
Balance Sheets
December 31, 1994 and 1993

Assets	1994	1993
Current Assets:		
Cash and cash equivalents	$ 11,000	$ 13,000
Accounts receivable (net)	92,000	77,000
Inventory	103,000	92,000
Prepaid expenses	6,000	5,000
Total current assets	$212,000	$187,000
Property, Plant, and Equipment:		
Land	$ 69,000	$ 66,000
Machinery and Equipment	172,000	156,000
Accumulated Depreciation, Machinery and Equipment	(113,000)	(102,000)
Total Property, Plant and Equipment	$128,000	$120,000
Total Assets	$340,000	$307,000

Liabilities and Stockholders' Equity		
Current liabilities:		
Accounts payable	$ 66,000	$ 78,000
Dividends payable	2,000	–0–
Income taxes payable	3,000	5,000
Total current liabilities	$ 71,000	$ 83,000
Long-term debt	75,000	42,000
Total liabilities	$146,000	$125,000
Stockholders' equity:		
Common stock, no par	$ 26,000	$ 26,000
Retained earnings	168,000	156,000
Total stockholders' equity	$194,000	$182,000
Total liabilities and stockholders' equity	$340,000	$307,000

The following additional information is available.

(a) Dividends declared during 1994 were $6,000.
(b) Market price per share of stock on December 31, 1994, was $14.50.
(c) Equipment worth $16,000 was acquired by the issuance of a long-term note ($10,000) and by paying cash ($6,000).
(d) Land was acquired for $3,000 cash.
(e) Depreciation of $11,000 was included in operating expenses for 1994.
(f) There were no accruals or prepaid amounts for interest.

Required: Prepare a statement of cash flows using (1) the indirect method and (2) the direct method.

Solution   **1. Indirect Method**

Cougar Corporation
Statement of Cash Flows (Indirect Method)
For the Year Ended December 31, 1994

Cash Flow from Operating Activities

Net income	$18,000	
Add (deduct) adjustments to cash basis:		
Depreciation expense	11,000	
Increase in accounts receivable	(15,000)	
Increase in inventory	(11,000)	
Increase in prepaid expenses	(1,000)	
Decrease in accounts payable	(12,000)	
Decrease in income taxes payable	(2,000)	
Net cash flow used in operating activities		$(12,000)

Cash Flow from Investing Activities

Cash payments for:		
Land	$(3,000)	
Machinery and equipment	(6,000)	
Net cash flow used in investing activities		(9,000)

Cash Flow from Financing Activities

Cash receipts from long-term borrowing	$23,000	
Cash payments for dividends	(4,000)*	
Net cash flow provided by financing activities		19,000
Net decrease in cash		$ (2,000)
Cash and cash equivalents at beginning of year		13,000
Cash and cash equivalents at end of year		$ 11,000

*Cash dividends declared ($6,000) less increase in dividends payable ($2,000).

Supplemental Disclosure

Cash payments for:
    Interest .... $ 4,000
    Income taxes 14,000
Noncash transaction
    Equipment was purchased by issuing a long-term note for $10,000.

    The statement of cash flows for Cougar Corporation shows that although reported net income was positive for 1994, the net cash flow generated from operating activities was negative. Only by borrowing cash was Cougar Corporation able to pay dividends and purchase land and equipment. Even then the Cash account decreased by $2,000 during the period.

2. Direct Method

Cougar Corporation
Statement of Cash Flows (Direct Method)
For the Year Ended December 31, 1994

Cash Flow from Operating Activities

Cash receipts from customers		$585,000
Cash payments for:		
Inventory	$523,000	
Operating expenses	56,000	
Interest expense	4,000	
Income tax expense	14,000	597,000
Net cash flow used in operating activities		$ (12,000)

Cash Flow from Investing Activities

Cash payments for:		
Land	$ (3,000)	
Machinery and equipment	(6,000)	
Net cash flow used in investing activities		(9,000)

Cash Flow from Financing Activities

Cash receipts from long-term borrowing	$ 23,000	
Cash payments for dividends	(4,000)	
Net cash flow provided by financing activities		19,000
Net decrease in cash and cash equivalents		$ (2,000)
Cash and cash equivalents at beginning of year		13,000
Cash and cash equivalents at end of year		$ 11,000

Supplemental Disclosure*

Equipment was purchased by issuing a long-term note for $10,000.

* A schedule reconciling net income with net cash flow used by operating activities would also be presented, either with the statement of cash flows or in the notes to the financial statements. The information provided in the schedule is the same as the operating activities section of the statement of cash flows prepared using the indirect method (see part 1).

A work sheet appears below although it is not required. The key to the items in the adjustment columns appears below the work sheet.

Cougar Corporation
Work Sheet for a Statement of Cash Flows (Direct Method)
For the Year Ended December 31, 1994

	Accrual Basis	Adjustments Debits	Adjustments Credits	Cash Basis
Revenues:				
Net sales	600,000	(1) 15,000		585,000
Expenses:				
Cost of goods sold	500,000	(2) 11,000		523,000
		(3) 12,000		
Operating expense	66,000	(4) 1,000	(5) 11,000	56,000
Interest expense	4,000			4,000
Income tax expense	12,000	(6) 2,000		14,000
	582,000			597,000
Net income	18,000			(12,000)

Key:
1. Increase in Accounts Receivable (sales not yet collected).
2. Increase in Inventory (inventory purchased this period but not yet sold).
3. Decrease in Accounts Payable (purchases paid for this period that were not expenses of the period).
4. Increase in Prepaid Expenses (cash paid this period to increase prepaid expenses not yet used).
5. Depreciation expenses (noncash item that must be eliminated).
6. Decrease in Income Taxes Payable (taxes paid this period that were recognized as an expense last period).

Discussion Questions

1. What are the main purposes of a statement of cash flows?
2. What are cash equivalents, and how are they treated on a statement of cash flows?
3. Distinguish among cash flows from operating, investing, and financing activities.
4. How are significant noncash investing and financing transactions to be reported?
5. Distinguish between the indirect and direct methods of reporting net cash flow provided by (used in) operating activities.
6. Describe the process of converting from accrual revenues to cash receipts.
7. How are depreciation and similar noncash items treated on a statement of cash flows?
8. What are the major differences between the traditional statement of changes in financial position (funds statement) and the statement of cash flows?
9. Why has the FASB decided to replace the statement of changes in financial position with the statement of cash flows?
10. What purpose does a statement of cash flows serve for investors and creditors?

Exercises

E15-1
Classification of Cash Flows

Indicate whether each of the following items would be classified as a cash inflow (I), cash outflow (O), or noncash item (N), and under which category each would be reported on a statement of cash flows: Operating Activities (OA); Investing Activities (IA); Financing Activities (FA); or not on the statement (NOS). An example is provided.

Item	Classified As	Reported Under
Example: Sales Revenue	I	OA

1. Fees for services
2. Interest paid
3. Proceeds from sale of equipment
4. Cash (principal) received from bank on long-term note
5. Purchase of treasury stock
6. Collection of loan made to company officer
7. Cash dividends paid
8. Taxes paid
9. Depreciation expense
10. Wages paid to employees
11. Cash paid for inventory purchases
12. Proceeds from sale of common stock
13. Interest received on loan to company officer
14. Purchase of land by issuing stock
15. Utility bill paid

E15-2
Adjustments to Cash Flow from Operations (Indirect Method)

Assume that you are using the indirect method of preparing a statement of cash flows. For the account balance changes listed, indicate which ones would be added to and which ones would be subtracted from net income in computing net cash flow provided by (used in) operating activities. If the change does not affect net cash flow provided by (used in) operating activities, so indicate.

1. Increase in Accounts Receivable
2. Decrease in Accounts Payable
3. Increase in Short-Term Investments in Marketable Securities
4. Gain on sale of equipment
5. Decrease in Inventory
6. Increase in Prepaid Insurance
7. Depreciation
8. Increase in Wages Payable
9. Decrease in Dividends Payable
10. Decrease in Interest Receivable

E15-3
Cash Flow from Operations (Direct Method)

Jane Ortiz is the proprietor of a small company. The results of operations for last year are shown, along with selected balance sheet data. From the information provided, determine the amount of net cash flow from operations using the direct method.

Sales revenue	$200,000	
Cost of goods sold	140,000	
Gross margin		$60,000
Operating expenses:		
Wages expense	$ 25,000	
Utilities expense	1,800	
Rent expense	12,000	
Insurance expense	3,000	41,800
Net income		$18,200

	Beginning of Year	End of Year
Accounts receivable	$22,000	$25,000
Inventory	35,000	30,000
Prepaid insurance	3,000	2,500
Accounts payable	14,000	17,000
Wages payable	4,000	2,000

E15-4
Cash Flow from Operations (Indirect Method)

Given the data in E15-3, show how the amount of net cash flow from operating activities would be calculated using the indirect method.

E15-5
Transaction Analysis

Following are the transactions of Dalta Company:

(a) Sold equipment for $1,000. The original cost was $15,700; the book value is $1,700.
(b) Purchased equipment costing $110,000 by paying cash of $20,000 and signing a $90,000 long-term note at 12 percent interest.
(c) Received $5,000 of the principal and $450 in interest on a long-term note receivable.
(d) Received $2,500 in cash dividends on stock held as a short-term investment. (Assume that the cost method is used.)
(e) Purchased treasury stock for $3,000.

Complete the following:

1. Prepare journal entries for each of the transactions. (Omit explanations.)
2. For each transaction, indicate the amount of cash inflow or outflow. Then, note how each transaction would be classified on a statement of cash flows.

E15-6 Cash Provided by Operations (Direct Method)

The following information was taken from the comparative financial statements of Imperial Corporation for the years ended December 31, 1993 and 1994:

Net income for 1994	$ 90,000
Sales revenue	500,000
Cost of goods sold	300,000
Depreciation expense for 1994	60,000
Amortization of goodwill for 1994	10,000
Interest expense on short-term debt for 1994	3,500
Dividends declared and paid in 1994	65,000

	Dec. 31, 1994	Dec. 31, 1993
Accounts receivable (net)	$30,000	$43,000
Inventory	50,000	42,000
Accounts payable	56,000	59,400

Use the direct method to compute cash provided by operating activities in 1994. (Hint: You need to calculate cash paid for operating expenses.)

E15-7 Cash Provided by Operations (Indirect Method)

Given the data in E15-6, show how the amount of cash provided by operations for 1994 is computed using the indirect method.

E15-8 Statement of Cash Flows (Direct Method)

Based on the following information, prepare a statement of cash flows using the direct method for Porter Corporation for the year ended December 31, 1994:

Cash received from interest revenue	$ 14,000
Cash paid for dividends	45,000
Cash collected from customers	349,000
Cash paid for wages	254,000
Depreciation expense for the period	25,000
Cash received from issuance of common stock	200,000
Cash paid for retirement of bonds at par	100,000
Cash received on sale of equipment at book value	5,000
Cash paid for land	85,000

E15-9 Statement of Cash Flows (Indirect Method)

Given the following selected data for Backman Corporation, use the indirect method to prepare a statement of cash flows for the year ended December 31, 1994:

Net income	$ 95,000
Depreciation	25,000
Other operating expenses	140,000
Cost of goods sold	240,000
Sales revenue	500,000
Increase in accounts receivable	10,000
Decrease in accounts payable	5,000
Decrease in inventory	3,000
Increase in prepaid assets	7,000
Increase in wages payable	15,000
Equipment purchased for cash	40,000
Increase in bonds payable	100,000
Dividends declared and paid	40,000
Decrease in dividends payable	2,000

Problem Set A

P15A-1
Cash Flow from Operations (Indirect Method)

Terminal Company reported a net loss of $25,000 for the year just ended. Relevant data for the company follows.

	Beginning of Year	End of Year
Cash and cash equivalents	$18,000	$ 7,000
Accounts receivable	34,000	24,000
Inventory	80,000	82,000
Prepaid expenses	4,000	3,500
Accounts payable	12,000	17,000
Accrued liabilities	8,000	2,000
Dividends payable	15,000	20,000

Depreciation for the year: $23,000
Dividends declared: $20,000

Required:
1. Using the indirect method, determine the net cash flow provided by (used in) operating activities for Terminal Company.
2. **Interpretive Question** Explain how Terminal Company can pay cash dividends during a year when it reports a net loss.

P15A-2
Cash Flow from Operations (Direct Method)

SPREADSHEET PROBLEM

The following combined income and retained earnings statement, along with selected balance sheet data, is provided for High Flying Company:

High Flying Company
Combined Income and Retained Earnings Statement
For the Year Ended December 31, 1994

Net sales revenue		$85,000
Other revenues		4,500[1]
Total revenues		$89,500
Expenses:		
Cost of goods sold	$51,000	
Selling and administrative expenses	14,700	
Depreciation expense	3,200	
Interest expense	1,400	
Total expenses		70,300
Income before taxes		$19,200
Income taxes		5,760
Net income		$13,440
Retained earnings, January 1, 1994		33,500
		$46,940
Dividends declared and paid		2,500
Retained earnings, December 31, 1994		$44,440

[1] Gain on sale of equipment (Cost $9,500; book value, $6,000; sales price $10,500).

	Beginning of Year	End of Year
Accounts receivable (net)	$10,500	$11,000
Inventory	19,300	18,000
Prepaid expenses	950	700
Accounts payable	7,200	8,000
Interest payable	1,500	1,000
Income taxes payable	500	2,500

Required: 1. Using the direct method, compute the amount of net cash flow from operations for High Flying Company for 1994.
2. What is the impact of dividends paid on net cash flow from operations? Explain.

P15A-3
Statement of Cash Flows
(Direct Method)

The following information was provided by the treasurer of Nichols, Inc., a manufacturer of voting machine equipment, for the year 1994:

(a) Cash sales for the year were $50,000; sales on account totaled $60,000.
(b) Cost of goods sold was 50 percent of total sales.
(c) All inventory is purchased on account.
(d) Depreciation on equipment was $31,000 for the year.
(e) Amortization of goodwill was $2,000.
(f) Collection of accounts receivable was $38,000.
(g) Payments on accounts payable for inventory equaled $39,000.
(h) Rent expense paid in cash was $11,000.
(i) 20,000 shares of $10 par stock were issued for $240,000.
(j) Land was acquired by issuance of a $100,000 bond that sold for $106,000.
(k) Equipment was purchased for cash at a cost of $84,000.
(l) Dividends of $46,000 were declared but not yet paid.
(m) $15,000 of dividends that had been declared the previous year were paid.
(n) A machine used on the assembly line was sold for $12,000. The machine had a book value of $7,000.
(o) Another machine with a book value of $500 was scrapped and was reported as an ordinary loss. No cash was received on this transaction.
(p) The Cash account increased $191,000 during the year.

Required: Use the direct method to prepare a statement of cash flows for Nichols, Inc., for the year ending December 31, 1994.

P15A-4
Statement of Cash Flows
(Direct Method)

Financial statement data for Continental Stores, Inc. are provided. (All numbers are shown rounded to the nearest thousand, with the final three zeros omitted.)

Continental Stores, Inc.
Income and Retained Earnings Statements
For the Year Ended December 31, 1994

Sales revenue	$1,290
Cost of goods sold	978
Gross margin	$ 312
Operating expenses:	
Depreciation expense	$ 14
Sales and administrative expenses	105
Other expenses	87
Total operating expenses	$ 206
Income before taxes	$ 106
Income taxes	51
Net income	$ 55
Dividends paid	10
Increase in retained earnings	$ 45

Continental Stores, Inc.
Balance Sheet
December 31, 1994 and 1993

Assets	1994	1993
Cash and cash equivalents	$ 752	$ 725
Accounts receivable	461	448
Inventory	226	953
Land	1,340	1,240
Stored fixtures	369	369
Accumulated depreciation, store fixtures	(51)	(37)
Total assets	$3,097	$3,698

Liabilities and Stockholders' Equity		
Liabilities:		
Accounts payable	$ 175	$ 378
Short-term notes payable	525	768
Long-term debt	804	1,004
Total liabilities	$1,504	$2,150
Stockholders' equity:		
Common stock	$ 448	$ 448
Paid-in capital in excess of par	500	500
Retained earnings	645	600
Total stockholders' equity	$1,593	$1,548
Total liabilities and stockholder equity	$3,097	$3,698

Required:
1. Compute the net cash flow from operations using the direct method.
2. **Interpretive Question** Comment on the difference between net income and net cash flow from operations.
3. Prepare a statement of cash flows for Continental Stores, Inc., for the period ended December 31, 1994.

P15A-5
Statement of Cash Flows (Indirect Method)

Using the data from P15A-4, do the following:

1. Prepare a statement of cash flows using the indirect method.
2. **Interpretive Question** What are the main differences between a cash flow statement prepared using the indirect method and one prepared using the direct method?

Problem Set B

P15B-1
Cash Flow from Operations (Direct Method)

Super Sales, Inc shows the following information in its accounting records at year end:

Sales revenue	$890,000
Interest revenue	12,000
Cost of goods sold	425,000
Wages expense	225,000
Depreciation expense	50,000
Other (cash) operating expenses	84,000
Dividends declared	40,000

Selected balance sheet data are as follows:

	Beginning of Year	End of Year
Accounts receivable	$ 55,000	$ 78,000
Interest receivable	10,000	12,000
Inventory	225,000	220,000
Accounts payable	42,000	35,000
Wages payable	20,000	25,000
Dividends payable	35,000	40,000

Required:
1. Using the direct method, compute the net cash flow provided by (used in) operating activities for Super Sales, Inc.
2. **Interpretive Question** Explain the main differences between the net amount of cash flow from operations and net income (loss).

P15B-2

Computation of Net Income from Cash Flow from Operations (Direct Method)

The following partially completed work sheet is provided for ATM Corporation, which uses the direct method in computing net cash flow from operations:

ATM Corporation
Partial Work Sheet—Cash Flow from Operations
(Direct Method)
For the Year Ended December 31, 1994

	Accrual Basis	Adjustments Debits	Adjustments Credits	Cash Basis
Net Sales Revenue				150,000
Other Revenues				–0–
Total Revenues				150,000
Expenses:				
Cost of Goods Sold				75,000
Depreciation				–0–
Other Expenses				26,000
Total Expenses				101,000
Net Income (Net Cash Flow from Operations)				49,000

Key:
(1) Decrease in Accounts Receivable, $4,500.
(2) Loss on sale of equipment, $1,500.
(3) Increase in Inventory, $10,000.
(4) Increase in Accounts Payable, $3,000.
(5) Depreciation for the year, $8,000.
(6) Decrease in Prepaid Expenses, $1,000.
(7) Increase in Accrued Liabilities, $2,500.

Required: What is the amount of net income (loss) to be reported by ATM Corporation on its income statement for 1994?

P15B-3
Statement of Cash Flows (Indirect Method)

The following data are from the 1994 and 1993 balance sheets for San Diego Corporation:

San Diego Corporation
Comparative Balance Sheets
December 31, 1994 and 1993

Assets	1994	1993
Cash and cash equivalents	$ 15,400	$ 8,000
Accounts receivable	37,000	30,000
Inventory	34,000	40,000
Equipment	40,000	28,000
Accumulated depreciation	(14,400)	(12,000)
Total assets	$112,000	$94,000
Liabilities and Stockholders' Equity		
Accounts payable	$ 20,000	$16,000
Long-term notes payable	20,000	10,000
Capital stock	50,000	50,000
Retained earnings	22,000	18,000
Total liabilities and stockholders' equity	$112,000	$94,000

The following additional information is available:

(a) Net income for the year as reported on the income statement was $17,000.
(b) Dividends of $13,000 were declared and paid.
(c) Equipment that cost $6,000 and had a book value of $400 was sold during the year for $1,400.

Required: Use the indirect method to prepare a statement of cash flows for San Diego Corporation for the year ended December 31, 1994.

P15B-4
Statement of Cash Flows (Direct Method)

Financial statement data for Richland Corporation are provided. (All numbers are shown rounded to the nearest thousand, with the final three zeros omitted.)

Richland Corporation
Income and Retained Earnings Statements
For the Year Ended December 31, 1994

Sales revenue		$1,233
Cost of goods sold		1,018
Gross margin		$215
Operating expenses:		
Depreciation expense	$ 56	
Administrative expenses	109	
Other expenses	42	
Total operating expenses		207
Income from operations		$ 8
Gain on sale of real estate		110
Income before taxes		$118
Income taxes		41
Net income		$ 77
Dividends paid		0
Increase in retained earnings		$ 77

Richland Corporation
Balance Sheets
December 31, 1994 and 1993

Assets	1994	1993
Cash and cash equivalents	$ 149	$ 761
Accounts receivable	163	151
Inventory	1,221	712
Land	1,159	1,639
Equipment	1,281	255
Accumulated depreciation, equipment	(81)	(25)
Total assets	$3,892	$3,493

Liabilities and Stockholders' Equity	1994	1993
Accounts payable	$ 371	$ 491
Long-term debt	1,189	1,402
Common stock ($1 par)	750	500
Paid-in capital in excess of par	840	435
Retained earnings	742	665
Total liabilities and stockholders' equity	$3,892	$3,493

Required:
1. Using the direct method, compute the net cash flow from operations.
2. Prepare a statement of cash flows for Richland Corporation for the period ended December 31, 1994.
3. **Interpretive Question** Comment on the impression an investor may have in comparing Richland's income statement with its cash flow statement.

P15B-5
Statement of Cash Flows (Indirect Method)

Using the data provided in P15B-4, prepare a statement of cash flows using the indirect method.

SPREADSHEET PROBLEM

Business Analysis Case 1   *Green Merchandise, Inc.*

Green Merchandise, Inc., a discount department store, has applied to its bankers for a loan. Although the company has been profitable, it is short of cash. The loan application includes the following information about current assets, current liabilities, net income, depreciation expense, and dividends for the past 5 years. (All numbers are rounded to the nearest thousand, with the 000's omitted.)

	Dec. 31, 1990	Dec. 31, 1991	Dec. 31, 1992	Dec. 31 1993	Dec. 31, 1994
Cash and cash equivalents	$ 5	$ 73	$ 10	$158	$(189)
Accounts receivable	403	555	516	576	654
Inventory	253	142	383	385	1,022
Accounts payable	19	17	281	253	52
Net income	454	492	467	440	481
Depreciation expense	50	50	55	60	60
Dividends paid	177	197	208	211	211

As a bank loan officer, you have been asked to review these figures in order to determine whether the bank should loan money to Green Merchandise, Inc.

Required:
1. Compute the net cash flow from operations for the last 4 years.
2. What caused the sudden decrease in cash flow from operations?
3. What factors would you focus on and what additional information would you need before deciding whether to make the loan?

Business Analysis Case 2 *High Tech Resources*

The following data show the account balances of High Tech Resources, Inc., at the beginning and end of the company's fiscal year.

Debits	Aug. 31, 1994	Sept. 1, 1993
Cash & cash equivalents	$ 88,200	$ 29,000
Accounts receivable	17,000	14,500
Inventory	10,500	12,700
Prepaid insurance	2,800	2,000
Long-term investments (at cost)	3,000	8,400
Equipment	40,000	33,000
Treasury stock (at cost)	5,000	10,000
Cost of goods sold	184,000	
Operating expenses	93,500	
Income taxes	18,800	
Loss on sale of equipment	500	
Total debits	$463,300	$109,600

Credits		
Allowance for uncollectible accounts	$ 2,000	$ 1,200
Accumulated depreciation—equipment	9,500	9,000
Accounts payable	3,500	5,600
Interest payable	500	1,000
Income taxes payable	6,000	4,000
Notes payable—long term	8,000	12,000
Common stock	55,000	50,000
Paid in capital in excess of par	16,000	15,000
Retained earnings	9,800*	11,800
Sales	352,000	
Gain on sale of long-term investments	1,000	
Total credits	$463,300	$109,600

*Pre-closing balance

The following information concerning this year was also available:

(a) All purchases and sales were on account.
(b) Equipment with an original cost of $5,000 was sold for $1,500; a loss of $500 was recognized on the sale.
(c) Among other items, the operating expenses included Depreciation Expense of $3,500; Uncollectible Accounts Expense of $1,000; Interest Expense of $1,400; and Insurance Expense of $1,200.
(d) Equipment was purchased by issuing common stock and paying the balance ($6,000) in cash.
(e) Treasury stock was sold for $2,000 less than it cost; the decrease in owners' equity was recorded by reducing Retained Earnings.
(f) No dividends were paid this year.

Required: 1. You are to examine High Tech's cash position by:
   (a) Preparing schedules showing the amount of cash collected from accounts receivable, cash paid for accounts payable, cash paid for interest, and cash paid for insurance.
   (b) Preparing a statement of cash flows for High Tech for the fiscal year 1994 using the direct method.
2. What are the major reasons why High Tech's cash and cash equivalents increased so dramatically during the year?
3. Does the dividend policy seem appropriate under the current circumstances?

Ethics Case *General Technology*

Maurice DeVoit is the president of General Technology, a diversified manufacturing company. The company makes several products, including wheelchairs. Maurice realizes that investors judge General Technology primarily on the basis of its reported net income and its cash flows. These are not good times for General Technology. In fact, every aspect of the company except the wheelchair division has lost money during the last two years. This year alone, total losses could exceed $60 million. Maurice is concerned about these losses for several reasons: (1) their stock price has fallen recently and will probably fall farther if such high losses are reported, (2) Maurice will not receive any bonus for the year if the company reports a net loss, and (3) reported cash flows will be negative for the third year in a row, which will put the company into default on some loan covenants that would require over $20 million in debt to be repaid.

Maurice believes the only way to report profits and positive cash flows for the year is to sell part of the company. A competitor has offered to purchase General Technology's wheelchair division for $110 million. This would provide a profit of $70 million and result in positive cash flows. Maurice knows that selling the wheelchair division will salvage this year's results, but it will jeopardize even further future cash flows and profits. However, he is 64 and retiring next year, and he could use the bonus. Besides, he reasons, if the debt covenants are violated and the debt must be repaid, the company won't make it anyway. He has asked the controller to determine the impact of the proposed transaction on the income statement and statement of cash flows. The controller has informed him that pretax income will be increased by $70 million on the income statement and that the result on the statement of cash flows will be as follows:

Increase in cash flow provided by operating activities:	
Increase in net income	$ 70,000,000
Less: Gain on sale	70,000,000
Net effect	$ 0
Increase in cash flow provided by investing activities:	
Sale of wheelchair division	$110,000,000

Based on this information, Maurice decides to sell the wheelchair division of the company.

Required: 1. Is the analysis correct; that is, has the controller correctly identified the impact of this transaction on the income statement and statement of cash flows?
2. Is selling the wheelchair division under these circumstances an ethical decision?

Chapter 16

Financial Statement Analysis

Learning Objectives

After studying this chapter, you should be able to:
1. Explain the reasons for financial statement analysis.
2. Identify and describe basic techniques and key relationships of financial statement analysis.
3. Measure and analyze operating performance.
4. Measure asset turnover and analyze asset utilization.
5. Measure and analyze the use of debt and equity in financing operations.
6. Measure and analyze return on stockholders' equity.
7. Calculate and explain return on total assets.
8. Understand the limitations of financial statement analysis.

SETTING THE STAGE

For years, McDonald's Corporation has been one of the strongest companies in the world. Its "Golden Arches" and hamburgers are well-known symbols of success, and its $6.6 billion in revenues is the highest of any fast-food company. Some observers even say that the McDonald's restaurant in Russia is one of the reasons the fall of communism was accelerated.

But how is McDonald's doing now? In 1990, its second-quarter earnings came in a penny under analysts' estimates. Its stock dropped 12% in two days, pulling the broader market down with it. Analysts and others are worried that the big fast-food company is running out of steam. They fear that competition is cutting into McDonald's market share, squeezing sales growth and profit margins. Observers appear mixed about whether McDonald's reign as fast-food king is over or whether it is poised for unparalleled growth and success from the proliferation of Golden Arches overseas.

How is McDonald's really doing? Analysts are trying every possible way to figure the company out. What they have discovered is that McDonald's started selling off company-owned restaurants as domestic sales went softer. Gains from the sales jumped from $37 million in 1989 to $61 million in 1990, accounting for most of McDonald's $75 million increase in net income. McDonald's says that these gains are ordinary income and are part of its long-term plan, but others argue that the company is merely selling off shareholder wealth to make McDonald's look better. As evidence that the company is hurting, critics cite the fact that McDonald's is getting an average of only $436,000 per store sold, or approximately 30% of previous year's revenues, in an industry where stores are usually sold for 50% to 90% of revenues. These critics also note that, through last year, the company was consuming cash faster than it was generating it. In fact, debt—as a percentage of capitalization—rose from a recent low of 39% in 1984 to 53%. One skeptic even believes McDonald's falls short of its AA credit rating on its debt. Others argue that, though recent numbers have been down, this period of tough competition will come to an end, and McDonald's will emerge again, this time as the international fast-food king throughout the 21st century.

Who is right? The skeptics? Or the believers?

Adapted from Dana Wechsler Linden, "R. McDonald, CPA," *Forbes,* September 16, 1991, p. 44.

In Chapter 15, you learned about cash flows and how the statement of cash flows can help you analyze a company. In this chapter, you will learn conventional techniques used in analyzing the balance sheet and the income statement. As you study this material, it is important to remember that applying the techniques is only the first step in financial analysis. The next, and most important, step is interpreting the information obtained. As indicated by the McDonald's case, financial information is sometimes subject to widely differing interpretations.

REASONS FOR FINANCIAL STATEMENT ANALYSIS

Objective 1
Explain the reasons for financial statement analysis.

The main purpose of financial analysis is to predict future performance. Although the primary financial statements are historical in nature, they usually provide indicators of how a firm is likely to perform in subsequent periods. These indicators may not be immediately evident, however, and interested users must analyze the statements carefully to obtain the particular information that suits their purposes.

There are several reasons why careful analysis of financial statements is necessary.

1. Financial statements are general-purpose statements. They are prepared for use by a variety of interested parties: stockholders, short- and long-term creditors, potential investors, government agencies, and management. These different users are involved in making different types of decisions, including whether to make an investment (potential owner) or lend money (potential creditor), whether opportunities exist for improving performance (manager), and whether the firm's activities require regulation (government agency). Each type of decision requires different information and therefore a different analysis.
2. The relationships between key figures on the income statement, on the balance sheet, or on both, and the relationships between amounts on successive financial statements, are not obvious without analysis. Accordingly, knowledgeable users develop ratios and percentages that reflect meaningful relationships and that show trends from previous years.
3. Users of financial statements may be interested in seeing how well a company is doing in comparison to (1) predetermined objective standards, (2) other companies in the industry, or (3) alternative opportunities for investment.

To a large extent, then, the amount of information one is able to draw from financial statements depends on the care and experience with which they are analyzed. Most people who analyze financial statements are interested in making investment, credit, managerial, or regulatory decisions. The types of financial information needed by these different users are discussed briefly in the following sections.

Investment and Credit Decisions

Owners and creditors of a company, and particularly potential owners and creditors, want to know what their return on investment is likely to be as well as the chances of their achieving that return. The probability of achieving a certain return on an investment is referred to as the degree of risk, or uncertainty, involved. The amount of return to be expected and the degree of uncertainty that is acceptable are likely to be different for each type of user: stockholder, short-term creditor, or long-term creditor.

Stockholders can gain a return on investment both from dividends and from proceeds on the sale of stock at an increased price. They want to be able to predict a firm's future profits because **profitability** is the best indicator of the ability to pay dividends and of the value the market is likely to place on the stock.

profitability *a company's ability to generate revenues in excess of the costs incurred in producing those revenues*

Short-term creditors, such as banks, are interested in a firm's ability to repay a loan promptly; hence, the short-term cash-generating ability of a firm, its degree of **liquidity**, is important to these creditors.

liquidity *a company's ability to meet current obligations with cash or other assets that can be quickly converted to cash*

Long-term creditors, such as bondholders, would like to be able to predict a firm's ability to pay the interest obligation regularly and to repay the principal at maturity. Such payments are made over periods of years, so these creditors are interested in judging a firm's **solvency**, its long-run ability to pay debts.

solvency *a company's long-run ability to meet all financial obligations*

Managerial Decisions

The managers of a company have a responsibility to all other users of the financial statements (creditors, owners, government agencies, and others such as financial analysts, customers, suppliers, and employees). They must constantly monitor the firm's financial position and performance and take corrective action where necessary. Before they can take action, however, they must understand the company's major strengths and weaknesses. Financial statement analysis is one of the tools management uses for identifying problems having to do with operating efficiency, asset utilization, and debt-equity management—problems that must be solved if a firm is to meet its short- and long-run profitability, liquidity, and solvency goals.

Regulatory Decisions

All firms are subject to some degree of government regulation. In discharging their oversight responsibilities, government agencies need to assess the operating results and financial status of companies under their jurisdiction. The Internal Revenue Service, for example, might want to determine whether related companies are avoiding income taxes by illegally shifting income. Or the IRS may use financial statement analysis to justify an assessment of taxes on the accumulated earnings of closely held corporations that forego dividends in order to save income taxes for their high-tax-bracket owners. Similarly, the Federal Trade Commission and the Justice Department may use financial statement analysis to determine whether too much economic power is concentrated in too few companies in an industry. The Securities and Exchange Commission, in executing its enforcement powers with respect to new stock offerings and annual reporting, may use financial statement analysis to judge whether a company is misleading potential investors by not disclosing all relevant data in its financial statements.

> **To Summarize** *Current and potential investors and creditors use financial statement analysis to help them judge the degree of profitability, liquidity, and solvency of a firm. Managers use financial statement analysis to identify problems having to do with operating efficiency, asset utilization, and debt-equity management. Government agencies use financial statement analysis in various ways, depending on their jurisdiction.*

OVERVIEW OF FINANCIAL STATEMENT ANALYSIS

Objective 2
Identify and describe basic techniques and key relationships of financial statement analysis.

Financial statement analysis clearly has many applications for a variety of users. In the remainder of this chapter, we will describe some of the most useful techniques of analysis. The experienced user begins an analysis by identifying an objective (assessing profitability, liquidity, or solvency) and choosing the techniques that will accomplish the objective. Such a careful approach usually provides valuable information, but it does not answer all questions. Financial statement analysis has limitations that must be kept in mind, as will be explained later.

Some Basic Techniques

Three techniques are widely used in analyzing the financial statements of profit-oriented companies. They are:

1. Ratio analysis: the appraisal of certain key relationships.
2. Vertical analysis: measuring relationships between items on a single year's income statement or balance sheet by expressing all items as percentages of net sales or as percentages of total assets.
3. Horizontal analysis: measuring changes in the same items on comparative statements over 2 or more years.

These techniques are sometimes described as alternative ways of assessing a company's status. A more logical approach is to consider each technique as an important part of a single, comprehensive analysis. This is the way financial statement analysis will be presented here. We will begin by presenting the four key relationships (ratios) for assessing a firm's profitability, liquidity, and solvency. Then, in a more detailed discussion of these assessment techniques, we will show how vertical and horizontal analyses are used along with more specific ratios to complete the analysis.

To illustrate the techniques, we will use hypothetical data from Sanford Company's financial statements for the calendar years ending December 31, 1994 and 1993, shown in Exhibits 16-1 and 16-2.

Exhibit 16-1

Sanford Company
Income Statements
For the Years Ended December 31, 1994 and 1993

	1994	1993
Net sales	$1,086,944	$988,417
Cost of goods sold	786,523	700,263
Gross margin	$ 300,421	$288,154
Expenses:		
Selling and administrative expenses	$ 190,090	$172,661
Interest expense	14,995	13,046
Total expenses	$ 205,085	$185,707
Income before taxes	$ 95,336	$102,447
Income taxes	54,961	50,197
Net income from operations	$ 40,375	$ 52,250
Extraordinary gain (net of tax)	–0–	12,400
Net income	$ 40,375	$ 64,650
Earnings per share of common stock:		
Income before extraordinary gain	$1.55	$2.01
Extraordinary gain	—	0.48
Net income	$1.55	$2.49

Exhibit 16-2

Sanford Company
Balance Sheets
December 31, 1994 and 1993

Assets	1994	1993
Current assets:		
Cash	$ 16,982	$ 9,020
Marketable securities	37,683	39,712
Accounts receivable (net)	127,544	121,614
Inventory	195,512	173,999
Other current assets	9,499	7,634
Total current assets	$387,220	$351,979
Property, plant, and equipment (net)	406,599	395,098
Other noncurrent assets	28,571	40,801
Total assets	$822,390	$787,878

Liabilities and Stockholders' Equity		
Current liabilities:		
Notes payable, bank	$ 24,658	$ 22,576
Current portion of long-term debt	1,919	3,320
Accounts payable and notes payable	78,967	69,475
Income taxes payable	15,090	14,656
Total current liabilities	$120,634	$110,027
Long-term debt	155,881	148,400
Deferred income taxes payable	31,361	29,210
Stockholders' equity (including capital stock and retained earnings)	514,514	500,241
Total liabilities and stockholders' equity	$822,390	$787,878

Key Relationships

Four key relationships serve as a basis for assessing a firm's profitability, liquidity, and solvency.

1. $\dfrac{\text{net income (earnings)}}{\text{net sales}}$ — a measure of operating performance for a period

2. $\dfrac{\text{net sales}}{\text{average total assets}}$ — a measure of asset utilization (or asset turnover)

3. $\dfrac{\text{average total assets}}{\text{average stockholders' equity}}$ — a measure of the management of debt and equity

4. $\dfrac{\text{net income (earnings)}}{\text{average stockholders' equity}}$ — a measure of performance from a stockholder's viewpoint

The first ratio relates two income statement items, net income and net sales. It provides a measure of operating performance, and hence of profitability, for a period by showing the amount of earnings generated by each sales dollar.

The second ratio relates an income statement amount (net sales) to a balance sheet amount (total assets). Since the income statement covers a period of time and the balance sheet presents the financial position at a given moment in time, the relationship will not be entirely valid unless the balance sheet amount is revised to cover a period of time. This can be accomplished by using the average of the total assets for the period selected. (For example, to obtain the annual average, take the total assets at the beginning and end of each year, add them, and divide by two.) This second key ratio, which indicates how efficiently assets are being utilized, is often called the asset turnover ratio. The more efficiently assets are used, the more profitable a firm is and the more likely it is to be able to pay its obligations on a timely basis.

The third ratio relates two balance sheet amounts and shows the degree to which debt and equity are used in financing the operations of a company. Average total assets divided by average stockholders' equity measures the firm's assets per dollar of its stockholders' equity. That is, the ratio shows the degree to which a firm is financing its total assets through the issuance of stock and the accumulation of past earnings. Since total assets minus total stockholders' equity is equal to total liabilities or debt, this ratio also shows the amount of debt used during a period to maintain assets. The amount of debt a firm has obviously relates directly to the amount of liquid resources it needs to remain solvent. The debt-equity relationship also bears on profitability through the use of leveraging, which allows a company to earn for stockholders a rate of return higher than the cost of borrowed money. This concept is discussed later in this chapter.

The fourth ratio relates an income statement amount (net income) to an average of balance sheet amounts (average stockholders' equity). It is a measure of the productivity of a company in terms of current earnings and stockholders' investments plus accumulated earnings. That is, the ratio shows how much income was earned during the period per dollar of investment and accumulated earnings. The greater the return on stockholders' equity, the more profitable a

Chapter 16 *Financial Statement Analysis* 671

firm is and the more likely it is to remain solvent. The fourth ratio, then, is an important indicator of a firm's overall performance.

If you think carefully about each of these ratios in terms of their components and their significance as indicators of profitability, liquidity, and solvency, you will notice that the first three can be chained together as a basis for explaining the fourth.

Operating Performance	Asset Turnover	Debt-Equity Management	Return on Stockholders' Equity
$\dfrac{\text{net income}}{\text{net sales}}$ ×	$\dfrac{\text{net sales}}{\text{average total assets}}$ ×	$\dfrac{\text{average total assets}}{\text{average stockholders' equity}}$ =	$\dfrac{\text{net income}}{\text{average stockholders' equity}}$

The return on stockholders' equity can be computed directly from the income statement and the comparative balance sheets. However, to understand the factors that contribute to this measure of overall performance, we must look again at each of the three areas of activity that influence it: operations, asset utilization, and management of debt and equity in financing operations.

To illustrate the relationships between these key ratios, Sanford Company's financial statements for 1994 and 1993 (Exhibits 16-1 and 16-2) were used in computing the following. Note that operating performance and return on stockholders' equity are usually expressed as percentages, whereas the asset turnover and the debt-equity management ratios are generally recorded as quotients.

	Operating Performance		Asset Turnover		Debt-Equity Management		Return on Stockholders' Equity
	$\dfrac{\text{net income}}{\text{net sales}}$	×	$\dfrac{\text{net sales}}{\text{average total assets}}$	×	$\dfrac{\text{average total assets}}{\text{average stockholders' equity}}$	=	$\dfrac{\text{net income}}{\text{average stockholders' equity}}$
1993:	$\dfrac{\$64{,}650}{\$988{,}417}$	×	$\dfrac{\$988{,}417}{\$764{,}306*}$	×	$\dfrac{\$764{,}306}{\$477{,}210*}$	=	$\dfrac{\$64{,}650}{\$477{,}210*}$
	6.54%	×	1.29 times	×	1.60 times	=	13.55%†
1994:	$\dfrac{\$40{,}375}{\$1{,}086{,}944}$	×	$\dfrac{\$1{,}086{,}944}{\$805{,}134*}$	×	$\dfrac{\$805{,}134}{\$507{,}378*}$	=	$\dfrac{\$40{,}375}{\$507{,}378*}$
	3.71%	×	1.35 times	×	1.59 times	=	7.96%

* These numbers are averages of beginning- and end-of-year balances. For average total assets, the beginning figure in 1993 was $740,734; for average stockholders' equity, the beginning figure in 1993 was $454,179.
† The factors may not multiply exactly to the products because of rounding.

OPERATING PERFORMANCE

Objective 3
Measure and analyze operating performance.

<u>operating performance ratio</u> *an overall measure of the efficiency of operations during a period; computed by dividing net income by net sales*

The relation of net income to net sales is known as a firm's **operating performance ratio,** or its profitability. For example, in 1994, Sanford Company earned for its stockholders approximately 3.71 cents on each net sales dollar. In 1993 the company had earned 6.54 cents per sales dollar on a smaller sales volume. The reasons for this decrease in profitability will be made clear in the following sections, as we analyze the elements that affect operating performance.

Comparing the current figure against previous years' ratios is one way of judging whether a particular ratio is satisfactory. However, such a comparison may not tell the whole story. The analyst should also compare the ratio against the company's expected operating performance ratio and against the operating performances of other companies in the same industry.

If the ratio is determined to be unsatisfactory, a company may improve it in one of two ways.

1. Increase net income and maintain the same level of sales revenue; that is, reduce costs without reducing sales revenue.
2. Maintain net income in spite of reduced revenues by eliminating the least profitable sales or products; in other words, by increasing the profit margin on each dollar of sales.

Two techniques used in assessing the likelihood of improving this ratio are vertical analysis of each year's income statement and horizontal analysis of the income statements of two or more periods.

Income Statement Vertical Analysis

vertical analysis of financial statements *a technique for analyzing the relationships between items on an income statement or balance sheet by expressing all items as percentages*

The **vertical analysis** of an income statement examines the relationship of each item to net sales. Generally, net sales is assigned 100 percent. This analysis reveals whether any particular revenue or expense item is out of line in its relationship to net sales. It also provides the analyst with clues as to the company's potential strengths and weaknesses in controlling costs and in achieving its profitability objectives. Exhibit 16-3 is a vertical analysis of the 1994 and 1993 income statements of Sanford Company. The percentages were obtained by dividing net sales into each item—for example, in 1994, $300,421 gross margin ÷ $1,086,944 net sales = 27.6%.

This vertical analysis reveals that Sanford's cost of goods sold was higher as a percentage of sales in 1994 than in 1993 (72.4 percent versus 70.8 percent).

Exhibit 16-3

Sanford Company
Vertical Analysis of Income Statements
For the Years Ended December 31, 1994 and 1993*

	1994		1993	
Net sales	$1,086,944	100.0%	$988,417	100.0%
Cost of goods sold	786,523	72.4	700,263	70.8
Gross margin	$ 300,421	27.6%	$288,154	29.2%
Expenses:				
Selling and administrative expenses	$ 190,090	17.5%	$172,661	17.5%
Interest expense	14,995	1.4	13,046	1.3
Total expenses	$ 205,085	18.9%	$185,707	18.8%
Income before taxes	$ 95,336	8.8%	$102,447	10.4%
Income taxes	54,961	5.1	50,197	5.1
Net income from operations	$ 40,375	3.7%	$ 52,250	5.3%
Extraordinary gain (net of tax)	—	—	12,400	1.3
Net income	$ 40,375	3.7%	$ 64,650	6.5%

* The percentages may not add (or subtract) to the totals because of rounding.

Chapter 16 *Financial Statement Analysis*

The combination of this increase and the lack of an extraordinary gain in 1994 was responsible for the significant drop in net income from 6.5 percent of sales to 3.7 percent of sales.

Income Statement Horizontal Analysis

horizontal analysis of financial statements a technique for analyzing the percentage change in individual income statement or balance sheet items from one year to the next

In contrast to vertical analysis, which compares each income statement item with net sales for each year, **horizontal analysis** computes the percentage change in income statement items from one year to the next. This analysis enables the user to determine whether any particular item has changed in an unusual way in relation to the change in net sales from one period to the next. Exhibit 16-4 is a horizontal analysis of Sanford Company's 1994 and 1993 income statements. Note that the change for each item between 1993 and 1994 is shown on a dollar basis in column (3) and on a percentage basis in column (4). The percentages were determined by dividing the dollar increase or decrease in an account by the amount in the account during the base year.

This horizontal analysis reveals that from 1993 to 1994 the cost of goods sold increased by 12.3 percent ($86,260 ÷ $700,263), and the total of other expenses increased by 10.4 percent ($19,378 ÷ $185,707), whereas net sales increased by only 10.0 percent. These changes resulted in a 6.9 percent decrease in income before taxes. Despite lower earnings, taxes on income were higher in 1994, probably due to the timing of reporting certain revenue and expense items. In addition, there were no extraordinary gains in 1994. The overall effect of these changes was that net income in 1994 was 37.5 percent less than in 1993.

Exhibit 16-4

Sanford Company
Horizontal Analysis of Income Statements
For the Years Ended December 31, 1994 and 1993

	1994 (1)	1993 (2)	Dollar Change (3) = (1) − (2)	Percentage Change (4) = [(3) ÷ (2)] ×100%
Net sales	$1,086,944	$988,417	+$98,527	+ 10.0
Cost of goods sold	786,523	700,263	+ 86,260	+ 12.3
Gross margin	$ 300,421	$288,154	+$12,267	+ 4.3
Expenses:				
Selling and administrative expenses	$ 190,090	$172,661	+$17,429	+ 10.1
Interest expense	14,995	13,046	+ 1,949	+ 14.9
Total expenses	$ 205,085	$185,707	+$19,378	+ 10.4
Income before taxes	$ 95,336	$102,447	− $ 7,111	− 6.9
Income taxes	54,961	50,197	+ 4,764	+ 9.5
Net income from operations	$ 40,375	$ 52,250	−$11,875	− 22.7
Extraordinary gain (net of tax)	—	12,400	− 12,400	−100.0
Net income	$ 40,375	$ 64,650	−$24,275	− 37.5

To Summarize *The operating performance ratio is a measure of a firm's overall profitability. It is computed by dividing net sales into net income. To determine whether this ratio can be improved, a company can employ two techniques: vertical analysis of each year's income statement and horizontal analysis of the income statements of two or more periods.*

ASSET TURNOVER

Objective 4
Measure asset turnover and analyze asset utilization.

asset turnover ratio *an overall measure of how effectively assets are used during a period; computed by dividing net sales by average total assets*

A measure of a company's efficiency in utilizing its resources is the **asset turnover ratio**; it is net sales divided by average total assets. This ratio shows the rate at which assets are "turned over." Stated another way, it is a measure of the amount of sales revenue generated with each dollar of assets owned by the company. Sanford Company increased its asset turnover from 1.29 times in 1993 to 1.35 times in 1994.

$$\text{Asset turnover} = \frac{\text{net sales}}{\text{average total assets}}$$

1993: $\dfrac{\$988,417}{\$764,306} = 1.29$

1994: $\dfrac{\$1,086,944}{\$805,134} = 1.35$

As we noted earlier, in this ratio the numerator (sales) is an income statement amount that covers a period of time, whereas the denominator relates to a particular date. To develop a reliable ratio, the analyst must convert the denominator into a figure that reflects a period of time. This is accomplished by averaging total assets for the period. Thus, for Sanford Company in 1994, the beginning- and end-of-year balances for total assets would be added and divided by 2 [($822,390 + $787,878)/2 = $805,134]. If more precise results are desired, quarterly or monthly totals can be used in computing the average.

The asset turnover ratios for 2 years can be compared to indicate how well a company performed in the current year in relation to the previous year. Similarly, the ratio for the current year can be compared with the projected turnover, or with competitors' turnovers.

In order to improve its asset turnover, a company must analyze how well each of its major types of assets is being utilized. To do so, management uses vertical, horizontal, and ratio analysis.

Balance Sheet Vertical Analysis

Vertical analysis of a balance sheet relates each account to total assets, or to total liabilities and stockholders' equity, with each amount being expressed as a percentage of the larger category. For example, cash would be expressed as a percentage of total assets, and accounts payable as a percentage of total liabilities and stockholders' equity. Exhibit 16-5 is a vertical analysis of the 1994 and 1993 balance sheets of Sanford Company.

Exhibit 16-5

Sanford Company
Vertical Analysis of Balance Sheets
December 31, 1994 and 1993*

Assets	1994		1993	
Current assets:				
Cash	$ 16,982	2.1%	$ 9,020	1.1%
Marketable securities	37,683	4.6	39,712	5.0
Accounts receivable (net)	127,544	15.5	121,614	15.4
Inventory	195,512	23.8	173,999	22.1
Other current assets	9,499	1.2	7,634	1.0
Total current assets	$387,220	47.1%	$351,979	44.7%
Property, plant, and equipment (net)	406,599	49.4	395,098	50.1
Other noncurrent assets	28,571	3.5	40,801	5.2
Total assets	$822,390	100.0%	$787,878	100.0%
Liabilities and Stockholders' Equity				
Current liabilities:				
Notes payable, bank	$ 24,658	3.0%	$ 22,576	2.9%
Current portion of long-term debt	1,919	.2	3,320	.4
Accounts payable and notes payable	78,967	9.6	69,475	8.8
Income taxes payable	15,090	1.8	14,656	1.9
Total current liabilities	$120,634	14.7%	$110,027	14.0%
Long-term debt	155,881	19.0	148,400	18.8
Deferred income taxes payable	31,361	3.8	29,210	3.7
Stockholders' equity	514,514	62.6	500,241	63.5
Total liabilities and stockholders' equity	$822,390	100.0%	$787,878	100.0%

*The percentages may not add to the totals because of rounding.

As illustrated, there has been only a small increase in the percentage of current assets in relation to total assets, with a corresponding decrease in property, plant, and equipment and other assets. Thus, this vertical analysis reveals no significant shifts in the turnover of assets between the 2 years.

Balance Sheet Horizontal Analysis

Horizontal analysis of two or more balance sheets indicates the dollar and percentage changes from year to year for individual accounts. Exhibit 16-6 is a horizontal analysis of Sanford Company's 1994 and 1993 balance sheets.

The accounts that had the most significant changes (in terms of dollars and percentages) were Inventory, Other Noncurrent Assets, Accounts Payable, and Notes Payable. Major percentage changes also occurred in balance sheet items that were small in size, such as Cash, Other Current Assets, and Current Installments of Long-Term Debt. When balance sheet accounts change significantly, it usually means that management has revised aspects of its financial policy. In such cases, the statement user should seek additional information to explain these policy changes—for example, by studying the policies reflected in the statement of cash flows.

Exhibit 16-6

Sanford Company
Horizontal Analysis of the Balance Sheets
December 31, 1994 and 1993

Assets	1994	1993	Dollar Change	Percentage Change
Current assets:				
Cash	$ 16,982	$ 9,020	$ 7,962	88.3%
Marketable securities	37,683	39,712	(2,029)	(5.1)
Accounts receivable (net)	127,544	121,614	5,930	4.9
Inventory	195,512	173,999	21,513	12.4
Other current assets	9,499	7,634	1,865	24.4
Total current assets	$387,220	$351,979	$35,241	10.0
Property, plant and equipment (net)	406,599	395,098	11,501	2.9
Other noncurrent assets	28,571	40,801	(12,230)	(30.0)
Total assets	$822,390	$787,878	$34,512	4.4
Liabilities and Stockholders' Equity				
Current liabilities:				
Notes payable, bank	$ 24,658	$ 22,576	$ 2,082	9.2
Current portion of long-term debt	1,919	3,320	(1,401)	(42.2)
Accounts payable and notes payable	78,967	69,475	9,492	13.7
Income taxes payable	15,090	14,656	434	3.0
Total current liabilities	$120,634	$110,027	$10,607	9.6
Long-term debt	155,881	148,400	7,481	5.0
Deferred income taxes payable	31,361	29,210	2,151	7.4
Stockholders' equity	514,514	500,241	14,273	2.9
Total liabilities and stockholders' equity	$822,390	$787,878	$34,512	4.4

With horizontal analysis, it is important to recognize that a large percentage change in an item with a small absolute dollar amount (such as Current Portion of Long-Term Debt) is probably not a very significant change, not only because the dollar amount is small but also because management may not have any immediate control over the item.

Balance Sheet Ratio Analysis

A number of ratios help explain why the asset turnover ratio changed as it did by indicating how well specific assets were utilized. These are the current ratio; the acid-test ratio; accounts receivable turnover; inventory turnover; working capital turnover; and property, plant, and equipment turnover. Each ratio is discussed separately and then related to the asset turnover ratio.

CURRENT RATIO. As you know, working capital is the excess of total current assets over total current liabilities. The amount of the excess is a measure of liquidity and represents a margin of safety for meeting current liabilities. The relative margin of safety is usually expressed as the ratio of current assets to current liabilities, which is called the **current (or working capital) ratio.**

current (or working capital) ratio a measure of the liquidity of a business; equal to current assets divided by current liabilities

Chapter 16 *Financial Statement Analysis*

The working capital totals and current ratios for Sanford Company for 1993 and 1994 are:

	1994	1993
Current assets	$387,220	$351,979
Current liabilities	120,634	110,027
Working capital	$266,586	$241,952
Current (working capital) ratio	$\dfrac{\$387,220}{\$120,634} = 3.21$	$\dfrac{\$351,979}{\$110,027} = 3.20$

Working capital increased by $24,634 ($266,586 − $241,952) from 1993 to 1994, which represents a 0.01 change in the current ratio. At the end of 1994, the firm had $3.21 of current assets for every $1.00 of current liabilities.

A particular current ratio is considered high or low depending on the nature of the business involved. Many financial statement readers use 2:1 as an acceptable ratio of current assets to current liabilities. However, companies in different industries have different liquidity needs, and a 2:1 ratio may not be good for every type of business. Rule-of-thumb guidelines for any ratio are arbitrary and cannot be appropriate for all companies in all industries. The important thing is for the current ratio to be at the right level to meet the particular company's needs. If the ratio is too low, the company may not be sufficiently liquid to pay current liabilities or to take advantage of discounts for prompt payment. If it is too high, the company probably has too many assets tied up in working capital for its current level of activity, and the excess assets are not earning an appropriate return.

acid-test ratio (or quick ratio) a measure of a firm's ability to meet current liabilities; more restrictive than the current ratio, it is computed by dividing net quick assets (all current assets, except inventories and prepaid expenses) by current liabilities

ACID-TEST RATIO. The **acid-test ratio** (sometimes called the **quick ratio**) is calculated because the current ratio does not reflect the fact that a large portion of current assets, specifically inventory and prepaid assets, may not be very liquid and therefore not readily available for paying current liabilities.

The acid-test ratio is computed by dividing cash, marketable securities, and notes and accounts receivable by current liabilities. To illustrate, we will calculate the acid-test ratios for Sanford Company for 1993 and 1994 using information from Exhibits 16-1 and 16-2.

$$\text{Acid-test ratio} = \frac{\text{cash, marketable securities, and accounts receivable}}{\text{current liabilities}}$$

1993: $\dfrac{\$170,346}{\$110,027} = 1.55$

1994: $\dfrac{\$182,209}{\$120,634} = 1.51$

These figures show a slight drop in the acid-test ratio. For both years, liquid current assets are approximately one and one-half times as large as current liabilities. The size of this ratio will help users judge whether the firm is maintaining an efficient level of liquid assets to meet its current obligations.

accounts receivable turnover *a measure used to determine a company's average collection period for receivables; computed by dividing net sales (or net credit sales) by average accounts receivable*

number of days' sales in receivables *a measure of the average number of days it takes to collect a credit sale; computed by dividing 365 days by the accounts receivable turnover*

ACCOUNTS RECEIVABLE TURNOVER. Accounts receivable turnover reflects a company's collection record. A trend toward a lower turnover could indicate a laxness in collection activity or a change in credit policy.

This ratio is computed by dividing net credit sales by average accounts receivable for a period. If net credit sales cannot be determined easily from the financial statements, then total sales are used as a substitute.

Accounts receivable turnover is often more useful if dollar amounts are converted into the number of days of uncollected sales, which reflects the average time taken to collect a credit sale. The easiest way to compute the **number of days' sales in receivables** is to divide the number of days in the period by the accounts receivable turnover.

To illustrate the calculation of accounts receivable turnover and the number of days' sales in receivables, we will use the following data for Sanford Company:

	1994	1993
Net credit sales	$1,086,944	$988,417
Accounts receivable (net):		
January 1	$ 121,614	$106,675
December 31	127,544	121,614
Total	$ 249,158	$228,289
Average (÷ 2)	$ 124,579	$114,145

$$\text{Accounts receivable turnover} = \frac{\text{net credit sales}}{\text{average accounts receivable}}$$

1993: $\dfrac{\$988,417}{\$114,145} = 8.66$

1994: $\dfrac{\$1,086,944}{\$124,579} = 8.72$

$$\text{Number of days' sales in receivables} = \frac{\text{number of days in a period}}{\text{accounts receivable turnover}}$$

1993: $\dfrac{365 \text{ days}}{8.66} = 42.1$ days

1994: $\dfrac{365 \text{ days}}{8.72} = 41.9$ days

Sanford Company increased its accounts receivable turnover from 8.66 times to 8.72 times between 1993 and 1994. This very small improvement in turnover reduced the number of days' sales in receivables from 42.1 to 41.9. An improvement in accounts receivable turnover and in the collection period means that less money is tied up in receivables, which, in turn, contributes to a higher asset turnover ratio. And as we have seen, Sanford's asset turnover increased from 1.29 times in 1993 to 1.35 times in 1994, showing a more efficient utilization of assets.

inventory turnover *a measure of the efficiency with which inventory is managed; computed by dividing cost of goods sold by average inventory for a period*

INVENTORY TURNOVER. Another influence on the asset turnover ratio is **inventory turnover.** This ratio, which is computed by dividing cost of goods sold for a period by the average inventory for the period, is useful in determining whether a company is managing its inventory efficiently. If the turnover is low, it means that the company is either overstocking or building up a stock of

Chapter 16 *Financial Statement Analysis*

obsolete merchandise. Whichever the case, too high an inventory indicates that excess resources are being tied up in working capital instead of being used to earn a return. If the turnover is too high, the company may lose sales because the goods are not in inventory when customers want them.

Inventory turnover is often more meaningful if dollar amounts are converted into **number of days' sales in inventory.** This ratio indicates the average time it takes to dispose of inventory. It is computed by dividing the number of days in a period by the inventory turnover.

number of days' sales in inventory *an alternative measure of how well inventory is being managed; computed by dividing 365 days by the inventory turnover ratio*

To illustrate the calculation of inventory turnover and the number of days' sales in inventory, we will use the following data from Sanford Company:

	1994	1993
Cost of goods sold	$786,523	$700,263
Inventories:		
January 1	$173,999	$167,286
December 31	195,512	173,999
Total	$369,511	$341,285
Average (÷ 2)	$184,756	$170,643

$$\text{Inventory turnover} = \frac{\text{cost of goods sold}}{\text{average inventory}}$$

1993: $\dfrac{\$700,263}{\$170,643} = 4.10$

1994: $\dfrac{\$786,523}{\$184,756} = 4.26$

$$\text{Number of days' sales in inventory} = \frac{\text{number of days in a period}}{\text{inventory turnover}}$$

1993: $\dfrac{365 \text{ days}}{4.10} = 89.0 \text{ days}$

1994: $\dfrac{365 \text{ days}}{4.26} = 85.7 \text{ days}$

Sanford Company increased its inventory turnover from 4.10 in 1993 to 4.26 in 1994. This had the effect of reducing the number of days' sales in inventory from 89.0 in 1993 to 85.7 in 1994. The improvement in inventory turnover, like the improvement in accounts receivable turnover, contributed to the improvement in Sanford's asset turnover ratio from 1993 to 1994.

working capital turnover *a measure of the amount of working capital used in generating the sales of a period; computed by dividing net sales by average working capital*

number of days' sales invested in working capital *an alternative measure of the amount of working capital used in generating the sales of a period; computed by dividing 365 days by the working capital turnover*

WORKING CAPITAL TURNOVER. A more general ratio, which includes both accounts receivable turnover and inventory turnover in the sense that they both involve use of current assets, is **working capital turnover.** It is computed by dividing net sales by average working capital for a period, and it indicates the amount of working capital used in generating the sales of that period.

Like the other ratios we have discussed, this ratio may be more useful if dollar amounts are converted to **number of days' sales invested in working capital.** A decrease in number of days' sales invested in working capital would suggest an improvement in the utilization of current assets, which, in turn, would contribute to an improvement in the key ratio, the asset turnover ratio.

To illustrate the method of calculating working capital turnover and the number of days' sales invested in working capital, we will use the following data for Sanford Company:

	1994	1993
Net sales	$1,086,944	$988,417
Working capital:		
January 1	$ 241,952	$217,848
December 31	266,586	241,952
Total	$ 508,538	$459,800
Average (÷ 2)	$ 254,269	$229,900

$$\text{Working capital turnover} = \frac{\text{net sales}}{\text{average working capital}}$$

1993: $\dfrac{\$988,417}{\$229,900} = 4.30$

1994: $\dfrac{\$1,086,944}{\$254,269} = 4.27$

$$\frac{\text{Number of days' sales}}{\text{invested in working capital}} = \frac{\text{number of days in a period}}{\text{working capital turnover}}$$

1993: $\dfrac{365 \text{ days}}{4.30} = 84.9 \text{ days}$

1994: $\dfrac{365 \text{ days}}{4.27} = 85.5 \text{ days}$

The working capital turnover for Sanford Company decreased very slightly from 1993 to 1994. This suggests that the small improvements in the accounts receivable and inventory turnovers were offset by larger investments in other current assets in relation to current liabilities. Sanford's overall improvement in asset turnover must therefore have been generated by an improvement in the turnover of property, plant, and equipment.

PROPERTY, PLANT, AND EQUIPMENT TURNOVER. *Property, plant, and equipment turnover* is computed by dividing net sales by property, plant, and equipment.[2] This ratio indicates how efficiently these assets are being utilized in generating sales volume.

To illustrate, we will calculate Sanford's property, plant, and equipment turnover for 1993 and 1994, using information from Exhibits 16-1 and 16-2.

property, plant, and equipment turnover a measure of how well property, plant, and equipment are being utilized in generating a period's sales; computed by dividing net sales by average property, plant, and equipment

$$\frac{\text{Property, plant, and}}{\text{equipment turnover}} = \frac{\text{net sales}}{\text{average net property, plant, and equipment}}$$

1993: $\dfrac{\$988,417}{\$395,098} = 2.50$

1994: $\dfrac{\$1,086,944}{\$406,599} = 2.67$

---

[2] The ending amounts of property, plant, and equipment were used to calculate this ratio because the information to compute the average amount for property, plant, and equipment is not available for 1993. An average amount for the year is preferable unless there has been little change in the account during the year.

The increase in property, plant, and equipment turnover from 2.50 times in 1993 to 2.67 times in 1994 was a primary contributor to the increase in the asset turnover ratio from 1.29 times in 1993 to 1.35 times in 1994.

> **To Summarize** *The asset turnover ratio is an important overall indicator of a company's efficiency in utilizing its assets. A number of ratios represent components of the asset turnover ratio: the current ratio; the acid-test ratio; accounts receivable turnover; inventory turnover; working capital turnover; and property, plant, and equipment turnover. Proper interpretation of these ratios not only helps managers determine how to improve asset turnover but also enables investors and creditors to assess the profitability and liquidity of a company.*

DEBT-EQUITY MANAGEMENT

Objective 5

Measure and analyze the use of debt and equity in financing operations.

debt-equity management ratio *a measure of the relative utilization of debt and equity; computed by dividing average total assets by average stockholders' equity*

The third key ratio, **debt-equity management,** indicates the extent to which debt and equity are used in financing a company's operations. It is computed by dividing average total assets by average stockholders' equity. The excess of average total assets over average stockholders' equity represents the average amount of debt outstanding during the year (Assets − Stockholders' Equity = Liabilities).

The debt-equity management relationship is used in determining the margin of safety for creditors by identifying the extent to which a company is leveraging, or trading on, equity. Leveraging, as you recall, refers to the use of stockholders' equity as a base for borrowing money. If a company can use borrowed funds to earn more than the funds cost, the excess return accrues to the stockholders. Thus, leveraging benefits both the company, by increasing its assets, and the stockholders, by increasing earnings.

The amount of leveraging a company can employ is limited, however. Banks and other lending institutions will expect a company, especially a young company without much of a borrowing history, to have a satisfactory debt-to-equity ratio in order to be eligible for a loan. Further, interest on borrowed funds has to be paid before any dividends can be paid to stockholders. If income before the interest deduction is not large enough to cover the interest charge, then the stockholders will be deprived of dividends.

A prudent management tries to keep the amount of borrowed funds at such a level that the interest charges will be considerably less than the income before the interest deduction. The more stable a company's earnings, the greater management's confidence in determining the level of borrowed funds it can maintain without taking undue risks. A public utility, for example, can maintain a relatively large amount of debt because, as a quasi-monopoly, its earnings are relatively stable. An automobile manufacturing company, on the other hand, has large fluctuations in its earnings and so should keep its debt small in relation to stockholders' equity. Otherwise, in a bad year, the fixed interest charges may exceed earnings and cause a serious liquidity problem.

Although the ratio of average total assets to average stockholders' equity is the key measure of debt-equity management used in this chapter, analysts also use other ratios to complement and supplement this ratio. Some of these are:

1. Long-term debt to total assets $= \dfrac{\text{long-term debt}}{\text{total assets}}$

This ratio provides an indication of what percentage of the firm's assets has been financed with long-term debt.

2. Times interest earned $= \dfrac{\text{income before interest and income taxes}}{\text{interest charges}}$

This ratio indicates the company's margin above the fixed interest charges to be paid to creditors.

3. Long-term debt to stockholders' equity $= \dfrac{\text{long-term debt}}{\text{stockholders' equity}}$

This ratio indicates the amount of funds supplied to a company by creditors as opposed to the amount provided by stockholders plus the accumulated earnings. Industry experience would dictate the maximum percentage of debt that would be reasonable.

These debt-equity management ratios are primarily measures of a firm's solvency. Thus, they indicate the degree of protection available to mortgage and bond holders, as well as the risk of common stockholders whose return becomes less certain as the proportion of debt increases.

To illustrate the calculations for these debt-equity management ratios, we will use data from Sanford's 1993 and 1994 financial statements (Exhibits 16-1 and 16-2).

		1994		1993	
1.	Long-term debt to total assets	$\dfrac{\$155,881}{\$822,390}$	= 18.95%	$\dfrac{\$148,400}{\$787,878}$	= 18.84%
2.	Times interest earned	$\dfrac{\$110,331}{\$14,995}$	= 7.36 times	$\dfrac{\$115,493}{\$13,046}$	= 8.85 times
3.	Long-term debt to stockholders' equity	$\dfrac{\$155,881}{\$514,514}$	= 30.30%	$\dfrac{\$148,400}{\$500,241}$	= 29.67%

As we showed on page 671, Sanford's ratio of average total assets to average stockholder's equity decreased from 1.60 times in 1993 to 1.59 times in 1994. This decrease, although slight, reflects a shift toward less use of leveraging, which is not confirmed by the trend in the debt-equity management ratios computed. This inconsistency results from the use of average assets and equity in the key ratio, whereas the debt-equity ratios use end-of-period amounts. Note that the percentage of debt in Sanford Company's financial structure is not large. The margin of safety of earnings in 1994 was comfortable (interest is earned 7.36 times) and was clearly sufficient to cover any fixed interest charges even though 1994 was not a good earnings year. Finally, note that the relationship of long-term debt to stockholders' equity is relatively unchanged.

Chapter 16 *Financial Statement Analysis* 683

> **To Summarize** *The various debt-equity management ratios are generally consistent with each other and provide a picture of the amount of debt in relation to total assets and to stockholders' equity, and a measure of the extent of fixed interest charges relative to the earnings available to cover those charges.*

RETURN ON STOCKHOLDERS' EQUITY

Objective 6
Measure and analyze return on stockholders' equity.

Each of the three key ratios—operating performance, asset turnover, and debt-equity management—gives an analyst important information about a company. However, as explained earlier, a view of a company's overall performance is provided only when the ratios are brought together. Thus, if all the key ratios are chained together, the **return on stockholders' equity** can be computed.

To illustrate, we again present the calculation for Sanford Company in 1994 and 1993.

	Operating Performance		Asset Turnover		Debt-Equity Management		Return on Stockholders' Equity*
	$\dfrac{\text{net income}}{\text{net sales}}$	×	$\dfrac{\text{net sales}}{\text{average total assets}}$	×	$\dfrac{\text{average total assets}}{\text{average stockholders' equity}}$	=	$\dfrac{\text{net income}}{\text{average stockholders' equity}}$
1993:	$\dfrac{\$64{,}650}{\$988{,}417}$	×	$\dfrac{\$988{,}417}{\$764{,}306}$	×	$\dfrac{\$764{,}306}{\$477{,}210}$	=	$\dfrac{\$64{,}650}{\$477{,}210}$
	6.54%	×	1.29 times	×	1.60 times	=	13.55%
1994:	$\dfrac{\$40{,}375}{\$1{,}086{,}944}$	×	$\dfrac{\$1{,}086{,}944}{\$805{,}134}$	×	$\dfrac{\$805{,}134}{\$507{,}378}$	=	$\dfrac{\$40{,}375}{\$507{,}378}$
	3.71%	×	1.35 times	×	1.59 times	=	7.96%

* The factors may not multiply exactly to the products because of rounding.

return on stockholders' equity *a measure of overall performance from a stockholder's viewpoint; includes management of operations, use of assets, and management of debt and equity, and is computed by dividing net income by average stockholders' equity*

Sanford's return on equity was lower in 1994 than in 1993, primarily because 1994 net income was only 3.71 percent of net sales, as compared with 6.54 percent in 1993.

Chaining the three key ratios is only one way of measuring the return to stockholders. Several others are useful. In this section, we will discuss four other commonly used methods: earnings per share, price-earnings ratio, dividend payout ratio, and book value per share.

Earnings per Share

earnings per share (EPS) *the amount of net income (earnings) related to each share of stock; computed by dividing net income by the number of shares of common stock outstanding during the period*

Earnings per share (EPS) is used to measure earnings growth and earnings potential. If a company has a simple capital structure, with only common stock outstanding, earnings per share would be computed by dividing net income by the average number of shares of common stock outstanding during the year. If the capital structure includes both preferred and common stock, the preferred dividend requirement must be subtracted from net income before earnings per share is computed.

For example, if total net income for the year is $130,000, and preferred stock is entitled to a current-dividend preference of $20,000, then earnings per share for common stock (assuming that 26,000 shares of common stock are outstanding) would be computed by dividing $110,000 of net income ($130,000 − $20,000) by 26,000 common shares to obtain earnings per common share of $4.23. To simplify our calculations, we will assume in the remainder of this section that the number of shares of common stock outstanding at the beginning of the year is the same as the number of shares outstanding at the end of the year—that is, no shares were issued or reacquired during the year.

To illustrate the computation for earnings per share, we will assume that Sanford Company's capital structure consists entirely of 26,000 shares of common stock. Earnings per share for 1993 and 1994 would be computed as follows:

$$\text{Earnings per share} = \frac{\text{net income}}{\text{(average) number of shares of common stock outstanding}}$$

1993: EPS, net income from operations $\dfrac{\$52{,}250}{26{,}000 \text{ shares}} = \$2.01$

EPS, extraordinary gain $\dfrac{\$12{,}400}{26{,}000 \text{ shares}} = \$0.48$

EPS, net income $\dfrac{\$64{,}650}{26{,}000 \text{ shares}} = \$2.49$

1994: EPS, net income $\dfrac{\$40{,}375}{26{,}000 \text{ shares}} = \$1.55$

Note that only one EPS number is needed for 1994 because there was no extraordinary gain. Earnings per share would be presented on the income statement in the following manner:

	1994	1993
Earnings per share of common stock:		
Income before extraordinary gain	$1.55	$2.01
Extraordinary gain	—	0.48
Net income	$1.55	$2.49

Price-Earnings Ratio

price-earnings (P/E) ratio
a measure of growth potential, earnings stability, and management capabilities; computed by dividing market price per share by earnings per share

Financial analysts use the **price-earnings (P/E) ratio** in judging the potential value of a company's stock in relation to that of other companies. This is because the price-earnings ratios of a company over a period of years indicate the stability of its earnings and are therefore assumed to reflect the capabilities of management and the growth potential of the company.

The ratio is computed by dividing the market price of a stock by its earnings per share. To illustrate, we will use the figures just calculated for Sanford Company. If the price of the stock was 18³⁄₈ ($18.375) when earnings were $1.55 per share, the stock would have a P/E ratio of 11.9.

$$\text{Price-earnings ratio} = \frac{\text{market price per share}}{\text{earnings per share}}$$

$$\frac{\$18.38}{\$1.55} = 11.9$$

Chapter 16 *Financial Statement Analysis*

A P/E ratio of 11.9 means that the stock is selling for 11.9 times annual earnings. To judge this ratio, the analyst will probably compare it with the price-earnings ratios for the stocks of Sanford's major competitors.

Dividend Payout Ratio

dividend payout ratio *a measure of earnings paid out in dividends; computed by dividing cash dividends by the net income available to each class of stock*

The **dividend payout ratio** indicates the percentage of earnings distributed to stockholders. It is computed by dividing cash dividends by the net income available to each class of stock.

To illustrate, we will assume that Sanford Company had the following dividend payout ratios on its common stock in 1993 and 1994:

$$\text{Dividend payout ratio} = \frac{\text{cash dividends}}{\text{net income available to common stockholders}}$$

1993: $\dfrac{\$26{,}000^*}{\$64{,}650} = 40\%$

1994: $\dfrac{\$26{,}000^*}{\$40{,}375} = 64\%$

* Assuming that there are 26,000 shares of common stock outstanding, the company paid dividends of $1.00 per share in both 1993 and 1994.

The numerators suggest that the company has a policy of paying a stable dividend. It appears that in 1994 the board of directors, in keeping with a stable dividend policy, decided not to reduce dividends despite a poor earnings performance. This resulted in a much higher payout ratio than would have been appropriate for that year's net income.

If an investor is interested in buying stocks that will provide a significant annual cash return, the dividend payout ratio is an important piece of information. A "growth company" usually reinvests a large percentage of its earnings and pays little or nothing in dividends. A more stable, mature company, such as a public utility, is likely to pay out a high percentage of its earnings in dividends.

Book Value per Share

book value per share *a measure of net worth; computed by dividing stockholders' equity for each class of stock by the number of shares outstanding for that class*

Book value per share is one measure of a company's net worth. Keep in mind that it usually will not reflect the fair market values of assets and liabilities because balance sheets generally report only historical costs. Therefore, the book value concept must be used with care in assessing a firm's financial condition.

Book value per share is computed by dividing stockholders' equity by the number of shares outstanding at year-end. If the capital structure contains both preferred and common stock, a portion of stockholders' equity must be assigned to preferred stock before the balance can be used in computing book value per share of common stock. Note that book value per share uses the number of shares outstanding at year-end rather than the average number of shares, as EPS does. This is because book value is a measure of net assets per share as of a balance sheet date, not for a period of time.

To illustrate the calculation of book value per share, we will now assume that Sanford Company's financial structure contains both preferred and common stock and that some of its stock has been reacquired and classified as treasury stock.

Sanford Company
Stockholders' Equity
December 31, 1994

Preferred stock (161 shares issued)		$16,100
Common stock (26,000 shares issued)		26,000
Paid-in capital in excess of par, common stock		47,067
Retained earnings		434,642
Total		$523,809
Less treasury stock at cost:		
Preferred stock (43 shares reacquired)	$3,986	
Common stock (193 shares reacquired)	5,309	(9,295)
Total stockholders' equity		$514,514

redemption value *the price, stated in the contract, to be paid by a company to repurchase preferred stock*

In computing book value per share, an analyst assigns to preferred stockholders the portion of stockholders' equity that represents the **redemption value** of the outstanding preferred shares, including any dividends in arrears. Assuming that there are no dividends in arrears on Sanford's preferred stock and that its redemption value is $102.75 per share ($12,125 ÷ 118*), the book value for preferred and common shares would be computed as follows:

Total stockholders' equity		$514,514
Less portion of equity assigned to preferred stock:		
Outstanding shares	118*	
Redemption value	×$102.75	12,125
Stockholders' equity applicable to common stock		$502,389

* 161 shares of preferred stock issued, less 43 shares in treasury.

$$\text{Book value per share} = \frac{\text{stockholders' equity}}{\text{number of shares of stock outstanding}}$$

Preferred stock: $\dfrac{\$12,125}{118} = \$102.75$

Common stock: $\dfrac{\$502,389}{25,807*} = \$19.47$

* 26,000 shares of common stock issued, less 193 shares in treasury.

Care must be taken in assigning the appropriate portion of stockholders' equity to preferred stock. The amount assigned is not identical to the equity accounts that have the word *preferred* in their titles. Rather, preferred stock is assigned a portion of stockholders' equity based on the claims of preferred shareholders in liquidation, including any premium to be paid above par value and dividends in arrears on cumulative preferred stock. Thus, the stockholders' equity clearly assignable to preferred stock should be used to compute the book value per share of preferred stock. The remainder should be assigned to common stock for the purpose of computing its book value per share.

Although the book value per share often bears little resemblance to the actual market price of the stock, it may provide some useful information about

Chapter 16 *Financial Statement Analysis*

a company's future. However, the other measures of overall performance—namely, return on stockholders' equity, earnings per share, dividend payout ratio, and price-earnings ratio—are better indicators of a company's expected performance.

> **To Summarize** *As illustrated in Exhibit 16-7 on page 688, the three key ratios of operating performance, asset turnover, and debt-equity management are chained together to determine the return on stockholders' equity. The return on stockholders' equity is a measure of overall performance from a stockholder's point of view. Several other ratios are useful in measuring the return to stockholders. They include earnings per share, price-earnings ratio, dividend payout ratio, and book value per share.*

RETURN ON TOTAL ASSETS

Objective 7
Calculate and explain return on total assets.

return on total assets *an overall measure of the return to both stockholders and creditors; includes operating performance and asset turnover*

The **return on total assets** is another measure of operating performance and efficiency in utilizing assets. Since this ratio is a measure of the return to both creditors and stockholders, the measure of operating performance is computed differently from when the three key ratios were chained together to compute the return on stockholders' equity. For the purpose of computing the return on total assets, the operating performance ratio includes not only the return to stockholders, that is, net income, but also the return to the creditors, that is, interest income net of income taxes. The return to creditors is interest income *net of income taxes* because the true cost to the company of the return to the creditors is the net interest cost since interest expense is deductible for income tax purposes. Therefore, the operating performance ratio that is used in computing return on total assets is computed as follows:

$$\frac{\text{net income} + \text{interest expense (net of tax)}^*}{\text{net sales}}$$

* Interest expense (net of tax) can be computed by multiplying interest expense by one minus the tax rate. Thus, if interest expense is $8,000 and the tax rate is 40%, the interest expense net of tax is $4,800 [$8,000 × (1 − .4) or $8,000 × 60%].

The calculation of this ratio for the Sanford Company for the years 1993 and 1994 is as follows:

1993: $\dfrac{\$64{,}650 + (13{,}046 \times 51\%)^*}{\$988{,}417} = \dfrac{\$71{,}303}{\$988{,}417} = 7.2\%$

1994: $\dfrac{\$40{,}375 + (14{,}995 \times 42.35\%)\dagger}{\$1{,}086{,}944} = \dfrac{\$46{,}725}{\$1{,}086{,}944} = 4.3\%$

* One minus the tax rate for 1993.
† One minus the tax rate for 1994.

As shown at the bottom of the next page, the recomputed operating performance ratios are then chained with the asset turnover ratios to compute the return on assets, which reflects the return to both creditors and stockholders.

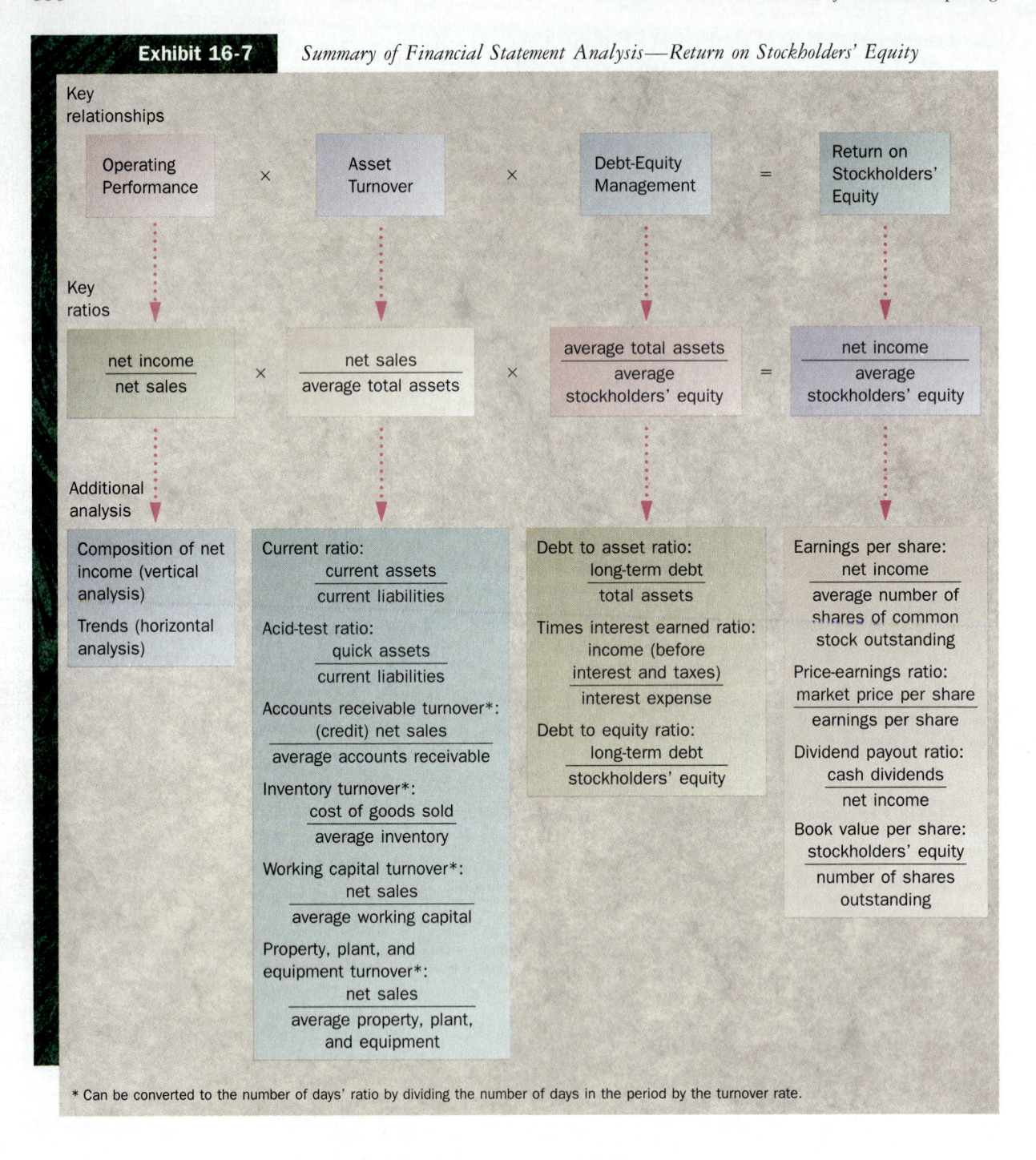

Exhibit 16-7 *Summary of Financial Statement Analysis—Return on Stockholders' Equity*

Key relationships:

Operating Performance × Asset Turnover × Debt-Equity Management = Return on Stockholders' Equity

Key ratios:

$$\frac{\text{net income}}{\text{net sales}} \times \frac{\text{net sales}}{\text{average total assets}} \times \frac{\text{average total assets}}{\text{average stockholders' equity}} = \frac{\text{net income}}{\text{average stockholders' equity}}$$

Additional analysis:

Composition of net income (vertical analysis)

Trends (horizontal analysis)

Current ratio:
$$\frac{\text{current assets}}{\text{current liabilities}}$$

Acid-test ratio:
$$\frac{\text{quick assets}}{\text{current liabilities}}$$

Accounts receivable turnover*:
$$\frac{\text{(credit) net sales}}{\text{average accounts receivable}}$$

Inventory turnover*:
$$\frac{\text{cost of goods sold}}{\text{average inventory}}$$

Working capital turnover*:
$$\frac{\text{net sales}}{\text{average working capital}}$$

Property, plant, and equipment turnover*:
$$\frac{\text{net sales}}{\text{average property, plant, and equipment}}$$

Debt to asset ratio:
$$\frac{\text{long-term debt}}{\text{total assets}}$$

Times interest earned ratio:
$$\frac{\text{income (before interest and taxes)}}{\text{interest expense}}$$

Debt to equity ratio:
$$\frac{\text{long-term debt}}{\text{stockholders' equity}}$$

Earnings per share:
$$\frac{\text{net income}}{\text{average number of shares of common stock outstanding}}$$

Price-earnings ratio:
$$\frac{\text{market price per share}}{\text{earnings per share}}$$

Dividend payout ratio:
$$\frac{\text{cash dividends}}{\text{net income}}$$

Book value per share:
$$\frac{\text{stockholders' equity}}{\text{number of shares outstanding}}$$

* Can be converted to the number of days' ratio by dividing the number of days in the period by the turnover rate.

Operating Performance × Asset Turnover = Return on Total Assets

1993: $\frac{\$71,303}{\$988,417}$ × $\frac{\$988,417}{\$764,306}$ = $\frac{\$71,303}{\$764,306}$

7.2% × 1.29 Times = 9.29%

1994: $\frac{\$46,725}{\$1,086,944}$ × $\frac{\$1,086,944}{\$805,134}$ = $\frac{\$46,725}{\$805,134}$

4.3% × 1.35 Times = 5.81%

This method of computing return on assets is preferred by financial analysts because it more accurately reflects the return to both creditors and investors as compared with computing the operating performance ratio by simply dividing net income by net sales. The chaining of the operating performance and asset turnover ratios reminds the analysts that the total return on assets is a function of both controlling expenses and efficiently utilizing assets. To judge how satisfactory the return on assets is, the analyst must compare it with the industry average and with the rate of return a company must earn to satisfy the demands of its creditors and owners.

> **To Summarize** *Exhibit 16-8 summarizes the relationship between operating performance, asset turnover, and return on total assets.*

Exhibit 16-8 *Summary of Financial Statement Analysis—Return on Total Assets*

Key relationships

$$\text{Operating Performance} \times \text{Asset Turnover} = \text{Return on Assets}$$

Key ratios

$$\frac{\text{net income + interest expense (net of income tax)}}{\text{net sales}} \times \frac{\text{net sales}}{\text{average total assets}} = \frac{\text{net income + interest expense (net of income tax)}}{\text{average total assets}}$$

LIMITATIONS OF FINANCIAL STATEMENT ANALYSIS

Objective 8
Understand the limitations of financial statement analysis.

Financial statement analysis serves an important function, but it must be used with care. Many people accept numbers computed by an expert without much question. Although ratios may be computed precisely, they are no better than the data on which they are based. Three areas of concern in computing ratios are (1) the use of estimates and judgments in measuring assets, liabilities, and income; (2) the fact that changing values and price levels frequently are not reflected in the financial statements; and (3) the fact that ratios are useful only when they can be related to comparable data, for example, industry statistics.

Use of Estimates

Estimates and judgments are used in allocating costs among periods—for example, in measuring depreciation, bad debts, warranty expenses, and prepaid

BUSINESS ENVIRONMENT ESSAY
Regulating Financial Planners

An important dimension of financial statement analysis is the qualifications of the person or group doing the analysis. In recent years, the fastest growing group of investment advisers has been financial planners. A financial planner is defined as anyone who provides comprehensive financial advice to help clients make investment decisions to achieve such goals as saving for retirement, reducing taxes, or providing for education. Financial planners are usually compensated for their advice by fees and commissions on products (often securities) they sell to customers. Financial planners now control nearly 25% of all invested assets owned by Americans, yet the laws governing them are far from adequate in protecting their clients from abuse. Accordingly, Congress is considering whether to impose stricter regulations on financial planners. Excerpts from an article in *The Washington Post* describe the situation.

Cracking Down on Advice Industry
Financial Planners Blamed for Up to $200 Million a Year in Fraud

Legislators are set to impose stricter regulations on a fast-growing group of investment advisers known as financial planners. . . . A report by the General Accounting Office found that some of these advisers and planners have been responsible for investment losses of about $90 million to $200 million a year due to fraud and abuse.

Although the estimated annual losses are low compared with the amount of assets these advisers manage, the GAO study said, many cases of fraud go unreported because, among other reasons, people are embarrassed when they lose money.

A bill introduced in the House April 2, designed to amend the Investment Advisers Act of 1940, would provide consumers with more information about the financial planners they hire and give consumers more powers to bring actions against planners who they believe have defrauded them.

The legislation would require all financial planners, investment advisers, or people with similar jobs to register as investment advisers under the 1940 law.

The bill seeks to include certain professionals, such as accountants, lawyers, and insurance agents, who also give their clients investment advice but are not covered by the 1940 law.

The bill would also require full written disclosure to the customer of direct or indirect compensation, including fees, commissions and other nonfinancial incentives, that the planner or adviser will receive by selling a customer a certain financial product.

Opposition to the bill came from accountants and insurance agents, who sometimes act as investment advisers to their clients.

The American Institute of Certified Public Accountants said the bill "does not properly focus on the problem areas associated with the investment advisory industry," adding that it "casts a wide net over an unduly large array of individuals and services."

Source: Adapted from Margie G. Quimpo, "Cracking Down on Advice Industry," *The Washington Post*, July 22, 1990.

expenses. The allocation judgments made by those who prepare the financial statements may result in different ratios. And since ratios are meaningful only when they are compared, care must be taken that the ratios being compared have been computed in the same way, or at least that they can be translated into common terms. Many analysts attempt to recast statements in order to provide comparable data for financial statement analysis.

Changes in Values and Price Levels

Financial statements are based on transactions that were recorded at cost when they were executed. Over time, gains and losses occur as the result of changes in values and changes in the purchasing power of the dollar. These changes in value and price level usually are not incorporated on a current basis into the primary financial statements and therefore may not be included in the analysis. The fact that unrealized gains and losses are not reflected is one reason that book value figures should be considered with care and in conjunction with other measurements.

Ratios as a Basis for Comparison

Even if an analyst is able to overcome the measurement problems caused by estimates and value changes, there are pitfalls in the use of ratios. A ratio by itself is neither good nor bad. Before it can be judged, it must be compared with the ratios of other years or other companies, or with a predetermined standard. Comparisons with rule-of-thumb guidelines are usually not desirable. Furthermore, ratios may not provide a precise picture of the company's financial situation. More specific analysis may be required.

Financial statement analysis is an important tool in learning about the operations of a firm, but the process of analysis should be performed, and the results evaluated, with its limitations always in mind.

Appendix

International Aspects of Financial Reporting

This text is primarily concerned with accounting concepts and procedures as they are understood and practiced in the United States. Many of the goods sold in this country by U.S. companies are not made here, however, and vice versa—many products made here are sold elsewhere. Even if a U.S. company's name is on a product, it, or some component of it, may have been imported. Almost every large U.S. company now has operations in other countries or at least conducts business with non-U.S. entities. A company that has operating units in more than one country is referred to as a **multinational company**. IBM, for example, has operations in over 80 countries and receives about 54 percent of its sales and income from foreign operations. Exhibit 16-9 shows the degree of foreign business of several large U.S. corporations.

multinational company *a company that has operating units in more than one country*

Like all other economic events, transactions with foreign companies or with foreign subsidiaries must be accounted for. In this appendix, we will take up the two aspects of international business that cause the most problems for accountants.

EXCHANGE RATES AND ACCOUNTING STANDARDS

There are two major accounting complexities of doing business in foreign countries. First, purchase and sales transactions usually involve foreign currencies, which need to be translated into U.S. dollars using exchange rates. An **exchange rate** is the value of one currency in terms of another. When IBM purchases or sells computer equipment in Japan, for example, the transactions are usually in yen, the currency of Japan. Translating the yen into U.S. dollars

exchange rate *the value of one currency in terms of another*

Exhibit 16-9 — Foreign Business of Selected U.S. Corporations

Company Name	Foreign Revenue (Millions)	Total Revenue (Millions)	Foreign Revenue as % of Total	Foreign operating Profit as % of Total	Foreign assets as % of Total
Exxon	$57,375	$76,416	75.1%	68.2%	51.0%
Mobil	31,633	52,256	60.5	60.9	48.9
IBM	29,280	54,217	54.0	63.3	54.1
Dow Chemical	7,431	13,377	55.6	55.2	49.0
Coca-Cola	4,185	7,644	54.7	74.4	26.0
Pepsico	1,970	11,485	17.2	10.8	33.2
Gillette	2,001	3,167	63.2	63.9	61.5
Kellogg	1,302	3,793	34.3	23.2	46.5

Source: "100 Largest Multinational Corporations," *Forbes*, July, 1988.

would be simple if exchange rates remained constant. However, foreign currencies, like other goods and services, change in price in response to changes in supply and demand and in the economies of the countries involved. During the past few years, for example, one U.S. dollar has purchased as many as 360 yen and as few as 125 yen. If you had deposited $10,000 in a Japanese bank when the exchange rate was 360 yen per dollar and withdrawn it when the rate was 140 yen, your profit would have been $15,714 (3,600,000 yen ÷ 140 yen = $25,714; $25,714 − $10,000 = $15,714). Exhibit 16-10 shows several examples of exchange rates.

The second major complexity is the varying accounting standards that exist throughout the world. Often, a multinational company will have to prepare at least four different sets of financial records. One set consists of reports independently prepared by each foreign operating unit on the basis of the accounting principles accepted in the country in which it is located. These reports are read by local tax authorities and other government officials and by stockholders in that country.

The second set is prepared in compliance with U.S. generally accepted accounting principles because the company's headquarters are here. These financial statements summarize the company's worldwide operations.

The third is simply the set prepared by all companies to comply with the regulations of the U.S. tax authorities because their requirements are generally quite different from those of GAAP.

Finally, separate financial reports may be prepared for individual segment managers. These reports highlight specific economic conditions, special problems, or unusual circumstances related to the country in which the operating unit is located.

Exhibit 16-10 *Selected Exchange Rates (March 1993)*

Country	$1 U.S. Buys	
Canada	1.25	Canadian Dollars
China	5.84	Chinese Yuans
Colombia	646.00	Colombian Pesos
England	0.70	English Pounds
France	5.64	French Francs
India	31.19	Indian Rupees
Italy	1607.23	Italian Lire
Japan	117.70	Japanese Yen
Mexico	3.10	Mexican Pesos
West Germany	1.67	Deutsche Marks

Source: *The Wall Street Journal*, March, 1993.

To Summarize *The two major accounting complexities of doing business with foreign companies involve fluctuating exchange rates and the existence of different accounting standards. Companies need to keep several different sets of financial records: (1) for each foreign operating unit, (2) for GAAP, (3) for the IRS, and (4) for segment managers.*

ACCOUNTING FOR TRANSACTIONS IN FOREIGN CURRENCIES

When a U.S. company transacts business with a foreign company in U.S. dollars, the accounting is the same as any other transaction. A manufacturer purchasing materials with dollars from a foreign company, for example, simply uses the amount on the invoice; it is the foreign company that has the translation problem. Only if the transactions are in a foreign currency must the U.S. company translate the amounts involved into dollars.

Foreign Purchases

To illustrate the accounting for foreign purchases, assume that a Honda dealer in Montana purchases a Honda Civic for $10,000 U.S. dollars from Japan and is billed at 1,500,000 yen. This price is based on an exchange rate of 150 yen to 1 dollar (1,500,000 ÷ 150 = $10,000). Since the purchase was billed in yen, the dealer will incur an **exchange gain or loss** if the exchange rate changes between the purchase and payment dates. For example, if the exchange rate is 160 yen to 1 dollar on the payment date, the dealer will realize a gain of $625 (1,500,000 ÷ 160 = $9,375; $10,000 − $9,375 = $625). Although the entry to record the purchase is standard, the payment entry is as follows:

exchange gain or loss the gain or loss incurred when the exchange rates are different on the purchase and payment dates or on the sale and receipt of payment dates

Accounts Payable	10,000	
Exchange Gain		625
Cash		9,375
Paid for Honda Civic previously purchased.		

Although the transaction was billed in yen, the U.S. automobile dealer used U.S. dollars in the journal entry. (Honda of Japan would use yen.)

Had the value of the dollar fallen—from 150 to 140 yen per dollar, for example—the automobile dealer would, of course, have incurred an exchange loss. As you can see, when the dollar is on the upswing in the foreign exchange market, it pays to purchase on credit goods that are billed in the foreign currency.

Foreign Sales

Sales are the opposite of purchases, and so credit sales result in exchange gains when the dollar weakens against foreign currencies and losses when it strengthens. Assume that a U.S. arms manufacturer sells 10 rifles to a Japanese company for 450,000 yen when the exchange rate is 150 yen to 1 dollar. The entry would be as follows:

Accounts Receivable	3,000	
Sales Revenue		3,000
Sold 10 rifles to Japanese company (450,000 yen ÷ 150 yen = $3,000).		

If the dollar gets stronger and the exchange rate is 160 yen per dollar on the collection date, the U.S. company will realize an exchange loss of $187.50, (450,000 ÷ 160 = $2,812.50; $3,000 − $2,812.50 = $187.50), and the entry would be:

Cash	2,812.50	
Exchange Loss	187.50	
Accounts Receivable		3,000.00

Received payment for 10 rifles sold to Japanese company.

Conversely, if the dollar had weakened, there would have been an exchange gain on this sales transaction.

Unrealized Exchange Gains and Losses

closed transaction *a transaction that is completed within the accounting period; both the purchase and payment or sale and receipt of payment occur within the same accounting period*

The transactions just described took place in the same accounting period, and so they are referred to as **closed transactions**. In such cases, the exchange gain or loss was actually realized during the period. If the accounting period ends between the date of the sale and its collection, however, or between the purchase and its payment, the exchange gain or loss will not have been realized (because payment has not yet been made or collected). In such a situation, should any unrealized gain or loss be recognized in the accounting records at the end of the period? For example, if the exchange rate per dollar is 150 yen at the time of a sale, 160 yen when the accounting period ends, and 155 yen when the bill is paid, should the difference between 150 and 160 yen be recognized on the financial statements? The FASB, in *Statement No. 52,* says "yes," even though the transaction was, at the end of the period, incomplete or **open**.[3]

open transaction *a transaction that is not completed at the end of the accounting period; a purchase that has not yet been paid for or a sale where payment is yet to be collected when the accounting period ends*

To illustrate, assume that the rifle transaction was open when the accounting period ended and that the facts are as stated here. The following three entries would be made:

Date of Sale

Accounts Receivable	3,000.00	
Sales Revenue		3,000.00

Sold 10 rifles to Japanese company (450,000 yen ÷ 150 yen = $3,000).

Financial Statement Date

Exchange Loss	187.50	
Accounts Receivable		187.50

Recognized exchange loss from strengthening of the dollar (450,000 ÷ 160 = $2,812.50; $3,000 − $2,812.50 = $187.50).

---

[3] *Statement of Financial Accounting Standards, No. 52,* "Foreign Currency Translation" (Stamford, Conn.: Financial Accounting Standards Board, 1981), par. 15.

> **Collection Date**
>
> Cash 2,903.23
>   Exchange Gain... 90.73
>   Accounts Receivable 2,812.50
>
> *Received payment for rifles sold to Japanese company (450,000 ÷ 155 = $2,903.23; $2,903.23 − $2,812.50 = $90.73).*

Because the exchange rate changed from 150 yen to 160 yen per dollar, an exchange loss of $187.50 had to be recognized on the financial statement date. The exchange rate had dropped back down to 155 yen per dollar by the date of payment, so $90.73 of the unrealized but recognized exchange loss of $187.50 had to be accounted for as an exchange gain.

The recognition of unrealized exchange gains and losses on open transactions is a topic of great debate. Those against such recognition contend that it results in a yo-yo effect on earnings. Supporters believe recognition is appropriate because using current rates reflects economic reality.

> **To Summarize** *When a transaction between a U.S. company and a foreign company is billed in U.S. dollars, there are no exchange gains or losses for the U.S. company. When a transaction is billed in a foreign currency, a gain or loss occurs if the exchange rate on the sale or purchase date is different from the rate on the collection or payment date. Exchange gains and losses must be recognized on both closed and open transactions. Exchange gains will be recognized by a U.S. company on credit purchase transactions when the dollar strengthens and on sale transactions when the dollar weakens.*

RESTATEMENT OF FOREIGN SUBSIDIARY FINANCIAL STATEMENTS

Many large companies have foreign subsidiaries, either established by the parent company or purchased, often to provide a cheaper source of materials or better access to an expanding marketplace.

As noted in Chapter 12 and explained later in the appendix on consolidations, if a parent company owns more than 50 percent of a subsidiary and exercises control over it, consolidated financial statements should be prepared. The consolidation procedure for foreign subsidiaries is the same as it is for U.S. subsidiaries, except that financial data reported in foreign currencies must be translated into U.S. dollars, the currency of the company's headquarters. This translation process is far from simple, however. Consider, for example, the basic question: What exchange rate should be used? The rate at the end of the accounting period would be simplest, but wouldn't the rates that existed at the time each of the foreign subsidiary's transactions took place be the most accurate? How about retained earnings, which is a total made up of the earnings accumulated over several years, what exchange rate would be appropriate? Such considerations make it necessary that the financial statements of foreign subsidiaries be restated in the process of translation.

Translation and Remeasurement

functional currency *the currency in which a subsidiary conducts most of its business; generally, but not always, the currency of the country where it does most of its spending and earning*

Type I subsidiary *a self-contained foreign subsidiary whose functional currency is different from the parent company's currency*

Type II subsidiary *a foreign subsidiary that is an extension of the parent company and whose functional currency is the same as the parent's*

reporting currency *the currency used by a company on its consolidated financial statements*

remeasurement *the process of restating a subsidiary's financial statements into its functional currency (used primarily for Type II subsidiaries)*

translation *the process of restating a subsidiary's financial statements from its functional currency to the reporting currency (used primarily for Type I subsidiaries)*

current exchange rate *the exchange rate that exists on the date the accounting period ends*

translation adjustment *perceived changes in value due only to exchange rate changes*

historical exchange rate *the exchange rate that existed on the date of a transaction*

The method of restatement depends on the **functional currency** of the foreign subsidiary, which is the currency in which the subsidiary conducts most of its business. Whether the functional currency is the currency of the country in which the subsidiary is located or the currency of its parent company (U.S. dollars) depends on the nature of the foreign subsidiary's operations. **Type I subsidiaries** are reasonably self-contained within a foreign country, usually both manufacturing and selling products there. **Type II subsidiaries** are merely extensions of the parent and are usually established only to market or buy goods. IBM, for example, derives about 90 percent of its non-U.S. revenues from Type I subsidiaries and only 10 percent from Type II subsidiaries.

Generally, the functional currency of Type I subsidiaries is the currency of the country in which they are located—that is, a Type I subsidiary located in Germany would use the Deutsche mark. The functional currency of Type II subsidiaries is the currency of the parent company. There is one major exception to this rule: Type I subsidiaries operating in countries with very high inflation (more than 100 percent cumulative inflation in 3 years) are accounted for in the same way as Type II subsidiaries, with the functional currency being the parent company's currency.

Whatever the subsidiary's functional currency, its financial statements generally must be restated in the **reporting currency,** the currency of the parent company (U.S. dollars for a U.S. company). Restatement for Type II subsidiaries therefore means that the subsidiary's statements based on the local currency must be **remeasured** in terms of the functional currency (which for Type II subsidiaries, is usually the reporting currency). Restatement for Type I subsidiaries means that the financial statements reported in the functional currency must be **translated** into the reporting currency.

Statement No. 52 makes a distinction between translation and remeasurement. The rationale behind using translation for Type I companies and remeasurement for Type II companies is based on the nature of these enterprises, as we will point out in a moment. The two methods of restating financial statements involve the use of different exchange rates. For a Type I subsidiary, all balance sheet accounts (except stockholders' equity) are translated from the functional currency to the reporting currency at the exchange rate that exists on the balance sheet date (the **current exchange rate**). All income statement accounts are translated at the average exchange rate for the period. Because of changes in exchange rates, the value of the parent's investment in the foreign subsidiary will appear to increase or decrease from year to year. These **translation adjustments,** or perceived changes in value due only to exchange rate changes, are reported separately in the stockholders' equity section of the consolidated balance sheet.

For Type II subsidiaries, only monetary assets and monetary liabilities are remeasured into the functional currency at the current exchange rate. The **historical rate**—the rate that existed at the time the transactions took place—is used for all other items on the balance sheet. Usually, several historical rates are used because transactions occur on varying dates: Inventory is usually purchased more recently than plant and equipment, for example. The average exchange rate for the year is used to remeasure most income statement accounts, except for cost of goods sold and depreciation expense, which use the same rates as the related asset accounts. Gains and losses that result from remeasurement are included in net income since Type II subsidiaries are considered an integral part of the parent.

Example of Restatement into U.S. Dollars

To illustrate the restatement of financial statements, assume that Nihon, Inc., is a wholly owned Japanese subsidiary of Marion Corporation. For Marion to prepare consolidated financial statements, Nihon's statements must be restated in U.S. dollars. Assume that the following exchange rates exist between Japan and the United States: historical rates, 200 yen per dollar for inventories, 360 yen per dollar for plant and equipment and contributed capital; current rate, 150 yen per dollar; average rate for the year, 170 yen per dollar.

In practice, the first step would be to determine whether Nihon, Inc., is Type I or Type II. For explanatory purposes, Exhibit 16-11 shows both types of financial statements.

Two items in Exhibit 16-11 need explanation. First, no exchange rates were used for retained earnings. Retained earnings cannot be directly remeasured or translated because it is made up of several year's net incomes that have already been remeasured or translated at different rates. Assuming begin-

EXHIBIT 16-11

Marion Corporation
Restatements of Nihon's Financial Statements

	Yen	Type I Translation Exchange Rate	Type I Translation U.S. Dollar	Type II Remeasurement Exchange Rate	Type II Remeasurement U.S. Dollar
Balance Sheet					
Cash	18,000	150	$ 120	150	$ 120
Accounts receivable	150,000	150	1,000	150	1,000
Inventories	450,000	150	3,000	200	2,250
Plant assets	900,000	150	6,000	360	2,500
Total assets	1,518,000		$10,120		$5,870
Accounts payable	36,000	150	$ 240	150	$ 240
Bonds payable	300,000	150	2,000	150	2,000
Common stock	750,000	360	2,083	360	2,083
Retained earnings	432,000		3,171		1,547
Cumulative translation adjustment			2,626		
Total liabilities and stockholders' equity	1,518,000		$10,120		$5,870
Income Statement					
Sales revenue	2,040,000	170	$12,000	170	$12,000
Cost of sales	986,000	170	$ 5,800	170	$ 5,800
Depreciation	90,000	170	529	360	250
Other expenses	850,000	170	5,000	170	5,000
Translation loss					403
Total deductions	1,926,000		$11,329		$11,453
Net income	114,000		$ 671		$ 547

ning retained earnings balances of $2,500 and $1,000 for Type I and Type II subsidiaries, respectively, we added net income ($671 and $547) to arrive at the ending retained earnings balances. Obviously, this assumes that there were no dividends or other transactions affecting retained earnings.

Second, the cumulative translation adjustment of $2,626 in the Type I restatement is the amount needed to make total liabilities and stockholders' equity equal to total assets. The calculation of the translation loss of $403 for the Type II subsidiary will be covered in more advanced accounting courses.

Looking at Exhibit 16-11, we see that these methods can produce very different results. When, as shown here, the dollar is weakening against the Japanese yen, the total asset figure is much higher under a Type I restatement than under Type II. The current year's translation adjustment is therefore needed in Type I restatements to bring total liabilities and stockholders' equity up to total assets. For a Type II restatement, the adjustment is included in net income.

Prior to *Statement No. 52*, only the Type II method was used, with the result that net income was influenced by exchange gains and losses. Though it makes sense to include exchange gains and losses in the net income of subsidiaries that are extensions of the parents, it is not useful or appropriate to do so with self-contained subsidiaries whose exchange gains and losses are seldom realized. Showing them as a cumulative adjustment to stockholders' equity allows companies to show a more realistic net income.

> **To Summarize** *The financial statements of Type I subsidiaries are translated from the company's functional currency into U.S. dollars, the reporting currency for U.S. companies. The statements of Type II subsidiaries are remeasured from the local currency into the functional currency, which for a U.S. company is the U.S. dollar.*

THE SEARCH FOR UNIFORMITY

Nations throughout the world have devised accounting principles and procedures that suit their own specific needs and requirements. For multinational corporations, this lack of uniformity can result in expensive and inefficient accounting. There have been several attempts to develop uniform international accounting standards, the most significant being the establishment of the International Accounting Standards Committee (IASC) in June 1973. The committee, which operates through a secretariat in London, includes representatives from the professional accountancy associations of some 40 countries. The members have pledged to comply with the committee's standards and to obtain the cooperation of both the business community and government authorities [the Securities and Exchange Commission (SEC) in the United States, for example]. The World Federation of Stock Exchanges requires that members comply with the IASC standards before they can have their stock listed. To date, the IASC has published over 30 standards, most of which are consistent with generally accepted accounting principles in the United States.

Review of Learning Objectives

Objective 1

Explain the reasons for financial statement analysis. The information that financial statement analysis provides about a company's performance is not readily apparent from a quick reading of the statements themselves. Although the statements are historical in nature, they are often useful in predicting future performance. Investors and creditors use financial statement analysis in judging the degree of profitability, liquidity, and solvency of a firm. Management uses it in identifying problems and measuring performance related to operations, asset turnover, and debt-equity management. Regulators use financial statement analysis in assessing operating results and financial status as it relates to taxing income, measuring concentrations of economic power, and so forth.

Objective 2

Identify and describe the basic technique and key relationships of financial statement analysis. Three techniques are commonly used in financial statement analysis: vertical analysis, horizontal analysis, and ratio analysis. The four key relationships (ratios) for assessing a firm's profitability, liquidity, and solvency with a focus on return on stockholders' equity are:

$$\underbrace{\frac{\text{net income}}{\text{net sales}}}_{\text{Operating Performance}} \times \underbrace{\frac{\text{net sales}}{\text{average total assets}}}_{\text{Asset Turnover}} \times \underbrace{\frac{\text{average total assets}}{\text{average stockholders' equity}}}_{\text{Debt-Equity Management}} = \underbrace{\frac{\text{net income}}{\text{average stockholders' equity}}}_{\text{Return on Stockholders' Equity}}$$

As this equation shows, the ratios that measure operating performance, asset turnover, and debt-equity management can be chained together to compute the return on stockholders' equity (which defines overall performance). Use of this approach helps the analyst understand how much each aspect of a company's activity contributed to the overall result.

Objective 3

Measure and analyze operating performance. An overall measure of a firm's operating performance, or profitability, is the operating performance ratio. Two techniques that are used to analyze operating performance in more detail are vertical and horizontal analysis of the income statement. Vertical analysis examines the relationship of each item to net sales for a particular year. Horizontal analysis compares individual income statement items for two or more periods.

Objective 4

Measure asset turnover and analyze asset utilization. An overall measure of how effectively a firm uses its assets is the asset turnover ratio. Detailed analysis of each major type of asset can be performed using vertical and horizontal balance sheet analysis and by computing additional ratios, including current ratio, acid-test ratio, accounts receivable turnover, inventory turnover, working capital turnover, and property, plant, and equipment turnover.

Objective 5

Measure and analyze the use of debt and equity in financing operations. The debt-equity management ratio measures the relative usage of debt and equity financing. It helps determine the margin of safety for creditors by identifying the extent to which a company is leveraging, that is, using stockholders' equity as a base for borrowing money. Additional ratios for measuring debt-equity management are the ratio of long-term debt to total assets, times interest earned, and the ratio of long-term debt to stockholders' equity.

Objective 6

Measure and analyze return on stockholders' equity. A measure of a firm's overall performance, from a stockholders' viewpoint, is provided by chaining the three key ratios (operating performance, asset turnover, and debt-equity management) to compute return on stockholders' equity. Other ratios can be computed to measure the return to stockholders, including earnings per share, price-earnings ratio, dividend payout ratio, and book value per share.

Objective 7

Calculate and explain return on total assets. Return on total assets is another measure of operating performance and asset utilization that measures the return to both creditors and stockholders. This ratio, which is favored by many financial analysts, is computed as follows:

$$\frac{\text{net income + interest expense (net of tax)}}{\text{net sales}}$$

Objective 8

Understand the limitations of financial statement analysis. Management and outsiders should recognize that information generated through the use of financial statement analysis has limitations because the underlying data are based on historical costs, estimates and judgments are used in allocating costs, accounting methods are not always comparable, and value and price-level changes may result in unrealized gains and losses that are not reflected in the financial statements.

Key Terms and Concepts

accounts receivable turnover *(678)*
acid-test ratio (or quick ratio) *(677)*
asset turnover ratio *(674)*
book value per share *(685)*
closed transaction *(695)**
current exchange rate *(697)**
current (or working capital) ratio *(676)*
debt-equity management ratio *(681)*
dividend payout ratio *(685)*
earnings per share (EPS) *(683)*
exchange gain or loss *(694)**
exchange rate *(692)**
functional currency *(697)**

historical exchange rate *(697)**
horizontal analysis of financial statements *(673)*
inventory turnover *(678)*
liquidity *(667)*
multinational company *(692)**
number of days' sales in inventory *(697)*
number of days' sales in receivables *(678)*
number of days' sales invested in working capital *(679)*
open transaction *(695)**
operating performance ratio *(671)*
price-earnings (P/E) ratio *(684)*
profitability *(667)*

property, plant, and equipment turnover *(680)*
redemption value *(686)*
remeasurement *(697)**
reporting currency *(697)**
return on stockholders' equity *(683)*
return on total assets *(687)*
solvency *(667)**
translation *(697)**
translation adjustment *(697)**
Type I subsidiary *(697)**
Type II subsidiary *(697)**
vertical analysis of financial statements *(672)*
working capital turnover *(679)*

* Related to Appendix.

Review Problem

Financial Statement Analysis

The comparative income statements and balance sheets for Montana Corporation for the years ending December 31, 1994 and 1993, are given here.

Montana Corporation
Income Statements
For the Years Ended December 31, 1994 and 1993

	1994	1993
Net sales	$600,000	$575,000
Cost of goods sold	500,000	460,000
Gross margin	$100,000	$115,000
Expenses:		
Selling and administrative expenses	$ 66,000	$ 60,000
Interest expense	4,000	3,000
Total expenses	$ 70,000	$ 63,000
Income before taxes	$ 30,000	$ 52,000
Income taxes	12,000	21,000
Net income	$ 18,000	$ 31,000

Earnings per share:
 1994 = $1.80
 1993 = $3.10

Montana Corporation
Balance Sheets
December 31, 1994 and 1993

Assets	1994	1993
Current assets:		
Cash	$ 11,000	$ 13,000
Accounts receivable (net)	92,000	77,000
Inventory	103,000	92,000
Prepaid expenses	6,000	5,000
Total current assets	$212,000	$187,000
Property, plant, and equipment:		
Land and building	$ 61,000	$ 59,000
Machinery and equipment	172,000	156,000
Total property, plant, and equipment	$233,000	$215,000
Less accumulated depreciation	113,000	102,000
Net property, plant, and equipment	$120,000	$113,000
Other assets	$ 8,000	$ 7,000
Total assets	$340,000	$307,000

Liabilities and Stockholders' Equity		
Current liabilities:		
Accounts payable	$ 66,000	$ 55,000
Notes payable	—	23,000
Dividends payable	2,000	—
Income taxes payable	3,000	5,000
Total current liabilities	$ 71,000	$ 83,000
Long-term debt	75,000	42,000
Total liabilities	$146,000	$125,000
Stockholders' Equity:		
Common stock ($1 par)	$ 10,000	$ 10,000
Paid-in capital in excess of par	16,000	16,000
Retained earnings	168,000	156,000
Total stockholders' equity	$194,000	$182,000
Total liabilities and stockholders' equity	$340,000	$307,000

Additional Information:	
Dividends declared in 1994	$6,000
Market price per share, December 31, 1994	$14.50

Required: Prepare a comprehensive financial statement analysis of Montana Corporation for 1994. Note that though financial statement analysts usually compare data from two or more years, we are more concerned here with the methods of analysis than the results, so we will use only 1 year, 1994.

Solution

1. Key Relationships

As shown in Exhibit 16-12, the computation of the four key ratios for 1994 provides the analyst with an overall view of the company's performance and gives an indication of how well management performed with respect to operations, asset turnover, and debt-equity management.

2. Analysis of Operating Performance

Operating performance is measured by means of vertical and horizontal analyses of the income statement.

Exhibit 16-12 Computation of Key Ratios (1994)

Operating Performance		Asset Turnover		Debt-Equity Management		Return on Stockholders' Equity*
$\dfrac{\text{Net Income}}{\text{Net Sales}}$	×	$\dfrac{\text{Net Sales}}{\text{Average Total Assets}}$	×	$\dfrac{\text{Average Total Assets}}{\text{Average Stockholders' Equity}}$	=	$\dfrac{\text{Net Income}}{\text{Average Stockholders' Equity}}$
$\dfrac{\$18,000}{\$600,000}$	×	$\dfrac{\$600,000}{\$323,500}$	×	$\dfrac{\$323,500}{\$188,000}$	=	$\dfrac{\$18,000}{\$188,000}$
3.00%	×	1.85 times	×	1.72 times	=	9.57%

* The factors do not multiply to the product because of rounding.

(a) Vertical analysis of the income statement. When the income statement is analyzed vertically, net sales is set at 100 percent, and each expense and net income are shown as percentages of net sales.

Montana Corporation
Vertical Analysis of Income Statement
For the Year Ended December 31, 1994

Net sales	$600,000	100.0%
Cost of goods sold	500,000	83.3
Gross margin	$100,000	16.7%
Expenses:		
Selling and administrative expenses	$ 66,000	11.0%
Interest expense	4,000	0.7
Total expenses	$ 70,000	11.7%
Income before taxes	$ 30,000	5.0%
Income taxes	12,000	2.0
Net income	$ 18,000	3.0%

(b) Horizontal analysis of the income statement. In horizontal analysis, the change in each income statement item from one period to the next is computed as a percentage increase or decrease using the earliest year as the base year. See Exhibit 16-13.

Exhibit 16-13

Horizontal Analysis of Income Statements
For the Years Ended December 31, 1994 and 1993

	1994	1993	$ Change	% Change
Net sales	$600,000	$575,000	+$25,000	+ 4.35
Cost of goods sold	500,000	460,000	+ 40,000	+ 8.70
Gross margin	$100,000	$115,000	−$15,000	−13.04
Expenses:				
Selling and administrative expenses	$ 66,000	$ 60,000	+ $ 6,000	+10.00
Interest expense	4,000	3,000	+ 1,000	+33.33
Total expenses	$ 70,000	$ 63,000	+ $ 7,000	+11.11
Income before taxes	$ 30,000	$ 52,000	−$22,000	−42.31
Income taxes	12,000	21,000	− 9,000	−42.86
Net income	$ 18,000	$ 31,000	−$13,000	−41.94

3. Analysis of Asset Turnover and Utilization

Asset turnover and utilization are analyzed by performing vertical and horizontal analyses of the balance sheets and computing some or all of the following: the asset turnover ratio and the ratios that together indicate efficient utilization of assets—current ratio; acid-test ratio; accounts receivable turnover; number of days' sales in receivables; inventory turnover; number of days' sales in inventory; working capital turnover; number of days' sales invested in working capital; and property, plant, and equipment turnover.

(a) Vertical Analysis—Balance Sheet

Montana Corporation
Vertical Analysis of the Balance Sheet
December 31, 1994

Assets

Current assets:		
Cash	$ 11,000	3.2%
Accounts receivable (net)	92,000	27.1
Inventory	103,000	30.3
Prepaid expenses	6,000	1.8
Total current assets	$212,000	62.4%
Property, plant, and equipment:		
Land and building	$ 61,000	17.9%
Machinery and equipment	172,000	50.6
Total property, plant, and equipment	$233,000	68.5%
Less accumulated depreciation	113,000	33.2
Net property, plant, and equipment	$120,000	35.3%
Other assets	$ 8,000	2.4%
Total assets	$340,000	100.0%

Liabilities and Stockholders' Equity

Current liabilities:		
Accounts payable	$ 66,000	19.4%
Dividends payable	2,000	0.6
Income taxes payable	3,000	0.9
Total current liabilities	$ 71,000	20.9%
Long-term debt	75,000	22.1
Total liabilities	146,000	42.9%
Stockholders' equity:	194,000	57.1
Total liabilities and stockholders' equity	$340,000	100.0%

(b) Horizontal Analysis—Balance Sheet (See Exhibit 16-14)

(c) Ratio Analysis—Asset Turnover
  (1) Asset turnover ratio:

$$\frac{\text{net sales}}{\text{average total assets}} = \frac{\$600,000}{\frac{\$340,000 + \$307,000}{2}} = \frac{\$600,000}{\$323,500} = 1.85$$

  (2) Current ratio:

$$\frac{\text{current assets}}{\text{current liabilities}} = \frac{\$212,000}{\$71,000} = 2.99$$

Chapter 16 *Financial Statement Analysis* 705

Exhibit 16-14 Horizontal Analysis—Balance Sheet (Montana Corporation)

Assets	1994	1993	$ Change	% Change
Current assets:				
Cash	$ 11,000	$ 13,000	−$ 2,000	− 15.4
Accounts receivable (net)	92,000	77,000	+ 15,000	+ 19.5
Inventory	103,000	92,000	+ 11,000	+ 12.0
Prepaid expenses	6,000	5,000	+ 1,000	+ 20.0
Total current assets	$212,000	$187,000	+$25,000	+ 13.4
Property, plant, and equipment:				
Land and building	$ 61,000	$ 59,000	+$ 2,000	+ 3.4
Machinery and equipment	172,000	156,000	+ 16,000	+ 10.3
Total property, plant, and equipment	$233,000	$215,000	+$18,000	+ 8.4
Less accumulated depreciation	113,000	102,000	+ 11,000	+ 10.8
Net property, plant, and equipment	$120,000	$113,000	+$ 7,000	+ 6.2
Other assets	$ 8,000	$ 7,000	+$ 1,000	+ 14.3
Total assets	$340,000	$307,000	+$33,000	+ 10.7
Liabilities and Stockholders' Equity				
Current liabilities:				
Accounts payable	$ 66,000	$ 55,000	+$11,000	+ 20.0
Notes payable	—	23,000	− 23,000	−100.0
Dividends payable	2,000	—	+ 2,000	—
Income taxes payable	3,000	5,000	− 2,000	− 40.0
Total current liabilities	$ 71,000	$ 83,000	−$12,000	− 14.5
Long-term debt	75,000	42,000	+ 33,000	+ 78.6
Total liabilities	$146,000	$125,000	+$21,000	+ 16.8
Stockholders' equity	194,000	182,000	+ 12,000	+ 6.6
Total liabilities and stockholders' equity	$340,000	$307,000	+$33,000	+ 10.7

(3) Acid-test ratio:

$$\frac{\text{cash and accounts receivable (net)}}{\text{current liabilities}} = \frac{\$103,000}{\$71,000} = 1.45$$

(4) Accounts receivable turnover:

$$\frac{\text{net sales}}{\text{average accounts receivable}} = \frac{\$600,000}{\frac{\$92,000 + \$77,000}{2}}$$

$$= \frac{\$600,000}{\$84,500} = 7.10 \text{ times}$$

(5) Number of days' sales in receivables:

$$\frac{365 \text{ days}}{\text{accounts receivable turnover}} = \frac{365}{7.10} = 51 \text{ days}$$

(6) Inventory turnover:

$$\frac{\text{cost of goods sold}}{\text{average inventory}} = \frac{\$500,000}{\frac{\$103,000 + \$92,000}{2}} = \frac{\$500,000}{\$97,500} = 5.13 \text{ times}$$

(7) Number of days' sales in inventory:

$$\frac{365 \text{ days}}{\text{inventory turnover}} = \frac{365}{5.13} = 71 \text{ days}$$

(8) Working capital turnover:

$$\frac{\text{net sales}}{\text{average working capital}} = \frac{\$600,000}{\frac{\$141,000 + \$104,000}{2}} = \frac{\$600,000}{\$122,500} = 4.90 \text{ times}$$

(9) Number of days' sales invested in working capital:

$$\frac{365 \text{ days}}{\text{working capital turnover}} = \frac{365}{4.90} = 74 \text{ days}$$

(10) Property, plant, and equipment turnover:

$$\frac{\text{net sales}}{\text{average net property, plant, and equipment}} = \frac{\$600,000}{\frac{\$120,000 + \$113,000}{2}} = \frac{\$600,000}{\$116,500} = 5.15 \text{ times}$$

4. Analysis of Debt-Equity Management

The management of debt and equity is measured by computing the following ratios: long-term debt to total assets, times interest earned, and long-term debt to stockholders' equity.

(a) Long-term debt to total assets:

$$\frac{\text{long-term debt}}{\text{total assets}} = \frac{\$75,000}{\$340,000} = 22.1\%$$

(b) Times interest earned:

$$\frac{\text{income before interest and tax expense}}{\text{interest expense}} = \frac{\$30,000 + \$4,000}{\$4,000} = \frac{\$34,000}{\$4,000} = 8.5 \text{ times}$$

(c) Long-term debt to stockholders' equity:

$$\frac{\text{long-term debt}}{\text{stockholders' equity}} = \frac{\$75,000}{\$194,000} = 38.7\%$$

5. Analysis of Return on Stockholders' Equity

Return on stockholders' equity is a key measure of overall performance. Other measures of overall performance are return on total assets, earnings per share, price-earnings ratio, dividend payout ratio, and book value per share.

(a) Return on stockholders' equity:

$$\frac{\text{net income}}{\text{average stockholders' equity}} = \frac{\$18,000}{\frac{\$194,000 + \$182,000}{2}} = \frac{\$18,000}{\$188,000} = 9.6\%$$

(b) Return on total assets:

$$\frac{\text{net income}}{\text{average total assets}} = \frac{\$18,000}{\frac{\$340,000 + \$307,000}{2}} = \frac{\$18,000}{\$323,500} = 5.6\%$$

(c) Earnings per share:

$$\frac{\text{net income}}{\text{average number of shares of common stock outstanding}} = \frac{\$18,000}{10,000 \text{ shares}} = \$1.80$$

(d) Price-earnings ratio:

$$\frac{\text{market price per share}}{\text{earnings per share}} = \frac{\$14.50}{\$1.80} = 8.1$$

(e) Dividend payout ratio:

$$\frac{\text{cash dividends}}{\text{net income}} = \frac{\$6,000}{\$18,000} = 33.3\%$$

(f) Book value per share:

$$\frac{\text{stockholders' equity}}{\text{number of shares outstanding}} = \frac{\$194,000}{10,000 \text{ shares}} = \$19.40 \text{ per share}$$

Discussion Questions

1. Why is financial statement analysis a desirable approach to studying financial statements?
2. How can the historical data reported by financial statements be used to make decisions affecting the future?
3. Who are the principal users of financial statements?
4. For what types of decisions is information from financial statements useful?
5. Identify and describe three common techniques of analyzing financial statements.
6. Identify the key ratios used to measure operating performance, asset turnover, debt-equity management, and return on stockholders' equity.
7. What are the components of the asset turnover ratio, and what does it measure?
8. Identify the components of the debt-equity management ratio. What does it measure?
9. What is the value of preparing a vertical analysis of an income statement?
10. What is the value of preparing a horizontal analysis of comparative income statements?
11. What types of financial statement analysis will help explain a trend in the asset turnover ratio?
12. Identify several ratios that will help explain how efficiently assets were utilized during a given period.
13. Show how the current ratio is computed, and explain its significance. What is considered to be an adequate current ratio?
14. Explain the different purposes of the current ratio and the acid-test ratio.
15. How is a firm's number of days' sales in receivables computed, and what is its significance?
16. How is the inventory turnover ratio computed, and what is its significance?
17. Explain the concept underlying property, plant, and equipment turnover.
18. What ratios might help explain changes over time in debt-equity management?
19. What is meant by the term *leveraging,* and what is its relationship to the management of debt?
20. Identify two alternative methods of measuring re-

Exercises

E16-1
Bad Debt Write-Off

Dixon Corporation wrote off a $400 uncollectible account receivable against the $2,400 credit balance in Allowance for Doubtful Accounts. How would this write-off affect its current ratio?

E16-2
Accounts Receivable and Inventory Turnovers

Selected data for Clark Corporation are as follows:

Balance Sheet Data

	December 31 1994	December 31 1993
Accounts receivable	$ 500,000	$ 470,000
Allowance for uncollectible accounts	25,000	20,000
Net accounts receivable	$ 475,000	$ 450,000
Inventories at cost	$ 600,000	$ 550,000

Income Statement Data

	1994	1993
Net credit sales	$2,500,000	$2,200,000
Net cash sales	500,000	400,000
Net sales	$3,000,000	$2,600,000
Cost of goods sold	$2,000,000	$1,800,000
Selling and general expense	300,000	270,000
Other expenses	50,000	30,000
Total operating expenses	$2,350,000	$2,100,000

What is the accounts receivable turnover for 1994? What is the inventory turnover for 1994?

E16-3
Inventory Turnover

On January 1, 1994, Hunt Company's beginning inventory was $200,000. During 1994 Hunt purchased $1,400,000 of additional inventory. On December 31 Hunt's ending inventory was $250,000. What is the inventory turnover for 1994?

E16-4
Number of Times Bond Interest Was Earned

The following data were abstracted from the financial records of King Corporation for 1994. How many times was bond interest earned in 1994?

Net sales	$3,600,000
Bond interest expense	200,000
Income tax expense	400,000
Net income	600,000

E16-5
The Effect of Transactions on the Current Ratio

Company B has a current ratio of 2:1. Describe the effect on the current ratio if the company:

1. Receives a 5 percent stock dividend on one of its marketable securities.
2. Pays a large account payable that had been a current liability.

Chapter 16 *Financial Statement Analysis* 709

3. Borrows cash on a 6-month note.
4. Sells merchandise for more than cost and records the sale using the perpetual inventory method.

E16-6
Accounts Receivable and Inventory Turnovers

Assuming that a business year consists of 300 days, what are the number of business days' sales in average receivables and the number of business days' sales in average inventories for 1994, based on the following information?

Net accounts receivable at December 31, 1993..	$ 900,000
Net accounts receivable at December 31, 1994..	$1,000,000
Accounts receivable turnover	5 times
Inventory at December 31, 1993	$1,100,000
Inventory at December 31, 1994	$1,300,000
Inventory turnover	5 times

E16-7
Acid-Test (Quick) Ratio

Information for Monet Company's balance sheet for December 31, 1994, is as follows:

Current assets:

Cash	$ 3,000,000
Marketable securities (at cost, which approximates market)	7,000,000
Accounts receivable (net of allowance for doubtful accounts)	100,000,000
Inventories (at lower or cost or market)	130,000,000
Prepaid expenses	2,000,000
Total current assets	$242,000,000

Current liabilities:

Notes payable	$ 4,000,000
Accounts payable	40,000,000
Accrued liabilities	30,000,000
Income taxes payable	1,000,000
Current portion of long-term debt	6,000,000
Total current liabilities	$ 81,000,000
Long-term debt	$180,000,000

What is the acid-test (quick) ratio?

E16-8
Dividends and the Current Ratio

1. Company A has a current ratio of 0.65. A cash dividend was declared last month but paid this month. What is the effect of this dividend payment on the current ratio and on working capital?
2. Company B has a current ratio of 1.60. An account payable was paid during this month. What is the effect of this payment on the current ratio and on working capital?

E16-9
Asset Turnover Ratio and Inventory Turnover

The following information was taken from the 1994 and 1993 financial statements of Levine Company:

	1994	1993
Net sales	$306,000	$225,000
Cost of goods sold	210,000	172,000
Average total assets	180,000	150,000
Average inventory	50,000	40,000
Average accounts receivable (net)	20,000	15,000
Average net working capital	75,000	60,000

1. Compute the asset turnover ratios for 1993 and 1994.
2. Compute the inventory turnover ratios for 1993 and 1994.
3. Compute the number of days' sales in inventory for 1993 and 1994.

E16-10
Accounts Receivable and Working Capital Turnovers

On the basis of the information presented for Levine Company in E16-9:

1. Compute the accounts receivable turnover and the average number of days' sales in receivables for 1993 and 1994.
2. Compute the working capital turnovers for 1993 and 1994.
3. What effect did the changes in the inventory, accounts receivable, and working capital turnovers from 1993 to 1994 have on the total asset turnover from 1993 to 1994?

E16-11
The Price-Earnings Ratio

Information concerning Bloom Company's common stock is as follows:

	Per Share
Book value at December 31, 1994	$12.00
Quoted market price on stock on December 31, 1994	18.00
Earnings per share for 1994	3.00
Par value	2.00
Dividend declared and paid in 1994	1.00

What was the price-earnings ratio on common stock for 1994?

E16-12
Exchange Rates *(Appendix)*

European Imports, Inc. (EII), an American company, contracted with Itol, Inc., a West German watchmaker, to make some collectors'-item Christmas watches. The contract required EII to sell Itol the watch casings and then buy back the completed watches before Christmas. To ensure that the proper specifications were followed, EII sent a consultant to help Itol get started, at Itol's expense. The following transactions occurred. (All transactions are in Deutsche marks.)

1993
Jan. 31   EII sold Itol 100 watch casings for 25,000 Deutsche marks. The sale was on account, and the exchange rate was $0.40 per mark.
Apr. 1   Itol pays the account in full (exchange rate = $0.375 per mark).
May   5   The EII consultant helped Itol work out the specifications and billed Itol 8,000 Deutsche marks (exchange rate = $0.375 per mark).
Sept. 1   Itol paid the consulting fee (exchange rate = $0.38 per mark).
Sept. 1   Itol sold the completed watches back to EII for 50,000 Deutsche marks, allowing EII to postpone payment until the watches were sold (exchange rate = $0.38 per mark).
Dec. 31   The exchange rate was $0.42 per mark.

1994
Jan. 31   EII paid Itol 50,000 Deutsche marks (exchange rate = $0.375 per mark).

How would EII and Itol account for the transactions given?

Problem Set A

P16A-1
Vertical Analysis

Below are income statements for Northern and Bishop Companies for the year ended 12/31/94.

Required:
1. Prepare a vertical analysis of the income statements for the two companies.
2. **Interpretive Question** Comment on the significant differences between the two companies.
3. **Interpretive Question** How would your comparison of the two companies be affected if you knew that Northern Company used the FIFO alternative of inventory costing and Bishop Company used the LIFO alternative?

	Northern	Bishop
Net sales	$360,000	$500,000
Cost of goods sold:		
Beginning inventory	$ 40,000	$ 80,000
Purchases (net)	290,000	320,000
Cost of goods available for sale	$330,000	$400,000
Ending inventory	60,000	60,000
Cost of goods sold	$270,000	$340,000
Gross margin	$ 90,000	$160,000
Operating expenses:		
Depreciation expense	$ 6,000	$ 15,000
Salaries and wages expense	24,000	40,000
Other expenses	12,000	30,000
Total operating expenses	$ 42,000	$ 85,000
Income before taxes	$ 48,000	$ 75,000
Income taxes	18,000	35,000
Net income	$ 30,000	$ 40,000

P16A-2
Asset Turnover Ratios

SPREADSHEET PROBLEM

Comparative balance sheets and income statements for Braun Company for the years 1993 and 1994 follow:

Braun Company
Balance Sheets
December 31, 1994 and 1993

Assets	1994	1993
Current assets:		
Cash	$ 15,000	$ 12,500
Marketable securities	45,000	32,500
Accounts receivable (net)	180,000	150,000
Inventories	160,000	130,000
Total current assets	$ 400,000	$ 325,000
Investments	$ 150,000	$ 162,500
Property, plant, and equipment	$1,000,000	$ 950,000
Less accumulated depreciation, plant and equipment	450,000	400,000
Total property, plant, and equipment	$ 550,000	$ 550,000
Intangible assets	$ 25,000	$ 12,500
Total assets	$1,125,000	$1,050,000

Liabilities and Stockholders' Equity	1994	1993
Current liabilities:		
Accounts payable	$ 62,500	$ 50,000
Notes payable	125,000	100,000
Accrued liabilities	100,000	75,000
Total current liabilities	$ 287,500	$ 225,000
Long-term debt:		
Bonds payable	362,500	325,000
Total liabilities	$ 650,000	$ 550,000
Stockholders' equity:		
Common stock (7,500 shares)	$ 75,000	$ 75,000
Paid-in capital in excess of par	275,000	275,000
Retained earnings	125,000	150,000
Total stockholders' equity	$ 475,000	$ 500,000
Total liabilities and stockholders' equity	$1,125,000	$1,050,000

Braun Company
Income Statements
For the Years Ended December 31, 1994 and 1993

	1994	1993
Net sales	$800,000	$675,000
Cost of goods sold	500,000	425,250
Gross margin	$300,000	$249,750
Expenses:		
Selling and administrative expenses	$187,200	$149,850
Interest expense	24,800	12,488
Total expenses	$212,000	$162,338
Income before taxes	$ 88,000	$ 87,412
Income taxes	44,000	43,706
Net income	$ 44,000	$ 43,706

Additional Information:

(a) Dividends paid in 1994 amounted to $28,600.
(b) The market price per share is 67½.

Required: Using the foregoing balance sheets and income statements, calculate the following ratios for 1994:

1. The current ratio.
2. The acid-test ratio.
3. The accounts receivable turnover.
4. The inventory turnover.
5. The working capital turnover.
6. The property, plant, and equipment turnover.
7. Return on assets.

Chapter 16 *Financial Statement Analysis*

P16A-3
Debt-Equity Management Ratios

Refer to the financial statements in P16A-2.

Calculate the following debt-equity management ratios for 1994:

1. Long-term debt to total assets.
2. Times interest earned.
3. Long-term debt to stockholders' equity.

P16A-4
Return on Stockholders' Equity

Refer to the financial statements in P16A-2.

Calculate the following ratios for 1994:

1. Return on stockholders' equity.
2. Earnings per share.
3. Book value per share (common).
4. Dividend payout ratio.
5. Price-earnings ratio.

P16A-5
Unifying Concepts: Key Ratios and Supplementary Ratios

SPREADSHEET PROBLEM

The balance sheets and income statements of Walton Supply Company for 1994 and 1993 are as follows:

Walton Supply Company
Balance Sheets
December 31, 1994 and 1993
(in thousands)

Assets	1994	1993
Current assets:		
Cash	$ 275	$ 450
Accounts receivable (net)	638	330
Inventories	907	660
Prepaid insurance	1,620	1,590
Total current assets	$3,440	$3,030
Property, plant, and equipment	$2,350	$2,250
Less depreciation	910	780
Total property, plant, and equipment	$1,440	$1,470
Total assets	$4,880	$4,500
Liabilities and Stockholders' Equity		
Current liabilities:		
Accounts payable	$ 666	$ 450
Notes payable	460	450
Other current liabilities	210	210
Total current liabilities	$1,336	$1,110
Long-term debt	270	240
Total liabilities	$1,606	1,350
Common stock ($10 par)	$1,000	$1,000
Retained earnings	2,274	2,150
Total stockholders' equity	$3,274	$3,150
Total liabilities and stockholders' equity	$4,880	$4,500

Walton Supply Company
Income Statements
For the Years Ended December 31, 1994 and 1993
(in thousands)

	1994	1993
Net sales*	$8,746	$7,950
Cost of goods sold	6,258	5,600
Gross margin	$2,488	$2,350
Expenses:		
Operating expenses	$ 862	$ 635
Depreciation expense	130	120
Interest expense	148	145
Total expenses	$1,140	$ 900
Income before taxes	$1,348	$1,450
Income taxes (50%)	674	725
Net income	$ 674	$ 725

* Assume that all sales were made on credit.

Additional Information:

(a) Dividends paid in 1994, $50,000 (on 100,000 shares of common stock outstanding).
(b) Market price per share at December 31, 1994, $60.67 per share.

Required:

1. Calculate the key ratios for measuring operating performance, asset turnover, and debt-equity management for 1994.
2. Using the ratios computed in part (1), assess the overall performance of the company from a stockholder's point of view.
3. Compute the following additional ratios to further analyze asset turnover, debt-equity management, and return on stockholders' equity:
   (a) Current ratio.
   (b) Acid-test ratio.
   (c) Accounts receivable turnover.
   (d) Number of days' sales in receivables.
   (e) Inventory turnover.
   (f) Number of days' sales in inventory.
   (g) Working capital turnover.
   (h) Property, plant, and equipment turnover.
   (i) Long-term debt to total assets.
   (j) Times interest earned.
   (k) Long-term debt to stockholders' equity.
   (l) Return on total assets.
   (m) Earnings per share.
   (n) Price-earnings ratio.
   (o) Dividend payout ratio (calculated for 1994).
   (p) Book value per share.
4. Classify each of the ratios listed in part (3) as to whether it is a measure of liquidity, solvency, or profitability.

P16A-6
Vertical and Horizontal Analyses

Mr. Gordon, manager of Sloan's Pickle Company, is pleased to see a substantial increase in 1994 sales. However, he has asked you, as the company's financial analyst, to evaluate the effects of this increase in sales on company operations and earnings. Following are the company's income statements for 1994 and 1993.

Chapter 16 *Financial Statement Analysis*   715

SPREADSHEET PROBLEM

Sloan's Pickle Company
Income Statements
For the Years Ended December 31, 1994 and 1993

	1994	1993
Net sales	$110,000	$ 80,000
Expenses:		
Cost of goods sold	$ 60,000	$ 48,000
Selling expenses	22,000	16,000
General and administrative expenses	10,000	8,000
Interest expense	2,000	2,000
Total expenses	$ 94,000	$ 74,000
Income before taxes	$ 16,000	$ 6,000
Income taxes (20%)	3,200	1,200
Net income	$ 12,800	$ 4,800

Required:
1. Perform a vertical and a horizontal analysis of the company's income statement.
2. **Interpretive Question** Note any significant changes that should be brought to Mr. Gordon's attention.

P16A-7
Measuring and Judging Profitability

The controller of Bookstone Company selected the following data from the company's 1994 financial statements for further analysis:

Preferred stock ($100 par, 1,000 shares issued and outstanding, 7% cumulative dividend, no dividends in arrears)	$100,000
Common stock ($10 par, 40,000 shares issued and outstanding)	400,000
Retained earnings at December 31, 1994	140,000
Net income for 1994	82,000
Dividends Declared and Paid During 1994:	
Preferred	7,000
Common	30,000
Market price per share of common stock at December 31, 1994	18

Required:
1. Compute the following amounts:
   (a) Book value per share for preferred and common stock.
   (b) EPS for preferred and common stock.
   (c) Dividend payout ratio for common stock.
   (d) Return on common stockholders' equity.
   (e) Price-earnings ratio for common stock.
2. **Interpretive Question** What information would you like to have to judge whether the current market price of the stock represents a good buy?

P16A-8
Unifying Concepts: Comprehensive Analysis of Financial Statements

Certain financial information relating to two companies, Thomas Clothes, Inc., and Corona Stores, Inc., as of the end of the current year is provided as follows:

Assets	Thomas Clothes	Corona Stores
Cash	$ 12,700	$ 18,100
Marketable securities (at cost)	12,900	45,300
Accounts receivable (net)	14,500	16,700
Inventory	75,500	38,400
Prepaid expenses	2,400	1,500
Plant and equipment (net)	68,000	57,000
Intangible and other assets	14,000	3,000
Total assets	$200,000	$180,000

Liabilities and Stockholders' Equity	Thomas Clothes	Corona Stores
Accounts payable	$ 35,500	$ 30,500
Accrued liabilities (including income taxes)	14,500	9,500
Bonds payable (7%, due in 10 years)	20,000	50,000
Capital stock ($10 par)	80,000	60,000
Paid-in capital in excess of par	15,000	25,000
Retained earnings	41,000	5,000
Treasury stock (1,000 shares, at cost)	(6,000)	–0–
Total liabilities and stockholders' equity	$200,000	$180,000
Analysis of retained earnings:		
Balance, beginning of year	$ 21,200	$ 2,000
Add net income	29,700	18,000
Subtract dividends	(9,900)	(15,000)
Balance, end of year	$ 41,000	$ 5,000
Market price per share of stock, end of year	$ 50	$ 40
Sales revenue (net)	$495,000	$450,000

Required:
1. Compute the key ratios (operating performance and asset turnover, for example) for each company using end-of-year balances.
2. Compute earnings per share for each company.
3. Compute the price-earnings ratio for each company.
4. Compute the book value per share for each company.
5. **Interpretive Question** What are some limitations in the use of a book-value computation when comparing two companies?

P16A-9

Journalizing Foreign Transactions and Restating Financial Statements *(Appendix)*

Mow Chemicals has decided to open a branch lab in Great Britain by purchasing all the common stock of the new lab for $150,000. The lab is an integral part of Mow Chemicals' operations (Type II subsidiary). The lab will require 6 months to set up its operations and will be open for business on January 1, 1994.

Required:
1. Prepare journal entries reflecting the following transactions for the British subsidiary. Entries should all be converted to British pounds.

    July 1 Received $150,000 in exchange for 10,000 shares of common stock (exchange rate = $1.50 per pound).

    1 Bought a lab building from a U.S. company for $90,000, paying $15,000 down and financing the balance with a long-term note. No interest will be charged on the loan until operations start.

    Oct. 1 Purchased lab equipment on account from a U.S. company for $42,000 when the exchange rate was $1.50 per pound.

    Nov. 1 Paid off lab equipment in full (exchange rate = $1.40 per pound).

    30 Bought inventory (for cash) from a British drug company for 25,000 pounds when the exchange rate was $1.55 per pound.

    Dec. 31 Bought $12,000 of inventory on account from a U.S. drug company when the exchange rate was $1.60 per pound.

2. Using these transactions, prepare a simple balance sheet for the subsidiary, in British pounds.
3. Convert the balance sheet prepared in (2) to U.S. dollars, and consolidate the results with the balance sheet for Mow Chemicals' American operations shown at the top of the next page.

Mow Chemicals
Balance Sheet
December 31, 1993

Assets

Cash	$100,000
Accounts receivable	150,000
Inventory	225,000
Equipment	75,000
Buildings	200,000
Other assets	50,000
Total assets	$800,000

Liabilities and Stockholders' Equity

Accounts payable	$120,000
Notes payable	200,000
Common stock	300,000
Retained earnings	180,000
Total liabilities and stockholders' equity	$800,000

Problem Set B

P16B-1
Calculation of Key Ratios

Trevino Company's 1994 and 1993 financial statements are presented here in summary form.

Trevino Company
Income Statements
For the Years Ended December 31, 1994 and 1993

	1994	1993
Net sales	$260,000	$220,000
Cost of goods sold	182,000	165,000
Gross margin	$ 78,000	$ 55,000
Selling and administrative expenses	52,000**	38,000*
Income before taxes	$ 26,000	$ 17,000
Income taxes	11,700	6,800
Net income	$ 14,300	$ 10,200

* Includes interest expense of $8,000.
**Includes interest expense of $5,000.

Trevino Company
Balance Sheets (condensed)
December 31, 1994 and 1993

Assets	1994	1993
Current assets	$ 30,000	$ 25,000
Property, plant, and equipment	40,000	28,000
Less accumulated depreciation	(6,000)	(4,000)
Other assets	5,000	3,000
Total assets	$ 69,000	$ 52,000

Liabilities and Stockholders' Equity	1994	1993
Current liabilities	$ 18,000	$ 14,000
Long-term liabilities	5,000	-0-
Capital stock	25,000	25,000
Retained earnings	21,000	13,000
Total liabilities and stockholders' equity	$ 69,000	$ 52,000

Required: Compute the following ratios for 1994:

1. Net income to net sales.
2. Asset turnover ratio.
3. Average total assets to average stockholders' equity.
4. Net income to average stockholders' equity.

P16B-2
The Current Ratio and Return on Total Assets

On the basis of the information presented for Trevino Company in P16B-1, answer these questions.

1. How much was declared in dividends during 1994, in dollars and as a percentage of income?
2. What is the return on average total assets for 1994?
3. What were the current ratios in 1993 and in 1994?

P16B-3
Horizontal Analysis

On January 1, 1994, Margie Alf, sales manager for Petro-Chemical Products Corporation, decided to discontinue the 1993 discount policy of 2/10, n/30. She believed that the company's cash flow and sales levels would not be affected by eliminating the discount. Selected data for 1994 and 1993 are as follows:

	1994	1993
Net sales	$655,000	$625,000
Cash on hand	237,500	312,500
Average accounts receivable for the year	45,000	30,000

Required:
1. Perform a horizontal analysis as a starting point for analyzing the effects of Ms. Alf's decision.
2. **Interpretive Question** Assume that all sales discounts in 1993 were taken by customers and that all sales were made on credit in both 1993 and 1994. What effect on accounts receivable can you see from discontinuing the discount policy? (Hint: What has happened to the accounts receivable turnover rate?).
3. **Interpretive Question** Using the same assumptions as in part (2), what was the effect of Ms. Alf's decision on net sales?

P16B-4
Debt-Equity Management Ratios

The following information was taken from the 1994 and 1993 financial statements of Glen Company:

	1994	1993
Average total assets	$300,000	$260,000
Average stockholders' equity	200,000	180,000
Interest expense	11,000	8,000
Net income after taxes	33,000	24,000
Tax rate	40%	40%

Chapter 16 *Financial Statement Analysis* 719

Required:
1. Compute the key ratio of average total assets to average stockholders' equity for 1993 and 1994.
2. Compute the ratio of average debt to average stockholders' equity for 1993 and 1994.
3. Compute the times interest earned in 1993 and 1994.
4. Did the company use more or less leverage in 1994 than in 1993?

P16B-5
Book Value per Share

Sooner Corporation's stockholders' equity at June 30, 1994, consisted of the following:

Preferred stock (10%, $50 par, liquidating value $55 per share, 12,000 shares issued and outstanding)	$ 600,000
Common stock ($10 par, 500,000 shares authorized, 150,000 shares issued and outstanding)	1,500,000
Retained earnings	700,000
Total stockholders' equity	$2,800,000

Required:
1. Compute the book value per share of the preferred stock, assuming that there are no dividends in arrears.
2. Compute the book value per share of the common stock. (Assume that common stock was the same at the beginning and the end of the year.)

P16B-6
Selected Profitability Ratios

Following are selected financial data for Mullin Realty Company for 1994 and some information about industry averages.

Financial Data for Mullin Realty Company

Net income		$ 164,000
Preferred stock (6%, 5,500 shares at $100 par)		$ 550,000
Common stock (25,000 shares at $1 par, market value $65 per share)		25,000
Paid-in capital in excess of par, common stock		400,000
Retained earnings		468,750
Total		$1,443,750
Less treasury stock:		
Preferred (500 shares)	$45,000	
Common (1,000 shares)	20,000	65,000
Total stockholders' equity		$1,378,750

Additional Information:

(a) Current year dividends on preferred stock, $30,000.
(b) Redemption value of preferred stock, $101.25 per share.

Industry Averages

Earnings per share	$6.00
Price-earnings ratio	9.0
Return on stockholders' equity	15.0%

Required:
1. Calculate the earnings per share, the price-earnings ratio, book value per share, and the return on stockholders' equity ratio for Mullin.
2. **Interpretive Question** Would you want to invest your money in the common stock of this company?

P16B-7

Unifying Concepts: Alternative Financing Plans

SPREADSHEET PROBLEM

Steele Company's balance sheet and additional information as of December 31, 1994, are as follows:

Steele Company
Balance Sheet
December 31, 1994

Assets

Current assets:
Cash	$ 30,000
Accounts receivable (net)	150,000
Notes receivable	65,000
Inventories	245,000
Prepaid expenses	10,000
Total current assets	$ 500,000

Property, plant, and equipment:
Land	$ 20,000
Building (net)	155,000
Equipment (net)	325,000
Total property, plant, and equipment	$ 500,000
Total assets	$1,000,000

Liabilities and Stockholders' Equity

Current liabilities:
Accounts payable	$ 80,000
Income taxes payable	60,000
Accrued liabilities	30,000
Total current liabilities	$ 170,000
Long-term note payable (10%)	150,000
Total liabilities	$ 320,000

Stockholders' Equity
Common stock ($10 par)	$ 400,000
Retained earnings	280,000
Total stockholders' equity	$ 680,000
Total liabilities and stockholders' equity	$1,000,000

Additional Information:

Net income for 1994, $54,400; effective tax rate, 40%.

The company's board of directors is considering several alternative plans for expanding its operations. It has been estimated that an additional investment of $500,000 will make it possible to increase the volume of operations by 60 to 75 percent. The $500,000 would be used to expand the present building, buy additional equipment, and increase working capital. Of the $500,000 needed, $200,000 would be used to increase working capital.

The two most viable alternatives are:

(a) Sell $500,000 of 20-year bonds at an estimated interest rate of 9 percent.
(b) Sell 15,625 shares of common stock at an estimated average price of $32 per share.

Required: 1. Assuming that one of these two alternatives were implemented in late 1994, prepare a balance sheet for each alternative as of December 31, 1994.

Chapter 16 Financial Statement Analysis

2. If net income before interest expense and income taxes is expected to be $190,000 for the year 1995, what would be the earnings per share for each of the above alternatives?
3. Compute the rate of return on stockholders' equity for 1995 under each alternative and compare these with the 1994 return. Assume that no dividends are paid in 1995.
4. Compute the debt-equity management ratio for each alternative and compare it with 1994.
5. **Interpretive Questions** Which alternative would you recommend to the board of directors? Why?

P16B-8
Unifying Concepts: Comprehensive Analysis of Asset Turnover

Douglas Stores has the comparative balance sheets for 1993, 1994, and 1995 shown below.

Douglas Stores, Inc.
Comparative Balance Sheets
December 31, 1995, 1994, and 1993

Assets	1995	1994	1993
Cash	$ 12,000	$ 15,000	$ 16,000
Accounts receivable (net)	183,000	80,000	60,000
Inventory	142,000	127,000	52,000
Other current assets	5,000	6,000	4,000
Plant and equipment (net)	60,000	80,000	70,000
Total assets	$402,000	$308,000	$202,000

Liabilities and Stockholders' Equity			
Accounts payable	$ 38,000	$ 51,000	$ 32,000
Federal income tax payable	30,000	14,400	28,000
Long-term liabilities	120,000	73,000	42,400
Common stock	110,000	110,000	80,000
Retained earnings	104,000	59,600	19,600
Total liabilities and stockholders' equity	$402,000	$308,000	$202,000

Additional Information:

(a) Net sales for 1994 and 1995 were $1,250,000 and $1,684,000, respectively.
(b) Cost of goods sold for 1994 and 1995 were $810,000 and $927,000, respectively.

Required:

1. You are asked to compute the following ratios for 1994 and 1995 as a basis for drawing some conclusions about the trends in asset turnover for Douglas Stores.
   (a) Number of days' sales in receivables.
   (b) Number of days' sales in inventory.
   (c) Working capital turnover.
   (d) Property, plant, and equipment turnover.
   (e) The key ratio for total asset turnover.
2. **Interpretive Question** Indicate the general trend in asset turnover from 1994 to 1995.

P16B-9
Restatement of the Financial Statements *(Appendix)*

Hansen Electric Company owns 100 percent of Tokyo Denki, a Japanese subsidiary. The following financial statements of Tokyo Denki will need to be converted to U.S. dollars in order to prepare consolidated statements. The historical exchange rate for plant assets and common stock is 250 Japanese yen (¥) per U.S. dollar. The historical rate for inventory and other assets is 225¥ per dollar, the average rate is 240¥ per dollar, and the current rate is 200¥ per dollar.

Tokyo Denki
Balance Sheet
December 31, 1994

Assets

Cash	¥ 2,000,000
Accounts receivable	17,000,000
Inventory	45,000,000
Net plant	15,000,000
Other assets	9,000,000
Total assets	¥88,000,000

Liabilities and Stockholders' Equity

Accounts payable	¥12,000,000
Notes payable	30,000,000
Common stock	28,000,000
Retained earnings	18,000,000
Total liabilities and stockholders' equity	¥88,000,000

Tokyo Denki
Income Statement
For the Year Ended December 31, 1994

Sales revenue		¥240,000,000
Cost of goods sold	¥144,000,000	
Depreciation	4,800,000	
General & administrative expense	84,000,000	232,800,000
Net income		¥ 7,200,000

Required:
1. Convert the financial statements of Tokyo Denki to U.S. dollars for consolidation purposes given the following two independent assumptions:
   (a) Assume that Tokyo is a self-contained subsidiary operating entirely within Japan (Type I) and that beginning retained earnings is $50,000.
   (b) Assume that Tokyo is an integral part of Hansen's operations and that beginning retained earnings is again $50,000 (Type II).
2. Why do the two assumptions result in different income or loss figures?

P16B-10
Journalizing Foreign Transactions and Translating Financial Statements *(Appendix)*

Gyrotech, a U.S. company, has a wholly-owned subsidiary in Germany. The subsidiary is self contained within Germany and manufactures and sells products there. The balance sheet for the German subsidiary is shown on the next page.

Required:
1. Prepare the journal entries reflecting the following 1994 transactions for the German subsidiary. Entries should all be converted to German marks.

   Jan. 27 Purchased on account inventory from Gyrotech U.S. for $200,000 (exchange rate = $2.50 per deutsche mark).
   Mar. 1   Sold on account $360,000 worth of manufactured inventory to Gyrotech U.S. (exchange rate = $2.40 per deutsche mark).

May 27   Purchased other assets (for cash) from an American company for $112,500 (exchange rate = $2.25 per deutsche mark).
July 6   Paid off inventory bought January 27 from Gyrotech U.S. (exchange rate = $2.60 per deutsche mark).
Aug. 28   Received payment for inventory sold March 1 to Gyrotech U.S. (exchange rate = $2.25 per deutsche mark).

2. Prepare a balance sheet for December 31, 1994, using prior year balances and accounting for the required journal entries. The balance sheet will be presented in deutsche marks. Assume the year-end exchange rate = $2.00 per deutsche mark. Historical rates = $2.50 per deutsche mark. Assume also retained earnings before translation equals 3,436,923 marks and after translation retained earnings equals 5,000,000 marks.

Gyrotech Subsidiary
Balance Sheet
December 31, 1993

Assets	German Marks
Cash	800,000
Accounts receivable	2,000,000
Inventory	4,000,000
Buildings	1,400,000
Other assets	800,000
Total assets	9,000,000

Liabilities and Stockholders' Equity	
Accounts payable	1,000,000
Notes payable	3,000,000
Common stock	2,600,000
Retained earnings	2,400,000
Total liabilities and stockholders' equity	9,000,000

Business Analysis Case 1   *Palmer Gourmet Restaurant*

The financial statements for Palmer Gourmet Restaurant are presented on the next page for the years 1992 to 1994. You have been asked to analyze these statements as a basis for advising a client who is thinking of making a significant investment in the restaurant. He is particularly interested in the firm's liquidity, solvency, and profitability, and in the efficiency and effectiveness of the company's management.

Required: In analyzing Palmer's financial statements, you are to answer the following questions:

1. What are the firm's current and acid-test ratios for the past 2 years?
2. What evidence is there that the firm is becoming more or less profitable?
3. How well is the firm managing its operations, its assets, and its debt? (In answering this question, assume that the amount of ending assets and equity at December 31, 1993, was the same as it was at December 31, 1994.)
4. Has the company been expanding? If so, how was the expansion financed?
5. What is your general assessment of the viability of this company?

Palmer Gourmet Restaurant
Income Statements
For the Years Ended December 31, 1994, 1993, and 1992

	1994	1993	1992
Revenues:			
Sales revenue	$19,153,000	$9,434,000	$7,937,000
Other revenues	689,000	355,000	111,000
Total revenues	$19,842,000	$9,789,000	$8,048,000
Operating expenses:			
Food and beverage expense	$ 9,081,000	$4,528,000	$3,847,000
Payroll expense	3,786,000	1,876,000	1,564,000
Depreciation and amortization expenses	477,000	222,000	175,000
General and administrative expenses	889,000	515,000	392,000
Interest expense	81,000	144,000	160,000
Miscellaneous expenses	1,710,000	792,000	647,000
Total operating expenses	$16,024,000	$8,077,000	$6,785,000
Income before taxes	$ 3,818,000	$1,712,000	$1,263,000
Income taxes	1,695,000	738,000	602,000
Net income	$ 2,123,000	$ 974,000	$ 661,000
Earnings per share	$ .52	$ .32	$ .28
Weighted-average shares outstanding	4,107,000	3,016,000	2,400,000

Palmer Gourmet Restaurant
Balance Sheets
December 31, 1994 and 1993

Assets	1994	1993
Current assets:		
Cash	$ 7,086,000	$3,192,000
Receivables	55,000	18,000
Inventories	237,000	152,000
Prepaid expenses	20,000	17,000
Total current assets	$ 7,398,000	$3,379,000
Property, plant, and equipment:		
Land	$ 3,020,000	$1,160,000
Buildings	5,801,000	3,133,000
Equipment	2,886,000	1,621,000
Less accumulated depreciation	(1,060,000)	(600,000)
Total property, plant, and equipment	$10,647,000	$5,314,000
Other assets, principally deferred charges (net of accumulated amortization)	$ 246,000	$ 102,000
Total assets	$18,291,000	$8,795,000

Liabilities and Stockholders' Equity		
Current liabilities:		
Accounts payable	$ 597,000	$ 645,000
Income taxes payable	110,000	356,000
Accrued liabilities	168,000	96,000
Total current liabilities	$ 875,000	$1,097,000
Long-term debt	867,000	1,332,000
Deferred income taxes	520,000	218,000
Total liabilities	$ 2,262,000	$2,647,000

Stockholders' Equity:
Common stock ($1.00 par, authorized
5,000,000 shares; issued and outstanding
4,116,426 and 1,261,820 shares in 1994 and
1993, respectively) .... $ 4,116,000 $1,262,000
Paid-in capital in excess of par 8,800,000   3,896,000
Retained earnings 3,113,000   990,000
   Total stockholders' equity $16,029,000 $6,148,000
   Total liabilities and stockholders' equity $18,291,000 $8,795,000

Business Analysis Case 2   *Virginia Wholesale Company*

Comparative balance sheets and an income statement for Virginia Wholesale Company are presented here. Following these statements are a series of questions relating to the company's operating and financial activities.

Virginia Wholesale Company
Comparative Balance Sheets
December 31, 1994 and 1993
(in Thousands)

Assets	1994	1993
Cash	$ 4,940	$ 800
Marketable securities (note 1)		3,440
Accounts receivable (net) (note 2)	6,600	6,000
Merchandise inventory (note 3)	4,800	5,200
Building and equipment	16,660	15,000
Less accumulated depreciation	(8,600)	(7,800)
Land	4,500	2,760
Total assets	$28,900	$25,400

Liabilities and Stockholders' Equity		
Accounts payable—merchandise suppliers	$ 8,420	$ 8,040
Notes payable (short-term)	800	1,800
Dividends payable	500	450
Taxes payable	1,000	1,300
Bonds payable	3,900	1,800
Other long-term debt	280	280
Preferred stock, 6%, $100 par	300	300
Common stock, $5 par	1,360	1,160
Additional paid-in capital	1,520	1,320
Retained earnings	10,940	9,020
Treasury stock (15,000 shares of common in 1994 and 10,000 shares common in 1993)	(120)	(70)
Total liabilities and stockholders' equity	$28,900	$25,400

Virginia Wholesale Company
Income Statement
For the Year Ending December 31, 1994
(in thousands)

Revenues:		
Sales	$40,000	
Less bad debt expense	(300)	$39,700
Gain on sale of marketable securities		1,000
Other revenues and gains		1,300
		$42,000
Operating expenses:		
Cost of merchandise sold		$22,400
Depreciation expense		950
Salaries and wages		11,050
Interest		1,200
Loss on sale of equipment		100
		$35,700
Income before taxes		$ 6,300
Income taxes		2,520
Net income		$ 3,780

Footnotes—Virginia Wholesale Company
Note: All numbers in the footnotes are in thousands.

Note #1—Marketable Securities
All marketable security holdings of Virginia Wholesale Company are equity securities, which are carried at the lower of cost or market. At December 31, 1993, the equity securities had an aggregate cost of $3,800 and aggregate market of $3,440. On that date, unrealized gains on certain equity securities amounted to $152, whereas unrealized losses on other equity securities amounted to $512. In 1994, Virginia Wholesale sold its entire portfolio of marketable equity securities on the open market and transferred the proceeds to various bank accounts.

Note #2—Accounts Receivable
Virginia Wholesale Company reports accounts receivable on its balance sheet net of estimated uncollectible accounts and uses the percent of sales method in estimating uncollectibles. The balance in the Allowance for Bad Debts account was $400 on December 31, 1994 and $440 on December 31, 1993.

Note #3—Inventories
Substantially all inventories are valued at the lower of cost or market using the LIFO inventory method. The estimated current replacement cost of these inventories exceeds their LIFO basis by $920 at December 31, 1994 and by $1,980 at December 31, 1993. The LIFO method of inventory valuation is used to better match costs and revenues.

Required:
1. Answer the following questions related to the marketable securities of the Virginia Wholesale Company:
    (a) What does the phrase *lower of cost or market* mean as applied to marketable securities?
    (b) Determine or compute the following amounts:
        (1) The realized gain or loss for 1994 from the sale of the securities.
        (2) The cash received from the sale of securities in 1994.
        (3) The balance in the Allowance for Market Decline account on December 31, 1993.

(4) The effect on the income statement for 1994 of both holding and trading marketable securities.
(c) Given that one of the purposes of financial statement analysis is to assess management's performance and future cash flows, what is one weakness of the method used to value marketable securities?

2. Answer the following questions concerning the company's accounts receivable:
   (a) What dollar amount was expensed for bad debts in 1994?
   (b) What dollar amount of accounts receivable were written off as uncollectible in 1994?
   (c) How much cash was collected in 1994 due to credit sales? (Assume all sales are on credit.)
   (d) What dollar effect did the write-off of specific accounts receivable have in 1994 on (a) cash and (b) net income before tax? Give the amount and whether it is an increase or decrease.
   (e) What dollar effect did the expensing of bad debts have on (a) cash and (b) net income before tax in 1994? Give the amount and whether it is an increase or decrease.
   (f) Assume that Virginia Wholesale began selling its products in 1994 to customers in developing countries. Further assume that at the end of 1994, the company significantly underestimated its bad debt expense related to these foreign sales and that the understatement is material in amount. How would this understatement of bad debt expense affect the following ratios: (a) accounts receivable turnover, (b) return on assets, and (c) the debt to equity ratio? Be specific. If there is no effect, so indicate.

3. Answer the following questions concerning Virginia Wholesale's inventory:
   (a) What does it mean to value inventory at the lower of cost or market?
   (b) If inventory prices have been rising in the past few years and the company is using the LIFO inventory method, are the inventories likely to be valued at cost or at market in computing total assets?
   (c) If prices have been rising in recent years, how does the use of the LIFO inventory method affect the inventory turnover ratio as compared with the use of the FIFO method? Why?
   (d) Would the company's banker prefer that the company use the LIFO or the FIFO method of inventory valuation?

4. Answer the following questions relating to Virginia Wholesale's fixed assets:
   (a) During 1994, Virginia Wholesale sold equipment that originally had cost $310 and recorded a loss. The equipment was several years old and no other buildings or equipment were disposed of during 1994. How much was the loss on the sale of the equipment?
   (b) How much cash did Virginia Wholesale receive for the equipment that was sold?
   (c) The original cost of the production line machinery was $2,300. This asset had a 25-year life and as of December 31, 1993, there was accumulated depreciation of $828 using the straight-line method of depreciation. Assuming the salvage value is zero, how old is the machinery?
   (d) Assume that Virginia Wholesale uses the straight-line method of depreciation for financial statement purposes. If the company used an accelerated method instead (assume accumulated depreciation would be higher), how would use of the accelerated method affect the fixed asset turnover ratio?

Ethics Case *Ferramo Furniture Company*

Assume you are the accountant for Ferramo Furniture Company. The company has been in existence for twenty-five years and employs nearly 1,000 people, some of whom are your friends. For the first twenty years the company was quite successful. Five years ago, Ferramo decided to expand and built a new manufacturing facility. During the time since construction, the company has not done so well and has borrowed additional funds on several occasions. Presently, the company owes $15,000,000 on the building mortgage and $10,000,000 in other loans. When signing the loan agreement for $10,000,000, Ferramo agreed to maintain its working capital ratio at 2:1 and its operating performance ratio at 10 percent. Loan covenants dictate that should either ratio fall below these amounts, the full $10,000,000 loan is payable immediately.

You have just finished preparing the financial statements for 1994. You are pleased because the current ratio is exactly 2:1 and the operating performance ratio is 10.1 percent. However, you also have some other information that is troubling you. The annual physical inventory revealed that inventory recorded on the books at $150,000 consisted of outdated and obsolete styles. You feel that the inventory could probably be sold for $80,000. In addition, included in receivables is $50,000 from Timp Furniture Company. Timp has just notified you in writing that they cannot pay and will probably be declaring bankruptcy. Finally, there is a lawsuit against the company claiming $500,000 in damages for a patent infringement. Ferramo's legal counsel believes the company would probably lose the suit but can settle out of court for $250,000.

If you recognize the $70,000 decline in the value of the inventory, the $50,000 uncollectible receivable, and the $250,000 loss from the lawsuit, net income will be wiped out completely. The result will be an operating performance ratio that is negative and a current ratio that falls to .9 to 1. This would mean an immediate call for payment of the $10,000,000 in loans.

You are troubled because if the loan is called, it will mean certain bankruptcy for the company. You and your friends will be out of work and the furniture company, one of the city's main industries, will be closed down. You wonder if it would be possible to delay recognition of these losses until next year. By then, the recession will probably be ended, profits should be up, and maybe the company could absorb the losses.

Required: 1. Describe the ethical dilemma facing the company and the accountant.
2. What would you do in this case?

Chapter 17

The Impact of Income Taxes on Business Decisions

Learning Objectives

After studying this chapter, you should be able to:
1. Explain the general procedures for determining income tax liability and how these procedures are applied to individuals and corporations.
2. Understand the tax treatment of proprietorships and partnerships and how the treatment differs from corporations.
3. Explain basic tax-planning guidelines.
4. Identify the income tax considerations in accounting for inventories.
5. Identify the income tax considerations in acquiring, depreciating, and disposing of long-term operating assets.

SETTING THE STAGE

No significant personal or business financial decision should be made without considering the impact of federal, state, and even local taxes, primarily income taxes. The reasons for this are many. First, federal income taxes represent a major cash outflow: up to 39 percent of taxable income for corporations and 31 percent for individuals. When state and local taxes are added, the total tax rate can be several percentage points higher than the federal rate alone. Second, income taxes usually do not affect each course of action equally. Congress has written the tax code in a way that provides incentives (lower taxes) for certain activities. Individuals are allowed, for example, to deduct from their income the interest cost on borrowings to make certain investments and for home ownership but not the interest on other personal debts. In this way, borrowing for the purpose of investing in securities and owning a home is encouraged and other kinds of indebtedness are not. A Business Environment Essay later in the chapter will suggest ways of avoiding income taxes by making wise investment decisions. Likewise, businesses are encouraged to execute transactions in certain ways to reduce the tax consequences, such as trading assets rather than selling them and buying new ones.

The financial press, such as *The Wall Street Journal,* and the business journals, such as *Business Week, Forbes,* and *Fortune,* regularly report on problems faced by businesses and individual taxpayers because they did not consider, or were not aware of, the tax laws that affect some of their business and investment decisions. One example recently reported was the fact that over one million American families fail to report payroll taxes for payments for maid service, yet are subject to severe penalties if discovered by the IRS. Another example is that pension plan deductions for the self-employed are becoming more complex than many self-employed taxpayers realize due to the differing wage bases that must be considered because of Social Security and Medicare taxes. These wage base changes affect the maximum deductible contribution by self-employed taxpayers to pension plans.

The solution to dealing with complicated tax problems is to either know the law yourself or obtain help from knowledgeable professional tax advisers. Some tax problems can be overcome by using the IRS electronic filing system or by using a dependable computer program to prepare your tax return. These programs provide added comfort that you have taken into consideration all the tax laws that affect your tax situation.

In this chapter, we examine some of the major provisions of the federal income tax law and the related tax-planning opportunities to minimize a company's tax liability. In fact, managers are expected to use whatever legitimate means are available to avoid, reduce, or postpone taxes. Although many of the tax-planning opportunities presented here are applicable to all types of businesses, we focus primarily on those most appropriate for corporations. We also restrict the discussion to federal income taxes.

As you read this chapter, bear in mind that this introduction to income taxes is limited by three factors. First, although the basic principles should have relevance for years to come, tax laws change frequently and sometimes dramatically, as they did in 1981, 1986, and are expected to do in 1993. Tax law changes may have an important effect on an individual's or a company's strategies for limiting taxes. Second, the basic principles are generalizations and may not apply equally to all situations. Third, the illustrations presented here are far from exhaustive; they provide only a sampling of the possible tax situations.

THE FEDERAL INCOME TAX LIABILITY

Objective 1

Explain the general procedures for determining income tax liability and how these procedures are applied to individuals and corporations.

The first federal income tax on individuals in the United States was levied in 1861 to raise funds to fight the Civil War. The Civil War ended in 1865, but the income tax continued until 1872. Another attempt was made to levy a personal income tax in 1895, but the law was declared unconstitutional because the tax levied on the income from real property was considered a "direct" tax, which had to be levied on the states in proportion to population. Therefore, a tax on personal income could not be levied directly on individual taxpayers until the U.S. Constitution was amended. The 16th Amendment to the Constitution was ratified in 1913 and stated that "The Congress shall have the power to lay and collect taxes on incomes, from whatever source derived, without apportionment among the several states, and without regard to any census or enumeration."

As soon as the 16th Amendment was ratified, Congress passed an income tax law effective March 1, 1913. The United States has levied an annual income tax on individuals' incomes on a continuous basis since the 1913 law was enacted.

The first federal income tax on corporate profits in the United States was levied by Congress in 1909 although similar taxes had been established by individual states during the previous century, and before that by the colonies. Then, as now, basing income taxes on income seemed to be one of the fairest ways to tap an individual's or a company's ability to provide financial support for governmental functions.

The subject of income taxes brings with it a whole new vocabulary. This section will serve as a brief introduction to individual and corporate income taxes, beginning with an overview of the general process for computing a tax liability and concluding with a discussion of key concepts.

The income tax law outlines the following general procedures for calculating a tax liability for individuals and corporations:

gross income *the taxable portion of a taxpayer's gross receipts*

1. Determine **gross income,** which includes all taxable receipts, such as salaries, interest, dividends, rents, gains on sales of assets, and gross margin from a business (service revenues and/or sales less cost of goods sold). An

Chapter 17 The Impact of Income Taxes on Business Decisions

exclusions *gross receipts that are not subject to tax and are not included in gross income, such as interest on state and local government bonds*

deductions *expenses or losses that are subtracted from gross income in computing taxable income*

taxable income *the income remaining after all deductions have been subtracted from gross income*

gross tax liability *the amount of tax computed by multiplying the tax base (taxable income) by the appropriate tax rates*

tax credit *a direct reduction in the tax liability, usually granted to encourage certain classes of taxpayers to take a particular action*

net tax liability *the amount of tax computed by subtracting tax credits from the gross tax liability*

adjusted gross income *an individual taxpayer's total income minus deductions (adjustments) for individual retirement plan contributions, alimony paid, and other specified items*

adjustments to gross income *amounts deducted from the gross income of an individual taxpayer in arriving at adjusted gross income; includes contributions to individual retirement plans and alimony paid*

itemized deductions *amounts paid by an individual taxpayer for personal expenses that can be deducted in computing taxable income, such as medical expenses, property and income taxes, mortgage and investment interest, charitable contributions, moving expenses, casualty and theft losses, and certain miscellaneous expenses*

example of a nontaxable receipt, or **exclusion,** is interest income from state and local government bonds.

2. Determine the allowable deductions from gross income. These **deductions** include expenses of a business that are ordinary and necessary and designated types of personal expenses and exemptions for individuals.
3. Subtract the allowable deductions from gross income to arrive at the tax base, or **taxable income.**
4. Multiply the increments of taxable income by the appropriate tax rates to arrive at the **gross tax liability.** The tax rates for both individuals and corporations are percentages that increase with the level of taxable income. These increasing percentage rates for higher levels of income result in what is referred to as progressive taxation. The philosophy of a progressive tax system is that individuals and businesses with higher incomes have a greater ability to support the functions of government.
5. When applicable, the gross tax liability is reduced by subtracting **tax credits** to arrive at the **net tax liability.** A tax credit is a benefit granted to taxpayers that directly reduces the gross tax liability.

This sequence of procedures for determining a tax liability applies somewhat differently to individuals than to corporations. The following section of this chapter will describe briefly the procedures for calculating the tax liability of individuals first and then corporations.

Calculating the Tax Liability for an Individual Taxpayer

Exhibit 17-1 summarizes the steps for calculating the federal income tax liability for an individual taxpayer. The first step is the determination of gross income. For individuals, gross income includes wages and salaries, interest and dividend income, alimony received, gains and losses on the sale of assets (such as investments in stocks and bonds), business income or loss from a sole proprietorship, share of income or loss from a partnership or S corporation, rent and royalty income, farm income or loss, and any other income that is subject to tax.

The next step is determining the allowable deductions from gross income to compute **adjusted gross income.** As you can see from Exhibit 17-1, several specific deductions, called **adjustments to gross income,** are allowed in computing adjusted gross income. These adjustments (subtractions) include amounts contributed to Individual Retirement Accounts (IRAs) and other qualified retirement plans, one-half of self-employment tax, penalties for early withdrawals of savings, and amounts paid for alimony. The total of these adjustments, if any, is subtracted from gross income to determine adjusted gross income. The adjusted gross income figure is important because it is used to determine limitations on certain types of deductions.

After adjusted gross income has been calculated, the next category of deductions for an individual taxpayer is for specific types of personal expenses. A taxpayer can itemize (list) the allowable expenses actually paid and deduct the total of those expenses from adjusted gross income. Generally, **itemized deductions** include medical and dental expenses; taxes paid during the year, including state and local income taxes and real and personal property taxes; interest paid on a home mortgage and interest related to investment property; charitable contributions; casualty and theft losses; qualified moving expenses

Exhibit 17-1 *Steps for Calculating the Federal Tax Liability for Individuals*

Gross income. Salaries and wages, dividend income, alimony received, business income, capital gains, pension and annuity income, rents and royalties, farm income, social security benefits, and other income.

Gross income
−

Adjustments to income. Subtractions from gross income to determine adjusted gross income; adjustments include contributions to individual retirement plans, one-half of self-employment tax, penalties on early withdrawal of savings, and alimony paid.

Adjustments to gross income
=

Adjusted gross income. An amount used to determine limitations on certain itemized deductions, such as medical expenses and charitable contributions.

Adjusted gross income
−

Itemized deductions or standard deduction. Itemized deductions are amounts actually paid during the year for certain types of personal expenses. Taxpayers itemize their deductions if the total is greater than the allowable standard deduction, a specified amount that varies with the taxpayer's filing status.

Itemized deductions or standard deduction
−

Personal exemptions. An exemption is a specified amount ($2,150 in 1991) allowed for the taxpayer, the taxpayer's spouse, and each dependent.

Personal exemptions
=

Taxable income. The amount to which tax rates are applied to arrive at the gross tax liability.

Taxable income
×

Tax rates. Percentages applied to taxable income to determine the gross tax liability; the rates are progressive and apply to income levels (brackets) that vary with filing status.

Tax rates
=

Gross tax liability. This is the amount due before deducting tax credits.

Gross tax liability
−

Tax credits and payments. Subtractions from the gross tax liability to determine the balance of taxes owed or the overpayment; includes taxes withheld, estimated taxes paid during the year, and specialized credits.

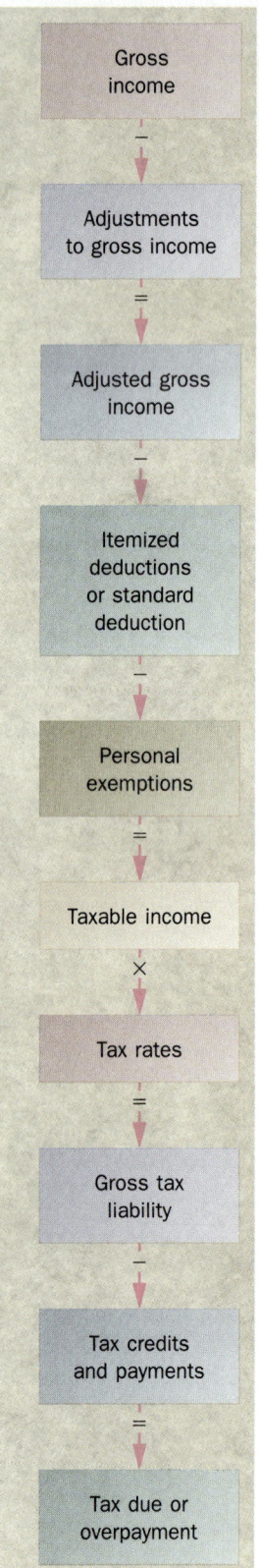

Tax credits and payments
=

Tax due or overpayment

incurred in connection with new employment; and certain miscellaneous expenses related to employment, investment activities, and education. Limitations, based on the taxpayer's adjusted gross income, are imposed on the amounts that can be deducted for some types of expenses. For example, the amount of medical expenses that can be included in itemized deductions is limited to the total medical expenses paid less 7½ percent of adjusted gross income. In addition, certain miscellaneous expenses are deductible only to the extent that they exceed 2 percent of adjusted gross income.

As an alternative to itemizing deductions, a taxpayer can use the **standard deduction,** an amount specified by the tax law. This amount varies according to the individual's filing status, that is, whether the taxpayer is single, married and filing a joint return, married and filing a separate return, or qualifies as head of household (an unmarried or legally separated taxpayer that maintains a household for a child or for another relative that qualifies as the taxpayer's dependent). For 1991, the standard deduction allowed for each filing status was as follows: single, $3,400; married filing jointly, $5,700; married filing separately, $2,850; and head of household, $5,000. An additional standard deduction is allowed if a taxpayer or spouse is age 65 or over or blind. A taxpayer should use the standard deduction if it is greater than the itemized deductions.

standard deduction *an amount that can be deducted on an individual's tax return in lieu of listing (itemizing) amounts actually paid for qualifying personal expenses; the amount varies with filing status*

The third category of deductions for an individual is called **personal exemptions.** An exemption is a specified amount allowed for the taxpayer, the taxpayer's spouse, and each person that qualifies as a dependent. For 1991, the amount of each exemption was $2,150. The amount of the exemption is adjusted each year for inflation. For 1991 and later years, the amount of the allowed exemption is reduced for taxpayers with high adjusted gross incomes.[1]

personal exemption *a deduction allowed to individual taxpayers for each qualifying person, including the taxpayer, taxpayer's spouse, and dependents*

As shown in Exhibit 17-1, the standard or itemized deductions and personal exemptions are subtracted from adjusted gross income to arrive at taxable income. This is the amount to which tax rates are applied to compute the gross tax liability. For 1991, the individual tax rates were 15%, 28%, and 31%. The income levels or "brackets" that are subject to each of the tax rates vary according to filing status. For example, the following rates are applied to the incomes of single taxpayers and married taxpayers filing joint returns:

Tax Rate	Single Taxpayer	Married, Filing Joint Return
15%	$0–$20,350	$0–$34,000
28%	$20,351–$49,300	$34,001–$82,150
31%	$49,301 and higher	$82,151 and higher

After the gross tax liability is computed, any applicable tax credits and payments are deducted to determine the balance of tax due or the overpayment of tax. Amounts withheld by employers for income taxes and any estimated tax payments made during the year are deducted, as well as any special credits that apply to the taxpayer. For example, special credits are allowed for elderly, disabled, and low-income taxpayers and for certain types of expenditures such as child care expenses and foreign taxes paid. If there is an overpayment after deducting the tax credits and payments, the taxpayer can either request a refund or apply the overpayment to next year's income tax liability.

---

[1] The details of calculating the reduction in the exemption when adjusted gross income is above specified amounts are explained in the instructions that accompany individual federal income tax forms and in textbooks on federal income taxation.

The following example is provided to help clarify how individuals compute their tax liabilities. We assume that the taxpayers are married, file a joint return, and have two children that qualify as dependents. We also assume that the taxpayers use the standard deduction instead of itemizing deductions. If their itemized deductions were greater than the allowed standard deduction, they would elect to itemize. The standard deduction and personal exemptions are based on amounts for 1991.

Gross income:		
Salaries: husband, $24,000; wife, $23,000		$47,000
Interest income (joint savings account)		800
Dividend income (jointly owned stock)		450
Capital gains (long-term) from sale of stock		865
Gross income		$49,115
Less deductions from gross income:		
IRA contribution by wife		600
Adjusted gross income		$48,515
Less: Standard deduction	$5,700	
Personal exemptions (4 × $2,150)	8,600	14,300
Taxable income		$34,215
Tax rate [(15% × $34,000) + (28% × $215)]		
Tax liability		$ 5,160
Less: Taxes withheld from salaries (husband,		
$2,650; wife, $2,265)		4,915
Tax due		$ 245

The preceding example shows that the first $34,000 of taxable income is taxed at the 15% rate, and the amount in excess of $34,000 ($215) is taxed at 28%. The taxpayers in this example had a gain from the sale of stock. This gain is distinguished from the other income and is called a **capital gain.** Capital gains are distinguished from ordinary income because such gains historically have been taxed at lower rates than other types of income, referred to as *ordinary income.* For the tax year 1991, long-term capital gains (gains on assets held more than one year) were taxable at a maximum rate of 28%. Thus, if the taxpayer in the example had been in the 31% tax bracket, the 31% would have applied only to ordinary income and short-term capital gains, whereas the long-term capital gain would have been taxed at not more than 28%. In the example, no distinction between ordinary income and capital gains was necessary because the maximum rate applicable to all the taxable income was 28%.

In the preceding discussion and illustration of individual income taxes, we have introduced only the basic rules and procedures applicable in determining the tax liability. There are many other aspects of individual taxation that are beyond the scope of this text. To accurately determine their tax liability, taxpayers need to know the law and keep good records. It is also important for taxpayers to understand the tax effects of transactions before the transactions are executed in order to minimize their tax liability or postpone the payment of taxes. The Business Environment Essay on the next page illustrates some of the considerations an investor must keep in mind in making wise investments and at the same time minimizing the tax impact of income from those investments.

capital gain *the excess of the selling price over the cost basis when assets, such as securities and other personal and investment assets, are sold*

BUSINESS ENVIRONMENT ESSAY
Smart Investing Is Tax-Wise Too

Taxpayers often do not pay a lot of attention to their income tax obligations until they prepare and file their tax returns. Furthermore, they read with only casual interest what Congress is discussing regarding changes in the tax law. Yet, investment adviser Terence Pare of *Fortune* magazine says that many taxpayers cannot afford *not* to think about taxes. According to a Federal Reserve survey of family finances, savings and investments make up about 28% of the average family's total assets, a close second to the 32% represented by the family residence. Earnings on savings and investments amount to about 10% of taxpayers' adjusted gross income. When federal, state, and local taxes can take away up to 40% of taxable income, failure to make an investment portfolio tax-effective is as sensible as failing to insulate your house!

How can a taxpayer keep more of his or her savings and investment earnings? The answer is to apply sound investment strategies that are also tax efficient. For example, buying and holding growth stocks enables a taxpayer to defer taxes. If capital gains rates are cut before the gains from the growth stocks are realized, the tax benefit is even greater. Keeping a portion of savings in municipal bonds permits the earning of tax-free interest and at the same time helps achieve a diversified portfolio. Yet only 14% of taxpayers with adjusted gross income between $75,000 and $100,000 reported earnings from tax-exempt interest. Yet this same group of taxpayers paid a significant amount of taxes on dividends and interest income.

You can also protect your liquid cash reserves from the tax bite by investing in a tax-exempt money market fund that buys short-term municipal securities. There are also many single state tax-free money market funds designed to avoid both federal and state income taxes.

Tax-savvy fund investing starts with defining investment goals and matching these goals with the right kind of fund. Look for those funds with the lowest rate of expenses in relation to invested assets. You cannot always avoid realizing capital gains when the fund manager decides to sell a security that has appreciated significantly and credits the investor for a share of the proceeds. Yet, you can try to avoid funds that reflect high turnover rates and concentrate on funds with low turnover rates and with consistency in the rate of earnings over time.

The bottom line is that smart investing in growth stocks and tax-exempt funds and staying away from stocks with high cash dividends is not only a good investment policy but is being tax-wise as well.

Source: Adapted from Terence Pare, "Smart Investing Is Tax-Wise Too," *Fortune*, March 9, 1992, pp. 127–136.

To Summarize *The income tax liability for individual taxpayers is determined as follows: (1) compute gross income, (2) subtract allowable adjustments to arrive at adjusted gross income, (3) subtract the higher of itemized deductions or the standard deduction and personal exemptions to arrive at taxable income, (4) multiply increments of taxable income by the appropriate tax rates to compute the gross tax liability, keeping in mind the maximum tax rate limit on long-term capital gains, and (5) subtract tax credits and payments to determine the net tax due or the amount of* *overpayment. Gross income includes salaries and wages, interest, dividends, business income (or loss), rents and royalties, and all other income subject to tax. Adjustments to gross income include deductions for retirement plan contributions, early withdrawal penalties on savings, a portion of the self-employment tax paid by proprietors, and alimony paid. The expenses allowed in computing itemized deductions include medical expenses, property taxes and state and local income taxes, mortgage and investment interest expense, charitable contributions, casualty and theft losses, moving expenses, and certain miscellaneous expenses. The standard deduction is an amount specified by law that varies with filing status, including single, married filing jointly, married filing separately, or head of the household. The deduction for personal exemptions is a specified amount allowed for the taxpayer, spouse, and each dependent. The tax rates are progressive and apply to different levels or brackets of taxable income depending on filing status. For the year 1991, income was taxed at 15%, 28%, and 31%, with a maximum rate of 28% on long-term capital gains.*

Calculating the Tax Liability for a Corporation

Exhibit 17-2 describes the steps for calculating a corporation's federal income tax liability. The steps are similar to those for calculating the tax liability for an individual taxpayer except that deductions for corporations are classified as ordinary and special deductions.

The first step is to compute the corporation's gross income, which includes gross profit (service revenue or net sales minus cost of goods sold), total dividends received, interest income (excluding any nontaxable interest), gross receipts from rents and royalties, gain or loss on the sale of assets, and any other income subject to tax. The next step is to determine the ordinary deductions. These are the operating expenses of the business and typically include salaries and wages, repairs and maintenance, bad debts, rent expense, taxes (other than federal income taxes), interest expense, depreciation, amortization, depletion, advertising, contributions to employee benefit plans, and any other ordinary and necessary expenses.

The third step is to compute the special deductions, if any, that are allowed to the corporation. Special deductions apply to certain types of dividends received by the taxpayer corporation and included in gross income. Generally, dividends received from another U.S. corporation qualify for the special deduction. The amount of the deduction is a percentage of the total dividends received and varies according to the percentage of stock owned. If the taxpayer corporation owns less than 20% of the investee's stock, the special deduction would be 70% of the dividends received; for ownership of at least 20%, but less than 80%, the special deduction is 80% of dividends received; with ownership of 80% or more, the special deduction is 100% of dividends received.

Ordinary and special deductions are subtracted from gross income to determine the corporation's taxable income, which is multiplied by the appropriate tax rate or rates to compute the gross income tax liability. Like individual tax rates, corporate income tax rates are progressive. The current tax rates for corporations start at 15% of the first $50,000 of taxable income and progress up to 39% of taxable income over $100,000 but revert to 34% of all taxable income when taxable income exceeds $335,000. Applying a 39% rate to all

Exhibit 17-2 — Steps for Calculating the Federal Income Tax Liability of a Corporation

Net receipts from services or sales less cost of sales; total dividends received, including nontaxable portion; interest income on U.S. obligations (including government bonds); other interest income, excluding nontaxable interest; gross rents and royalties; other income.

→ **Gross income**

Less

Salaries and wages, repairs, bad debts, rent, taxes (other than federal income tax), interest expense, contributions (limited), amortization, depreciation, depletion, advertising, contributions to employee pension and profit-sharing plans (limited), and other "ordinary" expenses.

→ **Ordinary deductions**

Less

Special deductions. A percentage (70%, 80%, or 100%) of dividends from investment in stock of other U.S. corporations subject to federal income tax.

→ **Special deductions**

Equals

Remember that taxable income is generally not the same as net income for financial reporting purposes because many income tax regulations are different from generally accepted accounting principles.

→ **Taxable income**

Times

The present corporation income tax rate on ordinary taxable income is 15% on the first $50,000 of taxable income, 25% on the next $25,000 of taxable income, 34% on taxable income of $75,000–$100,000, 39% on taxable income of $100,001–$335,000, and 34% on all taxable income when taxable income exceeds $335,000.

→ **Tax rates**

Equals

This is the amount a corporation would pay if there were no special tax credits.

→ **Gross tax liability**

Less

Special tax credits include the foreign tax credit and the targeted jobs credit.

→ **Tax credits**

Equals

All corporations must make installment payments of their estimated net tax liability for the coming year if the amount is expected to be $500 or more. The date the corporation can reasonably expect its tax to be $500 determines the number of installments, due dates, and amounts.

→ **Net tax liability**

taxable income between $100,000 and $335,000 is a procedure for phasing out the 15% and 25% rates so that all income is taxed at 34% when it exceeds $335,000.

Special tax credits available to corporations are deducted from gross tax liability to arrive at the net tax liability. Examples include credits for income taxes paid to foreign governments and a general business credit, which is the total of various types of individual credits. Generally, corporations are required to make quarterly payments of taxes during the year if the estimated net tax liability for the year is expected to be $500 or more. The total estimated tax payments are subtracted from the actual net tax liability for the year to determine the balance of tax owed or the overpayment. Like individual taxpayers, corporations can request a refund or apply an overpayment to the subsequent year's tax liability.

The following example illustrates the procedures for calculating the tax liability for a corporation. Assume the corporation reports the following income, before income taxes, on its income statement for the year ending December 31, 1994:

Net sales	$340,000	
Cost of goods sold	162,000	
Gross margin		$178,000
Dividend revenue		10,000*
Interest revenue		16,000**
Total revenues		$204,000
Less total operating expenses		100,000
Income before income taxes		$104,000

* Dividends were received from investments in the stock of several U.S. corporations; all the investments represent ownership of less than 20%.
** Interest revenue includes $12,000 of tax-free interest from local government bonds.

Using this information and assuming the corporation is entitled to a $1,650 general business credit, the corporation's 1994 federal income tax liability would be computed as follows:

Total revenues	$204,000
Less exclusion, nontaxable interest	(12,000)
Gross income	$192,000
Less ordinary deductions:	
Operating expenses	(100,000)
Less special deduction for dividends received ($10,000 × 70%)	(7,000)
Taxable income	$ 85,000
Tax calculations with assumed tax rates:	
15% × $50,000 = $7,500	
25% × $25,000 = 6,250	
34% × $10,000 = 3,400	
Gross tax liability	$ 17,150
Less tax credits:	
General business credit	(1,650)
Net tax liability	$ 15,500

Chapter 17 The Impact of Income Taxes on Business Decisions

It is important to note that taxable income often differs from pretax financial income reported in the income statement. In the example, taxable income was only $85,000, compared with pretax income on the income statement of $104,000. The difference is caused by the exclusion from gross income of $12,000 of tax-exempt interest and the special deduction of $7,000 for dividends received. Further, the gross tax liability was reduced by tax credits of $1,650 to determine the net tax liability of $15,500. Although the corporation's taxable income was taxed at assumed rates of 15%, 25%, and 34%, the effective tax rate is only 14.9%, computed as follows:

$$\frac{\text{Net tax liability}}{\text{Financial (book) income before taxes}} = \frac{\$15,500}{\$104,000} = 14.9\%$$

effective tax rate *a tax rate that reflects the percentage of the actual tax liability to the accounting income generated by the company, that is, net tax liability ÷ financial (book) income before taxes*

The **effective tax rate** is the actual tax liability as a percentage of the financial income reported by the company. The effective tax rate, as well as other income tax information, must be disclosed by corporations in the notes to their financial statements.

Some Considerations in Calculating Taxable Income

The first two steps in computing a tax liability are to determine gross income and deductible expenses. Because gross income for income tax purposes may not be the same as total revenues for accounting purposes and not all accounting expenses are deductible for income tax purposes (or some may be deductible in another period), these steps require calculations different from those used to prepare financial statements. The following considerations are involved.

THE REALIZATION PRINCIPLE. Gross income includes all taxable receipts. (Exclusions are nontaxable receipts.) However, amounts received are not considered gross income until they are realized. Realization, you will recall, means that a transaction has taken place in which assets have been given up in exchange for the cash or other assets received. Realization may also occur when an exchange of property is determined to be a taxable transaction. For example, if an operating asset (land, building, or equipment) is exchanged for inventory, the fair market value of the operating asset would be realized.

CASH-BASIS VERSUS ACCRUAL-BASIS ACCOUNTING. The calculation of gross income also depends on the accounting system used—cash or accrual. On a cash basis, gross income is the amount received; on an accrual basis, it is the amount earned regardless of when it is received. Note that "receipt of cash" is defined in a specific way for income tax purposes. That is, the tax law employs the **constructive receipt rule**, which states that cash is considered to have been received when a taxpayer can exercise control over it, whether or not the cash has actually been received. For example, interest deposited by a bank in a cash-basis taxpayer's saving account before year-end is considered to be gross income in the year of deposit, even if the taxpayer does not withdraw it until the next year.

constructive receipt rule *cash is considered to have been received when a taxpayer can exercise control over it, whether or not the cash has actually been received*

The timing of a business expense as a deduction follows the same pattern. With a cash-basis system, an expense is recognized and deducted when it is paid. On an accrual basis, an expense is recognized when it is incurred, which can be before or after the period in which it is paid. In an accrual-based system, for example, employees' wages are expenses in the period they are earned regardless of when they are paid. Likewise, an insurance premium paid in advance is an expense over the duration of the periods in which the policy provides protection.

Historically, the government allowed companies to use either cash- or accrual-basis accounting, except in cases where inventories are a significant factor in the measurement of income. Then, accrual-basis accounting had to be used for purchases and sales. Under the Tax Reform Act of 1986, many more companies have been required to use the accrual method.

The reasons for requiring accrual-basis accounting when significant inventories exist are probably apparent to you. Suppose, for example, that Ernie's Machine Company is in its first year of operation. During the year, management pays cash for 100 widgets at $10 each. By the end of the first year, Ernie's has sold 90 widgets and has 10 in inventory. On a cash basis, the company would show revenues for the 90 widgets sold and expenses for the 100 widgets purchased; income therefore would be understated by $100 (10 widgets × $10), which is significant in this case. The ending inventory of 10 units would have a zero cost. Since it is misleading to match expenses for 100 widgets with revenues for 90 widgets, Ernie's should use accrual-basis accounting, which matches expenses for 90 widgets with revenues for 90 widgets. This matching more appropriately measures income for the period and automatically provides for an ending inventory of 10 units at $10 each. In this example, accrual-basis accounting is appropriate for financial reporting purposes, as well as being required for income tax purposes.

DEDUCTIONS FOR EXPENSES AND LOSSES. As we have indicated, not all expenses are deductible for corporate federal income tax purposes. In general, expenses that are directly related to the operations of a company are deductible from gross income if they are ordinary and necessary, reasonable in amount, and paid or incurred. There are exceptions, however. For example, only a portion of the expense of business meals and entertainment for business purposes is deductible.

Some types of losses, such as the sale or exchange of operating assets at a loss, bad-debt losses, and casualty losses, are deductible expenses. But as we shall see later, there are restrictions on the deductibility of certain losses, such as those derived from the sale of capital assets.

To Summarize *A corporation's gross income is its taxable receipts (exclusions are nontaxable receipts) less the cost of sales. Business deductions and any special deductions are subtracted from gross income to arrive at taxable income. Currently, the tax rate increases with the level of taxable income to $335,000 and then reverts to 34% for all income as a device to phase out the lower tax rates of 15% and 25%. The increments of taxable income multiplied by the appropriate tax rates give the gross tax liability. The timing of the recognition of gross income and expenses depends on whether* *cash-* or *accrual-basis accounting is used. Only specified types of companies can choose either method, and the accrual basis is required for purchases and sales when inventories are a significant factor in computing income.*

HOW EACH FORM OF BUSINESS IS TAXED

Objective 2

Understand the tax treatment of proprietorships and partnerships and how the treatment differs from corporations.

As we explained in Chapters 13 and 14, the three basic types of business organizations—proprietorships, partnerships, and corporations—are treated differently from a tax point of view. In fact, the income tax consequences to the company and its owners are usually a key consideration in selecting which type of organization a new business is to be. Of course, other factors, such as the desire for limited liability and the ability to raise capital, are essential considerations as well.

How Proprietorships Are Taxed

conduit principle *the idea that all income earned by an entity must be passed through to the owners and reported on their individual tax returns; applicable to proprietorships, partnerships, and S corporations*

Because a proprietorship is not considered a legal entity separate from its owner, it is taxed under the **conduit principle.** This means that all income earned by the proprietorship is reported on the owner's personal income tax return. The owner lists the revenues and expenses of the business on Schedule C of his or her personal tax return. The income reported on this schedule is added to any other income the proprietor may have received from outside the company, both of which are taxed as personal income. The Schedule C income is taxed whether or not any of the income was withdrawn from the business for personal use. Since the owner of the proprietorship is not considered an employee of the business, his or her salary cannot be deducted as an expense on Schedule C.

Keogh plan *a pension plan for a self-employed individual taxpayer who has earned income; the annual contribution is limited to 20% of earned income, but it is not to exceed $30,000*

Besides having to report all business income as personal income, owners of proprietorships are considered to be self-employed and so cannot take advantage of tax-free fringe benefits such as group life insurance, medical expense reimbursement, certain death benefits to surviving relatives, and stock option plans—all of which can be made available to employees of corporations. However, a self-employed proprietor has the opportunity to create a pension plan, either in the form of a **Keogh Plan** or a simplified employer pension plan. These plans provide for self-employed individuals to contribute varying amounts (with designated limits) to a retirement plan and to deduct the amount contributed from their gross income. Readers are referred to income tax publications for the details of these types of pension plans.

The primary advantage of a proprietorship is its ease of formation and the fact that its income is taxed only to the owner; the proprietorship is not taxed as a separate legal entity as well. This avoids the double taxation that occurs with regular corporations, when corporate income is taxed, and then that portion of it paid out in dividends is again taxed as income to the stockholders.

How Partnerships Are Taxed

Like a proprietorship, a partnership is taxed under the conduit principle. Each partner's personal tax return includes that person's share of partnership income.

Unlike a proprietorship, a partnership is required to file a separate annual tax return. However, since the partnership is not required to pay a tax on its income, this return is for information purposes only.

The partnership return includes a Schedule K, which shows the breakdown of income, expenses, and credits by type: ordinary income, capital gains and losses, dividends from domestic corporations, charitable contributions, tax credits, and tax-preference income. These items are divided among the partners and are reported on a Schedule K-1 for each partner. Individuals then report the items in appropriate categories on their personal tax returns. The entire partnership income is taxed to the partners regardless of whether it remains in the business or is distributed to the partners. Like a proprietorship, the primary advantages of a partnership are the ease of formation and the avoidance of double taxation.

How Corporations Are Taxed

The tax law recognizes three types of corporations: regular corporations, S corporations, and tax-exempt corporations.

REGULAR CORPORATIONS. A regular corporation is a legal entity separate from its owners and, as such, is required to file its own tax return and pay its own taxes. Because dividend payments to stockholders are not allowable deductions for federal income tax purposes, corporate taxes are calculated on income before dividend distributions. As a result, earnings are taxed at the corporate level, and distributed earnings (dividends) are taxable income to stockholders. In other words, dividends are taxed twice, first as corporate income and again as dividend income to the stockholder.

This double taxation of a portion of earnings is a characteristic of the corporate form of business that makes it less attractive than proprietorships or partnerships. However, corporations also provide important tax advantages. For example, owner-managers are considered to be employees, so their salaries are deductions from the corporation's gross income. In addition, owner-managers may receive tax-free fringe benefits that are not available to proprietors and partners, such as life insurance, medical insurance, and pension and profit-sharing benefits. In general, the key advantages of the corporate form of organization are the tax advantages of fringe benefits and such nontax benefits as limited liability, ease of raising capital, and ease of ownership transfer.

S CORPORATIONS. An *S corporation* is a regular corporation in all respects, except for its special tax status. Most of the income of an S corporation is not taxed to the corporation but passes through to the individual stockholders in a manner similar to the conduit principle applied to proprietorships and partnerships. All income and deductions passed through to the stockholders are allocated on the basis of the number of shares owned, prorated on a daily basis of ownership. Thus, the owners of an S corporation have the advantage of limited liability while avoiding the problem of double taxation. If the owners are also employees, they receive many of the tax-free fringe benefits mentioned earlier for employees of regular corporations.

S corporation a domestic corporation that is recognized as a regular corporation under state law but is granted a special status for federal income tax purposes

Only certain companies qualify as S corporations. Some of the governing rules are[2]:

1. The corporation must elect to be taxed as an S corporation.
2. It must be a domestic corporation.
3. It can have only one class of stock outstanding.
4. It cannot have more than 35 stockholders. Note that this could involve as many as 70 individuals since spouses are considered to be one stockholder without regard to the manner in which the stock is held.
5. All stockholders must be U.S. citizens or resident aliens.
6. The company's income from investments (dividends, interest, rents, and so on) cannot exceed 25% of gross receipts in any one year.
7. All new stockholders are considered to have consented to the election to be an S corporation if they do not formally refuse within 60 days after the stock is acquired.
8. S corporation status is automatically terminated if any event occurs that would have prevented the corporation from qualifying in the first place—for instance, if a thirty-sixth stockholder (other than a stockholder's spouse) is added.
9. The corporation's status may be voluntarily revoked by election by stockholders owning more than 50 percent of the shares.

Regular corporate income and special items of income and deductions are passed through the S corporation to the stockholders to be reported on their individual tax returns. Dividends from unaffiliated domestic corporations, net long-term capital gains, charitable contributions (which have a deduction limitation), and tax credits, are examples of such special items that must be reported by stockholders, in addition to income from the same items that the individuals may have generated on their own behalf. The stockholders must report their appropriate share of each of these S corporation items regardless of whether the corporation makes a distribution to the stockholders in the form of a dividend. Dividends paid by the S corporation are generally not taxable to each stockholder up to the amount of the stockholder's share of the corporation's taxable income.

One of the most important benefits of the S corporation is that operating losses are passed through to the stockholders, thus offsetting other types of personal income and reducing the stockholders' tax liability. Often, when a company is established, it elects to be taxed as an S corporation in its formative years, when losses are likely. This reduces the financial burden on those who have invested in the new venture because their personal taxes due to income from other sources will be reduced by their share of the fledgling corporation's losses. In later years as profits are realized, the company may decide to terminate its S corporation status and become a regular corporation.

TAX-EXEMPT CORPORATIONS. Corporations that are formed for scientific, religious, educational, charitable, or other socially beneficial purposes are eligible for tax-exempt status if they meet certain conditions. In general, a **tax-exempt corporation** must be operated for the benefit of society, and no part of the corporation's net income may accrue to the benefit of an individual.

tax-exempt corporation a legal entity chartered by a state for scientific, religious, educational, charitable, or other purposes deemed beneficial to society

[2] *Internal Revenue Code,* Section 1361(b).

Choosing the Form of Organization

A number of factors must be considered when individuals are choosing the form of organization that will minimize the business entity's income taxes and best meet its objectives. Some of these factors are:

Nontax Factors:
1. Ease of raising new capital.
2. Extent of owners' liability.
3. Transferability of ownership.

Tax Factors:
1. Availability of tax-free fringe benefits.
2. Ease of disposing of the business. The tax effect of selling shares of corporate stock is different from that of selling an interest in a proprietorship or a partnership.
3. Disposition of net operating losses. Net operating losses pass through to the owners of proprietorships, partnerships, and S corporations. They do not pass through in regular corporations.

> **To Summarize** *The IRS recognizes three forms of business organizations: proprietorships, partnerships, and corporations (regular, S, and tax-exempt). Tax planning attempts to minimize taxes for the company, the owners, and the employees (including owner-employees). Several tax factors, such as the availability of tax-free fringe benefits, and nontax factors, such as the extent of the owner's liability, should be considered in determining which form of organization to select.*

TAX-PLANNING GUIDELINES

Objective 3
Explain basic tax-planning guidelines.

Tax consequences continue to be an important consideration after a business has been established. To the extent that management has some control over the timing of a tax liability, its objective is to pay the least amount of tax at the latest possible time. In essence, management should take advantage of all legal approaches to avoiding a tax, and if the tax cannot be avoided, all legal means should be used to postpone its payment as long as possible. Judge Learned Hand expressed it well: "Nobody owes any duty to pay more than the law demands."

To accomplish the "least and latest" objective, individual taxpayers and the management of businesses should follow a number of tax-planning guidelines in executing transactions that may have tax consequences:

1. *Know the tax law.* Only through knowledge of the law can taxpayers take advantage of its favorable provisions. If an individual or company cannot afford a full-time tax advisor, the individual or company management should ask a CPA or a tax lawyer for advice on special transactions and for help in preparing the tax returns.
2. *Plan transactions to minimize the tax effect.* The tax impact of a transaction is often determined by how it is executed because the method chosen may dictate when and how the transaction will be reported. For example, if a

used operating asset is *sold* and a new, similar operating asset is purchased, the gain or loss is included in income in the year of sale. However, if the old asset is *traded* for a similar asset, some or all of the gain or loss may be postponed to future years. Whether a gain or a loss should be reported in the current year or in future years will depend on the taxpayer's circumstances.

3. *Keep adequate records.* Adequate records are necessary to justify the deduction of legitimate expenses and the exclusion of receipts that are not taxable. Records not only provide proof that the expense was incurred, but they also ensure that the taxpayer does not overlook deductible expenses.

Several tax-planning opportunities have been eliminated in recent years. One of the most significant provisions of the Tax Reform Act of 1986 was the elimination of preferential tax treatment for capital gains. As indicated earlier in the chapter, preferential treatment has been partially restored by limiting the tax on capital gains for individuals to a maximum of 28%, and there is considerable debate about whether further preferential treatment should be provided for capital gains.

Another tax advantage eliminated by the 1986 act was the option to use either the allowance method or the direct write-off method for bad debts. As we explained in an earlier chapter, under the allowance method, companies can estimate the amount of uncollectible accounts and deduct the estimated expense in the year the sales were made. Under the direct write-off method, which is now required for income tax purposes, bad debt expense is not recognized until specific accounts are determined to be uncollectible and are written off. Given the required use of the direct write-off method, businesses should review their accounts receivable on a regular basis to identify uncollectible accounts and write them off as early as possible.

Although several tax advantages and planning opportunities have been eliminated, tax considerations are still important in many areas of business activity. Two of these areas, inventories and long-term operating assets, are discussed in the following sections.

> **To Summarize** *To the extent that management has control over the timing of a tax liability, the tax objective should be to pay the least legal tax at the latest possible time, since no one owes a duty to pay more than the law requires. Three important tax planning guidelines to meet this "least and latest" objective include (1) knowing the tax law, (2) planning transactions to minimize the tax effect, and (3) keeping adequate records. Tax considerations for businesses that continue to be important are the choice of inventory method (FIFO, LIFO, or weighted average) and the choice of depreciation method for long-term operating assets.*

TAX CONSIDERATIONS IN ACCOUNTING FOR INVENTORIES

When inventories first become a material factor in determining a company's net income, the taxpayer is permitted to select among a number of inventory costing alternatives (see Chapter 7): FIFO, LIFO, weighted average, and spe-

Objective 4

Identify the income tax considerations in accounting for inventories.

cific identification. Once an inventory costing alternative has been selected and used, however, the taxpayer must obtain approval from the Internal Revenue Service before changing to a different method. If LIFO is used in calculating income taxes, it must also be used for financial reporting. If another alternative is chosen for income tax purposes, the taxpayer is free to use any alternative for financial reporting.

Choosing an inventory alternative is a form of tax planning because each alternative has a different impact on the firm's income tax liability. FIFO and LIFO generally produce the highest and lowest taxable incomes, whereas the weighted-average alternative usually results in a taxable income figure somewhere in between. Whether FIFO or LIFO will result in the lowest or highest taxable income depends on the pattern of replacement prices over a period of time. During periods of rising prices, LIFO will result in the lowest taxable income. During periods of falling prices, FIFO will produce the lowest taxable income. From a historical perspective, prices have tended to rise far more often than they have fallen; as a result, many companies have chosen, or switched to, LIFO, when prices were expected to rise in the near future.

The following example presents the effects of FIFO, LIFO, and weighted average on taxable income during a time of rising prices:

	Units	Unit Cost	Total Cost
Beginning inventory	10	$10	$100
Purchases (in chronological order)	10	$11	$110
	10	12	120
	10	13	130
	10	14	140
Total purchases	40		$500
Inventory available for sale	50		$600
Ending inventory	10		

If the product has a selling price of $18 per unit, the three inventory methods compare as shown:

	FIFO	LIFO	Weighted Average
Sales revenue (40 × $18)	$720	$720	$720
Cost of goods sold:			
Cost of goods available for sale	$600	$600	$600
Less ending inventory:			
FIFO (10 at $14)	(140)		
LIFO (10 at $10)		(100)	
Weighted average (10 at $12)			(120)
Cost of goods sold	460	500	480
Gross margin	$260	$220	$240

As you can see, LIFO shows the lowest gross margin, and therefore the lowest income, during a period of rising prices, FIFO the highest, and weighted average falls between FIFO and LIFO.

For the best tax situation, a company should switch from FIFO to LIFO only when prices are at a low point and are expected to rise. A substantial number of companies shifted to LIFO in 1976, for example, when the United States was in an economic recession. A similar situation existed in the early 1990s. Despite the potential savings by shifting to LIFO at an opportune time, a few companies usually choose not to make the shift because they would be required to use LIFO for financial reporting as well. In times of rising prices, this would result in the reporting of lower earnings and hence lower earnings per share. Further, the tax laws impose limitations on frequent shifting of inventory methods.

If prices rise for one or more periods and then fall to their original levels in subsequent periods, FIFO and LIFO will result in the same total taxable income over the entire span of time, assuming that sales remain the same each year. For example, suppose that prices are rising in 1993 and 1994. LIFO will produce the lowest taxable income, and FIFO the highest. If prices fall in 1995 and 1996, FIFO will produce the lowest income, and LIFO the highest. Over the 4-year period, if the prices in 1996 return to 1993 levels and if the same number of units are sold each year, the total taxable income will be the same under either method. Note that the taxpayer using LIFO will be better off than the one using FIFO because the former paid lower taxes in the earlier years and thus had use of the tax savings during that time.

Two other observations are significant regarding the choice of an inventory costing alternative. First, if prices rise because of inflation and do not return to earlier levels, the firm using LIFO will pay less in total taxes over a long period of time. Second, if prices fluctuate without any identifiable pattern of increases and decreases, the weighted-average alternative may be the most useful method for smoothing out the price fluctuations.

To Summarize *The inventory costing method selected by a company is a form of tax planning because each alternative inventory method has a different impact on a company's tax liability. The tax impact depends on the pattern of changes in replacement prices over a period of time. During periods of rising prices, the LIFO method will produce the lowest taxable income. During periods of falling prices, FIFO will produce the lowest taxable income. Once an inventory method has been selected and used, the company is required to continue using that method for tax purposes until the IRS approves a request for a change. For the best tax situation, a company should switch from FIFO to LIFO only when prices are at a low point and are expected to rise. If prices rise because of inflation and do not return to earlier lower levels, the company using LIFO will pay less total tax over a long period of time. Using the FIFO method saves taxes during periods of declining prices. The weighted average method may be the best method for tax purposes when prices fluctuate significantly without any identifiable pattern.*

INVESTMENTS IN LONG-TERM OPERATING ASSETS

A company's income tax liability is affected by the way long-term operating assets are acquired, depreciated, and disposed of. Operating assets, as you recall, include such resources as land, buildings, and equipment. In this section, we

Objective 5

Identify the income tax considerations in acquiring, depreciating, and disposing of long-term operating assets.

focus on the tax effects resulting from various methods of acquiring long-term operating assets, of calculating depreciation, and of disposing of these assets.

Tax Effects of Ways of Acquiring Long-Term Operating Assets

Operating assets may be acquired directly by paying cash, issuing securities, leasing, or construction, or they may be acquired indirectly by buying the stock of a corporation. Each of these types of transactions has a different tax effect.

ACQUISITION BY PURCHASE. When an operating asset is acquired by paying cash, the important tax-related question is: What should be included in the cost of the asset? In principle, it should include all costs incurred to prepare the asset for its intended use—for example, the invoice price, sales tax, freight in, installation, and start-up costs. The total of these costs is the cost base used for recording and depreciating the asset.

ACQUISITION BY ISSUING SECURITIES. Assets acquired by issuing stocks or bonds are usually major assets, such as buying a building or another company. When such assets are acquired, a key question is: At what cost should the asset be recorded? Generally, the asset should be recorded at its fair market value or at the fair market value of the securities traded for the asset. The fair market value assigned to the asset would then be used as the basis for calculating the depreciation if the asset is a depreciable asset.

ACQUISITION BY LEASING. A company may choose to lease assets rather than to buy them possibly because the company does not want its capital tied up in that type of operating asset. Leasing can have important tax ramifications as well. For example, the rental payment for the use of leased land is a deductible expense, whereas land that is owned cannot be depreciated for tax purposes.

The tax situation is somewhat different for a lease arrangement that is in substance an installment purchase of an asset. As explained in Chapter 9, this type of lease is called a **capital lease**. Under a capital lease, title to the asset may pass to the lessee at the end of the lease term without any payment beyond the final period's rent. Or the lessee may have the option to buy the asset for substantially less than its estimated fair market value at the end of the lease. In such cases, the lease payments cannot be treated as rental expense. Instead, the asset must be recorded on the company's books at its fair market value with a related liability shown for the future rental payments. This treatment provides an annual tax deduction for the depreciation of the asset and for the interest on the installment loan. Usually, the sum of the depreciation and interest expenses will be larger than the rental payment in the early years of the lease and smaller in the later years, as Exhibit 17-3 illustrates.

capital lease *a leasing transaction that is recorded as a purchase by the lessee*

ACQUISITION BY CONSTRUCTION. When a company constructs its own assets, such as a building, the primary tax consideration is: Which costs must be recorded as part of the building, and which can be written off as an immediate expense? For instance, should interest expense and the property taxes incurred during the construction period be allocated to the building cost, as generally accepted accounting principles specify in certain cases, or can they be deducted as normal operating expenses? Likewise, must overhead costs be allocated to the construction activity, or can they be assigned to work-in-process as costs of

Exhibit 17-3   *A Lease as an Installment Purchase*

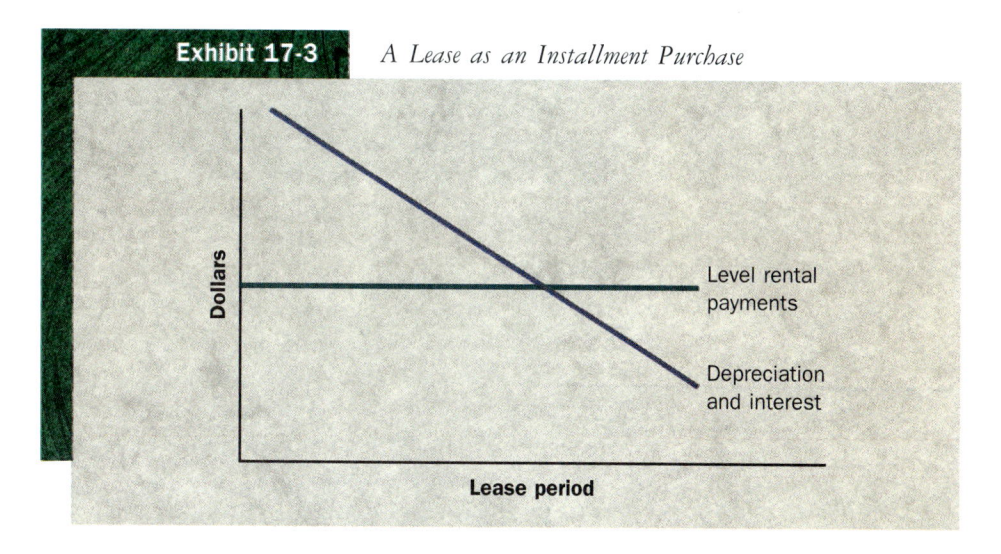

producing goods for sale? In general, when an asset is constructed, an allocated portion of the costs must be capitalized as part of the cost of the building. These costs are then included in the calculation of the annual depreciation expense.

Tax Effects of Alternative Ways of Depreciating Long-Term Operating Assets

modified accelerated cost recovery system (MACRS) *IRS regulations that allocate the cost of an asset according to predefined recovery percentages*

recovery period *the time period designated by Congress for depreciating business assets for tax purposes*

The primary tax consequence of using an operating asset is the amount and timing of depreciation expense. In Chapter 9, we described several methods of calculating depreciation for financial reporting purposes. We also introduced the **modified accelerated cost recovery system (MACRS)**, the depreciation system established by Congress for income purposes in 1981 and modified in 1986. MACRS is a plan for allocating the cost of an asset according to predefined percentages based on the **recovery period** for each type of asset.

As shown in Exhibit 17-4, MACRS defines 8 categories, or classes, of depreciable property, with recovery periods from 3 to 31.5 years. For most businesses, depreciable assets fall into one of four classes: 3-year, 5-year, 7-year,

Exhibit 17-4   *Asset Categories Under the Modified Accelerated Cost Recovery System (MACRS)*

Cost Recovery Period	Depreciation Method Allowed	Examples of Assets Included
3 years	200% declining balance	Race horses, special tools
5 years	200% declining balance	Automobiles, light trucks, computers
7 years	200% declining balance	Office furniture and fixtures, machinery and equipment
10 years	200% declining balance	Barges and vessels
15 years	150% declining balance	Billboards, land improvements
20 years	150% declining balance	Utilities and sewers
27.5 years	Straight line	Residential rental property
31.5 years	Straight line	Commercial and industrial real property

or 31.5-year property. For each class of property, a depreciation method is specified. All assets, other than real property, can be depreciated using a declining-balance method (200% or 150%), with a switch to straight-line in the year when the straight-line method results in a larger depreciation deduction. As an alternative, a taxpayer may elect to use straight-line depreciation over specified recovery periods. Real property (buildings and their structural components) must be depreciated using the straight-line method.

Whichever method is used, salvage value is ignored for purposes of computing tax depreciation. Further, in the year an asset, other than real property, is acquired or disposed of, a "half-year convention" must be applied. Under this convention, an asset is always assumed to be acquired (or disposed of) in the middle of the tax year. For real property, depreciation in the year of acquisition or disposal is based on the number of months the property was in service, and a midmonth convention applies. For example, if a building was purchased on September 5, for tax purposes it is assumed to have been acquired on September 15, the middle of the month of acquisition.

To illustrate the MACRS rules, we will assume that a company paid $12,000 for a new computer with a cost recovery period of 5 years. Although the computer has an estimated salvage value of $2,000, this amount is ignored for the purpose of these calculations. The allowable depreciation deductions for each year under the 200% declining-balance method and the alternative straight-line method are shown in the following table. With the 200% declining-balance method, a switch is made to straight-line depreciation in year 5. For both methods, the midyear convention is used in computing the deduction for the first and last year.

Year	Accelerated Cost Recovery Amount	200%-Declining-Balance Computation	Straight-Line ($12,000 ÷ 5 years)
1	$ 2,400	[($12,000 − $0) ÷ 5 × 2] × ½ year	$ 1,200
2	3,840	[($12,000 − $2,400) ÷ 5 × 2]	2,400
3	2,304	[($9,600 − $3,840) ÷ 5 × 2]	2,400
4	1,382	[($5,760 − $2,304) ÷ 5 × 2]	2,400
5	1,382	Convert to straight-line: ($3,456 − $1,382) ÷ 1½ years	2,400
			1,200
6	692	Straight-line (½ year)	$12,000
	$12,000		

SELECTING THE COST RECOVERY PERIOD FOR AN ASSET. In choosing a cost recovery period for depreciable assets, the taxpayer has two options: (1) select the appropriate MACRS recovery class, or (2) select the optional, longer period and use straight-line depreciation. The taxpayer's choice will depend on the type of asset and the taxpayer's expected income. If a taxpayer is already in the 34% corporate tax bracket, the company should select the method and period that provide the maximum depreciation deduction at the earliest time. Thus, the taxpayer would select the 200% declining-balance method rather than the optional straight-line method. An optional straight-line method would usually be selected if the taxpayer is paying less than 34% in taxes and wants to delay some depreciation deduction until the 34% tax bracket is reached in a later year.

Chapter 17 *The Impact of Income Taxes on Business Decisions* 753

With MACRS, taxpayers are likely to use a more rapid recovery period for income tax purposes than would be allowed for financial reporting. Whatever period and method are used for tax purposes, the taxpayer must use the same method throughout the life of the asset, except when a switch to the straight-line method is allowed or the Commissioner of Internal Revenue gives permission to change the method.

ELECTION TO EXPENSE CERTAIN BUSINESS ASSETS. If certain qualifications are met, business taxpayers can elect to take an expense deduction for the cost of **tangible personal business property** instead of treating the cost as a capital expenditure. To qualify for the expense deduction, the property must be tangible personal property purchased for use in a trade or business. If the expense deduction is taken, the maximum amount that can be expensed is $10,000. This $10,000 expense deduction is reduced a dollar for every dollar the cost of the qualified property exceeds $200,000 in any one year. Generally, the taxpayer will benefit from expensing since it provides an earlier deduction than if the cost was depreciated.

tangible personal business property depreciable operating assets of a business, other than real property, including machinery, furniture and fixtures, automobiles and trucks, and equipment

Tax Effects of Disposing of Long-Term Operating Assets

Long-term operating assets can be disposed of by sale, by exchange for another asset, or by abandonment. We briefly discuss each of these methods of disposal.

DISPOSAL BY SALE. When an operating asset is sold, a gain or loss is recorded for the difference between selling price and book value (cost minus accumulated depreciation) and reported as part of operating income on the income statement. Gains and losses on sales of assets are also included in gross income on the tax return. If depreciation on the asset has been the same for both tax and financial reporting purposes, the gain or loss on the income statement will be the same as the amount included in gross income. If tax depreciation is not the same as book depreciation, the gain or loss included in gross income will be different because the tax basis, or unrecovered cost, for tax purposes will not be the same as book value.

DISPOSAL BY EXCHANGE. When assets are exchanged for similar assets, some gains and all losses are recognized for financial reporting purposes. For income tax purposes, however, the exchange of similar assets is treated as a continuation of the original asset acquisition and is therefore considered a nontaxable transaction. Thus, if a taxpayer expects to have a gain on the disposal of an asset, the gain can be postponed for tax purposes by exchanging the asset for a similar one. If a loss is expected on the disposal of the asset, the loss cannot be deducted if the asset is exchanged for a similar asset but can be deducted if the asset is sold. When dissimilar assets are exchanged, the transaction is considered a taxable exchange. In that case, the tax law requires that the gain or loss be recognized in the year of the exchange, just as it is for financial reporting purposes.

DISPOSAL BY ABANDONMENT. If an asset is no longer usable and has no market value, a taxpayer may choose to abandon or scrap the asset and write off the remaining book value as a loss. The taxpayer has control over the timing of the loss deduction by choosing when to abandon the asset.

> **To Summarize** *A taxpayer has a variety of tax-planning opportunities with respect to the purchase, use, and disposal of long-term operating assets. The timing and the method of executing a transaction have an influence on when a gain or loss is reported.*
>
> *When an asset is acquired by purchase, its basis for depreciation is the total cost incurred to make the asset ready for its intended use, including the invoice cost, freight, sales tax, and installation cost. When an asset is acquired by issuing securities, it should generally be recorded at fair market value as a basis for determining depreciation. If an asset is leased, the lessee may deduct the rent as an expense; if the lease arrangement is an installment purchase, the lessee is allowed to take depreciation on the asset under MACRS or the optional straight-line method. When a company constructs its own building, it should determine which costs must be included as part of the building and which costs can be written off immediately as normal operating expenses.*
>
> *For income tax purposes, a company may elect to use the modified accelerated cost recovery system (MACRS) or straight-line depreciation with an optional recovery period to depreciate its assets. MACRS is an IRS plan for allocating the cost of an asset according to predefined recovery periods and percentages.*
>
> *An asset can be disposed of by exchange, sale, or abandonment, depending on the situation. The method of disposal will determine whether it is possible to postpone the gain or when to deduct the loss.*

Review of Learning Objectives

Objective 1

Explain the general procedures for determining income tax liability and how these procedures are applied to individuals and corporations. The income tax liability for individual taxpayers is determined as follows: (1) compute gross income, (2) subtract allowable adjustments to arrive at adjusted gross income, (3) subtract the higher of itemized deductions or the standard deduction and personal exemptions to arrive at taxable income, (4) multiply increments of taxable income by the appropriate tax rates to compute the gross tax liability, and (5) subtract tax credits and payments to determine the net tax due or the amount of overpayment. Gross income includes salaries and wages, interest, dividends, business income (or loss), rents and royalties, and all other income subject to tax. Adjustments to gross income include deductions for retirement plan contributions, one-half of self-employment tax, early withdrawal penalties on savings, and alimony paid. The expenses allowed in computing itemized deductions include medical expenses, property taxes, state and local income taxes, certain types of interest expense, charitable contributions, casualty and theft losses, moving expenses, and certain miscellaneous expenses. The standard deduction is an amount specified by law that varies with filing status and age or blindness. The deduction for personal exemptions is a specified amount allowed for the taxpayer, spouse, and each dependent. The tax rates are progressive and apply to different levels of income depending on filing status. For example, taxable income was taxed at rates of 15%, 28%, and 31% in 1991.

A corporation's gross income is its taxable receipts from service revenues or sales revenues less cost of sales. (Exclusions are nontaxable receipts.) Business deductions and any special deductions are subtracted from gross income to arrive at taxable income. The tax rate increases with the level of taxable income to $335,000 and then reverts to 34% for all income as a device to phase out the lower tax rates of 15% and 25%. The increments of taxable income multiplied by the appropriate tax rates give the gross tax liability, from which tax credits are subtracted to determine net tax liability. The timing of the recognition of gross income and expenses depends on whether cash- or accrual-basis accounting is used. Only specified types of companies can choose either method, and the accrual basis is required for purchases and sales when inventories are a significant factor in computing income.

Objective 2

Understand the tax treatment of proprietorships and partnerships and how the treatment differs from corporations. Tax consequences are an important consideration in selecting the form of business organization. Proprietorships and partnerships are not taxed as separate entities; their income is taxed to the proprietor or to the partners under the conduit principle. Because corporations are separate legal entities, corporate earnings are taxed to the corporation, and then the distributed portion of the earnings is taxed as dividends to the stockholders. However, income from S corporations, a special type of taxable entity, whether the income is distributed or not, is taxed to stockholders only. Both regular and S corporations can provide special tax benefits to employees in the form of tax-free fringe benefits that may not be available to the owners of partnerships and proprietorships.

Objective 3

Explain basic tax-planning guidelines. The basic objective of tax planning is to pay the least amount of tax at the latest possible time. Three important tax guidelines that will help individuals and management meet this objective are (1) knowing the law, (2) planning transactions to minimize the tax effect, and (3) keeping adequate records.

Objective 4

Identify the income tax considerations in accounting for inventories. The methods selected for measuring the cost of inventories will influence the amount of income reported and taxes paid in any one year. FIFO and LIFO generally produce the highest and lowest taxable incomes, and the weighted-average method usually produces a figure somewhere between FIFO and LIFO. During periods of rising prices, LIFO will result in the lowest taxable income. During periods of falling prices, FIFO will produce the lowest taxable income.

Objective 5

Identify the income tax considerations in acquiring, depreciating, and disposing of long-term operating assets. The way in which the acquisition of a long-term operating asset is recorded will affect the amount and timing of expenses to be charged for the purchase of an asset. Similarly, the depreciation method and recovery period selected to measure the use of an operating asset will determine the timing of the write-off of the asset's cost to expense. And finally, the method of disposing of an operating asset will be a factor in the timing of the recognition of the gain or loss.

Key Terms and Concepts

adjusted gross income *(733)*
adjustments to gross income *(733)*
capital gain *(736)*
capital lease *(750)*
conduit principle *(743)*
constructive receipt rule *(741)*
deductions *(733)*
effective tax rate *(741)*

exclusions *(733)*
gross income *(732)*
gross tax liability *(733)*
itemized deductions *(733)*
Keogh Plan *(743)*
modified accelerated cost recovery system (MACRS) *(751)*
net tax liability *(733)*
personal exemption *(735)*

recovery period *(751)*
S corporation *(744)*
standard deduction *(735)*
tangible personal business property *(753)*
taxable income *(733)*
tax credit *(733)*
tax-exempt corporation *(745)*

Review Problem 1

Computation of Individual's Taxable Income

Pete and Susan Barnes are married, file a joint return, and have two dependent children. Following is a list of their total receipts and additional information for determining their tax liability for the year just ended:

Receipts:

Pete's salary	$35,000
Susan's salary	28,000
Interest received on municipal bonds	2,000
Interest received on certificates of deposit	1,400
Dividends received on ABC Corporation stock	600

Additional information:

Federal income taxes withheld by employers	$ 6,000
Total allowable itemized deductions	16,250*
Standard deduction allowed	5,700
Amount allowed for each personal exemption	2,150
Tax credit for qualified child-care expenses	650
Penalty on early withdrawal of savings	375

*It is assumed that this is the net allowable itemized deductions after considering limitations.

Required: Compute Pete and Susan's taxable income for the year.

Solution

Gross income:	
Pete's salary	$35,000
Susan's salary	28,000
Interest income on certificates of deposit	1,400
Dividends on ABC stock	600
Gross income	$65,000
Adjustments to gross income:	
Penalty on early withdrawal of savings	(375)
Adjusted gross income	$64,625
Itemized deductions	(16,250)
Personal exemptions ($2,150 × 4)	(8,600)
Taxable income	$39,775

Note that gross income does not include interest on municipal bonds because it is nontaxable. Further, itemized deductions are used because they exceed the allowable standard deduction. The federal income taxes withheld and the credit for child-care expenses are not included in the computation of taxable income. These amounts are deducted from the gross tax liability to determine the balance of tax due or the overpayment.

Review Problem 2

Computing a Corporation's Tax Liability

Arce Corporation collected the following revenue, expense, and other information for computing its annual tax liability:

Gross receipts from services	$280,000
Excludable income (tax-exempt interest)	5,000
Gain on the sale of machinery (total depreciation taken, $15,000)	8,000
Ordinary business expenses	150,000
Taxes paid during the year on estimated income	35,000

Required: Compute Arce Corporation's tax liability for the year.

Solution

Gross receipts from services	$280,000
Gain on sale of machinery	8,000
Gross income	$288,000
Less ordinary business expenses	150,000
Taxable income	$138,000

Tax on income of $138,000:

15% × $50,000	$ 7,500
25% × $25,000	6,250
34% × $25,000	8,500
39% × $38,000	14,820
Gross tax liability	$37,070
Less estimated taxes paid	35,000
Tax due	$ 2,070

Discussion Questions

1. Distinguish between the following terms as they are used for tax purposes.
   (a) Gross receipts and gross income.
   (b) Exclusions and deductions.
   (c) Deductions and credits.
2. What characteristics of a business expense would allow it to be a deduction in the determination of taxable income?
3. Distinguish between revenues per income statement and gross income per tax return.
4. What is meant by the constructive receipt rule in measuring taxable income?
5. What types of losses are deductible for tax purposes?
6. From a tax point of view, what are the three types of corporations?
7. Describe the philosophy of the conduit principle as it relates to the taxation of proprietorships, partnerships, and S corporations.
8. What are the key tax and nontax factors to consider in choosing the appropriate form of business organization?
9. What is the objective of following good tax-planning guidelines?
10. What are three tax-planning guidelines?
11. Why is it important to keep good records as a basis for preparing a tax return?
12. Describe the acceptable method of accounting for bad debts for tax purposes.

13. In a period of rising prices, which inventory valuation alternative will result in the lowest taxable income for a business? Why?
14. Under the modified accelerated cost recovery system, what is the recovery period and depreciation method for each of the following assets?
    (a) Furniture.
    (b) Automobiles.
    (c) Machinery.
    (d) Buildings used for commercial purposes.
15. What primary factor should the taxpayer consider in choosing between accelerated and straight-line depreciation for an asset?
16. Explain the tax effects of the choice between selling an old asset and buying a new one versus trading an old asset for a new one.

Exercises

E17-1
Classifying Individual Receipts and Payments

Indicate whether each of the following items would be classified on an individual's tax return as (1) gross income, (2) an adjustment to gross income, (3) an itemized deduction, or (4) a credit against the gross tax liability. If an item is not part of the computation of net income tax liability, indicate "not included."

(a) A cash donation to a charitable organization.
(b) Interest received on a savings account.
(c) Dividends received on an investment in common stock.
(d) Interest paid on a home mortgage.
(e) Salaries received from employer.
(f) Interest received on municipal bonds.
(g) Federal income taxes withheld by employer.
(h) Contribution to an Individual Retirement Account.
(i) Refund of previous year's overpayment of federal income taxes.
(j) Loss on sale of stock.
(k) Income from operating a sole proprietorship.
(l) Rental income from an apartment building.
(m) State and local income taxes paid.
(n) Penalty incurred on early withdrawal of savings.
(o) Estimated taxes paid for the current year.

E17-2
Computing an Individual's Taxable Income

Emily Richards, a single taxpayer, is collecting data to file her tax return and is trying to determine whether she should itemize her deductions or take a standard deduction. She has determined that her adjusted gross income will be $25,000 and that she has made the following expense payments during the year:

Medical expenses	$1,400
Taxes: state and local income taxes $950; personal property tax $180; real property tax on condominium $700	1,830
Interest expense: mortgage interest	850

Assuming that the standard deduction for a single individual is $3,400, should Emily compute her taxable income using the standard deduction or itemized deductions? Assuming a personal exemption of $2,150 per taxpayer, what is the amount of Emily's taxable income?

Chapter 17 *The Impact of Income Taxes on Business Decisions*

E17-3
Computing Taxable Income for a Corporation

Taggert, Inc. reported the following amounts in its 1994 income statement:

Gross profit on sales	$175,000
Dividends received on 30% investment in the common stock of Holder Company	15,000
Gain on the sale of land held as an investment	28,000
Selling expenses	32,500
General and administrative expenses	46,200

Based on this information, compute the 1994 taxable income for Taggert, Inc.

E17-4
Computation of Corporate Tax Liability

Pioneer Corporation files its tax return on a calendar-year basis. Its gross revenues for 1994 were $280,000, and its deductible business expenses were $165,000. Compute the corporation's gross tax liability for 1994 using the tax rates in Exhibit 17-2 (page 739).

E17-5
Reporting of S Corporation Income by Stockholders

An S corporation reported taxable income of $90,000 on its 1994 tax return. During 1994, the corporation had distributed $30,000 in dividends to its stockholders. If the corporation has five stockholders, each owning 20 percent, how much income must each stockholder report on his or her 1994 individual income tax return?

E17-6
Depreciation Expense Under MACRS

On July 1, 1994, Broome Company paid $10,000 for a new light truck to be used to deliver merchandise to customers. If the company uses MACRS, how much is the depreciation deduction for 1994? How much is the depreciation deduction on a straight-line basis?

E17-7
Partnership Income

Crosby, Stills, and Nash are partners in Young Company. They share profits in the ratio of Crosby, 60%; Stills, 30%; Nash, 10%. This past year, the partnership income totaled $89,000. Crosby withdrew $15,000, Stills withdrew $9,000, and Nash withdrew no funds from the company during the year.

What share of partnership income will the partners in Young Company be required to report on their individual tax returns?

E17-8
Gain on the Sale of Machinery

On December 1, 1994, Wells Company sold a machine for $11,000 that it had purchased in 1984 for $47,000. Depreciation expense from the date of purchase to the date of sale amounted to $42,000 for both book and tax purposes.

1. What is the amount of gain on the sale?
2. How is the gain reported for tax purposes?
3. **Interpretive Question** If the company had wanted to postpone the gain, how should the asset have been disposed of?

Problem Set A

P17A-1
Computing Taxable Income for an Individual

Robert Blake is married, files a joint return with his spouse, Carolyn, and has two dependent children. The Blakes collected the following information regarding their 1994 federal income tax return:

Robert's salary	$19,900
Carolyn's income from self-employment (net income from business operated as sole proprietorship)	12,900
Itemized deductions (net of applicable limitations)	4,800
Contribution by Carolyn to a Keogh plan	500
Tax credit relating to Carolyn's business income	300
Income taxes withheld by Robert's employer	2,250
Estimated taxes paid by Carolyn on self-employment income	1,300

Required: Determine the 1994 taxable income for Robert and Carolyn Blake. Assume personal exemptions are $2,150 each and the standard deduction for a married couple filing a joint return is $5,700.

P17A-2
Computing the Tax Liability for a Corporation

Norton Corporation reported the following revenues and expenses, before income taxes in its income statement for the year ending December 31, 1994.

Net sales	$265,000
Cost of goods sold	105,000
Interest on notes receivable	9,800
Dividends on short-term investments in marketable equity securities (stock ownership did not exceed 5% for any investee corporation)	14,200
Total operating expenses	86,000

Additional Information:

During 1994, Norton paid estimated taxes of $19,600. Further, Norton declared and paid dividends of $30,000 to its common stockholders during 1994.

Required:
1. Compute the net tax liability for Norton Corporation using the tax rates in Exhibit 17-2.
2. Determine the amount of tax owed or the overpayment for 1994.

P17A-3
Inventory Valuation Alternatives

For 1994, its second year of operation, Parker Company had revenues of $300,000 from the sale of 600 mopeds at an average price of $500 per unit. Parker Company uses the periodic inventory method, and inventories and purchases of mopeds for 1994 were as follows:

Beginning inventory	60 units at $300
Purchases:	
January	130 units at $300
March	150 units at $310
July	140 units at $315
October	170 units at $320
Ending inventory	50 units

Required:
1. Compute the cost of goods sold and the total cost of the ending inventory using the FIFO, LIFO, and weighted-average inventory alternatives. (Round the weighted-average figures to two decimal places.)
2. Which alternative shows the highest profit in a period of rising prices?
3. **Interpretive Question** If a company has been using FIFO, when should it consider converting to LIFO in order to get the most benefit from the tax laws?

Chapter 17 The Impact of Income Taxes on Business Decisions

P17A-4
Maximum Deduction in Year of Asset Acquisition

On April 2, 1994, Flint Company purchased machinery for $24,000. The machinery has an estimated useful life of 8 years and a $2,000 salvage value. The company plans to take maximum advantage of the tax law in computing deductions.

Required:
1. What is the maximum amount of the asset's cost that can be deducted in the year of acquisition?
2. If the machinery was purchased for cash, how much of the initial outlay was recovered in the form of tax savings in the first year by means of the maximum deduction taken? (Assume an effective tax rate of 40 percent, including federal and state taxes.)

P17A-5
Unifying Concepts: Partnerships and S Corporations

Liliana Padilla is a partner in a venture that reports net income of $86,000 for the current taxable year. Her share is 25 percent. Her withdrawals from the partnership during the year were $18,000.

Required:
1. In preparing her income tax return for the year, what amount is Liliana required to report as income from the partnership?
2. **Interpretive Question** What are the advantages of an S corporation over a partnership? What are the disadvantages?

P17A-6
The S Corporation

Florida Corporation was organized on January 2, 1993, as an S corporation. Its taxable income for calendar year 1994 was $74,000, and its dividends distributed to stockholders in the same year were $36,000, as shown. Its taxable income in 1993 was $56,000, of which $25,000 was distributed to stockholders. The corporation made the following distributions during 1994:

March 1	$13,000
June 15	11,000
November 10	12,000

Required: Explain how these distributions will be treated by stockholders on their 1994 tax returns.

P17A-7
Bad-Debt Expense

Brand Corporation uses the allowance method of accounting for bad debts for financial reporting and the direct write-off method for tax purposes. In 1994, the corporation added $4,800 to Allowance for Uncollectible Accounts and wrote off $6,000 of uncollectible accounts receivable. Allowance for Uncollectible Accounts had a balance of $1,500 on January 1, 1994.

Required:
1. Calculate the bad-debt deduction allowed on the corporation's 1994 tax return.
2. Determine the balance in Allowance for Uncollectible Accounts on December 31, 1994, for financial reporting purposes.
3. Which method of accounting for bad debts is more consistent with the tax-planning objective of paying the least legal tax at the latest possible time? Why?
4. Could Brand Corporation use the same method for both income tax and financial reporting purposes? Explain.

P17A-8
Unifying Concepts: Depreciation and Salvage Value

Carter Trucking Company acquired the following assets in 1994. All the assets were placed in service in 1994.

Asset	Cost	Salvage Value
Office furniture	$14,000	$2,000
Light truck	9,000	1,000
Equipment	10,000	1,200
Computer	3,000	500
Building (new)*	60,000	4,000

*Acquired and put into use for commercial purposes on October 10, 1994.

Required: Answer the following questions concerning depreciation and salvage values of the assets:

1. For each asset listed, what is the maximum depreciation deduction allowed in the year of acquisition?
2. For each asset, how much salvage value must be considered in computing the tax deduction for depreciation?
3. **Interpretive Question** Explain the advantage to a taxpayer of being allowed to ignore the salvage value in computing the depreciation deduction.

Problem Set B

P17B-1
Computation of Individual Income Tax Liability

Stephanie Harris is divorced with one dependent and qualifies as head of household for federal income tax purposes. Her salary for 1994 was $47,000. During the year, she received $325 of dividend income from stock investments. She sold some of her stock during the year at a gain of $1,400. Stephanie had itemized deductions (net of applicable limitations) of $5,500. Federal income taxes withheld from her salary during the year amounted to $4,800, and she did not make any estimated tax payments. For the previous tax year, 1993, Stephanie had overpaid her taxes by $250 and applied this amount to her 1994 tax liability rather than requesting a refund.

Required: Based on this information, compute the following amounts for Stephanie's 1994 federal income tax return. Assume the allowable standard deduction for head of household taxpayers is $5,000 and each personal exemption is $2,150.

1. Gross income and adjusted gross income.
2. Taxable income.
3. Gross tax liability assuming the following tax rates apply for a head of household taxpayer: 15% of the first $25,000 of taxable income and 28% for income above $25,000 up to $65,000.

P17B-2
Computation of Corporation's Taxable Income

Woodlawn Corporation's 1994 income statement reports the following revenues and expenses before income taxes:

Sales	$480,000
Sales discounts and returns and allowances	62,900
Cost of goods sold	206,500
Interest income from city of Cincinnati bonds	7,000
Loss on sale of short-term investment in marketable securities	14,640
Operating expenses:	
Depreciation expense	37,880
Uncollectible accounts expense (2% of net sales)	8,360
Other operating expenses	68,540

Chapter 17 *The Impact of Income Taxes on Business Decisions*

For financial statement purposes, Woodlawn uses the FIFO method of inventory valuation; for income tax purposes, the weighted-average method is used. For 1994, cost of goods sold using the weighted-average method is $22,000 more than cost of goods sold using FIFO. Depreciation reported in the income statement is computed using the straight-line method. For the income tax return, depreciation is calculated under the MACRS rules, and for 1994, amounts to $52,600. During 1994, accounts receivable totaling $5,500 were determined to be uncollectible and were written off by Woodlawn.

Required:
1. Compute the income before taxes that should be reported on Woodlawn Corporation's 1994 income statement.
2. Compute the gross income tax liability for 1994.
3. **Interpretive Question** Why are different methods used for financial reporting and income tax purposes?

P17B-3
Inventory Valuation Alternatives

Regal Television Company was established this year. Management has asked you to determine which inventory alternative would result in the lowest taxable income: LIFO, FIFO, or weighted average.

Purchases during the year	20 televisions at $385	=	$ 7,700
	42 televisions at 375	=	15,750
	49 televisions at 370	=	18,130
	63 televisions at 365	=	22,995
	12 televisions at 395	=	4,740
Total purchases..................	186 televisions at 395	=	$69,315
Ending inventory	29 televisions		
Average selling price: $500			

Required: Answer the following questions concerning Regal's inventory valuation alternatives:

1. Assuming no other receipts, what is the gross income using each of the three inventory alternatives? (Round the weighted-average per television cost to two decimal places.)
2. **Interpretive Question** If a company has been using the LIFO inventory alternative during a period of rising prices, what will be the effect on the company's profits in a year in which the ending inventory is substantially less than the beginning inventory?
3. **Interpretive Question** Under what circumstances would weighted-average be more desirable than either LIFO or FIFO?

P17B-4
Calculating MACRS Depreciation

On May 10 of the current year, Palmer Company purchased a new machine for $40,000. The machine has an estimated useful life of 10 years and a salvage value of $4,000. The MACRS recovery period is 7 years.

Required: Compute the depreciation expense for the year of purchase and the subsequent years under MACRS on both an accelerated and a straight-line basis.

P17B-5
Calculating Maximum Deduction in Year of Asset Acquisition

Calliope Mills acquired a textile machine in early January at a cost of $88,000. The machine is classified as 7-year property under MACRS and has an estimated salvage value of $7,000.

Required: Determine how much total cost recovery is allowable in the calendar year of acquisition under MACRS using (1) an accelerated depreciation basis and (2) a straight-line depreciation basis. Calliope Mills uses the maximum expense election allowed.

P17B-6
Unifying Concepts: Expense Election and Regular Depreciation

Regent Corporation acquired a machine on January 3, 1994, for $75,000. Assume that the machine has an estimated life of 8 years and no salvage value. The company has an effective tax rate of 40 percent.

Required: Answer the following questions pertaining to Regent Corporation's 1994 tax liability:

1. What is the maximum tax saving in 1994 if the corporation uses the maximum expense election allowed and uses MACRS on an accelerated basis?
2. **Interpretive Question** When would it be to the company's advantage not to take the expense election and not to use accelerated depreciation?

P17B-7
Partner's Shares of Profits

Beth Wright and Roger Becker formed a partnership to operate a flower center. For the calendar year 1994, the net income of the partnership amounted to $60,000.

Required: Answer the following questions concerning the partners' tax liabilities:

1. If Beth and Roger share profits and losses on a 60/40 percent basis, what amount would each report as income for the year 1994 if Beth withdraws $800 per month and Roger withdraws $500 per month for each month during 1994?
2. **Interpretive Question** What effect on the partners' income taxes would there be if all the income were left in the business?

P17B-8
MACRS Depreciation for Buildings

On August 10, 1994, Windham Corporation acquired land and a building for $800,000. The property is to be used for commercial purposes. The portion of the cost assignable to the land was $90,000.

Required: Using this information, answer the following:

1. What is the maximum depreciation Windham Corporation is entitled to for each of the years 1994, 1995, and 1996?
2. Is the company entitled to elect an expense deduction in 1994? Why?
3. **Interpretive Question** Ordinarily, the cost of land is not eligible for a depreciation expense deduction. Are there any circumstances when the cost of land is deductible for income tax purposes? Explain.

Business Analysis Case *Easy Gasoline Company*

In March 1994, Easy Gasoline Company acquired land and a building along the highway. The company plans to sell gasoline and a general line of convenience items. Robert Easy, the owner, has asked his accountant to answer the following questions regarding options for income tax deductions on the property. The purchase price was $120,000, and an appraisal, made prior to the purchase, showed market values of $40,000 for the land and $120,000 for the building.

Required:
1. How should the $120,000 cost be divided between the land and the building?
2. Can the cost of the land be deducted for tax purposes?
3. Would the company be allowed to deduct $10,000 of the building's cost under the MACRS expensing election?
4. If the building has an economic life of 30 years, what depreciation method is required for income tax purposes? What will the annual depreciation be?

Ethics Case *Employee Expenses**

Peter Harris is a traveling salesperson with the Exeter Manufacturing Company. He received a travel allowance of $2,500 per month to cover his travel expenses in calling on customers and attending professional meetings to meet potential new customers. If he spends more than his allowance, he is reimbursed for the additional expenses when he submits his monthly expense report. After an extended period of travel in the past month, he returned to his office at the company headquarters on the first day of the next month and began to compile his expense report for the previous month. In the process, he discovered that he had lost all of his airline, taxi, and hotel receipts for attending a professional meeting early in the previous month. He decided to walk across the hall to the office of another salesperson, Amy Smith, who had attended the same professional meeting and ask her for some "ballpark" figures for his hotel room, food, and taxi fares for attending that meeting. Amy gave Peter the expenses she incurred, but pointed out that her hotel room cost ($189) was higher because she had a suite for entertaining potential customers and that her taxi fare ($18) was lower because she did not go during the rush hour. Peter indicated that he did go during the rush hour and that he was going to add another $10 to the taxi fare. Peter made no comment about what he would put down on his report for hotel cost. He then asked Amy if she was going to include her theater tickets in the expense report. Amy asked if Peter thought it was right to do so. Peter replied that he didn't think the company would expect them to stay in their hotel rooms and watch TV. He indicated that he would just add to his meal costs $5 for each meal until he had the theater tickets covered. Amy asked if it was right to do that. Peter said, "I could have eaten meals that cost $5 more than they did. Is the company going to quibble over an extra $5 on a meal in the big city?" He then said that he did such things all the time and felt that the company owed it to him since he had to be on the road so much.

Required:
1. What are the ethical issues in this case?
2. Who are the parties that are affected by Peter's actions?
3. What are Amy's alternatives in light of the knowledge she has that Peter is padding his expense report?
4. What would you do if you were in Amy's position?

* Case adapted from ethics cases prepared for publication by the American Accounting Association.

Illustrative Financial Statements
General Mills, Inc. and Subsidiaries

Report of Management Responsibilities

The management of General Mills, Inc. includes corporate executives, operating managers, controllers and other personnel working full time on company business. These managers are responsible for the fairness and accuracy of our financial statements. The Audit Committee of the Board of Directors meets regularly to determine that management, internal auditors and independent auditors are properly discharging their duties regarding internal control and financial reporting.

The financial statements have been prepared in accordance with generally accepted accounting principles, using management's best estimates and judgments where appropriate. The financial information throughout this report is consistent with our financial statements.

Management has established a system of internal controls that provides reasonable assurance that, in all material respects, assets are maintained and accounted for in accordance with management's authorization, and transactions are recorded accurately on our books. Our internal controls provide for appropriate separation of duties and responsibilities, and there are documented policies regarding utilization of company assets and proper financial reporting. These formally stated and regularly communicated policies demand high ethical conduct from all employees.

We maintain a strong audit program that independently evaluates the adequacy and effectiveness of internal controls. The independent auditors, internal auditors and controllers have full and free access to the Audit Committee at any time.

KPMG Peat Marwick, independent certified public accountants, are retained to audit the consolidated financial statements. Their report follows.

H. B. Atwater, Jr.
Chairman of the Board and Chief Executive Officer

J. R. Lee
Vice Chairman and Chief Financial Officer

Report of the Audit Committee

The Audit Committee of the Board of Directors is composed of six outside directors. Its primary function is to oversee the Company's system of internal controls, financial reporting practices and audits to ensure their quality, integrity and objectivity are sufficient to protect stockholder assets.

The Audit Committee met twice during fiscal 1992 to review the overall audit scope, plans and results of the internal auditor and independent auditor, the Company's internal controls, emerging accounting issues, officer and director expenses, audit fees, goodwill and other intangible values, and the audits of the pension plans. The Committee also met separately without management present and with the independent auditors to discuss the audit. Acting with the other Board members, the Committee reviewed the Company's annual financial statements and approved them before issuance. Audit Committee meeting results were reported to the full Board of Directors. The Audit Committee recommended to the Board that KPMG Peat Marwick be reappointed for fiscal 1993, subject to the approval of stockholders at the annual meeting.

The Audit Committee is satisfied that the internal control system is adequate and that the stockholders of General Mills are protected by appropriate accounting and auditing procedures.

M. D. Rose
Chairman, Audit Committee

Independent Auditors' Report

The Stockholders and the Board of Directors of
General Mills, Inc.:

We have audited the accompanying consolidated balance sheets of General Mills, Inc. and subsidiaries as of May 31, 1992 and May 26, 1991, and the related consolidated statements of earnings and cash flows for each of the fiscal years in the three-year period ended May 31, 1992. These consolidated financial statements are the responsibility of the Company's management. Our responsibility is to express an opinion on these consolidated financial statements based on our audits.

We conducted our audits in accordance with generally accepted auditing standards. Those standards require that we plan and perform the audit to obtain reasonable assurance about whether the financial statements are free of material misstatement. An audit includes examining, on a test basis, evidence supporting the amounts and disclosures in the financial statements. An audit also includes assessing the accounting principles used and significant estimates made by management, as well as evaluating the overall financial statement presentation. We believe that our audits provide a reasonable basis for our opinion.

In our opinion, the consolidated financial statements referred to above present fairly, in all material respects, the financial position of General Mills, Inc. and subsidiaries as of May 31, 1992 and May 26, 1991, and the results of their operations and their cash flows for each of the fiscal years in the three-year period ended May 31, 1992 in conformity with generally accepted accounting principles.

KPMG Peat Marwick
Minneapolis, Minnesota
July 1, 1992

Consolidated Statements of Earnings

	Fiscal Year Ended		
Amounts in Millions, Except per Share Data	**May 31, 1992**	May 26, 1991	May 27, 1990
Continuing Operations:			
Sales	**$7,777.8**	$7,153.2	$6,448.3
Costs and Expenses:			
Cost of sales	**4,123.2**	3,722.1	3,485.1
Selling, general and administrative	**2,504.5**	2,386.0	2,138.0
Depreciation and amortization	**247.4**	218.4	180.1
Interest, net	**58.2**	61.1	32.4
Total Costs and Expenses	**6,933.3**	6,387.6	5,835.6
Earnings from Continuing Operations before Taxes	**844.5**	765.6	612.7
Income Taxes	**338.9**	301.4	239.0
Earnings from Continuing Operations	**505.6**	464.2	373.7
Discontinued Operations after Taxes	**(10.0)**	8.5	7.7
Net Earnings	**$ 495.6**	$ 472.7	$ 381.4
Earnings per Share:			
Continuing operations	**$ 3.05**	$ 2.82	$ 2.27
Discontinued operations	**(.06)**	.05	.05
Net Earnings per Share	**$ 2.99**	$ 2.87	$ 2.32
Average Number of Common Shares	**165.7**	164.5	164.4

See accompanying notes to consolidated financial statements.

General Mills, Inc., and Subsidiaries

Consolidated Balance Sheets

In Millions	**May 31, 1992**	*May 26, 1991*
Assets		
Current Assets:		
Cash and cash equivalents	$ **.5**	$ 39.8
Receivables, less allowance for doubtful accounts of $6.4 in 1992 and $6.0 in 1991	**291.9**	306.3
Inventories	**487.2**	493.6
Prepaid expenses and other current assets	**106.3**	98.5
Deferred income taxes	**148.7**	144.1
Total Current Assets	**1,034.6**	1,082.3
Land, Buildings and Equipment, at cost	**2,648.6**	2,241.3
Other Assets	**621.8**	578.2
Total Assets	**$4,305.0**	$3,901.8
Liabilities and Stockholders' Equity		
Current Liabilities:		
Accounts payable	$ **632.5**	$ 578.7
Current portion of long-term debt	**32.6**	129.0
Notes payable	**169.3**	23.4
Accrued taxes	**127.9**	159.2
Accrued payroll	**165.0**	154.7
Other current liabilities	**244.4**	227.4
Total Current Liabilities	**1,371.7**	1,272.4
Long-term Debt	**920.5**	879.0
Deferred Income Taxes	**231.5**	239.4
Deferred Income Taxes – Tax Leases	**203.0**	215.8
Accrued Postretirement Benefits	**103.6**	109.5
Other Liabilities	**103.8**	72.2
Total Liabilities	**2,934.1**	2,788.3
Stockholders' Equity:		
Cumulative preference stock, none issued	**—**	—
Common stock, 204.2 shares issued	**343.6**	320.2
Retained earnings	**2,049.0**	1,795.5
Less common stock in treasury, at cost, shares of 38.7 in 1992 and 39.1 in 1991	**(802.9)**	(777.4)
Unearned ESOP and restricted stock compensation	**(172.3)**	(177.6)
Cumulative foreign currency adjustment	**(46.5)**	(47.2)
Total Stockholders' Equity	**1,370.9**	1,113.5
Total Liabilities and Stockholders' Equity	**$4,305.0**	$3,901.8

See accompanying notes to consolidated financial statements.

Consolidated Statements of Cash Flows

	Fiscal Year Ended		
In Millions	May 31, 1992	May 26, 1991	May 27, 1990
Cash Flows – Operating Activities:			
Earnings from continuing operations	**$505.6**	$464.2	$373.7
Adjustments to reconcile earnings to cash flow:			
Depreciation and amortization	**247.4**	218.4	180.1
Deferred income taxes	**13.5**	.9	12.5
Change in current assets and liabilities★	**20.0**	(96.7)	113.3
Other, net	**3.9**	(38.2)	(22.5)
Cash provided by continuing operations	**790.4**	548.6	657.1
Cash used by discontinued operations	**(18.8)**	(4.2)	(29.3)
Net Cash Provided by Operating Activities	**771.6**	544.4	627.8
Cash Flows – Investment Activities:			
Purchases of land, buildings and equipment	**(695.3)**	(554.6)	(540.0)
Investments in businesses, intangibles and affiliates	**(30.6)**	(91.6)	(.5)
Cash from disposal of land, buildings and equipment	**8.1**	9.8	12.1
Proceeds from dispositions	**77.7**	114.6	32.6
Other, net	**(7.9)**	(33.9)	(34.4)
Net Cash Used by Investment Activities	**(648.0)**	(555.7)	(530.2)
Cash Flows – Financing Activities:			
Increase (decrease) in notes payable	**150.3**	(80.0)	(24.5)
Issuance of long-term debt	**188.7**	373.0	142.4
Payment of long-term debt	**(248.0)**	(132.8)	(60.7)
(Increase) decrease in marketable investments and time deposits	—	67.7	(.6)
Cash flows from tax leases	**(7.9)**	(8.4)	(2.3)
Common stock issued	**39.3**	41.5	168.9
Purchases of common stock for treasury	**(40.1)**	—	(149.9)
Dividends paid	**(245.2)**	(210.6)	(180.8)
Net Cash Provided (Used) by Financing Activities	**(162.9)**	50.4	(107.5)
Increase (Decrease) in Cash and Cash Equivalents	**$ (39.3)**	$ 39.1	$ (9.9)

★Cash Flow from Changes in Current Assets and Liabilities:			
Receivables	**$ 2.1**	$ (47.4)	$ (1.5)
Inventories	**.6**	(109.8)	(22.4)
Prepaid expenses and other current assets	**(8.9)**	(19.0)	(6.6)
Accounts payable	**54.5**	63.1	79.1
Other current liabilities	**(28.3)**	16.4	64.7
Change in Current Assets and Liabilities	**$ 20.0**	$ (96.7)	$113.3

See accompanying notes to consolidated financial statements.

Notes to Consolidated Financial Statements

Note One: Summary of Significant Accounting Policies

A. Principles of Consolidation

The consolidated financial statements include the following domestic and foreign operations: parent company and 100% owned subsidiaries, and General Mills' investment in and share of net earnings or losses of 20-50% owned companies.

Our fiscal year ends on the last Sunday in May. Fiscal year 1992 consisted of 53 weeks, and fiscal years 1991 and 1990 each consisted of 52 weeks.

B. Land, Buildings, Equipment and Depreciation

Buildings and equipment are depreciated over estimated useful lives ranging from three to 50 years, primarily using the straight-line method. Accelerated depreciation methods are generally used for income tax purposes.

When an item is sold or retired, the accounts are relieved of cost and the related accumulated depreciation; the resulting gains and losses, if any, are recognized.

C. Inventories

Inventories are valued at the lower of cost or market. Certain domestic inventories are valued using the LIFO method, while other inventories are generally valued using the FIFO method.

D. Intangible Assets

Goodwill represents the difference between purchase prices of acquired companies and the related fair values of net assets acquired and accounted for by the purchase method of accounting. Goodwill acquired after October 1970 is amortized on a straight-line basis over 40 years or less.

Intangible assets include an amount that offsets a minimum liability recorded for a pension plan with assets less than accumulated benefits as required by Financial Accounting Standard No. 87.

The costs of patents, copyrights and other intangible assets are amortized evenly over their estimated useful lives. Most of these costs were incurred through purchases of businesses.

The Audit Committee of the Board of Directors annually reviews goodwill and other intangibles. At its meeting on April 27, 1992, the Board of Directors affirmed that the remaining amounts of these assets have continuing value.

E. Research and Development

All expenditures for research and development are charged against earnings in the year incurred. The charges for fiscal 1992, 1991 and 1990 were $62.1 million, $57.0 million and $48.2 million, respectively.

F. Income Taxes

Income taxes include deferred income taxes that result from timing differences between earnings for financial reporting and tax purposes.

G. Earnings per Share

Earnings per share has been determined by dividing the appropriate earnings by the weighted average number of common shares outstanding during the year. Common share equivalents were not material.

H. Foreign Currency Translation

For most foreign operations, local currencies are considered the functional currency. Assets and liabilities are translated using the exchange rates in effect at the balance sheet date. Results of operations are translated using the average exchange rates prevailing throughout the period. Translation effects are accumulated in the foreign currency adjustment in stockholders' equity.

Gains and losses from foreign currency transactions are generally included in net earnings for the period.

We selectively utilize foreign exchange contracts to hedge foreign currency exposure related to operating activities and net investments in foreign operations. Realized and unrealized gains and losses on contracts that hedge operating activities are recognized currently in net earnings. Realized and unrealized gains and losses on contracts that hedge net investments are recognized in the foreign currency adjustment in stockholders' equity. At May 31, 1992, we had forward contracts maturing in fiscal 1993 to sell $297.8 million and purchase $15.5 million of foreign currencies.

I. Statements of Cash Flows

For purposes of the statement of cash flows, we consider all investments purchased with a maturity of three months or less to be cash equivalents.

Note Two: Discontinued Operations

No operations were discontinued in fiscal 1992. However, we recorded a net after-tax charge related to previously discontinued operations of $10.0 million ($.06 per share). This charge primarily relates to a lease adjustment with the R.H. Macy Company which is operating under bankruptcy law protection.

In fiscal 1990, we sold Vroman Foods, our frozen novelties operation, for proceeds of $24.5 million and adjusted our estimated disposition loss recorded in fiscal 1989, recording after-tax income of $9.6 million ($.06 per share).

Other minor adjustments were made during fiscal 1992, 1991 and 1990 for previously discontinued operations.

Sales for the discontinued operations were $9.5 million in fiscal 1990.

Note Three: Unusual Items

In fiscal 1992, we recognized a gain on the sale of the stock of our Spanish frozen food subsidiary, Preparados y Congelados Alimenticios, S.A. (PYCASA) and also recorded charges primarily related to restructuring our Betty Crocker packaged mixes production, European food operations, Consumer Foods national sales organization and the call of our 9⅜% sinking fund debentures. These transactions resulted in no net effect on earnings.

In fiscal 1991, we recognized gains on the sale of the net assets of our O-Cel-O Division, a cellulose sponge operation, and Lancia Bravo, our Canadian pasta operation. We also recorded charges primarily related to restructuring our Yoplait yogurt and hot oatmeal cereal operations. These transactions resulted in an increase in net earnings of $26.5 million ($.16 per share).

Note Four: Investments in Affiliates and Intangibles

During fiscal 1992, we made additional capital contributions and advances of $24.3 million to Cereal Partners Worldwide (CPW), our joint venture with Nestlé S.A.

During fiscal 1991, we invested $88.2 million in CPW. This investment consisted primarily of capital contributions and advances of $70.1 million, and our purchase of intangible assets related to RHM Breakfast Cereals (RHM) for $18.1 million. CPW purchased the RHM business in the United Kingdom.

Note Five: Inventories

The components of inventories are as follows:

In Millions	May 31, 1992	May 26, 1991
Raw materials, work in process and supplies	**$202.0**	$227.4
Finished goods	**290.3**	274.6
Grain	**61.9**	67.5
Reserve for LIFO valuation method	**(67.0)**	(75.9)
Total inventories	**$487.2**	$493.6

At May 31, 1992 and May 26, 1991, respectively, inventories of $266.3 million and $241.4 million were valued at LIFO. If the FIFO method of inventory accounting had been used in place of LIFO, reported earnings per share would have been lower by $.03 in fiscal 1992 and higher by $.02 in fiscal 1991 and 1990.

Note Six: Balance Sheet Information

The components of certain balance sheet items are as follows:

In Millions	May 31, 1992	May 26, 1991
Land, Buildings and Equipment:		
Land	**$ 253.9**	$ 215.2
Buildings	**1,302.2**	1,116.6
Equipment	**1,903.2**	1,701.6
Construction in progress	**450.0**	303.7
Total land, buildings and equipment	**3,909.3**	3,337.1
Less accumulated depreciation	**(1,260.7)**	(1,095.8)
Net land, buildings and equipment	**$2,648.6**	$2,241.3
Other Assets:		
Prepaid pension	**$ 217.4**	$ 173.5
Marketable investments, at cost	**170.4**	167.9
Intangible assets	**81.0**	79.2
Investments in and advances to affiliates	**70.2**	70.2
Miscellaneous	**82.8**	87.4
Total other assets	**$ 621.8**	$ 578.2

Note Seven: Notes Payable

The components of notes payable are as follows:

In Millions	May 31, 1992	May 26, 1991
U.S. commercial paper	**$ 58.0**	$ 70.0
Canadian commercial paper	**103.1**	83.7
Financial institutions	**158.2**	19.7
Amount reclassified to long-term debt	**(150.0)**	(150.0)
Total notes payable	**$169.3**	$ 23.4

To ensure availability of funds, we maintain bank credit lines sufficient to cover our outstanding commercial paper. As of May 31, 1992, we had $225.0 million fee-paid lines and $295.8 million uncommitted, no-fee lines available in the U.S. and Canada. In addition, other foreign subsidiaries had unused credit lines of $79.8 million.

We have a revolving credit agreement expiring in fiscal 1994 that provides for the fee-paid credit lines. This agreement provides us with the ability to refinance short-term borrowings on a long-term basis, and therefore we have reclassified a portion of our notes payable to long-term.

We have U.S. and Canadian interest rate swap agreements with commercial banks that convert variable interest rates to fixed interest rates as follows:

In Millions			Notional Amount	
Expiration Date	Fixed Rate	Type	May 31, 1992	May 26, 1991
June 1994	8.83%	Swap	**$ 25.0**	$ 25.0
November 1993	9.53	Swap	**74.0**	74.0
November 1993	7.00	Option	**50.0**	—
May 1992	9.38	Swap	—	25.0
April 1992	9.79	Swap	—	50.0
January 1992	11.04	Swap	—	26.1
August 1991	12.28	Swap	—	21.8
Total notional amount			**$149.0**	$221.9

We have an interest rate swap agreement that converts the fixed interest rate to a variable interest rate on $13.0 million of nine-month commercial paper notes (3.68% at May 31, 1992).

We have a forward agreement to enter into a 10-year interest rate swap to pay 40.5 basis points over 10-year U.S. Treasury securities on a notional amount of $50.0 million with an expiration date of May 1993.

Any interest rate differential on interest rate swaps is recognized as an adjustment of interest expense over the term of the agreement. We are exposed to credit loss in the event of nonperformance by the other parties to these agreements. However, we do not anticipate any losses.

Note Eight: Long-term Debt

In Millions	May 31, 1992	May 26, 1991
Zero coupon notes, yield 11.14%, $481.6 due August 15, 2013	**$ 49.2**	$ 48.4
9⅜% sinking fund debentures due March 1, 2009	—	109.9
ESOP loan guaranty, variable rate (3.2% at May 31, 1992), due December 31, 2007	**50.0**	50.0
8.31% ESOP loan guaranty, due through June 30, 2007	**85.5**	89.8
Zero coupon notes, yield 11.73%, $67.8 due August 15, 2004	**17.0**	15.1
6.24% to 9.14% medium-term notes, due 1993 to 2007	**571.6**	391.3
Currency purchase obligation, yield 9.29%, due through November 15, 1993	**12.5**	19.9
12% notes due December 19, 1991	—	63.7
Zero coupon notes, yield 14⅝%, $49.3 due June 30, 1991	—	48.7
Notes payable, reclassified	**150.0**	150.0
Other, no individual item greater than $3.1	**17.3**	21.2
	953.1	1,008.0
Less amounts due within one year	**(32.6)**	(129.0)
Total long-term debt	**$920.5**	$ 879.0

Our shelf registration statement permits the issuance of up to $307.1 million net proceeds in unsecured debt securities to reduce short-term debt and for other general corporate purposes. This registration authorizes a medium-term note program that allows us to issue debt quickly for various amounts and at various rates and maturities.

In fiscal 1992, we issued $181.3 million of debt under our medium-term note program with maturities from three to 15 years and interest rates from 6.24% to 8.13%. In fiscal 1991, $310.6 million of debt was issued under this program with maturities from three to 15 years and interest rates from 8.46% to 9.14%.

We have an interest rate swap agreement that converts the fixed interest rate to a variable interest rate on $100.0 million of medium-term notes (3.88% at May 31, 1992).

In fiscal 1992, we called our 9⅜% sinking fund debentures due March 1, 2009 (see note three). This transaction resulted in a decrease in net earnings of $3.5 million ($.02 per share).

The Company has guaranteed the debt of the Employee Stock Ownership Plans; therefore, the loans are reflected on our consolidated balance sheets in long-term debt with a related offset in stockholders' equity, "Unearned ESOP and restricted stock compensation."

The currency purchase obligation had a variable rate at May 31, 1992 of 3.86%. The obligation is secured by $13.0 million of corporate commercial paper, which is held under a trust agreement.

The sinking fund and principal payments due on long-term debt are (in millions) $32.6, $49.3, $37.2, $72.8 and $94.1 in fiscal years ending 1993, 1994, 1995, 1996 and 1997, respectively. The notes payable that are reclassified under our revolving credit agreement are not included in these principal payments.

Our marketable investments consist of corporate commercial paper and zero coupon U.S. Treasury securities. These investments are intended to provide the funds for the payment of principal and interest for the zero coupon notes due August 15, 2013 and 2004, and the currency purchase obligation.

Certain debt issues have been removed from our consolidated balance sheets through the creation of irrevocable trusts. The principal and interest of the securities deposited with the trustee will be sufficient to fund the scheduled principal and interest payments of these debt issues. At May 31, 1992, there was $58.6 million of this debt outstanding.

Note Nine: Stock Options

The following table contains information on stock options:

	Shares	Average Option Price per Share
Granted		
1992	**2,574,008**	**$58.29**
1991	2,931,372	42.50
1990	2,777,196	34.71
Exercised		
1992	**1,026,760**	**$19.64**
1991	1,578,774	16.32
1990	1,101,120	15.58
Expired		
1992	**175,804**	**$39.12**
1991	272,910	27.33
1990	193,458	23.76
Outstanding at year-end		
1992	**13,030,720**	**$35.88**
1991	11,659,276	29.55
1990	10,579,588	23.93
Exercisable at year-end		
1992	**8,938,384**	**$28.71**
1991	7,202,248	24.19
1990	6,139,424	19.15

A total of 9,372,246 shares are available for grants of options or restricted stock to officers and key employees under our 1988 and 1990 stock plans through September 30, 1995. The options may be granted at a price not less than 100% of fair market value on the date the option is granted. Options now outstanding include some granted under the 1980 and 1984 option plans, under which no further options or other rights may be granted. All options expire within 10 years plus one month after the date of grant. The plans provide for full vesting of the option in the event there is a change of control.

The 1988 plan permits awards of restricted stock to key employees subject to a restricted period and a purchase price, if any, to be paid by the employee as determined by the Compensation Committee of the Board of Directors. In fiscal 1992, grants of 79,918 shares of restricted stock were made and on May 31, 1992, there were 256,415 of such shares outstanding.

The 1988 plan also permits the granting of performance units corresponding to stock options granted. The value of performance units will be determined by return on equity and growth in earnings per share measured against preset goals over three-year performance periods. For seven years after a performance period, holders may elect to receive the value of performance units (with interest) as an alternative to exercising corresponding stock options. On May 31, 1992, there were 4,315,214 outstanding options with corresponding performance units or performance unit accounts.

The 1988 plan provides for the granting of incentive stock options as well as non-qualified options. No incentive stock options have been granted.

A total of 62,400 shares are available for grants of options and restricted stock to non-employee directors until September 30, 1995 under a separate 1990 stock plan. An option to purchase 2,500 shares is granted upon becoming a member of the Board of Directors at fair market value on the date of grant. Options expire 10 years after the date of grant. Each year 400 shares of restricted stock will be awarded to each non-employee director, restricted until the later of the expiration of one year or completion of service on the Board of Directors.

General Mills, Inc., and Subsidiaries

Note Ten: Stockholders' Equity

In Millions, Except per Share Data	Issued Shares	Issued Amount	Treasury Shares	Treasury Amount	Retained Earnings	Unearned ESOP and Restricted Stock Compensation	Cumulative Foreign Currency Adjustment	Total
Balance at May 28, 1989	204.2	$222.3	(43.0)	$(781.9)	$1,327.8	$ —	$(36.3)	$ 731.9
Net earnings					381.4			381.4
Cash dividends declared ($1.10 per share), net of income taxes of $2.2					(178.6)			(178.6)
Stock option, profit sharing and ESOP plans		74.8	6.5	119.1				193.9
Shares purchased on open market			(4.5)	(149.9)				(149.9)
Unearned compensation related to:								
Guaranties of ESOPs debt						(142.4)		(142.4)
Note receivable from ESOP						(25.0)		(25.0)
Earned compensation						2.7		2.7
Translation adjustments, net of income taxes of $7.2							(4.3)	(4.3)
Balance at May 27, 1990	204.2	297.1	(41.0)	(812.7)	1,530.6	(164.7)	(40.6)	809.7
Net earnings					472.7			472.7
Cash dividends declared ($1.28 per share), net of income taxes of $2.8					(207.8)			(207.8)
Stock option, profit sharing and ESOP plans		23.1	1.9	35.3				58.4
Unearned compensation related to:								
Note receivable from ESOP						(10.0)		(10.0)
Restricted stock awards						(8.2)		(8.2)
Earned compensation						5.3		5.3
Translation adjustments, net of income taxes of $1.4							(6.6)	(6.6)
Balance at May 26, 1991	204.2	320.2	(39.1)	(777.4)	1,795.5	(177.6)	(47.2)	1,113.5
Net earnings					495.6			495.6
Cash dividends declared ($1.48 per share), net of income taxes of $3.1					(242.1)			(242.1)
Stock option, profit sharing and ESOP plans		23.4	1.1	21.5				44.9
Shares purchased on open market			(.7)	(47.0)				(47.0)
Unearned compensation related to restricted stock awards						(4.3)		(4.3)
Earned compensation						9.6		9.6
Translation adjustments, net of income taxes of $.7							(6.7)	(6.7)
Amount charged to gain on sale of foreign operation							7.4	7.4
Balance at May 31, 1992	**204.2**	**$343.6**	**(38.7)**	**$(802.9)**	**$2,049.0**	**$(172.3)**	**$(46.5)**	**$1,370.9**

Cumulative preference stock of 5.0 million shares, without par value, is authorized but unissued.

We have a shareholder rights plan that entitles each outstanding share of common stock to one-fourth of a right. Each right entitles the holder to purchase one one-hundredth of a share of cumulative preference stock (or, in certain circumstances, common stock or other securities), exercisable upon the occurrence of certain events. The rights are not transferable apart from the common stock until a person or group has acquired 20% or more, or makes a tender offer for 20% or more, of the common stock. If the Company is then acquired in a merger or other business combination transaction, each right will entitle the holder (other than the acquiring company) to receive, upon exercise, common stock of either the Company or the acquiring company having a value equal to two times the exercise price of the right. The rights are redeemable by the Board in certain circumstances and expire on March 7, 1996. At May 31, 1992, there were 41.4 million rights issued and outstanding.

The Board of Directors has authorized the repurchase, from time to time, of common stock for our treasury, provided that the number of shares in the treasury shall not exceed 50.0 million.

Note Eleven: Interest Expense

The components of net interest expense are as follows:

In Millions	Fiscal Year 1992	1991	1990
Interest expense	**$89.5**	$94.0	$75.5
Capitalized interest	**(13.6)**	(9.9)	(14.2)
Interest income	**(17.7)**	(23.0)	(28.9)
Interest expense, net	**$58.2**	$61.1	$32.4

During fiscal 1992, 1991 and 1990, we actually paid interest (net of amount capitalized) of $70.7 million, $64.7 million and $54.6 million, respectively.

Note Twelve: Retirement Plans

We have defined benefit plans covering most employees. Benefits for salaried employees are based on length of service and final average compensation. The hourly plans include various monthly amounts for each year of credited service. Our funding policy is consistent with the funding requirements of federal law and regulations. Our principal plan covering salaried employees has a provision that any excess pension assets would be vested in plan participants if the plan is terminated within five years of a change in control. Plan assets consist principally of listed equity securities and corporate obligations, and U.S. government securities.

Components of the net pension credit are as follows:

In Millions	Fiscal Year 1992	1991	1990
Service cost—benefits earned	**$ 14.2**	$ 12.8	$ 13.0
Interest cost on projected benefit obligation	**51.2**	49.4	46.1
Actual return on plan assets	**(75.0)**	(70.6)	(84.8)
Net amortization and deferral	**(26.1)**	(26.1)	(8.8)
Net pension credit	**$(35.7)**	$(34.5)	$(34.5)

The weighted-average discount rate and rate of increase in future compensation levels used in determining the actuarial present value of the benefit obligations were 9.5% and 6% in fiscal 1992, and 9.73% and 6% in fiscal 1991, respectively. The expected long-term rate of return on assets was 11.35%.

The funded status of the plans and the amount recognized on the consolidated balance sheets (as determined as of May 31, 1992 and 1991) are as follows:

In Millions	May 31, 1992 Assets Exceed Accumulated Benefits	May 31, 1992 Accumulated Benefits Exceed Assets	May 26, 1991 Assets Exceed Accumulated Benefits	May 26, 1991 Accumulated Benefits Exceed Assets
Actuarial present value of benefit obligations:				
Vested benefits	**$453.6**	**$ 11.3**	$425.4	$ 7.7
Nonvested benefits	**41.7**	**2.2**	37.4	3.3
Accumulated benefit obligation	**495.3**	**13.5**	462.8	11.0
Projected benefit obligation	**568.3**	**19.3**	526.1	17.5
Plan assets at fair value	**824.8**	**—**	786.7	—
Plan assets in excess of (less than) the projected benefit obligation	**256.5**	**(19.3)**	260.6	(17.5)
Unrecognized prior service cost	**28.3**	**.4**	26.9	.5
Unrecognized net loss	**97.9**	**7.1**	67.6	4.9
Recognition of minimum liability	**—**	**(11.4)**	—	(9.6)
Unrecognized transition (asset) liability	**(165.3)**	**9.7**	(181.6)	10.7
Prepaid (accrued) pension cost	**$217.4**	**$(13.5)**	$173.5	$(11.0)

We have defined contribution plans covering salaried and non-union employees. Contributions are determined by matching a percentage of employee contributions. Such plans had net assets of $658.2 million at May 31, 1992. Expense recognized in fiscal 1992, 1991 and 1990 was $12.7 million, $16.1 million and $18.8 million, respectively.

Within our defined contribution plans we have Employee Stock Ownership Plans (ESOP). These ESOPs borrowed funds guaranteed by the Company with terms described in the long-term debt footnote, and borrowed $35.0 million from the Company at a variable interest rate (4.07% at May 31, 1992) with $10.0 million due June 15, 2015 and $25.0 million due December 15, 2014. Compensation expense is recognized as contributions are accrued. Our contributions to the plans, plus the dividends accumulated on the common stock held by the ESOPs, are used to pay principal, interest and expenses of the plans. As loan payments are made, common stock is allocated to ESOP participants. In fiscal 1992, 1991 and 1990, the ESOPs incurred interest expense of $11.3 million, $13.4 million and $12.1 million, respectively, and used dividends received of $7.8 million, $6.4 million and $5.4 million and contributions received from the Company of $7.1 million, $12.1 million and $11.7 million, respectively, to pay principal and interest on their debt.

Note Thirteen: Other Postretirement Benefits

We sponsor several plans that provide health care benefits to the majority of our retirees. The salaried plan is contributory with retiree contributions based on years of service.

We fund a plan for certain employees and retirees on an annual basis. In fiscal 1992, 1991 and 1990 we contributed $4.2 million, $4.0 million and $19.8 million, respectively, to a trust with plan assets consisting principally of listed equity securities and U.S. government securities.

Components of the postretirement health care expense are as follows:

		Fiscal Year	
In Millions	1992	1991	1990
Service cost—benefits earned	$3.5	$ 3.8	$ 3.4
Interest cost on accumulated benefit obligation	9.7	10.5	9.7
Actual return on plan assets	(3.0)	(2.3)	—
Net amortization and deferral	(1.2)	(.9)	(.9)
Net postretirement expense	$9.0	$11.1	$12.2

We initially adopted accrual accounting for the expense of these plans in fiscal 1989 by setting up a liability of $115.7 million. The amount accrued on the consolidated balance sheets as of May 31, 1992 is $103.6 million. The table below indicates this liability and the funded status of the plans.

In Millions	May 31, 1992	May 26, 1991
Accumulated benefit obligation:		
Retirees	$ 56.3	$ 57.6
Fully eligible active employees	16.2	15.5
Other active employees	46.4	40.4
Accumulated benefit obligation	118.9	113.5
Plan assets at fair value	28.5	23.8
Accumulated benefit obligation in excess of plan assets	90.4	89.7
Unrecognized prior service cost	16.4	18.4
Unrecognized net gain (loss)	(3.2)	1.4
Accrued postretirement benefits	$103.6	$109.5

There are assumptions used in determining the accumulated postretirement benefit obligation and related expense. The discount rate used in determining the benefit obligation was 9.5% and 8.75% in fiscal 1992 and 1991, respectively. The expected long-term rate of return on assets was 9.6%.

The health care cost trend rate increase in the per capita charges for benefits ranged from 9.4% to 15.4% for fiscal 1993 depending on the medical service category. The rates gradually decrease to 4.5% to 5.8% for fiscal 2017 and remain at that level thereafter. If the health care cost trend rate were increased by one percentage point in each future year, the aggregate of the service and interest cost components of postretirement expense would increase for fiscal 1992 by $2.3 million and the accumulated postretirement benefit obligation as of May 31, 1992 would increase by $15.3 million.

Note Fourteen: Profit-sharing Plans

We have profit-sharing plans to provide incentives to key individuals who have the greatest potential to contribute to current earnings and successful future operations. These plans were approved by the Board of Directors upon recommendation of the Compensation Committee. The awards under these plans depend on profit performance in relation to pre-established goals. The plans are administered by the Compensation Committee, which consists solely of outside directors. Profit-sharing expense, including performance unit accruals, was $8.8 million, $11.0 million and $11.2 million in fiscal 1992, 1991 and 1990, respectively.

Note Fifteen: Income Taxes

The components of earnings before income taxes and the income taxes thereon are as follows:

In Millions	Fiscal Year 1992	1991	1990
Earnings before income taxes:			
U.S.	**$818.3**	$710.4	$584.9
Foreign	**26.2**	55.2	27.8
Total earnings before income taxes	**$844.5**	$765.6	$612.7
Income taxes:			
Current:			
Federal	**$254.0**	$238.3	$183.8
State and local	**55.1**	49.9	37.6
Foreign	**16.3**	12.3	5.1
Total current	**325.4**	300.5	226.5
Deferred (principally U.S.)	**13.5**	.9	12.5
Total income taxes	**$338.9**	$301.4	$239.0

During fiscal 1992, 1991 and 1990, we paid income taxes of $326.4 million, $257.7 million and $231.3 million, respectively.

In prior years we purchased certain income tax items from other companies through tax lease transactions. Total current income taxes charged to earnings in fiscal 1992, 1991 and 1990 reflect the amounts attributable to operations and have not been materially affected by these tax leases. Actual current taxes payable on fiscal 1992, 1991 and 1990 operations were increased by approximately $10 million, $9 million and $4 million, respectively, due to the effect of tax leases. These tax payments do not affect taxes for statement of earnings purposes since they repay tax benefits realized in prior years. The repayment liability is classified as "Deferred Income Taxes–Tax Leases."

Deferred income taxes result from timing differences in the recognition of revenue and expense for tax and financial statement purposes. The tax effects of these differences follow:

In Millions	Fiscal Year 1992	1991	1990
Depreciation	**$ 6.5**	$10.8	$13.8
Prepaid pension asset	**16.8**	16.1	14.8
Accrued expenses	**(1.1)**	(28.0)	(30.6)
Other	**(8.7)**	2.0	14.5
Total deferred income taxes	**$13.5**	$ .9	$12.5

The following table reconciles the U.S. statutory income tax rate with the effective income tax rate:

	Fiscal Year 1992	1991	1990
U.S. statutory rate	**34.0%**	34.0%	34.0%
State and local income taxes, net of federal tax benefits	**4.9**	4.3	4.2
Other, net	**1.2**	1.1	.8
Effective income tax rate	**40.1%**	39.4%	39.0%

Provision has been made for foreign and U.S. taxes that would be payable on foreign operations' earnings that are not considered permanently reinvested. Additional income taxes have not been provided on unremitted earnings of foreign operations amounting to $106.4 million that are expected by management to be permanently reinvested. If a portion were to be remitted, income tax credits would substantially offset any resulting tax liability.

Note Sixteen: Leases

An analysis of rent expense by property leased follows:

In Millions	Fiscal Year 1992	1991	1990
Restaurant space	**$33.9**	$27.8	$22.9
Warehouse space	**12.6**	11.8	9.7
Equipment	**8.3**	5.9	5.5
Other	**5.4**	4.8	5.2
Total rent expense	**$60.2**	$50.3	$43.3

Some leases require payment of property taxes, insurance and maintenance costs in addition to the rent payments. Contingent and escalation rent in excess of minimum rent payments and sublease income netted in rent expense were insignificant.

Noncancelable future lease commitments are (in millions) $57.0 in 1993, $52.0 in 1994, $50.1 in 1995, $46.5 in 1996, $42.9 in 1997 and $263.9 after 1997, with a cumulative total of $512.4.

General Mills, Inc., and Subsidiaries

Note Seventeen: Segment Information

In Millions	Consumer Foods	Restaurants	Unallocated Corporate Items (a)	Consolidated Total
Sales				
1992	**$5,233.8**	**$2,544.0**		**$7,777.8**
1991	4,939.7	2,213.5		7,153.2
1990	4,520.3	1,928.0		6,448.3
Operating Profits				
1992	**744.3(b)**	**190.8**	**$ (90.6)**	**844.5**
1991	689.5(c)	172.2	(96.1)	765.6
1990	533.9	154.2	(75.4)	612.7
Identifiable Assets (d)				
1992	**2,481.2**	**1,419.3**	**404.5**	**4,305.0**
1991	2,189.2	1,256.4	456.2	3,901.8
1990	1,834.2	1,038.2	417.1	3,289.5
Capital Expenditures				
1992	**397.1**	**297.0**	**1.2**	**695.3**
1991	277.6	273.0	4.0	554.6
1990	298.2	239.1	2.7	540.0
Depreciation Expense				
1992	**140.3**	**99.4**	**2.3**	**242.0**
1991	131.7	79.7	2.0	213.4
1990	110.2	64.2	1.7	176.1

	U.S.A.	Foreign	Unallocated Corporate Items (a)	Consolidated Total
Sales				
1992	**$7,039.6**	**$738.2**		**$7,777.8**
1991	6,376.8	776.4		7,153.2
1990	5,796.1	652.2		6,448.3
Operating Profits				
1992	**896.3(b)**	**38.8(b)**	**$ (90.6)**	**844.5**
1991	805.8(c)	55.9(c)	(96.1)	765.6
1990	655.9	32.2	(75.4)	612.7
Identifiable Assets (d)				
1992	**3,452.2**	**448.3**	**404.5**	**4,305.0**
1991	3,001.5	444.1	456.2	3,901.8
1990	2,543.3	329.1	417.1	3,289.5

(a) Corporate expenses reported here include net interest expense and general corporate expenses.
(b) Consumer Foods operating profits include a net gain of $17.5 million (U.S.A. $20.5 million loss; Foreign $38.0 million gain) for unusual items described in note three.
(c) Consumer Foods operating profits include a net gain of $48.2 million (U.S.A. $20.9 million; Foreign $27.3 million) for unusual items described in note three.
(d) Identifiable assets for our segments consist mainly of receivables, inventories, prepaid expenses, net land, buildings and equipment, and other assets. Corporate identifiable assets consist mainly of cash, cash equivalents, deferred income taxes and marketable investments.

Note Eighteen: Quarterly Data (unaudited)

Summarized quarterly data for fiscal 1992 and 1991 follow:

In Millions, Except per Share and Market Price Amounts	First Quarter 1992	1991	Second Quarter 1992	1991	Third Quarter 1992	1991	Fourth Quarter 1992	1991	Total Year 1992	1991
Sales	**$1,916.5**	$1,739.5	**$1,992.5**	$1,836.8	**$1,868.3**	$1,747.6	**$2,000.5**	$1,829.3	**$7,777.8**	$7,153.2
Gross profit (a)	914.6	828.5	946.9	874.1	884.9	870.5	908.2	858.0	3,654.6	3,431.1
Earnings after taxes —										
Continuing operations	**142.1**	123.8	**128.3**	118.2(b)	**132.1**	131.3(c)	**103.1**	90.9	**505.6**	464.2
Earnings per share —										
Continuing operations	**.86**	.75	**.77**	.72	**.80**	.80	**.62**	.55	**3.05**	2.82
Discontinued operations after taxes	—	5.7	—	—	—	2.8	**(10.0)**	—	**(10.0)**	8.5
Net earnings	**142.1**	129.5	**128.3**	118.2	**132.1**	134.1	**93.1**	90.9	**495.6**	472.7
Net earnings per share	**.86**	.79	**.77**	.72	**.80**	.81	**.56**	.55	**2.99**	2.87
Dividends per share	**.37**	.32	**.37**	.32	**.37**	.32	**.37**	.32	**1.48**	1.28
Market price of common stock:										
High	**64**	47½	**68⅝**	45⅜	**75⅞**	54¾	**70⅛**	60⅞	**75⅞**	60⅞
Low	**54¼**	37⅞	**58⅝**	39½	**64⅛**	43½	**58¾**	52⅛	**54¼**	37⅞

(a) Before charges for depreciation.
(b) Includes a net after-tax gain of $9.2 million ($.06 per share) from the sale of our Lancia Bravo pasta operation and a restructuring charge for Yoplait yogurt operations.
(c) Includes a net after-tax gain of $17.3 million ($.10 per share) from the sale of our O-Cel-O sponge operation and restructuring charges primarily for hot cereal operations.

Eleven Year Financial Summary as Reported

Amounts in Millions, Except per Share Data	May 31, 1992	May 26, 1991	May 27, 1990	May 28, 1989	May 29, 1988	May 31, 1987	May 25, 1986	May 26, 1985	May 27, 1984	May 29, 1983	May 30, 1982
Financial Results											
Earnings (loss) per share (a)	$ **2.99**	$ 2.87	$ 2.32	$ 2.53	$ 1.63	$ 1.25	$ 1.03	$ (.41)	$ 1.24	$ 1.22	$ 1.11
Return on average equity	**39.9%**	49.2%	49.5%	60.0%	41.1%	31.4%	21.5%	(6.5)%	19.0%	19.9%	19.1%
Dividends per share (a)	**1.48**	1.28	1.10	.94	.80	.625	.565	.56	.51	.46	.41
Sales (b)	**7,777.8**	7,153.2	6,448.3	5,620.6	5,178.8	5,189.3	4,586.6	4,285.2	5,600.8	5,550.8	5,312.1
Costs and expenses:											
Cost of sales (b)	**4,123.2**	3,722.1	3,485.1	3,114.8	2,847.8	2,834.0	2,563.9	2,474.8	3,165.9	3,123.3	3,081.6
Selling, general and administrative (b)	**2,504.5**	2,386.0	2,138.0	1,808.5	1,710.5	1,757.5	1,547.2	1,443.9	1,841.7	1,831.6	1,635.5
Depreciation and amortization (b)	**247.4**	218.4	180.1	152.3	140.0	131.7	113.1	110.4	133.1	127.5	113.2
Interest (b)(c)	**58.2**	61.1	32.4	27.5	37.7	32.9	38.8	60.2	61.4	58.7	75.1
Earnings before income taxes (b)	**844.5**	765.6	612.7	517.5	442.8	433.2	323.6	195.9(d)	398.7	409.7	406.7
Net earnings (loss)	**495.6**	472.7	381.4	414.3(e)	283.1	222.0	183.5	(72.9)(f)	233.4	245.1	225.5
Net earnings (loss) as a percent of sales	**6.4%**	6.6%	5.9%	7.4%	5.5%	4.3%	4.0%	(1.7)%	4.2%	4.4%	4.2%
Weighted average number of common shares (a)	**165.7**	164.5	164.4	163.9	174.0	177.5	178.5	179.0	187.5	200.4	202.4
Taxes (income, payroll, property, etc.) per share (a)(b)	**3.09**	2.77	2.29	1.98	1.66	1.80	1.33	1.00	1.56	1.43	1.47
Financial Position											
Total assets	**4,305.0**	3,901.8	3,289.5	2,888.1	2,671.9	2,280.4	2,086.2	2,662.6	2,858.1	2,943.9	2,701.7
Land, buildings and equipment, net	**2,648.6**	2,241.3	1,934.5	1,588.1	1,376.4	1,249.5	1,084.9	956.0	1,229.4	1,197.5	1,054.1
Working capital at year end	**(337.1)**	(190.1)	(263.1)	(197.1)	(205.5)	(57.1)	41.6	229.4	244.5	235.6	210.7
Long-term debt, excluding current portion	**920.5**	879.0	688.5	536.3	361.5	285.5	458.3	449.5	362.6	464.0	331.9
Stockholders' equity	**1,370.9**	1,113.5	809.7	731.9	648.5	730.4	682.5	1,023.3	1,224.6	1,227.4	1,232.2
Stockholders' equity per share (a)	**8.28**	6.74	4.96	4.54	3.88	4.14	3.81	5.76	6.76	6.42	6.13
Other Statistics											
Cash provided by operations (b)	**790.4**	548.6	657.1	527.3	329.9	442.9	466.5	150.4	236.1	438.8	280.2
Total dividends	**245.2**	210.6	180.8	154.4	139.3	110.8	100.9	100.4	96.0	92.7	82.3
Gross capital expenditures (g)	**695.3**	554.6	540.0	442.4	410.7	329.1	244.9	209.7	282.4	308.0	287.3
Research and development (b)	**62.1**	57.0	48.2	41.2	40.7	38.3	41.7	38.7	63.5	60.6	53.8
Advertising media expenditures (b)	**426.8**	419.6	394.9	336.5	345.9	330.0	317.0	274.3	349.6	336.2	284.9
Wages, salaries and employee benefits (b)	**1,398.5**	1,331.6	1,171.5	987.1	911.3	958.6	895.8	860.2	1,121.6	1,115.2	1,028.4
Number of employees (b)	**111,501**	108,077	97,238	83,837	74,453	65,619	62,056	63,162	80,297	81,186	75,893
Accumulated LIFO reserve	**67.0**	75.9	71.4	65.5	53.0	51.5	45.8	47.5	79.7	79.7	75.5
Common stock price range (a)	**75⅞**	60⅞	39⅝	33⅞	31	28	20	15⅛	14¼	14⅜	10½
	54¼	37⅞	31⅜	22⅜	20⅜	18½	13	11⅞	10⅜	9⅝	8⅛

(a) Years prior to fiscal 1991 have been adjusted for the two-for-one stock splits in November 1990 and 1986.
(b) Includes continuing operations only; years prior to fiscal 1989 include the discontinued cafeteria-style restaurant and frozen novelties operations, years prior to fiscal 1988 include the discontinued specialty retailing apparel operations, years prior to fiscal 1987 include the discontinued furniture operations, and years prior to fiscal 1985 include the discontinued toy, fashion and specialty retailing non-apparel operations.
(c) Interest expense is net of interest income; amounts for years prior to fiscal 1986 are interest expense only with interest income included in selling, general and administrative expenses.
(d) Includes pretax redeployment charge of $75.8 million.
(e) Includes after-tax discontinued operations income of $169.0 million and cumulative effect of accounting change charge of $70.0 million.
(f) Includes after-tax discontinued operations charge of $188.3 million.
(g) Includes capital expenditures of continuing operations and discontinued operations through the date disposition was authorized.

Financial Data For Continuing Operations

	Fiscal Year Ended				
Amounts in Millions, Except per Share Data	May 31, 1992	May 26, 1991	May 27, 1990	May 28, 1989	May 29, 1988
Sales	**$7,777.8**	$7,153.2	$6,448.3	$5,620.6	$4,979.6
Earnings after taxes	**505.6**	464.2	373.7	315.3	282.2
Earnings per share	**3.05**	2.82	2.27	1.92	1.62

Glossary

A

account. An accounting record in which the results of transactions are accumulated; shows increases, decreases, and a balance

account payable. An amount owed to a supplier for goods or services purchased on credit; payment is due within a short time period, usually 30 days or less

account receivable. A current asset representing money due for services performed or merchandise sold on credit

accounting. A service actively designed to accumulate, measure, and communicate financial information about economic entities for decision-making purposes

accounting cycle. The procedures for analyzing, recording, classifying, summarizing, and reporting the transactions of a business.

accounting equation. An algebraic equation that expresses the relationship between assets (resources), liabilities (obligations), and owners' equity (net assets, or the residual interest in a business after all liabilities have been met): Assets = Liabilities + Owners' Equity

accounting model. The basic accounting assumptions, concepts, principles, and procedures that determine the manner of recording, measuring, and reporting an entity's transactions

accounts receivable turnover. A measure used to determine a company's average collection period for receivables; computed by dividing net sales (or net credit sales) by average accounts receivable

accrual basis. Gross income is recognized when earned

accrual-basis accounting. A system of accounting in which revenues and expenses are recorded as they are earned and incurred, not necessarily when cash is received or paid

accumulated depreciation. The total depreciation recorded on an asset since its acquisition; a contra account deducted from the original cost of an asset on the balance sheet

acid-test ratio (or quick ratio). A measure of a firm's ability to meet current liabilities; more restrictive than the current ratio, it is computed by dividing net quick assets (all current assets, except inventories and prepaid expenses) by current liabilities

adjusted gross income. An individual taxpayer's total income minus deductions (adjustments) for individual retirement plan contributions and alimony paid

adjusting entries. Entries required at the end of each accounting period to recognize, on an accrual basis, revenues and expenses for the period and to report proper amounts for asset, liability, and owners' equity accounts

adjustments to gross income. Amounts deducted from the gross income of an individual taxpayer in arriving at adjusted gross income; includes contributions to individual retirement plans and alimony paid

aging accounts receivable. The process of categorizing each account receivable by the number of days it has been outstanding

Allowance for Uncollectible Accounts. A contra account, deducted from Accounts Receivable, that shows the estimated losses from uncollectible accounts

allowance method. The recording of estimated losses due to uncollectible accounts as expenses during the period in which the sales occurred

American Institute of Certified Public Accountants (AICPA). The national organization of CPAs in the United States

amortization. The process of cost allocation that assigns the original cost of an intangible asset to the periods benefited

annuity. A series of equal amounts to be received or paid at the end of equal time intervals

arm's-length transactions. Business dealings between independent and rational parties who are looking out for their own interests

articulation. The interrelationships among the financial statements

asset turnover ratio. An overall measure of how effectively assets are used during a period; computed by dividing net sales by average total assets

assets. Economic resources that are owned or controlled by an entity

audit report. A report issued by an independent CPA that expresses an opinion about whether the financial statements present fairly a company's financial position, operating results, and cash flows in accordance with generally accepted accounting principles

authorized stock. The amount and type of stock that may be issued by a company, as specified in its articles of incorporation

B

bad debt. An uncollectible account receivable

balance sheet (statement of financial position). The financial statement that shows the assets, liabilities, and owners' equity of an entity at a particular date

bank reconciliation. The process of systematically comparing the cash balance as reported by the bank with the cash balance on the company's books and explaining any differences

board of directors. Individuals elected by the stockholders to govern a corporation

bond. A contract between a borrower and a lender in which the borrower promises to pay a specified rate of interest for each period the bond is outstanding and repay the principal at the maturity date

bond carrying value. The face value of bonds minus the unamortized discount or plus the unamortized premium

bond discount. The difference between the face value and the sales price when bonds are sold below their face value

bond indenture. A contract between a bond issuer and a bond purchaser that specifies the terms of a bond

bond maturity date. The date at which a bond principal or face amount becomes payable

bond premium. The difference between the face value and the sales price when bonds are sold above their face value

book value. The net amount shown in the accounts for an asset, liability, or owners' equity item

book value per share. A measure of net worth; computed by dividing stockholders' equity for each class of stock by the number of shares outstanding for that class

business. An organization operated with the objective of making a profit from the sale of goods or services

business documents. Records of transactions used as the basis for recording accounting entries; includes invoices, check stubs, receipts, and similar business papers

business expenses. Expenses that have been paid or incurred in the course of business and that are ordinary, necessary, and reasonable in amount

C

calendar year. An entity's reporting year, covering 12 months and ending on December 31

callable bonds. Bonds for which the issuer reserves the right to pay the obligation before its maturity date

capital. The total amount of money or other resources owned or used to acquire future income or benefits

Capital account. An account in which a proprietor's or partner's interest in a firm is recorded; it is increased by owner investments and net income and decreased by withdrawals and net losses

capital expenditure. An expenditure that is recorded as an asset because it is expected to benefit more than the current period

capital gain. The excess of the selling price over the cost basis when assets, such as securities and other personal and investment assets are sold

capital lease. A leasing transaction that is recorded as a purchase by the lessee

capital stock. The portion of a corporation's owners' equity contributed by investors (owners) in exchange for shares of stock

cash basis. Gross income is recognized when cash is received

cash-basis accounting. A system of accounting in which transactions are recorded and revenues and expenses are recognized only when cash is received or paid

Cash Disbursements Journal. A special journal in which all cash paid out for supplies, merchandise, salaries, and other items is recorded

cash dividend. A cash distribution of earnings to shareholders

cash equivalents. Short-term, highly liquid investments that can be converted easily into cash

cash inflows. Any current or expected revenues or savings directly associated with an investment

cash outflows. The initial cost and other expected outlays associated with an investment

Cash Over and Short. An account used to record overages and shortages in petty cash

Cash Receipts Journal. A special journal in which all cash received, from sales, interest, rent, or other sources, is recorded

ceiling. The maximum market amount at which inventory can be carried on the books; equal to net realizable value

Glossary

Certified Public Accountant (CPA). A special designation given to an accountant who has passed a national uniform examination and has met other certifying requirements; CPA certificates are issued and monitored by state boards of accountancy or similar agencies

chart of accounts. A systematic listing of all accounts used by a company

charter (articles of incorporation). A document issued by a state that gives legal status to a corporation and details its specific rights, including the authority to issue a certain maximum number of shares of stock

classified balance sheet. A balance sheet in which assets and liabilities are subdivided into current and noncurrent categories

closed transaction. A transaction that is completed within the accounting period; both the purchase and payment or sale and receipt of payment occur within the same accounting period

closing entries. Entries that reduce all nominal, or temporary, accounts to a zero balance at the end of each accounting period, transferring their preclosing balances to a permanent balance sheet account

common stock. The most frequently issued class of stock; usually it provides a voting right but is secondary to preferred stock in dividend and liquidation rights

comparative financial statements. Financial statements in which data for two or more years are shown together

compound journal entry. A journal entry that involves more than one debit or more than one credit or both

compounding period. The period of time for which interest is computed

conduit principle. The idea that all income earned by an entity must be passed through to the owners and reported on their individual tax returns; applicable to proprietorships, partnerships, and S corporations

consignee. A vendor who sells merchandise owned by another party, known as the consignor, usually on a commission basis

consignment. An arrangement whereby merchandise owned by one party (the consignor) is sold by another party (the consignee), usually on a commission basis

consignor. The owner of merchandise to be sold by someone else, known as the consignee

consolidated financial statements. Statements that report the combined operating results, financial position, and cash flows of two or more legally separate but affiliated companies as if they were one economic entity

consolidation. The combining of two or more companies into a new legal corporation, with the original companies going out of existence

constructive receipt rule. The idea that cash has been received when a taxpayer can exercise control over it, whether or not the cash has been physically received

contingent liability. A potential obligation, dependent upon the occurrence of future events

contra account. An account that is offset or deducted from another account

contributed capital. The portion of owners' equity contributed by investors (the owners) in exchange for shares of stock

control account. A summary account in the General Ledger that is supported by detailed individual accounts in a subsidiary ledger

convertible bonds. Bonds that can be traded for, or converted to, other securities after a specified period of time

convertible preferred stock. Preferred stock that can be converted to common stock at a specified conversion rate

corporation. A legal entity chartered by a state; ownership is represented by transferable shares of stock

cost method of accounting for investments in stocks. Method used to account for an investment in the stock of another company when less than 20 percent of the outstanding voting stock is owned

cost of goods sold. The expenses incurred to purchase or manufacture the merchandise sold during a period

cost principle. The idea that transactions are recorded at their historical costs or exchange prices at the transaction date

coupon bonds. Unregistered bonds for which owners receive periodic interest payments by clipping a coupon from the bond and sending it to the issuer as evidence of ownership

credit. An entry on the right side of an account

credit card. A plastic card that represents an individual's right to make purchases on credit; examples are VISA, MasterCard, American Express, and store-issued cards

credit card draft. The part of the multiple-page credit form that is sent by the retailer to the credit card company for reimbursement of the stated amount

cumulative-dividend preference. The right of preferred stockholders to receive current dividends plus all dividends in arrears before common stockholders receive any dividends

current assets. Cash and other assets that may reasonably be expected to be converted to cash within a year or during the normal operating cycle

current (or working capital) ratio. A measure of the liquidity of a business; equal to current assets divided by current liabilities

current exchange rate. The exchange rate that exists on the date the accounting period ends

current liabilities. Debts and other obligations that will be paid in cash or satisfied with other assets or services within one year

current-dividend preference. The right of preferred shareholders to receive current dividends before common shareholders receive dividends

D

date of record. The date selected by a corporation's board of directors on which the shareholders of record are identified as those who will receive dividends

debentures (unsecured bonds). Bonds for which no collateral has been pledged

debit. An entry on the left side of an account

debt-equity management ratio. A measure of the relative utilization of debt and equity; computed by dividing average total assets by average stockholders' equity

debt financing. Acquiring funds by borrowing money from creditors in the form of long-term notes, mortgages, leases, or bonds

declaration date. The date on which a corporation's board of directors formally decides to pay a dividend to shareholders

declining-balance depreciation method. An accelerated depreciation method in which an asset's book value is multiplied by a constant depreciation rate (such as double the straight-line percentage, in the case of double-declining-balance)

deduction. Business expenses or losses that are subtracted from gross income in computing taxable income

Deferred Income Taxes. An account used to record the difference between income tax expense on the income statement and income taxes payable for the year to federal and state governments

depletion. The process of cost allocation that assigns the original cost of a natural resource to the periods benefited

depreciation. The process of cost allocation that assigns the original cost of plant and equipment to the periods benefited

direct method. A method of reporting net cash flow from operations that shows the major classes of cash receipts and payments for a period of time

direct write-off method. The recording of actual losses from uncollectible accounts as expenses during the period in which accounts receivable are determined to be uncollectible

discount. The amount charged by a bank when a note receivable is discounted; calculated as maturity value times discount rate times discount period

discount period. The time between the date a note is sold to a financial institution and its maturity date

discount rate. The interest rate charged by a financial institution for buying a note receivable

discounting a note receivable. The process of the payee's selling notes to a financial institution for less than the maturity value

dividend payment date. The date on which a corporation pays dividends to its shareholders

dividend payout ratio. A measure of earnings paid out in dividends; computed by dividing cash dividends by the net income available to each class of stock

dividends. Distributions to the owners (stockholders) of a corporation

dividends account. The account used to reflect periodic distributions of earnings to the owners (stockholders) of a corporation

dividends in arrears. Missed dividends for past years that preferred stockholders have a right to receive under the cumulative-dividend preference if and when dividends are declared

double-entry accounting. A system of recording transactions in a way that maintains the equality of the accounting equation

drawings. Distributions to the owner(s) of a proprietorship or partnership; similar to dividends for a corporation

drawings account. The account used to reflect periodic withdrawals of earnings by the owner (proprietor) or owners (partners) of a proprietorship or partnership

E

earnings per share (EPS). The amount of net income (earnings) related to each share of stock; computed by dividing net income by the number of shares of common stock outstanding during the period

economic income. The maximum amount a person or a firm can consume during an accounting period and still be as well off at the end of the period as at the beginning

effective-interest amortization. A method of systematically writing off a bond premium or discount that takes into consideration the time value of money and results in an equal rate of amortization for each period

effective tax rate. A tax rate that reflects the percentage of the actual tax liability to the accounting income generated by the company, that is, net tax liability/financial (book) income before taxes

effective (yield or market) rate of interest. The actual interest rate earned or paid on a bond investment

electronic data processing (EDP). A term referring to the use of computers in recording, classifying, manipulating, and summarizing data

entity. An organizational unit (a person, partnership, or corporation) for which accounting records are kept and about which accounting reports are prepared

equity financing. Acquiring funds in the form of investments by owners (proprietor, partner, or stockholder)

equity method of accounting for investments in stocks. Method used to account for an investment in the stock of another company when significant influence can be imposed (presumed to exist when 20 to 50 percent of the outstanding voting stock is owned)

exchange gain or loss. The gain or loss incurred when the exchange rates are different on the purchase and payment dates or on the sale and receipt of payment dates

exchange rate. The value of one currency in terms of another

exclusions. Gross receipts that are not subject to tax and are not included in gross income, such as interest on state and local government bonds

expense. Costs incurred in the normal course of business to generate revenues

extraordinary items. Nonoperating gains and losses that are unusual in nature, infrequent in occurrence, and material in amount

F

FIFO (first-in, first-out). An inventory cost flow whereby the first goods purchased are assumed to be the first goods sold so that the ending inventory consists of the most recently purchased goods

financial accounting. The area of accounting concerned with reporting financial information to interested external parties

Financial Accounting Standards Board (FASB). The private organization responsible for establishing the standards for financial accounting and reporting in the United States

financing activities. Transactions and events whereby resources are obtained from, or repaid to, owners (equity financing) and creditors (debt financing)

fiscal year. An entity's reporting year, covering a 12-month accounting period

floor. The minimum market amount at which inventory can be carried on the books; equal to net realizable value minus a normal profit

FOB (free-on-board) destination. A business term meaning that the seller of merchandise bears the shipping costs and maintains ownership until the merchandise is delivered to the buyer

FOB (free-on-board) shipping point. A business term meaning that the buyer of merchandise bears the shipping costs and acquires ownership at the point of shipment

freight-in. An account used with the periodic inventory method for recording the costs of transporting into a firm all purchased merchandise intended for sale; added to purchases in calculating cost of goods sold

functional currency. The currency in which a subsidiary conducts most of its business; generally, but not always, the currency of the country where it does most of its spending and earning

G

general-purpose financial statements. The financial reports intended for use by a variety of external groups; they include the balance sheet, the income statement, and the statement of cash flows

generally accepted accounting principles (GAAP). Authoritative guidelines that define accounting practice at a particular time

going concern. The idea that an accounting entity will have a continuing existence for the foreseeable future

goodwill. An intangible asset that exists when a business is valued at more than the fair market value of its net assets, usually due to strategic location, reputation, good customer relations, or similar factors; equal to the excess of the purchase price over the fair market value of the net assets purchased

gross income. The taxable portion of a taxpayer's gross receipts

gross margin. The excess of net sales revenue over the cost of goods sold

gross margin method. A procedure for estimating the amount of ending inventory; the historical relationship of cost of goods sold to sales revenue is used in computing ending inventory

gross sales. Total recorded sales before deducting any sales discounts or sales returns and allowances

gross tax liability. The amount of tax computed by multiplying the tax base (taxable income) by the appropriate tax rates

H

historical cost. The dollar amount originally exchanged in an arm's-length transaction; an amount assumed to reflect the fair market value of an item at the transaction date

historical exchange rate. The exchange rate that existed on the date of a transaction

horizontal analysis of financial statements. A technique for analyzing the percentage change in individual income statement or balance sheet items from one year to the next

I

imprest petty cash fund. A petty cash fund in which all expenditures are documented by vouchers or vendors' receipts or invoices; the total of the vouchers and cash in the fund should equal the established balance

income statement (statement of earnings). The financial statement that summarizes the revenues generated and the expenses incurred by an entity during a period of time

income summary. A clearing account used to close all revenues and expenses at the end of an accounting period; the preclosing balance of the income summary account represents the operating results (income or loss) of an accounting period

income taxes payable. The amount expected to be paid to the federal and state governments based on the income before taxes reported on the income statement

indirect method. A method of reporting net cash flow from operations that involves converting accrual-basis net income to a cash basis

inflation. An increase in the general price level of goods and services; alternatively, a decrease in the purchasing power of the dollar

intangible assets. Long-lived assets without physical substance that are used in business, such as licenses, patents, franchises, and goodwill

intercompany transaction. A transaction between a parent company and a subsidiary company

interest. The payment (cost) for the use of money

interest rate. The cost of using money, expressed as an annual percentage

inventory cutoff. The determination of which items should be included in the year-end inventory balance

inventory turnover. A measure of the efficiency with which inventory is managed; computed by dividing cost of goods sold by average inventory for a period

investing activities. Transactions and events that involve the purchase and sale of securities (excluding cash equivalents), property, plant, equipment, and other assets not generally held for resale, and the making and collecting of loans

issued stock. Authorized stock originally issued to stockholders; it may or may not still be outstanding

itemized deduction. Amounts paid by an individual taxpayer for personal and quasi-business expenses that can be deducted in computing taxable income, such as medical expenses, property and income taxes, mortgage and investment interest, charitable contributions, moving expenses, casualty and theft losses, and certain miscellaneous expenses

J

journal. An accounting record in which transactions are first entered; provides a chronological record of all business activities

journal entry. A recording of a transaction where debits equal credits; usually includes a date and an explanation of the transaction

K

Keogh Plan. A pension plan for a self-employed individual taxpayer who has earned income; the annual contribution is limited to 20 percent of earned income, but it is not to exceed $30,000

L

lapping. A procedure used to conceal the theft of cash by crediting the payment from one customer to another customer's account on a delayed basis

lease. A contract that specifies the terms under which the owner of an asset (the lessor) agrees to transfer the right to use the asset to another party (the lessee)

ledger. A book of accounts in which data from transactions recorded in journals are posted and thereby classified and summarized

legal capital. The amount of contributed capital not available for dividends; usually equal to the par or stated value of outstanding capital stock

lessee. The party that is granted the right to use property under the terms of a lease

lessor. The owner of property that is rented (leased) to another party

liabilities. Obligations measurable in monetary terms that represent amounts owed to creditors, governments, employees, and other parties

LIFO (last-in, first-out). An inventory cost flow whereby the last goods purchased are assumed to be the first goods sold so that the ending inventory consists of the first goods purchased

limited liability. The legal protection given stockholders whereby they are responsible for the debts and obligations of a corporation only to the extent of their capital contributions

line of credit. An arrangement whereby a bank agrees to loan an amount of money (up to a certain limit) on demand for short periods of time, usually less than a year

liquid. Readily convertible into cash

liquidation. The process of dissolving a business by selling the assets, paying the debts, and distributing the remaining equity to the owners

liquidity. A company's ability to meet current obligations with cash or other assets that can be quickly converted to cash

long-run planning. The process of establishing goals that extend 3-5 years into the future; involves decisions about products, labor, facilities and financial resources

long-term investment. An expenditure to acquire a nonoperating asset that is expected to increase in value or generate income for longer than 1 year

long-term liabilities. Debts or other obligations that will not be paid within 1 year

losses. Costs that provide no benefit to an organization

lower of cost or market (LCM). A basis for valuing certain assets at the lower of original cost or current market value

M

maker. A person (entity) who signs a note to borrow money and who assumes responsibility to pay the note at maturity

management accounting. The area of accounting concerned with providing internal financial reports to assist management in making decisions

marketable securities. Short-term investments in securities (stocks, bonds, and so on) made with temporarily idle cash to earn a return

market price. The price of which goods are exchanged in arm's-length transactions in the marketplace

matching principle. The concept that all costs and expenses incurred in generating revenues must be recognized in the same reporting period as the related revenues

maturity date. The date on which a note or other obligation becomes due

maturity value. The amount of an obligation to be collected or paid at maturity; equal to principal plus any interest

merger. The acquisition of one company by another company whereby the companies combine as one legal entity, with the acquired company going out of existence

minority interest. The interest owned in a subsidiary by stockholders other than those of the parent company; occurs when the acquiring company has less than a 100 percent ownership interest

modified accelerated cost recovery system (MACRS). IRS regulations that allocate the cost of an asset according to predefined recovery periods and percentages

monetary measurement. The idea that money, as the common medium of exchange, is the accounting unit of measurement, and that only economic activities measurable in monetary terms are included in the accounting model

mortgage amortization schedule. A schedule that shows the breakdown between interest and principal for each payment over the life of a mortgage

mortgage payable. A written promise to pay a stated amount of money at one or more specified future dates; a

Glossary

mortgage is secured by the pledging of certain assets, usually real estate, as collateral

moving average. A perpetual inventory cost flow alternative whereby the cost of goods sold and the cost of ending inventory are determined by using a weighted-average cost of all merchandise on hand after each purchase

multinational company. A company that has operating units in more than one country

multiple-step income statement. An income statement that separates cost of goods sold from other expenses and reports a gross margin figure

mutual agency. The right of all partners in a partnership to act as agents for the normal business operations of the partnership, with the authority to bind it to business agreements

N

natural resources. Assets that are physically consumed or waste away, such as oil, minerals, gravel, and timber

net income (or net loss). A measure of the overall performance of a business entity; equal to revenues minus expenses for the period

net proceeds. The difference between maturity value and discount when a note receivable is discounted

net realizable value of accounts receivable. The net amount that would be received if all receivables considered collectible were collected; equal to total accounts receivable less the allowance for uncollectible accounts; also called the book value of accounts receivable

net realizable value. The selling price of an item less reasonable selling costs

net sales. Gross sales less sales discounts and sales returns and allowances

net tax liability. The amount of tax computed by subtracting tax credits from the gross tax liability

no-par stock. Stock that does not have a par value printed on the face of the stock certificate

nominal accounts. Accounts that are closed to a zero balance at the end of each accounting period; temporary accounts generally appearing on the income statement

noncash items. Items included in the determination of net income on an accrual basis that do not affect cash; examples are depreciation and amortization

noncash transactions. Investing and financing activities that do not affect cash; if significant, they are disclosed below the statement of cash flows or in the notes to the financial statements

nonprofit organization. An entity without a profit objective, oriented toward providing services efficiently and effectively

note payable. A debt owed to a creditor, evidenced by an unconditional written promise to pay a sum of money on or before a specified future date

note receivable. A claim against a debtor, evidenced by an unconditional written promise to pay a certain sum of money on or before a specified future date

notes to financial statements. Explanatory information considered an integral part of the financial statements

NSF (not sufficient funds) check. A check that is not honored by a bank because of insufficient cash in the customer's account

number of days' sales in inventory. An alternative measure of how well inventory is being managed; computed by dividing 365 days by the inventory turnover ratio

number of days' sales in receivables. A measure of the average number of days it takes to collect a credit sale; computed by dividing 365 days by the accounts receivable turnover

number of days' sales invested in working capital. An alternative measure of the amount of working capital used in generating the sales of a period; computed by dividing 365 days by the working capital turnover

O

open transaction. A transaction that is not completed at the end of the accounting period; a purchase that has not yet been paid for or a sale where payment is yet to be collected when the accounting period ends

operating activities. Transactions and events that enter into the determination of net income

operating assets. Long-term, or noncurrent, assets acquired for use in the business rather than for resale; includes property, plant, and equipment; intangible assets; and natural resources

operating lease. A simple rental agreement

operating leverage. The extent to which fixed costs are part of a company's cost structure; the higher the proportion of fixed costs, the faster income increases or decreases with sales volume

operating performance ratio. An overall measure of the efficiency of operations during a period; computed by dividing net income by net sales

outlay cost. In transfer pricing, the variable cost of providing the product or service, if fixed costs are covered, or, if they are not, the total cost

outstanding stock. Issued stock that is still being held by investors

owners' equity (net assets). The ownership interest in the assets of an entity; equals total assets minus total liabilities

P

par-value stock. Stock that has a nominal value assigned to it in the corporation's charter and printed on the face of each share of stock

parent company. A company that owns or maintains control over other companies, known as subsidiaries, which are themselves separate legal entities; control generally refers to more than 50 percent ownership of the stock of another company

partnership. An association of two or more individuals or organizations to carry on economic activity

partnership agreement. A legal agreement between partners; it usually specifies, among other things, the capital contributions to be made by each partner, the ratios in which partnership earnings and losses will be distributed, the management responsibilities of the partners, and the partners' rights to transfer or sell their individual interests

patent. An exclusive right granted for 17 years by the federal government to manufacture and sell an invention

payee. The person (entity) to whom payment on a note is to be made

payback method. A capital budgeting technique that determines the amount of time it takes the net cash inflows of an investment to repay the investment cost

payback reciprocal method. A capital budgeting technique in which the reciprocal of the payback period is used in computing an investment's approximate internal rate of return

pension plan. A contract between a company and its employees whereby the company agrees to pay benefits to employees after their retirement

period costs. Nonmanufacturing costs that are charged to the income statement in the period in which they are incurred

periodic inventory method. A system of accounting for inventory in which cost of goods sold is determined and inventory is adjusted at the end of the accounting period, not when merchandise is purchased or sold

perpetual inventory method. A system of accounting for inventory in which detailed records of the number of units and the cost of each purchase and sales transactions are prepared throughout the accounting period

personal exemption. A deduction allowed to individual taxpayers for each qualifying person, including the taxpayer, taxpayer's spouse, and dependents

petty cash fund. A small amount of cash kept on hand for making miscellaneous payments

pooling of interests. The acquisition of one company by another whereby the acquiring company issues voting stock to the acquired company's stockholders in exchange for at least 90 percent of the acquired company's outstanding voting stock (and when 11 other conditions are met)

pooling-of-interests method. A method used to prepare consolidated financial statements when one company issues common stock to acquire at least 90 percent of the common stock of another company and when 11 other specific conditions are met

post-closing trial balance. A listing of all real account balances after the closing process has been completed; provides a means of testing whether total debits equal total credits for all real accounts prior to beginning a new accounting cycle

posting. The process of transferring amounts from the journal to the ledger

preemptive right. The right of current stockholders to purchase additional shares of stock in order to maintain their same percentage of ownership if new shares are issued

preferred stock. A class of stock that usually provides dividend and liquidation preferences over common stock

premium on stock. The excess of the issuance (market) price of stock over its par or stated value

prepaid expenses. Payments made in advance for items normally charged to expense

present value of $1. The value today of $1 to be received or paid at some future date given a specified interest rate

present value of an annuity. The value today of a series of equally spaced, equal-amount payments to be made or received in the future given a specified interest rate

price-earnings (P/E) ratio. A measure of growth potential, earnings stability, and management capabilities; computed by dividing market price per share by earnings per share

principal (face value or maturity value). The amount that will be paid on a bond at the maturity date

principal on a note. The face amount of a note; the amount (excluding interest) that the maker agrees to pay the payee

prior-period adjustments. Adjustments made directly to Retained Earnings in order to correct errors in the financial statements of prior periods

pro-forma. A projected financial statement

pro rata. A term describing an allocation that is based on a proportionate distribution of the total

profitability. A company's ability to generate revenues in excess of the costs incurred in producing those revenues

property dividend. The distribution to shareholders of assets other than cash

property, plant, and equipment. Tangible, long-lived assets acquired for use in business operations; includes land, buildings, machinery, equipment, and furniture

property, plant, and equipment turnover. A measure of how well property, plant, and equipment are being utilized in generating a period's sales; computed by dividing net sales by average property, plant, and equipment

proprietorship. A business owned by one person

purchase. The acquisition of one company by another whereby the acquiring company exchanges cash or other assets for more than 50 percent of the acquired company's outstanding voting stock

purchase discount. A reduction in the purchase price, allowed if payment if made within a specified period

purchase method. A method used to prepare consolidated financial statements when one company has acquired a controlling interest in another company with similar activities by exchanging cash or other assets for more than 50 percent of the acquired company's outstanding voting stock

Purchase Returns and Allowances. A contra-purchases account used for recording the return of, or allowances for, previously purchased merchandise

purchases. An account in which all inventory purchases are recorded; used with the periodic inventory method

Purchases Journal. A special journal in which credit purchases are recorded

R

real accounts. Accounts that are not closed to a zero balance at the end of each accounting period; permanent accounts appearing on the balance sheet

receivables. Claims for money, goods, or services

Glossary

recourse. The right to seek payment on a discounted note from the payee if the maker defaults

recovery period. The time period designated by Congress for depreciating business assets

redemption value. The price, stated in the contract, to be paid by a company to repurchase preferred stock

registered bonds. Bonds for which the names and addresses of the bondholders are kept on file by the issuing company

relative fair market value method. A way of allocating a lump-sum or "basket" purchase price to the individual assets acquired based on their respective market values

remeasurement. The process of restating a subsidiary's financial statements into its functional currency (used primarily for Type II subsidiaries)

reporting currency. The currency used by a company on its consolidated financial statements

residual income. The amount of net income an investment center is able to earn above a specified minimum rate of return on assets

retail inventory method. A procedure for estimating the dollar amount of ending inventory; the ending inventory at retail prices is converted to a cost basis by using a ratio of the cost and the retail prices of goods available for sale

retained earnings. The portion of a corporation's owners' equity that has been earned from profitable operations and not distributed to stockholders

return on sales revenue. A measure of operating performance; computed by dividing net income by total sales revenue

return on stockholders' equity. A measure of overall performance from a stockholder's viewpoint; includes management of operations, use of assets, and management of debt and equity, and is computed by dividing net income by average stockholders' equity

return on total assets. An overall measure of the return to both stockholders and creditors; includes operating performance and asset turnover

return on investment (ROI). A measure of operating performance and efficiency in utilizing assets; computed in its simplest form by dividing net income by average total assets

revenue recognition principle. The idea that revenues should be recorded when (1) the earnings process has been substantially completed and (2) an exchange has taken place

revenues. Increases in a company's resources from the sale of goods or services

reversing entry. A journal entry made at the beginning of a year that exactly reverses an adjusting entry made at the end of the previous year

S

S corporation. A domestic corporation that is recognized as a regular corporation under state law but is granted special status for federal income tax purposes

sales discount. A reduction in the selling price that is allowed if payment is received within a specified period

Sales Journal. A special journal in which credit sales are recorded

Sales Returns and Allowances. A contra-revenue account in which the return of, or allowance for, reduction in the price of merchandise previously sold is recorded

sales tax payable. Money collected from customers for sales taxes that must be remitted to local governments and other taxing authorities

salvage, or residual, value. Estimated value or actual price of an asset at the conclusion of its useful life, net of disposal costs

secured bonds. Bonds for which assets have been pledged in order to guarantee repayment

Securities and Exchange Commission (SEC). The government body responsible for regulating the financial reporting practices of most publicly owned corporations in connection with the buying and selling of stocks and bonds

serial bonds. Bonds that mature in a series of installments at specified future dates

single-step income statement. An income statement that lists all expenses together, including cost of goods sold

sinking fund bonds. Bonds for which the borrowing company agrees to accumulate cash to retire the bonds

social security (FICA) taxes. Federal Insurance Contributions Act taxes imposed on employee and employer; used mainly to provide retirement benefits

solvency. A company's long-run ability to meet all financial obligations

special journal. A book of original entry for recording similar transactions that occur frequently

special order. An order that may be priced below the normal price in order to utilize excess capacity and thereby contribute to company profits

specific identification. A method of valuing inventory and determining cost of goods sold whereby the actual costs of specific inventory items are assigned to them

standard deduction. An amount that can be deducted on an individual's tax return in lieu of listing (itemizing) amounts actually paid for qualifying personal expenses; the amount varies with filing status

stated rate of interest. The rate of interest printed on the bond

stated value. A nominal value assigned to no-par stock by the board of directors of a corporation

statement of cash flows. The financial statement that shows an entity's cash inflows (receipts) and outflows (payments) during a period of time

statement of partners' capital. A partnership report showing the changes in the capital balances; similar to a statement of retained earnings for a corporation

statement of retained earnings. A report that shows the changes in the Retained Earnings account during a period of time

statement of stockholders' equity. A financial statement that reports all changes in stockholders' equity

stock certificate. A document issued by a corporation to stockholders evidencing ownership in the corporation

stock dividend. A pro rata distribution of additional shares of stock to shareholders

stock split. The replacement of outstanding shares of stock with a greater number of new shares that have a proportionately lower par or stated value

stockholders (shareholders). Individuals or organizations that own a portion (shares of stock) of a corporation

straight-line amortization. A method of systematically writing off a bond discount or premium in equal amounts each period until maturity

straight-line depreciation method. The depreciation method in which the cost of an asset is allocated equally over the periods of the asset's estimated useful life

subsidiary company. A company owned or controlled by another company, known as the parent company

subsidiary ledger. A grouping of individual accounts that in total equal the balance of a control account in the General Ledger

sum-of-the-years'-digits (SYD) depreciation method. The accelerated depreciation method in which a constant balance (cost minus salvage value) is multiplied by a declining depreciation rate

supplies. Materials used in a business that do not generally become part of the sales product and were not purchased to be resold to customers

T

T-account. A simplified depiction of an account in the form of a letter T

tangible personal business property. Depreciable operating assets of a business, other than real property, including machinery, furniture and fixtures, automobiles and trucks, and equipment

tax credit. A direct reduction in the tax liability, usually granted to encourage certain classes of taxpayers to take a particular action

taxable income. The income remaining after all deductions have been subtracted from gross income

tax-exempt corporation. A legal entity chartered by a state for scientific, religious, educational, charitable, or other purposes deemed beneficial to society

term bonds. Bonds that mature in one lump sum at a specified future date

time period (or periodicity) concept. The idea that the life of a business is divided into distinct and relatively short time periods so that accounting information can be timely

transactions. Exchanges of goods or services between entities (whether individuals, businesses, or other organizations), as well as other events having an economic impact on a business

translation adjustment. Perceived changes in value due only to exchange rate changes

translation. The process of restating a subsidiary's financial statements from its functional currency to the reporting currency (used primarily for Type I subsidiaries)

treasury stock. Issued stock that has subsequently been reacquired by the corporation

trial balance. A listing of all account balances; provides a means of testing whether total debits equal total credits for all accounts

Type I subsidiary. A self-contained foreign subsidiary whose functional currency is different from the parent company's currency

Type II subsidiary. A foreign subsidiary that is an extension of the parent company and whose functional currency is the same as the parent's

U

Uncollectible Accounts Expense. An account that represents the portion of the current period's receivables that are estimated to become uncollectible

unearned revenues. Amounts received before they have been earned

units-of-production depreciation method. The depreciation method in which the cost of an asset is allocated to each period on the basis of the productive output or use of the asset during the period

unlimited liability. The lack of a ceiling on the amount of liability a proprietor or partner must assume; meaning that if business assets are not sufficient to settle creditor claims, the personal assets of the proprietor or partners may be used to settle the claims

unrecorded expenses. Expenses incurred during a period that have not been recorded by the end of that period

unrecorded revenues. Revenues earned during a period that have not been recorded by the end of that period

useful life. The term used to describe the life over which an asset is expected to be useful to the company; cost is assigned to the periods benefited from using the asset

V

vertical analysis of financial statements. A technique for analyzing the relationships between items on an income statement or balance sheet by expressing all items as percentages

W

weighted-average. A periodic inventory cost flow alternative whereby the cost of goods sold and the cost of ending inventory are determined by using a weighted-average cost of all merchandise available for sale during the period

work sheet. A columnar schedule used to summarize accounting data

working capital turnover. A measure of the amount of working capital used in generating the sales of a period; computed by dividing net sales by average working capital

Index

A

ABC. *See* Activity-based costing
Account, *def.*, 62
Account balances, 78–79
Account(s) payable, 407–408
　def., 407
Account(s) receivable, 315–322
　aging of, *def.*, 319
　aging of, *illus.*, 320
　credit card sales, 320–321
　def., 211, 315
　net realizable value of, *def.*, 317
Accounts receivable turnover, *def.*, 678
Accounting:
　career opportunities in, 19–21
　career opportunities in, *illus.*, 20
　cash-basis versus accrual-basis, 741–742
　def., 6
　educational preparation for, 21
　environment of, 13–18
　ethics in, 16–18
　financial, *def.*, 8
　management, *def.*, 7
　public, 19
　purpose of, 4–6
　relationship of, to business, 6
Accounting cycle:
　def., 6, 60
　first four steps in, 66–79
　illus., 80–82
　output of the, *illus.*, 8
　sequence of, *illus.*, 61, 153
　steps in the, *illus.*, 67
　summary of the, 152–155
Accounting equation:
　basic, 61–66
　def., 12
　elements of, *illus.*, 30
　expanded, *illus.*, 65
　expanding, to include revenues, expenses, and dividends, 64–66
Accounting information, users of, 6–9
Accounting model:
　characteristics of, 102–105
　def., 9
Accounting Principles Board (APB), 15
Accounting Research Bulletins (ARBs), 15
Accounting standards and exchange rates, 692–693
Accounting system, 332
Accrual to cash basis, guidelines for converting from, *illus.*, 634
Accrual-basis accounting:
　def., 103, 208
　versus cash-basis accounting, 104–105, 741–742
Accumulated depreciation, *def.*, 365
Acid-test ratio (or quick ratio), *def.*, 677
Acquisition(s):
　of bonds, accounting for, 485–486
　by leasing, 360–362
　of property, plant, and equipment, 359–363
　by purchase, 359–360
　of stocks, 493–494
Adjusted gross income, *def.*, 733
Adjusting entries, 105–115
　alternative approaches for, 115–118
　def., 106
Adjustments:
　for depreciation and other noncash items, 630
　for gains and losses, 630–631
　to gross income, *def.*, 733
　for payables and other current liabilities, 630
　prior-period, *def.*, 537
　for receivables and other current operating assets, 629–630
Aging accounts receivable:
　def., 319
　illus., 320
Aging method, 319
AICPA (American Institute of Certified Public Accountants):
　def., 15
　Code of Professional Conduct of, 16–18
　Committee on Accounting Principles of, 15
Allowance for uncollectible accounts:
　def., 317
　estimating, 318–320
　　using aging method, 319
　　using percentage of sales method, 318–319
　　using percentage of receivables method, 319
Allowance method, *def.*, 316
American Institute of Certified Public Accountants. *See* AICPA

793

Amortization:
  of bond discounts and premiums, accounting for, 487–491
  def., 380
  effective-interest, 464–465, 490–491
    def., 460, 490
  straight-line, 488, 490
    def., 460, 488
Amortization schedule, *def.*, 422
Analysis:
  of asset turnover, 674–681
  of business documents and transactions, 66, 68
  of current assets, 637–638
  of current liabilities, 640
  of land, buildings, and equipment, 638–640
  of long-term liabilities, 640
  of retained earnings, 635–637
Annuity:
  def., 418
  present value of, *def.*, 418
APB (Accounting Principles Board), 15
APB Opinion No. 19, 644–645
ARBs (Accounting Research Bulletins), 15
Arm's-length transactions:
  assumption of, 11
  def., 11
Articles of incorporation, *def.*, 518
Articulation, *def.*, 38
Asset(s):
  acquired by leasing, 360–362
  acquired by purchase, 359–360
  acquiring other, 71
  analysis of current, 637–638
  business, election to expense, 753
    def., 29
  dissimilar, exchange of, 379
  intangible,
    accounting for, 380–382
    def., 358
  operating,
    def., 358
    long-term,
      investments in, 749–753
    tax effects of acquiring, 750–751
    tax effects of alternative ways of depreciating, 751–753
    tax effects of disposing of, 753
  nature of, 358
  and records, physical control over, 334
  selecting cost recovery period for, 752–753
  similar, gain on the exchange of, 377–378
  similar, loss on the exchange of, 378–379
  tax effects of
    acquisition by construction, 750–751
    acquisition by issuing securities, 750
    acquisition by leasing, 750
    acquisition by purchase, 750
    disposal by abandonment, 753
    disposal by exchange, 753
    disposal by sale, 753
  summary of exchanges of, *illus.*, 379
  total, summary of financial statement analysis of return on, *illus.*, 689
  useful life of, *def.*, 358
Asset categories under MACRS, *illus.*, 751
Asset turnover, analysis of, 674–681
Asset turnover ratio, *def.*, 674
Audit committee, 330
Audit report, 39–41
  def., 40
Auditing, 19
Authorization, proper procedures for, 333
Authorized stock, *def.*, 520

B

Bad debt, *def.*, 316
Bad-debt loss, 316
Balance sheet(s), 28–29
  classified and comparative, 31–32
  classified, *def.*, 31
  comparative, *illus.*, 32, 636
  condensed, *illus.*, 542, 550
  consolidated:
    illus., 540
    preparation of, 545, 551–553
    using pooling-of-interests method, 549–554
    illus., 554
    using purchase method, 542–548
    using purchase method, *illus.*, 546
  format of, 30–31
  horizontal analysis, 675–676
  illus., 31, 82, 146, 539, 669
  limitations of, 32–33
  partnership, *illus.*, 592
  ratio analysis, 676–681
  reporting stock on, 528–529
  vertical analysis, 674–675
Bank account, reconciling, 306–311
Bank reconciliation:
  def., 309
  illus., 308
Board of directors, *def.*, 519
Bond(s):
  acquisition of, accounting for, 485–486
  callable, *def.*, 453
  characteristics of, 453–454
  def., 452
  determining issuance price of, 454–458
  issued at,
    a discount, 456
    a discount, accounting for, 460–462
    face value, 455–456
    face value, accounting for, 459–460
    a premium, 456–458
    a premium, accounting for, 460, 462–464
  issued between interest dates,
    accounting for, 465–467
    interest for, *illus.*, 467
  long-term investments in, accounting for, 484–493
  payable, accounting for, 458–469
  purchased between interest dates, accounting for, 486–487
  types of, 452–453
  valuation of long-term investments in, 492
Bond carrying value, *def.*, 464
Bond discount(s):
  amortization of, accounting for, 487–491
  def., 455
Bond indenture, *def.*, 453
Bond investments, accounting for the sale or maturity of, 491–492
Bond maturity date, *def.*, 453
Bond premium(s):
  accounting for the amortization of, 487–491
  def., 455
Bond retirements:
  at maturity, 468
  before maturity, 468–469
Book value:
  consolidations involving payments in excess of, 545–547
  def., 365
Book value per share, 685–687
  def., 685
Book(s) of original entry, 68
Business:
  def., 5
  how different forms of are taxed, 743–746
  international, 16
  relationship of accounting to, 6
Business document(s):
  analysis of transactions and, 66, 68
  def., 66
  illus., 68
Business organizations:
  activities common to, *illus.*, 7

C

Calendar year, *def.*, 103
Callable bonds, *def.*, 453
Capital, 29
  contributed, *def.*, 520
  legal, *def.*, 521
  statement of partners', *def.*, 591
Capital account, *def.*, 586
Capital expenditure, *def.*, 374
Capital gain, *def.*, 736
Capital investment ratio, 594–595

Index

795

Capital lease, 750
  def., 360, 426
  schedule of payments, *illus.*, 425
Capital stock, *def.*, 29, 520
Career opportunities in accounting, 19–22
Cash:
  acquiring either from owners or by borrowing, 70
  and cash equivalents, increase in, 640
  collecting, and paying obligations, 73–75
  control of, 302–304
  controlling and accounting for, 302–311
  flow of, *illus.*, 626
  handling of, 303
  petty, accounting for, 304–306
  recording of, 303
Cash-basis accounting:
  def., 104, 207
  versus accrual-basis accounting, 104–105, 741–742
Cash disbursements journal, 165–169
  def., 165
  illus., 168–169
Cash dividend, *def.*, 530
Cash equivalents, *def.*, 625
Cash flow(s):
  direct method of preparing a statement of, *illus.*, 642–644
  general format for statement of, *illus.*, 625
  illus., 37
  indirect method of preparing a statement of, *illus.*, 635–642
  information reported in the statement of, 625–628
  major classifications of, 625–627
  from operating activities using indirect method, *illus.*, 631
  operating, indirect method of reporting, 629–631
  preparing a statement of, 635–644
  purpose of statement of, 624–625
  statement of using direct method, *illus.*, 641
  statement of, 36–38
  def., 36, 624
  illus., 38
  using direct method, *illus.*, 643
  and supplemental disclosures, statement of, 641–642
  work sheet for statement of, using direct method, *illus.*, 642
Cash flow analysis, importance of, 645
Cash flow statements, usefulness of, 644–645
Cash fund, imprest petty, *def.*, 304
Cash fund, petty, *def.*, 304
Cash over and short, *def.*, 305
Cash receipts journal, 163–165
  def., 163
  illus., 166–167
Cash voucher, petty, *illus.*, 304
Ceiling, *def.*, 275
Certified public accountant (CPA), 16, 39–40
  def., 40
Chart of accounts:
  def., 76
  illus., 78
Charter, *def.*, 518
Classified balance sheet:
  and comparative balance sheet, 31–32
  def., 31
Closed transactions, *def.*, 695
Closing entries, 148–149
  for cost of goods sold, 224–226
  def., 148
Closing process, 147–151
  illus., 150
  for proprietorships and partnerships, the, 151
Code of Professional Conduct, 16–18
Committee on Accounting Principles, 15
Common stock, *def.*, 520
Communication methods, 330
Company:
  multinational, *def.*, 692
  parent, *def.*, 541
  subsidiary, *def.*, 541
Comparative balance sheet:
  and classified balance sheet, 31–32
  illus., 32, 636
Comparative financial statements, *def.*, 32
Compound journal entry, *def.*, 72
Compounding period, *def.*, 417
Computers, effects of on internal control, 335–336
Condensed balance sheets, *illus.*, 542, 550
Condensed income statements, *illus.*, 548
Conduit principle, *def.*, 743
Consignee, *def.*, 264
Consignment, *def.*, 264
Consignor, *def.*, 264
Consolidated balance sheet(s):
  illus., 540
  preparation of, 545, 551–553
  using pooling-of-interests method, 549–555
  illus., 554
  using purchase method, 542–548
  illus., 546
Consolidated financial statements, 541–555
  def., 41, 494, 541
  need for, 541
  preparation of, 541–555
Consolidated income statement(s):
  illus., 555
  using purchase method, 548–549
  illus., 549
  using pooling-of-interests method, 554–555
Consolidated work sheet:
  illus., 543, 547, 552
  preparation of, 543–545
Consolidation(s):
  def., 541
  involving payments in excess of book value, 545–547
Constructive receipt rule, *def.*, 741
Contingent liability(-ies), 427–428
  def., 427
Contra account, *def.*, 212
Contributed capital, *def.*, 520
Control:
  elements of, *illus.*, 335
Control account, *def.*, 160
Control environment, the, 328
Convertible bonds, *def.*, 453
Convertible preferred stock, *def.*, 521
Corporate stock, 518–522
Corporation(s), 10–11, 518–522
  characteristics of, 518–520
  and corporate stock, 518–522
  def., 10, 518
  distribution to owners of, 29
  regular, taxation of, 744
  S,
    def., 520, 744
    taxation of, 744–745
  stock of, 520–522
  tax-exempt, 745
    def., 745
  taxation of, 744–746
  tax liability for, calculating, 738–743
  tax liability for, federal, steps for calculating, *illus.*, 739
Cost(s):
  calculating with the periodic method, 222–223
  calculation of, *illus.*, 220
  closing entries for, 224–226
  def., 72, 214
  expense, 215
  historical, *def.*, 11
  of plant and equipment, allocating to expense, 363–373
Cost and equity methods of accounting for long-term investments in stocks, 497–500
  illus., 494, 498
Cost flow assumptions, comparison of, using the periodic inventory method, 269–271
Cost method of accounting for investments in stocks, 494–496, 497–500
  def., 494
  illus., 494, 498
Cost principle, 11–12
  def., 12
Costing system:
CPA (certified public accountant), 16, 39–40
  def., 40

Index

Credit, 62–64
  def., 62
  and investment decisions, 666–667
  line of, *def.*, 311
Credit card:
  def., 320
  draft, *def.*, 320
  sales, 320–322
Credit sales, recognizing revenue on, 211–214
Creditors, short-term obligations to, 406–410
Cumulative-dividend preference, *def.*, 533
Current (or working capital) ratio, *def.*, 676
Current-dividend preference, 532–533
  def., 532
Current exchange rate, *def.*, 697
Current liabilities, 406–415
  def., 406
Current ratio, 676–677

D

Date of record, *def.*, 531
Debentures, *def.*, 452
Debit, 62–64
  def., 62
Debt:
  bad, *def.*, 316
  long-term,
    current maturities of, 410
    current portion of, 410
Debt financing, *def.*, 452
Debt-equity management, analysis of, 681–683
Debt-equity management ratio, *def.*, 681
Declaration date, *def.*, 531
Declining-balance depreciation method, 366–367
  def., 366
Deductions:
  def., 733
  for expenses and losses, 742
  itemized, *def.*, 733
  standard, *def.*, 735
Deferred income taxes, 426–427
  def., 426
Depletion, *def.*, 383
Depreciation:
  accumulated, *def.*, 365
  change(s) in estimates of, 371–372

comparison of expense of, using different depreciation methods, *illus.*, 370
declining-balance method of, 366–367
  def., 366
def., 363
for income tax purposes, 372–373
and other noncash items, adjustments for, 630
partial-year, calculations for, 371
  illus., 371
straight-line method of, 364–366
  def., 364
sum-of-the-years'-digits (SYD) method of, 367–369
  def., 367
units-of-production method of, *def.*, 369, 369–370
Depreciation methods, comparison of, *illus.*, 365
Depreciation schedule:
  with a change in estimate, *illus.*, 372
  with double-declining-balance depreciation, *illus.*, 367
  with straight-line depreciation, *illus.*, 366
  with sum-of-the-years'-digits depreciation, *illus.*, 368
  with units-of-production depreciation, *illus.*, 370
Direct method:
  def., 631
  of preparing a statement of cash flows, *illus.*, 642–644
  of reporting operating cash flows, 631–633
  for statement of cash flows, *illus.*, 641
  using for statement of cash flows, *illus.*, 643
  using for work sheet for statement of cash flows, *illus.*, 642
Direct write-off method, *def.*, 316
Directors, board of, *def.*, 519
Discarding property, plant, and equipment, 375–376
Discount, *def.*, 324
Discount period, *def.*, 324

Discount rate:
  def., 324
Discounting note(s) receivable, 324–325
  def., 324
Disposal:
  by discarding, 375–376
  by exchanging, 377–380
  by selling, 376–377
  of property, plant, and equipment, 375–380
Dissimilar assets, exchange of, 379
Distributions to owners, 29
Distributions to stockholders, 529–536
Dividend(s):
  in arrears, *def.*, 533
  cash, *def.*, 530
  def., 29, 529
  property, *def.*, 530
  stock,
    accounting for, 534–535
    def., 530
  types of, 530
Dividend payment date, *def.*, 531
Dividend payout ratio, *def.*, 685
Dividend preferences, 532–534
Dividends account:
  closing the, 150
  def., 65
Documents and records, adequacy of, 333–334
Double-declining-balance, 366
  depreciation schedule for, *illus.*, 367
Double-entry accounting, 12–13, 63
  def., 13
Draft, credit card, *def.*, 320
Drawings, 29
  def., 151
Drawings account(s):
  def., 65, 586
  partners', 590–591
Duties, adequate segregation of, 333

E

Earnings, retained:
  accounting for, 536–539
  analysis of, 635–637
  reporting the ending balance, 143–147

restrictions on, 537–539
statement of,
  def., 537
  illus., 538
Earnings per share (EPS), 230–231, 683–684
  def., 34, 230, 683
Economic income, *def.*, 206
EDP (electronic data processing), *def.*, 158
Effective-interest amortization, 464–465, 490–491
  def., 460, 490
Effective rate of interest, *def.*, 455
Effective tax rate, *def.*, 741
Electronic data processing (EDP), *def.*, 158
Elements of control, *illus.*, 335
Employee(s):
  performance review and supervision of, 331
  selection of, 331
  supervision and performance review of, 331
  training of, 331
Entity, *def.*, 9
Entity concept, 9–11
EPS (earnings per share), 230–231, 683–684
  def., 34, 230, 683
Equity financing, *def.*, 452
Equity method of accounting for investments in stocks, 496–500
  def., 494
  illus., 494, 496
Equity, stockholders', statement of, 539–540
  def., 539
Equivalent units of production:
Estimates, use of in financial statement analysis, 689–691
Ethics in accounting, 16–18
Exchange gain(s) or loss(-es):
  def., 694
  unrealized, 695–696
Exchange rate(s)
  and accounting standards, 692–693
  current, *def.*, 697
  def., 692
  historical, *def.*, 697
  illus., 693
Exchange transactions, 60

Index

Exchanges of assets, a summary of, *illus.*, 379
Exchanges of dissimilar assets, 379
Exchanging property, plant, and equipment, 377–380
Exclusions, *def.*, 733
Exemption, personal, *def.*, 735
Expenditure, capital, *def.*, 374
Expense(s), 33–34, 230
   allocating the cost of plant and equipment to, 363–373
   deductions for, 742
   def., 33, 64, 214
   depreciation, comparison using different depreciation methods, *illus.*, 370
   other operating, 226–227
   prepaid, 110–113
      alternative approach to adjustments for, 116–117
      def., 110
   recognizing, 214–227
   unrecorded, 108–110
      def., 108
Extraordinary items, *def.*, 230

F

Face value, *def.*, 453
FASAC (Financial Accounting Standards Advisory Council), 15
FASB (Financial Accounting Standards Board):
   def., 15
   Interpretations issued by, 15
   Statement No. 95, recommendation of, 633
   Statements of Financial Accounting Concepts issued by, 15
Federal income tax liability, 732–743
FICA (social security) taxes, *def.*, 410
Fidelity bonding, 332
FIFO (first-in, first-out):
   def., 267
   inventory costing,
      periodic, 267–268
      perpetual, 271
Financial accounting:
   basic concepts and assumptions underlying, 9–13
   def., 8
Financial Accounting Federation, 15

Financial Accounting Standards Advisory Council (FASAC), 15
Financial Accounting Standards Board (FASB). *See* FASB
Financial position, statement of. *See* Balance sheet
Financial reporting, international aspects of, 692–699
Financial statement(s):
   comparative, *def.*, 32
   consolidated, 541–555
      def., 41, 494, 541
      need for, 541
      preparation of, 541–555
   general-purpose, 28–38
      def., 28
   horizontal analysis of, 673
   how they tie together, 38–39
   notes to, *def.*, 39
   preparing, 147
   foreign subsidiary, restatement of, 696–699
      example of, 698–699
      illus., 698
   vertical analysis of, 672
Financial statement analysis:
   basic techniques of, 668–669
   effect of changes in values and price levels on, 691
   key relationships as basis of, 670–671
   limitations of, 689–691
   overview of, 668–671
   reasons for, 666–673
   using ratios as basis for comparison in, 691
Financing activities, *def.*, 627
First-in, first-out (FIFO). *See* FIFO
Fiscal year, *def.*, 103
Floor, *def.*, 275
FOB (free-on-board) destination, *def.*, 264
FOB (free-on-board) shipping point, *def.*, 264
Foreign business of selected U.S. corporations, *illus.*, 692
Foreign currencies, accounting for transactions in, 694–696
Foreign purchases, 694
Foreign sales, 694–695

Foreign subsidiary, restatement of financial statements of, 696–699
   example of, 698–699
   illus., 698
Form of organization, choosing, 746
Franchise(s):
   def., 381
   and licenses, 380
Free-on-board. *See* FOB
Freight-in, *def.*, 222
Functional currency, *def.*, 697
Future value and present value, concepts of, 416–418
Future value table, 417–418

G

GAAP (generally accepted accounting principles), 41
   def., 15
   significance and development of, 13–15
Gain(s):
   on the exchange of similar operating assets, 377–378
   and losses, adjustments for, 630–631
Garbage in, garbage out (GIGO), 158
General journal, 68–69
   illus., 69
General ledger, 76–78
   posting to, *illus.*, 76, 77
   and subsidiary ledgers, *illus.*, 161
General-purpose financial statements, 28–38
   def., 28
Generally accepted accounting principles. *See* GAAP
GIGO (garbage in, garbage out), 158
Going concern, *def.*, 12
Going concern assumption, 12
Goods and services, obligation to provide, 414–415
Goods, selling, 72–73
Goodwill, 380–381
   def., 380, 546, 597
Government and other non-profit organizations, accounting career opportunities in, 21
Gross income:
   adjustments to, *def.*, 733
   def., 732

Gross margin(s):
   def., 214, 261
Gross margin method, *def.*, 278
Gross sales, *def.*, 213
Gross tax liability, *def.*, 733

H

Historical cost, *def.*, 11
Historical exchange rate, *def.*, 697
Horizontal analysis of balance sheets, 668, 673, 675–676
   def., 673
   illus., 673, 676

I

IASC (International Accounting Standards Committee), 699
IMA (Institute of Management Accountants), 16
Imprest petty cash fund, *def.*, 304
Income:
   adjusted gross, *def.*, 733
   definition of, 206–207
   gross,
      adjustments to, *def.*, 733
      def., 732
   methods of measuring, 207–210
   taxable,
      considerations in calculating, 741–742
      def., 733
Income statement(s), 33–36, 227–231
   condensed, *illus.*, 548
   consolidated,
      illus., 555
      using pooling-of-interests method, 554–555
      using purchase method, 548–549
      illus., 549
   def., 33
   format of, 34–36
   illus., 35, 82, 146, 215, 229, 637, 669
   multiple-step, *def.*, 214
   partnership, *illus.*, 592
   single-step, *def.*, 214
Income statement horizontal analysis, 673
Income statement vertical analysis, 672–673
Income summary, *def.*, 149

Income summary account, using, 149–150
Income tax(-es):
  deferred, 426–427
    def., 426
  depreciation for purposes of, 372–373
  federal, liability for, 732–743
  payable, *def.*, 413
Incorporation, articles of, *def.*, 518
Indenture, bond, *def.*, 453
Independent checks on performance, 334–335
Indirect method:
  def., 629
  of preparing a statement of cash flows, *illus.*, 635–642
  of reporting cash flows from operating activities, *illus.*, 631
  of reporting operating cash flows, 629–631
Individual taxpayer, calculating tax liability for, 733–738
  illus., 734
Industry, accounting career opportunities in, 19
Inflation, *def.*, 210
Institute of Management Accountants (IMA), 16
Intangible assets:
  accounting for, 380–382
  def., 358
Intercompany transaction, *def.*, 544
Interest:
  for bonds issued between interest payment dates, *illus.*, 467
  def., 322
  effective rate of, *def.*, 455
  market rate of, *def.*, 455
  stated rate of, *def.*, 455
  yield rate of, *def.*, 455
Interest date(s):
  accounting for bonds purchased between, 486–487
  def., 322
  investing between, *illus.*, 487
Interest-bearing notes, 419–420
Internal audit function, 331
Internal control, 327–336
  def., 328
  effects of computers on, 335–336
  elements of, 329–335
  procedures for, 332–335
International Accounting Standards Committee (IASC), 699
International accounting, search for uniformity in, 699
International business, 16
International financial reporting, 692–699
Interpretations (FASB), 15
Inventory(-ies):
  accounting for in manufacturing firms, 280
  def., 72, 112, 207
  factors in accounting for, 264–265
  methods of estimating, 277–280
    using gross margin method, 278–279
    using retail inventory method, 279
  proper measurement of, 260–265
  reporting at amounts below cost, 274–277
  specific identification costing of, 265–266
  taking a physical count of, 223–224
  tax considerations in accounting for, 747–749
  using a work sheet in accounting for, 233–237
  valued at lower of cost or market, 275–277
  valued at net realizable value, 274–275
Inventory cost flows, 265–274
  assumed, 266–267
Inventory cost flow assumptions:
  periodic, 267–271
  perpetual, 271–273
Inventory costing, 223
  comparison of all alternatives, 273–274
  comparison of LIFO and FIFO values, *illus.*, 270
  periodic average, 268–269
  periodic FIFO, 267
  periodic LIFO, 268
  perpetual FIFO, 271
  perpetual LIFO, 272
  using the average costing alternative,
    with the periodic method, 268–269
    with the perpetual method, 273
Inventory cutoff, *def.*, 260
Inventory errors, effects of, 260–264
Inventory turnover, 678–679, *def.*, 678
Inventory values, comparison of LIFO and FIFO, *illus.*, 270
Investing activities, *def.*, 626
Investing between interest dates, *illus.*, 487
Investment(s):
  long-term,
    in bonds, accounting for, 484–493
    def., 484
    in stocks, *illus.*, 498
    in stocks, accounting for, 493–500
    in stocks, valuation of, 492
    return on. *See* ROI
  in marketable securities, recording of, 312–313
  short-term, accounting for, 311–326
  in stocks,
    cost method of accounting for, 495–496, 497–500
    def., 494
    equity method of accounting for, 496–500
    def., 494
    long-term, accounting for, using the cost and equity methods, 497–500
    illus., 494, 498
Investment and credit decisions, 666–667
Investment decisions, strategic and capital:
Investments in long-term operating assets, 749–753
Issuance of no-par stock without a stated value, 524–525
Issuance of par-value stock and no-par stock with stated value, 522–524
Issuance price of a bond, determining, 454–458

Issued stock, *def.*, 520
Itemized deductions, *def.*, 733

J

JIT. *See* Just-in-time inventory system
Journal(s):
  computerized, 158–159
  def., 68
  general. *See* General journal
  special, 158–169
Journal entry(-ies)
  compound, *def.*, 72
  def., 69
  post to accounts, 75

K

Keogh plan, *def.*, 743

L

Land, buildings, and equipment, analysis of, 638–640
Lapping, *def.*, 303
Last-in, first-out (LIFO), *def.*, 268
LCM (lower-of-cost-or-market), *def.*, 313
LCM (lower-of-cost-or-market) rule, *def.*, 275
Lease:
  capital,
    def., 360, 426
    schedule of payments, *illus.*, 425
  classifying of, 362–363
  def., 426
  as an installment purchase, *illus.*, 751
  obligations of, 423–426
  operating, *def.*, 360, 426
Ledger:
  def., 76
  general. *See* General ledger
Legal capital, *def.*, 521
Lessee, *def.*, 360, 423
Lessor, *def.*, 360, 426
Liability(-ies):
  contingent, 427–428
  def., 427
  current, 406–415
  analysis of, 640
  def., 406
  def., 29, 406
  limited, *def.*, 518
  long-term, 415–427
  analysis of, 640
  def., 415
  measuring of, 415–419

Index

payroll, 410–411
pension, 427
tax, 412–413
unlimited, *def.*, 585
LIFO (last-in, first-out)
  def., 268
  inventory costing,
    periodic, 268
    perpetual, 272
Limited liability, *def.*, 518
Line of credit, *def.*, 311
Liquidation, *def.*, 606
Liquidation of a partnership, 605–606
Liquidity, *def.*, 667
Long-term debt:
  current maturities of, 410
  current portion of, 410
Long-term investment(s):
  in bonds,
    accounting for, 484–493
    valuation of, 492
  def., 484
  in stock(s),
    accounting for, 493–500
    illus., 498
Long-term liability(-ies), 415–427
  accounting for, 419–427
  analysis of, 640
  def., 415
  measuring of, 415–419
Loss(es):
  deductions for, 742
  on the exchange of similar operating assets, 378–379
  and gains, adjustments for, 630–631
  per share, *def.*, 34
  from uncollectible accounts, 213–214
    accounting for, 316
    allowance method of, 316
    direct write-off method of, 316
Lower of cost or market (LCM), *def.*, 313
Lower-of-cost-or-market (LCM) rule, *def.*, 275

M

MACRS (modified accelerated cost recovery system):
  asset categories under, *illus.*, 751
  def., 751
Maker, *def.*, 322
Management accountant(s), *def.*, 7
Management advisory services, 19
Management control methods, 331
Management philosophy and operating style, 329
Managerial decisions, 667
Margin of safety (MOS):
Market rate of interest, *def.*, 455
Marketable securities:
  def., 312
  recording investments in, 312–313
  valuing at lower of cost or market, 313–315
Matching principle, 103–104
  def., 103, 226, 316
Maturity date, *def.*, 322
Maturity value, *def.*, 323, 453
Merger, *def.*, 541
Minority interest, *def.*, 542
Modified accelerated cost recovery system. *See* MACRS
Monetary measurement:
  concept of, 12
  def., 12
Mortgage amortization schedule:
  def., 422
  illus., 423
Mortgage bonds, 452
Mortgage(s) payable, 422–423
  def., 422
MOS. *See* Margin of safety
Moving average, *def.*, 273
Multinational company, *def.*, 692
Multiple-step income statement, *def.*, 214
Mutual agency, *def.*, 589

N

Natural resources:
  accounting for, 382–383
  def., 358
Net assets, *def.*, 29
Net income, *def.*, 34, 261
Net loss, *def.*, 34
Net proceeds, *def.*, 324
Net realizable value:
  of accounts receivable, *def.*, 317
  def., 274
Net sales, *def.*, 213
Net tax liability, *def.*, 733
No-par stock:
  def., 521
  issuance of, with stated value, 522–524
  issuance of, without a stated value, 524–525
Nominal accounts, 147–148
  def., 147
Noncash investing and financing activities, 627
Noncash items:
  adjustments for, 630
  def., 630
Noncash transactions, *def.*, 627
Noninterest-bearing notes, 420–421
Nonprofit organization, *def.*, 5
Not sufficient funds (NSF) check, *def.*, 307
Note(s):
  to financial statements, *def.*, 39
  interest-bearing, 419–420
  noninterest-bearing, 420–421
  payable, 408–410
    def., 408
  principal on, *def.*, 322
  receivable, 322–326
    def., 322
    discounting, 324–325
      def., 324
    typical, *illus.*, 323
NSF (not sufficient funds) check, *def.*, 307
Number of days' sales:
  in inventory, *def.*, 679
  in receivables, *def.*, 678

O

Obligations:
  lease, 423–426
  paying, and collecting cash, 73
  to provide goods and services, 414–415
  short-term, to creditors, 406–410
Open transaction, *def.*, 695
Operating activities, *def.*, 626
Operating assets:
  acquisition of,
    by construction, tax effects of, 750–751
    by issuing securities, tax effects of, 750
    by leasing, tax effects of, 750
    by purchase, tax effects of, 750
  def., 358
  disposal of,
    by abandonment, tax effects of, 753
    by exchange, tax effects of, 753
    by sale, tax effects of, 753
  long-term,
    acquiring, tax effects of, 750–751
    depreciating, alternative ways of, tax effects of, 751–753
    disposing of, tax effects of, 753
    investments in, 749
  nature of, 358
  similar,
    gain on the exchange of, 377–378
    loss on the exchange of, 378–379
Operating lease, *def.*, 361, 426
Operating performance, analysis of, 671–674
Operating performance ratio, *def.*, 671
Operating style and management philosophy, 329
Organization, choosing form of, 746
Organizational structure, 329–330
Outstanding stock, *def.*, 520
Overhead:
Owners' equity (net assets), 29–30
  def., 29

P

P/E (price-earnings) ratio, 684–685, *def.*, 684
Par-value stock:
  def., 521
  issuance of, 522–524
Parent company, *def.*, 494, 541
Partial-year depreciation:
  calculations of, 371
  illus., 371
Partner(s):
  capital, statement of, *def.*, 591

799

Index

Partner(s): *(cont.)*
  death of, 604
  departing, payment to from the partnership's assets, 603–604
  drawings accounts, 590–591
  new, admission of, 598–601
    illus., 602
  purchasing an interest from, 598–599
  selling an interest to an outsider by, 602–603
  selling an interest to the other partners by, 603
  statement of partner's capital, *def.*, 591
  withdrawal of, 601–604
    illus., 605
Partnership(s), 10
  accounting for changing members of, 597–605
  admission of a new member to, 598–601
    illus., 602
  agreement, *def.*, 585
  balance sheet, *illus.*, 592
  basic accounting for, 589–593
  characteristics shared by proprietorships and, 584–586
  characteristics unique to, 588–589
  def., 10, 584
  distribution to owners of, 29
  ease of formation of, 584–585
  forming, 590
  income statement of, *illus.*, 592
  investing directly in, 599–601
  limited life of, 585
  liquidation of, 605–606
  members of, accounting for changing of, 597–605
  selling of partner's interest, to an outsider, 602–603
    to the other partners, 603
  payment to a departing partner from the assets of, 603–604
  profits, sharing of, 589
  profits and losses of, accounting for, 593–597
    allocation of, using allowance for salaries with the remainder at stated ratio, 595–596
    allocation of, using capital investment ratio, 594–595
    allocation of, using stated ratio, 593–594
  property of, co-ownership of, 589
  taxation of, 743–744
  unlimited liability of, 585
  withdrawal of a partner from, 601–604
    illus., 605
Patents, 380–381
  def., 380
Payables and other current liabilities, adjustments for, 630
Payee, *def.*, 322
Payroll liabilities, 410–411
Pension:
  liabilities of, 427
  plan, *def.*, 427
Percentage of receivables method, 319
Percentage of sales method, 318–319
Performance, independent checks on, 334–335
Periodic average inventory costing, 268–269
Periodic inventory cost flow assumptions, 267–271
  using FIFO inventory costing, 267–268
  using LIFO inventory costing, 268
Periodic inventory method, 219–223
  comparison of cost flow assumptions, using, 269–271
  comparison of with perpetual method, *illus.*, 228
  def., 219
  work sheet for using, *illus.*, 236–237
Periodic reporting, 102–103
Periodicity concept, *def.*, 102
Perpetual average inventory costing, 273
Perpetual inventory cost flow assumptions, 271–273
  using FIFO inventory costing, 271
  using LIFO inventory costing, 272
Perpetual inventory method, 215–219
  comparison of with periodic method, *illus.*, 228
  def., 215
  illus., 216
  work sheet for using, *illus.*, 234–235
Personal exemption, *def.*, 735
Personnel policies, 331–332
Petty cash, accounting for, 304–306
Petty cash fund, *def.*, 304
Petty cash voucher, *illus.*, 304
Physical control over assets and records, 334
Physical inventory form, *illus.*, 224
Planning:
  tax, guidelines for, 746–747
Plant and equipment:
  allocating the cost of to expense, 363–373
  repairing and improving of, 374–375
Pooling of interests, *def.*, 542
Pooling-of-interests method, using for consolidated balance sheet(s), 549–554
  illus., 554
  using for consolidated income statements, 554–555
Post-closing trial balance:
  def., 152
  illus., 153
  preparing, 151–152
Posting, *def.*, 75
Preemptive right, *def.*, 520
Preference(s):
  cumulative-dividend, *def.*, 533
  current-dividend, 533
    def., 532
  dividend, 532–534
Preferred stock:
  convertible, *def.*, 521
  def., 520
Premium on stock, *def.*, 521
Prepaid expenses, 110–113
  alternative approach to adjustments for, 116–117
Prepaid expenses, *def.*, 110
Present value:
  of an annuity, *def.*, 418
  and future value, concepts of, 416–418
  of $1, *def.*, 416
Present value table(s), 417, 446–448
Price-earnings (P/E) ratio, 684–685
  def., 684
Principal:
  def., 453
  on a note, *def.*, 322
Prior-period adjustments, *def.*, 537
Pro-rata, *def.*, 529
Profitability:
  def., 667
Property, tangible personal business, *def.*, 753
Property, plant, and equipment:
  accounting for, 358–373
  acquisitions of, 359–363
  def., 358
  discarding of, 375–376
  disposal of, 375–380
  exchanging of, 377–380
  selling of, 376–377
  turnover of, 680–681
    def., 680
Property dividend, *def.*, 530
Property taxes payable, 412–413
Proprietorship(s), 10
  accounting for, 586–588
  characteristics shared by partnerships and, 584–586
  def., 10, 584
  distribution to owners of, 29
  ease of formation of, 584–585
  limited life of, 585
  taxation of, 743
  unlimited liability of, 585
Public accounting:
  career opportunities in, 19
  services to clients, 19
Purchase, *def.*, 219, 542
Purchase discount(s), 220–221
  def., 218
Purchase method:
  using for consolidated balance sheet(s), 542–548
  illus., 546
  using for consolidated income statement(s), 548–549
  illus., 549

Index

Purchase returns and allowances, *def.*, 222
Purchases journal, 160–163
  def., 160
  posting, *illus.*, 164
  a sample page in, *illus.*, 163
Purchasing an interest, 598–599

Q

Quantity count, 223
Quick ratio, *def.*, 677

R

Ratio analysis:
  of balance sheets, 676–681
  of financial statements, 668
Real accounts, 147–148
  def., 147
Realization principle, 741
Receivables, 315–326
  accounting for, 315
  adjustments for, and other current operating assets, 629–630
  def., 315
Reconciling the bank account, 306–311
Records:
  and assets, physical control over, 334
  and documents, adequacy of, 333–334
Recourse, *def.*, 325
Recovery period:
  cost, selecting for asset, 752–753
  def., 751
Redemption value, *def.*, 686
Registered bonds, *def.*, 453
Regular corporations, taxation of, 744
Regulatory decisions, 667
Relative fair market value method, *def.*, 359
Remeasurement:
  def., 697
  and translation, 697–698
Repairing and improving plant and equipment, 374–375
Reporting currency, *def.*, 697
Residual value, *def.*, 363
Resources, natural:
  accounting for, 382–383
  def., 358

Restatement of financial statements of a foreign subsidiary:
  example of, 698–699
  illus., 698
Retail inventory method, *def.*, 279
Retained earnings:
  accounting for, 536–539
  analysis of, 635–637
  def., 30
  reporting the ending balance of, 143–147
  restrictions on, 537–539
  statement of,
    def., 35, 537
    illus., 36, 538
Return on investment. *See* ROI
Return on stockholders' equity, 683–687
  def., 683
  summary of financial statement analysis of, *illus.*, 688
Return on total assets, 687–689
  def., 687
  summary of financial analysis of, *illus.*, 689
Revenue(s):
  def., 33, 64, 210
  recognition of, 210–214
  on credit sales, 211–214
  unearned, 113–115
    alternative approach to adjustments for, 117–118
    def., 113, 414
  unrecorded, 106–108
    def., 106
Revenue recognition, 103, 210–214
Revenue recognition principle, *def.*, 103, 210
Reversing entry(-ies), 155–157
  def., 155
  preparing, 155–157

S

S corporation(s):
  def., 520, 744
  taxation of, 744–745
Sales discount(s), 211–212
  accounting for, *illus.*, 212
  def., 211
Sales invoice, *illus.*, 68

Sales journal, 159–160
  def., 159
  posting from, *illus.*, 162
  sample page in, *illus.*, 159
Sales returns and allowances, 212–213
  def., 213
Sales tax payable, *def.*, 412
Salvage value, 367
  def., 363
Schedule of capital lease payments, *illus.*, 425
Scrapping. *See* Discarding
Secured bonds, *def.*, 452
Securities, marketable:
  def., 312
  recording investments in, 312–313
  valuing at lower of cost or market, 313–315
Securities and Exchange Commission (SEC), *def.*, 15
Segregation of duties, adequate, 333
Selling property, plant, and equipment, 376–377
Serial bonds, *def.*, 453
Services, providing, 72–73
Shareholders. *See* Stockholders
Short-term investments, accounting for, 311–326
Short-term obligations to creditors, 406–410
Single-step income statement, *def.*, 214
Sinking fund bonds, *def.*, 453
Small-business accounting, 19
Social security (FICA) taxes, *def.*, 410
Solvency, *def.*, 667
Special journal(s), 158–169
  def., 158
Specific identification, *def.*, 265
Specific identification inventory costing, 265–266
Standard deduction, *def.*, 735
Stated rate of interest, *def.*, 455
Stated ratio, 593–594
  allowance for salaries with the remainder at, 595–596
Stated value, *def.*, 521
Statement of cash flows, 36–38
  def., 36, 624
  general format for, *illus.*, 625

  illus., 38
  information reported in, 625–628
  preparing, 635–644
  purposes of, 624–625
  and supplemental disclosures, 641–642
  using direct method, *illus.*, 641, 643
  work sheet for, using direct method, *illus.*, 642
Statement of earnings, *def.*, 33
Statement of financial position. *See* Balance sheet
Statement of partners' capital, *def.*, 591
Statement of retained earnings:
  def., 35, 537
  illus., 36, 538
Statement of stockholders' equity, 36, 539
  def., 539
Statements of Financial Accounting Concepts, 15
Statements of Financial Accounting Standards, 15
Stock(s):
  accounting for, 522–529
  accounting for long-term investments in, 493–500
  using the cost and equity methods of, *illus.*, 494, 498
  acquisition of, 493–494
  capital, *def.*, 520
  common, *def.*, 520
  convertible preferred, *def.*, 521
  corporate, 518–522
  investments in,
    cost method of accounting for, 495–496, 497–500
    def., 494
  equity method accounting for, 496–500
    def., 494
  issued, *def.*, 520
  long-term investments in, *illus.*, 498
  no-par,
    def., 521
    with stated value, issuance of, 522–524
    without stated value, issuance of, 524–525
  outstanding, *def.*, 520

Stock(s): *(cont.)*
  par-value,
    def., 521
    issuance of, 522–524
  preferred, *def.*, 520
  premium on, *def.*, 521
  reporting of on the balance sheet, 528–529
  stages in the status of, *illus.*, 521
  treasury,
    accounting for, 525–528
    def., 520
Stock certificate, *def.*, 519
Stock dividend(s):
  accounting for, 534–535
  def., 530
Stock split(s), *def.*, 536
Stockholders (shareholders), 10–11
  def., 10, 519
  distributions to, 529–536
Stockholders' equity, 29
  return on, 683–687
    def., 683
  statement of, 36, 539
    def., 539
  summary of financial statement analysis of return on, *illus.*, 688
Straight-line amortization, 488, 490
  def., 460, 488
Straight-line depreciation method, 364–366
  def., 364
Straight-line depreciation schedule, *illus.*, 366
Strategic investment decisions:
Subsidiary company, *def.*, 494, 541
Subsidiary ledger, *def.*, 160
Sum-of-the-years'-digits (SYD) depreciation method, 367–369
  def., 367
Sum-of-the-years'-digits depreciation schedule, *illus.*, 368
Supplies, *def.*, 112
SYD. *See* Sum-of-the-years'-digits

T

T-account, 62–64
  def., 62
  illus., 63

Tangible personal business property, *def.*, 753
Tax(-es):
  of corporations, 744–746
  of different forms of business, 743–746
  FICA (social security), *def.*, 410
  income. *See* Income tax(es)
  of partnerships, 743–744
  of proprietorships, 743
Tax accounting, 19
Tax considerations in accounting for inventories, 747–749
Tax credit, *def.*, 733
Tax effects of:
  acquisition of
    long-term operating assets, 750–751
      by construction, 750–751
      by issuing securities, 750
      by leasing, 750
      by purchase, 750
  alternative ways of depreciating long-term operating assets, 751–753
  disposing of
    long-term operating assets, 751
      by abandonment, 751
      by exchange, 751
      by sale, 751
Tax liability(-ies), 412–413
  calculating for corporation, 738–743
  calculating for individual taxpayer, 733–738
  federal, steps for calculating for corporation, *illus.*, 739
  for individual taxpayer, *illus.*, 734
  gross, *def.*, 733
  income, federal, 732–743
  net, *def.*, 733
Tax(-es) payable:
  income, *def.*, 413
  property, 412–413
  sales, *def.*, 412
Tax-exempt corporation(s), 745
  def., 745
Tax-planning guidelines, 746–747
Taxable income:
  considerations in calculating, 741–742

def., 733
Taxpayer, individual:
  calculating tax liability for, 733–738
  steps for calculating federal tax liability for, *illus.*, 734
Term bonds, *def.*, 453
Time period concept, *def.*, 102
Trade payable(s). *See* Account(s) payable
Trade receivables, 315
Transaction(s):
  analysis of business documents and, 66, 68
  arm's-length, assumption of, 11
    def., 11
  def., 11
  exchange, 60
  journalizing, 68–75
  using accounts to categorize, 62–64
Transaction data, process of transforming into useful accounting information, 60–61
Translation:
  def., 697
  and remeasurement, 697–698
Translation adjustment, *def.*, 697
Transportation costs, 218–219, 222
Treasury stock:
  accounting for, 525–528
  def., 520
Trial balance:
  def., 79, 138
  determining and preparing, 78–79
  illus., 79, 81
  post-closing,
    def., 152
    illus., 153
  preparing, 151–152
Type I subsidiary, *def.*, 697
Type II subsidiary, *def.*, 697

U

Uncollectible accounts:
  accounting for losses from, 316
  allowance method of, 316
  direct write-off method of, 316

allowance for, *def.*, 317
  estimating the allowance for, 318–320
    aging method of, 319
    percentage of receivables method of, 319
    percentage of sales method of, 318–319
  losses from, 213–214
Uncollectible accounts expense, *def.*, 317
Unearned revenues, 113–115
  alternative approach to adjustments for, 117–118
  def., 113, 414
Units-of-production depreciation method, *def.*, 369, 369–370
Units-of-production depreciation schedule, *illus.*, 370
Unlimited liability, *def.*, 585
Unrecorded expenses, 108–110
  def., 108
Unrecorded revenues, 106–108
  def., 106
Unsecured bonds, *def.*, 452
Useful life:
  def., 358

V

Value:
  residual, *def.*, 363
  salvage, *def.*, 363
Vertical analysis:
  of balance sheets, 674–675
    illus., 675
  of financial statements, 668
    def., 672
  of income statements, 672–673
    illus., 672

W

Weighted average, *def.*, 268
Withdrawals, 29
Work sheet, 138–147
  adjustment for income taxes, 142–143
  consolidated, *illus.*, 543, 547, 552
  def., 138
  eight-column, *illus.*, 140–141

Index

preparing, 138–142, 551–553
special considerations in using, 142–147
for statement of cash flows using direct method, *illus.*, 642
ten-column, *illus.*, 144–145
for using in accounting for inventory, 233–237
for using the periodic inventory method, *illus.*, 236–237
for using the perpetual inventory method, *illus.*, 234–235

Work-in-process inventory, *def.*, 763
Working capital ratio, *def.*, 676
Working capital turnover, 679–680
def., 679

Write-off method, direct, *def.*, 316

Y

Yield rate of interest, *def.*, 455

Checklist of Key Figures

Chapter 1 No check figures

E2-1	Owners' Equity Company C $30,000	**P2B-6**	2. Liabilities on Sept. 1 $8,000
E2-2	Owners' Equity 12/31/94, Z Co. $220	**P2B-7**	Net Cash Flow, Operating Activities $274,000
E2-3	1. Capital Stock 12/31 $55,000	**P2B-8**	Retained Earnings 1/1/94 $28,680
E2-5	Owners' Equity 12/31/94 $166,000	**P2B-9**	3. Total Assets $172,200
E2-6	1. Income Before Taxes $52,500	**P2B-10**	2. Net Income for 1994 $6,000
E2-7	Income Before Taxes $114,800	**E3-8**	Trial Balance Totals $95,600
E2-9	2. Net Cash Flow, Financing Activities $27,000	**E3-10**	Revenues for 1994 $240,000
E2-10	1. Net Income $380,000	**P3A-1**	Ending Cash Balance $28,700
E2-11	Net Income 1994 $80,000	**P3A-2**	Ending Cash Balance $15,900
E2-12	Ret. Earnings 6/30/94 $83,900	**P3A-4**	3. Trial Balance Totals $95,000
E2-13	2. Net Income $28,400	**P3A-5**	Ending Cash Balance $27,950
P2A-1	2. Total Liabilities $33,000	**P3A-7**	Ending Cash Balance $24,500
P2A-2	Total Long-Term Assets $56,000	**P3B-1**	2. Trial Balance Totals $139,500
P2A-3	1. Total Assets $69,200	**P3B-3**	Ending Cash Balance $14,350
P2A-4	Income Before Taxes $11,200	**P3B-4**	2. Ending Cash Balance $22,700
P2A-6	Total Assets $40,000	**P3B-5**	Trial Balance Totals $300,900
P2A-7	Net Cash Flow, Financing Activities ($40,000)	**P3B-7**	3. Trial Balance Totals $357,400
P2A-8	1. Total Expenses $71,650	**E4-3**	1.(a) Cash-Basis Net Loss ($7,600)
P2A-9	2. Retained Earnings 12/31/94, $173,600	**E4-4**	1. Interest Revenue $4,000
P2A-10	1. Total Expenses $53,800	**E4-5**	3. Salaries Expense $6,000
P2B-1	Cash $26,000	**E4-8**	2. Property Tax Expense $1,650
P2B-2	Retained Earnings $13,050	**E4-9**	1. Prepaid Insurance $6,000
P2B-3	Total Current Liabilities $15,960	**E4-10**	3. Interest Revenue $2,000
P2B-4	Earnings Per Share $21.20	**E4-11**	2. Unearned Rent Revenue $800
P2B-5	Net Income $34,515	**E4-12**	5. Unearned Revenue Balance $625
		P4A-1	1. Net Income $399,300
		P4A-6	1. Cash Paid for Insurance $5,800

P4A-8	2. Net Income $81,450
P4B-1	3. Accrual-Basis Net Inc. $2,600
P4B-5	3. Total Interest Expense $2,060
P4B-6	2. Rent Revenue for 1993 $11,500
P4B-8	Subtotal — Liabilities $56,999
E5-1	Trial Balance Totals $112,470
E5-2	Net Loss $6,000
E5-3	Total Assets $72,000
E5-4	Adjustments Totals $6,030
E5-8	Income Summary Closing Amount $48,900
E5-9	Ending Balance in Ret. Earnings After Closing Entries $19,200
E5-10	Income Summary Closing Amount $60,830
E5-11	2. Jane Stewart Capital $14,765
E5-12	2. Post-Closing Trial Balance Totals $149,970
P5A-1	2. Net Income $25,000
P5A-2	2. Adjustments Totals $5,750
P5A-5	2. Income Summary Closing Amount $5,200
P5A-6	2. Income Summary Closing Amount $3,205
P5A-7	1. Adjustments Totals $952
P5A-8	2. Net Income $290,000
P5A-9	4. Net Income $43,000
P5B-1	Unadjusted Trial Balance Totals $80,660
P5B-2	Adjustments Totals $4,380
P5B-4	1. Income Summary Closing Amount $8,200
P5B-5	2. Income Summary Closing Amount $28,140
P5B-6	1. After-Tax Net Income $11,718
P5B-7	2. Income Summary Closing Amount $13,800
P5B-8	Liabilities Corrected Balance $27,800
P5B-9	3. Net Income $11,210
E6-3	(9) $635
E6-4	(2) Gross Purchases $203,000
E6-5	Cost of Goods Available for Sale $352,560
E6-6	Net Purchases $263,880
E6-8	1.(b) 1994 income $300 overstated
E6-9	(5) $267,000
E6-10	Income from operations $2,020
P6A-1	1. Cash Basis Net Loss ($184,000)
P6A-2	1. Accrual Basis Gross Margin $44,000
P6A-4	(5) $150
P6A-5	(17) $212,500
P6A-6	2. Income Summary Closing Amount $66,600
P6A-7	Gross Margin $124,938
P6A-8	Adjusted Trial Balance Totals $397,600
P6B-1	1. Cash Basis Revenues $40,000
P6B-2	Net Cash Outflow $53,197
P6B-4	(13) $21,000
P6B-5	(4) $89,400
P6B-6	3.(a) Debit to Inventory Shrinkage $12,000
P6B-7	Income from operations $342,100
P6B-8	Net Income $48,300

E7-1	1.(b) Cost of Goods Sold $51,000
E7-2	1. Ending Inventory $30,300
E7-3	1. Ending Inventory $32,000
E7-4	2. Cost of Goods Available for Sale $103,100
E7-5	1. Cost of Goods Available for Sale $24,450
E7-6	1. Cost of Goods Available for Sale $89,500
E7-7	1.(c) July 17 Cost of Goods Sold $6,150
E7-8	4. Loss on Write-Down of Inventory to LCM $150
E7-9	2.(a) Loss on Write-Down of Inventory to LCM $9,800
E7-10	1. Cost of Goods Sold $240,000
E7-11	Cost Ratio 68%
P7A-1	2. Corrected Purchases $84,600
P7A-2	1994 Inventory Overstatement, Beginning of Year $3,000
P7A-3	1.(a) Income Before Taxes $2,600
P7A-4	1.(c) Aug. 13 New Cost Per Unit $10.699
P7A-5	3. Cost of Goods Available for Sale $2,490
P7A-6	1.(c) Average Cost $30.67
P7A-7	1994 Cost of Goods Available for Sale $108,500
P7A-8	1.(b) Ratio 72%
P7B-1	1.(a) No Effect on Gross Margin
P7B-2	Cost of Goods Sold $254,900
P7B-3	1. Net Income 1995 $305,000
P7B-4	(8) $122,200
P7B-5	1.(b) Cost of Goods Available for Sale— Plaster $8,400
P7B-6	Ending Inventory $22,500
P7B-7	1. Cost of Goods Sold $72,000
P7B-8	1. Cost of Goods Sold—Situation C $1,400
E8-1	2. Total Cash $3,125
E8-4	Dec. 31 Cash Credit $394
E8-5	1. October Deposits in Transit $5,100
E8-6	Adjusted Bank Balance $71,416
E8-7	2/20/95 Cash Debit $3,700
E8-8	Sept. 28 Marketable Securities, Eli Corp. Stock, Credit $20,940
E8-9	(3) Entry Amount $63,500
E8-12	Oct. 1 Cash Debit $12,715
P8A-1	1. Dec. 31 Cash Credit $707
P8A-2	Adjusted Book Balance $84,250
P8A-3	(5) Outstanding Checks $700
P8A-4	Ending Cash Balance ($16,150)
P8A-5	May 22 Cash Debit $30,000
P8A-6	1. Uncollectible Accounts Expense Debit $320
P8A-7	1. Oct. 1 Cash Debit $9,763
P8A-8	June 16 Cash Debit $28,610.96
P8B-2	4. Cash Debit $4,540
P8B-3	1. Adjusted Balance $168,594
P8B-4	1. Cash Debit Dec. 1 $14,800
P8B-5	Oct. 10 Gain on Sale of Marketable Securities Credit $1,607
P8B-6	4.(b) Accts. Rec. Credit $64,000
P8B-7	1. Apr. 11 Interest Revenue Credit $17.22
P8B-8	3. Special Receivable Credit $24,781.80

Checklist of Key Figures

E9-1	1. Total Cost $83,000	P10B-4	2. Salaries Payable Debit $8,289.70
E9-2	Building Debit $262,500	P10B-6	1.(d) $44,955
E9-5	2.(a) $8,182	P10B-7	2. Dec. 31 Interest Expense Debit $1,998
E9-6	1.(b) Depreciation Expense Debit $16,000	P10B-8	4. Interest Exp. Debit $2,595
E9-7	3. Machine Debit $400	P10B-9	Total Long-Term Liab. $714,000
E9-8	1.(c) 1993 $3,750	P10B-10	2. Total Current Liab. $43,336
E9-9	3. 1994 $12,800		
E9-10	3. 1995 $122,825	E11-1	2. July 1 Bond Interest Expense Debit $30,000
E9-12	1. Loss on Exchange $500	E11-2	1.(a) Premium on Bonds Credit $2,000
E9-13	4. Gain on Trade of Truck $4,000	E11-3	June 30, 1993 Discount on Bonds Debit $9,000
E9-14	2. Total Intangible Assets $138,000	E11-5	Total price $89,404
E9-15	4. Depletion Expense, Coal Mine Debit $100,000	E11-6	3. $2,608
P9A-1	Land, Total $99,500	E11-7	3. Bond Interest Expense Debit $8,267
P9A-2	1. Net Invoice Price $153,745	E11-8	2. Premium on Bonds Debit $125
P9A-3	3. Lease Liability—Computer Debit $39,118	E11-9	2. Bond Premium Debit $17,920
P9A-4	1. Depreciable Amount $30,000	P11A-2	1.(c) Premium on Bonds Credit $4,500
P9A-5	3. Book Value $17,600	P11A-3	2. Premium on Bonds Debit $675
P9A-6	2.(a) $58 per hour	P11A-4	2. Total Interest Expense $86,039
P9A-7	1. Equipment Debit $44,444	P11A-5	Bond Carrying Value Case 3 $205,500
P9A-8	1.(b) 12/31/92 Depreciation Expense Debit $16,000	P11A-6	4. Bond Discount Debit $7,722
P9A-9	3. Machine (new) Debit $77,000	P11A-7	3. Bond Interest Expense Debit $8,400
P9A-10	5. Truck (new) Debit $84,333	P11A-8	2. Gain on Retirement of Bonds Credit $7,800
P9B-2	3. 1994 Depr. Expense $1,600	P11B-1	3. Premium on Bonds Debit $600
P9B-4	1.(d) 1993 $2,400	P11B-2	1. Issuance Price of Bonds $112,463
P9B-5	2. Equipment Debit $45,000	P11B-3	2. Total Interest Expense $24,759
P9B-6	1. Depr. Expense Debit $1,980	P11B-4	2. Interest Expense 1994 $25,706
P9B-7	1.(b) Depr. Expense Debit $950	P11B-6	1. Issuance price of bonds $171,156
P9B-8	1.(c) Loss on Trade-In Debit $15,000	P11B-7	2. Total Principal Amortization $32,336
P9B-9	1. Double-Declining Balance Totals (1993–95) $85,440	E12-2	1. Bond price $31,461.33
P9B-10	2. Amort. Expense Debit $750	E12-3	2. Dec. 31 Bond Interest Revenue Credit $1,545
P9B-11	3.(c) Total Depletion $36,000	E12-4	Total Interest Earned $6,294
		E12-5	Total Amortization $1,706
E10-2	1. 12/31/94 Interest Expense Debit $2,333	E12-7	Oct. 5, 1995 Loss on Sale of Investments Debit $25,000
E10-3	4. Cash Credit $10,296	E12-8	1. Dec. 31, 1994 Revenue from Investments Credit $90,000
E10-5	1. Second Month, Warranty Expense Debit $400	P12A-1	1. Feb. 1, 1993 Bond Interest Receivable $1,000
E10-6	10/1/94 Interest Expense Debit $2,250	P12A-2	2. Total Interest Actually Earned $10,123
E10-7	1. 7/1/93 Discount on Note Payable Debit $2,200	P12A-3	2. Bond Interest Receivable Debit $899.59
E10-9	1. $10,209	P12A-5	1. Total market value $575,000
E10-10	3. $9,500	P12A-8	1. Oct. 15 Gain on Sale of Investments $6,625
E10-11	2. $30,326	P12B-2	2. Selling Price of Bonds $280,598
E10-12	2. Lease Obligation Debit $7,172	P12B-4	3. Loss on Sale Debit $15,000
P10A-2	(b) 1/1/93 Discount on Note Payable $24,870	P12B-8	3. Dec. 31, 1994 Investment Balance $210,000
P10A-3	Sept. 23 Interest Expense Debit $444		
P10A-4	2. Payroll Tax Expense Debit $10,322	E13-2	2. Stockholders' Equity $820,800
P10A-5	2. Income before Taxes $9,750	E13-3	(c) Dividends, Preferred Stock Debit $4,000
P10A-7	1. 12/31/95 Interest Expense and Discount Amort. $4,091	E13-4	5. Dividends Payable Credit $38,600
P10A-8	1.(c) Lease Obligation Debit $3,782	E13-5	(d) Treasury Stock Credit $40,000
P10A-9	Total Current Liabilities $158,700	E13-6	6. Paid-in Capital, Treasury Stock Debit $3,200
P10A-10	2. Total Assets $364,200	E13-7	(5) $789,000
P10B-1	5. Interest Payable Debit $800		
P10B-2	2. 3/1/93 Discount on Notes Payable Debit $500		
P10B-3	Sept. 23 Interest Expense Debit $222		

E13-8	Total Contributed Capital $975,000	E15-3	Total Cash Receipts $197,000
E13-9	Total Dividends Declared $50,000	E15-4	Decrease in Prepaid Insurance $500
E13-10	3. $1.69 per share	E15-6	Net Cash Flow Provided by Operating Activities $161,600
E13-11	Common Stock Case A $66,000	E15-7	Net Cash Flow Provided by Operating Activities $161,600
E13-12	1. Nov. 6 Dividends Payable Debit $77,275	E15-8	Net Cash Flow Provided by Financing Activities $55,000
E13-13	3. Retained Earnings Debit $750,000	E15-9	Net Cash Flow Provided by Operating Activities $116,000
E13-16	2. Investment in Missouri Company Credit $230,000	P15A-1	1. Net Cash Flow Provided by Operating Activities $5,500
E13-17	Additional Expense $8,250	P15A-2	1. Net Cash Flow from Operations $15,490
P13A-1	4.(a) Paid-in Capital, Treasury Stock Debit $1,000	P15A-3	Net Cash Flow Used in Investing Activities <$72,000>
P13A-2	2. Total Contributed Capital $1,802,200	P15A-4	Net Cash Flow from Operations $580
P13A-3	(d) Retained Earnings Debit $50,000	P15A-5	1. Net Increase in Cash and Cash Equivalents $27
P13A-4	(c) Total Preferred Dividends $64,000	P15B-1	Cash Collected from Customers $867,000
P13A-5	2. Total Common Dividends $103,000	P15B-2	Net Income $38,500
P13A-6	3. Total Contributed Capital $3,700,000	P15B-3	Net Cash Flow Provided by Operating Activities $27,000
P13A-7	1. Dec. 31, 1994 Retained Earnings $121,000	P15B-4	Net Cash Flow Provided by Financing Activities $442
P13A-8	2. Total Contributed Capital & Retained Earnings $805,000	P15B-5	Net Cash Flow Used in Investing Activities ($436)
P13A-9	2. Total Stockholders' Equity $1,311,760	E16-3	Cost of Goods Sold $1,350,000
P13A-10	2. Investment in Sawyer Credit $250,000	E16-4	Income Before Interest & Taxes $1,200,000
P13A-11	2. Total Consolidated Assets $435,000	E16-6	Sales Per Business Day $15,833
P13B-1	2. Total Contributed Capital $279,250	E16-7	Acid-Test Ratio 1.36
P13B-2	2. Total Stockholders' Equity $268,100	E16-8	1. New current ratio 0.30
P13B-3	Mar. 15 Retained Earnings Debit $76,000	E16-9	2. 1994 4.2 times
P13B-4	1. 1995 Preferred Stock Dividends Declared $24,000	E16-10	1. Accounts Receivable Turnover 1994 15.3 times
P13B-5	2. Par Value of Common Stock Issued $1,890,000	P16A-1	Income before Taxes-Northern $48,000 or 13.3%
P13B-6	2. Dividends in Arrears at end of 1994 $100,000	P16A-2	4. 3.45 times
P13B-7	1. Total Net Income $46,000	P16A-3	2. 4.55 times
P13B-8	2. Total Retained Earnings $134,300	P16A-4	3. $63.33 per share
P13B-9	2. Total Contributed Capital $48,200	P16A-5	3.(h) 6.01 times
P13B-10	Pooling of Interests Net Income $127,000	P16A-6	1. Gross Margin 1993 Vertical Analysis 40%
E14-1	Net Income $8,500	P16A-7	1.(b) Preferred Earnings per share $7.00
E14-2	2. Total Capital, Dec. 31, 1994 $246,200	P16A-8	3. Corona's Price-Earnings Ratio 13.3 times
E14-4	Total Income to Smith $36,000	P16A-9	2. & 3. Mow Chemicals Total Consolidated Assets $1,038,750
E14-5	Deficiency Allocated to Pound $8,333	P16B-1	2. 4.3 times
E14-6	2. Total Capital $81,000	P16B-2	1. Dividends as a percentage of income 44.1%
E14-7	1. Harrison, Capital Credit $57,600	P16B-3	3. Increase in gross sales $17,245
P14A-1	2. Capital, Dec. 31 $76,000	P16B-4	1. 1993 1.4 times
P14A-2	3. Total Capital $89,200	P16B-5	2. Book value per share $14.27
P14A-3	1.(c) 1993 Muley $6,164	P16B-6	1. Earnings per share $5.58
P14A-4	1. Total Capital $150,000	P16B-7	1. Total Liabilities Alternative 1 $820,000
P14A-5	1. Total Partners' Capital, Ending Balance $340,000	P16B-8	1.(e) 1995 4.74 times
P14A-7	3. Total Assets $50,950	P16B-9	1.(b) Tokyo Denki Type II Net Income $23,000
P14A-8	3. Total Capital Dec. 31 $92,000	P16B-10	2. Total Assets, dollars, $18,326,154
P14B-1	2. Capital Dec. 31 $179,000		
P14B-2	2. Total Partners' Capital, Ending Balance $39,870		
P14B-3	1. Total Average Capital $134,000		
P14B-4	3. Total Capital Dec. 31 $232,000		
P14B-6	1. Jones Capital Balance $71,000		
P14B-7	1. Gross margin $138,000		
P14B-8	1.(b) Smith, Capital Credit $82,000		

Checklist of Key Figures

E17-2	Total Itemized Deductions $2,680	**P17A-8**	1. Light Truck $1,800
E17-3	Gross Income $218,000	**P17A-9**	1. After-Tax Cash Flow Savings $40,848
E17-4	Taxable Income $115,000	**P17B-1**	2. Taxable Income $38,925
E17-6	MACRS Depreciation Expense Year 3 $1,920	**P17B-2**	2. Gross Profit $188,600
E17-8	1. Book Value $5,000	**P17B-3**	1. Cost of Goods Sold FIFO $58,370
P17A-1	Adjusted Gross Income $32,300	**P17B-4**	MACRS Depreciation Year 4 $4,998
P17A-2	Taxable Income $88,060	**P17B-5**	1. Accelerated Depreciation $11,143
P17A-3	1. Cost of Goods Sold LIFO $187,000	**P17B-7**	1. Partnership Income Reported by Wright $24,000
P17A-4	1. MACRS Depreciation $2,000	**P17B-8**	1. 1994 MACRS Depreciation $8,452
P17A-6	Total S corporation income reported $74,000	**P17B-9**	1. Net present value at 12% $(7,522)